CW00517365

ISBN 978-1-5279-9366-2
PIBN 10974005

REPORTS

OF

CASES

ARGUED AND DETERMINED

IN

The Court of Queen's Bench:

WITH TABLES OF THE NAMES OF THE CASES ARGUED AND CITED, AND THE PRINCIPAL MATTERS.

BY

JOHN LEYCESTER ADOLPHUS, OF THE INNER TEMPLE,

AND

THOMAS FLOWER ELLIS, OF THE MIDDLE TEMPLE,

ESQRS. BARRISTERS AT LAW.

VOL. VIII.

CONTAINING THE CASES OF PART OF HILARY TERM,
AND OF EASTER, TRINITY, AND MICHAELMAS TERMS,
IN THE FIRST AND SECOND YEARS OF VICTORIA. 1838.

LONDON:

PRINTED FOR SAUNDERS AND BENNING,

(SUCCESSORS TO J. BUTTERWORTH AND SON,)

43. FLEET-STREET.

1840.

London:
Printed by A. Spottiswoode,
New-Street-Square.

JUDGES

OF

THE COURT OF QUEEN'S BENCH,

DURING THE PERIOD OF THESE REPORTS.

The Right Hon. THOMAS LORD DENMAN, C. J.
Sir JOSEPH LITTLEDALE, Knt.
Sir JOHN PATTESON, Knt.
Sir JOHN WILLIAMS, Knt.
Sir JOHN TAYLOR COLERIDGE, Knt.

ATTORNEY GENERAL.

Sir JOHN CAMPBELL, Knt.

SOLICITOR GENERAL.

Sir ROBERT MOUNSEY ROLFE, Knt.

A

TABLE

OF

THE NAMES OF CASES

REPORTED IN THIS VOLUME.

Harris,

N

O

P

R

Regina

Wain-

TABLE OF CASES REPORTED.

TABLE OF CASES CITED.

C

D

M

N

O

P

S

T

Y

Z

ERRATA.

Page 240. note (*a*), for "15" read "11."
336. line 17. omit "which the defendants have."
468. line 13. for "plaintiff" read "defendant."
470. marg. note, for "1835" read "1825."
686. line 5. from bottom, for "plaintiffs" read "defendants."
743. last line, for "defendant" read "plaintiff."
779. marg. note, in beginning, dele one "in fee."

CASES

ARGUED AND DETERMINED

1838.

IN THE

Court of QUEEN's BENCH,

AND

UPON WRITS OF ERROR FROM THAT COURT TO THE

EXCHEQUER CHAMBER,

IN

Hilary Term,

In the First Year of the Reign of VICTORIA.

The Judges who usually sat in Banc in this term were

Lord DENMAN C. J. WILLIAMS J.
LITTLEDALE J. COLERIDGE J.

(Continued from Vol. VII.)

DOE on the Demise of REED *against* ALICE HARRIS.

Testator, intending to destroy his will, threw it on the fire; but a devisee under the will snatched it off, and took it away, a corner of the envelope only being burnt. The testator was displeased at her having taken it, and she, being urged by him to give it back, promised to burn it, and pretended to do so in his presence, but did not. Testator afterwards told another person that the devisee had thrown the will on the fire; but, on that party expressing a doubt, testator said that he did not care, and that, if he was alive and well, he would make another. He took no further step either to destroy the old will, or to make a new one. A jury having found that the testator had revoked the will by burning,

Held, in a case of copyhold, to which the Statute of Frauds, 29 *Car.* 2. *c.* 3. *s.* 6. does not extend, and before stat. 7 *W.* 4. & 1 *Vict.* c. 26., that the will was revoked by the attempt to burn, and was not revived after such revocation.

ON the trial of this ejectment, before *Coleridge* J., at the *Glamorganshire* Spring assizes, 1836, it appeared that the action was brought by the heir at law

 against

1838.

Doe dem. Reed against Harris.

against the same devisee who was defendant in *Doe dem. Reed* v. *Harris*, reported, 6 *A. & E.* 209.: and the question, as in that case, was, whether the will had been revoked by the testator's throwing it on the fire, where the envelope had been partially burnt. The evidence was, in all material points, the same as in the former case (*a*); but the lands for which that ejectment was brought were freehold; in the present case the lands were copyhold. The learned Judge left it to the jury to say whether that which the testator did was an actual revocation of the will, and so intended by him; reserving leave, however, to move to enter a nonsuit or a verdict for the defendant, if the verdict should be for the plaintiff and this Court should be of opinion that the Judge ought to have directed a contrary verdict or a nonsuit. The jury said that they thought the will revoked by the burning; and a verdict was taken for the plaintiff. In the ensuing term *John Evans* obtained a rule to shew cause why a verdict should not be entered for the defendant. In *Michaelmas* term, 1837 (*b*),

Chilton and *W. M. James* shewed cause. First, a will of copyhold is not strictly a devise, but rather an appointment or declaration of uses; it is not within the Statute of Wills (*c*); and the enactments of the Statute of Frauds, 29 *Car.* 2. *c.* 3. *s.* 5., do not apply to the execution of such a will. (This point was not contested in argument, and was taken for granted in the judgment of the Court. The authorities cited upon it were, *Tuff-*

(*a*) See *Doe dem. Reed* v. *Harris*, 6 *A. & E.* 209, and the introductory part of the judgment in this case, p. 9. post.

(*b*) *November* 16th. Before Lord *Denman* C. J., *Patteson*, *Williams*, and *Coleridge* Js.

(*c*) 32 *H.* 8. *c.* 1. And see 4 & 35 *H.* 8. *c.* 5.

nell

nell v. *Page* (*a*), *Doe dem. Cook* v. *Danvers* (*b*), 1 *Scriven on Copyhold*, 291, Part I. c. 5. (*c*), *Peake's Law of Evidence*, 457 [426], Part II. c. 17. (*d*), *Royden* v. *Malster* (*e*), *Carey* v. *Askew*, and Mr. *Belt's* note (3) to that case (*g*)). Then, if wills of copyhold may be executed without the formalities required by stat. 29 *Car.* 2. *c.* 3. *s.* 5., they may also be revoked in other ways than those prescribed by sect. 6, which clearly refers to wills executed according to the previous section. In *Mortimer* v. *West* (*h*) a devise of an annuity out of copyhold estates was held to be revoked by a codicil not witnessed according to stat. 29 *Car.* 2. *c.* 3. *s.* 6. In *Vawser* v. *Jeffery* (*i*) it was contended at the bar, and does not seem to have been disputed, that a devise of copyhold lands may be revoked by parol. The authorities there cited, namely, 1 *Roll. Abr.* 614, *Devise*, (O), pl. 1. (*k*), pl. 4. (*l*), *Ford's Case* (*m*), *Burton* v. *Gowell* (*n*), and *Coke* v. *Bullock* (*o*), shew that, before the Statute of frauds, wills of freehold might be revoked by parol, or by act of the testator: *Ex parte the Earl of Ilchester* (*p*) also illustrates this position. Wills of copyhold, having never been operated upon by the statute, must stand upon the same footing. Sect. 22, which enacts that no will in writing "concerning any goods or chattels, or personal estate," shall be repealed "by any words, or will by word of mouth only," unless

(*a*) 2 *Atk.* 37.
(*b*) 7 *East*, 299.
(*c*) 3d ed.
(*d*) 5th ed.
(*e*) 2 *Roll. Rep.* 383.
(*g*) 2 *Bro. C. Ch.* 58. 5th ed.
(*h*) 2 *Sim.* 274.
(*i*) 3 *B. & Ald.* 462.
(*k*) Same placitum, as *Brook* v. *Warde*, *Dyer*, 310. *b.*
(*l*) *Frenche's Case.*
(*m*) 1 *Sid.* 73.
(*n*) *Cro. Eliz.* 306.
(*o*) *Cro. Jac.* 49.
(*p*) 7 *Ves.* 348.

 committed

1838.

Doe dem. Reed against Harris.

committed to writing in the testator's lifetime, &c., does not apply to copyhold property; and, even if it did, the revocation here is by more than words. A question on this clause, as to the personalty, is still depending in the Ecclesiastical Court. In *Walcot* v. *Ochterlony* (*a*), decided by Sir *Herbert Jenner*, in the Prerogative Court of *Canterbury*, *July* 19th, 1837, the deceased, having made a will, which remained in the hands of Mr. *George*, one of the persons appointed executors, caused a letter to be written desiring that the will might be destroyed. The executor did not destroy it; and the deceased was never informed, down to the time of her death, whether her desire had been complied with or not; but she died without having altered her intention to revoke, and in the belief that she had done so; and this (in a case within the Statute of frauds) was held a good revocation. Where the alleged revocation is by an act, it is

(*a*) Not yet published. The reporters are indebted to Dr. *Curteis* fo a note of Sir *H. Jenner's* judgment, from which the following is an extract. After stating that the first question was the intention of the deceased, and that the animus revocandi was clear, the learned Judge said: —

"What does the law require to give effect to such intention? The Statute of Frauds provides that no will in writing of personal estate shall be repealed, nor any clause or bequest therein altered or changed, by any words. Is this a revocation by words? I apprehend not. The deceased did not say, 'I revoke my will,' but in effect says, 'Mr. *George* is in possession of my will; I am not able to destroy it myself, but I desire that he will destroy it;' and this amounted to a present intention absolutely to revoke, which was written down at the time, approved by the deceased, and by her direction communicated to the person in whose custody the will was. It was an absolute direction to revoke, reduced into writing in the deceased's lifetime. There is nothing in the Statute of frauds which prevents such revocation having effect; and it is clear that, prior to that statute, a will might be so revoked. Further, the deceased subsequently directed a letter to be written to Mr. *George*, intimating that is a question upon the evidence, whether or not a revocation was intended; as, in *Frenche's Case* (*a*), where the testator devised lands to one, and then devised the same lands to the poor of the parish, that was held to be a revocation, though the second devise was void. In the present case there was evidence for the jury of an intent to revoke. It is not necessary that that intent should be declared by words; although there were, in this case, words intimating that such an intention had existed. [*Patteson* J. Is there any case in which an act without words has been held a sufficient revocation at common law?] *Frenche's Case* (*a*) is one. [*Patteson* J. In that case there was a writing inconsistent with the prior devise.] A party may shew the intent to destroy by acts as unequivocal as any words. The former decision in *Doe dem. Reed* v. *Harris* (*b*), where the act was held insufficient, proceeded strictly on sect. 6 of the Statute of Frauds. Parol revocations have been held good, not upon any technical principle, but only because they shewed conclusively that the testator had changed his mind. But the same inference may be drawn from any other fact which shews clearly that the testator's former intention cannot have continued: as a feoffment not effectual for want of a good livery of seisin, or a bargain and sale not properly enrolled; or a change in the testator's estate or circumstances, as by

that she would give her reasons thereafter, and evinced anxiety for a reply to that letter down to the time of her death. There could be no doubt that she died in the intention to revoke the will, and in the belief that it was revoked. I am of opinion that the will in this case is revoked, and that the deceased is dead intestate."

(*a*) 1 *Roll. Abr.* 614, *Devise* (O), pl. 4.

(*b*) 6 *A.* & *E.* 209. *S. C.* 1 *N.* & *P.* 405.

1838.

Doe dem. Reed against Harris.

marriage and the birth of a child (*a*). The authorities on these points are collected in 2 *Sheppard's Touchstone* (*b*) pp. 410, 411. *c.* 23.; 8 *Vin. Abr.* 134; tit. *Devise*, (P); 2 *Roberts on Wills*, 20 (*c*); part IV. c. 1. s. 4. If the intention be not wholly unequivocal in the alleged act of revocation, still the construction of it is for the jury. In stat. 7 *W.* 4. & 1 *Vict. c.* 26. *s.* 20. the legislature, in altering the provisions of stat. 29 *Car.* 2. *c.* 3. *s.* 6., as to revocation of wills, has made the animus revocandi essential, while it allows the revocation to take place, not only by burning or tearing, but by "otherwise destroying," the will.

Maule, *John Evans*, and *E. V. Williams*, contrà. The Statute of frauds did not introduce any new modes of revocation, but prohibited some, leaving the rest to be governed by the same rules as before. Where it enacts that burning shall be a revocation, it does not mean any burning, but such as would have been equivalent to a cancellation before the statute. A burning which would now be insufficient is so, not by reason of the statute, but because the animus revocandi is not clearly shewn. It is immaterial, therefore, that the present is a case of copyhold: the former judgment in *Doe dem. Reed* v. *Harris* (*d*) is decisive here. In *Bibb dem. Mole* v. *Thomas* (*e*) the testator had done all that he intended to do, and could do, as to burning and tearing the will. Here, if there was evidence of an intention to destroy the will, there was no proof of any thing done by the testator or by his direction to carry that design into effect. His declarations, after the supposed burning, are no

(*a*) See the next case. (*b*) 7th (*Preston's*) ed. (*c*) 3d ed.
(*d*) 6 *A.* & *E.* 209. (*e*) 2 *W. Bl.* 1043.

evidence

1838.

Doe dem. Reed against Harris.

evidence of any fact to which they relate. Declarations of a testator are not evidence to invalidate his own will; *Provis* v. *Reed* (a). [*Coleridge* J. There were also declarations of the defendant herself.] The expressions of the testator upon the whole imply a supposition by him that the will was still extant when he used them: there was nothing which shewed, at any time, a present intention in him to revoke. The case therefore differs from that in 1 *Roll. Abr.* 614, *Devise*, (O), pl. 1. (b), where a man revoked his will by parol in the presence of certain persons, requiring their testimony of his present revocation, and saying that he would alter the will when he came to *D.*, which, however, he did not live to do. So in *Walcot* v. *Ochterlony* (c) the testatrix had made a present intimation of her desire that the will should be destroyed: she had done every thing that lay in her for that purpose. In *Cranvel* v. *Sanders* (d) it was held that a testator's saying he has made his will, but it shall not stand, is no revocation, these being "words but in futuro." [*Patteson* J. *Burton* v. *Gowell* (e) seems a contrary decision.] *Thomas dem Jones* v. *Evans* (g) and *Doe dem. Perkes* v. *Perkes* (h) are instances in which the revocation has been held not to have gone beyond intention, and therefore to have been incomplete. [*Patteson* J. What do you say to the cases in which a will has been held to be revoked by an imperfect conveyance?] They are anomalous, and of a class which perhaps would not now be introduced into the law. They are attempts to take away

(a) 5 *Bing.* 435.
(b) Same placitum, as *Brook* v. *Warde*, *Dyer*, 310 b.
(c) Antè, p. 4., note (a).
(d) *Cro. Jac.* 497.
(e) *Cro. Eliz.* 306.
(g) 2 *East*, 488.
(h) 3 *B. & Ald.* 489.

the

1838.

Doe dem. Reed against Harris.

the subject-matter upon which the will was to operate, but are not, in a proper sense, revocations. At all events, however, there is, in those cases, a present execution of an intent, as far as lies in the testator. [*Patteson* J. The expressions of Lord *Eldon* in *Vawser* v. *Jeffery* (*a*) are strong, and put the point differently. "If this proceeds to a case, my notion would be to suggest" "whether, if the testator had attempted to convey his copyhold estate in the same manner as he has conveyed his freehold estate, that would not afford evidence of his intention, however incomplete the conveyance may be?"] That means "evidence of his intention" to pass the copyhold by the act he was then doing. The law as to words or acts expressing an intention to revoke at the time or in future is summed up in 8 *Vin. Abr.* 133—136., *Devise*, (O), (P), and note (4) to *Duppa* v. *Mayo* (*b*). [*Patteson* J. In 1 *Powell on Devises*, 516, c. 13. (*c*) it is said, "If one, saying that he had made his will, added that it should not stand; or that he would alter it; these words would not have been a revocation; for they are words but *in futuro* (*d*)." But it is laid down in the same page that, "if a man said, *animo revocandi*, 'my will made at *A.* shall not stand,' that had been an immediate revocation; for it referred to a present resolution (*e*)."] In 2 *Shepp. Touchst.* 411. c. 23. (*g*) it is said, "But note here, that revocations in general are not favoured in law; and therefore he that will avoid a former will by revocation, must see he prove it [the revocation] well." It is a mixed question of law and fact,

(*a*) 2 *Swanst.* 274.

(*b*) 1 *Wms. Saund.* 278 *h.*

(*c*) 3d (*Jarman's*) ed.

(*d*) Citing *Cranvell* v. *Sanders*, *Cro. Jac.* 497.

(*e*) Citing *Burton* v. *Gowell*, *Cro. Eliz.* 306.

(*g*) 7th (*Preston's*) ed.

1838.

DOE dem. REED against HARRIS.

fact, to be laid before the jury, who are to decide, under all the circumstances, whether there was a determined intention to revoke. A mere throwing on the fire is not sufficient. [*Patteson* J. This Court has held that, under the Statute of Frauds, there must be some actual burning of the will itself. It does not follow that, at common law, throwing it on the fire in the envelope may not be sufficient.] A particular mode of cancellation may not be requisite at common law, as it is under the statute: but, if the testator chooses any mode, he must pursue it effectually. Here the facts of the case, and among them the testator's declarations after the attempt to burn, shew that the act was merely inchoate. And, further, as a will not affected by the Statute of frauds may be republished by parol, those declarations, even if the will had been cancelled, amounted to a republication: *Brotherton* v. *Hellier* (*a*), and *Slade* v. *Dr. Friend* (*b*), there cited. [*Patteson* J. The testator here never asserted, after the attempt to burn the paper, that it was his will. He expressed a wish to have it back, but that was for the purpose of destroying it.] He permitted it to remain in existence, and made no other will.

Cur. adv. vult.

Lord DENMAN C. J. in *Hilary* term, 1838 (*January* 20th), delivered the judgment of the Court.

This was an action of ejectment for copyhold premises by the heir at law of the person last seised against one who claimed as his devisee. The plaintiff succeeded at the trial; but leave was given to the defendant

(*a*) 2 *Sir G. Lee's Judgments* (edited by Dr. *Phillimore*), 55.

(*b*) 2 *Sir G. Lee's Judgments*, 84.

to

1838.

Doe dem. Reed against Harris.

to move for a nonsuit, or for a verdict in his favour. On discussing a rule granted in conformity to this permission, the question was, whether the will (admitted to have been duly executed) had been well revoked. The facts lay in a narrow compass. The testator was much under the influence of the devisee, who lived with him as his housekeeper, but, according to the testimony of a witness to whom the jury gave credit, he had frequent quarrels with her, often complained of her behaviour towards him, and on one occasion, when irritated, he threw the will upon the fire: she rescued it without his knowledge, at which he expressed his displeasure when informed of it. The paper in which it was wrapt was thereby partially burnt; but the will itself was not affected by the fire. The devisee kept it till after the testator's death.

These circumstances being established in evidence, the learned Judge asked the jury whether what was then done by the testator was an actual revocation of the will and so intended by him. In another case tried between the same parties (*a*) the same question had arisen; and upon the same facts the Court was of opinion that the will was not revoked. That ejectment was, however, brought to recover freehold lands; and our decision proceeded wholly on the express enactment of the Statute of Frauds. [His Lordship here read sect. 6 of stat. 29 *Car.* 2. *c.* 3.]

There the will itself was not burnt: we therefore thought that the statute prevented it from being revoked, and that no evidence whatever of what was said, proving an intention to revoke, could supply that deficiency. But, the property now in question being copyhold, to

(*a*) *Doe dem. Reed* v. *Harris*, 6 *A.* & *E.* 209.

which

1838.

Doe dem. Reed against Harris.

which the Statute of Frauds does not apply, because it is not devisable within the Statute of Wills, the point is different, and must be treated as if the first-mentioned act had never passed. In that case, the law would have required clear evidence of a positive declaration of the intent to revoke at the time such declaration was made; or some act done with the intent thereby to revoke; and the jury would have had to determine whether in fact such declaration was made or act done.

Some doubt has been entertained whether any declaration could be sufficient without the word "revoke;" but, upon full consideration, we think it impossible so to limit the testator's power of revocation, and that any equivalent word or words and expressions would be sufficient for that purpose.

But, further, we are now required to consider whether, without any language at all, a testator may revoke a will by the conduct he exhibits. And this appears to be tantamount to an inquiry whether conduct *can* give a positive declaration of intent. If it can, there can be no more *necessity* for words than for the use of a particular expression. Now, nothing is easier than to imagine such gestures and proceedings, connected with the will, as must fully convince every rational mind that the testator intended to revoke his will, and thought he had done so by the means he took for that purpose. But if he who has power to revoke by declaring a present resolution then to do so does in fact make that resolution manifest, it seems clear that the act of revocation is complete in every essential part.

This proposition is not inconsistent with any authority in our books. Any doubt that may rest upon it may probably be the result of our habit of considering the

subject

1838.

Doe dem. Reed against Harris.

subject since the Statute of Frauds. That law, one of the wisest in principle, though far from being complete in its details or fortunate in its execution, enacts certain formalities for giving effect to the revocation of a will; and the obvious good sense of that provision has in some way embodied itself with our ideas of revocation. But the law with respect to wills not within that statute is the same as it was before the statute.

This use was made of our former decision between the same parties:—the will was intended to be revoked by burning, but the burning was not complete, and the will was held not to be revoked; it follows, as the revoking act was not performed, that there was no revocation. But this is clearly a fallacy. Burning the will is one of the modes of revocation permitted by the Statute of Frauds: it follows that there must be burning of the will to some extent to satisfy the enactment: but this is a case of revocation at common law, which only requires evidence of intention; and that evidence may be found in an imperfect act or a mere attempt. The duty then of the judge, in trying a question as to such revocation of a will, was to lay before the jury the facts proved, and ask whether they amounted to a revocation. This was done on the present occasion: there was certainly evidence from which the inference might be drawn, and by which we think it was warranted. On this point, then, there is no ground for a new trial.

There was one other argument which requires notice. The testator was aware that his devisee had taken the will off the fire; he expressed his annoyance that she had recovered possession of it, and his intention to make a new will instead of it; yet he took no further steps towards its destruction or the making a new will. He

was

1838.

Doe dem. Reed against Harris.

was therefore said to acquiesce in its continuance; the revocation itself was said to be revoked and the will revived. This state of things may certainly exist: and, if there was evidence of it, such evidence ought to have been submitted to the jury. But we cannot think that the mere knowledge of the continuing existence in specie of a will intended to be destroyed, when accompanied with no wish to restore its efficacy, but, on the contrary, with great displeasure at its rescue from the flames, does constitute such evidence.

The recent act (*a*) for amending the law of wills will propably prevent any future agitation of a question like the present, as the third section makes all property devisable, and the twentieth and twenty-second prescribe the mode of revoking wills and of reviving such as may have been revoked.

Rule discharged (*b*).

(*a*) 7 *W.* 4. & 1 *Vict. c.* 26.

(*b*) See the next case.

1838.

IN THE EXCHEQUER CHAMBER.

(Error from the Queen's Bench.)

WILLIAM MARSTON *against* ROE on the several Demises of WILLIAM JOHN FOX and WILLIAM HALTON. And ROE, on the same Demises, *against* WILLIAM MARSTON.

In the case of a will made before stat. 7 *W.* 4. & 1 *Vict.* c. 26. the following points were decided by the Judges of the Queen's Bench (absente Lord *Denman* C. J.), Common Pleas, and Exchequer, in the Exchequer Chamber.

Where an unmarried man, without children by a former marriage, devises all the property he has at the time of making his will, and leaves no provision for any child of a future marriage, the law annexes to such will the tacit condition that, if he afterwards marries and has a child born of such marriage, the will shall be revoked.

And evidence (not amounting to proof of republication) cannot be received in a court of law to shew that the testator meant his will to stand good, notwithstanding the subsequent marriage and birth of issue.

Such revocation is not prevented by a provision in the will, or otherwise, for the future wife only: the children of the marriage must also be provided for.

Semble, that such revocation is not prevented if property acquired by the testator after making his will descend upon the child of such marriage on the testator's death.

It is not prevented if the child takes a legal estate only, and no beneficial interest, in the property so descending.

F. made a will as above-mentioned. Before that event, *J.* had contracted for the purchase of an estate at *M.*; possession was given, but no conveyance executed. *J.* then died intestate, leaving *F.* his heir at law and sole next of kin. *F.* then made his will, and afterwards the estate was conveyed to him. Held, that the estate was not after-acquired property, but that, by reason of *F.*'s equitable interest, derived from *J.*, it was one of the subjects of devise in the will made and revoked as above stated.

In an action of ejectment by *F.*'s heir at law against the devisee under such will, for the devised estates: Held, that the plaintiff might give parol evidence that *J.* purchased the property at *M.* as agent for *F.*, the testator, although *J.* had contracted, in writing, for the purchase, in his own name.

Held also, upon bill of exceptions, that the following evidence was admissible for the defendant, the devisee, in the same cause, the bill not stating for what purpose it was tendered.

Two former wills of the testator; the first devising all his estates to *J.*, subject to an annuity to *A. B.* (whom testator afterwards married); for raising which annuity a term in certain lands was granted to defendant: the second devising certain lands to *A. B.* for life, and all the residue of his estates to defendant.

A verbal direction given by the testator, after the will made, and shortly before his marriage, that a clause barring dower should be omitted in the conveyance to him, then preparing, of certain premises.

THIS case was brought by three writs of error from the Court of Queen's Bench, where judgment had been given for the lessor of the plaintiff on a special verdict. The plaintiff below brought ejectment to recover certain lands in *Staffordshire*, the trial of which action

was

1838.

Marston *against* Roe dem. Fox.

was removed, by a suggestion on the record, to *Gloucester*, where it took place before *Alderson* B. (*a*). Upon the trial, cross bills of exceptions were tendered to, and allowed by, the learned Judge; that on the part of the lessor of the plaintiff containing exceptions, as well against admissions of evidence given by the defendant below, as also for the rejection of evidence which he had offered; that on the part of the defendant below for the rejection of evidence only. One of the writs of error was sued out by the defendant below to bring up the judgment which was given for the plaintiff, without argument, on the special verdict; and each party brought up his own bill of exceptions by a writ of error sued out by himself.

The jury found for the plaintiff as to the premises stated in the declaration to have been demised by *William Halton*. And, as to the residue of the premises, alleged to have been demised by *W. J. Fox*, they found a special verdict. The verdict stated:—

That on *January* 17th, 1835, *John Fox* made his last will, duly executed &c., and thereby devised as follows. "I give and devise" &c. (specifying certain messuages and lands) "unto and to the use of my friend *Anne Bakewell*, of *Uttoxeter* aforesaid, spinster, and her assigns, for and during the term of her natural life, or so long thereof as she shall remain sole and unmarried, subject, nevertheless, to impeachment of waste: and, from and after the decease or marriage of the said *Anne Bakewell*, which shall first happen, I give and devise the said messuages, dwelling-houses or tenements, buildings, yards, gardens, farms, lands and hereditaments, with the appurtenances, to my

(*a*) At the Spring assizes, 1836.

relation

1838.

MARSTON against ROE dem. FOX.

relation *William Marston*, of *Manchester* in the county palatine of *Lancaster*, cork merchant, his heirs and assigns for ever." "And" (after some further devises not material here, to relations and others) "I give, devise and bequeath all my messuages, farms, lands, tenements, tithes, rents, hereditaments and real estate, and parts and shares of such (not hereinbefore given, devised, and disposed of), wheresoever situate in *Great Britain*, and whether freehold, copyhold or customary, and whether in possession, reversion, remainder, contingency or expectancy, with all rights, members and appurtenances thereto respectively belonging; and also all my monies, securities for money, goods, cattle, chattels, rights, credits, effects and personal estate whatsoever and wheresoever, and of what nature, kind or quality soever, unto the said *William Marston*, his heirs, executors, administrators and assigns for ever, according to the respective natures and tenures thereof; nevertheless subject" to debts &c.

That from *March* 25th 1834, down to the time when he executed the said will, the testator contemplated a marriage with the said *Anne Bakewell*. That he married her on *February* 21st, 1835, and lived with her until the time of his death. That from the time of his marriage until his death he was in a bad state of health; and that on *May* 11th, 1835, he was taken ill, and died in about two hours. And that at the time of his death he was seised in fee-simple in possesion of the residue of the hereditaments and premises mentioned in the will, and demised by the said *William John Fox*.

That the said will was, in a short time after the death of the said *John Fox*, found in his bedroom in an oak chest of which he had kept the key; and that *Elizabeth Stone*,

1838.

MARSTON *against* ROE dem. FOX.

Stone, the person who had found the will, had been told by the testator, ten weeks before his death, where he had deposited his will.

That, on 16th *October* 1835, the said wife of *John Fox* was delivered of the said *William John Fox*, one of the lessors of the plaintiff, who is the only son and heir at law of the said *John Fox*.

That the said *John Fox* was seised in fee of certain lands, tenements, and hereditaments, and continued so seised until the time of his death, out of which lands, tenements, and hereditaments his widow would be entitled to dower, unless she was deprived thereof by the operation of his will, or by operation of law.

That the testator, on 20th *November* 1834, had agreed to purchase a house for 690*l.* for the purpose of residing in it when married. That in the draft of conveyance sent to the testator for his perusal was inserted a declaration that "any wife testator might take should not be entitled to dower." That testator requested that such clause should be struck out; and that, upon its being explained to him as he was on the point of marriage, that, if, after he was married, he wished to resell the property, he could not do so without the consent of his wife, he said he was perfectly aware of that, and that he did not intend to debar his wife of dower.

That, on the 30th *September* 1829, *Joseph Fox*, the brother of the said *John Fox*, entered into a written contract for the purchase of some property at *Marston Montgomery*, in the county of *Derby*, at the sum of 463*l.* 14*s.* 6*d.*, with *Thomas Harrison* and others, trustees under the will of *John Etches* deceased. That, on 25th *March* following, the said *John Fox* was let into possession of the last mentioned premises; but, the

1838.

MARSTON *against* ROE dem. FOX.

titles not being then complete, it was agreed that he should receive the rents and profits from that period, and should pay interest to the said trustees on the purchase-money, until the purchase was completed.

That, after this agreement, the said *John Fox*, in like manner as the purchasers of other parts of the same estate, which was sold in lots, was let into possession of the property so contracted for by the said *Joseph Fox*, and let the same to *John Deaville*, who held the same as tenant, and paid rent half yearly to *John Fox*, from the said 25th of *March* 1830 until the time of his decease, some of which payments were made in the presence of his brother *Joseph*. That no other contract than the one before mentioned to have been entered into, by the said *Joseph Fox* with the said *Thomas Harrison* and others, was made for the sale of the said last mentioned property.

That, on 17th *November* 1834, the said *Joseph Fox* died unmarried and intestate, seised of considerable real estates in fee simple in possession, which thereupon descended to the said *John Fox* as his only brother and heir at law; and that *John Fox* was the sole next of kin of *Joseph Fox*, and entitled to administration of the personal estate of which he died possessed.

That by lease and release, bearing date 6th and 7th *March* 1835, the said property at *Marston Montgomery* was conveyed by the surviving trustees under *John Etches*'s will to the said *John Fox*, in consideration of 463*l.* 14*s.* 6*d.*, and he thereupon paid the said purchase-money, and interest thereupon from 25th *March* 1830.

That, in *August* 1835, the said *John Deaville* paid half a year's rent, due for the same premises on the 25th *March*

1838.

MARSTON against ROE dem. FOX.

March preceding, to *John Hordern*, who was one of the executors of the said *John Fox*.

That the value of the real estate left by the said *John Fox* amounts to about 49,000*l*.

Error was assigned upon the judgment in the common form; and the plaintiff below joined in error.

The plaintiff below (the defendant in error), in his bill of exceptions, stated that the defendant below, on the trial, admitted the title of *W. J. Fox* as heir at law, and consented to a verdict for the plaintiff below as to the premises stated to have been demised by *W. Halton*; but that, as to the residue of the premises, he insisted on his own title as devisee under the will of *John Fox*, dated *January* 17th, 1835. The plaintiff below then stated the following grounds of exception.

First, that the defendant below (before putting in the will of *January* 1835), offered in evidence a will of *John Fox*, dated *March* 25th, 1834, in which he bequeathed to *William Marston* (the defendant below) and another, for the life of *Anne Bakewell*, an annuity of 40*l*., upon trust to pay the same to her, and not to any husband or assignee, &c.; and he made the annuity payable out of the rents of certain lands, which he bequeathed to the trustees for the term of ninety-nine years (if *Anne Bakewell* should so long live) for that purpose; and, subject to the above bequests, he devised all his estates, lands, &c., and personalty, to his brother, *Joseph Fox*, his heirs, executors, &c., for ever. That the defendant below likewise offered in evidence a will of *John Fox*, dated *December* 1st, 1834, whereby he devised certain messuages and lands to *Anne Bakewell* for her life, and from and after her decease to the said *William Marston* in fee; he also bequeathed certain legacies; and,

1838.

Marston *against* Roe dem. Fox.

and, subject &c. he left all the residue of his real and personal estates to *W. Marston*, the defendant below, his heirs, executors, &c., for ever; and he appointed *W. Marston* and another his executors. That the counsel for the plaintiff below objected to the admission of these wills of 1834, but that the learned Judge received them, whereupon the plaintiff's counsel excepted, &c.

The second ground of exception was the admission in evidence of *John Fox*'s declaration, under the circumstances stated in the special verdict (antè, p. 17.), that he did not intend to debar his wife of dower. The bill of exceptions stated this evidence to have been objected to at the trial, on behalf of the plaintiff below, but received; whereupon &c.

Thirdly, the bill of exceptions stated that the plaintiff below, at the trial, proved the contract entered into by *Joseph Fox* with *Harrison* and others, for the purchase of property at *Marston Montgomery*, as stated in the special verdict; and it set out the contract as follows: "*Joseph Fox*, of *Uttoxeter*, in the county of *Stafford*, tanner, doth hereby acknowledge himself to be the highest bidder for the purchase of the premises described in the annexed particulars, in lots 2 and 3, under the above conditions, at the price or sum of" &c.; "and he hereby agrees to pay the said purchase monies pursuant to these conditions, and in all other respects to be bound by and perform the same; and the vendors" (naming them) "do hereby agree to sell the said tenements and premises mentioned in this contract, to the said *Joseph Fox*, under the above conditions, at the prices aforesaid. Dated the 30th day of *September*, 1829. *Joseph Fox*. *Benjamin Carnell*. *Thomas Carnell*." Then followed a specification of the lots. The bill then

1838.

MARSTON *against* ROE dem. FOX.

then stated, as in the special verdict (antè, p. 17.), the facts proved, from the letting of *John Fox* into possession to the payment of rent by *Deaville*. It then proceeded: "And the counsel for the said *Richard Roe*, further to prove the said issue on his part, and for the purpose of shewing that it was the said *John Fox* who entered into the said contract for the purchase of the said premises at *Marston Montgomery*, and that the said *Joseph Fox* was the agent for the said *John Fox* in that behalf, and had signed the contract as such agent, then and there tendered and proposed to give parol evidence that, on the 30th day of *September* 1829, the said *Joseph Fox* (the brother of the said *John Fox*) was appointed by the said *John Fox* his agent, for the purpose of making the agreement aforesaid for the purchase of the said premises; and that, in consequence of such appointment, the said *Joseph Fox* did, in his own name, but as such agent as aforesaid and on behalf of the said *John Fox*, sign the said agreement; and that both the said *Joseph Fox* and *John Fox*, in the year 1830, within three months after the said agreement was so signed as aforesaid by the said *Joseph Fox*, gave instructions to one *James Blair*, the attorney who prepared the deed of conveyance of the same hereditaments and premises, that the same should be conveyed to the said *John Fox*, and not to the said *Joseph Fox*; and that the same were so conveyed accordingly." And the bill of exceptions stated that this evidence was objected to by the counsel for the defendant below, and that the learned Judge rejected it, whereupon &c.

The plaintiff below assigned for error that the evidence objected to by him "ought not," and that the evidence tendered by him as above mentioned "ought to have

1838.

Marston against Roe dem. Fox.

have been admitted and allowed." The defendant below joined in error.

The defendant below, in his bill of exceptions, stated that it was admitted, on the trial, that the testator contemplated marriage when he made his will of *January* 17th, 1835. That the counsel for the defendant below offered in evidence certain letters of the testator to him, which were set out, written subsequently to the will, and expressing much kindness to the defendant. Also a letter written to the defendant after the marriage, announcing it, but stating that no act of the testator's should ever prejudice the interest of relatives, and subscribed, "Your truly sincere and affectionate cousin, *John Fox*." Also a verbal declaration of the testator, a week or ten days before his death, that he had made his will and that he would not alter it, as it was so it should stand; that he had left the chief part of his property to his friend, Mr. *William Marston;* and that he had taken care the *Bakewells* should not have any part of his property; and other expressions to a similar effect between the marriage and death of the testator. Also a statement by him, about a month before his marriage, that he was going to be married to *Ann Bakewell;* that he had made his will; that he had left her a very handsome fortune whether he married her or not; and that he had left Mr. *Marston* the biggest bulk of his property, by the wish of his brother: and other declarations, both before and after the marriage, importing that his property would fall into the hands of *Marston*, the defendant below.

The bill of exceptions then stated that the counsel for the plaintiff below objected to the reception of these letters and declarations, and the learned Judge excluded them; whereupon &c.

The

1838.

MARSTON *against* ROE dem. FOX.

The defendant below assigned for error that the evidence "ought to have been admitted and allowed, to entitle the said defendant to a verdict." Joinder.

An action of trover for the title-deeds of the same estate had been brought by the lessor of the plaintiff against the defendant below in the Court of Exchequer, and came on for trial before *Alderson* B. at the same assizes; and, as the same question arose in both actions, a course precisely similar was pursued in both; and, for the purpose of avoiding as well unnecessary expense to the parties as loss of time to the respective Courts of error, it was thought convenient that the argument of the writs of error in the first mentioned cause should take place in the presence of all the Judges of the three Courts of *Westminster Hall*, the parties having consented that both cases should abide the decision of the present.

This case was argued *June* 13th, and *November* 1st and 27th, 1837, before *Tindal* C. J., Lord *Abinger* C. B., *Littledale, Patteson, Williams, Coleridge, Park, Bosanquet, Vaughan* and *Coltman* Js., and *Parke, Bolland, Alderson* and *Gurney* Bs.

Sir *J. Campbell*, Attorney-General, for the plaintiff in error (the defendant below). As to the special verdict. The plaintiff in error is entitled under the will of *January* 17th, 1835, unless it has been revoked. There has been no revocation under the Statute of Frauds. Marriage and the birth of a child after the execution of a will undoubtedly revoke it under some circumstances; *Overbury* v. *Overbury* (*a*) decides this as to personalty, and *Christopher* v. *Christopher* (*b*) as to realty: but there is

(*a*) 2 *Show.* 242.

(*b*) 4 *Burr.* 2182. *S. C.* 2 *Dickens*, 445. See 1 *Williams on Executors*, 106. notes (*f*), (*g*). Part I. B. II: c. 3. s. 5. 2d ed.

1838.

MARSTON against ROE dem. FOX.

is no rule that they shall do so at all events. In the first place, the Court will look at the testator's intention as appearing on the face of the will, and in acts done and declarations made by him before and after he executed it, and will not consider the will revoked, if a clear intention appears to keep it alive. If, for instance, the testator were to say in express terms, that he intended the will to stand although, after executing it, he should marry and have a child of the marriage, the will would hold good notwithstanding those events, and though the wife and child should be unprovided for. Secondly, the will is not revoked by marriage and the birth of a child, if there be a provision made for the wife and child, though it should not appear that such provision is made by the will itself.

As to the first point, it will be contended on the other side that marriage and the birth of a child revoke a will by the operation of law; that is, either the law supposes a tacit condition annexed to the devise, that those events shall revoke it, or the occurrence of those events is of itself a revocation in law. But the cases shew that there is no rule which excludes consideration of the testator's intent. In *Overbury* v. *Overbury* (a) the decision was merely "that if a man make his will and dispose of his personal estate amongst his relations, and afterwards has children and dies, that this is a revocation of his will, according to the notion of the civilians, this being an *inofficiosum testamentum*." In *Lugg* v. *Lugg* (b) (where a common lawyer, *Treby* C. J. of C. P., was one of the Delegates) marriage and birth of children were held to be a presumptive revocation only

(a) 2 *Show.* 243. (b) 1 *Ld. Ray.* 441. *S. C.* 2 *Salk.* 592.

of

1838.

MARSTON *against* ROE dem. FOX.

of a will of personalty, and not a revocation, "if by any expression, or any other means, it had appeared that the intent of *A.*" (the testator) "was that this will should continue in force." The rule on this subject is borrowed from the spiritual courts, where the circumstances in question are held to raise a presumption only, capable of being rebutted. In *Spraage* v. *Stone* (*a*) those circumstances were deemed to be a revocation; but there the intent was clear, and a second will, unattested, appears to have been relied on as evidence of it. And in *Brown* v. *Thompson* (*b*), where the testator devised to *E. C.*, whom he purposed to marry, and afterwards married her, and died leaving her pregnant, the will was held not to be revoked, reference being evidently had to the presumable intention. *Thompson* v. *Sheppard* (*c*) appears to have been decided on the same principle. The testator there, a widower having children, made a will of personalty, and afterwards married, had a child born of that marriage, and died leaving real and personal estates. The will was held not to be revoked, the offspring of the second marriage not being unprovided for. In *Brady, Lessee of Norris,* v. *Cubitt* (*d*) (where memorandums, and a verbal declaration of the testator, were admitted as shewing his intention) Lord *Mansfield* said (referring to *Shepherd* v. *Shepherd* (*e*)), "In that case" "the child was totally unprovided for. A subsequent marriage, and the birth of a child, affords a mere presumption. There may be many circumstances where a revocation may be presumed." "But, upon

(*a*) *Ambl.* 721.

(*b*) 1 *Eq. Ca. Abr.* 413. pl. 15. *S. C.* 1 *P. Wms.* 304. note †, 6th ed.

(*c*) Cited in *Sheath* v. *York*, 1 *Ves. & B.* 391. and 394.; and note (*a*) to p. 394. Also in *Emerson* v. *Boville*, 1 *Phillim.* 343.

(*d*) 1 *Doug.* 31.

(*e*) 5 *T. R.* 51. note (*a*).

my

1838.

MARSTON against ROE dem. FOX.

my recollection there is no case in which marriage and the birth of a child have been held to raise an implied revocation, where there has not been a disposition of the *whole* estate." "In such cases, the inference is excessively strong in favour of the wife and children." Lord *Mansfield* then argues upon the intention of the testator in the case before the Court, and continues: — "Suppose a man had given several legacies by a will, and had devised all his real estate to the use of his children when he should have any: would a subsequent marriage and the birth of a child have revoked a will of that sort? — But I am clear on the other ground, that this presumption, like all others, may be rebutted by every sort of evidence." And *Buller* J. says, "Implied revocations must depend on the circumstances at the time of the testator's death." In *Doe dem. Lancashire* v. *Lancashire* (a) it was decided that marriage and the birth of a posthumous child revoked a will of lands: and the Court there rejected parol evidence; but that evidence consisted of direct declarations by the testator of his intention to revoke, the reception of which would have been contrary to the Statute of frauds. In *Ex parte the Earl of Ilchester* (b) marriage and birth of children were held not to revoke a will, the testator having provided, by a settlement, for the children of that marriage. [Lord *Abinger* C. B. The will, there, though made during a former marriage, gave the real estates to the heirs male of the testator's body, generally.] The principle of the decision is, that there may be a provision, by means of a settlement made after the will, which shall prevent its being revoked by marriage and birth of children: and the point is so stated by Sir

(a) 5 *T. R.* 49.

(b) 7 *Ves.* 348.

John

1838.

MARSTON *against* ROE dem. FOX.

John Nicholl, in *Johnston* v. *Johnston* (*a*). In *Sheath* v. *York* (*b*) the testator, when he made his will (of real and personal estate), had a son living who would have been his heir: and it was held that a subsequent marriage, and the birth of a child, who would not have been the testator's heir, did not revoke the will. That decision proceeded wholly on the ground of intent. The judgment of Lord *Ellenborough* in *Kenebel* v. *Scrafton* (*c*) does not impugn the doctrine of intent; and the circumstance there relied upon was, that the wife and children were parties provided for by the testator. The argument from "a total want of provision" for the new family (p. 542.) did not arise. And it is not denied there that evidence, even of parol declarations by the testator, may be admitted to rebut the implied revocation. *Johnson* v. *Wells* (*d*) (in the Ecclesiastical Court) shews that, to prevent revocation from taking place, the provision for the new family need not be by the will itself; the wife there was provided for by a settlement upon her, after marriage, of property left to her separate use by her father. *Talbot* v. *Talbot* (*e*) (also in the spiritual court) is to the same effect; and it would seem that the amount of provision is not material. And, on the question how far circumstances may rebut a presumptive revocation, decisions in the ecclesiastical courts are as strong authority as those in the courts of common law, since, by stat. 29 *Car.* 2. *c.* 3. *s.* 22., a will of personalty cannot be revoked by parol merely.

In the present case, then, according to the authorities, if any presumption arises of a revocation, it is rebutted

(*a*) 1 *Phillim.* 447. See p. 471.
(*b*) 1 *Ves. & B.* 390.
(*c*) 2 *East*, 530.
(*d*) 2 *Hagg. Ecc. Rep.* 561.
(*e*) 1 *Hagg. Ecc. Rep.* 705.

by

1838.

Marston against Roe dem. Fox.

by the facts. The testator, when he executed his will of *January* 1835, contemplated marriage with *Anne Bakewell*, and therefore could not intend that the marriage should revoke his will. [*Parke* B. Contemplation of marriage is a vague phrase. He might not know that she would accept him.] He left her the estate for so long time as she should remain unmarried, evidently intending her to hold, as his widow, dum sola et casta; or, at any rate, if she did not marry him, then as his devisee so long as she married no other person.

But, further, the will is unrevoked, on the ground that the future wife and child are otherwise provided for. The testator's direction, on purchasing a house in 1834, that the conveyance should not contain a clause to bar dower, shews that he then meant the wife to be provided for in that manner: and the verdict finds that he died seised of lands out of which she was dowable, unless deprived of dower by the will or by operation of law. Stat. 3 & 4 *W.* 4. *c.* 105. *s.* 4. may be relied upon as having such an effect: but that enacts "that no widow shall be entitled to dower out of any land which shall have been absolutely disposed of by *her husband* in his life-time, or by his will." A statute taking away a right which existed, and was favoured, at common law must be construed strictly. Now a will speaks from the time of execution; and at that time the testator was not the "husband" of *Anne Bakewell*. Sects. 5 and 10 also speak of acts done by the "husband;" both those sections, and sect. 4, evidently contemplating transactions during the coverture. The object of sect. 4 was to enable a husband to bar dower without fine, or such other equivalent proceedings as were formerly necessary.

It

1838.

MARSTON *against* ROE dem. FOX.

It has been held, in one case (*a*), that provision for the wife alone was sufficient to prevent revocation. But here the child also was provided for by the property conveyed to *John Fox* on *March* 6th and 7th, 1835. *Joseph Fox*, the testator's brother, agreed for the purchase of that property on *September* 30th, 1829. It is not shewn that he made the agreement otherwise than on his own account. *Joseph* died intestate in *November* 1834, leaving the testator his heir at law; but *Joseph* had not, at that time, such an equitable estate in the property as would descend to an heir at law; and therefore the testator had no interest in it until the legal estate was conveyed to him by lease and release in *March* 1835; but that was after the execution of his will. He, therefore, was intestate as to this property; and it descended to the lessor of the plaintiff, *William John Fox*, as his heir at law. *William John Fox*, therefore, the child born of the testator's marriage with *Anne Bakewell* was provided for as heir at law of the undevised property; and the will was not revoked. [*Parke* B. Do we know enough from the special verdict to say what equitable interest passed by the contract of 1829?] It is sufficient if the verdict does not shew that there was such an interest as would pass to *Joseph*'s heir at law.

Then as to the exceptions tendered by the plaintiff below. First, it is objected, generally, that the wills of *March* and *December* 1834 were not admissible. No reference is made to any purpose for which they were put in. The exception cannot avail if they were re-

(*a*) *Brown* v. *Thompson*, 1 *Eq. Ca. Abr.* 413. pl. 15. *S. C.* 1 *P. Wms.* 304. note †, 6th ed.

ceivable

1838.

Marston against Roe dem. Fox.

ceivable for any imaginable purpose. Now it is clear that the defendant (who is a trustee under the first, and residuary devisee under the second) might have made title under them if he had failed under the will of 1835. So, secondly, as to the declaration made when the conveyance of a house was executed. That also is excepted to generally; and the exception fails if the evidence was admissible for any purpose. Now the declaration was made before the will of 1835 was executed; and what was then said may be strictly proper evidence if the question is, whether or not the testator annexed a tacit condition to his will. [*Parke* B. It might be admissible even to shew that the testator was of competent understanding to transact business]. Thirdly, parol evidence was not admissible to shew that *Joseph* purchased the property at *Marston Montgomery* as trustee for *John*. The object of such evidence was to prove a trust of lands created by parol, contrary to the Statute of frauds, 29 *Car*. 2. *c*. 3. *s*. 7. If *Joseph* had the legal estate in him, it could not be proved by parol that he held as trustee; and, if his interest was only equitable, the same objection applies, it being an interest in land. Nor can it make any difference whether the party is called a trustee or an agent. There is not, indeed, any proof that he did sign as an agent. The contract is simply executed by *Joseph Fox* in his own name; and the attempt is, in effect, to shew by parol that he made the agreement as trustee. [Lord *Abinger* C. B. Agency would not make him a trustee, in the sense in which you state it. *Parke* B. May not a man be authorized by parol to make an executory agreement for another? *Tindal* C. J. As an auctioneer is made by parol the authorised agent of the parties to the sale.] Here the purchaser,

1838.

MARSTON against ROE dem. FOX.

purchaser, by writing, professes to contract on his own behalf. *Joseph* acquired an equitable interest; and he had it either beneficially or as trustee: and in the latter case it could not pass by parol. At all events the question as to the admissibility of this evidence does not affect the case of the plaintiff in error upon the special verdict.

Then, as to the bill of exceptions tendered by the defendant below. The letters and verbal declarations of the testator were admissible to shew that he intended his will to stand: what weight they were entitled to is not now material. If marriage and the birth of a child are a presumptive revocation, the presumption is not one of law, and it may be rebutted by facts. It is raised by extrinsic evidence, and may be met in the same manner. Acts of the testator may clearly be given in evidence to shew a non-revocation; thus, if he had provided for his widow or children by deed, that fact might be proved, as shewing his intent. Then may not the intent be also shewn by his words or letters? Again, if the revocation depend upon a tacit condition annexed to the will, it is not a pure condition of law, that the testator shall not marry and have a child born after the execution of the will, because the will is clearly not revoked if the testator has provided for the wife and child, thereby declaring his intent that the will shall stand. It may, then, be stated generally, that the implied condition is subject to the qualification, that the testator shall not have made an effectual declaration of his intent that the will shall remain unrevoked: and, on principle, any circumstance which shews that the qualification has taken effect, so that the condition loses its force, may be proved as well by parol evidence as otherwise. No objection arises from the Statute

1838.

MARSTON against ROE dem. FOX.

Statute of frauds. Notwithstanding the statute, a will may be revoked, not only by a formal writing, but by circumstances (as by the events in question, of marriage and birth); and there is no statute law which lays down that the conclusion from those circumstances may not be rebutted by parol evidence. On the other hand, many decisions establish that it may be met by evidence shewing, not that the will has been republished, but that it never was revoked. The doctrine of the ecclesiastical courts on this subject is laid down in *Lugg* v. *Lugg* (a), *Emerson* v. *Boville* (b), *Thompson* v. *Sheppard*, there cited (c), *Johnston* v. *Johnston* (d), and *Wright* v. *Samuda* and *Calder* v. *Calder*, there cited (e), and *Gibbens* v. *Cross* (g): in which cases the question is uniformly treated as one of intent, to be explained by the facts in evidence; and among these facts the ecclesiastical courts constantly admit declarations and letters of the testator. [*Alderson* B. Suppose the testator, after marriage, has clearly declared his intention that the will shall be revoked, and he afterwards changes his mind, and declares his intention that it shall take effect, is the will ambulatory in the mean time? and where are such changes to stop?] Any declaration, before his death, that he intended the will to operate, would be proof that he never meant it to be revoked, and would rebut evidence adduced, from other circumstances, to shew the contrary. The mere declaration of an intent to revoke would be excluded, as in *Doe dem. Lancashire* v. *Lancashire* (h). The decisions on this point in the ecclesiastical courts, shewing

(a) 1 *Ld. Ray.* 441. *S. C.* 2 *Salk.* 592.
(b) 1 *Phillim.* 342.
(c) 1 *Phillim.* 343: and see p. 472. See also 1 *Ves. & B.* 391, 394., and note (a) to p. 394.
(d) 1 *Phillim.* 447.
(e) Page 472.
(g) 2 *Add.* 455.
(h) 5 *T. R.* 49.

that

1838.

MARSTON *against* ROE dem. FOX.

that revocation or non-revocation is a question of intent, may (as was before pointed out) be referred to as authority at common law; but the principle that the testator's intention shall be looked to, and ascertained from the facts of the particular case, is as much recognized by the temporal as by the spiritual courts. In *Brady, lessee of Norris*, v. *Cubitt* (*a*), Lord *Mansfield* held it clear that the presumption of revocation from marriage and birth of a child might be "rebutted by every sort of evidence;" and *Ashhurst* J. relied upon a "strong case" (*Rogers* v. *Longfield*) (*b*) in *K. B.*, *Easter T.* 13 *G.* 3., "as to the admission of parol evidence to rebut an equity, or implication." In *Kenebel* v. *Scrafton* (*c*) Lord *Ellenborough* said it was unnecessary to consider whether the presumptive revocation could be rebutted by parol declarations in favour of the will; but it seems probable, from what follows, that, if it had been necessary, he would have grounded his judgment on the declarations there proved. In *Pole* v. *Lord Somers* (*d*) Lord *Eldon* says, "I now allude to *Brady* v. *Cubitt* (*a*) and those cases upon an implied revocation of a will; in which it was said, evidence of declarations was admitted, because it is to rebut an equity. If they meant to say, that parol evidence is admitted, to get the better of a presumption, that is accurate: but it is perfectly inaccurate to say, that any thing like an equity is to be rebutted." "It is, not rebutting an equity, but answering a presumption."

The cases which may be cited as impugning the admissibility of parol evidence for this purpose do not

(*a*) 1 *Doug.* 31.

(*b*) Or *Goodright dem. Hodges* v. *Clanfield*. See note (*b*) to *Kenebel* v. *Scrafton*, 2 *East*, 534. (*c*) 2 *East*, 543. (*d*) 6 *Ves.* 326.

 apply.

1838.

Marston *against* Roe dem. Fox.

apply. In *Parsons* v. *Lanoe* (*a*), where evidence of this kind was disregarded, the will had been made subject to a contingency, and had been completely revoked by the contingent event happening. The revocation was not matter of presumption, but a fact established. In *Doe dem. Lancashire* v. *Lancashire* (*b*) none of the Judges contradicted the doctrine now contended for. The declarations which Lord *Kenyon* laid out of consideration in that case were offered, not as circumstances rebutting a presumption, but as direct evidence of revocation, which was contrary to the Statute of frauds. The revocation there was established independently of those declarations. And Lord *Kenyon* thought that such cases turned upon an implied condition annexed to the will, rather than an intent of the testator to be inferred from circumstances. *Buller* J., who agreed with Lord *Kenyon* in rejecting the declarations (saying, "if there be any revocation at all of this will, it is so by presumption of law, independently of express declarations"), was one of the Judges who decided *Brady, lessee of Norris*, v. *Cubitt* (*c*); and he refers to this case with approbation in *Goodtitle dem. Holford* v. *Otway* (*d*), subsequently to the determination in *Doe dem. Lancashire* v. *Lancashire* (*b*). In *Goodtitle dem. Holford* v. *Otway* (*d*) the attempt was to alter, by declarations of the testator, the effect of deeds which he had executed. For that purpose the parol evidence was clearly not admissible. Sir *R. P. Arden*, M. R., in *Gibbons* v. *Caunt* (*e*), disapproved of the reception of evidence to rebut the presumption

(*a*) *Ambl.* 557. *S. C.* 1 *Ves.* sen. 189.; 1 *Wils.* 243.

(*b*) 5 *T. R.* 49.

(*c*) 1 *Doug.* 31.

(*d*) 2 *H. Bl.* 516.

(*e*) 4 *Ves.* 848.

of

1838.

MARSTON against ROE dem. FOX.

of a will being revoked by marriage and the birth of a child; but he did not dispute that the rule of evidence was established. A dictum of Lord *Loughborough*, when referring the case of *Kenebel* v. *Scrafton* (a) to a court of law, may be cited: but his Lordship's observation, "that the parol evidence" (against the supposed intention to revoke) "did not weigh at all," applies only to evidence of conversations, as distinguished from formal proof of republication; and the dictum is uttered only incidentally, and is probably not one which his Lordship intended to be bound by. The judgment of Sir *Herbert Jenner*, in the present case (b), as to the personal property, supports the reception of this evidence, unless a valid distinction can be drawn between realty and personalty. The defendant below is entitled, if not to judgment, at least to a venire de novo.

Sir *W. W. Follett* for the defendant in error (the plaintiff below). The essential points of this case are only two. First, on the special verdict, taking it to be conceded that marriage and the birth of a child revoke a will of land in the absence of other circumstances, are there such other circumstances in the present case as rebut the ordinary presumption? Secondly, on the bills of exceptions, could parol evidence be received to set up the will by shewing an intention in the testator that it should still operate?

As to the first point. It is contended, on the other side, that marriage and the birth of a child revoke a

(a) 5 *Ves.* 664.

(b) In the Prerogative Court, *March* 21st, 1837. The case (*Fox* v. *Marston*) will be published in the first volume of Dr. *Curteis's Reports*.

will,

1838.

MARSTON *against* ROE dem. FOX.

will, because the testator is supposed, in those events, to intend revoking it; but that his intention is a matter of fact to be enquired into, and may be elucidated by any circumstances, including even declarations by the testator. But the question does not turn upon intent. In *Christopher* v. *Christopher* (a), where it was decided that marriage and the birth of a child revoke a will of real property, *Perrot* B. differed from the rest of the Court of Exchequer, thinking it a contravention of the Statute of frauds that a revocation should take effect even by these events; and *Adams* B., who delivered a contrary opinion, distinguished between express revocations and those to be implied from facts, holding that the one class was excluded by the statute, but the other left as before: and he said, "Declarations made by a testator lie open to perversion; but in this case, it is not declarations, but facts (as a subsequent marriage, and having children), are to be proved, which are notorious matters." The distinction between declarations and the class of facts alluded to was evidently the ground on which the majority of the Court decided. An imperfect settlement, made after the will, revokes it; and such revocation would not be defeated by any number of letters which the testator might write, stating that he did not mean the settlement to have that effect. [*Tindal* C. J. referred to *Goodtitle dem. Holford* v. *Otway* (b).] In *Forse and Hembling's Case* (c), where the Court of Common Pleas held that the marriage of a woman revokes a will previously made by her, it was said that "her proper act shall amount to a countermand in law." It is the changing of her status that makes the

(a) 2 *Dickens*, 445. *S. C.* 4 *Burr.* 2182.

(b) 2 *H. Bl.* 516.

(c) 4 *Rep.* 60 *b*.

will

1838.

MARSTON *against* ROE dem. FOX.

will no longer effectual. Lord *Kenyon*, in *Doe dem. Lancashire* v. *Lancashire* (*a*), was of opinion that marriage and the birth of a child revoked a will by a tacit condition which the law annexed to the will, and not in consequence of a presumable change of intention. Since the Statute of frauds, the most direct expression of an intent to revoke avails nothing, unless intimated by the means there pointed out. And, further, if a question like the present depends on intent, the intent is a matter of fact on which a jury, and not the Court, should draw the requisite conclusion from the evidence. But the true ground of revocation is the operation of law; and it was so considered in *Spraage* v. *Stone* (*b*), where the marriage and birth were held to be "in point of law an implied revocation of the will," and no inference was drawn as to intention from a will which the testator had made after the marriage, but which was not duly attested. This last circumstance is noticed in 1 *Powell on Devises*, 533. *c*. 13 (*c*). The parol evidence rejected in *Doe dem. Lancashire* v. *Lancashire* (*d*) was relied upon by the defendants' counsel as rebutting the proof of revocation; and the remark of Lord *Kenyon*, that "letting in that kind of evidence would be in direct opposition to the Statute of frauds," may be extended to evidence offered for the purpose of meeting a case of revocation; for, if that could be admitted, parol evidence must also be received to support the revocation; and, if receivable in answer, it would be so in the first instance, for the order of proof could make no difference.

There are, indeed, cases in which marriage and the birth of a child have been held no revocation, because

(*a*) 5 *T. R.* 49.

(*b*) *Ambl.* 721.

(*c*) 3d (*Jarman's* ed.).

(*d*) 5 *T. R.* 49.

the

1838.

Marston against Roe dem. Fox.

the attendant facts were such that the testator was not placed in the situation in which a will is revoked. But (as Sir J *Nicholl* lays down in *Gibbens* v. *Cross* (*a*)) it is revoked primâ facie; the onus of shewing the contrary lies upon the party contesting the revocation. Then what evidence is sufficient for this purpose? The doctrine as to revocation originates in the civil law, and is founded on the duty which a man lies under, of providing for his children. There is no case in which the revocation by marriage and birth of a child has been held not to take place, except where the child was fully provided for, or where the revocation would not have been for his benefit. *Brown* v. *Thompson* (*b*) is not an exception; for there the testator had, before the marriage, devised to *E. C.*, whom he married, and her heirs; the son born of the marriage was her heir; and the Lord Keeper (*Wright*), after admitting that "alteration of circumstances might be a revocation of a will of lands," proceeded to say, "no such alteration appears here, for no injury is done any person; and those are provided for whom the testator was most bound to provide for;" and he established the will. The ground of decision in this case is stated by Sir *John Nicholl* in *Johnston* v. *Johnston* (*c*) to be, "that the will made a provision for the wife, and through her for the son." In *Kenebel* v. *Scrafton* (*d*) (and there is no case to a different effect between that and *Brown* v. *Thompson* (*b*)) Lord *Ellenborough* states it as "a general proposition of law, that marriage and the birth of a child, without provision made for the objects of those relations,

(*a*) 2 *Add. Rep.* 455.

(*b*) 1 *Eq. Ca. Abr.* 413. pl. 15. *S. C.* 1 *P. Wms.* 304. note †. 6th ed.

(*c*) 1 *Phillim.* 470.

(*d*) 2 *East*, 541.

of

1838.

MARSTON against ROE dem. FOX.

of themselves operate a revocation of a will of lands." But he adds that the rule does not apply "where the same persons, who after the making of the will stand in the legal relation of wife and children, were before specifically contemplated and provided for by the testator, though under a different character and denomination." In the same passage he approves of Lord *Kenyon's* doctrine in *Doe dem Lancashire* v. *Lancashire* (*a*), that the revocation should be ascribed rather to a tacit condition than to a presumed change of intention, "which alteration of intention," he observes, "should seem in legal reasoning not very material, unless it be considered as sufficient to found a presumption in fact, that an actual revocation has followed thereupon." But such actual revocation could not be presumed, consistently with the Statute of frauds. In *Ex parte The Earl of Ilchester* (*b*) marriage and the birth of children were held not to revoke the will (Lord *Eldon* relying on the circumstances of the particular case), because the wife and children were provided for by a settlement, and there was a son of the testator by the first marriage living, who, in case of a revocation, would have taken as heir at law. So in *Sheath* v. *York* (*c*), where the testator left children by two marriages, his will made between the first and the second marriage was held not revoked as to real estate, because the children of the second marriage could not have benefited by such revocation, but revoked as to personalty, because, as to that, the rights of the second family were affected if the will remained in force. The latter point in that case had already been decided by the Ecclesiastical Court;

(*a*) 5 *T. R.* 49. (*b*) 7 *Ves.* 348. (*c*) 1 *Ves. & B.* 390.

and

1838.

MARSTON against ROE dem. FOX.

and the principle of that decision was recognised in the Prerogative Court by Sir *J. Nicholl* in *Talbot* v. *Talbot* (*a*) and *Johnson* v. *Wells* (*b*), where the wills were upheld.

Then are the circumstances stated in this verdict sufficient to rebut the presumption that the will is revoked, on the principle of former decisions? The testator, by his will, disposes of his whole property. He makes no provision for the heir, and gives to *Anne Bakewell*, afterwards his wife, a life estate only in certain premises, and that subject to the condition that she remain unmarried. It is stated in the verdict that the testator contemplated marriage with her down to the time of his executing this will. The restriction, " so long thereof as she shall remain sole and unmarried," seems inconsistent with a design to provide for her in case of her marriage with him. It is suggested that he wished the devise to operate so long as she did not marry any other person; and it may be presumed that the devise was not meant to take effect if she had married another man who had died in the testator's lifetime. Neither could it operate after she had married the testator. It was not a forfeiture that he imposed, but a condition, that she should be sole and unmarried. By marrying her he shewed that he no longer intended to provide for her in this way (*c*). Then it is said that she is provided for by dower, stat. 3 & 4 *W.* 4. *c.* 105. *s.* 4. only excluding the widow from dower out of lands disposed of by " her husband." But the sense of the clause is, that the widow, when she becomes such, is not to have dower of lands which the person lately her

(*a*) 1 *Hagg. Ecc. Rep.* 705. (*b*) 2 *Hagg. Ecc. Rep.* 561.

(*c*) But see *Smith* v. *Cowdery*, 2 *Sim. & St.* 358.

husband

1838.

MARSTON *against* ROE dem. FOX.

husband shall have disposed of. The contemplation of marriage spoken of in the verdict is not one of those facts which can properly be attended to as rebutting a presumed revocation. This will, however, was not made in contemplation of marriage, but in case the testator should die before the marriage. At all events, the child was not provided for. The purchase of a few acres at *Marston Montgomery*, after leaving the bulk of the property so that it passed from the heir, could not make such a difference as to prevent the ordinary rule of law from attaching. But neither did this purchased property descend to the child of the marriage. If *Joseph Fox* made the contract for it on his own account, he had the equitable estate in it. "Equity looks upon things agreed to be done, as actually performed; consequently, when a contract is made for sale of an estate, equity considers the vendor as a trustee for the purchaser of the estate sold, and the purchaser as a trustee of the purchase-money for the vendor." 1 *Sugd. Vend. and Purch.* 171. c. 4. s. 1. (*a*). The equitable estate vested in *Joseph* would, at his death, in *November* 1834, go to his heir at law. *John Fox*, the testator, was his heir at law; and he, after the death of *Joseph*, made his will, giving all his property to the devisees mentioned in the verdict. The son of *John Fox* would not, therefore, inherit the property at *Marston Montgomery*; and, though the legal estate in it might pass to him under the deeds of *March* 1835, a court of equity would have decreed a conveyance. In fact, however, *Joseph* purchased as the agent of *John*. In either case the child of the testator's marriage took nothing in the purchased estate, but as trustee for the residuary de-

(*a*) 9th ed.

visee.

1838.

Marston against Roe dem. Fox.

visee. The bill of exceptions was rightly tendered on the exclusion of evidence that *Joseph* was an agent, appointed by parol, to purchase the estate at *Marston Montgomery*. An agent might be so appointed for that purpose; and *Joseph's* signature to the contract bound *John*.

Then, secondly, as to the other points raised by the bills of exceptions. The parol declarations were all inadmissible; and among these are to be reckoned the first two wills. It is said that they might have been evidence for other purposes than as shewing intent; but that is an evasion of the point which the parties consented to raise, and, if necessary, leave should be given to amend the bill of exceptions in this particular. It is clear, however, from the contents of these wills, that they could have no bearing on the case, except as shewing the testator's disposition towards particular parties. The parol declarations stated in the special verdict ought not to have been introduced there; if they were admissible at all, their result should have been found by the jury. In *Brady, lessee of Norris*, v. *Cubitt* (a) there was no parol declaration stated in the verdict, except the desire expressed by the testator to have a pen drawn through a passage in one of the memorandums. If the case decides that that expression was properly introduced as a declaration of the testator, the judgment is, so far, erroneous. And the evidence was not necessary to the decision. Of the documents subsequent to the will, set out in that verdict, the first was a regular testamentary paper as to personalty; the second was, in effect, a re-publication of the will, and was properly executed for that

(a) 1 *Doug.* 31.

purpose.

1838.

MARSTON *against* ROE dem. FOX.

purpose. The point argued at the bar was, whether or not there had been a revocation by operation of law; and on this question the defendant was entitled to succeed. Lord *Mansfield*, indeed, says in his judgment that the presumption of a will being revoked by marriage and birth of a child "may be rebutted by every sort of evidence;" but that must be legal evidence; the dictum means only that the presumption is not unbending. To hold that, on the subject of implied revocation, parol evidence is admissible, and the question of revocation to be determined by the jury, would be over-ruling all the cases from *Christopher* v. *Christopher* (a) downwards. Of the two cases cited in *Brady, lessee of Norris,* v. *Cubitt* (b), as supporting the admissibility of parol evidence, *Rogers* v. *Longfield* (c) is not found in any report, and *Lake* v. *Lake* (d) related to personalty, which is dealt with by the Ecclesiastical Courts upon principles different from those of the common law. A revocation by matter in pais would be for the consideration of a jury; but then it must be executed according to stat. 29 *Car.* 2. *c.* 3. *s.* 6. A revocation not so executed takes effect by operation of law; and it is for the Court, not the jury, to say when it so operates, and when the operation is defeated. This was the doctrine of *Eyre* C. J. in *Goodtitle dem. Holford* v. *Otway* (e), where direct evidence of intention was offered, but rejected; and the Lord Chief Justice said it was difficult to understand *Brady* v. *Cubitt* (b), supposing the revocation there to have been by operation of law, and not within the Statute of frauds. *Buller* J. acquiesced in the

(a) 2 *Dickens*, 445.

(b) 1 *Doug.* 31.

(c) See note (b) to *Kenebel* v. *Scrafton*, 2 *East*, 534.

(d) *Ambl.* 126. *S. C.* 1 *Wils.* 313. *Bul. N. P.* 298.

(e) 2 *H. Bl.* 516.

1838.

MARSTON *against* ROE dem. FOX.

the general doctrine of *Eyre* C. J., but supported the decision in *Brady* v. *Cubitt* (*a*) by a distinction, which, however, appears rather adverse than favourable to it. And in *Doe dem. Lancashire* v. *Lancashire* (*b*) *Buller* J. held that the testator's declarations were not to be regarded, saying, "If there be any revocation at all of this will, it is so by presumption of law, independently of express declarations."

In cases where the reception of such parol evidence has been incidentally discussed, it has not been supported. In *Kenebel* v. *Scrafton* (*c*) a decision on this point became unnecessary; but Lord *Loughborough*, in sending the case (*d*) to this Court, expressed his opinion "that the parol evidence" (of declarations shewing an intent not to revoke) "did not weigh at all." In *Christopher* v. *Christopher* (*e*), the judgments of *Adams* B. and *Smith* B., who decided in favour of the revocation by marriage and birth of a child, are, in principle, opposed to the admissibility of declarations as evidence on the subject of revocation. Lord *Alvanley*, in *Gibbons* v. *Caunt* (*g*), expressed disapprobation of parol evidence being received against a revocation by marriage and birth of offspring. In *Martin* v. *Savage* (*h*) Lord *Hardwicke* held that a testator's declaration of intent that his will should stand, after a primâ facie revocation by marriage and birth of a child, could not operate as a republication. Lord *Eldon*, in the dictum uttered by him in *Pole* v. *Lord Somers* (*i*), cannot be considered as

(*a*) 1 *Doug.* 31.

(*b*) 5 *T. R.* 61.

(*c*) 2 *East*, 530.

(*d*) 5 *Ves.* 663.

(*e*) 2 *Dickens*, 445. *S. C.* 4 *Bur.* 2182.

(*g*) 4 *Ves.* 848.

(*h*) *Barn. Chanc. Rep.* 189. Cited in *Potter* v. *Potter*, 1 *Ves.* sen. 440. and *Gibson* v. *Lord Montfort*, 1 *Ves.* sen, 489.

(*i*) 6 *Ves.* 326. Antè, p. 33.

pronounc-

1838.

MARSTON against ROE dem. FOX.

pronouncing on the admissibility of such evidence. The law on this subject is laid down, and the authorities collected, in note (4) to *Duppa* v. *Mayo* (a), where the doubt expressed (p. 278 *e.*), whether or not such parol evidence be receivable, seems to arise chiefly from the case of *Brady, lessee of Norris,* v. *Cubitt* (b). It is stated in that note, as the argument in favour of such proof, that, as "marriage and the birth of a child amount only to a presumptive revocation, and as the circumstances from which the presumption is inferred, arise out of parol evidence, they may be repelled by the same kind of evidence." It does not follow, however, that evidence of declarations may be received for this purpose.

The intention to revoke or republish is, in fact, immaterial, where it is not carried into effect. If an unmarried woman devises land and then marries, the will is revoked, because her status is altered; if the husband dies, her will is not set up again; and if, during or after coverture, she declares her intent that the will shall have effect, it is not revived unless she republishes it with the attestation of three witnesses; otherwise the Statute of frauds would be repealed. If a lease is surrendered, the Court will not receive parol evidence of the intent. If a lessor makes a second lease, so that a former one is vacated by operation of law, his declaration that he did not intend to revoke that can avail nothing. If a man makes a will, not knowing that his wife is pregnant, yet the birth of a child revokes the will so made. It would be the same if he said that he meant his will to stand although a child should be born. [*Patteson* J. No kind of revocation seems to

(a) 1 *Wms. Saund.* 277 *f.*

(b) 1 *Doug.* 31.

depend

1838.

MARSTON *against* ROE dem. FOX.

depend more on intent than that caused by executing an imperfect conveyance; but there parol evidence in support of the will is not received. But whether or not such conveyances are revocations by operation of law may be a question. His Lordship here referred to the observations of *Eyre* C. J. in *Goodtitle dem. Holford* v. *Otway* (*a*).]

As to the decisions in the Ecclesiastical Courts, there has been an appeal from Sir *Herbert Jenner's* judgment in the present case, as to the personalty, which shews that even in those courts the law is not settled. But, further, the ecclesiastical courts always admit testamentary declarations of the testator, where a will is disputed. The ground of that practice is, that a will of personalty need not be written or signed by the testator; it is sufficient if he has recognised it; and it may often be necessary to ascertain that fact by proof which would not be necessary or admissible as to a devise of realty. The same observation applies to proof of revocation or alteration of a will. Stat. 29 *Car.* 2. *c.* 3. *s.* 22. only requires, in case of a will of personalty being repealed or altered, that such repeal or alteration shall, if verbal, be committed to writing, read over to the testator and allowed by him, and proved to be so by three witnesses. And the will may be adopted or republished without such attestation. So, in *Emerson* v. *Boville* (*b*), Sir *William Wynne* says that, where a will has been revoked by marriage and birth of a child, "the death of the child does not revive the will; — but it requires some act, some recognition, or something to shew the deceased's intention that it should take effect." In

(*a*) 2 *H. Bl.* 522, 523.

(*b*) 1 *Phillim.* 342.

Sullivan

1838.

MARSTON against ROE dem FOX.

Sullivan v. *Brooke* (*a*), there cited, Sir *George Hay* made a similar observation. And again in *Thompson* v. *Sheppard* (*b*) proof by letters and declarations was received, to shew that the testator did not intend his will to be revoked by marriage and the birth of a child. But in each of those cases the will, being of personalty, might be republished by a mere verbal declaration. For the same reason the verbal declarations were admissible in *Braddyl* v. *Jehen* (*c*), and *Lewis* v. *Bulkeley*, there cited (*d*). *Johnston* v. *Johnston* (*e*), and *Gibbens* v. *Cross* (*g*), where parol declarations were held to be receivable, were also cases in the ecclesiastical courts, concerning wills of personalty. The same observation applies to *Lugg* v. *Lugg* (*h*).

The result is, that, in the case of a devise of real property, marriage and the birth of a child being of themselves a revocation in law, their effect cannot be defeated by shewing the intent of the testator, unless that intent be expressed by an instrument executed conformably to the Statute of Frauds.

Sir *J. Campbell*, Attorney-General, in reply. It is contended that the revocation of a will by marriage and the birth of a child takes effect, not by a presumption or condition, but by a rule of law, founded on duty. But the testamentary power is altogether dependent on intention. By the law of *England* a testator has, in the first instance, unlimited power, and may leave the whole property

(*a*) 1 *Phillim.* 343.

(*b*) Cited in 1 *Phillim.* 343. And see 1 *Ves. & B.* 391, 394; and note (*a*) to p. 394.

(*c*) 2 *Sir G. Lee's Judgments*, 193.

(*d*) Page 213.

(*e*) 1 *Phillim.* 447.

(*g*) 2 *Add.* 455.

(*h*) 1 *Ld. Ray.* 441. *S. C.* 2 *Salk.* 592.

1838.

MARSTON *against* ROE dem. FOX.

property to one child, or to a stranger. The decisions in the courts of law have proceeded on the ground, not that a duty would be violated if the will took effect, but that the testator did not mean it to operate after the change of circumstances. If a revocation took place in all cases where the testator married afterwards and a child was born, his intent would often be defeated, as if he made his will, intending at the time to marry a particular person, and did marry her. If the will provides for the future wife and child, a revocation is clearly prevented. The cases in which it has been held to take effect have been where the will was made without contemplation of marriage, or where all the property was devised and no provision made for the future wife and child, no intention appearing in such cases that the will should remain valid notwithstanding the marriage. The question of revocation is one of law; but the question of law arises on facts; and those are to be found by a jury, though the result of them is for the consideration of the Court. In the three cases of *Christopher* v. *Christopher* (a), *Spraage* v. *Stone* (b), and *Doe dem. Lancashire* v. *Lancashire* (c), where marriage and the birth of a child were held to be a revocation, the will was made without contemplation of the subsequent marriage, and the issue were unprovided for. But in *Brown* v. *Thompson* (d), where the testator made his will in contemplation of marriage with *E. C.*, and devised to her and her heirs, and in *Brady, lessee of Norris*, v. *Cubitt* (e), *Ex parte Lord Ilchester* (g), *Sheath* v. *York* (h),

(a) 2 *Dickens*, 445. *S. C.* 4 *Burr.* 2182. (b) *Ambl.* 721.
(c) 5 *T. R.* 49.
(d) 1 *Eq. Ca. Abr.* 413. pl. 15. *S. C.* 1 *P. Wms.* 304. note * †. 6th ed.
(e) *Doug.* 31. (g) 7 *Ves.* 348. (h) 1 *Ves. & B.* 390.

and

1838.

MARSTON against ROE dem. FOX.

and *Kenebel* v. *Scrafton* (a), where there were other incidents, varying the cases from the three first mentioned, the Courts looked at all the circumstances, and, concluding from them as to the intention in each case, held the wills not revoked. The ecclesiastical courts proceeded on the same principle in *Talbot* v. *Talbot* (b) and *Johnson* v. *Wells* (c). The narrative, in the present special verdict, of the testator's declaration as to dower, might be dismissed without materially altering the case. And the statement as to his contemplating marriage sufficiently shews that he had it in view at the time of executing the will. Upon this state of facts, as appearing on the special verdict, there is nothing which supports an implication that the will was revoked.

As to the provision for the widow and child. The words "for and during the term of her natural life, or so long thereof as she shall remain sole and unmarried," provide for the widow if she should marry the testator and survive him, or even if she should marry, and survive, another person. The will would be ambulatory during the testator's life, and would take effect at his death in the literal sense of the words. Further, the widow was entitled to dower out of lands of which the testator died seised. Stat. 3 & 4 *W*. 4. *c*. 105. *s*. 4. enables a husband, during the marriage, to alien lands of which the wife, formerly, would have been entitled to dower. The testator here did not exercise that power, but intentionally died intestate as to the third part of which the wife was dowable. It was as if he had said, in terms, that he meant his wife to take that third part. This, therefore, was a provision for her by his voluntary

(a) 2 *East*, 530. (b) 1 *Hagg. Ecc. Rep.* 705.
(c) 2 *Hagg. Ecc. Rep.* 561.

1838.

Marston *against* Roe dem. Fox.

act; and he shewed by that, as well as by the devise in her favour, that he meant the will to remain unrevoked. It is for the defendant in error to establish that, where the widow is provided for, the will is nevertheless revoked if there be no provision for the issue. But, in this case, there was such a provision, by means of the after-purchased property; and *Brady, lessee of Norris*, v. *Cubitt* (*a*), and other cases, shew that a will may be kept alive by such provision, though arising independently of the will. Neither the testator nor *Joseph Fox* had any legal estate in the property at *Marston Montgomery* till after the will was made; and the verdict does not shew that either had, before that time, even an equitable estate. There was only an executory contract made by *Joseph* in his own name; no purchase-money had been paid, nor any possession given to *Joseph*; and the possession by *John*, the testator, is not shewn to be connected with *Joseph*'s contract. If the vendors had refused to convey, *Joseph* might have sued at law for damages, or in equity for a specific performance; but he had no interest in the premises which could pass to *John* at his death. The passage cited on this point from Mr. *Sugden* is only the opinion of a contemporary writer. The legal estate, then, which the testator acquired in these premises, descended to his heir at law, as undisposed of by the will. Its value to the heir is immaterial; if there be any provision, the Court will not measure its sufficiency.

Then as to the bill of exceptions tendered by the plaintiff below. The two former wills were admissible if they tended to shew the testator's disposition towards parties named in the third will, or the intention he had

(*a*) 1 *Doug.* 31.

of

1838.

MARSTON *against* ROE dem. FOX.

of marrying. [*Parke* B. The question raised by the plaintiff's bill of exceptions is simply whether these wills "ought to have been admitted and allowed." We must decide upon the bill of exceptions as it is worded.] The declaration as to dower was at least admissible with reference to the fact of the testator having contemplated marriage. The tender of parol evidence as to *Joseph Fox*'s agency was an attempt to set up a parol declaration of trust, contrary to stat. 29 *Car.* 2. *c.* 3. *s.* 7. [*Parke* B. cited *Wilson* v. *Hart* (*a*) and *The Duke of Norfolk* v. *Worthy* (*b*).]

As to the bill of exceptions for the defendant below. The testator's declarations there referred to were admissible, and shewed his intention that the defendant below should take, whether a child were born or not. It is suggested that in a case like the present declarations are to be excluded, though facts may be evidence. If it is supposed that proof of facts is less calculated to let in fraud and perjury than proof of declarations, the difficulties which arose, in the *Douglas* and *Berkeley* cases, on the very facts of birth and marriage, afford a strong argument to the contrary. But, in any view of the subject, evidence of declarations is admissible. If the revocation by marriage and birth of a child be matter of presumption (as it was considered in the earlier cases, and still is in the Ecclesiastical Courts), they are clearly evidence to rebut the presumption, which can subsist only till the contrary is proved. If it depend on a condition (a doctrine first introduced in *Doe dem. Lancashire* v. *Lancashire* (*c*)), the condition is created either by law

(*a*) 7 *Taunt.* 295.

(*b*) 1 *Camp.* 337.

(*c*) 5 *T. R.* 49.

or

1838.

Marston against Roe dem. Fox.

or by the testator's act. If by law, it may be asked whether the same condition is annexed to every will made by an unmarried person without provision for a future wife and child? If by the testator, evidence must be receivable to shew whether the party really annexed it or not. Supposing a condition to be annexed, it is not merely that the testator shall not afterwards marry and have a child born; two further terms are to be added, that the wife and children shall not have been provided for, and that the testator shall not have contemplated marriage when he made his will. The defendant in error seeks only to add another term, which, like the former, may be supposed for the purpose of effecting the testator's intent, namely, that the testator shall not have declared that he means his will to stand although he may marry and have a child born. If that were expressed in the will itself, undoubtedly there would be no revocation; and the intention may be proved by extrinsic evidence. The principle is admitted when it is allowed that evidence may be given of the party's status, as of his being a bachelor, or being about to marry. Supposing that the revocation takes place by a rule of law, still that rule must admit of being expanded, in the same manner as the condition. In any view of the subject the testator's intent must be the guide to a decision.

It is not correct to say that the ground on which declarations have been received in the Ecclesiastical Courts is, that they constitute a republication. The evidence was received as illustrative of intent in *Lugg* v. *Lugg* (*a*) and the other cases cited on this point for the plaintiff in error. The argument here, as in those

(*a*) 1 *Ld. Ray.* 441. *S. C.* 2 *Salk.* 592.

cases,

cases, is, not that the will is republished, but that it was never revoked; and the cases cited shew that the evidence in question is applicable to that point. *Braddyl* v. *Jehen* (*a*), where the will was considered as revoked, does not establish the contrary.

1838.

MARSTON *against* ROE dem. FOX.

The decision in *Brady, lessee of Norris*, v. *Cubitt* (*b*) turned, in part, on evidence of a declaration: and the marginal note (which is that of a very accurate reporter) states that "an implied revocation of a will by a subsequent marriage and the birth of a child, may be rebutted by parol evidence." In *Kenebel* v. *Scrafton* (*c*) and *Doe dem. Lancashire* v. *Lancashire* (*d*) the parol evidence was not relied upon by the Court, but it was not laid down that such evidence, generally, is inadmissible; nor has any instance of such a decision been pointed out. In *Martin* v. *Savage* (*e*), where it was held that a declaration of the testator could not support the will, there had been "a settlement by fine, which had revoked the will by altering the estate (*g*)." In such a case mere declarations could not avail; but there was not, properly speaking, a revocation of the will; it was an ademption of the subject-matter. So, if a single woman makes a will and then marries, the will is not revoked, but the condition of the party, and that of the estate, are altered. No question of intent can any longer arise. [*Patteson* J. No power remains in the testatrix to revoke.] In *Goodtitle dem. Holford* v. *Otway* (*h*) there had been a clear revocation de facto; and there was no room, therefore, for evidence to explain the intent. Lord *Loughborough*'s observation in *Kenebel* v. *Scraf-*

(*a*) 2 *Sir G. Lee's Judgments*, 193.
(*b*) 1 *Doug.* 31.
(*c*) 2 *East*, 530.
(*d*) 5 *T. R.* 49.
(*e*) *Barn. Rep. Ch.* 189.
(*g*) *Potter* v. *Potter*, 1 *Ves. sen.* 440.
(*h*) 2 *H. Bl.* 516.

 ton

1838.

MARSTON against ROE dem. FOX.

ton (a) was a mere dictum thrown out without hearing any argument; and Lord *Alvanley*, in *Gibbons* v. *Caunt* (b), did not say that he refused to be bound by the rule which he disapproved.

Cur. adv. vult.

TINDAL C. J. in this term (*January* 26th) delivered the judgment of the Court. After stating (as at pp. 14, 15, 23, antè) the manner in which the writs of error came before the Court, his Lordship proceeded. This case has accordingly been argued in the presence of all the Judges of *England*, with the exception of Lord *Denman*.

On the part of the plaintiff in error (the defendant below), it was contended that, admitting the general rule to be established, that marriage and the birth of a child operated as the revocation of a will made before the marriage, where the wife and child were left without provision, yet such revocation was grounded on an implied intention of the testator to revoke his will under the new state of circumstances which had taken place since the will made, and upon such implied intention only, and consequently that any evidence was admissible on the part of the devisee which shewed a contrary intention, in order to rebut such presumption.

On the part of the defendant in error it was contended that such revocation, under the circumstances above supposed, is the consequence of a rule of law, or of a condition tacitly annexed by law to the execution of a will, that, when the state of circumstances under which the will is made becomes so materially, or rather entirely, altered by a subsequent marriage and the birth

(a) 5 *Ves.* 663.

(b) 4 *Ves.* 848.

of

1838.

MARSTON *against* ROE dem. FOX.

of a child, the will should become void; and that the operation of this rule of law was altogether independent of any intention on the part of the testator. The broad question therefore which has been argued between the parties has been, whether evidence of the testator's intention that his will should not be revoked is admissible to rebut the presumption of law that such revocation should take place? And we all concur in the opinion that the revocation of the will takes place in consequence of a rule or principle of law, independently altogether of any question of intention of the party himself, and consequently that no such evidence is admissible. The plaintiff in error, in support of the proposition for which he contends, has relied on the authority of various decisions of cases as well in the Ecclesiastical Courts as in the courts of common law. With respect to the former we cannot but entertain considerable doubt whether their authority can be held to apply to the present question. For, whilst we are entirely convinced of the importance of an uniformity of decision between the courts of ecclesiastical and of common law jurisdiction, where the same state of facts is under investigation, or the same principle of law is under discussion in each; and entertaining, as we do, at the same time, the highest respect for the learning and ability of those by whom justice is administered in the Ecclesiastical courts, we cannot forget that in the question now before us *we* have to deal with the provisions of a statute with which the questions ordinarily coming before *them* are wholly unincumbered. The question now before us relates to the revocation or non-revocation of a will *devising real property;* it is a question whether such revocation shall be allowed to depend upon evidence of intention, that

 is,

1838.

Marston *against* Roe dem. Fox.

is, upon evidence of which parol declarations of the testator may confessedly form a part; whilst the Statute of Frauds has anxiously and carefully excluded evidence of that nature, with respect both to the original making and the revoking of wills of land. The Ecclesiastical Courts, on the other hand, are concerned in the granting probate of wills and testamentary papers, *relating to personalty only*, in which cases no statutory enactment has excluded parol evidence of the intention of the testator as to what shall or shall not be a testamentary paper, or what shall or shall not amount to a revocation or republication of a will. On the contrary, the evidence bearing on those points is generally mixed up with declarations of the party, and frequently consists of such declarations alone. The decisions therefore in the ecclesiastical courts, referred to by the counsel for the plaintiff in error, may be sound decisions with respect to the subject-matter to which they relate, and may yet furnish no authority on the case now in judgment before us. And, if that question is to be decided, as we think it is, by the weight of the authorities to be found in the courts of common law, the balance preponderates greatly in favour of the proposition that no evidence of intention is to be admitted to rebut the presumption of law that a will is revoked by subsequent marriage and the birth of a child. The cases relied upon principally by the plaintiff in error (the defendant below) are those of *Brady, lessee of Norris*, v. *Cubitt* (a) and *Kenebel* v. *Scrafton* (b); those which are appealed to by the defendant in error (the lessor of the plaintiff) are *Doe dem. Lancashire* v. *Lancashire* (c) and *Goodtitle dem. Holford* v. *Otway* (d). Now, with respect to the case of

(a) 1 *Doug.* 31.

(b) 2 *East*, 530.

(c) 5 *T. R.* 49.

(d) 2 *H. Bl.* 516.

1838.

MARSTON *against* ROE dem. FOX.

of *Brady*, *lessee of Norris*, v. *Cubitt* (*a*), it must be admitted that the opinion of Lord *Mansfield* is expressed in terms the most explicit and unreserved, that the presumption of revocation from marriage and the birth of children, like all other presumptions, "may be rebutted by every sort of evidence." But it must, at the same time, be observed that the decision of that case rests also upon other grounds, which are altogether satisfactory and free from objection; viz., first, that the disposition made by the will was of *part only* not *the whole* of the estate; and, secondly, that the instrument executed after the birth of the child operated *as a republication* of the devise contained in the will. And, as to the case of *Kenebel* v. *Scrafton* (*b*), it affords no authority whatever for the position that such implied revocation can be rebutted by parol evidence of a contrary intention existing in the testator's mind, because, in that case, the objects of the marriage were contemplated and provided for by the will, so that there was no implied revocation whatever of the will; and, next, because the question as to the admissibility of such evidence is expressly declared by Lord *Ellenborough*, in giving the judgment of the Court, to be left entirely untouched by the decision of that case.

And, looking, on the other hand, at the cases relied upon on the part of the lessor of the plaintiff, we agree entirely with Lord *Kenyon* as to the ground upon which the doctrine of implied revocation, under the circumstances now before us, ought to be rested. That very learned Judge, in giving his judgment in the case of *Doe dem. Lancashire* v. *Lancashire* (*c*), treats it as a

(*a*) 1 *Doug.* 31. (*b*) 2 *East*, 530. (*c*) 5 *T. R.* 58, 59.

principle

1838.

Marston *against* Roe dem. Fox.

principle of law, of which he suggests the foundation to be a tacit condition annexed to the will itself when made, that it should not take effect if there should be a total change in the situation of the testator's family; and this foundation of the rule is confirmed by the judgment of Lord *Ellenborough* in the case above referred to (*a*), where he says this ground is to be preferred to "any presumed alteration of intention; which alteration of intention should seem in legal reasoning not very material, unless it be considered as sufficient to found a presumption in fact, that an actual revocation has followed thereupon." The case, again, of *Goodtitle dem. Holford* v. *Otway* (*b*), although not the same in circumstances, yet establishes the very same principle as that contended for by the defendant in error. That case did not indeed relate to the revocation of a will by subsequent marriage and the birth of a child, but to revocation of a will by a subsequent conveyance of lease and release executed for a limited purpose only. But the same principle was laid down, that parol evidence shall not be admitted to shew that the testator meant his will to remain in force against the revocation implied by law from the execution of such subsequent conveyance, the Lord Chief Justice *Eyre* stating his opinion to be, "that, in cases of revocation by operation of law," "the law pronounces upon the ground of a *presumptio juris et de jure*, that the party did intend to revoke, and that *presumptio juris* is so violent, that it does not admit of circumstances to be set up in evidence to repel it. And this makes it difficult," he says, "to understand the case in *Douglas*" (*Brady, lessee of Norris*, v. *Cubitt* (*c*)) supposing that to be a

(*a*) 2 *East*, 541. (*b*) 2 *H. Bl.* 516. (*c*) 1 *Doug.* 31.

case

case of revocation by operation of law, and not within the Statute of Frauds."

And we think this opinion, at which we have arrived, not only supported by the authority of the decided cases, but the only one which is consistent with the provisions of the Statute of Frauds. For, if, against the intention to revoke, which is presumed by law, parol evidence of a contrary intention could be admitted, such as evidence of conduct of the testator leading to the inference that he meant the will to stand, or of declarations to that effect, then it would be but reasonable to allow such evidence to be met and encountered by evidence of conduct of the testator, leading to a different inference, and of declarations contradictory to the former. And, again, the admission of such evidence leads to this further difficulty, that, if the testator changes his first intention, and adopts a contrary one, which of the two intentions is to prevail? Is it to be the first, which is clearly expressed and proved, or is the latest formed intention, like the last will, to be allowed to predominate? It was precisely to preserve us from the perplexity and uncertainty of such conflicting evidence, both in the making and revoking of wills, that some of the provisions of the Statute of Frauds were expressly framed. We think, therefore, such evidence was inadmissible; and that the rejection of it, when offered by the plaintiff in error (the defendant below), was right; and that the bill of exceptions, tendered upon that ground by the defendant below, and allowed by the learned Judge, has entirely failed.

But the plaintiff in error contends that the rule of law, to which we have adverted, does not apply to the case before us. It becomes necessary, therefore, to determine

1838.

MARSTON against ROE dem. FOX.

determine what is the precise rule of law upon this subject, and to consider the objections urged against its application to the present case. And, upon a careful examination of the several cases which have been decided on this point, we take the rule of law, so far as it is material to the present enquiry, to be this; that, in the case of the will of an unmarried man having no children by a former marriage, whereby he devises away the whole of his property which he has at the time of making his will, and leaves no provision for any child of the marriage, the law annexes the tacit condition that subsequent marriage and the birth of a child operates as a revocation.

Now, with respect to the rule so laid down, the plaintiff in error objects that the exception to it is not confined to the single case where a provision is made by the will for the children of the marriage, but that the case is also excepted in which a provision is made by the will for either the wife, *or* the children; and, still further, he contends that, if it is necessary that provision should be made for both wife *and* children, it is enough that it is made either by the will itself or any subsequent provision; and that, upon the facts of this case, it appears a provision is made for both in the one way or the other; and that the estate, which was conveyed to the testator after the making of his will, being an after-purchased estate, did not pass thereby, but descended to the child of the marriage as his heir at law, and thereby formed such a provision for him.

With respect to the first objection, we are all of opinion that, under the circumstances above supposed, in order to prevent the revocation of the will, and to take the case out of the general rule, it is not sufficient that

1838.

MARSTON *against* ROE dem. FOX.

that a provision is made for the *wife only*, but that such provision must also extend to the children of the marriage.

The children of the marriage, both in the consideration of our law, and of the civil law, from which the rule itself has been adopted, are the subjects of the marked anxiety of both codes of law. This is evident from the preamble to the Statute of Wills, 32 *H.* 8. *c.* 1., which recites, as the object of the statute, the enabling the king's subjects to further "the good education and bringing up of their lawful generations," and "to discharge their debts, and, after their degrees set forth, advance their children:" and, still further, the observation of Lord Chancellor *Nottingham*, in the case of *Pitt* v. *Pelham and Another* (*a*), is direct upon the point: "The ground of the Statute of Wills, 32 *H.* 8., is the good of children and posterity." And no case has been decided, in which the will has been held to be not revoked, where the courts have not acted on the principle that the provision was not made for the wife only, but extended to the children also. In the case of *Eyre* v. *Eyre*, cited in 1 *Peere Williams* (*b*), the will appears to have been held to be revoked upon the ground that no provision is made for the child. And the case of *Brown* v. *Thompson* (*c*), which at first seems to lead to a contrary conclusion, does in fact support the principle now laid down. In that case, the testator had devised an estate to the woman whom he afterwards married, *and her heirs;* and Sir *John Trevor*, M. R., held the will to be

(*a*) *Freeman's Rep. Ch.* 134. The case was temp. Lord Keeper *Bridgman*. See *S. C.* in *Dom. Proc.* 1 *Lev.* 304.

(*b*) 1 *P. Wms.* 304.

(*c*) 1 *Eq. Cas. Abr.* 413. pl. 15. *S. C.* 1 *P. Wms.* 304., note †, 6th ed.

revoked

1838.

Marston against Roe dem. Fox.

revoked by the subsequent marriage and the birth of a child; which must necessarily have been on the ground that no provision was made for *the child;* and, although this decree was afterwards reversed by the Lord Keeper *Wright*, yet such reversal (the propriety of which seems very doubtful) expressly recognises the principle that the children of the marriage must be provided for by the will; for he assigns, as the reason for the reversal, that "no injury is done any person; and those are provided for, whom the testator was most bound to provide for," meaning thereby that the child was to be considered as provided for, by reason of an estate of inheritance having been given to the mother. And the case of *Kenebel* v. *Scrafton* (a) (before referred to) confines the exception to the case where both wife *and* children are provided for by the will.

Taking therefore the rule of law to be, that *the children* of the marriage must be provided for in order to prevent the revocation of the will, it is obvious that no provision whatever is made by this will for any child of the marriage; and whether any provision whatever is made for *the wife* by the devise to her of the estate for life, upon the condition expressed in the will, or whether she could claim a provision by her right to dower, we give no opinion whatever, because it is obvious that such provision for the wife, if it exists at all, is limited to her for life only, and cannot be extended in any way to form a provision for the children of the marriage.

But it is further objected that an after-purchased estate did not pass by the will, but descended upon the son in fee, and thereby became a provision for him, and prevented the revocation of the will. In the first place

(a) 2 *East*, 530.

we

we answer that no case can be found in which after-acquired property, descending upon the child, has been allowed to have that effect. And indeed such a proposition seems incompatible with the nature of a condition annexed to the will, which, so far as relates to the existence or extent of the provision, must, in its own nature, have reference to the existing state of things at the time the will itself was made. But, secondly, it appears to us a conclusive answer to the objection, that, upon the statement of facts in the special verdict, the testator had in him, at the time of making his will, an equitable interest in the estate in question, which equitable interest passed to the devisee under his will, so that the subsequent conveyance of the legal estate to the testator would give no real or beneficiary interest to his heir at law, but would make him a trustee for the devisee. For it is well established that an estate contracted for will pass under general words of devise in a will, even though the agreement to purchase is not to be carried into execution until a future day, which does not occur until after the time when the will bears date. See *Potter* v. *Potter* (*a*); *Greenhill* v. *Greenhill* (*b*): see also the case cited from the Rolls in 7 *Ves.* Jun., 436, 16 *Ves.* Jun., 253 (*c*). And, in this special verdict, it appears that the contract to purchase so entered into by *Joseph Fox*, upon his dying intestate and unmarried, descended upon and came to *John Fox*, his elder brother and heir at law, and sole next of kin, and the person entitled to take out administration of his personal estate;

(*a*) 1 *Ves.* sen. 437. (*b*) *Pre. Chanc.* 320.

(*c*) *Lawes* v. *Bennett*, 1 *Cox*, 167, cited in *Ripley* v. *Waterworth*, 7 *Ves.* 436, in *Townley* v. *Bedwell*, 14 *Ves.* 596, and (as *Douglas* and *Witterwronge*) in *Daniels* v. *Davison*, 16 *Ves.* 252.

1838.

MARSTON against ROE dem. FOX.

estate: *John Fox*, therefore, at any time after his brother's death, had the right to file a bill in equity for the specific performance of the contract, and was therefore seised of the equitable estate at the time of making his will.

Holding therefore, as we do, that the beneficiary interest in this estate passed under the devise, we consider the descent of the legal estate upon the child of the marriage to have formed no provision for him, but that he was left wholly unprovided for, as he neither took anything under the will, nor anything (if that would have been sufficient) by descent from his father.

We therefore think the will revoked, and that the lessor of the plaintiff is entitled to have the judgment affirmed which has been already given for him on the special verdict. And this makes it unnecessary for us to give any judgment upon the bill of exceptions tendered by the lessor of the plaintiff: for, as he is entitled to our judgment on the facts found by the jury, that bill of exceptions may for the present be considered as wholly immaterial, or as if it had never been tendered at the trial; although, at the same time, we have no hesitation in declaring our opinion to be, that the learned Judge was right in admitting the evidence therein mentioned, but wrong in rejecting the evidence which was offered to prove that *Joseph Fox* entered into the agreement of purchase stated in the bill of exceptions as the agent of *John Fox*.

Upon the whole, therefore, we are of opinion that the judgment of the Queen's Bench must be affirmed.

Judgment affirmed.

END OF HILARY TERM.

CASES

ARGUED AND DETERMINED

1838.

IN THE

Court of QUEEN's BENCH,

AND

UPON WRITS OF ERROR FROM THAT COURT TO THE

EXCHEQUER CHAMBER,

IN

Easter Term,

In the First Year of the Reign of VICTORIA.

The Judges who usually sat in Banc in this term were

Lord DENMAN C. J. PATTESON J.
LITTLEDALE J. COLERIDGE J.

The QUEEN *against* The Mayor, Sheriffs, Citizens, and Commonalty of the City of LINCOLN.

A party who is liable, by prescription, to repair a bridge, is also primâ facie liable to repair the highway, to the extent of 300 feet, from each end.

Such presumption is not rebutted by proof that the party has been known only to repair the fabric of the bridge, and that the only repairs known to have been done to the highway have been performed by commissioners under a turnpike road act.

THIS indictment (removed into K. B. by certiorari) was tried at the *Lincoln* Summer assizes, 1834, when a verdict was taken, by consent, for the Crown, subject to the opinion of this Court upon the following case.

 The

1838.

The QUEEN against The Mayor, &c., of LINCOLN.

The indictment stated that, from time immemorial, there was and yet is a common and public bridge called the *Great Bar Gates Bridge*, over a certain drain &c., which bridge is in the parish &c., in the city of *Lincoln*, and the county of the same city, in a common and ancient King's highway, leading from &c., over the said bridge, toward and unto &c., used from time immemorial for all the liege subjects, &c.; and that a certain part of the said highway next adjoining the north end of the said bridge, and within the distance of 300 feet thereof, beginning at the north end of the said public bridge, and extending from thence northwards, containing in length &c., and in breadth &c., and a certain other part of the said highway lying next adjoining the south end of the said bridge, and within the distance of 300 feet, beginning at the south end of the said bridge and extending from thence southwards, containing in length &c., and in breadth &c., on &c., at &c., were, and from thence hitherto have been, and still are, very ruinous &c., in great decay, and much out of repair, for want &c., to the great damage and common nuisance of all the liege &c., in and along the same parts of the same highway going &c., against the peace &c., and against the form of the statute &c.; and that the mayor, sheriffs, citizens, and commonalty of the city of *Lincoln* the said bridge have immemorially been bound, and been used and accustomed, to repair and amend, and still of right &c.; and that the said mayor, &c., being so liable as aforesaid, have not repaired, and still refuse to repair, the said parts of the said last-mentioned highway, so as aforesaid being in decay. (There were other counts, not materially vary-

ing

1838.

The QUEEN *against* The Mayor, &c., of LINCOLN.

ing from the above, some of which stated a prescriptive liability in the defendants to repair the parts of the highway, describing them as within 300 feet of the ends of the bridge respectively.)

Plea, Not Guilty.

The defendants are the corporation of the city of *Lincoln*, which is an immemorial corporation. The city of *Lincoln* is a county of itself, and is not comprised in any other county. The bridge mentioned in the indictment is an ancient public bridge; and the said corporation have, from time immemorial, exclusively repaired the fabric of the said bridge, and are liable by prescription to repair it. The fabric of the bridge is not out of repair; but there is a public highway passing over the bridge; and the said highway, extending from the said bridge from each end of it for more than 100 yards both ways, within the city and county of the city of *Lincoln*, is out of repair; which is the highway mentioned in the indictment. There was no evidence that any part of the said highway had ever been repaired by the defendants, or their predecessors, or by the parish in which it is situated; but the whole of the said highway, including the part of it which passes over the bridge, has, as far back as the memory of living witnesses can go, been repaired by the commissioners for the south east and south west district of the *Lincoln* turnpike road, which commissioners were first appointed by a public act of parliament, 29 *G.* 2. *c.* 84.

The question for the opinion of the Court was, whether the defendants were liable to repair the part of the said highway so out of repair.

 The

1838.

The Queen against The Mayor, &c., of Lincoln.

The case was argued last term (*a*).

Balguy, for the Crown. The defendants, being liable to repair the fabric of the bridge, are bound also to repair 300 feet of the road leading to it, on each side; *Rex* v. *The West Riding of York* (*b*). That was the case of a riding, liable by the common law as defined by the Statute of Bridges, 22 *H.* 8. *c.* 5. *s.* 9.; but the present case is not distinguishable in principle. The counsel for the prosecution there cited 43 *Assis.* 275 B. pl. 37., where the *Abbot of Combe* was presented for non-repair of a bridge, and it had been found by a jury on a previous record that he was bound to repair only two arches, and the bridge beyond the course of the stream, "et non fines ejusdem pontis:" but *Knivet* said that the Court would intend him liable to repair the bridge and the highway adjoining (*c*) to each end, although it were the soil of another. That was a case of prescription; and it was relied on in *Rex* v. *The West Riding of Yorkshire* (*d*), by Lord *Ellenborough*, who said, "I consider it as having been laid down long ago by Lord *Coke*, that the 300 feet of highway at the ends of the bridge are to be taken as part of the bridge itself," referring to *Coke's Commentary* on stat. 22 *H.* 8. *c.* 5., in 2 *Inst.* 705.

Sir *F. Pollock*, contrà. It is true that, where the general law of the land casts upon parties a duty to repair the fabric of a bridge, the same parties are bound also to repair the 300 feet of highway at each end. But that

(*a*) *January* 17th, 1838. Before Lord *Denman* C. J., *Littledale*, *Williams*, and *Coleridge* Js.

(*b*) 7 *East*, 588.; affirmed in *Dom. Proc. The West Riding of Yorkshire* v. *Rex*, 5 *Taunt*, 284.

(*c*) "Appleant."

(*d*) 7 *East*, 598.

1838.

The QUEEN against The Mayor, &c., of LINCOLN.

that rule cannot apply to a prescription, which supposes a grant upon condition, or some arrangement creating a duty, and where, therefore, the only question is as to the precise duty created by such grant or arrangement. The nature of the duty may be limited: whether it be so, is a question of fact. And here the case expressly confines the liability to the fabric of the bridge. The dictum in 43 *Ass.* 275 B. pl. 37. was not necessary to the decision of the case; the doctrine, as Lord *Eldon* remarks (*a*), is hard: and he seems to consider that the liability to repair the two arches was merely evidence as to the rest. Why should there not be a prescriptive liability to repair a single arch? *Rex* v. *The West Riding of Yorkshire* (*b*) was a case of liability of a riding under the general law of the land. An indictment charging only a non-repair of a bridge will not be supported by proof of non-repair of the highway adjacent. [Sir *J. Campbell*, Attorney-General, *amicus curiæ*, stated that this had been decided in a case tried in *Gloucestershire*.] That shews that the highway adjacent is not, in all cases, a part of the bridge. [*Coleridge* J. The language of stat. 22 *H.* 8. *c.* 5. seems to shew that prescriptive as well as other liability is comprehended; as appears, for instance, by the second and fifth sections: then it should seem that sect. 9 must apply to all kinds of liability.]

Balguy in reply. Lord *Coke*, in 2 *Inst.* 705., clearly considers the adjacent highway to be connected with the bridge as much in the case of prescriptive liability as in any other.

Cur. adv. vult.

(*a*) In *The West Riding of Yorkshire* v. *Rex*, 5 *Taunt.* 299.

(*b*) 7 *East*, 588.; affirmed in *Dom. Proc.* 5 *Taunt.* 284.

Lord

1838.

The QUEEN against The Mayor, &c., of LINCOLN.

Lord DENMAN C. J., in this term (*April* 25th), delivered the judgment of the Court.

This is an indictment for the non-repair of certain portions of the common highway, to which the defendants have pleaded Not Guilty. A verdict for the Crown has passed by consent, subject to our opinion upon a special case, which raises this question, whether a prescriptive liability to the repair of a public bridge, in the absence of any evidence to the contrary, and by itself, includes a liability to repair the highways at the ends of it within the distance of 300 feet. The prescriptive liability to repair the bridge is not contested on the one hand; and it is found on the other that there is no evidence of any actual repair done to the highways at the ends of it by the defendants, or their predecessors, within living memory: the only repairs proved have been done by a body of turnpike commissioners created by act of parliament, 29 *G.* 2. *c.* 84.

Since the case of *Rex* v. *The West Riding of Yorkshire* (*a*), it has been considered settled that, where the liability to repair a bridge attaches by the general law, as declared by the Statute of bridges, the liability to repair the approaches to the bridge for the space of 300 feet follows the same rule. It is contended, however, that a prescriptive liability is independent of the common law, and must in each case be measured by its own exact limits, which in the present instance are confined to the bridge itself. We think that the proposition of law is here correctly laid down; but that the facts found in the present case do not warrant the conclusion drawn from it.

(*a*) 7 *East*, 588.; affirmed on error, in *Dom. Proc. The West Riding of Yorkshire* v. *Rex*, 5 *Taunt.* 284.

Nothing

1838.

The QUEEN against The Mayor, &c., of LINCOLN.

Nothing appears here by which the liability to repair the approaches, *as parcel* of the prescriptive liability to repair the bridge itself, is excluded; there is no evidence of any conflicting liability. The non-repair by the parish, or the inhabitants of the county, and the non-repair de facto by the defendants, when explained by the repairs having been done for a great number of years by a body created by a modern act of parliament, are both consistent with a prescriptive charge *de jure* having been all the time existing and binding on the defendants. The jury, therefore, if this issue had gone to them for a decision, would have been properly directed to draw all such inferences in fact from the admitted liability to repair the bridge as that liability unexplained and unrestricted contains by intendment of law within itself.

The question then returns; what, by intendment of law, is the extent of a prescriptive liability to repair a bridge? Does it include the approaches or not? The dictum of *Knivet* J., in the *Abbot of Combe's Case* (a), answers this question, if it be law. There, to an indictment for the non-repair of a bridge, the Abbot had pleaded that he was only bound to repair two arches of it; and the jury had found that he was bound only to the repair of two arches, and the bridge over the stream of the water, *et non fines ejusdem pontis*. This was pleaded by him to a second indictment, and the record read: yet *Knivet* J. said, "We intend that you are bound to repair the bridge, and *the highway applying to the one end and to the other, although the soil be in another, because the easement shall be preserved for the people.*" This is a

(a) 43 *Ass.* 275 B. pl. 37.

1838.

The QUEEN against The Mayor, &c., of LINCOLN.

strong case, because the jury had negatived the liability to repair any more than the bridge: but they had not shewn in certain any other person or body liable: it was a case, therefore, like the present, of a prescriptive charge to repair a bridge, unexplained and unrestricted in fact; and the judges considered that the charge to repair the approaches was legally parcel of such a prescription. This case was mainly relied on in the judgment of this Court in the case first mentioned (*a*), as shewing that, so early as the reign of *Edward* 3., the judges understood the approaches to the bridge to be, as it were, excrescences of the bridge itself, and that the charge of repairing them was considered as belonging primâ facie to the party charged with the repair of the bridge itself. In the House of Lords, also, in the argument on the same case in error (*b*), this dictum was again relied on: and Lord *Eldon*, though he called it "*hard doctrine*," yet expressed no dissatisfaction with it as a lawyer, and assigned a satisfactory legal reason for it. It would be difficult for us, therefore, to say that this case, so recognised, is not law; and, being a case of prescription, it is certainly more directly applicable to the present case than it was to that of *Rex* v. *The West Riding of Yorkshire* (*c*), which was a case of common law liability. But, independently of authority, we think it maintainable on principle, the same principle which has united the approaches of the bridge to the bridge itself in the case of a common law liability, that, namely, of rendering complete the benefit to the public from the repair of the bridge itself. It is, besides, re-

(*a*) *Rex* v. *The West Riding of Yorkshire*, 7 *East*, 588.

(*b*) *The West Riding of Yorkshire* v. *Rex*, 5 *Taunt.* 284.

(*c*) 7 *East*, 588.; affirmed in *Dom. Proc.*, 5 *Taunt.* 284.

pugnant

pugnant to the genius of our law to multiply distinctions unnecessarily, and much more convenient and reasonable to hold that the same general rule should prevail, whoever may be charged with the repair of the bridge itself.

1838.

The QUEEN *against* The Mayor, &c., of LINCOLN.

We do not, therefore, break in upon the well established rules of law as to the extent of prescriptive liabilities, but lay down this only, that, in the absence of any evidence to the contrary, the prescription to repair the bridge must be intended to include within it the repair of the approaches to it. The verdict for the Crown therefore will stand.

Judgment for the Crown.

The QUEEN *against* The CAMBRIDGE Gas Light Company.

ON appeal against a poor-rate for the parish of *St. Mary the Great* in the town of *Cambridge*, wherein the *Cambridge* Gas Light Company was assessed at 70*l.*, for "the mains and other pipes and other apparatus for the conveyance of gas, belonging to the company, situate, being, lying, and fixed in the ground in the parish of *St. Mary the Great*," the sessions confirmed the rate, subject to the opinion of this Court upon a case, which was substantially as follows.

A company, under an act of parliament, erected in the parish of *A.*, in *Cambridge*, a gasometer and other gas apparatus, and laid down mains and pipes in that and other parishes, and also in extra-parochial land belonging to certain colleges in the University. The company supplied light by means of such pipes, &c., to the several parishes and colleges.

Held, that the company were rateable as occupiers of the land in the different parishes by their apparatus, pipes, &c.; and were properly assessed upon the sum which a tenant would pay yearly for the apparatus, pipes, &c., deducting the annual average expense of renovating the same, but not profits of the trade (though profits in trade were not assessed in any of the parishes); and deducting also the annual value of the apparatus and pipes lying in extra-parochial land.

And that the resulting amount was to be distributed among the assessments of the several parishes, in proportion, not to the payments made for lights in the respective parishes, but to the quantity of land occupied by the apparatus, &c., in each parish.

By

1838.

The QUEEN against The CAMBRIDGE Gas Light Company.

By stat. 4 & 5 *W.* 4. *c.* xxiv., local and personal, public, entitled "An act to incorporate a company for better supplying with gas the town of *Cambridge*" &c., certain persons, and their successors, were incorporated by the name of the *Cambridge* Gas Light Company, for the purpose of making coal-gas, coke, &c., and for lighting and supplying with gas all persons, and all colleges, halls, public places, roads, streets, &c., and any churches, chapels, theatres, &c., and private houses, shops, counting-houses, warehouses, manufactories, &c., within the town and university of *Cambridge*, or the precincts and neighbourhood thereof respectively, and they were empowered to sell such coal-gas, coke, &c., in such manner as they might think proper (*a*). The company was also empowered (*b*) to erect retorts, gasometers, &c., upon any lands which they might purchase for that purpose, and to break up the soil and pavement of any of the footways and carriage ways of any roads, streets, &c., and other public passages and places, and also (with consent of owners and occupiers) of any private ground, &c., in the said town, and to make culverts, &c., and to dig trenches and drains, and to lay mains and other pipes, and put stopcocks from such pipes, from the gasometer and other works, in, under, and along such public places, &c., as aforesaid, in such manner as should be necessary for carrying the act into execution, or supplying such lights as aforesaid.

Powers were also given (*c*) to the company to contract for lighting with the commissioners for lighting and paving the town of *Cambridge*, and with any persons,

(*a*) Sect. 1. (*b*) Sect. 58. (*c*) Sect. 69.

bodies

bodies politic, corporate, or collegiate, &c., within the town and university of *Cambridge* respectively.

It was also provided (*a*) that, for all the purposes of the act, the town and university of *Cambridge* should comprise and be deemed co-extensive with the fourteen parishes in the said town.

In pursuance of the said act, the company have purchased lands and premises in the parish of *St. Andrew the Less*, within the town of *Cambridge*, and erected thereon buildings, gasometers, retorts, and other necessary works and apparatus, for making gas and coke, and have broken up the soil and pavement of the several public streets and ways, and (with the consent of owners and occupiers) of divers of the private grounds, &c., in the several parishes, and have fixed therein proper mains and pipes for the conveyance of gas along the streets and into the several colleges, halls, shops, &c., of the university and town. They also manufacture for sale a considerable quantity of coke and tar at their said works and premises in *St. Andrew the Less*.

The several colleges and halls in the university were all founded before 43 *Eliz.* (1601), except *Downing* College, which was founded in 1800; and, with the exception of *Downing* College (and of some modern additions to others), no college or hall in the university is, or ever has been, rated to the relief of the poor. The various parishes, however, in which the colleges and halls are locally situate, in perambulating their respective boundaries, have been accustomed to go into and pass through the colleges and halls, and to affix their boundary marks therein. Several of the colleges

(*a*) Sect. 102.

and

1838.

The QUEEN *against* The CAMBRIDGE Gas Light Company.

and halls are lighted by the company with gas, which is supplied from their works by the mains and pipes fixed in the ground, and which pass into and through various parishes as aforesaid, and, among others, into and through the parish of *St. Mary the Great.*

The lands, buildings, gasometers, retorts, and other works and apparatus for making gas, coke, and tar, together with the mains and pipes for conveying gas through the town, colleges, and halls, would let to a responsible tenant at a rent of 2400*l.* a year, the tenant paying all rates and outgoings for making the subject of occupation productive, and doing all the ordinary repairs required, but not providing for the renewal of the various works when necessary, which renovation would cost, upon an average, 500*l.* a year; viz., for the buildings and main pipes, 300*l.*; and, for the gasometers and other more perishable articles, 200*l.*

The rent of 2400*l.* also includes the mains, pipes, and apparatus in those colleges and halls which are not assessed to the relief of the poor, the value of which mains, &c., so included, is 350*l.* a year.

The gas consumed in *St. Mary the Great* is conveyed into and through it by mains and service pipes sunk and affixed in the soil. The sum received by the company for gas thus conveyed and consumed by the parish is 763*l.* 18*s.* 8*d.* per annum. The assessment in *St. Mary the Great* has been confirmed, upon the assumption that 2400*l.* is the sum at which the works, mains, pipes, and apparatus of the company are liable at law to be rated to the relief of the poor, and that that sum, after deducting 150*l.* for the value of the buildings and works at the manufactory, ought to be distributed amongst the different parishes through which the mains and

1838.

The QUEEN against The CAMBRIDGE Gas Light Company.

and pipes are laid, with reference to the annual receipts by the company for gas supplied in each parish respectively. If this be correct, 70*l.* is the amount at which the company should be assessed in *St. Mary the Great.*

The company contend that, assuming the sum for which the works, &c., would let, to furnish the proper criterion of the annual value for the purpose of rating, they are entitled to make from the said sum of 2400*l.* the following deductions.

	£	s.	d.
For the annual cost of the renovation of the various works as before mentioned	500	0	0
For the annual value of their mains, pipes, and apparatus within those colleges and halls which are not rated to the relief of the poor - - -	350	0	0
For the profits in trade of the company	600	0	0

The company, however, contend that the above criterion is not the proper one; but that they should be rated upon the actual productive value of the works &c., the amount of which should be ascertained by a calculation of the company's total receipts and expenditure, according to the following statement.

The annual receipts of the company were stated as follows.

	£	s.	d.
For gas supplied to shops and private buildings - - -	3301	3	6
For gas supplied to colleges and halls not rated to the poor - - -	814	17	4
For public lights - -	1300	0	0
For coke sold - - -	500	0	0
For tar sold - -	50	0	0
	£5966	0	10

The

1838.

The QUEEN against The CAMBRIDGE Gas Light Company.

	£	s.	d.
The expenses for purchase of coals, lime, labour, salaries, ordinary repairs, and poor-rates and other taxes, were then stated (specifying the respective amounts) at the total sum of - -	3595	18	10
Leaving a profit balance of	£2370	2	0

From which balance the company deducted,

	£	s.	d.
For renovation of buildings and works (500*l.*); bad debts; law expenses; interest on a capital of 3000*l.* employed in the works; and 20 per cent. allowance for profits in trade: in the whole	1325	0	0
The company also claimed to deduct gross annual receipts for gas supplied to the colleges and halls not rated to the poor - - -	814	17	4
In all - - - -	2139	17	4
Leaving the annual amount of the rateable property of the company - -	230	4	8

Personal estate, or the profits of trade, are not assessed to the poor rate in any parish within the town of *Cambridge*.

The questions for the opinion of the Court were,

1. Whether the principle upon which the assessment has been made, or that contended for by the company, be the right.

2. Whether, supposing the principle adopted by the parish to be upheld, the company may make any and which of the deductions claimed from the sum of 2400*l.*

3. Whether, if the company's principle be adopted, they are entitled to all or any of the deductions which they

1838.

The Queen against The Cambridge Gas Light Company.

they claim to make from their gross receipts beyond their ordinary expenses.

4. The total rateable value being ascertained, upon what principle it ought to be distributed amongst the several parishes in and through which the mains and pipes are laid, after deducting 150*l.* for the value of the buildings and works in *St. Andrew the Less?*

The order of sessions was to be confirmed, or the rate to be adjusted, according to the opinion of this Court upon the above questions. The case was argued in last *Hilary* term (*a*).

Kelly and *Bodkin*, in support of the order of sessions. First, the general principle, upon which the rate is founded, is correct; namely, that of ascertaining the sum for which the lands, buildings, and pipes, would let to a tenant; *Rex* v. *The Birmingham Gas Light and Coke Company* (*b*). The sum suggested as the proper criterion, on behalf of the company, is the amount of their net profits. But no rate could be made upon such a principle with any certainty. This criterion was contended for unsuccessfully in *Rex* v. *The Birmigham Gas Light and Coke Company* (*b*); and that decision was in conformity with *Rex* v. *The Brighton Gas Light Company* (*c*), where the company were held to be rateable as occupiers of the land by their pipes. The same doctrine was laid down, in the case of a canal, in *Rex* v. *Chaplin* (*d*), where Lord *Tenterden* said that the canal was, in effect, let; and the rent was made the

(*a*) *January* 20th, 1838; before Lord *Denman* C. J., *Littledale*, *Williams*, and *Coleridge* Js.

(*b*) 1 *B. & C.* 506.

(*c*) 5 *B. & C.* 466.

(*d*) 1 *B. & Ad.* 926.

criterion

1838.

The QUEEN *against* The CAMBRIDGE Gas Light Company.

criterion of value. So in *Rex* v. *Lower Mitton* (*a*) this was taken as the criterion in the first instance, subject to deductions. It is true that the rent which a tenant gives is rather evidence of value than the absolute value itself; for there may be an excessive rent. But here the finding shews what would be a fair rent.

Next, as to the deductions. The company claim a deduction of 500*l.* for the average annual expense of renewing the works. *Rex* v. *Lower Mitton* (*a*) will probably be relied on. There such a deduction was incidentally said to be proper: the decision of the Court turned upon a previous point, which made the order of sessions bad. It was said, "a further deduction should be allowed from that rent, where the subject is of a perishable nature, towards the expense of renewing or reproducing it." If this dictum be adopted to the full extent, it comprehends every thing but the actual land: therefore, not only the repairs of buildings and works of every kind, but an annual repairing fund, must always be deducted; a rule which cannot be upheld. Indeed, land itself requires renovation, in some sense. If, in addition to a rent, the landlord exacted a renovating fund, no doubt the rate ought to be laid on the aggregate, as shewing the value of the property to the tenant: therefore the expense in question, when mixed up with the rent, is not to be deducted. [*Littledale* J. Any tenant who was required to renew works would estimate this, and deduct from his rent accordingly.] Besides, this is an occasional expense, not an annual one. In *Rex* v. *Tomlinson* (*b*) the sessions had assessed houses and a coal mine at a lower proportion of the net

(*a*) 9 *B.* & *C.* 810.

(*b*) 9 *B.* & *C.* 163.

rent

1838.

The QUEEN *against* The CAMBRIDGE Gas Light Company.

rent than the land: and the Court held that they could not take upon themselves to say that the rate was necessarily unequal; assigning, as a reason, that the houses and the works of the colliery would require renovation. That case does not go the length of shewing that the sessions were bound to make a deduction on that ground. In point of fact, the annual value is always estimated without going into a calculation how long buildings, &c., will last. The next deduction claimed is in respect of the mains and pipes in land of the colleges and halls which is not assessed to the poor rate. Now the case does not find that the land, when occupied by the company by means of their mains and pipes, is not rateable, whatever may be its exemption so far as it is occupied by the colleges and halls. The land is not found to be extra-parochial: indeed it appears to have been comprehended in the parish perambulations. [*Coleridge* J. It appears that the exemption from rateability cannot arise from the land being held by the colleges, inasmuch as the colleges are rated for land which they have recently taken. And this agrees with *Rex* v. *Gardner* (*a*).] The deductions for the interest and profits in trade will probably not be insisted upon.

Next, as to the distribution of the value of the whole among the parishes. The assessment is made so that in each parish the company are rated for what they earn by their occupation in that parish. [*Littledale* J. Suppose they have pipes laid in a parish where they supply no

(*a*) 1 *Cowp.* 79. See *Downing College, Cambridge,* v. *Purchas,* 3 *B. & Ad.* 162. *Harrison* v. *Bulcock,* 1 *H. Bl.* 68.

1838.

The QUEEN against The CAMBRIDGE Gas Light Company.

gas.] If the fact were so, that might make it necessary to adopt a different principle. But, as the facts are here, no other method of distribution appears practicable. In the case of a canal where different tonnage dues are earned in different parishes, the rate is determined by what is earned in each parish; *Rex* v. *Kingswinford* (*a*). The cases are collected in *Gunning on the Law of Tolls*, 201–9. ch. VII. s. 3.

Sir *W. W. Follett* and *Byles*, contrà. It is true that the company are to be rated, as occupying the land by their mains and pipes, according to the improved value: that appears from *Rex* v. *The Birmingham Gas Light and Coke Company* (*b*) and *Rex* v. *The Brighton Gas Light Company* (*c*). But the question is, how this value is to be ascertained? Sometimes the rent is a fair test; under some circumstances it is no test at all. The rent might be the best criterion, if all were in a single parish. But, when the property is distributed through different parishes, as here, the rent of the whole furnishes no test as to the amount to be assessed in each parish. It is contended, on the other side, that, for the purpose of apportioning the value, the sums earned in the several parishes must be looked to. If so, it follows that the whole sum assessed must be the whole sum earned; in other words, the profits. The two principles contended for on the other side are therefore inconsistent. *Rex* v. *The Corporation of Bath* (*d*) and *Rex* v. *The New River Company* (*e*) shew that the profits earned

(*a*) 7 *B. & C.* 236.
(*b*) 1 *B. & C.* 506.
(*c*) 5 *B. & C.* 466.
(*d*) 14 *East*, 609.
(*e*) 1 *M. & S.* 503.

by

1838.

The QUEEN against The CAMBRIDGE Gas Light Company.

by the distribution of water from reservoirs and springs to different parishes constitute the amount to be assessed in the parish where the reservoirs and springs are situate, except so far as a proportion of the profits arises from the actual occupation of land in other parishes by the pipes. Further, this rate, in fact, includes the value of the gasometer and other fixtures; but, as the case does not find that other such property is rated in the parish, the rate is bad for inequality; *Rex* v. *The Birmingham and Staffordshire Gas Light Company* (*a*). Then, as to the deduction claimed for renovation. Unless the renovations were allowed, the annual rent would no longer be the same; in order to keep it up to 2400*l.* there must be an expenditure of 500*l.* That is therefore a diminution of the annual value. As to this, *Rex* v. *Tomlinson* (*b*), *Rex* v. *Lower Mitton* (*c*), *Rex* v. *The Trustees of the Duke of Bridgewater* (*d*), are conclusive authorities. The same principle was adopted in *Rex* v. *Woking* (*e*); and it is embodied in the late statute, 6 & 7 *W.* 4. *c.* 96. *s.* 1. As to the deduction claimed for the land which is within the colleges, and not rated, there can be no doubt that the sessions meant to find that the land is extra-parochial, otherwise it would have been rateable; *Rex* v. *Gardner* (*g*); where Lord *Mansfield* said that, in fact, most of the old colleges were extra-parochial. As to the tenant's profits, *Rex* v. *Joddrell* (*h*) and *Rex* v. *Woking* (*e*) shew that a rack rent does not include them:

(*a*) 6 *A.* & *E.* 634.
(*b*) 9 *B.* & *C.* 163.
(*c*) 9 *B.* & *C.* 810.
(*d*) 9 *B.* & *C.* 68.
(*e*) 4 *A.* & *E.* 40.
(*g*) 1 *Cowp.* 84.
(*h*) 1 *B.* & *Ad.* 403.

if,

1836.

The QUEEN *against* The CAMBRIDGE Gas Light Company.

if, therefore, the rack rent generally has been taken as the criterion throughout the parish, and it has here been estimated without making the deduction for tenant's profits, the rate is unequal. The distribution among the parishes has been shewn to be inconsistent with the general principle, assumed by the sessions, of rating according to the rent; and it cannot be justified. It would clearly be absurd if any one parish, in which the pipes lay, had no lights; and the same reason applies where the lights paid for are not exactly in proportion to the land occupied. Besides, the most remote parish probably pays a higher price on account of the length of pipe necessary to reach it; but this does not increase the value of the land occupied by the pipes in that parish. The safe principle is to take the profits, subject to the deductions, as in *Rex* v. *Woking* (a), and to distribute them, as there, in proportion to the land occupied.

Cur. adv. vult.

Lord DENMAN C. J., in this term (*April* 25th), delivered the judgment of the Court.

This was an appeal against a rate made for the relief of the poor of the parish of *St. Mary the Great*, in the town of *Cambridge*. The sessions confirmed the rate, subject to the opinion of this Court upon a case, stating that the said company, by virtue of an act of parliament containing the usual powers, had erected a gasometer and other apparatus in the parish of *St. Andrew the Less*, in the said town of *Cambridge*, and had also laid down

(a) 4 *A.* & *E.* 40.

mains

1838.

The QUEEN against The CAMBRIDGE Gas Light Company.

mains and pipes through the various parishes, and, also, colleges and halls (which upon the statement we consider to be extra parochial), including the said parish of *St. Mary the Great*, and thereby supply the public and private buildings in the said town with gas. The company has been assessed in the latter parish in the sum of 70*l.* upon the amount of 2400*l.*, which is stated to be what a responsible tenant would give for the whole apparatus for a year, after making some deductions and disallowing others hereafter to be noticed. Upon the hearing of the appeal, two questions mainly arose. 1. Whether the above principle of ascertaining the sum to be assessed be correct, or whether it ought to have been made upon the total receipts of the company deducting their expenditure. And, 2., Whether due allowance has been made of all proper deductions, supposing the first principle to be correct.

Now that the general principle adopted by the parish officers, and confirmed by the sessions, as contrasted with that contended for by the appellants, is correct, we consider it to be now too late to doubt. The decisions of *Rex* v. *The Trustees of the Duke of Bridgewater* (*a*), of *Rex* v. *Tomlinson* (*b*), and *Rex* v. *Lower Mitton* (*c*), have, we think, settled the question. The former case is an express authority against the appellants, and the latter in favour of the decision of the sessions, upon this point. We are of opinion, therefore, that the sessions were quite right in the adoption of the general principle, but not equally so in allowing the deductions which ought to be made.

(*a*) 9 *B.* & *C.* 68. (*b*) 9 *B.* & *C.* 163.
(*c*) 9 *B.* & *C.* 810.

1838.

The Queen *against* The Cambridge Gas Light Company.

Three were claimed by the company. 1st, for the renewal of the works 500*l.*; 2dly, for the value of mains and pipes within the colleges and halls 350*l.*; and, 3dly, for the profits in trade of the company 600*l.*

As to the first. The rule laid down in the case of *Rex* v. *Lower Mitton* (*a*), before mentioned, is, we think, in point. Amongst other deductions there mentioned, which ought to be made from that rent which is to be the criterion for ascertaining the proper amount of the rate, there is specified a "further deduction," which ought to be allowed, "where the subject is of a perishable nature, towards the expense of renewing or reproducing it." It was observed at the bar that, until the case of *Rex* v. *Lower Mitton* (*a*), this doctrine is not to be found. The Court, however, in their judgment, for which time was taken, referred to other cases as the foundation of it: and the reasonableness of allowing such a deduction is, we think, obvious; because the estimated rent at the supposed time of letting manifestly could not be continued at the same amount unless the apparatus be maintained in as good a state and condition. And this view of the subject receives confirmation, if it had been requisite, from the recent stat. 6 & 7 *W.* 4. *c.* 96. *s.* 1., which prescribes the manner in which property shall thereafter be assessed. The language there used, in describing one of the deductions to be allowed, is almost in terms the same as that employed by the Court in the last mentioned case.

The second ground of deduction may be more conveniently considered hereafter.

The third claim of deduction is, for the profits in trade

(*a*) 9 *B.* & *C.* 810.

of

1838.

The QUEEN against The CAMBRIDGE Gas Light Company.

of the company, 600*l.* This claim, it is presumed, has arisen from the fact stated, that profits in trade are not assessed in any parish in the town of *Cambridge.* Nor are they in this instance. The rent, which it is found a tenant would give by the year after certain deductions (viz. 2400*l.*), is not the amount of *profits.* Those, necessarily, are something independent of and beyond the rent, upon which the person taking the apparatus must calculate, or nobody would become tenant at all: they are, therefore, perfectly distinct. The rent which a tenant would give for lands after certain deductions, which is the criterion for the due assessment of it, is one outgoing; the expense of cultivation, another: and all beyond, whatever that may be, obviously comes under the denomination of profits. Since, therefore, the profits are in their nature wholly distinct from the rent, and are, not only not a deduction from it, but the reverse, something beyond and in addition to it, we cannot perceive that this claim rests upon any just principle, and are of opinion that it has been properly disallowed.

We come now to the fourth question, upon what principle the total rateable value, being ascertained, ought to be distributed amongst the parishes in and through which the mains and pipes are laid, after deducting 150*l.* for the value of the buildings and works in the parish of *St. Andrew the Less:* and it is one of considerable general importance. The sessions have adopted, as their criterion, the amount of the receipts for gas supplied in each parish, and have assigned to the respondent parish the sum of 763*l.* 18*s.* 8*d.*, being such amount within it; and, if the principle be correct, it is admitted that 70*l.* is the proper assessment upon the

1838.

The QUEEN *against* The CAMBRIDGE Gas Light Company.

company in that parish. In determining this point, it is necessary to consider, *in respect of what* the company is rateable, according to the decisions. And from the case of *Rex* v. *The Corporation of Bath* (a), and various other authorities in conformity thereto, including *Rex* v. *The Brighton Gas Light Company* (b), and the still later case of *Rex* v. *The Trustees of the Duke of Bridgewater* (c), and many others which might be cited, it appears that they are rateable as occupiers of land *for the improved value of the land, from the gas pipes being laid in it.* This therefore, being, as we think it is, the acknowledged principle, it seems to follow that the criterion before mentioned, which has been adopted by the sessions, cannot be the true one. Suppose (adopting their own rule) the value of the whole works to be 2400*l.* per annum, minus certain deductions, and the quantity of apparatus in the soil of each of the several parishes to be equal, but the sale of gas and the receipts for it to be confined to one; the cases of *Rex* v. *The Corporation of Bath* (a), before referred to, and *Rex* v. *The New River Company* (d), and *Rex* v. *Foleshill* (e), are express authorities to shew that a rate upon the company in that particular parish where all the profits are received could not be sustained. The *New River* Company was rated in the parish of *Little Amwell*, at the sum of 300*l.*, the value of the land, independent of the water, being 5*l.* only: and this Court held the rate to be proper, though it was expressly stated that *no part of the profits accrued in the parish of Little Amwell*, nor indeed until the distri-

(a) 14 *East*, 609.
(b) 5 *B.* & *C.* 466.
(c) 9 *B.* & *C.* 68.
(d) 1 *M.* & *S.* 503.
(e) 2 *A.* & *E.* 593.

bution

1838.

The QUEEN *against* The CAMBRIDGE Gas Light Company.

bution of the water in *London*. Since, therefore, in the present case, the land occupied by the apparatus in each parish through which it passes contributes to the whole value to let, it follows that the company must be rated in respect of its occupation in each parish; and, if so, we are aware of no rule which can be laid down as to the amount, except that it must be in proportion to the quantity of apparatus situate in each parish. It is true that, in the case of a canal where the tolls varied in different parts of the line, it was decided that a rate could not be made upon the company in each parish, according to the length of the canal in it, and *for that reason; Rex* v. *Kingswinford* (a); but in a case very recently before this Court, where the tolls were the same throughout the whole line, it was held that the proportion to be paid by the company, in any given parish along the line, must be ascertained by a mileage calculation; *Rex* v. *Woking* (b). And, as it is impossible to suppose any superiority in one part of the apparatus over another, the same principle, we think, should be applied in the present instance; and that the assessment upon the amount of profits received in the respondent parish was wrong.

It remains only to consider whether the deduction of 350*l*., being the annual value of that part of the apparatus which lies within the colleges and halls, ought to be made. And we purposely reserved the consideration of this point to the last, because it is connected with the principle which regulated our answer to the last question. For, inasmuch as the rate is imposed upon the

(a) 7 *B.* & *C.* 236.

(b) 4 *A.* & *E.* 40.

land

1838.

The Queen *against* The Cambridge Gas Light Company.

land used for the apparatus, and as none can be imposed upon that part which lies in those extra-parochial places, the amount which would otherwise have arisen therefrom (the aforesaid sum of 350*l.*) must, we think, be deducted.

Upon the whole, therefore, in those particulars as to which the sums are agreed upon, the amendment of the rate will be of course; but, as we have no materials for ascertaining the proportion between the parishes, it must (as, according to the statement, was intended) in that respect be "adjusted."

Rate to be amended accordingly.

Thursday, April 19th.

Field and Another *against* Joseph Robins.

Plaintiffs, on becoming sureties for defendant, took a joint and several indemnity bond from defendant and *J.* Plaintiffs afterwards became liable, as such sureties, to pay, and paid, 1098*l.* They then sued *J.* on the indemnity bond, and obtained a verdict for 1098*l.*, but accepted 215*l.* from him in compromise, giving him a receipt as follows: — "Received of *J.* 215*l.*, being the sum we have agreed to accept in discharge of the damages and costs in this action." Plaintiffs afterwards sued defendant on the same bond, and he pleaded payment by *J.* of 215*l.* in full satisfaction.

Held, that proof of the compromise with *J.*, as above stated, did not support the plea.

DEBT on bond. The condition of the bond, set forth in the declaration, recited a previous bond, whereby the plaintiffs and defendant became jointly and severally bound to his then Majesty in a penalty of 2000*l.* for the faithful discharge by defendant of the office, to which he had been appointed, of a storekeeper of the Ordnance; and it was declared by the condition of the present bond that, if the defendant and one *James Robins*, or either of them, their or either of their heirs, executors, &c., should indemnify the plaintiffs and each of them, &c., from and against all actions, suits, costs, charges, &c., by reason of the recited obligation, then the

1838.

FIELD *against* ROBINS.

the obligation now declared upon was to be void, otherwise &c. The declaration then stated that the defendant entered upon and did not faithfully discharge the office, by reason whereof the recited bond became forfeited, and the plaintiffs were sued thereupon in two several actions in the Court of Exchequer, and, to compromise the same, were forced and obliged to pay one *James Smith*, on behalf of his Majesty, 1098*l.* Breach, that defendant and *James Robins*, although requested, did not nor would indemnify plaintiffs, &c.

Plea. That the said *James Robins*, after the making of the writing obligatory declared upon in this action, and after the forfeiture of the same by the breach of the condition thereof in the declaration mentioned, and whilst the damages sustained by the plaintiffs by reason of the said breach remained and were wholly unliquidated, and before the commencement of this suit, viz., on &c., paid to plaintiffs 215*l.* in full satisfaction and discharge of the last-mentioned damages, which sum of 215*l.* plaintiffs then accepted and received of and from the said *James Robins* in full satisfaction of the last mentioned damages: by means whereof defendant then became and still is fully and absolutely discharged and exonerated from the said damages sustained by the plaintiffs by reason of the said breach of the said condition of the writing obligatory (declared upon in this action), and from all claims and demands by plaintiffs in respect thereof. Verification.

Replication, traversing the payment and acceptance of 215*l.*, in the same terms in which they were pleaded. Issue on the traverse.

On the trial before Lord *Denman* C. J., at the *London* sittings after last *Hilary* term, it appeared that the indemnity

1838.

Field against Robins.

indemnity bond was given by the defendant and his brother, *James Robins*; that, after the forfeiture of the previous bond to the Crown, and payment of 1098*l.* by the plaintiffs, as above stated, the plaintiffs sued *James Robins* upon the indemnity bond, and, in 1827, obtained a verdict for 1098*l.* damages on the breach assigned in that suit. *James Robins* then paid the plaintiffs 215*l.* in satisfaction of the damages and costs in that action, and the plaintiffs gave him a receipt as follows.

"*Chichester, January* 15*th*, 1828.

"*Field and Another* v. *Robins.*

"Received of Mr. *James Robins* the sum of two hundred and fifteen pounds, being the sum we have agreed to accept in discharge of the damages and costs in this action. £215.

"*George Field.*

"*J. P. Hayllar.*"

On the trial of the present cause the plaintiffs had a verdict for 1098*l.*, but leave was given to move to enter a verdict for the defendant, on the ground stated in the following motion.

Sir *F. Pollock* now moved according to the leave reserved. The defendant and *James Robins* were liable jointly (though severally also), upon their bond, to the plaintiffs; and, they having sued *James* and received a sum from him in full satisfaction, this was a complete settlement of the cause of action against both *James* and *Joseph*, and their bond could not be put in suit again. *Watters* v. *Smith* (*a*), which was cited for the

(*a*) 2 *B. & Ad.* 889.

plaintiffs

1838.

FIELD *against* ROBINS.

plaintiffs at the trial, does not apply. All that the Court there relied upon was the apparent intention of the plaintiff to take from the joint debtor, whom he permitted to compound, the proportion due from that debtor, and to discharge him only. Here no such intention is expressed in the receipt, nor is there any other evidence of it.

Lord DENMAN C. J. I think the verdict ought not to be disturbed, though *Watters* v. *Smith* (*a*) does not quite come up to the point for which it was cited at the trial. The defendant, on this issue, was to prove payment in full satisfaction. I think that the principle of *Watters* v. *Smith* (*a*) applies, and that the defendant here cannot be said to have proved such payment.

LITTLEDALE J. I am of the same opinion. The 215*l*. was not likely to have been accepted in full satisfaction of 1098*l*.

PATTESON J. I think there ought to be no rule. The onus of proving payment in full satisfaction lay on the defendant; and the facts stated did not prove it.

COLERIDGE J. concurred.

Rule refused.

(*a*) 2 *B. & Ad.* 889.

1838.

Thursday, April 19th.

BAKER *against* WILLIAM DENING and Others.

Under the Statute of Frauds, 29 *C.* 2. *c.* 3. *ss.* 5, 6., the making of a mark by the devisor, to a will of real estate, is a sufficient signing; and it is not necessary to prove that he could not write his name at the time.

TRESPASS for breaking and entering defendant's close. Plea, that the locus in quo was the soil and freehold of the defendant *Dening;* and justification in *Dening's* right. Replication, that the locus in quo was not the soil and freehold &c.: and issue thereon.

On the trial before Lord *Denman* C. J., at the last *Devonshire* assizes, it appeared that the locus in quo was part of an estate of which one *John Dening* died seized in fee. The defendants' case rested on a will, regularly signed and attested, by which *John Dening* devised the estate to the defendant *W. Dening* in fee. The plaintiff put in a codicil, dated subsequently to the will, revoking the will, and devising the estate to another party. The codicil was duly attested, but had only the devisor's mark, instead of his signature. Evidence was given to shew that the devisor, at the time of putting his mark, could have written his name: and the defendants' counsel contended that, under the Statute of Frauds, 29 *C.* 2. *c.* 3. *ss.* 5. 6., a mark could operate as a signature only where the party was unable to write his name. The Lord Chief Justice directed a verdict for the plaintiff, reserving leave to the defendants to move for a nonsuit.

Rogers now moved accordingly. Upon the evidence, it must be assumed that the devisor could have written his name at the time when he made his mark. [He then went into the evidence.] Sect. 6 of stat. 29 *C.* 2. *c.* 3.

1838.

BAKER *against* DENING.

c. 3. provides that no devise in writing of lands shall be revocable otherwise than by some other will or codicil in writing, or other writing declaring the same, or by burning &c.; and that all devises of lands shall remain in force until the same be burnt &c., "or unless the same be altered by some other will or codicil in writing, or other writing of the devisor signed in the presence of three or four witnesses, declaring the same." It has been considered (*a*) that the words "signed in the presence" &c. refer not to "will" and "codicil," but only to "other writing" &c.; on this construction the material question here arises upon sect. 5, which enacts that all devises and bequests of lands "shall be in writing, and signed by the party so devising the same, or by some other person in his presence and by his express directions, and shall be attested &c." It may be conceded that, where a party is unable to write, the affixing of his mark is a sufficient signature. Where a party cannot write, his mark is, in fact, his only signature; and therefore the case may fall within the equity of the statute. It is, however, remarkable that no express decision, even to this extent, can be found. In *Lemayne* v. *Stanley* (*b*) there is an obiter dictum by *North*, *Wyndham*, and *Charlton*, that "the putting of his seal had of itself been a sufficient signing within the statute; for *signum* is no more than a mark, and sealing is a sufficient mark that this is his will: but *Levinz* doubted of this upon the case in *Roll.* 1 *Abridgm.* 245." (*c*). In the report of the same case in *Freeman* (*d*) the dictum is reported as sanctioned by the whole Court, and is as

(*a*) See *Ellis* v. *Smith*, 1 *Ves.* jun. 12. (*b*) 3 *Lev.* 1.

(*c*) *Arbitrement*, (B), pl. 25.

(*d*) *Lemaine* v. *Stanelcy*, *Freem.* (*K. B.* and *C. P.*) 538.

follows:

1838.

BAKER against DENING.

follows: "And it is not necessary to write his name, *for some cannot write, and there their mark is a sufficient signing.*" The dictum, as reported in *Levinz*, that sealing is a sufficient signing, was held to be bad law in *Smith* v. *Evans* (a), and has long been so considered; *Grayson* v. *Atkinson* (b), (where Lord *Hardwicke* observes (c), "the statute requiring the will to be signed, undoubtedly meant some evidence to arise from the handwriting; then how can it be said, that putting a seal to it would be a sufficient signing? For any one may put a seal; no particular evidence arises from that seal: common seals are alike, and one man's may be like another's; no certainty or guard therefore arises from thence;"), *Ellis* v. *Smith* (d), *Wright* v. *Wakeford* (e); in which last case Lord *Eldon* alludes to the inference having been drawn from the notion that a person may sign by his mark. The object of the enactment was to perpetuate evidence of the act of the devisor. Now, if the statute allowed that the requisite of signing could be satisfied by any visible indication of intent, except writing the name, surely so solemn an act as affixing a seal would have been held enough. If, again, a mark be a signature, why should not a mark made, not by the devisor himself, but by another "by his express directions," be sufficient? [Lord *Denman* C. J. May a devisor direct another to sign his own name instead of the devisor's?] The intention of the legislature was that the devisor's name should appear. [*Coleridge* J. You must contend that, wherever a mark appears, there must be a collateral enquiry whether the party could write at the time.] That will

(a) 1 *Wils.* 313.

(b) 2 *Ves.* sen. 454. See note (4) ibid. 4th (*Belt's*) ed.

(c) P. 459.

(d) 1 *Ves.* jun. 11.

(e) 17 *Ves.* 459.

certainly

1838.

BAKER against DENING.

certainly follow: and it is reasonable that any one claiming under the statute should bring the case within its provisions. There are express decisions that the mark of an attesting witness is enough; *Harrison* v. *Harrison* (*a*), where it was pointed out that the statute does not apply the word "signed" to the witnesses; *Addy* v. *Grix* (*b*).

Lord DENMAN C. J. If there were any doubt at all on this question, it would be very fit that it should be considered; but, if there be none, we ought not to create any by granting a rule. It has been urged that sealing is insufficient: but sealing is one thing, signing another. The mark of a person who is not capable of writing is allowed to be sufficient: and I never heard of any enquiry being made whether the party making the mark was, at the time, capable of writing. Here it was certainly a matter of doubt whether the party could, or could not, write at the time: it is not clear that he could. I think it much better that there should be no enquiry on such a point.

LITTLEDALE J. Mr. *Rogers* admits that, in some cases, a mark is sufficient; and that cannot be disputed. Under the statutes 3 & 4 *Ann.* *c.* 9. *s.* 1. and 17 *G.* 3. *c.* 30. *s.* 1., the requisite of *signing* is satisfied by a mark. The only doubt now suggested is, whether the rule apply to cases where the party can write at the time. I never heard of an enquiry into that point: it might be a very difficult and unsatisfactory one. It does not follow that, because a man can write at the time, he can write

(*a*) 8 *Ves.* 185. (*b*) 8 *Ves.* 504.

 legibly,

1838. Baker against Daniel.

legibly. I think that no collateral enquiry of this sort ought to take place. In this case it is doubtful how the fact was: but I think it better not to disturb the general understanding.

Patteson J. It is conceded that, in all the clauses of the Statute of Frauds respecting wills, the requisite of signing is satisfied by making a mark; for Mr. *Rogers* admits that the practice cannot be disputed. Now, if it be once conceded that a mark, by way of signature, is a signing within the act, it is too much to say that in every particular case we are to enquire minutely into the ability of the party to write his name. It would be inconvenient to enter into such a question: and there is always the attestation; so that, when a mark appears, there are means of enquiry into the circumstance; and the enquiry in such a case is of course more close than in ordinary cases. But I am not prepared to say that a man may not at any time sign by merely putting his mark, whether he can write his name or not.

Coleridge J. I should be sorry if our decision were to lead to the practice of substituting a mark for a name, for this might give much opportunity for fraud. But here we are on the question of law, whether, if a party make his mark, that be a signature, although he could have written his name. How can we say that it is not, when we look at the statute and find what is admitted in argument? The statute has only the word "signed;" and it is admitted that. in some cases, this is satisfied by a mark. When I consider the inconvenience which would result from enquiring, in all cases, whether the party who has made a mark could write at all, or could write

write at the particular time, I think it would be wrong to raise a doubt by granting a rule.

Rule refused (*a*).

(*a*) The provisions in stat. 7 *W.* 4. & 1 *Vict.* c. 26. ss. 20, 9. appear not to vary the law on this point.

BARRACLOUGH and Others *against* JOHNSON and Another.

Friday, April 20th.

On an issue whether or not certain land, in a district repairing its own roads, was a common highway, it is admissible evidence of reputation, (though slight,) that the inhabitants held a public meeting to consider of repairing such way, and that several of them, since dead, signed a paper on that occasion, stating that the land was not a public highway; there being at the time no litigation on the subject.

In determining whether or not a way has been dedicated to the public, the proprietor's intention must be considered. If it appear only that he has suffered a coutinual user, that may prove a dedication; but such proof may be rebutted by evidence of acts shewing that he contemplated only a license resumable in a particular event.

Thus, where the owner of land agreed with an Iron company, and with the inhabitants of a hamlet repairing its own roads, that a way over his land, in such hamlet, should be open to carriages, that the company should pay him 5*s.* a year and find cinder to repair the way, and that the inhabitants of the hamlet should lead and lay down the cinder, and the way was thereupon left open to all persons passing with carriages for nineteen years, at the end of which time, a dispute arising, the passage was interrupted, and the interruption acquiesced in for five years: Held, that the evidence shewed no dedication, but a license only, resumable on breach of the agreement.

DECLARATION (*February* 1838) in trespass for breaking and entering plaintiff's close, &c. Pleas: 1. Not guilty. 2. That, before and at the times when &c., there was and of right ought to have been a certain common and public highway into, through, over and along the said close in which &c., for all the liege subjects, &c., on foot and with cattle and carriages at all times of the year, &c.: justification under such right of way. Verification. Replication to this plea, traversing the right of way as pleaded. Issue on the traverse.

On the trial before *Patteson* J. at the *York* Spring assizes, 1838, it appeared that the alleged road, called the *Green Gate Lane*, lay in the hamlet of *Mortomley*,

which

1838.

BARRACLOUGH *against* JOHNSON.

which repairs its own highways. A witness for the plaintiffs proved that, forty years ago, a public meeting of the inhabitants of *Mortomley* was held, and a document there signed by the witness, and by twelve others of the inhabitants present, who were since dead: this writing was tendered as evidence of reputation, and objected to, but admitted by the learned Judge. It purported to be made by the inhabitants of the hamlet assembled for the purpose of considering whether or not the road should be repaired; and it stated their opinion that it was not, and ought not to be, a public highway; and that the site was the property of a Mr. *Parkin*, and subject only to a public bridle-way. The paper remained with the surveyor of the highways. The plaintiffs also proved that, in 1814, the executors of *Parkin* (being then the proprietors of the soil in question) entered into an agreement with the *Thorncliffe* Iron Company, and the inhabitants of the hamlet by their surveyors, that the lane should be open to carriages; that the company should pay an acknowledgment of 5*s.* a year, and supply cinders for the repair of the road; and that the hamlet should lead and spread them. It further appeared that, before that time, there was a gate across the road, which was kept locked, and excluded carriages; but that, from the time of the agreement till 1832, there was no longer any obstruction, and the lane was used as a carriage road. In 1832, disputes arose, and the passage along the lane with carriages was interrupted by the then proprietor. The defendants' counsel objected to the reception of evidence as to the agreement, but the learned Judge received it, as explanatory of the user. And he stated to the jury that the user from 1814 to 1832 appeared to have been by

1838.

BARRACLOUGH *against* JOHNSON.

by convention between the *Thorncliffe* Company and *Parkin*'s representatives: that, although user was evidence of a dedication to the public, yet the question always was what the land-owner intended, and, if it appeared that he had not intended absolutely to dedicate, the inference from user failed: and that in the present case, unless the jury thought that the proprietor, in 1814, intended absolutely to dedicate the carriage road to the public, he might resume it if the bargain was broken by the other parties. A verdict was given for the plaintiffs on the general issue, and on the second plea so far as regarded a carriage way; for the defendants, on that plea, as to a way on foot and with horses.

Atcherley Serjt. now moved for a new trial. First, the paper signed by the inhabitants of *Mortomley* was not evidence of reputation, because it was drawn up by persons assembled, not to settle any matter of reputation, but to consider whether or not they should undertake repairs. Such a document, to be admissible as suggested, should be framed in the course of a transaction shewing, by its nature, that it was reputation, strictly, which the parties met to pronounce upon. And the document should be, in effect, an assertion of something which the parties have received, as reputation, from others. Here the thing stated is mere opinion. And the parties were interested. [*Patteson* J. It was urged at the trial that the declaration was against as well as for their interest; for, if it exempted them from repairs, it took from them the benefit of the road.] They met to consider whether they should repair or not; and decided in favour of their own exemption.

1838.

BARRACLOUGH against JOHNSON.

[*Coleridge* J. referred to *Nicholls* v. *Parker* (*a*).] There the parties made a statement of something which they considered reputation. Here nothing is pronounced but a resolution, or declaration of opinion. Secondly, the direction of the learned Judge as to dedication was not correct. The owner of land must, in such a case, be supposed aware of the consequence of his own acts. If he allows free and unqualified use of a way over his premises, he subjects himself to the loss of that which he has led the public to believe he intended to grant. Here the representatives of *Parkin* gave persons to understand that they meant all the King's subjects to use the road with carriages, provided they themselves were exempted from repairs. It was for them to see that the condition was made available; but, if it ceased to be so, they could not resume the road. If they meant to create a limited right only, they should have restrained the user accordingly. The observation of Lord *Ellenborough* in *Rex* v. *Lloyd* (*b*) applies. "If the owner of the soil throws open a passage, and neither marks by any visible distinction, that he means to preserve all his rights over it, nor excludes persons from passing through it by positive prohibition, he shall be presumed to have dedicated it to the public. Although the passage in question was originally intended only for private convenience, the public are not now to be excluded from it, after being allowed to use it so long without any interruption." The plaintiffs here say that the dedication was not meant to be absolute, but subject to the condition that certain persons should observe a private bargain. It cannot be contended, after nineteen years'

(*a*) 14 *East*, 331; note (*a*) to *Outram* v. *Morewood*.

(*b*) 1 *Camp.* 260.

user

1838.

BARRACLOUGH against JOHNSON.

user by the public, that their right is to depend on what may have passed in the mind of the land-owner with reference to such a proviso at the time of the dedication. If there could be a provisional dedication, such as the plaintiffs contend for, at least there should have been some notice of the limitation. And, if a qualified dedication was originally contemplated, a change of intention may be inferred from the unrestricted user during nineteen years. Lastly, the verdict was against the weight of evidence. [*Patteson* J. There was evidence that the defendants had acquiesced in the road being treated as not public, during the five years from 1832.]

Lord DENMAN C. J. There is no ground for this application. As to the first point, the evidence of reputation was very slight, but there was some. I do not agree that it is necessary for persons giving an opinion as to the publicity of a way to state that they found themselves on reputation, although their statement ought in reality to be founded on some reputation. The statement of each of the deceased persons was reputation, to some extent. As to the other point, the agreement between the land-owner and the township, if it could be considered a conditional dedication, was as public as it can be expected that such a dedication should be: and it was for the convenience of both parties. Then, can there be a conditional dedication of the kind here supposed? Perhaps not. A dedication must be made with intention *to dedicate*. The mere acting so as to lead persons into the supposition that the way is dedicated does not amount to a dedication, if there be an agreement which explains the transaction: and, referring to the agreement here, it is

 plain

1838.

Barraclough against Johnson.

plain that there was only a license to use. There was a permissive enjoyment from 1814; but it was put an end to in 1832. If such an enjoyment may be permitted by means of the way being left open to every one, the leaving it so is not in itself evidence of a dedication. In *Wood* v. *Veal* (a) the public had used a way over the locus in quo as long as could be remembered; but the land had been under a ninety-nine years' lease during the whole time, and *Abbott* C. J. left it as a question for the jury whether there had been a dedication to the public before the term commenced, saying that, if not, there could be no dedication except by the owner of the fee, and the lease explained the user as not being referable to a dedication by him. Yet there was strong evidence there to shew that the landlord could not have been ignorant of the user; and Lord *Tenterden* did not dispute the doctrine of Lord *Ellenborough* in *Rex* v. *Lloyd* (b). Therefore there is nothing in the cases to establish that a permissive user may not be consistent with a right to resume the way. As to the weight of evidence, the learned Judge is not dissatisfied with the verdict.

Littledale J. The document put in was evidence, though very slight, of reputation. The common case as to reputation is that the witness has heard old persons make a statement. Here, the plaintiffs put in a resolution subscribed by several persons since dead. It is as if each had been heard to say that the lane was not a public highway. The supposed dedication was, I think, a mere permission. When the circumstances under which it arose are stated, the idea of a dedication is rebutted. It is said that an intention to dedicate must

(a) *5 B. & Ald.* 454.

(b) 1 *Camp.* 260.

be

1838.

BARRACLOUGH against JOHNSON.

be inferred from the acts of a proprietor; and it is true that the question is not decided by what he says. A man may say that he does not mean to dedicate a way to the public, and yet, if he had allowed them to pass every day for a length of time, his declaration alone would not be regarded, but it would be for a jury to say whether he had intended to dedicate it or not. The facts may warrant them in believing that the way was dedicated, though he has said that he did not so intend: and, if his intention be insisted upon, it may be answered that he should have shewn it by putting up a gate, or by some other act. The intent is a proper ingredient in the decision of such a question as this; but here I think it was shewn by acts that a dedication was not contemplated.

PATTESON J. I had some difficulty as to the document; but I thought it was evidence, to be admitted, valeat quantum. On the other point, I think that the intention to dedicate or not must be left to the jury. The very term dedication shews that the intent is material. There cannot be such a thing as turning land into a road without intention on the owner's part. The facts here are strong in disproof of such an intention. The payment of *5s.* yearly could only be for a leave. The real transaction was, that the company wanted to go upon this road, and the land-owner had no objection, provided they would repair the road, which he himself had occasion for as an occupation way: they were to give the cinders, and the inhabitants of the hamlet to carry and spread them; but this was not to continue when the annual payment ceased. No person, probably, came along that road within the year but those who had occasion

1838.

Barraclough against Johnson.

occasion to pass from the hamlet or the company's works; except, in short, those who were included in the agreement. And for five years from 1832 they submitted to its being no road.

Coleridge J. As to the objection that the inhabitants who declared the lane to be no road were parties interested, *Nicholls* v. *Parker* (a) shews that persons, who might by their declaration take a burden upon themseves, may also declare that the road in respect of which the burden would attach is not public, provided there be no litigation depending at the time. Here there was no evidence of any litigation depending when the declaration was made; it appeared only that the parties met to talk over the subject of repairing. Then, as to the dedication. A party is presumed cognizant of the consequences following his own acts; and, if he permits user of a way over his land, a jury may presume that he intended to dedicate such way to the public. But you cannot exclude evidence of the circumstances under which the user commenced. And it appears here that an agreement took place between the land-owner, the surveyors of the hamlet, and the proprietors of the iron-works, that these last were to pay 5*s.* a year and to find cinders, which the inhabitants of the hamlet were to lead and spread: these are circumstances which, if not to be excluded, throw a strong light upon the commencement of user, and shew that no dedication was intended, provisional or absolute. And again, after nineteen years, we find an alleged breach of contract by the parties using the way,

(a) 14 *East*, 331; note (a) to *Outram* v. *Morewood*.

and

1838.

BARRACLOUGH *against* JOHNSON.

and a consequent interruption of the user. Suppose that, after nineteen days, the *Thorncliffe* Company had refused to fulfil their engagement; could not the land-owner have resumed the right of way? And, if so, why might not he after nineteen years?

Rule refused.

HURST *against* ORBELL.

Friday, April 20th.

A. bought horses of *B.*, paying 80*l.*, with liberty to return them within a month, allowing *B.* 10*l.* out of the 80*l.*, and with a stipulation that, if he kept them beyond the month, he should pay *B.* 10*l.* above the 80*l.*

Held, that *A.*, on returning the horses within a month, might recover the 70*l.* in an action for money had and received.

ASSUMPSIT for money had and received. The plaintiff, by his particular of demand, claimed 80*l.* Plea, non assumpsit. On the trial before *Tindal* C. J. at the last assizes for *Kent*, it appeared that the plaintiff had agreed to buy a pair of horses of the defendant, paying 80*l.*; but the bargain was, that plaintiff should be at liberty to return the horses within a month, allowing defendant 10*l.* out of the 80*l.*; and that, if plaintiff kept them beyond the month, he was to pay 10*l.* above the 80*l.* Defendant gave plaintiff a receipt as follows:— "80*l.*—Received of —— *Hurst*, Esq., eighty pounds for two grey horses, warranted sound and quiet in harness. Ten pounds more if the horses are kept. *Henry Orbell.*" The plaintiff returned the horses within the month, and brought the present action. It was not proved that the plaintiff had been ready, before action brought, to allow the 10*l.* For the defendant it was urged that the action ought to have been brought on the special contract, or at least that the plaintiff should have proved his readiness to pay the 10*l.*, before attempting to recover back any part of the 80*l.* as money had and received to his use. The Lord Chief Justice directed a verdict

1838.

Hurst against Oakley.

a verdict for the plaintiff, giving leave to move to enter a nonsuit; and the plaintiff had a verdict for 70*l.*

Peacock now moved according to the leave reserved. This action cannot be supported without shewing that the money claimed was the plaintiff's, as is laid down by Lord *Ellenborough* in *Thurston* v. *Mills* (*a*). That does not appear in the present case. The property in the horses had passed to the plaintiff, that in the money to the defendant. How then did the 70*l.* become the plaintiff's? If the contract was rescinded, he was entitled to the whole 80*l.* "Where a contract is to be rescinded at all, it must be rescinded in toto, and the parties put in statu quo:" per Lord *Ellenborough* in *Hunt* v. *Silk* (*b*). [Lord *Denman* C. J. Here they were to be put into a situation which they had themselves agreed upon in the event of rescinding]. This was, in effect, an agreement that the defendant should repurchase the horses at 70*l.*, if the plaintiff returned them within a month; it was not an agreement for rescinding, or putting the parties in statu quo. The distinction taken by *Buller* J., in *Towers* v. *Barrett* (*c*), applies here; the contract remained open, and the action should have been for damages, not for money had and received.

Lord Denman C. J. The objection is too refined. The defendant held the 70*l.* to the use of the party who should be entitled at the time when the option was to be determined.

Littledale J. concurred.

(*a*) 16 *East*, 274. (*b*) 5 *East*, 452. (*c*) 1 *T. R.* 136.

1838.

HURST *against* ORRELL.

PATTESON J. I am of the same opinion. The 70*l.* remained in the defendant's hands during the month, to be paid back or retained according to the event.

COLERIDGE J. concurred.

Rule refused.

RANDLESON *against* MURRAY and Another.

Saturday, April 21st.

A warehouseman at *Liverpool* employed a master porter to remove a barrel from his warehouse. The master porter employed his own men and tackle; and, through the negligence of the men, the tackle failed, and the barrel fell and injured plaintiff: Held, that the warehouseman was liable in case for the injury.

CASE. The declaration stated that, before and at the time &c., defendants were the possessors and occupiers of a certain warehouse, situate at *Liverpool*, for the reception, custody, and transmission of goods and merchandize; and therefore it became and was the duty of defendants to have, use, and employ, within and upon their said warehouse, good, proper, and sufficient tackle, implements, and materials, in and about the receiving and sending away the said goods and merchandize, and in and about the raising and lowering the same; and also to use and employ due and proper skill and care in fastening and securing, with the tackle, &c. aforesaid, the said goods and merchandize whilst the same were being so received or sent away, and raised or lowered as aforesaid, and to use due and proper care and attention in raising or lowering the same, so that the said goods and merchandize might be received and sent away, and raised and lowered, without damage or injury to the persons employed in delivering or receiving the same: yet the defendants, well knowing &c., and whilst they were so possessors &c., to wit on &c., and whilst the said defendants, by their servants in that behalf, were sending

1838.

RANDLESON against MURRAY.

sending away and lowering from their said warehouse and premises certain goods and merchandize, to wit a barrel filled with flour, to and into a certain cart there standing ready to receive the same, not regarding &c., wrongfully, &c., by their said servants, had, used and employed such bad, improper, and insufficient tackle, implements, and materials in sending away and lowering the said barrel, and by their said servants used and employed so little and such bad skill and care in fastening and securing, with the said tackle, implements, and materials, the said barrel, and by their said servants used so little care and attention in lowering the said barrel, that, by means of the use and employment of the bad, improper, and insufficient tackle, implements and materials aforesaid, and of the want of due and proper skill and care in fastening and securing the said barrel, whilst the said barrel was being sent out and lowered from the said warehouse and premises to or into the cart aforesaid, the same slipped and fell from the said tackle and implements aforesaid unto and upon the said plaintiff, and thereby greatly bruised &c. (describing the damage to the plaintiff), and other injuries &c. Pleas: 1. Not guilty. 2. That the defendants were not, at the time in the declaration in that behalf mentioned, sending away or lowering the said goods and merchandize in manner and form as in the declaration above alleged: conclusion to the country. Issues thereon.

On the trial, before *Coleridge* J., at the last *Liverpool* assizes, it appeared that the defendants were the occupiers of a bonded warehouse in *Liverpool*; and that, for the purpose of removing some barrels of flour from their warehouse, they had employed one *Wharton*, who was a master porter in *Liverpool*, and who used his own

tackle,

1838.

RANDLESON against MURRAY.

tackle, and brought and paid his own men. *Taylor*, a master carter, was employed by *Wharton* to carry the barrels away; *Taylor* also sent his own carts, &c., and his own men, one of whom was the plaintiff. The injury to the plaintiff was occasioned by a barrel falling on him in consequence of part of *Wharton's* tackle failing while it was being used by *Wharton's* men. On this evidence, the defendants' counsel contended that the plaintiff's remedy was against *Wharton;* not against the defendants. The learned Judge reserved leave to move for a nonsuit on this point, and directed the jury to find for the plaintiff, if they considered that there had been carelessness in the use of the tackle. Verdict for the plaintiff.

Alexander now moved according to the leave reserved. It must be admitted that the defendants would be liable, if *Wharton* and his men could be considered as their servants; *Bush* v. *Steinman* (*a*). Admitting that case (which, however, has been questioned) to be law, it is to be distinguished from the present upon the ground that here *Wharton*, though undoubtedly employed by the defendants, is rather a bailee for a particular purpose than a servant. In *Laugher* v. *Pointer* (*b*) the owner of a carriage hired horses of a stable-keeper, who also provided a driver; and the Judges were equally divided on the question whether the owner was liable for an accident caused by the negligent driving. There *Littledale* J. said that, upon principle, the rule making a party responsible for his servants could not be carried so far as to hold him liable for the acts of all employed and chosen by his agent. *Harris* v. *Baker* (*c*) is also in

(*a*) 1 *B. & P.* 404. (*b*) 5 *B. & C.* 547. (*c*) 4 *M. & S.* 27.

favour

1838.

RANDLESON *against* MURRAY.

favour of the more limited rule. In *Witte* v. *Hague* (a) an engineer had contracted with a sugar-refiner to erect a steam-boiler for him; the boiler burst, and injured the property of a third party, the plaintiff: and, the jury having found that the engineer was, by himself or his servants, conducting and managing the operations of the apparatus when the accident happened, the engineer was held liable, though the Court intimated that, if the jury had found the other way, there might have been some weight in the objection that the action should have been brought against the party employing the engineer. Here the facts are substantially the same as in the last-cited case. Is the owner of a bale of goods, who sends it by a common carrier, liable for every injury which may arise from the carrier allowing the bale, through negligence, to fall on another person during its transport? Or is the owner of a house liable for an injury caused by a chimney-sweeper who carelessly knocks a brick from the chimney top? Yet both the carrier and the chimney-sweeper are employed by the owner. Probably the only satisfactory rule in cases of this description would be that the jury, rather than the Judge, should decide whether the offending individual be or be not the servant of the party sued. That was directed by Lord *Abinger* C. B. in *Brady* v. *Giles* (b). The learned Judge ought therefore to have put that question to the jury instead of merely asking their opinion upon the point of carelessness in using the tackle.

Lord DENMAN C. J. Had the jury in this case been asked whether the porters, whose negligence occasioned

(a) 2 *D. & R.* 33. (b) 1 *Mo. & Ro.* 494.

the

1838.

RANDLESON *against* MURRAY.

the accident, were the servants of the defendant, there can be no doubt they would have found in the affirmative. I can see no reason for granting a rule.

LITTLEDALE J. It seems to me to make no difference whether the persons whose negligence occasions the injury be servants of the defendant, paid by daily wages, or be brought to the warehouse by a person employed by the defendant. The latter frequently occurs in a large place like *Liverpool*, where many persons exercise the occupation of a master porter. But the law is the same in each case.

PATTESON J. The case of a carrier is quite distinct. He has goods in his custody as bailee.

COLERIDGE J. concurred.

Rule refused (*a*).

(*a*) See *Chandler* v. *Broughton*, 1 *C. & M.* 29. *S. C.* 3 *Tyrwh.* 220. *Hussey* v. *Field*, 2 *C. M. & R.* 432. *S. C.* 5 *Tyrwh.* 855.

CARRUTHERS *against* HOLLIS and CHURCH.

Saturday, April 21st.

Trespass for driving plaintiff's sheep, and leaving them in a highway, by which they were injured. Plea, that they were wrongfully in defendant's close depasturing, wherefore defendant drove them into a highway adjoining the close. Replication, that they escaped into defendant's close from an adjoining close of plaintiff through defect in the fence between the two closes, which fence defendant was bound to repair. Rejoinder, traversing the escape of the sheep through defect in the fence. The issue being found for the plaintiff: Held, on motion in arrest of judgment, that the replication answered the plea.

TRESPASS. The declaration contained two counts. The second count stated that the defendants chased and drove about certain sheep of the plaintiff, then being upon a certain close in the county of *Monmouth*,

 from

1838.

CARRUTHERS *against* HOLLIS.

from and off the said close into a certain highway in the county aforesaid, when and where the defendants left the said last-mentioned sheep, whereby they were damaged &c.

Plea to the second count. That, before and at the said times when &c., the defendant *Hollis* was lawfully possessed of the said close; and, because the last-mentioned sheep, before and at the said several times when &c., were wrongfully in the said close of the defendant *Hollis*, eating and depasturing his herbage there then growing, and doing damage there to him, defendant *Hollis* in his own right, and defendant *Church* as his servant and by his command, at the said times when &c., chased and drove the said last-mentioned sheep from and out of the said close in which they were then doing such damage, into a certain highway adjoining the said close, and there left the same for the plaintiff, doing no unnecessary damage to the plaintiff on that occasion &c., which are the same &c.

Replication. That the plaintiff heretofore, to wit at the said times when &c., was and still is possessed of a close, situate &c., and contiguous to the said close of defendant *Hollis;* and that defendant *Hollis*, and all other the tenants &c. of the said close in which &c. for the time being, from time whereof &c., have repaired, and of right ought to have repaired, &c., and defendant *Hollis* still of right ought to repair, &c., the hedges between the said close of defendant *Hollis* and the said close of plaintiff, as often as need hath been or required, that cattle being, feeding, and depasturing in those closes respectively might not escape &c.: and, because the said hedges between the said closes of defendant *Hollis* and plaintiff, before and at the said time when &c.,

1838.

CARRUTHERS *against* HOLLIS.

&c., were ruinous &c., for want of needful repair &c., the said sheep being, feeding, and depasturing in the said close of plaintiff, a little before the said time when &c., escaped from and out of plaintiff's said close into the said close of defendant *Hollis*, in which &c., through the defects of the said hedges, and on that occasion were in the said close of defendant *Hollis*, in which &c., until the defendants, at the same time when &c., of their wrong, chased and drove about the said sheep from and off the said closes in the second count of the declaration mentioned, into the said highway in the said declaration also mentioned, when and where the defendants left the said last-mentioned sheep, in manner and form &c. Verification.

Rejoinder. That the said sheep, or any part thereof, did not escape from the said close of plaintiff in the replication mentioned into the close of the defendant *Hollis*, in which &c., nor, at the said time when &c., were the said sheep, or any of them, in the said close of the defendant *Hollis*, through the defects of the said hedges between those closes, in manner and form &c.; and of this &c. Conclusion to the country. Issue thereon.

On the trial before *Gurney* B., at the last *Monmouthshire* assizes, a verdict was found for the plaintiff on the above issue, and for the defendants upon another issue joined on the first count.

R. V. Richards now moved for a rule to shew cause why judgment should not be arrested, or a repleader awarded. The plea to the second count discloses a defence which is not answered. The defendant was justified in driving the sheep out of his own close, although he

1838.

CARRUTHERS against HOLLIS.

was bound to repair the fence: the only consequence of the obligation to repair is that he is not entitled to complain of their coming upon his close; he could not therefore have brought an action, or distrained damage feasant, without giving notice: on giving notice, he might do either; note (4) to *Poole* v. *Longuevill* (a). There is no express authority for saying that a party who has not given notice may, under such circumstances, drive back the sheep to the close from which they have strayed; but it seems clear, upon principle, that he may. Now the record does not shew that the defendant has done more than this: it is only said that the defendant drove the sheep into a certain highway adjoining his close. The highway may be the plaintiff's close from which the sheep strayed into the defendant's. It appears from many authorities (as, for instance, *Dovaston* v. *Payne* (b)) that the highway may be the close of an individual, inasmuch as the public right of passage does not exclude private property in the soil. The highway, again, might be the nearest road to the plaintiff's close: or it might be the only one by which it was practicable to drive the sheep back. If the acts of the defendants, as they appear on the declaration and pleas, are not illegal, the plaintiff should have new assigned, in order to avail himself of any answer furnished by facts not necessarily to be collected from the record.

LORD DENMAN C. J. The plea justifies the trespass complained of, by stating that the sheep were wrongfully in the defendant's close. Then the replication alleges that the sheep were not there wrongfully, be-

(a) 2 *Wms. Saund.* 284 *e*.

(b) 2 *H. Bl.* 527.

cause

1838.

CARRUTHERS *against* HOLLIS.

cause the defendant *Hollis* was bound to repair the fence, and had not done so, which occasioned the escape of the sheep into his close. The plaintiff denies that the escape was so occasioned; and the verdict is found for him on that issue. Then may the owner of a close, under such circumstances, drive sheep into the highway and leave them there? There is no authority on this point: but none is necessary. It is perfectly clear that the least to be expected from a party in the situation of the defendant here is, that he should put back the sheep into the place in which they were before they quitted it in consequence of his neglect.

LITTLEDALE J. concurred.

PATTESON J. The plea, taken by itself, might furnish a good answer to the declaration: but the replication is good. It answers the justification in the plea by alleging that the sheep came from the plaintiff's close into that of the defendant *Hollis* through defect in the fence, which defendant was bound to make good. The defendant was driven to meet this by denying that the escape had been caused by his default: he does so, and the issue is found against him.

COLERIDGE J. concurred.

Rule refused.

1838.

Saturday, April 21st.

GORE *against* WRIGHT.

Debt for 63*l.*, rent for two years and one quarter, due 25th *March* 1837, reserved on a demise for forty-five years, at 28*l.* per annum.

Plea, that, before any of the sum claimed became due, and more than two years and a quarter before 25th *March* 1837, and before 25th *December* 1834, viz. 17th *April* 1834, plaintiff and defendant agreed that defendant should give up, and plaintiff take, possession of the premises before 25th *December* 1834, in consideration whereof defendant should be discharged from the rent which would have become due for the occupation after 25th *December* 1834; that possession was given up by defendant and accepted by plaintiff accordingly; and that plaintiff entered on 17th *April* 1834, and had held ever since, and defendant had not held since; "and the said tenancy and the defendant's said interest were thereby then surrendered and extinguished."

Held that, on this plea, the objection did not arise whether the term was shewn upon the record to be regularly surrendered according to the Statute of frauds, 29 *C.* 2. *c.* 3. *s.* 3.; the defence being merely an executed contract that, in consideration of defendant's giving up possession, plaintiff should abandon his claim to the rent; and that such defence was valid.

DEBT. The declaration stated that plaintiff, on 29th *April* 1814, demised to defendant a messuage &c., for a term of forty-five years and three quarters, to be computed from 29th *September* 1812, at a yearly rent of 28*l.*, payable quarterly, viz. 25th *March* &c.: that defendant entered, and that, on 25th *March* 1837, 63*l.* was due for two years and a quarter's rent.

Plea 1. Nunquam indebitatus.

Plea 2. That the plaintiff claims and seeks to recover the said sum of 63*l.*, being the sum above demanded and alleged to be due to the plaintiff for the rent of the said messuage &c. in the said declaration mentioned, for the space of two years and one quarter of a year, ending upon 25th *March* 1837, as in the said declaration mentioned: That defendant held the said messuage and tenements at the said rent of 28*l.*, payable quarterly on the days and at the times in that behalf in the declaration mentioned; That, before the said sum of 63*l.* above mentioned, or any part thereof, accrued or became due, and more than two years and a quarter before the said 25th *March* 1837, being the day when the said sum of 63*l.* is supposed to have been due and payable to plaintiff, and before 25th *December* 1834,

viz.

viz. on 17th *April* 1834, it was agreed by and between plaintiff and defendant that defendant should quit and deliver up to plaintiff, and that plaintiff should take possession of, the said messuage &c., before the said 25th *December* 1834, and that, in consideration thereof, defendant should be discharged from all liability to pay any further rent, or any other compensation which would otherwise become due for the occupation of the messuage &c. after the said 25th *December* 1834: That, in pursuance of the said agreement, defendant afterwards, viz. 17th *April* 1834, being before the commencement of this suit, and before the said sum of 63*l.* or any part thereof accrued or became due, and more than two years and a quarter before the said 25th of *March* 1837, and before the said 25th of *December* 1834, did quit and deliver up possession of the said messuage &c. to plaintiff, and plaintiff then accepted such possession thereof, in pursuance and on the terms of the said agreement, and in discharge of the liability of defendant to pay any more or further rent or compensation for the said messuage &c.; and that plaintiff then, to wit on 17th *April* 1834, accordingly entered into and upon the said messuage &c., and thenceforth hitherto hath remained and continued in possession thereof; and defendant hath not, at any time since he so quitted and gave up possession of the said messuage &c., held, used, or enjoyed the same; and the said tenancy, and defendant's said interest, were thereby then surrendered and extinguished. Verification.

Replication. That defendant did not, in pursuance of the said agreement in the said last plea mentioned, quit and deliver up possession of the said messuage &c.

1838.

Goar against Wright.

to plaintiff, nor did plaintiff accept such possession thereof, in pursuance and on the terms of the said agreement, and in discharge of the liability of defendant to pay any more or further rent or compensation for the said messuage &c.; nor did plaintiff then enter &c., in manner &c. Conclusion to the country.

On the trial before *Williams* J., at the *Middlesex* sittings in this term, a verdict was found for the plaintiff on the first issue, and for the defendant on the second.

Platt now moved (*a*) for judgment non obstante veredicto. The plea shews no contract binding upon the parties, and therefore no sufficient discharge from the rent. The term could not be surrendered without writing, by sect. 3 of the Statute of frauds, 29 *C.* 2. *c.* 3.; and there is no pretext for saying that it was surrendered by operation of law. Besides, this is an agreement which could not be performed within one year from the making; and therefore the action does not lie, by sect. 4. The plea should allege a writing, so as to satisfy the statute, though that might be unnecessary in a declaration; note (2) to *Duppa* v. *Mayo* (*b*). [*Coleridge* J. Suppose the term to be in existence, may not the landlord agree that, if the tenant will go out without insisting on the remainder of the term, he will not claim the rent? Then, after such an agreement is executed, there is an end of the difficulty.] The Defendant here pleads the agreement as a surrender; therefore, unless there be a legal surrender shewn on the record, he must

(*a*) Before Lord *Denman* C. J., *Littledale*, *Patteson*, and *Coleridge* Js.

(*b*) 1 *Wms. Saund.* 276 *e.*

fail.

fail (*a*). [*Patteson* J. referred to *Thomas* v. *Cook* (*b*), *Whitehead* v. *Clifford* (*c*), and *Grimman* v. *Legg* (*d*).]

Cur. adv. vult.

1838.

GORE *against* WRIGHT.

Lord DENMAN C. J., on a subsequent day of the term (*May* 2d), delivered the judgment of the Court.

This motion was made on the ground that no surrender could be effected by the transaction between these parties, as set out in the plea. But we think that the plea does not set up a surrender as the defence, but simply a contract by the landlord to excuse payment of rent in consideration of the defendant giving up possession; which possession has actually been given up by the defendant, and accepted by the plaintiff his landlord.

Rule refused.

(*a*) See note (2) to *Chester* v. *Willan*, 2 *Wms. Saund.* 97 *b.*

(*b*) 2 *B. & Ald.* 119. See note [*n*] to *Thursby* v. *Plant*, 1 *Wms. Saund.* 236 c. (5th ed.).

(*c*) 5 *Taunt.* 518.

(*d*) 8 *B. & C.* 324.

ASHBY *against* MINNITT and Others.

Monday, April 23d.

Trespass for taking plaintiff's goods; plea, that the goods were not plaintiff's. Plaintiff proved that the sheriff had seized the goods, being the property of *B.*, under an execution against *B.*, and had sold them to plaintiff: Held, that defendant might shew, on the issue here joined, that the sale was fraudulent as against creditors, that he himself had taken the goods under an execution against *B.*, and that this was the alleged trespass.

TRESPASS for seizing and taking goods, chattels, and effects of the plaintiff. Pleas, 1. Not Guilty. 2. That the goods, chattels, and effects, &c., were not the goods, &c., of the plaintiff. Issue joined on both pleas.

On the trial before *Littledale* J., at the last *Nottingham* assizes, the plaintiff proved that the goods in question had been the property of one *Brennan*, and had been

seized

1838.

ASHBY against MINNITT.

seized under a fi. fa. upon a judgment obtained against *Brennan* by a person named *Beadle*; that, upon that seizure, *Brennan* sent to the plaintiff, who purchased the goods from the sheriff's officer, while in his possession, the sale being verbal only. The plaintiff paid the purchase-money, which the sheriff's officer handed over to *Beadle*. The goods were left upon *Brennan*'s premises by the plaintiff, until the time of the alleged trespass. The case for the defendants was, that this transfer to the plaintiff was fraudulent as against creditors. Evidence was adduced to prove the fraud; and, to shew that the defendants were entitled to avail themselves of this defence, proof was offered that the defendant *Minnitt* had obtained a judgment in a local court (the *Peverell* Court), and had sued out execution there; that the other defendants were officers of the Court charged with the execution; and that the alleged trespass was in the course of such execution. The plaintiff's counsel objected that, on the issues joined, the defendants were not entitled to justify the seizure under an execution. The learned Judge received the evidence, and directed the jury to say whether they considered the transfer fraudulent against creditors. The jury found that the transfer was "fraudulent against creditors." The learned Judge then directed a verdict to be entered for the plaintiff on the first issue and the defendant on the second, reserving leave to move to enter a verdict for the plaintiff on the second issue.

Hildyard now moved accordingly. On the finding of the jury, the defendants must fail unless they set up *Minnitt*'s title as creditor. But they cannot do so on this issue, which simply brings in question the plaintiff's

title.

1838.

ASHBY against MINNITT.

title. Under the new rules, fraud must be specially pleaded (*a*): the second plea raises, therefore, only the question of the sale in fact to the plaintiff; *Howell* v. *White* (*b*). But here the defendants seek, not only to shew fraud in the plaintiff, but to do so by means of a special title in themselves, which they have not pleaded. On this record, they are mere wrong-doers. [*Coleridge* J. What does a defendant undertake to shew when he traverses a plaintiff's title?] He undertakes to negative the title shewn by the plaintiff; not to set up a special one in himself. [*Littledale* J. I do not see what plea but the present one could raise this question of fraud as against the defendants, without being specially demurrable: unless perhaps colour were given.]

Cur. adv. vult.

Lord DENMAN C.J. now said that the Court were of opinion that the evidence had been properly received, and the case rightly left to the jury.

Rule refused (*c*).

(*a*) See, as to assumpsit, *R. Hil.* 4 *W.* 4. *Pleadings in Particular Actions*, I. 3. 5 *B.* & *Ad.* viii.

(*b*) 1 *M.* & *Rob.* 400.

(*c*) See *Lewis* v. *Alcock*, 3 *M.* & *W.* 188.

1838.

Monday, April 23d.

NEWMAN *against* The Earl of HARDWICKE and Another.

A conviction under stats. 11 *G.* 4. & 1 *W.* 4. *c.* 64., sects. 14, 25., and 4 & 5 *W.* 4. *c.* 85. *s.* 6., for allowing beer to be consumed in a licensed house at other hours than those prescribed by order of petty sessions, must state the time fixed by the justices at which houses may be kept open, and the hour at which the beer was consumed. It is not enough to say, "at a time declared to be unlawful by an order of the justices."

If goods be seized upon a warrant founded on a conviction so improperly framed, the magistrates issuing the warrant are liable in trespass.

TRESPASS for seizing and carrying away plaintiff's cart, and detaining it till he paid 3*l.* 10*s.* 6*d.* Plea, Not Guilty.

On the trial before *Parke* B., at the last *Cambridgeshire* assizes, it appeared that the defendants were justices of the peace of *Cambridgeshire*, and that the goods had been seized under their warrant, which was founded on a conviction under stat. 11 *G.* 4. *c.* 64. *s.* 14. and stat. 4 & 5 *W.* 4. *c.* 85. *s.* 6. (*a*).

The

(*a*) Stat. 11 *G.* 4. & 1 *W.* 4. *c.* 64. *s.* 1. enacts that every person licensed under the act may sell beer, &c., by retail in the house, &c., specified in the licence.

Sect. 2 regulates the obtaining of licences.

Sect. 14 enacts, "That no person licensed to sell beer by retail under this act shall have or keep his house open for the sale of beer, nor shall sell or retail beer, nor shall suffer any beer to be drank or consumed, in or at such house, at any time before the hour of four of the clock in the morning nor after ten of the clock in the evening of any day in the week, nor" &c. (regulations as to *Sundays*, and certain other days). The clause imposes a penalty, which, by sect. 15, may be recovered on information before two justices in petty sessions.

Sect. 25 enacts, "That a conviction in the form or to the effect following, mutatis mutandis, as the case may be, shall be good and effectual to all intents and purposes whatsoever, without stating the case or the facts or evidence in any more particular manner; (that is to say,)

"   } Be it remembered, that on this   day of   , in
to wit. } the year   , *A. B.* of   was duly convicted before us, *C. D.* and *E. F.*, two of his Majesty's justices of the peace in petty sessions for the   of   , for that [*here state the offence, and the time and place when committed,*] whereby the said *A. B.* has forfeited" &c. The rest of the form is not material here.

Sect. 27 enacts that no conviction under the act shall be quashed for want of form.

Stat.

The parts of the conviction material to the present decision were as follows.

" *Cambridgeshire*, to wit. } Be it remembered that, on this 30th day of *October*, in the year of our Lord 1837,

---

Stat. 4 & 5 *W.* 4. *c.* 85. is entitled " An act to amend an act passed" &c. (stat. 11 *G.* 4. & 1 *W.* 4. *c.* 64.).

Sect. 1 gives the power of granting licences for the sale of beer &c.

Sect. 6 enacts, " That it shall be lawful for the justices of the peace of every county, riding," &c., " in petty sessions assembled, and they are hereby required, to fix once a year " (at times prescribed in the act) " the hours at which houses and premises licensed to sell beer under this act shall be opened and closed : provided always, that any person thinking himself aggrieved by any such order " may appeal to the quarter sessions ; the decision of quarter sessions to be final and conclusive : " provided also, that the hour so to be fixed for opening any such house shall not in any case be earlier than " &c., " nor for closing the same later than " &c. ; " and the hours so fixed from time to time by such justices, with reference to the districts and places within their respective jurisdictions, shall be deemed and taken to be the hours to be observed and complied with under this act as fully as if the same had been specially appointed by this act."

Sect. 11 enacts, " that all the powers, regulations, proceedings, forms, penalties, forfeitures, and provisions contained in" stat. 11 *G.* 4. & 1 *W.* 4. *c.* 64. " with reference to persons licensed under the said act, and to the offences committed by such persons against the said act, or against the tenor of any licence granted under the said act," &c., " shall (except where they are altered by this act or are repugnant thereto) be deemed and taken to be applicable to all persons licensed under this act, and to all offences committed by such persons of the same description as the offences mentioned in the said act," &c., " as fully and effectually as if" here re-enacted.

Sect. 12 enacts that all the provisions of stat. 11 *G.* 4. & 1 *W.* 4. c. 64. " shall be deemed and taken to be in full force, save and except where the same are altered by this act."

The schedule to the act gives the form of licence, which purports to be upon condition that the party licensed shall observe certain regulations, and, among others, that he do not " sell any beer, ale, or porter," " nor suffer the same to be drunk or consumed in or at such house or premises at any time which, by any order of the justices of the peace made in pursuance of an act " &c. (the present act) " shall be declared to be unlawful."

Robert

1838.

NEWMAN *against* The Earl of HARDWICKE.

Robert Newman, of" &c., "was duly convicted before us, the Right Honorable the Earl of *Hardwicke*, and the Honorable and Reverend *Henry Yorke*, two of Her Majesty's justices of the peace in and for the said county, acting in petty sessions in and for the division of *Arrington* in the said county, for that he, the said *Robert Newman*, being a seller of beer, ale and porter, cyder and perry by retail, and licensed to sell the same by retail to be drunk and consumed in and upon the dwelling-house and premises thereunto belonging of him the said *R. N.*, hereinafter mentioned, under the provisions of the statutes in that case made and provided, did, on the 7th day of *October* in the year of our Lord 1837, at the parish" &c., "*at a time declared to be unlawful by an order of the justices of the peace* for the said county acting in and for the said division of *A.*, permit beer to be drunk and consumed in the house and premises mentioned in such licence, and situate in the said parish, in the division of *A.* aforesaid, in the said county, against the tenor of such licence granted to the said *R. N.* under the provisions of the said statutes, and contrary to the form of the said statutes; whereby the said *R. N.* has forfeited" (40*s.* and 1*l.* costs); &c.

"Given" &c. Signed and sealed by the two defendants.

The following objections were taken, among others, to the conviction; first, that it did not state what order the sessions had made as to the time at which the houses should be kept open, and closed; secondly, that it did not state at what time the plaintiff's house had been, in fact, kept open. The learned Judge directed a verdict

1838.

NEWMAN *again* The Earl of HARDWICKE.

a verdict for the plaintiff, reserving leave to move to enter a verdict for the defendants.

Byles now moved accordingly (*a*). The offence described in the conviction, permitting beer to be drunk "at a time declared to be unlawful by an order of the justices" &c., exactly corresponds with the provision in the licence, in the schedule to stat. 4 & 5 *W.* 4. *c.* 85., —"nor suffer the same to be drunk or consumed in or at such house or premises at any time which, by any order of the justices" &c., "shall be declared to be unlawful." It was argued, at the trial, that the exact time specified by the justices ought to appear on the conviction, in order that it might be seen that there was no excess of jurisdiction: but, in fact, there could be no such excess, since sect. 6 of stat. 4 & 5 *W.* 4. *c.* 85. prescribes a limit only to the time during which the houses may be allowed to be open: the justices may order them to be opened as late, and closed as early, as they think fit. And, as to the hour at which the house was actually kept open, the allegation of the offence is sufficient, inasmuch as it is expressly alleged that the house was kept open at a time declared to be unlawful. [Lord *Denman* C. J. Would it be enough if the conviction merely stated that the party offended against the order, without saying how?] A conviction for keeping open "at unlawful hours" would be good. The objection is merely formal; and sect. 27 of stat. 11 *G.* 4. & 1 *W.* 4. *c.* 64. (which act is incorporated in stat. 4 & 5 *W.* 4. *c.* 85. by sect. 11) cures defects of form. [*Patteson* J. The form in sect. 25 of stat. 11 *G.* 4. & 1 *W.* 4. *c.* 64. says,

(*a*) Before Lord *Denman* C. J., *Littledale*, *Patteson*, and *Coleridge* Js.

1838.

Newman *against* The Earl of Hardwicke.

says, "here state the offence, and the time and place when committed."] That refers to the day and the parish. (He then argued against the other objections.)

Cur. adv. vult.

Lord Denman C. J., on a subsequent day (*May* 9th), delivered the judgment of the Court.

This was an action against two justices of peace of the county of *Cambridge*, for seizing the plaintiff's goods by a warrant of distress. The defence was a conviction of the plaintiff, by the same magistrates, for having kept open his beer-shop at times prohibited by the order of justices in execution of the power vested in them by stat. 11 *G.* 4. & 1 *W.* 4. *c.* 64. *s.* 14., and stat. 4 & 5 *W.* 4. *c.* 85. *s.* 6. By the clause last referred to, the petty sessions are required to issue an order for closing the beer shops during the year, which order has the force of a parliamentary enactment: and the present conviction was for keeping the plaintiff's house open at a time so made illegal.

Various objections were taken to it. Two appear to us to be fatal. There is no averment that the sessions made such order, nor at what time the house was kept open.

These are substantial defects in the conviction; and the plaintiff is entitled to keep his verdict.

Rule refused (*a*).

(*a*) See *Ashby* v. *Harris*, 2 *M.* & *W.* 673.

1838.

LEVY *against* YATES.

Monday, April 23d.

ASSUMPSIT. The declaration stated that plaintiff, before and at the time of the making of the agreement and promise after mentioned, was lawfully possessed of certain premises, to wit the *Victoria* theatre; and during that time defendant had treated with plaintiff for the opening of the said theatre by defendant; and thereupon, to wit &c., it was agreed by and between plaintiff and defendant that defendant should open at the said theatre on *Whit-Monday*, 15th *May* 1837, with *J. R.*, &c. (naming certain actors and actresses), with a new piece, the authorship to be paid for by defendant, for one month certain, and, unless renewed by defendant on or before 27th *May* 1837, for one month further; defendant to furnish &c. (then followed stipulations as to pieces to be performed, dresses, &c.); the terms, that defendant should have one clear half of each night's clear receipts, &c., save &c.: Allegation of mutual promises, and of plaintiff's readiness to perform the agreement on his part: breach, that defendant did not nor would open at the said theatre, &c. (as in the agreement, with breaches of the several stipulations): matters of special damage were added.

Entertainments of the stage cannot be exhibited for gain within twenty miles of *Westminster* or *London*, the place of exhibition not being in *Westminster* or its liberties, or some place in which the sovereign resides.

By stat. 10 *G.* 2. *c.* 28., neither the Crown, by letters patent, nor the Lord Chamberlain, by licence, can authorize such performance.

Nor can the county magistrates, under either stat. 25 *G.* 2. *c.* 36. or stat. 28 *G.* 3. *c.* 30.

No action can be maintained on an agreement to exhibit entertainments of the stage for gain in a place where, by the above statutes, a licence or patent cannot be obtained.

A plea shewing that the intended place of exhibition was so situated is an answer to a declaration on the breach of such an agreement.

Pleas. 1. Non assumpsit: and issue thereon.

2. That the said theatre is situate in the parish of *St. Mary, Lambeth*, in the county of *Surrey*, and within less than twenty miles, that is to say within two miles, of the cities of *London* and *Westminster* respectively,

 and

1838.

Levy *against* Yates.

and not in the city of *Westminster*, nor within the liberties thereof, nor in any place where his late Majesty or her present Majesty has resided, during any portion of the time during which such agreement was to be acted upon, or to be in force: and that neither plaintiff nor defendant, nor any other person or persons, had been, or were, or was, during such time as last aforesaid, that is to say, during the months of *May*, *June*, and *July*, 1837, or any part thereof, or during any period of the said year, duly licensed or authorized, under or by virtue of letters patent or otherwise, from his or her said Majesty, or by licence from the Lord Chamberlain of his or her Majesty's household for the time being, or by any other competent authority whatsoever, to act, represent, or perform, for hire, gain, or reward, any interlude, tragedy, comedy, opera, play, farce, or other entertainment of the stage, or any part or parts therein, in or at the said theatre, as by law required: nor was the said theatre, during any part of the said year, duly licensed for such representations, performances, or entertainments as aforesaid: and that neither plaintiff nor defendant, nor any other person on their or either of their behalf, could or would have procured such licence or authority as was and is by law required for such representations, performances, and acting as aforesaid, during the whole or any part of the time aforesaid, to wit &c.: nor did defendant at any time tender or offer to procure such licence or authority: and defendant says that the pieces, representations, parts, and performances to be and intended to be acted, represented, and performed, under and in pursuance of the said agreement, were and would have been interludes, &c., or other entertainments of the stage, or some

one

one or other of the same, for the acting, representing, and performing whereof such licence or authority was, and would have been, and is, so required by law as aforesaid: and that the pieces in and by the said supposed agreement mentioned were, and each of them was, such interludes or an interlude, tragedies or a tragedy, &c., or other entertainments or entertainment of the stage, or some one or other of the same; and that the same were to be acted, &c., at the said theatre, during such time as aforesaid, for hire, gain, and reward (*a*); of all which premises the plaintiff, before and at the time of the making of the said supposed agreement, to wit on &c., had notice. Verification.

Replication, de injuriâ.

On the trial before Lord *Denman* C. J., at the *Middlesex* sittings after last term, it appeared that the theatre was licensed only by the magistrates of the county. The pieces intended to be performed came within the description in the plea. By consent of the parties, the jury were discharged from giving a verdict on the issue joined on the first plea, and a verdict was taken for the defendant on the second, with liberty to move to enter a verdict for the plaintiff: the questions as to the promise and damages to be referred, in the event of such a rule, or a rule for judgment non obstante veredicto, being made absolute.

Sir

(*a*) Stat. 10 *G.* 2. *c.* 28. *s.* 1. enacts that "every person who shall, for hire, gain, or reward, act, represent, or perform, or cause to be acted," &c., "any interlude, tragedy, comedy, opera, play, farce, or other entertainment of the stage, or any part or parts therein, in case such person shall not have any legal settlement in the place where the same shall be acted," &c., "without authority by virtue of letters patent from his Majesty, his heirs, successors or predecessors, or without licence from the

1838.

Levy *against* Yates.

Sir *F. Pollock* now moved accordingly. The issue on the second plea raises the question whether an annual licence from the magistrates be sufficient to authorize the performances mentioned in the plea, or whether there

the lord chamberlain of his Majesty's household for the time being, shall be deemed to be a rogue and a vagabond within the intent and meaning of the said recited act:" (12 *Ann.* stat. 2. *c.* 23.)

Sect. 2 enacts, "that if any person having or not having a legal settlement as aforesaid shall, without such authority or licence as aforesaid, act," &c., "or cause to be acted," &c., "for hire, gain, or reward, any interlude," &c., "or any part or parts therein, every such person shall for every such offence forfeit the sum of *50l.*"

Sect. *5* enacts, "that no person or persons shall be authorised by virtue of any letters patent from his Majesty, his heirs, successors or predecessors, or by the licence of the lord chamberlain of his Majesty's household for the time being, to act," &c., "for hire," &c., "any interlude," &c., "or any part or parts therein, in any part of *Great Britain*, except in the city of *Westminster*, and within the liberties thereof, and in such places where his Majesty, his heirs or successors, shall in their royal persons reside, and during such residence only."

Stat. 25 *G.* 2. *c.* 36. (made perpetual by stat. 28 *G.* 2. *c.* 19. *s.* 1.) *s.* 2. enacts that "any house, room, garden, or other place kept for public dancing, music, or other public entertainment of the like kind, in the cities of *London* and *Westminster*, or within twenty miles thereof, without a licence had for that purpose, from the last preceding *Michaelmas* quarter sessions of the peace, to be holden for the county," &c., "in which such house," &c., "is situate, (who are hereby authorised and empowered to grant such licences as they in their discretion shall think proper) signified under the hands and seals of four or more of the justices there assembled, shall be deemed a disorderly house or place." The section then directs proceedings against persons found in, or keeping such house, &c.

Sect. 4 provides "that nothing in this act contained shall extend, or be construed to extend, to the theatres royal in *Drury Lane* and *Covent Garden*, or the theatre commonly called the *King's Theatre* in the *Hay-Market*, or any of them; nor to such performances and public entertainments as are or shall be lawfully exercised and carried on under or by virtue of letters patents, or licence of the crown, or the licence of the lord chamberlain of his Majesty's household."

Stat. 28 *G.* 3. *c.* 30. *s.* 1. enacts, "That it shall and may be lawful to and for the justices of the peace of any county, riding, or liberty, in general

1838.

LEVY against YATES.

there must also be a licence from the Lord Chamberlain, or a patent. It must be admitted that the letter of the statute, 28 *G.* 3. *c.* 30. s. 1. is against the plaintiff; and the performances intended cannot, perhaps, be said to fall within the class of entertainments pointed out by stat. 25 *G.* 2. *c.* 36.: but the universal practice has been to treat the licence of the magistrates as sufficient; and, as very valuable property is in question, there ought at least to be a rule granted for the purpose of finally determining the question. [Lord *Denman* C. J. Lord *Tenterden* seems, in *Rodwell* v. *Redge* (a), to have allowed some weight to the argument from continued performances, as authorizing presumption of a licence]. It has been held that "tumbling" is not an "entertainment of the stage"

neral or quarter sessions assembled, at their discretion, to grant a licence to any person or persons, making application for the same by petition, for the performance of such tragedies, comedies, interludes, operas, plays, or farces, as now are, or hereafter shall be acted, performed, or represented, at either of the patent or licensed theatres in the city of *Westminster*, or as shall, in the manner prescribed by law, have been submitted to the inspection of the lord chamberlain of the King's household for the time being, at any place within their jurisdictions, or within any city, town, or place, situate within the limits of the same, for any number of days, not exceeding sixty days, to commence within the then next six months, and to be within the space of such four months as shall be specified in the said licence, so as there be only one licence in use at the same time within the jurisdiction so given, and so as such place be not within twenty miles of the cities of *London*, *Westminster*," &c.

Stat. 5 *G.* 4. *c.* 83. *s.* 1. enacts, "that all provisions heretofore made relative to idle and disorderly persons, rogues and vagabonds, incorrigible rogues or other vagrants, in *England*, shall be and the same are hereby repealed, except only as to any offence committed before the passing of this act," "and save and except as hereinafter excepted." The exception is in sect. 22, and does not apply to the enactments above set out: but the repealing clause is inapplicable to ss. 2. and 5. of stat. 10 *G.* 2. *c.* 28. Per Lord *Cottenham*, in *Ewing* v. *Osbaldiston*, 2 *Myl.* & *Cr.* 84.

(a) 1 *C.* & *P.* 220.

1838.

Levy against Yates.

under stat. 10 *G.* 2. *c.* 28.; *Rex* v. *Handy* (*a*): the precise effect of the several statutes seems not to have been fully defined. *Ewing* v. *Osbaldiston* (*b*) appears to be an authority for the defendant; but that was merely a refusal by a court of equity to enforce an agreement: it does not follow that a court of law, where the point is doubtful, will refuse a rule. The statute 10 *G.* 2. *c.* 28. is penal; and the consequences now sought to be deduced from it are still more so. Then, as to the application for judgment non obstante veredicto, it does not appear by the record that the plaintiff was bound to obtain the licence rather than the defendant: if it was incumbent on the defendant, he cannot take the objection.

Lord Denman C. J. If there were any doubt in the case, the great extent of the consequences would induce us to grant a rule. But I can see no doubt; and we shall do no good by creating one. The decision in *Ewing* v. *Osbaldiston* (*b*) by Lord Chancellor *Cottenham*, affirming that of the Vice-Chancellor Sir *L. Shadwell*, is precisely in point; and the matter is, indeed, perfectly clear, independently of authority. The plea shews that this agreement could not be carried into effect without a contravention of the law. The question which party was to procure the licence does not arise. If it were the defendant's duty, he could not take the objection. But the plea alleges that neither could procure a proper licence, and that the plaintiff had notice of this before the agreement. And by the terms of the acts it is plain that neither could procure a licence. By

(*a*) 6 *T. R.* 286.

(*b*) 2 *Myl. & Cr.* 53.

stat.

stat. 28 G. 3. c. 30. s. 1. the power of the justices to license does not extend to any place within twenty miles of *London* or *Westminster*: and by stat. 10 G. 2. c. 28. s. 5. neither the Crown, by letters patent, nor the Lord Chamberlain, by licence, can authorize performances, except in *Westminster* or its liberties, or in places where the sovereign resides. Therefore the illegality created by sect. 2 of the last mentioned act could not be cured.

LITTLEDALE J. concurred.

PATTESON J. It is almost conceded that no licence could be granted under stat. 28 G. 3. c. 30. s. 1. Then can a licence protect under stat. 25 G. 2. c. 36. s. 2? It is clear that this last-mentioned act does not apply to theatrical entertainments. Then under stat. 10 G. 2. c. 28. s. 5. the magistrates clearly had no power to license. *Ewing* v. *Osbaldiston* (a) is exactly in point. As to the motion for judgment non obstante veredicto, the plea alleges that the theatre is within twenty miles of *London* and *Westminster*, and not in the city of *Westminster*, nor within the liberties thereof, nor in any place where his late or her present Majesty resided during any portion of the term during which the agreement was to be acted upon. That is, I think, a sufficient answer to the declaration; for it is a legal consequence that neither the defendant, nor any one else, could obtain a licence authorizing the performance: so that the plea need not have made the allegations which follow. How then can we give judgment for the breach of such an agreement?

(a) 2 *Myl. & Cr.* 53.

1838.

Levy *against* Yates.

Coleridge J. The plea clearly shews a good defence under stat. 10 G. 2. c. 28. The second point does not arise; for the plea alleges that no one could have obtained a sufficient licence. And no licence could have authorized the performance.

Rule refused (a).

(a) See *Rex* v. *Neville*, 1 *B. & Ad.* 489.

Monday, April 23d.

Catton *against* Simpson.

Defendant and plaintiff gave a joint and several promissory note to *A.*, plaintiff signing as defendant's surety. Afterwards, *A.* pressing defendant for payment, time was allowed upon *L.* adding his signature as additional security. No new stamp was put on the note. Plaintiff afterwards paid *A.* the money. Held, that he might sue defendant for money paid, and that the payment was not voluntary, the addition of *L.*'s name not annulling plaintiff's original liability on the note.

ASSUMPSIT for money paid, and on an account stated. Plea, non assumpsit.

On the trial before *Patteson* J., at the last *York* assizes, it appeared that in 1831 the defendant was indebted to a person named *Allen*, since deceased, in the sum of 120*l.*; and that the plaintiff and defendant gave *Allen* a promissory note for the amount. The note was in the words "we jointly and severally promise, &c.;" and to plaintiff's signature, which followed defendant's, were added the words "as his surety." After *Allen*'s death, the defendant was called on by *Allen*'s executors to pay the money. Time was allowed him, at his request, upon a person named *Laybourne* adding his signature as additional security: it did not appear that this was done in pursuance of any understanding which had existed at the time of making the note. Plaintiff and *Laybourne*, being afterwards called on by the executors, paid each one half of the note. This action was brought to recover from the defendant the amount so paid by the plaintiff. The defendant's counsel contended that the addition of *Laybourne*'s name vitiated the note. The

1838.

CATTON *against* SIMPSON.

The learned judge directed a verdict for the plaintiff, and reserved leave to the defendant to move for a nonsuit.

Cresswell now moved accordingly. The defendant merely indemnified the plaintiff against the legal consequences of the note. Now the plaintiff was not legally bound to pay the note, if it was vitiated by the addition of *Laybourne's* name. That was a material alteration; for, though the note, in its altered state, was still, as before, the several note of the plaintiff, yet it was formerly the joint note of two, whereas, after the alteration, it was no longer the joint note of two, but of three, and the two could no longer have been sued without joining *Laybourne* (*a*). The additional name having been affixed after the note was issued, and not in pursuance of any agreement entered into when the note was originally made, the note is void for want of a fresh stamp; *Clerk* v. *Blackstock* (*b*). It is true that in that case the action was brought against the party who added his name. [*Coleridge* J. Then *Laybourne* was not bound, by adding his name?] That is immaterial: a note with an altered date does not bind any one to the new contract, yet the old contract is void.

Lord DENMAN C. J. In the absence of all authority, we shall hold that this was not an alteration of the note, but merely an addition which had no effect.

LITTLEDALE, PATTESON, and COLERIDGE Js. concurred.

Rule refused.

(*a*) See note (4) to *Cabell* v. *Vaughan*, 1 *Wms. Saund.* 291 *f.*

(*b*) *Holt's N. P. C.* 474.

Tuesday, April 24th.

MURLY *against* M'DERMOTT.

1. Trespass for breaking, &c., a wall of plaintiff, bounded on the north by a workshop of defendant. Plea, that the wall was not the wall of plaintiff. The wall was a party wall, standing partly on plaintiff's, and partly on defendant's, land. The roof of defendant's workshop rested on the top of the wall on defendant's side, and the trespass was committed partly on the plaintiff's half of the wall. Held, that defendant was entitled to the verdict, for that the plaintiff must be understood to have brought his action for the whole wall, and, even if the party wall were treated as two walls, defendant's part could not be considered as part of the workshop, and therefore the description in the declaration, with the abuttals, comprehended the whole wall, and, consequently, the plaintiff had not proved his property in the wall described in the declaration.

2. Defendant also pleaded, that the wall was a party wall, partly on the land of plaintiff, and partly on the land of defendant. A verdict having been found for the defendant on this plea, *quære*, whether plaintiff was entitled to judgment, non obstante veredicto, for so much of the party wall as belonged to him.

3. On trial of the issues on the above pleas, it appeared that the plaintiff and defendant occupied contiguous premises bounded by the wall, which premises they had severally purchased, at the same auction, from the then owner of the whole. The lots were afterwards conveyed to plaintiff and defendant by separate deeds, in which the premises were described as being in the occupation respectively of *H.* and *R.*, together with all buildings, ways, &c., known or reputed to be parcel thereof. Held, that defendant might give in evidence conditions of sale distributed at the time of the auction, describing the premises by measurement, there being probable evidence that these conditions were seen by the plaintiff's agent at the sale; inasmuch as the conditions were used, not to controul or construe, but to apply, the language of the deeds.

TRESPASS. The second count (*a*) charged that defendant broke and entered a wall of plaintiff, bounded towards the north by a certain workshop and building of defendant, and towards the south by a certain building of plaintiff, broke down &c. twenty perches of the said wall of plaintiff, and twenty perches of the thatch of and belonging to the said wall, and with which the said wall of plaintiff was covered, and the materials of the said wall and the said thatch seized, took, and carried away, and converted &c. To this count the defendant pleaded, Secondly, that the wall was not, at the time when &c., nor at any time from thence hitherto, nor is, the wall of the plaintiff, in manner &c., concluding to the country; Fourthly, that the said wall was, at the said time when &c., a party wall, standing, being, erected and built partly on land of plaintiff, and partly

(*a*) Money was brought into Court, and accepted in satisfaction, on the first count.

on

1838.

MURLY against M'DERMOTT.

on land of defendant; wherefore defendant committed &c. The replication joined issue on the second plea, and traversed the fourth plea in terms; on which traverse the plaintiff joined issue.

On the trial before *Bosanquet* J., at the last *Somersetshire* assizes, other issues, not mentioned above, were found for the plaintiff. As to the issues above mentioned, it appeared that the plaintiff and defendant occupied adjoining premises, separated by the wall in question; plaintiff on the south, defendant on the north. The whole premises, including those of plaintiff and those of defendant and the wall, were the property of a person named *Budge*, until *March* 1837, when *Budge* sold the whole by auction, and the plaintiff and defendant purchased their respective premises: and, by lease and release of 28th and 29th *September* 1837, the release made between *Budge* of the first part, plaintiff of the second, a trustee for plaintiff of the third, and defendant of the fourth, *Budge* conveyed plaintiff's premises to him in fee simple by the description of "all that messuage and dwelling house, with the garden, workshop, and buildings behind the same, situate in" &c., "many years heretofore in the possession of" &c. (naming successive occupiers), "and now in the occupation of *George Howe*, as tenant thereof," together with all houses, outhouses, edifices, buildings, ways, paths, passages, &c., thereto belonging or appertaining, or accepted, reputed, deemed, taken, or known as or to be part or parcel of the same. Each party, at the trial, claimed the whole of the wall. It appeared that the roofs covering the buildings both of plaintiff and defendant rested on the top of the wall on their respective sides. The alleged trespass was committed both

1838.

Murly *against* M'Dermott.

both on the half of the wall nearest to the plaintiff's premises, and on the half nearest to those of the defendant. The defendant put in the conveyance to him by *Budge*, which was also of 28th and 29th *September* 1837, between *Budge* of the first part, the defendant of the second, and a person named *Hoskins* of the third, and was framed in similar terms with the conveyance to the plaintiff, except as to the names of the occupiers, the premises being described as now in the occupation of one *Riddle*. The defendant also offered in evidence the printed advertisement of the sale, containing the conditions of sale distributed in the sale room before and at the time of the auction in *March*, and during the time when the agent, who purchased for the plaintiff at the auction, was present. In these conditions the frontages of the lots respectively purchased by the plaintiff and defendant, running east and west at right angles to the wall in question, were described by their dimensions. And the defendant contended that his frontage, thus described, included the wall. The plaintiff's counsel objected to the reception of these conditions of sale; but the learned Judge received the evidence. The jury found that the wall was a party wall: and the learned Judge directed the verdict to be entered for the defendant on the issues on the second and fourth pleas.

Erle now moved (*a*) for a rule to shew cause why the verdict should not be entered for the plaintiff on the issue on the second plea, and why the plaintiff should not have judgment, non obstante veredicto, on the issue

(*a*) Before Lord *Denman* C. J., *Littledale*, *Patteson*, and *Coleridge* Js.

on

1838.

MURLY against M'DERMOTT.

on the fourth plea, or why there should not be a new trial on account of the improper reception of evidence (a). First, as to the fourth issue, the justification applies only to the northern half of the wall. In a case tried in *Devonshire*, before Lord *Denman* C. J., where the declaration was for trespass on the bed of a river, and the plea was as to so much as was within the southern moiety of the bed, it was held that the plaintiff was entitled to recover. [*Patteson* J. I doubt whether you can have judgment here, non obstante veredicto. The plea does cover a part of the trespass complained of. It would be bad on demurrer]. The plaintiff should have judgment for so much as is not covered by the plea. [Lord *Denman* C. J. Evidence of a trespass on any part of the wall supports your declaration]. If the parties had been tenants in common of the wall, the justification would have extended to the whole wall; but it is otherwise in the case of a party wall, built partly on the land of one proprietor, and partly on the land of another: *Matts* v. *Hawkins* (b), *Cubitt* v. *Porter* (c). As to the issue on the second plea, the plaintiff is entitled to treat so much of the wall as is covered by the defendant's roof as distinct from the plaintiff's wall, and as part of the defendant's workshop and building, in which view of the case the description in the abuttals applies only to the plaintiff's moiety of the wall; and then the evidence, as to this last moiety, shews that it belongs to the plaintiff. As to the conditions of sale, they were merely a declaration to a third party. At any rate, they cannot be admitted to contradict or vary

(a) Also on the ground that the verdict was against the weight of evidence.

(b) 5 *Taunt.* 20.

(c) 8 *B. & C.* 257.

the

1838.

MORLY *against* M'DERMOTT.

the descriptions in the conveyances, under which the only question is, how much was occupied by *Howe* and how much by *Riddle*.

Cur. adv. vult.

Lord DENMAN C. J., on a subsequent day of this term (*May* 10th), delivered the judgment of the Court. After stating the pleadings, and the nature of the motion, his Lordship proceeded:

The foundation of the motion as to the second issue is that, regard being had to the finding on the fourth, it must be taken that there are two walls, one on the plaintiff's land, and his property, the other on the defendant's, and his property: and, as a trespass has been proved on that wall, or that portion of the two united walls which stands on plaintiff's land, and is his property, the second plea is negatived, and the issue should be found for him. And it is said that the abuttals in the declaration present no difficulty in the way of this finding, for that the portion of wall on the north of the plaintiff's wall is only the back wall of the defendant's workshop and building.

But we are of opinion that this reasoning cannot prevail: it is clear that the plaintiff brought his action for an alleged trespass on the *whole* of that which the jury have found to be a party wall, as one entire building, erected on his own land; and the struggle in the cause was as to the property in the whole wall. And, *assuming* that, from the jury's finding, we must take these to be two walls, one on the land of each party, that same finding shews that these two walls abut on each other, and the plaintiff consequently has failed to prove his property in the wall described by its abuttals in the declaration.

1838. MURLY *against* McDERMOTT.

declaration. The fact that the defendant's workshop and other buildings of the defendant, mentioned in the declaration, are built against, with their roof resting on, the top of the united walls, does not make that wall which stands on the defendant's land a portion of themselves: *they* are not, therefore, the abuttals, but the wall itself is the abuttal to the plaintiff's wall.

If the verdict is rightly entered on the second issue, it is unnecessary to grant any rule for the purpose of considering whether the fourth be a good plea. Nothing would depend on that plea but the costs of the issue, which must be inconsiderable, as all the evidence applicable to it is also material to the second. Upon the defendant's allowing the plaintiff the costs of this issue, there will therefore be no rule on this point.

A motion was also made for a new trial on the ground that the verdict was against the evidence; and that some evidence had been improperly received.

We have seen the learned Judge's note. There appears to have been much evidence offered on both sides; and he is satisfied with the verdict.

The evidence said to have been improperly received was a handbill, advertising the properties both of plaintiff and defendant for sale; and it was urged that this was received in order to construe the deed by which the plaintiff's property was conveyed to him. The plaintiff and defendant had purchased of the same owner. The lot which each purchased was described in his deed by a reference to the occupation of the then tenant; and there were words to pass all that *was known or reputed parcel* of such occupation. There was evidence to shew that the hand-bill in question was circulated in the sale-room before and at the time of the sale, and that

1838.

Murly *against* M'Dermott.

that it was seen by the person who attended as the plaintiff's agent and bid and bought for him. Looking then at these facts, and the language of the deed, we think this hand-bill properly received, not to control the language of the deed, or to construe it, but to apply it. It was evidence to shew what it was that, at the time of the sale, was known or reputed to be parcel of that tenant's occupation which the plaintiff purchased, and which was conveyed to him by the deed.

For these reasons, we think there should be no rule on any of the grounds taken by Mr. *Erle*.

Rule refused.

Tuesday, April 24th.

WRIGHT *against* GODDARD and Others.

Declaration on the following covenants in a lease. To repair and keep in repair the premises, *reasonable use and wear only excepted*, and to leave the same in repair, with the like exception. That the lessor might enter and view, &c., and, in case of defect, the defendants should repair within one month after notice *in writing*. That defendants might put an end to the lease in three years, giving six months' notice *in writing*.

Averment, that the demise was put an end to, defendants having given plaintiff *six months' notice* of their desire to end the demise in three years; and that plaintiff, during the said demise, gave defendants *notice* of certain defects.

Breach, that defendants did not within one month after such last-mentioned notice, or at any other time before or afterwards during the demise, and while they were in possession, repair, &c., or keep in repair; nor did they leave in repair &c. at the determination of the term as aforesaid, according to the indenture; but, on the contrary, after the making of the same, and during the continuance of the demise and of their possession, and until the determination of the term as aforesaid, they suffered the premises to be out of repair, and so left the same, &c., contrary to the indenture, whereby &c.

Plea, payment of money into Court generally. Replication of damages ultrà: Issue thereon: Held:

1. That the declaration would have been bad on special demurrer (but was not so after verdict) for mixing the claim of damages on the breach of covenant to repair after notice with the claim for breach of the covenant to repair generally.

2. That the breach was demurrable (though sufficient, *semble*, after verdict) for not noticing the exception of reasonable wear and tear.

3. and 4. That the averments of notice were demurrable for not stating that the notices were in writing. But

5. That the defendants, by pleading payment into Court generally, had acknowledged something to be due on every part of the breach, and could not, therefore, allege the last three objections in arrest of judgment.

COVENANT on an indenture of lease made by plaintiff to two of the defendants. The declaration stated the demise of a messuage &c., and a covenant by

all

1838.

WRIGHT *against* GODDARD.

all the defendants that the lessees should, at their own expense, well and efficiently and substantially repair, maintain, paint, cleanse, and preserve the demised premises, and would keep the same "in a good and substantial state of repair, condition, and preservation in all things, reasonable use and wear thereof only excepted." Also a covenant that the lessees should, "at the expiration or other sooner determination of the said term," yield up the premises to plaintiff in good, substantial, and tenantable repair, &c., reasonable use and wear thereof only excepted. Also, that it should be lawful for plaintiff at certain times to enter on the premises to view their state and condition, and that, "in case of any defects or want of reparation or painting as aforesaid," &c., the lessees should, "within one calendar month next after notice in writing should have been given" to them, or left on the premises, cause the repairs to be done. Also, that, if the lessees should wish to put an end to the demise at the expiration of the first three years (the term being seven), and should for that purpose deliver to plaintiff, or leave at his place of abode, "six calendar months' previous notice in writing of such desire," and should pay all arrears of rent and perform all the covenants, &c., the lease should, at the expiration of the three years, become void. Averment, that the lessees entered under the demise, and were possessed &c., and continued in possession till &c., when the said demise was ended and determined according to the tenor and effect &c. of the said indenture, the lessees having theretofore, viz. on &c., "in pursuance of the provision in the said indenture in that behalf contained, given to the plaintiff six calendar months' notice of their desire to put an end to the said demise at the

 expiration

Tuesday, April 24th.

MURLY *against* M'DERMOTT.

1. Trespass for breaking, &c., a wall of plaintiff, bounded on the north by a workshop of defendant. Plea, that the wall was not the wall of plaintiff. The wall was a party wall, standing partly on plaintiff's, and partly on defendant's, land. The roof of defendant's workshop rested on the top of the wall on defendant's side, and the trespass was committed partly on the plaintiff's half of the wall. Held, that defendant was entitled to the verdict, for that the plaintiff must be understood to have brought his action for the whole wall, and, even if the party wall were treated as two walls, defendant's part could not be considered as part of the workshop, and therefore the description in the declaration, with the abuttals, comprehended the whole wall, and, consequently, the plaintiff had not proved his property in the wall described in the declaration.

2. Defendant also pleaded, that the wall was a party wall, partly on the land of plaintiff, and partly on the land of defendant. A verdict having been found for the defendant on this plea, *quære*, whether plaintiff was entitled to judgment, non obstante veredicto, for so much of the party wall as belonged to him.

3. On trial of the issues on the above pleas, it appeared that the plaintiff and defendant occupied contiguous premises bounded by the wall, which premises they had severally purchased, at the same auction, from the then owner of the whole. The lots were afterwards conveyed to plaintiff and defendant by separate deeds, in which the premises were described as being in the occupation respectively of *H.* and *R.*, together with all buildings, ways, &c., known or reputed to be parcel thereof. Held, that defendant might give in evidence conditions of sale distributed at the time of the auction, describing the premises by measurement, there being probable evidence that these conditions were seen by the plaintiff's agent at the sale; inasmuch as the conditions were used, not to controul or construe, but to apply, the language of the deeds.

TRESPASS. The second count (*a*) charged that defendant broke and entered a wall of plaintiff, bounded towards the north by a certain workshop and building of defendant, and towards the south by a certain building of plaintiff, broke down &c. twenty perches of the said wall of plaintiff, and twenty perches of the thatch of and belonging to the said wall, and with which the said wall of plaintiff was covered, and the materials of the said wall and the said thatch seized, took, and carried away, and converted &c. To this count the defendant pleaded, Secondly, that the wall was not, at the time when &c., nor at any time from thence hitherto, nor is, the wall of the plaintiff, in manner &c., concluding to the country; Fourthly, that the said wall was, at the said time when &c., a party wall, standing, being, erected and built partly on land of plaintiff, and partly

(*a*) Money was brought into Court, and accepted in satisfaction, on the first count.

on

on land of defendant; wherefore defendant committed &c. The replication joined issue on the second plea, and traversed the fourth plea in terms; on which traverse the plaintiff joined issue.

On the trial before *Bosanquet* J., at the last *Somersetshire* assizes, other issues, not mentioned above, were found for the plaintiff. As to the issues above mentioned, it appeared that the plaintiff and defendant occupied adjoining premises, separated by the wall in question; plaintiff on the south, defendant on the north. The whole premises, including those of plaintiff and those of defendant and the wall, were the property of a person named *Budge*, until *March* 1837, when *Budge* sold the whole by auction, and the plaintiff and defendant purchased their respective premises: and, by lease and release of 28th and 29th *September* 1837, the release made between *Budge* of the first part, plaintiff of the second, a trustee for plaintiff of the third, and defendant of the fourth, *Budge* conveyed plaintiff's premises to him in fee simple by the description of "all that messuage and dwelling house, with the garden, workshop, and buildings behind the same, situate in" &c., "many years heretofore in the possession of" &c. (naming successive occupiers), "and now in the occupation of *George Howe*, as tenant thereof," together with all houses, outhouses, edifices, buildings, ways, paths, passages, &c., thereto belonging or appertaining, or accepted, reputed, deemed, taken, or known as or to be part or parcel of the same. Each party, at the trial, claimed the whole of the wall. It appeared that the roofs covering the buildings both of plaintiff and defendant rested on the top of the wall on their respective sides. The alleged trespass was committed both

1838.

MURLY *against* M'DERMOTT.

both on the half of the wall nearest to the plaintiff's premises, and on the half nearest to those of the defendant. The defendant put in the conveyance to him by *Budge*, which was also of 28th and 29th *September* 1837, between *Budge* of the first part, the defendant of the second, and a person named *Hoskins* of the third, and was framed in similar terms with the conveyance to the plaintiff, except as to the names of the occupiers, the premises being described as now in the occupation of one *Riddle*. The defendant also offered in evidence the printed advertisement of the sale, containing the conditions of sale distributed in the sale room before and at the time of the auction in *March*, and during the time when the agent, who purchased for the plaintiff at the auction, was present. In these conditions the frontages of the lots respectively purchased by the plaintiff and defendant, running east and west at right angles to the wall in question, were described by their dimensions. And the defendant contended that his frontage, thus described, included the wall. The plaintiff's counsel objected to the reception of these conditions of sale; but the learned Judge received the evidence. The jury found that the wall was a party wall: and the learned Judge directed the verdict to be entered for the defendant on the issues on the second and fourth pleas.

Erle now moved (*a*) for a rule to shew cause why the verdict should not be entered for the plaintiff on the issue on the second plea, and why the plaintiff should not have judgment, non obstante veredicto, on the issue

(*a*) Before Lord *Denman* C. J., *Littledale*, *Patteson*, and *Coleridge* Js.

on

1838.

MURLY against M'DERMOTT.

on the fourth plea, or why there should not be a new trial on account of the improper reception of evidence (*a*). First, as to the fourth issue, the justification applies only to the northern half of the wall. In a case tried in *Devonshire*, before Lord *Denman* C. J., where the declaration was for trespass on the bed of a river, and the plea was as to so much as was within the southern moiety of the bed, it was held that the plaintiff was entitled to recover. [*Patteson* J. I doubt whether you can have judgment here, non obstante veredicto. The plea does cover a part of the trespass complained of. It would be bad on demurrer]. The plaintiff should have judgment for so much as is not covered by the plea. [Lord *Denman* C. J. Evidence of a trespass on any part of the wall supports your declaration]. If the parties had been tenants in common of the wall, the justification would have extended to the whole wall; but it is otherwise in the case of a party wall, built partly on the land of one proprietor, and partly on the land of another: *Matts* v. *Hawkins* (*b*), *Cubitt* v. *Porter* (*c*). As to the issue on the second plea, the plaintiff is entitled to treat so much of the wall as is covered by the defendant's roof as distinct from the plaintiff's wall, and as part of the defendant's workshop and building, in which view of the case the description in the abuttals applies only to the plaintiff's moiety of the wall; and then the evidence, as to this last moiety, shews that it belongs to the plaintiff. As to the conditions of sale, they were merely a declaration to a third party. At any rate, they cannot be admitted to contradict or vary the

(*a*) Also on the ground that the verdict was against the weight of evidence.

(*b*) 5 *Taunt.* 20.

(*c*) 8 *B. & C.* 257.

1838.

Wright *against* Goddard.

exception, and the declaration would be bad upon demurrer. But it would probably be good after verdict, according to an *Anonymous Case* in Sir *Thomas Jones* (a).

Another defect in the declaration is, that it does not state that the term was determined at the end of three years by a notice *in writing* (b), and, as damages are claimed for not *leaving* the premises in repair, it ought to be shewn that the term is well determined. That also would be bad on demurrer. Another defect is, that it is not stated that the notice to repair at the end of *one* month was *in writing*, and, as damages are claimed for the breach of covenant upon that branch of the lease, that also would be bad upon demurrer.

But the defendants pleaded payment of 12*l.* into Court, and that the plaintiff had not sustained damages to a greater amount than the said sum &c. in respect of the causes in the said declaration mentioned, or any of them. To which the plaintiff has replied that he has sustained damages to a greater amount than the said sum of 12*l.* in respect of the causes of action in the declaration mentioned. Upon the whole, we think that this general plea of payment of money into Court must be taken to admit some damage upon every part of the breach of covenant in the declaration; and that the allegations as to the different notices, and as to the exception of reasonable use and wear, must be taken to be admitted: and that therefore there should be no rule to shew cause for arresting the judgment.

Rule refused.

(a) *T. Jones*, 125. See *Archer* v. *Marsh*, 6 *A.* & *E.* 959.

(b) On this point *Patteson* J., upon the motion, cited *Everard* v. *Paterson*, 6 *Taunt.* 625.

1838.

DOE on the Demise of NEALE *against* SAMPLES.

Tuesday, April 24th.

A document more than thirty years old is admissible in evidence without proof of execution, if produced by persons whose possession of it may be reasonably accounted for, although their custody be not the strictly proper one.

A conveyed lands to trustees by way of marriage settlement, the deed containing a proviso that it should be void if the marriage did not take place in six months. The marriage did so take place. Afterwards *A.* executed a mortgage of the same lands in fee. On his death, the mortgagee brought ejectment against *A.*'s son, then in possession. The son, in defence, produced the deed of settlement, which appeared to have remained among his father's papers ever since the execution, and was more than thirty years old.

Held, that the deed might be read in evidence without proof of the execution.

ON the trial of this ejectment, before Lord *Denman* C. J., at the last *Winchester* assizes, it appeared that the lessor of the plaintiff claimed under a mortgage to him in fee, by lease and release, executed in 1821 by *John Samples*, the defendant's father, since deceased. The defendant's case was, that, in 1785, the father, being then seised of the premises in question, executed a conveyance of them to trustees, by way of marriage settlement; the limitations being for the benefit of himself for his life, then of his intended wife for her life, and, after the death of the survivor of them, to the use of the children of the marriage, one of whom was the defendant: and consequently that, at the time of the supposed mortgage, the mortgagor had only a life-estate. The defendant's attorney produced the deed of settlement, which he had found among the papers of *John Samples* the father, at his late residence. It bore date *November* 9th, 1785, and contained a proviso avoiding it if the marriage should not be solemnized within six calendar months. The marriage was proved to have taken place within that time. No evidence was given as to the execution of the deed; but it was put in as proving itself, being more than thirty years old. The plaintiff's counsel objected that proof of execution could not be dispensed with on this ground, the deed not coming from the proper custody. The Lord Chief

1838.

Doe dem. Neale against Samples.

Justice admitted the document, reserving leave to move to enter a verdict for the plaintiff on the objection taken; the case went to the jury on the question whether the deed was actually delivered, or remained an escrow (a), and a verdict was given for the defendant.

Erle now moved according to the leave reserved. The deed produced did not come from the proper custody. The right custody is that of the party claiming under the deed, not that of the party against whom its provisions operate. Although a deed be thirty years old, the execution must be proved, "if the deed import a fraud; as where a man conveys a reversion to one, and after conveys it to another, and the second purchaser proves his title; because in such case the presumption arising from the antiquity of the deed is destroyed by an opposite presumption; for no man shall be supposed guilty of so manifest a fraud:" *Chettle* v. *Pound* (b). The objection arises à fortiori where the tenant in fee remains in possession of the deed after execution, and then conveys for a valuable consideration, and the former deed is produced from his repository after his death. In *Forbes* v. *Wale* (c) a bond more than thirty years old was produced, with no appearance of interest having been paid, and without any other mark of authenticity; it was urged that "if the length of date was alone sufficient to establish it, a knave has nothing to do, but to forge a bond with a very ancient date;" and the objection was allowed. The authority of that decision is

(a) *Murray* v. *The Earl of Stair*, 2 *B. & C.* 82, was cited.

(b) *Bull. N. P.* 255. *S. C. Gilb. Evid.* 90. (6th ed.); 3 *Bac. Abr.* 304, *Evidence* (F). 7th ed.

(c) 1 *W. Bl.* 532.

recognised

1838.

Doe dem. Neale against Samples.

recognised in *The Chelsea Water Works Company* v. *Cowper* (a). In 12 *Vin. Abr.* 84, *Evidence* [A. b. 5.] pl. 7., it is said, "An ancient writing that is proved to have been found amongst deeds and evidences of land, may be given in evidence, although the executing of it cannot be proved; for it is hard to prove ancient things, and the finding them in such a place is a presumption they were honestly and fairly obtained, and preserved for use, and are free from suspicion of dishonesty." Here the production of the deed tends to shew that the father must have been guilty of a fraud in selling property already conveyed, and suppressing the deed which conveyed it; and that deed is now produced by the son to maintain his possession of the property against the vendee. The trustees under the marriage settlement would have been guilty of a breach of trust, which the Court will not presume, in leaving this deed with the future husband, for he was thereby enabled to destroy it, or to commit a fraud by suppressing it. [*Patteson* J. If he had had any fraudulent intention he would most likely have destroyed it.] The probability is, that it never was looked upon as a valid deed, the marriage having been uncertain when it was executed. [*Patteson* J. That uncertainty may account for its having remained in the settlor's possession.] The broad principle which supports the present application is, that this deed comes from the hands of an improper party, and one who, if the verdict stands, is enabled to give effect to a fraud. [Lord *Denman* C. J. The view I took was that this was not an improper custody.]

(a) 1 *Esp. N. P. C.* 275. The report of *Forbes* v. *Wale* in 1 *W. Bl.* 532. states that the bond was found among the papers of the obligee; the note read by Lord *Kenyon*, in *The Chelsea Water Works Company* v. *Cowper*, seems to intimate the contrary.

LITTLEDALE

1838.

Doe dem. Neale against Samples.

Littledale J. I think this was not the best custody, because that of the trustees was the fit one; but it was a sufficiently proper custody to make the evidence admissible.

Patteson J. This deed was executed on the 9th of *November* 1785, with a proviso that it should become void if the marriage did not take place within six months; and it was proved that the marriage did take place within that time. Then the question is, whether the deed comes from the proper custody. I never understood that the custody to be shewn, for the purpose of making a document evidence without proof of execution, was necessarily that of a person strictly entitled to the possession. It is enough if the person be so connected with the deed that he may reasonably be supposed to be in possession of it without fraud, no such fraud being proved. The evidence, therefore, was rightly admitted.

Coleridge J. It is sufficient that the custody be one which may be reasonably and naturally explained, though not the strictly proper custody in point of law: this principle was laid down, and two documents held admissible in conformity to it, in *Bishop of Meath* v. *Marquess of Winchester* (a).

Lord Denman C. J. concurred.

Rule refused.

(a) 3 *New Ca.* 183.

1838.

MIDELTON *against* GALE, STONE, and KING, Esquires.

Wednesday, April 25th.

Under stat. 1 & 2 *W*. 4. c. 32. s. 30., it is not necessary that a conviction for a trespass in search of game should purport to be, or should in fact be, at the instance or on the information of the owner or occupier of the land, or of a party interested in the game, or of a person authorised by such owner, occupier, or party.

THE first count of the declaration stated that the plaintiff was summoned to appear before *Gale* and other justices for *Somersetshire*, to answer the complaint and information on oath of *William Sparks* for having unlawfully committed a trespass by entering and being in and upon certain waste land called *Pickeridge Hill*, being part of the waste land of the manor of *Taunton Dean*, in *Somersetshire*, the property of the lord of the said manor, in search and in pursuit of game: that the plaintiff appeared before *Gale* and other justices &c., to answer the complaint and information; and that the defendants, being three justices for the county, did, as such justices, claim and exercise pretended jurisdiction over the said pretended offence, and hear and determine the said pretended complaint and information, whereas in truth the defendants had not any right or power by law so to do, nor any jurisdiction whatever over such pretended complaint and information, the said *W. Sparks* not being, at the time of the committing of the said supposed offence, nor at the time of the hearing and determining of the said pretended complaint and information as aforesaid, nor at the time when the said *W. Sparks* made such complaint and gave such information as aforesaid, the occupier of the said land on which the said trespass was so alleged to have been committed as aforesaid, nor being the lord of the said manor of *Taunton Dean*, nor then having the right of killing game upon such land, nor having been proved to

the

1838.

MIDDLETON against GALE.

the said defendants, or any or either of them, to have been such occupier or person having the right of killing game as aforesaid, or to have been the lord of the said manor of *Taunton Dean*, or to have been authorised to institute proceedings with respect to the said supposed trespass by such occupier, or such person having the right of killing game upon the said land, or by the lord of the manor of *Taunton Dean*, whose property the said last-mentioned land was at the time of the plaintiff's committing the said supposed offence, and of the said information being given, and of the hearing and determining of the said pretended complaint and information as aforesaid; the said last-mentioned land then being part of the waste land of the said manor, and it not having been proved before the said defendants, or any or either of them, that such information as aforesaid was laid, instituted, or prosecuted, at the instance or with the concurrence or assent of the lord of the said manor. Yet the defendants, well knowing &c., did, as justices, on the oath of the said *W. Sparks*, without any charge by any other person, hear and determine the said complaint and information, and knowingly, &c., cause the plaintiff to be convicted of unlawfully trespassing on &c. in pursuit of game, and to be unlawfully fined, &c., a large sum &c.; by means whereof the plaintiff was forced and obliged to, and did, pay a large sum &c. There was a second count like the first, except that it stated the complaint and information of *W. Sparks* for a trespass in search and pursuit of game, on certain lands, parcel of *Hayne Farm*, in the occupation of *Jacob Westlake*, and who had not authorised the proceeding, with other negative averments as before, mutatis mutandis. The death of *Stone* was suggested on the record; and *Gale* and *King* pleaded Not Guilty.

On

1838.

MIDELTON against GALE.

On the trial before Lord *Denman* C. J., at the last *Somersetshire* assizes, the convictions were produced, They began: "Be it remembered that, on" &c., "at" &c., "*G. M.*" &c. "is convicted" &c., "on the oath of *William Sparks*, of unlawfully trespassing" &c. They were signed by *Gale* and *Stone* only. The summonses were also produced, and purported to be each a summons "to answer the complaint and information upon oath of *William Sparks*, of *Corfe*, labourer." One of the informations was lost: the other was produced, and corresponded with the summons and one of the convictions. It appeared that both the convictions took place the same day; the prosecution, in each case, being conducted by an attorney named *Mills*, who stated, in the presence of the plaintiff, that he appeared on behalf of the lord of the manor as regarded the trespass on *Pickeridge Hill;* and also that he rented the shooting on *Hayne* farm of *Westlake*. It was proved that *Sparks* had no interest in the land or game in either case. The Lord Chief Justice expressed an opinion that, under the Game Act, 1 & 2 *W.* 4. *c.* 32. *s.* 30., it was not necessary that the information should be laid either by the lord of the manor or by the owner or occupier of the land, or at the instance of any party interested: but he left it to the jury whether *Sparks* was authorised by any of the above parties; and, the jury finding in the affirmative, his Lordship directed a verdict for the defendants.

Cockburn now moved (*a*) for a new trial, on the ground of misdirection. First, the information must be laid

(*a*) Before Lord *Denman* C. J., *Littledale*, *Patteson*, and *Coleridge* Js.

by

1838.

MIDDLETON against GALE.

by the owner or occupier of the land, or person interested in the game, or at least by his agent, as a gamekeeper, &c. Stat. 1 & 2 *W.* 4. *c.* 32. *s.* 30. first authorized the sale of game, which, in sect. 30, is stated to be the reason for providing "more summary means" "for protecting the same from trespassers." The public at large have no interest; the protection was merely for the party who, till the summary means were created, must have brought an action of trespass. There was no intention of protecting the revenue, as in the provisions for certificates. By a later act, 5 & 6 *W.* 4. *c.* 20. *s.* 21., half the penalty goes to the informer; but the informer should be the party interested, since the penalty is in lieu o. damages in trespass. By sect. 30 of stat. 1 & 2 *W.* 4. *c.* 32. it is provided that the occupier's leave shall be no defence where the landlord, &c., has reserved to him the right of killing the game: "but such landlord, lessor, or other person shall, *for the purpose of prosecuting,*" "be deemed to be the legal occupier of such land, whenever the actual occupier thereof shall have given such leave or licence." Hence it appears that the legislature intended the prosecution to be by the party really interested in the preservation of the game. [*Patteson* J. Sect. 31 gives power both to the occupier and to the party having the right of killing game to demand names.] It limits the power to such parties: and, as the occupiers are expressly mentioned there, the inference is that in sect. 31, where they are not so mentioned, the right to inform is given only to the party interested in the preservation of the game. Secondly, assuming that the information must be laid by some party interested, there was no evidence that it had been so here. The account given by *Mills* did

1838.

MIDDLETON against GALE.

did not prove enough; but, even if it did, it was not on oath, and the jury ought not to have been allowed to take notice of it. And, further, the conviction states the information to have been upon the oath of *Sparks*, who is not stated to have an interest. In *Rex* v. *Corden* (*a*) a conviction, under stat. *5 G. 3. c.* 14. (*b*), for fishing in a private water, was held bad for not shewing that it was on the complaint of the owner, and that the fishing had taken place without his leave; although it was stated, not on oath, who was the owner (*c*). *Rex* v. *Daman* (*d*) is to the same effect. Here, therefore, positive evidence that the information was on the part of the owner could not have supplied the defect. [*Coleridge* J. Where would you insert the allegation?] The conviction purports to be on the oath of *William Sparks*. [*Coleridge* J. But that is not required according to the form in sect. 39.] If the informant's name be inserted, it should appear that he is the proper party. But, further, it was proved that *Sparks* was not the party interested in either case. [*Coleridge* J. If a conviction drawn according to the form in sect. 39 would be a good defence, could you have met it by parol evidence that the informant was not the party interested?] Possibly not, if the conviction had been enforced by imprisonment or distress, and thereupon trespass had been brought. But in the present case the fine was paid on the conviction, and an action on the case is brought for the illegal conviction. On the trial, the information was produced by the plaintiff; and, as it did not appear on the face of it that the complaint was preferred by any party

(*a*) 4 *Bur.* 2279. (*b*) Sect. 3. The penalty goes to the owner.
(*c*) A different person from the informant.
(*d*) 2 *B. & Ald.* 378.

interested,

1838.

MIDELTON *against* GALE.

interested, or any person properly authorized by such party, it follows, upon the authorities, if the proposition first contended for be correct, that the justices had no jurisdiction over the alleged offence. The information which is the groundwork of their jurisdiction was bad; and parol evidence could not be admitted to supply its defects. [Lord *Denman* C. J. *Mills*'s statement was certainly not receivable as evidence: if, therefore, the conviction must be at the instance of the party interested, this requisite was not satisfied.]

Cur. adv. vult.

Lord DENMAN C. J. in this term (*May* 10th) delivered the judgment of the court.

The question was, whether it was necessary that a complaint, under stat. 1 & 2 *W.* 4. *c.* 32. *s.* 30., for a trespass committed in search of game, should be made by an owner or occupier of the land, or a person authorised by such owner or occupier. We do not find that any decision has taken place on this point; but we have considered it, and are of opinion that any person may make such complaint, and that the conviction was therefore good.

Rule refused.

Wednesday, April 25th.

BAILEY *against* APPLEYARD.

Under stat. 2 & 3 *W.* 4. c. 71. *s.* 1., proof of a thirty years' enjoyment of common of pasture is not complete if proof be given of an enjoyment for twenty-eight years immediately preceding an action in which the right is disputed, and it appear that twenty-eight years back the enjoyment was interrupted, but that the right was exercised before the interruption.

And the party disputing the right is not bound to shew that such interruption was adverse: it lies upon the party prescribing, under the statute, to prove thirty years' uninterrupted enjoyment.

Semble, that, under sect. 2 of the statute, prescription for a right, every year, and at all times of the year, to put and turn the party's cattle into and upon a certain close, is too vague, and may be demurred to.

If there be no demurrer, and the issue on such plea be tried, the party prescribing, and relying on sect. 2, must give proof applicable to some definite easement.

And he will fail if the evidence entitle him not to an easement, but to a profit à prendre.

Per *Coleridge* J. A plea of prescription is supported if the party prove a right more extensive than that pleaded; but the right proved must be of such a nature that it may comprehend the right pleaded.

DECLARATION (*December* 30th 1837), in replevin for cattle. Avowry, that the locus in quo was defendant's close, soil and freehold, and that the cattle were damage-feasant.

Pleas in bar. 1. That, before and at the time when &c., plaintiff was, and still is, the occupier of a certain messuage and of certain closes of land with their respective appurtenances, situate and being in the township of *Thornton*, &c.; "and that he the said plaintiff and the occupiers for the time being of the said messuage," &c., "for thirty years next before the said time when" &c., "and before the commencement of this suit, have continually had, and have been used and accustomed to have, and of right ought" &c., "and the plaintiff still of right ought, to have, for himself and themselves, and his and their tenants, occupiers of the said messuage and land with the appurtenances, a right of pasture in, upon, over, and throughout a certain close called *Toadholes Lane*, situate and being in the said township of *Thornton*," &c., "for his and their cattle, every year and at all times of the year, as to the said messuage and land with the appurtenances belonging and appertaining;" that the locus in quo was next adjoining

1838.

Bailey *against* Appleyard.

Toadholes Lane; that defendant was bound by prescription to repair the fence between the locus in quo and *Toadholes Lane*; and that the fence was out of repair; by means whereof plaintiff's cattle, then lawfully feeding and being in and upon *Toadholes Lane*, escaped into the locus in quo, &c. Verification.

2. That, before and at &c., plaintiff was, and still is, the occupier of a messuage and closes of land with the appurtenances, situate &c., and that plaintiff and the occupiers for the time being of the last-mentioned messuage, &c., "for twenty years next before the said time when &c., and before the commencement of this suit, have continually had, and have been used" &c., "and of right" &c., "and the said plaintiff still of right ought to have, for himself and themselves, and his and their tenants, occupiers of the said last-mentioned messuage," &c. "a right, every year and at all times of the year, to put and turn his and their cattle into and upon the said close called *Toadholes Lane*, as to the said last-mentioned messuage and land with the appurtenances belonging and appertaining." The plea then stated, as before, the duty of the defendant to repair fences, and that, by reason of the fence being out of repair, the cattle in the declaration mentioned, "lawfully being in and upon the said close called *Toadholes Lane*," erred and strayed, &c. Verification.

3. Like the second plea, but substituting "forty" for "twenty" years.

The replication traversed the prescriptive rights of the plaintiff, as pleaded, and issues were joined on the traverses.

On the trial before *Patteson* J., at the last spring assizes at *York*, evidence was given of the enjoyment of

1838.

BAILEY against APPLEYARD.

of pasture in *Toadholes Lane* by the occupier of plaintiff's farm for the time being, from 1809 downwards, and before the interruption next mentioned; but that, in 1809, a stang (rail) had been erected, which prevented the access of cattle from plaintiff's land to the *Toadholes Lane*. The stang was removed in consequence of an agreement; and then the plaintiff's cattle depastured in the lane. The learned Judge was of opinion, as to the first issue, that, under stat. 2 & 3 *W.* 4. *c.* 71. (for shortening the time of prescription in certain cases), the plaintiff was bound to shew an uninterrupted enjoyment of pasturage for thirty years; and that, if there had been an interruption, the plaintiff could not aid himself by proof of a prior enjoyment. And he left it to the jury to say, whether there had been, substantially, an enjoyment for thirty years, or for twenty-eight only. His Lordship held that the second and third pleas were unsupported, inasmuch as the plaintiff, by them, claimed an easement, whereas the evidence tended to establish a right to a profit à prendre. A verdict was found for the defendant on all the issues; and now,

Alexander moved for a new trial on the ground of misdirection. The first plea in bar was sufficiently proved. [*Patteson* J. That plea says that the plaintiff, and the occupiers &c., had been used and accustomed to have "a right of pasture" upon the lane "for his and their cattle;" but it does not say whether the cattle were to be levant and couchant.] The learned Judge laid it down that the plaintiff was bound to give strict evidence of an uninterrupted enjoyment for thirty years. He gave such evidence as to twenty-eight years; and from that the jury

1838.

Bailey *against* Appleyard.

might have presumed an enjoyment for thirty. [*Patteson* J. Stat. 2 & 3 *W.* 4. *c.* 71. *s.* 1. requires, in the case of a profit á prendre, enjoyment "without interruption for the full period of thirty years;" and sect. 6 enacts that no presumption shall be made in favour of any claim on proof of enjoyment "for any less period of time or number of years" than that specified in the act as applicable to the particular claim. I thought that the most undoubted exercise of enjoyment for twenty-nine years and three quarters would not have been sufficient]. The defendant ought to have shewn that the stang was adversely put up. [Lord *Denman* C. J. It was for you to prove the uninterrupted enjoyment]. At all events, the second plea was proved. [*Patteson* J. I am unable to understand what was claimed by that plea]. The plea would have been made out by proof of a right to turn cattle on the close for any purpose; as if the owner of a stage-coach had acquired a right to place his relay of horses there till they were wanted. If there is any objection to the manner of claiming the right, it should have been taken by demurrer. The evidence applicable to this plea was, that for more than twenty years cattle had been turned upon the lane and had depastured there. In the case of prescription, a party "will not be precluded from recovering, because he proves a more ample right than what he claims:" 1 *Phillips on Ev.* 857 (*a*). [*Patteson* J. If any right was proved, it was a right of common. But a plea of right of common enjoyed for twenty years is bad in law, because, by stat. 2 & 3 *W.* 4. *c.* 71. *s.* 2., such a plea could avail only as to a "way or other easement, or to any water-course, or the use

(*a*) 8th ed. part 3. c. 1. s. 3. An earlier edition was cited.

of

of any water." As to the third plea, if the proof bore upon a right of common, and that proof failed as to thirty years' enjoyment, it failed of course as to forty.] In *The Bailiffs, &c. of Tewkesbury* v. *Bricknell* (*a*) the plaintiff claimed under a more limited prescription than he proved, and was held entitled to recover. [*Patteson* J. Your argument would shew that a profit à prendre includes an easement. *Coleridge* J. You say that the second plea claims a right to turn on for all purposes, and therefore that proof of a right to depasture supports the plea. But a right, for instance, to turn on for the purpose of washing would be something quite different from a right to common of pasture.]

Lord DENMAN C. J. The plaintiff is not entitled to a rule. As to the first issue, the enjoyment of pasture for thirty years was not proved as the statute requires, because, during two of the thirty, there was an interruption. Then, as to the second plea in bar, without discussing the goodness of such a plea, it is sufficient to say that the defendant, claiming a right to put and turn his cattle upon the close, was at any rate bound to shew in what respect he had exercised that right. But the only right of which an exercise could appear from the evidence was a right to pasture. If the plaintiff by his plea claimed a right to turn on cattle for all purposes, including pasture, he did not claim less than he proved, but more. The evidence failed as to a right of pasture, and did not apply to any claim of easement.

LITTLEDALE J. It is clear that, on the first issue, no sufficient proof was given under stat. 2 & 3 *W.* 4.

(*a*) 1 *Taunt.* 142.

 c. 71.

1838.

BAILEY *against* APPLEYARD.

c. 71. *s.* 1. If the claim had been made by virtue of immemorial user, or of a non-existing grant, as was done before the statute, twenty-eight years' enjoyment would have been some evidence; but the late act, while it dispenses with the necessity of setting up such user or grant, and limits proof to a thirty years' enjoyment, requires that that enjoyment shall be proved to the full extent. The second plea in bar alleges a right to turn cattle on the close, not saying for what purpose. This might have been demurred to, but was not, and the case went to trial. Then, to make a twenty years' enjoyment suffice, it was necessary to shew in evidence some particular easement enjoyed. It was not requisite perhaps to prove such an unlimited right of easement as the words of the plea seem to imply: but at all events there ought to have been some easement of which definite proof could be given; as, for instance, if it had been for the purpose suggested, to place the horses of a coach in the close; or to turn cattle upon it for the purpose of their going upon some other close of the plaintiff, or a common, or a highway. Even in those cases there might have been a difficulty, because the plaintiff has pleaded the right in himself and the other occupiers for "his and their cattle," generally. Still it might be sufficient if he proved a right exercised to put on all the cattle he ever had. But it was necessary to prove that they were put on with a view to some definite easement which might be claimed under the statute in virtue of twenty years' enjoyment. Here the twenty years' enjoyment was proved in respect of a right which, by the statute, requires thirty years to confirm it, that is, the right of pasture. The plaintiff, therefore, was not entitled to recover on any of the issues.

COLERIDGE

1838.

BAILEY *against* APPLEYARD.

COLERIDGE J. The words of stat. 2 & 3 *W.* 4. *c.* 71. s. 6. are explicit; and the construction is assisted by sect. 4, which enacts, "that each of the respective periods of years hereinbefore mentioned shall be deemed and taken to be the period next before some suit or action wherein the claim or matter to which such period may relate shall have been or shall be brought into question;" thus making the thirty or other numbers of years before spoken of entire periods. And there is reason for this. Before the passing of the act, a prescriptive claim was a claim of immemorial right; the evidence in support of it was such as a party might be able to give in such a case; and the jury were to draw their inference from such proof as could be produced. Now, the burden of establishing an immemorial right is withdrawn, and the proof is limited to thirty years. When that was done, the legislature might reasonably say that the party prescribing should prove his right for that whole period, and that no presumption should be drawn from evidence as to a part. As to the second issue, we must take the plea to be founded on sect. 2 of the act. That clearly distinguishes between easements and common or profit à prendre; and a different limitation is established for the first and the latter cases. Here all the evidence went to shew that the right to be exercised was right of pasture. How, then, could it be said that proving the right actually contended for was, inclusively, proving the right claimed by the second plea? A party may prescribe for less than he proves; but that implies that the lesser right claimed is included in the greater. The rule, therefore, ought not to be granted.

PATTESON J. I am of the same opinion. The act keeps up a distinction between easements and profit à

 prendre

1838.

BAILEY against APPLEYARD.

prendre. I regret that such pleas should have been put on the record.

Rule refused (a).

(a) See (as to the point on the first issue) *Lawson* v. *Langley*, 4 *A. & E.* 890. And, as to the difference between easement and profit à prendre, *Manning* v. *Wasdale*, 5 *A. & E.* 758. Also see *Jones* v. *Richard*, 5 *A. & E.* 413.

Friday, April 27th.

The QUEEN *against* BALDWIN.

In moving for a criminal information for libel, a prosecutor need not adopt the statutory mode of proof (see stats. 38 *G.* 3. *c.* 78., 6 & 7 *W.* 4. *c.* 76.); but it is not sufficient to produce an affidavit, stating merely that the defendant, on &c., printed and published a libel in a newspaper, called &c., a copy of which libel is hereunto annexed; and to annex such copy.

The prosecutor cannot use a statement in the defendant's affidavits to supply a defect in his own, where the latter are so imperfect that the Court, if aware of their defectiveness, would not have granted a rule nisi.

A RULE nisi was obtained in a former term for a criminal information against the defendant for an alleged libel on the mayor of *Lichfield*. The mayor made affidavit in support of the rule, beginning as follows: — "*Thomas Rowley*" &c. maketh oath and saith that *Charles Baldwin* of" &c., "the printer of a certain newspaper called the *Standard*, on the 8th day of *November* instant, did insert and print in the said newspaper a certain scandalous and defamatory libel relating to this deponent in his office of mayor," &c., "and a copy of which said libel is hereunto annexed and stands near the middle of the fifth column of the second page of the said newspaper, and a copy of which said libel, marked B., is hereinafter contained." The newspaper, containing the alleged libel, was annexed to the affidavit. The affidavits filed in opposition to the rule admitted that the article complained of had been inserted in the *Standard*, and that the defendant was then proprietor of that paper.

Sir *W. W. Follett* now shewed cause. There is no sufficient proof that the defendant printed and published this libel. The prosecutor has not given the evidence required

1838.

The QUEEN *against* BALDWIN.

required by statute (*a*), nor has he effectually supplied its place. He merely states that the defendant inserted and printed a libel in the paper; and that a copy of such libel is annexed.

Sir *J. Campbell*, Attorney-General, contrà. This is not the statutory evidence, but better. The prosecutor avers that the defendant inserted and printed a libel; and he annexes the very libel to his affidavit. [*Patteson* J. At common law is it sufficient to state merely that a person printed in a paper something, of which the annexed is a copy?] It is sufficient primâ facie evidence. At all events the affidavits in opposition to the rule supply the necessary facts.

Lord DENMAN C. J. We have decided before that affidavits on shewing cause cannot assist the party moving, where the affidavits in support of the motion are defective; because the Court, if it had known that fact, would not have granted a rule. The prosecutor's affidavit here is not sufficient. There should be proof of publication by the defendant distinctly given. If the affidavits offered here did contain primâ facie evidence, I do not think we should be satisfied with it, where conclusive evidence is so easily attainable.

LITTLEDALE J. The affidavits in answer cannot be gone into, because, if our attention had been drawn to the defect now pointed out in the former affidavits, we should not have granted a rule. And, as to the evidence offered by the prosecutor, if this were received, affidavits for a criminal information in cases of libel would never be made in any other form.

(*a*) See stats. 38 *G.* 3. *c.* 78. (now repealed), and 6 & 7 *W.* 4. *c.* 76.

PATTESON

1838.

The Queen against Baldwin.

Patteson J. There is an express statutory provision as to the proof in such cases. If parties will not adopt that, they must shew publication by some direct proof, as that a party bought the libel in the defendant's shop.

Coleridge J. concurred.

Rule discharged (a).

(a) See *Murray* v. *Souter*, cited in *Cook* v. *Ward*, 6 *Bing*. 414.; *Rex* v. *Donnison*, 4 *B.* & *Ad.* 698.; *Rex* v. *Franceys*, 2 *A.* & *E.* 49.; *Watts* v. *Fraser*, 7 *A.* & *E.* 223.

Friday, April 27th.

Merrick *against* Wakley, Esquire, M.P.

A register of attendances, &c., kept by the medical officer of a poor-law union, and laid before the board of guardians weekly for inspection, in obedience to rules made by the commissioners under stat. 4 & 5 *W.* 4. c. 76. s. 15., is not receivable in evidence for the party making it, as a public official book.

CASE for a libel imputing mala praxis to the plaintiff as a surgeon employed to attend the poor of a parochial union under sat. 4 & 5 *W.* 4. *c.* 76. The defendant pleaded the general issue and pleas of justification, to which the plaintiff replied de injuriâ, and issues were joined thereupon. On the trial, before *Alderson* B., at the last *Herefordshire* assizes, it appeared that the plaintiff, at the time in question, was employed as a medical officer of the *Kington* union, *Herefordshire*, by appointment of the guardians; and that the poor-law commissioners, acting under stat. 4 & 5 *W.* 4. *c.* 76. s. 15., had duly made rules and regulations for the government of the workhouse (a) of the above union, prescribing, among other things, the duties of the medical officer. One of these was stated as follows: —

(a) It appeared that the pauper, to whose case the libel here in question related, was not in the workhouse at the time in question, but no reference was made to this fact on the present motion.

"To

1838.

MERRICK against WAKLEY.

"To make a weekly return to the board of guardians in a book prepared according to the form I. (*a*)" (subjoined); "in which book he shall insert the date of every attendance at the workhouse, and make any reports relative to the sickness prevalent within his district which the board of guardians or the poor-law commissioners may require; and shall attend the board of guardians when summoned by them for that purpose." The plaintiff kept such a book, which was laid on the table of the guardians at their weekly meetings, to be inspected by them. The book was produced and identified at the trial; and the plaintiff's counsel proposed to read some entries in it, for the purpose of shewing what had been the plaintiff's attendance upon, and treatment of, a person whose case was commented upon in the libel, and whom the plaintiff was therein alleged to have neglected. The learned Judge held this evidence inadmissible for the plaintiff. A verdict was given for one farthing damages, and the learned Judge certified to deprive of costs, under stat. 43 *Eliz.* *c.* 6. *s.* 2. In this term (*b*),

Ludlow Serjt. moved for a new trial, stating, as one ground, the rejection of the above evidence. The commissioners are authorized by stat. 4 & 5 *W.* 4. *c.* 76. *s.* 15. to make rules "for the guidance and control of all guardians, vestries, and parish officers, so far as relates to the management or relief of the poor;" and the word "officer," by sect. 109, extends to any "person duly licensed to practise as a medical man," who

(*a*) The form had columns headed, — Name. Age. In-door. Out-door. Nature of disease. Days when attended. Wine and other necessaries ordered to be given to the patient. Observations.

(*b*) *April* 23d. Before Lord *Denman* C. J., *Littledale*, *Patteson*, and *Coleridge* Js.

shall

1838.

Merrick against Wakley.

shall be employed under the act. And sect. 42 enacts that all rules to be made by the commissioners under this act shall be binding, and be observed as if embodied therein. The book made up and left for inspection at the meetings of guardians, in pursuance of such rules, was admissible in evidence as a public book, kept under the direct authority of an act of parliament. It may indeed be considered as embodied in the rules, and sanctioned by the act in the same degree as they are. The entries were made before any dispute on the matters involved in this action.

Cur. adv. vult.

Lord Denman C. J. now delivered the judgment of the Court. A point of evidence which arose in this case was, whether certain entries could be read from a book kept by the plaintiff as a medical officer, under rules of the poor-law commissioners, which book contained entries of professional visits, and was produced at the weekly meetings of the guardians. The endeavour was to put this document upon the same footing with the register of the Navy-office, the log-book of a man of war, the books of the Master's office, and other public books which are held to be admissible in evidence. But in these cases the entries are made by an officer in discharge of a public duty; they are accredited by those who have to act upon the statements; and they are made for the benefit of third persons. Here, it is true, the book is kept by a public officer; but no credit is given him in respect of the entries: they are merely a check upon himself. If we held this book admissible, we should make the entries of any public accountant evidence on a similar occasion. There will therefore be no rule.

Rule refused.

The QUEEN *against* The Justices of SHROPSHIRE. (TIBBERTON *against* NEWPORT.)

Friday, April 27th.

Where an act is required by statute to be done so many days *at least* before a given event, the time must be reckoned, excluding both the day of the act and that of the event.

A statement of grounds of appeal under stat. 4 & 5 *W.* 4. c. 76. s. 81. is not duly served unless fourteen days elapse between the day of service and the first day of the sessions at which the appeal is to be tried.

A RULE nisi was obtained, in *Hilary* term 1837, for a mandamus to the justices of *Shropshire* to enter continuances, and hear the appeal of the inhabitants of the parish of *Tibberton, Shropshire,* against an order removing *Anne Bate* to that parish from the parish of *Newport* in the same county. The statement of grounds of appeal was served upon the parish officers of *Newport* on *December* 19th, 1836. The ensuing quarter sessions began on *January* 2d, 1837. The appeal being called on for trial at those sessions, it was objected that there had not been fourteen clear days between the delivery of the statement and the first day of the sessions, and therefore that, by stat. 4 & 5 *W.* 4. *c.* 76. *s.* 81., the appellants could not be heard. The sessions, on this ground, dismissed the appeal.

Whateley now shewed cause. Sect. 81 of stat. 4 & 5 *W.* 4. *c.* 76. requires notice of the grounds of appeal "fourteen days at least" before the first day of the sessions at which the appeal is intended to be tried. That means fourteen clear days. Here either *December* 19th or *January* 2d must be included to make up fourteen days. By the general rule of practice, as stated in *Rex* v. *The Justices of the West Riding* (*In re Bower*) (*a*), the fourteen days would be reckoned, one inclusive and one exclusive of the day of notice or the first day of the

(*a*) 4 *B.* & *Ad.* 685. And see *Rex* v. *Goodenough*, 2 *A.* & *E.* 463.

sessions;

1838.

The Queen against The Justices of Shropshire.

sessions; but that is in the absence of express words of regulation to a different effect. In *Rex* v. *The Justices of Herefordshire* (a), where notice was required by statute (49 *G.* 3. *c.* 68. *s.* 5.) "ten clear days before" the sessions, it was held that "ten perfect intervening days" were required "between the act done and the first day of the sessions." Even in a case affecting liberty, this Court held (under the Lords' Act, 32 *G.* 3. *c.* 28. *s.* 13.) that "fourteen days at least must mean fourteen clear days;" *Zouch* v. *Empsey* (b). In *Hardy* v. *Ryle* (c) the time limited by stat. 24 *G.* 2. *c.* 44. *s.* 8., for bringing an action against a magistrate, was reckoned, in a case of false imprisonment, exclusively of the last day of imprisonment, the words of the statute being "within six calendar months after the act committed." The expression "at least" is significant, because not always used for defining spaces of time, in stat. 4 & 5 *W.* 4. *c.* 76. On applications in bastardy, sect. 73 requires only "fourteen days' notice," which would be reckoned one inclusively, and the other exclusively.

Sir *F. Pollock*, contrà. The words "fourteen days at least" mean only that the shortest notice must be fourteen days, but that the party may give a longer notice if he pleases. In the absence of such an enactment, the person receiving a longer notice than that prescribed might say that it tended to mislead, and that he was not bound to pay attention to it. One day's notice would mean a notice to be given on the day before the sessions; so fourteen days' notice means a notice on the fourteenth day preceding that of the sessions, not a day

(a) 3 *B. & Ald.* 581. (b) 4 *B. & Ald.* 522.

(c) 9 *B. & C.* 603. *S. C.* 4 *Mann. & Ry.* 295.

before

1838.

The QUEEN against The Justices of SHROPSHIRE.

before the fourteenth. Where the words "clear days" are used, the meaning evidently is different. In *Hardy* v. *Ryle* (a) it is said that where the act from which the computation is made is one to which the party against whom the time runs is privy, the day of the act done may reasonably be included. Here the act done is giving notice; and the party giving it, and against whom the time runs, is privy to the act. *Zouch* v. *Empsey* (b) does not appear to have been much considered by the Court, and no reason is given for the decision. If "fourteen days" would mean one inclusive and one exclusive, why should "fourteen days at least" be construed as requiring a day more? [*Patteson* J. Do you know of any decision contrary to that in *Zouch* v. *Empsey* (b)?] None has been found; but the construction there adopted is not the natural one. [*Coleridge* J. On the Rule of Court, *Hil.* 6 *W.* 4. *s.* 5. (c), as to examinations of attorneys, we determined (d) that "three days at the least" should be held to mean clear days].

Lord DENMAN C. J. We may regret the decision we have to pronounce in the particular instance; but it is much best not to shake a rule settled by former decisions. The writ, therefore, must not go.

LITTLEDALE J. We must abide by what has been already decided, though it appears to me that a day is a day, whether "at least" be added or left out.

(a) 9 *B.* & *C.* 603. *S. C.* 4 *Mann.* & *Ry.* 295.
(b) 4 *B.* & *Ald.* 522. (c) 4 *A.* & *E.* 747.
(d) *In re Prangley*, 4 *A.* & *E.* 781.

PATTESON

1838.

The QUEEN *against* The Justices of SHROPSHIRE.

PATTESON J. In a matter wholly indifferent, it is best to abide by former decisions: that is the ground of my judgment.

COLERIDGE J. I think, for the same reason, that the rule must be discharged: but, on principle, I should be of a different opinion.

Rule discharged.

Friday, April 27th.

The QUEEN *against* The Mayor, Aldermen, and Burgesses of the Borough of LIVERPOOL.

Stat. 5 & 6 *W.* 4. c. 76. *s.* 68., directing that stipends, which, for seven years before *June* 5th 1835, have been usually paid to *the minister* of any church or chapel, shall be secured by bond under the corporation seal to the person *entitled or accustomed* to receive the same, extends to a person appointed lecturer of a church in such borough by the corporation, and having read prayers, preached, and administered the sacrament of the Lord's Supper, and occasionally solemnized baptisms, marriages, and burials; although there is an incumbent of the same church duly appointed under a local act of parliament, which constitutes him, and not such lecturer, the minister of that church.

It is sufficient, under stat. 5 & 6 *W.* 4. *c.* 76. *s.* 68., that the claimant has performed the duties of minister, according to the general acceptation of that term, and been accustomed for seven years to receive the stipend.

SIR *W. W. FOLLETT*, in *Easter* term, 1837, obtained a rule calling on the above parties to shew cause why a mandamus should not issue, "commanding them to secure to *Thomas Moss*, clerk, by bond or obligation under the common seal of the said borough in a sufficient penalty, the yearly sum of 180*l*., being the allowance or stipend which, during seven years next before the 5th day of *June* 1835, has been usually paid and granted to the said *Thomas Moss* as minister or lecturer of the church of *St. John* in *Liverpool*." The facts of the case, stated on affidavit, were as follows.

By virtue of stat. 2 *G.* 3. *c.* 68. (public), two new churches, *St. Paul's* and *St. John's*, were built in the town and parish of *Liverpool*; and it was enacted by that statute (*s.* 34.) that the right of presentation and perpetual advowson and patronage of the two churches should be,

and

1838.

The QUEEN *against* The Mayor, &c., of LIVERPOOL.

and the same thereby was, vested in the mayor, bailiffs, and burgesses of the town of *Liverpool* for ever; and the mayor, aldermen, bailiffs, and common council of the borough and corporation of *Liverpool* and their successors, or the major part of them, in common council assembled, were authorised and empowered and required to appoint under the common seal "a proper person duly qualified to be the minister and ministers of each of the said churches," and also in like manner to appoint a minister to and for each of the said churches on every vacancy, such ministers respectively to be licensed by the Bishop of *Chester* and his successors.

The church of *St. John* was completed and consecrated in 1784; and the corporation thereupon nominated and appointed a minister or incumbent thereof, and presented such minister or incumbent to the Bishop under the common seal of the borough and corporation; they at the same time nominated and appointed a lecturer of the said church with a yearly stipend or salary payable by the corporation; and they presented such lecturer to the Bishop under the common seal. Such nominations and appointments have been ever since regularly kept up by the corporation, such ministers or incumbents and lecturers respectively having been regularly licensed by the bishop, and no objection having been made to such appointment of lecturers, either by the rector for the time being of the parish of *Liverpool*, or the minister or incumbent for the time being of the church of *St. John*, to the knowledge or belief of the party making affidavit.

Mr. *Moss* was appointed lecturer of *St. John's*, *February* 1st, 1815, by a resolution of the corporation in common council,

1838.

The Queen against The Mayor, &c., of Liverpool.

council, stating him to be elected, nominated, and appointed to be lecturer of the said church of *St. John* in the place of Mr. *Loxham* appointed minister. The presentation of Mr. *Moss* to the bishop was under the common seal. It recited the clause of stat. 2 *G.* 3. *c.* 68., above mentioned, and that the church of *St. John* had from time to time been supplied with a minister and also with a lecturer to the same; that the office of lecturer was now vacant by the resignation of *Loxham;* that the mayor, bailiffs, &c., had elected and chosen, and did, by those presents, under the common seal, elect and choose, and present to the bishop, the said *Thomas Moss* (being a minister of the church of *England* as by law established) to be lecturer of the said church of *St. John* in the place and stead of *Loxham,* "to officiate and serve therein as lecturer as aforesaid according to the rites and usage of the Church of *England,* and to preach the word of God, and duly administer the holy sacraments therein;" beseeching the bishop to license the said *T. M.* to officiate in the said church as the lecturer thereof in such manner as other lecturers within the diocese were licensed to do &c. The bishop granted Mr. *Moss* his licence accordingly, "to perform the office of lecturer of the church of *St. John,*" vacant &c., of which the mayor, bailiffs, &c., were the patrons, as was asserted, "in preaching the word of God, and in reading the common prayers, and performing all other ecclesiastical duties belonging to the said office according to the form prescribed in the Book of Common Prayer," &c. (he the said *T. M.* having first, before the bishop's commissary, read and subscribed the Articles and taken the oaths, and made and subscribed the declaration which in that case were by law required); and the licence

1838.

The QUEEN against The Mayor, &c., of LIVERPOOL.

licence authorised him "to receive and enjoy all and singular stipends, profits, and advantages whatsoever belonging to the said office. Mr. *Moss* (after reading and subscribing the Articles &c.) entered upon and discharged the duties of lecturer, which were described as follows.

"That such duties consist in the celebration of divine service and reading prayers, and preaching morning and evening, and solemnizing the sacrament of the Lord's Supper on *Sundays* and the usual holidays, feasts, and festivals of the church, in conjunction with the incumbent of the said church of *St. John*, the occasional duty of weddings, churchings, baptisms, and funerals, having been usually discharged by the incumbent of the said church and his curate, though deponent" (Mr. *Moss*) "and his curate" (Mr. *Moss* being also vicar of the vicarage of *Walton*) "have frequently performed the same; and that, except as above-mentioned with respect to the discharge of the occasional duty, the respective duties of the incumbent and lecturer of the said church are in all respects similar."

The governing body of the corporation was changed under stat. 5 & 6 *W.* 4. *c.* 76.; and, after *December* 26th, 1835, payment of Mr. *Moss*'s salary as lecturer (which had been regularly paid until that time) was discontinued. Mr. *Moss* applied to the corporation to secure his salary by a bond, and they refused.

By stat. 2 *G.* 3. *c.* 68. *s.* 32., 50*l.* is to be paid out of the corporate stock to the minister of *St. Paul*'s, and, by *s.* 33, 50*l.* out of the parochial levies to the minister of *St. John*'s. Stat. 7 *G.* 3. *c.* 80. (public), for enlarging the term and powers granted by the former act, &c., recites (sect. 14) the before-mentioned clauses of that act, and,

 after

1838.

The QUEEN against The Mayor, &c., of LIVERPOOL.

after stating that the duty of *St. Paul's* is expected to be too much for one minister to undertake, enacts that the mayor, &c., may nominate and present two ministers to the church of *St. Paul*, and supply vacancies; and sect. 15 provides for payment to the second minister of *St. Paul's*, and also a payment, by way of addition, to the first.

Sir *J. Campbell*, Attorney-General, *Wightman* and *Crompton*, now shewed cause. Stat. 5 & 6 *W.* 4. *c.* 76. *s.* 68., under which this claim is made, directs that "all stipends and allowances which during seven years next before the said 5th day of *June*" (1835) "have been usually paid and granted to the minister or late minister of any church or chapel," "within such borough" (which words include *Liverpool*), "shall be secured, as soon as conveniently may be after the passing of this act, to every person entitled or accustomed to have and receive the same, by bond or obligation under the common seal of the borough out of whose funds the same shall be payable." And it is contended that, by the interpretation clause, sect. 142, the singular, "minister," may be construed to mean more than one. This is not denied: but the party now applying was not a minister within sect. 68. He was so, in the sense in which "the minister" is spoken of in the Rubrick; but he was not the minister of the church of *St. John*, mentioned or contemplated by stat. 2 *G.* 3. *c.* 68. [This point was argued on the sections, above referred to, of stats. 2 *G.* 3. *c.* 68. and 7 *G.* 3. *c.* 80. A more particular notice of the observations on these clauses is not thought necessary.] The lecturer, here, was appointed by a voluntary act of the corporation, like a domestic chaplain; the stipend might have been withdrawn at any

1838.

The QUEEN *against* The Mayor, &c., of LIVERPOOL.

any time. [*Patteson* J. That may be so; but the statute, 5 & 6 *W.* 4. *c.* 76. *s.* 68., points at a person not having permanent title, when it directs the stipend to be secured to every person "entitled *or accustomed* to have and receive the same."] He must be a "minister." [*Coleridge* J. That only shews the large sense in which the word "minister" is used.] The lecturer, properly, means only a person who is to deliver lectures, and it is so understood in popular acceptation; here the party has administered the sacraments and solemnized marriages, but not in discharge of his duty as lecturer; he assisted the incumbent, but his own function was distinct in character from that of minister; and the claimant ought to shew that he was minister in respect of his office, not of the duties he discharged. The lecturership, as here described, is not, properly, an office at all. The private appointment of lecturers, and their intrusion into churches, became matter of complaint at an early period after the Reformation: stat. 13 & 14 *Car.* 2. *c.* 4. *s.* 19., which corrects the practice in this particular, shews the difference, which the legislature recognised, between lecturers and other ministers: and the nature of such an appointment is illustrated by the argument, and judgment of the Court, in *Rex* v. *The Bishop of London* (*a*).

Sir *W. W. Follett* and *Tomlinson* contrà, were stopped by the Court.

Lord DENMAN C. J. I think this rule ought to be made absolute. The question is not whether the party was, correctly speaking, the "minister of any church or

(*a*) Mr. *Downey's Case*, 1 *Wils.* 11.

 chapel,"

1838.

The Queen against The Mayor, &c., of Liverpool.

chapel," but whether he was so under sect. 68 of stat. 5 & 6 *W.* 4. *c.* 76. We have always given a liberal construction to such enactments in the statute; and we are not called upon to say here what the lecturer was entitled to as matter of strict right, but what he has been "accustomed to have and receive" for seven years next before the day mentioned in the act. Construing the clause in the same spirit in which we have before given effect to these enactments, I think that the applicant is a person entitled to the relief prayed for.

Littledale J. I am of the same opinion. The provisions of this act are of general application; and I think that we are bound to construe the word "minister," not merely according to the sense which it may have in *Liverpool*, but as it is understood throughout the country.

Patteson J. The legislature, in using the word "minister," seems to have chosen the largest term possible, as suited to an enactment which was to have effect throughout the country. We are not to construe the word merely as occurring in the local act. The sixty-eighth section would apply if the lecturer had been appointed as he is here, and called a chaplain.

Coleridge J. Mr. *Moss* was not a minister within the meaning of the local acts; but he was so for the purpose of stat. 5 & 6 *W.* 4. *c.* 76. *s.* 68. The legislature has framed that clause for a general purpose, and has used the word "minister" as the most comprehensive. In providing for pensions, for stipends, and for charitable allowances, the enactment speaks

speaks of that which the person has been entitled "or accustomed" to receive. Now, here, the lecturer had been in the habit of performing certain duties, had reason to expect that his functions would continue for life, and had been accustomed for more than seven years to receive the salary which he claims to have secured. The rule, therefore, ought to be made absolute.

1838.

The QUEEN *against* The Mayor, &c., of LIVERPOOL.

Rule absolute.

The QUEEN *against* JOSHUA THOMAS.

Monday, April 30th

The borough of *T.*, until *May* 1st, 1836, had its own quarter sessions, and *W.* held the offices of town clerk and clerk of the peace. He resigned; and thereupon, by a resolution of town council on *July* 20th, 1836, *S.* was elected town clerk; but no step was taken towards investing him with the office. At an adjourned meeting of the council, *July* 25th, 1836, a resolution was passed, rescinding that of *July* 20th, and, by another resolution, *T.* was elected town clerk. In *August* 1836, the borough obtained a grant of quarter sessions; and, on *August* 15th, *T.* was, by resolution of the council, elected clerk of the peace: Held, on motion for a quo warranto information against *T.* at the instance of *S.*, for claiming to exercise the two offices,

That *T.* was legally appointed town clerk on *July* 25th, and clerk of the peace on *August* 15th.

That the offices were not full at the times of such respective elections.

That *T.* could not be presumed to claim the office of clerk of the peace as incidental to the office of town clerk, by the appointment of *July* 25th, no specific act appearing to have been done by him in the capacity of clerk of the peace between that time and *August* 15th; though it was alleged generally on affidavit that he had acted as clerk of the peace from *July* 25th.

That the prosecutor could not allege that notice had not been given to him, or to the councillors (according to stat. 5 & 6 *W.* 4. *c.* 76. *s.* 69.), of the business to be done at the meeting of *July* 25th, inasmuch as the prosecutor was bound to prove that fact by his affidavits, and had not done so. And, per *Coleridge* J., because by analogy to the General Rule, *Hil.* 7 & 8 *G.* 4., the objection could not be urged on motion unless specified in the rule nisi, which had not been done here.

That the resolutions rescinding that of *July* 20th, and appointing *T.* town clerk, were, under the circumstances, a sufficient removal of *S.* from that office.

A RULE nisi was obtained, in *Hilary* term 1837, for a quo warranto information against *Joshua Thomas*, to shew by what authority he claimed to be town-clerk and clerk of the peace of the borough of *Tewksbury*, on the following grounds. 1. That he has not been duly elected to those offices or either of them. 2. That *Thomas Jelf Sandilands* was duly elected to those offices, and has

1838.

The Queen *against* Thomas.

never been legally removed. 3. That both the said offices were full at the time of the supposed election of the said *Joshua Thomas*. 4. That the said *Joshua Thomas* has never been elected or appointed to the office of clerk of the peace of the said borough.

The affidavits in support of the rule stated that *Sandilands* was elected town-clerk on *July* 20th, 1836, at an adjourned quarterly meeting of the council, in the room of *George Edmunds Williams*, who resigned the offices of town-clerk and clerk of the peace in *July* 1836. *Sandilands*, when elected, understood and still believed that he was to hold the office of clerk of the peace with that of town-clerk, as *Williams* had done; and he cited entries in the minutes of the town council relating to *Williams*, as shewing that the two offices had been looked upon as conjoint. On *July* 22d, some members of the council urged *Sandilands* to relinquish the office of town-clerk, several councillors having threatened to resign if he held it: and he thereupon said that he would put himself into the hands of the friends by whose favour he had obtained the office, and would give it up if they were of opinion that he ought to do so. An adjourned quarterly meeting of the council was holden, *July* 25th, 1836 (no official communication having been made to *Sandilands* in the mean time as to his entry on the office of town-clerk), and it was there resolved, "That the resolution of the last meeting appointing Mr. *Sandilands* town-clerk be rescinded." An amendment, to the effect that *Sandilands* should be sent for, was negatived by ten votes to three. It was then resolved (an amendment being again negatived by ten votes to three,) that Mr. *Joshua Thomas* be appointed town-clerk: and it was stated (on information and belief)

1838.

The QUEEN *against* THOMAS.

belief) that *Thomas* had "acted as town-clerk and clerk of the peace of the said borough, under the last-mentioned appointment, from that time to the present." Of nine councillors who voted for the election of *Sandilands*, three only voted against the resolution for rescinding his election: a fourth was stated to have been absent. *Sandilands* was never directly called upon by those friends in the council to whom he had referred himself to give up the town-clerkship. The salary paid to *Williams*, while town-clerk, had been 100*l.*; but, at the meeting of *July* 20th, the salary was reduced to 50*l.*, which was declared to be the salary for all the offices which *Williams* had held.

The affidavits against the rule alleged that the election of *Sandilands* had resulted from a mistake; and they contained some statements, which are not here material, as to the notice which he had of the intention to move that his appointment should be rescinded (*a*). They further stated that neither on *July* 20th, nor *July* 25th, was it intended to appoint to the office of clerk of the peace; that such office, though it had usually been held with the town-clerkship, was distinct, and had reference only to the existence of a separate Court of Quarter Sessions; that by stat. 5 & 6 *W.* 4. *c.* 76. *s.* 107. the sessions jurisdiction which the borough justices had under the former corporation expired on *May* 1st, 1836; that Mr. *Williams*, the late town-clerk and clerk of the peace, acted in the latter capacity till *May* 1st, but not afterwards;

(*a*) Sir *J. Campbell*, Attorney-General, in moving for the rule, admitted that his affidavits did not sufficiently shew a want of notice to *Sandilands*, or to others, of the motion to be made on *July* 25th. He also admitted that, under sect. 58 of stat. 5 & 6 *W.* 4. *c.* 76., the town clerk might be dismissed at the will of the council; but he contended that the mode, supposed to have been here adopted, of determining the will was irregular.

1838.

The QUEEN against THOMAS.

afterwards; that the council of the new corporation applied for a separate Court of Quarter Sessions, under sect. 103, but had not, on the 20th or 25th of *July*, any assurance that it would be granted: and it was not till *August* 15th, 1836, that the council were informed that such grant had issued. That on that day, at an adjourned quarterly meeting of the council, it was resolved that the said *Joshua Thomas*, the town-clerk, should be elected clerk of the peace, no opposition being made, though all but two of the persons who had voted for *Sandilands* on *July* 20th were present. That the resolution of *July* 20th as to salary was not intended to determine that the offices of town-clerk and clerk of the peace should continue to be held together. That *Sandilands* did not apply to the mayor, or, as far as the mayor was informed, to any other person, to call a council to invest him with the office of town-clerk or clerk of the peace; that he never acted in either office, or made or offered to make the declaration required by the statute in respect of either, but that *Thomas* had made the declaration in respect of each office, after being appointed, namely on *July* 30th and *August* 19th., and had acted as town-clerk, and acted also as clerk of the peace after *August* 19th, when he took the oaths and qualified himself in respect of the latter office.

Sir *W. W. Follett* now shewed cause. The offices of town-clerk and clerk of the peace were held together down to 1836, but in that year, by the operation of stat. 5 & 6 *W.* 4. *c.* 76., the office of clerk of the peace expired, together with the jurisdiction to hold sessions, on *May* 1st, and there was no grant of sessions till *August*. After the passing of this act, the two offices were clearly separate,

separate, and the subject of distinct elections: and in *July*, when *Sandilands* was elected town-clerk, there could be no election of a clerk of the peace. He was chosen town-clerk on *July* 20th; but that office, under sect. 58, was determinable at pleasure, and it was determined on *July* 25th. A quo warranto information in respect of two distinct offices is at least unusual.

Sir *J. Campbell*, Attorney-General, and *R. V. Richards*, contrà. There is nothing unusual in granting a quo warranto information for two offices (as alderman and justice of the peace (*a*)) or even more. It is true that the office of town-clerk is held at the will of the corporation; but the will is not determined by merely carrying a motion for rescinding the resolution to appoint. There must be some formal mode of determination, as in the case of the offices held under the Crown, that, for instance, of Attorney-General, which is determined under the Great Seal. The meeting of *July* 25th was holden by adjournment from *July* 20th; but it does not follow that the resolution passed on the 20th might be rescinded on the latter day. Even at the same meeting the resolution could not properly have been rescinded, if some of the parties to that resolution had gone away. [They also observed that no regular notice was given to any person of the intention to move for this vote at the second meeting, nor any summons issued, pursuant to stat. 5 & 6 *W.* 4. *c.* 76. *s.* 69.; and they cited *Rex* v. *Harris* (*b*) and *Rex* v. *The Mayor, &c. of Doncaster* (*c*): but the decision of the Court renders any further mention of the argument on this point unnecessary (*d*).]

(*a*) *Rex* v. *Patteson*, 4 *B. & Ad.* 9. (*b*) 1 *B. & Ad.* 936.
(*c*) 2 *Burr.* 738. (*d*) And see p. 185, note (*a*), antè.

With

1838.

The Queen against Thomas.

With respect to the office of clerk of the peace, it is immaterial whether that had any legal existence or not on the 25th of *July*: if a party usurps an office against the Crown, a quo warranto lies. [*Coleridge* J. *Thomas* was duly elected in *August*.] He might adopt whichever election he chose; and, having acted under the appointment of *July*, he must be supposed to have recognised that, and rested his claim upon it.

Littledale J. (*a*). This rule must be discharged. With regard, first, to the office of clerk of the peace, on the 25th of *July*, when *Thomas* is supposed to have been elected, there was no such office; but still a man may be liable to a quo warranto information for acting as if he were an officer, if the office, though not existing in the particular instance, is one known to the country at large, and he pretends to exercise it. But the defendant here was legally elected clerk of the peace in *August*, and has, therefore, a lawful cause for exercising the office. He is not called upon to account for having done so from *July* to *August*, but for claiming to exercise the office now. It is said that he ought to shew under which appointment he acted; but there are no specific acts to prove that he disclaimed exercising the office under the second appointment; and, if there are two claims of right under which a man may be acting, a good and an invalid one, we must take it that he acts under the good unless the contrary be shewn: as a man putting in force execution against person or goods, if he was furnished with legal process, although he was likewise armed with an illegal authority, may justify in

(*a*) Lord *Denman* C. J. was attending the Privy Council.

virtue

1838.

The QUEEN against THOMAS.

virtue of the good process, unless it appear in point of fact that he did not really act under that: *Lucas* v. *Nockells* (*a*), *Groenvelt* v. *Burwell* (*b*). As to the appointment of town-clerk, there is more doubt. It has been objected that there was no notice of the meeting on *July* 25th, or summons to the councillors for that day, as required by stat. 5 & 6 *W.* 4. *c.* 76. *s.* 68. But the want of notice was a fact to be laid before this Court on affidavit by the prosecutor, who insists that the election was illegal. There has been an election in fact; and the prosecutor's affidavits are defective in not shewing the irregularity relied upon. The question then is, whether *Sandilands* was ever properly displaced. It is true that there was no formal determination to this effect, the resolution having been only that the former resolution, appointing *Sandilands*, be rescinded. That is not a displacing in so many words; but he is in fact displaced by the resolution being rescinded, and another party elected in his stead. *Thomas*, therefore, was properly elected. With respect to costs, I think that, if the application had related to the office of town-clerk only, there would not have been sufficient reason to grant them against the prosecutor; but, as there was no ground for calling upon the defendant with respect to the office of clerk of the peace, the rule must be discharged with costs.

PATTESON J. Four grounds for a quo warranto are stated in the rule. As to the last, that *Thomas* has never been elected clerk of the peace, he clearly was elected in last *August*, and there is nothing to affect the validity of that election. It is said, indeed, that he

(*a*) 4 *Bing.* 729. Affirmed in *Dom. Proc.* 10 *Bing.* 157.
(*b*) 1 *Ld. Raym.* 454.

acted

1838.

The Queen against Thomas.

acted as clerk of the peace on the appointment of *July* 25th; but we are not called upon to conclude so merely because the prosecutor's affidavit states generally that *Thomas* acted in the two offices from that period. It was impossible in law that he could perform any functions as clerk of the peace before the grant of quarter sessions; and no instance is given of anything in fact so done by him. The prosecutor appears to suppose that the appointment of clerk of the peace is incidental to that of town-clerk, and that the will of the corporation might be determined as to this last, and yet the incidental appointment remain: but no one looking at the act of parliament can reasonably come to that conclusion. The third ground stated is, that both the offices were full at the time of *Thomas's* election. But I think it is clear that neither was so. Sect. 58 of stat. 5 & 6 *W.* 4. *c.* 76, requires that security be taken from the town-clerk for the due execution of his office. That office, therefore, was not full till the security was given. The first two objections resolve themselves into one. As to the want of notice and summons to the members of the council, it is observable that sect. 69 prohibits, where the meeting is called by the mayor, the transacting of any business not specified in the notice of meeting, and yet, in directing such notice to be given, it does not enact that the notice shall state the business, though it is required that the summons, and the notice when given by members of the council, shall do so. Perhaps the intention was to enact that no business not stated in the summons should be entered upon. It may be necessary, not only that a notice and summons should be given to the members of the council, but also a summons to the party whom it is intended to remove. Still we come to the question whether, in fact, the notice and summons, alleged

1838.

The QUEEN *against* THOMAS.

alleged here to have been wanting, were or were not given; and the Attorney-General admitted, in moving for the rule, that his affidavits were not sufficiently positive on this point. I think that he was correct in so stating, and that, on the statements before us, it must be taken that the notices were properly given. Then, was *Sandilands* properly removed by the resolution of *July* 25th? It is difficult to say that he could have been removed in any other manner. He could not be formally removed till he had been invested with the office; and there was not only a rescinding of his appointment, but a formal appointment of another person. As to costs I agree with my brother *Littledale*.

COLERIDGE J. There is no doubt as to the office of clerk of the peace. It is true, *Thomas* does not deny that he acted under the appointment of *July* 25th; but it was not necessary to deny it: that could not be a valid appointment to the office of clerk of the peace; and it is not shewn that *Thomas* did any act in that character between *July* 25th and *August* 15th, when he was regularly appointed. It is idle, therefore, to say that he acted under the invalid appointment. Then, as to the removal of *Sandilands*. He was elected, but the appointment was never carried into effect. It would have been difficult in explicit terms to vote a removal, where it was doubtful if the party had been effectually appointed. And rescinding the former resolution was in substance a removal, if there was notice. On that point I have had most doubt. If it had appeared as a fact on the affidavits that notice was not given of the purposes of the adjourned meeting, and this had been stated as an objection in the rule nisi, I question if it could have been got over. But parties who take such an objection

1838.

The Queen against Thomas.

objection must shew it by their affidavits and on their rule; and that is not done here. The rule of Court, *Hil.* 7 & 8 *G.* 4. (*a*), as to quo warranto informations, orders that no objection to the defendant's title, not specified in the rule to shew cause, shall be raised (without special leave) on the pleadings. That being so, it ought not to be urged on the motion. The rule must be discharged on the grounds already stated: and I think also that, as the prosecutor had been distinctly informed of the proceedings contemplated, and had put himself into the hands of his friends, who did not support him, this must be considered a vexatious application.

Rule discharged with costs.

(*a*) 6 *B.* & *C.* 267.

Wednesday, May 2d.

The Queen *against* William Lloyd Roberts.

This case is reported, 7 *A.* & *E.* 433.

Wednesday, May 2d.

The Queen *against* The Inhabitants of St. John in Bedwardine.

Under stat. 6 *G.* 4. *c.* 57. *s.* 2., a settlement is acquired by renting a tenement for 10*l.*, though the landlord agree to pay, and do pay, tithes to an amount which, if deducted from the rent, would reduce it below 10*l.*; and though it appear that the rent demanded would have been only 9*l.* if the landlord had not so agreed.

ON appeal against an order of two justices, whereby *Thomas Bryan* was removed from the parish of *Upton-upon-Severn* to the parish of *St. John in Bedwardine*, both in the county of *Worcester*, the sessions confirmed the order, subject to the opinion of this Court on the following case.

The

1838.

The QUEEN *against* The Inhabitants of ST. JOHN in BEDWARDINE.

The pauper, being legally settled in the parish of *St. John in Bedwardine*, did, at *Michaelmas* 1829, take a house and buildings, two gardens, and an orchard, in *Upton-upon-Severn*, for a year, of one *Edward Perrins*, at 10*l*., the landlord agreeing to discharge all taxes and payments for that period. Before entering into this arrangement, *Perrins* had offered to let the premises to the pauper for 9*l*., the latter satisfying the taxes and payments: but the tenant preferred to take at 10*l*. upon the terms above stated. The premises were occupied for a year under that hiring; and 10*l*. paid to the landlord in respect of them. Under the head of payments, the landlord satisfied a claim for tithe becoming due in the course of the year, to the amount of 6*s*.

If this Court should be of opinion that the pauper obtained a settlement in *Upton-upon-Severn*, the order of removal was to be quashed; otherwise to be confirmed.

Whitmore, in support of the order of sessions. It is true that in *Rex* v. *Framlingham* (*a*) and *Rex* v. *St. Paul's, Deptford* (*b*) this Court held that, under stat. 13 & 14 *C.* 2. *c.* 12. *s.* 1., a settlement is gained by occupying a tenement for which 10*l*. rent is paid, though the landlord pays the rates and charges to an amount which, if deducted, would reduce the rent below 10*l*. Afterwards, in *Rex* v. *Thurmaston* (*c*), the same principle was held applicable to stat. 59 *G.* 3. *c.* 50. and stat. 6 *G.* 4. *c.* 57. *s.* 2. Here the question arises under the latter statute. But the payment for tithes distinguishes the present case from those above mentioned. The

(*a*) *Bur. S. C.* 748. (*b*) 13 *East*, 320.
(*c*) 1 *B. & Ad.* 731.

1838.

The QUEEN against The Inhabitants of St. JOHN in BEDWARDINE.

tithe is not, like other charges and rates, simply on house and land, but is defined to be "the tenth part of the increase, yearly arising and renewing from the profits of lands, *the stock upon lands, and the personal industry of the inhabitants*;" 2 *Bla. Comm.* 24. Therefore the payment here made by the landlord does not merely represent the value of the land, but relieves the tenant from a liability independent of the land. The rent is merely a criterion of the value of the land; and the value cannot be 10*l.*, when a part of the 10*l.* is paid in consideration of something quite independent.

W. J. Alexander, contrà. The case cannot be distinguished from *Rex* v. *Thurmaston* (*a*). It is said that tithe arises partly from the personal industry of the tenant: but so do the profits of the land. The legislature has, in stat. 6 & 7 *W.* 4. *c.* 96. *s.* 1., recognised, as the criterion of rateable value, the rent at which the hereditaments will let, "free of all usual tenant's rates and taxes, and tithe commutation rent-charge." [*Patteson* J. Under stat. 6 *G.* 4. *c.* 57. *s.* 2. and stat. 1 *W.* 4. *c.* 18. *s.* 1., the criterion for the purpose of settlement is rent, not value.] That shews that the amount bargained for is to be looked to. According to the argument on the other side, a settlement might be destroyed by the landlord agreeing to perform repairs. [*Coleridge* J. The question is, whether this was a bonâ fide renting for 10*l.*] In *Rex* v. *Thurmaston* (*a*) Lord *Tenterden* said, "The cases put, of collateral benefit wholly unconnected with the occupation of the tenement, are not in point. In those instances, if they occurred, there might be ground for

(*a*) 1 *B.* & *Ad.* 731.

saying

saying that the house was not bonâ fide rented at 10*l.* a year. But here, the benefit conferred on the tenant was in its nature connected with the occupation. We cannot say that he has not, bonâ fide, paid 10*l.* rent." (He was then stopped by the Court.)

1838.

The QUEEN *against* The Inhabitants of ST. JOHN in BEDWARDINE.

LITTLEDALE J. (*a*) I cannot distinguish this case from *Rex* v. *Thurmaston* (*b*). Tithes are, in this respect, like other taxes and charges.

PATTESON J. *Rex* v. *Thurmaston* (*b*) is not distinguishable. If a party were to rent a tithe-free farm at 10*l.*, he would gain a settlement.

COLERIDGE J. I am of the same opinion. I am always unwilling to encourage nice distinctions; and I think we must adhere to *Rex* v. *Thurmaston* (*b*).

Order of sessions quashed.

(*a*) Lord *Denman* C. J. had left the Court during the argument.
(*b*) 1 *B.* & *Ad.* 781.

THORN *against* LESLIE, Bart.

Thursday, May 3d.

Plaintiff signed judgment against defendant in *Michaelmas* term 1836. Defendant rendered in discharge of his bail in the vacation after *Michaelmas* term 1837, and gave notice to plaintiff. He was not charged in execution in *Hilary* term, 1838: Held, that he was supersedeable under R. *Hil.* 2 *W.* 4. I. 85.

Semble, per *Patteson* J., that, if a trial be had, and judgment entered, in vacation, and afterwards the defendant render in the same vacation, the plaintiff has the two following terms for charging the defendant in execution.

THE plaintiff obtained a verdict against the defendant at the third sitting in *Michaelmas* term 1836. Judgment was entered up in the same term. On 5th *December* 1837, the defendant rendered in discharge of his

1838.

Thorn *against* Leslie.

his bail, and gave notice thereof to the plaintiff (*a*). The defendant not having been charged in execution, he was brought into court to be discharged on a former day in this term. *Wordsworth* then opposed the discharge on affidavit of the above facts; and time was given to defendant to answer the affidavit. The defendant being now brought up,

Humfrey was heard in support of the application. The defendant, having been rendered in *Michaelmas* vacation 1837, must be considered as having been in custody during *Michaelmas* term 1837, and *Hilary* term 1838, the judgment having preceded both these terms; for the render in the vacation has relation back to the preceding term, in which judgment was signed; *Neill* v. *Lovelass* (*b*). [*Patteson* J. Certainly that was the practice before the new rules.] It is true, that under the rules *Hil.* 4 *W.* 4. *General Rules and Regulations*, 3. (*c*), the judgment has no relation back: but that is immaterial here, the judgment having been entered up four terms before the render. And the practice, since R. *Hil.* 2 *W.* 4. I. 85. (*d*), is, in this respect, the same as under R. (Excheq.) *Trin.* 26 & 27 *G.* 2., which entitles the prisoner to his discharge unless he has been charged within two terms next after the surrender, of which the term of the surrender is one (*e*), as was stated by *Parke* B. in *Baxter* v. *Bailey* (*g*).

(*a*) Some discussion took place as to the service of the notice: but, as the Court were of opinion that the particular circumstances of the case precluded the party from taking the objection, the arguments on this point are not reported.

(*b*) 3 *B. Moore*, 8.

(*c*) 5 *B.* & *Ad.* ii.

(*d*) 3 *B.* & *Ad.* 386.

(*e*) 1 *Tidd's Pr.* 362. (9th ed.).

(*g*) 3 *M.* & *W.* 415.

Wordsworth,

1838.

THORN *against* LESLIE.

Wordsworth, contrà. In *Smith* v. *Jefferys* (a) it was held, under R. (K. B.) *Hil.* 26 *G.* 3. (b), that a surrender in the vacation after verdict did not relate back. [*Patteson* J. That applied to the case where the trial was in the vacation in which the render took place. The render was not allowed to relate back to a term preceding the trial. Here the judgment is signed of a term earlier than that preceding the vacation in which the render is made. Must not the surrender be considered to be as of *Michaelmas* term 1837?] Judgments are now to be dated of the day on which they are signed: the same rule, by analogy, must apply to a render.

LITTLEDALE J. (c) The judgment was signed a year before the render. Then has the prisoner been in custody for two terms? That depends upon the question, whether the render relates back to the term preceding the vacation in which it is made. By the practice, it does so relate, when the judgment is of an earlier term. We cannot extend the rule, as to dating judgments from the day on which they are signed, to the render.

PATTESON J. The rule as to the relation of the render is decisive, unless the New rules have made any alteration. Mr. *Wordsworth* cites no authority to shew that they have: but he relies on the analogy of the judgment being no longer allowed to have relation. That argument I cannot accede to. *Smith* v. *Jefferys* (a) shews merely that, if the trial be in a vacation and the render afterwards in the same vacation, the plaintiff has the two following terms. It does not apply here. There is in-

(a) 6 *T. R.* 776. (b) 1 *Tidd.* 360. (9th ed.)

(c) Lord *Denman* C. J. was absent.

 deed

1838.

THORN *against* LESLIE.

deed a case, *Borer* v. *Baker* (a), in which it was held that, in the case of a surrender after trial, both being in the same vacation, the plaintiffs had only one term. I cannot accede to that decision, except upon the ground that the judgment there, from what cause does not appear, was entered up as of the term preceding the trial; so that perhaps, by the same fiction, the verdict also may be considered as having taken place in that term.

COLERIDGE J. concurred.

Defendant superseded.

(a) 1 *A. & E.* 860.

Thursday, May 3d.

BRISCO *against* LOMAX and Another.

In trespass for breaking plaintiff's close, issues were joined on two pleas. 1. that the close was not the plaintiff's: 2. that the close was parcel of the manor of *O.*, and the close of the lord of the said manor. Plaintiff was owner of an estate conterminous with the manor of *W.* in *Yorkshire.* Manor *O.* was in *Lancashire;* the boundary between manors *W.* and *O.* was the boundary between *Yorkshire* and *Lancashire;* another manor, *I.*, was in *Yorkshire,* next adjoining to *W.*, and also abutting on *O.;* and the boundary between manors *I.* and *O.* was also the boundary between *Yorkshire* and *Lancashire.*

Plaintiff's case was, that the boundary between manors *W.* and *O.* was the ridge of a mountain, from which the waters descended in opposite directions. Held,

1. That he might shew, in support of this, that the boundary between manors *O.* and *I.* was the ridge of the same line of mountain from which the waters descended in opposite directions.

2. That he might prove this fact by the finding of a jury summoned under a commission from the Duchy Court of *Lancaster,* for the purpose of determining the boundary between manors *I.* and *O.*, on the petition of former owners of *I.* and *O.*, who had represented that the boundary was uncertain, and that suits were likely to grow between them. And this, though it did not appear that any steps had been taken after the return of the verdict to the Duchy Court, and though another commission had issued in the next year to ascertain the boundary of *O.* For that on a question of boundary reputation was evidence; and, where reputation is evidence, a verdict between third parties is evidence; and the Duchy Court must be taken to have had authority to issue the commission.

TRESPASS for breaking and entering the plaintiff's close, in the parish of *Halifax* in the county of *York,* abutting, towards the west, partly on land in the parish of *Rochdale* in the county of *Lancaster,* and partly &c.

First

First plea. That the close in which &c. is not, nor at the said several times when &c. was, the close of the plaintiff. Conclusion to the country.

Third plea. As to all the trespasses except &c. (certain trespasses not mentioned here): That the close in which &c. now is, and at the said several times when &c. was, and from time immemorial hath been, within and parcel of the manor of *Rochdale* in the county of *Lancaster*; and that the said close in which &c. now is, and at the said several times when &c. was, the close, soil, and freehold of *James Dearden*, lord of the said manor of *Rochdale*: with justification by the defendants as servants of *Dearden*. Replication, that the close in which &c. was not, at the time of pleading the plea, or at the said several times when &c., or any of them, nor from time immemorial, within or parcel of the said manor of *Rochdale*, nor was, at the time of pleading &c., or the said several &c., the close, soil, or freehold of *Dearden*, in manner &c. Conclusion to the country. Similiter.

On the trial before *Parke* B., at the *Yorkshire* Summer assizes, 1836, it appeared that the plaintiff was a copyhold tenant of the manor of *Wakefield*, and that the boundary of his property towards the west was identical with that of the manor of *Wakefield*, which was bounded on the west by the manor of *Rochdale*; and that the common boundary of *Rochdale* and *Wakefield* manors formed the common boundary of *Lancashire* and *Yorkshire*. The dispute at the trial, on the issues above mentioned, was as to the exact line of boundary between *Rochdale* and *Wakefield* manors, the plaintiff contending that it lay more to the west than the defendants admitted. It was agreed that this boundary was the boundary between the property of the plaintiff

1838.

BRISCO *against* LOMAX.

and that of *Dearden*, as well as between the two counties. The boundary ran, upon the supposition of either party, nearly north and south, over a mountain district. The plaintiff produced parol evidence of acts of user up to the present time, and that the boundary had been always understood to be the highest line of the ridge, separating the land whence the water descended westward from that whence the water descended eastward. It was further proved that the manor of *Rishworth*, which had been a subinfeudation from the lord of the manor of *Wakefield*, and anciently part of the said manor, lay immediately to the south of *Wakefield* manor, in *Yorkshire*, and that its western boundary was identical with the western boundary of *Yorkshire*, and also with the eastern boundary common to the county of *Lancaster* and the manor of *Rochdale*. The eastern boundary of *Rochdale* manor, therefore, was first, and northward, the manor of *Wakefield*, and next, immediately southward, the manor of *Rishworth*. The plaintiff offered parol evidence that the boundary between *Rishworth* and *Rochdale* manors had been always understood to be the ridge parting the waters which descended eastward from those which descended westward. This was objected to as irrelevant, but admitted by the learned Judge.

The plaintiff then proved that *Rishworth*, *Wakefield*, and *Rochdale* manors were held of the Duchy of *Lancaster*; and he then offered in evidence the following documents, which were proved to have been duly received from the records of the Duchy.

First, a document under the seal of the Duchy of *Lancaster*, dated 1st *July*, 13 *Car.* 1., entitled a commission to set out the manors of *Rishworth*, *Rochdale*, and *Butterworth*, in the counties of *York* and *Lancaster*, with

1838.

BRISCO *against* LOMAX.

with metes and bounds. It was directed to seven commissioners; and recited that Sir *William Savile* and Sir *John Byron* had petitioned the Chancellor of the Duchy, shewing that Sir *William Savile's* manor of *Rishworth*, and the lands, wastes, and commons thereof, were adjacent to and bordering upon Sir *John Byron's* manor of *Rochdale* and *Butterworth* (*a*), and upon divers of the lands &c. of Sir *John Byron* within his manor and parish of *Rochdale*, "the boundaries whereof being uncertain, suits are likely to grow between the said parties and their tenants; for prevention whereof" the Chancellor, willing that the boundaries thereof should be discovered and made known, assigned and appointed the commissioners, or any two or more of them, to repair to the said manors &c., or to any other place &c., and to call before them the parties interested in the said manors &c., and all such persons as they should think meet, diligently, &c., "to enquire, search, try, and find out, as well by survey, view, oath, evidence, perambulation, admeasurement, examination of witnesses, impannelling and swearing of a substantial jury or juries, as by all other good ways" &c., "the true metes and boundaries of the said manors and lands above mentioned, and the same to set forth with meeres, stones, and other mounds and notorious marks in such manner and sort as the same may evidently be known, distinguished, and severed one from the other for the time to come;" and the sheriff of *Yorkshire* was commanded, at the time and place to be notified by the commissioners, to cause to come before them such and so many lawful men of his bailiwick as would make up

(*a*) *Butterworth* is a township in the parish of *Rochdale*; *Rochdale* parish is conterminous with *Rochdale* manor.

a substantial

1838.

Brisco against Lomax.

a substantial jury or juries: "and of your faits, doings, and proceedings herein, with these our letters, and all surveys, interrogatories, examinations, and depositions hereby taken, fair ingrossed into parchment, we will and require ye, or any two or more of ye, to certify our Chancellor and Council of our said Duchy in our Duchy chamber" &c.

Secondly, the certificate (dated 16th *October* 1637) of three of the commissioners, that, for the execution of the commission, they had assembled themselves at *Baytinge's* in the parish of *Halifax* in the county of *York*, to which place "the parties interested came" &c., and the sheriff returned and caused to come before them a jury of freeholders of *Yorkshire*, who "being elected, impannelled, and solemnly sworn to enquire, and true verdict give, concerning the boundaries betwixt the manors in the said commission specified," witnesses were produced, sworn, and examined, and the place viewed by the jurors, and the jury gave their verdict, which the commissioners caused to be put in writing, subscribed by the jurors &c.: and the commissioners certified that they had caused the said commons, wastes, and moors, bordering betwixt either of the manors, to be set forth &c., and returned and certified the commission, verdict, interrogatories &c., "unto your good Lordship (*a*) into this honourable Court, referring the same to your grave consideration." This was signed by the three commissioners.

Thirdly, the above mentioned verdict of the jury, as follows. "The jury, upon full evidence on both parts, and view of the commons and wastes in question, do

(*a*) Apparently the Chancellor of the Duchy.

find

1838.

BRISCO against LOMAX.

find and say upon their oaths, that the rain water falling upon the mountains, wastes, and hills betwixt the manor of *Rishworth* and the manors of *Rochdale* and *Butterworth* is or causeth the bounder, and divideth betwixt the said manors, that is to say, for so much of the said commons as through which the said rain water descendeth towards the *West Sea*, the same wastes are parcel of the manor of *Rochdale* and *Butterworth*, and for such part of the said wastes as the said rain water descendeth and passeth through towards the *East Sea*, the same wastes are parcel of the manor of *Rishworth*: and also find that one heap of stones at the upper end of *Blagegate* is a bounder betwixt the said manors."

The defendants' counsel objected that, even supposing evidence of the boundary between *Rishworth* and *Rochdale* to be admissible, these documents could not be received. His lordship received the evidence.

The defendants gave parol evidence to shew that the boundary between *Wakefield* and *Rochdale* lay to the east of the ridge separating the eastward and westward drainages; and also put in another commission duly proved, from the Duchy Court of *Lancaster*, of 14 *Car.* 1., reciting the grant of the manor and lordship of *Rochdale* to *Edward Ramsay* and *Robert Ramsay* in fee farm, and that doubts and questions had arisen and were likely to arise touching its boundaries, by the neighbouring lords, who pretended parcel of the wastes of the said manor to belong to their manors adjoining; and that there was no perfect and exact survey extant, whereby the boundaries were not known, for want whereof inconveniences were likely to ensue; and directing commissioners to make a survey of *Rochdale* manor, &c., call witnesses, impannel juries &c.: and the sheriff was directed to

summon

1838.

BRISCO *against* LOMAX.

summon a jury. The defendants also produced the return to the commission last mentioned, with the verdict of the jury, describing the boundary, which, as the defendants contended, supported their case. These documents were duly authenticated as records of the Duchy coming from the proper custody.

Verdict for the plaintiff on the above and other issues.

In *Michaelmas* term, 1836, *Coltman* obtained a rule for a new trial, on the ground of the reception of improper evidence.

Cresswell now shewed cause. There are two questions: first, whether any evidence of the boundary between *Rishworth* and *Rochdale* was admissible; secondly, whether the commission, certificate, and inquisition of 13 *C.* 1. were proper evidence of such boundary. First, the fact, that the division of the drainage formed the boundary between *Rochdale* and *Rishworth*, was strong evidence of the probability that the same division constituted the boundary between *Rochdale* and *Wakefield*, *Wakefield* and *Rishworth* being contiguous manors, both lying to the east of *Rochdale*. The case resembles *Jones* v. *Williams* (*a*). But, further, the question being as to the limits of *Rochdale* manor, a perambulation of that manor might be given in evidence; and it could not be contended that so much only of the perambulation as applied to the boundary between *Rochdale* and *Wakefield* could be shewn. Then any evidence of the boundary must be subject to the same rule as a perambulation. It is clear that the defendants, who were to shew affirmatively that *Rochdale* included the locus in

(*a*) 2 *M.* & *W.* 326.

quo,

quo, might have proved the whole boundary of *Rochdale*: the plaintiff, therefore, was entitled to do the same. Further, if *Rishworth* be considered as part of *Wakefield* manor, the boundary to which the evidence related is in fact part of the boundary between *Wakefield* and *Rochdale*. Secondly, considering the question as between the manors of *Rochdale* and *Rishworth*, the commission and proceedings under it were evidence of the boundary. In a suit for tithes (*a*), the question being as to the existence of a modus, it was held that interrogatories and answers in an ecclesiastical suit for tithes, between a former rector and a former owner of the same lands, might be given in evidence, the libel and answer in that suit being lost. Here the former owners of *Rochdale* and *Rishworth* appear to have been parties to the proceeding. *Richards* v. *Bassett* (*b*) will be cited on the other side. There a presentment of the homage of a manor, that certain land was common within the manor, and that a tenant of a farm in the manor had no exclusive right to the land, as he claimed, was held not to be evidence against a subsequent tenant of the same farm now claiming such exclusive right. The issue there was not on a question of boundary, but on a claim to a definite piece of land. And the question as to the right claimed was not public, as that between the two manors in this case: neither was the former tenant a party to the proceeding, as here the former owners of the two manors were; so that it could not be considered as an award, for want of mutuality. Reputation is evidence of the boundary of a manor, though there may

(*a*) Perhaps *Miller* v. *Jackson*, 1 *Y. & J.* 65. See pp. 74, 93. See *Byam* v. *Booth*, 2 *Price*, 231., and note at p. 234. *Illingworth* v. *Leigh*, 4 *Gwil.* 1615.

(*b*) 10 *B. & C.* 657.

1838.

Brisco *against* Lomax.

may have been disputes on the matter for a long time; *Nicholls* v. *Parker* (*a*) and, had the question in *Richards* v. *Bassett* (*b*) been a public one, or relating to a boundary, the evidence might have been receivable as of reputation. [*Coleridge* J. The objection to evidence of reputation was, that it appeared to be post litem motam.] Here the question seems to have been amicably raised: if there was any lis mota, it was not that now before the Court; so that the case falls within the principle of *Freeman* v. *Phillipps* (*c*). The doctrine as to lis mota may perhaps, upon the authority of the case last cited, be considered to have been carried too far in *Richards* v. *Bassett* (*b*). Verdicts are evidence in the nature of reputation; they are post litem motam; but it is not the same lis as that in which they are made evidence. Further, the homage, in *Richards* v. *Bassett* (*b*), had no power to try the right of the individual to the land; but the Crown was undoubtedly competent to issue this commission to ascertain the boundaries of its own manors upon petition. [*The Court* expressed a doubt whether the evidence shewed that the manors had been held under the Duchy at the time of the commission issuing.] The case may be put upon the general power of the Duchy Court to issue such commissions. The verdict, therefore, goes farther than reputation; *Reed* v. *Jackson* (*d*). In *Rogers* v. *Wood* (*e*) a document offered as a decree was held not admissible, as not proceeding from a Court known to the law: here the commission acted under the recognised authority of the Duchy Court. [*Coleridge* J. The power of a

(*a*) 14 *East*, 331, note.
(*b*) 10 *B. & C.* 657.
(*c*) 4 *M. & S.* 486.
(*d*) 1 *East*, 355.
(*e*) 2 *B. & Ad.* 245.

Court

1838.

BRISCO *against* LOMAX.

Court of Equity to issue commissions for ascertaining boundaries, is shewn in *Maddock's Practice of the Court of Chancery* (a).] There was good ground here for exercising that power, as the owners of the contiguous manors both petitioned on account of the difficulty of ascertaining the boundary. (*Starkie* and *Joseph Addison*, on the same side, were stopped by the Court.)

Alexander and *Tomlinson*, contrà. First, the question was not as to the boundary of *Rochdale* manor generally, but as to the boundary between it and *Wakefield*. The evidence should have been confined to the locus in quo. To infer the physical nature of the boundary of *Wakefield* from that of the boundary of *Rishworth* would be as incorrect as to infer the existence of a custom in one manor from its existence in a manor adjoining, which cannot be done; *Doe dem. Foster* v. *Sisson* (b). Secondly, the proceedings under the commission of 13 *C.* 1. were not evidence, either as an award, or as being in the nature of a decree or verdict, or as reputation. They could not be evidence as an award, for want of mutuality between the present litigants, even admitting the parties to the proceedings to have mutually submitted to the decision of the Duchy Court. The defendants here could not have treated the proceedings as an award; for the lord of the manor of *Wakefield* was not a party to them. Neither, therefore, could the lord of the manor of *Wakefield* have used them against the lord of the manor of *Rochdale*. It is not enough that the claim of the present plaintiff may be analogous to that of the former owners of *Rishworth*. In *Doe dem. Foster* v. *The Earl of Derby* (c)

(a) Vol. I. p. 38. Book II. ch. i. (3d ed.)

(b) 12 *East*, 62.

(c) 1 *A.* & *E.* 783.

the

1838.

BRISCO *against* LOMAX.

the party, against whom the evidence taken on the former ejectment was offered, was much more nearly privy to the party who gained the former verdict than these defendants are to the former owners of *Rishworth*, even taking into consideration the fact of *Rishworth* having formerly been a subinfeudation of *Wakefield*. The fact that the party offering the evidence had had no power to cross-examine on the first occasion was relied on as shewing it to be inadmissible on the second. [*Patteson* J. On the assumption that evidence as to the boundary between *Rishworth* and *Rochdale* was admissible, must we not allow all that would be evidence in a dispute as to that boundary?] The objection arises, at this step, not simply from the question being varied, but from the parties not being privy to the former proceedings. *Doe dem. Foster* v. *The Earl of Derby* (a) shews that the same objection exists to a verdict as to depositions; for in that case the question as to the admissibility of the evidence was treated as if the former verdict itself had been offered; and in 1 *Phil. on Ev.* 327 (b), where the admissibility of a verdict with reference to the parties is discussed, it is said, "The same rule applies to depositions as well as to verdicts." And, further, a verdict is admissible only where judgment has followed: in the case of a feigned issue there must be a decree; *Bull. N. P.* 234, and *Montgomerie* v. *Clarke* (c), there cited: and depositions are admissible only where they have been followed by a decree: but here nothing has been done since the return of the verdict. The certificate of the commissioners concludes with referring the matter to the Chancellor of the Duchy: and the defend-

(a) 1 *A. & E.* 783. (b) 7th ed. (c) *Bull. N. P.* 234.

ants

1838.

BRISCO *against* LOMAX.

ants proved that a commission issued the next year to ascertain the boundary of *Rochdale* manor, which shews that the previous proceedings were incomplete. In *Reed* v. *Jackson* (*a*) the record seems to have been completed. Next, the proceedings, if not admissible as a verdict simply, were not admissible as reputation. The verdict is a finding on evidence: the depositions therefore are the evidence of reputation: the verdict is only the inference which a jury, taken from the whole county, draw from evidence of reputation given to them. This was the view taken in *Rogers* v. *Wood* (*b*). [*Coleridge* J. In cases where a verdict has been held to be evidence, was it ever inquired whether the jurors had personal knowledge of the matter?] A verdict is given in evidence as part of proceedings followed by judgment. [*Coleridge* J. Was such enquiry ever made as to the knowledge of the Judges?] A verdict and judgment are not received as evidence of reputation at all: if they were, such an inquiry would be necessary. They are received as substantive proof of a fact: but here the proceedings cannot be so received, from their incompleteness. Further, there was, on the face of the former proceedings, a lis mota; therefore *Richards* v. *Bassett* (*c*) applies; and *Rex* v. *Cotton* (*d*) is to the same effect. It is questionable whether the case of *Nicholls* v. *Parker* (*e*) would now be supported to the full extent of the inference sought to be drawn from it. *Lawrence* J., in the *Berkeley Peerage Case*, objects to "declarations *post litam motam*, not merely after the commencement of the law suit, but *after the dispute has arisen* (*g*)." In

(*a*) 1 *East*, 355. (*b*) 2 *B. & Ad.* 245.

(*c*) 10 *B. & C.* 657. (*d*) 3 *Campb.* 444.

(*e*) 14 *East*, 331. note. See *Barraclough* v. *Johnson*, p. 99. antè.

(*g*) 1 *Phil. Ev.* 245, (7th ed.); p. 275, (8th ed.). 4 *Camp.* 411.

1838.

BRISCO *against* LOMAX.

Freeman v. *Phillipps* (*a*) the custom litigated was different from the custom in dispute in the former case. Again, this was not a matter of public interest, but merely a question between the owners of two adjacent manors: reputation therefore was not evidence. In *Weeks* v. *Sparke* (*b*) Lord *Ellenborough* questioned the principle on which evidence of reputation had been admitted even in cases of public right: the line ought, at least, not to be extended. [*Litttledale* J. referred to *Tooker* v. *Duke of Beaufort* (*c*).] There the Crown was interested: and inquisitions returned, where the Crown is party, are held to be conclusive if not traversed (*d*).

LITTLEDALE J. (*e*). The question is not as to the effect of the evidence, but whether it was admissible. I think it was. The case is very like *Tooker* v. *Duke of Beaufort* (*c*). In Chancery it has always been customary to issue commissions for ascertaining boundaries: it was therefore competent to the Duchy Court to do so, the proceedings there being in the same nature with those in Chancery. The commission, then, went down, directing the sheriff to issue his precept to return a jury, who were to hear the evidence and determine the fact. It is true that their verdict, when found, was not followed up by any decree: and, perhaps, to make the proceeding conclusive between the parties, there should be a decree. But, without being conclusive, it is evidence between the owners of the manors of *Rishworth* and *Rochdale*. On a question of boundary, mere reputation is evidence. But I put this as a verdict, not as reputation. It is a trial by witnesses competent to speak to

(*a*) 4 *M.* & *S.* 486.

(*b*) 1 *M.* & *S.* 686.

(*c*) 1 *Bur.* 146.

(*d*) 1 *Stark. Ev.* 261. (2d ed.).

(*e*) Lord *Denman* C. J. was absent.

the

1838.

BRISCO *against* LOMAX.

the fact. Now, reputation being evidence, the verdict must be evidence, as was said in *Reed* v. *Jackson* (*a*); and this, though the former proceeding was between different parties. It is not reputation; but it is as good evidence as reputation. But then it is contended that the verdict was found after the dispute had arisen, and is therefore objectionable by analogy to the rule as to reputation, because the jury or witnesses were liable to prejudice. This might be objected in all cases where a verdict is given in evidence. But here, in fact, it does not appear that any dispute was actually depending, only that the parties wished to prevent disputes which were likely to arise. That is not an uncommon case: parties often resort to Chancery in a similar manner to prevent disputes. Here then was not a lis mota; consequently, I think this verdict is evidence between the owners of the manors of *Wakefield* and *Rochdale*. We know that, when there is a dispute whether a piece of land belongs to a waste or to the owner of the land adjoining, evidence is allowed respecting the land to a great distance. This was lately carried very far in the Common Pleas (*b*). Evidence that the boundary between *Rishworth* and *Rochdale* is continuous with that which the plaintiff asserts to be the boundary between *Wakefield* and *Rochdale* was evidence for the jury in support of the plaintiff's claim, resting upon the extreme improbability of the boundary being varied. The rule must therefore be discharged.

PATTESON J. The first question is, whether evidence of the boundary between *Rishworth* and *Rochdale* was admissible.

(*a*) 1 *East*, 355. See the judgment of *Lawrence* J.

(*b*) The learned Judge probably alluded to *Doe dem. Barrett* v. *Kemp*, 7 *Bing*. 332. *S. C.* in error, on a bill of exceptions at the second trial, 2 *New Cases*, 102.

1838.

Brisco against Lomax.

admissible. This cannot be decided on the ground of *Rishworth* manor having been a subinfeudatim of *Wakefield*, without more distinct proof whether *Wakefield* and *Rishworth* were separated at the time to which the evidence as to the boundary of *Rochdale* relates. Had there been evidence clearly applicable to a time before the separation, there could have been no doubt that it would have been admissible. But still we have this strong circumstance: that the line to which the evidence applies does abut on the boundary of *Rochdale;* and certainly the dispute here is as to the boundary of *Rochdale.* I feel great difficulty in rejecting evidence of any part of the boundary of *Rochdale.* For, as was urged by Mr. *Cresswell*, a perambulation of *Rochdale* might be proved; and the proof might begin at any point; it would not be necessary to begin at the particular spot in dispute. I think, therefore, that evidence might be given of a line forming the boundary between *Rishworth* and *Rochdale*, pursued up to the spot in question here. The second question is, how this boundary between *Richworth* and *Rochdale* may be proved. On this I have felt more difficulty. It is not easy to distinguish *Tooker* v. *The Duke of Beaufort* (*a*) from the present case. There the inquisition was not between the parties to the subsequent litigation; and the evidence was objected to on that ground, but admitted. Now it is certainly difficult to say that a verdict can be received merely as evidence of reputation; for a jury are summoned from the body of the county at large, and are not themselves likely to know the matter. But that argument, if it were to prevail, would exclude all evidence of verdicts: for a jury do not find upon knowledge of their own; so

(*a*) 1 *Bur.* 146.

that

1838.

BRISCO *against* LOMAX.

that the verdict never could be reputation, nor quite analogous to it. Yet, where a matter has been before a jury, the verdict is generally given in evidence as a sort of reputation, if I may so term it. I confess that it does not stand on the footing of a verdict between the parties, and conclusive upon them, where it is not followed by a decree. But I do not think that, in order to make the verdict admissible between the owners of *Rishworth* and *Rochdale*, it was necessary that there should be a decree. Then, as between the owners of *Wakefield* and *Rochdale*, whatever is admissible must no doubt be mutually admissible: so that, if the evidence would not be admissible against the plaintiff, it is not evidence for him. But the verdict here would be, though not on the same footing as a verdict inter partes, admissible evidence on either side.

COLERIDGE J. I think that, as between the owners of *Rochdale* and *Wakefield*, evidence might be given of the boundary between *Rochdale* and *Rishworth*. The objection confounds the question, what the issue is, with the question, what is applicable to it: whereas evidence is not strictly confined to the direct issue. Some facts prove an issue directly, some incidentally. But whatever throws light on the question at issue is evidence, if properly proved. Thus here, the question is, what is the boundary of the plaintiff's property? And it was proved that his property was conterminous with the manor of *Wakefield*: thus the boundary of the manor of *Wakefield* became evidence. Then did the evidence of the boundary between *Rishworth* and *Rochdale* throw light on the question at issue? Clearly it did.

1838.

Brisco against Lomax.

did. In numerous cases a natural boundary between two estates is also the natural boundary between the next adjoining estates, as in the instance of an arm of the sea, or a navigable river. So here, the evidence that the ridge separating the fall of the water was the boundary between *Rishworth* and *Rochdale* was also evidence that it was the boundary between *Wakefield* and *Rochdale*. Mr. *Cresswell* urged that the defendants might have shewn the whole boundary of *Rochdale*, and that therefore the plaintiff was entitled to give opposite evidence to the same extent; and this argument was not answered. Then comes the question, whether this documentary evidence was admissible. That must be tried exactly as if the collateral matter of inquiry were the actual issue. Now it appears that the owners of *Rishworth* and *Rochdale* applied to the Duchy Court, which has the same authority as the Crown, and stated that disputes had arisen, and that, upon their petition, a commission issued directing the sheriff to summon jurors, who attended, and found the verdict. Then, first, did the question admit of such proof? And, secondly, was the proof given in an authentic way? First, on the question of a boundary between two owners, no doubt reputation is admissible. And verdicts are evidence where reputation is admissible, as between third parties. This distinguishes the case from *Doe dem. Foster* v. *The Earl of Derby* (a). For, though here the defendants had no power of cross-examining the witnesses on the former proceeding, that is no more than occurs, for instance, in questions as to tolls, where payment of

(a) 1 *A. & E.* 783.

tolls

1838.

BRISCO *against* LOMAX.

tolls by third parties is evidence. Then, secondly, as to the necessity of a decree or judgment to render the verdict admissible. That necessity exists only where it is sought to bind parties conclusively by the finding. But here the verdict is not offered as conclusive evidence, but as evidence in the nature of reputation. It is not precisely evidence of reputation: but it has always been held that, in questions where reputation is admissible, verdicts may be given in evidence against third parties; and mutuality is then not essential. Then is this in the nature of a verdict? If it were merely a verdict found by a jury summoned by the parties, it would amount to nothing. But here we must assume that the Duchy Court had power to issue the commission. If so; the verdict is as complete as if it were given at Nisi Prius. Therefore the inquiry was relevant: and, this being a question upon which reputation was admissible, a verdict, found under competent authority, was good evidence.

Rule discharged.

KNIGHT *against* CLEMENTS and Another.

Friday, May 4th.

Where a bill of exchange, produced on a trial, appears to have been altered, the jury cannot, on inspection of such bill, without other proof, decide whether it was altered at the time of making or at a subsequent period.

Where a bill was drawn upon a two months' stamp, and had begun with the words "*Three* months after date," but the word "three" had been defaced (as if blotted while the ink was wet), and "two" written upon it, and "two" written again underneath, and the plaintiff, who put in the bill at nisi prius, offered no evidence to account for these alterations: Held, that the document, by itself, was no evidence to go to the jury of the alterations having been made at the original writing of the bill. And (issue having been joined on a plea of non accepit), that the plaintiff must be nonsuited.

ASSUMPSIT by indorsee, against defendants as acceptors, of a bill of exchange, payable two months after date. Plea, that defendants did not accept. Issue

1838.

KNIGHT against CLEMENTS.

thereon. At the trial, before *Coleridge* J., at the *Liverpool* Summer assizes, 1836, the bill was produced. The acceptance appeared to have been written before the bill. The bill began, "Two months after date, pay" &c.; but it appeared, on inspection, that the first word had originally been "three;" traces of that word were visible, as if blurred while the ink was wet, and upon them the word "two" was written; and "two" was again written underneath. The stamp was sufficient only for a bill at two months. The defendants' counsel insisted that the plaintiff must shew, by extrinsic evidence, that the bill was altered before it was negotiated. For the plaintiff it was contended that the jury might form an opinion on this point from an inspection of the bill itself, without other proof; and no further evidence was given. The learned Judge placed the bill in the hands of the jury, and desired them to say whether the alteration had been made before or after the instrument was negotiated, giving leave to move for a nonsuit if the Court should be of opinion that there was no evidence to go to the jury on this point. The jury found that the bill was altered in time; and the plaintiff had a verdict.

Cresswell, in the next term, moved for a nonsuit, on the ground taken at the trial. He admitted that the appearances on the bill, if there had been other evidence, could not have been withdrawn from the attention of the jury; but he contended that those appearances, by themselves, though they might entitle the jury to say that an alteration had taken place, could not be evidence of the time at which it was made. A rule nisi was granted.

Tomlinson

1838.

KNIGHT *against* CLEMENTS.

Tomlinson now shewed cause. It must be admitted that the question as to the time of altering might be raised under a plea of non-acceptance, according to *Cock* v. *Coxwell* (*a*), and consistently with *Sibley* v. *Fisher* (*b*). Then, is it an invariable rule that, if an instrument be produced for the plaintiff with an apparent alteration, he must account for it by extrinsic evidence, or be non-suited? Or, where the appearances are such as on the present bill, may not the jury form a judgment, by their own inspection, as to the circumstances under which it was altered? There is much difference between the case in which an instrument has evidently been complete once, and then altered, and that in which it may reasonably be inferred that the writing never was complete except in its present form, as where the party writing the document has drawn his pen through a word and substituted another, currente calamo. [Lord *Denman* C. J. Here the bill may have been altered when wet, or else after it was complete. That is the difficulty of going into any speculation on the mere appearance.] The latter supposition is very improbable here. The probability is that the drawer first wrote "three," and then, observing that the stamp was insufficient, blotted the word and wrote "two" upon it, and then, thinking that not plain enough, wrote "two" again underneath. The first "two" is perfectly legible. It was competent to the jury to say, on these appearances, whether the alteration was made at once in the course of writing, or whether the bill had ever had complete existence in a form differing from its present one. In *Johnson* v. *The*

(*a*) 2 *Cro. M. & R.* 291. *S. C.* 5 *Tyr.* 1077.
(*b*) 7 *A. & E.* 444. *S. C.* 2 *Nev. & P.* 430.

Duke

1838.

KNIGHT against CLEMENTS.

Duke of Marlborough (a), where the plaintiffs, suing as indorsees, produced a bill which had apparently been altered in date, *Abbott* J. required them to prove that the alteration had been made before acceptance; but he laid down no inflexible rule. In *Henman* v. *Dickinson* (b) it was held that the party producing an altered bill must account for the alteration; but there it seems to have been clear that the bill, when produced, was in a state different from that in which it had once existed. In *Bishop* v. *Chambre* (c) there was some doubt whether or not the note had been altered after completion; and Lord *Tenterden* left it to the jury to judge of this point from inspection. Had there been no doubt, a nonsuit must have been directed. The question, whether a bill had been altered or not, and whether certain words had been added before or after acceptance, was left to the jury on inspection, in *Taylor* v. *Mosely* (d).

Cresswell and *Crompton* contrà. There was no evidence for the jury that the alteration of this bill was made before it was negotiated. In *Bishop* v. *Chambre* (c) the note was submitted to the jury; but that was to ascertain whether there had, in fact, been an alteration or not. If it appears that the bill was altered, the party relying on the instrument must account for the alteration. Every person who takes such a bill must know the burden with which he takes it, and should be prepared to account for any thing suspicious in its appearance. The acceptor may not have it in his power to do so; for he may have had no reason to expect that it would be produced in the altered form. Conjectures may be made

(a) 2 *Stark. N. P. C.* 313.
(b) 5 *Bing.* 183.
(c) *M. & M.* 116.
(d) 6 *Car. & P.* 273.

variously

1838.

KNIGHT *against* CLEMENTS.

variously on each side; and a jury should not be asked to form them without evidence. If they may be resorted to, the defendant here may suggest that, after the bill was made, the word "three" was smeared intentionally, to create the appearance of a contemporary alteration. The time when the blot was made requires proof as much as any other fact. There is no instance where a jury has been called upon in such a case to decide any thing by eye-sight, except whether the instrument was or was not altered. In *Johnson* v. *The Duke of Marlborough* (a) it might have been conjectured that the alteration was made uno flatu with the drawing of the bill; but *Abbott* J. required evidence to be given that the alteration took place before the acceptance. [*Coleridge* J. Suppose, here, the word "three" had been written, and a pen drawn through it, and then the word "two" written continuously after it.] It would appear there that the word "three" had never formed part of the instrument. The words, if both were read, would be "three two months." It would be evident, on inspection, that the instrument had not, at any time, been a three months' bill. But to allow inspection by a jury, for the purpose of ascertaining when an alteration was made, is, in effect, shifting the onus of proof to a dangerous extent.

Cur. adv. vult.

Lord DENMAN C. J., in this term (*May* 10th), delivered the judgment of the Court. This was an action on a bill of exchange at two months: plea, non accepit. The plaintiff produced the bill, which had the word

(a) 2 *Stark. N. P. C.* 313.

two

1838.

KNIGHT *against* CLEMENTS.

two (before *months*); but the letters of that word were written over those of the word *three*, and the strokes composing the letters of the latter word appeared to have been blotted. The stamp was good for a two months' bill, bad for one at three months. The defendants' counsel objected that the party producing a document is bound to explain such an ambiguity appearing on the face of it, and to shew distinctly that the alteration was made before the bill was negotiated. The plaintiff's counsel, not disputing this rule, argued that the inspection of the bill was alone sufficient to prove the alteration so made, inasmuch as the word *three* plainly appeared to have been blotted out while wet and in the course of the writing: and my learned brother who tried the cause placed the bill in the hands of the jury, and asked their opinion whether they thought so, directing a verdict for the plaintiff if they did. They found that the alteration was completed in time; and their verdict was entered for the plaintiff, subject to a motion for a nonsuit if the question was improperly submitted to them. This point was argued and has been considered by us. We think the rule for a nonsuit must be made absolute.

The plaintiff was bound to prove a bill accepted payable at two months: that which he produced was accepted, payable either at two or three months, with no evidence whether it was the one or the other. The mode of obliteration might have furnished arguments in favour of one or the other supposition, and material confirmation to any proof adduced as to that fact. But, standing by itself, it was obviously no better than a conjecture; for the alteration might have been too late, and accompanied with a fresh marking by wet ink

rubbed

1838.

KNIGHT *against* CLEMENTS.

rubbed over on the instant. The case of *Bishop* v. *Chambre* (*a*) was cited on the trial for the plaintiff, and the marginal note appears favourable to him. But Lord *Tenterden*'s proceeding on that occasion was, in truth, the other way: he permitted the jury to inspect the bill, to see if there had been any alteration, which there manifestly had, and then decided against the party producing it for want of proof that it was made before the instrument was complete.

Rule absolute.

(*a*) *M. & M.* 116. Lord *Denman* C. J. in the course of the argument referred to S. C. at Nisi Prius, 3 *Car. & P. 55.*, and in *Banc, Danson & Lloyd*, 83.; in which latter case the point taken in *Knight* v. *Clements*, suprà, as to the question to be considered by the jury, does not appear to have come under discussion.

ROUTLEDGE *against* RAMSAY.

Saturday, May 5th.

J. R., a debtor, having sums due to him, handed the accounts to his creditor, and wrote " I give the above accounts to you, so you must collect them and pay yourself, and you and I will then be clear. *J. R.*" Held, that this acknowledgment did not imply a promise to pay, and was no answer, under stat. 9 *G.* 4. *c.* 14., to a plea of the Statute of Limitations.

Per Lord *Denman* C. J. Whether such a written acknowledgment be conditional or unconditional is a question for the Court, not the jury, except where the document is connected with other evidence affecting the construction.

ASSUMPSIT on a promissory note for 40*l.*, and for goods sold and delivered to the same amount. Plea, that the causes of action did not accrue within six years. Issue thereon. On the trial before *Coleridge* J. at the *Carlisle* Summer assizes, 1836, the plaintiff put in a paper dated less than six years before the commencement of this action, addressed to the plaintiff and signed by the defendant. It contained a list of names, opposite to which various sums were set down, and below was written,

" *Aldstone*, 1 *June*, 1830. Mr. *Jas. Routledge*, I give the above accounts to you, so you must collect them and pay yourself, and you and me will then be clear. *John Ramsay*."

The

1838.

ROUTLEDGE *against* RAMSAY.

The plaintiff had a verdict; but leave was given to move to enter a nonsuit, if the Court should think the above document no evidence in bar of the statute. In *Michaelmas* term, 1836, *W. H. Watson* moved for a rule to shew cause why a nonsuit should not be entered or a new trial had, on the ground that the document produced was no answer to the plea (*a*), and he cited *Tanner* v. *Smart* (*b*) and *Whippy* v. *Hillary* (*c*). A rule nisi was granted.

Knowles now shewed cause. The plaintiff was entitled to recover, having proved an unqualified acknowledgment of the debt within six years. The question whether this was a conditional or an unconditional acknowledgment was for the jury. [Lord *Denman* C. J. It is for the Court to construe a written document.] The meaning is sometimes a question for the jury. [Lord *Denman* C. J. That is where the document is connected with other evidence affecting the construction (*d*).] Then, the effect of the writing was an absolute engagement to pay. An acknowledgment by one of two joint acceptors in these terms, "I beg leave to refer you to my trustee" "on this complicated business," "I should be glad to be informed how you have settled it with Lord *Cork*" (the other acceptor), was held sufficient, in *Baillie* v. *Lord Inchiquin* (*e*), to take the case out of the statute. The rule is, that, if there be an unqualified acknowledgment of the debt, the law will imply

(*a*) He also contended, that the paper (which bore no stamp) should have been stamped as an assignment; but no rule was granted on this point.

(*b*) 6 *B. & C.* 603.

(*c*) 3 *B. & Ad.* 399.

(*d*) See *Morrell* v. *Frith*, 3 *M. & W.* 402. *Bird* v. *Gammon*, 3 *New Ca.* 883. *Power* v. *Barham*, 4 *A. & E.* 473. *Dodson* v. *Mackey*, p. 225, note (b), post.

(*e*) 1 *Esp. N. P. C.* 435.

a pro-

1838.

ROUTLEDGE against RAMSAY.

a promise to pay; at least if the admission be not accompanied by a specific promise different from the implied one which the plaintiff seeks to set up. *Tanner* v. *Smart* (*a*) was decided on the principle that an acknowledgment is only evidence of a promise to pay, and that a declaration stating an absolute and unconditional promise is not supported by proof of a qualified one, as "I will pay as soon as I can." The ground of decision in *Whippy* v. *Hillary* (*b*) was, that the promise was not contained in a writing signed "by the party chargeable thereby," according to stat. 9 *G.* 4. *c.* 14. *s.* 1.; the defendant did not undertake on his own behalf, but referred the plaintiffs to his trustees. [Lord *Denman* C. J. Here the defendant makes the plaintiff himself his trustee. *Patteson* J. The letter may be construed, "Here are the accounts, you may pay yourself out of the proceeds; I will not undertake it."] That appears a forced construction. The meaning is, "I have a sum due to me; go and take it, and we shall be clear." No condition is annexed. In *Dodson* v. *Mackey* (*c*) an acknowledgment not less qualified than the present was held to be unconditional.

W. H. Watson, contrà, was stopped by the Court.

Lord DENMAN C. J. *Whippy* v. *Hillary* (*b*) is quite in point. In cases like the present there is clearly an acknowledgment, but the question is whether the party charges himself. Here the effect of the letter was only, "there are certain amounts due to me; get them in if you can." In *Baillie* v. *Lord Inchiquin* (*d*) it was certainly

(*a*) 6 *B.* & *C.* 603. (*b*) 3 *B.* & *Ad.* 399.
(*c*) 4 *Nev.* & *M.* 327. See the end of this case.
(*d*) 1 *Esp. N. P. C.* 435.

1838.

ROUTLEDGE *against* RAMSAY.

tainly held by Lord *Kenyon* that a letter from the defendant, referring the creditor to his trustee, was a sufficient acknowledgment. But *Whippy* v. *Hillary* (a) decides that a letter containing such words is not an acknowledgment in writing signed by the party chargeable thereby, within stat. 9 *G.* 4. *c.* 14. *s.* 1.: and that case governs the present.

LITTLEDALE J. There is so far an acknowledgment here that the defendant does not deny the debt; but, whether or not such an acknowledgment implies a promise, depends upon the words used. In the present instance the defendant only makes an admission of the debt, pointing out to the plaintiff a mode in which to get paid.

PATTESON J. An acknowledgment without any thing more may raise an implied promise since stat. 9 *G.* 4. *c.* 14., as it did before. But, where something else is added, the effect of that must be taken into consideration. In this case there is matter added to the acknowledgment, namely, "Take these accounts and pay yourself." The effect of that is to enable the plaintiff to use the rights of the defendant; but the defendant does not bind himself. The case falls within the principle of *Whippy* v. *Hillary* (a). I do not know whether, in the discussion on that case, *Baillie* v. *Lord Inchiquin* (b) was brought before the Court; but the ruling there was before stat. 9 *G.* 4. *c.* 14.

COLERIDGE J. An acknowledgment is only evidence from which a promise may be inferred; we must look

(a) 3 *B. & Ad.* 399. (b) 1 *Esp. N. P. C.* 435.

at

1838.

ROUTLEDGE against RAMSAY.

at all that is said, to ascertain whether a promise is implied or not. In *Whippy* v. *Hillary* (*a*) there was a clear acknowledgment, but the defendant pointed to a particular fund in the hands of trustees. This is a similar case. We cannot infer, from the defendant's words, a promise that if the fund referred to failed he would himself be liable. On principle and authority I think that the verdict for the plaintiff in this case was wrong.

Rule absolute (*b*).

(*a*) 3 *B. & Ad.* 392.

(*b*) ANNE DODSON *against* MACKEY.

Monday, January 12th, and *Wednesday, January* 14th, 1835.

In assumpsit on a bill of exchange, a letter was produced, to take the case out of the statute of limitations, from defendant to plaintiff, stating that plaintiff should be informed immediately it was settled how defendant's affairs should be arranged; and adding, "Your account is quite correct; and O! that I were now going to enclose the amount." No amount of debt was stated; and no proof was given, from the letter or otherwise, to what account the letter referred, nor whether the letter applied to the bill.

It being left to the jury whether this was an unconditional acknowledgment of the debt, and they having found that it was: Held that there was no ground for a nonsuit; for that the acknowledgment was unconditional, and that the jury, if it was a question for them, had decided it rightly.

Quære, whether the plaintiff was entitled to more than nominal damages: And whether the effect of the acknowledgment was a question for the Court or jury.

DECLARATION (*April* 12th, 1834) in assumpsit, by drawer against acceptor of two bills of exchange, dated respectively 1st *July* 1826, and 15th *September* 1826, payable at six and three months. The declaration stated promises, on *April* 20th, 1828, to pay the bills respectively. Pleas, 1. Non assumpsit. 2. The statute of limitations. Replication, that the causes did accrue within &c. On the trial before Lord *Denman* C. J., at the *London* sittings after *Michaelmas* term 1834, the plaintiff put in a letter from the defendant to herself, dated 21st *April* 1828, part of which was as follows.

"I am deputed by my brother, who is gone to *London*, to answer yours." — "I never can be happy until I have not only paid you every thing, but all to whom I owe money; and whatever privations I suffer in endeavouring to liquidate my debts, they will be borne patiently." — "It is impossible to state to you what will be done in my affairs at present; it is difficult to know what will be best, but immediately it is settled you shall be informed. It will give me much pleasure to see you when you visit *Bath*. Your account is quite correct; and O! that I were now going to enclose you the amount of it!" — "As my brother will write to or see you when something is settled, I shall now only beg you still to retain that friendship," &c.

 "The

1838.

DODSON *against* MACKEY.

The account referred to was not in evidence; and the letter contained no express reference to the bills. Another letter, from the defendant to a third person, was also put in; but counsel, on making the motion after mentioned, stated that it carried the case no further. The Lord Chief Justice left it to the jury to say whether the letter amounted to an unconditional acknowledgment as to the bills. The plaintiff had a verdict for the amount of both bills: and the Lord Chief Justice reserved leave to move for a nonsuit or a reduction of damages. In *Hilary* term, 1835,

Wordsworth moved accordingly. To take a case out of the statute, an acknowledgment must be unqualified; *Fearn* v. *Lewis* (6 *Bing.* 349.): or, if it is conditional, the performance of the condition must be proved; *Haydon* v. *Williams* (7 *Bing.* 163.): there ought to be a promise implied; *Brigstocke* v. *Smith* (1 *Cr. & M.* 483; *S. C.* 3 *Tyrwh.* 445.): and the amount payable ought to be specified; *Kennett* v. *Milbank* (8 *Bing.* 38.). All these requisites are here wanting; and the case ought not to have gone to the jury. At any rate, as there is no reference to the bills, and as the amount is not specified, the damages can be only nominal; *Dickenson* v. *Hatfield* (5 *C. & P.* 46.). In that case the acknowledgment was connected by evidence with the note on which the action was brought: here was no such evidence.

Lord DENMAN C. J. It seemed to me that the point made, whether the acknowledgment in the letter to the defendant was absolute or conditional, raised a fair argument. That question was put to the jury, and they found that it was not conditional. My learned brothers think that it was not conditional. If it was proper to leave that to the jury, no doubt they decided rightly. The other letter may be laid out of the question. There will, therefore, be no rule on that point. But, as to the other, it seems to me that *Dickenson* v. *Hatfield* (5 *C. & P.* 46.) goes the length of shewing that, when a written acknowledgment does not state the amount due, there can only be nominal damages: for, in that case, there was proof aliundè of the amount. I should have thought the acknowledgment evidence which the jury might take into consideration, to determine what was due; but, as Lord *Tenterden* entertained a different opinion, we will take time to consider whether a rule should be granted.

LITTLEDALE J. The jury came to the right conclusion: there was nothing like a condition.

WILLIAMS J. concurred.

(*Patteson* J. was in the Bail Court; and no successor had been appointed to the late Mr. Justice *Taunton*).

Rule on first point refused; as to the other,

Cur. adv. vult.

Afterwards,

1838.

DODSON *against* MACKEY.

Afterwards, (*January* 28, 1835,) a rule nisi was granted on the other point for a new trial or reduction of damages. No cause was ever shewn, the parties having agreed to a stay of proceedings.

See, as to the second point, *Lechmere* v. *Fletcher*; 1 *Cro.* & *M.* 623., *S. C.* 3 *Tyr.* 450; *Dabbs* v. *Humphries*, 10 *Bing.* 446. And, generally, as to the points in this case and that in the text, *Linsell* v. *Bonsor*, 2 *New Ca.* 241; *Bird* v. *Gammon*, 3 *New Ca.* 883; *Edmunds* v. *Downes*, 2 *Cro.* & *M.* 459. *S. C.* 4 *Tyr.* 173. And p. 222, note (*d*), antè.

The QUEEN *against* TOKE, Clerk, and Another.

Monday, May 7th.

Under stats. 43 *Eliz.* c. 2. s. 7., and 59 *G.* 3. c. 12. s. 26., which authorise the making of orders on children, having sufficiency, to maintain their parents, such maintenance to be assessed by justices of the county where the sufficient parties dwell, an order describing the party as *T. G.* "*of*" the parish of *M.*, in the county, &c. (for which the justices act), shews, distinctly enough, that he dwells within that county.

And, where the order recited a complaint made by the parish officers against *T. G.*, described as above, a summons issued against *the said T. G.*, and his appearance before the justices, &c.; and then went on to adjudge that *the said T. G.* is of sufficient ability, and shall forthwith pay &c.; Held, that the dwelling of *T. G.* in the county was sufficiently stated, by reference, in the adjudication.

Absente Lord *Denman* C. J.; dubitante *Littledale* J.

PERRY, in *Hilary* term last, obtained a rule calling on the Reverend *Nicholas Toke* and another, justices of the county of *Kent*, to shew cause why a certiorari should not issue, directed to them, to remove into this Court an order made by them in petty sessions. The order was as follows.

"County of *Kent*, to wit. The order of the Reverend *Nicholas Toke*, clerk, and *George Edward Sayer*, Esq., two of Her Majesty's justices of the peace in and for the said county, one whereof is of the quorum, made at a petty sessions held at the *Saracen's Head* Inn, *Ashford*, in the said county, on *Saturday* the 2d day of *December*, A. D. 1837. Upon an application to us, the said justices, at the said petty sessions, by the churchwardens and overseers of the poor of the parish of *Mersham*, in the county of *Kent*, to have an order made on *Thomas Gilbert*, of the parish of *Mersham* in the said county, woolsorter, for him to maintain his father *James Gilbert*, who is poor and un-

1838.

The Queen against Toke.

able to work so as to maintain and support himself, and chargeable to the said parish of *Mersham*, he the said *Thomas Gilbert* being a person of sufficient ability to maintain and provide for his said father, and the said *Thomas Gilbert* having been duly summoned to appear before us the said justices at the said petty sessions, to the end that we might examine into the cause and circumstances of the premises, and now appearing before us the said justices in pursuance of the said summons, but he has not shewn any sufficient cause why such order should not be made; and we, having heard the parties so complaining, and duly considering the circumstances of the said complaint, as well as the want of any adequate defence on the part of the said *Thomas Gilbert*, do adjudge and determine that the said *James Gilbert* is poor and unable to work so as to maintain and support himself, and actually chargeable to the said parish of *Mersham*, and that the said *Thomas Gilbert* is a person of sufficient ability to maintain and provide for his said father: And therefore we order that the said *Thomas Gilbert* shall and do forthwith, upon notice of this our order, pay, or cause to be paid, to the churchwardens and overseers of the poor of the said parish of *Mersham* for the time being, or to some or one of them, weekly and every week from this present time, the sum of 2*s.* 6*d.* for and towards the sustentation, relief, maintenance, and support of the said *James Gilbert*, for and during so long time as the said *James Gilbert* shall be chargeable to the said parish of *Mersham*, or until the said *Thomas Gilbert* shall be legally directed to the contrary. Given under our hands and seals the day and year first above written.

N. Toke. *George Edward Sayer.*

Deedes,

1838.

The QUEEN against TOKE.

Deedes now shewed cause. The only question will be, whether or not this order be on the face of it informal. Stat. 43 *Eliz. c.* 2. *s.* 7. directs that the maintenance of parents by children having sufficiency shall be "according to that rate, as by the justices of peace of that county where such sufficient persons dwell," shall be assessed. Stat. 59 *G.* 3. *c.* 12. *s.* 26. gives to justices "for the county or other jurisdiction in which any such sufficient person shall dwell" the power of making such assessment in petty sessions as, by the former act, might be made by the justices in quarter sessions. The objection taken to this order is, that it does not any where shew that *Thomas Gilbert* dwells within the county of *Kent*, or therefore, that he is within the jurisdiction of the justices (*a*). But, in stating the application made by the parish officers, he is described as "*Thomas Gilbert* of the parish of *Mersham*, in the said county;" and that description is carried on by reference through the order, the party being always termed "the said *Thomas Gilbert*." In affidavits it is necessary to state the party's residence; but "of" such a place is held a sufficient description. [*Coleridge* J. The order does not adjudge that he is resident within the jurisdiction.] That need not appear in the adjudication: *Rex* v. *Fox* (*b*). [*Littledale* J. The description recited here is merely that given by the parish officers.] The whole must be taken as the order of the justices; and the Court will make intendment in

(*a*) It was also objected, in moving for this rule (before *Patteson* J. in the Bail court), that the magistrates did not appear by the order to be justices usually acting for the division in which *Mersham* was situate; but the learned Judge refused to grant a rule on this ground, saying that they appeared to be justices for the county, and divisions were mere matter of arrangement.

(*b*) Cited in *Rex* v. *Price*, 6 *T. R.* 148.

favour

1838.

The Queen against Toke.

favour of such orders. They are not construed as rigidly as convictions or indictments; *Rex* v. *Bissex* (*a*), *Rex* v. *Middlehurst* (*b*), *Rex* v. *Lloyd* (*c*). The forms of an order of maintenance upon a parent or child, given in 4 *Chit. Burn*, 1067, *Poor*, *Appendix* (28th ed.), and in 4 *D'Oyl. & Wms. Burn*, 238, *Poor*, iii. (1), do not materially differ from the present. *Rex* v. *Woodford* (*d*) and *Rex* v. *Reve* (*e*) were cited in moving for the rule; but it does not appear, in the first case, what the form of the order was, or, in the second, that the warrant was considered bad on the face of it.

Perry contrà. By sect. 59 *G.* 3. *c.* 12. *s.* 26., a jurisdiction is taken from the court of quarter sessions, and given to the less public one of the justices in petty session, with special words limiting the jurisdiction. That limitation ought to be strictly observed. There is no ground for saying that intendments are to be made in favour of an order more than of a conviction. It is often difficult to draw any distinction between them. Whether the present be an order or a conviction, the jurisdiction does not appear. In *Rex* v. *Fox* (*g*) the words in the title of the order, which described the child as born in the parish, were words of the justices themselves: here, the words which it is attempted to incorporate in the adjudication are those of the parish officers. And, even if the adjudication mentioned "*Thomas Gilbert* of the parish of *Mersham*," that would

(*a*) 1 *Chitt. Burn*, (28th ed.) 1129, note (*a*): *Distress for Rent*, *s.* V. 1 *D'Oyl. & Wms. Burn*, 969: *Distress*, V. *S. C. Sayer's Rep.* 304.

(*b*) 1 *Burr.* 399.

(*c*) 2 *Stra.* 996.

(*d*) 1 *Bott.* 400. pl. 434. 6th ed.

(*e*) 2 *Bulst.* 344.

(*g*) Cited in *Rex* v. *Price*, 6 *T. R.* 148.

not

1838.

The QUEEN *against* TOKE.

not be sufficient. "Late of" is a proper description in an indictment, because, for the purpose of such description, it is sufficient if the party has ever been in the parish. So in the direction of a writ of summons, under stat. 2 *W.* 4. *c.* 39. *s.* 1., it is sufficient to style the party "of" &c., though he may not, in the ordinary sense, reside in the place; actual dwelling, in that case, not being material, as the statutes make it in this. *Rex* v. *Reve* (*a*) shews the strictness maintained on this point in the application of stat. 43 *Eliz.* *c.* 2. *s.* 7. A person who, in an affidavit, has styled himself "of" &c. cannot afterwards deny what he has so stated on his oath. But, in an adjudication by justices, any thing in the description of a party which is essential to the proceeding must be expressly found. In *Day* v. *King* (*b*) it was held that an order of justices for payments to a member of a friendly society must find, by way of adjudication, that he is a member; the statement of it in reciting the party's complaint not being sufficient. So in *Rex* v. *Pennoyer* (*c*) an order on defendant to maintain his daughter in law was held insufficient, because it did not adjudge her to be poor and impotent, but stated the fact by way of recital only. In 2 *Nol. P. L.* 263, *c.* 30. *s.* 4. (*d*) it is said that an order for maintenance of relations "must state" several particulars, and "1st, that the person upon whom it is made lives within the jurisdiction of the justices." Intendment will be made in favour of an order of justices if the jurisdiction be shewn, not otherwise. And formerly there was a laxity on this subject which would not prevail now. Thus in

(*a*) 2 *Bulst.* 344.

(*b*) 5 *A.* & *E.* 359.

(*c*) 1 *Bott.* 400. pl. 433. 6th ed.

(*d*) 4th ed.

Rex

1838.

The QUEEN against TOKE.

Rex v. *Venables* (a), where justices had made an order of commitment for keeping open an alehouse contrary to former orders, the Court said they would intend (though it was not stated in the order of commitment) that the party had been summoned.

LITTLEDALE J. (b). This is an order made by justices in petty sessions under the authority given to them by stat. 59 *G.* 3. *c.* 12. *s.* 26. That clause extends the provisions of stat. 43 *Eliz. c.* 2. *s.* 7., as to the persons by whom the powers are to be exercised; but the powers themselves are the same under both enactments. The objection here taken is, that the party is not sufficiently shewn by the order to "dwell" in the county for which the justices act. I have great doubt whether it is sufficiently averred that he dwells there; but my brothers *Patteson* and *Coleridge* think the allegation sufficient, and I cannot say that my own doubt goes so far as to induce me to pronounce the order bad. The order recites an application by the churchwardens and overseers of *Mersham* in *Kent*, against *Thomas Gilbert*, "of the parish of *Mersham* in the said county." "Of" does not necessarily imply that the party dwells in the place of which he is described to be, according to several instances in *Com. Dig. Abatement* (F 25.). The order next states that the justices summon the said *Thomas Gilbert*; which they may have done, though he was not resident in the county; and it then states an adjudication that *the said Thomas Gilbert* is a person of sufficient ability, and that he do pay, &c. If that adopts what the parish officers say as to the party's description,

(a) 2 *Ld. Ray.* 1405. *S. C.* 1 *Stra.* 630.

(b) Lord *Denman* C. J. was attending the Privy Council.

the

1838.

The QUEEN against TOKE.

the order is good; and it is contended that, when *Thomas Gilbert* is described as "of" a parish in *Kent*, and a statement then comes, that "the said" *Thomas Gilbert* is summoned, and an adjudication follows against "*the said*" *Thomas Gilbert*, he is sufficiently identified in all respects. I must say that, according to the rule stated in 2 *Nol. P. L.* 263 (*a*), I think it should be distinctly adjudged that the party lives within the jurisdiction. In *Rex* v. *Woodford* (*b*), however, which is there cited, the form of the order does not appear. Upon the whole, I think that the sufficiency of this order may be questioned; but, as my brothers consider it maintainable, the rule will be discharged.

PATTESON J. I have had doubts on this point; but the word "of" very generally does import dwelling, and I think it may be taken primâ facie to do so here. Then, in the present case, do the justices by their order merely recite a description given them by some one else? If so, it would be carrying intendment to a length hitherto unknown to say that the justices, by their order, ascertain the place of dwelling. But I think that, in their adjudication, they adopt the statement given in the recital; and, if they do so, the only question is whether "of" imports dwelling, which I think it may be considered to do here.

COLERIDGE J. The rule of intendment is correctly stated by Mr. *Perry*. The Court must see, beyond dispute, that the magistrates have jurisdiction; they must not give it to themselves by doubtful words; but, when

(*a*) C. 30. s. 4. 4th ed.

(*b*) 1 *Bott.* 400. pl. 434. 6th ed.

the

1838.

The QUEEN against TOKE.

the jurisdiction once appears, reasonable intendment will be made in favour of the order, as to the facts stated. It will be construed candidly and liberally. The question here, however, is not one of intendment, but turns on the meaning of the word "of." Now that, in ordinary cases, is taken to mean that the party dwells in the place named. If then, in the present case, *Thomas Gilbert* of the parish of *Mersham*, in the recital, means that he dwells at *Mersham*, who is "the said *Thomas Gilbert*" mentioned in the adjudication? I think that the justices adopt there in effect the words used in the recital, and may be taken to mean "the said *Thomas Gilbert* of the parish of *Mersham*." *Day* v. *King* (a) is a distinguishable case. There the order set out the direction and recital of the information, which stated, among other facts, that *John Day* and *Matthew Diver* were the stewards of the Friendly society; and in the adjudication they were mentioned as "the said *John Day* and *Matthew Diver*," without any other reference to the preceding statement. That did not shew that the parties were stewards, which was one of the very facts the justices had to decide upon. *Day* v. *King* (a) was rightly decided; and our present determination will not trench upon it.

Rule discharged without costs.

(a) 5 *A.* & *E.* 359.

Doe on the several Demises of Madkins and Long, *against* Horner and Roupell.

Monday, May 7th.

On motion to set aside a judgment on an award, advantage may be taken of objections apparent on the face of the award, but of none other.

Ejectment being brought on two demises, all matters in difference in the cause were referred by a Judge's order, which directed that the costs of the suit and of the reference and award should abide the event of the award; that the party in whose favour the award should be might sign judgment in the same manner as if the cause had been tried at Nisi Prius; and that, if it was in plaintiff's favour, he might issue a writ of possession thereon and proceed in the usual way for costs on such judgment.

The arbitrator awarded that the plaintiff was entitled to the possession "of a certain part of the lands sought to be recovered," which he set out by boundaries. The award stated nothing as to the residue; did not say on which demise the plaintiff was entitled; and gave no damages. Held,

1. That the award was bad for not stating on which demise the plaintiff was entitled.
2. Also for not expressly deciding as to the residue. Per *Littledale* and *Patteson* Js., dubitante *Coleridge* J.
3. But not for giving no damages. Per *Coleridge* J.

THE plaintiff declared against the defendants on the above demises, in *Easter* term 5 *W.* 4. Issue was joined; and the plaintiff delivered particulars describing the premises claimed by abuttals. After issue joined, all matters in difference in the cause were referred to arbitration by a Judge's order, which directed that the costs of the suit and of the reference and award should abide the event of the said award; that, if the award should be in favour of the plaintiff, he should be at liberty to sign judgment against the defendants in the same manner as if the cause had been tried at Nisi Prius, and to issue a writ or writs of possession thereon, and also to proceed in the usual way for costs on such judgment; and that, if the award should be in favour of the defendants, they should be at liberty to sign judgment as if the cause had been tried at Nisi Prius. The order contained the usual clause prohibiting either party from bringing error.

The arbitrator, on the 26th *August* 1837, made and published his award, in which, after reciting in part the order

1838.

Doe dem. Madkins against Horner.

order of reference; he proceeded: — "I," &c., "do make and publish this my award in writing of and concerning the matters referred to me as follows, that is to say, I do award and adjudge that the said plaintiff was, on the 1st day of *March*, A.D. 1834, and still is, entitled to the possession of a certain part of the lands sought to be recovered in the said action, that is to say," &c.: he then set out the part so adjudged to the plaintiff by boundaries, referring to a map annexed to the award; and concluded his award without any further adjudication.

Ogle, in *Hilary* term 1838, obtained a rule to shew cause why the judgment, which had been signed for the plaintiff, should not be set aside, and why the lessors of the plaintiff should not be restrained from issuing execution, on the grounds, "That the arbitrator has not finally decided the matters in difference referred to him; that he has not awarded any damages to the lessors of the plaintiff; and that the award purporting to have been made by the said arbitrator is not in favour of the said lessors of the plaintiff, so as to entitle them to enter up judgment pursuant to the terms of the order of reference." The rule directed that proceedings should be stayed in the mean time, but that the lessors of the plaintiff should, nevertheless, be at liberty to move for an attachment if they should think fit.

Cresswell and *Armstrong* now shewed cause. The present application would be too late if it were for setting aside the award; but it will be said that the defendants may still take advantage of any defect on the face

1838.

Doe dem. Madkins against Horner.

face of it: *Manser* v. *Heaver* (a). This award, however, shews no such defect. It professes to be made "of and concerning the matters referred." Those matters are certain lands which are set out by metes and bounds, and the right to which is disputed between the parties. Then the arbitrator adjudges that the plaintiff is entitled to a certain part of those lands, which he marks out by boundaries. That means that the plaintiff is entitled to so much and no more: the defendants are entitled, under the award, to retain possession of the rest. It is as if assumpsit were brought for 100*l.*, and an arbitrator awarded 10*l.* to the plaintiff. No adjudication would be necessary as to the residue. In ejectment, a verdict as to any part of the premises claimed entitles the lessor of the plaintiff to enter up judgment generally. The Court will not institute a comparison between what was claimed and what is to be recovered, *Doe dem. Drapers' Company* v. *Wilson* (b); it is for the lessor of the plaintiff to see that he does not take out execution for more than he is entitled to. The award, therefore, is final in this respect. As to damages, it was not necessary that the award should give them. The object of an action of ejectment is not damages but possession. An award of damages was not necessary here to give costs. The costs were to abide the event of the award; and that is substantially for the plaintiff. [*Littledale* J. Can you enter up judgment for costs, unless there are nominal damages at least to warrant taxing them (c)?] The title to costs here does not depend upon the statute of *Gloucester*, but on the order of reference; and that directs that, if the award shall be in favour of the plain-

(a) 3 *B. & Ad.* 295.

(b) 2 *Stark. N. P. C.* 477.

(c) See stat. *Gloucest.* 6 *E.* 1. c. 1. s. 2.; 2 *Inst.* 288.

 tiff,

1838.

Doe dem. Madkins against Horner.

tiff, he shall be at liberty to sign judgment in the same manner as if the cause had been tried at Nisi Prius, and to issue a writ of possession thereon. Suppose the lessors of the plaintiff entered up a judgment, simply, that the plaintiff should recover his term; by the order of reference no writ of error could be brought: nor would it be error; for he is not bound to enter up judgment for damages and costs. And, further, the order of reference directs that he shall be at liberty "to proceed in the usual way for costs on such judgment;" that clause gives him power to enter up judgment for nominal damages, assuming that it were necessary. The arbitrator had no express authority, by the order of reference, to direct a verdict to be entered; and there was none on the record. *Hutchinson* v. *Blackwell* (*a*) shews that he could not, under the submission, order a verdict for damages. In *Wykes* v. *Shipton* (*b*), which may be cited, the plaintiff was entitled to damages on the new assignment; and, the arbitrator not having given them, there were no means of supplying the defect: the Court could not do so. But the present case is more like the *Anonymous* (*c*) case there cited from *Smith's* Reports, where the costs of a cause referred were to abide the event of the award, and, the arbitrator having ordered something to be done which shewed the event to be in favour of the plaintiff, the latter was held entitled to costs, though the award did not direct a verdict to be entered.

It will be further objected to the present award, that the arbitrator does not say on which demise the plaintiff is entitled. But he virtually finds for him on both. Intendment will be made in favour of this award, as it

(*a*) 8 *Bing*. 331. (*b*) 3 *Nev. & M*. 240. See the end of this case.
(*c*) 1 *Smith's Rep*. 426.

was

1838.

Doe dem. Madkins *against* Horner.

was of the judgment in ejectment after verdict in *Morris* v. *Barry* (*a*).

Sir *W. W. Follett* and *Ogle*, contrà. First, the award does not include all the matters in difference. According to the argument on the other side, an award would be good which decided the title as to a single inch of land only, though the submission was of a dispute as to a thousand acres. [*Coleridge* J. Suppose no evidence had been offered as to any part, but that respecting which the arbitrator has decided.] The arbitrator should then have awarded that the defendant was entitled to the possession of the remainder. [*Coleridge* J. The only effect of such an award would be that the plaintiff's right to possess that part would be negatived. Is not that substantially done by this award?] Suppose the claim referred were partly on account of goods sold and delivered, and partly for some other cause perfectly distinct: would it be sufficient to confine the award to the latter cause, on the ground that the claim on account of goods sold and delivered was impliedly negatived? [*Patteson* J. If assumpsit were brought in respect of a great many articles, and the arbitrator simply ordered a verdict for 50*l*., that would be final.] That might perhaps be, where the award did not shew that there was a part as to which no decision was given; for it might be intended that the 50*l*. applied to the whole. But here it appears, on the face of the award, that it omits to decide at all as to one part of the claim. *In the matter of Robson and Railston* (*b*) and *Samuel* v. *Cooper* (*c*)

(*a*) 1 *Wils*. 1. 2 *Stra*. 1180.

(*b*) 1 *B. & Ad*. 723.

(*c*) 2 *A. & E*. 752. See *In the Matter of Gillon* v. *The Mersey and Clyde Navigation Company*, 3 *B. & Ad*. 493.

shew

1838.

Doe dem. MADKINS against HORNER.

shew that this defect is fatal; and that, even if the plaintiff had expressly abandoned his claim as to the residue of the land here, the award ought to contain a decision upon that part of the claim. As it now stands, it is not final. The defendants might still be sued in ejectment for the residue, on the demise of the same lessors. It is attempted on the other side to put the award, in this respect, on the footing of a verdict at Nisi Prius: but a verdict is often good where an award would be bad; the object of a reference is to place parties in a situation different from that in which a verdict could place them. The reference is, not of the cause, but of all matters in difference in the cause. The award, if properly made, would be conclusive as to the whole; *Doe dem. Morris* v. *Rosser* (a). Secondly, the award ought to have shewn on which demise the plaintiff is to recover. Both lessors cannot be entitled; but this award is conclusive against the defendants as to both demises. If one lessor were to convey his interest to the defendants, would they have a title or not? Or, if, instead of execution issuing, two separate actions of ejectment, on the respective demises, were brought against the defendants, would this award be conclusive evidence on each? Besides, the taxation of costs must be guided by the event of the evidence on each demise; *Doe dem. Smith* v. *Webber* (b). Thirdly, damages ought to have been awarded. On what can the costs be taxed? They were to abide the event of the award: but what is the event of the award? *Wykes* v. *Shipton* (c) is in point. [*Patteson* J. referred to *Steeple* v. *Bonsall* (d).] *In the matter of Leeming and Fearnley* (e) shews that this award determines nothing

(a) 3 *East*, 15. (b) 2 *A.* & *E.* 448. (c) Post, p. 246., note (a). (d) 4 *A.* & *E.* 950. (e) 5 *B.* & *Ad.* 403.

1838.

Doe dem. Madkins against Horner.

as to costs. It is contended that there was no power here to award a verdict: but damages might have been awarded: in contemplation of law every ejectment implies damage; every verdict is for damages: and the parties, by the submission, were to be at liberty to sign judgment as upon a verdict at Nisi Prius. These objections are all on the face of the award: the judgment therefore must be set aside. In *Wrightson* v. *Bywater* (a), on a motion to set aside a judgment entered upon an award, the Court discussed the validity of the award.

Littledale J. (b). Although the time for setting aside the award be expired, yet on motion for an attachment cause might have been shewn on the ground that the award was bad on the face of it (c). It is true that the defendants here are not shewing cause against a rule by which it is sought to enforce the award, but endeavouring to get rid of the judgment founded upon it. I think, however, that under such circumstances advantage may be taken of any objection on the face of the award. Then as to the objections. The order of reference does not give any description of the premises: it refers "matters in difference in the cause." But the award shews, with the aid of the map, what was in difference in the cause; and it professes to be "of and concerning the matters referred," that is, the matters in difference in the cause. Now the arbitrator does not profess to make his award of all these matters, but distinctly confines it to a "part of the land sought to be recovered." The counsel for the plaintiff say that this is, in effect, an

(a) 3 *M. & W.* 199.

(b) Lord *Denman* C. J. was attending the Privy Council.

(c) See *Macarthur* v. *Campbell*, 2 *A. & E.* 52.

1838.

Doe dem. Madkins against Horner.

award of the rest to the defendants; or, at least, an award that the plaintiff has no title to the rest. That may be the arbitrator's meaning: but is such meaning expressed? Suppose assumpsit were brought for 50*l.*, for the price of a horse, and 50*l.* more for the price of a bale of cloth; and that the award shewed this, and then gave the first 50*l.* to the plaintiff: it may possibly be said that this would be awarding for the defendant as to the other 50*l.* But I think that, when, in ejectment, all matters in difference in the cause are referred, the arbitrator, after deciding as to one part, and so expressing himself, should do something as to the other. I do not say what he ought to do: whether he should set out the residue by metes and bounds, or may describe one part specifically, and then award as to the remainder in general terms. But I think his omitting of all mention of the remainder is not tantamount to deciding that the plaintiff has no title to it. On this ground, therefore, the rule must be made absolute. I think also that the arbitrator ought to have said on which of the two demises the plaintiff was entitled to recover. It is indeed possible that part of the land which is awarded to the plaintiff might be recoverable under one demise, and part under the other. Still the arbitrator should state how the right is. I own that it is not usual to take a verdict so: but a verdict may find that as to 100 acres the plaintiff is entitled on the demise of *A.*, and as to another 100 acres on the demise of *B.* It may make a difference in the taxation of costs. A verdict might be set right in this respect by the Judge's notes: here there is nothing upon which to proceed.

Patteson

1838.

Doe dem. Madkins against Horner.

Patteson J. This is an application to set aside a judgment on an award: it would be too late to set aside the award itself. No objection can now be taken which does not arise on the face of the award. *Wrightson* v. *Bywater* (a) does not shew that any other objection can be noticed. Then, as to what is on the face of the award. To make this award good, we must import what the Court never does import. We cannot say that the plaintiff is to recover costs as to one part, and the defendants as to another. The ejectment is for certain premises; and these appeared on the particulars of demand. The reference is of all matters in difference in the cause; and the parties are to be at liberty to sign judgment as if the cause had been tried at Nisi Prius. The arbitrator professes to decide only as to a part of the premises in dispute, which he sets out by metes and bounds: he says nothing of the residue: he does not even add, after stating to what the plaintiff is entitled, that he is entitled to no more. If this, by implication, be an award for the defendants as to the residue, the Master will be at liberty to tax costs for the defendant as to all that the award does not mention; and the defendants may set up the award in a future action brought for the residue on the same demises; for it is conceded that an award for a defendant in ejectment is a bar. Now it is difficult to say that the defendants can do so here. There should have been an express decision as to the residue. Whether it was necessary to set it out by metes and bounds we need not determine: I should say that this ought to have been done. But we cannot see that the arbitrator has determined at all as to the residue. At any rate,

(a) 3 *M. & W.* 199.

the

1838.

Doe dem. Madkins against Horner.

the defendants are entitled to a determination of their right under the arbitrator's hand. Otherwise this awkwardness arises: if the defendants bring ejectment for the part to which the award declares the plaintiff entitled, they are at once concluded by the award; if they are sued for the residue, then, to avail themselves of the award, they must shew, first, that there was a residue in difference; secondly, what the residue is. I do not, however, say that this last suggestion is quite conclusive. I also think the award bad for not shewing on which title the plaintiff has a right to the part named. The costs are to abide the event. But the award does not say on which demise the event is in favour of the plaintiff: it can hardly be so on both. It may be that some of this part is recoverable under one demise, some under the other; but, if so, that should be said: if the plaintiff recovers on one demise only, the defendants are entitled to costs on the other. We must therefore set this award aside, or at least do that which is tantamount to setting it aside. I agree that the Court ought not to be astute in finding objections to an award.

Coleridge J. The defendants can be in no better position than they would be in upon motion for an attachment; and it has been long settled that, on such motion, no objections can be taken which are not on the face of the award. After an award has been left unquestioned for a long time, a party who lies by is not to be in a more favourable situation than if the opposite party had attempted to enforce it by attachment. I agree that *Wrightson* v. *Bywater* (a) determines nothing here, because in that case the point was not decided, and the

(a) 3 *M. & W.* 199.

Court

1838.

Doe dem. Madkins against Horner.

Court sustained the award. If the fate of this award had depended upon the point which has been principally discussed, I should have wished to take time before I decided that it was bad. For, though I assent to the general principle that there must be a decision on all that is referred, yet, taking into consideration the anxiety which the courts feel to uphold awards, I should doubt whether the arbitrator, though he has not expressly decided on all the matters, has not done all that is necessary. If he had expressly said that the plaintiff was not entitled to the residue of the premises claimed, the defendants would have had the full benefit of the award: yet then they would have been as much compelled to resort to parol evidence in a future proceeding as now. I agree, however, that, as the arbitrator does not profess to go into the question as to more than one part of the premises claimed, that may constitute a material distinction: and, if I were bound to decide upon this part of the case, I should perhaps agree with the rest of the Court. As to the other point, here is an award respecting a portion of land claimed on two demises. But the arbitrator does not say on which demise the plaintiff is to recover. That is, in substance, he does not say which party is to recover the land. The award is therefore uncertain. Besides, the costs cannot be taxed upon such an award. As to the arbitrator having awarded no damages, I think the award is nevertheless good: because, with the disposition which I have already expressed to uphold awards, I think the plaintiff would be entitled to all costs which a verdict at the assizes would have given him. And, though I have some doubt whether the arbitrator could expressly award

damages

1838.

Doe dem. Madkins against Horner.

damages upon this reference, I think the plaintiff in signing judgment might enter it for 1*s*. damages.

Rule absolute (*a*).

(*a*) Wykes *against* Shipton and Another.

January 21*st*. 1834.

In trespass, quare clausum fregit, &c., defendant pleaded several pleas, to some of which plaintiff replied, and issue was joined on the replication; as to others, the plaintiff new assigned, and signed judgment for want of a plea. The cause went to the assizes for an assessment of damages on the new assignment, and for trial on the issues joined. A verdict was taken for the plaintiff, subject to a reference of the cause and all matters in difference; the costs to abide the event of the award. The arbitrator awarded in defendant's favour as to the matter disputed on the issues, and directed a verdict to be entered for him, instead of the former verdict; but he took no notice of the new assignment.

Held, that the award was therefore bad, and that the Court could not remedy the defect.

Trespass for breaking and entering plaintiff's dwelling-house, and pulling down a flue therein, and fixing a plate across an opening through which smoke from the said dwelling-house was accustomed to pass through the said flue, &c. There were several counts, to which special pleas were pleaded. The plaintiff new assigned as to some of the pleas, and signed judgment on the new assignment for want of a plea. Issues were joined on the replication as to other pleas. Notice of trial was given as to the issues in fact, and for an assessment of damages on the new assignment. On the trial, before *Park* J., at the *Essex* Summer assizes, 1834, it was ordered that a verdict should be entered for the plaintiff for the damages in the declaration, subject to the award of a barrister, to whom the cause, and an indictment against the plaintiff for an assault, and all matters in difference between the parties, were referred, and who was to order that verdicts should be entered therein as he, the arbitrator, should think proper, and to direct what should be done between the parties to secure to both the enjoyment of an exit for the smoke &c. : and that the plaintiff should pay such compensation, if any, as the arbitrator should think fit to award to the prosecutor of the indictment; the arbitrator to order what should be done respecting the matter in dispute; the costs of the first-mentioned cause to abide the event of the award, and the costs of the reference and all other costs to be in the discretion of the arbitrator. The arbitrator made his award "of and concerning the several matters so as aforesaid referred," as follows: — That the plaintiff had no right to use the flue, in respect of a disturbance of which use the action was brought; and that therefore the verdict entered in the cause should be set aside and a verdict entered for the defendants; that the plaintiff should be at liberty to place an iron pipe as described in the award; that he should pay to *Shipton* 10*l*. as a compensation for the assault; and that each party should pay his own costs of the reference, and a moiety of the costs of the award. The award did not notice the new assignment, or the judgment thereon. Before any judgment was entered on this award, in *Michaelmas* term 1833, *Channell* obtained a rule to shew cause why the award should not be set aside, on the ground that it did not put a final end to the cause, but, at most, only disposed of the issues in fact; that it assessed no damages, and did not adjudicate upon, or put an end to, the residue, viz. the damages to which plaintiff might be entitled on the judgment on the new assignment, or the plaintiff's

1838.

Doe dem. MADKINS against HORNER.

plaintiff's rights as regarded that judgment: that it appeared that the only reason why the arbitrator ordered a verdict for the defendant was that he found that plaintiff had no right to use the flue as in the award mentioned, whereas, as appeared by the pleadings, the obstruction thereto was not the point in dispute in the cause, nor one of the points in dispute between the parties, nor a matter the determination of which for the defendant entitled him to a verdict.

On behalf of the defendants it was sworn that the action was brought for obstructing the flue which plaintiff claimed to use, and that the whole of plaintiff's evidence applied thereto: and that the judgment on the new assignment was not brought before, nor mentioned to, the arbitrator.

Thesiger now shewed cause. The statement that this action was brought for obstructing the flue is merely the arbitrator's mode of describing the gravamen, and is sufficient, being substantially correct. [*Taunton* J. He has described it according to the substance.] As to the omission to give damages on the new assignment, it is clear that, in effect, all matters in dispute between the parties have been settled. *Cross* v. *Johnson*, 9 *B. & C.* 613., shews that a recovery of damages on the new assignment was not necessary to give the defendants their costs of the trial. *Broadbent* v. *Shaw*, 2 *B. & Ad.* 940., also bears upon this point. [*Patteson* J. The difficulty is in saying whether or not the defendants can have their costs taxed on the new assignment, no damages having been assessed upon it.] That difficulty may be removed, the application here being to the discretion of the Court. In a case, *Anonymous*, 1 *Smith's Rep.* 426, where the costs of a cause were ordered to abide the event of an award, and the arbitrator awarded in favour of the plaintiff as to the enjoyment of rights, but omitted to give him costs, or direct a verdict to be entered, this Court made a rule absolute to tax the plaintiff his costs.

Channell, contrà. Assuming that the plaintiff here was entitled only to one shilling on the new assignment, that cannot be given without an inquiry. It is true that the Court, where it has power, will endeavour to supply the defects of an award; but here no such power exists. The present is not an application to its discretion. The award ought to have been such that the Court could give final judgment; but, as to the new assignment, that cannot be done.

Lord DENMAN C. J. A good objection has been taken, namely, that the arbitrator has awarded nothing on the new assignment; and we find no means of getting over that objection. The rule must therefore be absolute.

LITTLEDALE J. I am of the same opinion. In *Com. Dig. Pleader*, Z. 1., it is laid down that, "If there be judgment by default or confession, and the certainty of the demand appears upon record, the Court may

1838.

Doe dem. Madkins *against* Horner.

may assess damages without awarding a writ of inquiry, if they will," "with the consent of the plaintiff:" but it is said afterwards, that, "where issue is joined, a writ of inquiry never issues; for the jury, which tries the issue, must assess the damages, and the omission cannot be supplied by a writ of inquiry." That applies to the present case.

Taunton J. We entertain no doubt as to the existence of the defect; the only question is, whether there be any mode of curing it; and I can find none.

Patteson J. concurred.

Rule absolute.

Tuesday, May 8th.

Mary Lant *against* Peace.

P. mortgaged land to *L.* for 400*l.* Afterwards *P.* borrowed 1000*l.* more from *L.*, and mortgaged other land to him as a security for the whole 1400*l.* Held, that, under stat. 55 *G.* 3. c. 184., the last mortgage required an *ad valorem* mortgage stamp, with progressive duty, on the 1000*l.*, and also a deed stamp on the fresh security upon the 400*l.*, as a deed not otherwise charged for.

DEBT on an indenture under seal of the defendant, dated 5th *April* 1837, whereby he covenanted to pay the plaintiff, on 5th *October* 1837, 1000*l.* with interest at 5 per cent.; plea, non est factum.

On the trial before *Park* J., at the last *Warwickshire* assizes, the plaintiff put in a deed of the date alleged in the declaration, under the defendant's seal. This deed recited two deeds, one of *November* 1834, the other of *December* 1836. By the recital it appeared that the deed of 1834 was a mortgage deed, by the defendant and a person named *Nicklin*, to secure the payment of 400*l.* then lent to the defendant and *Nicklin* by one *W. Lant*, each of the borrowers covenanting for himself to pay the whole, and each having power to redeem; and that the deed of 1836 was a transfer of that mortgage by *W. Lant* to the plaintiff, *Mary Lant*. By the deed on which the action was brought, the defendant, having borrowed 1000*l.* more from the plaintiff, mortgaged certain property, not included in the former mortgage, to the plaintiff as a security for the 1000*l.* newly

1839.

LANT *against* PEACE.

newly borrowed, and also as an additional security for the 400*l.* previously lent. This deed had four skins. The first skin had two stamps, one of 5*l.*, the other of 1*l.* 15*s.*; the second, third, and fourth skin had each a stamp of 1*l.* But the four together contained 5430 words. It was admitted that the recited deeds were duly stamped with the *ad valorem* and other stamps required: but it was contended that the stamps on the deed in question were insufficient. The learned Judge received the deed in evidence, and the plaintiff had a verdict, leave being reserved to move for a nonsuit. In this term, *Whitehurst* obtained a rule accordingly.

Humfrey now shewed cause. Considering the deed simply as a mortgage deed for 1000*l.*, the stamp required by stat. 55 *G.* 3. *c.* 184. sched. part. 1. *Mortgage* (*a*) would be

(*a*) "Where the same respectively shall be made, as a security for the payment of any definite and certain sum of money, advanced or lent at the time, or previously due and owing, or forborne to be paid, being payable," &c., "Exceeding 300*l.* and not exceeding 500*l.*, — 4*l.* Exceeding 500*l.* and not exceeding 1000*l.*, — 5*l.*" "And where any such mortgage or wadset, or other instrument hereby charged with the same duty as a mortgage or wadset, together with any schedule, receipt or other matter, put or indorsed thereon, or annexed thereto, shall contain 2160 words or upwards, then for every entire quantity of 1080 words contained therein, over and above the first 1080 words, a further *progressive* duty of 1*l.*" "Exemptions from the said *ad valorem* duty on mortgages, &c., but not from any other duty to which the same may be liable." "Any deed or other instrument, made as an additional or further security for any sum or sums of money," "already secured by any deed or instrument, which shall have paid the said *ad valorem* duty hereby charged," "to be exempt from the said *ad valorem* duty hereby charged, so far as regards such sum or sums of money," "before secured, in case such additional or further security shall be made by the same person or persons who made the original security; but if any further sum of money" "shall be added to the principal money" "already secured, or shall be thereby secured to any other person," "the said *ad valorem* duty shall be charged in respect of such further sum of money." "Where any

1838.

LANT *against* PEACE.

be 5*l.* for the first 1080 words, and 1*l.* more for every 1080 words in addition. The 5*l.* stamp, and the three 1*l.* stamps, would therefore cover only a mortgage in which there were fewer words than 5400, whereas here there are 5430. It must therefore be admitted that the stamps are insufficient, unless the 1*l.* 15*s.* stamp can be applied to the progressive duty. It can be so applied, unless wanted for some other purpose. The question, therefore, is whether the deed, as a further security for the 400*l.*, require the 1*l.* 15*s.* stamp. Now, as far as regards the 400*l.*, the deed operates simply as an additional security for money already secured by the deeds of 1834, 1836, which have paid the *ad valorem* duty. The defendant, who makes the additional security, is the same person who made the original security: it is immaterial that another party joined in the first security,

any deed or writing shall operate as a mortgage or other instrument hereby charged with the *ad valorem* duty on mortgages, and also as a conveyance of the equity or right of redemption or reversion of any lands, estate or property therein comprised, to, or in trust for, or according to the direction of a purchaser, such deed or writing shall be charged not only with the said *ad valorem* duty on mortgages, but also with the *ad valorem* duty hereinbefore charged on a conveyance upon the sale of any property; but where the equity or right of redemption or reversion shall be thereby conveyed or limited in any other manner, such deed or writing shall be charged only as a mortgage; And in all other cases where a mortgage or other instrument hereby charged with the *ad valorem* duty on mortgages shall be contained in one and the same deed or writing with any other matter or thing (except what shall be incident to such mortgage or other instrument), such deed or writing shall be charged with the same duties (except the progressive duty), as such mortgage or other instrument and such other matter or thing would have been separately charged with if contained in separate deeds or writings. And where any such deed or writing, as is mentioned in the two preceding clauses, together with any schedule, receipt or other matter, put or indorsed thereon, or annexed thereto, shall contain 2160 words or upwards, then for every entire quantity of 1080 words contained therein, over and above the first 1080 words, a further *progressive* duty of 1*l.*"

no

1838.

LANT *against* PEACE.

no new party being added by the last. The case therefore falls within the express words of the exemption. If the deed had contained simply the additional security on the 400*l.*, the *ad valorem* stamp would not have been necessary at all. This view is confirmed by stat. 3 *G.* 4. *c.* 117. *ss.* 1, 2.; those sections exempt from the *ad valorem* duty transfers of mortgages which have already paid such duty: their intention was clearly to put transfers on the same footing as fresh securities on debts formerly secured; and this furnishes an inference as to the regulations which the legislature considered to be already imposed on the latter. Upon any view but that now taken, it is impossible to suppose that fresh securities would not have been expressly protected as well as transfers. The duty regards the sum secured, not the security. If a transfer of the 400*l.* mortgage had been made to a person who at the same time advanced the additional 1000*l.* on the new security, no *ad valorem* duty would have been payable on the 400*l.*; *Doe dem. Bartley* v. *Gray* (*a*). *Doe dem. Brame* v. *Maple* (*b*) assumes the same principle. Therefore the 1*l.* 15*s.* was not payable in respect of the 400*l.*, and may be applied to the progressive duty.

Whitehurst, contrà. The argument for the plaintiff establishes that no *ad valorem* duty is payable in respect of the new security for the 400*l.* The defendant admits this, but contends that, in respect of the 400*l.*, a deed stamp was necessary, under stat. 55 *G.* 3. *c.* 184. sched. part 1. *Deed* (*c*), the new security on the

(*a*) 3 *A.* & *E.* 89.

(*b*) 3 *New Ca.* 832.

(*c*) "DEED of any kind whatever, not otherwise charged in this schedule, nor expressly exempted from all stamp duty — 1*l.* 15*s.*" (with a progressive duty).

 400*l.*

1838.

Lant against Peace.

400*l.* being a deed "not otherwise charged." The exemption from the *ad valorem* duty, in stat. 55 *G.* 3. *c.* 184. sched. part 1. *Mortgage*, is expressly declared not to extend to other duties to which the deed may be liable. If this instrument had simply contained the additional security upon the original debt of 400*l.*, there must have been a deed stamp: this liability is not removed by its containing a security for the 1000*l.*, requiring distinct stamps. By stat. 55 *G.* 3. *c.* 184. sched. part 1. *Mortgage*, if the deed in question contains a conveyance of the equity of redemption of the land mortgaged previously as a security for the 400*l.*, the *ad valorem* duty on "conveyances" is expressly made requisite, which is another ground of objection; and, if the equity of redemption is not conveyed, then this is clearly, as to the 1000*l.*, "a mortgage, or other instrument" "charged with the *ad valorem* duty on mortgages," and contained in a deed with other matter, viz. the additional security for the 400*l.*, and liable, therefore, to be charged as if the further security had been by a separate deed. There are also strong grounds for presuming that the legislature intended such a deed to be stamped with a deed stamp, from analogy to the provisions of stat. 3 *G.* 4. *c.* 117., which, by sect. 3., exempts additional securities, where *a bond* has paid the *ad valorem* duty, from a new *ad valorem* duty, but expressly provides that they shall be liable to the ordinary deed stamps: the intention of this is, to put additional securities for money advanced on *bonds*, upon which the *ad valorem* duty has been paid, on precisely the same footing as additional securities for money advanced on *indentures* upon which the *ad valorem* duty has been paid; and the obvious inference is, that the legislature understood that in the

latter

1838.

LANT against PEACE.

latter case a deed stamp was necessary on the new security. *Doe dem. Bartley* v. *Gray* (*a*) is inapplicable, for there the Court expressly abstained from deciding whether a deed stamp was necessary, and confined themselves to the question of the *ad valorem* duty. In *Doe dem. Brame* v. *Maple* (*b*) there was a deed stamp: the decision was only that an *ad valorem* stamp was not required. Here, therefore, the 1*l.* 15*s.* stamp was required on the new security for 400*l.*, as a deed; and therefore there is not a stamp sufficient to cover the progressive duty on the mortgage for the 1000*l.*

Lord DENMAN C. J. The stamps are sufficient, if the 1*l.* 15*s.* be not required as a duty on the new security for the 400*l.*; if it be, then the progressive duty on the security for 1000*l.* is not satisfied: and I think that it is required. Stat. 55 *G.* 3. *c.* 184. expressly provides that the exemptions from the *ad valorem* stamp on mortgages shall not exempt from any other duty to which the instrument shall be liable. Here the instrument was liable as a deed creating an additional security for the 400*l.*; and, as to this, the exemption does not apply.

LITTLEDALE J. I think this instrument is not protected from duty as a new security for the 400*l.*, by the part of the schedule which is relied on for the plaintiff. The deed is properly stamped, so far as regards the 1000*l.*, but for the odd words. That deficiency cannot be supplied by the 1*l.* 15*s.*, which is required for the instrument in the character of a deed creating a new security for the 400*l.*

(*a*) 3 *A.* & *E.* 89. (*b*) 3 *New Ca.* 832.

1838.

LANT against PEACE.

PATTESON J. I feel no doubt on this point. Looking at the heading of the exemptions, we find them refer only to the ad valorem duty. If this instrument contained only the additional security on the 400*l.*, there would be nothing to exempt it from a deed stamp. Then the other security which it contains, for the 1000*l.*, does not swallow up the security as to the 400*l.* In *Doe dem. Bartley* v. *Gray* (*a*) the question was, whether the transfer duty was swallowed up by an additional advance having been made; and we held that it was so, under the express words of stat. 3 *G.* 4. *c.* 117. *s.* 2. Here there are no such words.

COLERIDGE J. concurred.

Rule absolute.

(*a*) 3 *A.* & *E.* 89.

DOE, on the several Demises of ANNE WRIGHT and ELIZABETH WRIGHT, *against* SMITH.

Tuesday, May 8th.

S. being in possession of lands, *B.* brought ejectment against him, and recovered; but, at *S.*'s request, forbore taking possession. It was proposed that *S.* should take a lease; but before this was done *B.* died, having devised the lands to *T. S.* then signed a paper, reciting the above facts, stating that he thereby attorned tenant to *T.* of the said lands, then in his, *S*'s, possession, and adding: "And I do become tenant thereof to *T.*, from," &c. "last past." Held, that this instrument did not require to be stamped as an agreement, though it was not strictly an attornment, no attornment being necessary where the new landlord comes in as devisee of the old.

Plaintiff gave defendant notice, under *Reg. Gen. Hil.* 4 *W.* 4. 20., that he might inspect, and would be required to admit, on trial, a "counterpart of lease" from *T.* to *S.*, dated &c.; and a Judge, on summons, made an order, by consent, for admitting the same. The instrument produced on the trial was in the form of a demise from *T.* to *S.* of the date specified, and was indorsed "counterpart," but was executed by landlord as well as tenant. No proof was given that any original or duplicate lease had or had not existed. The stamp was sufficient for a counterpart, but not for a lease.

Held, that the defendant, having consented to admit a counterpart of lease, corresponding in date and parties with that produced, could not now contend that the instrument produced was a lease, and therefore improperly stamped.

And this, whether before such consent he had actually inspected the document mentioned in the notice, or not.

On motion to enter a nonsuit, the plaintiff is not entitled to shew cause in the first instance as a matter of right, even on giving notice of his intention to the defendant.

EJECTMENT for messuages, &c., in *Middlesex*. On the trial before Lord *Denman* C. J., at the sittings at *Westminster* after *Hilary* term 1837, it appeared that the ejectment was brought on a forfeiture alleged to have been incurred by breach of covenants in a lease. The parties had attended before *Patteson* J., on a summons taken out by the lessors of the plaintiff (under *Reg. Gen. Hil.* 4 *W.* 4. *s.* 20. (*a*)), requiring the defendant to shew cause why he should not admit certain documents. The notice of intention to produce such documents was in the form given by the rule; and one of them was described as follows. "Counterpart of lease from *Elizabeth Taylor* of *Pailton*, in the parish of *Monks Kirby*, in the county of *Warwick*, to the defendant, date 26th *December* 1829." *Patteson* J. made the following indorsement on the summons: — "Take order by consent for admitting all but the three wills and probates, as to which I do not think it reasonable to require the admission." The lessors of the plaintiff, at the trial, produced

(*a*) 5 *B.* & *Ad.* xvii.

1838.

Doe dem. Wright against Smith.

produced, as the counterpart in question, an instrument in the form of an indenture of lease from, and executed by, *Elizabeth Taylor*, and also executed by the defendant, indorsed "counterpart," and having a 1*l.* 10*s.* stamp, which was sufficient, assuming the instrument to be a counterpart, but not so if it was a lease (*a*). It did not appear whether or not any corresponding document had been executed. It was objected, for the defendant, that the instrument produced was a lease, not a counterpart, and was therefore not receivable in evidence. The plaintiff's counsel answered that the admissions excluded this objection. The Lord Chief Justice admitted the evidence (*b*), reserving the point.

The lessors of the plaintiff claimed as devisees of *Elizabeth Taylor*, who was devisee of the Rev. *John Banks*. In 1829, Mr. *Banks* had brought an action of ejectment against the defendant for the premises now in question, and recovered, but did not take possession, it being proposed that the defendant should accept a lease. In the same year, *Banks* having in the mean time died, before any lease was executed, the defendant signed the following paper.

"In the King's Bench.—Between *John Doe* on the demise of *John Banks*, clerk, plaintiff, and *Richard Roe*, defendant.—Whereas a judgment against the casual ejector in this action of ejectment was obtained in *Easter* term last past, and I the undersigned, being tenant of the several messuages &c., situate &c., do hereby admit that possession thereof hath been stayed and not taken, under the said judgment, at my request:" the document then recited that *Banks* had since died, and had devised the premises to —— *Taylor* of *Pailton*, spinster:

(*a*) Stat. 55 G. 3. c. 184. *Sched. Part* 1. *Lease.*

(*b*) See *Doe dem. Wright* v. *Smith*, 2 *M.* & *Rob.* 7.

1838.

Doe dem. Wright *against* Smith.

ter: and it proceeded: "Now know all men, by these presents, that, in consideration of the premises, I do hereby attorn tenant to the said —— *Taylor* for the said messuages," &c., "which are now in my possession, and have this day paid to" *F. R.*, of &c., "the agent of the said —— *Taylor*, the sum of one shilling upon that attornment, on account and in part of the rent due and to become due from me for and in respect of the said premises. And I do become tenant thereof to the said —— *Taylor* from the 29th day of *September* last past. As witness my hand, this 4th day of *December* 1829. *Wm. Smith.*" Miss *Taylor* afterwards executed the instrument before mentioned of the date of *December* 26th, 1829. The writing of *December* 4th was produced as an attornment. It was unstamped; and the defendant's counsel therefore contended that it was inadmissible. The Lord Chief Justice received the evidence, and the plaintiff had a verdict: but leave was reserved to move to enter a nonsuit, on the last as well as on the first point.

Sir *W. W. Follett*, in *Easter* term, 1837, moved accordingly (*a*). As to the first objection, the documents were admitted, under the Judge's order, "saving all just exceptions." The want of a proper stamp is one. The defendant agreed to admit that the instrument mentioned in the notice was executed, but not that it was a counterpart and therefore rightly stamped. The lessors of the plaintiff could not require him to admit that which might be contrary to the fact, that the lease had been executed with a counterpart or duplicate. They failed to identify the document produced at the trial with that described in their notice and admitted

(*a*) *April* 15th. Before Lord *Denman* C. J., *Littledale*, *Patteson*, and *Coleridge* Js.

 by

1838.

Doe dem. Wright against Smith.

by the defendant. As to the second point, the writing of *December* 4th, 1829, if it was a mere attornment, required no stamp. Now an attornment, according to the definition by *Holroyd* J. in *Cornish* v. *Searell* (a), "is the act of the tenant's putting one person in the place of another as his landlord." "Where the original landlord parts with his estate, and transfers it to another, and the tenant consents to hold of that other, the tenant is said to attorn to the new landlord" (a). But, where the party becomes tenant for the first time, the instrument creating that relation is a lease, not an attornment. The provision of stat. 4 *Ann.* c. 16. s. 9. is consistent with this view of the subject. Attornment does not mean merely that the party confesses himself to be tenant to a particular person. It implies a change of tenancy. The mere acknowledgment of a tenancy is a creation of a tenancy. By attornment no interest is *created*. This is the effect of the decision in *Cornish* v. *Searell* (b), as stated in the marginal note. In the present case there was judgment in ejectment against the defendant; he therefore had, at that time, no interest in the premises; he was there as a wrong-doer, and liable to be turned out; but he consented to become tenant to the party recovering in the ejectment. That was, not an attornment, but an agreement to hold as tenant, which, being reduced to writing, required a stamp. [*Manning*, for the plaintiff, mentioned *Doe dem. Linsey* v. *Edwards* (c).] That was a case of pure attornment. The landlord had entered, as devisee, upon premises held by the parties attorning. [*Patteson* J. The form of the instrument was, We "do hereby severally attorn and become tenants" of the premises in our respective

(a) 8 *B. & C.* 476.

(b) 8 *B. & C.* 471.

(c) 5 *A. & E.* 95. See *Doe dem. Chawner* v. *Boulter*, 6 *A. & E.* 675, 683.

occupations,

occupations, "at and under the several yearly rent and rents now paid by us, and under which we now hire and occupy the same." The parties there appeared to be already tenants to some one. Here the defendant was in the situation of a wrong-doer, judgment having been recovered against him in ejectment.]

1838.

DOE dem. WRIGHT against SMITH.

Manning, for the plaintiff, proposed to shew cause in the first instance (*a*), alleging, as a reason, the injury to the lessors of the plaintiff from the delay which must ensue if the case went into the new trial paper. And he cited 1 *Tidd's Practice*, 499. (9th ed.), where it is said that, "when a rule nisi is moved for, the party called upon may either shew cause against it in the first instance, or on a subsequent day." [Lord *Denman* C. J. It is only said that he *may*, not that he has the right; and, that being so, the Court will adhere to its course, without looking to the consequences suggested. We will consider whether or not a rule nisi should be granted.]

Cur. adv. vult.

Lord DENMAN C. J., in the same term (*April* 25th), delivered the judgment of the Court as follows. On the first point made in this case we think there should be a rule to shew cause. On the second question, whether the instrument produced was an attornment or an agreement for a lease, *Doe dem. Linsey* v. *Edwards* (*b*) was referred to, where an instrument of a similar kind was considered to be an attornment merely. And we think that is the character of the writing in question here.

(*a*) Notice had been given to the defendant's attorney of the intention to shew cause immediately in case of a motion being made.

(*b*) 5 *A.* & *E.* 95.

One

1838.

Doe dem. Wright against Smith.

One circumstance only raised some doubt. The landlord who devised to *Elizabeth Taylor* had recovered in ejectment against *Smith*, the now defendant, so that his attornment to Miss *Taylor* had the appearance of accepting a new title under a new party. But, taking the view which common sense points out, I think that is not so. The former landlord had claimed a right to eject *Smith*, but had not availed himself of that right. He afterwards died, having devised to *Elizabeth Taylor*; and to her *Smith* made the acknowledgment now in question. The term "acknowledgment" is more suitable to this transaction than "attornment," which relates to cases of transfer, and not to those of devise or descent. To an heir or devisee attornment is unnecessary. This agrees with the language of *Holroyd* J. in *Cornish* v. *Searell* (*a*), and with the law of attornment as stated by *Littleton* (*b*), who expressly lays it down that attornment to the devisee of a reversion is not requisite. It

(*a*) 8 *B. & C.* 476.

(*b*) See, as to a devisee, sect. 586. Also Mr. *Butler's* note (1) to *Co. Litt.* 309 *a*, as to the effect of the statutes of wills, 32 *H.* 8. c. 1.; 34 & 35 *H.* 8. c. 5.

In 2 *Shepp. Touchst.* c. 13. p. 256. (7th, *Preston's*, ed.) it is said that "an attornment is not necessary in these cases following, viz. Where one doth grant a rent, reversion, remainder, service, or seigniory to another by way of devise by a last will and testament:" and *Fitz. N. B.* 121, *M.* (*N.*) is cited. In 2 *Shepp. T.*, same chapter, p. 257., it is added: "So where one doth come to any such thing by title or seigniory paramount, as by escheat, surrender, or forfeiture, or by descent, [under a title which did not require attornment to its perfection;] in all these cases, and the rest before, the attornment of the tenant is to no purpose, neither to pass the thing as to the estate; nor to make a privity to distrain or bring action of debt." "If a reversion descend to an heir from his ancestor; in this case it will vest in the heir without attornment, and attornment in this case is not necessary, [even to entitle the heir to distrain; for the law gives a perfect title to the heir, and he is in under the old title, and a continuance of the same seisin; and if attornment were necessary, it would give the tenant the option of repudiating the heir. And there is the continuance of the same seisin, and a change of person only, and not of estate]."

may,

1838.

Doe dem. Wright against Smith.

may, however, be desirable to such a devisee to obtain an acknowledgment from the tenants; and that appears to have been done here. There will, therefore, be no rule on this point. The first raises a mere question of practice.

Erle and *Manning* now shewed cause. The document was described as a counterpart in the notice to admit; and the defendant, by his consent, referred to in the order of *Patteson* J., admitted it to be a counterpart, having previously had an opportunity of inspecting it if he thought proper. The document itself was indorsed "counterpart," and agreed in other respects with the description given in the notice. Where a deed is executed between several persons, it is to be supposed that as many parts are made as there are parties, and that each is executed by those only who are to be bound by that part. That the part here produced by the lessors of the plaintiff was only a duplicate or a counterpart must be presumed from its being in their custody. "That part of the indenture which belonged to the lessee, doth after the term ended belong to the lessor;" *Co. Litt.* 47 b.: during the term, therefore, the lessor holds the counterpart only. To give him the original during that period would tend to frustrate the grant. The lessee would not have the lease to assign, if he wished to do so. And, if the part in question was merely that belonging to the lessor, the execution of it by her was mere surplusage: it was not the less a counterpart by reason of that circumstance.

Sir *W. W. Follett* and *R. S. Richards*, contrà. An instrument may be stamped as a counterpart with a

1*l.* 10*s.*

1838.

Doe dem. Wright against Smith.

1*l.* 10*s.* stamp, if there be an original lease bearing a stamp exceeding 1*l.*; but this must be proved, to make the 1*l.* 10*s.* stamp sufficient. [*Manning* referred to *Quin* v. *King* (*a*). *Patteson* J. There it appeared by the document produced that there was another deed, upon which the *ad valorem* duty in question would have been charged.] In this case there appears a complete lease, executed by landlord and tenant, and there is no evidence, or ground for presuming, that any counterpart or duplicate ever existed. It is true that the word "counterpart" is written on the outside of this document; but it does not appear when that indorsement was made; it is not part of the deed; and an original lease might be so indorsed to defraud the revenue. As to the admission, the defendant might undertake, if the instrument described were produced, to admit its execution; but he was not therefore bound to admit that the instrument to be produced answered the description given. He might admit the execution of a counterpart, if produced, but not that anything to be tendered in evidence was a regular counterpart, which would involve the admission that an original had been executed and duly stamped. If such an acknowledgment was required, the defendant's attention should have been called to it by the notice. Suppose he consented to admit a probate, and a plain paper were produced, which was manifestly a mere copy, would he be precluded from objecting to this as evidence? It is said that the defendant had an opportunity of inspecting the documents; but, if he did so (and of that there is no evidence), it was only with a view to admitting that

(*a*) 1 *Mee.* & *W.* 42. *S. C. Tyr.* & *Gr.* 407.

such

such documents, whatever might be their character, had in fact been executed. 1838.

Doe dem. Wright against Smith.

LITTLEDALE J. I am of opinion that this rule must be discharged. Supposing the Stamp Act to be out of the question, it would have been sufficient here if the landlord had put in a lease under the defendant's seal, whether any other instrument had been executed or not. But the question now arises on the stamp. I think that the document would not, independently of the Judge's order, be admissible as properly stamped, for that the defendant could not call it a counterpart. The subjects of duty mentioned in the schedule (part 1.) to stat. *55 G. 3. c.* 184. are "Lease," "Counterpart," and "Duplicate." This is not a counterpart, because it bears the seal of the lessor. A counterpart is, properly, executed by the grantee only. If the instrument is executed by both parties, it is either the only document that exists, or a duplicate: but, to use it as a duplicate, you must shew that there was an original, properly stamped. This, at least, would be the course of observation, if no admission had been made. But then, in the present case, notice has been given to the defendant to inspect certain instruments with a view to admission, and, among them, what is termed a counterpart. Suppose it had been called a duplicate. The defendant in such a case may inspect if he chooses. If he consents to the order for admission without looking at the document, he must take the consequence, and be considered as admitting that it is a duplicate; for, by not objecting, he prevents the landlord from giving notice to produce the original. The term used here is "counterpart;" and a counterpart is not strictly the same as a duplicate; but

1838.

Doe dem. Wright against Smith.

but the stamp which is proper for one is so for the other, and both are under the seal of the lessee. I think, therefore, that it would be too great a formality in this case to insist upon the difference.

Patteson J. There appeared some difficulty in this case at first. Without the admission, we must have considered this instrument as a lease. But here the defendant has received a notice that he will be required to admit that certain documents, and among them a "counterpart of lease," were "respectively written, signed, or executed as they purport respectively to have been;" and he has consented to make the admission as required; that is, that the particular instrument in question was written, signed, and executed as it purports to have been. It is true that this instrument does not purport to have been executed as a counterpart; for the term "counterpart" indorsed is no part of it, and cannot be taken into consideration. But the consent given by the defendant, after the notice, must be taken as an admission that there is such a document as the notice describes, and properly executed. If the defendant examined it, and found that it differed from the description, he should have objected then; if he did not examine, it is his own fault. It is very necessary that a party, who has an opportunity of inspecting documents and does not trouble himself to do so, should be in the same situation as if he had. A counterpart and a duplicate, though not the same, are stamped alike; and the effect of the admission is, that a document was executed of the same character with that described in the notice.

Coleridge

1838.

Doe dem. Wright against Smith.

Coleridge J. It is urged that the defendant was not proved to have inspected the particular document produced at the trial; but who ever heard that it was necessary to prove, on such an occasion, that the document in Court was the same with that seen at the Judge's Chambers? To require such evidence would be multiplying proofs so as to defeat the rule of Court. It is also said that the defendant is not proved to have inspected any document at all; but he is not competent to allege this. If, having opportunity given, he did not inspect, he stands in the same situation as if he had. The instrument in question was indorsed "counterpart"; if he looked at it, that word would stare him in the face; and at any rate he must have seen the paper described as a counterpart in the plaintiff's notice. Then was he not bound to make his objection at the time when inspection was offered? If he had then said, "I cannot admit this as a counterpart," he would thereby have given the opposite party notice to prove that there was an original properly stamped. By the conduct now pursued he has lulled asleep the caution of that party; and he must be taken to have said, "I agree to admit the instrument in the manner in which you have described it." It is asked what would be the case if a probate were mentioned in the notice, and nothing produced but a plain paper. Such a paper could never have been a probate at all; it manifestly wants the legal authority; but the instrument here produced may have been a counterpart, and would not cease to be so because the landlord signed it. There is no similitude between the case supposed and the present. This is a case in which we may say that a party, having consented to admit the execution of an instrument in a particular character,

1838.

Doe dem. Wright against Smith.

character, shall not afterwards object that the instrument has not that character.

Lord Denman C. J. I never doubted on this point. The defendant agreed to admit the document described as a counterpart; and it was properly stamped for a counterpart. I agree that persons might, as has been suggested, attempt to defraud the revenue by calling that a counterpart which was really an original lease; but, if that were done, the party opposing its production would have his opportunity of stating in Court the fact as it really occurred, and so far defeating the fraud.

Rule discharged.

Wednesday, May 9th.

The Queen *against* The Mayor and Town Clerk of Evesham.

Under stat. 5 & 6 *W.* 4. c. 76. *s.* 69., the minutes of proceedings in town-council should be entered and signed by the chairman at the meeting, and not afterwards.

TALFOURD Serjt., in *Easter* term, 1837, obtained a rule nisi for a mandamus to the mayor and town-clerk of the borough of *Evesham*, "to enter in the minute-book of the Court of the said borough the resolution passed at a meeting of the council of the said borough, held on the 3d day of *December*," 1836. The following facts were stated, among others, as grounds for the rule.

Evesham is an ancient borough, governed by a mayor, aldermen, and burgesses, and subject to the regulations of stat. 5 & 6 *W.* 4. *c.* 76. In *July* 1836, a committee, appointed by the town council to inquire into the charitable

1838.

The QUEEN *against* The Mayor of EVESHAM.

charitable and other trusts with which the corporation was charged under the statute, made a report to the council, which was duly entered in the minute-book of the council by the town-clerk. The report contained certain statements respecting a charity founded by *John Deacle;* and, in consequence of these, seven councillors sent a requisition to the mayor to convene a special meeting of the council on a day stated, for the purpose of taking the report into consideration. The mayor, for reasons which he gave, declined to call a meeting at that time; whereupon five of the requisitionists, by notice, under sect. 69 of the act, convened a meeting of the council on *December* 3d, 1836, to consider the report on *Deacle's* charity, and the right of nominating persons who should partake of it, and to make such resolutions and orders thereon as should seem proper. Eight of the council (the whole number being fifteen) attended the meeting, *Edward Rudge*, alderman, taking the chair. They passed certain resolutions, and appointed a committee to report at an adjourned meeting, which was ordered for *April* 5th; and it was also ordered, at the meeting of *December* 3d, that the resolutions then passed should be entered on the minutes of the corporation. The affidavits stated "that the town-clerk, at such meeting, caused a draft to be made in writing of such resolutions and orders, and of the exhibits, which the chairman took home to revise before entering; and, the chairman having so revised such draft, he caused a fair copy thereof, signed by himself, to be delivered to the town-clerk on the day after the meeting." The town-clerk, on that day, gave a memorandum in the following words: "*Evesham*, 4th *December* 1836. Received of *Edward Rudge*, Esq., the chairman of the special meeting of council yesterday,

1838.

The QUEEN against The Mayor of EVESHAM.

the minutes of that meeting signed by him as chairman, for the purpose of the same being regularly entered by me in the minute-book of the corporation. *James Taylor*, town-clerk." He did not, however, so enter them, having (as he stated at the next quarterly meeting of the town council, *February* 8th) been warned by the mayor not to do so; nor did he issue summonses for the meeting of *April* 5th, in consequence of which it was not held. At the said quarterly meeting of *February* 8th, it was voted that the proceedings of *December* 3d were illegal, and the town-clerk was ordered not to enter any minute of them in the minute-book; and an order, made by the town council, *November* 23d, 1836, that the book should remain in the town-clerk's possession, was rescinded, and the book ordered to be thereafter kept in the muniment chest.

In opposition to the rule, an affidavit was made, among others, by the town-clerk, who stated that he, in that capacity, attended the meeting of *December* 3d, where divers matters were discussed and resolutions come to, respecting *Deacle's* charity; "and a draft of the minutes of such proceedings was made in writing, partly by this deponent and partly by one of the members of the council; but such minutes were not, as this deponent verily believes, signed by the chairman; and when the meeting was over, such minutes were taken away by one of the council present, and, this deponent believes, the said *John Mosley Gilbert Cheek*" (a councillor and one of the above-mentioned requisitionists), "for the purpose of being revised by him; and that several papers and exhibits, referred to in such minutes, were taken away at the same time, and never returned to this deponent; and, on the day following such meeting, a paper,

1838.

The QUEEN *against* The Mayor of EVESHAM.

a paper, purporting to be a copy of the said minutes (which paper was, as deponent believes, in the handwriting of *Thomas White*, a clerk of the said *J. M. G. Cheek*, and *Oswald Cheek*, his son and copartner, and which said *Oswald Cheek* is the attorney employed by the persons applying for the mandamus against the said *Thomas Beale Cooper*," the mayor, "and this deponent, and was signed *Edward Rudge*, chairman), was brought to him, this deponent, by the said clerk *Thomas White*; and this deponent saith that he asked the said clerk for the original minutes, when the said clerk said that he had not got them; and this deponent hath never received the same." The town-clerk further stated that, having doubts as to the legality of the meeting of *December* 3d, and having received a protest from the mayor, and moreover not having the original minutes, he delayed entering the minutes until the quarterly meeting of *February* 8th, when he asked the directions of the council as to the course he should pursue; and that, in obedience to the resolution then passed, he refrained from entering the minutes in the minute-book. In this term (*a*),

Sir *W. W. Follett* and *C. Cooper* shewed cause. The mayor and town-clerk are called upon to enter resolutions which have been rescinded. [Lord *Denman* C. J. Although that be so, why should not the minutes be entered?] There are no minutes which can be relied upon as genuine. The draft is made up by one of the councillors at his own house after the meeting. There is no evidence that it contains the actual resolutions and

(*a*) The case was heard, *May* 8th and *May* 9th.

1838.

The QUEEN against The Mayor of EVESHAM.

and proceedings. The town-clerk, it is true, acknowledged the receipt of "the minutes;" but that does not ascertain their genuineness. [*Coleridge* J. In all cases, some person reduces the rough minutes into form, though they ought then to be read over at the next meeting.] Stat. 5 & 6 *W.* 4. *c.* 76. *s.* 69. directs that minutes of the proceedings in town council "shall be drawn up and fairly entered into a book to be kept for that purpose, and shall be signed by the mayor, alderman, or councillor presiding at such meeting." It does not say who shall make the entry; but the legal mode evidently is, that it should be made at the meeting, and signed by the councillor who presides. There was no reason for including the mayor in this rule; he has no peculiar control over the books. And it does not appear that the town-clerk has ever been requested to make the entry.

Talfourd Serjt., contrà. There is nothing to shew that the meeting of *December* 3d was not legally held. The minutes were taken away to be revised by the chairman with the town-clerk's consent, and returned to him on the following day; and he gave a receipt for them as "the minutes" of the meeting. There is, therefore, no ground for supposing them not genuine; and the town-clerk's reason for not entering them when received appears to have been merely that he was desired not to do so by the mayor.

Lord DENMAN C. J. The parties making this application are themselves in fault. The act says that "minutes of the proceedings of all such meetings shall be drawn up and fairly entered into a book to be kept for

1838.

The QUEEN *against* The Mayor of EVESHAM.

for that purpose," and that they "shall be signed by the mayor, alderman, or councillor presiding at such meeting." That has not been complied with here. The receipt given by the town-clerk for the minutes admits merely that he has received the paper, not that its contents are correct. If the admission were sufficient for that purpose, it would conclude the meeting in a manner which the act did not contemplate. The rule must therefore be discharged.

LITTLEDALE J. concurred.

PATTESON J. The words of the act imply that the minutes shall be drawn up at the time of the meeting, and signed at that time. It may be inconvenient; and perhaps, if the town-clerk had drawn up the minutes, and had them signed, after the meeting, we might not say that the thing was incorrect when so *done*. But we cannot order a thing to be done in an irregular manner.

COLERIDGE J. We are called upon here to give a direction. I do not see that we have a right to give it, as to the mayor. And, if it was the duty of the town-clerk to make this entry, he should have done it at the time of the meeting. However important it may be that what is done at such meetings should appear in the minute-book, it is still more important that nothing should find its way there but what actually did pass. If we once allow that a party may take away the minutes, and send back afterwards what appears to be an account of the proceedings, we can never be sure that there will be a statement of that which really occurred.

Rule discharged.

Thursday, May 10th.

BAYLEY *against* POTTS.

Plaintiff having signed judgment for 23*l.* debt and costs, took out a fi. fa. for 24*l.*, the 1*l.* being claimed for costs of execution, under stat. 43 *G.* 3. c. 46. *s.* 5. An attempt was made to levy, which failed, defendant having no goods. Defendant then tendered 23*l.*, which plaintiff refused, and issued an elegit for the 24*l.*

Held, that the tender was insufficient, the plaintiff being entitled, under the statute, to the costs claimed above 23*l.*: and the Court refused to set aside the elegit.

THE plaintiff signed final judgment for 2*l.* 10*s.* damages and 20*l.* 10*s.* costs, and issued a fi. fa. for 24*l.*, including the costs of the writ, warrant, &c.; but the defendant (who lived with his father) had no goods on which the sheriff could levy. The sheriff was ruled to return the writ. Afterwards, and after it had been found that no levy could be made, the defendant's attorneys tendered 23*l.* to the plaintiff's attorneys; but they declined receiving it unless 1*l.* was also paid for costs of the fi. fa. This was refused, it being alleged that the plaintiff was not entitled to such costs, as no levy could be made. The plaintiff's attorneys then issued an elegit for the debt and costs. A rule was obtained in this term, calling on the plaintiff to shew cause why, on the defendant's undertaking to pay into Court, or as the Court should direct, 23*l.*, the amount of damages and costs recovered, the elegit should not be set aside with costs, and satisfaction entered on the roll.

Bayley now shewed cause. Although no effectual levy has been made, the defendant is bound to pay the costs of the execution, and these include the costs of the levy, under stat. 43 *G.* 3. *c.* 46. *s.* 5., which enacts that "in every action in which the plaintiff or plaintiffs shall be entitled to levy under an execution against the goods of any defendant, such plaintiff or plaintiffs may also levy the poundage fees and expenses of the execution

over

1838.

BAYLEY *against* POTTS.

over and above the sum recovered by the judgment." The object of this clause was that where a party could pay, and did not until levy made, the costs thereby incurred should fall on him. In *Rumsey* v. *Tuffnell* (a) *Best* C. J. said, "I cannot think that 'expenses of execution' means only the costs of the writ." And in 2 *Tidd's Practice*, 997. (9th ed.), it is said, referring to that case, "It seems that, under this act, the expenses of execution include the expenses of levying." [*Patteson* J. Could you, under the elegit, recover the costs of a fi. fa. which had been abortive? Would you be entitled to levy more than the judgment money?] The process isued bonâ fide, and the sheriff was entitled to enforce it for all the costs of the fi. fa. and rule to return the writ; those costs, therefore, may be recovered under the elegit.

Platt, contrà. It was clear that the defendant had no goods to be levied upon; the proceeding, therefore, was a trick to charge him with the costs of a levy. [*Coleridge* J. Do you shew that the plaintiff knew the issuing of a fi. fa. to be useless?] He ought to have ascertained that it was likely to be effectual, and should now shew some grounds on which he resorted to it. The costs in question cannot be recovered under the elegit; it is only by the express provision of stat. 43 *G.* 3. *c.* 46. *s.* 5. that the costs of execution can be levied under a fi. fa.

Lord DENMAN C. J. The rule must be discharged. A fi. fa. issued, under which the plaintiff had endea-

(a) 2 *Bing.* 256.

1838.

BAYLEY *against* POTTS.

voured to levy. The debtor then asks him to accept the debt without the costs of the fi. fa. He refuses to do so; and he had a right to refuse; for he might, by law, recover the whole under the writ. Then, the tender being insufficient, he was at liberty to issue any other writ that would give him what he was entitled to.

LITTLEDALE J. concurred.

PATTESON J. The tender was insufficient under the statute, though it would have been otherwise at common law.

COLERIDGE J. The plaintiff has not shewn that the defendant was bound to accept the 23*l.* without the 1*l.* The plaintiff had issued his fi. fa., and was entitled to try whether he could not levy.

Platt then proposed that the elegit should be set aside on the payment of 24*l.*, but

The Court refused to make such order.

Rule discharged.

1838.

The QUEEN *against* BURGESS.

Thursday, May 10th.

Where a party has been arrested on *February* 3d, it is too late to move for his discharge, by reason of irregularity, on *April* 18th (the eleventh day of the ensuing term); though the process is an attachment for non-payment of costs on final judgment, and the irregularity complained of is that the party was arrested redeundo after his discharge from custody on a former attachment for the same costs.

The Court will not refuse to entertain such motion because the attorney whose name is used in the proceeding deposes that he never acted, or sanctioned the use of his name, in it.

BURGESS was taken into custody by the sheriff of *Suffolk*, on an attachment for nonpayment of costs taxed on setting aside a judgment obtained by him in a cause, *Burgess* v. *Baker*. On 31st *January* 1838, a rule was made absolute for his discharge, on the ground of irregularity; and on *February* 3d he was discharged from prison. Shortly afterwards, on the same day, he was again taken on an attachment for the same contempt, and recommitted to prison. A rule nisi for his discharge was moved for and granted in the ensuing term, *April* 28th, on the ground that he was taken the second time while going from the gaol to his home on being discharged by order of the Court, and that, on such occasion, he was privileged from arrest. The affidavit was sworn on the 20th of *February*.

Knowles now shewed cause, on an affidavit by the person represented as *Burgess*'s solicitor in obtaining the rule nisi, and in other proceedings referred to upon this application, who stated that he had never been employed, or acted, as the solicitor, or permitted his name to be used, on the motion or in any part of the proceedings.

Archbold contrà. The party who had used the name may be liable to punishment; but the misconduct cannot prejudice the client, who might have applied without employing any attorney. [Lord *Denman* C. J. I think that is the rule we have acted upon.]

Knowles

1838.

The Queen *against* Burgess.

Knowles then contended that the application, though made by a prisoner, came too late, the rule nisi not having been moved for till the eleventh day of the term following the arrest; that event having taken place on the 3d of *February*, and the affidavit being sworn on the 20th. And he cited *Primrose* v. *Baddeley* (*a*).

Archbold, contrà. There the arrest was on mesne process: here the process is in its nature final; and in such a case there is no authority for restricting a prisoner as to time. [*Patteson* J. I discharged a rule last term, where the irregularity complained of was in a capias ad satisfaciendum, thinking, on the authority of one or two former cases, that it was applied for too late.] The party here has been arrested in violation of his privilege redeundo, after a discharge from prison.

Lord Denman C. J. That is the very thing, of all others, that should be complained of in good time. The rule must be discharged.

Littledale, Patteson, and Coleridge Js., concurred.

Rule discharged.

(*a*) 2 *Cro.* & *M.* 468. *S. C.* 4 *Tyrwh.* 370. See *Fowell* v. *Petre*, 5 *A.* & *E.* 818.

END OF EASTER TERM.

CASES

ARGUED AND DETERMINED 1838.

IN THE

Court of QUEEN's BENCH,

AND

UPON WRITS OF ERROR FROM THAT COURT TO THE

EXCHEQUER CHAMBER,

IN

Trinity Term,

In the First Year of the Reign of VICTORIA.

The Judges who usually sat in Banc in this term were

Lord DENMAN C. J. PATTESON J.
LITTLEDALE J. WILLIAMS J.

REGULÆ GENERALES.

(Read in Court, *Saturday, May* 26th.)

Trinity Term, 1 *Vict.*

IT IS ORDERED, that, in future, in any action against an acceptor of a bill of exchange or the maker of a promissory note, the defendant shall be at liberty to stay proceedings on payment of the debt and costs in that action only.

(Signed by the fifteen Judges.)

Trinity

1838.

Trinity Term, 1st Vict.

WHEREAS it is expedient that certain of the rules and regulations made in *Hilary* term in the fourth year of his late Majesty King *William* the Fourth, pursuant to the statute of the 3 & 4 *W.* 4. *c.* 42. *s.* 1., should be amended, and some further rules and regulations made pursuant to the said statute:

IT IS THEREFORE ORDERED, that, from and after the first day of *Michaelmas* term next inclusive, unless parliament shall in the mean time otherwise enact, the following rules and regulations made pursuant to the said statute shall be in force.

1st. IT IS ORDERED, that the seventeenth and nineteenth of the general rules and regulations made pursuant to the statute 3 & 4 *W.* 4. *c.* 42. *s.* 1. (*a*) be repealed, and that in the place thereof the two following amended rules be substituted, viz.

For the seventeenth rule.

Payment of money into Court:

When money is paid into Court, such payment shall be pleaded in all cases and as near as may be in the following form, mutatis mutandis.

Form of.

C. D. ats. *A. B.* The day , the defendant by his attorney (*or* in person, &c.), says (*or in case it be pleaded as to part only, add* as to £ , being part of the sum in the declaration *or* count mentioned; *or* as to the residue of the sum of £) that the plaintiff ought not

(*a*) *General Rules and Regulations*, 5 *B.* & *Ad.* vi.

further

1838.

further to maintain his action, because the defendant now brings into Court the sum of £ ready to be paid to the plaintiff: and that the defendant further says that the plaintiff has not sustained damages (*or, in actions of debt,* that he never was indebted to the plaintiff) to a greater amount than the said sum, &c., in respect of the cause of action in the declaration mentioned (*or* in the introductory part of this plea mentioned): and this he is ready to verify: wherefore he prays judgment if the plaintiff ought further to maintain his action thereof.

For the nineteenth rule.

Proceedings by plaintiff after payment of money into Court.

The plaintiff, after delivery of a plea of payment of money into Court, shall be at liberty to reply to the same by accepting the sum so paid into Court in full satisfaction and discharge of the cause of action in respect of which it has been paid in, and he shall be at liberty in that case to tax his costs of suit; and, in case of nonpayment thereof within forty-eight hours, to sign judgment for his costs of suit so taxed; or the plaintiff may reply that he has sustained damages (*or* that the defendant was and is indebted to him, *as the case may be*) to a greater amount than the said sum; and, in the event of an issue thereon being found for the defendant, the defendant shall be entitled to judgment and his costs of suit.

General issue by statute.

IT IS FURTHER ORDERED, that, in every case in which a defendant shall plead the general issue, intending to give the special matter in evidence by virtue of any act of parliament, he shall insert in the margin of such plea the words "By Statute;" otherwise such plea shall be taken not to have been pleaded by virtue of any act of parliament.

1838.

parliament. And such memorandum shall be inserted in the margin of the issue and of the Nisi Prius record.

Payment credited in particular of demand need not be pleaded.

In any case in which the plaintiff (in order to avoid the expense of a plea of payment) shall have given credit in the particulars of his demand for any sum or sums of money therein admitted to have been paid to the plaintiff, it shall not be necessary for the defendant to plead the payment of such sum or sums of money.

Rule not to apply to claim of balance.

But this rule is not to apply to cases where the plaintiff, after stating the amount of his demand, states that he seeks to recover a certain balance, without giving credit for any particular sum or sums.

Payment in reduction of damages or debt not to be allowed.

Payment shall not in any case be allowed to be given in evidence in reduction of damages or debt, but shall be pleaded in bar.

(Signed by the fifteen Judges.)

1838.

The QUEEN *against* ARCHDALL, D.D.

On a motion for a quo warranto information, calling on the Vice-Chancellor of the University of *Cambridge* to shew by what authority he granted alehouse licences within the borough of *Cambridge*, it appeared that the first exercise and origin of the franchise were too remote to be traced; that it had been exercised both within the borough of *Cambridge* and without it to the extent of the University liberties, but not in pursuance of statutory authority, or according to the statutable form of granting licences; that the franchise was recognised in stat. 9 *Ann.* c. 23. s. 50., and later statutes, though not in stat. 5 & 6 *Ed.* 6. c. 25.; that, till very recently, no serious dispute had arisen on the subject between the borough and the University, nor had any licences been granted by the charter justices of the borough, or those of the county at large; that in early times the assise of bread and ale was in the borough, not the University; that the Vice-Chancellor, in licensing, had always acted with another head of a house, both being styled justices of peace, but the licence being under the single seal and signature of the Vice-Chancellor; and that his course of proceeding had not been in all respects uniform.

Held that, sufficient doubt not being thrown on the legality of the franchise by these circumstances, the Court would not assist in questioning it by granting an information.

AMOS, in *Hilary* term 1837, obtained a rule calling on the Rev. *George Archdall*, Doctor of Divinity, to shew cause why an information in the nature of a quo warranto should not be exhibited against him, to shew by what authority he did, as Vice-Chancellor of the University of *Cambridge*, together with one *William Webb*, Doctor of Divinity, as his assistant, grant licences (*a*) to divers persons to keep common inns, alehouses,

(*a*) The following is the form of the licence.

To all Christian people to whom these presents shall come to be read. *George Archdall*, Doctor of Divinity, and Vice-Chancellor of the University of *Cambridge*, sendeth greeting: Know ye that I, the said Vice-Chancellor, with mine assistant the worshipful *C. D.*, two of his Majesty's justices of the peace within the university and town of *Cambridge* and the precincts thereof, have admitted and allowed *E. F.* of *Cambridge*, in the county of *Cambridge*, to keep a common inn, alehouse, or victualling house, and to utter and sell, in the house in which he now dwelleth, and in the premises thereunto belonging, and not elsewhere, victuals and all such exciseable liquors as he shall be licensed and empowered to sell under the authority and permission of any excise licence which shall be duly granted by the Commissioners of Excise, or persons to be employed by them for that purpose, or by any collector and supervisor of excise respectively; I having before taken bond by recognisance (as in ordinary licences),

1838.

The Queen against Archdall.

houses, and victualling houses, within the borough of *Cambridge;* and by what warrant he did then take bond by recognisance of such persons respectively, and of their respective sureties, for the due observation of all and singular the statutes in that behalf theretofore made and provided for the good ordering of common alehouses, and for the observing and keeping of the clauses and articles under the said licences respectively written; and by what warrant he granted such licences respectively, under his seal of office as Vice-Chancellor of the University of *Cambridge*, to continue during the good will of him and his successors; and by what warrant he took upon himself, as such Viçe-Chancellor, to transfer

---

licences), in the name of our Sovereign Lord the King's Majesty, that now is, for the due observation of all and singular the statutes and acts of parliament in that behalf heretofore made and provided for the good ordering of common alehouses, and also for the observing and keeping the clauses and articles hereunder written. In witness whereof I have unto these presents set my seal of office, to continue during the good will and pleasure of me and my successors. Given at *Cambridge*, the day of , in the year of our Lord .

1. That you take no horse belonging to any scholar of this University to stand at livery in your stables, without the permission of the master of the college. 2. That you suffer no scholar, no neighbour's children, nor servants, nor any dwelling in your parish, to tipple in your house. 3. That you suffer none to tipple in your house on *Sundays*, holy-days, or thanksgivings days, in the time of sermon or service, or at any time after nine of the clock at night. 4. That you suffer no carding, dicing, or other gaming in your house. 5. That, if any vagabonds or suspicious persons come to your house, you shall acquaint the officers therewith, and so shall you likewise do if any goods be offered in your house to be sold by any. 6. That you suffer no drunkenness nor dissolute disorder in your house; and, if any happen to be, to acquaint the constables of your town and parish with it, that the offender may be punished. 7. That you draw your beer by ale quart, or pint, and not by jugs or cups.— N.B. No licence will be granted for the future, except the party it is to be granted to attend in person, to enter into a recognisance for keeping an orderly house.

George Archdall. (Seal of Office).

such

1838.

The QUEEN *against* ARCHDALL.

such licences as aforesaid from persons to whom the same had been granted, to other persons (*a*) being desirous to keep inns, &c., within the said borough; and particularly (specifying two transfers of licences); and by what warrant he, as such Vice-Chancellor, did, at each of the days and times aforesaid, take upon himself to charge and receive a fee or sum of money upon each of such licences and transfers. The grounds stated for an information were, that the said Vice-Chancellor was not a justice of the peace when he granted such transfers and took such recognisances; that, when he granted such licences, and took such recognisances upon such grants, he had no power to act as a justice of the peace out of Special Sessions; that he had no power to receive any fees upon the occasions aforesaid; and that there is no valid custom for the said Vice-Chancellor to do the acts aforesaid. In *Easter* term last (*b*),

Sir *W. W. Follett*, *Starkie*, and *Cowling*, shewed cause against the rule, which was supported by Sir *John Campbell*, Attorney-General, *Kelly*, and *Waddington*. The material points are so fully discussed in the judgment of the Court that a detail of the arguments at the bar is unnecessary.

Cur. adv. vult.

(*a*) The form of transfer was as follows.

Cambridge, 27th *June* 1836.

I do hereby allow *M. N.* to keep a common public house at the sign of , in the parish of , to which *E. F.* was licensed the day of last, having first taken bond by recognisance of the said *M. N.*, &c., for his keeping a regular and orderly house, during the goodwill of me and my successors.

George Archdall, Vice-Chancellor.

(*b*) *April* 30th and *May* 2d, 1838. Before *Littledale*, *Patteson*, and *Coleridge* Js.

1838.

The Queen against Archdall.

Littledale J. in this term (*June* 14th) delivered judgment as follows.

This was a rule for a quo warranto information to be filed against the Reverend Doctor *Archdall*, Master of *Emmanuel College* in, and lately Vice-Chancellor of, the University of *Cambridge*, to shew by what authority he had taken on himself to grant alehouse licences. It was moved on the part of the justices of the borough of *Cambridge*, for the purpose of contesting the right, claimed by the Vice-Chancellor, of granting such licences within the liberties and precincts of the University. It was argued in the last term, before my brothers *Patteson*, *Coleridge*, and myself, at great length and with great ability and research: we have taken time to look into the affidavits; and I am now to pronounce our judgment.

In the course of the argument, principally in consequence of a doubt thrown out by the Court, the question, whether this was a proper subject for a quo warranto, was much considered by the counsel who argued in support of the rule (*a*); but it is unnecessary for us to pronounce

(*a*) The following authorities were cited on this point. *Case of the Archbishop of York*, 2 *Inst.* 497.; *Rex* v. *Breton*, 4 *Bur.* 2260.; *Rex* v. *Williams*, 1 *Bur.* 402.; *Rex* v. *The Aldermen of New Radnor*, 2 *Ld. Kenyon's Cases*, 498; *Rex* v. *The Mayor and Aldermen of Hertford*, 1 *Salk.* 374.; *S. C.* 1 *Ld. Raym.* 426.; *Rex* v. *Stanton*, *Cro. Jac.* 259.; *Rex* v. *Badcock*, cited in *Rex* v. *The Corporation of Bedford Level*, 6 *East*, 359.; *Rex* v. *Nicholson*, 1 *Str.* 299.; *Rex* v. *Beedle*, 3 *A.* & *E.* 467.; *Rex* v. *Ramsden*, 3 *A.* & *E.* 456.; *Rex* v. *Hall*, 1 *B.* & *C.* 123, 237.; *Rex* v. *Boyles*, 2 *Str.* 836.; *S. C.* 2 *Ld. Raym.* 1559.; *Rex* v. ——, 2 *Chit. Rep.* 368.; *Rex* v. *Hubball*, 6 *B.* & *C.* 139.; *Rex* v. *Patteson*, 4 *B.* & *Ad.* 9.; *Rex* v. *Mashiter*, 6 *A.* & *E.* 153.; *Stat.* 12 *E.* 4. c. 8.; 4 *Inst.* 261.; *The Count of Shrewsbury's Case*, 17 *Vin. Abr.* 263, 264, *Prescription*, (E), pl. 3, 4.; *Jacob's Law Dict.* art. *Prisage*; *Rex* v. *Mein*, 3 *T. R.* 596.; *Rex* v. *The Duke of Bedford*, 1 *Barnard.* (K. B.) 280. *Co. Ent.* 537 a. pl. 5. (*Reg.* v. *Inhabitants of Denbigh*); *Com. Dig. Quo Warranto*

1838.

The QUEEN against ARCHDALL.

pronounce any opinion on that question, as our judgment will not proceed upon it; and we decline to do so the rather because the counsel who shewed cause against the rule scarcely noticed the point in argument, relying entirely upon the facts.

Turning then to the affidavits, it appears to be unquestionable that the Vice-Chancellor of *Cambridge* has exercised this franchise from a very remote period, from a period, indeed, so remote, that the first exercise of it cannot be distinctly traced, nor the origin to which it is referable at all certainly assigned; that he has exercised it, not merely within the borough of *Cambridge* but without it, and in the county, to the extent of the known liberties of the University. The history of alehouse licences, as granted by justices of the peace, is well known; it takes its commencement from stat. *5* & 6 *Ed.* 6. *c.* 25.; but the mode of proceeding by the Vice-Chancellor has never borne express reference to any authority given by the statute, nor squared with its provisions in form or substance. He has described himself indeed as a justice of the peace, and he has acted with another head of a house described in the same way; but the latter is called his assistant only; the licence is stated to proceed from himself, and is under his single seal and signature; it is granted during good pleasure, is subject to other conditions than those of a magistrate's licence; and the recognisance has never been certified to the quarter sessions. It further appears that this privi-

Warranto (A.); *Rex* v. *Gregory*, 4 *T. R.* 240, note (*a*) to *Rex* v. *The Master and Fellows of St. Catherine's Hall*; *Rex* v. *Bingham*, 2 *East*, 308.; *Rex* v. *Highmore*, 5 *B. & Ald.* 771.; *Rex* v. *Harrison*, 8 *Mod.* 135; *Rex* v. *Mayor &c. of London*, 8 *How. St. Tr.* 1039.; *Rex* v. *Holland*, 1 *T. R.* 692.; *Rex* v *Filewood*, 2 *T. R.* 145.

 lege

1838.

The Queen against Archdall.

lege has been recognised, with more or less distinctness, in a great number of public statutes, some of them going back to a distant period; one, stat. 9 *Ann.* c. 23. s. 50., passed considerably more than a century since, in very clear language recognising and confirming it. Lastly, it appears that, during the whole of this period, the University has been placed side by side, as it were, with a municipal body of considerable power, and that between the two differences have from time to time prevailed, and much jealousy been manifested as to the conflicting privileges; yet, until very modern times, no resistance entitled to serious consideration has been made by the borough to the exercise of this franchise; and no licences have been granted by the charter justices; and it may be collected from the silence of the affidavits for the rule that the same acquiescence and abstinence have been displayed by the justices of the county at large.

We purposely abstain from noticing many smaller circumstances of detail, which appear in the affidavits, and would not be without their weight in a balance of conflicting testimony, because in our judgment we shall not rely upon them. We have noticed only the great and undisputed features of the evidence in support of this franchise; and, before we pass to our conclusion, we observe that what we here find is exactly what we might have expected to find. In early times, it is well known that the number of students at the University, as at our Inns of Court, was much greater than at present; they were also younger in age, and yet for the most part lived, not within the restraint of college walls, nor under that discipline, almost of a domestic character, which now prevails in our universities, but in lodging-houses, inns, or hostelries,

1838.

The QUEEN *against* ARCHDALL.

hostelries, scattered through the town. In those times, too, the ordinary beverage, even for the educated classes, especially of the moderate means of the majority of students, was ale and beer, not wine or spirits. A control over the houses of resort in which these articles were sold, a control of the most absolute kind, was in some sort necessary for the preservation of discipline and morals, and for the prevention of those brawls and street riots, and fierce contentions with the inhabitants of the town, which the age and dispositions of the parties, and the manners of the times, would otherwise have made inevitable. Such a control, therefore, was highly expedient, if not necessary; the University, generally a favoured body, was not unlikely to procure from the Crown what might be so reasonably asked for; and, being a learned body, was likely to procure it in such form and with such sanction as would render the grant valid. And, if granted, there was no officer in whom it would so reasonably be vested as in the Vice-Chancellor, the great resident governor of the whole body.

We are now called upon, however, to subject this franchise to inquiry as an usurpation upon the Crown; not because any of the facts above stated are disputed, but because the University cannot shew the precise charter or statute to which the grant of the franchise can be expressly referred; because at an early period the assize of bread and ale was in the borough, and not in the University; because the first licensing statute, *5 & 6 Ed. 6. c. 25.*, does not notice the franchise as existing in the University, nor save it; because the Vice-Chancellor appears always to have styled himself and his assistant justices of the peace; because the course of proceeding by the Vice-Chancellor has not always been

 uniform;

1838.

The QUEEN *against* ARCHDALL.

uniform; and, generally and principally, because ingenious objections, objections at this day difficult to answer, may be raised against the evidence in support of any legal origin, whether prescriptive, by lost charter, or lost statute, which may be theoretically assigned for the franchise.

By stating these objections thus generally, we do not intend to take from their legitimate force; still less do we intend to be influenced in our decision upon them by the consideration that they are urged against a great and venerable body like the University. But, equally in this as in the case of any individual lord of a manor, we would ask any lawyer, whether he has ever known a franchise of equal antiquity in its exercise, though most undoubted in right, against which ingenious minds might not raise similar objections. It follows almost necessarily, from the imperfection and irregularity of human nature, that a uniform course is not preserved during a long period: a little advance is made at one time, a retreat at another; something is added, or taken away, from indiscretion, or ignorance, or through other causes: and, when by the lapse of years the evidence is lost which would explain these irregularities, they are easily made the foundation of cavils against the legality of the whole practice. So also with regard to title: if that which has existed from time immemorial be scrutinised with the same severity which may properly be employed in canvassing a modern grant, without making allowance for the changes and accidents of time, no ancient title will be found free from objection: that, indeed, will become a source of weakness, which ought to give security and strength. It has therefore always been the well-established principle of our law to presume

1838.

The QUEEN against ARCHDALL.

sume every thing in favour of long possession; and it is every day's practice to rest upon this foundation the title to the most valuable properties.

We should be departing from this principle and practice if we were now to institute the inquiry prayed for, and call upon the Vice-Chancellor to justify the exercise of this ancient franchise. It is possible that it may rest upon no legal foundation, and that, upon a full examination, it may turn out to be incapable of being supported. By refusing this rule, we do not prevent the parties from raising the question, if they shall be so advised, nor prejudice its determination; we decline only to render any assistance in originating the proceeding, which may imply a suspicion in our minds that what has existed unquestioned for centuries is referable only to usurpation on the Crown.

Upon these grounds, we do not examine minutely the several objections above enumerated. They are of more or less weight, and have received answers more or less satisfactory; the principle of our decision would lead us to the same conclusion, even if we should think that many of them remained entirely unanswered.

We were pressed with the anomalous nature and inconvenience of this jurisdiction under the altered circumstances of the times; especially that the power claimed was irresponsible in its exercise and liable to no appeal. This, however, is a matter with which we have no concern. If abuses are found to exist for which the law gives no remedy, or if the franchise be found objectionable in theory, or unsuited to the present times, application must be made elsewhere. The only question for us is, whether, under the circumstances, sufficient doubt has been raised in our minds, as to the lawfulness of its

 present

1838.

The QUEEN *against* ARCHDALL.

present title, to make it proper for us to direct the information to be filed. That has not been done; and this rule will therefore be discharged.

Rule discharged (*a*).

(*a*) See *The Mayor of Leicester* v. *Burgess*, 5 *B.* & *Ad.* 246.

Thursday, May 24th.

Ross *against* BOARDS.

A. agreed to purchase land of *B.*, the title to be made out to the satisfaction of *B.*'s attorney. The agreement being uncompleted, and disputes arising, all matters in difference between the parties, and the settlement of all questions on the agreement, were referred to arbitration. The arbitrator awarded that *B.* should convey to *A.* the title to the above land, contained in two abstracts given in evidence on the arbitration; he also prescribed the boundary of the land so to be conveyed, and ordered that *B.* should execute an indemnity bond to *A.*, to be forfeited if *A.* should be evicted by reason of defect in the title; and that, on execution of the premises, *A.* should pay the purchase-money. Nothing further was awarded as to the validity of the title. The goodness of the title had been a matter of dispute before the arbitrator.

Held, that the award was bad, as not finally determining the questions referred.

ISSUES being joined between these parties in an action of trespass, Lord *Denman* C. J. made an order "that all matters in difference in this action, and all other matters in difference between the parties, and the settlement of all questions on an agreement existing between them, including" &c. (subjects of dispute not material here), "be referred to the award," &c., of &c., barrister at law; and "that the said arbitrator shall have the power of inspecting the premises at *Edmonton* of both parties, and of laying down the boundary-line between the property of the plaintiff and the lands of which the defendant is the owner or occupier, and to award such damages and costs to either party as he shall think fit," &c. By the agreement referred to, it was recited that defendant, being the proprietor of certain ground at *Edmonton*, had agreed, and did thereby agree, with plaintiff for the sale to him of a part of the said ground afterwards described, for 100*l.*; the title to be made out to the satisfaction of Mr. *Blunt*: and plaintiff, in pursuance of the said agreement, did thereby agree to pay defendant the 100*l.*, at or before the time of executing the conveyance.

The

1838.

Ross *against* Boards.

The arbitrator made his award, the material parts of which were these. "I do award, of and concerning the matters to me referred, as follows, that is to say: Touching an agreement, the subject of evidence before me, I do award that the said *William Boards* do, at the expense of the said *Robert Ross*, convey to the said *Robert Ross* the title, contained in the two abstracts which have been given in evidence before me, to the parcel of ground particularly specified in such agreement; and, pursuant to the intention of the parties to the said agreement, such parcel is to extend unto a certain brook, the subject of evidence before me, so that the boundary-line between the respective properties of *Robert Ross* and *William Boards* shall be the line marked A B in the accompanying plan." "And I do hereby further award that the said *William Boards* shall, at the expense of the said *Robert Ross*, execute a bond to the said *Robert Ross* in the penal sum of 200*l.*, to be forfeited in case of the eviction of the said *Robert Ross* from any part of the premises so conveyed as aforesaid by reason of any defect of the title so to be conveyed as aforesaid: And I do further award that, upon execution of the premises, the said *Robert Ross* do pay to the said *William Boards* 100*l.*, as mentioned in the said agreement." "And I do further award that the said *William Boards* do pay to the said *Robert Ross* his costs incurred in the investigation of the title to the piece of ground specified in the said agreement, as far as the same may exceed the sum of 10*l.* 10*s.*"

In *Hilary* term, 1837, a rule nisi was obtained for setting aside the award, on the grounds: 1. That the arbitrator has exceeded his authority with respect to the agreement mentioned in his award, and to the estate the

1838.

Ross *against* Boards.

the subject of the agreement. 2. That the arbitrator has not decided whether the title to the said estate be good or bad, or such as the plaintiff was bound to accept. 3. That the award is not final with respect to the questions on the said agreement. 4. That the arbitrator has directed a bond of indemnity to be accepted by the plaintiff, without deciding as to the title to the said estate. 5. That, if the plaintiff should be evicted from the said estate, another suit would arise, and no sufficient security is given to the plaintiff as purchaser of the said estate.

The affidavit in support of the rule stated that, before the parties agreed to refer, it had been a matter of dispute between Mr. *Blunt*, as the plaintiff's attorney, and the defendant, whether the defendant could make a good title to the land in question, and whether the title to such land, set forth in certain abstracts furnished by the defendant to Mr. *Blunt*, was such as he could properly accept on the plaintiff's behalf; that the principal matter in difference before the arbitrator was whether the title, as set forth on such abstracts, was good, and such as the plaintiff and *Blunt* ought to be satisfied with; and that evidence was given of the insufficiency of such title. The affidavit further stated that the defendant, as the plaintiff's attorneys were advised, could not make a good title. The affidavit in opposition represented that, although, upon the arbitration, a question of identity arose, namely, whether the land in dispute was parcel of certain lands formerly purchased by and allotted to the defendant, or of adjoining lands purchased by and allotted to the plaintiff, yet no real question existed as to the power to make a good title, on a conveyance by defendant to plaintiff of the land in question;

1838.

Ross against Boards.

question; that defendant had, as the deponent (his attorney) believed, made out a good title; and that the direction as to a bond of indemnity was given, as the deponent believed, not because the arbitrator thought the title defective, but in consequence of an attempt by plaintiff to prove an adverse holding of part of the land thirty-five or forty years ago by one *Davies*; and that the case, as to such holding, had been satisfactorily answered before the arbitrator by evidence, which the affidavit stated.

Sir *W. W. Follett*, with whom was *Halcombe*, now shewed cause. The real dispute on the reference was on the subject of identity. The arbitrator has, in effect, found that the land to be conveyed is the property of the defendant; and the award is final, though an indemnity is directed. It appears from *Fisher* v. *Pimbley* (a) that an award is not vitiated by an indemnity bond being ordered, between parties to the reference, against claims to be made on account of matters submitted to the arbitrator. It is very common to award a conveyance with a covenant for title.

Sir *J. Campbell*, Attorney-General, and *Shee*, contrà. The arbitrator has not decided whether the defendant's title is good or bad. He calls upon the plaintiff to take a title which is not marketable. The order of reference empowered him to decide certain matters in dispute, not generally to direct what should be done between the parties. The matters brought before him as the subject of dispute were, whether the defendant could

(a) 11 *East*, 188.

make

1838.

Ross
against
Boards.

make a good title, and whether the title, as shewn on the abstracts, was such as Mr. *Blunt* ought to be satisfied with. Instead of determining these points, he has made an order which shews that he doubted whether or not the title was one which Mr. *Blunt* ought to have approved. This deviation from the line prescribed to the arbitrator vitiates the award, as in *Bonner* v. *Liddell* (a). A covenant for title occurs in all conveyances, and does not throw a suspicion on the title, as a bond of indemnity does.

Lord Denman C. J. The objection insisted upon must prevail. The agreement between these parties was, that the defendant should sell the land to the plaintiff, the title to be made out to the satisfaction of Mr. *Blunt*. It was referred to the arbitrator to settle all questions between the parties, on the agreement. He does not decide the questions arising on the agreement, but awards, of and concerning the matters referred, that the defendant shall convey to the plaintiff the title, contained in the abstracts, to the parcel of ground specified in the agreement, such parcel to extend, and be bounded, as the award points out. He leaves it in doubt whether the title is good or bad, and, in effect, orders that it shall be taken with all faults. The doubt is rendered stronger by the direction that an indemnity bond shall be executed, which is more than the arbitrator had a right to order. The award is not final, because, instead of deciding the questions referred, it sets on foot new ones; and, instead of ascertaining a right for the plaintiff, gives him a new action for the recovery of damages.

(a) 1 *Brod. & B.* 80.

Littledale

1838.

Ross *against* Boards.

LITTLEDALE J. The arbitrator should have stated in his award whether the title was good or bad. It is said that he has in effect done so. I have had some doubt; but I am of opinion that he ought to have proceeded in a direct way to determine the question as it arose out of the agreement. He should have said whether the title was good or not.

PATTESON J. The plaintiff agreed to purchase land, the title to be made out to Mr. *Blunt's* satisfaction; that is, he agreed to take a good title, not a doubtful title with an indemnity. Then a reference is made of all questions on the agreement. Upon the arbitration, a question is raised on the sufficiency of the title. If no such point had arisen, the case would have been different. Then the arbitrator awards, not that the title is good or bad, but that there shall be a conveyance of the title, and a bond executed; in effect, that the plaintiff shall take a doubtful title, with an indemnity. The award, therefore, is bad. The arbitrator was not empowered to order what should be done between the parties.

WILLIAMS J. The language of the order of reference decides this case. The arbitrator has not settled the question between the parties according to the terms of their submission to arbitration. He has merely directed a conveyance, and stated what shall be done in case of its proving ineffectual.

Rule absolute.

1838.

Friday, May 25th.

EMPSON *against* FAIRFAX and WEAVER.

Case for publishing a libel. Pleas: 1. Not guilty. 2. Justification, that the supposed libel was true; replication, de injuriâ. The publication was proved, and defendant offered no evidence. The jury found for the defendant on the first issue: Held, that (at any rate, in default of directions to the contrary from the Judge) the verdict should be entered on the postea for the defendant on the first issue, and the plaintiff on the second; such entries not being necessarily inconsistent; and that the plaintiff should have his costs of the second issue.

CASE for publishing a libel. Pleas: 1. Not guilty; and issue thereon. 2. A justification, averring the truth of the alleged libel. Replication, de injuriâ; and issue thereon.

On the trial before Lord *Denman* C. J., at the *London* sittings after *Michaelmas* term, 1836, a verdict was found for the defendants on the first issue, and for the plaintiff on the second.

On 27th *January* 1837, the defendants not having brought in the postea, the plaintiff obtained a Judge's order that the defendants' attorney, &c., should attend the Master with the postea, to tax the plaintiff's costs on the issue found for him. The parties attended accordingly, when the plaintiff's costs on the second issue were taxed at 188*l.* 2*s.* The defendants withholding the postea, and taking no steps to have the defendants' costs on the first issue taxed, the plaintiff, on 20th *February* 1837, obtained a Judge's order that the defendants should attend with the postea before the Master, and that the Master should be at liberty to tax their costs, and decide for whom the judgment ought to be given. The Master, on such attendance, taxed the defendants' costs on the first issue at 47*l.* 8*s.* 4*d.*; but, on the defendants' agent producing the postea, it appeared that the entry thereon was that, as to the second issue, the jurors were, by consent of the parties on both sides, discharged

1838.

EMPSON against FAIRFAX.

discharged from giving any verdict (*a*). The Master declared his inability to proceed further. The plaintiff then obtained a summons from Lord *Denman* C. J., to shew cause at chambers why the postea should not be delivered to the plaintiff to be amended, and why he should not be at liberty to enter up judgment thereon, and to retain the same until payment by the defendants of the taxed costs due to the plaintiff; but, on the parties attending the summons, his Lordship referred them to the full Court. In last *Easter* term, *Bompas* Serjt., on affidavit of the above facts (*b*), obtained a rule to shew cause why the Nisi Prius record, with the marshal's indorsement on the panel, should not be delivered up to the plaintiff, to enable him to prepare the postea and enter up final judgment thereon, and why the Master should not tax the plaintiff's costs of this application to be added to his costs of the second issue.

(*a*) The entry was as follows. "The jurors" &c., "as to the first issue herein joined between the parties aforesaid, upon their oath say that the defendants are not guilty of the grievances within laid to their charge, or any or either of them, or any part thereof, in manner and form as the plaintiff hath within complained against them; and therefore the jurors aforesaid, although no evidence whatever was given by the within named defendants in support of the issue secondly within joined between the parties aforesaid, cannot find, return, or say that the defendants, at the said time when &c., of their own wrongs did commit the grievance in the said second plea mentioned; wherefore the jurors aforesaid, by the consent of the said parties respectively, are discharged from giving any verdict whatever on the last issue herein joined between the parties aforesaid. Therefore" &c.

(*b*) The affidavit did not state the form of the postea, otherwise than as in the text; and it was assumed, in argument, that the plaintiff proved the publication, and that the defendants' counsel offered no evidence, but contended that the publication was not a libel.

Sir

1838.

EMPSON *against* FAIRFAX.

Sir *J. Campbell*, Attorney-General, and *W. H. Watson*, now shewed cause. *Spencer* v. *Hamerton* (a) may be cited as an authority to shew that, if the postea can be amended as prayed, the plaintiff is entitled to the costs of the issue found for him. But the amendment would introduce an absurdity. The finding as to the consent of the parties perhaps ought not to have been introduced. But the Judge at Nisi Prius had power to discharge the jury on the second issue. If a verdict be entered for the plaintiff on that issue, the finding will be, first, that the defendants have not published the libel complained of; secondly, that they have published it without the cause alleged in justification. Where an issue becomes immaterial, the Judge may discharge the jury from finding on it; *Cossey* v. *Diggons* (b), *Cook* v. *Caldecot* (c), *Dibben* v. *The Marquess of Anglesey* (d), *Powell* v. *Sonnett* (e), *Rex* v. *Johnson* (g). [*Patteson* J. Where there is only an affirmative plea on the record, and the defendant does not appear, the plaintiff must have judgment.] That is different from this case, where there is also a plea of Not Guilty, by which the burthen of proof is thrown on the plaintiff, and the defendant merely undertakes to prove the affirmative plea in the event of its becoming necessary by the plaintiff succeeding on the first issue. [*Patteson* J. Then the issues would have to be tried separately. In *Dibben* v. *The Marquess of Anglesey* (d) the case seems to have turned on the parties not having insisted upon a finding on the issues in question.] The

(a) 4 *A.* & *E.* 413. And see *Bird* v. *Higginson*, 5 *A.* & *E.* 83.
(b) 2 *B.* & *Ald.* 546. (c) 4 *C.* & *P.* 315.
(d) 10 *Bing.* 568. See *Norris* v. *Daniel*, 10 *Bing.* 507.
(e) 3 *Bing.* 381. *S. C.* in *D. P.* 1 *Bligh, N. S.* 545.
(g) 5 *A.* & *E.* 488.

question,

1838.

EMPSON against FAIRFAX.

question, however, was whether they were or were not immaterial. Suppose there were a plea of non assumpsit; and a plea of set-off. If the defendant succeeded on the first, he would offer no evidence on the set-off: then, if the plaintiff had a verdict on the second, the defendant would be barred of his cross action, although he had no benefit from his claim. This Court indeed said, in *Spencer* v. *Hamerton* (a) (adverting to the case of *Hart* v. *Bush* (b)), "It has been objected, that the consequence of holding that decision to be right will be, that issues, which have become immaterial by the decision of some one, will always be tried out for the mere sake of costs, and that great waste of time and inconvenience and delay to other suitors will be occasioned. We do not think these consequences at all necessary; but, even if they were, they are not sufficient to prevent the statute of *Anne*," 4 *Ann. c.* 16, *ss.* 4, 5., "from having that construction which appears most consonant to the intention of the legislature and to reason and justice." The objection there noticed is not met. [Lord *Denman* C. J. Suppose, in such a case as the present, the result of the first issue is doubtful, and the plaintiff is prepared with a great number of witnesses on the second, and the jury find that the publication is not a libel, but that the justification is a mass of falsehood, is not the plaintiff to have the costs of disproving the justification?]

Bompas Serjt., *Humfrey*, and *Hughes*, contrà, were stopped by the Court.

Lord DENMAN C. J. The argument in support of the rule must go the length of shewing that the Judge, not

(a) 4 *A. & E.* 418. (b) 2 *Dowl. P. C.* 456.

1838.

EMPSON against FAIRFAX.

not only may, but must, discharge the jury. Therefore the only question is, whether there be an apparent incongruity in entering one issue for the defendant and another for the plaintiff, there being an affimative and a negative. Now, when we see that the alleged contradiction may be satisfactorily explained on one supposition, we must assume that the jury acted as supposed: that is, that they found, not that there was no publication, but that there was no libel. And, as we know that really was the fact here, we must construe the finding, so as to make it consistent; as if they had said that the defendant was not guilty of reflecting on the character of the plaintiff, but that the imputation of the truth of the charges was unfounded. There is no great violence done to the language of the finding by so interpreting it.

LITTLEDALE, PATTESON, and WILLIAMS Js. concurred.

Rule absolute.

1838.

WHITWILL *against* SCHEER.

Friday, May 25th.

ASSUMPSIT. The declaration stated that, by a charter-party made between the plaintiff, therein described as owner of a ship called *The City of Genoa,*

Declaration, in assumpsit, set out a charter-party, between plaintiff, owner and master of a ship, and defendant, whereby it was agreed that the ship should proceed to *Constantinople* for orders whether she should load at *Odessa* or the *Crimea* from defendant's factors, and that she should then proceed with the cargo to *Falmouth,* &c., at the master's option: and that, by a memorandum endorsed on the charter-party, the ship was to be addressed to *S.* at *Odessa,* and, should she not arrive at *Constantinople* before 15th *November,* defendant's agents should have the option of annulling the contract: that defendant promised to perform the charter-party, and that there should be some agent of *S.,* or of defendant, at *Constantinople,* to give orders to plaintiff whether the ship was to load at *Odessa* or the *Crimea,* or, in the event of her not arriving at *Constantinople* before 15th *November,* to exercise the option of annulling the contract, and that the option should be exercised in a reasonable time after the ship's arriving at *Constantinople* and notice thereof to the agents of *S.* or defendant there: Averment, that she arrived after 15th *November* at *Constantinople,* and was ready to proceed to *Odessa* or the *Crimea,* as plaintiff should be ordered by *S.,* or defendant, or their agents: that plaintiff, on the ship's arriving at *Constantinople,* made due search to find, but could not find, *S.,* or any agent of *S.,* or defendant, nor could discover any orders, or information whether the option would be exercised: that the ship remained at *Constantinople,* waiting for orders or notice, for a long and reasonable time, after which plaintiff received notice from *S.* that he cancelled the contract: that this notice was not given in a reasonable time after the ship's arrival at *Constantinople* and the period at which plaintiff would and could have given notice of the arrival had *S.,* or any agent of *S.,* or defendant, been at *Constantinople,* or could plaintiff have discovered them: that plaintiff was ready to receive a cargo, but, by reason of defendant's neglect in not having *S.* or an agent at *Constantinople,* and of the option not being exercised *by reason thereof* in a reasonable time, plaintiff was prevented from proceeding to *Odessa,* or the *Crimea,* and there receiving such a cargo as aforesaid, or seeking a cargo elsewhere.

Pleas, 1. Non assumpsit. 2. That notice was given by *S.* in reasonable time after the ship's arrival at *Constantinople.* 3. That she did not remain at *Constantinople* waiting for such orders or notice, from the time of her arrival, for a reasonable time. Issues thereon.

On the trial, no evidence was given of any express promise that *S.,* or any agent, should be at *Constantinople,* or that the option should be exercised in a reasonable time after the vessel's arrival. Defendant objected that such promise did not arise from the charter-party, and applied for a nonsuit. The Judge left it to the jury, whether the notice of the exercise of option was reasonable; and, upon their finding in the negative, directed a verdict for plaintiff, and allowed him to amend the declaration by substituting a promise that defendant, or *S.,* in a reasonable time after the ship's arrival at *Constantinople* and notice thereof, would give orders whether she was to load at *Odessa* or the *Crimea,* or, if she arrived after 15th *November,* would, in a reasonable time after her arrival and notice thereof, communicate to plaintiff the exercise of the option: and the Judge reserved to the full Court the question whether he had the power to allow the amendment, and on what terms it should be made.

Held, that, the allegation of the promise being intended only as a statement of the legal effect of the charter-party, the Judge had power, under stat. 3 & 4 *W.* 4. *c.* 42. *s.* 23., to amend, by either striking out the allegation, or substituting a correct statement of the legal effect; that the promise as amended was such a correct statement; and that the amendment should be allowed, without any terms as to costs.

Although affidavit was made that defendant had gone to trial with the intention and expectation (grounded on circumstances which were stated) of contesting the allegation as it stood originally.

1838.

WHITWILL against SCHEER.

whereof he was master, then lying at *Gravesend*, and the defendant, it was mutually agreed between plaintiff and defendant that the ship should, with all convenient speed after delivering her then present cargo at *Alexandria* in *Egypt*, proceed, either in ballast or with goods (provided there should be no unnecessary detention thereby), to *Constantinople, for orders whether she should load at Odessa, or a safe port in the Crimea, or so near thereto as she might safely get*, and there load from the factors of the defendant a full and complete cargo of tallow, &c., and that, being so loaded, she should therewith proceed to *Falmouth* or *Cork*, at the master's option, for orders to discharge at a safe port in *Great Britain*, upon being paid for freight, &c.; cash for ship's use to be advanced to the master at *Odessa*, or at the port of loading, by defendant's agents, against his draft on the owners or brokers in *London*; that forty running days should be allowed defendant for loading at *Odessa* or at the other port, and unloading at the port of discharge; and ten days on demurrage, over and above the said laying days, at 4*l.* per day. There was also an agreement for an intermediate voyage at the defendant's option; but no question arose on this. There was also a penalty of 500*l.* for nonperformance of the agreement. The declaration then set out several memoranda on the charter-party; amongst others, one by which it was declared that the ship was to be addressed to *L. Stieglitz* and Co., *Odessa*; and another by which it was declared that the defendant was not to be responsible for detention by frost, unless his agent had twenty clear days for loading, after the arrival of the vessel, before the frost set in; and that, *should the vessel not arrive at Constantinople*

before

1838.

WHITWILL against SCHEER.

before 15th *November then next, the defendant's agents were to have the option of annulling the contract.* Then followed an averment that, in consideration that plaintiff had promised defendant to perform the charter-party on his part, defendant promised to perform it on his part; *and that there should be some factor, agent, or assign of L. Stieglitz and Co., or of the defendant, at Constantinople, to give orders to the plaintiff whether the vessel was to load at Odessa or at some safe port in the Crimea; or, in the event of the vessel not arriving at Constantinople until after* 15*th November in the charter-party mentioned, to exercise the option given by the charter-party to annul the contract; and that such option should be exercised within a reasonable time after the arrival of the vessel at Constantinople, and notice thereof to the agents, factors, or assigns, of L. Stieglitz and Co., or the defendant, at Constantinople, in the event of the vessel not arriving at Constantinople until after* 15*th November, in the charter-party mentioned.*

Averment, that the vessel, with all convenient speed, set sail from *Gravesend* for *Alexandria*, but was prevented from arriving there until 24th *October;* that she, with all convenient speed, delivered her cargo and proceeded in ballast to *Constantinople*, but was prevented by the dangers and accidents of the seas from arriving there *until after the said* 15*th day of November*, to wit until and on 10th *December* in the year aforesaid, on which last mentioned day she arrived at *Constantinople:* and that the plaintiff was then ready to proceed either to *Odessa*, or to a safe port in the *Crimea*, as he should be ordered by *L. Stieglitz* and Co., their factors, agents, or assigns at *Constantinople*, or the

1838.

WHITWILL against SCHEER.

defendant, or his factors, agents, or assigns at *Constantinople*, according to the true intent of the charter-party, and there, to wit at *Odessa* as aforesaid, or such safe port in the *Crimea* as aforesaid, to receive on board the ship a full and complete cargo, according to the terms of the charter-party. Averment, that the plaintiff forthwith upon and after arrival of the ship at *Constantinople* made due and diligent search and inquiry for, and took all due and proper means to find out and discover, *L. Stieglitz* and Co., or the agents, factors, or assigns, at *Constantinople*, of *L. Stieglitz* and Co., and of the defendant, for the purpose of receiving orders, whether the said ship should be loaded at *Odessa*, or at a safe port in the *Crimea*, or learning and being informed whether the agents, factors, or assigns of the defendant would exercise the option given by the charter-party of annulling the contract by reason of the vessel not arriving at *Constantinople* until after 15th *November*; but that, notwithstanding such diligent search, &c., he could not find out or discover at *Constantinople* the said *L. Stieglitz* and Co., or any factor, agent, or assign of *L. Stieglitz* and Co., or any factor, &c., of the defendant, or any person or persons who could give him orders as to whether the ship was to load at *Odessa*, or at a safe port in the *Crimea*, or any orders or directions whatever touching or relating to the ship, or any notice or information whether the said *L. Stieglitz* and Co., or any agent, factor, or assign of *L. Stieglitz* and Co., or the defendant, or any agent, &c., of the defendant, at *Constantinople* or elsewhere, would exercise the option given by the charter-party to annul the contract in consequence of the vessel not arriving at *Constantinople* before 15th *November*. Averment, that the ship remained at *Constan-*

1838.

WHITWILL *against* SCHEER.

Constantinople waiting for such orders, or notice of the exercising such option, for a long and reasonable time, to wit until 1st *February* 1833, when the plaintiff received a notice from *L. Stieglitz* and Co. that, in consequence of the arrival of the ship at *Constantinople* after 15th *November*, they cancelled the charter-party, and would not make use of the ship. Averment, that the said notice was not given in a reasonable time after the arrival of the vessel at *Constantinople*, and the period at which plaintiff would and could have given notice of such arrival of the vessel at *Constantinople*, had *L. Stieglitz* and Co., or any agent, factor, or assign of *L. Stieglitz* and Co., or of the defendant, been at *Constantinople*, or could he have found or discovered the said *L. Stieglitz* and Co., or such agent, factor, or assign as aforesaid, on such diligent search and inquiry as aforesaid. The plaintiff then averred his readiness to receive a cargo, &c., but that, by reason of the neglect and default of defendant, in not having at *Constantinople L. Stieglitz* and Co., or some of them, or some factor, agent, or assign of *L. Stieglitz* and Co., or of himself, the defendant, or some proper person or persons to give plaintiff orders as to the port to which the vessel was to proceed from *Constantinople* for orders, and of the said refusal of *L. Stieglitz* and Co. as aforesaid, and of such option as aforesaid not being exercised *by reason thereof* within such reasonable time as aforesaid, the plaintiff was prevented from proceeding from *Constantinople* to *Odessa*, or such other port in the *Crimea* as aforesaid, and there receiving such cargo as aforesaid, or seeking a cargo elsewhere, &c.

There was a second count for money paid.

Pleas. 1. Non assumpsit. 2. To the first count, that

1838.

WHITWILL against SCHEER.

that the notice in the declaration mentioned to have been received by the Plaintiff from *L. Stieglitz* and Co. was given in a reasonable time after the arrival of the vessel at *Constantinople*. 3. To the first count, that the ship did not remain at *Constantinople*, waiting for such orders as aforesaid, or notice of the exercising such option as aforesaid, from the time of her arrival at *Constantinople* aforesaid, for a reasonable time in that behalf, in manner and form &c. On these pleas issue was joined.

On the trial before Lord *Denman* C. J., at the *London* sittings after *Hilary* term, 1836, the Plaintiff gave no proof of an express promise that there should be *some factor, agent, or assign of L. Stieglitz and Co., or of the defendant, at Constantinople*, to give orders as to loading, or as to exercising the option reserved by the charter-party. The defendant's counsel objected that there was a variance, inasmuch as no such promise was implied by law. For the plaintiff it was insisted that such a promise was implied by the charter-party, but leave was prayed to amend, if the Lord Chief Justice should take a different view. His Lordship gave the plaintiff leave to alter the declaration in such manner as his counsel should think necessary, so as to make it consistent with the proof, subject to the opinion of this Court as to the power of amendment under stat. 3 & 4 *W.* 4. *c.* 42. *s.* 23., and as to the terms on which it ought to be made; and reserving to defendant leave to move for a nonsuit. His Lordship then directed the jury to find for the plaintiff, if they thought that reasonable notice of the exercise of option had not been given. Verdict for the plaintiff.

The plaintiff afterwards altered the declaration, by striking out the allegation of the defendant's promise

to

to have an agent of *L. Stieglitz* and Co. or himself at *Constantinople;* and also of his promise that the option should be exercised in a reasonable time, and stating, instead, a promise, merely, *that the defendant or L. Stieglitz and Co. should, within a reasonable time after the arrival of the vessel at Constantinople, and notice thereof given, give or cause to be given orders to the plaintiff whether the vessel was to load at Odessa aforesaid, or some safe port in the Crimea, or, in the event of the said vessel not arriving at Constantinople until after 15th November, should, within a reasonable time after such arrival and notice, communicate to the plaintiff the exercise of the option given by the charter-party to annul the contract.*

Kelly, in *Easter* term, 1837, obtained a rule to shew cause why the verdict should not be set aside and a nonsuit entered, or why the Court should not make such rule or order in the cause as they should think fit. This rule was obtained on an affidavit of the defendant's attorney, which stated, in substance, that the plaintiff had twice before amended the declaration, so as to make it necessary for the defendant to plead anew, and that the last amendment was made for the very purpose of inserting the promise which it was now sought to alter. And the deponent stated that he always understood from his client that a principal ground of complaint to be insisted on by the plaintiff was, that there was no agent of the defendant at *Constantinople*, at the time of the arrival there of the said vessel, to whom the plaintiff could cause notice to be given of such arrival: and that the deponent was induced to believe that such, in fact, was the ground of complaint which the plaintiff meant to insist

1838.

WHITWILL *against* SCHEER.

insist on, as well because the plaintiff would not go to trial on an issue which had been joined upon an allegation that *Stieglitz* and Co. had, within a reasonable time, elected to cancel the contract and given notice thereof to the plaintiff as by the nature of the several amendments made by the plaintiff in his declaration. That the defendant always insisted that he was not bound to have an agent at *Constantinople*, at the time of the vessel's arrival there. That the counsel before whom the declaration was laid to advise on the pleas was instructed accordingly, and had given it as his opinion that the general issue was the most important plea, inasmuch as it raised the question whether a promise could be implied on the defendant's part to have an agent at *Constantinople* to give orders as to loading the vessel, or to exercise the option of annulling the contract; and that the counsel further expressed his opinion that such promise was stated too loosely. And that the defendant's attorney accordingly went to trial in the full expectation that the defendant's liability to have an agent at *Constantinople*, for the purposes mentioned in the declaration, would be a material and principal question on the trial.

Sir *W. W. Follett* and *Petersdorff* now shewed cause (*a*). There can be no doubt that both parties meant to try the question whether the vessel had or had not been improperly detained; that is, whether notice of abandonment of the contract was given in reasonable time. Before the new rules, the pleader would have shaped the complaint in several ways: the question

(*a*) Before Lord *Denman* C. J., *Littledale*, *Patteson*, and *Williams* Js.

now

1838.

WHITWILL *against* SCHEER.

now is, whether the plaintiff is to suffer from the restrictions imposed by the rules, without having the benefit of amendment. If the Judge had power to amend, there is no question before the Court; for he has already exercised his discretion by amending. The first question is, whether the amendment be necessary at all; whether the charter-party does not imply a contract on the part of the defendant to have some person to act for him at *Constantinople* on the arrival of the vessel, and whether the mutual promises be not sufficient without more? But, secondly, supposing this not to be so, the amendment is correct. Stat. 9 *G.* 4. *c.* 15. applies only to variances between written or printed evidence and the record. But stat. 3 & 4 *W.* 4. *c.* 42. *s.* 23. gives the Judge power, if he "shall see fit so to do," to make the amendment "when any variance shall appear between the proof and the recital or setting forth on the record" "of any contract," &c., if the variance, in the judgment of the Judge, be one "not material to the merits of the case, and by which the opposite party cannot have been prejudiced in the conduct of his action," defence, &c. Here the variance cannot be material, nor could the defendant be prejudiced; the whole of the charter-party, from which the promise is implied, is set out. The amendment affects merely the statement by the pleader of the legal effect of the instrument. Similar cases have occurred at Nisi Prius, though such questions can rarely be discussed in banc. [*Patteson* J. You might find such authorities in banc, where the question has been whether the Judge was entitled to make an amendment which he actually has made. Where he refuses, the statute gives no power to apply in banc, but leaves the party to his motion for a new trial

1838.

WHITWILL against SCHEER.

trial in the ordinary way.] In *Moilliet* v. *Powell* (*a*) an instrument was declared on as a bill of exchange, which turned out to be a promissory note; and *Alderson* J. amended the record. In *Hemming* v. *Parry* (*b*) the same learned Judge amended a count stating an absolute warranty of a horse, by substituting an allegation of a qualified warranty; and he referred to the case of *Jones* v. *Cowley* (*c*), which, he said, "was a great disgrace to the *English* law." In *Parry* v. *Fairhurst* (*d*) the declaration was on a duty arising from an undertaking to carry, convey, and deliver goods: the jury found that the undertaking was to forward; and, the Judge having indorsed the special finding, under sect. 24 of stat. 3 & 4 *W.* 4. *c.* 42., the Court ordered the amendment, *Parke* B. saying that he would have allowed the amendment at Nisi Prius. In *Parks* v. *Edge* (*e*), under stat. 9 *G.* 4. *c.* 15., a count stating a bill to have been drawn payable to order of the drawer was amended, and a statement substituted that it was payable to order of the defendant, an indorser. In *Hanbury* v. *Ella* (*g*) "guarantee" was substituted for "pay;" that was, like the present, a mistake, if any, of the pleader as to the legal effect. [*Patteson* J. referred to *Lamey* v. *Bishop* (*h*), under stat. 9 *G.* 4. *c.* 15.] *Guest* v. *Elwes* (*i*) was a case under sect. 24 of stat. 3 & 4 *W.* 4. *c.* 42. There the declaration was for an escape: the proof was of a neglect to arrest; and, the verdict being indorsed, the Court gave judgment for the plaintiff. There *Patteson* J. said that sect. 24 was not intended to apply to cases where the

(*a*) 6 *C.* & *P.* 233.

(*b*) 6 *C.* & *P.* 580.

(*c*) 4 *B.* & *C.* 445. See *Second Report of Commissioners on Courts of Common Law*, p. 38., et seq., and p. 85.

(*d*) 2 *C. M.* & *R.* 190. *S. C.* 5 *Tyrwh.* 685.

(*e*) 1 *C.* & *M.* 429. *S. C.* 3 *Tyrwh.* 364.

(*g*) 1 *A.* & *E.* 61.

(*h*) 4 *B.* & *Ad.* 479.

(*i*) 5 *A.* & *E.* 118.

Judge

1838.

WHITWILL *against* SCHEER.

Judge at Nisi Prius thought there ought not to be an amendment. The case is therefore an authority as to amendments at Nisi Prius under sect. 23. The breach here applies equally well to each form of the declaration. Further, the Court will impose no terms for the amendment. Formerly the practice was for a party to swear he had defended with a view to the particular allegation; and then, if he submitted to a verdict, he had costs; but here the defendant did not submit.

Cooper contrà. First, if the amendment be not allowed, the plaintiff must be nonsuited. The promise alleged was not proved to have been expressly made: the only question, therefore, is whether it be implied by the charter-party and the promise to perform the terms. The ship was to be addressed to *L. Stieglitz* and Co., *Odessa*. How could a duty arise of providing an agent at *Constantinople?* It is said that this allegation may be neglected, and the breach still be good. But the breach, admitting that notice of the option was given, alleges that it was not given in a reasonable time from the period of the arrival at *Constantinople, and the period at which the plaintiff could have given notice of the arrival had there been an agent at Constantinople.* The complaint, therefore, essentially depends upon the promise in question. It is not a complaint of unreasonable notice generally, but of an infraction of the contract, as laid in an allegation which was not proved. Secondly, there can be no amendment. The case is not like that of misdescription of an instrument, as where a promissory note is called a bill of exchange. It is a statement of a contract which never existed, and which the defendant went to trial with the intention of disputing. In

1838.

WHITWILL *against* SCHEER.

trying that point upon a writ of error, after having attempted a defence upon the merits on the other pleas.

Rule discharged.

Afterwards, in this term (*June* 6th), *Kelly* applied for costs to be made part of the terms of the amendment. The Court (Lord *Denman* C. J., *Littledale*, *Patteson*, and *Williams* Js.) took time to consider; and, in the same term (*June* 12), refused the rule.

WILLIAMS *against* WILCOX and Another.

A weir appurtenant to a fishery, obstructing the whole or part of a navigable river, is legal, if granted by the crown before the commencement of the reign of *Edward* the First.

Such a grant may be inferred from evidence of its having existed before that time.

If the weir, when so first granted, obstruct the navigation of only a part of the river, it does not become illegal by the stream changing its bed, so that the weir obstructs the only navigable passage remaining.

Trespass for breaking down a weir appurtenant to a fishery. Justification, that the weir was wrongfully erected across part of a public and navigable river, the *Severn*, where the king's subjects had a right to navigate, and that the rest of the river was choked up so that defendants could not navigate without breaking down the weir. Replication, that the part where the weir stood was distinct from the channel where the right of navigation existed, and was not a public navigable river. Rejoinder, that the part was a part of the *Severn*, and the king's subjects had a right to navigate there when the rest was choked up, and that the rest was choked up. Surrejoinder, traversing the right. Held, that in support of this traverse plaintiff might shew user to raise presumption of such a grant as above, and was not bound, for the purpose of introducing such proof, to set out his right more specifically on the record.

Where the crown had no right to obstruct the whole passage of a navigable river, it had no right to erect a weir obstructing a part, except subject to the rights of the public; and therefore, in such a case, the weir would become illegal upon the rest of the river being so choked that there could be no passage elsewhere.

A party objecting to the production of a copy, on account of due search not having been made for the original, must make the objection, at the time of the trial, distinctly on that ground; if he does not, the Court will not afterwards entertain it.

TRESPASS for throwing down a weir of plaintiff, appurtenant to his fishery, and seizing, taking, and carrying away the materials thereof, to wit 1000 stakes and 1000 yards of pleaching work of wood of plaintiff, and converting &c., and thereby hindering plaintiff from having the benefit and enjoyment of the weir, &c.

Pleas,

1838.

WILLIAMS *against* WILCOX.

Pleas, 1. Not Guilty.

2. That the said weir, stakes, and pleaching work of wood of the plaintiff, before the said times when &c., had been wrongfully erected, and placed and set up, in and across part of a public navigable river called the *Severn;* that the said part of the said river in which &c. was a part of the said river situate between *Worcester* and *Shrewsbury*, and that the said river now is, and at the said several times when &c. was, a public and common navigable river for all the liege &c. to navigate and pass with barges on the said river between *Worcester* and *Shrewsbury*, and that all the liege &c., before and at the said times when &c., of right ought to have navigated and passed, and still of right &c., with barges in and along the said river from *Worcester* to *Shrewsbury* at all times of the year, at their free will and pleasure; that defendants, being liege &c., at the said times when &c., had occasion to use the said river, and to navigate and pass in and along the said river between *Worcester* and *Shrewsbury*, with a certain barge of defendants, in going and passing from *Worcester* to *Shrewsbury*, and had navigated and passed with the said barge in and along the said river from *Worcester* to the said part of the said river in which &c.; and, because the said weir, &c., had, before the said several times when &c., been wrongfully erected, &c., and were then wrongfully remaining and standing in and across the said part of the said river in which &c., and obstructing the same, and because a certain other part of the said river, near and adjoining to the said part of the said river in which &c. was, at the said times when &c., choked and stopped up, so that, without breaking down, throwing down, prostrating, and destroying the said

1838.

WILLIAMS *against* WILCOX.

weir &c., defendants could not then navigate or pass with their said barge through, over, and along the said river from *Worcester* to *Shrewsbury* as they ought to have done, and because defendants could not then remove the obstructions in, or open, the said other part of the said river which was so choked and stopped up, or pass over or navigate the said part of the said river in which &c., defendants, at the said several times when &c., in order to remove the said obstruction in the said part of the said river in which &c., and to enable themselves to pass with and navigate their said barge in and upon the said part of the said river in which &c., broke down, &c., the weir, and the materials thereof, to wit &c., and took and carried away the same to a small and convenient distance, &c., which are the same &c.

Replication. That true it is that the river *Severn* was and is a public navigable river, as in the plea mentioned, and that the said weir, &c., before the said times when &c., had been erected, &c., in and across a part of the said river, as in the plea mentioned; but the plaintiff in fact says that the said part of the said river, in and across which the said weir, &c., had been so erected &c., was a part of the said river other than, and wholly distinct from, the channel of the same in which the liege &c. had navigated and passed and of right ought &c., as in the plea in that behalf mentioned, and lying between the said channel of the said river and the north eastern bank thereof: and that the said part of the said river in and across which the said weir, &c., had been so erected, &c. is not, and at the said several times when &c. was not, a public common navigable river for all the liege &c. to navigate &c. on the said part of the said river, in which &c., from *Worcester* &c., nor ought

1838.

WILLIAMS *against* WILCOX.

ought the liege &c., before or at the said times when &c., of right to have navigated &c., nor still of right &c., in and along the said part of the said river in which &c., from *Worcester* &c., at all times &c., in manner and form &c.

Rejoinder. That the said part of the said river, in and across which the said weir, &c., had been so erected and placed, is, and at the said several times when &c. was, part of the said river *Severn*; and that the liege &c., before and at the said times when &c., ought of right to have navigated and passed with barges in and along the said part of the said river in which &c., from *Worcester* to *Shrewsbury*, at all times of the year, at their free &c., when and so often as the channel of the said river had been or was choked or stopped up so as to prevent the liege &c. from navigating and passing with barges in, through, over, or along the said river except by navigating and passing in, through, or along the said part of the said river in which &c.; and that the said channel of the said river, being the said part of the said river in the plea mentioned to have been near to the said part of the said river in which &c., and to have been so choked up as aforesaid, was, at the said times when &c., choked and stopped up so as to prevent the liege &c. from navigating and passing with barges in, over, through, or along the said river except by navigating and passing in, over, through, and along the said part of the said river, in which &c. Verification.

Surrejoinder. That the liege &c., before and at the said times when &c., ought not of right to have navigated and passed with barges in and along the said part of the said river in which &c., from *Worcester* &c., at

 all

1838.

Williams against Wilcox.

all times &c., when and so often as the channel &c., in manner and form &c. Conclusion to the country: and issue thereon.

On the trial before *Williams* J., at the *Shropshire* Spring assizes, 1836, the plaintiff proved the trespass, and, in support of his issue on the second plea, produced evidence to shew the antiquity of the weir and fishery, beginning with an extract from Domesday book, in which the fishery is mentioned. A great number of documents were put in by him: among others, an extract from the chartulary of *Haghmon* Abbey, containing copies of grants of the fishery to the church, and of a way to the fishery; the earliest appearing to have been made in the year 1172–3. This chartulary appeared to contain copies of the deeds and charters relating to the property of the abbey: but no evidence was given of search for the originals. A judgment was also put in of *Mich. T.* 1 *H.* 6., in a cause wherein the Abbot of *Haghmon* was indicted for obstructing the navigation of the *Severn*, and pleaded an immemorial right of taking fish in the weir, that the navigation was not obstructed, and that the weir was not made since 3 *Ed.* 1.; all which was found in his favour. The counsel for the defendants objected that no ancient right could be paramount to the right of navigation; and that, at any rate, the antiquity of such a special right could not be given in evidence under this issue, but its nature or origin, by grant or otherwise, should have been expressly pleaded. The learned Judge received the evidence, and left it to the jury to say whether there had been an immemorial right, under a grant from the crown, of obstructing the navigation by the weir, even when the rest of the channel was obstructed. The jury

1838.

WILLIAMS *against* WILCOX.

jury found for the plaintiff. In *Easter* term 1836, *Maule*, on the objections urged at the trial, and for misdirection, and also on the ground that no search for the originals of the deeds in the chartulary had been shewn, obtained a rule *nisi* for arresting the judgment, or for a new trial. In *Michaelmas* term last (*a*),

Talfourd Serjt. and *R. V. Richards*, shewed cause. The first question is, whether the Crown had, before Magna Charta, power to grant the right of erecting a weir for a fishery which might afterwards obstruct the navigation of a river. It is not absolutely necessary to contend that a weir could have been granted which created an obstruction at the time of the grant. Then, could there be a legal grant to erect a weir obstructing any part of a navigable river? If there could, would the weir become illegal by an alteration of circumstances, as by such a change in the bed of the river that the obstruction entirely prevented the passage? It is impossible to decide this point by the analogy of a right of highway. Before Magna Charta, the king was understood to be owner of the soil of navigable rivers, as high as the tide flows; *Com. Dig. Navigation*, (A), (B); but he never had such a right as to highways. In the case of highways, as of rivers not navigable, the presumption is that the soil belongs to the owners of the adjoining land. The right of passage along navigable rivers, like that of fishery in them, so far as the tide rises, was originally subject to the right of the Crown

(*a*) *November* 16th, 1837: Before Lord *Denman* C. J., *Patteson*, *Williams*, and *Coleridge* Js.

to

1838.

WILLIAMS *against* WILCOX.

to obstruct (*a*). The right of passing along a highway arises from a presumed dedication to the public by a private proprietor; nothing of this kind is applicable to a navigable river. It will be said that the language of Magna Charta (9 *H.* 3. *c.* 23.) is in favour of the defendants: "Omnes kidelli deponantur de cetero penitùs per Tamisiam et Medweyam et per totam Angliam nisi per costeram maris." But it cannot be inferred from this that weirs were illegal before the statute. Indeed it may be rather inferred that until that time such erections were legal; and this inference is strengthened by 4 stat. 25 *Ed.* 3. *c.* 4., which recites that the passage of boats and ships in the great rivers of *England* is annoyed by the inhancing (*le lever*) of, among other obstructions, weirs and kiddles, and enacts that all set up in the time of *Ed.* 1., and since, whereby ships and boats were impeded from passing the river, should be out and utterly pulled down, without being renewed. This statute is confirmed and enforced by stat. 45 *E.* 3. *c.* 2., and by stat. 1 *H.* 4. *c.* 12. This last statute, *s.* 10., directs that such weirs and kiddles as are too much enhanced or straitened should be corrected, pulled down, and amended: but it contains a saving of a reasonable substance of weirs, kiddles, &c., so in old times (before *Ed.* 1.) made and levied. The statute of sewers, 23 *H.* 8. *c.* 5., does not authorise the abatement of any erection which has not been made or enhanced since the commencement of the reign of *Edward* the First; *The Case of Chester Mill upon the River of Dee* (*b*). So in *Callis on*

(*a*) *Talfourd* Serjt. referred to the case of the *Minsterworth* fisheries in the *Severn* (mentioned in *Evans* v. *Taylor*, 7 *A.* & *E.* 617.), as illustrating the rights in navigable rivers.

(*b*) 10 *Rep.* 137 *b.*

Sewers,

1838.

WILLIAMS *against* WILCOX.

Sewers, p. 266 (*a*), it is said (speaking of the same statute), "All mills, mill-dams, flood-gates, weres, stanks, stakes, kiddels, and such like, are not to be put down and overthrown: but such as are ancient and are thereby grown to be the proper inheritances of men, and such also which are useful and necessary are to be maintained, kept, and repaired;" and, at p. 267, the power of the Commissioners of Sewers is limited as follows: "If one do erect and build a were, mill, mill dam, or other thing on a river navigable, to the hindrance of navigation; or if there was an ancient were which was enhanced of late years." In *Hale de Jure Maris* (*b*) it is said, "A subject may by prescription have the interest of fishing in an arm of the sea, in a creek or port of the sea, or in a certain precinct or extent lying within the sea; and these not only free fishing, but several fishing. Fishing may be of two kinds ordinarily, viz. the fishing with the net, which may be either as a liberty without the soil, or as a liberty arising by reason of and in concomitance with the soil, or interest or propriety of it; or otherwise it is a local fishing, that ariseth by and from the propriety of the soil. Such are *gurgites*, weares, fishing-places, *borachiæ stachiæ*, &c. which are the very soil itself, and so frequently agreed in our books." The existence of the weir from time immemorial furnishes in itself evidence that whatever right of navigation existed at any time has been legally put an end to; *Rex* v. *Montague* (*c*). *Rex* v. *Clark* (*d*) is an instance of a modern obstruction to a navigable river being held illegal. Then what limit can be assigned to the right of the Crown to grant such weirs before the time

(*a*) 4th ed.

(*b*) Part 1. Ch. 5. P. 18.

(*c*) 4 *B. & C.* 598.

(*d*) 12 *Mod.* 615.

of

1838.

Williams *against* Wilcox.

of *Ed.* I.? The course of a river is liable to change from physical circumstances, which again distinguishes the case from that of a highway; but such change cannot make unlawful an erection which was previously lawful. In *Callis on Sewers*, 78, it is said that the use of the banks of the sea and of great rivers is common to all the King's liege people, as to tie ships to the trees, to tow them, to lade and unlade merchandise, and to dry nets. But, in *Ball* v. *Herbert* (a), *Buller* J. denies that this principle prevails in *English* law; and he says, "*Callis* compares a navigable river to an highway; but no two cases can be more distinct. In the latter case, if the way be founderous and out of repair, the public have a right to go on the adjoining land: but if a river should happen to be choked up with mud, that would not give the public a right to cut another passage through the adjoining lands." If the public have such right of passage as is contended for, they must have the right of using the banks for towing up the stream, since they can use the passage upwards in no other way; but that they have no such right of towing appears from *Ball* v. *Herbert* (a). In an earlier case, *Zangers* v. *Whiskard* (b), the same point was raised, but not decided. In most of the cases respecting weirs the question has been only whether a party, entitled to a weir of one sort, can convert it into a weir of another sort; as in *Weld* v. *Hornby* (c). If it had appeared here that the plaintiff had done so, he must have failed; but the jury found that the weir had existed from time immemorial in its present state. At what time then could the public acquire a right? Suppose a vessel, requiring more

(a) 3 *T. R.* 263.

(b) Cited in *Ball* v. *Herbert*, 3 *T. R.* 259.

(c) 7 *East*, 195.

room

room than the unobstructed part of the channel could give, had come into use; can it be said that the weir would thereupon have become illegal? The right of fishery in navigable rivers, for all the king's subjects, appears from *Carter* v. *Murcot* (*a*): it seems to follow that the Crown had a right, at common law, to erect a weir in aid of the fishing. Secondly, the question is properly raised on these pleadings. The plaintiff traverses the right of the public to the passage, and sets up his right to a weir appurtenant to a fishery. The right of the public was negatived, and the plaintiff's right affirmed, by evidence of immemorial user, from which a grant by the Crown might be presumed. It was not necessary to aver a grant; and, if it was, the defect is cured by verdict; note (1) to *Stennel* v. *Hogg* (*b*). *Yarborough* v. *The Bank of England* (*c*) and *Tilson* v. *The Warwick Gas Light Company* (*d*) shew how far the Court will carry the doctrine of presumption after verdict. But here a right of way is traversed generally; and, in support of the traverse, evidence is given of the particular circumstances which may have put an end to it. [They also proceeded to discuss the question as to the admissibility of the chartulary; but the judgment of the Court renders it unnecessary to report this part of the argument.]

Maule and *Whateley*, contrà. First, the weir was illegal. The analogy between the right of passing along a navigable river and the right of passing along a highway is not impeached by the tests suggested on the other side. There is no right to deviate, in case of

(*a*) 4 *Burr.* 2162.
(*b*) 1 *Wms. Saund.* 228 *a.* note (1).
(*c*) 16 *East*, 6.
(*d*) 4 *B. & C.* 962.

stoppage;

1838.

Williams against Wilcox.

stoppage; but that is because a deviation by going upon the adjoining shore could not be an exercise of the right of passage. The analogy would arise if the stream shifted its bed; and in that event the right of passage would follow. It is said that the way up the stream could not be used except by towing; but the way down the stream might nevertheless be used. There is no authority for the position that the soil of navigable rivers is in the Crown. It is indeed said, in *Com. Dig. Navigation* (A), that "The king has the property *tam aquæ quam soli*, and all profits in the sea, and all navigable rivers." For this, however, he cites *Callis on Sewers*, 17, and Sir *J. Davies*, 56, 57 (*a*); and the passage in *Callis* (*b*) which seems to be referred to is as follows: "And Sir *John Davies*, in his *Irish* Reports in the said case of *Banne*, saith, 'That so far as *the sea* doth flow and reflow, it is a royal stream, and the fishings therein belong to the Crown.'" And the note on the same passage is, "So the soil of all other rivers," that is of all navigable, "as high as there is flux and reflux of *the sea*, is in the king, if no other claim it by prescription, *Siderfin*, 1. 149." (*c*). These authorities clearly refer only to such estuaries as may be termed arms of the sea. Even if the plaintiff had a right to maintain the weir while it did not impede the passage of the river, that would be a qualified right, subject to be devested as soon as there was no other passage; per *Holroyd* J. in *Rex* v. *Montague* (*d*). It is difficult to see how the plaintiff, upon any supposition, can maintain trespass for a weir not on his own soil; but,

(*a*) *Le Case del Royall Piscarie de la Banne.* (*b*) Page 77.

(*c*) *Bulstrode* v. *Hall.*

(*d*) 4 *B.* & *C.* 604., where the dictum of *Thorp* (C. J. of K. B.) is cited, from 22 *Ass.* pl. 93. fol. 106 A.

1838.

WILLIAMS against WILCOX.

but, supposing that he can, he is at any rate in no better situation than the owner of the adjacent land, who has, of course, a right to erect a wall on his own land, but who loses that right as soon at the land becomes part of the course of the river. Even where the soil undoubtedly is in the Crown, as where the locus in quo is in an arm of the sea, the King cannot exercise his ownership so as to deprive the subject of his rights. In *Weld* v. *Hornby* (a) Lord *Ellenborough* says, "The right set up by the defendant to have a stone weir is plainly founded upon encroachment. The erection of weirs across rivers was reprobated in the earliest periods of our law. They were considered as public nuisances." In that case the alteration of a weir was complained of as injurious to the plaintiff's fisheries. But a navigable river, *ex vi termini*, is a river subject to a right of public navigation. Magna Charta is in the nature of a declaratory act throughout. *Glanville* (b), as cited in 2 *Inst.* 38., treats weirs as a nuisance at common law; and in *Hale de Jure Maris* (c) it is said, "All nuisances and impediments of passages of boats and vessels, though in the private soil of any person, may be punished by indictments, and removed; and this was the reason of the statute of Magna Charta cap. 23." It is true that there may be found statutory savings of ancient weirs. But the intention of such clauses is merely to protect such weirs from the extraordinary powers granted under the acts, and not to recognise their general legality. Weirs existing before *Edward* the First might be legal or not; so far as the fishery was concerned, perhaps they were legal: but it cannot be inferred that they could be legal

(a) 7 *East*, 195.

(b) Lib. IX. c. 11.

(c) Part 1. c. 3. p. 9.

if

1838.

WILLIAMS *against* WILCOX.

if they obstructed navigation. As to 4 stat. 25 *E.* 3. *c.* 4., it does not follow from the language there used that weirs were legal up to that time. It is known that early statutes often originated in complaints that the law was not observed; and they were then passed, not to alter the law, but to meet the grievance in the particular case. In stat. 9 *H.* 6. *c.* 5. there is an express enactment that there shall be free passage by the *Severn;* and stat. 12 *E.* 4. *c.* 7. is directed against impediments by weirs. The remarks of *Buller* J. in *Ball* v. *Herbert* (*a*), so far as they can be sustained, apply to rights claimed on the adjacent land by virtue of the supposed analogy to a common highway. *The Case of Chester Mill upon the river of Dee* (*b*) is inapplicable, not being the case of a navigable river. If the passage cited from *Hale de Jure Maris*, part i. c. 5., be applicable, it cannot be supported; for it would shew that a subject may have a right to obstruct the navigation of an arm of the sea. The prerogative of the Crown is limited by law: if it were not so in this respect, the King might stop up a highway. He cannot dispense with a nuisance to the highways; *Thomas* v. *Sorrell* (*c*). In *Callis on Sewers*, p. 266., the sentence before the passage referred to on the other side shews that, in that author's opinion, all walls, banks, sewers, &c., were not to be maintained, "because in tract of time some may prove unnecessary and unuseful, which for that cause may be pulled down." A fortiori, a weir, which has become, not simply useless, but a complete obstruction to navigation, may be pulled down. It is not necessary here to contend that an ancient weir, partially obstructing the river, may not be legal; though the legality is at least very questionable. But here is

(*a*) 3 *T. R.* 263.

(*b*) 10 *Rep.* 137 *b.*

(*c*) *Vaugh.* 339.

a total

1838.

WILLIAMS against WILCOX.

a total stoppage. From the judgment read at the trial, it appears that the Abbott of *Haghmon* pleaded, not merely the antiquity of the weir, but that it was no nuisance. Had the antiquity of the right been a defence, this plea would have been double; which is an argument of much weight in the case of pleadings of that age. In the present case, the evidence at the trial shewed only a right to have some weir, not a weir which obstructed the navigation. It is true that a subject may have, by prescription, an exclusive right of fishing in a navigable river; *Lord Fitzwalter's Case* (*a*), *Carter* v. *Murcot* (*b*): but that is subject to the right of navigation; *Anonymous* case in 1 *Campbell* (*c*). But, supposing the plaintiff to have the right contended for, he cannot avail himself of it on this record. It is not denied that the weir is erected in a public navigable river; nor is the erection justified. There is merely a traverse of the right of navigation in this particular part. That is either a general denial of the right of the public to pass along navigable rivers, which is a mere question of law; or it admits that the river is public and navigable, without shewing any thing to deprive the public of the right of navigation in the locus in quo when the rest of the channel is stopped. The finding of the jury on such an issue is ineffectual: it is as if issue were joined on an allegation that a bond did not "thereby" become void. [They then argued against the admissibility of the chartulary; on which point *Bullen* v. *Michel* (*d*) was cited.]

Lord DENMAN C. J., in this term (*June* 13th), delivered the judgment of the Court.

(*a*) 1 *Mod.* 105.

(*b*) 4 *Burr.* 2162. See note (*a*) to *Rogers* v. *Allen*, 1 *Campb.* 312.

(*c*) Note to *Harmond* v. *Pearson*, 1 *Campb.* 517. (*d*) 4 *Dow*, 297.

This

1838.

WILLIAMS *against* WILCOX.

This was a case tried before my brother *Williams* at the *Shrewsbury* Spring assizes for 1836. A verdict passed for the plaintiff for 1*s.* damages; and the defendants contend that the judgment should be arrested, or a verdict entered for themselves, or, at all events, that they are entitled to a new trial, on account of the improper reception of evidence objected to. Their objection under the last head appears to be two-fold; first, they deny that any evidence was receivable to shew the antiquity of a weir mentioned in the pleadings; secondly, they object to the admissibility of a particular document tendered for that purpose on a specific ground.

In the view which we take of this case, it will be necessary to dispose of all these grounds.

(His lordship here shortly stated the pleadings, and then proceeded.) Subject to the questions upon the evidence hereafter to be discussed, the case between the parties is this. The plaintiff has established the existence of the weir in question by a royal grant made at some period prior to the time of *Edward* 1.; but it stands across part of a public navigable river, a part, indeed, not required for the purposes of navigation at the date of the grant, but, at the time of the commission of the trespass, necessary for those purposes, by reason of the residue of the channel having become choked up. He contends that, at the date of the grant, the Crown had the power of making it, even to the disturbance, or total prevention, of the right of navigation by the subject; or that, at all events, it had the power of making such a grant, if, in the then existing state of circumstances, it did not interfere with the rights of the subject: and that such a grant, valid in its inception, will not become invalid by reason of any change of circumstances

1838.

WILLIAMS *against* WILCOX.

cumstances which may afterwards affect the residue of the channel.

This latter point, although argued with much ingenuity, does not present any serious difficulty to our minds; and we may conveniently dispose of it in passing. If the subject (which this view of the case concedes) had by common law a right of passage in the channel of the river, paramount to the power of the Crown, we cannot conceive such right to have been originally other than a right locally unlimited to pass in all and every part of the channel. The nature of the highway which a navigable river affords, liable to be affected by natural and uncontroulable causes, presenting conveniences in different parts and on different sides according to the changes of wind or direction of the vessel, and attended by the important circumstance that on no one is any duty imposed by the common law to do that which would be analogous to the ordinary repair of a common highway to remove obstructions, namely, clear away sand banks and preserve any accustomed channel, — all these considerations make it an almost irresistible conclusion that the paramount right, if it existed at all, must have been a right in every part of the space between the banks. It cannot be disputed that the channel of a public navigable river is a King's highway, and is properly so described; and, if the analogy between it and a highway by land were complete, there could be no doubt that the right would be such as we now lay down; for the right of passage in a highway by land extends over every part of it. Now, although it may be conceded that the analogy is not complete, yet the very circumstances pointed out by the counsel for the plaintiff in which it fails, are strong to

1838.

WILLIAMS *against* WILCOX.

to shew that in this respect at least it holds. The absence of any right to go extra viam in case of the channel being choked, and the want of a definite obligation on any one to repair, only render it more important, in order to make the highway an effectual one, that the right of passage should extend to all parts of the channel. If then, *subject to this right*, the Crown had at any period the prerogative of raising weirs in such parts as were not at the time actually required by the subject for the purposes of navigation, it follows, from the very nature of a paramount right on the one hand and a subordinate right on the other, that the latter must cease whensoever it cannot be exercised but to the prejudice of the former. If, in the present case, the subject has not at this moment the right to use that part of the channel on which the weir stands, it is only because of the royal grant; and that grant must then be alleged at its date to have done away for ever, in so much of the channel, the right of the public: but that is to suppose the subordinate right controuling that which is admitted to be paramount, which is absurd. On the other hand, there is nothing unreasonable or unjust in supposing the right to erect the weir subject to the necessities of the public when they should arise: for, the right of the public being supposed to be paramount by law, the grantee must be taken to be cognizant of such right: and the same natural peculiarities, and the same absence of any obligation by law on any one to counteract those peculiarities above-mentioned, would give him full notice of the probability that at some period his grant would be determined. We do not therefore think that the plaintiff can sustain his second point.

To the first point, on which his case must now rest,

two

1838.

WILLIAMS *against* WILCOX.

two objections are made by the defendants. They deny that, by the law of *England*, the Crown ever had the power of interfering with the navigation of public navigable rivers; and they contend, secondly, that, if any such power existed, and the plaintiff relies upon an exercise of it, that specific exercise should have been replied to the plea, the allegations of which shewed, primâ facie, that the weir in question was a wrongful erection. For want of this, they say, the plea has received no answer; it alleges the obstruction of the channel of a navigable river, that is admitted; but no lawful cause for such obstruction is shewn.

We are of opinion, however, that this second objection is not sustainable; and that, upon the face of the record, a sufficient answer in substance appears to the plea, if the Crown had the power of making the supposed grant. It is an elementary rule in pleading, that, when a state of facts is relied on, it is enough to allege it simply, without setting out the subordinate facts which are the means of producing it, or the evidence sustaining the allegation. Thus, in a case very familiar, and almost identical with the present, if a trespass be justified by a plea of highway, the pleader never states how the locus in quo became highway; and, if the plaintiff's case is that the locus in quo, by an order of justices, award of inclosure commissioners, local act of parliament, or any other lawful means, had ceased to be such at the time alleged in the declaration, he simply puts in issue the fact of its being a highway at that time, without alleging the particular mode by which he intends to shew, in proof, that it had before then ceased to be such. So, here, the defendants, relying on the common law, allege that the weir is wrongfully placed in part of a

 common

1838.

WILLIAMS *against* WILCOX.

common navigable river; the plaintiff, relying on a grant, which, as he contends, in effect took the site of the weir out of the public and navigable channel of the river, properly, as it appears to us, abstains from setting out that grant, and with substantial correctness replies only that that part of the river was other than, and wholly distinct from, the channel in which the right and user of navigation existed, and was not a public common navigable river. It is true that this mode of pleading does not disclose to the defendants the case on which the plaintiff relies: but, to object to it on this ground, is to misconceive one object of pleading, and to forget another: the certainty or particularity of pleading is directed, not to the disclosure of *the case* of a party, but to the informing the Court, the jury, and the opponent, of *the specific proposition* for which he contends; and a scarcely less important object is the bringing the parties to issue on a single and certain point, avoiding that prolixity and uncertainty which would very probably arise from stating all the steps which lead up to that point.

Having then thus disposed of the subordinate matters on each side, we come to that on which the argument mainly turned, that is to say, the power of the Crown at common law to interfere with the channels of public navigable rivers. On the one side the contention is that, prior to Magna Charta, the power of the Crown was absolute over them; and that this weir, by the antiquity assigned to it by the finding of the jury, is saved from the operation of that or any succeeding statute; while, on the other, it is alleged that they are and were highways to all intents and purposes, which the Crown had no power to limit or interfere with, and that as well the restraints enacted by, as the confirmations implied

from,

1838.

WILLIAMS *against* WILCOX.

from, the statutes alluded to have nothing to do with the present question.

After an attentive examination of the authorities and the statutes referred to in the argument, we cannot see any satisfactory evidence that the power of the Crown in this respect was greater at the common law before the passing of Magna Charta than it has been since. It is clear that the channels of public navigable rivers were always highways: up to the point reached by the flow of the tide the soil was presumably in the Crown; and above that point, whether the soil at common law was in the Crown or the owners of the adjacent lands (a point perhaps not free from doubt), there was at least a jurisdiction in the Crown, according to Sir *Matthew Hale*, "to reform and punish nuisances in all rivers, whether fresh or salt, that are a common passage, not only for ships and greater vessels, but also for smaller, as barges or boats:" *De Jure Maris*, Part I. C. 2. (*a*). In either case the right of the subject to pass up and down was complete. In *The Case of the Bann Fishery* (*b*), where the reporter is speaking of rivers within the flux and reflux of the tide, it is stated that this right was by *the King's permission*, for the ease and commodity of the people: but, if this be the true foundation, and if the same may be also properly said of the same right in the higher parts of rivers, still the permission supposed must be coeval with the monarchy, and anterior to any grant by any particular monarch of the right to erect a weir in any particular river. It is difficult, therefore, to see how any such grant made in derogation of the public right previously existing, and in direct opposition to that

(*a*) Page 8.

(*b*) *Davies's Rep.* 57 *a.*

1838.

WILLIAMS *against* WILCOX.

duty, which the law casts on the Crown, of reforming and punishing all nuisances which obstruct the navigation of public rivers, could have been in its inception valid at common law. Nor can we find, in the language of the statutes referred to, anything inconsistent with this conclusion. They speak indeed of acts done in violation of this public right; but they do not refer them to any power legally existing in the Crown, which for the future they propose to abridge. We are, therefore, of opinion that the legality of this weir cannot be sustained on the supposition of any power existing by law in the Crown in the time of *Edward* 1., which is now taken away.

But this does not exhaust the question; because that which was not legal at first may have been subsequently legalised. The question of fact was submitted to the jury most favourably for the defendants, whether any such grant had been made before Magna Charta as the plaintiff relied on. And the jury, upon the evidence, have found in the affirmative. If, therefore, upon an examination of the statutes relied on by the plaintiff, such a grant, whether valid or not at common law, appears to be saved by their operation, the objection of the defendants falls to the ground. And we think that to be the true construction of the statutes.

The learned counsel for the defendants is probably correct in saying that the twenty-third chapter of Magna Charta may be laid out of the case. The kidelli there spoken of appear, from the 2 *Inst.* p. 38., and the *Chester Mill Case* (*a*), to have been open weirs erected for the taking of fish; and the evil intended to be remedied by

(*a*) 10 *Rep.* 137 *b.*

the

1838.

WILLIAMS *against* WILCOX.

the statute was the unlawful destruction of that important article of consumption. That statute, therefore, being pointed at another mischief, might leave any question of nuisance by obstruction to the passage of boats exactly as it stood at common law. But the same remark does not apply to 4 stat. 25 *Ed.* 3. *c.* 4. That begins by reciting that the common passage of boats and ships in the great rivers of *England* is oftentimes annoyed by the inhansing (a mistranslation of the word *lever* for levying or setting up (*a*)) of gorces, mills, weirs, stanks, stakes, and kiddles, and then provides for the utter destruction of all such as have been levied and set up in the time of *Edward* 1. and after. It further directs that writs shall be sent to the sheriffs of the places where need shall be, to survey and inquire, and to do thereof execution; and also the justices shall be thereupon assigned at all times that shall be needful. It is clear, we think, that, in any criminal proceeding for the demolition of this weir which had been instituted immediately after the passing of this statute, it would have been a sufficient defence to have shewn its erection before the time of *Edward* 1.: and, considering the concise language of statutes of that early period, we think the statute would equally have been an answer in any civil proceeding at the suit of a party injured. Assuming the weir to have been illegally erected before the date of Magna Charta, it is not unreasonable to suppose that a sort of compromise was come to: similar nuisances were probably very numerous; but they were probably, many of them, of long standing: it may have been impossible to procure, or it may well have been

(*a*) Corrected in the translation of stat. 45 *Ed.* 3. *c.* 2. (recital).

1838.

WILLIAMS *against* WILCOX.

thought unreasonable to insist on, an act which should direct those to be abated which had acquired the sanction of time: and a line was therefore drawn, which, preventing an increase of the nuisance for the future, and abating it in all the instances which commenced within a given period, impliedly legalised those which could be traced to an earlier period. This appears to us the proper effect to be attributed to the statute; and, if it be, it disposes of any difference between a criminal and civil proceeding. The earlier weirs were not merely protected against the specific measures mentioned in the act, but rendered absolutely legal. If this would have been a good answer immediately after the act passed, it is at least equally good now; and therefore, of stat. 45 *Ed.* 3. *c.* 2. and stat. 1 *H.* 4. *c.* 12., it is unnecessary to say more than that they do not at all weaken the defence which the defendants have under the former statute.

We are of opinion, therefore, that there is no ground for arresting the judgment or entering a verdict for the defendants: and the conclusion to which we have come on these points decides, of course, that the learned Judge was quite right in receiving evidence of the antiquity of the weir.

A single point, however, still remains to be mentioned, on which the defendants claim a new trial.

In order to establish the antiquity of the weir, the plaintiff tendered in evidence what purported to be a copy of an ancient grant found in a chartulary of *Haghmon Abbey;* the single objection now relied on against its reception is, that no search was proved to have been made for the original. The note of the learned Judge is very specific as to the objections made at the trial,

and

1838.

WILLIAMS *against* WILCOX.

and his memory clear as to what then occurred; but he has no minute or recollection of this point having been pressed; and it is an objection so much upon the surface, that, if brought clearly to his notice, it is scarcely conceivable but that it must have prevailed; indeed we think that it must have been acquiesced in by the counsel on the other side. We do not doubt that it was in fact made; but, as the whole class of that evidence, of which this document formed a single item, was also objected to, and the attention of the learned Judge was naturally directed to that more general and important objection, it is probable that this was not so made as to attract his notice. In all cases, and especially in one so circumstanced as this, it is the business of the counsel to take care that the Judge's attention is drawn to any objection on which he intends afterwards to rely. Justice requires this, not so much to the Judge, as to the opposite party, who may be willing, as in the present case would probably have been done, rather to waive the benefit of the evidence than put his verdict in peril on the issue of the objection. If, by inadvertence, this was not done at the trial, we think we ought not, either upon general principles or with a view to the particular circumstances of this case, to allow the objection now to prevail. The admitted document was but one of many to prove what in the end was unquestionable and unquestioned, the very great antiquity of the weir: its admission, therefore, occasioned no injustice: its rejection could not and ought not to have varied the verdict.

The rule, therefore, on all points will be discharged.

Rule discharged.

1838.

The QUEEN *against* Lord GODOLPHIN and Another, Justices of CAMBRIDGESHIRE.

A Friendly Society enrolled its rules in 1794, under stat. 33 G. 3. c. 54. In 1804 alterations were made in them, but, by a neglect for which the society was not to blame, the altered rules were never enrolled. They were, however, acted upon, and the original ones disused, till 1835, when the omission to enrol was for the first time discovered. On motion for a mandamus to justices to hear the complaint of a member who had been expelled in 1836,

Held: 1. That the rules as altered could not legally be acted upon.

2. That it was at least doubtful whether the original rules continued in force, and, consequently, that the Court could not issue a mandamus to the justices, but must leave the applicant to his remedy in equity.

IN *Hilary* term, 1837, a rule nisi was obtained for a mandamus to *Francis* Lord *Godolphin* and *John Hailstone*, clerk, two of the justices in and for the county of *Cambridge*, acting within the division of *Cambridge*, commanding them to issue their summons to the president and stewards of a certain Friendly Society established in the town of *Cambridge*, called the *Old Club*, and to hear and determine the complaint of *Thomas Lupson* against the said society and the officers thereof for having expelled him from the said society, and to make such order therein as to them should seem just. The affidavits used on application for the rule stated the following facts.

The society was established in 1755. Its rules were enrolled with the clerk of the peace for the county in 1794, and remain so enrolled, and unaltered. Those rules were acted upon till 1804, when they were altered and reprinted (*a*). The society directed one *Driver*, an attorney's clerk, to get the amended rules enrolled; *Lupson* paid him money for that purpose; and *Lupson* and the rest of the members understood and believed that it had been done. Under that impression the amended rules were acted upon till 1835; and, since 1804, various applications have been made to magistrates, by persons

(*a*) The nature of the alterations was not specified by the affidavits on either side.

expelled,

1838.

The QUEEN *against* Lord GODOLPHIN.

expelled, for readmission, all which have been adjudicated upon. In 1835 it was discovered, and the society informed, that the amended rules had never been enrolled; but no step has hitherto been taken for enroling them. In *September* 1836, *Lupson* was expelled the society for alleged misconduct. He thereupon laid an information before the magistrates of the division of *Cambridge*, who issued a summons to *Massey*, the president, and *Briggs*, one of the stewards, to answer the information. On the hearing, *November* 12th, 1836, before the magistrates named in the present rule, and two others, *Massey* and *Briggs* contended that the magistrates had no jurisdiction, because the rules, as amended in 1804, had, in effect, and in point of law, annulled the rules of 1794. The magistrates thought that, under these circumstances, they had not jurisdiction, and therefore they refused to adjudicate. The affidavits stated that *Massey* himself, in 1830, after being expelled the society, had obtained readmission by an order of justices; and that, in *December* 1836, he, being the president, and two other persons, the stewards, had drawn 75*l.* out of the society's funds, stating to the treasurer at the time (in answer to a question from him) that they applied as officers of the society, and under its rules as enrolled.

The affidavits in answer stated that, in 1804, certain "rules and articles, differing most materially and essentially from the original ones," were adopted by the society; and that, in 1820 (with the sanction of *Lupson*, who was then president), certain other rules or articles were adopted by the society, and have been acted upon (with some alteration as to allowances) ever since, but were never exhibited at sessions or enrolled. Several members of the society, admitted at various periods

1838.

The QUEEN *against* Lord GODOLPHIN.

periods from 1816 downwards, stated that, since they had been members, the rules of 1794 had not been acted upon by the society, nor had their existence been known to the deponents, or, as they believed, to any of the present society, till about 1834; and the general belief of the members, until then, had been "that the present rules of the said society were enrolled," which belief originated "in the representations made to the society to that effect by the said *Thomas Lupson*." Counsel were heard for and against the rule in last *Hilary* and *Easter* terms (*a*).

Kelly, against the rule. The justices had no jurisdiction to give relief under stat. 33 *G.* 3. *c.* 54. *s.* 15., unless the rules to be acted upon in pursuance of that clause had been enrolled according to sects. 2 and 3; *Rex* v. *Gilkes* (*b*). That was not a case where it appeared, as here, that the society had had rules enrolled which they had subsequently departed from; but *Ex parte Norrish* (*c*) was such a case. There, on a petition to the Master of the Rolls, under sect. 8 of the statute, for the transfer of funds from an old to a new trustee, it appeared that amended rules had been enrolled in 1813; that soon afterwards dissatisfaction had arisen, and a committee had been appointed to regulate the society's affairs; but that since that time (the case being heard in 1821) "the rules had not been attended to; meetings had not been held, or payments made, and officers had not been regularly appointed;" and that "the new trustee had not been chosen according to the rules."

(*a*) *January* 11th, before Lord *Denman* C. J., *Littledale*, *Williams*, and *Coleridge* Js. And *April* 26th, before Lord *Denman* C. J., *Littledale*, *Patteson*, and *Coleridge* Js.

(*b*) 8 *B.* & *C.* 439.

(*c*) *Jac. Rep.* 162.

Sir

1838.

The QUEEN *against* Lord GODOLPHIN.

Sir *T. Plumer*, M. R., said there, "that it was a great misfortune to these societies, that they were in the habit of deviating from their rules. Here, since the year 1813, they had ceased to act upon the rules that had been registered; and had proceeded upon a different plan. What had been done since, had been done by agreement, and not under the regulations. They had become dissolved; and the Court had no longer any jurisdiction under the act; if any relief could be given it must be upon bill." The same observations apply here: if a society ceases to act upon its rules, much more if, in practice, it adopts new ones, the magistrates, being bound to administer justice according to rules existing, have no ground to proceed upon. Here, there were rules in force, under sect. 2, till 1804; when altered in that year, they should, according to sect. 3, have been enrolled; but the society, while it abandoned the old rules, omitted to enrol those which they meant to proceed upon for the future. Enrolment does not depend on mere ministerial acts: it implies that the rules have been submitted to the justices in quarter sessions, to be reviewed and allowed or disallowed by them. The effect of an omission like the present was discussed, and the validity of rules altered but not enrolled was held doubtful at least, in *Rex* v. *The Witham Savings' Bank* (*a*). *Battey* v. *Townrow* (*b*) is an express authority on the point now raised. If the question be even doubtful, the Court will not issue a mandamus to justices (*c*). [*Gunning*, on the same side, was stopped by the Court.]

(*a*) 1 *A. & E.* 321. *S. C.* 3 *Nev. & M.* 416. (*b*) 4 *Camp.* 5.

(*c*) It was further contended, that the motion ought to have been for a mandamus to four justices; and *Rex* v. *Sillifant*, 4 *A. & E.* 354., was cited; but nothing ultimately turned on this point.

B. Andrews

1838.

The QUEEN *against* Lord GODOLPHIN.

B. Andrews and *W. H. Watson*, contrà. If the amended rules were of no effect for want of enrolment, those enrolled in 1794 must be still the governing rules of the society. If neither are in force, the effect is virtually a dissolution of the club; but, by sect. 12, a society of this kind can be dissolved only with the consent of five sixths of the members, and on other conditions there specified; such a dissolution cannot be indirectly brought about by an alteration of the rules. An alteration, without enrolment, is by sect. 3 not to have "any force or effect," and cannot therefore operate to the dissolution of the society. [*Littledale* J. The society has been acting on the unenrolled rules for thirty-four years, and probably distributing the funds in a manner quite different from that originally directed. Can you still say that they are governed by the old rules?] The Court might reasonably suppose that, in the long period of time since the new rules were made, they have been enrolled. [*Littledale* J. That is impossible.] Then it must follow that the old rules continue, whatever has been the lapse of time. [*Littledale* J. If so, the magistrates may be called upon to overturn all the payments made since 1804.] They must do justice as well as they can. *Massey*, the president, against whom the present application is directed, has shewn, by application to the justices, and otherwise, that he considers the society as still subsisting, and governed by rules. Other members have made similar admissions. If the effect of an alteration in the rules be to destroy the society, how do they become operative for that purpose? By the mere making, or by being acted on? And, in the latter case, what length of time is necessary? Could not a member of this society have enforced the old

1838.

The QUEEN against Lord GODOLPHIN.

old rules in 1805 or 1806? [*Coleridge* J. On the other hand it may be asked how long the old rules are to continue in force after the society has ceased to act upon them? Are they to be valid at the end of fifty years, when there is perhaps an entirely new body of members?] That may be inconvenient; but there is also great inconvenience if those rules are to be held invalid while the new ones also are not in force. The funds are in the hands of a person called the treasurer: if there are no rules on which the society can act, those funds can be recovered only by an equity suit, to which all the members must be parties. [*Coleridge* J. If new rules were enrolled, they would perhaps have a retrospective effect. There must always be an interval between the making of new rules and the enrolment. Suppose that were to be a week, it could not be said that the society was dissolved.] If the parties resisting this application contend that the old rules were abrogated, they should have shewn the alterations which are supposed to have that effect. If any practical variation, however slight, will produce it, few friendly societies in the kingdom can be governed by their original rules. [*Littledale* J. How are the magistrates to know what the alterations are? Lord *Denman* C. J. You know them, and should have explained them, if necessary.] As to the cases cited. The point decided in *Rex* v. *Gilkes* (*a*) is not in dispute here. In *Battey* v. *Townrow* (*b*) a rule had been altered, but without fresh enrolment, and Lord *Ellenborough* clearly thought the original rule still binding. In *Rex* v. *The Witham Savings' Bank* (*c*) the persons claiming to be the officers

(*a*) 8 *B. & C.* 439.
(*b*) 4 *Camp.* 5.
(*c*) 1 *A. & E.* 321.

of

1838.

The Queen against Lord Godolphin.

of the benefit society had been in fact expelled; the question was, which of two contending parties legally represented the persons who were depositors in the savings' bank; and this Court merely refused to issue a mandamus to the bank until that question was settled. The decision in *Ex parte Norrish* (a) was merely that a society could not petition under the statute in the name of a trustee not regularly appointed under any rules.

Cur. adv. vult.

Lord Denman C. J. in this term (*June* 2d) delivered the judgment of the Court.

This was a rule for a mandamus to justices to issue a summons to the president, &c., of a Friendly Society, and to hear and determine the complaint of *Thomas Lupson* against the society for having expelled him. The cause shewn was, that, under the circumstances hereinafter stated, the Friendly Society in question was no longer within the provisions of stat. 33 *G.* 3. *c.* 54., and consequently that the magistrates had no jurisdiction. In answer to this, it was, amongst other things, urged that some of the members had recently declared that the society was still existing within and governed by the provisions of the act. We mention this in the first place, to dispose of it at once, because we can attach no importance to the opinion or declarations of all or any portion of the members of this society as to the legal character now to be attributed to it. In order to make the rule absolute, we must satisfy ourselves that the magistrates have jurisdiction to make a legal order in the matter in which their interference is required: an

(a) *Jac. Rep.* 162.

order

1838.

The QUEEN *against* Lord GODOLPHIN.

order that may be enforced if resisted, and the enforcement of which will not expose the magistrates to the payment of damages. It appears from the affidavits that the society was established in 1755: in 1794 their rules were duly enrolled, and continued to be acted upon until 1804: at that time new rules were made in many respects essentially different from the former; these were intended to be enrolled, but, in fact, were not; they were, however, acted on till 1820, when further alterations were made, which, like the former, never have been enrolled. In both instances the omission to enrol appears to have been unintentional, and the misfortune rather than the fault of the society. The application to the magistrates is upon the footing that the rules enrolled in 1794 are still the governing rules of the society. In support of this, the third section of 33 *G. 3. c.* 54. is relied upon. That section enacts that no rule once confirmed by the justices at sessions shall be altered, rescinded, or repealed, except in the manner there provided, and then proceeds thus, "and *such* alteration or repeal shall be subject to the review of the justices," "and shall be filed in the manner hereinbefore directed; and that no *such* rule, order," &c., "shall be binding, or *have any force or effect*, until the same shall have been agreed to and confirmed by such justices, and filed as aforesaid." It is contended, therefore, upon these words, that, as the new rules by which the former enrolled rules were intended to be repealed have never been confirmed or filed at sessions, they have no force or effect whatever; and it is thence inferred that the old rules are still in operation, and the society, in point of law, still governed by them, and so within the protection of the statute.

As

1838.

The QUEEN *against* Lord GODOLPHIN.

As far as respects the new rules, it appears to us that the argument is well founded; whether the inference drawn as to the present binding power of the old rules be correctly drawn, is the question. The section under consideration is manifestly framed to regulate the manner in which any society of this sort shall proceed in the formal repeal or alteration of a confirmed rule, specifying the notices and proportion of consenting members which shall be necessary; and when, in compliance with these requisitions, an old rule shall have been altered or repealed by a new rule, it *further*, and in addition, provides that *such* new rule shall not be binding or have any effect until confirmed and filed at sessions. For any thing, therefore, intended to be effected by the new rules, it is enough to say that, for want of confirmation and filing, they are at present inoperative; but, as it must be taken upon these facts that, by common consent of the then existing members, the old rules were abandoned in 1804, and have practically had no operation since, and, further, as it must be presumed that, in an interval of thirty-three years, many of the then existing members must have died, and many new members must have been added, who have become so upon the faith that the new rules were the governing rules of the society, and who may have been in entire ignorance of the old rules, it is by no means a clear consequence that the old rules can, at this moment, be resorted to as in existence, even for the purpose of holding the society together under the statute. If they are binding rules for that purpose, they are so for all purposes; they may, for any thing we know, provide different rates of contribution and relief from those now acted on, and may vary the rights of the members in other

1838.

The Queen against Lord Godolphin.

other material points; and there would arise the gross injustice, that members added since 1804 may find themselves now upon a totally different footing from that on which they understood themselves to stand when they joined the society. The only decided case exactly in point, which was cited, is *Ex parte Norrish* (a). That was an application made in 1821 to the Master of the Rolls, by petition, in order to a summary proceeding against a late trustee of a Friendly Society under the eighth section of the statute; that mode of proceeding could only be adopted in case the society was existing under the statute; the same point, therefore, arose as here. The facts were, that the rules had been allowed and filed in 1813: soon after, some dissatisfaction with the conduct of the officers having arisen, a committee had been formed to regulate the affairs of the society; and from that time the rules had not been attended to, the meetings not held, nor payments made, nor officers regularly appointed. The Master of the Rolls said: [His Lordship here read the words already cited, p. 341, antè, ending, "jurisdiction under the act."] In this case, it is true, the third section does not appear to have been noticed; and, in the view which we have taken, it was not applicable, because there had been no attempt by new rules formally to alter or repeal the old ones. The Master of the Rolls decides upon the effect of a practical abandonment of the old rules, which is the difficulty that presses upon our minds in the way of issuing the mandamus prayed for.

We are aware of the extreme inconvenience of putting the claimant in the present case to seek his relief

(a) *Jac.* 162.

 in

1838.

The QUEEN *against* Lord GODOLPHIN.

in a Court of Equity: but, with the authority of *Ex parte Norrish* (a) before us, and the serious doubts (to say no more) which we entertain whether the magistrates have the jurisdiction which the writ would command them to exercise, we should violate our well established rules if we were to make the rule absolute: and, whatever may be the amount of inconvenience in the particular case, we perhaps do that which is more than proportionably convenient in general, if by discharging the rule we cause it to be generally understood that these societies cannot depart from their established rules, or neglect to comply with the statute in the mode of altering or repealing them, without exposing their property to danger, and themselves to great expense, loss, and inconvenience.

Rule discharged (b).

(a) *Jac.* 162. (b) See stats. 10 *G.* 4. c. 56. 4 & 5 *W.* 4. c. 40.

Saturday, May 26th.

GREEN *against* SALMON.

In an action by an undertaker for funeral expences, against a person not the executor, a residuary legatee is a competent witness for the plaintiff. For, although a person, other than the executor, may have rendered himself liable to the undertaker, the estate is ultimately answerable for so much of the cost as an executor might reasonably pay, and no more, and the witness, therefore, has no disqualifying interest.

ASSUMPSIT for work, labour, care, diligence, and attendance, and for hearses, coaches, horses, materials, chattels, and other necessary things used and applied in and about the furnishing and conducting of a certain funeral by the plaintiff before that time found and provided for the defendant at his request &c.; and for goods sold and money paid. Plea, non assumpsit. On the trial before *Coleridge* J. at the sittings in *Middlesex* in this term, it appeared that the action was brought by an undertaker against the brother of the deceased, to recover

461.

1838.

GREEN *against* SALMON.

46*l.* for expenses of the funeral. A creditor had taken out administration cum testamento annexo. The plaintiff's case was, that defendant had retained plaintiff as the undertaker, and made himself liable for the expenses. The plaintiff called a witness, whose wife was a residuary legatee under the will. He was objected to as having an interest in discharging the estate of this demand by throwing it on the defendant. *Coleridge* J. received the evidence, and left it to the jury, whether or not the defendant had contracted with the plaintiff. The jury were of opinion that he had, and found a verdict for the plaintiff for 46*l.*

Alexander now moved for a new trial (*a*). The administrator was liable for these expenses, at least to the amount of 20*l.* (*b*), which must have been paid out of the estate unless the defendant had taken the liability on himself. That fact, therefore, was one which the husband of a residuary legatee was interested in proving. [*Patteson* J. Would not the defendant, if he paid, have an action against the administrator for the reasonable expenses?] *Brice* v. *Wilson* (*c*) seems to render that doubtful.

(*a*) Before Lord *Denman* C. J., *Littledale*, *Patteson*, and *Williams* Js.

(*b*) See *Hancock* v. *Podmore*, 1 *B.* & *Ad.* 260.

(*c*) BRICE *against* WILSON. *Jan.* 31st, 1834.

If an executor ratifies orders given by another person for an extravagant funeral, he may be sued by the undertaker individually, and not as executor, for the whole expence.

ASSUMPSIT by an undertaker for funeral expences. The defendant was the executor, but was not sued in that character. He suffered judgment by default, and a writ of inquiry was executed before the sheriff of *Middlesex*. The plaintiff had a verdict for 52*l.* *Butt*, in *Hilary* term, 1834 (*January* 14th), moved (in the full court) for a rule to shew cause why the inquisition should not be set aside and a new writ of inquiry issued. By the under-sheriff's notes taken on the inquiry, it appeared that the funeral, in the opinion of two witnesses, was too expensive for the station and circumstances of the deceased; that the deceased had died insolvent; and that the widow had ordered the funeral. Evidence, however,

1838.

GREEN *against* SALMON.

doubtful. [*Patteson* J. The judgment there probably means that the executor, where credit has been given to another person, is not liable *to the undertaker;* if it lays down more, the law stated is extrajudicial. Is not there

---

ever, had been given to shew that the defendant knew of the expence after it was incurred, and sanctioned it. It appeared he had attended the funeral, and that, after being called upon for payment, he had sent letters to the plaintiff, apologising for his not immediately paying the whole demand, and stating his expectations of being able to do so. The defendant's counsel contended that, not having ordered the funeral, he was liable only to an amount which would be reasonable for a person in the testator's station in life, and which an executor would be entitled to charge as against the creditors on the estate. But the under-sheriff told the jury that the defendant was liable to all the expences, if the charges were (in themselves) reasonable. Cause was shewn in the Bail Court, before *Patteson* J., in the course of the term.

Cur. adv. vult.

PATTESON J. now delivered judgment in the full Court. After stating the facts of the case which shewed a ratification by the defendant, and referring to two letters, above mentioned, his lordship said: Here then is an express promise of payment by the defendant, after he knew of the expence incurred. It is said that the defendant can be liable only as far as the assets can be rendered so for a funeral suited to the station of the deceased. The under-sheriff thought he was liable for the whole charge, supposing it reasonable. Several cases shew that an executor is liable for a funeral, though not ordered by him, so far as it is suited to the testator's degree, where credit has not been given to any other person. But, where credit has been given to some other person, no case shews that the executor can be liable. It might be said here that the credit had been given to the defendant in his character of executor, if there had been nothing but the common legal liability to be looked to. But by the conduct stated in evidence, and by the letters which he has sent, he has adopted the acts of the widow, has made her his agent, and ratified her order. This, therefore, is not the case of an executor's common law liability; the defendant has made himself individually the party ordering the funeral, by adopting the acts of another.

Lord DENMAN C. J. As the rule was moved for in the full court, I may say that I concur in the judgment which has been delivered.

LITTLEDALE and TAUNTON Js. concurred.

Rule discharged.

The case was cited, on the present motion, from 3 *Nev. & M.* 512.

another

1838.

GREEN *against* SALMON.

another case, bearing on this subject, as to the common law liability of executors?] Perhaps *Rogers* v. *Price* (*a*) is the case meant (*b*).

Cur. adv. vult.

Lord DENMAN C. J., on a subsequent day of the term (*June* 2d), delivered the judgment of the Court.

In this case a residuary legatee was called by the plaintiff, an undertaker, to prove that the defendant had expressly employed the plaintiff to conduct his brother's funeral, at a cost of 46*l.* The question was, whether he was not interested to relieve the residue by charging the defendant. We think he was not: for the estate must at all events pay the reasonable expenses of the funeral, and can in no event be liable beyond them.

Rule refused.

(*a*) 3 *Y.* & *J.* 28.

(*b*) *Littledale* J. referred to *Burghart* v. *Hall*, then under consideration in the Court of Exchequer. See 4 *Mee* & *W.* 727. note (*c*).

JAMES *against* SARAH ASKEW.

Saturday, May 26th.

To entitle a defendant to costs under stat. 43 *G.* 3. *c.* 46. *s.* 3., there must have been an arrest in fact. It is not sufficient that the sheriff's officer called on defendant's attorney with a warrant, and required special bail to be put in, which was done after communication between such attorney and the defendant.

J. HENDERSON, in last *Michaelmas* term, obtained a rule nisi for costs in this cause, pursuant to stat. 43 *G.* 3. *c.* 46. *s.* 3., under the following circumstances. The plaintiff issued a capias against the defendant, indorsed "bail for 25*l.*, by affidavit." The sheriff's officer called on the defendant's attorney with the warrant, and required bail to the sheriff: the attorney, in consequence, procured from the defendant the names of her bail; and the sheriff's officer, on being afterwards furnished therewith, and paid his fee, sent a bail-bond to the attorney to be filled up and executed. This was done, and the bond

1838.

James *against* Askew.

delivered to the officer, and special bail afterwards put in and perfected according to the writ. The cause being tried, the plaintiff recovered only 8*l.* 8*s.*

Wightman and *Crompton* now shewed cause (*a*). Stat. 43 *G.* 3. *c.* 46. *s.* 3. does not apply where the party has not been actually arrested (*b*). The introductory statement in the declaration, that the party has been arrested, cannot estop the plaintiff on this point: it has no more substantial effect than the averment formerly used, that the defendant was in the custody of the marshal. The preamble of the act states it to be for the prevention of frivolous *arrests*, and for the relief of persons *imprisoned* on mesne process. Sect. 1 enacts, that no person shall be "arrested *or* held to special bail" for a cause of action not originally amounting to the sum for which such person is by law liable to be arrested and held to bail, over and above costs. Sect. 2 is confined to the case of persons *arrested* on mesne process. Then sect. 3 gives costs where the defendant is "arrested *and* held to special bail," and the plaintiff does not recover the amount for which the defendant shall have been so "arrested and held to special bail." To bring this case within sect. 3, "or" must be read for "and." It appears to have been the opinion of *Tindal* C. J., in *Amor* v. *Blofield* (*c*), that an arrest at all events was necessary. In *Preedy* v. *M'Farlane* (*d*) Lord *Abinger* C. B. thought an arrest equivalent, under sect. 3, to "an arrest and holding to bail." Arrest and holding

(*a*) Before Lord *Denman* C. J., *Littledale*, *Patteson*, and *Williams* Js.

(*b*) It was also contended that there was probable cause for an arrest.

(*c*) 9 *Bing.* 91. (*d*) 1 *Cro. M. & R.* 819. *S. C.* 5 *Tyr.* 355.

1838.

JAMES *against* ASKEW.

ing to bail seem to have been considered synonymous in *Edwards* v. *Jones* (*a*), where, however, no actual decision took place on this point: Lord *Abinger* C. B. said, "Where a party voluntarily gives special bail, he can in no sense be said to be arrested; but when he is arrested, he is taken into custody only *until* he gives special bail; so that in one sense he is *held* to special bail. If the terms can be considered synonymous, there is no necessity to read it *or* instead of *and*." And *Parke* B. asked, "Does not the being actually arrested, and so brought under an obligation of putting in special bail, satisfy all that the statute intended?" It is true that the same learned Judge said there, with reference to *Bates* v. *Pilling* (*b*), which had been cited, "If the defendant accepts his release from arrest on the terms of putting in special bail, he himself waives the benefit of the statute:" but it was expressly decided in that case, that, to bring a party within sect. 3, there must be not only an arrest but a giving of special bail; and that decision is unimpeached. *Parke* B., in *Wilson* v. *Broughton* (*c*), thought that such a construction would be inconvenient, but he admitted that he was not aware of *Bates* v. *Pilling* (*b*) (which had not then been reported); and the case did not require a decision on this point. In none of the cases has it been questioned (unless by the doubt of *Parke* B., just referred to) that an arrest was necessary. [*Patteson* J. referred to *Small* v. *Gray* (*d*).] There an action was considered maintainable for holding to bail though there had been no arrest; but such an action would be grounded on sect. 1, which enacts that

(*a*) 2 *M.* & *W.* 416, 417. (*b*) 2 *Cro.* & *M.* 374. *S. C.* 4 *Tyr.* 231.
(*c*) 2 *Dowl. P. C.* 631. (*d*) 2 *Car.* & *P.* 605.

1838.

JAMES *against* ASKEW.

no person shall be arrested *or* held to special bail for certain causes of action.

Cresswell and *J. Henderson*, contrà. The real question is, whether *Bates* v. *Pilling* (a) was rightly decided or not. The statute is remedial, and to be liberally construed. Lord *Abinger* C. B., in *Preedy* v. *M'Farlane* (b), and *Parke* B. in *Wilson* v. *Broughton* (c), inclined to such a construction of sect. 3. If the judgment in *Bates* v. *Pilling* (a) is to be put upon the ground that the statute must be literally construed, then, if a party were arrested and unable to give special bail, he could not recover costs under sect. 3. That case is the only direct authority for a literal construction. Lord *Abinger* C. B. and *Parke* B., in *Edwards* v. *Jones* (d), and *Parke* B. in *Wilson* v. *Broughton* (c), clearly intimated their opinion that arrest and holding to bail, as distinct proceedings, were not necessary. In *Edwards* v. *Jones* (d) *Alderson* B. said (as the dictum is reported in 5 *Dowl. P. C.* (e)), "If you look at the act, it is clear the legislature contemplated an arrest; the reasons upon which the Judges decided *Bates* v. *Pilling* (a) are utterly irreconcilable with the point before them." In *Berry* v. *Adamson* (g), there cited, the plaintiff declared against the defendant for maliciously arresting, but failed, because it appeared that he had given a bail-bond without having been actually arrested. That case is no authority for the present plaintiff: there the party had chosen to state, by his pleading, that the defendant ar-

(a) 2 *Cro. & M.* 374. *S. C.* 4 *Tyr.* 231.
(b) 1 *Cro. M. & R.* 819. *S. C.* 5 *Tyr.* 355.
(c) 2 *Dowl. P. C.* 631.
(d) 2 *M. & W.* 416, 417.
(e) 5 *Dowl. P. C.* 588.
(g) 6 *B. & C.* 528.

rested

1838.

JAMES *against* ASKEW.

rested him: if he had declared for maliciously holding to bail, he might have recovered; *Small* v. *Gray* (*a*). *Amor* v. *Blofield* (*b*) is inapplicable, because there the party had not been arrested, and had never put in special bail. Upon the authorities, therefore, the Court may still be asked to consider what is the natural construction of the statute. And that is, that, where there is an improper issuing of bailable process, which may subject the defendant to imprisonment at any time, the third section shall take effect. When a party, though not actually arrested, gives bail, the bail are supposed to have him in custody. Even if they rendered the defendant, as they might the next day, still, as the case is argued on the other side, he would be without remedy. It may be contended here, on the express words of sect. 3, without seeking to read "or" for "and," that the defendant was arrested; for that, although there was no taking by actual contact, the facts amounted to a virtual arrest, as in *Grainger* v. *Hill* (*c*). [Lord *Denman* C. J. That case is not applicable; the facts were different.] If the circumstances of this case do not amount to an arrest, a person situated as the defendant here was could not make a deposit in lieu of bail under stat. 43 *G.* 3. *c.* 46. *s.* 2., which gives that relief only to persons "arrested."

Cur. adv. vult.

Lord DENMAN C. J., on a subsequent day of the term (*June* 2d), delivered judgment as follows.

The question in this case was, whether costs could be given, under stat. 43 *G.* 3. *c.* 46. *s.* 3., to a party who had

(*a*) 2 *Car.* & *P.* 605.

(*b*) 9 *Bing.* 91.

(*c*) 4 *New Ca.* 212.

not

1838.

JAMES *against* ASKEW.

not been actually arrested, but who had given an undertaking to put in special bail, which had afterwards been perfected. On consideration of the cases cited, we think that we are not warranted in giving costs, unless under circumstances which would authorise a finding that the party had been arrested in point of fact.

Rule discharged.

Monday, May 28th.

The QUEEN *against* The Rector, Churchwardens, and Parishioners of ST. MARY, LAMBETH.

In the election of churchwardens, if a poll be demanded, the votes are to be given by the qualified inhabitants present; but all qualified inhabitants (whether they were present or not at the shew of hands) have a right to be admitted into the vestry-room and vote during such poll: Although the qualified inhabitants present at the time of granting the poll resolve that the poll shall be confined to those then present.

It is not a sufficient ground for impeaching such election (on motion for a mandamus to elect) that the poll was taken with closed doors, unless it be expressly sworn that some qualified person who meant to vote was thereby prevented from doing so.

Semble, per Lord *Denman* C. J., that, if such an instance were shewn, the Court would grant a mandamus, without inquiring strictly whether the number of persons excluded was in fact such as to affect the result of the election.

A RULE nisi was obtained in the last term, calling upon the above parties to shew cause why a mandamus should not issue, commanding them to hold a vestry meeting for the purpose of electing proper persons to be churchwardens for the remainder of the present year. The facts stated on affidavit in support of the rule were as follows.

On *April* 17th, 1838, being *Tuesday* in *Easter* week, a vestry meeting of the parishioners was held at the Boys' School House, *Lambeth Green*, pursuant to notice, for the purpose, among others specified in the notice, of appointing churchwardens. One churchwarden having been appointed on the part of the rector, according to custom, certain persons were proposed to the parishioners to be the three other churchwardens, it being the

custom

1838.

The QUEEN *against* The Rector of LAMBETH.

custom to have three nominated and appointed in addition to the rector's warden. Six appearing as candidates, and a shew of hands being taken, *Saunders*, *Hunt*, and *Barton* were declared to be elected, whereupon two rated inhabitants handed the following notice in writing to the chairman (who was appointed in the rector's absence, according to stat. 58 *G.* 3. *c.* 69. *s.* 2.). "We demand a poll of the whole parish, on behalf of" &c. (the unsuccessful candidates), proposed as churchwardens." Some of the rate-payers then required that the poll should be confined to the vestrymen present; others insisted that a poll of the inhabitants at large should be taken. The chairman took a shew of hands (though protested against by many of the rate-payers) on this question; the majority was in favour of polling (as was stated on affidavit) "the inhabitants rate-payers then present only;" and such mode of polling only was allowed by the chairman to take place, two of the rate-payers, however, giving in a written protest against it in the following terms. "We protest against the polling of the inhabitants assembled in vestry only on the election of churchwardens, and require the poll to be taken of the whole parish." *Saunders*, *Hunt*, and *Barton* again had the majority, and were declared to be elected. During the poll, the doors of the vestry-room were closed by order of the chairman. One of the parties making affidavit stated that, while the doors were closed, he saw several persons assembled against them on the outside, three or four of whom he knew to be inhabitants, and among them an aged gentleman, a rate-payer, who knocked repeatedly, but could not gain admittance till the poll was over; and that the time during which the said persons remained

1838.

The QUEEN *against* The Rector of LAMBETH.

mained excluded was half an hour. Another rate-payer deposed that, having left the vestry-room during the meeting (after the appointment of the rector's warden, and when the proposal had been made for the choice of three others), but with the intention of returning to the vestry, he came back and found the doors shut, and several persons standing near them on the outside: that, finding the doors shut, he therefore remained in the road twenty minutes, during which time several persons came out of the room, but none entered; that he remained until the doors opened, and then entered the room, with other persons, and found that the poll had just closed. One of the affidavits stated, on information and belief, that the number of persons in the parish assessed to the poor-rate exceeded 8000. No affidavit was filed in opposition to the rule.

Sir *W. W. Follett* and *G. Hayes* now shewed cause. The question here is not, as in *Campbell* v. *Maund* (*a*), whether or not a poll might be demanded, but whether the vestry was not competent to determine, by shew of hands, that the poll should be confined to the persons present at that meeting. The vestry was held at the usual time for electing churchwardens, and on proper notice. The general rule is, that the majority of rate-payers assembled in vestry bind the rest of the parishioners. The majority assembled in this vestry were the proper persons to elect churchwardens; and no one had a right to demand, against the opinion of the greater number, that the proceedings should stop, and the meeting be adjourned, to take the sense of the parish at

(*a*) 5 *A.* & *E.* 865.

large.

large. [Lord *Denman* C. J. Was that demanded here? The assembly might be a continuing one, and no adjournment necessary.] It seems established by *Campbell* v. *Maund* (*a*) that, if the vestry continues, any one, though not present at the shew of hands, may come in and vote. But that, if then settled, was established for the first time. The language of stat. 58 *G.* 3. *c.* 69. *s.* 3. is, "that in all such vestries every inhabitant present," who shall have been assessed, &c., shall vote as is there pointed out. In *Prideaux's Directions to Churchwardens*, p. 46 (*b*), it is said that, when the inhabitants properly qualified are duly assembled in vestry "at the time and place appointed, the present include the absent, and the major part of the present include all the rest. For those who absent themselves after such public notice given do it voluntarily, and therefore do thereby devolve their votes upon those who are present, and every act of the major part of the present in all such meetings, is in construction of law the act of the whole parish." And 4 *Burn's Ecc. Law*, 8, 9, tit. *Vestry*, sects. 1, 5, is to the same effect. [Lord *Denman* C. J. The question is what the word "present" implies.] It may be inferred from *Rex* v. *The Archdeacon of Chester* (*c*) and *Rex* v. *The Churchwardens of St. Mary, Lambeth* (*d*) that, in ordinary cases, the poll, if demanded, is to be taken immediately, and the votes to be given by the inhabitants in vestry, in the place previously pointed out by notice; the protest here offered against the manner of taking the poll would have required an adjournment to some new place, where all rate-payers in the parish might

(*a*) 5 *A.* & *E.* 865. See p. 874.
(*b*) 10th ed.
(*c*) 1 *A.* & *E.* 342.
(*d*) 1 *A.* & *E.* 346. note (*b*).

have

1838.

The QUEEN *against* The Rector of LAMBETH.

have an opportunity of voting. [Lord *Denman* C. J. It is complained here that the chairman, when proceeding to a poll, ordered the doors to be closed. *Patteson* J. If the poll had been taken with open doors, there would have been nothing objectionable in it.] To make this an objection it must be shewn that some particular person, who wished to vote, was prevented from doing so by the doors being closed. In parliamentary committees on elections, where obstruction is complained of, the inquiry always is, whether persons were actually prevented from voting whose votes would have turned the election. Here the act of closing the doors was not in itself unlawful; and a poll was taken of the persons present in vestry, in the proper sense of those words.

Sir *J. Campbell*, Attorney-General, contrà. No adjournment was demanded; the only question was, whether the right of voting should be limited to those present at the shew of hands, or whether all the qualified inhabitants should have an opportunity of voting, which, according to *Campbell* v. *Maund* (*a*), and to the judgment of Sir *William Scott* in *Anthony* v. *Seger* (*b*), there cited, they ought to have had. Lord *Abinger* C. B. said, in *Campbell* v. *Maund* (*c*), "Do you say that a person not present at the shew of hands could not afterwards vote on a poll being granted?" "The practice is against your position." The poll is a continuation of the vestry, and is like an election by freeholders at the county court. Here a resolution was passed, limiting the

(*a*) 5 *A.* & *E.* 865.
(*b*) 1 *Hagg. Consist. Rep.* 13. 5 *A.* & *E.* 871.
(*c*) 5 *A.* & *E.* 874, 875.

right

right of voting to the persons actually present; and in pursuance of that resolution the doors were closed. [Lord *Denman* C. J. The meeting decided in their own favour. But I want to see that some one actually suffered by it]. It is clearly to be inferred from the statements that persons who would have voted were shut out; and it cannot be necessary for the purpose of this motion to shew that as many were excluded as would have turned the election. (He then commented on the affidavits). No affidavits are offered in contradiction.

Lord DENMAN C. J. This rule must be discharged. There is no doubt of the law; that the rate-payers in vestry are to elect, and that, if a poll be demanded, it should be kept open for all qualified persons. If any single person had been excluded in the present case, it might have been a reason for demanding that the election should be set aside; but I do not find, by the affidavits, that any person who would have voted was shut out; and, if so, nothing has been done to render the case different from what it would have been if the election had been decided at once. If it had appeared that any one person had been excluded, we would have gone a good way in supposing that the resolution had affected the result of the election.

LITTLEDALE J. I am of the same opinion. It does not appear that any one was in fact prevented from voting.

PATTESON J. I am of the same opinion. It is not proved that any one came to vote and was shut out; and

1838.

The QUEEN *against* The Rector of LAMBETH.

and the chairman was not bound to wait many hours to see if any person would come.

WILLIAMS J. concurred.

Rule discharged.

Monday, May 28th.

EVANS *against* DAVIES and LUCAS.

D. and *L.* being defendants in replevin, the Court allowed *D.* to avow, for a distress damage feasant, in his own right as tenant from year to year to *W.*, tenant in fee, and also to make cognizance as bailiff of *C.*, tenant in fee; and *L.* to make cognizance as bailiff of *D.*, tenant to *W.* as above, and also as bailiff of *C.* tenant in fee.

SIR *JOHN CAMPBELL*, Attorney-General, (with whom was *R. V. Richards*,) moved (*a*) for a rule to shew cause why the defendants should not be allowed to avow and make cognizance doubly. The plaintiff had declared in replevin for taking his cattle. Leave was now asked that, first, *Davies* might avow, and *Lucas* make cognizance as his bailiff, for taking the cattle damage-feasant, stating that *James Watt*, being seised of the closes in which &c. in his demesne as of fee, had demised to *Davies* from year to year; and that, secondly, both *Davies* and *Lucas* might make cognizance, stating that the late king, *William* IV., was seised in his demesne as of fee, in right of his crown, of the close in which &c., and that the defendants, as his bailiffs, distrained the cattle damage-feasant. It appeared that the locus in quo was part of the waste of the manor of *Iscoed* in *Radnorshire*: that the plaintiff, as was alleged, had encroached on the waste in 1815 or 1816, while it was the property of the Crown, and had held the locus in

(*a*) Before Lord *Denman* C. J., *Littledale*, *Patteson*, and *Williams* Js. The application had previously been made at chambers, before *Williams* J., who had declined to give leave, but stayed proceedings in order that an application might be made to the full Court.

quo

1838.

EVANS *against* DAVIES.

quo ever since. In 1826, *Watt* purchased from the Crown, and took a conveyance from the commissioners of woods and forests. *Watt* had recovered the land by ejectment from the plaintiff; but he, subsequently to the decision of *Doe dem. Watt* v. *Morris* (*a*), which related to another encroachment on the same manor, had sent his cattle into the close, with the view of again trying the title. *The Attorney-General* now pointed out that *Doe dem. Watt* v. *Morris* (*a*) had decided that the right of the Crown did not pass, under circumstances in many respects resembling the present, to a vendee: but that it was still doubtful whether the more advisable method of resisting the encroachment was by relying on the title of the Crown or on that of *Watt*; and that the defendants ought not to be driven to put their defence on either title exclusively. The Judge could not amend, if the title were wrongly set out; and it must be traced to the fee. (He was stopped by the Court.)

E. V. Williams shewed cause in the first instance. In the rules of *Hil.* 4 *W.* 4., *General Rules and Regulations*, 5. (*b*), it is said, "Nor shall several pleas, or avowries, or cognizances, be allowed, unless a distinct ground of answer or defence is intended to be established in respect of each." This is an express prohibition; and it places the defendant in replevin in the same situation as before stat. 4 *Ann. c.* 16. *s.* 4., unless he can establish that he intends a distinct ground of answer or defence. It is afterwards said (*c*), "Pleas, avowries, and cognizances, founded on one and the same principal matter, but varied in statement, description, or circumstances only," "are not to be allowed." Here the

(*a*) 2 *New Ca.* 189.

(*b*) 5 *B.* & *Ad.* ii.

(*c*) 5 *B.* & *Ad.* iii.

1838.

EVANS *against* DAVIES.

principal matter is the same in each of the proposed answers, namely, that the cattle were damage-feasant on a single occasion, and that the defendants had the authority of the owner of the soil to distrain: it is attempted to vary the description of the circumstances under which the authority exists. It is not like several justifications under the authority respectively of several commoners; for there the rights of all the commoners to authorise may well co-exist; there may, therefore, be several real distinct answers: here, if the Crown was seised, *Watt* was not seised. This is merely an attempt to evade the necessity, imposed by the rules, of electing on what ground a single defence shall be put. A plaintiff is now compelled, by the express words of the rules, to elect whether he will treat a given contract as conditional or unconditional; whether he will rely on a particular transaction as a sale and delivery of goods, or only a bargain and sale: and a defendant must elect whether he will plead a given right of common as a common at all times of the year, or at particular times; a given right of way as a way for convenient enjoyment of his house, or for farming and watering cattle; a given transaction as a discharge or a suspension of his liability. [*Patteson* J. He may plead agreements to accept the security of two different persons (*a*).] Those are distinct agreements which may co-exist: here, it is attempted to give two inconsistent descriptions of the same fact. It is not allowed to plead, to a bond, solvit ad diem and solvit post diem, there being but one payment. Avowries for rent arrear, laying the reservation quarterly and half yearly, are not allowed. The power of the Judge to amend at Nisi Prius is not a correct test of the right to multiply defences. It is true that the

(*a*) *Reg. Gen. Hil.*, 1834, *General Rules*, &c., 5. 5 *B. & Ad.* iv.

commencement

1838.

EVANS *against* DAVIES.

commencement of the rule in question alludes to the enlarged power of amendment; but it refers also to the more distinct knowledge which the party pleading now has of the facts. Supposing, in a case like *Hanbury* v. *Ella* (*a*), where it is doubtful whether the contract be a purchase or a guarantee, a plaintiff should choose to treat the contract as a guarantee, and the defendant, instead of denying it, should plead that there is no writing to satisfy the Statute of Frauds, and the replication should set out the writing, and the defendant demur; there, if the Court should hold the writing insufficient to satisfy the act, as a guarantee, the plaintiff would fail, though he might have succeeded if he had treated the contract as a purchase. Now, in such a case, there would be no opportunity for amendment at Nisi Prius: yet that would not be a sufficient reason for allowing the plaintiff to declare on the contract both as a purchase and as a guarantee. *Jenkins* v. *Treloar* (*b*), *Bastard* v. *Smith* (*c*), and *Cholmondeley* v. *Payne* (*d*) shew the strictness with which the Courts prohibit different descriptions of the same subject-matter. [*Patteson* J. Why may not *Lucas* have authority both from the Crown and from *Davies*?] The Crown and *Davies* could not both have the authority, as described in the two proposed avowries. *Davies*'s power to authorise is deduced from the seisin of *Watt*, which is inconsistent with the seisin of the Crown. [*Patteson* J. I have often allowed cognisances for rent as bailiff to *A.* and bailiff to *B.*] *The Attorney-General* referred to *Leuckhart* v. *Cooper* (*e*) as shewing that two defences were to be allowed, if they were different defences on the

(*a*) 1 *A.* & *E.* 61. (*b*) 1 *M.* & *W.* 16. *S. C.* *Tyrwh.* & *Gr.* 316.
(*c*) 5 *A.* & *E.* 827. (*d*) 3 *New Ca.* 708.
(*e*) 3 *Dowl. P. C.* 415.

 face

1838.

EVANS *against* DAVIES.

face of the pleas: and he suggested, as to the rule in favour of pleading securities from different parties, that it would not necessarily appear whether there were two securities or one. [*Patteson* J. I think the rule seems to assume that there are two]. *R. V. Richards* referred to *James* v. *Bourne* (a).

Lord DENMAN C. J. We will see the other Judges; and, if necessary, will call on the defendants' counsel to support the rule.

Cur. adv. vult.

Afterwards, in this term (*June* 2d), Lord *Denman* C. J. said that the avowry and cognisances might be pleaded as prayed.

Rule absolute.

(a) 4 *New Ca.* 420.

Tuesday, May 29th.

SLACK *against* SHARPE.

A lessee, under an unwritten contract reserving rent on 6th *April* and 6th *October*, became bankrupt, and a fiat issued in *March*, the rent due in the previous *October* having been paid. Upon the assignees refusing to accept the premises, the bankrupt offered, within fourteen days after his receiving notice of such refusal, and one day before 6th *April*, to deliver up possession to the lessor. Held that, under stat. 6 *G.* 4. *c.* 16. *s.* 75., he was not liable in assumpsit for use and occupation to pay any thing in respect of the time subsequent to 6th *October*.

Where the bankrupt holds by an unwritten lease, offering possession is a delivery within sect. 75.

THE following case was stated for the opinion of this Court, according to stat. 3 & 4 *W.* 4. *c.* 42. *s.* 25.

The defendant was tenant to the plaintiff of certain premises, from 1st *January* 1833 until the time of the bankruptcy and fiat hereinafter mentioned. The tenancy was from year to year, at the rent of 50*l.*, payable on 6th *April* and 6th *October* in every year. On 25th *March*, 1834, the defendant committed an act of bankruptcy; and, on 31st *March* 1834, a fiat in bankruptcy issued

against

1838.

SLACK *against* SHARPE.

against him. The defendant requested the assignees to accept the premises, which they declined: whereupon the defendant, conformably to stat. 6 *G.* 4. *c.* 16. *s.* 75., offered to deliver up possession of the premises to the plaintiff, on 5th *April* 1834; and the plaintiff accepted the possession on 7th *April* 1834. The plaintiff claimed compensation for the defendant's enjoyment of the premises from 6th *October* 1833 until the issuing of the fiat on 31st *March* 1834. Each party was to be at liberty to avail himself, in support of his case, of sect. 75 of the bankrupt act, according as the Court should consider that it went to maintain or defeat the demand, without reference to the pleadings (*a*). If the Court should be of opinion that the plaintiff was entitled to a verdict, the rent was to be considered the measure of damages in proportion to the time of occupation.

Wightman for the plaintiff. First, independently of stat. 6 *G.* 4. *c.* 16. *s.* 75., the bankrupt is liable for the rent which accrued before the fiat. In *Auriol* v. *Mills* (*b*)

(*a*) The action was assumpsit for use and occupation, and on an account stated. Pleas, 1. Non assumpsit; and issue thereon. 2. To the first count, that defendant was tenant to plaintiff under a rent payable 6th *April* and 6th *October*; the plea then stated defendant's trading and bankruptcy, the fiat and adjudication, and further proceedings, the appointment of the assignees, his application to them, their refusal to accept, his delivery of possession to plaintiff within fourteen days of notice of refusal, and plaintiff's acceptance; and averred that the sum claimed in the first count was for the occupation up to 6th *April* next after the fiat. 3. Payment of 25*l.* in accord and satisfaction, and acceptance. The plaintiff new assigned, as to the 2d plea, that the action was for the use and occupation from 6th *October* 1833 to the issuing of the fiat: and, as to the 3d plea, he denied the acceptance in satisfaction. The defendant pleaded non assumpsit to the new assignment, and joined issue on the replication to the 3d plea. The plaintiff joined issue on the plea to the new assignment.

(*b*) 4 *T. R.* 94., affirming *Mills* v. *Auriol*, in C. P., 1 *H. Bl.* 433. See *S. C.*, and notes, 1 *Smith's Leading Cases*, 436.

1838.

Black *against* Sharpe.

it was held that a bankrupt was not discharged from payment of rent under a covenant, the rent accruing after the bankruptcy. In *Boot* v. *Wilson* (a) the same point was decided in assumpsit for use and occupation, the bankruptcy having occurred before the day on which the rent claimed became due. There Lord *Ellenborough* remarked that *Wadham* v. *Marlowe* (b) "only decided that the action of *debt* on the reddendum would not lie against the lessee, for rent accruing after his bankruptcy, when he had ceased to occupy the premises, and the assignee was in possession under the commissioners' assignment." In *Boot* v. *Wilson* (a) the facts were specially pleaded, and there was a special demurrer: and Lord *Ellenborough* remarked (c) "that the plea either denied the occupation of the defendants as tenants, and then it was bad on the demurrer, as amounting only to the general issue; or it did not; and then it was bad, as being no answer in law to the declaration." Now here the occupation up to 25th *March* at least is admitted: so far, therefore, the plaintiff must be entitled to recover. Secondly, as to stat. 6 *G.* 4. *c.* 16. *s.* 75. The offer to deliver up was made on the day before that on which the rent accrued: if that is to discharge the defendant, it will open the way to frauds upon landlords, for they will lose all their remedy. If the assignees had not elected till after the 6th of *April*, when the rent became due, the case would have been like *Tuck* v. *Fyson* (d), where, upon the authority of *Copeland* v. *Stephens* (e), it was decided that the term vested in

(a) 8 *East*, 311.

(b) Note (c) to *Boot* v. *Wilson*, 8 *East*, 314. *S. C.* note (a) to *Mills* v. *Auriol*, 1 *H. Bl.* 437.

(c) Page 313.

(d) 6 *Bing.* 321.

(e) 1 *B. & Ald.* 593.

in the bankrupt till the election was made, and therefore his surety was liable for breach of covenant between the bankruptcy and the acceptance by the assignees or delivery up to the lessor. If it be argued that here no rent was due till the 6th of *April*, and that therefore the whole liability accrued after the offer to deliver possession, the answer is that here the action is not for rent, upon the reddendum of a lease, but for use and occupation, which went on up to the offer to deliver possession; the plaintiff is entitled to compensation at least for the use and occupation down to the act of bankruptcy. [*Patteson* J. Is there any such apportionment independent of statute? The recital of stat. 11 *G.* 2. *c.* 19. *s.* 15. seems to state the contrary expressly.] The bankruptcy does not so extinguish the contract that the lessor is deprived of his remedy for the use and occupation down to the bankruptcy. [*Littledale* J. Suppose the occupation had been wholly of arable land, the benefit from which accrues only at particular times of the year; might the defendant have been liable for an occupation merely at other times?] This is the case of a house: and the damages are agreed upon. [*Patteson* J. referred to *Manning* v. *Flight* (a).] That case shews that the term is not extinguished for all purposes. Sect. 75 of stat. 6 *G.* 4. *c.* 16. was intended for the benefit of landlords rather than of tenants: it enacts that the bankrupt shall not be liable for rent accruing after the date of the commission; that, by a reasonable interpretation, would shew that he was liable for use and occupation until that time. [*Patteson* J. If the rent be due before the commission, will it not be barred by the certificate?]

(a) 3 *B.* & *Ad.* 211.

Ogle,

1838.

SLACK *against* SHARPE.

Ogle, contrà. It is understood that the case is to be treated as if there were a regular plea of bankruptcy and certificate. *Auriol* v. *Mills* (a) was decided before stat. 49 *G.* 3. *c.* 121. Sect. 19 of that act exonerated the lessee in cases where the assignees accepted the lease. Then sect. 75 of stat. 6 *G.* 4. *c.* 16. extended the protection by enabling the lessee to deliver up the lease where the assignees declined to accept. Under each act the landlord may require the assignees to elect immediately, and will be protected by the Chancellor against any fraudulent delay or refusal: that answers the suggestion on the other side as to the risk of fraud. *Grimman* v. *Legge* (b) shews that use and occupation cannot be maintained for occupation during part of a quarter, if the contract be put an end to before the quarter day, and the landlord accept possession. That was a case of express contract to pay on stated days, as here. *Turner* v. *Robinson* (c) establishes a similar principle as to wages. In *Thomas* v. *Williams* (d) this principle was not disputed, though held to be qualified by a subsequent contract to pay pro ratâ. *Tuck* v. *Fyson* (e) is in the defendant's favour: for there the Court, though they held that the surety was not discharged, said that "the bankrupt himself would not be liable to be sued now for the non-payment of the rent, or non-observance of the covenant to repair stated in the declaration, inasmuch as those breaches accrued subsequently to the date of the commission." There being here an express agreement, no implied agree-

(a) 4 *T. R.* 94.
(b) 8 *B.* & *C.* 324.
(c) 5 *B.* & *Ad.* 789.
(d) 1 *A.* & *E.* 685.
(e) 6 *Bing.* 321.

ment

1838.

SLACK *against* SHARPE.

ment to pay pro ratâ can be assumed in a Court of law: but the Court of Review might have relieved equitably by making such order as it thought fit (according to sect. 75), to meet the justice of the case; as appears from *Ex parte Benecke* (a).

Wightman, in reply. The rent may be apportioned. "It seems extremely reasonable, that if the use of the thing be entirely lost or taken away from the tenant, the rent ought to be abated or apportioned, because the title to the rent is founded upon this presumption, that the tenant enjoys the thing during the contract:" 7 *Bac. Ab.* 63., *Rent* (M), 2. (b). [*Patteson* J. That is, apportioned with respect to a division, not of time, but of the land demised.] The principle applies to a division of time also. The actual contract, not having been carried into effect, may be disregarded, except as an element in the estimate of damages, as in *Tomlinson* v. *Day* (c). That is also in accordance with the principle of stat. 11 *G.* 2. *c.* 19. *s.* 14. *Thomas* v. *Williams* (d) is in favour of the plaintiff; for there the Court inferred from the facts of the case a second contract to pay pro ratâ. This case is not like that of a tenancy for life, where the contract is made with the knowledge that the performance depends upon a contingency. Here the bankruptcy is a termination of the tenancy which could not be contemplated. The tenant has had the benefit of a partial enjoyment, for which he ought to pay.

(a) 2 *Mont. & Ayr.* 692.

(b) 7th ed.

(c) 2 *Br. & B.* 680. See *Neale* v. *Mackenzie*, 2 *Cr. M. & R.* 84. *S. C.* 5 *Tyr.* 1106.

(d) 1 *A. & E.* 685.

Lord

1838.

SLACK against SHARPE.

Lord DENMAN C. J. Sect. 75 of stat. 6 G. 4. c. 16. provides that the bankrupt "shall not be liable to pay any rent accruing after the date of the commission," if the assignees accept the lease: "and if the assignees decline the same, shall not be liable as aforesaid, in case he deliver up such lease or agreement to the lessor," "within fourteen days after he shall have had notice that the assignees shall have declined as aforesaid." We have felt some doubt on a point which has not been argued; namely, whether a parol contract be within this clause. We think, however, that the clause does comprehend the case; and that the offer to deliver up possession is, in such a case, equivalent to a delivery of the lease or agreement. Then the remaining question admits of a very simple answer. This rent accrued after the date of the commission; it was not due before. But it is argued that it may be apportioned. Had the clause so said, there could have been no doubt; but it does not say so: it says only that the bankrupt is not to be liable for rent accruing due after the date of the commission. There is therefore no ground for holding the defendant liable for any thing.

LITTLEDALE J. I agree that this case is within sect. 75. The words "deliver up such lease or agreement" might indeed seem to contemplate some writing: still, considering that the clause is framed for the benefit of the tenant, I think that delivering up possession is delivering up the lease. Then does this rent accrue after the date of the commission? The whole rent becomes due after that date. For, although up to that date the time in respect of which the rent becomes due goes on accumulating,

accumulating, yet the rent is an entire thing, and becomes due all at once. It is unquestionable that no liability exists for the time after the delivering up. Then how is the defendant to be liable for any part of the time? It is said that this construction will produce a hardship upon landlords, because they cannot prove for this rent under the commission. That may sometimes be the effect of the clause; but its object clearly is to protect the bankrupt from payment of what was merely tending to become due before the date of the commission. With respect to Mr. *Wightman*'s argument that the rent may be apportioned, there is in *Viner's Abridgment*, title *Apportionment* (a), a long list of instances in which the rent may be apportioned; but they all relate to cases in which there has been some division of the land into distinct portions. There is no instance in which the apportionment is made in respect of time.

PATTESON J. The question is merely when the rent accrued. Rent accrues when it becomes due, and at no other time. If there be no demise, and an action be brought merely for use and occupation, then the compensation due for such actual occupation accrues, like interest, de die in diem. But where there is an actual demise, and an express reservation, the rent accrues on the day named in the reservation, and on no other. Here then I take it that the rent accrued on the 6th of *April*, and not before. The bankrupt is relieved from all rent accruing after the date of the commission; and he has paid what accrued before. On the plain words of the act, therefore, he is not liable. Had the act intended

(a) Vol. iii. p. 10., &c. And see *William Clun's Case*, 10 *Rep.* 128 *a.* "The third reason was," et seq.

that

1838.

BLACK against SHARPE.

that there should be an apportionment (or, to speak more properly, a payment of rent pro ratâ), one might have expected to find that intention expressed. The act says nothing of the bankrupt giving up possession; but, where there is no written contract, giving up possession is giving up the lease. Why there should be a difference between a written and an unwritten contract, in this respect, I cannot see. That would narrow the intended remedy. It does seem, at the first sight, as if giving up a lease, and giving up possession, were different things; but, looking at the whole statute, I cannot but construe the giving up possession, in the case of an unwritten contract, to be tantamount to giving up the lease where there is one. Mr. *Ogle* seems to think that it is for the landlord to proceed upon the provisions of sect. 75.: but I think that is not so. By the earlier part of the section, the tenant is exempted altogether if the assignees accept the lease; if they decline, the tenant may deliver up. In neither of these cases does the landlord act. Then the section directs that, if the assignees will not elect, "upon being thereto required," the landlord may proceed as is there pointed out. In this last case, no doubt, it is for him to act; but in the two earlier cases the tenant may proceed without him.

WILLIAMS J. The plaintiff's counsel was driven to contend that something was due at the date of the commission; for, if all became due after, the case falls within the express words of the act. But then, upon reference to the contract of the parties, it is clear that nothing was due on the 31st of *March*, nor before the 6th of *April*. The doctrine in *Grimman* v. *Legge* (a)

(a) 8 *B. & C.* 324.

goes

1838.

SLACK *against* SHARPE.

goes very nearly the length of deciding this case. Where parties have made one contract for themselves, we cannot imply another: but we should be doing so, if we held that the rent became due pro ratâ. Whether there be a remedy for the plaintiff in any other shape, I cannot say. I agree also that, where there is no written contract, delivering up possession satisfies the statute.

Judgment for defendant.

The QUEEN *against* The Inhabitants of BRIXHAM.

Wednesday, May 30th.

Where an order of removal has been served upon a parish under stat. 4 & 5 *W.* 4. c. 76. s. 79., but without notice of chargeability, the parish may take advantage of such omission as a ground of appeal against the order.

ON appeal against the after-mentioned order of removal, the sessions confirmed the same, subject to the opinion of this Court on the following case.

An order was made by two justices of the county of *Devon*, dated 7th *October* 1836, for the removal of *Elizabeth Thomas*, single woman, from the parish of *Tormoham* to the parish of *Brixham*, both in the county of *Devon*. A copy of the order of removal, and a copy of the examination upon which the order was made, were served on the parish officers of *Brixham*, on 7th *October*, 1836, by the overseers of *Tormoham;* but no notice in writing of the pauper being chargeable to *Tormoham*, or relieved therein, was sent with the said notices by the overseers or guardians of *Tormoham* to the overseers of *Brixham*. On 25th *October*, 1836, the parish officers of *Brixham* gave notice of appeal against the order of removal, and on 2d *December* following they sent to the overseers of *Tormoham* a statement in writing, under their hands, of the grounds of their appeal.

The

1838.

The Queen *against* The Inhabitants of Brixham.

The two grounds first stated regarded the settlement of the pauper; the last stated was, that the overseers of *Tormoham* had omitted to send with the beforementioned order of removal any notice of the said *Elizabeth Thomas* having become chargeable to or having been relieved by the parish of *Tormoham*, as directed by stat. 4 & 5 *W.* 4. *c.* 76. *s.* 79. On the hearing of the appeal, the appellants contended that the respondents were bound to prove that they had given the above notice. The sessions were of opinion that the omission to send the above notice with the copy of the order was no ground for quashing the order; and, after hearing evidence and counsel on the other grounds of appeal, they confirmed the order of removal, subject to the opinion of this Court on the question, whether the omission to send notice of chargeability as above was a ground for quashing the order.

Montague Smith, in support of the order of sessions. The appellants, if they meant to avail themselves of this irregularity, should have taken no notice of the order. The object for which sect. 79 requires notice of chargeability to be served with a copy of the order and examination is, that the parish receiving notice may dispute the order before actual removal. Here the appellants were not bound to litigate until the pauper was removed, or proper notice given; but they have attended to the notice which they received, and tried their appeal on the merits. They cannot now allege want of notice. The order is the judgment of the two justices; formerly no other step was necessary to a removal: sect. 79 has rendered another necessary, but the omission of that is ground only for disregarding the order,

1838.

The QUEEN against The Inhabitants of BRIXHAM.

order, not for disputing it at sessions. The want of notice of chargeability does not affect the order itself. *Rex* v. *Englefield* (a) is an analogous case. There an order for removing a pauper and his family had been suspended, under stat. 35 *G.* 3. *c.* 101. *s.* 2.; and, the pauper dying, an order was made for costs during the suspension, and the wife and children were removed under the first order, none, however, being made for taking off the suspension; and on this ground the orders for the last-mentioned removal, and for costs, were appealed against, and all quashed. But this Court held that the neglect to take off the suspension did not invalidate the several orders, which, upon the face of them, were good. *Rex* v. *Alnwick* (b) is consistent in principle with that case, and illustrates the distinction between objections to an order itself and objections to service of notice. In *Rex* v. *Penkridge* (c) it was held that a suspended order of removal was voidable where notice of it was not given within a reasonable time; but there the want of notice was a fact bearing upon the order itself: no notice having been given of the order for fifteen months, the sessions might presume that it had been abandoned, and the reasonableness of the time was a question of which, Lord *Tenterden* said, they were the proper judges. The present case is like those in which an irregularity in a civil action is waived by taking a step; *Fraas* v. *Paravicini* (d). The appellants should have waited till there was an actual removal. [*Patteson* J. What could they have done then, if the order could not be contested?] The removal would be bad, though the order was valid.

(a) 13 *East*, 317.
(b) 5 *B.* & *Ald.* 184.
(c) 3 *B.* & *Ad.* 538.
(d) 4 *Taunt.* 545.

1838.

The QUEEN *against* The Inhabitants of BRIXHAM.

valid. [*Patteson* J. Sect. 79 of stat. 4 & 5 *W.* 4. *c.* 76. enacts that no poor person "shall be removed or removable, under any order of removal," without the notice of chargeability; the notice, therefore, is necessary, to make the pauper removable.] The meaning is, that without notice of chargeability the order shall not operate for the purpose of removal. [*Patteson* J. But that is the whole object of the order. I should be very much disposed to uphold this enactment as strictly as possible.]

Elliot, contrà, was stopped by the Court.

Lord DENMAN C. J. The course pursued by the appellants was the only one by which the enactment could be taken advantage of, unless we were to multiply distinctions in a manner not desirable. Section 79 clearly makes the notice of chargeability necessary to give effect to an order of removal.

LITTLEDALE, PATTESON, and WILLIAMS Js. concurred.

Order of Sessions quashed.

The QUEEN *against* WALL LYNN.

Wednesday, May 30th.

A servant occupying a house cannot be said to hold it *as* servant, if it be not the master's house.
R., a brewer, engaged *L.* as clerk, at a yearly salary, and agreed to permit him to occupy a certain house as his residence, free from rent, rates, and taxes, another clerk being also boarded and lodged in the same house if *R.* should require it, but paying for his board: and such salary and house-accommodation were to be in full satisfaction to *L.* for all perquisites, and for his expenses in the service. Either party might give the other three months' notice of determining the service. *L.* occupied the house for some time, and then, his health being impaired, he removed to another. *L.* agreed with the landlord for this house, but the latter considered *R.* as his tenant. The furniture of the first house, belonging to *R.*, was removed to the second. *L.* was assessed to the poor-rates and window duty; and these, as well as the rent, were paid by *R.* at the brewery. *L.* once objected to being registered as a voter by reason of occupying the house, but afterwards acquiesced, and voted at the election of a borough member. Subsequently, *L.* appealed against a poor-rate in which he was assessed as the occupier, alleging that he held as servant only; and *R.* appeared on the hearing of the appeal, and claimed to be the party rateable. The sessions confirmed the rate, but stated the above facts for the opinion of this Court.
Held that *L.*, the clerk, and not *R.*, was the rateable occupier.

ON the appeal of *Wall Lynn* against a poor-rate, made *July* 1st 1835, for the township of *Sheffield*, the sessions confirmed the rate, subject to the opinion of this Court upon a case which stated the following facts.

Wall Lynn was assessed as the occupier of a house and garden, of which *George Rodgers* was named in the rate as proprietor.

Catherine Eyre and Hannah Rawson are the proprietors of a brewery in the township of *Sheffield*. The appellant is their servant and head-brewer. From 1828 to *February* 1833 he resided in a house situate in the brewery-yard, under an agreement dated 1st *November* 1828, made between him and the said *Hannah Rawson* (for herself and her partners), a copy of which was annexed to the case. By that agreement, the appellant, in consideration of the salary and privileges after mentioned, agreed to serve *Hannah Rawson*, and her partners, &c., in the capacity of a clerk, brewer, and maltster, in the brewing, &c., upon their premises in *Pond Lane*, *Sheffield*, and in the management of their trade as common brewers, under their

1838.

The QUEEN *against* LYNN.

direction and control; and *Hannah Rawson* for herself and her partners agreed to take him into their service in the capacity aforesaid on the terms and conditions after mentioned. Then, after agreements by *Wall Lynn* for the due performance of his service, *Hannah Rawson*, in consideration of the premises, and of the service to be duly performed, did, for herself and her partners, &c., agree with *Wall Lynn* to pay him at the rate of 150*l.* a-year during his continuance in the service, by quarterly or monthly payments, &c.; and also that she and her partners "shall and will permit the said *Wall Lynn* to occupy and enjoy the house adjoining the buildings and brewery of the said co-partners, in *Pond Lane*, *Sheffield*, aforesaid, lately occupied by *Joseph Henry Streatfield*, as and for the place of his residence, free and clear of and from all rents, rates, and taxes, and find and provide coals, candles, and beer for the use of the said *Wall Lynn*; *Thomas Birks*, another clerk in the said brewery, being also provided with board and lodging in the same house, if required by the said co-partners or any of them; the said *Thomas Birks* also defraying the expenses of his board; which salary and house-accommodation are to be in full satisfaction and compensation for all other perquisites of every description, and for every expense incurred by him, the said *Wall Lynn*, in the service of the said employers in the town of *Sheffield* aforesaid, or in the immediate neighbourhood thereof, either in soliciting orders or otherwise in and about the business and concerns of the said co-partners, save and except such expenses as shall be specifically agreed upon between the said parties." After some further stipulations (not material here), it was agreed that, if either party should be desirous of determining the service, such party

party should give the other three months' previous notice in writing.

In *February* 1833, the appellant's health being impaired, he removed from the house in the brewery-yard to one with a garden attached to it at *Farm Bank*, about a quarter or half a mile from it, belonging to one *Edward Whitehead Drury*, who, upon the trial of the appeal, stated that he made the agreement with the appellant, and saw no one else upon the matter, and that the rent was 35*l.* per annum, but that he considered *Rawson* and Co. as his tenants. Upon sale of the said house and garden by *Drury* to one *George Rodgers*, the same tenancy was continued. When appellant removed from the house in the brewery-yard to the house at *Farm Bank*, the furniture, which belonged to the proprietors of the brewery, was removed to the house at *Farm Bank*, and another servant of *Rawson* and Co. was then put by them into the occupation of that house, in the brewery-yard, which up to that time had been occupied by the appellant. The appellant's salary was at the same time increased. The rent and rates were paid by *Rawson* and Co. at the brewery. The assessment for window duty for the house at *Farm Bank* was regularly made in the name of the appellant from the time of his entering upon the house down to the trial of the appeal, and paid at the brewery without any objection to the form of assessment. The appellant had also been assessed to the poor's rate in every rate since his entry upon the house and garden at *Farm Bank*, in respect of those premises. An objection was made to the last rate but two before that appealed against, on the ground that *Rawson* and Co., and not the appellant, ought to have been rated; but the last two rates had been in the same form as before, and they had been

1838.

The QUEEN against LYNN.

paid without objection. In 1833 the appellant was summoned for payment of the registration shilling under the provisions of the Reform Act, which he paid, together with the costs of the summons. In 1832 and 1833, when the name of the appellant was inserted in the list of voters for the election of members of parliament for the borough of *Sheffield*, as the occupier of the house at *Farm Bank*, the appellant objected to his name being inserted in the list; no formal objection, however, had been made according to the provisions of the Reform Act, and the appellant's name remained upon the register. In 1834 the appellant's name was again inserted in the list of borough voters; a regular objection was made to its being inserted, but was disallowed by the revising barrister, after hearing evidence; and the name was retained. At the election of borough members in *January* 1835, the appellant tendered his vote, and, on being asked whether he voted for the house in *Shrewsbury Road* (*Farm Bank*), replied that he did, and accordingly voted.

The appellant, at the trial of the appeal, insisted, in conformity with his notice of appeal, that he lived in the house at *Farm Bank* as a servant only, and was not liable to be rated to the poor, but that *Catherine Eyre* and *Hannah Rawson* ought to have been rated for the house. On the hearing of the appeal, *Catherine Eyre* and *Hannah Rawson* appeared by their counsel, and contended that they were the parties liable to be rated, and that the appellant occupied the house and garden at *Farm Bank* as their servant only. The sessions decided that the appellant was liable to be rated as the occupier of the house and garden, subject to the opinion of this Court on all the facts of the case.

Baines,

1838.

The QUEEN *against* LYNN.

Baines, in support of the order of sessions, was stopped by the Court. [Lord *Denman* C. J. The sessions have set out a good deal of evidence; can we say that they have not decided rightly on it?]

Wortley, contrà. The employers, and not the appellant, ought to have been rated. The occupation was not by him independently, but by the employers, through him, for the purposes of the service. He did not pay the rent; and his holding depended on the continuance of the service, which either party might put an end to at three months' notice. And, further, the contract provided that his enjoyment of the house should not be exclusive, for another clerk was to have board and lodging there if the partners so required. There are several cases applicable in principle, where the real question has been, whether the primary object of a servant's occupation was the service or a tenancy; *Rex* v. *Field* (*a*), *Rex* v. *Cheshunt* (*b*). The first case shews that this Court may examine the evidence stated in a special case, where their opinion is desired by the sessions, although the sessions have themselves decided on the facts, subject to such opinion (*c*). And it appears from the second case that, if the occupation be necessarily connected with the service, though it may not be absolutely necessary for the performance of such service, the party occupying is not to be considered a tenant. The same doctrine may be collected from *Rex* v. *Seacroft* (*d*), *Rex* v. *Minster* (*e*), *Rex* v. *Kelstern* (*g*), *Rex* v. *Iken* (*h*). *Bayley* J., in *Rex* v. *Kelstern* (*g*), when

(*a*) 5 *T. R.* 587.
(*b*) 1 *B. & Ald.* 473.
(*c*) See *Rex* v. *Snape*, 6 *A. & E.* 278.
(*d*) 2 *M. & S.* 472.
(*e*) 3 *M. & S.* 276.
(*g*) 5 *M. & S.* 136.
(*i*) 2 *A. & E.* 147.

stating

1838.

The Queen *against* Lynn.

stating what occupation will confer a settlement by reason of its being necessarily connected with the service, says, "*as* if it be necessary for the due performance of the service;" putting that by way of instance only. The test, "what was the primary object of the agreement?" has been usefully applied in a case of apprenticeship; *Rex* v. *Crediton* (*a*); and may be adopted here. *Rex* v. *Melkridge* (*b*) may be cited as favourable to the respondents; but that case was not fully argued; it did not appear that the occupation was necessarily connected with the service; and there was an exclusive enjoyment. [*Patteson* J. It is not stated in this case, as a fact, that the second house was substituted for the first. The landlord's opinion that *Rawson* and Co. were his tenants is no proof that they took it.] No fresh agreement appears to have been made; the presumption is that *Lynn* and his employers went on upon the former terms. [*Patteson* J. The second house was not the house of the employers. Does not it appear in all the cases on this point that the house in which the servant lived was the master's house?] It is so virtually, if the master hires it and pays the assessments. [*Patteson* J. They were paid in *Lynn*'s name; and he has taken advantage of it by voting at an election.] Stat. 2 *W.* 4. *c.* 45. *s.* 27. makes payment of rates the test of substance in a voter for a borough; if payment of them, under the circumstances of this case, be sufficient, a large proprietor may create as many votes as he pleases. On the other hand, a case like that of the respondents might be injuriously set up to take the privilege of voting from a party who was the substantial occupier, and wished to retain it.

(*a*) 2 *B.* & *Ad.* 493. See p. 497. (*b*) 1 *T. R.* 598.

Lord

Lord DENMAN C. J. This case does not involve any doubtful doctrine. I think that the appellant was an independent holder of the premises. He took them, and agreed to pay the rent; and, by the universal consent of those interested, was assessed to the rates and window duty. He was the party liable to a distress. The cases which have been cited do not come in question. It would be strong, however, to say that an allowance by the master, as in this case, in part payment for services, made the occupation of a house auxiliary to the service. Any house he might occupy while he was servant might be so in some sense; but the cases where a party has been held to occupy such premises as a butler's pantry or a coach-house in the character of servant are very different from this.

LITTLEDALE J. Whatever view might be taken by some of the parties, I am of opinion that *Lynn* was tenant to *Drury* of these premises. He was clearly occupier. Was that occupation his own? He had the absolute dominion; no person could say to him, "you now hold so many rooms; in future you shall have only half the number." It is said that the employers might have sent another servant to lodge in the house; but still *Lynn* had dominion over the whole. There was nothing to prevent a complete occupation by him. The house was not that of the master.

PATTESON J. Our decision of this case does not affect any other; for I am satisfied that *Lynn* was the tenant of the house, and that his employers had nothing to do with it.

1838.

The QUEEN *against* LYNN.

WILLIAMS J. *Rex* v. *Field* (a) and the other cases cited do not govern this. *Lynn* took the house and occupied it; whether he paid the rent or not is immaterial.

Order of sessions confirmed.

(a) 5 *T. R.* 587.

Wednesday, May 30th.

The QUEEN *against* RUSCOE.

A turnpike act contained a clause giving certain exemptions from toll, but excepted from it, by a proviso, all horses drawing *any stage coach, diligence, van, caravan, or stage waggon, or other stage carriage*, conveying passengers or goods for pay.

R. was a wharfinger and agent to a company, who were carriers of goods by canal. *R.* kept waggons and horses, which he employed in carrying out goods brought by the company to his wharf, situate at *S.*, for persons in the neighbourhood, and bringing goods from the neighbourhood to his wharf, for transit by the canal. For such his conveyance of goods he made charges on each parcel. His waggons were so employed in carrying goods to and from persons residing at or near a place called *L.*, or places intermediate between that and *S.*, almost every day except *Sundays*. The waggons went out and returned at different hours according to circumstances; on some days they made more journeys than on others, and they seldom omitted going altogether. *R.* had no office or receiving house at *L.*

Held, that *R.*'s waggons were not *stage* waggons or carriages within the terms of the proviso, and therefore were not excluded from the exempting clause.

THOMAS PEARSON was convicted, by a justice of the peace for *Staffordshire*, of having, as toll-gate keeper, at a certain toll-gate, demanded and taken from *Ralph Ruscoe* certain sums as the toll of two waggons belonging to him, *R. R.*, for repassing through the said gate, the said waggons not being stage waggons or stage carriages, and being respectively drawn by one horse, the said waggons being exempt as having passed through the said gate before on the same day, and paid toll, and such exemption having been claimed; contrary to stat. 4 *G.* 4. *c.* li., local and personal, public, "for improving and maintaining in repair divers roads in the county of *Stafford*," &c., and to stat. 4 *G.* 4. *c.* 95. (a). On appeal, the sessions quashed the conviction, subject to the opinion of this Court on the following case.

(a) Sect. 30.

The

1838.

The QUEEN against RUSCOE.

The appellant, *Thomas Pearson*, the toll collector at a turnpike gate called *Fenton Gate*, in the parish of *Stoke-upon-Trent*, demanded and received from *Ralph Ruscoe*, for the toll on the horses drawing two waggons belonging to him, returning about twelve at noon on 29th *March* last, 4½*d.* for each waggon, the said two waggons having, with the same two horses, passed the said turnpike gate about eight on the morning of the same day, and for which the like toll had been demanded and paid to the said *Thomas Pearson*. The said *R. R.* claimed to be exempt by reason of such previous payment. *R. R.* is a wharfinger at *Stoke-upon-Trent*, and is agent to *Henshall* and Co., carriers upon the *Trent* and *Mersey* canal, and employs his said waggons and horses in carrying out goods, brought by the said canal carriers, from his wharf, on the said canal, for persons in the neighbourhood, and in collecting crates and other goods from the neighbourhood to his wharf for transit by the said canal. *R. R.* is paid for each and every package of goods which he so carries; and his waggons were so loaded each time on the said 29th *March* last. His said waggons are so employed almost every day, except *Sundays*, in carrying goods to persons residing at or near *Lane End*, or places intermediate between it and *Stoke*, and in carrying goods from such persons to the said wharf. His journeys are made at different hours, according to circumstances; but he generally commences before eight in the morning. On some days his journeys are more in number than on others; and the days when he omits his journeys altogether seldom occur. The times of his return vary, being regulated by the facility or otherwise in collecting loads. *R. R.* has

1838.

The QUEEN *against* RUSCOE.

has no office or receiving house at *Lane End*. The case then set out the following provisions of the local act.

"That if any person shall upon any day have paid the toll hereby authorised to be taken for the passing of any horse, cattle, beast, or carriage (*a*), through any one of the toll-gates or turnpikes herein before authorised to be continued or erected upon any part of the said roads, such horse," &c. "shall, upon a ticket denoting the payment thereof on that day being produced, be permitted to pass toll-free through the same toll-gate or turnpike, and also through all the other toll-gates and turnpikes erected or to be erected upon the whole line of the said roads, at any time or times during the same day, to be computed" &c. (*b*). "Provided also, and be it further enacted, that the tolls hereby made payable shall be paid for and in respect of all horses or beasts of draught drawing any stage coach, diligence, van, caravan, or stage waggon, or other stage carriage, conveying passengers or goods for pay or reward, every time of passing or repassing along the said roads, or any of them" (*c*).

If the Court should be of opinion, from the facts stated in the case, that the above-mentioned waggons of the appellant come under the denomination of stage waggons or other stage carriages, the order of sessions was to stand confirmed; if of a contrary opinion, the order to be quashed.

(*a*) The act, sect. 26., authorises the road trustees to take, on every day, to be computed from twelve at night to twelve the next night, "For every horse or other beast drawing any carriage of any description, the sum," &c.

(*b*) Sect. 29.

(*c*) Sect. 30.

Talfourd

1838.

The QUEEN *against* RUSCOE.

Talfourd Serjt. and *Whitmore*, in support of the order of sessions. The question is, whether the waggon in question comes within the terms of the local act, s. 30. Undoubtedly it is within the meaning. If it be contended that a "stage waggon" means one passing and repassing between the same points, the clause taking away the exemption could scarcely operate; for it would probably be found that a stage coach or waggon so passing and repassing within the limits of this local act seldom is drawn twice through the same gate within a day. It may be said that "stage waggon" means a waggon travelling between ascertained points; but the word "stage" is a popular term, and not customarily used for the purpose of ascertaining liabilities, but differently applied in different instances. In stat. 50 *G.* 3. *c.* 104. *s.* 6. an exemption from duties is given to "every cart having the name and place of residence of the owner, and the words 'common stage cart' legibly painted thereon, which shall be kept truly and without fraud to be used wholly in the affairs of husbandry, or in the carriage of goods in the course of trade;" although such cart shall be used for riding therein on certain specified occasions; provided it be not let to hire for such occasions. The word "stage," there, cannot be used in the sense which will here be given to it on the part of the appellant. It is probably meant to denote a somewhat similar use of the carriage in both enactments. In stat. 2 & 3 *W.* 4. *c.* 120. *s.* 5. it is expressly enacted that every carriage used for conveying passengers for hire, and travelling at a certain rate, shall be deemed "a stage carriage" within that act, if the passengers, or any of them, pay distinct fares. Stat. 6 & 7 *W.* 4. *c.* 65. *s.* 7. also makes the rate of travelling essential to the character of a "stage carriage." These instances shew, at least,

1838.

The Queen *against* Roscoe.

least, that the term "stage" is used by the legislature arbitrarily, and variously in different instances. It is observable, also, that in the excepting clause now in question the term "stage waggon" is used after the words "stage coach, diligence, van, caravan;" "stage," therefore, when used the second time, may have a different meaning from that which it bore at the beginning of the enumeration.

F. V. Lee, contrà. "Stage coach" is defined in *Johnson's Dictionary*, "A coach that keeps its stages (*a*); a coach that passes and repasses on certain days for the accommodation of passengers." The mention of "stage coach," in the beginning of the enactment just adverted to, fixes the meaning of "stage," when afterwards applied to other similar carriages. The definition of a "stage cart," in stat. 50 *G. 3. c.* 104. *s.* 6., was given for the purpose of ascertaining what carriages should be liable to or exempt from certain taxes, but not to determine the application of the word "stage" for other purposes. The definition of a "stage carriage" in 2 & 3 *W.* 4. *c.* 120. *s.* 5. begins, "Every carriage used or employed for the purpose of conveying passengers for hire to or from any place in *Great Britain;*" agreeing, so far, with the description in *Johnson;* and the licence, by sect. 11, is to state "the names of the extreme places from which and to which such carriage shall be authorised by such licence to go." The facts here stated shew that the waggons could not be, in the ordinary acceptation, stage carriages. They do not travel every day, but only on occasion; nor do they pass at stated times or between any fixed points; and there is no house for re-

(*a*) "Stage" is defined in the same book, "as much of a journey as is performed without intermission."

ceiving

ceiving or booking the goods sent. Enactments tending to impose a public burden should be quite clear; *Gildart* v. *Gladstone* (a). The question now under consideration was raised in 1824, under the same local act, 4 *G.* 4. *c.* li., and a case submitted to a barrister, afterwards a Judge of this court, whose opinion may be read as part of the present argument. (He then read the opinion of *Taunton* J., which will be found at the end of this case.)

Lord DENMAN C. J. I should apprehend that the legislature did not intend to exempt carriages of this description; but, if that was so, the proviso should not have been qualified by the word "stage," used as it is here; and we must find some meaning for that expression. Now the lowest description of a "stage" would be a vehicle that starts from some one point at certain stated intervals, as an errand cart may do; anything below this cannot, in my opinion, answer to the term. But the carriages described in this case do not go at stated intervals, and may never go at all.

LITTLEDALE J. I think these waggons are not within the meaning of the proviso. The definition of a stage-coach, which has been cited, may probably be accurate. They are carriages which travel generally, but do not go always, and may sometimes make many journeys in a day. Their hours of travelling vary on different days. I think, therefore, that we cannot say they are stage carriages.

PATTESON J. We must put some meaning on the term "stage," used in this proviso. The same word as

(a) 11 *East*, 675.; see p. 685.

applied

1838.

The QUEEN against RUSCOE.

applied to the carts mentioned in stat. 50 *G.* 3. *c.* 104. *s.* 6. throws no light upon it, the regulation there having reference merely to the particular purposes of the clause with regard to taxation. Here a terminus is given from which the complainant goes into a certain neighbourhood to collect parcels. I suppose that, if he had gone from the wharf to a particular public house only, and had collected the parcels there, his carriages would have been stage waggons; but I should think that, to make them such, there must be some determinate place to and from which they travel.

WILLIAMS J. We must assign some meaning to the word "stage;" and I think that the carriages in question do not come within it. Their times of setting out are utterly undetermined; and, if there were no crates to carry, they would not go at all. We cannot then say that they fall within the language used in this proviso.

Order of sessions quashed (*a*).

(*a*) The case and opinion alluded to in the argument were as follows.

The case, after mentioning the clauses of stat. 4 *G.* 4. *c.* li. above referred to, proceeded as follows. "A doubt has arisen upon which your opinion is desired, whether carts drawn by one horse, under the following circumstances, are to be considered as coming within the above description of stage carriages conveying goods for pay or reward; and, if so, how often the toll may be considered to attach upon them in the course of a day.

Several carts drawn by one horse each are kept and employed by Messrs. *Pickford* and Co. (who are carriers to a great extent on inland canals as well as by land carriage) at their wharf on the *Grand Trunk Canal*, at *Stoke-upon-Trent*; to which wharf goods are brought by them along the canal for different persons in the Potteries and neighbourhood; and to which wharf other goods are brought by land carriage in order to be dispatched along the canal to different destinations. When goods arrive at the wharf by the boats, they are generally, but not invariably, delivered out by these carts, and are often obliged to pass along the turnpike road to be delivered according to their respective destinations; and the

1838.

The QUEEN *against* RUSCOE.

the same cart frequently conveys at one and the same time different packages of goods addressed to many different owners. Sometimes the cart returns to the wharf, after delivering its load, without a fresh load; but more frequently it brings back on its return to the wharf fresh packages of goods, received either from the parties to whom the former load had been consigned, or from other persons in the neighbourhood, for the purpose of such fresh packages being dispatched by the canal to a variety of distant destinations. In this occupation such carts are almost daily employed. The journeys which they take are seldom more than one or two miles from the canal wharf, and in various directions; but in almost every instance they have to pass twice through one of the toll-gates belonging to this road, viz. once in going from the wharf and once in returning to it; and they frequently take not less than three or four journeys from the wharf and back again in the course of a day. There is no regular stage for the carts to travel to, nor any particular times or places appointed for their resting, except only at the wharf when they happen to be at home. Their rounds are quite uncertain, and depend wholly on the quantity of goods to be delivered out from the wharf at different places, or to be collected at different places for the purpose of being brought to the wharf. Messrs. *Pickford* and Co. make an additional charge per cwt. for delivering goods from the wharf: and it frequently happens that the parties to whom such belong send their own carriages to convey their goods from the wharf, to save the cartage; for instance, if a hogshead of sugar comes by the boat from *Liverpool* to the wharf at *Stoke*, the charge is 11*d.* per cwt., and, if the same is delivered out by the carts, they charge an additional sum per cwt. according to the distance, from 1*d.* upwards."

(The case then stated a claim of toll to have been made for the horses drawing the carts in question for every time of their passing or repassing through a toll-gate, or at least as often as they passed or repassed not empty, but laden with a fresh cargo of goods; which claim the owners of the carts disputed, alleging that they could not be considered as stage carriages, and therefore did not come within the scope of the clause taking away the exemption. The Hackney Coach Acts, 48 *G.* 3. *c.* 87., and 12 *G.* 3. *c.* 49., were referred to for the distinction between stage and other coaches, and *Johnson's Dictionary* for a definition of the words "stage" and "stage coach.")

Opinion.

"The exemption under the local act in question is, in the first instance, general, being in favour of every "horse, cattle, beast, or carriage," passing through the toll-gates with a ticket denoting the payment on that day of the toll. The exception which follows is secondary or subordinate to the exemption; and it is clear that, if the carts of Messrs. *Pickford* do not come within the terms of the exception, they are entitled to the benefit of the clause of exemption. And I am of opinion, on the whole, after referring

1838.

The QUEEN *against* RUSCOE.

referring to the acts cited above, and to the various cases on the post horse duty, in which travelling by the stage has sometimes been discussed, but which contain no decision on this point, and more particularly on considering the popular sense of the term "stage carriage," which is defined by Dr. *Johnson* to be one that "keeps its stages," that the carts of Messrs. *Pickford* are not excepted from the exemption.

The words of the exception are "stage-coach, diligence, van, caravan, or stage waggon, or other stage carriage, conveying passengers or goods for pay or reward." These words appear to me to import public carriages which travel certain stages, or at least one certain stage. But Messrs. *Pickford*'s carts do not go backwards and forwards to any certain place, but their rounds are altogether irregular, depending on the places of abode whereat the consignees of the goods brought by the canal to the wharf reside. It is true that Messrs. *Pickford* charge the consignees with something extra for the cartage; but the exception requires, not merely that the carriage should convey passengers or goods for pay or reward, but that it should be a stage carriage. On the ground, therefore, that the carts are not stage carriages, I think that they do not come within the description to which the exception applies, and consequently that they are exempt from a second payment of a toll on the same day on which they have already paid, on producing a ticket denoting the payment.

"*W. E. Taunton*,

"*Serjeant's Inn*, 18th *September* 1824."

Wednesday, May 30th.

The QUEEN *against* The Inhabitants of ABERGELE.

On appeal against an order of removal, the respondents contended that no sufficient notice had been given of the grounds of appeal. The justices in sessions held, assuming that to be so, that the objection had been waived. The respondents then declined to try the appeal, and the order was quashed. The justices refused a case. The respondents then obtained a certiorari to bring up all orders of sessions made in the case, with all things touching the same. The sessions returned the orders, with the notice of grounds and other papers relating to the appeal: and the respondents moved, on the return, and on affidavit, that the order of sessions might be quashed.

Held, that the return was irregular in setting out more than the order of sessions, that this Court could not look to the other matter in the return and affidavits, and that the return ought to be quashed.

But, as a new return, if properly made, would not support a motion to quash the order of sessions, the Court discharged the rule without quashing the return.

A CERTIORARI issued to the justices of *Denbighshire*, to remove into this Court all orders, with all things touching the same, as fully, &c., as made by them between the inhabitants of *Eglwys Rhos*, otherwise

Llanrhos,

1838.

The QUEEN *against* The Inhabitants of ABERGELE.

Llanrhos, in the county of *Carnarvon*, appellants, and the inhabitants of *Abergele*, in *Denbighshire*, respondents, touching the settlement of *Evan Evans*. The certiorari having been duly allowed (*a*), the justices made a return, annexing thereto an order for the removal of *Evan Evans* from *Abergele* to *Llanrhos;* the pauper's examination; a notice of appeal against the order, not stating the grounds of such appeal except by the following words, "the said *Evan Evans*," &c. "not having any legal settlement in the said parish;" a notice of motion to be made at the ensuing sessions to adjourn such appeal; a further notice of appeal, stating the grounds more fully; the motion-papers signed by the advocate for the respondents on the motion after-mentioned, at the *Easter* quarter sessions, 1836; and an order made by the justices at those sessions, quashing the order of removal. A rule was afterwards obtained, calling on the churchwardens and overseers of *Abergele* to shew cause why the order of sessions should not be quashed, and the original order confirmed. The following facts appeared by the affidavits in support of the rule.

The order of removal, examination, and notice of chargeability, were served, *November* 4th, 1835. The first notice of appeal was served, *November* 21st, 1835; the appeal was respited, without objection, at the *Epiphany* sessions, 1836; and the further notice of appeal was served, *March* 21st, 1836. At the ensuing *Easter* sessions, in *April* 1836, the respondents moved that the order of removal should be confirmed, because the statement of the grounds of appeal in the notice of *November* 21st was insufficient, and no other statement had been delivered before the *Epiphany* sessions; and because the notice of *March* 21st was too late. The

(*a*) See *Rex* v. *Abergele*, 5 *A.* & *E.* 795.

 Justices

1838.

The QUEEN *against* The Inhabitants of ABERGELE.

Justices said they were of opinion that the first notice was bad, and that, if the objection had been made at the *Epiphany* sessions, the order would have been confirmed; but they thought that the respondents had waived the objection by not taking it at those sessions; and that, as the subsequent notice of appeal contained a sufficient statement of grounds, the respondents were bound to go into their case. They, however, declined to do so; and the sessions then quashed the order. The respondents asked the chairman to state, in the order of sessions, that the justices thought the first notice insufficient; but he said that it was unnecessary, as the file of proceedings would shew that they had so decided. The respondents observing that it would not appear otherwise than by the motion-papers filed in the court, the chairman said that was sufficient. The order of sessions, quashing the order of removal, was drawn up with the following commencement. "Upon hearing Mr. *Horne*, attorney for the appellants, and Mr. *Thomas Oldfield*, attorney for the respondents, refusing to enter upon the respondents' case, on the alleged ground that no sufficient notice of the grounds of the appeal had been given by the appellants to the respondents, notwithstanding the decision of the justices assembled at the said court that sufficient notice had been given: it is ordered," &c. The affidavit (by the appellants' attorney), in opposition to the rule, represented that the justices in sessions had refused a case; that they had only said, as to the insufficiency of the first notice, that, "if they were of opinion that the notice of 21st *November* might be insufficient," the objection was waived: and that the course pursued by them was, according to the deponent's understanding and belief, conformable to the practice of their court.

W. H. Watson

1838.

The QUEEN *against* The Inhabitants of ABERGELE.

W. H. Watson now shewed cause. No defect appears in the order of sessions; and the justices have not stated a case. The merits of the order cannot be discussed on affidavit, and on matter, beside the order, which ought not to have appeared on the return.

Humfrey, *contrà*. The sessions have returned documents from which it appears that the order ought not to have been made. They do not in terms ask the opinion of this Court, but they do so in effect, by submitting the materials on which an opinion is to be formed. [*Patteson* J. They have returned a great deal that cannot be matter for the opinion of this Court at all, such as the motion papers.] The writ requires them to return the orders "with all things touching the same," in the usual form. In stating a case, the sessions transmit the order, and with it all the facts upon which this Court may form a judgment. [*Patteson* J. There the order is made in a qualified form, subject to the opinion of the Court on a case. Here it is without qualification, but they return that which led to the making of it.] Still, if it appears on the face of the return that the sessions have done wrong, this Court must decide upon it. If the respondents object to such a return, they should have moved to quash it. [*Patteson* J. That might be done now, to prevent an irregular practice.]

Lord DENMAN C. J. To entertain this application would be introducing a new practice, and would tend to let in a motion for a new trial upon every order of sessions. I think that the return ought to be quashed.

W. H. Watson then contended that the proper course under these circumstances would be, not that the return

 should

1838.

The QUEEN *against* The Inhabitants of ABERGELE.

should be quashed, but that the rule should be discharged. [*Patteson* J. If we quashed the return on account of the impertinent matter introduced, and the sessions made another return, simply of the order of sessions, we could not then quash the order, but must discharge the rule. We may as well discharge the rule at once.]

Per Curiam (*a*),

Rule discharged (*b*).

(*a*) Lord *Denman* C. J., *Littledale*, *Patteson*, and *Williams* Js.

(*b*) See the next case.

The following case, decided in *Michaelmas* term, 1838, may conveniently be added here.

Thursday, November 15th.

The QUEEN *against* The Justices of CHESHIRE.

On appeal against an order of removal, the respondents, at sessions, objected to the statement of grounds, and the Court held the statement bad. The respondents demanded to have the order confirmed, but the sessions quashed it for a defect in the order. On motion for a certiorari to bring up the order of sessions, founded upon affidavit of the above facts: Held,

That the facts did not shew want of jurisdiction in the sessions; and that this Court, therefore, would not notice objections not appearing on the face of the order.

Especially as the respondents, after the statement of grounds had been held insufficient, had asked for a confirmation of the removal.

Although the affidavits showed that the objection to the order of removal was supported by no proof except an assertion, made at the hearing, by a magistrate on the bench.

EVANS had obtained a rule, in *Trinity* term, 1837, calling upon the defendants to shew cause why a certiorari should not issue, to remove into this Court all orders made by them at the *Nether Knutsford* sessions of *March* 1837, for quashing an order whereby *William Jepson* was removed from the township of *Yeardsley cum Whaley*, in *Cheshire*, to the parish or township of *Chapel-en-le-Frith*, otherwise called *Combs Edge*, in *Derbyshire*, and all proceedings relating thereto.

The affidavits on which the rule was obtained stated the following facts. The order of removal was appealed against by *Chapel-en-le-Frith*, and the appeal

came

1838.

The QUEEN *against* The Justices of CHESHIRE.

came on for hearing at the *March* sessions, 1837. The appellants, being called upon so to do, put in the notice and statement of grounds of appeal, when it appeared that the latter was given in the name of "the churchwarden and overseer of the poor of the township, district, or place, known by the name of *Combs Edge*, and sometimes called *Chapel-en-le-Frith*." The respondents thereupon objected that the statement of grounds of appeal was invalid for not being signed by two overseers of *Combs Edge;* and the court held that it was so. One of the justices then looked at the order of removal, which was to remove to "the parish, township, or place, of *Chapel-en-le-Frith;*" and he stated that there was no township of *Chapel-en-le-Frith*, but that the parish of *Chapel-en-le-Frith* was divided into three townships, one of which was *Combs Edge*, each maintaining its own poor. The court thereupon decided that the order was misdirected, and a nullity, and quashed it: "although it was contended by the respondents' counsel that the order ought to have been confirmed, as the appellants were out of court in consequence of the invalidity of the notice containing the grounds of appeal."

There was no affidavit in answer.

Cottingham now shewed cause. There is a preliminary objection to this rule. The case has been heard and disposed of; and the certiorari, if granted, could be of no avail, as the order of sessions, when brought up, will appear to be perfectly legal, and the Court can notice only what appears upon the order: *Rex* v. *The Justices of Carnarvon* (*a*); the two cases of *Rex* v. *The Justices of Monmouthshire* (*b*); *Reginâ* v.

(*a*) 4 *B. & Ald.* 86. See *In the Matter of Pratt*, 7 *A. & E.* 27.

(*b*) 4 *B. & C.* 844.; and 8 *B. & C.* 137.

 Abergele

1838.

The QUEEN *against* The Justices of CHESHIRE.

Abergele (*a*); which last case closely resembles the present. The Court then called upon

Evans and *Townsend*, contrà. It is true that, where the sessions have jurisdiction, their decision cannot be impeached upon certiorari, unless they have granted a case. But the jurisdiction may be negatived by affidavit. *Rex* v. *The Justices of Carnarvon* (*b*) is qualified by *Rex* v. *The Justices of Cumberland* (*c*). [Lord *Denman* C. J. There the sessions had disclaimed jurisdiction, and refused to hear; and this Court, considering that they had jurisdiction, directed them to hear.] In *Rex* v. *The Parishioners of St. James, Westminster* (*d*) the Court allowed the question, whether the justices had exceeded their jurisdiction, to be discussed on affidavit; and *Taunton* J. said that it had been constantly done. *Rex* v. *The Justices of Somersetshire* (*e*) and *Rex* v. *The Justices of the North Riding* (*g*), there cited, fully establish the principle. *Rex* v. *Great Marlow* (*h*) (and the authorities there cited by *Lawrence* J.), *Rex* v. *The Justices of the West Riding* (*i*), *Rex* v. *The Justices of Oxfordshire* (*k*), *Rex* v. *The Justices of Buckinghamshire* (*l*), *Rex* v. *Overseers of Bridgewater* (*m*), are to the same effect. So in *Rex* v. *The Justices of Cambridgeshire* (*n*) the Court allowed that there were exceptions to the rule that, on certiorari, objections to the order could not be made by affidavit. In *Rex* v. *Wakefield* (*o*) the ques-

(*a*) Antè, p. 394.

(*b*) 4 *B.* & *Ald.* 86.

(*c*) 4 *A.* & *E.* 695. See *Ex parte The Inhabitants of Broseley*, 7 *A.* & *E.* 423.

(*d*) 2 *A.* & *E.* 241.

(*e*) 5 *B.* & *C.* 816. See Ib. p. 818. note (*a*).

(*g*) 6 *B.* & *C.* 152.

(*h*) 2 *East*, 244.

(*i*) 5 *T. R.* 629.

(*k*) 1 *M.* & *S.* 446.

(*l*) 3 *East*, 342.

(*m*) 1 *Cowp.* 139.

(*n*) 4 *A.* & *E.* 111.

(*o*) 2 *Ld. Ken.* 164.

tion

1838.

The QUEEN against The Justices of CHESHIRE.

tion of jurisdiction was discussed entirely on affidavit. In *Rex* v. *The Justices of Carnarvon* (a) and the two cases of *Rex* v. *The Justices of Monmouthshire* (b) the question of jurisdiction was not raised by the affidavits. In *Regina* v. *Abergele* (c) it was not an undisputed fact that the sessions had themselves come to a decision which ousted them of jurisdiction. The question then is, whether, in the present case, the affidavits do not shew that the sessions were without jurisdiction. In 2 *Nol. P. L.* 515. (4th ed.) it is said that notice is in the nature of process. By stat. 9 *G.* 1. *c.* 7. *s.* 8. no appeal against an order of removal "shall be proceeded upon in any Court or quarter-sessions, unless reasonable notice be given." By stat. 4 & 5 *W.* 4. *c.* 76. *s.* 81. "it shall not be lawful for the overseers of such appellant parish to be heard in support of such appeal," unless the notice of appeal, and statement of grounds, be duly given. The power of the sessions to hear, therefore, arises only upon proof of due notice and statement. In *Rex* v. *The Justices of Oxfordshire* (d) Lord *Ellenborough* said that the giving notice was a condition annexed to the right of appeal, which had not there been complied with; and he added, "Of course, therefore, the appeal has never been duly entered; and if so, it could not be adjourned; for the sessions cannot acquire to themselves a jurisdiction by an act of their own." In the present case, the magistrates first decide that the condition which is essential to give them the power to hear is not satisfied; and then they go on to hear, and decide the case; and that, not upon evidence,

(a) 4 *B. & Ald.* 86. (b) 4 *B. & C.* 844.; and 8 *B. & C.* 137.

(c) Antè, p. 394.

(d) 1 *M. & S.* 448. See the remarks on this case, and on *Rex* v. *The Justices of Lincolnshire*, 3 *B. & C.* 548., in *Rex* v. *Kimbolton*, 6 *A. & E.* 603.

1838.

The QUEEN *against* The Justices of CHESHIRE.

but upon the assertion of one of the bench; which assertion too is incorrect, as appears from *Rex* v. *The Justices of Derbyshire* (*a*). [*Coleridge* J. The respondents did not decline the jurisdiction, but insisted on having the order confirmed.] That could only mean that the order should be allowed to stand, and no objection be entertained against it. In 4 *Burn's Just.* 1202. *s.* xvii. (2.*i.*) (ed. *D'Oyl.* and *Wms.*) it is said, "It is usual, in some places, for the overseers who made the removal to bring the original order to the next sessions, and there make oath that they removed the party in pursuance of such order; and if then there appeared to be no appeal against it, the order is confirmed by the Court, and filed amongst the records. And although such confirmation is merely void, because the sessions have no jurisdiction therein, unless in the case of appeal, which here is not; yet such confirmation is also superfluous and needless, for the order not appealed against is final without more." Therefore the expression "confirmed" cannot be interpreted as recognising the jurisdiction of the sessions. If this rule be refused, the respondents are without remedy; for they connot quash the order of sessions for any thing on the face of it; *Rex* v. *Cottingham* (*b*); and it will afterwards be intended that the order of removal was quashed on the merits. [*Patteson* J. If the magistrate's assertion be correct, you are not prejudiced, as you may still remove to the proper place.] It is incorrect, and therefore the respondents will be concluded.

Lord DENMAN C. J. Certainly the circumstances of this case are very peculiar: and we cannot approve of the conduct of the magistrates. But this Court is al-

(*a*) 6 *A.* & *E.* 885.

(*b*) 2 *A.* & *E.* 250.

ways

ways extremely scrupulous in interfering with magistrates where they have jurisdiction. Therefore the first question for us here is, whether the magistrates had jurisdiction. I think they had. The appeal was duly lodged; but, upon its coming on for hearing, it appeared that the notice was bad. I think it is a fallacy to say that upon this the magistrates were without jurisdiction. As a test of this, could they not at any time have given costs? I think the appeal continued before them as long as the sessions lasted. And the respondents themselves applied to have the order confirmed. Had they withdrawn, upon the notice being declared bad, they might perhaps have more consistently contended that the magistrates were without jurisdiction. But, when the respondents demanded the confirmation of the order, it was not unnatural for the magistrates to look at it, in order that they might see what it was that they were called on to confirm. Then the order is quashed upon the mere assertion of a magistrate, and that, no doubt, an erroneous one: but this we cannot look into. I do not say that, in the event of another removal, these circumstances may not be open to discussion: for I will not pronounce that what has taken place is final. The argument from the impropriety of the proceedings would have equally arisen, on whatever ground the order had been quashed. But, supposing it had been quashed on the merits, there could have been no doubt as to the jurisdiction. The sole question for us is, whether, at the time when the Court decided, they had power to decide.

PATTESON J. If one were to enter into the question whether the sessions were right or wrong, there can be no

1838.

The QUEEN *against* The Justices of CHESHIRE.

no doubt that they were wrong, and that they acted very inconsistently and very absurdly. But we cannot say that they had no jurisdiction, because they throw out an opinion on which they have not acted.

WILLIAMS J. Upon the affidavits, it appears that the magistrates had jurisdiction in the matter, not only at the first, but up to the time of their order. For the respondent's counsel insisted on the order being confirmed, on account of the badness of the notice; upon which a magistrate, before assenting to this, pointed out what he considered a fatal objection to the order.

COLERIDGE J. The rule that, where the sessions have jurisdiction and have decided, this Court will not interfere may, perhaps, in this particular case, produce a hardship. Yet, if it exist, and especially since it is a sensible rule, we must adhere to it. As to the general principle, we do not differ from the respondents. It never has been laid down that in all cases the Court, upon issuing a certiorari, are precluded from looking into affidavits. We might of course look into affidavits as to the fact whether the party making an order was a magistrate or not. Then here the question is, whether it appears that the magistrates had jurisdiction; and they certainly had. The appeal was properly lodged. Then an objection, which is held good, is made to the notice. It is contended that, upon this, the appeal was put an end to. But the argument is not supported by the words of the act. The appellants could not be heard: but the respondents might; for they might ask for costs. And, if there really was a difficulty, the sessions were relieved from it by the respondents praying to have the

1838.

The QUEEN against The Justices of CHESHIRE.

the order confirmed, which would place it on the files of the Court. If they had power to confirm the order, they had jurisdiction.

Rule discharged.

The QUEEN *against* STOCK and Another.

Wednesday, May 30th.

The church-building act, 59 *G.* 3. *c.* 134. *s.* 39., empowers the commissioners to order the stopping up of footways, which appear to them unnecessary, in churchyards, provided the same be done with the consent of two justices, and on notice being given in the manner and form prescribed by stat. 55 *G.* 3. c. 68. Schedule (A.) of that statute gives a form of notice of an order for stopping up a useless road; and the form states that such order will be enrolled at sessions, unless, *upon an appeal against the same to be then made*, it be otherwise determined. Sect. 3 of the same act empowers any party aggrieved by such order to appeal to the sessions, upon giving ten days' notice to the *surveyor of the highways*.

Held, that stat. 59 *G.* 3. *c.* 134, *s.* 39. though incorporating the form of notice annexed to stat. 55 *G.* 3. *c.* 68., did not thereby give an appeal against an order of the commissioners for stopping a footway: for that an appeal cannot be given by implication only.

Held also that, if such power had been given by reference to stat. 55 *G.* 3. *c.* 68., the repeal of that statute would not have taken it away.

ON appeal against an order of her Majesty's commissioners for building new churches, the court of quarter sessions quashed the order, subject to the opinion of this Court upon the following case.

The commissioners were made a corporation by stat. 59 *G.* 3. *c.* 134. Sect. 39 of that act empowers the commissioners to stop up and discontinue, or alter or vary, or order to be stopped, &c., such footways and passages through or over any churchyard "as to them may appear useless and unnecessary, or as they shall think fit to alter or vary; provided that the same be done with the consent of any two justices of the peace of the county, city, town or place, where any such" "path or passage shall be stopped up;" "and on notice being given in the manner and form prescribed by an act passed" &c. (55 *G.* 3. *c.* 68. (*a*)), intituled "An act to amend an act of

(*a*) Stat. 55 *G.* 3. *c.* 68. *s.* 2. empowers two or more justices to order footways to be stopped, which appear to them unnecessary, provided that notices be given in the manner there directed; and enacts that, after publication

1838.

The QUEEN against STOCK.

of the 13th year of his present Majesty, for the amendment and preservation of the public highways, in so far as the same relates to notice of appeal against turning or diverting a public highway; and to extend the provisions of the same act to the stopping up of unnecessary roads."

The last-mentioned act was repealed by stat. 5 & 6 *W.* 4. *c.* 50. *s.* 1.

The commissioners made an order under their seal, with the requisite consent of justices, dated *March* 2d, 1837, for stopping up certain footways within the outward walls of the churchyard of the parish church of *St. Philip, Birmingham*, which footways, as the order stated, appeared to the commissioners useless and unnecessary. The appellants, being aggrieved by the order, gave notice of appeal, ten days before the sessions, to the commissioners, the consenting magistrates, and the surveyor of the highways of the parish of *Birmingham*, of which *St. Philip's* for this purpose forms part, and affixed such notice to the door of the church of *St. Philip*, and of the parish church of *St. Martin, Birmingham*. The appeal was entered at the sessions; but the respondents objected to its being heard, on the ground that there was not, in point of law, any appeal to the quarter

publication of such notices, the order shall be returned to the clerk of the peace at the quarter sessions next after &c., and there confirmed and enrolled. Sect. 3 proceeds as follows. "Provided always, and be it further enacted, that where any such" footway shall be ordered to be stopped up as before mentioned, "it shall and may be lawful for any person or persons injured or aggrieved by any such order" "to make his or their complaint thereof, by appeal to the justices of the peace at the said quarter sessions, upon giving ten days' notice" &c. (as the section points out); and the sessions are thereby authorised to hear and finally determine the appeal.

1838.

The QUEEN *against* STOCK.

quarter sessions from an order made by the commissioners for building new churches, under stat. 59 *G.* 3. *c.* 134. *s.* 39. The sessions held that the appeal lay, and proceeded to hear it.

The respondents proved the publication of notices (set out in the case, and framed according to sched. (A) of stat. 55 *G.* 3. *c.* 68.), bearing date *March* 4th, 1837, and stating that an order had been made by the commissioners, on *March* 2d, 1837, with the consent, &c., for stopping up the under-mentioned footways (which were then described), and that such order would be lodged with the clerk of the peace at the sessions to be holden, &c., and would, at those sessions, be confirmed and enrolled, "unless, upon an appeal against the same to be then made, it be otherwise determined." But, it appearing that two orders had been made by the commissioners, and that the notices did not refer to the order then produced by the respondents, the Court quashed the order.

If this Court should be of opinion that the sessions had jurisdiction to entertain the appeal, the order of sessions was to be confirmed; otherwise to be quashed.

Sir *J. Campbell*, Attorney-General, *Balguy*, and *Mellor*, in support of the order of sessions. The questions are, 1. Whether an appeal is given by stat. 59 *G.* 3. *c.* 134. *s.* 39.? 2. Whether, if given, it is taken away by stat. 5 & 6 *W.* 4. *c.* 50. *s.* 1.? As to the first point: stat. 59 *G.* 3. *c.* 134. *s.* 39. empowers the commissioners to stop up footways, "on notice being given in the manner and form prescribed by" stat. 55 *G.* 3. *c.* 68. Now the form given by that statute, sect. 2, and sched.

(A)

1838.

The QUEEN *against* STOCK.

(A) there referred to, states that the order will be confirmed and enrolled at sessions, unless "upon an appeal against the same to be then made," it be otherwise determined. Taking these several enactments together, it is clear that sect. 39 of stat. 59 *G.* 3. *c.* 134. gives an appeal. The object of such a notice is, that any aggrieved party may appeal; it would be idle to publish the notice, if the thing done could not be altered. In *Rex* v. *St. James, Westminster* (*a*), where a statute (2 *G.* 3. *c.* 58.) authorised the making of rates, and then enacted that, if any person found himself aggrieved thereby, he should first apply to two justices for the city and liberty of *Westminster*, and, if not relieved, should pay the rate, and might then appeal to the sessions, *Patteson* J. said, "I cannot understand that the legislature should do so absurd a thing as to direct an application to justices, and then oblige the justices to say to the person applying, 'We have no power to relieve you, therefore you must go to the sessions.'" That course of reasoning may be adopted here. It appears, by the recital of stat. 55 *G.* 3. *c.* 68. *s.* 1., that one specific purpose of that act was to give more public notice of orders for stopping highways, and "a greater facility of appeal" against them; and the directions as to notices of orders were no doubt intended to promote those objects. It is reasonable to suppose that an appeal to sessions would be given against such large powers as are conferred by the act of 59 *G.* 3. A clause giving an appeal is to be construed liberally; *Rex* v. *The Justices of Salop* (*b*) is an instance of such a construction.

(*a*) 2 *A.* & *E.* 241.

(*b*) 2 *B.* & *Ad.* 145.

struction. Secondly, it may be objected that stat. 55 *G.* 3. *c.* 68. is repealed. But stat. 59 *G.* 3. *c.* 134. is still in force; and that which, by incorporation, has become part of it is not affected by the repeal of another act.

1838.

The QUEEN *against* STOCK.

Waddington, contrà. No case has been cited in which an appeal has been held to be given by implication. The rule is, that it can be given only by express words; per *Abbott* C. J. in *Rex* v. *Hanson* (*a*). Such an effect cannot be attributed to a clause in stat. 59 *G.* 3. *c.* 134., merely directing a notice to be given conformably to stat. 55 *G.* 3. *c.* 68. The reference to a form there set forth in a schedule does not incorporate the appeal clause, sect. 3, of the same act: the form itself is not of a notice of appeal, or a notice to be given by the party who would become appellant. If, indeed, the appeal clause of stat. 55 *G.* 3. *c.* 68. were incorporated in the subsequent act, there would be an end of this case. There is no instance, unless the present be one, in which an appeal to sessions is given against any act of the commissioners, by stat. 59 *G.* 3. *c.* 134., or the previous church-building act, 58 *G.* 3. *c.* 45., although many more important powers are conferred than those now in question, as, for instance, by stat. 59 *G.* 3. *c.* 134. sect. 36. The power now in question is restricted by the provision that two justices must consent to the order. In stat. 55 *G.* 3. *c.* 68. the right of appeal is not left to be inferred from the terms of the schedule, but is expressly given by sect. 3. It is true that the mention of an appeal is improper in a notice under stat. 59 *G.* 3.

(*a*) 4 *B.* & *Ald.* 521.

c. 134.,

1838.

The QUEEN against STOCK.

c. 134., if no appeal is given by the act; but that circumstance alone is not sufficient to authorize it. The retention of that part of the notice was probably an inadvertence. The appeal clause of stat. 55 *G.* 3. *c.* 68., if imported into the other statute, is incongruous; for it requires notice to be given to the surveyors of the highways, who have nothing to do with the ways to be stopped under stat. 59 *G.* 3. *c.* 134. *s.* 39.; and it furnishes no provision for notice to the commissioners for building churches, or to the consenting magistrates. [*The Attorney-General* suggested that the notice would be sufficient if given as nearly in accordance with that referred to as the circumstances would permit; *Regina* v. *The Recorder of Carmarthen*(*a*).] It is asked what use there is in giving notice of the order to stop, if there be no appeal; but the order informs the public that the way is no longer to be used. [*Patteson* J. Is the consent of justices ministerial or otherwise? If it be more than ministerial, it is an order of justices and may be appealed against as such.] It is an order of the commissioners, though with the justices' consent. The consent would be inoperative of itself. And the appeal here is against an order of the commissioners, not of the justices. *Rex* v. *St. James, Westminster* (*b*). does not apply: the Court there merely adopted the best decision that offered itself, in the difficulty created by the words of the particular act.

Lord DENMAN C. J. The objection arising from the repeal of stat. 55 *G.* 3. *c.* 68. is not insisted upon, and does not seem tenable. As to the question, whether

(*a*) 7 *A.* & *E.* 756. *S. C.* 3 *Nev.* & *P.* 19. (*b*) 2 *A.* & *E.* 241.

or

1838.

The Queen *against* Stock.

or not an appeal is given by the reference in stat. 59 *G.* 3. *c.* 134, *s.* 39, to the former statute, I confess I am strongly of opinion that it was intended; but, on the whole, I cannot say that it is done. *Abbott* C. J. says, in *Rex* v. *Hanson* (*a*), speaking, not from any authority, but from his own observation, that a right of appeal cannot be implied, but must be given by express words. Here it is not so given. The notice of the order certainly appears by its form to challenge an appeal; but the direction as to notice of appeal in stat. 55 *G.* 3. *c.* 68. does not point out the parties who, in this case, ought to receive it; and there is nothing in *Regina* v. *The Recorder of Carmarthen* (*b*) that adequately meets this objection. The reason why a power of appeal ought not to be implied is, that the appeal brings a new set of parties into action, and it is necessary that the persons to be affected and the machinery to be employed should be distinctly pointed out. The reference to stat. 55 *G.* 3. *c.* 68. in stat. 59 *G.* 3. *c.* 134, *s.* 39, falls infinitely short of this object.

Littledale J. We cannot here intend a power of appeal. I admit that the words of stat. 55 *G.* 3. *c.* 68. sched. (A.) must be considered as if introduced in stat. 59 *G.* 3. *c.* 134, *s.* 39, and perhaps, if a power of appeal could be implied, it would be so here; but *Abbott* C. J. says, in *Rex* v. *Hanson* (*a*), that that power cannot be given by implication. And the notice in 55 *G.* 3. *c.* 68. sched. (A.), where it mentions an appeal, refers to sect. 3 of the same act, which relates to the stopping of ways that are under the jurisdiction of a surveyor.

(*a*) 4 *B.* & *Ald.* 521. (*b*) 7 *A.* & *E.* 756.

1838.

The QUEEN against BROCK.

When that notice is incorporated in stat. 59 *G.* 3. *c.* 134, *s.* 39, the words relating to an appeal seem to be surplusage.

PATTESON J. The act of 59 *G.* 3. stops short of expressly giving an appeal. The dictum in *Rex* v. *Hanson* (*a*), that a certiorari lies unless expressly taken away, but an appeal does not lie unless expressly given, seems to be clear law. The provision as to notice, in stat. 59 *G.* 3. *c.* 134, *s.* 39, is made after giving power to the commissioners to stop or alter, or vary such paths, footways, and passages "as to them may appear useless and unnecessary, *or* as they shall think fit to alter or vary;" provided the same be done with consent of two justices, and on notice given as prescribed by stat. 55 *G.* 3. *c.* 68.: but it is not added that in such cases the party aggrieved may appeal. If it was intended that an appeal should lie, it has not been said.

WILLIAMS J. There are innumerable instances where an appeal is given in terms; but no case has been mentioned in which it has been given by implication. By the reference to stat. 55 *G.* 3. *c.* 68. on the subject of notice, an appeal seems to have been contemplated; but it should have been expressly given.

Rule absolute for quashing the order of sessions and confirming the order of the commissioners.

(*a*) 4 *B.* & *Ald.* 521.

The QUEEN *against* The MANCHESTER and LEEDS Railway Company.

Thursday, May 31st.

A certiorari will not be granted to bring up the inquisition of a compensation jury, unless defects in the inquisition be positively sworn to. Thus, where a statute (6 & 7 *W.* 4. *c.* cxi.) directed that a railway company should not take lands, unless set out in a schedule to the act, or certified by justices to have been omitted by mistake, it was held not sufficient to shew that lands which were the subject of the inquisition were not in the schedule, without negativing the fact of the certificate.

Nor to assert generally, in addition to such statement, that the act did not authorise taking the lands.

Nor to allege further that certain objections were made in a protest delivered before the taking of the inquisition, which were now in general terms sworn to be true.

If the objection be to the form of the inquisition, a copy should be set out, or it should be sworn that the deponent could not procure a copy; and he should in the latter case swear positively on information and belief.

It is not enough to swear that he "objects" that the inquisition does not contain certain requisites pointed out.

The granting a certiorari is matter of discretion, though there are fatal defects on the face of the proceedings which it is sought to bring up.

It is an almost invariable rule that, where a party applying for a certiorari fails from incompleteness in his affidavits, he will not have a certiorari granted to him upon fresh affidavits supplying the defect; as in the case of the defects above mentioned.

Especially if he appears to have suffered no injury;

Or to have assented to the proceeding below.

Semble, per Lord *Denman* C. J., that the rule requiring that, in proceedings by an inferior jurisdiction, the facts giving the jurisdiction should appear on the face of such proceedings, is not confined to facts necessarily within the knowledge of the party exercising the jurisdiction.

SIR *F. POLLOCK* obtained a rule, in *Easter* term last, calling upon the *Manchester* and *Leeds* Railway Company to shew cause why a certiorari should not issue to remove an inquisition taken for the purpose of inquiring, assessing, and giving a verdict for the money to be paid to *Henry Taylor* and others for the purchase of certain lands, &c., taken by the company under stat. 6 & 7 *W.* 4. *c.* cxi. (local and personal, public (*a*)), and all proceedings had thereon.

The act empowered the company to make a railway, &c., over the lands delineated on the plans, and described in books of reference, deposited &c. (sect. 3); and over lands delineated on the maps and plans, "although such lands or any of them, or the situation thereof respectively, or the name of the owners or of the occu-

(*a*) "An Act for making a Railway from *Manchester* to *Leeds*."

 piers

1838.

The QUEEN against The MANCHESTER and LEEDS Railway Company.

piers thereof respectively, may happen to be omitted, mis-stated, or erroneously described in this act or in the schedule thereto, or in the said books of reference, if it shall appear to any two or more justices of the peace" of *Lancashire*, the West Riding of *Yorkshire*, or the borough of *Leeds*, (in case of dispute), "and be certified by writing under their hands, that such omission, mis-statement, or erroneous description proceeded from mistake" (sect. 5); and that they should not take, &c., any house or other building erected on or before 30th *November* 1835, or any garden, orchard, &c., other than and except such as were specified in the schedule to the act, without the consent in writing of the owners and occupiers, unless the omission in the schedule should have proceeded from mistake, and should be so certified as before provided (sect. 7). Owners and occupiers might agree to receive satisfaction and recompense for their lands; and, if they should not agree with the company, the amount was to be settled by a jury (sect. 137). Sect. 138 enacted that, if any person, &c., interested or entitled should not agree with the company as to the amount of purchase-money or compensation; or should refuse the purchase-money &c. offered by them, and should give notice as in that section was specified, and request that the dispute should be determined by a jury; or should, for twenty-one days after notice given to such person, &c., neglect or refuse to treat; and in other cases (some of which were specified) where agreement for compensation could not be made; the company should issue a warrant to the sheriff, &c., to summon a jury, who should inquire of, and assess and give a verdict for, the sum to be paid for purchase or compensation, "and the said sheriff," &c., "shall

1838.

The QUEEN *against* The MANCHESTER and LEEDS Railway Company.

"shall accordingly give judgment for such purchase-money, satisfaction, recompence, or compensation as shall be assessed by such jury; which said verdict and the judgment thereon to be pronounced as aforesaid shall be binding and conclusive to all intents and purposes upon all persons and corporations whatsoever:" provided that seven days' notice of the time and place at which the jury were to be returned should be given by the company to the party. Sect. 140 enacted, "that the said verdicts and judgments, being first signed by the said sheriff," &c., "presiding at the taking of such verdict and pronouncing such judgment respectively, shall be kept by the clerk of the peace for the county or riding in which the matter in dispute shall have arisen among the records of the quarter sessions of such county or riding, and shall be deemed records to all intents and purposes; and the same or true copies thereof shall be allowed to be good evidence in all courts whatsoever; and all persons shall have liberty to inspect the same, paying for such inspection" &c.

The affidavits in support of the rule stated that the company claimed to take part of *Taylor's* land, and issued their warrant to the sheriff; that a jury was summoned to assess the value, and that the company gave notice accordingly to *Taylor*; that he served them, and the sheriff, with a notice or protest, denying their right to take certain parts of the land, for reasons alleged in the notice, which (as appeared by the description of the notice in the affidavit) were, that some parts were not specified in the act of parliament, or in the schedule, "and that two justices had not jurisdiction to grant a certain certificate as to the omission;" and that other parts named (some of which fell, as explained, within the de-

 scription

1838.

The QUEEN against The MANCHESTER and LEEDS Railway Company.

scription in sect. 7), were not described in the book of reference, or the act, or the schedule (not negativing the certificate of the justices): That the jury were impannelled, &c., the deponent appearing under protest, and gave their verdict for the sum to be paid for premises of *Taylor*, which, in the inquisition, were stated to be particularised in the warrant to the sheriff, and to be by the act of parliament authorised to be taken, "but which this deponent asserts is not the fact." The affidavit then added, "*and this deponent further objects* that the said inquisition does not set forth," &c. (certain particulars supposed to be requisite). The deponent then alleged that the only description of his property in the books of reference was as set forth in an extract contained in the affidavit, "and that all the facts set forth in the said protest, so served upon the said company, and upon the sheriff of *Lancashire*, as aforesaid, are true, as deponent verily believes," with some trifling exceptions, which were stated.

Cresswell, Sir *W. W. Follett*, and *Tomlinson*, now shewed cause, and contended, first, that the objections were invalid in themselves; secondly, that the facts raising them were not positively sworn to in the affidavits.

Sir *F. Pollock* and Sir *G. A. Lewin*, contrà, contended that the objections were fatal, and that the deponent must be understood as swearing to the facts, and that the affidavits stated them with sufficient positiveness, at any rate, to induce the Court to have the inquisition brought up for examination.

Lord DENMAN C. J. We should issue the certiorari if it distinctly appeared that the jury had comprehended

in

1838.

The QUEEN *against* The MANCHESTER and LEEDS Railway Company.

in their verdict any thing which they were not authorised to include. But we cannot assume that the fact is so, unless the affidavits positively state it. They should either set out the inquisition, or shew that the deponent has no copy, and then distinctly state that he is informed of and believes the facts raising the objection. Here all that appears as to the inquisition is, that the party "objects" that certain deficiencies exist. It is said that this is an objection upon oath; but suppose he had actually said, "I object upon oath," that would merely be a solemn form of stating the objection. Then, as to the authority of the company to take the lands, and of the jury to assess the value. This should be distinctly negatived. Here all that is positively sworn to is the description in the books of reference, which is alleged to be insufficient, and the statement by Mr. *Taylor* in his protest, that the lands were not properly described in the act or schedule. It should be shewn positively that the justices have not certified; for their certificate would give the power. To assert, generally, that it is not the fact that the statute authorises the proceeding, is not enough; it should be stated how it fails to do so. Even if the misdescription in the schedule raised a primâ facie case, the want of authority should be fully shewn. We are bound to see that all facts have been brought before us. I disclaim the principle that we are to issue a certiorari to bring up the inquisition on the ground that there may probably be defects; we must clearly see that facts do exist, which will bring the defects before us. I would further observe, as a warning, that we cannot encourage applications of this sort; otherwise they would be made by every person who might be dissatisfied with the verdict of the jury. We must

1838.

The QUEEN *against* The MANCHESTER and LEEDS Railway Company.

hold parties strictly to the rules by which the issuing of writs of certiorari is restrained.

LITTLEDALE J. Either there should be a regular copy of the inquisition, or, if that cannot be procured, the fact should be stated, and then the party should swear directly to his information and belief.

PATTESON J. As to the statement of supposed defects in the inquisition by merely saying that the party objects that they exist, it is urged that any person of common sense must see that he means to swear to the fact. Then why does he not swear to it? I never will encourage a man to use other language, and that purposely, for so I must take the fact to be here. I know that, in proceedings in other places, the language of a deposition is, "deponent further submits:" but that must be only, I presume, in the case of a proposition of law. As for the other objections to the proceedings, I agree with my Lord Chief Justice that we should be cautious how we grant a certiorari without positive affidavit of facts. It is not sufficient for a deponent to say he asserts generally that it is not the fact that the statute authorises the proceedings: he should shew how it fails to do so.

WILLIAMS J. It is true that we are not called upon, at this stage, to quash the inquisition; but we ought to see clearly that the affidavits state facts raising the objections. The practice is, I believe, the most lax in the instance of removing convictions by certiorari. But there the conviction is not made up till the last moment, whereas the error has arisen upon the hearing (a).

(a) See *Massey* v. *Johnson*, 12 *East*, 67.

It

1838.

The QUEEN *against* The MANCHESTER and LEEDS Railway Company.

It is expected, in such a case, that the affidavits should shew some error committed by the magistrate; and then, although the conviction may be drawn up afterwards, credit is given to the justice that he will return a conviction agreeable to the facts which took place at the hearing where the affidavit shews an error committed; if that were not so, a certiorari never could be granted in such a case. But here nothing is distinctly sworn to, shewing an error in any part of the proceedings; and as, in this case, there is a regular record to which recourse might be had, I see a difficulty in saying how this inquisition could be sufficiently brought before us except by verifying it fully, which could be easily done by a copy.

Rule discharged.

Sir *F. Pollock*, in the same term, *June* 14th, moved for a rule similar to that which had been discharged. The former affidavits were read in support of the rule, with new ones, verifying a copy, which was annexed, of the inquisition and warrant, stating that the company had given *Taylor* notice to treat, and also deposing positively to the alleged defects before complained of. The inquisition did not shew that any notice to treat had been given to *Taylor;* nor did it state that any of the events had arisen, upon which, under sect. 138, the company were to issue the warrant. It ran as follows. "An inquisition, verdict, and judgment, held, taken, and given, at" &c., "on" &c., "before me, *Thomas Bright Crosse*, Esq., Sheriff" &c., "pursuant to an act of parliament made" &c., "on the oaths" &c., "duly empannelled, summoned, and returned by the said sheriff," "in pursuance of, and in obedience to, a warrant made

and

1838.

The QUEEN against The MANCHESTER and LEEDS Railway Company.

and issued under the common seal of the *Manchester* and *Leeds* Railway Company, to me directed and delivered, and hereunto annexed; who, being sworn and charged as in and by the said warrant directed, upon their oaths present and say that they have inquired of, found, and assessed," &c. The annexed warrant was in the name of the company, incorporated by an act &c.; it said nothing of any notice to treat, or of any event pointed out in sect. 138 as ground for a warrant, but was described only as "this our warrant pursuant to the powers for that purpose given us by the said act." The inquisition assessed the purchase-money to be paid to *Taylor* at the gross sum of 17,000*l*., and found that no compensation was to be paid for any damage. The Court took time to consider; and afterwards, in *Michaelmas* term, 1838, granted a rule nisi. The rule was drawn up to shew cause (as before), on notice to the clerk of the company. In *Michaelmas* term (*November* 26th), 1838,

Cresswell shewed cause. The first question is, whether the Court, in its discretion, will grant the certiorari, on a second application, the first having failed. If this be now done, what limit can be assigned to the practice? In *Rex* v. *Orde* (*a*) this Court discharged a rule

(*a*) The KING *against* ORDE.

A rule for a quo warranto information against a mayor, on the ground that he did not reside as the charter required, was discharged on affidavits shewing residence. Afterwards a second rule was obtained, on the same ground, on affidavits impeaching the former opposing affidavits, and tending to shew that the residence was colourable. The rule was discharged, on the ground that a second application ought not to have been made after the former decision; but without costs, as the Court had granted the rule nisi.

IN *Michaelmas* term, 1830, *Denman* obtained a rule nisi for an information in the nature of quo warranto, calling upon *J. B. Orde*, Esq. to shew by what authority he claimed to be mayor of the borough of *Berwick*-

a rule for a quo warranto, which had been obtained after a previous rule against the same party had been discharged, though the second rule was obtained on affidavits explaining and contradicting those upon which the former rule had been discharged. Here the case is the weaker, because it does not appear that

---

wick-upon-Tweed, on the ground (among others) that, at the time of his election, he was incapable of being elected by reason that he did not reside and inhabit within the said borough, nor was at scot and lot, or partaker of the assessments there. The affidavits in support of the rule alleged the facts, as above, and also set out a clause of the charter for the purpose of shewing that residence, &c., were essential: the affidavits in answer stated that Mr. *Orde* was tenant of a house in *Berwick-upon-Tweed*, at which he generally slept; and that no rates, &c., had been made or levied since he came to reside. The rule was discharged with costs, in the same term (27th *November*). Present Lord *Tenterden* C. J., *Parke*, *Taunton*, and *Patteson* Js. *Campbell* and *Ingham* against the rule; Sir *T. Denman*, Attorney-General, in support of it.

In *Hilary* term, 1831, Sir *T. Denman*, Attorney-General, obtained a rule nisi to the same effect, on the ground above specified. The rule was drawn up on reading some of the affidavits filed on the previous occasion, and also affidavits impeaching those filed in opposition to the former rule, and tending to shew that the residence of Mr. *Orde* was colourable. Cause was shewn in the same term (31st *January*); and, upon its being opened that the application was against the same party, and on the same alleged defect, as before, Lord *Tenterden* C. J. interposed, and said that the rule ought not to have been granted, that the objection to the mayor's title was a captious one, and that to allow it to be raised on a second application would be to encourage parties to come before the Court in the first instance with an imperfect case, and then eke it out on a second application by picking out inconsistencies in the opposing affidavits. *The Court* accordingly discharged the rule without hearing any answer to it on the merits; but gave no costs, inasmuch as it had been the error of the Court, in granting the second rule nisi, which occasioned the defendant to appear.

Present Lord *Tenterden* C. J., *Littledale*, *Taunton*, and *Patteson* Js.

Campbell and *Ingham* against the rule.

Sir *T. Denman*, Attorney-General, in support of it.

Ex relatione *Ingham*.

the

1838.

The QUEEN against The MANCHESTER and LEEDS Railway Company.

the party applying has been injured; the inquisition itself gives no title. [*Patteson* J. By sect. 140, the judgment is to be recorded, and to be deemed a record to all intents and purposes. If it be a judgment of record, is not the remedy by error rather than certiorari?] That is another objection to the rule, if these proceedings be treated as the act of a court of record; and, if they be not in the nature of proceedings of a court, how can there be a certiorari at all? In *Rex* v. *The Trustees of the Norwich and Watton Road* (a) the inquisition was not a record. [Sir *F. Pollock* referred to *Rex* v. *The Nottingham Old Water Works Company* (b).] There the question was merely whether a mandamus was rendered unnecessary by the verdict and judgment being made records. Next, admitting that the certiorari lies, and that the Court will examine into the regularity of the inquisition, the first objection is, that it does not recite that the company had given *Taylor* notice to treat. It has often been laid down that this is necessary for the purpose of shewing jurisdiction; but the notice to treat is not here essential to the jurisdiction; it is sufficient, by sect. 138, that the parties should not agree as to the amount; and that fact appears by one of the parties having issued a warrant to have the amount assessed. Further, the instances in which an averment of the facts raising the jurisdiction was required have occurred where the party holding the inquisition, or making the adjudication, had cognisance of the facts which were to be stated. Thus, under stat. 11 *G.* 2. *c.* 19, *s.* 16, justices putting landlords into premises on a vacant possession themselves ascertain the facts. The same principle applies to an

(a) 5 *A.* & *E.* 563.

(b) 6 *A.* & *E.* 355.

order

1838.

The Queen against The Manchester and Leeds Railway Company.

order for stopping up a highway as unnecessary, under stat. 55 *G.* 3. *c.* 68, *s.* 2. (*a*). So in *Kite and Lane's Case* (*b*) the conviction was held bad, for not shewing a fact essential to the jurisdiction, and of which the convicting magistrates were to take cognisance. In *Rex* v. *The Mayor, &c., of Liverpool* (*c*), the sheriff, before whom the inquisition was holden, was himself to give the notice; and therefore the inquisition was quashed for not shewing such notice. In *Rex* v. *Bagshaw* (*d*) the jury was summoned, and the order upon the inquisition made, by the trustees, who were to give the notice. So in *Rex* v. *The Trustees of the Norwich and Watton Road* (*e*) the trustees, who were to give the notice, were the parties before whom the inquisition was holden. There, *Patteson* J. would not express a positive opinion whether the notice should appear, but said that his impression was "that it should appear, not as the finding of the jury, but in the nature of a caption." Now, a caption is the statement by the court or magistrate of that which is within their own knowledge, and upon which they act. But what knowledge could the sheriff here have of the fact of notice? It was not to be found by the jury; and, indeed, the jury could find nothing except upon the assumption of the facts essential to the jurisdiction. If it lay with the sheriff to state the fact, his statement would be conclusive, even though false, according to the principles laid down by *Holroyd* J. in *Basten* v. *Carew* (*g*). But that will not be contended for here. (He then argued

(*a*) See *Rex* v. *Justices of Cambridgeshire*, 4 *A.* & *E.* 111.
(*b*) 1 *B.* & *C.* 101.
(*c*) 4 *Burr.* 2244.
(*d*) 7 *T. R.* 363.
(*e*) 5 *A.* & *E.* 563.
(*g*) 3 *B.* & *C.* 649.

upon

1838.

The QUEEN against The MANCHESTER and LEEDS Railway Company.

upon the other objections taken; but the decision of the Court renders it unnecessary to go into these (a).)

Sir *F. Pollock*, contrà. The Court will not discharge the rule upon the ground of this being a second application, after they have, upon consideration, determined to entertain the question in its present shape. The powers granted by the act are in derogation of the common law; and, however necessary they may be, this Court has always watched the exercise of such powers very strictly. It is said that no injury is suffered, because the inquisition gives no title. But, if the inquisition includes lands which the company has no power to take, then, the whole purchase-money being assessed in a gross sum, Mr. *Taylor* is unable to separate the portion that belongs to the lands which ought not to have been taken: he cannot therefore receive any of the purchase-money without subjecting himself to a kind of estoppel against his claim to the lands in dispute, from his consent to the assessment so made for all. Next, it does not follow from the judgment having become a record that certiorari will not lie. Instances of certiorari being granted in such cases may be found in 4 *Vin. Abr.* 330, *Certiorari* (A.) and (B.). In *Groenvelt* v. *Burwell* (b) it was held, by *Holt* C. J., "That

(a) One point made against the rule was, that the sheriff or undersheriff should have been called on to shew cause, as being the party summoning the jury, and giving judgment, under sect. 138. 4 *Vin. Abr.* 339, 340, *Certiorari*, (B. 3.), was cited.

Mr. *Dealtry* stated, that it was not the practice to give notice to any one except the party interested; that, in removing an indictment, notice of a rule to shew cause was given only to the prosecutor: but that, in removing an order or a conviction, notice was given to the justice as well as the party, because the justice is interested in supporting it, as there may be an action against him if the order or conviction be illegal.

The Court gave no judgment on this point.

(b) 1 *Salk.* 263. *S. C.* 1 *Ld. Raym.* 454.

wherever

1838.

The Queen against The Manchester and Leeds Railway Company.

wherever a new jurisdiction is erected by act of parliament, and the court or judge that exercises this jurisdiction acts as a court or judge of record according to the course of the common law, a writ of error lies on their judgments; but where they act in a summary method, or in a new course different from the common law, there a writ of error lies not, but a *certiorari*." The case of a removal of proceedings of commissioners of sewers, which was there mentioned by Lord *Holt* (a), is a strong instance. Again, sect. 140 of this local act has not the effect suggested. The words were as strong in the corresponding enactment in *Rex* v. *The Nottingham Old Water Works Company* (b); and it is clear, from the judgment of *Patteson* J. there, that the effect of judgments of record will not be given, for all purposes, to such proceedings. Here there is nothing analogous to an ordinary judgment of a court of record: there could be no arrest of judgment: and it is difficult to see how error could be brought. The case rather falls within the rule of *Holt* C. J. in *Crosse* v. *Smith* (c), that "there is no jurisdiction which can withstand a certiorari." Next, it is argued that the notice to treat need not be alleged, inasmuch as it was not necessary that the jurisdiction should have arisen in that way: but that renders it more essential to shew what origin, if any, the jurisdiction had. The argument, that such an allegation is requisite only where the party holding the inquisition has personal knowledge of the fact, raises a distinction which has never been recognised: and the circumstance is not adverted to in the cases where the allegation has been held necessary. (He also argued on the other points of the case.)

(a) 1 *Ld. Raym.* 469.

(b) 6 *A. & E.* 355. See p. 369.

(c) 3 *Salk.* 80.

Lord

1838.

The QUEEN *against* The MANCHESTER and LEEDS Railway Company.

Lord DENMAN C. J. Two objections are urged in support of this rule. The first is, that the inquisition does not shew that there was notice to treat; the second, that it comprises land which the company had no power to take. Against the rule, it has been urged, first, that no certiorari will lie. For my own part, I beg to say that I express no doubt that it will lie. As to the objections arising upon the absence of a statement of notice to treat, I cannot say that I am satisfied with the distinction for which Mr. *Cresswell* contended; and, as to the land taken, I cannot say I perceive it to be clearly shewn that the land in question was subjected to the company's use. But it is clear that we must exercise a discretion as to granting a certiorari. The conduct of the party applying may be such as to preclude him from being entitled to it. On a recent occasion (*a*), we would not allow a party to take advantage of a defect on the face of the inquisition which arose from his having himself requested that the provisions of the act should be deviated from. Here it does not appear that the party applying has been injured by either of the defects to which he objects, nor that he had not in fact full notice, nor that he was misled. He went down to the inquisition; he was fully heard by counsel (*b*); but he is disappointed by the amount eventually awarded. [Sir *F. Pollock* here pointed out that *Taylor* protested, at the taking of the inquisition.] I do not mean that he formally waived his objection; but, in fact, he had every advantage that a party can obtain in conducting such an enquiry; and, if the Court is quite satisfied that the

(*a*) *Regina* v. *The Committee Men for the South Holland Drainage*, post, p. 429.

(*b*) This was assumed in the argument on both sides.

sum

1838.

The QUEEN *against* The MANCHESTER and LEEDS Railway Company.

sum awarded is as large as he can reasonably expect, and has not been less on account of the defects pointed out, that also may be a circumstance to convince the Court that a certiorari ought not to issue. But here we have, in addition to the facts already noticed, the fact that the very same application was made under circumstances such that the Court thought proper to dismiss it. Now, if the Court can, in any case, be deprived of discretion as to granting a certiorari, it is under such circumstances as these. For the rule of practice, if not altogether universal and inflexible, is as nearly so as possible, that the Court will not allow a party to succeed, on a second application, who has previously applied for the very same thing without coming properly prepared. We are constantly acting on this principle, of which the convenience and the justice are apparent. I feel, indeed, that there is something ungracious in discharging the rule on this ground, after the encouragement held out to a second application. In particular, I take blame to myself for my share in it, having taken the affidavits home with me for the purpose of examining, with no little trouble and consumption of time, whether they shewed in themselves legal objections sufficient to entitle the party to a certiorari. I then assumed that, if these should appear, the Court would have no choice, but must grant the rule as a matter of course. My view now is, however, quite opposite to this. I must say (as I should have said in the first instance had this view occurred to me) that a party after once failing in consequence of a defect in the way in which he brought his case forward, is not entitled to renew the same application. I regret the expense incurred by the party; but it is some con-

1838.

The QUEEN *against* The MANCHESTER and LEEDS Railway Company.

solation to remember that, in the case which Mr. *Cresswell* cited, Lord *Tenterden* thought that the rule ought to be discharged, but without costs, as the Court had sanctioned, to a certain extent, the second application, by granting the rule nisi. That I think forms a precedent which we may properly follow here. In the first place, then, I think it most important that we should assert our right to a discretion in granting the writ of certiorari. And, secondly, I think that every party is to come at first fully prepared with a proper case, and, if he fails to do so, must not afterwards renew the application with an amended case (*a*).

PATTESON J. I quite agree. I recollect the case alluded to by Mr. *Cresswell*; and I believe I am the only Judge now present who took a part in that decision. As to what fell from me during the argument in the present case, respecting the effect of the inquisition considered as a judgment, I merely wished to inquire whether, if it have the effect of a judgment of a Court of record, error would not lie, and a certiorari be excluded. But I think that, in fact, this cannot be considered as a judgment. The section is drawn very loosely; but it does not, as far as I can understand it, give these proceedings an effect analogous to that of judgments of a court of record (*b*).

WILLIAMS and COLERIDGE Js. concurred.

Rule discharged without costs (*c*).

(*a*) See the authorities in *Todd* v. *Jeffery* (7 *A.* & *E.* 519.), and *Rex* v. *Eve* (5 *A.* & *E.* 780.)

(*b*) See *Rex* v. *The Nottingham Old Waterworks Company* (6 *A.* & *E.* 369, 370.), *Regina* v. *Trustees of Swansea Harbour*, p. 448, post.; judgment of *Littledale* J.

(*c*) See the next two cases.

1838.

The following case, decided in *Michaelmas* term, 1838, may conveniently be inserted here.

The QUEEN *against* The Committee Men for the SOUTH HOLLAND Drainage.

Thursday, November 15th, 1838.

On application for a certiorari, the Court will take into consideration the conduct of the party applying.

A party, whose land had been taken under the *South Holland* Drainage act (57 *G.* 3. c. lxix.), applied for a certiorari to bring up the inquisition held before a compensation jury on the grounds, 1. That the inquisition did not state such a notice to treat for compensation as was requisite under the act to give jurisdiction; 2. That the jury had ordered a fence to be erected for the benefit of the applicant, in addition to a money compensation, instead of giving him the whole compensation in money; 3. That the applicant held in right of his wife, and that the tenure was copyhold, and no compensation was made to the wife or lord.

This Court refused a certiorari, it appearing, on affidavit, 1. That the applicant had consented to waive the notice, and requested that the jury might be summoned for a day too near to admit of proper notice under the act; 2. That he had discussed the amount of compensation proper to be given, upon the supposition of the fence being erected, and, 3. That he did not now swear to his belief that the jury had awarded less money in consequence of the award as to the fence; 4. That, in the dispute respecting the land, he had not mentioned his wife's interest, or the nature of the tenure, but had acted as if the property was his own freehold.

W. *H. WATSON* obtained a rule in *Michaelmas* term, 1837, calling upon the committee men under stat. 57 *G.* 3. *c.* lxix, (local and personal, public), "for amending and rendering more effectual an act of his present Majesty (*a*), for draining lands in *South Holland*," &c., to shew cause why a certiorari should not issue, to remove a verdict and inquisition, and judgment thereon, given on 16th *August* 1837, before and by the said committee men, touching the compensation to be made to *Philip Copeman* for certain lands adjudged by the said committee men to be taken from him for the purpose of the act.

Sect. 2 of the local act appoints trustees for the purposes of the act. Sect. 11 directs the appointment of committee men for the purposes of the act; in whom, by

(*a*) Stat. 33 *G.* 3. *c.* 109. Stat. 35 *G.* 3. *c.* 166. was also referred to in the Act.

1838.

The QUEEN against The Committee Men for the SOUTH HOLLAND Drainage.

by sect. 20, certain powers or authorities of the trustees are vested. Sect. 35 authorises the committee men to execute certain works. Sect. 36 enacts that they shall have power to agree, on behalf of the trustees, with the proprietors of, or persons interested in, any lands, &c., which the committee men shall adjudge necessary to be taken or made use of for the purposes of the act, for the purchase of such lands, &c., or for recompense to the proprietors, &c., for damage, &c.; and also to settle in what proportions the sum or sums so agreed for shall be paid to the several persons interested; and power is given to bodies politic, tenants for life or in tail, husbands, &c., to contract with the committee men; but if any such body politic, &c., or other person or persons interested, &c., "shall, for the space of forty days after notice in writing given to the principal officer or officers of such body politic," &c., or to such "person or persons respectively," "neglect or refuse to treat, or shall not agree with the said committee men for the time being," then the committee men are empowered to issue their warrant to the sheriff, &c., to summon a jury to appear before the committee men, who may also summon witnesses; and the jury, "upon their oaths (which oaths, as also the oaths to such person or persons as shall be called upon to give evidence, the said committee men for the time being are hereby empowered to administer) shall inquire of, assess," &c., the sums "to be paid for the purchase," &c., "or the recompence to be made for damages," &c., "and to (*a*) settle and ascertain in what proportions" the sums assessed shall be paid to the several persons interested; and the committee men

(*a*) Sic.

shall

1838.

The QUEEN against The Committee Men for the SOUTH HOLLAND Drainage.

shall give judgment for such purchase monies or recompence so to be assessed by such juries; which verdict and judgment shall be binding and conclusive to all intents and purposes against all parties," &c., "and all persons whomsoever." Sect. 38 prescribes a form for sales, conveyances, and assurances of lands, &c., and enacts that every such sale, &c., so made, shall vest the premises conveyed in the trustees, freed and discharged from all claims, rights, &c., of all persons whomsoever.

Copeman, in his affidavit made in support of the rule, deposed that his wife was seised in her own right of a close of land, copyhold of inheritance, holden by her of the manor of *Sutton Holland*, part of which close was, at the time of the giving of the verdict and judgment afterwards mentioned, in his possession. That the committee men, determining to adversely purchase part of the close, summoned a jury before them, on 16th *August* 1837, to assess, as they alleged, the money to be paid for the purchase of the land, and the recompence to be made for damage to be sustained thereby. The affidavit then set out the verdict and judgment, the material parts of which were as follows.

"*Lincolnshire* to wit. An inquisition indented and taken at" &c., "on" &c., "before us the undersigned," &c. (naming four persons who were stated to be committee men duly appointed, &c.), "on the oath of" &c., "honest and lawful men of" &c., "who, being sworn" &c., "say that they assess and ascertain the sum of *56l.* to be the true value of, and a proper sum to be paid by the said committee men for the purchase of, one rood," &c., "being the property or reputed property of *Philip Copeman*, of" &c., "and which land has been

 adjudged

1838.

The QUEEN against The Committee Men for the SOUTH HOLLAND Drainage.

adjudged by the said committee men necessary to be taken and made use of for the purposes of the said recited act; and for the recompence to the said *P. C.* for the damage he may sustain; which sum of 56*l.*, so assessed and ascertained as aforesaid, shall be wholly paid to the said *P. C.*; and the said committee men shall, moreover, at the expense of the *South Holland* drainage trust, plant young white-thorn quicksets on the bank reserved or retained by the said *P. C.*, four feet distant from the edge of the land purchased and taken by the said committee men as aforesaid, and place and fix, within side the said quicksets, a post and three-rail fence for the protection thereof, and use due means, for the next ensuing seven years, to prevent the same quicksets from being injured by cattle or otherwise on the side thereof next to the said purchased land and main drain aforesaid," &c. "We, the committee men above said, do hereby give judgment for the sum of 56*l.*, the purchase money assessed and ascertained by the said jury, to be paid as in the above inquisition mentioned." (Signed by the four committee men.)

Copeman further deposed "that no notice in writing, as prescribed by the said act, was given previously to the impannelling, summoning, and returning of the said jury;" that he was advised and believed that the inquisition founded on the verdict was defective and bad in form, inasmuch as it did not set forth that any notice in writing, as required by the act, was given previously to the impannelling &c., or shew any legal authority by which the committee men or jury have jurisdiction; and, also, inasmuch as no compensation was awarded to the lords of the manor in respect of their interest; and also that it appeared by the inquisition that the jury, instead

1838.

The QUEEN *against* The Committee Men for the SOUTH HOLLAND Drainage.

instead of awarding to the deponent recompence in money for the whole damages which he would sustain, has assumed to authorise the committee men to commit trespasses upon other land of the deponent, and do certain works thereon, as part of such recompence.

From the affidavits in answer it appeared that *Copeman*, after the land required had been pointed out to him, wrote to the clerk of the committee men, on 4th *July* 1837, as follows. "Inclosed I transmit, agreeable to your request, the particulars of valuation of a plantation belonging to me, which the committee men of the *South Holland* drainage are desirous to purchase: the average of profit is taken at twenty years' purchase, which I hope will prove satisfactory." Annexed to the letter was a statement of the price required by *Copeman* for the land, with an additional charge for trees standing thereon. On 12th *July* 1837, *Copeman*, by appointment, met the clerk of the committee men and their valuers: the valuers afterwards drew up a minute, stating the value they assigned to the land and trees, and containing the following clause: "The committee men, at the expense of the trust, to plant a quick fence on the land reserved by the several proprietors, four feet from the edge of the land to be purchased by the committee men; and the committee men are to place and fix, within side the said quick, a post and three rail fence to protect the same; and shall use means to prevent the quick for the next seven years being injured by cattle or otherwise on the drain side thereof." The contents of this minute were, on the same day, communicated to *Copeman*, who refused to accept the sum named: and a discussion ensued between him and the committee men then present and their valuers. It being then re-

1838.

The QUEEN *against* The Committee Men for the SOUTH HOLLAND Drainage.

presented to *Copeman* that the lapse of forty days, and the subsequent time before a jury could be impannelled, would carry the time for executing the required works too far into the autumn, *Copeman* stated that, as the question must go to a jury, he did not care how soon; and, with his expressed consent, the 16th of *August* then next was appointed. The clerk then entered in a minute book this memorandum: "Mr. *Copeman* and Mr. *Prest*" (another landholder) "refused to accept the sums offered to them respectively, but agreed that a tender thereof should be considered to have been made; and they further agreed to dispense with any notice required by the provisions of the act of parliament in this behalf: and it was consented and agreed by all parties that the jury, for the ascertainment of the amount of purchase or compensation money to be paid, shall be summoned for *Wednesday*, 16th *August* next, at eleven o'clock in the forenoon, to sit at this place: and the clerk is directed to prepare a warrant to the sheriff accordingly." This memorandum was read audibly in *Copeman*'s presence, and he was cognizant of and assenting to it. The inquisition was, accordingly, holden on 16th *August*; and *Copeman* attended, addressed the jury, and called witnesses. *Copeman* never disclosed, until some time after the inquisition had been taken, that he was seised only in right of his wife, or that the land was copyhold; and he never made any objection to the proposed arrangement as to the fence.

Humfrey now shewed cause. First, as to the objection that the inquisition does not state such notice in writing to have been given as the act requires. Where such an objection has been sustained, there was, in fact, no

1838.

The QUEEN against The Committee Men for the SOUTH HOLLAND Drainage.

no notice given: *Rex* v. *Mayor, &c., of Liverpool* (a), (citing *Rex* v. *Manning* (b)), *Rex* v. *Bagshaw* (c). This distinction was taken in *Rex* v. *The Trustees of the Norwich and Watton Road* (d). Here, though the forty days' notice required by sect. 36 has not been given, it appears that, on the 12th *July*, *Copeman* assented to the inquisition being holden on the 16th *August*, and to the forty days' interval being dispensed with. Such a waiver debarred him from insisting on the want of notice, and, at the same time, made it impossible to draw the inquisition with the averment in question, which would not be true. If the waiver had been stated, the inquisition would equally have failed to allege that the requisites of sect. 36 had been satisfied. Secondly, it is objected that the jury have directed a fence to be made. But the committee men might have taken the whole land in which the fence is to be made, which is for the protection of *Copeman;* he cannot complain of a benefit thus given up to him by the committee men. And, further, on the 12th *July*, *Copeman* assented to the erection of the fence; the only difference between him and the committee men was as to the money to be paid besides. Thirdly, it is objected that the land is copyhold. If it be, the committee men, and those whom they represent, are the losers, and *Copeman* is a gainer, having the price fixed on the supposition that he can convey a fee simple. The lord, if his right be interfered with, may apply for compensation hereafter; so may the wife, if she be interested. But, at any rate, *Copeman* cannot make this objection; for, by his letter of 4th *July*, he gives the committee men to understand that the land is absolutely his.

(a) 4 *Burr.* 2244.
(b) 1 *Burr.* 377.
(c) 7 *T. R.* 363.
(d) 5 *A. & E.* 563. See p. 571.

W. H. Watson,

1838.

The QUEEN *against* The Committee Men for the SOUTH HOLLAND Drainage.

W. H. Watson, contrà. First, as to the want of allegation of notice, the objection is that the inquisition is, in this respect, a defective instrument. The decisions cited on this point all proceeded on the ground that facts shewing the jurisdiction must appear by the inquisition itself, and not on the ground suggested, that there was actually no notice. Such a defect on the face of a proceeding cannot be cured by the parol waiver of an individual; for the instrument is, by sect. 36, to conclude all parties and persons whomsoever, to all intents and purposes. But, if such a waiver be equivalent to notice, then a statement of the waiver on the face of the inquisition would be equivalent to a statement of notice. It is said that this would not satisfy the act; but the statement would satisfy the act, if the waiver itself cured the want of notice. This is a notice essential to give jurisdiction, and cannot therefore be treated like a notice of trial, or of executing an inquiry. On such an inquisition as this the witnesses could not be indicted for perjury. Secondly, as to the fence. The jury are to give full compensation in money: here they have assumed to protect *Copeman* against damage by ordering the erection of a fence. He was entitled to an award of money instead. The direction on this point cannot be considered as surplusage, for it is obvious that less money must have been awarded in consequence. Besides, as the jury had no power to order the fence to be made, *Copeman* has not the means of securing himself by enforcing this part of the verdict; and at the end of seven years he will have to repair the fence himself. Thirdly, the land being copyhold, and *Copeman*'s wife having an interest, the inquisition is bad for not awarding compensation to the lord and the wife. It is even doubtful whether an act of this kind apply to copyhold

1838.

The QUEEN against The Committee Men for the SOUTH HOLLAND Drainage.

copyhold lands at all; and whether, under the conveyance directed by sect. 38, copyhold lands will pass; *Coke's Copyholder*, sect. 53; 1 *Scriven on Copyholds*, pp. 99 to 110, part I. c. 2. (3d edit.).

Lord DENMAN C. J. It is not to be understood that I am deciding this case on the ground that this inquisition is good in itself; for I think there are perhaps two fatal objections; one, that no notice appears upon it; the other, that the jury have made it part of their award that the fence should be erected. To the objection suggested as arising from the land being copyhold I do not advert; for it does not appear on the face of the inquisition, nor is the fact of its being copyhold said to have been previously communicated. But the ground of my decision is that this party is not competent to make the objections which he now brings before us. We cannot doubt that the inquisition would have been free from the defect created by want of due notice, if the party had not himself waived it, requesting for his own benefit that the enquiry might take place at an earlier period than that which a regular notice would have assigned. As to the suggestion that the jury have awarded a smaller compensation in money on account of their unlawfully giving directions to erect the fence, it is open to the same answer; for the party discussed the amount of the estimate on the supposition that a fence was to be made for him; and no doubt he might waive his right to a full money compensation on that account. But it also admits of this further answer, that he does not swear to his belief that the jury have in fact given him less money than they would have given if they had omitted

all

1838.

The QUEEN *against* The Committee Men for the SOUTH HOLLAND Drainage.

all that respects the fence. As that is not expressly stated, he may not have suffered. I cannot, therefore, consider him to be in a situation to take advantage of defects, one of which he caused in the hope of obtaining an ampler remuneration, and the other he waived at the inquiry.

PATTESON J. This case must not be cited to shew that notice, and all things necessary to give authority, need not be on the face of the inquisition. Several cases have been cited to shew that this is requisite: and, for the purpose of the present case, I assume them to be right. But I agree with my Lord that this party cannot take the objection. Perhaps, as Mr. *Watson* argues, the witnesses could not be indicted for perjury. But whose fault is that? The party himself has occasioned it. So as to the objection that the estate is copyhold: he himself has treated it as freehold. And, again, with respect to his wife's interest, he keeps that fact back, and acts as if the property were entirely his own. He has so conducted himself that he is not entitled to ask anything.

WILLIAMS and COLERIDGE Js. concurred.

Rule discharged (*a*).

(*a*) See the next case.

1839.

The following case, decided in *Hilary* term, 1839, may conveniently be inserted here.

The QUEEN *against* The Trustees of SWANSEA Harbour.

Wednesday, Jan. 30th, 1839.

By a statute (6 & 7 *W.* 4. c. cxxvi.) empowering trustees of a harbour to purchase lands for certain purposes, it was enacted that, in case of difference between the trustees and any landholder as to compensation, and if the same could not be agreed for, or the landholder should refuse &c. to treat, after twenty-one days' notice, the trustees might issue their warrant to the sheriff to summon a jury, who should appear before the justices at quarter sessions, and should there assess the compensation, and the justices should accordingly give judgment for the same: And that the verdict and judgment should be kept by the clerk of the peace among the records of sessions, and should be deemed records: Also that, if the verdict should be for a sum exceeding, or the same as, that offered by the trustees, they should pay costs to the landholder; if for a less sum, then the costs should be borne equally by the parties: such costs, if necessary, to be recovered under a justice's warrant of distress; the amount to be ascertained by a justice.

The trustees offered money for certain land; the landholder did not accept it, but desired that the amount might be settled by a jury. In the mean time, at their request, he consented that they should take possession, agreeing to pay him interest on the amount of the future compensation. The inquiry was held, and compensation assessed. An inquisition was drawn up, purporting to be taken at sessions under the statute, and stating that, the trustees and landlord appearing by their counsel, the jurors, being sworn to inquire of the purchase-money of the lands (specified), and recompense for damage, did assess and give a verdict for the sum of &c. for the land, and the sum of &c. for damage: whereupon the said Court did adjudge and order the said sums to be paid by the trustees.

On cross motions, for a mandamus to pay, and a certiorari to bring up the inquisition, Held,

That the non-statement in the inquisition of any preliminary requisite to the taking of it (as twenty-one days' notice to treat) could not be insisted upon by the trustees, whose business it was to institute the proceedings.

That the fact of differences having existed sufficiently appeared by the inquisition.

That the inquisition was not irregular in omitting to state whether or not the sum assessed exceeded or equalled the sum offered by the trustees.

The Court granted a mandamus, and discharged the rule for a certiorari. Per *Littledale* J. The statute requiring no regular form of an inquisition, the enactment that such inquisitions should be kept among the records of sessions, and should be records, did not render it necessary to draw them up with the formality required in setting out the judgment of an inferior court.

BY stat. 6 & 7 *W.* 4. *c.* cxxvi, local and personal, public, entitled "An act to alter and amend several acts for the improvement of the harbour of *Swansea*, in the county of *Glamorgan*, and for further improving the said harbour," the trustees of the harbour are empowered to purchase certain lands for the purposes of the act. Sect. 33 enacts that, in case of any

difference

1839.

The QUEEN *against* The Trustees of SWANSEA Harbour.

difference or dispute between the trustees and any body politic, &c., or person interested in or entitled to any lands to be taken or used for the purposes of the act, relative to price, damages, or recompence, and in case the same cannot be agreed for; or if such body, &c., or person, shall refuse, on tender, such purchase-money as shall be offered by the trustees; or shall, for twenty-one days next after notice, neglect or refuse to treat; or if any person shall, by absence or otherwise, be prevented from treating, and shall not, within twenty-one days, produce title to the premises he is in possession of, and the interest he claims therein; then and in every such case the trustees are empowered and required to issue their warrant to the sheriff of *Glamorganshire* (or the undersheriff or coroner in certain cases) commanding him to impannel, summon, and return a jury (and he is, by the same clause, required so to do), to appear before the justices in quarter sessions; and such jury, upon their oaths, and upon the oaths of witnesses, whom the sheriff is also empowered and required to summon, shall inquire of, assess, and ascertain the sum to be paid for purchase of lands or recompence for damage; "and the said justices shall accordingly give judgment for such purchase-money or recompence so to be assessed;" which verdict and judgment shall be binding and conclusive to all intents and purposes against all bodies politic &c., trustees, and other persons. Sect. 36 enacts that, where a verdict shall be given for the same or more money than the trustees shall have offered, the costs of the inquisition, &c. (specified in the clause), shall be borne by the trustees; such costs, in case of non-payment, to be levied by distress under a warrant issuable by a justice for the county on application by the party entitled; that, where a less sum shall be recovered

1839.

The QUEEN *against* The Trustees of SWANSEA Harbour.

covered than was offered, the costs shall be borne equally by the parties; but where a party shall have been prevented from treating by absence, the costs shall be borne by the trustees: And that the amount of costs shall be ascertained by any justice for the county, not interested, who is authorised and required to examine into and settle the same, and appoint a time and place for payment. Such costs, when payable to the trustees, are to be deducted from the sum due to the other party; or otherwise, if not paid on demand when ascertained, may be recovered by action of debt or on the case. Sect. 39 enacts "That all the said verdicts and judgments shall be kept by the clerk of the peace for the said county among the records of the quarter sessions for such county, and shall be deemed records to all intents and purposes; and the same, or copies thereof, shall be evidence," &c.

A difference of opinion arising between the trustees and *Thomas Starling Benson*, Esquire, touching the value of, and recompence for, certain lands belonging to him, which the trustees required for the purposes of the harbour, and were authorised by the act to take, they issued their warrant to the sheriff to summon a jury who should assess the purchase-money, and the recompence to be paid for damage by reason of the works authorised by the act. A jury was accordingly summoned, and an inquisition held. The record filed at quarter sessions was as follows.

"*Glamorganshire.*

"At the general quarter sessions of the peace" &c., held at &c., on &c., before &c., justices &c.

"*Thomas Starling Benson*
and
"The Trustees of the *Swansea* Harbour.

"Claim

1839.

The QUEEN *against* The Trustees of SWANSEA Harbour.

"Claim for compensation, &c., under the provisions of an act passed in the 6 & 7 *W.* 4.

"An inquisition taken by virtue and under the powers of an act of parliament made and passed" &c., "intituled" &c., "on the oaths of" &c., "good and lawful men" &c. "The trustees of the said harbour by their counsel, *William Milbourne James*, Esquire, and the said *Thomas Starling Benson* by his counsel, *Edward Vaughan Williams*, Esquire, duly appearing before this Court (the said *Thomas Starling Benson* being the owner of, or the person otherwise interested in, the lands and premises hereinafter described); the said jurors, being sworn to inquire of, assess, and ascertain the sum of money to be paid by the said trustees for the purchase of certain pieces or parcels of land" &c., "containing" &c., "being part of certain lands and hereditaments situate" &c., "now or late in the several occupations of *Edward Griffiths* and *William Williams*, or in which the said several parties or some or one of them have or claim to have some estate or interest, about to be taken and used in the execution of certain of the powers granted by the said act or by certain other acts therein recited or referred to; and also the sum of money to be paid by way of recompence to be made for the damage which shall or may be sustained by reason of the execution of any of the works by the said acts authorised; do assess and give a verdict for the sum of 2865*l.*, to be paid by the said trustees for the fee-simple and inheritance of and in the lands" &c., "hereinbefore particularly described, and do also assess and give a verdict for the further sum of 7476*l.*, to be paid by the said trustees by way of recompence for the damage which shall or may be sustained by reason of the execution of any of the works by the said acts authorised. Whereupon this Court

Court doth adjudge and order the said several sums of 2865*l.* and 7476*l.* to be paid by the said trustees according to the provisions of the said act.

1839.

The QUEEN *against* The Trustees of SWANSEA Harbour.

"By the Court,

"*Wood*, clerk of the peace."

In the margin was written, "The jury, on returning their verdict, added that, had it not been a waste water cut, they would not have given so much. *Tho. Dalton*, Dy C. P."

The sums awarded not having been paid, a rule nisi was obtained, in *Michaelmas* term 1838, for a mandamus to the trustees to pay the several sums awarded by the jury and adjudged by the Court, at the said quarter sessions, to be paid to the said *Thomas Starling Benson*. And in the same term the trustees obtained a rule nisi for a certiorari to remove into this Court the inquisition, verdict, and judgment.

The solicitor to the trustees, in his affidavits against and for the above rules respectively, stated, as an objection to the verdict, that the jury had, as he was advised and believed, exceeded their powers in giving damages with reference to the cut mentioned in the inquisition being a waste water cut and not navigable. He also stated that, as he was advised and believed, the inquisition was defective and illegal, because it did not shew on the face of it that the proceeding thereunder was warranted by the act, and did not recite or state either the existence of differences between Mr. *Benson* and the trustees, the issuing of a warrant to impannel and summon the jury, nor any of the circumstances necessary under the act to give the jury and quarter sessions jurisdiction; and did not state any thing on which a decision as to costs could be pronounced.

1839.

The QUEEN *against* The Trustees of SWANSEA Harbour.

By the affidavits on Mr. *Benson's* part it appeared that, after some negotiation between him and the trustees, they offered a certain sum per acre for the land to be taken, but proposed at the same time that, to avoid delay, the trustees should have immediate possession, paying 5 per cent. interest, from the day of the offer, on the amount thereafter to be ascertained. Mr. *Benson* consented to the proposal as to possession and interest, but requested that a jury might be summoned to ascertain the value. An agreement was made, as suggested by the trustees; and, in pursuance of the arrangement between them and *Benson*, a jury was summoned, and the inquisition held, the trustees, by their counsel and solicitor, taking part in the proceedings. Mr. *Benson* stated in his affidavit that the trustees had, as he was informed and believed, taken possession of the lands and exercised acts of ownership over them.

The two rules were now discussed together.

Sir *J. Campbell*, Attorney-General, and *J. Henderson*, for the trustees. The act creates a jurisdiction with a limited authority, which must be strictly pursued. The inquisition, by sect. 39, is made a record; and, being a record of an inferior court, it must shew that such proceedings were taken as gave the Court jurisdiction. That, in the present case, would depend upon the circumstances, enumerated in sect. 33, under which the trustees are empowered to summon a jury. The record here does not shew that any of those circumstances had occurred. In *Rex* v. *The Trustees of the Norwich and Watton Road* (a) the objection, that a notice to treat,

(a) 5 *A.* & *E.* 563.

which

1839.

The QUEEN *against* The Trustees of SWANSEA Harbour.

which was necessary to give jurisdiction, did not appear on the inquisition, was countenanced by the majority of the Court. Here the same defect exists. *Rex* v. *Bagshaw* (*a*), and *Rex* v. the *Mayor*, *&c.*, *of Liverpool* (*b*), are decisive authorities in support of this objection, which is also sustained by *Rex* v. *Manning* (*c*). Further, the record of quarter sessions ought to have shewn how the costs were to be disposed of: but it does not appear by the inquisition whether the sum awarded by the jury was greater or less than that offered by the trustees, or the same. A mandamus ought not to issue, because the trustees have not yet obtained any valid title to the land. All the facts stated on the inquisition may be true, and yet it may not constitute an available title-deed. The trustees have possession; but they entered under an agreement to pay interest on the amount of purchase-money and recompence to be afterwards ascertained. That has not yet been ascertained conclusively.

Sir *W. W. Follett* and *E. V. Williams*, contrà. The sheriff's jury are not called upon to inquire what sum was originally offered, nor have they any thing to do with the costs: those, when payable by the trustees, are to be recovered before a justice; and it is for him to inquire what offer was made. Nor is it necessary that the jury should examine or decide as to the twenty-one days' notice. The inquisition, in this case, is contested by the very parties at whose instance it was taken: they themselves have entered up, or caused to be entered up, the judgment, and cannot, therefore, impeach its correct-

(*a*) 7 *T. R.* 363. (*b*) 4 *Burr.* 2244.
(*c*) 1 *Burr.* 377.

 ness

1839.

The QUEEN against The Trustees of SWANSEA Harbour.

ness to the prejudice of the opposite party. This line of argument was taken, and adopted by the Court, in the case *In the Matter of the London and Greenwich Railway Company* (a). Where the Court has appeared to countenance such objections, they have been raised by the party against whose property the proceedings were instituted; as in *Regina* v. *The Manchester and Leeds Railway Company* (b). It cannot be stated as an invariable rule that the inquisition must disclose the facts which led to its being taken. Parties may expressly agree to go before a jury, waiving any reference to the preliminary circumstances; those circumstances would then not appear on the inquiry; yet the inquisition would be good. [Lord *Denman* C. J. mentioned *Regina* v. *The Committee Men for the South Holland Drainage* (c).] Here the parties went before the jury in pursuance of an arrangement, under which the trustees were let into possession. On the inquiry the trustees appeared, and were heard. Can they now object to the assessment? A justice, before he can convict, should summon the party charged; and the conviction should state that he did so: but, if the party appears voluntarily, a summons need not be issued or alleged. The only point material, as a preliminary to this inquisition being taken, was, that the parties should have disagreed about price; and that sufficiently appears by the record. In *Rex* v. *Bagshaw* (d) and *Rex* v. *The Trustees of the Norwich and Watton Road* (e) the trustees, who set the proceedings in motion, had something to do for the purpose of creating a jurisdiction; and the opposite party objected that that had not been

(a) 2 *A.* & *E.* 678.

(b) Antè, p. 413.

(c) Antè, p. 429.

(d) 7 *T. R.* 363.

(e) 5 *A.* & *E.* 563.

done.

1839.

The QUEEN *against* The Trustees of SWANSEA Harbour.

done. But in *Rex* v. *Bagshaw* (a) it is clear that the objection would have been unavailing, if it had distinctly appeared that the objecting parties had attended the inquiry. No particular form of record is required by stat. 6 & 7 *W.* 4. *c.* cxxvi. The want of jurisdiction, in this case, would be matter of evidence, if it could be entered into. The form here used is one which has been ordinarily adopted; the objection, if admitted, would overthrow inquisitions affecting a great amount of property. *Rex* v. *The Nottingham Old Water-works Company* (b) shews that a mandamus lies to enforce this judgment. There the local act contained a clause like sect. 39 of stat. 6 & 7 *W.* 4. *c.* cxxvi., directing that the verdicts and judgments should be kept among the records of the quarter sessions, and should be deemed records to all intents and purposes: but this Court said it was not clear that a remedy other than mandamus could be enforced on such judgments, and they granted the writ. (*E. V. Williams* was stopped by the Court.)

Lord DENMAN C. J. This is an inquisition obtained by the trustees, who were bound to set in motion the necessary machinery for obtaining the land. They, therefore, cannot object that the inquisition is defective. In the other cases which have been cited, the applications were made by the parties whose lands were taken. In *Rex* v. *Bagshaw* (a) it did not appear that the objecting party had been heard on the inquiry. Here it is otherwise; and I am not prepared to say that this inquisition is not good. The rule for a mandamus will be absolute: the rule for a certiorari discharged.

(a) 7 *T. R.* 363. (b) 6 *A.* & *E.* 355.

 LITTLEDALE

1839.

The QUEEN *against* The Trustees of SWANSEA Harbour.

LITTLEDALE J. The trustees, who allege the want of notice, were the persons who ought to have given it. It is evident from the inquisition that the parties differed as to price or recompence; else why was the jury summoned? As to the necessity of the record being drawn in a particular form to shew jurisdiction, it states that, the parties appearing, the jury give their verdict for certain amounts as purchase-money and recompence to be paid by the trustees, and the Court adjudge the said sums to be paid by them: and the statute does not require any regular form. It is said that, because this inquisition is to be kept among the records of the quarter sessions, it ought, as the record of an inferior court, to set forth every thing which was necessary to give jurisdiction. But the enactment is merely directory, that the judgment, having been given, shall be kept among the records of sessions (*a*); and, as to the judgment itself, nothing is prescribed, except that the jury shall ascertain the sum to be paid for purchase or recompence, and the justices shall accordingly give judgment for such purchase-money or recompence so to be assessed.

WILLIAMS J. (*b*) The objection from the alleged want of preliminary circumstances is completely answered. Both parties appeared on the inquiry; and, if there had not been a disagreement, such an inquiry would not have taken place. It was suggested that the inquisition ought to shew the facts which ascertain the liability to costs; but it is obvious that that is not so, because the

(*a*) See *Rex* v. *Nottingham Old Water-works Company*, 6 *A.* & *E.* 369, 370. *Regina* v. *Manchester and Leeds Railway Company*, p. 428., *antè*, judgment of Patteson J.

(*b*) *Patteson* J. was sitting at Nisi Prius.

costs

costs are not a matter for the consideration of the jury: they are recovered by a proceeding quite independent of the inquiry; and there is no reason that any thing respecting them should appear by the inquisition.

Rule absolute for a mandamus.

Rule for a certiorari discharged (*a*).

(*a*) The mandamus issuing, a return was made, but quashed on motion, no cause being shewn.

CODRINGTON *against* LLOYD, Gent., One, &c.

Friday, June 1st.

Where an arrest is made under process which is afterwards set aside for irregularity, the attorney in the suit is liable in trespass, as well as the plaintiff.

And if, in an action of trespass, he justifies under the process, it is a good replication, that the process was irregularly sued out, and was afterwards set aside, by rule of Court, for irregularity.

Where issues are joined in fact and in law on the same count, and the plaintiff obtains judgment on the issue in law, and then proceeds to try the issue in fact, the jury process must be awarded to assess damages on the issue in law as well as to try the issue in fact; although the latter issue goes to the whole cause of action in the count.

Where the plaintiff in such a case delivered an issue and notice of trial with a venire only to try the issue in fact, the Court set them aside for irregularity, with costs.

TRESPASS for an assault and false imprisonment. Pleas, Not Guilty, and a justification. Replication, to the first plea, similiter; to the second, a new assignment. Pleas to the new assignment, 1. Not Guilty. 2. A special plea in excuse of the arrest, which it is unnecessary to set out. 3. That defendant was an attorney of the Court of Exchequer; that plaintiff was indebted to *Francis Paiplief* in the sum of 112*l.*; that *F. P.*, for the recovery of the debt, retained defendant to sue out an alias capias for him against plaintiff: whereupon defendant, as *F. P.*'s attorney in that behalf, sued out of the Exchequer a writ of alias capias against plaintiff at the suit of *F. P.*, directed to the sheriff of *Hants*, commanding him &c., which writ was duly indorsed for bail, &c.; and by defendant, as *F. P.*'s attorney, and by his command, delivered to the sheriff to be executed; and by virtue of which writ, afterwards, &c., plaintiff was duly arrested by the said sheriff, and imprisoned &c. Verification. Repli-

1838.

CODRINGTON against LLOYD.

cation: 1. To the first plea to the new assignment, similiter. To the second, a traverse of the matter of excuse, on which traverse issue was joined. 3. To the third, that the said writ, under which the defendant attempts to justify, was, on &c., irregularly sued and prosecuted out of the said Court of Exchequer; and that afterwards, to wit on &c., by a certain order then made by the Right Hon. Sir *J. Parke*, Knight, one of the Barons &c., bearing date &c., and which order was afterwards duly made a rule of the said Court, it was, upon hearing &c. (counsel on each side), and reading the affidavits &c., ordered that the said writ of capias should be set aside for irregularity, as by the said rule and order, now remaining &c., will more fully appear. Verification. General demurrer, and joinder.

E. James, for the defendant. An attorney is not liable in trespass for procuring execution of a writ which is afterwards set aside, if he acted bonâ fide, and the writ was not originally void, as if issued for recovery of a debt after the debt had been paid. It is not even alleged here that the writ was void, or not issued bonâ fide, but merely that it was set aside for irregularity. In *Barker* v. *Braham* (*a*), cited in *Bates* v. *Pilling* (*b*), the process was unjustifiably issued in the first instance; here the writ was good, till invalidated by some act of the defendant.

Kinglake, contrà. Where process is set aside for irregularity, both the attorney and the party who have put it in force are liable in trespass, though the officer

(*a*) 3 *Wils.* 368.

(*b*) 6 *B. & C.* 38. See *Sowell* v. *Champion*, 6 *A. & E.* 407.

who

who executed it may still justify. This distinction was admitted in *Philips* v. *Biron* (a), which case was acted upon by the Court of Common Pleas in *Parsons* v. *Lloyd* (b). The law, as to the distinction between the party and officer, and the remedy against a party, is discussed, and authorities cited, in a note to *King* v. *Harrison* (c). It is a frequent practice, when process is set aside for irregularity, to require, as a condition, that the defendant shall bring no action. [*Patteson* J. Against the party; but is the condition extended to the attorney?] He is the acting party. [*Patteson* J. In *Loton* v. *Devereux* (d) the attorney's liability was not discussed with reference to this point.]

E. James, in reply. The point decided in *Philips* v. *Biron* (a) was only that the officer had forfeited the protection which he would otherwise have had, by pleading jointly with the principal party in the former suit. An attorney who issues process does not stand on the same footing with the party, but with the officer, who is not liable if the process be set aside. It would be very hard if the attorney could be held responsible when the process is vitiated, perhaps by some slight technical defect. [Lord *Denman* C. J. What distinction is there, in favour of the attorney, between him and the party? The party knows nothing of the writ.] There is, at least, no act done here by the defendant for which trespass can be brought. If a bailable writ were sued out without an affidavit of debt, trespass might be the remedy: here it only appears that the writ, which may have been good unless properly invalidated, was

(a) 1 *Stra.* 509.
(b) 2 *W. Bl.* 845.
(c) 15 *East*, 615. note (c).
(d) 3 *B. & Ad.* 343.

ultimately

1838.

CODRINGTON *against* LLOYD.

ultimately set aside for an irregularity. In *Noel* v. *Isaac* (*a*) Lord *Abinger* C. B. was clearly of opinion that trespass would not lie for holding an attorney to bail in violation of his privilege; but that the action, if maintainable, must be on the case. [Lord *Denman* C. J. In *Philips* v. *Biron* (*b*) the judgment on which the writ had issued was set aside for irregularity. *Littledale* J. In *Barker* v. *Braham* (*c*) and *Bates* v. *Pilling* (*d*) there was no plea of justification; the attorney pleaded the general issue jointly with the party.]

Lord DENMAN C. J. The plaintiff here was arrested on a writ which was afterwards declared by the Court irregular. It was, therefore, as if there had been none. Then is the attorney liable in this action for the arrest? A similar question was very fully discussed in *Barker* v. *Braham* (*c*), and the attorney was held liable as well as the client; and in *Bates* v. *Pilling* (*d*) no doubt was entertained that if the action lay against the principal it lay also against the attorney. Indeed there is a stronger reason for holding the attorney liable; since the party cannot be expected to know whether the process is regular in point of law or not. If there were any such distinction in favour of the attorney as has been suggested, there would most probably be some case in which it would appear.

LITTLEDALE J. The attorney is not in the situation of an officer to whom process is directed, and who knows nothing of its regularity or irregularity. It is true that in *Barker* v. *Braham* (*c*) and *Bates* v. *Pilling* (*d*)

(*a*) 1 *Cro. M. & R.* 753. *C. S.* 5 *Tyrwh.* 376.
(*b*) 1 *Stra.* 509.
(*c*) 3 *Wils.* 368.
(*d*) 6 *B. & C.* 38.

the

1838.

CODRINGTON *against* LLOYD.

the attorney did not justify, the only plea, by both defendants, being Not Guilty. But, if the principal was liable for a trespass, I do not see how the attorney could have protected himself. There appears to me no distinction between them.

PATTESON J. Mr. *James*'s argument would go the length of shewing that this action did not lie against the principal. But it lies against him because the process, when set aside, is as if it had never existed: and, if the party therefore cannot justify under it, neither can the attorney. If, indeed, the attorney had done no act beyond what his duty required, that might be made a defence, as in a case in *Espinasse* (a); but that would be under the general issue. If the attorney is liable where the proceedings are void from the beginning, he is so à fortiori where they fail from a subsequent irregularity. The first defect may be unknown to him; he or his clerk must know of the other.

WILLIAMS J. The foundation of the action of trespass is the taking without authority. There is no distinction between the party and the attorney. Indeed, the proceedings may be more emphatically said to be under the attorney's conduct; the party in general merely tells the attorney that he wishes the action to be prosecuted.

Judgment for the plaintiff.

On a subsequent day of this term the plaintiff delivered the issue and notice of trial to the defendant.

(a) See *Sedley* v. *Sutherland*, 3 *Esp. N. P. C.* 202. Also *Carrett* v. *Smallpage*, 9 *East*, 330.

In

1838.

CODRINGTON *against* LLOYD.

In the same term, *June* 13th, *Humfrey* obtained a rule to shew cause why the issue and notice of trial should not be set aside for irregularity, with costs, on the ground that, in the award of jury process in the issue, the venire was only to try the issues in fact, and not to assess damages on the demurrer.

Wightman, in the same term (*June* 14th), shewed cause (*a*). It was needless to assess damages on the demurrer; for the judgment on that did not entitle the plaintiff to any damages, the issues in fact going to the whole ground of action. In 2 *Tidd's Practice*, 895 (*b*), it is laid down that, "if there be a demurrer to part, and an issue upon other part," "the jury who try the issue shall assess the damages for the whole." But "when the issue, as well as the demurrer, goes to the whole cause of action, the damages shall be assessed upon the issue, and not upon the demurrer." Here no part of the cause of action was finally found in the plaintiff's favour: though successful on the demurrer, he might fail on the pleas not demurred to, and, in that case, could recover no damages. The effect of the judgment on demurrer, in such a case, is merely that one ground of defence is out of the question. It may be inferred from *Pepper* v. *Whalley* (*c*) that a judgment on demurrer in a case like the present need not be noticed on the Nisi Prius record.

Humfrey, contrà. The established practice is, where there are issues both in fact and in law, to award a venire tam ad inquirendum quam ad triandum. There

(*a*) Before Lord *Denman* C. J., *Littledale*, *Patteson*, and *Williams* Js.

(*b*) 9th ed.

(*c*) 4 *A.* & *E.* 90.

cannot

1838.

CODRINGTON against LLOYD.

cannot be two taxations. [*Littledale* J. Only one is proposed here, of damages on the issues in fact, which go to the whole cause of action.] In 2 *Tidd*, 722 it is said that, where there are issues in fact and in law, "if the issues in law" "are first determined, and the plaintiff is in consequence entitled to damages upon part of the declaration," "there is an entry of an *unica taxatio*, to postpone the assessment of such damages, until the trial of the issues in fact. But if the issues in fact are first tried, an *unica taxatio* is unnecessary; for in such case, the jury who try these issues, will of course assess the damages." [*Patteson* J. Here it is denied that, on the demurrer, the plaintiff is entitled to damages on any part of the cause of action.] *Pepper* v. *Whalley* (a) shews merely that a plea in abatement and judgment thereon need not be set out on the issue delivered by the plaintiff; it proves nothing as to the purpose for which the jury process should be awarded.

Cur. adv. vult.

Lord DENMAN C. J., in *Michaelmas* term 1838 (*November* 3d), delivered the judgment of the Court.

The question in this case, in substance, amounts to this: Whether it be necessary that the jury process should be as well to try the issue in fact as to assess damages on the issue in law, in a case where two pleas are pleaded to the same count, to one of which the plaintiff replies, and to the other demurs, so that an issue in fact, and another in law, arise out of the same count. It is said that a venire tam quam cannot be requisite, because, if the jury find the issue in fact

(a) 4 *A.* & *E.* 90.

for

1838.

CODRINGTON *against* LLOYD.

for the plaintiff, they will of course assess the damages also, which must obviously be the same as would be assessed on the issue in law; and, if they find it for the defendant, the action is defeated, and no damages can be recovered. This argument is quite just in the event of the jury finding for the plaintiff; but, if they should find for the defendant, it is still possible that the plea may be held bad, and that the Court may give judgment for the plaintiff notwithstanding the verdict: if they should do so, and also give judgment for the plaintiff on the demurrer, he will be entitled to damages, and a second jury must be summoned to assess them; whereas, if the venire in the first instance had been tam quam, they would have been assessed by the first jury.

The practice has uniformly been to award a venire tam quam in similar cases; and, as there is a possible state of circumstances which may lead to the necessity of summoning a second jury if that form be not adopted, this issue is incorrect in not adopting it; and the rule to set it aside, as irregular, must be made absolute.

Rule absolute.

Friday, June 1st.

HALL *against* MAULE and STREAT.

This case is reported, 7 *A. & E.* 721.

1838.

REBECCA SWANN *against* ANDREW PHILLIPS.

Friday, June 1st.

ASSUMPSIT. The declaration stated that defendant, being an attorney, requested plaintiff to lend *William John Jellicorse* 300*l.* at 5 per cent. interest; and that defendant, contriving, &c., to defraud and deceive plaintiff, and wrongfully, deceitfully, and fraudulently to induce, persuade, and encourage her to lend and advance to the said *W. J. J.* the said sum of 300*l.* upon interest as aforesaid, and to take no further security from the said *W. J. J.* for the repayment, &c., than the promissory note of the said *W. J. J.* for the said sum of 300*l.* with interest as aforesaid, falsely, fraudulently, and deceitfully asserted and represented to plaintiff "that she, the plaintiff, might safely lend and advance to the said *W. J. J.* the said sum of 300*l.*, and take no further security for the repayment thereof than such promissory note as aforesaid, because the title deeds to a certain estate, which he, the defendant, then asserted and represented that the said *W. J. J.* had just bought, were in the possession of him, the defendant, and that nothing could be done without the knowledge of the defendant, and the plaintiff would be perfectly safe in making such loan and advance to the said *W. J. J.* upon the terms aforesaid." By means of which false, &c.,

Declaration, in assumpsit, that defendant, an attorney, requested plaintiff to lend *J.* 300*l.*, and, to encourage plaintiff to do so, and to take no further security than *J.*'s promissory note, falsely and fraudulently represented to plaintiff that she might safely lend *J.* the 300*l.*, and take no further security than such note, *because the title deeds to a certain estate, which defendant then asserted that J. had bought, were in defendant's possession, and nothing could be done without defendant's knowledge, and plaintiff would be perfectly safe in making such loan to J. on the terms aforesaid*; that defendant by the representation induced plaintiff to lend, and plaintiff did lend, *J.* the 300*l.* on *J.*'s note only, whereas plaintiff could not safely lend, &c. (negativing the representations as above stated); all which defendant, at the time he made such representations, well knew: that *J.* had not paid or been able to pay, the 300*l.*, and had become bankrupt.

Plea, that defendant's representations were representations concerning the ability of *J.* to repay, and were not in writing.

Held good on demurrer, the representations being within stat. 9 *G.* 4. *c.* 14. *s.* 6.

1838.

Swann *against* Phillips.

&c., assertions and representations, defendant fraudulently and deceitfully induced plaintiff to lend *W. J. J.* the said 300*l.* on the said interest, and to take no further security, &c.; and plaintiff, confiding &c., did lend, &c., and did take from *W. J. J.* a promissory note, &c.: whereas, in truth and in fact, at the time defendant made such assertions, &c., "the plaintiff could not safely lend and advance to the said *W. J. J.* the said sum of 300*l.* without taking further security for the repayment thereof, with such interest as aforesaid, than such promissory note as aforesaid, and the said title deeds were not, at the time of the making of the said assertions and representations by the defendant as aforesaid, in the possession of him, the defendant, and the said plaintiff was not then perfectly safe in making such loan and advance to the said *W. J. J.* upon the terms aforesaid: all which he, the defendant, at the time he so made such assertions and representations as aforesaid, well knew." Averment, that *W. J. J.* never paid, but became bankrupt, &c., and the 300*l.* and interest are still unpaid.

Plea, that the said assertions and representations of the defendant in the declaration mentioned were representations and assurances concerning and relating to the ability of the said *W. J. J.*, to wit to his ability to repay to the plaintiff the said sum of money in the declaration mentioned to have been lent and advanced by her to the said *W. J. J.*, with interest thereon; and that the said assertions and representations were not, nor was any part thereof, ever made in writing signed by the defendant. Verification.

General demurrer and joinder.

R. V. Richards,

1838.

SWANN *against* PHILLIPS.

R. V. Richards, for the plaintiff. The representation set out in the declaration is not within stat. 9 *G.* 4. *c.* 14. *s.* 6. It is, in substance, only an assertion that the defendant had possession of the title deeds of the estate bought by *Jellicorse*: it is not a "representation or assurance made or given concerning or relating to the character, conduct, credit, ability, trade, or dealings" of *Jellicorse*. It is indeed, strictly speaking, a representation concerning the defendant himself. Even admitting it to be a representation concerning *Jellicorse*, it is one equally consistent with his solvency and insolvency. A representation that a party was in *London*, he being really in *Cornwall*, might perhaps be said to relate to the probability of his paying; but that would not be within the statute. *Haslock* v. *Fergusson* (*a*) does not apply; because there the verbal representation did affect the ability of the party, and the whole question was, whether the action could be maintained by treating the representation as a circumstance, only, of a fraudulent transaction by the defendant. In *Lyde* v. *Barnard* (*b*) the Judges of the Court of Exchequer were divided in opinion as to the question, whether the verbal representation was within the statute; the facts were not like those of the present case; but there seems to have been little question that the test was, whether the representation made regarded the credit and ability of the party: and it was said that the statute was passed in consequence of the evasion of the Statute of Frauds, as to guarantees, introduced by the decision in *Pasley* v. *Freeman* (*c*). It is impossible here to treat the representation as separate

(*a*) 7 *A.* & *E.* 86. *S. C.* 2 *N.* & *P.* 269.

(*b*) 1 *Mee.* & *W.* 101. *S. C. Tyrwh.* & *G.* 250.

(*c*) 3 *T. R.* 51.

from

1838.

SWANN against PHILLIPS.

from the reason given for it. But, if that could be done, the plea would be bad, as not being confined to that part: and the defendant would be bound by that part which did not need writing. The breach alleges that the representation as to the possession of the title deeds was false.

Wightman, contrà. The representation relates to "dealings;" and its effect is, that the party obtains credit. Suppose it had been simply that the plaintiff might safely lend the money; no doubt, then, the statute would have been applicable. A bad reason is added: but that does not alter the effect of the representation. If nothing had been proved but the representation as to the possession of the deeds, the plaintiff must have failed. The language of the judges who held that the representation in *Lyde* v. *Barnard* (*a*) was not within the statute shews that they would have held differently in a case like this, where there is an express assertion of the safety of the advances (*b*).

R. V. Richards in reply. An action might have been maintained simply on the representation as to the possession of the title deeds. It is said that this relates to the party's "dealings:" if that were so, any statement as to any transaction whatever of *Jellicorse* would be within the statute

Lord DENMAN C. J. The only question is, what do the words in the declaration mean? If they amount only to an assertion that the defendant, being in possession

(*a*) 1 *Mes. & W.* 101. *S. C. Tyrwh. & Gr.* 250.

(*b*) See the conclusions of the judgments of *Alderson* and *Parke* Bs.

of

of the title deeds, would know what *Jellicorse* was doing, the statute does not apply. If they mean that *Jellicorse* might be trusted, then they constitute a representation as to his credit and ability. Now, here is a loan contemplated, and the plaintiff is told that he may safely make it because the title deeds are in the defendant's custody. That is clearly a representation as to *Jellicorse's* credit.

LITTLEDALE J. The defendant, an attorney, wants to get money advanced to his client: and, to induce the plaintiff to make the advance, tells her that she may safely do so, taking no further security than the client's promissory note, because he, the defendant, has possession of that party's title deeds. I think that is within the statute. The representation is entire: no one part can be separated from the rest. In the ordinary course of things, if a man states another to be a man of ability, he is asked why he says so: he may answer, "because he has had a legacy left to him," by way of enforcing his representation as to the ability. Here, the substance of the conversation is similar; the defendant says, "You may trust him; and my reason for saying so is, that I know the estate which he has bought, and have his title deeds." That is one entire representation concerning his credit.

PATTESON J. The only doubt in my mind arose from the words, "that nothing could be done without the knowledge of the defendant." Had the representation been merely that the plaintiff might trust *Jellicorse*, because the defendant had possession of *Jellicorse's* title deeds, there could have been no doubt. That could have been understood only as a representation as to the

 ability

1838.

SWANN *against* PHILLIPS.

ability of the party, with regard to his sufficiency in respect of property. But the following words might be thought to mean that the defendant engaged to protect the plaintiff by means of the property to which the title deeds related. I think, however, that that would be a strained construction. Taking all together, the meaning (though I do not fully understand all the words) seems to be, " You may lend the money, for he has an estate, and I have the deeds."

WILLIAMS J. I think this is a representation concerning the party's ability. If the defendant had said that he had in his hands a purse belonging to *Jellicorse*, with 1000*l.* in it, that would have tended to satisfy the plaintiff of *Jellicorse*'s ability. We must understand the words as parties generally would understand them. Any income, whether from land or any other source, increases personal credit.

Judgment for the defendant.

1838.

HOPKINS *against* HELMORE.

Friday, June 1st.

Declaration, in covenant, that, by indenture of 21st *March* 1828, plaintiff demised a messuage to defendant, habendum from 25th *March* then instant, for the term of seven years then next ensuing, wanting seven days, *yielding and paying yearly and every year during the term the yearly rent of* 285*l.* by four equal quarterly payments on 25th *March*, 24th *June*, 29th *September*, and 25th *December*, *in every year, commencing from 25th March then instant:* and defendant covenanted to pay the said yearly rent of 285*l.* on the days and in manner appointed. Breach, that in the last year defendant paid only half the yearly rent, and on 25th *March* 1835 two quarters became payable, and were in arrear.

Defendant, paying into Court so much *as became due as and for the first of the two quarterly payments alleged to have become due on 25th March* 1835, demurred to so much of the breach *as respected the non-payment of the second and last quarterly payment alleged to have become due on 25th March* 1835.

Held, that 285*l.* was payable for each year; and that either the first payment was to be made on 25th *March* 1828, or a payment on 25th *March* 1835, though after the expiration of the term.

Judgment for plaintiff.

COVENANT. The declaration stated that, by indenture of *March* 21st, 1828, between plaintiff and defendant, plaintiff demised a messuage to defendant, habendum to him, his executors, &c., from 25th *March* then instant for the term of seven years thence next ensuing, wanting seven days; yielding and paying therefore, yearly and every year during the said term, to the plaintiff, his executors, &c., the yearly rent of 285*l.*, by four equal quarterly payments on the 25th day of *March*, 24th *June*, 29th *September*, and 25th *December* "in every year, commencing from the said 25th day of *March* then instant." And defendant did thereby, for himself, his heirs, executors, &c., covenant and agree with plaintiff, his executors, &c., that defendant, his executors, &c., should and would, yearly and every year during the continuance of the said demise, pay to plaintiff, his executors, &c., the said yearly rent of 285*l.*, on the days and in the manner therein-before appointed for payment thereof. Breach, that defendant did not, in every year during the continuance of the said demise, pay or cause to be paid to plaintiff the said yearly rent of 285*l.*; but, on the contrary thereof, in the last year of the said term by the said indenture demised, defend-

1838.

HOPKINS *against* HELMORE.

ant wholly omitted and neglected to pay plaintiff any greater part of the said yearly rent of 285*l.* than one half part thereof; and, on 25th *March* A.D. 1835, a large sum, to wit 140*l.* of the rent aforesaid, for two quarterly payments of the said yearly rent of 285*l.*, "on that day in that year became and was due and payable from the said defendant to the said plaintiff, and is still in arrear."

Plea, as to 71*l.* 10*s.*, parcel of the 140*l.*, being so much as became due as and for the first of the two quarterly payments alleged to have become due on *March* 25th, 1835, payment into Court. And, as to the alleged breach of covenant in respect of the non-payment of the second and last quarterly payment in the declaration alleged to have become due on the said 25th *March*, general demurrer. Joinder. The cause of demurrer stated in the margin of the paper-book was, that it appears on the face of the declaration that there was no day within the term upon which the second quarter's rent mentioned in the breach became due.

Ogle, for the defendant. The lease expired on 18th *March* 1835; therefore the 25th of *March* 1835 was not within the term. The covenant is only to pay on the days specified, during the term. It will be said that the parties intended the rent to be paid for the whole time: but the language of the covenant must be followed.

J. Bayley, contrà. The covenant is for seven years' rent, for a term of seven years wanting seven days. In *Hill* v. *Grange* (*a*) rent was reserved, payable at the

(*a*) *Plowd.* 164. See p. 171.

feasts

1838.

HOPKINS against HELMORE.

feasts of *Annunciation* and *Michaelmas*, on a twenty years' lease, commencing in *August*; and, though it was objected that the *Annunciation*, being first named, was to be the first day of payment, it was held that payment was to be made on the first *Michaelmas*, and so on each of the two feasts throughout the twenty years. Here, therefore, the rent would be payable on the 25th of *March* 1828, and so forward. But, if that suggestion be inadmissible, and the first 25th *March* be excluded, still there is no reason that a tenant should not covenant to pay rent on a day after the expiration of the term; as in *Hutchins* v. *Scott* (*a*); although perhaps a difficulty might then arise as to distraining. [*Littledale* J. But the rent is made payable "during the said term."] The rent of 285*l.* is to be paid for every year of the term, yearly: it need not be paid on a day in the term. (He also referred to *Baden* v. *Flight* (*b*) and *Long* v. *Burroughs* (*c*).)

Ogle, in reply. When it is meant that there shall be a payment on a day occurring in less than a quarter of a year, &c., there is usually an express clause for a forehand rent. Here there was probably a compensation for the loss of one quarter. In *Hill* v. *Grange* (*d*) it was not pretended that rent could be recoverable up to a day after the expiration of the term. As to the suggestion that this covenant may be interpreted to be for payment beginning with the first 25th of *March*, there is, on the record, a payment up to the last 25th of *December*, and the sum claimed is rent supposed to become due on 25th *March* 1835. Nothing is due since the preceding *December*; *Stevenson* v. *Lambard* (*e*).

(*a*) 2 *Mee. & W.* 809. See *Parke* B. at p. 810. (*b*) 3 *New Ca.* 685.
(*c*) 1 *Ld. Ken.* 247. (*d*) *Plowd.* 164. (*e*) 2 *East*, 575.

 Lord

1838.

Hopkins *against* Helmore.

Lord Denman C. J. The defendant has contracted to pay 285*l.* in each year: one year wanting seven days is one of the years in popular language. Take this as a forehand rent: then there will be an equal quantity payable on each of the four days in each year, beginning with 25th *March* 1828. That will reconcile the whole.

Littledale J. The defendant contracts to make four quarterly payments in every year. It is not intended to strike off the rent by striking off seven days of the last year. It is difficult to reconcile the whole: but I think there is one way, namely, by making the first day of payment the 25th day of *March* 1828. We may assume that the days of payment are enumerated in the order in which they were to occur. The payments may be considered to commence on 25th *March* 1828, by reading the words "commencing *from* the said 25th day of *March* then instant," as if the words were "*on* the 25th" &c. I do not say that this may not be rather a forced construction.

Patteson J. On reading so much of the indenture as is in the declaration, I have no doubt that the defendant was to pay 285*l.* seven times. The words are, "yearly and every year." Had the contract stopped there, no question could have arisen. But then it is added, "by four equal quarterly payments on the 25th day of *March*," &c., "in every year, commencing from the said 25th day of *March* then instant." Now, it being clearly meant that there should be seven annual payments of 285*l.*, the question is whether that meaning can be collected. There are two ways of effecting this.

First,

1838.

HOPKINS *against* HELMORE.

First, we may treat the rent as a forehand rent, the first payment to be made on entering. But, secondly, I think that a good deal may be said for the other construction suggested by Mr. *Bayley*: that the rent is to be paid for every year during the term, and on the days named, one of which occurs after the expiration of the term. If this be admissible, there is no doubt: and I cannot see why the payment should not be covenanted to be made after the expiration of the term.

WILLIAMS J. There is no doubt of the meaning of the parties; and every reasonable mode of construction should be resorted to, for the purpose of furthering it. The term commencing on the 25th of *March*, and that being the first day of payment named, we may take it that the first payment was to be on the day on which the term commenced.

Judgment for plaintiff.

JOHN MEYER *against* SARAH HAWORTH.

Friday, June 1st.

Coverture being pleaded to a declaration in assumpsit for goods sold and delivered, plaintiff replied that defendant was, at the time of the contract, separated from her husband and living in open adultery, that plaintiff did not know of the marriage or adultery, and that defendant, after her husband's death, and before action brought, in consideration of the premises, promised to pay. Held,

1. That no consideration appeared for the promise in the replication.

2. That the replication was a departure, the promise therein being distinct from that alleged in the declaration.

ASSUMPSIT for goods sold and delivered, goods bargained and sold, and, at defendant's request, delivered to *W. J. R.*, work and labour, money paid, and interest, and on an account stated.

Plea, coverture at the time of the promise.

Replication, that defendant, at the time when the

debts

1838.

MEYER against HAWORTH.

debts were contracted, was living separate from her husband, and in open adultery with *W. J. R.*; that the husband was not liable to pay, nor did pay, the debts so contracted by defendant while she was so living separate &c.; that plaintiff, at the time of the sale and delivery &c., did not know that defendant was the wife of &c., nor that she was living in open adultery &c., and dealt with her as a feme sole; and that, after the death of the husband, and before action brought, defendant, in consideration of the premises, promised to pay. Verification.

General demurrer, and joinder.

Streeten, for the plaintiff. A married woman is not liable for the debts she contracts, though she be living in open adultery and separate from her husband. [*Patteson* J. I presume the defendant does not mean to impugn *Marshall* v. *Rutton* (*a*), and other cases to the same effect. The subsequent promise will probably be relied on.] The replication, if it insist on the subsequent promise, is a departure. It admits the promises stated in the declaration to have been made during coverture, and sets up a new promise. The considerations are different: the delivery of the goods, &c., form the consideration in the declaration: the consideration for the promise in the replication is "the premises," which seems to point to a moral consideration. Such a consideration appears not to be sustainable; *Littlefield* v. *Shee* (*b*). *Barden* v. *De Keverberg* (*c*) shews what is necessary to make a feme covert liable as a feme sole.

(*a*) 8 *T. R.* 545. See *Lean* v. *Schutz*, 2 *W. Bl.* 1195; *Boggett* v. *Frier*, 11 *East*, 301.; *Lewis* v. *Lee*, 3 *B. & C.* 291.

(*b*) 2 *B. & Ad.* 811.

(*c*) 2 *Mee. & W.* 61.

Humfrey,

1838.

MEYER against HAWORTH.

Humfrey, contrà. In *Littlefield* v. *Shee* (*a*) the husband was originally liable: here he never was so; *Rex* v. *Flintan* (*b*). *Lee* v. *Muggeridge* (*c*) supports the validity of such a moral consideration as this. Then this is not a departure: if it were, every replication to a plea of the Statute of Limitations, setting up an acknowledgment, would be so; for such an acknowledgment is merely evidence of a fresh promise; *Tanner* v. *Smart* (*d*). [*Patteson* J. That is a promise to pay an existing debt: here there was no debt from the wife.] If there be any state of facts in which the debt would not be absolutely null in the first instance, that distinction would not apply. Now suppose the husband had been transported. [Lord *Denman* C. J. That should be part of the statement of consideration. *Patteson* J. You are to support your declaration.]

Streeten, in reply. The declaration states the supply of goods at the request of the wife, who could not then contract. The doctrine in *Lee* v. *Muggeridge* (*c*) has been qualified by later decisions (*e*): and there, too, the special contract was set out in the declaration.

Lord DENMAN C. J. The record states that goods were supplied to a married woman, who, after her husband's death, promised to pay. That is not sufficient. The debt was never owing from her. If there was a moral obligation, that should have been shewn.

LITTLEDALE J. If there was any moral obligation, it should have been stated. The replication does not

(*a*) 2 *B. & Ad.* 811.
(*b*) 1 *B. & Ad.* 227.
(*c*) 5 *Taunt.* 36.
(*d*) 6 *B. & C.* 603.
(*e*) See note [*b*] to *Barber* v. *Fox*, 2 *Wms. Saund.* 137. c., 5th ed.

support

1838.

MEYER *against* HAWORTH.

support the declaration. The promise in the declaration, was altogether void. This is not like the case of an infant, whose promise is voidable only.

PATTESON J. For the reasons given this replication is bad as a departure. The promise originally stated was not one merely voidable, like that of an infant. There is another fault in the replication: it does not allege positively the death of the husband.

WILLIAMS J. concurred.

Judgment for defendant.

YOUNG *against* RISHWORTH.

To an action for money had and received, it is a good plea (under stat. 6 G. 4. c. 16. s. 127), that, plaintiff became bankrupt and obtained his certificate in 1822; that a second commission issued against him, May 20th, 1825, under which his effects were assigned in July 1825, and he obtained his certificate in 1826, but did not pay 15s. in the pound, whereby, and by force of the statute, the debt demanded in the declaration hath vested in the assignees.

Stat. 6 G. 4. c. 16. s. 127. (*September* 1, 1825), operates in such a case retrospectively.

Where the estate of a bankrupt after certificate is vested in the assignees by stat. 6 G. 4. c. 16. s. 127., he cannot sue for an after-accruing debt, though the assignees do not interpose.

ASSUMPSIT for money received to plaintiff's use, and on an account stated. Plea, that plaintiff, before and on 15th *July* 1822, and from thence continually until the suing out of the commission after mentioned, was a merchant, &c.; that he became indebted, &c.; and, being so indebted, and trading, he became and was a bankrupt within the true intent, &c.: the plea then stated the issuing of a commission on the day and year aforesaid, and the proceedings on it, and that the plaintiff duly obtained his certificate under the said commission, which certificate was allowed by the Lord Chancellor on *November* 14th, 1822. The plea then stated that plaintiff, afterwards, and before and on *May* 20th, 1825, and from thence continually until the suing out

of

1838.

YOUNG *against* RISHWORTH.

of the commission after mentioned, exercised trade, &c.; that plaintiff, so exercising trade, &c, became indebted, &c.; and, being so indebted, he, on the day and year last aforesaid, became bankrupt within the true intent, &c., and, thereupon, on the same day and year, a commission of bankruptcy issued against him, &c.: the plea then stated the proceedings on the second commission down to *July* 5th, 1825, when the commissioners assigned all plaintiff's present and future personal estate to *Stanislaus Dartez* and *Basil Caroline Montagu*, for the benefit of plaintiff's creditors. The plea then proceeded as follows. "And, although the said plaintiff duly surrendered himself," &c., "and submitted himself," &c., "and duly conformed himself" &c., "and although the said plaintiff afterwards, and after the making of the act of parliament," (6 *G.* 4. *c.* 16.), "to wit on the 1st day of *April*, A. D. 1826, duly obtained his certificate of conformity under the last mentioned commission, nevertheless the defendant says that the estate of the plaintiff under the last mentioned commission did not produce, nor hath as yet produced, sufficient to pay every creditor or any of the creditors under the last mentioned commission 15*s.* in the pound on the amount of their several debts proved under the last mentioned commission; and none of the said creditors have as yet received 15*s.* in the pound on the amount of their said debts: whereby, and by force of the statute in such case provided, the debt in and by the declaration demanded hath vested in the said *Stanislaus Dartez* and *Basil Caroline Montagu*, as assignees under the last mentioned commission, according to the form of the statute in such case provided." Verification.

Demurrer, assigning several special causes which were not

1838.

YOUNG *against* RISHWORTH.

not discussed on the argument. Joinder. The demurrer was argued in last *Hilary* term (*a*).

Knowles, for the plaintiff. The defence in this plea is founded on the supposed title of the assignees under stat. 6 *G.* 4. *c.* 16. *s.* 127., which enacts that, if any person who shall have been discharged by certificate as before mentioned, or discharged by any insolvent act, shall be or become bankrupt and have obtained or shall hereafter obtain his certificate, then, unless his estate shall produce sufficient to pay, under that commission, 15*s.* in the pound, such certificate shall only protect his person from arrest, "but his future estate and effects (except his tools of trade and necessary household furniture, and the wearing apparel of himself, his wife and children), shall vest in the assignees under the said commission, who shall be entitled to seize the same in like manner as they might have seized property of which such bankrupt was possessed at the issuing the commission." This enactment varies from the previous one in stat. 5 *G.* 2. *c.* 30. *s.* 9., which left the future estate and effects of the bankrupt, in the like case, "liable to his" "creditors," the tools of trade, &c., excepted. Then, First; by stat. 6 *G.* 4. *c.* 16. *s.* 127. the effects of a party, bankrupt for the second time, who has obtained a certificate but has not paid 15*s.* in the pound, are subject to the same liabilities as attach by sect. 63 to the effects of a party, bankrupt for the first time, who has obtained no certificate. In the latter case, the bankrupt's after-ac-

(*a*) *January* 19th. Before Lord *Denman* C. J., *Littledale*, *Williams*, and *Coleridge* Js. For a point decided in this case on a previous day of the term, see p. 479. note (*c*), post.

quired

1838.

YOUNG against RISHWORTH.

quired property vests in the assignees; this appears from the decisions, on the prior statutes, in *Kitchen* v. *Bartsch* (a) and *Nias* v. *Adamson* (b). That being so, there are other decisions which shew that an uncertificated bankrupt may sue in respect of after-acquired property, if the assignees do not interpose (as they did in the two cases just cited), and that, not only where the action is for work, labour, and materials, as in *Silk* v. *Osborn* (c), or for money which may be supposed the produce of the bankrupt's labour, as in *Evans* v. *Brown* (d), but in other instances also, on the general principle of his right to claim property except as against his assignees; *Fowler* v. *Down* (e), *Webb* v. *Fox* (g), *Drayton* v. *Dale* (h). The analogy between the cases of an uncertificated bankrupt and a certificated bankrupt under a second commission who has not paid 15*s*. in the pound was urged at the bar in *Robertson* v. *Score* (i). Secondly, it has long been a question whether stat. 6 *G*. 4. *c*. 16. *s*. 127. took effect where the certificate or certificates had been obtained before the act passed; *Robertson* v. *Score* (i), *Carew* v. *Edwards* (k). In the latter case, where the defendant had both been discharged under an insolvent act and obtained his certificate as a bankrupt before the passing of stat. 6 *G*. 4. *c*. 16., this Court held that sect. 127 had not a retrospective operation. It is true that in *Elston* v. *Braddick* (l), where a party had been discharged as an insolvent before, and had become bankrupt after, the statute came into operation, sect. 127 was held

(a) 7 *East*, 53.
(b) 3 *B. & Ald.* 225.
(c) 1 *Esp. N. P. C.* 140.
(d) 1 *Esp. N. P. C.* 170.
(e) 1 *B. & P.* 44.
(g) 7 *T. R.* 391.
(h) 2 *B. & C.* 293.
(i) 3 *B. & Ad.* 338.
(k) 4 *B. & Ad.* 351.
(l) 2 *Cro. & M.* 435. *S. C.* 4 *Tyr.* 122.

1838.

YOUNG against RISHWORTH.

held to operate retrospectively: but in *Ex parte Hawley, in re Richards* (a), where there had been a like discharge, and a certificate without payment of 15s. in the pound, both before the act, Lord Chancellor *Brougham* decided against a retrospective construction. Further, it does not appear by this plea that the money now claimed is not property within the exception of sect. 127; and it was for the defendant to shew that. [Lord *Denman* C. J. The declaration claims a debt; was it necessary to state that this was not an excepted article? *Coleridge* J. If a bankrupt reduces his tools to money, does not that vest in the assignees? *Littledale* J. If you relied on the money being the produce of excepted articles, it was for you to shew it.] The plaintiff declares in the regular form. The defendant does not assert that the debt is one which vests in the assignees, so as to give the plaintiff an opportunity of traversing that fact. The plaintiff may be entitled to the debt as trustee. [*Littledale* J. In *Winch* v. *Keeley* (b) that fact was replied to a general plea of the plaintiff's bankruptcy.]

Sir *W. W. Follett*, contrà. Stat. 6 *G.* 4. *c.* 16. *s.* 127. alters the old law. By stat. 5 *G.* 2. *c.* 30. *s.* 9. the after-acquired property where the estate did not pay 15s. in the pound under a second commission was to "remain liable" to the creditors, the bankrupt being discharged from arrest, only, by the certificate: under this statute, *s.* 126, he is discharged, not only from arrest but from action for any debt proveable under the commission:

(a) 2 *Mont. & Ayr.* 426.; *Elston* v. *Braddick*, 2 *Cro. & M.* 435, *S. C.* 4 *Tyr.* 122, (not then reported) was cited from a short-hand writer's note, which the Lord Chancellor refused to admit as authority.

(b) 1 *T. R.* 619.

but

1838.

YOUNG *against* RISHWORTH.

but sect. 127 directs that his future estate "shall vest in the assignees under the said commission." The argument that, as between the bankrupt and a creditor, the property is in the same situation as where the bankrupt has failed to obtain his certificate under a first commission, and that such property may be treated as the bankrupt's where the assignees do not interfere, was urged without success in *Robertson* v. *Score* (*a*); some of the cases cited as to this point on the other side were there mentioned, but were not thought applicable under the present act. [*Coleridge* J. The plaintiff there might have proved under the second commission]. The argument of the Court was, that the effects, where not discharged by the second certificate, were vested in the assignees; and that, if the certificate were no bar, the plaintiff would, in effect, be recovering against their goods. In *Elston* v. *Braddick* (*b*), which was an action for money had and received, brought by assignees for sums paid by the bankrupt into the Bank of *England*, the plaintiff relied on sect. 127: one point made by the defendant was, that the action did not lie, there being no privity between the assignees and the Bank. But *Bayley* J. said (*c*), "Assuming that the act is retrospective, the act says that the future property of the bankrupt shall vest in the assignees; and it vests in the assignees *ab initio*: and when the money was paid in by the bankrupt, it was money had and received to the use of the assignees. In reality, this never was the property of the bankrupt. It appears to me, therefore, that money had and received is the proper form of action." And there the Court of Exchequer, after an elaborate discussion, held that sect. 127 applied retro-

(*a*) 3 *B. & Ad.* 338. (*b*) 2 *Cro. & M.* 435. *S. C.* 4 *Tyr.* 122.
(*c*) 2 *Cro. & M.* 438.

1838.

YOUNG *against* RISHWORTH.

spectively. In *Ex parte Robinson, in re Freer* (a), Sir *L. Shadwell*, V. C. held that, under sect. 127, after-acquired estate "vests absolutely, and *ab initio*, in the assignees." In *Fowler* v. *Coster* (b), where the question was on the validity of a third commission, the bankrupt having paid no dividend under the second, the third was held void, because, when it issued, the effects were already vested in the assignees formerly appointed. The difference between stat. 6 *G.* 4. *c.* 16. *s.* 127. and stat. 5 *G.* 2. *c.* 30. *s.* 9. was there noticed by the Court. Even in the cases previous to stat. 6 *G.* 4. *c.* 16., cited on the other side, where uncertificated bankrupts were allowed to sue, some peculiar state of circumstances was requisite, to prevent the operation of the general rule that the right of action is in the assignees; and, if it was necessary to shew such circumstances, even in the former state of the law, to defeat a plea like the present, they should have been specially replied here, the plea shewing the property to be, primâ facie, in the assignees. But, since the late act, no distinction can arise upon which the bankrupt can found a right to sue as in those cases, the property vesting absolutely and ab initio in the assignees. It has been held, and no doubt properly, that, an uncertificated bankrupt, having possession of his property with the consent of the assignees, might bring trover in respect of it against a wrong doer: the nature of his right under such circumstances is illustrated by *Nias* v. *Adamson* (c), and *Hull* v. *Pickersgill* (d), cited in *c.* 14. *s.* 20. of Lord *Henley's* bankrupt law (e): but the present case does not raise any similar point. It is true that in *Elston* v. *Braddick* (g) the insolvency and commission

(a) 1 *Mont. & Mac.* 44.

(b) 10 *B. & C.* 427. And see *Phillips* v. *Hopwood*, 1. *B. & Ad.* 619.

(c) 3 *B. & Ald.* 225.

(d) 1 *Brod. & B.* 282.

(e) Page 256. 3d ed.

(g) 2 *Cro. & M.* 435. *S. C.* 4 *Tyr.* 122.

1838.

YOUNG *against* RISHWORTH.

commission were not both prior to the act coming into operation (*a*); but the principle of the decision applies where both are so.

Knowles in reply. *Elston* v. *Braddick* (*b*) was a case where the assignees interfered, as it is admitted they may do. The decision in *Robertson* v. *Score* (*c*) does not show that the bankrupt might not have been sued, if the debt had not been proveable under the second commission. Where an uncertificated bankrupt relies merely on his right to dispose of property if the assignees do not interfere, it is not necessary to plead such non-interference. In *Drayton* v. *Dale* (*d*) the plaintiffs, indorsees of a note, founded their title on the indorsement of a bankrupt; the bankruptcy was pleaded, and the plaintiffs replied consent of the assignees to the indorsement; this was negatived by verdict; but the Court nevertheless gave judgment non obstante veredicto, on grounds, one of which was that the bankrupt's indorsement was valid because it did not appear that the assignees had interposed.

Cur. adv. vult.

Lord DENMAN C. J., in this term (*June* 13th), delivered the judgment of the Court.

This was an action brought in assumpsit upon counts for money had and received, and an account stated. The defendant pleaded, in substance, that the plaintiff, in the year 1822, became bankrupt and obtained his certificate; and again that, in the year 1825, he became bankrupt, and, on the first of *April* 1826, obtained his certificate, but that the estate of the plaintiff under the

(*a*) *September* 1st, 1825. See sect. 136.

(*b*) 2 *Cro.* & *M.* 435. *S. C.* 4 *Tyr.* 122.

(*c*) 3 *B.* & *Ad.* 338.

(*d*) 2 *B.* & *C.* 293.

 latter

1838.

YOUNG against RISHWORTH.

latter commission was not sufficient to pay his creditors fifteen shillings in the pound, and had not paid them or any of them that sum.

To this there was a demurrer: and the question is, whether, under the circumstances disclosed in that plea, the plaintiff is entitled to bring this action; and that mainly depends (as was admitted in argument on both sides) upon the proper construction of the 127th section of stat. 6 *G.* 4. *c.* 16: because, if that statute applies to the cases of bankruptcy which took place before it passed, it was hardly contended but that the plea does amount to an answer to the action. And we think that, after the decisions which have taken place, the question can no longer be considered as open. The language of the 127th section is as follows. "If any person who shall have been so discharged by such certificate as aforesaid," &c., "shall be or become bankrupt, and have obtained or shall hereafter obtain such certificate as aforesaid," unless his estate shall pay fifteen shillings in the pound, his future estate and effects (except &c.) "*shall vest* in the assignees" under the commission. And upon this point, whether the bankrupt act does apply to commissions sued out and certificates thereunder obtained before it passed, or, in other words, whether the section just quoted be in its effect retrospective, the Court of Exchequer, after deliberation, and a careful comparison of the language of the two statutes (5 *G.* 2. *c.* 30. and the present act), have come to a decision in the affirmative (*a*). That being so, we consider ourselves bound by that decision, being of opinion that it is most inconvenient to question the authority of cases deliberately decided, except for the strongest and clearest reasons. In this

(*a*) *Elston* v. *Braddick*, 2 *Cro.* & *M.* 435. *S. C.* 4 *Tyr.* 122.

case,

1838.

YOUNG *against* RISHWORTH.

case, however, we approve of the reasons given as well as of the decision itself, which is indeed fortified by the cases of *Fowler* v. *Coster* (*a*) and *Robertson* v. *Score* (*b*).

The section, therefore, being (as we think it is) applicable to the present case, what is its effect? The words are "his future estate and effects" shall vest "in the assignees," and his person only be protected. The language of the former act 5 *G.* 2. *c.* 30. *s.* 9., is different: it is there said that the future effects shall remain liable to his creditors as before the passing of that act; that is (according to the construction put by this Court in *Fowler* v. *Coster* (*a*)), liable to his individual creditors. Here however they are vested absolutely in the assignees, and by consequence devested from the bankrupt under the circumstances disclosed in the plea, which we therefore think contains a sufficient answer to the action: and that judgment must be for the defendant.

Judgment for the defendant (*c*).

(*a*) 10 *B.* & *C.* 427. (*b*) 3 *B.* & *Ad.* 338.

(*c*) Before the argument of this demurrer, in the same term, the following motion was heard, in the same cause.

January 18th, 1838.

Defendant on the eve of trial at the assizes, *March* 1836, obtained leave to add a plea. Plaintiff thereupon countermanded notice of trial, and demurred to the plea; and the demurrer was set down for argument, *May* 1836. Plaintiff in *October* 1836 became insolvent, and in *December* obtained his discharge. In the beginning of *Michaelmas* term, 1837 (the demurrer then standing near the head of the special paper), defendant moved that plaintiff might give security for costs.

Held, too late.

A rule nisi was obtained in *Michaelmas* term, 1837, for a stay of proceedings until the plaintiff should give security for costs. By the affidavits for and against the rule, it appeared that the defendant was arrested in the action (for 23*l.* 10*s.*) on *January* 26th, 1836, and a declaration delivered, *February* 4th; that, the cause being at issue, notice of trial was given for the *Kingston* Spring assizes, 1836, the commission day being *March* 28th; that, on *March* 25th, defendant obtained leave of a Judge to add a plea, which he delivered on *March* 26th, whereupon plaintiff countermanded his notice of trial; that, in the following *Easter* term, plaintiff demurred to the plea, and the demurrer (the judgment upon which is above reported) was set down for argument, *May* 26th, 1836; that plaintiff, on 1st *October* 1836, petitioned the Court for relief of insolvent debtors, and, on 22d *December* following, obtained his discharge; and that a summons, taken out on 25th *April* 1837, for the purpose

of

1838.

YOUNG *against* RISHWORTH.

of obtaining from the plaintiff security for costs, was heard by a single Judge, and dismissed. The present rule nisi was obtained on the same grounds as the summons, *November* 4th, 1837, a demand of security having been made on the previous 26th *October*. At the beginning of *Hilary* term, 1838, the demurrer was expected to stand No. 9. in the special paper.

Cresswell and *Knowles* shewed cause. The defendant makes no affidavit of merits. Such an affidavit was made in *Heaford* v. *Knight* (2 *B. & C.* 579.). The application comes late, and no special excuse is made for the delay. Nor is this in itself a case in which security for costs can be demanded, *Snow* v. *Townsend* (6 *Taunt.* 123.).

Sir *W. W. Follett*, contrà. This is not a question of indulgence, but of right, under the practice of the Court. No affidavit of merits is required in such cases. [*Littledale* J. I never heard of its being necessary.] *Heaford* v. *Knight*, (2 *B. & C.* 579.), cited in 1 *Tidd's Practice*, 536 (9th ed.), is an authority supporting this application, in the case of an insolvent. As to the delay, no step has been taken in the cause between the insolvency and the making of this motion.

Lord DENMAN C. J. The defendant has been a long time in making this application; and, if the rule is discharged, no material expense will be ultimately sustained in addition to that which was incurred before making the motion. There is no ground for making the rule absolute.

LITTLEDALE J. I am of the same opinion. There has been great delay.

WILLIAMS and COLERIDGE Js. concurred.

Rule discharged.

1838.

The QUEEN *against* MARTIN and Wife.

Saturday, June 2d.

An indictment, under stat. 7 & 8 G. 4. c. 29. s. 53., for obtaining goods by false pretences, must state to whom the goods belonged.

Otherwise it will be bad on error; the omission not being cured after verdict by the last clause of stat. 7 G. 4. c. 64. s. 21., that provision relating to the description of the offence, not of the subject-matter.

THE defendants were indicted at the quarter sessions for the parts of *Kesteven*, in *Lincolnshire*, for that they, contriving and intending, &c., to cheat and defraud *William James Holt* of his goods, on &c., at &c., unlawfully did falsely pretend to *George Ingle*, then and there being an apprentice to the said *W. J. Holt*, that &c. (stating and negativing the pretences); and that the said *G. M.* and *E.* his wife, by the false pretences aforesaid, did then and there unlawfully, knowingly, and designedly obtain from the said *W. J. Holt* divers goods and merchandizes, that is to say, six dozen pounds weight of candles of the value &c., with intent then and there to cheat and defraud the said *W. J. Holt* of the same, against the form of the statute, &c. Plea, Not Guilty. Verdict, Guilty: and judgment of transportation.

Error was brought on the judgment, on the ground, among others, that it was not stated in the indictment that the goods alleged to have been fraudulently obtained were the property of any person. Joinder in error.

Curwood for the plaintiffs in error. Sect. 53 of stat. 7 & 8 *G.* 4 *c.* 29., reciting that "a failure of justice frequently arises from the subtle distinction between larceny and fraud," enacts "that if any person shall by any false pretence obtain from any other person any chattel," &c., "with intent to cheat or defraud any per-

1838.

The Queen *against* Martin.

son of the same," he shall be guilty of a misdemeanor: "provided always, that if upon the trial of any person indicted for such misdemeanor it shall be proved that he obtained the property in question in any such manner as to amount in law to larceny, he shall not by reason thereof be entitled to be acquitted of such misdemeanor;" "and no person tried for such misdemeanor shall be liable to be afterwards prosecuted for larceny upon the same facts." The indictment therefore should be so framed as to be pleadable in bar, or to be evidence in a plea of auterfois acquit, upon a subsequent prosecution for larceny on the same facts. The indictment here could not be so used, because it does not furnish the means of identifying the transaction by means of the name of the owner of the chattels. In *Regina* v. *Norton* (a), *Alderson* B. (with the concurrence of *Williams* and *Coltman* Js.) directed an indictment for obtaining money under false pretences to be quashed for this defect, and upon the ground now suggested; and this, although the defendant's counsel wished to waive the objection. [*Lord Denman* C. J. The defendant, in pleading auterfois acquit, would aver the identity; and it must always be proved.] Where it is possible, the indictment should state the facts fully. The identity should appear on collation of the indictments. [*Lord Denman* C. J. Have you any authority for saying that identity is shewn primâ facie by collation of the indictments? A defendant may have stolen the goods of the same party twenty times.] In *Rex* v. *Parry* (b) auterfois acquit was pleaded to an indictment for rape: *Bolland* B. ruled that the proof lay on the defendant, and he thereupon put in a previous in-

(a) 8 *C. & P.* 196.

(b) 7 *C. & P.* 836.

dictment,

1838.

The QUEEN *against* MARTIN.

dictment, consisting of four counts, which corresponded with four counts of the indictment in question; and upon this proof only the jury found for the defendants: and, the case being afterwards argued before fourteen judges, it was held that the verdict was final. [Lord *Denman* C. J. The point as to the sufficiency of proof was not decided by the fourteen judges.] It will be argued that the defect is cured by the verdict. But, in *Regina* v. *Norton* (*a*), *Alderson* B. said that it would be waste of time to go on with the trial, clearly intimating, therefore, that the defect would be fatal at any stage. The defect is one of substance. Stat. 7 *G.* 4. *c.* 64. *s.* 21. enacts, "That where the offence charged has been created by any statute, or subjected to a greater degree of punishment, or excluded from the benefit of clergy by any statute, the indictment or information shall after verdict be held sufficient to warrant the punishment prescribed by the statute if it describe the offence in the words of the statute." But that does not protect an omission of any substantive matter of description. [Lord *Denman* C. J. Surely, in an indictment for burglary, the omission to state whose the house or goods were would not be protected.] Neither here would it be enough to charge that the defendant "by a false pretence obtained from another person a chattel, with intent to cheat that person of the same." The cases upon the Polish notes (*Rex* v. *Harris* (*b*), *Rex* v. *Moses* (*c*), *Rex* v. *Balls* (*d*),) are instances of the curing of a defect by verdict under stat. 7 *G.* 4. *c.* 64. *s.* 21.: but it would not there have been held sufficient if the indictment had merely charged

(*a*) 8 *C.* & *P.* 196.

(*b*) 7 *C.* & *P.* 416, 429. *S. C.* 1 *Moo. Cr. Ca.* 470.

(*c*) 7 *C.* & *P.* 423, 429. *S. C.*, as *Rex* v. *Warshaner*, 1 *Moo. Cr. Ca.* 466.

(*d*) 7 *C.* & *P.* 426, 429. *S. C.* 1 *Moo. Cr. Ca.* 470.

 that

1838.

The QUEEN *against* MARTIN.

that the defendant "knowingly had in his custod va plate upon which a promissory note of a foreign prince was engraved without the authority of the said foreign prince;" though such are the words of stat. 11 *G.* 4. & 1 *W.* 4. *c.* 66. *s.* 19.

Archbold, contrà. As to an indictment for burglary, stat. 7 & 8 *G.* 4. *c.* 29. *s.* 11. simply (except as to the case of breaking out) uses the word "burglary," leaving the meaning as it stood at common law, which meaning therefore the words of the indictment must meet. [*Littledale* J. Sect. 12 of the same statute enacts the punishment for stealing in a dwelling house: would you say it was enough to use those words without naming the owner?] There, again, the word "stealing" throws the meaning back upon the common law definition: the words of the statute, therefore, are not sufficient in an indictment: "stealing," or larceny, necessarily is taking the goods of another, that is, either of *A. B.*, or of a person unknown. It is said in *Hawkins*, *Pl. Cr.*, *B.* 1. *c.* 33. *s.* 38. (*a*), "It seems agreed, that the taking of goods whereof no one had a property at the time, cannot be felony." [Lord *Denman* C. J. What do you say of stat. 7 & 8 *G.* 4. *c.* 29. *s.* 22., as to destroying a will?] A charge that the defendant "destroyed a will" would be sufficient after verdict. *Alderson* B., in *Regina* v. *Norton* (*b*), merely intimated what he thought the most eligible mode of disposing of the indictment, to which objection was made at the trial. [*Littledale* J. Does sect. 21 of stat. 7 *G.* 4. *c.* 64. apply to more than the description *of the offence*, that is, the obtaining by false pretence? Does it

(*a*) Vol. i. p. 215. 7th ed.

(*b*) 8 *C.* & *P.* 196.

1838.

The QUEEN *against* MARTIN.

it apply at all to the description of the goods or person?] The goods are in fact described here; it is not material whose property they were: a man might be guilty of obtaining his own goods under false pretences from the prosecutor, with intent to defraud him. *Rex* v. *M'Gregor* (*a*), which may appear to support the objection to this indictment, was a case of embezzlement under stat. 39 *G.* 3. *c.* 85., which made the offence felonious *stealing* from the master. As to the supposed difficulty in case of a future indictment for larceny, it would not, in any case, lie on the prosecutor to make it appear that the offences were not identical: the defendant must aver identity. *Hawkins*, speaking of the plea of auterfois acquit (B. 2. *c.* 35. *s.* 3. (*b*)), says, "I take it to be clear, that if the nature of the crime be in substance the same, a variance may generally be helped by proper averments."

Curwood was heard in reply.

Lord DENMAN C. J. This indictment is clearly bad on the face of it. For aught that appears, the defendant may only have obtained his own goods. Perhaps he might even do that under circumstances which would render it criminal: but, primâ facie, it would not be criminal; and the circumstances which rendered it so should be stated. Suppose, for instance, he obtained his own goods under false pretences from a carrier in whose possession they were, in order to defraud the carrier; the possession would make them the carrier's goods; and the fact that the goods were the property of the defendant would only appear upon evidence,

(*a*) *Russ. & R. C. C. R.* 23. *S. C.* 3 *B. & P.* 106.
(*b*) Vol. iv. p. 313. 7th ed.

1838.

The QUEEN *against* MARTIN.

dence, and would not constitute a defence. Then is the defect cured by verdict? The act, 7 *G.* 4. *c.* 64. *s.* 21., says, that after verdict the indictment shall be sufficient, "if it describe the offence in the words of the statute;" and here the indictment does certainly pursue the words of the statute. But it is not enough to state the offence in general terms: the enactment assumes that the words shall be so employed as to shew that some offence has been committed. In indictments for larceny the ownership of the goods is always stated. There may be some question as to the validity of the argument urged respecting a plea of auterfois acquit; for the same difficulty would arise on pleas of auterfois acquit at common law. Still it furnishes a reason for requiring strictness; and this is, I think, all that was meant by *Alderson* B. in *Regina* v. *Norton* (a). The Court there interfered on the ground that there must be certainty, else the defendant could never use the indictment at all, no offence being charged. There are many instances in which, if merely the statutory form were followed, no offence would be charged. For instance, if a man destroyed his own will, would that be an offence under sect. 22 of stat. 7 & 8 *G.* 4. *c.* 29.? Or would it be an offence, under sect. 33., if he took his own house-doves or pigeons? We must put a reasonable construction on the act, and not go the length of holding an indictment good, after verdict, which charges only what may be no offence at all.

LITTLEDALE J. I am entirely of the same opinion. No doubt this indictment would be bad on judgment by

(a) 8 *C.* & *P.* 196.

default,

1838.

The QUEEN *against* MARTIN.

default, for want of stating whose the property was. Then, as to the operation of stat. 7 *G.* 4. *c.* 64. *s.* 21., after verdict. Stat. 7 & 8 *G.* 4. *c.* 29. *s.* 53. punishes the obtaining by false pretence any chattel, &c., with intent to cheat or defraud any person of the same. That description is followed in the indictment; and the offence is therefore described in the words of the statute. But the subject-matter must be described with the same particularity as in a common law indictment. Thus it would not be enough to charge the stealing goods in a dwelling house, the destroying a will, the taking pigeons, without adding whose goods, whose will, whose pigeons.

PATTESON J. I think this indictment bad; and that it is not cured by stat. 7 *G.* 4. *c.* 64. *s.* 21. after verdict. I agree that, after verdict, it is sufficient if the offence be described in the terms of the statute; but here the omission is of the statement whose the goods were. I cannot see how, if we held that such a defect was cured, we could hold that a verdict did not cure an omission, in an indictment for burglary, of any statement whose the house or goods were. It is said this argument would not apply to a case where "stealing" is a part of the description of the offence, inasmuch as that word necessarily implies taking the goods of another. If that were the meaning in the act, it would be the meaning in the indictment: therefore an indictment for stealing goods, without describing the owner, would be cured after verdict. But it is not cured. In fact, stat. 7 & 8 *G.* 4. *c.* 29. seldom does, in words, make it requisite that the goods, &c., should be those of another: yet that must be always meant. Thus

 sect.

1838.

The Queen against Martin.

sect. 31 must mean that the offence is stealing the dog, &c., of another. Then it is argued that the offence charged in this indictment may be committed though the chattels belonged to the defendant, for that the real intent of sect. 53 is to punish the obtaining of *any* chattel, under false pretences, with intent to cheat or defraud any person of the same. Now, on looking through the whole act, it is clear that the goods meant are those of another. If a party obtained his own goods from another by false pretences, with intent to defraud him, the goods would be, in a legal sense, the goods of that other. The case would be like what is sometimes erroneously called the larceny of the defendant's own goods; the goods being, in such an instance, the goods of another. The word "any" is used throughout stat. 7 & 8 *G.* 4. *c.* 29.; but the person, the pretence, the chattel, &c., must always be described.

Williams J. The only question is, whether the defect be cured by stat. 7 *G.* 4. *c.* 64. *s.* 21.; for it is almost admitted that the indictment is wrong. Long as the offence has existed, the allegation of property has never been omitted. Mr. *Archbold* was pressed with analógies from other offences, in which omissions would be cured by verdict, if here. He answered, that "burglary" and "stealing" had ascertained meanings by common law: that they involved the idea of the house and property belonging to another. But what is the meaning of "by any false pretence obtain?" Surely the words mean something which excludes the case of there being no offence at all. To do that, you must describe the chattel

as

as belonging to another. Therefore the reasoning will be the same in this case as in that of larceny.

1838.

The QUEEN *against* MARTIN.

Judgment reversed.

MORGAN *against* HALLEN and Another, Executors of SARAH ANN IRONMONGER.

Monday, June 4th.

There is no rule of law which prevents an apothecary from making distinct charges for attendances and for medicines.

Whether the patient be liable to a separate demand for attendances, is a question to be decided by the jury in each case, on the facts proving or disproving a contract to that effect; as the prior dealing between the same parties; or the reasonableness or unreasonableness, under the circumstances in the particular case, of making a charge for attendances, as well as for medicines.

ASSUMPSIT. The declaration stated that the testatrix in her lifetime, viz. on &c., was indebted to plaintiff in the sum &c., "for the price and value of the work and labour, care and attendance of the plaintiff as a surgeon and apothecary before that time performed and bestowed by him, and of medicines and other necessary things found and provided by him," &c., and in a further sum on an account stated: and that in consideration thereof she promised &c. There was also a count on an account stated between plaintiff and the executors. Particulars of demand were annexed, beginning with a statement of medicines supplied during the year 1829, setting forth every article with its price, and concluding the account for that year as follows: "To attendances, advice, and applications by myself and assistant almost every day, and very frequently many times a day, during the year 1829: 18*l.*" Then followed charges for medicines, made out in the same manner, for the five ensuing years, with a concluding item in each year for attendances, expressed as before, the demand in every instance being 18*l.* The whole amount was, for medicines, 96*l.* 16*s.* 6*d.*: attendances, 108*l.* Total 204*l.* 16*s.* 6*d.* Plea, payment into court, generally, of 124*l.* 10*s.* 2*d.* Replication, damage to a greater amount. Issue thereon.

On

1838.

MORGAN *against* HALLEN.

On the trial before *Littledale* J., at the *Stafford* summer assizes, 1836, it appeared that the testatrix died in *May* 1835, and that, during the last six years of her life, medicines had been supplied as charged in the particular. No part of the demand arose in respect of surgery. The testatrix lived at *Lichfield*, within a few hundred yards of the plaintiff: she was between eighty and ninety years old; and, during the period in question, was in the habit of requiring the plaintiff's personal attendance very often, and on very trivial occasions, sending for him generally once, and occasionally three or four times in a day. The quantity of medicines supplied bore a very small proportion to the number of attendances, the plaintiff often advising her not to take medicine. It was stated in evidence that apothecaries in the neighbourhood of *Lichfield* had been in the practice of charging for attendances as well as medicines; and that the plaintiff's charges for medicine were such as might reasonably be made where attendances also were set down as an item (*a*). The plaintiff had sent to the testatrix, in her lifetime, a bill for several years ending on *December* 30th 1828, in which was an item for attendances in 1823 and 1826 only, but no charge was made for them, a blank being left, to be filled up by the testatrix (*b*); and she paid him on this item 20*l*.

(*a*) It appeared that in the present case the price of medicines had been moderated by sending in a large quantity at a certain charge, as a "mixture," which, if divided into "draughts," would have cost a much greater sum.

(*b*) The rate of charge for medicines in this bill was not discussed, the bill being handed to the jury at their request, and by consent of the plaintiff's counsel, after the learned Judge had finished his summing up. In the course of his address, however, the learned Judge made some observations on that bill hypothetically, and tending to shew that, if that bill were in evidence, the absence of a direct charge there for attendances would not of itself be conclusive against the present demand.

His

1838.

MORGAN against HALLEN.

His attendances down to the end of 1828 were much less frequent than afterwards; and in 1827 and 1828 she was taking medicine under the advice of a physician. The bill now in question was sent to the executors after the testatrix's death, and a specific sum charged therein for "extraordinary attendance and advice." The defendants' counsel objected that, in point of law, an apothecary charging for medicines had no right to charge for attendances also. The learned Judge reserved leave to move to enter a verdict for the defendant, or a nonsuit; and stated, as the question for the jury, whether, assuming that the two demands could be made together, it was reasonable in this case that any thing should be claimed for attendances, taking into consideration the charge made for medicines; and how much should be given for the attendances, supposing the charge for medicines not a sufficient compensation. The plaintiff had a verdict for 80*l.*

Sir *W. W. Follett*, in the ensuing term, obtained a rule to shew cause why a nonsuit or a verdict for the defendant should not be entered, or a new trial had. He cited *Towne* v. *Lady Gresley* (*a*), *Handey* v. *Henson* (*b*), and stat. 55 *G.* 3. *c.* 194. *s.* 5.

Talfourd Serjt., *M'Mahon* and *R. V. Richards* now shewed cause. An apothecary is entitled to a reasonable compensation for his attendances and medicines: he may include the one in his charge for the other, or he may charge for both, so that he does not claim more, in all, than a proper compensation. Here the latter mode has been adopted; and the defendants have sanctioned

(*a*) 3 *Car.* & *P.* 581. (*b*) 4 *Car.* & *P.* 110.

it

1838.

MORGAN *against* HALLEN.

it in principle, by paying into Court more than suffices for either head of charge by itself. The matter of fact was properly left to the jury; and there is no authority of law for saying that an apothecary, although he may charge for attendances under the head of medicines, may not charge for them specifically. If he may lawfully attend, he may recover for so doing, like any other person who has rendered services. Stat. *55 G. 3. c.* 194. *s. 5.* does not shew the contrary. To "prepare" and "dispense" medicines are mentioned there as duties of an apothecary; and he is also to "administer." As to *Towne* v. *Lady Gresley* (*a*), *Best* J. said there, "I am inclined to think that there is something in some of the acts of parliament upon the subject of attendances; but if there is not any express provision, yet the practice is so inveterate that I cannot allow the plaintiff to charge in both ways. An apothecary may charge for attendances if he pleases, and then the jury will say what is reasonable for those attendances, or he may charge for the medicine he sends, but he cannot be permitted to make a charge for both." But there is no such statutory provision as the learned Judge mentions; and, unless he intended to say merely that an apothecary shall not recover full remuneration twice by means of the double charge, there is no authority for his ruling. And in *Handey* v. *Henson* (*b*) Lord *Tenterden* held that the plaintiff might recover for attendances (the charge being reasonable) as well as for medicines. In principle, the two demands may as properly be separated as charges for work and materials. This point was raised, but not decided upon, in *Gens-*

(*a*) 3 *Car. & P.* 581.

(*b*) 4 *Car. & P.* 110.

ham

1838.

MORGAN against HALLEN.

ham v. *Germain* (*a*). To say that an apothecary must always recover his remuneration in the form of a charge for medicines, is obliging him to fix different prices upon the same medicine in each case according to the trouble and loss of time which it occasions him. If a double claim be made, as here, a jury can always ascertain whether or not it is reasonable upon the whole. If the plaintiff here had delivered his bill to the executors, as he did to the testatrix, without a specific charge for attendance, he would have been bound to accept the sum they offered; *Tuson* v. *Batting* (*b*): but here a sum has been specified, and the jury has thought it reasonable.

C. Phillips and *Busby* contrà. That which *Best* C. J., in *Towne* v. *Lady Gresley* (*c*), called the inveterate practice is against these charges. And the plaintiff himself, in his former bill, did not make a demand in respect of attendances, but received payment for them as a gratuity. The defendants have made a gratuitous payment into court for attendances, in addition to the whole amount claimed for medicines. They do not thereby recognise the right now disputed. If the plaintiff had sent in his bill as he did in the testatrix's lifetime, *Tuson* v. *Batting* (*b*) would have been directly applicable; and he ought not to be placed in a more advantageous situation by having waited for her death and then made a charge on the executors, instead of leaving a blank in the account. If this demand were supported, an apothecary would be more favourably circumstanced than a physician; for he might not only charge for his skill and labour, but likewise

(*a*) 11 *B. Moore*, 1.

(*b*) 3 *Esp. N. P. C.* 192.

(*c*) 3 *Car. & P.* 581.

demand

1838.

Morgan against Hallen.

demand a sum much above the intrinsic value for his medicines, which he is permitted to do at present on the supposition that he cannot charge in any other form. It is true that in *Handey* v. *Henson* (a) Lord *Tenterden* did not follow the ruling of *Best* C. J. in *Towne* v. *Lady Gresley* (b); but neither that case, nor *Tuson* v. *Batting* (c), was brought to his attention. Both the summing up and the verdict in the present case were delivered on the assumption merely, that the charge for attendance was legal. The duty of an apothecary, according to stat. *55 G. 3. c.* 194. *s.* 5., is to superintend the preparing and giving of medicine; but for so doing he is allowed to charge a higher price for the drugs; and his practice differs wholly from that of the physician, who has nothing to do with the preparing and administering of medicine. Even supposing that no general question of law arises in this case (though all parties at the trial assumed the contrary), it was a question what contract between the plaintiff and the testatrix was to be inferred from their former course of dealing; and that was not left to the jury. (They also entered into the merits of the case on the particular charges.)

Lord Denman C. J. On the learned Judge's report, he does not appear to me to have actually held that a question of law arose, but to have put the case to the jury, subject to the question of law, if it arose. I think the case really turned upon questions of fact: first, whether any contract could be inferred which precluded the plaintiff from charging for attendances: secondly, whether, if not, his charges were reasonable. If

(a) 4 *Car. & P.* 110. (b) 3 *Car. & P.* 581.
(c) 3 *Esp. N. P. C.* 192.

the

the jury were, in point of law, at liberty to infer from the former dealings, and from the other facts, that such a contract existed as would allow of a charge for attendances, they have found, upon the facts, that this was the case; that the attendances were such as the plaintiff was entitled to charge for, and that the amount claimed was reasonable. If they have been liberal in the view they have taken, the question was of fact only, and was for them.

LITTLEDALE J. I do not say, as matter of law, that an apothecary may in every instance charge for attendances, or that there may not, in some cases, be circumstances which would prevent it. An apothecary may have to take journeys of many miles, where he may find that, as a conscientious man, he ought not to send medicine; in such a case it may be quite reasonable that a demand should be made for the attendances; on the other hand, if he has no great distance to go, attends but once a day, and sends a great deal of medicine, the price of the medicine may be a sufficient remuneration. It depends, therefore, upon circumstances whether he may charge for attendances or not; and those circumstances are for a jury. Here it was for the jury, whether the plaintiff was precluded from such a claim by the former course of dealing between him and the testatrix: they thought he was not: and there may be many cases where such a charge, though not specifically made in one bill, may be reasonably introduced in the next.

PATTESON J. No case occurs to me at the present moment in which a question like this could be a matter of law. The right to charge for attendances must be the subject of contract, express or implied; the existence

of

1838.

MORGAN *against* HALLEN.

of the first must clearly be determined upon by the jury; and so must the existence of the other. If, in point of fact, there is such a contract that attendances may be charged for, the question of reasonable remuneration which then arises is a question of fact also. If the price demanded for medicines is so high that the jury think it ought to include attendances, they will disallow the claim for these: but the circumstance of attendances and medicines being split into several items cannot make any difference.

WILLIAMS J. I think the case was correctly left to the jury. There is nothing to shew that, in point of law, attendances may not form a proper item in some supposable case. And, the jury having found that they were properly charged for here, the plaintiff was entitled to recover.

Rule discharged.

Monday, June 4th.

The QUEEN *against* The Inhabitants of MAWGAN, in MENEAGE.

Under stat. 13 *G.* 3. *c.* 78. *s.* 24, a magistrate presented the inhabitants of a parish for non-repair of a highway. The proceedings having been removed by certiorari, the defendants pleaded, and issues of fact were joined, which were tried and found against the defendants. The issues were joined before, but the cause was tried after, 20th *March* 1836, on which day stat. 5 & 6 *W.* 4. *c.* 50., repealing stat. 13 *G.* 3. *c.* 78., came into operation.

Judgment was arrested, on the ground that the Court could not now give judgment upon a conviction founded on a magistrate's presentment.

THE defendants, inhabitants of the parish of *Mawgan* in *Meneage*, were indicted, at the *Cornwall* quarter sessions, on the presentment of a justice, for non-repair of a highway. The record was removed by certiorari. Several issues of fact were joined. The case was tried before *Williams* J., at the *Cornwall* summer assizes 1836, when some of the issues were found for the crown, and

some

1838.

The QUEEN *against* The Inhabitants of MAWGAN.

some for the defendants. The issues found for the defendants applied only to part of the highway indicted. After the cause had been removed, and after the defendants had pleaded, but before replication, stat. 5 & 6 *W.* 4. *c.* 50. passed (31st *August* 1835). The issues were joined before 20th *March* 1836, from which day stat. 5 & 6 *W.* 4. *c.* 50. is, by sect. 119, to "commence and take effect." In *Michaelmas* term, 1836, *Erle* obtained a rule to shew cause why judgment should not be arrested.

Crowder and *Rowe* now shewed cause. The presentment is under stat. 13 *G.* 3. *c.* 78. *s.* 24., which enables a justice to present, and gives the presentment the same force as a presentment and finding by the oaths of twelve men. It will be contended on the other side that, stat. 5 & 6 *W.* 4. *c.* 50. having, by sect. 1, repealed stat. 13 *G.* 3. *c.* 78., the presentment is of no effect. But the repeal of a statute does not invalidate what has been done under its authority before the repeal. The effect of the repeal is merely to prevent any step being taken under the authority of the repealed act; thus, in *Kay* v. *Goodwin* (*a*), an enrolment of proceedings on a commission of bankruptcy, under stat. 5 *G.* 2. *c.* 30. *s.* 41., that statute having been repealed by stat. 6 *G.* 4. *c.* 16. *s.* 1. before the enrolment, and the commission itself being anterior to stat. 6 *G.* 4. c. 16., was held not to make the proceedings so enrolled available in evidence. *Surtees* v. *Ellison* (*b*) and *Maggs* v. *Hunt* (*c*) were decided on a similar principle; which also seems to have been recognised in *Ex parte*

(*a*) 6 *Bing.* 576.
(*b*) 9 *B.* & *C.* 750.
(*c*) 4 *Bing.* 212.

1838.

The QUEEN *against* The Inhabitants of MAWGAN.

Lowe (*a*). So in *Miller's Case* (*b*) it was held that an insolvent who, under stat. 1 *G.* 3. *c.* 17. *s.* 46., had been compelled to give up his effects, could not be discharged, stat. 2 *G.* 3. *c.* 2. having passed since the signing of the schedule, sect. 1 of which repeals the compulsory clauses in the former act. So, if a specific punishment be imposed for an offence, a prisoner cannot, after the act, be tried for an offence committed before; though by a previous statute, repealed by the act in question, benefit of clergy was taken away from the offence; *Rex* v. *M'Kenzie* (*c*). So an application for costs under stat. 13 *G.* 3. *c.* 78. *s.* 81. was refused, being made after the repeal of that statute by stat. 5 & 6 *W.* 4. *c.* 50.; *Charrington* v. *Meatheringham* (*d*). But here the effect of the repealed act was simply to bring the defendants into Court; after issue is joined, at any rate, the assistance of the repealed act is no longer required: it is as if issue had been joined on a presentment by a grand jury. The liability to repair was not created by stat. 13 *G.* 3. *c.* 78.; the non-repair was a misdemeanor before the act: the judgment therefore does not proceed on the statute: and this also appears from the presentment, No. xxxii., in the schedule to 13 *G.* 3. *c.* 78., which does not conclude "against the form of the statute." The intention of the legislature, in stat. 5 & 6 *W.* 4. *c.* 50., cannot have been to stop proceedings already commenced by presentment; especially as sect. 99 enacts, "that *from and after the commencement of this act* it shall not be lawful to *take or commence* any legal proceeding, by presentment, against the inhabitants of any parish, or other person, on account

(*a*) *Mont. C. Bank.* 392.
(*b*) 1 *W. Bl.* 451.
(*c*) *Russ. & R. C. C. R.* 429.
(*d*) 2 *M. & W.* 228.

of

1838.

The QUEEN against The Inhabitants of MAWGAN.

of any highway or turnpike road being out of repair." The repeal of stat. 13 *G.* 3. *c.* 78. *s.* 24. is to prevent future presentments by justices, but nothing more. In 2 *Dwarris on Statutes*, 675, it is said, "The word 'repealed' is not to be taken in an absolute, if it appear upon the whole act to be used in a limited, sense." *Rex* v. *Rogers* (*a*) and *Camden* v. *Anderson* (*b*), there cited, are instances of restricting the absolute meaning of the word "repeal." Here, if stat. 13 *G.* 3. *c.* 78. were absolutely repealed by stat. 5 & 6 *W.* 4. *c.* 50., sect. 99 of the latter act would be superfluous. *Hitchcock* v. *Way* (*c*) is in favour of the prosecutor. Sect. 3 of stat. 5 & 6 *W.* 4. *c.* 50. provides that nothing in the act contained shall be so construed as to defeat any prosecution commenced. [*Patteson* J. Prosecution "for such offence;" that is, for any offence against the provisions of the recited acts.] Then, if this be an offence under the acts, the prosecution is not to be defeated; if not, the judgment is independent of the acts, and must be given notwithstanding their repeal.

Erle and *Montague Smith* contrà. The words of repeal in sect. 1 of stat. 5 & 6 *W.* 4. *c.* 50. are unqualified. It is said that, upon this supposition, sect. 99 would have been superfluous; but that argument assumes that there could be no presentment except under stat. 13 *G.* 3. *c.* 78. *s.* 24., whereas a constable, for instance, could present (*d*), independently of the statute. The language of *Tindal* C. J., in *Kay* v.

(*a*) 10 *East*, 569. (*b*) 6 *T. R.* 723. (*c*) 6 *A.* & *E.* 943.

(*d*) See 1 *Burn's Just.* 836, *Constable*, IV. 28th (*Chitty's*) ed. 3 *Burn's Just.* 59, *Assizes*, (ed. *D'Oy.* & *W.*). And see stat. 7 & 8 *G.* 4. c. 38.

1838.

The QUEEN against The Inhabitants of MAWGAN.

Goodwin (*a*), is, "I take the effect of repealing a statute to be, to obliterate it as completely from the records of the parliament as if it had never passed; and it must be considered as a law that never existed, except for the purpose of those actions which were commenced, prosecuted, *and concluded* whilst it was an existing law." So in *Surtees* v. *Ellison* (*b*) Lord *Tenterden* said, "It has been long established, that, when an act of parliament is repealed, it must be considered (except as to transactions past *and closed*) as if it had never existed. That is the general rule; and we must not destroy that, by indulging in conjectures as to the intention of the legislature." It is argued that the effect of the presentment is already complete; but the Court is called on to give effect to it by pronouncing judgment. The judgment rests upon the presentment, especially as sect. 24 of stat. 13 *G.* 3. *c.* 78. enables the justices to pay the expenses out of the county rate. And, under that section, it may be doubtful whether judgment for more than a fine could be given upon a presentment; whereas the common law punishment might be fine or imprisonment. Therefore the judgment on a conviction upon presentment was statutable. *Charrington* v. *Meatheringham* (*c*) has not been distinguished; and that case was confirmed by *Warne* v. *Beresford* (*d*), where *Alderson* B. said, "The question is, upon the facts found on this record, what must be the judgment of the Court, according to the law now in existence." The legislature no doubt meant that there should be but one statute on the subject. Stat. 6 &

(*a*) 6 *Bing.* 582.
(*b*) 9 *B.* & *C.* 752.
(*c*) 2 *M.* & *W.* 228.
(*d*) 2 *M.* & *W.* 848.

7 *W.* 4.

1838.

The QUEEN *against* The Inhabitants of MAWGAN.

7 *W.* 4. *c.* 63. recites the repeal of the statutes relating to highways by stat. 5 & 6 *W.* 4. *c.* 50., and provides that the surveyor may recover rates &c. due under the repealed acts: which shews that the repeal was understood to be without qualification. As to sect. 3 of stat. 5 & 6 *W.* 4. *c.* 50, it provided for the case of offences under the previous acts: it is clear that, but for that provision, the offences would not have been liable to prosecution, nor the prosecutions for them kept alive: here, therefore, the prosecution is not kept alive, inasmuch as it is for a common law offence, though a peculiar process was given by statute.

Lord DENMAN C. J. If the question related merely to the presentment, that, no doubt, is complete. But, dum loquimur, we have lost the power of giving effect to any thing which takes place under that proceeding. The rule, therefore, must be made absolute.

LITTLEDALE J. I am of the same opinion. The case seems to be as it would have been if sect. 24 of stat. 13 *G.* 3. *c.* 78. had expressly said that the Court should give judgment in the case of a presentment by a magistrate as in the case of a presentment by a grand jury. Then, as the act is repealed which conferred on us the power to give the judgment, our power is gone. I do not say that what is already done has become bad, but that no more can be done.

PATTESON J. I have little doubt that the legislature meant such prosecutions to go on; but they have not said so.

1838.

The QUEEN *against* The Inhabitants of MAWGAN.

WILLIAMS J. Stat. 13 *G.* 3. *c.* 78. is repealed in unambiguous words. How then can we pronounce judgment? But that is what the plaintiff seeks.

Rule absolute.

Monday, June 4th.

DOE on the Demise of BOULTBEE and Others *against* ADDERLEY.

DOE on the Demise of BATCHELOR and Wife *against* BOWLES and Others.

In ejectment by or against parish officers claiming to hold premises for the parish under stat. 59 *G.* 3. *c.* 12. *s.* 17., rated inhabitants of the parish are competent witnesses for the officers, under stat. 54 *G.* 3. *c.* 170. *s.* 9.

THE first of these actions was ejectment for premises in *Staffordshire.* On the trial before *Littledale* J., at the *Staffordshire* summer assizes, 1836, it appeared that the lessors of the plaintiff were the churchwardens and overseers of the parish of *Gnosall*, in *Staffordshire*, who claimed as owners under stat. 59 *G.* 3. *c.* 12. *s.* 17. All the material witnesses called in support of the plaintiff's case were rated inhabitants of *Gnosall.* It was objected that they were incompetent from interest. The learned Judge was of this opinion; but, at his suggestion, it was agreed that the witnesses should be allowed to give their evidence, and the opinion of the jury be taken; and, the jury having expressed themselves satisfied that the plaintiff's case was proved, his Lordship directed a nonsuit, giving leave to move to enter a verdict for the plaintiff. In *Michaelmas* term, 1836, *R. V. Richards* obtained a rule accordingly.

The second action was ejectment for premises in *Gloucestershire.* On the trial before *Littledale* J., at the *Gloucestershire* summer assizes, 1836, it appeared that the defendants were the churchwardens and overseers of the

1838.

Doe dem. Boultbee against Adderley.

Doe dem. Batchelor against Bowles.

the parish of *Cowhoneyborne*, in *Gloucestershire*, claiming to hold under stat. 59 G. 3. *c.* 12. *s.* 17. The defendants called witnesses who were rated inhabitants of *Cowhoneyborne*. The learned Judge, upon objection taken, rejected their evidence; and the plaintiff had a verdict. In *Michaelmas* term, 1836, *Maule* obtained a rule nisi for a new trial.

Ludlow Serjt. and *Godson* on this day shewed cause against the rule in the first case, and argued against the admissibility of the evidence; and *Talfourd* Serjt. and *R. V. Richards* argued in support of the rule, and in favour of the admissibility of the evidence. And *Talfourd* Serjt. and *Godson* shewed cause against the rule in the second case, and argued against the admissibility of the evidence; *Maule* and *W. J. Alexander* contrà (*a*).

Arguments against admitting the evidence. The evidence is clearly inadmissible at common law, the witness being one of the parties really interested; *Rex* v. *Woburn* (*b*), *Rex* v. *Hardwick* (*c*). He diminishes the rate to be laid hereafter on himself; and he is, on principle, as inadmissible as if he were the only rated inhabitant. In *Rhodes* v. *Ainsworth* (*d*) a nonresident owner of land in a parish, whose tenant was rated, was held inadmissible on an issue whether the inhabitants were bound to repair the chapel. In *The Bailiffs of Godmanchester* v. *Phillips* (*e*) a freeman was held not to be admissible for a corporation in an action of trespass for breaking and entering lands of the corporation. Then the question is whether

(*a*) Both cases were argued before Lord *Denman* C. J., *Littledale*, *Patteson*, and *Williams* Js.

(*b*) 10 *East*, 395.

(*c*) 11 *East*, 578.

(*d*) 1 *B. & Ald.* 87.

(*e*) 4 *A. & E.* 550.

1838.

Doe dem. Boultbee against Adderley. — Doe dem. Batchelor against Bowles.

whether stat. 54 G. 3. c. 170. s. 9. removes the objection. The words relied on are these: "That no inhabitant or person rated or liable to be rated to any rates or cesses of any district, parish, township, or hamlet," "shall, before any court or person or persons whatsoever, be deemed and taken to be by reason thereof an incompetent witness for or against any such district, parish, township or hamlet, in any matter relating to such rates or cesses." In *Doe dem. Hobbs* v. *Cockell* (a) a rated inhabitant was admitted to give evidence: but that was decided, not on the statute, but on the general ground that the witness was not shewn to be interested in the event, inasmuch as the premises which were the subject of the action were in the hands of the defendants as tenants, and they paid a rent which was not shewn to be less than a rack rent. The circumstance of the witness being ultimately liable to be rated for the costs, if the action failed, was not adverted to: if that point had been taken, the question on the statute would have arisen. And there *Littledale* J. clearly considered that, in a case of ejectment by overseers where the defendant was not a tenant, the reception of the evidence must depend on stat. 54 G. 3. c. 170. s. 9. being applicable or not. *Meredith* v. *Gilpin* (b) is certainly in favour of the applicability of the statute; but that case is, in effect, overruled by *Oxenden* v. *Palmer* (c), which was acted upon in *Rex* v. *Bishop Auckland* (d). In *Marsden* v. *Stansfield* (e) a rated inhabitant was admitted on an issue as to boundary; but that is within the express words of the statute. In *Tothill* v. *Hooper* (g) it

(a) 4 *A.* & *E.* 478.

(b) 6 *Price*, 146.

(c) 2 *B.* & *Ad.* 236. See p. 243.

(d) 1 *A.* & *E.* 744.; and, at N.P., 1 *Mo.* & *R.* 287. note (d).

(e) 7 *B.* & *C.* 815.

(g) 1 *Mo.* & *R.* 392.

1838.

Doe dem. Boultbee against Adderley.

Doe dem. Batchelor against Bowles.

it was held that the statute did not make a rated parishioner admissible for the defendant in an action against an overseer for medical attendance bestowed on a pauper: yet, if the mere fact, that the result of the verdict would ultimately increase the rate on the individual, made the action one relating to the rates or cesses, the statute clearly would have applied. The argument on the other side must go the length of insisting that every thing at all connected with parish property is within the act. But the question must, in itself, relate immediately to the rates and cesses: *Prewit* v. *Tilly* (a), *Jones* v. *Carrington* (b). Sect. 100 of stat. 5 & 6 *W.* 4. *c.* 50. would have been unnecessary, if stat. 54 *G.* 3. *c.* 170. *s.* 9. had the extensive application suggested. The interest created by stat. 59 *G.* 3. *c.* 12. *s.* 17. did not exist when stat. 54 *G.* 3. *c.* 170. passed, which therefore was probably not intended to apply to such an interest.

Arguments for admitting the evidence. It may be granted that the witnesses would be incompetent at common law, on the ground that they would at some time be more highly rated if the party calling them failed. But this objection assumes that the question at issue ultimately relates to the rates and cesses, and then the statute applies; if it did not, there would be no objection at common law. It is suggested that, to render the statute applicable, the question must have an immediate, and not merely an ultimate, relation to the rates and cesses. If the legislature had intended this restriction, they would certainly have expressed it. The present is exactly the kind of difficulty contemplated by the statute; for, if this ob-

(a) 1 *C.* & *P.* 140.

(b) 1 *C.* & *P.* 327.

jection

1838.

Doe dem. Boulter against Adderley.

Doe dem. Batchelor against Bowles.

jection prevail, proof can never be given of parish property, since the parties who shew occupation, repairs, receipt of rents, and the like, will almost invariably be rated inhabitants. The legislature, when stat. 59 *G.* 3. *c.* 12. passed, must have supposed the difficulty to be provided for, else they would have added the necessary provision to sect. 17. [*Littledale* J. Many particular cases are enumerated in sect. 9 of stat. 54 *G.* 3. *c.* 170., in which the evidence is to be admitted; all these would be included in the first words, "any matter relating to such rates or cesses," if the words had the general meaning contended for.] It is not unusual for the legislature to add unnecessary particular words to a general provision; if the words relied on had followed the rest, such an answer could not have been made; yet the place in whch they occur cannot make an essential difference. In *Doe dem. Hobbs* v. *Cockell* (*a*) it is clear that the Court would have held the party incompetent, if interested at all, only on the ground that the event ultimately related to the rates; therefore, if the costs had been adverted to, that would not have introduced a new question; and consequently the case is an authority. In the same case, at Nisi Prius (*b*), *Alderson* B. expressly held the statute applicable. *Meredith* v. *Gilpin* (*c*) is a direct authority for the admission of the evidence; *Holroyd* J. decided that case at Nisi Prius, as it was afterwards decided in the Exchequer; and it has not been overruled, though it was questioned by the dictum in *Oxenden* v. *Palmer* (*d*). This last case must be supported, if at all, on the ground that the question, whether inhabitants could take shingle from the beach to repair the roads, did not affect the inhabitants simply

(*a*) 4 *A.* & *E.* 478. (*b*) *Doe dem. Higgs* v. *Cockell*, 6 *C.* & *P.* 525.
(*c*) 6 *Price*, 146. (*d*) 2 *B.* & *Ad.* 243.

as

1838.

Doe dem. Boulter against Adderley.

Doe dem. Batchelor against Bowles.

as a question relating to rates or cesses. The words of stat. 54 *G. 3. c.* 170. *s.* 9. are "be deemed and taken to be *by reason thereof* an incompetent witness." The inhabitants would be liable to more statute labour if they could not take the shingle; therefore they would not suffer merely by being more heavily rated; and the Court seemed to consider the statute as relating more properly to poor rates. In *Rex* v. *Bishop Auckland* (*a*) the Court scarcely noticed the point; and the party making the objection succeeded, on another ground, in arresting the judgment; whereas the objection to the evidence went only to a new trial. Besides, there the witnesses were, in fact, defendants on the record; and the case also comes under the distinction already pointed out with respect to *Oxenden* v. *Palmer* (*b*). *Marsden* v. *Stansfield* (*c*) is an authority here; for *Bayley* J., the only judge who is reported to have given his reasons, rested the applicability of the statute on the ground, not merely that the case related to boundary, but that it was "a question relating to the rates or cesses of the district." *Rex* v. *Hayman* (*d*) and *Heudebourck* v. *Langston* (*e*) are also authorities in favour of the evidence (*g*).

Cur. adv. vult.

Lord DENMAN C. J. in this term, *June* 14th, delivered the judgment of the Court.

(*a*) 1 *A. & E.* 744. (*b*) 2 *B. & Ad.* 236.

(*c*) 7 *B. & C.* 815. (*d*) *Mo. & M.* 401.

(*e*) Note (*b*) to *Rex* v. *Hayman*, *Mo. & M.* 402.

(*g*) *Maule* mentioned that in a case (not reported) of *Doe dem. Harrison* v. *Murrell*, at the *Gloucestershire* Summer assizes, 1837, Lord *Abinger* C. B., upon argument, admitted a rated inhabitant to prove that a cottage was parish property, and no objection to the ruling was taken in banc.

On

1838.

Doe dem. Boultbee against Adderley.

Doe dem. Batchelor against Bowles.

On the question, whether a rated inhabitant was admissible to prove that the house sought to be recovered in ejectment was parish property, we do not feel it necessary to enter upon a discussion of the numerous and conflicting cases which have arisen on the construction of stat. 54 *G.* 3. *c.* 170. *s.* 9. We content ourselves with saying that the case of *Meredith* v. *Gilpin* (*a*) appears to us to be well decided, and that, on consideration, we cannot agree with *Oxenden* v. *Palmer* (*b*) and the decisions to which it has given birth.

Both rules absolute.

(*a*) 6 *Price*, 146.

(*b*) 2 *B.* & *Ad.* 236.

Tuesday, June 5th.

The Queen *against* Goodburn.

Under the pawnbrokers' act, stat. 39 & 40 *G.* 3. *c.* 99., where the pledge is redeemed after several months, and the interest, according to the terms of the act, is a sum which is not an exact number of farthings, the pawnbroker is not entitled to calculate the interest on each month separately, taking upon each month the benefit of the fraction of the farthing. *Quære*, whether he be entitled to the benefit of the fraction at all.

ON appeal by *William Goodburn*, a pawnbroker, against a conviction by a justice, under stat. 39 & 40 *G.* 3. *c.* 99., for unlawfully taking from *Daniel Byrne* more than the legal interest upon a pledge, the sessions confirmed the conviction, subject to the opinion of this Court upon the following case.

The appellant, on *March* 1836, received in pledge two tablecloths, upon which he advanced 4*s.* On 16th *February* 1837, *Byrne* applied to the appellant to be permitted to redeem the goods; whereupon the appellant demanded and took from him 11½*d.*, as profit, over and above the principal sum of 4*s.* which had been lent.

The

1838.

The QUEEN *against* GOODBURN.

The question for the opinion of the Court was, whether the taking the said 11½*d.* as aforesaid was taking more than the appellant was entitled to take, and was an offence against the statute.

The case was argued on a former day of this term (*a*).

C. C. Jones in support of the conviction. By sect. 2 of stat. 39 & 40 *G.* 3. *c.* 99., the pawnbroker is not obliged to redeliver unless he receives principal and interest as limited by the act; that is, one halfpenny per month on 2*s.* 6*d.*, 1*d.* per month on 5*s.*, 4*d.* on one pound, &c.; and, by sect. 3, where any intermediate sum lent exceeds 2*s.* 6*d.* and does not exceed 40*s.*, the pawnbroker may take "at and after the rate of 4*d.* and no more, for the loan of 20*s.* by the calendar month, including the current month," although not expired, in which the pledge is redeemed. Sect. 5 enacts that the pledge may be redeemed without paying any thing for the current month, if applied for in the first seven days of such current month: if it be applied for afterwards and within the first fourteen days, then half of the interest for the current month is to be paid. Here the application was made after the first seven and within the first fourteen days of the twelfth month: the interest therefore was claimable on eleven months and a half. The monthly interest on 4*s.*, at 4*d.* in the pound, is four fifths of a penny: that, in eleven months and a half, amounts to 9⅕ of a penny: giving the pawnbroker the benefit of the fraction of the farthing, the interest is 9¼*d.* The sum taken is 11½*d.*, which is at the rate of

(*a*) *Saturday, June* 2d, before Lord *Denman* C. J., *Littledale, Patteson,* and *Williams* Js.

1*d.*

1838.

The QUEEN against GOODBURN.

1*d.* per month on the 4*s.*, that is, of 5*d.* on the pound. The attempt on the other side will be to give the pawnbroker the fraction of the farthing in each month; but, inasmuch as the interest is to be paid, not necessarily every month, but "*at and after the rate* of 4*d.* and no more, for the loan of 20*s.* by the calendar month," the necessity which gives the pawnbroker the benefit of the fraction arises only once, at the time when it is necessary to redeem the goods.

Sir *W. W. Follett* and *Adolphus* contrà. The pawnbroker is entitled to four fifths of a penny per month. Now that exceeds three farthings, but is less than a penny: the interest is therefore 1*d.* per month. It is not denied, on the other side, that the benefit of the fraction is claimable; but the attempt is to give the benefit only once. If the goods were redeemed at the end of the first month, there could be no question that the pawnbroker would be entitled to a penny. Therefore, for eleven months and a half, "at and after" that rate, he is to have 11½*d.* A loan of 3*s.* 9*d.* would entitle to an interest of three farthings per month (since 1*s.* 3*d.* is one sixteenth of a pound): the additional 3*d.* is entitled to additional interest; and less than one farthing cannot be added. Sect. 4 shews that the pawnbroker is bound to give change where that can be done by a farthing, but not to carry the division farther. By sect. 2 he is not bound to redeliver till the interest is paid: therefore the pawner must lose the fraction of the farthing.

Cur. adv. vult.

Lord DENMAN C. J. now delivered the judgment of the Court. After stating the substance of the case, his Lordship

1838.

The QUEEN *against* GOODBURN.

Lordship said: An ingenious argument was raised on the defendant's behalf, that the act considers the sum lent as advanced by the month: that, if the 4s. had been repaid at the end of the first month, the 20 per cent. would be three farthings and one fifth, which sum the defendant could not have received, as there are no fifths of a farthing, so that he must have either received a penny or lost a portion of his 20 per cent.: that the act requires a similar mode of paying for every succeeding month: that, therefore, a penny for each month must have been paid; and, adding all these for the eleven months and upwards, the amount actually received by the defendant is warranted by the act.

But, supposing this argument to be valid if the loan were repaid while the interest is less than a farthing, from the necessity of the case, inasmuch as it must otherwise be less than 20. per cent. (which we are by no means prepared to admit, the words being so much "and no more"), still, as soon as that period arrived when the interest so calculated amounted to a current coin, that necessity is at an end.

Nothing prescribes that rests must be made monthly, the effect of which in the present case would entitle the pawnbroker to 25 per cent. We think, therefore, that the sessions did right in affirming the conviction; and the rule for setting it aside must be discharged.

Judgment of sessions affirmed.

1838.

Tuesday, June 5th.

LYONS *against* MARTIN.

A master is answerable in trespass for damage occasioned by his servant's negligence in doing a lawful act in the course of his service; but not so if the act is in itself unlawful and is not proved to have been authorised by the master. As if a servant, authorised merely to distrain cattle damage-feasant, drives cattle from the highway into his master's close and there distrains them.

TRESPASS for seizing, distraining, and impounding plaintiff's horse. Pleas, 1. Not Guilty. 2. That defendant took and distrained the horse on his close, damage-feasant. Replication to the second plea: That the close adjoined the highway, and that the horse was wrongfully driven by defendant from the highway into the close, and was, by means thereof, damage-feasant there; wherefore defendant of his own wrong seized &c. Rejoinder, denying that defendant drove the horse into the close. Issue thereon. On the trial, before *Coleridge* J., at the sittings in *Middlesex* during this term, it appeared that the defendant occupied land adjoining a highway, and not fenced; that horses kept by persons in the neighbourhood had sometimes, and shortly before the act in question, trespassed on the land and been distrained by the defendant's servants, and impounded; that the plaintiff's horse, being on the highway, was intentionally driven from it by a servant of the defendant into the defendant's ground, and there immediately seized by the same servant and taken to the pound. The learned Judge was of opinion that, as the act of seizure under these circumstances was not within the scope of a servant's ordinary authority, some direct authority from the master ought to be proved: and, this not being done, the plaintiff was nonsuited.

Humfrey now moved for a new trial. The defendant's servants had been used to distrain horses with his authority:

1838.

LYONS *against* MARTIN.

authority: that was a primâ facie case of authority in the present instance; and the defendant should have been called upon to rebut it. The conclusion, in such a case, is to be drawn by a jury from all the facts. If the master has adopted his servant's act, the case of authority is clear. If the act was for his benefit, that circumstance, among others, will tend strongly to prove sanction, as was pointed out by *Bayley* B. in *Attorney-General* v. *Siddon* (*a*). The servant here does not appear to have thought that he was doing wrong in making the seizure; and, if a servant acting under the directions of his master uses ordinary care, but nevertheless, by accident or mistake, does some injury which the master did not mean to authorize, an action of trespass lies against the master: *Gregory* v. *Piper* (*b*). The present was such a case; or at least the jury should have been allowed to decide whether it was so or not. *Brucker* v. *Fromont* (*c*), *Turberville* v. *Stamp* (*d*) (there cited), *Michael* v. *Alestree* (*e*), and *Goodman* v. *Kennell* (*g*), shew the liability of a master on the ground of implied authority, where a servant, acting under his general order, does an injury through negligence. Besides, in this case the defendant has pleaded a justification; that is a fact which may be looked at in trying the question of guilty or not guilty on the first issue; and it shews an adoption of the servant's act. [Lord *Denman* C. J. There is a case of *Woolf* v. *Tollemache* (*h*) now depending in this Court, where a second

(*a*) 1 *Tyr.* 41. *S. C.* 1 *Cro. & J.* 220. (*b*) 9 *B. & C.* 591.

(*c*) 6 *T. R.* 659. (*d*) 1 *Ld. Ray.* 264.

(*e*) 2 *Lev.* 172., cited in *Brucker* v. *Fromont*, 6 *T. R.* 661.

(*g*) 1 *Moore & Payne*, 241.

(*h*) This was an action for goods sold and delivered. Pleas, non assumpsit, and infancy. Replication to the latter plea, that the goods were necessaries.

1838.

LYONS against MARTIN.

second plea was referred to in the manner now suggested; but I have much doubt whether it was right to do so.] At all events the principle is, that, where a person acting as the servant of another does a thing which is not for his own benefit but that of the master, an authority from the master is shewn, not conclusively, but with sufficient probability to make a case for the jury.

Lord DENMAN C. J. I think the learned Judge ruled rightly. It is clear that the wrongful act could not be traced to the master. He had authorised nothing that was not lawful. He has pleaded a special plea; but that is out of the question. The case here is of an act in itself unlawful; and the question then is, whether that particular act was authorised; the instances where an injury has resulted from negligence in performing a lawful service do not apply. In *The Attorney-General* v. *Riddle* (a), where the wife of a paper-maker had il-

necessaries. Issue thereon. On the trial before Lord *Denman* C. J. at the sittings in *Middlesex* after *Michaelmas* term, 1836, evidence was given of the goods having been ordered by a person supposed to have been the defendant; but it was doubtful whether he was sufficiently identified. The Lord Chief Justice thought that the plea of infancy identified the defendant with the party giving the order, and might be looked at for this purpose, though not for others, in trying the issue on the plea of non assumpsit; but he gave leave to move to enter a nonsuit if this ruling should be wrong. The defendant's counsel offered no evidence on the plea of infancy; and the plaintiff had a verdict. In *Hilary* term 1837, Sir *W. W. Follett* moved according to the leave reserved, contending that, where several pleas are pleaded, they are distinct for all purposes, and each must be tried as if there were no other on the record; and that to hold otherwise would in a great measure put an end to the practice of pleading different pleas. *The Court* (Lord *Denman* C. J., *Littledale*, *Williams* and *Coleridge* Js.) granted a rule nisi. No cause was ever shewn.

(a) 2 *Cro.* & *J.* 493. *S. C.* 2 *Tyr.* 523.

legally

1838.

LYONS *against* MARTIN.

legally delivered out paper without proper stamps, the Court of Exchequer held it to be a fit question for the jury whether or not the husband was chargeable with her acts, as done under his authority; but that decision proceeded on the supposition that the husband was generally presiding over the business, and that any thing done in the management of it by a person usually acting in it under his control, as the wife was shewn to have been, might be referred to him.

LITTLEDALE J. concurred.

PATTESON J. *Brucker* v. *Fromont* (*a*), and other cases, where the master has been held liable for the consequences of a lawful act negligently done by his servant, do not apply. Here the act was utterly unlawful. A master is liable where his servant causes injury by doing a lawful act negligently, but not where he wilfully does an illegal one. Every person is to be taken to know the law.

WILLIAMS J. concurred.

Rule refused.

(*a*) 6 *T. R.* 659.

1838.

The QUEEN *against* The Honourable HENRIETTA BARBARA MANNERS SUTTON, Widow, and Others.

On indictment for non-repair of a bridge, charging the defendants ratione tenuræ, they produced at the trial a record setting forth a presentment, in the time of *Ed.* 3., against a Bishop of *L.* (not connected with the present defendants), who was thereby charged with non-repair of the same bridge, and liability to repair. The record stated a trial of this presentment at the Spring assizes, in the year 20 *Ed.* 3., and an acquittal of the Bishop as not liable; it further stated that the jury, being asked who was bound to repair, said they did not know; and, being asked when and by whom it was first built or repaired, said, about sixty years since, and then of alms, and that a bishop of *L.* bestowed 40*s.* on the workmen repairing it, of his alms, and not otherwise.

In addition to this record, the defendants put in a writ of privy seal of *June* 28th, 20 *Ed.* 3., for a grant of pontage to the town of *K.* (where the bridge was), reciting, as the cause of the grant, that the bridge was ruinous, and no person bound to repair in certain, according to that which was found by inquest. They also put in the grant of pontage, dated in the same year.

Held, that the evidence was admissible on behalf of the present defendants.

Semble, that the special findings of the jury may have been regular, according to the practice in the time of *Ed.* 3. But

Held, that at all events the acquittal of the Bishop, followed by the writ and grant of pontage, was evidence to negative the existence of a prescriptive liability in any person.

INDICTMENT for non-repair of *Kelham* bridge, in the county of *Nottingham*, averring that the defendants were bound to repair the same "by reason of their tenure of certain lands in the parish of *Kelham*" (*a*). Plea, Not Guilty.

On the trial before *Bosanquet* J., at the *Warwick* Spring assizes 1836, the defendants offered in evidence a record from the treasury of the Court of the Receipt of the Exchequer, commencing, "Pleas before our Lord the King at *York*, of the term of *St. Hilary*, in the eighteenth year of King *Edward* the Third after the Conquest." It set forth a writ of certiorari, tested *July* 6th, 17 *Ed.* 3., directed to the sheriff of *Nottingham*, reciting the

(*a*) Lady *Henrietta Barbara Manners Sutton* occupied the mansion, and the other defendants were tenants of premises, all forming part of the estate in respect of which the liability was supposed to attach. See *Rex* v. *J. H. Manners Sutton, Esq.*, 3 *A.* & *E.* 597.

1838.

The QUEEN *against* Lady H. B. M. SUTTON.

the complaint of the Bishop of *Lincoln* that certain presentments had been unjustly made against him in the sheriff's tourn, by which it was charged, among other things, that the Bishop ought to repair and uphold the bridge of *Kelm*, which was in decay and broken, to the damage of the men passing by the same bridge," &c.; by reason of which premises the sheriff had amerced and distrained upon the Bishop, whereupon he had supplicated the King to afford relief. The writ then commanded the sheriff to return the presentments, with all things touching the same, into the King's Bench in eight days of *St. Michael*. The sheriff returned the proceedings as follows.

"The great turn of *Thur* and *Lyth* at *Scarthorp*, on *Thursday* next before the feast of the Ascension of our Lord in the seventeenth year of the reign of King *Edward* of *England*, after the conquest the Third.

Kelum, to wit. The vill of *Kelum* present that the Bishop of *Lincoln* ought and is accustomed to repair the bridge of *Kelum*, which is decayed and broken by default of the same Bishop, to the damage of the men passing by the same bridge.

Duhm, to wit. The vill of *Duhm* present that the Bishop of *Lincoln* made a certain pool in the water of *Trente* at *Shoredayles*, to the injury of the ships passing by the same water."

The record then proceeded. "And now, that is to say in eight days of the purification of the Blessed *Mary*, in the eighteenth year of the reign of the now King, before the King at *York* comes *Thomas*, Bishop of *Lincoln*, by *Adam* of *Lound* his attorney, and is asked by him if he, for himself, has or can say any thing why he should not repair, &c., the aforesaid

 bridge

1838.

The QUEEN against Lady H. B. M. SUTTON.

bridge so broken down, and also why he made the aforesaid pool in the aforesaid water, to the injury, when &c.: Who says, that as to repairing the aforesaid bridge, that neither he nor his predecessors the aforesaid bridge ever repaired, nor are they bound to repair or uphold the aforesaid bridge, &c.: he says also, that as to the aforesaid pool, that he has not caused any pool to be made in the aforesaid water: and hereupon he puts himself upon the country; and *John* of *Lincoln*, who prosecutes for the king, does the like. Therefore" &c. The record then set out an award of jury process, continuances, and a respite of the jury, ultimately, until fifteen days of *Easter*, 20 *Ed.* 3., unless *W. Scot* of *Thorp*, *W. Basset*, and *R.* of *Bankwell*, three or two of them, shall first come at *Retford* on *Tuesday* next after *Palm Sunday*, &c.

"On which day, that is to say on" &c. "before the Lord the King, come as well the aforesaid *John* who prosecutes for the King, as the aforesaid Bishop by his attorney aforesaid; and the aforesaid *William* of *Thorp* and *Roger* of *Bankwell*, before whom &c., took here in Court the verdict of the jury aforesaid delivered before them in these words.

"Afterwards, at the day and place within contained, before the aforesaid *William* of *Thorp* and *Roger* of *Bankwell*, associating to themselves *John* of *Bolyngbrook*, came as well *John* of *Lincoln*, who prosecutes for our Lord the King, as the aforesaid Bishop by *Robert* of *Totel* his attorney, and in like manner the jury come, who, being chosen and sworn, say upon their oath that the aforesaid Bishop or his predecessors the aforesaid bridge never repaired nor are bound of right to repair or uphold that bridge; and, as to the pool aforesaid, they

1838.

The Queen *against* Lady H. B. M. Sutton.

they say that the aforesaid Bishop never caused any pool to be made in the water aforesaid to the injury of the ships passing by the aforesaid water, as above in the aforesaid presentment contained. The same jury, being asked if there were any bridge at *Kelm*, say there is. Also, being asked who of right is bound the aforesaid bridge to repair and uphold, say they are entirely ignorant. Being also asked at what time and by whom the aforesaid bridge was first built or repaired, say about sixty years since, and then of alms of the men of the country passing that way; and in the building and repairing of the bridge aforesaid there came a certain *Oliver*, formerly Bishop of *Lincoln*, the predecessor of the same bishop who now is, passing through the country, and of his alms charitably bestowed on the workmen of the aforesaid bridge 40*s.*; and not in any other manner. The said jurors, being also asked if there has been made any pool at the aforesaid place of *Shortdayles*, and at what time and to whose injury, say that a certain pool there was made at the time to which the memory of man does not extend; and they say that the pool aforesaid is not injurious to the ships passing there or in any other ways. The same jurors, being asked the breadth of the course of the water of *Trent*, say that the course of the water aforesaid there contains in breadth ninety feet, and that the passage for ships in the water there passing is sufficiently large. Therefore it is considered that the aforesaid Bishop depart without a day, saving always the King's right, &c."

Sir *F. Pollock*, for the Crown, objected that this document was not admissible as the record of a judicial proceeding, the presentment being res inter alios; and that the statement of the jury could not be received as

1838.

The QUEEN *against* Lady H. B. M. SUTTON.

evidence of reputation. The learned Judge admitted the evidence (*a*).

The defendants also put in the following writ, under the privy seal, from among the records of the Court of Chancery preserved in the Tower of *London*, that is to say, writs under the Privy Seal of 20 *Ed.* 3.

"*Edward*, by the grace of God," &c., "to our dear clerk, Master *John* of *Offord*, Dean of *Lincoln*, our Chancellor, greeting. Whereas we have heard that the bridge below the town of *Kelm*, near *Newark*, is broken and ruinous to the great peril of the people passing by the same, which bridge no one is bound to repair in certain, according to that which is found by inquest . . . . (*b*), and returned into our chancery; wherefore we have granted to the good people of the town before named a pontage, according to the course of our chancery, to last for three years: therefore we command you that you cause to be made to the said good people letters under our great seal, in due form, without fine being made therefore. Given under our Privy Seal, at *Porchester*," 28th *June*, 20 *Ed.* 3.

The grant was also put in, from amongst the records of the Court of Chancery preserved in the Tower of *London*, that is to say, the patent rolls of 20 *Ed.* 3.; and began as follows.

" Grant of pontage to the men of the town of *Kelm*. } The King to his well beloved faithful men of the town of *Kelm*, near *Newark*, greeting. Know ye that, in aid of mending and repairing the

(*a*) By a shorthand writer's note, his Lordship appears to have said: "I think I ought to receive it, to shew the course of litigation that was then proceeding;" (that) "any liability of the persons, occupiers of the land, was not certainly ascertained at that time; that is the ground on which it is offered, and I receive it; that there was litigation about it." See p. 524, post.

(*b*) Words not legible.

broken

1838.

The QUEEN against Lady H. B. M. SUTTON.

broken bridge at *Kelm*, near *Newark*, and the decayed and ruined causeways between the same towns, to the great danger of the men there passing, to the repair of which no one is bound unless from his own mere will, as we are informed: we, of our special grace, have granted to you that, from the day of making these presents to the end of three years next following fully to be completed, you take by the hands of those whom you may depute for this purpose, and for whom you shall be willing to answer, for things for sale passing the bridge and causeways aforesaid, whether over, under, within, or without, the following customs, that is to say" (then followed a list of the customs): "and therefore we command you that you take the said customs unto the end of the said three years fully to be completed as is aforesaid, so that the money arising therefrom be employed about the repair and support of the bridge and footways aforesaid, and not for other purposes; but, the said term of three years being completed, the same custom shall entirely cease and be disused. In witness" &c. Dated 12th *August*.

A verdict was found for the defendants; and in *Easter* term, 1836, Sir *F. Pollock* moved for a new trial, or that the entry of judgment might be stayed (*a*), on account of the admission of the first mentioned document in evidence, repeating the objections urged at the trial. A rule *nisi* was granted in the alternative.

Sir *J. Campbell*, Attorney-General (with whom were *Adams* Serjeant, and *Starkie*), shewed cause (*b*). The question turns on the admissibility of the evidence, not

(*a*) See *Rex* v. *Sutton*, 5 *B. & Ad.* 52.

(*b*) *Michaelmas* term, 1837, *Nov.* 20 and 21. Before Lord *Denman* C. J., *Patteson*, *Williams*, and *Coleridge* Js.

the

1838.

The Queen *against* Lady H. B. M. Sutton.

the weight it should have. The special findings of the jury were legitimate according to the practice in the time of *Edward* III. At that period, and long after, the jurors were considered as witnesses; and, coming from the vicinage, spoke from their own knowledge. It was not till the times of *Edward* VI. and Queen *Mary* that this practice was completely altered; 2 *Reeves's Hist. Eng. Law.* 269—272. (*a*). Accordingly, it is said in 2 *Hale's P. C.* 300., that "if a man be arraigned upon an inquest of murder or manslaughter taken by the coroner, and be found *not guilty*, the jury that acquits him ought to inquire, who committed the fact, and that shall serve as an indictment against that person, that the jury find did the fact." And afterwards, at p. 301, it is said, as to indictments for robbery, that, "if the petit jury acquit the prisoner, they do not inquire who did it, and the reason of the difference is, that for the most part in *Eyre* the petit jury were all of the same hundred, where the offence was committed, and then upon the statute of *Winton* the hundred were to answer *de corporibus malefactorum*, and therefore it was reason to put them upon the inquiry, who committed the robbery, if it appears to the court, that a robbery was committed," "but now the jury, that tries, as well as inquires, is for the most part of the rest of the county, and therefore they answer only the point of *guilty* or *not guilty*."

But, further, in the time of *Edward* III., if there was no person bound by tenure to repair, the crown might grant pontage; but before such grant there would be an inquisition, which was a proceeding as much known to the law as an ad quod damnum now is: and the proceeding

(*a*) Chap. xi. 3d ed. See 1 *Stark. on Ev.* 5. note (*e*), 2d ed.

1838.

The QUEEN against Lady H. B. M. SUTTON.

ceeding referred to by the grant in question may be taken to have been an inquisition of that kind. Then the question is, whether this record could be wholly excluded? For the present motion assumes that the whole was inadmissible. The learned judge received it merely as evidence of certain proceedings having been taken, not as evidence that the facts found were true: and no objection is made to his manner of leaving it to the jury. Besides, it was not only evidence of a lis mota; it was proof at least of reputation, tending to negative a prescriptive obligation on certain parties: and it was more than this; for it was evidence of a verdict on the subject; and, wherever proof of reputation is admissible, so too, à fortiori, is evidence of a verdict or judgment on the same point: *Reed* v. *Jackson* (*a*). Evidence of reputation is not admissible where the subject matter is strictly private; *Morewood* v. *Wood* (*b*): but here the disputed liability is of general concern. It may be said that, to let in evidence of reputation, an exercise of the right within living memory must be proved (*c*); but that is not so where the subject does not admit of such proof; 1 *Phill. on Ev.* 271. Part I. *c.* 13. *s.* 2. (8th ed.): as here, where the subject-matter is merely a negation of liability. In *Rex* v. *Cotton* (*d*), which may be cited for the crown, the award, which was held to be no evidence of reputation, had been made post litem motam. *Rex* v. *Antrobus* (*e*) may also be cited, where the defendant's counsel proposed to

(*a*) 1 *East*, 355. See *Brisco* v. *Lomax*, antè, p. 198.

(*b*) 14 *East*, 327, note (*a*).

(*c*) Sir *F. Pollock*, in moving for the rule, cited, on this point, the judgment of *Dampier* J. in *Weeks* v. *Sparke*, 1 *M.* & *S.* 690.: but *Coleridge* J. referred to *Crease* v. *Barrett*, 1 *Cro. M.* & *R.* 919. *S. C.* 5 *Tyrwh.* 458, as at least qualifying that rule.

(*d*) 3 *Camp.* 444.

(*e*) 2 *A.* & *E.* 793.

shew,

1838.

The QUEEN *against* Lady H. B. M. SUTTON.

shew, by declarations of old persons, that the corporation of *Chester*, and not the sheriffs, were bound to execute criminals; and such evidence was rejected. But that was because it did not interest the public which party was bound to execute. *Patteson* J. is indeed reported to have asked, there, whether a liability to repair a bridge ratione tenuræ could be supported by evidence of reputation because the whole country is interested in the repair; but the dictum is thrown out incidentally, and probably would not have been followed up on further consideration: and the case of a bridge was not at all in point. The question here was not simply of tenure; because, if the defendants were not liable ratione tenuræ, it became matter of inquiry who was liable; and that affects the public.

In *Weeks* v. *Sparke* (*a*) the evidence of reputation (as to rights over a common) was held admissible because the claim concerned many persons. In *Reed* v. *Jackson* (*b*) the evidence of reputation, admitted on the same ground, consisted of a record which was inter alios. *Berry* v. *Banner* (*c*), where the question related to a custom, is a similar case. If it be said that the record in question here is a matter post litem motam, so is every judicial decision. And, if the record was admissible in evidence at all, the defendants were entitled to have the whole read, subject to the direction of the learned Judge as to the effect which any particular part ought to have. And the objection taken was, not that some part of the document ought not to have been read, but that it was altogether inadmissible. [Lord *Denman* C. J. My Brother *Bosanquet* reports that he admitted the document only as evidence that the subject

(*a*) 1 *M.* & *S.* 679. (*b*) 1 *East*, 355.
(*c*) 1 *Peake*, *N. P. C.* 212, 3d ed.

of

1838.

The QUEEN *against* Lady H. B. M. SUTTON.

of liability had been litigated; and I do not well see how, for that purpose, it could have been excluded. We will hear the other side.]

Sir *F. Pollock* in support of the rule. The evidence was not put in for the purpose of shewing that a litigation had existed; if it had been so offered, no more of the document should have been read than that object required. But it was produced to support a case of reputation; and it ought not to be available for a purpose not contemplated in offering it. The document was not good evidence of reputation. In cases where that effect has been given to a record, as against persons not parties to it, the point to be proved has been the same with that formerly in issue; *Reed* v. *Jackson* (*a*), *Berry* v. *Banner* (*b*). Here that is not so: the parties are not the same, nor claimants in the same right, as those on the former record; and the question is different. This is a dispute as to a private liability; and evidence of reputation is not applicable. But, if it were, the evidence shews no reputation affecting that liability. The record, so far as the verdict goes, merely shews that the Bishop of *Lincoln*, with whom the present defendants have no connection, was not bound to repair. The other answers stated on that record (and for the sake of which it was, in reality, produced) have no bearing on the present cause, and should not have been submitted to the jury without an express warning to that effect from the Judge. It is said that the document was admissible to shew the fact of a lis mota: but, to make it admissible on that ground, the lis mota should have been the same with that which is now

(*a*) 1 *East*, 355. (*b*) 1 *Peake, N. P. C.* 212. 3d ed.

before

1838.

The Queen against Lady H. B. M. Sutton.

before the Court, and between persons connected in some manner with the parties to the present record; otherwise the proof is irrelevant, and belongs to no head of evidence which has ever been held admissible. [*Patteson* J. This objection was not raised in moving for the rule]. The learned Judge had not then explained, as he has since, the ground on which he admitted the evidence. [*Patteson* J. Should not the ground have been ascertained, and the objection taken, at the trial ?] If evidence has been improperly received, that is at the risk of the parties tendering it; and they must be prepared to support it. The Court will inquire whether justice has been done upon the whole case. [Lord *Denman* C. J. I do not agree that we can go into that speculation. Parties may chuse, at the trial, to acquiesce in a particular course of proof].

The Court, however, thought that the opponents of the rule ought to be heard on this point: and the case was adjourned. In *Hilary* term 1838 (*a*),

Sir *J. Campbell*, Attorney-General, *Adams* Serjt. and *Starkie* resumed the argument against the rule. The evidence, as proving a lis mota, was relevant and material. The present indictment charges an immemorial liability. It is at least some evidence against such a liability, that in the time of *Edward* III. it was a disputed question whether the public or an individual were bound to repair. The inhabitants of a county, when indicted for non-repair of a bridge, may shew that individuals have repaired it; *Rex* v. *The Inhabitants of Northampton* (*b*), where *Le Blanc* J.

(*a*) *January* 22d. Before Lord *Denman* C. J., *Littledale*, *Williams*, and *Coleridge* Js.

(*b*) 2 *M.* & *S.* 262.

said:

said: "It was for the prosecutor to shew it a public bridge; and the defendants had a right to give every species of evidence to shew the contrary." So, on the other hand, an individual, charged ratione tenuræ, may give any evidence which shews either that the bridge is not repairable by individuals, or that the public prosecutor has formerly attempted to charge persons unconnected with the present defendant. But, further, the lis mota here connects itself with the grant of pontage. The writ for that grant is tested on the 28th of *June* in the same year in which the presentment against the Bishop was tried at the Spring assizes; and it states the bridge of *Kelm* to be ruinous, "which bridge no one is bound to repair in certain, according to that which is found by inquest." And the grant thereupon issues on the 12th of *August*. It thus appears, at least, that the pontage was not granted in aid of the estate which the prosecutors now seek to charge. The inquest was probably that to which the record of 20 *Ed.* 3. relates: it is not likely that a commission would be granted for taking an inquisition pendng the proceedings against the Bishop; and afterwards it would not have been necessary. In *Com. Dig. Toll.* (E.), it is said that, "if a man builds a new bridge," "the King may grant to him to take pontage," "for it is for the ease of the people." Here the jury found that the bridge was new, but that they did not know who was liable to repair. The verdict, if it is to be taken into consideration only as far as regards the acquittal, shewed that the Bishop was not liable; and it did not appear who was. The record of such a finding might have been removed into Chancery, (as, according to the writ, this was,) either for the purpose of shewing an acquittal, as is

1838.

The Queen *against* Lady H. B. M. Sutton.

is pointed out in 2 *Hale's P. C.* 242, or, if there had been a conviction, for the purpose of enforcing the repair by writ and distress, *Fitz. N. B.* 127, tit. *Writ de reparatione facienda*, E. (a). [*Coleridge* J. Do you say that the writ and grant would have been of any weight without the preceding evidence ?] They would, inasmuch as the recital concerning the inquisition would have shewn the motive of the grant. Further, the special findings of the jury on this record, as negativing a prescriptive liability, affected the public interest; and therefore, although the opposing interest was a private one, they were legitimate evidence of reputation, according to the opinions of Lord *Kenyon* and *Lawrence* J. in *Reed* v. *Jackson* (b) and *Morewood* v. *Wood* (c). The answers, so affecting the public, were given in an authorised proceeding, and by parties who had opportunities of knowing the facts. Such findings, when the jurors came from the vicinage, had the authority of an inquest of office; and a party might have been tried upon them, as on an indictment: 2 *Hale's P. C.* 300. According to 3 *Hawk. P. C.* 113., Book 2. c. 9. s. 33. (d), a jury acquitting of homicide on the coroner's inquisition were anciently compellable to say who did the fact; and on indictments generally they might have stated it. *Buller* J., in *Rex* v. *Jolliffe* (e), approved of the doctrine that "if to an action for slander in charging the plaintiff with felony a justification be pleaded, which is found by the jury, that of itself amounts to an indictment, as if it had been found by the grand inquest." [*Littledale* J. I never heard of that being acted upon, nor saw any instance of it.] In *The Duke of Newcastle* v. *The Hundred*

(a) See note (b), 9th ed.

(b) 1 *East*, 355.

(c) 14 *East*, 327. note (a).

(d) 7th ed.

(e) 4 *T. R.* 293.

of

1838.

The QUEEN against Lady H. B. M. SUTTON.

of Broxtowe (*a*) orders of justices in quarter sessions were held to be evidence of reputation that *Nottingham Castle* was within the hundred. The present declaration was against the interest of those making it, because, if no person was liable ratione tenuræ, the burden fell on the county. The degree of knowledge which the jurors might possess would affect only the weight attributable to the evidence, not its admissibility. *Reed* v. *Jackson* (*b*) shews that their finding, though upon the testimony of witnesses, is some evidence of reputation; à fortiori, the finding of a jury on their own knowledge would be so. "If a bishop or prior, &c. hath at once or twice of alms repaired a bridge, it bindeth not (and yet is evidence against him, until he prove the contrary) but if time out of mind, they and their predecessors have repaired it of alms, this shall bind them to it:" 2 *Inst.* 700: the finding of the jury, therefore, upon the matter of reputation in this case might have been available to charge the Bishop and exonerate the public: if so, it should be equally admissible for the opposite purpose; *Drinkwater* v. *Porter* (*c*). As to the argument that the finding was not upon the matter now in controversy, reputation, to be admissible in evidence, need not be upon the very point under litigation; *Price* v. *Littlewood* (*d*); *Doe, Lessee of Foster*, v. *Sisson* (*e*). There is no analogy between the finding here, that the jury do not know who is bound to repair, and the ignoring of a bill; because that never becomes matter of record. Nor is it like the finding of ignoramus as to a lunatic's estate; because here the statement is not a mere matter

(*a*) 4 *B. & Ad.* 273.
(*b*) 1 *East*, 355.
(*c*) 7 *Car. & P.* 181.
(*d*) 3 *Camp.* 288.
(*e*) 12 *East*, 62.

of

1838.

The Queen *against* Lady H. B. M. Sutton.

of course, but results, as the context shews, from an inquiry into the facts.

Sir *F. Pollock*, *Clarke*, and *Waddington*, contrà. There was no sufficient evidence to connect this record with the grant of pontage. The writ recites that the inquest is "returned into our chancery;" but there is no proof that this inquisition ever was so returned, or that search has been made for one there. The present inquisition is kept in a different place, and does not appear to be such a one as would properly be returned into chancery. As to the suggestion that this document was evidence of a lis mota; if that ground of admissibility was not disputed at the trial, it was because the defendant's counsel wished the whole document to go to the jury, in order that it might produce an effect as to other points than the lis mota; and the counsel for the prosecution, desiring to prevent that, would have excluded it altogether. When the learned Judge decided on receiving it for the limited purpose, the counsel for the prosecution did not make any further opposition; but they did not on that account waive their objection to the evidence as ultimately received. That objection is, that the lis mota between the Bishop and the vill of *Kelham* was not relevant to the dispute whether the *Sutton* family or the county are liable to repair the bridge. The defendants attempt to give this record the force of an inquisition; for which purpose they cite the passage in 2 *Hale's P. C.* 300., stating that, if a man be arraigned on a coroner's inquest of murder or manslaughter, and found not guilty, the jury ought to inquire who did the fact, and their finding shall serve for an indictment. From the whole context, that appears to have been a consequence

1838.

The QUEEN against Lady H. B. M. SUTTON.

sequence of the liability of the hundred (from which the jurors anciently came) in cases of felony, under the statute of *Winchester* (a); if so, the same law would not hold in cases of misdemeanor. In 3 *Hawk. P. C.* 113. *Book* 2. *c.* 9. *s.* 33. the practice is limited to cases of death; and a doubt is justly expressed as to its reasonableness. But, assuming that in some cases such a finding would be equivalent to an indictment, or would be a foundation for one, that could not apply here, where the finding consists merely in an acquittal of the bishop, a declaration of ignorance as to the liability, and a statement, apparently on hearsay, of some facts which were not properly in question before the jury. If the bishop had been convicted on the presentment, or even if there had been a finding that some other party was liable, the evidence might have had greater weight; but to hold it relevant as it now stands would be carrying the doctrine of *Rex* v. *The Inhabitants of Northampton* (b) much too far. The men of the county (whom the acquittal in the present case tends to charge) were not parties either to the presentment or to the application for a grant of pontage. As to the admissibility of this record on the ground that it proves reputation, it may be observed, in addition to the former arguments, that, although a verdict may be proof of reputation, it is not evidence where the parties are not the same as on the former litigation; because in such a case the verdict may have been obtained on the evidence of those under whom the party now adducing it claims. Here the inhabitants of *Kelham* were interested in the former inquiry, and may have furnished the evidence on which the special

(a) 13 *Ed.* 1. *stat.* 2. *c.* 2. See 2 *Hale's P. C.* 301.
(b) 2 *M.* & *S.* 262.

 findings

1838.

The Queen against Lady H. B. M. Sutton.

findings proceeded. And, further, reputation is evidence on general points only, not on particular facts; 1 *Stark. on Ev.* 34, 35., citing *Harwood* v. *Sims* (a); *Chatfield* v. *Fryer* (b). Here there is no affirmative finding except of particular facts, or of the jury's ignorance.

Cur. adv. vult.

Lord Denman C. J., in this term (*June* 11th), delivered the judgment of the Court.

On the last trial of this long pending question, whether the defendant is liable to the repair of *Kelham Bridge* over the *Trent*,] ratione tenuræ, objection was taken by the prosecutor to the admission of an ancient document brought from the Exchequer of Pleas at *York* (c), purporting to be the record of pleas in *Hilary* term, 18 *Ed.* 3. It is a complaint by the Bishop of *Lincoln* that he was unjustly distrained upon for the repair of the bridge in consequence of a presentment by the men of *Kelham* in the following form: "The vill of *Kelham* present that the Bishop of *Lincoln* ought and is accustomed to repair the bridge of *Kelum*, which is decayed and broken by default of the same Bishop, to the damage of the men passing by the same bridge."

The Bishop pleaded that he and his predecessors were not liable; and, upon issue joined between *John* of *Lincoln*, who prosecuted for the King, and the Bishop, the jury found their verdict in favour of the Bishop. The same jury, being asked whether there is any bridge at *Kelm*, say there is: Also, being asked who of right is bound the aforesaid bridge to repair and uphold, say they are entirely ignorant. Being also asked at what time

(a) *Wightw.* 112.

(b) 1 *Price*, 253. See 2 *Stark. on Ev.* 665. note (*l*), 2d ed.

(c) See p. 516. antè.

and

and by whom the aforesaid bridge was first built or repaired, say about sixty years since, and then of alms of men of the country passing that way; and in the building and repairing of the bridge aforesaid, there came a certain *Oliver*, Bishop of *Lincoln*, passing through the country, and of his alms charitably bestowed on the workmen of the said bridge 40*s*., and not in any other manner.

This verdict was found in *Easter* term, 20 *Ed.* 3.; and among the records of the *Tower* was found a writ of Privy Seal, dated *June* 28th in the same year, which, reciting that the bridge was dangerous, and that no one was bound to repair it as was found by inquest, directed a grant of pontage for reparation of the same, to be made under the great seal to the men of *Kelm*. Lastly, the grant of pontage to the men of *Kelm*, bearing date *August* 12th in the same year, was produced.

Much discussion appears to have taken place at the trial, as well as in this Court, respecting the purpose for which this evidence was received, as if it might be admissible in some points of view, though not in others. We find it unnecessary to consider any distinctions of this kind, because we are clearly of opinion that these documents, all and each of them, were material to the issue and good evidence towards proving it. They testablished that, in the time of *Edward* the Third, the men of *Kelham*, acting for the public, and represented by *John* of *Lincoln*, an officer of the Crown, proceeded against the party whom they conceived chargeable with repairing the bridge. Him the jury acquitted of the charge: and it was argued that this was all they had a right to do, and that their ignorance of any other liability, and their statement of the origin of the bridge and the

1838.

The QUEEN against Lady H. B. M. SUTTON.

manner in which the Bishop had contributed, by way of charity and not upon compulsion, were beyond their province. We think it cannot be assumed that at the remote period of this inquiry the functions of a jury were bounded within the same limits as at present; every lawyer, indeed, knows that the contrary is the fact; with the reasonable presumption, therefore, which must always be made in favour of the regularity of proceedings conducted by proper authority, it might not be too much to hold that this inquest was a public proceeding in which the jury might properly inquire, not only whether the person charged, but also in general who, and whether any one, was liable to the repairs. At the same time we find no necessity for going this length; because, even if there should be some irregularity in setting forth some particulars not inquired of, that cannot vitiate what was correctly done. The facts, then, that the Bishop was presented as chargeable by the men of *Kelham*, acting for the public, that such presentment ended with his acquittal on that ground, and was shortly followed by the grant of pontage to the men of *Kelham* for the same repairs, were strong to negative any immemorial liability ratione tenuræ; because we must suppose that the presentment would rather have been made against the person so liable than against the Bishop, and that the grant of pontage would not have been made at all.

Rule discharged.

The QUEEN *against* LEDGARD.

Tuesday, June 5th.

On trial of a quo warranto information for exercising the office of councillor for a ward having nine, the issue being whether defendant was duly elected, the prosecutor's case was, that nine other candidates at the election had a majority over the defendant: Held, that the prosecutor was not bound to prove, in the first instance, that the nine were qualified to be councillors, but might make a case by shewing simply that they had the actual majority.

Papers, purporting to be voting papers given in at the election, were produced from the town clerk's office; and it appeared that he had been elected town clerk some days after the election, and had not received the voting papers in the first instance, but that they had been delivered to him shortly after his own appointment: Held that, under stat. 5 & 6 *W.* 4. *c.* 76. *ss.* 32, 35., the papers were not sufficienly identified to be evidence of the votes given.

INFORMATION in the nature of a quo warranto for using and exercising the office of a councillor of the town and borough of *Poole*, from 28th *December*, 6 *W.* 4., to 31st *December* in the same year.

Pleas. 1. That, at the time of the election after mentioned, the borough was divided into two wards, the South East Ward and the North East Ward, having each nine councillors: that 28th *December* 1835 was fixed for the election of councillors, and an election duly made on that day before the mayor: that defendant was duly qualified to be elected and to be a councillor, and was a candidate for the South East Ward, and was at the conclusion of the election "duly ascertained, according to the provisions of" stat. 5 & 6 *W.* 4. *c.* 76., "to be one of so many of the several persons then voted for at the said election, being equal to the number of persons then to be chosen, to wit to the number of nine, who then and there had the greatest number of votes at the said election, and were deemed accordingly to be elected councillors for the said town and borough of *Poole*, under and according to the provisions and directions of the said act; and that he, the said *George Ledgard*, was thereupon duly declared to be and was elected a councillor" for the borough, according to the act; that he made and subscribed the declaration, and was duly admitted, and

1838.

The QUEEN *against* LEDGARD.

became and was a councillor &c. Replication, that defendant was not at the conclusion &c. duly ascertained &c., and was not duly declared to be and was not elected &c., in manner &c. Similiter.

2. That, on 28th *December* 1835, an election was duly made, before the mayor, of nine councillors for the South East Ward; that defendant was a candidate, being duly qualified; and that after the election he was duly declared by the mayor to have been elected one of the nine councillors for the said ward, and accepted the office, and complied in all things with the provisions of the statute, and took upon himself the duties; that on 1st *January* 1836, he was elected an alderman, and took upon himself that office, and ceased to be councillor. Replication, that defendant was not duly elected one of the councillors for the said ward. Rejoinder, that defendant was duly elected &c. Similiter.

On the trial, before *Alderson* B., at the *Dorsetshire* Summer assizes, 1836, the defendant, who began, proved that he had been declared duly elected by the mayor. The case for the prosecution was, that there were nine candidates, the number of councillors to be elected for the ward, who had, in fact, a majority over the defendant: that fraud had been practised in the handing in and receipt of the voting papers, and that some votes had been recorded for the defendant which had really been given for opposing candidates. To prove this, it was proposed to shew that among the voting papers, now remaining in the town clerk's office, there were some duplicates containing on the face of them opposite votes by the same voters; that in other instances the voting papers remaining were not those actually handed in; and that in other instances the voting papers handed in had been destroyed.

This

1838.

The QUEEN against LEDGARD.

This it was proposed to prove by parol evidence of the voters. The learned Judge, however, ruled that the voting papers were in the nature of a poll book, and must be considered as conclusive evidence, in this inquiry, of the side on which the voter, whose name was on the paper, had voted; but that, where duplicates were among the voting papers, the parol evidence was admissible. The counsel for the prosecution called Mr. *Arnold*, who was town clerk at the time of the trial, and who produced a bundle of papers purporting to be the voting papers. He stated that a person named *Parr* had been town clerk at the time of the election: that he himself had been elected town clerk on the 1st of *January* 1836: that, on that day, one *Cole*, who was in the employ (and, as the witness supposed, a clerk) of *Parr*, brought him a box, locked up, with a key, as from *Parr*: that the witness refused to receive it, because he could not then take a schedule of the contents: that the box was left at his office, *Cole* taking away the key: that, on the 4th of *January*, *Cole* brought back the key, and that, on the same day, witness saw the box, then open, in the possession of his own clerk, *Bury*: that he directed *Bury* to examine the contents, but did not do so himself: that, by his authority, *Bury* received and kept the key, and the box remained in witness's office: that the papers in the box were afterwards treated as the voting papers, burgesses being allowed to examine them as such under the inspection of *Bury* (a): that the witness himself had not personally received the papers till *March* 5th, when *Bury* handed them over to him, with a view to their being produced before a committee of the House of Commons: and that

(a) See *Rex* v. *Arnold*, 4 *A.* & *E.* 657.

on

1838.

The Queen against Ledgard.

on *March* 6th the witness did produce them before that committee as the voting papers. The defendant's counsel objected that the identity of the papers was not proved. His lordship expressed his opinion that they were not traced: but he admitted them, because they came from the custody of the town clerk who had treated them as the voting papers. The defendant's counsel also contended that the prosecutor was bound to shew that the candidates, whom he alleged to have the real majority, were qualified to be elected as councillors: but the learned Judge held this to be unnecessary. No evidence was offered to disprove their qualification; and it was shewn that all the names of the nine candidates whom the prosecutor asserted to have the majority above the defendant were on the burgess list, and that seven of them had been returned by the mayor as elected. Verdict for the crown. Leave was given to move to enter a verdict for the defendant, on the last point. In *Michaelmas* term 1836, *Bompas* Serjt. obtained a rule to enter a verdict accordingly, or for a new trial on either point (*a*).

Erle, *Crowder*, and *Newman* now shewed cause. First, as to the admissibility of these voting papers in evidence. For the present purpose, it is sufficient to shew that they were primâ facie evidence, no proof having been tendered by the defendant that the votes were not given as the papers represented. Sect. 32 of stat. 5 & 6 *W.* 4. *c.* 76. provides the mode of electing by voting papers: sect. 35 enacts "that the mayor and assessors shall

(*a*) Several other questions were raised in support of the motion for a new trial, which the judgment of the Court renders it unnecessary to notice.

examine

1838.

The QUEEN against LEDGARD.

examine the voting papers so delivered as aforesaid, for the purpose of ascertaining which of the several persons voted for are elected; and so many of such persons, being equal to the number of persons then to be chosen, as shall have the greatest number of votes, shall be deemed to be elected;" "and the mayor shall cause the voting papers to be kept in the office of the town clerk during six calendar months at the least after every such election; and the town clerk shall permit any burgess to inspect the voting papers of any year, on payment of one shilling for every search." These papers, then, are documents of a public nature, brought from the place where they are appointed to be kept for public resort. It is true that the six months, during which the statute requires the town clerk to keep the papers, had expired before the trial; but that does not make the custody improper. They are to be kept six months "at the least;" the town clerk would not be justified in destroying them at the expiration of that time; and the town clerk here identified the papers as those which he had kept throughout. In *Webb* v. *Smith* (a) it was holden that a precept for an election was sufficiently proved by a copy from the Crown office, that being the proper place for the custody of the original. It is never considered necessary to trace custody back from an officer through his predecessors. The Courts have admitted as evidence copies from the *Custom House* of the searcher's account of a cargo under stat. 12 *C.* 2. *c.* 19., *Johnson* v. *Ward* (b); of entries in the books of commissioners of excise (c); of transfers of stock in the Bank books (d); of books kept at the

(a) 4 *New Ca.* 373. (b) 6 *Esp. N. P. C.* 47.

(c) See *Fuller* v. *Fotch*, *Carth.* 346.

(d) See *Breton* v. *Cope*, *Peake*, *N. P. C.* 43. (3d ed.).

Sick

1838.

The QUEEN against LEDGARD.

Sick and Hurt Office, containing copies of the returns of naval officers, *Wallace* v. *Cook* (*a*); of the entry in the Master's office, containing copies of the roll of attorneys, *Rex* v. *Crossley* (*b*). So copies of ships' registers, properly kept, are admissible, under stat. 6 *G*. 4. *c*. 110. *s*. 43.; of parish rates, under stat. 17 *G*. 2. *c*. 38. *s*. 13.: so also are the minutes of parish indentures under stat. 42 *G*. 3. *c*. 46. *s*. 3. *Bullen* v. *Michel* (*c*) shows how far the mere fact of proper custody authenticates a copy of an ancient deed. If, in such cases, it were necessary to call every person who has superintended the custody, there would be a constant failure of justice. It is enough that the party filling the office has the custody in that character; by sect. 65 of stat. 5 & 6 *W*. 4. *c*. 76. the town clerk's predecessor was to hand the papers in question to the council, and the succeeding town clerk was to have the custody of them. As to the objection that the prosecutor was bound to prove the qualification of the nine candidates who ought, as he contends, to have been elected, the defendant must contend that, in case of their not being qualified, the votes given for them were thrown away. But no notice of want of qualification was given to the electors. (On this point they were stopped by the Court.)

Bompas Serjt., *Barstow*, *Bond*, and *Butt*, contrà. First, there was no evidence that the papers produced as voting papers were such. The papers are accessible to burgesses demanding inspection: it is therefore the more important that the evidence of identity should be watched. The cases cited shew only that, when documents

(*a*) 5 *Esp*. 117. (*b*) 2 *Esp*. 526.

(*c*) 2 *Price*, 399.; affirmed in *Dom. Proc.* 4 *Dow*, 297.

1838.

The QUEEN *against* LEDGARD.

ments are directed to be kept in any place for a specific purpose, then the custody makes them evidence for that purpose. Here the statute does not indicate that the papers are to be preserved in order to make them evidence. In the case of rate books, stat. 17 *G.* 2. *c.* 38. *s.* 13. directs that they shall be preserved by the parish officers "for the time being." The books of parish indentures are made evidence in all courts of law by the express words of stat. 42 *G.* 3. *c.* 46. *s.* 3.; and that only "in case it shall be proved to the satisfaction of such Court that the said indentures are lost or have been destroyed." So copies of ships' registers are made evidence by the express words of stat. 6 *G.* 4. *c.* 110. *s.* 43. In the case of ancient deeds, the death of parties makes it necessary to rely more on the custody than where, as in this case, no difficulty exists as to calling the parties: and the books of the *Sick and Hurt Office* (*Wallace* v. *Cook* (*a*)) are also evidence from necessity. The argument from the public nature of the documents would go too far; for it would shew that copies of the voting papers would be evidence: 1 *Stark. Ev.* 192. 2d ed. The corporate officers, under sect. 65 of the statute, have custody of muniments; but a copy of a deed less than thirty years old, coming from such custody, could not be evidence; nor would the original, without proof of execution. As to the other point. The prosecutor's case was that nine other candidates were elected. He was bound to prove this election as much as if he had expressly pleaded it instead of traversing the election of the defendant and offering proof of the election of the other nine in support of the traverse. This is not like a case where the right to elect has been created, and then a subsequent

(*a*) 5 *Esp.* 117.

statute

1838.

The Queen *against* Ledgard.

statute creates a positive disability: the right to elect at all is created by sect. 30, which gives power only to "elect from the persons qualified to be councillors." Suppose an officer were, by statute, to be elected from the councillors, would it not be necessary to plead and prove that he was a councillor at the time of the election? Here the case is the stronger, because the proceeding is of a criminal nature. [*Patteson* J. Is it not enough here to shew that the defendant had not the majority? Were the votes for the others thrown away if they were not qualified?] A mere protest against the swearing in of a particular candidate, not followed up by a vote, was holden not to invalidate the swearing in, which afterwards was administered by competent persons, in *Rex* v. *Courtenay* (*a*): in *Regina* v. *Boscawen* (*b*) votes given for an incapable candidate were holden to be thrown away: in *Rex* v. *Withers* (*b*) six persons refused to vote, five voted for the defendant; and it was held that the defendant was nevertheless elected. [*Patteson* J. But there is nothing to shew that the votes there, if given, would have been thrown away.] Here, the act having given an election only out of qualified persons, the case resembles those in which there had been notice of a candidate not having taken the test under 2 stat. 13 *Car.* 2. *c.* 1. *s.* 12., and where the votes given after notice were thrown away, and an opposite candidate with an apparent minority was held to be elected; *Rex* v. *Hawkins* (*c*), *Taylor* v. *Mayor of Bath* (*b*), *Rex* v. *Parry* (*d*). In cases of that class, the individual, till notice, must be presumed to have obeyed the law: here the qualification is the preliminary condition. It is as if votes were given for a

(*a*) 9 *East*, 246. (*b*) Cited in *Rex* v. *Monday*, 2 *Cowp.* 537.

(*c*) 10 *East*, 211. Affirmed in error in *Dom. Proc. Hawkins* v. *Rex*, 2 *Dow*, 124. (*d*) 14 *East*, 549.

dead

1838.

The Queen against Ledgard.

dead person. [Lord *Denman* C. J. Does the act contain any positive qualification; or is there merely the disqualification in sect. 28?] Sect. 30 has the same effect as if the words had been "from persons not disqualified." In *Regina* v. *Hiorns* (a) the disqualification arose on a subsequent statute. Besides, here the proceedings afford no opportunity for a notice of disqualification.

Lord DENMAN C. J. The argument for entering a verdict for the defendant is that, if the replication, which denies that the defendant is duly elected, were expanded by adding the supposed reason of his not being duly elected, it would aver that others were so, and on such a replication it would be clear that the prosecutor must prove the qualification of the parties whom he asserts to have been elected. Therefore it is said that the replication, as it now stands, must require the same proof. By sect. 30 of stat. 5 & 6 *W.* 4. *c.* 76. the burgesses are to "elect from the persons qualified to be councillors." That appears to involve, in the description of the persons eligible, the fact of qualification. But, when we look at the whole course of proceeding, and especially at the twenty-eighth section, which describes only what are disqualifications, it seems that the proper construction of sect. 30 is, that the election is to be from persons not disqualified. It does not appear that at this election any objection to qualification was made by the returning officer, or by any elector or rival candidate. The mayor, therefore, was to assume that the candidates were not disqualified. Consequently, the prosecutor was not bound to prove the absence of disqualification of the

(a) 7 *A. & E.* 960.

rejected

1838.

The Queen *against* Ledgard.

rejected candidate, but only that the candidates returned were in an actual minority. The other question is, whether the supposed polling papers were properly received. Sect. 35 makes the custody of the town-clerk the proper custody; and this, it is said, makes the fact of the custody evidence as to the identity of the voting papers. I think that is not so; and that we cannot engraft so much upon the words of the section as to hold that this is any evidence at all, without some further proof. We will not suppose any fraud. Had the town clerk done any thing, as, for instance, if he had made up the whole poll, perhaps some ground might have been laid for the argument; but it is too much to say that, when the papers are produced to shew the whole poll, they are sufficiently identified by the custody. I doubt whether the mere custody makes them evidence at all; for the consigning them to the town clerk's custody, which is what the act does, is very different from making them public documents. I think, therefore, that the evidence was improperly admitted, and that there must be a new trial.

Littledale J. I am entirely of the same opinion. There is clearly no ground for entering a verdict for the defendant. As to the other point, I think there must be a new trial on the ground that the papers were not traced. Sect. 35 says that the papers are to be lodged in the town clerk's office, and kept at least six months. The original town clerk was not called to shew that the papers which had come into his office were the same as those which the present town clerk had. Therefore, without considering whether the papers would have been conclusive or not, I think the evidence inadmissible, because the continuity of the custody was not shewn.

Patteson

1838.

The QUEEN *against* LEDGARD.

PATTESON J. I agree on both points. It cannot be the true construction, that a prosecutor must prove the qualification of the candidates who, he says, ought to have been returned. It is argued that the prosecutor must take on himself this burthen, because there is no opportunity of notice. But that shews that the vote must be received without question as to the candidate's qualification. For, where the notice causes votes given for the unqualified candidate to be thrown away, and the returning officer has to take the responsibility, there the question is obtruded upon him by the elector who takes the objection at the time. Here the provisions of the act, as to the mode of voting, prevent this course; and, if the returning officer were to take it on himself to decide on the qualification, no better mode of fraud could be devised: for he might assume the want of qualification, and put the borough to a quo warranto. The act studiously makes the returning officer ministerial for the purpose of summing up the votes, and declaring the party who has the greatest number to be elected. It is no business of his whether the candidate be qualified or not; I do not know that he would be bound to notice his not being on the burgess roll. I think therefore that, even if the replication had set out the matter specially, the Crown need not have shewn the qualification. It would have been enough to prove that the defendant had the minority of votes. As to the other point, I cannot find that the act makes the voting papers in the town clerk's custody any thing like a record. I can easily conceive that, where so many persons have access, much trickery may take place. Still the officer, who accepts the situation, and to whom the act gives the custody, must take care that no fraud is practised. But here

1838.

The Queen *against* Ledgard.

here the question is, whether these are *the* papers. For, if they are shewn to be so, I agree with the learned Judge who tried the cause, that they are evidence how the parties voted. It is said that it would be very difficult to trace them. I do not see that. One town clerk has handed them to another; why could not the former, or his clerk who actually gave them to the clerk of the second town clerk, be called? If the first town clerk had said, I received the papers from the mayor, and handed over all I got to my successor, and the successor had said, these are as they were when I received them, perhaps that would have been enough; or perhaps the mayor should have been called also. This is no more than the kind of evidence which is given at every assizes, when, in criminal cases, it is proved that the property has been handed from *A.* to *B.*, from *B.* to *C.*, and so on. Every link is required to be made good. Why should that not be so here? Whether the voters must be called, to identify the papers, I need not determine. But here all the evidence is, that the second town clerk says, here is my box, and my clerk tells me that it was brought to him from my predecessor. All we know is, that the second town clerk treated them as the voting papers, and that the burgesses inspected them. That they did on the faith that no change had taken place; and probably there had been none; but this should have been proved.

Williams J. I am of the same opinion. As to the evidence, no doubt the custody of the papers was right at the time of the trial; but the question is as to the custody up to that time. The identity up to *Arnold*'s time was left uncertain. To rest on mere proof of the use made of them, or even proof of correspondence

in

1838.

The QUEEN *against* LEDGARD.

in number, would be very unsafe compared with an actual tracing of the identity. On the other point; the act entrusts the returning officer only with the reporting on the actual majority. Nothing gives him any discretion; and it would be highly dangerous if he had the power to take objections which were not suggested to him; but that is required by the argument in support of entering a verdict for the defendant.

Rule absolute for a new trial.

ANN WILDER *against* SPEER, GRAVES, WINCH, and Others.

Wednesday, June 6th.

In an action for abusing a distress, by putting the animals distrained into a muddy pound, whereby they were injured, it is no defence that the place was the manor pound, and was *generally* in a proper state. The distrainer must, at his peril, put the distress into a pound which is, not only in general, but at the particular time, fit for it. And, if the common pound be unfit (though by reason of a casualty, as rain or snow), he must find another.

To trespass for distraining sheep, and injuring them by impounding them in a muddy pound, defendants pleaded distress damage-feasant, and that the sheep were impounded in a common pound, with no unnecessary damage to them. Replication, that defendants, after the distress, at the time when &c., impounded them in the pound in the declaration mentioned, which was *then* too small, and which was *then* muddy, and thereby injured them. Rejoinder, that the pound was not too small, nor muddy *in manner* &c. Held, that this was an issue on the state of the pound *at the time of the impounding*; and that, on proof that the pound was *then* muddy, plaintiff was entitled to recover.

TRESPASS. The declaration stated that defendants, on &c., and on divers other days &c., with force and arms, seized, took, and distrained divers, to wit 174 ewes and 60 wethers of plaintiff, of great value, to wit &c., and then, with force &c., chased, drove, and hurried about the said ewes and wethers, the same ewes being then with lamb, and then impounded the said ewes and wethers in a small wet, muddy, and dirty pound, and then kept and detained them in the said pound for a long space of time, to wit &c., during all which time the said ewes and wethers, by reason of their having been so impounded and kept &c., were greatly squeezed and injured; and, by means and in consequence

 of

1838.

WILDER *against* SPEER.

of the premises, divers, to wit 100, of the said ewes yeaned and brought forth their lambs prematurely, and divers of the lambs which were brought forth by the said first-mentioned ewes were brought forth dead, and divers, to wit four others, of the said lambs which were brought forth by the said ewes were drowned and trampled to death in the said pound, and the rest of the said lambs which were brought forth by the said ewes have since died, and the said ewes and wethers have been and are by means of the premises greatly injured, &c.; and defendants, on the same day &c., converted and disposed of divers, to wit 50, of the said ewes and wethers to their own use, &c.

Pleas, by *Speer*. 1. Not guilty. 2. That the ewes and wethers were not plaintiff's property in manner &c. 3. That defendant *Speer* was seised in fee of the manor of *Weston*, with the appurtenances, in *Surrey*, and of a waste, situate &c., parcel of the said manor: and, because the said ewes and wethers, at the said times when &c., were in the said waste feeding &c. and doing damage &c., he, at the said times when &c., seized and distrained the same for a distress for the said damage &c., and under such distress a little chased &c., and impounded the same in a certain common pound within the said manor, and kept and detained them under such distress there for the said space of time, &c., doing no unnecessary damage, &c. Verification. 4. That defendant, being lord of the said manor, took the ewes and wethers surcharging the common, and drove and impounded them, &c. Verification.

Pleas, by *Graves* and two others. 1. and 2. As by *Speer*. 3. That defendants, as *Speer*'s servants and by his command, took and distrained the ewes &c. damage-feasant on the waste, parcel of *Speer*'s manor of *Weston*, and

and drove and impounded them in a common pound within the manor, &c. Verification. 4. That defendants, as servants, and by command, of *Speer*, the lord of the manor, distrained the ewes &c. surcharging &c., and drove and impounded them (as in the third plea).

Pleas, by *Winch* and eight others. 1. and 2. As by *Speer*. 3. Justification by some of the defendants as commoners, and by others as their servants, that they distrained the ewes &c. damage-feasant, and drove them to a certain common pound in the parish of *Thames Ditton* (where the locus in quo was situate), the same being a safe and proper pound in that behalf, and there impounded &c. Verification. 4. That defendants, as servants, and by command, of *Speer*, the lord of the manor, distrained the ewes &c. surcharging &c., and drove them to a certain common pound within the manor, and there impounded &c.

Replication. To the pleas by *Speer*. 1. and 2. Similiter. 3. That defendant, after he had distrained the said ewes &c. for the damage in the third plea mentioned, "to wit at the said times when &c. in the said declaration mentioned, chased, drove and hurried about the said ewes and wethers, under the said distress, in a wanton and cruel manner, and to a greater degree, and with more force and violence, and at a greater and more furious rate, than was necessary, and then impounded the same under the said distress in the said pound in the said declaration mentioned, which was then too small to hold or contain the same in a fit and proper manner, and which was then very wet, muddy, and dirty, and wholly improper for impounding the same, and thereby greatly injured the said ewes and wethers as in the said declaration mentioned, and abused the said distress."

 Verification.

1838.

Wilder against Speer.

Verification. 4. A similar replication, adapted to *Speer's* fourth plea. There were similar replications to the pleas, respectively, pleaded by the other defendants.

Rejoinder, by *Speer*, to the replication to the third plea: that he did not chase &c. under the said distress in a wanton or cruel manner, or to a greater degree &c. than was necessary: "nor was the said pound in the said declaration mentioned, in which he impounded the same, too small to hold or contain the same in a fit and proper manner, nor was the same wet, muddy, or dirty, and improper for impounding the same, in manner and form as in the said replication to the said third plea is alleged." Conclusion to the country. There was a similar rejoinder by *Speer* to the replication to the fourth plea.

Rejoinder by *Graves* and others to the replication to the third and fourth pleas, in the same terms, mutatis mutandis.

Rejoinder by *Winch* and others to the same pleadings: that, after they had distrained &c., they did not injure the said ewes and wethers, or abuse the said distress, in manner and form &c. Conclusion to the country. Issues were joined on the several rejoinders.

On the trial before Lord *Abinger* C. B. at the *Guildford* Summer assizes, 1836, the plaintiff's case was abandoned (on terms) as against *Speer*. By the evidence given against the other defendants, it appeared that 160 of the plaintiff's sheep had been put at one time into the manor pound. Witnesses for the plaintiff alleged that the pound was much too small to contain that number; but the defendants' witnesses denied this. There had been snow and rain shortly before, which had formed such a depth of mud and water in the pound that the sheep sank up to their bellies: and

and in consequence of the state of the pound several lambs were lost, and other injury done, within the averments of the declaration. The Lord Chief Baron, in his summing up, said that the plaintiff's right to a verdict on the third and fourth issues in each set of pleadings would depend upon the question whether or not the pound was generally fit for impounding such a number of sheep as the defendants had put in; and not whether at the time in question it was, from particular circumstances, unfit: and he advised the jury to find for the defendants if they thought that the sheep were not overdriven, that the pound was not too small, and that it was generally a proper place, although it might have been in an unfit state at the time of taking this distress. He was of opinion that the right of impounding could not be made dependent on the state of the weather; but he also intimated a doubt whether the question as to the temporary condition of the pound was raised by these pleadings. And he said that the defendants would have had no right to put the sheep into any other place than the manor pound. Verdict for *Speer* on the first issue: and the jury discharged as to the other issues between him and the plaintiff. As to the other defendants; verdict for the plaintiff on the first and second issues, for the defendants on the third and fourth. In *Michaelmas* term, 1836, a rule nisi was obtained for a new trial, on the ground of misdirection.

Andrews Serjt. and *M. Chambers* now shewed cause on behalf of *Winch* and those who joined in pleading with him. The defendants put the distress into the manor pound, and they were not bound to place it elsewhere, which, if they had done it, would have been at

 their

1838.

WILDER *against* SPEER.

their own risk. The distress, when taken to the public pound, is in the custody of the law; if such pound be, in its ordinary state, a proper one, the distrainer is not liable because, at the time of impounding the particular distress, it is, by the accident of weather, in a bad condition. The question here was, whether the pound, in its general state, was a fit one, and of sufficient size: no issue could properly be raised on its temporary state, which the plaintiff has relied upon in her replication. [Lord *Denman* C. J. You have taken issue upon that replication. Should not you have stated that the unfitness was temporary and the act of God, if such was your defence? That, if made out, would, according to your view of the question, have given you the verdict.] But upon an immaterial issue. [*Patteson* J. If so, the plaintiff, in such a case, could not move for judgment non obstante veredicto: but, if the plaintiff succeeded, the defendant might move to arrest the judgment.] The issue which the defendants really intended to join was on the general state of the pound. If that issue is, in strictness, not raised by the rejoinder, still the Court, in the exercise of its discretion, will not send the parties to a new trial, and expose the defendants to the risk of paying damages, on a point beside the merits. There is no authority for saying that a distrainer putting cattle into a public pound is liable, if it happens at the time to be in an unfit state. It is indeed said in argument, in *Vaspor* v. *Edwards* (*a*), "The distress must be in a convenient pound, and if it be not such, and a distress is put into it and abused, though it be what is called a common pound, the distrainer shall answer for it. And

(*a*) 12 *Mod.* 659.

therefore

1838.

WILDER *against* SPEER.

therefore if a live beast be put into a place in which there are sharp spikes, by which the beast is stuck, though it be a public pound, the distrainer shall answer for it, for it is his pound, and it is he shall have a *parco fracto* for the breach of it, and not the lord; *vide Doct. and Stud.*, c. 27." But in *Doctor and Student*, Dialogue 2. c. 27., there referred to, no corresponding passage appears (*a*). And in *Doct. and Stud.* 14., Dial. 1. c. 5., it is said that, if "a man for a just cause taketh a distress, and putteth it in the pound overt, and no law compelleth him that distrained to give them meat, then it seemeth of reason, that if the distress die in pound for lack of meat, that it died at the peril of him that oweth the beasts, and not of him that distrained; for in him that distrained there can be assigned no default, but in the other may be assigned a default, because the rent was unpaid." On the same grounds it may be said that the distrainer is not liable if the cattle perish from the state of the weather.

Shee, for *Graves* and the two other defendants. The issue actually taken on the third and fourth pleas was, that the pound was generally in a fit state. The replication states that the defendants, at the times when &c., chased and drove the sheep, and impounded them in the said pound, which was *then* too small to contain the same in a proper manner, and which was *then* very wet, muddy, and wholly improper. "*Then*" is not to be limited in construction to the particular moment; the pound was not small then, more than in general; and, if the sense is not to be limited with reference to that averment, the allegations that the pound was muddy and

(*a*) P. 192. 18th ed. See the report in 1 *Ld. Ray.* 720, (*Vasper* v. *Eddowes*).

dirty

1838.

Wilder against Speer.

dirty are not important enough to vary the construction of the whole. And the rejoinder (rightly, according to the view now pointed out) states, generally, that the pound was not too small, nor was the same wet, muddy, dirty, and improper for impounding, in manner and form &c. [*Patteson* J. It is too much to assume that the allegations of the pound being wet and muddy are immaterial. Those circumstances might be trifling or important in their effect, as the pound was good or bad in other respects.]

Platt, *Clarkson*, and *Channell*, contrà, were not heard.

Lord DENMAN C. J. It is clear that the ruling of the Lord Chief Baron cannot be maintained. It is immaterial what the pound habitually was, if, at the time of the impounding, it was in a bad condition. Suppose the distress had been taken at a time of flood; could the defendants have justified putting the sheep into the pound when it was covered with water? The question must be, what the condition of the pound was at the particular time. A party distraining is to impound for safe custody, but not so as to destroy the subject of distress.

LITTLEDALE J. The distrainer must, at his peril, find a proper pound; generally the manor pound would be the proper place; but, if that is not in a fit state, he must find another. The pound must be in a proper condition at the time of impounding: and the issues here referred to that time.

PATTESON J. concurred (*a*).

Rule absolute.

(*a*) *Williams* J. had left the Court.

1838.

KEABLE *against* PAYNE.

Wednesday, June 6th.

In assumpsit for goods sold and delivered, plaintiff's case was, that defendant had received them of *M.*, who had obtained them from plaintiff, the owner, by pretending to purchase and pay for them by a cheque drawn on a party who, as *M.* knew, would dishonour the cheque: Held that, in support of this case, the cheque was admissible in evidence, though not duly stamped.

ASSUMPSIT for goods sold and delivered, and on an account stated. Plea, Non Assumpsit.

On the trial before *Bosanquet* J., at the *Suffolk* Summer assizes, 1836, the case for the plaintiff was, that he had exposed to sale six bullocks, his property, at *Woodbridge* market; and that a person named *Mann* agreed with him to purchase them at the price of 100*l.* 7*s.* 6*d.*, for which sum he gave a check on Messrs. *Mills, Bawtree*, and Co., *Hadleigh* Bank, payable to the plaintiff or bearer, dated *Hadleigh, Lawford.* The cheque was presented, and dishonoured for want of funds. Afterwards the defendant bought the bullocks of *Mann;* and the action was for the value of the bullocks. It was contended, for the plaintiff, that *Mann* knew that the cheque would not be paid, and that therefore, his transaction with the plaintiff being fraudulent, no property in the bullocks passed to *Mann*, nor, consequently, to the defendant. On production of the cheque, it appeared to be without a stamp; and it was shewn to have been issued by *Mann* to the plaintiff at *Woodbridge*, which is more than ten miles from the place where it was made payable. The defendant's counsel objected to the admission of the cheque in evidence; but the learned Judge received it, and directed the jury to find for the plaintiff if they were of opinion that *Mann*, at the time of the transaction, knew that the cheque would not be paid. Verdict for the plaintiff. Leave was given to move to enter a nonsuit. In *Michaelmas*

1838.

KEABLE *against* PAYNE.

chaelmas term, 1836, *Kelly* obtained a rule nisi for a nonsuit or new trial, on the question as to the stamp, and on the evidence.

B. Andrews and *O'Malley* now shewed cause. This cheque was certainly not within the exemption given to drafts on bankers in stat. *55 G. 3. c.* 184. Sched. Part I. But the provisions of the stamp acts, making unstamped instruments inadmissible in evidence (*a*), apply only to cases where the instrument is produced in order to carry it into effect, not where the effect is disputed; otherwise the stamp acts would operate to protect fraudulent instruments. In *Scott* v. *Jones* (*b*) it was said by the Court, "The meaning of the act is, that" the instrument "shall not without a stamp be available as between the parties, so as to enable them to enforce the agreement." It was held by *Abbott* C. J., in 1822, that an unstamped agreement is admissible in a civil action to prove usury (*c*); and afterwards his Lordship admitted such evidence in *Nash* v. *Duncomb* (*d*). So an unstamped bill is evidence on an indictment for forgery, *Rex* v. *Hawkeswood* (*e*), *Rex* v. *Teague* (*g*), *Rex* v. *Reculist* (*h*); or in debt for bribery at an election, *Dover* v. *Maestaer* (*i*); or to prove the larceny

(*a*) By stat. 31 *G. 3. c.* 25. *s.* 19., no draft, &c., "shall be pleaded or given in evidence in any court, or admitted in any court to be good, useful, or available in law or equity," unless the paper, &c., on which such draft, &c., shall be made, "shall be stamped or marked with a lawful stamp or mark." This provision is incorporated in stat. 55 *G.* 3. c. 184. by sect. 8. See *Field* v. *Woods*, 7 *A. & E.* 114.

(*b*) 4 *Taunt.* 865.

(*c*) 2 *Stark. Ev.* 772. (2d ed.).

(*d*) 1 *Moo. & R.* 104.

(*e*) *Bayley on Bills*, 80, note (7), (5th ed.). Note (*c*) to *Crosley* v. *Arkwright*, 2 *T. R.* 606.

(*g*) *Bayley on Bills*, 547. note (12), (5th ed.).

(*h*) 2 *Leach, C. C.* 703. (4th ed.).

(*i*) 5 *Esp.* 92.

1838.

KEABLE against PAYNE.

larceny of a letter in which it was inclosed, *Rex* v. *Pooley* (a); and generally for a collateral purpose, *Gregory* v. *Fraser* (b). [*Williams* J. referred to *Rex* v. *Gillson* (c).] Here the gist of the plaintiff's case was, that the instrument was not available. In *Rex* v. *Freeth* (d) it was held that to obtain goods by a forged note was obtaining under false pretences, though the note was void on the face of it. Then, as to the evidence, the question was for the jury. *Shelley* v. *Ford* (e) shews that, if *Mann* contemplated fraud, the defendant's ignorance would be no answer to this action (g). (They then went into the evidence.)

Kelly and *Gunning*, contrà. The attempt is, not to invalidate a fraudulent transaction, but to defeat a bonâ fide purchase by the defendant; for there was no evidence to shew that the defendant was a party to *Mann*'s fraud, even if *Mann* did in fact commit any fraud, which was not satisfactorily proved. (The observations on the weight of evidence are omitted.) The argument for the admissibility of this evidence would tend to a virtual repeal of the Stamp Act. The cases respecting forgery rest on this principle, that a party shall not avoid punishment for a forgery by committing it on unstamped paper: that is supported by the general policy of the law; and the same observation applies to cases of usury.

(a) 3 *B. & P.* 310.; see p. 316. *S. C. Russ. & R. C. C. R.* 31.

(b) 3 *Campb.* 454. (c) 1 *Taunt.* 95. (d) *Russ. & R. C. C. R.* 127.

(e) 5 *C. & P.* 313. See *Earl of Bristol* v. *Wilsmore*, 1 *B. & C.* 514.; *Peer* v. *Humphrey*, 2 *A. & E.* 495.

(g) It was stated that the jury, in answer to a question from the learned Judge, expressed their opinion that the defendant was aware of the way in which the property had been obtained; his lordship, however, intimating that he thought the case complete against the defendant without that fact, if *Mann* knew that the cheque would be dishonoured.

[*Patteson*

1838.

KEABLE against PAYNE.

[*Patteson* J. *Rex* v. *Fowle* (*a*) shews that this note would have been admissible upon an indictment of *Mann* for the fraud.] But here it is sought to make it evidence against a third party. Even in a criminal case against *Mann*, if he were indicted for obtaining the property under false pretences, the representation charged would be, that the money was at the banker's; and then the giving the cheque would be of the essence of the crime charged, and the case would fall under the principle already stated: if the indictment were for larceny on the supposition that the taking was animo furandi (as in *Rex* v. *Semple* (*b*)), it does not seem clear that the cheque would be admissible to prove the intention. [*Littledale* J. The want of stamp might be part of the fraud.] In *Nash* v. *Duncombe* (*c*) the evidence was only received doubtfully, and subject to the objection; which could not be afterwards raised, because the verdict was against the party in whose favour the evidence was given. *Rex* v. *Gillson* (*d*) is a very strong case. There an unstamped policy of insurance was held not admissible in support of an indictment for burning a house to defraud the insurer: the objection arose on stat. 10 *Ann.* *c.* 19. *s.* 105. (*e*), of which the material words are similar to those of stat. 31 *G.* 3. *c.* 25. *s.* 19. *Bayley* J. ruled (*g*) that, on an indictment against a clerk for embezzlement, effected by obtaining money due to the master, an unstamped receipt given by the clerk to the debtor was not admissible.

(*a*) 4 *C.* & *P.* 592.

(*b*) 1 *Leach, C. C.* 420. 4th ed.

(*c*) 1 *Moo.* & *R.* 104.

(*d*) 1 *Taunt.* 95.

(*e*) Perpetuated, and applied to policies of insurance, by stat. 10 *Ann.* *c.* 26. *s.* 73.

(*g*) 2 *Stark. Ev.* 772. (2d ed.).

Lord

1838.

KEABLE against PAYNE.

Lord DENMAN C. J. I think what was done at the trial was right. As to the question of the stamp, there is no authority against the reception of the evidence. It is not contended that the words of the statute are in all cases to be literally adhered to. Here the plaintiff had to shew that *Mann* had committed a fraud: it is, consequently, as if *Mann* had been on his trial for obtaining the cattle under false pretences. The case, therefore, falls under the rule which prevails in cases of usury: the unstamped paper may be given in evidence to shew the criminal act. On the other point, the rule cannot be supported. (The part of the judgments relating to the weight of evidence is omitted.)

LITTLEDALE J. I am of the same opinion. The cheque was produced to shew that *Mann* had committed the fraud. Although stat. 31 *G. 3. c. 25. s.* 19. uses the words "available in law or equity," yet these must be understood with some qualification, as indeed is admitted by the counsel who support the rule, in the cases of forgery and usury. They contend, however, that the evidence is receivable only where the instrument is the immediate subject of prosecution. But, the question here being whether *Mann* committed the fraud, the act of *Mann* is admissible in evidence, though it consist in writing on unstamped paper.

PATTESON J. I think this cheque was properly received in evidence. I cannot recognise the distinction for which Mr. *Kelly* and Mr. *Gunning* contend. Whether against the person accused of the fraud, or a third party, the principle must be the same, if the question turn on the fact of fraud. If it were necessary, in a civil

1838.

KEABLE *against* PAYNE.

civil action, to shew that there had been a felony, or an obtaining by false pretences, the evidence would be admissible as if the case were that of an indictment for the felony or fraud: and it is conceded that here the giving the cheque was an ingredient in the fraud. There is indeed one qualification of this principle: an admission by *Mann* would not be evidence against this defendant. On an indictment for receiving goods feloniously taken, the felony must be proved: and neither a judgment against the felon, nor his admission, would be evidence against the receiver. In such a case (*a*) I once admitted evidence of a plea of guilty by the taker: and it was held that I did wrong. Here it is clear, from all the authorities, that, if *Mann* had been indicted, the cheque would have been admissible. In *Rex* v. *Gillson* (*b*) the validity of the instrument was essential to the offence charged: if the policy did not bind, there was no fraud upon the assurer. Here the validity of the instrument is no point in the plaintiff's case.

WILLIAMS J. The cheque was an ingredient in the fraud, whether stamped or not: it is as if the fraud had been committed by giving a flash note.

Rule discharged.

(*a*) Perhaps *Rex* v. *Turner*, 1 *Moo. C. C. R.* 347.; where, however, the evidence received was of a confession.

(*b*) 1 *Taunt.* 95.

1838.

The QUEEN *against* The Guardians of the DOLGELLY Union.

On motion for a mandamus to guardians of a poor law union, to admit *J.* to the office of their clerk, it appeared that *J.* and *R.* had been candidates for the clerkship, but that, at a meeting of the persons acting as guardians to elect, *R.* had the majority of votes, and was declared elected. *J.* suggested, as a ground for the rule, that several of the guardians whose votes gave *R.* the majority were themselves not duly elected.

Assuming that the Court would grant a mandamus to admit to this office,

Held, that they would not grant it for the purpose of scrutinizing the elections of guardians who had voted. And that if this enquiry were open, the Court could not grant the writ, since it did not appear who were the proper persons to make a return; and, if the guardians de facto might make it, they might also appoint a clerk.

The Court will not take judicial notice of the rules made by the Poor law commissioners, for the government of a union, under stat. 4 & 5 *W.* 4. *c.* 76. *s.* 15.

A RULE nisi was obtained in *Easter* term, 1837, for a mandamus to the guardians of the poor of the *Dolgelly* Union, in *Merionethshire*, to swear in *John Jones* as their clerk. By the affidavits in support of the rule, it appeared that the board of guardians, acting under stat. 4 & 5 *W.* 4. *c.* 76., and constituted by order of the Poor Law Commissioners, partly stated in the affidavits, met on *February* 22d, 1837, for the appointment of officers, when *John Jones* and *Richard Jones* were respectively proposed to fill the office of clerk to the guardians; and, votes being taken, *Richard Jones* was declared to be elected, having a majority of one. The affidavits represented that four of the guardians who voted for *Richard Jones* had not been legally chosen at the election of guardians in *January* 1837. There were statements on this subject, applying to each of the cases severally. In last *Easter* term (a),

R. V. Richards shewed cause. By analogy to the practice in corporation cases, the Court will not, on this motion for a mandamus, investigate the title of electors who have for some time exercised the office of guardians;

(a) *May* 8th. Before Lord *Denman* C. J., *Littledale*, *Patteson*, and *Coleridge* Js.

1838.

The QUEEN *against* The Guardians of the DOLGELLY Union.

guardians; especially where objections are taken to the title of each individual. The Court, last year, refused to grant a quo warranto information for the purpose of scrutinizing the election of guardians under stat. 4 & 5 *W.* 4. *c.* 76. (*a*). [Lord *Denman* C. J. to *Jervis*, who supported the rule. Is there any authority for our entering into this question, the office of clerk being full, and no public inconvenience being occasioned by the election?]

Jervis, contrà. In *Rex* v. *The Trustees of Cheshunt Roads* (*b*) this Court made a rule absolute for a mandamus to admit to the office of clerk to turnpike trustees; and the decision was grounded on the valuable and lasting nature of the office. And in 1829 they granted a rule nisi for a mandamus in respect of a similar office, in *Rex* v. *The Trustees of the Hincksey Roads* (*c*), and, on cause being shewn, directed a feigned issue to try the right. As to the title of the guardians, in a corporation case each separate title may be tried by a distinct information: here the titles can be examined only in the mode now proposed. [*Littledale* J. In that mode you might carry on the investigation six deep; for if you examined the title of the electors you might examine that of the persons who elected them, and so on.] That, if proposed, would be an inconvenience; on the other hand, it is hard that a person should be deprived of a valuable office, without opportunity of trying the right. Magistrates are guardians ex officio. Suppose persons

(*a*) *In the Matter of the Aston Union*, 6 *A.* & *E.* 784. *Rex* v. *Ramsden*, 3 *A.* & *E.* 456. was relied upon.

(*b*) 5 *B.* & *Ad.* 438. (*c*) 5 *B.* & *Ad.* 439, note (*a*).

interfere

1838.

The QUEEN *against* The Guardians of the DOLGELLY Union.

interfere in the election, pretending to be magistrates, who are not so: cannot that be inquired into? [Lord *Denman* C. J. I am unwilling to say that, where a party is de facto elected and acting, another shall be admitted to allege that the electors were not qualified. On the other hand, it is difficult to say that, if strangers were to interfere as electors, there should be no inquiry.] (*R. V. Richards*. Strangers would not be de facto exercising any office.) [*Patteson* J. Stat. 4 & 5 *W.* 4. *c.* 76. says nothing of a clerk to the guardians. We know nothing of the office without the order of the commissioners. That should have been brought before us.] The rules and orders of the commissioners are made under the direct authority of the statute (*a*). [*Patteson* J. We cannot take judicial notice of them.] The office is shewn to exist; the Court will not presume that it is irregularly created. [*Patteson* J. The order of the commissioners, if produced, might take away the very ground of the application. It might direct that the guardians de facto for the time should elect the clerk. *Coleridge* J. You are not entitled to assume that this is a general order.] The applicant then asks for time to bring the order before the Court. [Lord *Denman* C. J. We are not disposed to give any facilities for trying the question in this way. It might perhaps be decided on an issue, upon terms.]

The rule was, however, enlarged. In this term (*June* 7th), no communication having in the mean time been made to the Court,

(*a*) 4 & 5 *W.* 4. *c.* 76. *s.* 15.

1838.

The QUEEN against The Guardians of the DOLGELLY Union.

Lord DENMAN C. J. delivered judgment as follows.

This was an application for a mandamus to the guardians of the *Dolgelly* Union to admit *John Jones* as their clerk, and permit him to perform the duties of that office. Another clerk, *Richard Jones*, has been admitted and is acting; but the applicant says that *R. Jones* was not duly elected. There was a contest and a poll; and, though *R. Jones* was returned, *John Jones* asserts that he had the majority of good votes, and ought to have been returned.

In effect, therefore, it is proposed to set on foot a scrutiny of all the votes given in the election of the guardians, in the shape of a mandamus to admit their own servant to a ministerial office. No precedent for such a course was quoted: the inconvenience of thus unravelling the rights of voters in an antecedent stage would be very great: and we think it ought not to be done.

There is a preliminary difficulty of no light importance. If we sent the writ, who must make the return? That question must be answered before the return can be made; yet the object of the proceeding itself is to settle that question. If the guardians de facto are to make the return, that must be because they are in possession, and competent to do the duties attached to their office. One of these is to appoint a clerk; they have done so, and the public suffer no inconvenience from a vacancy of the office. The rule must be discharged.

Rule discharged.

Raphael and Illidge, Esquires, *against* Goodman.

Friday, June 8th.

To an action by a sheriff against an execution creditor, on a bond of indemnity for seizing goods under a fi. fa., defendant pleaded that the bond was obtained from defendant, *by plaintiff and others in collusion with him*, by fraud and misrepresentation: Held, that defendant supported this plea by proof that the sheriff's officer, who executed the process, obtained the bond by fraud and misrepresentation, though the plaintiff did not appear to have been personally cognizant of any part of the transaction.

DEBT by the sheriff of *Middlesex* on a bond.

The defendant set out the condition on oyer. It recited that the sheriff, by virtue of a fi. fa. against the goods of *John Hayward* at the suit of defendant, had seized goods as of *J. H.*, and that he had received notice that they were not *J. H.*'s goods; it further recited that doubt had arisen whether *J. H.* had become bankrupt; that defendant insisted that the goods were *J. H.*'s and liable to be seized under the writ and that *J. H.* had not become bankrupt nor done any act which could affect defendant's right under the writ; and that defendant had requested the sheriff to proceed to a sale, and pay him the proceeds, and had proposed to indemnify the sheriff, to which the sheriff had agreed: then followed a condition for indemnifying the sheriff. Defendant then pleaded, 1. and 2. Pleas which led to issues of fact; 3. That the bond "was obtained from defendant, *by the said plaintiffs and others in collusion with them*, by fraud, covin, and misrepresentation," and was therefore void. Replication to the third plea, that the bond "was obtained fairly and honestly by the plaintiffs, and not by fraud," &c., in manner &c. Similiter.

On the trial before *Coleridge* J. at the *Middlesex* sittings after *Michaelmas* term, 1836, a verdict was found for the plaintiff on the issues arising on the first two pleas. With respect to the issue on the third, it appeared that, on 24th *December*, 1834, *Levy*, a sheriff's

 office

1838.

RAPHAEL *against* GOODMAN.

officer, employed by the plaintiffs, seized the goods under the fi. fa., and told the execution creditor, the present defendant, that he had left a man in possession. In fact, however, *Levy*, on the same day, quitted possession of the goods, receiving money from *Hayward* for so doing, and did not resume possession till after 30th *December*, on which day *Hayward* became bankrupt, and notice of the fiat was immediately served on *Levy*. *Levy*, being afterwards called upon by the present defendant to sell the goods, refused to do so, unless the defendant would give the sheriff an indemnity bond, telling the defendant, at the same time, that he, *Levy*, had constantly kept possession. Under these circumstances the bond in question was given, the goods sold, and the proceeds paid to the defendant. Afterwards, the assignees of *Hayward* recovered against the sheriff. The counsel for the plaintiffs contended that the issue on the third plea could be supported only by shewing that they were personally parties to the fraud. The learned Judge left to the jury, whether *Levy* had obtained the bond by fraud; and, upon their finding in the affirmative, directed a verdict for the defendant on the third issue, reserving leave to move to enter a verdict for the plaintiffs. In *Hilary* term, 1837, Sir *F. Pollock* obtained a rule accordingly.

Thesiger and *Ball* now shewed cause. The sheriff is answerable for the fraud of his officer; and here the sheriff is endeavouring to put in suit a bond obtained through that very fraud, and is thus adopting the officer's act. It will be said that the plea should have stated the fraud to have been committed by the officer; but that really leaves the question as before; for, if the sheriff

is

is liable for the officer's fraud, or loses his right of suing on the bond obtained by the officer's fraud, the reason must be that the law so far fixes the sheriff with the fraud of his officer, and treats the fraud as if committed by the sheriff himself. The civil liability of the sheriff for the acts of all those employed by him "has been carried so far, that a return made by a sheriff that the person arrested was rescued out of the custody of the bailiff has been held to be bad; the return must be that the person was rescued out of *his* custody;" per *Buller* J. in *Woodgate* v. *Knatchbull* (*a*). If it be said that the sheriff is not to suffer the imputation of misconduct from acts to which he is not personally a party, the answer is that he does not so suffer, and the issue is never so understood. Under stat. 23 *H.* 6. *c.* 10. it may be pleaded that a sheriff's bond was taken for ease and favour; yet that might be termed an imputation on the sheriff. In fact, however, this is manifestly the action of the sheriff's officer himself, from whom the sheriff always takes security. In *Woodgate* v. *Knatchbull* (*b*) it was held that, under stat. 29 *Eliz. c.* 4., the sheriff was liable even to a penalty for excessive fees taken by his officer, though the sheriff himself was not personally cognisant of the transaction. In *Sturmy* v. *Smith* (*c*) it was held that the sheriff was liable to a suit by a common informer, under stat. 44 *G.* 3. *c.* 13. *ss.* 1, 4., for the act of his officer in discharging a seaman arrested by him. The sheriff places the officer in a situation of trust; and therefore the loss should fall on the sheriff, according to the principle of *Fitzherbert* v. *Mather* (*d*), and

(*a*) 2 *T. R.* 156.
(*b*) 2 *T. R.* 148.
(*c*) 11 *East*, 25.
(*d*) 1 *T. R.* 12.

1838.

RAPHAEL *against* GOODMAN.

Doe dem. Willis v. *Martin* (*a*). In *Laicock's Case* (*b*) it is said the sheriff shall be fined and amerced (though not imprisoned or indicted) for any default in the execution of the office, though it be by the neglect *or fraud* of the under-sheriff; and there is no distinction in this respect between the under-sheriff and sheriff's officer; *Sanderson* v. *Baker* (*c*). In *Smart* v. *Hutton* (*d*) it was held that trespass lay against a sheriff for an arrest made by his

(*a*) 4 *T. R.* 39. (*b*) *Latch.* 187. *S. C. Noy*, 90.
(*c*) 2 *W. Bl.* 832. *S. C.* 3 *Wils.* 309. (*d*) 2 *N. & M.* 426.

Nov. 22d, 1833.

SMART *against* HUTTON, Esquire.

The sheriff is civilly liable for misconduct of his officer in executing a writ, though the act done be contrary to the express terms of the writ; as if he take the person under a fi. fa.

THIS was an action against the sheriff of *Lincoln* for false imprisonment, tried at the *Lincoln* Spring assizes, 1833, before *Denman* C. J. The facts were, that a writ of fi. fa. had been directed to the sheriff, whose officer, *Solomon Woodroffe*, attempted to levy on the plaintiff's goods. The produce being insufficient to satisfy the debt, *Woodroffe* took the plaintiff himself, and lodged him in the county gaol, from which he was afterwards released by order of the defendant. The Lord Chief Justice thought that the conduct of *Woodroffe* was such an excess of authority that the sheriff could not be affected by his act as in ordinary cases; and the plaintiff was nonsuited. In the ensuing term, *Humfrey* moved for a new trial, and cited *Ackworth* v. *Kempe* (1 *Doug.* 40.); *Parrot* v. *Mumford* (2 *Esp. N. P. C.* 585.); *Sanderson* v. *Baker* (2 *W. Bl.* 832. 3 *Wils.* 309.); *Woodgate* v. *Knatchbull* (2 *T. R.* 148.). The case being now called on, and counsel in opposition to the rule not being present,

Humfrey supported the rule, and cited, in addition to the above authorities, the judgment of *Taunton* J. in *Balme* v. *Hutton* (9 *Bing.* 483, 484.). [*Denman* C. J. The Court is entirely with you at present; but we will hear what counsel can say on the other side. *Parke* J. The sheriff and his officer are one as to every thing done under the writ. *Taunton* J. It is sufficient that the officer acted under colour of the writ.]

Adams Serjt. afterwards (on the same day) shewed cause, and cited 2 *Roll. Abr.* 552. *Trespass*, (O) pl. 10.; where it is said that, if a man is arrested by the sheriff's bailiffs, and thereupon shews them a supersedeas, and they refuse it, and detain him afterwards in prison, he shall have false imprisonment against the bailiffs and not against the sheriff. [*Parke* J. The sheriff is liable for whatever the bailiff does under colour of

1838.

RAPHAEL *against* GOODMAN.

his officer under a fi. fa.; and *Parke* J. said, "If the sheriff puts into the hand of his officer a writ, he and the officer are to be considered as one person, for every thing the officer does under colour of that writ." Even what the bailiff says is evidence against the sheriff in an action for a false return; *North* v. *Miles* (a). Where the sheriff sues an execution creditor who has colluded with the bailiff, and thereby subjected the sheriff to an action, and verdict against him, there, as between those parties, the act of the bailiff is not the act of the sheriff; *Crowder* v. *Long* (b): but *Bayley* J. said that such a case was an exception to "the general rule," that "the act of the officer is, in point of law, the act of the sheriff."

Sir *F. Pollock* and *Hoggins*, contrà. To fix the sheriff with the fraud of his officer in this case would produce great hardship. The sheriff is compelled to undertake the office. If the plea here had alleged that the sheriff had said so and so, could that be supported by shewing such words uttered by a bailiff? It is admitted that the liability for the acts of the officer does not go so far as to make the sheriff indictable for what the officer does. At the least, the plea should have stated generally that the bond was obtained by fraud; not that it was so obtained by the plaintiffs; but indeed, if the sheriff be liable at all, it would be enough to plead the fraud of the officer according to the fact. In *Fitzherbert* v.

---

of the writ. The officer is delegated by him to execute the writ; and the officer's acts are his: it is as if the sheriff himself delivered the party to the gaoler's custody.]

Per Curiam (*Denman* C. J., *Parke*, *Taunton*, and *Patteson* Js.).

Rule absolute.

(a) 1 *Campb.* 389. (b) 8 *B.* & *C.* 598.

Mather

1838.

RAPHAEL *against* GOODMAN.

Mather (*a*) the point, that the assured was liable for misrepresentations of the party procuring the policy, could not have been raised by pleading a misrepresentation by the assured. The issue here was, whether the plaintiffs had been guilty of a fraud. In *Woodgate* v. *Knatchbull* (*b*) the declaration against the sheriff was supported on the sheriff's own return. *Sturmy* v. *Smith* (*c*) is explainable on the same principle.

Lord DENMAN C. J. There is no doubt that, in all matters relating to the execution, the sheriff's officer is the same as the sheriff; and most especially so where the sheriff seeks to recover on a bond obtained by the officer's fraud. We should be contradicting the plainest principles of law if we authorised a doubt on this point.

LITTLEDALE J. The fraud is committed by the officer; but the sheriff is the person to whom the law looks. He cannot attend personally to all the duties of his office, and therefore employs an officer; but that is for his own convenience. He is himself identified with the officer, as is clear from all the cases, except where, as in *Crowder* v. *Long* (*d*), the party opposed to the sheriff is colluding with the officer.

PATTESON J. This is the clearest case I ever heard discussed. It is contended that, if we do not assent to the argument urged for the plaintiff, we are making one man responsible for the fraud of another. I, on the contrary, think that, if we did assent to it, we should be enabling a sheriff to recover by means of the fraud of his officer.

(*a*) 1 *T. R.* 12.
(*b*) 2 *T. R.* 148.
(*c*) 11 *East*, 25.
(*d*) 8 *B. & C.* 598.

The

1838.

RAPHAEL *against* GOODMAN.

The argument on the language of the plea rests upon a misrepresentation of its meaning. It does not mean, nor does any one suppose it to mean, that the sheriff personally has been guilty of a fraud.

COLERIDGE J. It does not appear to be very strongly disputed that the sheriff is responsible for the fraud of the officer: but the language of the plea is objected to. That objection, however, is answered by the principle which makes the sheriff responsible; namely, that the act of the officer is, according to law and sense, the act of the sheriff. If we upheld such an objection, we should be departing from one of the most sensible of all rules, that a transaction is to be pleaded according to its effect.

Rule discharged.

DOE on the Demise of BRIDGER *against* WHITEHEAD.

Saturday, June 9th.

In ejectment by landlord against tenant, on an alleged forfeiture by breach of a covenant to insure in some office in or near *London*, the omission to insure must be proved by the plaintiff.

It is not sufficient proof of such omission that the defendant, being asked to shew a policy, or receipt for premium, refused (after which the plaintiff accepted rent, and made no further enquiry till the action was commenced), and that the plaintiff gave notice to produce such policy or receipt at the trial, which was not done on demand.

EJECTMENT on a demise of *March* 25th, 1836. Plea, Not Guilty. On the trial before *Littledale* J., at the sittings in *Middlesex* after *Michaelmas* term, 1836, it appeared that the action was brought by a ground landlord against a tenant, on alleged forfeitures by breaches of covenants, in the lease, to repair and to insure against fire in some office in or near *London*. The only evidence for the plaintiff as to the latter breach was that, in *September* 1834, a person acting for the

lessor

1838.

Doe dem. Bridger against Whitehead.

lessor of the plaintiff asked the defendant if the premises were insured, and, if so, in what office, and whether the defendant would shew him the receipt: but the defendant said he would give neither the witness nor any one else any information. Notice was served on the defendant, before the trial, to produce all and every policy or policies of insurance against fire at any time effected by him on the premises in question in any insurance office or offices, and all and every receipts and receipt for the premiums or annual payments on such policy or policies, &c. It appeared that the lease did not contain any covenant to produce such vouchers. On *March* 25th, 1836, the lessor of the plaintiff received rent from the tenant in possession, due at the preceding *Christmas*. This action was commenced on *March* 26th, 1836. The learned Judge left it to the jury to say whether the premises were out of repair on *March* 25th, 1836, the day of the demise in the declaration; and whether they were then uninsured. He observed, as to the want of evidence on the latter point, that, the covenant being to insure in some office in or near *London*, it would be impossible for the landlord to make enquiry at all the offices; and he said that the defendant, when questioned on the subject in *September* 1834, ought to have given the required information. He was proceeding to observe upon the effect of the receipt of rent as a waiver, when the jury interposed and found a verdict for the defendant. In *Hilary* term 1837, *Platt* moved for a new trial, on the ground that no evidence had been given by the defendant of an insurance effected by him; and that it lay on him to furnish that evidence, and not on the landlord to prove the contrary, for the reason given by

1838.

Doe dem. Bridger against Whitehead.

by *Littledale* J. at the trial. He also moved on the ground that the verdict was against the evidence as to non-repair. And he contended that neither breach of covenant had been waived. A rule nisi was granted.

Kelly now shewed cause. The plaintiff founds his action upon a breach of covenant; and he ought to have given at least primâ facie evidence of it; as a formal demand of the policy, and refusal to produce it, since *Christmas* 1835; any breach previous to that time being waived by the receipt of rent. Or he might have proved some inquiry at the insurance offices. It is true that slight evidence would have been suffcent, because the plaintiff's allegation is of a negative kind, and the affirmative is easily proved on the other side. But here none was given. And this is not a motion to set aside a nonsuit, in which case it would be sufficient to shew that there was some evidence to go to the jury, but an application for a new trial, the jury having found for the defendant; it ought, therefore, to appear satisfactorily that the jury have done wrong.

Platt and *Peacock*, contrà. It would be a very inconvenient rule that the onus of proving non-insurance in a case like this should lie upon the plaintiff. The tenant, and not the landlord, must be expected to know where the insurance was effected. The premises were to be insured in some office in or near *London*. Was the plaintiff to subpœna clerks from all the offices to shew that no insurance was effected? [*Patteson* J. No doubt, if he began such a course of proof, he must go through with it. Lord *Denman* C. J. It is easy to avoid such a difficulty by a clause in the lease requiring the

1838.

Doe dem. Bridger against Whitehead.

the tenant to produce a policy when called for.] Notice was given to produce the policy and receipts for premium at the trial; and this was not done. [*Patteson* J. You received the rent to *Christmas* 1835. The inference was that you were satisfied of the premises having been insured in the mean time. After that, you should have demanded again to see the policy and receipts.] The refusal to shew them in 1834 was evidence of non-insurance at that time. The receipt of rent afterwards might be a waiver of forfeiture, but was not an acknowledgment that the insurance had been effected. And the covenant, having been broken, might be presumed to continue so, in the absence of proof to the contrary. As to the onus of proof, the case is substantially the same as if the declaration had been for breach of covenant, and the plea had alleged performance. In that case the defendant must have averred, and proved, that he insured in a particular office. [*Patteson* J. At any rate his plea there would have consisted of an affirmative, which would have cast the onus of proof on him.] Where the proposition relied upon by a plaintiff is in fact a negative, and the defendant contests it, the burden of proof must fall upon the defendant. Lord *Mansfield*, in *Spieres* v. *Parker* (a), treats this as a matter of course in the instance there referred to, of actions on the game laws. The Court was divided on this point in *Rex* v. *Stone* (b); but in *Rex* v. *Turner* (c) it was clearly settled that, in a prosecution on the game laws, where want of qualification is alleged, possession of it must be proved by the defendant; and *Bayley* J. said, " I have always understood it to be a general rule, that if a negative averment

(a) 1 *T. R.* 141. (b) 1 *East*, 640. (c) 5 *M. & S.* 206.

be

1838.

Doe dem. Bridger against Whitehead.

be made by one party, which is peculiarly within the knowledge of the other, the party within whose knowledge it lies, and who asserts the affirmative is to prove it, and not he who avers the negative." In *The Apothecaries' Company* v. *Bentley* (a), which was a penal action for practising as an apothecary without a certificate, *Abbott* C. J. held that the defendant was bound to prove his qualification. That was a stronger case than the present or those on the game laws, because the plaintiffs could easily have furnished the negative proof.

Lord DENMAN C. J. This was an action of ejectment, founded on alleged breaches of covenants to insure and to repair. There was no direct proof of non-insurance, but the defendant, when called upon at the trial to produce a policy, after notice, did not do so. I think that quite insufficient. Then it is said that the fact of insurance ought to have been proved by the defendant. I am not of that opinion. The estate was vested in him; and his title could be got rid of only by proving a forfeiture. I do not dispute the cases on the game laws which have been cited; but there the defendant is, in the first instance, shewn to have done an act which was unlawful unless he was qualified; and then the proof of qualification is thrown upon the defendant. Here the plaintiff relies on something done or permitted by the lessee, and therefore takes upon himself the burden of proving that fact. The proof may be difficult where the matter is peculiarly within the defendant's knowledge; but that does not

(a) *Ry. & M.* 159.

vary

1838.

DOE dem. BRIDGER *against* WHITEHEAD.

vary the rule of law. And the landlord might have had a covenant inserted in the lease, to insure at a particular office, or to produce a policy when called for, on pain of forfeiture. If he will make the conditions of his lease such as render the proof of a breach very difficult, the Court cannot assist him. As to non-repair, the question was for the jury, and the learned Judge expresses no dissatisfaction.

LITTLEDALE J. In the cases cited, as to game, the defendant had to bring himself within the protection of the statutes which prohibited any person from using an engine to destroy game, or from having it in his possession, unless properly qualified or authorised. A like observation applies to *The Apothecaries' Company* v. *Bentley* (a). But here, where a landlord brings an action to defeat the estate granted to a lessee, the onus of proof ought to lie on the plaintiff. It is true that, if the action had been in covenant, the onus would have lain on the defendant; but that does not shew that it will so lie in a different form of action. As to the notice to produce, the only effect of such a notice is that the party serving it may give secondary evidence of the document if it is not produced. If he does not think proper to do so, there is no further result. As to the non-repair, I think there is no ground for a rule.

PATTESON and WILLIAMS Js. concurred.

Rule discharged.

(a) *Ry. & M.* 159.

BLUNT, Gent., One, &c., *against* HESLOP.

Saturday, June 9th.

Under stat. 2 *G.* 2. *c.* 23. *s.* 23., which directs that no attorney shall commence an action for his fees until *the expiration of one month or more after* he shall have delivered his bill, the month is to be reckoned exclusively of the days on which the bill is delivered and the action brought.

ASSUMPSIT for business done as an attorney. Plea (among others not material here) that the action was commenced before the expiration of a month after delivery of the bill. Issue thereon. At the trial before Lord *Denman* C. J., at the sittings in *London* after last *Michaelmas* term, it appeared that the action was brought for charges within stat. 2 *G.* 2. *c.* 23. *s.* 23.; that the bill was delivered on *January* 12th, 1836; and that the action was commenced on the ensuing 9th of *February*. The defendant's counsel therefore contended that the plaintiff had proceeded before the time prescribed by the statute. The Lord Chief Justice reserved the point; and the plaintiff had a verdict on this issue. *Alexander*, in the next term, moved for a rule to shew cause why a verdict should not be entered for the defendant on this issue; insisting that, on a right construction of the statute, a lunar (*a*) month ought to elapse between the days of delivering the bill and commencing an action, exclusive of both days. *The Court* granted a rule nisi.

Channell now shewed cause. The words of stat. 2 *G.* 2. *c.* 23. *s.* 23. are, that no attorney or solicitor shall commence any action for the recovery of any fees, charges, or disbursements at law or in equity, "until the expiration of one month or more after such attorney

(*a*) *Hurd* v. *Leach*, 5 *Esp. N. P. C.* 168.

1838.

BLUNT against HESLOP.

or solicitor respectively shall have delivered unto the party or parties to be charged therewith, or left for him, her or them, at his, her or their dwelling house or last place of abode, a bill" &c. Here the bill was delivered after the expiration of a month, if the month be taken to include the 12th of *January*, and not the 9th of *February*. The general rule is that, where time is computed *from an act done*, the day of doing the act is included; *Castle* v. *Burditt* (*a*) (which is nearly in point, for the delivery of a bill is in the nature of a notice of action), *Glassington* v. *Rawlins* (*b*), *Rex* v. *Adderley* (*c*). A distinction was indeed introduced in *Lester* v. *Garland* (*d*). Sir *W. Grant*, Master of the Rolls, there seemed to approve of the suggestion made at the bar, that, where the day is to be included, the act done is "an act, to which the party, against whom the time runs, is privy." Here that party is so, unless it can be said that the client is not privy to the delivery of the bill because it may be left at his dwelling house or last place of abode. But the same argument would apply to a notice of action; yet in that case the day is included. In *Pellew* v. *The Hundred of Wonford* (*e*) the act, or event (and Sir *W. Grant* puts an event on the same footing as an act), was a fire; and the day was excluded, partly, it seems, on the principle adverted to in *Lester* v. *Garland* (*d*), that the party to be affected was not privy to the occurrence. *Bayley* J., in *Hardy* v. *Ryle* (*g*), recognises that principle, and cites from Sir *W. Grant* the instance of a notice of action among those in which the day should be included. In *Ex parte Farquhar* (*h*),

(*a*) 3 *T. R.* 623.
(*b*) 3 *East*, 407.
(*c*) 2 *Doug.* 463.
(*d*) 15 *Ves.* 248.
(*e*) 9 *B. & C.* 134.
(*g*) 9 *B. & C.* 603.
(*h*) *Mont. & Mac.* 7.

which

1838.

BLUNT *against* HESLOP.

which turned upon the words of stat. 6 *G.* 4. *c.* 16. *s.* 81., rendering conveyances and contracts by a bankrupt valid, if "made and entered into more than two calendar months before the date and issuing of the commission," Sir *John Leach*, Vice-Chancellor, held that one of the days must be included; and the Lord Chancellor (Lord *Lyndhurst*) confirmed that ruling. That case was recognised and acted upon by this Court in *Godson* v. *Sanctuary* (*a*). There is indeed a late case, *Webb* v. *Fairmaner* (*b*), in which the Court of Exchequer decided that, goods being sold "to be paid for in two months," the day of the contract was excluded; but neither *Ex parte Farquhar* (*c*) nor *Godson* v. *Sanctuary* (*a*) was noticed there; nor was the criterion of privity referred to. The case seems hardly reconcilable with former decisions.

Alexander and *Butt* contrà. The words of the statute here ("the expiration of one month or more after" &c.) imply exclusion. It may have been properly held that one day should be included, where either the words prescribing the time have been quite general, as in *Rex* v. *Goodenough* (*d*), or the direction has been that the thing should be done "within" a certain time (*e*). But here the words "or more" are equivalent to "at least," which has been held to operate exclusively; *Zouch* v. *Empsey* (*g*), *Regina* v. *The Justices of Shropshire* (*h*). The cases of *Castle* v. *Burditt* (*i*) and

(*a*) 4 *B.* & *Ad.* 255.

(*b*) Reported since this argument, 3 *Mee.* & *W.* 473.

(*c*) *Mont.* & *Mac.* 7.

(*d*) 2 *A.* & *E.* 463. *S. C.*, as *Rex* v. *The Justices of Cumberland*, 4 *N.* & *M.* 378.

(*e*) See *Rex* v. *Adderley*, 2 *Doug.* 463.

(*g*) 4 *B.* & *Ald.* 522.

(*h*) Antè, p. 173.

(*i*) 3 *T. R.* 623.

 Glassington

1838.

BLUNT *against* HESLOP.

Glassington v. *Rawlins* (*a*) cannot any longer be considered as furnishing a general rule on this subject; the authority of the first was questioned by *Parke* B. in *Webb* v. *Fairmaner* (*b*). In *Watson* v. *Pears* (*c*), where a patent was to be enrolled "within one calendar month next and immediately after the date thereof," which was *May* 10th, an enrolment on *June* 10th was held to be in time, the month including that day, and not *May* 10th. *Pellew* v. *The Hundred of Wonford* (*d*) and *Hardy* v. *Ryle* (*e*) are in favour of excluding the day of the act or event. As to the criterion of privity; in *Lester* v. *Garland* (*g*) the Master of the Rolls expressly declined laying down any general rule; but, if the reckoning of time were to depend, as was there suggested, on the privity of that person against whom the time is to run, the plaintiff here would not be entitled to recover, for no privity appears between him and his client as to the delivery of the bill. The authority of *Ex parte Farquhar* (*h*) must be considered as shaken, at least, by *Webb* v. *Fairmaner* (*b*), which, if correctly decided, must determine the present case. The reasonableness of the defendant's construction here will be apparent, if it be supposed that the statute had given two days only instead of a month for bringing the action. Might the action, in that case, have been commenced the next day but one after delivering the bill? The object of stat. 2 *G.* 2. *c.* 23. *s.* 23. was that the client should have due time to examine the charges, and take advice upon them; *Brooks* v. *Mason* (*i*): the con-

(*a*) 3 *East*, 407.
(*b*) 3 *Mee.* & *W.* 473.
(*c*) 2 *Camp.* 294.
(*d*) 9 *B.* & *C.* 134.
(*e*) 9 *B.* & *C.* 603.
(*g*) 15 *Ves.* 248.
(*h*) *Mont.* & *Mac.* 7.
(*i*) 1 *H. Bl.* 290.

struction

struction which lengthens the time is most agreeable to this intention.

Lord DENMAN C. J. I do not see how it is possible to give the full benefit of this statute without saying that there shall be, before the action is commenced, twenty-eight days, and so many hours over as there may happen to be of the day on which the act takes place, after it is performed.

LITTLEDALE J. The words being "one month or more," we must suppose that the client was intended to have a full month after the delivery of the bill.

PATTESON J. Whatever may be the case where the thing is to be done "within" such a time after an act done, Mr. *Alexander's* construction is correct here, where the action is not to be brought "until the expiration of one month or more after" the delivery of the bill.

WILLIAMS J. concurred.

Rule absolute for entering a nonsuit (*a*).

(*a*) A rule in this form was agreed upon for reasons which it is not material to state.

1838.

Saturday, June 9th.

Josiah Thomas Poole and David Charles Poole *against* Warren.

Defendant, in an action for double value under stat. 4 G. 2. c. 28. s. 1., had notice to produce the original notice to quit, but refused. Plaintiff then produced and proved a copy, by which it appeared that there was an attesting witness. Held, that the attesting witness need not be called.

K., being beneficially interested in the reversion, joined with the trustee, who was legally entitled, in mortgaging it to plaintiff; and K., by the mortgage deed, with the approbation of plaintiff, testified by plaintiff's executing the deed, appointed G. to be receiver, agent, and attorney of K., to demand and collect rents, to adjust accounts, to sue or distrain for rent, give notice to quit, and eject on refusal, and to do all that K. could have done if the deed had not been made. K., the trustees, and plaintiff, executed the deed. Held, that G. was an agent lawfully authorised to give the notice required by the statute.

DEBT. The declaration stated that defendant, before and at the time of giving the notice and making the demand after mentioned, held a messuage, &c., as tenant thereof to plaintiffs for the remainder of a certain term of years, viz. seven years ending on 25th *June* 1834, which term and tenancy then ended, at a certain yearly rent, viz. the yearly rent of 180*l*., payable &c., the reversion belonging to the plaintiffs; and thereupon, and whilst the defendant so held, viz. on 24th *March* 1834, and oftentimes afterwards, viz. upon the expiration of the said term and tenancy, plaintiffs gave notice in writing to defendant, and in writing demanded of him and required him to deliver up possession of the messuage, &c., to plaintiffs, viz. on the determination and ending of the said term and tenancy: yet defendant did not on the determination, &c., deliver up the possession to plaintiffs according to the notice and demand, but neglected &c., and wilfully held over the said &c., for a long time after the determination and ending of the said term as aforesaid, and after the said notice and demand, viz. from thence until and upon 18th *August* 1835; during all which time the defendant wrongfully and wilfully kept the plaintiffs out of the possession &c., they during all that time being entitled to possession, contrary to the statute, &c. Averment, that

that the tenements holden over were of great yearly value, viz. the yearly value of 200*l.* And thereby, and by force of the statute, the defendant became liable to pay to the plaintiffs a large sum, viz. 400*l.*, being at the rate of double the yearly value &c.

The first plea led to a demurrer. Plea 2. That defendant held over the said tenements under a fair claim of title to hold the same, and not contumaciously: verification. Replication, that defendant wrongfully, wilfully, and contumaciously held over, without any fair claim of title &c.: conclusion to the country. Issue thereon. Plea 3. That plaintiffs did not give notice in writing to defendant, nor did they in writing demand of him or require him to deliver up possession of the said messuage, &c., in manner &c.: conclusion to the country. Issue thereon.

On the trial before Lord *Denman* C. J., at the *London* sittings after *Michaelmas* term, 1836, the plaintiffs put in and proved the execution of a deed of 1833, whereby certain trustees, entitled to the legal reversion on the defendant's term, and *Arthur Keating* and *Ann Keating* his wife, the parties beneficially interested in the reversion, assigned the reversion to the plaintiffs, to secure the payment of 4000*l.* This deed contained the following clause. "And the said *Arthur Keating* and *Ann Keating*, with the approbation of the said *Josiah Thomas Poole* and *David Charles Poole*, testified by their respectively executing these presents, have, and each and every of them hath, nominated, constituted, and appointed, and by these presents do" &c., "*Samuel John Grellett* to be the receiver, agent, and attorney of the said *Arthur K.* and *Ann K.*, for them and their respective executors and administrators, and in their

 respective

1838.

POOLE *against* WARREN.

respective names and stead, to ask, demand, collect, and receive all and singular the rents and profits of the said leasehold" &c., "and premises hereby assigned or expressed so to be, from the present and future tenants and occupiers thereof respectively, or other the person or persons liable to pay the said rents and profits, as and when the same shall from time to time become due, until the said sum of 4000*l.* and all interest thereof shall be fully satisfied and discharged, and for that purpose to settle and adjust all accounts and differences relating to the said rents and profits, and to make such allowances therefrom as occasion shall from time to time require, and, in case of non-payment of the said rents and profits, or any part thereof, to take and use such lawful remedies for the recovery and obtaining payment of the same respectively by action, suit, distress, or otherwise, as shall be thought necessary or expedient, and also to give notice to the tenants or occupiers of the said leasehold premises, or any part of them, to quit possession of the same or of such parts thereof as may be in their respective occupation, and, on refusal or neglect so to do, to eject them respectively therefrom, and also to demise or let," &c., "and further to do, perform, and execute all other matters and things requisite or proper in or concerning the said premises as fully and effectually to all intents and purposes as the said *Arthur K.* and *Ann K.*, their executors, administrators, or assigns respectively could or might themselves do, or might have done if these presents had not been made." The trustees, *Arthur* and *Ann Keating* and the plaintiffs were parties to this deed. The plaintiffs then put in a copy of a notice (having given the defendant notice to produce the original, which he refused at the trial to do),

1838.

POOLE *against* WARREN.

do), and proved the service of the original on the defendant. The notice, according to the copy, was dated *March* 24th, 1834, signed by *Grellett;* and there was one attesting witness to the signature. The notice recited the deed of 1833: and *Grellett* thereby gave notice to yield quiet possession of the premises, on or before 24th *June* 1834, in good condition, &c., "and to do all things necessary in fulfilment of the clauses contained in your lease, or you will be called upon to pay double rent (*a*)." Secondary proof was given of the execution of the original notice; but the attesting witness was not called. The lease to the defendant was not proved. It was shewn that the defendant had held on to the 18th *August* 1835. The annual value was proved to be 200*l.* The defendant's counsel objected, first, that the attesting witness to the notice ought to have been called; secondly, that the authority given to *Grellett* by the deed of 1833 did not entitle him to give the notice required by stat. 4 *G.* 2. *c.* 28. *s.* 1.; thirdly, that, the lease to the defendant not being proved, it did not appear how long the defendant had held over; for that, although the record admitted a lease and a holding over, the dates specified in the declaration were not admitted, so that no more than nominal damages could be recovered. No evidence being given on the part of the defendant, the Lord Chief Justice directed a verdict to be entered for the plaintiffs on the first issue, for 1*s.*, and for the defendant on the second; and likewise reserved leave to move to enter a verdict for the plaintiffs on the second issue, and

(*a*) That this is a sufficient notice for double *value*, see Lord *Mansfield's* judgment in *Doe lessee of Matthews* v. *Jackson*, 1 *Doug.* 175.

to

1838.

Poole *against* Warren.

to increase the damages to 400*l*. In *Hilary* term, 1837, *Kelly* obtained a rule accordingly.

E. V. Williams now shewed cause. First, the attesting witness should have been called. In proving the execution of the original document this would have been necessary; and it has never been decided that less proof will suffice in the case of a copy. The fact of there being such a witness was proved by the plaintiffs themselves. If notice were given to produce a bond, and, on its not being produced, secondary evidence of it were put in, which shewed that there was an attesting witness, then (unless the opposite party had an interest under the bond) the witness must be called. Where a bond has been burnt, the attesting witness must be called, if proof of the execution be essential; *Gillies* v. *Smither* (*a*). In *Call* v. *Dunning* (*b*) it was held that the attesting witness must be produced or accounted for, though the defendant, the obligor of a bond, had admitted the execution, on oath, in an answer in chancery. In *Higgs* v. *Dixon* (*c*) it was held that the general rule applied to a warrant of distress. *Doe dem. Sykes* v. *Durnford* (*d*) has been understood to be a case in which the original notice was produced; but it rather seems, considering the party producing, that there were two duplicate originals: if the notice produced was a copy, the case is a decisive authority here; and, even if the notices were duplicates, there does not appear to be any sound distinction in principle. Indeed the rule must be considered general, though cases

(*a*) 2 *Stark. N. P. C.* 528.
(*b*) 4 *East*, 53.
(*c*) 2 *Stark. N. P. C.* 180.
(*d*) 2 *M. & S.* 62.

may

1838.

Poole against Warren.

may occur, as in other branches of the law of evidence, where evidence which is legally insufficient may be more convincing than that which the law requires. Secondly, *Grellett* was not duly authorised by the plaintiffs. Stat. 4 *G.* 2. *c.* 28. *s.* 1. requires the notice to be given by the landlord or lessor, or reversioner, or "his or their agent or agents thereunto lawfully authorised." *Grellett* here has not the authority of the plaintiffs, who are the legal reversioners, but of the persons assenting, in the character of parties beneficially interested, to the conveyance of the legal interest to the plaintiffs. In *Wilkinson* v. *Colley* (*a*) it was held that a receiver in chancery was an agent lawfully authorised within the statute; but the question in that case seems to have been discussed with reference to the power of the receiver to turn out the tenant; and the authority to give notice, so as to create a liability for double value, appears to have been discussed merely as incidental to that power. Here the term expired by efluxion of time. It is true that the Court there intimated that the law was remedial: but at the end of sect. 1 the double value is called a "penalty." Thirdly, there is nothing to shew how long the defendant held over, unless the days named in the declaration are material. They are not laid traversably. But, if they are, then the notice is bad; for, according to the time named in the declaration, the term expires on the 25th of *June*, whereas the notice requires possession to be given up on the 24th of *June*. In *Cutting* v. *Derby* (*b*) a party gave notice to quit on the last day of the term; and the Court held it good, refusing to take into consideration what *Blackstone* J. termed the fraction

(*a*) 5 *Bur.* 2694. (*b*) 2 *W. Bl.* 1075.

of

1838.

Poole *against* Warren.

of a second. But here the notice required the tenant to quit while a whole day was unexpired.

Kelly (with whom was *Moody*) contrà. First, it was not necessary to produce the attesting witness. [Lord *Denman* C. J. We need not trouble you on that point; *Cooke* v. *Tanswell* (*a*), which has the sanction of *Gibbs* C. J., a very high authority on points of evidence, is decisive in your favour.] Secondly, the authority here is stronger than in *Wilkinson* v. *Colley* (*b*). There the receiver had no authority from the plaintiff, but only from the Court of Chancery; and the receiver was appointed only to take the rents and profits, and to let and set the premises with the approbation of the Master. Here the plaintiffs assent, under seal, to the appointment, which authorises *Grellett* to give notice to quit and to do whatever the *Keatings* could have done. [Lord *Denman* C. J. That case is too strong to be got over; though I thought, at the trial, that many plausible reasons might be suggested for considering a more strict and specific authority to be requisite. *Littledale*, *Patteson*, and *Williams* Js. concurred.] As to the third point, the discrepancy between the notice and declaration was not objected to at the trial.

Lord Denman C. J. I would suggest that the parties agree that the verdict shall stand for the single value.

The counsel for the plaintiffs and defendant assented (*c*).

Verdict to stand accordingly.

(*a*) 8 *Taunt.* 450.

(*b*) 5 *Bur.* 2694.

(*c*) See *Doe dem. Marsack* v. *Read*, 12 *East*, 57. *Doe dem. Earl Manvers* v. *Mizem*, 2 *Mo. & Rob.* 56.

The Queen *against* ——.

Monday, June 11th.

An indictment charging that defendant assaulted *J. S.*, and unlawfully, indecently, &c. (not adding publicly), exposed his person to *J. S.*, with intent to incite *J. S.* to commit an unnatural offence with defendant, is not within st. 7 *G.* 4. *c.* 64. *s.* 23., and the Court cannot give the prosecutor his expenses under that clause.

A BILL was found against the defendant at the *Middlesex* quarter sessions for assaulting *A. B.*, and unlawfully and indecently exposing his person to him, with intent to incite him to commit unnatural practices with the defendant. There was a second count for a common assault. The defendant removed the indictment into this court by certiorari. On the trial before Lord *Denman* C. J., at the *Middlesex* sittings after *Easter* term, 1837, the defendant was acquitted. The Lord Chief Justice made an order directing the Treasurer of *Middlesex* to pay the prosecutor, or his attorney, the costs and expenses of the prosecution and his witnesses: and in *Easter* term the order was made a rule of this Court. In *Trinity* term, 1837, *Joseph Addison* obtained a rule to shew cause why the rule of *Easter* term should not be discharged. By affidavit in answer, it appeared that the prosecutor and witnesses attended the trial on subpœna.

Hughes now shewed cause (*a*). Under stat. 7 *G.* 4. *c.* 64. *s.* 23. any Court before which any prosecutor or other person appears on recognizance or subpœna to prosecute or give evidence against any person indicted of the offences there mentioned, among which is "wilful and indecent exposure of the person," is authorised and empowed to order payment of costs to the pro-

(*a*) Before Lord *Denman* C. J., *Littledale*, *Patteson*, and *Williams* Js.

secutor

1838.

The QUEEN against

secutor and his witnesses. The order being made, this Court will not set it aside, any more than they will review the decision of a judge who has refused to grant the order. [Lord *Denman* C. J. The doubt here is whether I had jurisdiction.] The words of the statute are "any Court." In *Rex* v. *Jeyes* (a), where this Court refused to issue a mandamus commanding the treasurer to pay the costs, *Littledale* J. remarked that, where the prosecutor had removed the indictment by certiorari, the statute had been held not to apply. The reason is that the statute was passed to indemnify parties unable to bear expense; but that such inability is not likely to exist where a party voluntarily removes an indictment to the superior Court. That reason does not apply when the defendant removes the indictment. The language of *Littledale* J., in *Rex* v. *The Treasurer of Exeter* (b), seems indeed to shew that in the case of indictments for felony there is no distinction as to this between removal by the prosecutor and by the defendant: but such a view is not supported by the language of the act, or by authority. (He also referred to *Rex* v. *Chadderton* (c), *Rex* v. *Clifton* (d), *Rex* v. *Johnson* (e).)

Joseph Addison contrà. First, this is not an indictment for an offence within stat. 7 *G.* 4. *c.* 64. *s.* 23. It is not for wilful and indecent exposure of the person, but for an assault with intent to incite to an unnatural crime: the exposure is not the gist of the offence. It is not charged as a public exposure. Nor does the indictment charge

(a) 3 *A.* & *E.* 416. See p. 419.
(b) 5 *Man.* & *R.* 167.
(c) 5 *T. R.* 272.
(d) 6 *T. R.* 344
(e) 4 *M.* & *S.* 515.

an

an "assault with intent to commit felony," or an "attempt to commit felony." Secondly, supposing the offence charged to be within the act, after removal by certiorari the statute ceases to apply. That was decided in *Rex* v. *Richards* (*a*), where no distinction is made as to the party removing. [*Hughes*. In *Archbold's Peel's Acts* (*b*), there is another report of that case, from which it appears that the removal was by the prosecutor, and that the ruling applied to such removals only.] In *Rex* v. *Johnson* (*c*) and *Rex* v. *Oates* (*d*) the prosecutor removed the indictment; and it was held that the statute did not apply. *Rex* v. *Clifton* (*e*) arose on the highway act, 13 *G.* 3. *c.* 78. *s.* 64., where the words are much more general. Thirdly, the prosecutor was not bound over by recognisance, and therefore was not entitled to costs; and, when the prosecutor is not entitled, the witnesses cannot be so (*g*).

Cur. adv. vult.

Lord DENMAN C. J., on a subsequent day of the term (*June* 13th), delivered the judgment of the Court.

We are of opinion that these costs cannot be allowed, the offence not being within the clause of the statute. The rule, therefore, must be made absolute.

Rule absolute.

(*a*) 8 *B.* & *C.* 420. (*b*) Vol. i. p. 214. ed. 3.

(*c*) 1 *Mood. C. C.* 173.

(*d*) Cited in *Rex* v. *Johnson*, 1 *Mo. C. C.* 175.

(*e*) 6 *T. R.* 344.

(*g*) As to this, see *Rex* v. *Jeyes*, 3 *A.* & *E.* 416. v.

1838.

Monday, June 11th.

ROUTLEDGE *against* ABBOTT, NIXON, and HOPE.

Trespass for breaking and entering plaintiff's house and taking and converting his goods, which were described by distinct parcels. Pleas. 1. Not guilty. 2. That the house and goods were not plaintiff's. Issues thereon. 3. That the goods were not plaintiff's, but the goods of a bankrupt; justifying the seizure under a warrant of the commissioners. Replication, traversing the pleas. Issue thereon. Verdict for plaintiff as to the trespasses in entering the house, and taking parcel *A.* of the goods, with 100*l.* damages; for defendant as to parcel *B.* of the goods: Held, that the second and third issues were divisible, and that the verdict must be entered up distributively, according to the special finding, for the purpose of an apportionment of costs according to *Reg. Gen. Hil.* 2 *W.* 4. I. 74.

TRESPASS for breaking and entering plaintiff's dwelling-house, and seizing and taking his goods (many distinct parcels of which, consisting of fixtures and other articles, were described), and converting &c. Pleas, 1. Not Guilty. 2. That the dwelling-house was not plaintiff's, nor were the goods and chattels, or any of them, the goods and chattels of plaintiff, in manner and form &c. Conclusion to the country. 3. As to seizing and taking the goods and chattels in the declaration mentioned, and as to the said converting and disposing thereof, that one *Francis Knowles*, being an inn-keeper, and being indebted &c., became bankrupt: the plea then stated a fiat and proceedings in the bankruptcy, and alleged that the goods and chattels were the goods &c. of *Knowles*, and that the commissioners issued their warrant, by virtue of which, and by force of the statute &c., *Nixon* as messenger, *Hope* as his assistant and by his command, and *Abbott* as official assignee and as assistant to *Nixon* and by his command, at the times when &c., and while the goods and chattels were *Knowles*'s, seized and took the same for the purpose mentioned in the warrant, as they lawfully &c. Verification. Replication, to pleas 1 and 2, joining issue; to plea 3, that the goods and chattels were not *Knowles*'s in manner and form &c., but were the plaintiff's, as stated in the declaration. Issue was joined on this traverse.

On

1838.

ROUTLEDGE against ABBOTT.

On the trial, before Lord *Denman* C. J., at the *London* sittings after *Hilary* term, 1837, it appeared that the house in question was the *City Hotel, King Street, Cheapside;* that, before the alleged trespasses, the plaintiff had taken possession of it for the purpose of carrying on the business of an innkeeper, bringing with him a quantity of furniture (mentioned in the declaration) from *Camberwell;* and that there were in the *City Hotel,* when the plaintiff entered, fixtures and furniture (also mentioned in the declaration) which had been bought for that house. The defendants endeavoured to shew that the plaintiff had been fraudulently set up in the business, to conduct it for *Knowles,* who was an uncertificated bankrupt. The jury found that the house and fixtures, and the goods brought from *Camberwell,* belonged to the plaintiff; and they assessed the damages at 100*l.* The associate indorsed on the jury panel, "Verdict for the plaintiff, damages 100*l.*, costs 40*s.*" The postea was drawn up by the plaintiff, and indorsed on the record as follows:

"That, as to the first issue, the defendants are guilty of the several trespasses within laid to their charge, in manner and form" &c.: "and, as to the second issue, that the dwelling-house in the declaration mentioned was the dwelling-house of the plaintiff, and that the goods and chattels in the declaration also mentioned were the goods and chattels of the plaintiff, in manner and form" &c.: "and, as to the last issue, that the goods and chattels in the declaration mentioned were not, at or during the time in the said declaration mentioned, the goods and chattels of *Francis Knowles,* in manner alleged by the defendants in the last plea; but that, on the contrary thereof, the said goods and chattels were and still are the goods and chattels of the plaintiff

as

1838.

ROUTLEDGE *against* ABBOTT.

as alleged in the declaration: And the jurors assess the damages of the said plaintiff on occasion of the trespasses to 100*l.*"

In *Easter* term, 1837, Sir *F. Pollock* obtained a rule to shew cause why the postea "should not be amended by making the same in conformity with the finding of the jury."

Sir *W. W. Follett* now shewed cause. The plaintiff was entitled to a verdict on each of the issues, and damages for so much loss as he proved. He was not bound to give evidence as to all the articles mentioned in the declaration. Before the New Rules (*a*) the postea would have been entered generally; and they do not warrant such an entry as that now proposed. Under the rule, *Hil.* 2 *W.* 4. I, 74. (*a*), the plaintiff is still to have the costs of those issues on which he has succeeded, and the defendant is to deduct the costs of all issues found for him from the plaintiff's costs, Here the plaintiff succeeded on all the issues. [*Littledale* J. If the chattels are specified in the declaration, and the finding on the issues be not divided, it will appear that all belonged to the plaintiff. Lord *Denman* C. J. The title to some of the things may be bound by the finding, in opposition to the evidence.] If the plaintiff gives proof only that a part of the goods belonged to him, there is no reason that that should be stated on the postea. The question is not one of disputed title. The complaint is that the defendant has done an injury to the plaintiff's chattels; the plaintiff is entitled to recover damages for that injury so far as he proves it: if he proves less than he alleges, the defendant is still guilty of a trespass, to

(*a*) *Reg. Hil.* 2 *W.* 4. I. 74: 3 *B. & Ad.* 385. And see *Reg. Hil.* 4, *General Rules and Regulations*, 7: 5 *B. & Ad.* iv.

which

1838.

ROUTLEDGE *against* ABBOTT.

which that issue relates. The case differs wholly from those in which the plaintiff seeks to recover given chattels, or a particular place. *Doe dem. Errington* v. *Errington* (*a*), where *Coleridge* J. held that an issue was divisible for the purpose of taxing costs, is an instance of the latter kind. In *Prudhomme* v. *Fraser* (*b*) (the authority of which was followed in that case) the single count, upon which issue was taken, raised, in effect, a number of issues, upon distinct libels. If the operation of the New Rules were to make issues divisible in the manner here contended for, the exact number of each description of goods mentioned in the declaration would be material; for, if the precise number of each kind were not proved, there must be a finding for the defendant. [*Patteson* J. mentioned *Bowen* v. *Jenkin* (*c*).] There, in case for disturbance of common, the defendant pleaded that the cattle were his commonable cattle levant and couchant; the replication was, that all the said cattle were not his commonable cattle levant and couchant; and issue was joined on that averment. It had been proposed to prove, at the trial, that the defendant, though entitled to turn some cattle on, had turned on an unreasonable number; but this Court held that on the pleadings, if the defendant had a right to put on any, the number was not material; and that the averment, that *all* the cattle were not levant and couchant, was not equivalent to a new assignment. That is an authority for the plaintiff. Nothing here raises the question whether the defendant took more or fewer chattels; the only matter of inquiry on each of the issues is, whether or not he took the property of the plaintiff. [*Littledale* J. Has not the defendant

(*a*) 4 *Dowl. P. C.* 602.

(*b*) 2 *A. & E.* 645.

(*c*) 6 *A. & E.* 911.

 proved

1838.

ROUTLEDGE *against* ABBOTT.

proved a part of the affirmative proposition in the third issue, which it lay on him to establish, that the goods were *Knowles*'s ?] If he had pleaded that part were *Knowles*'s the plea would have been bad, unless he had let judgment go by default as to the rest. [*Patteson* J. If he had pleaded as to part only, there would have been judgment by default as to the rest.]

Sir *F. Pollock* and *Butt*, contrà. The action is not merely for an injury to the property, but for a conversion. The verdict binds the property, as it would in an action of trover. The chattels here are as completely distinguished as if the action had been in respect of a horse and a bale of goods. In such a case, there might have been a decision in favour of the plaintiff at very little expense as to the one article of claim, and for the defendant at great expense as to the other. Ought the defendant there to pay the whole costs of the issue? *Doe dem. Errington* v. *Errington* (*a*), and *Cox* v. *Thomason* (*b*), *Knight* v. *Brown* (*c*) and *Prudhomme* v. *Fraser* (*d*), there referred to, decide that, where Not Guilty is pleaded to any number of counts, it raises as many issues as there are counts; and where it is pleaded to a single count consisting of several allegations, each of which contains a cause of action, it raises a number of issues equal to the number of such allegations. It is said here that the plaintiff was not obliged to give evidence as to all the parcels of goods specified in the declaration; but in *Phythian* v. *White* (*e*), where the plaintiff declared in trespass quare clausum fregit, and, by her replication, on which the parties went to issue, made

(*a*) 4 *Dowl. P. C.* 602. (*b*) 2 *Cro. & J.* 498. *S. C.* 2 *Tyr.* 411.
(*c*) 1 *Dowl. P. C.* 730. (*d*) 2 *A. & E.* 645.
(*e*) 1 *M. & W.* 216. *S. C. Tyr. & Gr.* 515.

1838.

ROUTLEDGE *against* ABBOTT.

made title to three closes, but at the trial gave evidence as to two only, the Court of Exchequer held that the issue was divisible, and that the verdict, as to one close, must be entered for the defendants. The defendants here will be satisfied to have the verdict entered distributively on the second and third issues; but, if it were important with a view to the amount of costs, they would be entitled to ask that the verdict on those issues should be entered entirely for them, according to *Bowen* v. *Jenkin* (a); for the plaintiff ought to have new assigned. (They were then stopped by the Court.)

Lord DENMAN C. J. The last point we may leave as we find it. On the other my mind is satisfied. The verdict must be entered for the plaintiff generally on the first issue, and distributively for the plaintiff and defendant on the second and third.

LITTLEDALE J. I am of the same opinion. As to a new assignment, none was necessary, the subject-matter being in its nature divisible.

PATTESON and WILLIAMS Js. concurred.

Ordered, that the postea be amended by directing the verdict to be entered according to the finding of the jury, dividing the second and third pleas (b).

(a) 6 *A. & E.* 911.

(b) The postea, as ultimately drawn up, stated the finding of the jury as follows.

As to the first issue, "that the defendants are guilty of the several trespasses within laid to their charge, in manner and form" &c.

As to the second issue, "that the dwelling-house in the declaration mentioned was the dwelling-house of the plaintiff, and that certain of the goods and chattels in the declaration mentioned, to wit two mahogany chests" &c. (setting forth all the articles found to belong to plaintiff),

"were

1838.

ROUTLEDGE *against* ABBOTT.

"were the goods and chattels of the plaintiff, in manner and form as the plaintiff hath within in that behalf alleged; and, as to the residue of the goods and chattels in the declaration mentioned, the jurors" &c. "say that the same were not the goods and chattels of the plaintiff, in manner and form" &c.

As to the last issue, "that divers of the goods and chattels in the declaration mentioned, to wit a feather-bed" &c. (setting forth the articles), "were the goods and chattels of the said *Francis Knowles*, in manner and form as the defendants have within in their last plea in that behalf alleged; and, as to the residue of the goods and chattels in the declaration mentioned, the jurors" &c. "say that the same were not the goods and chattels of the said *Francis Knowles*, in manner and form" &c. "And the said jurors assess the damages of the plaintiff on occasion of the trespasses within-mentioned, over and above his costs," &c. "to 100*l.*" &c.

The defendants obtained, by the Master's allocatur, 57*l.* costs, after deduction of the plaintiff's costs and damages.

Monday, June 11th.

THOMAS *against* DAVIES.

Trespass for breaking and entering plaintiff's house, and taking away a sign-board affixed thereto, and goods not affixed. Pleas. 1. Not guilty. 2. As to the breaking, &c., and taking away the sign-board, that the house and sign-board were not the plaintiff's. 3. As to the same trespasses, that the house and sign-board were defendant's. Replication, that defendant demised the house, with the sign-board affixed, to plaintiff, who entered and was possessed, and that defendant during the continuance of the demise committed the trespasses. Rejoinder, traversing the demise. Issues on the pleas and rejoinder. Verdict for plaintiff on all the issues, with 20*s.* damages.

Held, that the Judge could not certify to deprive plaintiff of costs under stat. 43 *Eliz.* c. 6. *s.* 2., and that the plaintiff might recover full costs without a certificate from the Judge, the case not being within stat. 22 & 23 *Car.* 2. *c.* 9. *s.* 136.

TRESPASS for breaking and entering plaintiff's dwelling-house, and seizing and carrying away a sign board of plaintiff affixed thereto, and other chattels (not affixed), &c. Pleas. 1. Not guilty. 2. As to breaking and entering the dwelling house and carrying away the sign board, that the dwelling house and sign board were not the plaintiff's, in manner and form &c. 3. As to the same trespasses, that before the time when &c. the sign board had been affixed to the dwelling-house, and the same at the time when &c. remained so affixed thereto and was parcel thereof, and that the dwelling-house was then defendant's dwelling-house and freehold: Verification. Replication, joining issue on

the

1838.

THOMAS *against* DAVIES.

the first and second pleas: To the third, that defendant demised the dwelling-house to plaintiff for a year and so on &c., by virtue of which demise plaintiff entered and was possessed &c., until defendant during the continuance of the demise of his own wrong committed the trespasses, &c.: Verification. Rejoinder, traversing the demise. Issue thereon. On the trial before *Coleridge* J., at the *Brecon* Spring assizes, 1837, the plaintiff had a verdict on all the issues, with 20*s.* damages. The learned Judge certified, under stat. 43 *Eliz.* *c.* 6. *s.* 2., to deprive the plaintiff of costs.

Evans, in the ensuing *Easter* term, moved that the full costs might be taxed, notwithstanding the certificate. He relied upon the words of the statute, sect. 2, confining the power of the Judge to "any action personal," "not being for any title or interest of lands, nor concerning the freehold or inheritance of any lands;" and he cited *Tyler* v. *Bennett* (*a*). [*Coleridge* J. The only trespass proved was taking down the sign-board.] The pleadings and postea must shew whether the Judge had power or not. [*Coleridge* J. cited *Smith* v. *Edwards* (*b*). *Patteson* J. There was an issue here on the demise. That must have been either admitted or proved.] A rule nisi was granted.

Chilton now shewed cause. By stat. 22 & 23 *Car.* 2. *c.* 9. *s.* 136., in all actions of trespass, &c., where "the Judge *at the trial*" shall not find and certify under his hand, upon the back of the record, "that the freehold or title of the land mentioned in the plaintiff's declaration *was chiefly in question*,"&c. or an assault and battery proved, the plaintiff, if the damages be under

(*a*) 5 *A.* & *E.* 377. (*b*) 4 *Dowl. P. C.* 621.

1838.

THOMAS *against* DAVIES.

40*s*., shall recover no more costs than the damages amount to. This, independently of the statute of *Elizabeth*, precludes the plaintiff from recovering full costs. There is a current of authorities against the application of this enactment to the present case; but, unless they are over-ruled, the statute becomes a dead letter, except in a very few instances. The statute of *Elizabeth*, from its wording, was found ineffectual in practice; and it was intended by the statute of *Charles* to remove that inconvenience by enabling the Judge to determine, from the facts appearing at the trial, what was the real matter "chiefly" in dispute. Before the New Rules of pleading, it had been established (against the evident meaning of the act), that the statute of *Charles* could not apply where there was a special plea which excluded *any* question as to the freehold, the provision being intended (as was supposed) for cases only where the freehold *might* come in question, but *in fact* did not: and, since those rules, the plain construction of the statute has been still further departed from, by holding that Not Guilty had the effect of a special plea in saving the plaintiff's costs, because, by the rule *Hil.* 4 *W.* 4. tit. *Pleadings in Particular Actions*, V. 2. (*a*), that plea now operates "as a denial that the defendant committed the trespass alleged in the place mentioned, but not as a denial of the plaintiff's possession or right of possession of that place;" *Hughes* v. *Hughes* (*b*), *Smith* v. *Edwards* (*c*). It was indeed observed, in argument, in *Dunnage* v. *Kemble* (*d*), that this application of the new rule could not take effect where, by statute, parties are enabled

(*a*) 5 *B.* & *Ad.* ix.

(*b*) 2 *Cro. M.* & *R.* 663. *S. C. Tyr.* & *Gr.* 4. *Dunnage* v. *Kemble*, 3 *New Ca.* 538., and *Purnell* v. *Young*, 3 *M.* & *W.*, appear to be contrà, but were decided before the rule of this term.

(*c*) 4 *Dowl. P. C.* 621. (*d*) 3 *New Ca.* 538.

to

1838.

THOMAS *against* DAVIES.

to plead the general issue and give special matter in evidence; but the exception is unimportant since the Rule *Trin.* 1 *Vict.* (*a*). Again, it appears now to be doubtful, from the different constructions which have been put upon the statute of *Charles*, whether a plea denying the close to be the plaintiff's will admit of a Judge's certificate or not: *Hughes* v. *Hughes* (*b*), *Howell* v. *Thomas* (*c*), *Purnell* v. *Young* (*d*). It has never been sufficiently remarked that by this statute the Judge is to certify that, at the trial of the cause, the freehold was *chiefly* in question. The state of authorities on the subject shews the necessity of reverting to the plain words of the statute. [*Patteson* J. You ask us to over-rule *Purnell* v. *Young* (*d*).] *Chilton* admitted that this was the effect of his argument.

Evans, contrà, was stopped by the Court.

Lord DENMAN C. J. We ought not to hear this further discussed. The current of authorities is too strong to admit of our over-ruling them. Mr. *Chitty* (*e*), in his edition of Statutes, urges the same doubts which have just been presented as to the construction that has been put upon the statute of *Charles*, citing the opinion of Sir *W. D. Evans* (*g*) against it, and disapproving of Lord *Kenyon*'s course of argument in *Peddell* v. *Kiddle* (*h*). But, after the decisions of so many years, and the judgment lately delivered, on consideration, by the Court of Exchequer, we cannot overrule the prevailing construction. The rule for taxing the full costs must be absolute.

LITTLEDALE, PATTESON, and WILLIAMS Js. concurred.

Rule absolute.

(*a*) Antè, p 279.
(*b*) 2 *Cro. M. & R.* 664. *S. C. Tyr. & Gr.* 5.
(*c*) 7 *Car. & P.* 342. (*d*) 3 *M. & W.* 288. See p. 296.
(*e*) 1 *Chitty's Statutes*, 219., tit. *Costs, in General*, note (*l*).
(*g*) 3 *Evans's Statutes*, 301. note (1), tit. *Costs.* 3d ed.
(*h*) 7 *T. R.* 659.

1838.

Monday, June 11th.

PURSELL *against* HORN and ELIZABETH, his Wife.

Trespass for assaulting plaintiff, and throwing water upon him, and also wetting and damaging his clothes. Pleas, 1. As to assaulting plaintiff, and wetting and damaging his clothes, a justification: Replication, de injuriâ. 2. As to the residue of the trespasses, not guilty. Issues thereon. Verdict for plaintiff on both issues; damages, a farthing.

Held that plaintiff could not recover more costs than damages, without a judge's certificate under stat. 22 & 23 *Car.* 2. c. 9. s. 136., since the declaration was for a *battery*, as well as an assault, and therefore the case was within the statute: and the special plea of justification did not extend to any alleged trespass in the declaration amounting to a battery.

TRESPASS. The declaration stated that defendant *Elizabeth*, on &c., assaulted plaintiff, "and then cast and threw divers large quantities of boiling water *on the plaintiff*, and also then wetted, damaged, and spoiled the clothes and wearing apparel, to wit one great coat," &c., of the value &c., "which the plaintiff then wore:" by means of which he was hurt, scalded, &c., and forced to expend money in endeavouring to cure himself.

Pleas. 1. "As to the said assaulting the said plaintiff as in the said declaration mentioned, and wetting, damaging, and spoiling the said clothes and wearing apparel of the said plaintiff, as therein also mentioned;" that plaintiff assaulted and would have beaten defendant *Elizabeth*, wherefore she defended herself as she lawfully &c., "and in so doing did necessarily and unavoidably a little assault the said plaintiff, and a little wet, damage, and spoil his said clothes and wearing apparel in the said declaration mentioned, doing no unnecessary damage," &c. Verification. 2. As to the residue of the trespasses in the declaration mentioned, Not Guilty. Replication to the first plea, de injuriâ. Issues joined on the replication and second plea.

On the trial before *Littledale* J., at the *Northampton* Spring assizes, 1837, the jury found a verdict for the plaintiff, damages one farthing. The learned Judge did not certify under stat. 22 & 23 *Car.* 2. *c.* 9. *s.* 136. The finding stated in the postea was, on the first issue, that *Elizabeth Horn* of her own wrong and without the cause &c. committed the said trespasses, in manner and form &c.;

1838.

PURSELL *against* HORN.

&c.; and, on the second issue, that, "as to the residue of the said trespasses, the said defendants are guilty thereof, in manner and form" &c.: and that the jury assess the plaintiff's damages, over and above his costs and charges &c., to one farthing, and, for those costs and charges, to 40*s*. *Waddington*, in *Trinity* term, 1837, obtained a rule nisi for amending the postea by substituting one farthing costs for 40*s*.

Humfrey now shewed cause. Stat. 22 & 23 *Car.* 2. *c.* 9. *s.* 136. deprives of costs "in all actions of trespass, assault and battery, and other personal actions," where the damages are found below forty shillings, and the Judge does not certify "that an assault and battery was sufficiently proved." This is not a case within the statute, because no battery was alleged. It is laid down in *Com. Dig. Battery*, (C), that, "If a man strike at another, and do not touch him, it is no battery, but it will be an assault." "So" "if he throws stones, water, or other liquor upon him" (*a*). [Lord *Denman* C. J. Is it no battery, if a man throws a stone at another and breaks his arm? The notion must have been that battery could not be committed except with something which the party held in his hand at the time; but that cannot be maintained (*b*).] If throwing water on the plaintiff be a battery, the justification here admits it, and then no certificate was necessary.

Waddington, contrà. The words "upon him," in *Com. Dig. Battery*, (C), must have been used by mistake.

(*a*) Citing *Reg. Brev.* 108 *b*.

(*b*) "A man cannot justify" "a *battery by throwing* stones *molliter* against a trespasser." *Com. Dig. Battery* (A); citing 2 *Roll. Abr.* 548., l. 45. *Trespas d'assalt et batterie* (G), 8. *Cole* v. *Maunder*.

This

1838.

PURSELL against HORN.

This may be inferred from other placita under the same head. (He was stopped by the Court on this point.) The justification here omits any reference to that which constitutes a battery. Nothing is justified but assaulting the plaintiff, and wetting, damaging, and spoiling his clothes. The latter averments are mere matter of gravamen, and ancillary to the main charge; they do not, therefore, take the case out of the statute; *Bannister* v. *Fisher* (a), *Mears* v. *Greenaway* (b), *Hamson* v. *Adshead* (c). In *Johnson* v. *Northwood* (d) the defendant, in his pleas, confessed a battery. In the present justification the fact to which the wetting and damaging are treated as the gravamen is not a battery, but merely "assaulting" the plaintiff. The clothes might be wetted and damaged without a battery.

Lord DENMAN C. J. I think that a battery does not necessarily mean something done cominus. But it must imply personal violence; and I think that the matter justified by this plea is not a battery. The rule must be absolute.

LITTLEDALE J. The argument for the plaintiff on the first point would go the length of saying that to shoot at a person and hit him would be no battery.

PATTESON and WILLIAMS Js. concurred.

Rule absolute (e).

(a) 1 *Taunt.* 357.

(b) 1 *H. Bl.* 291. And see *Atkinson* v. *Jackson*, there cited; p. 295.

(c) *Bull. N. P* 329. *S. C. Sayer's Rep.* 91.

(d) 7 *Taun.* 689.

(e) See *Bone* v. *Daw*, 3 *A. & E.* 711.

1838.

HEAD *against* BALDREY.

Tuesday, June 12th.

The Court will not, before taxation of costs, make an order as to the principle upon which they are to be taxed, if objection be taken to that course.

W. *H. WATSON* obtained a rule, in *Easter* term last, calling upon the plaintiff to shew cause why he should not pay the defendant or his attorney the said defendant's costs, pursuant to *R. Hil.* 4 *W.* 4., *General Rules and Regulations*, 7. (*a*), to be taxed by the Master, and why the plaintiff should not be deprived of the costs of the issue upon which he had succeeded.

By the affidavits in support of the rule, it appeared that there had been several counts in this case, and several issues of law relating to the first count only, and several of fact; that the defendant had obtained judgment on demurrer on all the issues of law (*b*), and that the plaintiff had afterwards obtained a verdict on all the issues of fact. The affidavits stated the circumstances under which particular evidence was produced, and other matters, which the judgment of the Court renders it unnecessary to state. Final judgment had not been entered up, and there had been no taxation.

Kelly now shewed cause, and suggested a preliminary objection, that the application was premature, inasmuch as the Master, on taxation, might take the view which the defendant contended was the correct one; in which case the application would be unnecessary: and that, in

(*a*) 5 *B. & Ad.* iv.

(*b*) See this argument and judgment in *Head* v. *Baldrey*, 6 *A. & E.* 459.

the

1838.

HEAD *against* BALDREY.

the mean time, the plaintiff was put to expense which might eventually turn out to be useless.

W. H. Watson, contrà. The Master has intimated that there is a difficulty in the case; and, as the question will ultimately come before the Court, it is unnecessary to incur the expense of taxing previously. In *Doe dem. Errington* v. *Errington* (*a*) the Court allowed the question of taxation to be discussed at this stage. [*Patteson* J. The objection was not taken.]

Per Curiam (*d*). Parties may find it convenient to agree to such a course; but the Court cannot, if the objection be before them, anticipate the decision of the Master, and presume that he will decide erroneously.

Rule discharged.

(*a*) 4 *Dowl. P. C.* 602. But see *Prudhomme* v. *Fraser*, 2 *A. & E.* 645.

(*b*) Lord *Denman* C. J., *Littledale*, *Patteson*, and *Coleridge* Js.

Tuesday, June 12th.

ROBINSON *against* MESSENGER.

Since the rules of *Hil.* 4 *W.* 4. a Judge may still certify, under stat. 4 *Ann.* c. 16. s. 5., that a defendant (who succeeds on an issue that goes on to the whole action) had probable cause to plead one of several pleas, which is found against him.

ASSUMPSIT for breach of warranty of a horse. Pleas. 1. Non assumpsit. 2. That the horse was sound, excepting as to a defect reserved in the warranty. On the trial before *Patteson* J., at the last *Appleby* assizes, a verdict was found for the defendant on the first issue, and for the plaintiff on the second. Afterwards, on 4th *May*, *Patteson* J., upon an ex parte application, certified on the back of the record that the defendant had a probable cause to plead the second plea. On the taxation, the Master refused to tax the plaintiff's costs of the second issue. The plaintiff afterwards

wards applied to the learned Judge that the certificate might be annulled, and the Master be at liberty to review his taxation. His Lordship declined to make the order prayed, and directed an application to the Court. *Dundas*, in this term, obtained a rule calling on the defendant to shew cause why it should not be referred back to the Master to review his taxation; and the defendant was ordered to produce the record on shewing cause.

Armstrong and Sir *G. A. Lewin* now shewed cause. Stat. 4 *Ann. c.* 16. which (sect. 4) allows several pleas, enacts by sect. 6 that, if a verdict in any issue be found for the plaintiff, costs shall be given at the discretion of the Court, "unless the Judge, who tried the said issue, shall certify, that the said defendant, or tenant, or plaintiff in replevin, had a probable cause to plead such matter which upon the said issue shall be found against him." Upon this statute it was held, in *Cooke* v. *Sayer* (*a*), that, if on the whole the plaintiff had no cause of action, he should not have costs of the issue upon which he succeeded. The issue there, on which the plaintiff succeeded, was one of fact: that on which he failed was one of law, which was decided on demurrer after the trial: so that there was no certificate. Here the Judge has certified. It will be said that stat. 4 *Ann. c.* 16. is, as to this matter, repealed by the rules of *Hil.* 4 *W.* 4. But those rules, though they have the force of an act of parliament, can repeal a statute only so far as they contain enactments repugnant to such statute: the judges had no direct power to repeal exist-

(*a*) 2 *Burr.* 753. *S. C.* 2 *Wils.* 85.

ing

1838.

ROBINSON *against* MESSENGER.

ing statutes; and there is no such repugnancy. The rule *Hil.* 4. *W.* 4., *General Rules and Regulations*, 7.(*a*), makes a defendant, pleading more than one plea, and failing to establish a distinct ground of defence, liable for the costs of the pleas, including the evidence. That applies, not to a case where the two pleas raise, as here, defences altogether distinct in their nature, but to cases where the same evidence will prove the two pleas. The supposition is that both the pleas are proved. The case of a defendant succeeding on one issue, and failing on another, is left to the former regulations, stat. 4 *Ann.* c. 16. s. 5. and *Reg. Hil.* 2 *W.* 4. I. 74. (*b*). Stat. 4 *Ann.* c. 16. was an enabling statute; and the rules of *Hil.* 4 *W.* 4., though they limit the power of shaping the same defence in different ways, compel the pleading of defences which are really distinct more specially than before.

Dundas, contrà. In *Bird* v. *Higginson* (*c*) the cases on stat. 4 *Ann.* c. 16. were before the Court, and *Cooke* v. *Sayer* (*d*) was over-ruled, on the ground that sect. 5 of stat. 4 *Ann.* c. 16. was not there adverted to; and it was held that the plaintiff must have the costs of the issues found for him, though the defendant has judgment on the whole record. *Spencer* v. *Hamerton* (*e*) is in accordance with *Bird* v. *Higginson* (*c*). As to the Judge's certificate, stat. 4 *Ann.* c. 16. s. 5. can no longer be in force, since a completely different set of regulations on the subject of double pleas has been established by the rules of *Hil.* 4 *W.* 4. The object of these rules was

(*a*) 5 *B.* & *Ad.* iv.
(*b*) 3 *B.* & *Ad.* 385.
(*c*) 5 *A.* & *E.* 83.
(*d*) 2 *Burr.* 753. *S. C.* 2 *Wils.* 85.
(*e*) 4 *A.* & *E.* 413. See *Empson* v. *Fairfax*, antè, p. 296.

to

1838.

ROBINSON *against* MESSENGER.

to make the pleading of several defences more perilous to the party pleading than before; and, with this view, such party is subjected to costs. The rule *Hil.* 2 *W.* 4. I. 74. (*a*) had the same object. In *Simpson* v. *Hurdis* (*b*) it was held that the rules of *Hil.* 4 *W.* 4. did not repeal stat. 43 *Eliz. c.* 6. *s.* 2.: but this latter statute was passed with a different intent; it does not relate to multiplicity of pleas, but to frivolous actions; and the Judge there deprives the plaintiff of costs. [*Patteson* J. In *Richmond* v. *Johnson* (*c*) it was held that stat. 4 *Ann. c.* 16. *s.* 5. did not destroy the effect of the Judge's certificate under stat. 43 *Eliz. c.* 6. *s.* 2., though there were several pleas.] The words of *Reg. Hil.* 4. *W.* 4., *General Rules and Regulations*, 7. (*d*) are very large.

Per Curiam (*e*). We think the rules of *Hil.* 4 *W.* 4. do not repeal stat. 4 *Ann. c.* 16. *s.* 5.

Rule discharged.

(*a*) 3 *B. & Ad.* 385.

(*b*) 5 *Dowl. P. C.* 304.

(*c*) 7 *East*, 583.

(*d*) 5 *B. & Ad.* iv.

(*e*) Lord *Denman* C. J., *Littledale*, *Patteson*, and *Williams* Js.

Tuesday, June 12th.

Blunt and Another *against* Harwood.

At a vestry meeting, certain plans were produced for improving the parish church, and were referred to a committee. At a subsequent vestry their report, recommending an enlargement, was received and adopted, and a resolution passed for borrowing money on the parish rates, under stats. 58 G. 3. c. 45. and 59 G. 3. c. 134., to carry the plans into execution. The notice of holding the latter vestry, published in pursuance of stat. 58 G. 3. c. 69. s. 1., stated the purpose of it to be "to receive a report from the church committee, and to adopt such measures as may appear necessary for carrying that report into execution."

Held, that this was a sufficient notice of the intention to propose borrowing money on the church-rates for the purpose of executing the plans.

Quære, whether it would have been sufficient to give notice of a vestry meeting, "to receive the report of the committee appointed to consider the plans produced to the vestry meeting held on" &c. (the first-mentioned vestry), "for affording additional accommodation to the parishioners desirous of attending divine worship in the said parish church."

A party being libelled in the Spiritual Court for non-payment of a rate made in pursuance of the above resolution, objected to the libel because it stated the notice to have been given in the form last above-mentioned, and he obtained a rule nisi for a prohibition. Afterwards the notice really given, which was in the form first above-mentioned, and had been lost, was discovered, and was submitted to this Court in shewing cause, with an affidavit that, by the practice of the Ecclesiastical Court (in the opinion of the deponent, a proctor), leave would be given to amend the libel by an additional article setting out the real notice.

Held that the rule nisi for a prohibition might be enlarged, to give opportunity for such amendment.

A RULE was obtained in last *Easter* term, calling upon the above-named plaintiffs and Sir *Herbert Jenner*, the official principal of the Arches Court of *Canterbury*, to shew cause why a prohibition should not issue to prohibit the said Court from further proceeding in the suit between the plaintiffs and *Harwood*. The affidavit in support of the rule stated the material parts of the libel and additional articles thereto filed in the Arches Court in the said suit. The libel was filed by the plaintiffs, as churchwardens, for non-payment of a rate made to repair the parish church of *Streatham*, and to repay certain portions of a principal sum of 3300*l.*, borrowed under stats. 58 *G.* 3. *c.* 45. and 59 *G.* 3. *c.* 134., and interest on a part of that sum. The libel alleged that the 3300*l.* was borrowed in 1830, in pursuance of resolutions passed at a vestry-meeting of the parish of *Streatham* on 2d *August* 1830; that a committee had been appointed at a previous vestry, holden *March* 17th, 1830, to consider

1838.

BLUNT *against* HARWOOD.

sider a plan then produced to the vestry, and report whether it would be expedient to adopt that or any other plan for affording additional accommodation to the parishioners in the church: that the committee, at the vestry of *August* 2d, presented a report recommending an enlargement of the church at an expense not exceeding 3300*l.*, agreeably to certain plans; and the vestry, at that meeting, resolved that the report should be adopted, and the plans carried into execution, if proper persons could be found who would give security to carry the same into execution at a sum not exceeding 3300*l.*, that the churchwardens and rector should be authorised to carry the plans into execution, and that the churchwardens should be authorised to borrow 3300*l.*, at certain interest, on the security of the parish rate. The additional articles (according to the affidavit) stated that a notice, published on 25th *July* 1830, "declared that a vestry was to be held in the vestry-room of the said parish on the 2d day of *August* then next, at nine o'clock in the forenoon, *to receive the report of the committee appointed to consider the plans produced to the vestry meeting held on the said 17th day of* March, *for affording additional accommodation to the parishioners desirous of attending divine worship in the said parish church*, or to that effect." The defendant's affidavit in support of the rule stated that the libel or additional articles did not allege or plead that the purpose for which the vestry was to be held was further or otherwise set out in the notice; and that it did not appear by the libel, or additional articles, or otherwise, that any other notice was given, and no other was in fact given, of the holding of such vestry. And the affidavit further alleged that no public notice was given of the special

 purpose

1838.

BLUNT *against* HARWOOD.

purpose of such last-mentioned vestry, three days before the said 2d of *August*, according to stat. 58 *G.* 3. *c.* 69., "for the regulation of parish vestries." It also stated that the defendant had appeared to the libel, and that Sir *H. Jenner* had admitted the same to proof, and assigned defendant to give an issue thereto, but no sentence had been given. And that the defendant was advised and believed that the issue of the matters depending would be determined or influenced by the construction of the acts of parliament in the libel mentioned, and that for want of proper notice the vestry of *August* 2d was illegally holden.

An affidavit was made in answer by *J. S. Yeats*, who was vestry clerk in 1830, setting out the notice of the vestry meeting on *March* 17th (as to which no question arose), and the notice actually published of the vestry to be holden on *August* 2d, which was as follows.

Streatham, 24th *July* 1830.

Notice is hereby given that a vestry will be held in the vestry room of this parish on *Monday* the 2d day of *August*, at nine o'clock precisely, to receive a report from the church committee, *and to adopt such measures as may appear necessary for carrying that report into execution;* and further that it is intended that such vestry do adjourn to the workhouse of this parish, there to transact the business of the day.

J. S. Yeats, Vestry clerk.

He further stated that the original notice, written by him, had been lost, and only recovered within twenty-four hours before the making of his affidavit; that the notice was published in church and affixed as stat. 58 *G.* 3. *c.* 69. *s.* 1. directs; that the vestry of *August* 2d was holden

holden in pursuance of it; and that the defendant was present, and proposed that the rector should be authorised, as well as the churchwardens, to carry into execution the plans approved of by the vestry. The proctor employed by the plaintiffs deposed that the original notice had not been discovered at the time of filing the amended articles, but that, if it had, its contents would have been inserted therein; and that, according to the practice of the Arches Court, if the rule for a prohibition were discharged, the Judge, in the deponent's opinion, would, on application, admit an amendment of the libel by a new additional article, setting forth the said notice. The contents of the notice, as now stated in the additional articles, were set forth, nearly as in the affidavit for the rule; but it was deposed that the articles stated the original to be lost.

Sir *W. W. Follett* and *Channell* now shewed cause. The objection to the proceedings before the Arches Court is, in effect, that the notice of holding the vestry of *August* 2d, as set out in the libel, states the purpose of the vestry to be "to receive the report of the committee," omitting the words (which, as it now appears, were actually inserted in the notice) "and to adopt such measures as may appear necessary for carrying that report into execution." It is contended, therefore, that the resolution for borrowing, upon which the prosecution wholly rests, is invalid. But first, the informality, if there be one, in the notice which appears on the libel, cannot annul all the proceedings taken since, more especially where innocent persons would be exposed to the loss of money which they have advanced on the faith of such proceedings, and where the party raising the ob-

1838.

BLUNT *against* HARWOOD.

jection was present at, and shared, in, the transactions which are impeached. The statute 58 *G.* 3. *c.* 69. *s.* 1. does not say that, if a vestry be holden without the notice there required, the proceedings may at any future time be treated as null and void. Further, the notice, even as stated in the libel, was sufficient. Taking it by itself, the announcement, that a vestry would be holden to receive the report of the committee, gave sufficient warning that the steps to be taken in pursuance of that report would likewise come under consideration: but the notice also refers to the circumstances under which the committee was appointed at a former vestry, and, by that reference, points out distinctly the nature of the business to be transacted on the presenting of the report. It cannot then be asserted (as it must be to warrant the issuing of a prohibition) that the Judge of the Arches Court will contravene stat. 58 *G.* 3. *c.* 69. by proceeding upon this libel. But, assuming that that would be so, the affidavits state that the original notice, which is correct in form, has now been found, and, by the practice of the Court, may be filed in an additional article.

Sir *F. Pollock* and *M. Smith* contrà. If there be a positive law on the subject of notice, it cannot be altered by the conduct of this defendant at the meeting of *August* 2d. The question is, whether the resolution then passed and the rate then made were good, not merely as against him, but as against every one. And this Court will interfere, if it sees that the ecclesiastical Judge, in the sentence he is about to pronounce, will be contravening the interpretation which would be given to a statute here. [Lord *Denman* C. J. That is not disputed

1838.

BLUNT against HARWOOD.

puted on the other side.] The Court, in disposing of this rule, will look only to the notice as stated in the libel itself; not to any representation of it on affidavit; *Ricketts* v. *Bodenham* (a). It is said that the libel can be amended; but, if the judgment of the Ecclesiastical Court is now in favour of the libel, it cannot be expected that the plaintiffs will amend. And, if they rely on doing so, they should have moved to have the rule enlarged till they could make the proper application. Even supposing leave given to amend, the notice now produced (if that can be considered here) would not sustain the libel. The power of borrowing money, which has been exercised in this case, is given by stat. 58 *G.* 3. *c.* 45. *s.* 58., which requires that such borrowing shall be "with the consent" of the vestry, and stat. 59 G. 3. *c.* 134. *s.* 14., which also makes the "consent of the vestry" necessary. Between those two acts, stat. 58 *G.* 3. *c.* 69. was passed, which enacts (sect. 1), that "no vestry or meeting of the inhabitants in vestry of or for any parish shall be holden until public notice shall have been given of such vestry, and of the place and hour of holding the same, and the special purpose thereof, three days at the least before the day to be appointed for holding such vestry," &c. Then, if it be intended, at such a meeting, to authorise borrowing money on the rates, this, which is clearly a special purpose, ought to be pointed out by the notice. By stat. 59 *G.* 3. *c.* 134. *s.* 24. (altering the provisions of stat. 58 *G.* 3. *c.* 45. *s.* 60.) it is enacted that no application and offer to build or enlarge any church shall be made, nor shall any church be built, rebuilt, or enlarged, by

(a) 4 *A.* & *E.* 433.

1838.

Blunt *against* Harwood.

means of any rates upon any parish, where one third part in value of the proprietors of lands, as there described, shall dissent therefrom. In order that such power of dissent may be exercised, a special notice ought to be given where it is proposed to do acts which may be so dissented from. Here the intention to authorise a borrowing of 3300*l.* on the parish rates is not intimated in the notice, as stated either in the libel or on affidavit. The words "to adopt such measures as may appear necessary" do not, as of course, imply it, even if reference be made to the proceedings of the vestry in *March* 1830, when the committee was appointed. The parishioners receiving this notice could not guess what the report would be: and they might suppose that, if money was to be raised, the purpose would be effected by raising the pew-rents, or by a subscription. It is contended that, even if the meeting was not duly summoned, the proceedings are not now to be set aside: but stat. 58 G. 3. *c.* 69. *s.* 1. forbids the holding any vestry without proper notice; if, therefore, the notice was insufficient, the meeting was only an assemblage of individuals, not a vestry. *Rex* v. *Dursley* (*a*) shews that, notwithstanding what has been done in pursuance of the proceedings on *August* 2d, a rate grounded upon them cannot legally have any force.

Lord Denman, C. J. It has not been questioned by the parties that we have that jurisdiction in the present case which the Court may exercise, according to *Gare* v. *Gapper* (*b*) and *Gould* v. *Gapper* (*c*), to correct the misconstruction of a statute by the

(*a*) 5 *A.* & *E.* 10. (*b*) 3 *East*, 472. (*c*) 5 *East*, 345.

ecclesiastical

1838.

BLUNT *against* HARWOOD.

ecclesiastical courts. I think it so doubtful whether the first notice is sufficient, that, in my opinion, a rule ought to go, if the libel could not be amended. But, supposing it to be amended by inserting the notice actually given of the purposes of the vestry, namely, "to receive a report from the church committee, and to adopt such measures as may appear necessary for carrying that report into execution," I think the libel will then shew a notice conveying substantially a full intimation of the business to be done. Referring to the former proceedings which led to the report, no one would suppose that it could be carried into execution without raising money; and I think the notice does, in effect, call upon the parishioners to consider of borrowing a sum for the purposes which the report would bring under consideration. The statutes 58 *G.* 3. *c.* 45. and 59 *G.* 3. *c.* 134. do not require any stricter notice than has been given here. Stat. 58 *G.* 3. *c.* 69. *s.* 1. does, indeed, require notice to be given of the vestry, "and the special purpose thereof;" but I think the word "special" carries us no farther than the word "purpose" alone would have done if we really and satisfactorily see that the parish has had notice of what was intended; especially as no particular form or other circumstance of distinction in the notice is introduced for the occasion on which borrowing is contemplated. I can see reasons why the act should have been more strict, but none for construing it more strictly as it now is. Then, as the amended statement of the notice would be sufficient, I think we ought not to make this rule absolute.

LITTLEDALE J. I am of the same opinion, since, if the additional article be introduced, the Ecclesiastical Court

1838.

BLUNT *against* HARWOOD.

Court will have jurisdiction. I agree that the notice, under stat. 58 *G.* 3. *c.* 69. *s.* 1., ought to inform the parishioners of the intention with which a vestry is called; but it was not necessary that this notice should say, in so many words, that a proposal would be made to borrow money, if it stated that that would be taken into consideration which necessarily includes such a proposal. Now the words "such measures as may appear necessary for carrying that report into execution" do so include it; and I therefore think that the parishioners had notice, impliedly, that a proposal would be made at the vestry for borrowing the money requisite for giving effect to the report.

PATTESON J. I am not quite satisfied that the notice as stated in the libel is not sufficient. But, assuming that the libel is to be amended, the notice, as it will then stand, will be sufficient beyond all doubt. No particular form of notice is directed by any of the three statutes: we have only to see that the notice published gives sufficient information to the inhabitants. Here no man applying common sense to the subject could have the slightest doubt that, if the vestry determined on building or enlarging, a rate must be laid, or money borrowed. The supposition that the expense might be met by a subscription is a mere fancy; and it does not appear to have been in contemplation to raise the pew rents, which could only be done in a particular manner directed by act of parliament (*a*). When it was stated that the report of the church committee was to be received, and measures adopted for carrying it into execution, no one could doubt that the bor-

(*a*) See stat. 58 *G.* 3. *c.* 45. *s.* 78. stat. 59 *G* 3. *c.* 134. *s.* 31.

rowing

1838.

BLUNT *against* HARWOOD.

rowing of money must come under consideration. The fact that, for so many years, no objection was made to the proceedings of this vestry, though followed up by the making of rates, and that the present defendant never complained till now, though it does not estop him, is strong evidence of the understanding which prevailed on the subject. The libel will be clearly sufficient when it sets out the notice properly, and for that purpose it will be amended. I am not satisfied of our authority to prohibit in such a case, and do not understand the decision in *Gare* v. *Gapper* (a) and *Gould* v. *Gapper* (b); but it is unnecessary to discuss that now.

WILLIAMS J. The case has been argued on the supposition that we can prohibit. There is no ground for saying that, on this notice, any one was taken by surprise. The parishioners were called upon to consider the report of the committee on the plan referred to them, and (which is more material) to adopt measures for carrying the report into execution. It could not be supposed that the intention was merely to consider of the beauty or convenience of the plan; the object, evidently, was to take measures for carrying it into effect by money.

Lord DENMAN C. J. then proposed that the rule should be enlarged, to give an opportunity for amending the libel; but, Sir *F. Pollock* not insisting upon this, his Lordship said: Then we discharge the rule, considering the amendment as actually made.

Rule discharged.

(a) 3 *East*, 472. (b) 5 *East*, 345.

1838.

Doe on the Demise of Merceron *against* Bragg.

Land was mortgaged with a proviso of redemption on payment of principal and interest, and the mortgagor covenanted by the deed to pay all taxes, rates, or assessments upon the premises. The proviso for redemption was made subject to the performance of this covenant.

Held, that such mortgage was not a "security for the repayment of money to be thereafter lent, advanced, or paid," to an amount "uncertain and without any limit," within the stamp act 55 *G.* 3. *c.* 184. sched. part 1. tit. *Mortgage.*

EJECTMENT by mortgagee against mortgagor of a house and land. On the trial before *Coleridge* J., at the sittings in *Middlesex* during this Term, it appeared that the mortgage deed, dated *March* 8th, 1825, contained a covenant by the mortgagor to pay the mortgagee 300*l.* (the sum borrowed), with interest, on *March* 8th, 1826; and, until full payment thereof, to pay all taxes, rates, duties, or assessments then imposed, or to be imposed, on the premises, or on the principal sum or interest, or on the lessor of the plaintiff, his executors, &c., for or in respect of the same. The proviso for redemption was subject to the performance of this covenant. The deed had a 3*l.* stamp. It was objected, on the defendant's part, that the deed required a 25*l.* stamp under stat. 55 *G.* 3. *c.* 184. *Schedule*, *Part* 1. tit. *Mortgage*, the total amount secured being "uncertain and without any limit." *Halse* v. *Peters* (*a*) was cited. The learned Judge directed a nonsuit, giving leave to move to enter a verdict for the plaintiff. *Wightman* in this term moved accordingly; and a rule nisi was granted. On a subsequent day of the term (*b*),

Byles shewed cause. *Halse* v. *Peters* (*a*) does not materially differ from this case; and the grounds of decision there stated by Lord *Tenterden* and *Parke* J. are

(*a*) 2 *B.* & *Ad.* 807.

(*b*) *June* 12th. Before Lord *Denman* C. J., *Littledale*, *Patteson*, and *Williams* Js.

applicable

1838.

Doe dem. MERCERON *against* BRAGG.

applicable here. [*Littledale* J. The rates and taxes would at all events be payable by the mortgagor, in respect of his occupation.] That makes the present case the stronger, since the payment in question is quite collateral to the mortgage debt, and yet is made part of the charge upon the land; for there can be no re-conveyance till it is satisfied. In *Halse* v. *Peters* (*a*) the insurance does not appear to have been made a charge upon the land. The payments here stipulated for are not those only which would be due in respect of occupation. The mortgagor is to pay all taxes and assessments to be imposed on the premises, or on the principal sum or interest, or on the lessor of the plaintiff in respect of the same. [*Littledale* J. That was introduced into such deeds on account of the property tax, but has been continued ever since.] In *Doe dem. Scruton* v. *Snaith* (*b*) the proviso of redemption was, if the mortgagor should pay the mortgagee 3000*l.*, and all sums which the mortgagee should expend or disburse for or in respect of those presents, with interest; and that was held not to be a mortgage for an uncertain amount, within the schedule. But it is a rule that the mortgagor indemnifies the mortgagee for all such expenses; therefore nothing was imposed upon him by these words of the proviso to which he would not have been liable in an ordinary case. [*Littledale* J. The provisions in the schedule do not seem to have in view expenses and outgoings in respect of the mortgaged premises, but fresh loans.] Such a construction would have been adverse to the decision in *Halse* v. *Peters* (*a*). In *Pruessing* v. *Ing* (*c*) it was held that the interest reserved on a promissory note was not a part of the sum

(*a*) 2 *B. & Ad.* 807. (*b*) 8 *Bing.* 146.
(*c*) 4 *B. & Ald.* 204.

secured,

1838.

Doe dem. Mercerow against Bragg.

secured, within the meaning of the schedule. *Dickson* v. *Cass* (a) shews that, in the case of a bond, if a contingent charge, beyond interest, be created in any part of it, the deed ought to be stamped as given for an uncertain amount. *Doe dem. Jarman* v. *Larder* (b) is not applicable, because the contingent expense there contemplated would not have been a charge upon the land; the mortgagee's remedy in respect of it would have been merely on the mortgagor's covenant.

Wightman contrà. *Doe dem. Scruton* v. *Snaith* (c) decides the present case. *Halse* v. *Peters* (d) is different, because there the payment to be secured beyond the principal and interest was for something in the nature of an advance to be made by the mortgagee; here the additional payment is only to secure the mortgagor against loss of any part of his existing debt; to give him the means of recovering his 300*l.* and interest clear. The words of the schedule imposing a 25*l.* duty where the sum secured is without limit shew the distinction between the two cases: the 25*l.* duty is imposed where the mortgage &c. "shall be made as a security for the repayment of money, to be thereafter lent, advanced or paid, or which may become due upon an account current, together with any sum already advanced or due, or without, as the case may be." Here nothing was to be done in the nature of loan or advance; the mortgagor only consented to a charge which properly devolved on him. *Tindal* C. J. said in *Doe dem. Scruton* v. *Snaith* (c) that, on looking at this clause, the only question was, "whether it was intended to effect a security against a contingent loss to

(a) 1 *B. & Ad.* 343.
(b) 3 *New Ca.* 92.
(c) 8 *Bing.* 146.
(d) 2 *B. & Ad.* 807.

the

1838.

Doe dem. Mercerон against Bragg.

the lender;" and he was of opinion there that the clause did not so operate. Here the necessity of paying rates and taxes, if it fell on the mortgagee, was such a contingent loss. If he had entered on nonpayment of the principal and interest, and had then been compelled to pay assessments, he might legally have insisted that the mortgagor should reimburse him for those payments: and the deed gives him the security of the land that this shall be done.

Cur. adv. vult.

Lord DENMAN C. J., in the same term (*June* 14th), delivered the judgment of the Court.

The plaintiff was nonsuited for the insufficiency of the stamp on a mortgage deed, on the authority of *Halse* v. *Peters* (*a*), decided in this Court in *Michaelmas* term 1831. In *Doe dem. Scruton* v. *Snaith* (*b*), *Hilary* term 1832, the Court of Common Pleas took a different view of this point, all the four Judges giving their reasons in detail for thinking the stamp sufficient. The former case was not at that time reported nor brought before the Court of Common Pleas; on the other hand a decision of Lord *Tenterden*'s in *Pruessing* v. *Ing* (*c*), on which that Court mainly relied, does not appear to have been cited in *Halse* v. *Peters* (*a*). We are of opinion that the authority of *Doe dem. Scruton* v. *Snaith* (*b*) ought to prevail.

The objection was, that the mortgage deed was stamped only to the extent of the sum advanced, and did not cover the amount of taxes and rates which might be charged on the premises, and which the mortgagor

(*a*) 2 *B. & Ad.* 807.

(*b*) 8 *Bing.* 146.

(*c*) 4 *B. & Ald.* 204.

covenanted

1838.

Doe dem. Mercercon against Bragg.

covenanted to pay, and until payment of which the proviso for redemption was not to operate. This amount is truly said to be uncertain and without limit; and hence the 25*l.* stamp is argued to be necessary instead of the ad valorem stamp. The answer is that to the amount of these taxes and rates the mortgagee is, at all events, entitled; that he required no stipulation in respect of them; and that the stamp is regulated by the amount advanced or agreed to be advanced. This distinction is made clear by the Chief Justice's remarks on *Dickson* v. *Cass* (*a*).

We are, therefore, of opinion that the rule for setting aside the nonsuit and entering a verdict for the plaintiff must be absolute.

Rule absolute.

(*a*) 1 *B. & Ad.* 343.

Tuesday, June 12th.

Suwerkrop, Administrator of Fox, *against* Day and Others.

K. being left executor, *M.*, as his attorney, obtained letters of administration to the testator's effects, with the will annexed, for the benefit of *K.*, who never took out probate. *K.* died, having appointed an executor, and *S.* took out administration with the will of the first testator annexed, and also administration with the will of *K.* annexed, for the benefit of *K.*'s executor, till that executor should himself obtain probate. *M.* was still living, and the goods of the first testator were not fully administered.

Held, that during the life-time of *K.* the goods of the first testator vested, not in him, but in *M.*, as the personal representative of the first testator: but that after *K.*'s death *M.* ceased to be such representative.

And consequently, that arrears of interest, becoming due to the estate of the first testator in *K.*'s life-time, were not recoverable in assumpsit by *S.* as his personal representative: but that *S.* might, by virtue of the administration taken out by him, bring assumpsit for such arrears accruing after the administration was granted.

ASSUMPSIT by plaintiff as administrator, with the will annexed, of the goods of *Hubert Fox*, deceased, left unadministered by *Owen Kernan*, who in his life-time was executor &c. The recital of title went on to state that *Kernan* was executor of the will of *Fox*, and

proved

1838.

SUWERKROP *against* DAY.

proved the same in the Prerogative Court of *Canterbury*, by *Allan Macdonald*, his certain attorney in that behalf, "to whom the said Court granted letters of administration, with the will of the said *Hubert Fox* annexed, for the benefit of the said *Owen Kernan*;" that *Kernan* (now deceased), by his will, appointed *John Macdowall* and *John Hicks Hewlings* executors thereof; and that *Macdowall* had since died: whereupon, on plaintiff's petition, "administration with the will annexed of the said *Hubert Fox* was granted" to plaintiff "for the benefit of *J. H. Hewlings*, until he shall legally apply for and obtain probate of the will of *Owen Kernan*." The first count stated that defendants, after the death of *Fox*, and in the lifetime of *Kernan*, were indebted to *Kernan* as executor as aforesaid in 500*l.* interest, for the forbearance by him, as such executor, to defendants of monies due from them to *Kernan* as such executor, and that they, in consideration of the premises, promised *Kernan*, as executor as aforesaid, to pay him &c. Breach, non-payment to *Kernan*, or to plaintiff, as administrator as aforesaid, since *Kernan*'s death. There were also counts for interest due to plaintiff as administrator as aforesaid for the forbearance by him as administrator for monies due to him as such; also for monies found due to him, as administrator as aforesaid, on an account stated. Profert of the letters of administration, "which give sufficient evidence to the Court of the grant of administration to the said *Allan Macdonald*, the attorney of the said *Owen Kernan*, with the will of the said *Hubert Fox* annexed as aforesaid." Profert also of the letters of administration granted to plaintiff after *Kernan's* death.

Pleas. 1. To the first count, that *Kernan* did not prove the will of *Fox*, as by the declaration is supposed, but,

1838.

SOWERKROP against DAY.

but, on the contrary, that after the death of *Fox*, to wit on &c., administration, with the will annexed, of the goods of *Fox*, was granted by the Archbishop of *Canterbury* to the said *Allan Macdonald*, and thereby he became and was the personal representative of *Fox*, and so continued from thence until and at the time of *Kernan*'s death; without this, that defendants were indebted to *Kernan* as executor &c., in manner and form &c. 2. To the first count, that defendants did not promise *Kernan* as executor, in manner and form &c. 3. To the second and third counts, that defendants did not promise plaintiff as administrator, in manner and form &c. Issues were joined on the several pleas.

On the trial before Lord *Denman* C. J., at the sittings in *London* after *Michaelmas* term, 1836, it appeared that the action was brought to recover 330*l.* 3*s.* 10*d.*, the interest of a debt which had been due to *Fox*, in his lifetime, from the defendants, and was paid, but without the interest, in *December* 1833. *Fox*, who was a merchant in *Demerara*, died in *May* 1830, and left *Kernan* his executor. *Kernan*, who was then in *Demerara*, sent a power of attorney to *Allan Macdonald* in *England*, to enable him to prove the will there. Administration with the will annexed was granted to *Macdonald* for *Kernan*'s benefit; and he acted in settling the affairs. *Kernan* died in *Demerara* in *August* 1831, not having administered all the effects of *Fox*, and left *Hewlings* and another his executors. In *September* 1833, *Hewlings* being then abroad, and the other executor of *Kernan* dead, administration, with the will annexed, to the goods of *Kernan* was granted to the plaintiff as *Hewlings*'s attorney, for the use and benefit of *Hewlings*. The like administration, with the will annexed, was

1838.

SOWERKROP *against* DAY.

was also granted him to the goods, not administered, of *Fox*. *Allan Macdonald* was living when this action was brought. There was evidence that the defendants had, by letter and otherwise, admitted *Kernan*, in his lifetime, to have a claim for principal and interest as executor of *Fox*. Objections were taken to the plaintiff's right, in point of law, to recover; on which the Lord Chief Justice gave leave to move as after-mentioned: and the plaintiff had a verdict on the first count for 125*l.* 10*s.* 5*d.*, the interest due when *Kernan* died, and on the second for 204*l.* 13*s.* 5*d.*, the interest accruing between that time and the payment of the principal.

Sir *J. Campbell*, Attorney-General, in *Hilary* term, 1837, moved for a rule to show cause why a nonsuit should not be entered, or a verdict entered for the defendants on the first count and the damages reduced, or why the judgment should not be arrested. First, by the letters of administration granted to *Macdonald*, he was legally constituted the personal representative of *Fox*; and, till those letters were revoked, the plaintiff could have no claim as administrator; he cannot therefore recover on any of the counts. And, as to the first count, the defendants could not be indebted to the plaintiff for money forborne by *Kernan* while *Macdonald* was the administrator. These objections appear on the record, and therefore judgment should be arrested. Secondly, assuming that *Macdonald*'s representative character was determined by *Kernan*'s death, the damages must at all events be reduced by the amount of interest which had become due in *Kernan*'s lifetime. A rule nisi was granted. In this term (*a*),

(*a*) *June* 8th. Before Lord *Denman* C. J., *Littledale*, *Patteson*, and *Williams* Js.

Platt

1838.

SUWERKROP *against* DAY.

Platt and *Petersdorff* shewed cause. The declaration is inartificial; and the averment as to *Macdonald* might have been altogether omitted, he having acted merely as agent to *Kernan*. The statement in the first count, that the debt accrued in respect of forbearance by *Kernan* of monies due to him as executor, is substantially true; and the plaintiff may sue upon promises made in consideration of that forbearance, by reason of the privity which subsists between an administrator de bonis non and a first executor, and the interest in the estate which devolves upon the administrator de bonis non as soon as he is invested with that character: *Hirst* v. *Smith* (*a*); *Catherwood* v. *Chabaud* (*b*). *Macdonald* had only a limited administration, which was determined by *Kernan*'s death. In the case "*In the Goods of Cassidy* (*c*)," where administration with the will annexed had been granted "for the use and benefit of *J. Cassidy*," an executor, "then at sea," the administration was held to have "ceased and expired" on his return. The death of the party for whose benefit administration was granted to another as attorney must have the same effect. *Taynton* v. *Hannay* (*d*) is not an authority to the contrary, because, in that case, the administrator's authority was specially regulated by act of parliament, 38 *G.* 3. *c.* 87. Then, after *Kernan*'s death, it was for the Ecclesiastical Court to grant administration of the remaining goods as it thought proper; administration has been granted to the plaintiff; and nothing has occurred to invalidate or revoke it. There cannot be a

(*a*) 7 *T. R.* 182. (*b*) 1 *B. & C.* 150. *S. C.* 2 *D. & R.* 271.

(*c*) 4 *Hagg. Ecc. Rep.* 360.

(*d*) 3 *B. & P.* 26. See *Rainsford* v. *Taynton*, *Taynton* v. *Hannay*, 7 *Ves.* 460.

nonsuit

1838.

SOWERKROP *against* DAY.

nonsuit on the facts, because the defendants have recognised the plaintiff as representative of *Fox*. Supposing that the defendants are improperly alleged to have been indebted for a forbearance by *Kernan*, the plaintiff is at any rate entitled to a verdict, since part of the interest claimed became due after *Kernan*'s death.

Sir *J. Campbell*, Attorney-General, and *Wightman*, contrà. *Macdonald*, not *Kernan*, was the representative of *Fox*; and administration was granted to him, not durante absentiâ, or with any other limit, but generally. *Kernan* himself had never proved; and, although an executor may do many things before proof, yet, if he dies without having proved, his acts are void. *Kernan*'s representative, therefore, was not the representative of *Fox*. There is an inconsistency in this record. By the declaration, *Kernan*, as the party for whose benefit *Macdonald* administers, is treated as the person representing the testator; the interest is said to accrue in respect of forbearance by *Kernan*: but *Hewlings*, for whose benefit the plaintiff administers, is not so treated, the plaintiff claiming as principal in respect of the sum accruing since *Kernan*'s death. Administration was granted to both on the same terms; the attorney and principal cannot both represent the testator; if the attorney does, *Kernan* did not; if the principal does, the present plaintiff does not. But it is, in fact, the attorney who represents the testator; *Macdonald*, therefore, was, and is, the representative. The declaration states, in the first count, a forbearance by *Kernan* as executor; and the plaintiff gave in evidence, on the trial, a letter of the defendants acknowledging him to be so; but that cannot vary the rights of parties, when it is shown that he, in fact, never proved, which is the substantial de-

1838.

SUWERKROP *against* DAY.

fence raised by the first plea. So as to the counts alleging a promise to the plaintiff as administrator; it might have been urged that there is a privity between a first executor and administrator de bonis non, if *Kernan* had taken out probate: but he did not; and *Macdonald*, who administered with the will annexed, is still living; therefore the pleas denying any promise to the plaintiff as administrator remain without answer. If, indeed, it were correctly alleged that on the death of *Kernan* the grant of administration to *Macdonald* was determined, there might, on that event, have been a grant of administration de bonis non to the plaintiff; but then he must have taken out such administration to *Fox*, not to *Kernan*, who never represented *Fox*. The principle of the decision in *Taynton* v. *Hannay* (*a*) is against the extinction of *Macdonald*'s representative character. In the case *In the Goods of Cassidy* (*b*) the administration seems to have been granted durante absentiâ. [Lord *Denman* C. J. There the person administering was the executor's attorney, and probably acted merely under a power from him. Then it would seem that what the attorney did during the absence of the principal was the principal's act.] Here, if *Macdonald* had been appointed to act merely as attorney for *Kernan*, he would have taken out probate, as *Kernan* himself would have done if in *England*; not administration cum testamento annexo. If, then, *Macdonald* has continued to be administrator ever since the death of *Kernan*, the plaintiff must be nonsuited upon the evidence; and, even if his administration ceased with *Kernan*'s life, the plaintiff cannot succeed on the first

(*a*) 3 *B. & P.* 26. See *Rainsford* v. *Taynton*, *Taynton* v. *Hannay*, 7 *Ves.* 460.

(*b*) 4 *Hagg. Ecc. Rep.* 360.

count,

1838.

SUWERKROP *against* DAY.

count, and must recover, on the second, only so much interest as accrued after *Kernan*'s death. But the judgment ought to be arrested, because it appears, from the body of the declaration, that *Kernan* never was executor, and, from the declaration and profert, that *Macdonald*, who took out administration with the will of *Fox* annexed for the benefit of *Kernan*, really was the party acting as *Fox*'s representative.

Cur. adv. vult.

Lord DENMAN C. J., in this term (*June* 14th), delivered the judgment of the Court.

This was an action by the plaintiff, describing himself as administrator, with the will annexed of *Hubert Fox*, of the goods left unadministered by *Owen Kernan*, who was executor of *Hubert Fox*, and who was alleged to have proved the will by *Allan Macdonald*, his attorney, to whom, as such attorney, administration with the will annexed, for the benefit of the said *Owen Kernan*, was granted, which *Owen Kernan* is since deceased, having left *Macdowall* and *Hewlings* his executors; and that on *Macdowall*'s death plaintiff took administration with the will of *Hubert Fox* annexed for the benefit of *Hewlings*. The first count states that the defendants were indebted to *Owen Kernan*, as executor as aforesaid, for interest of money forborne by him as such executor, and lays the promise to *Owen Kernan* as such executor. The second count states that the defendants were indebted to the plaintiff, as such administrator, for interest of money forborne by him as such administrator, and lays the promise to the plaintiff as such administrator. Profert is made of the letters of administration both to *Macdonald* and to the plaintiff.

 The

1838.

SOWERBY *against* DAY.

The first plea traverses the being indebted to *Owen Kernan* as such executor. The second traverses the promise to *Owen Kernan*. The third traverses the promise to the plaintiff.

The question in the cause is, what is the legal effect of these different letters of administration.

We are of opinion that, by the first grant, *Allan Macdonald* became the legal representative of *Hubert Fox* during the life of *Owen Kernan*, or, at all events, until he should himself take out probate, which he never did; but that on the death of *Owen Kernan* that grant was ipso facto at an end, and the subsequent grant to the plaintiff is good. The consequence is, that the plaintiff is entitled to recover on the second count all interest accruing subsequent to the grant to him; and the rule must be absolute to reduce the verdict on that count to that amount. But the defendants are entitled to a verdict on both the issues on the first count, because the defendants never were indebted to *Owen Kernan* as executor for interest, nor promised him as executor. Their debt and their promise in law for interest during *Owen Kernan*'s life was to *Allan Macdonald*, as administrator, and not to *Owen Kernan*. This appears on the face of the declaration itself, and therefore would be a ground for arresting the judgment on the first count; but, as we are of opinion that the issues on that count are proved in favour of the defendant, the rule will be absolute to enter the verdict accordingly.

Rule absolute, to enter a verdict for the defendants on the first two issues; for the plaintiff on the other two, with 204*l*. 13*s*. 5*d*. damages.

1838.

The QUEEN *against* The Mayor, Aldermen, and Burgesses of the City and Borough of NORWICH.

Wednesday, June 13th.

The steward of a borough, removed under stat. 5 & 6 *W.* 4. *c.* 76., demanded compensation under sect. 66, as for an office held for life. The town council allowed compensation as for an annual office only. The Lords of the Treasury, on appeal, and after hearing the parties, awarded compensation on the former principle. On motion for a mandamus to the corporation to execute a compensation bond, there appeared evidence, on the one hand, that the office was not, legally, holden for life, and, on the other, that it had usually been so holden, and that the appointment was accepted on that understanding.

Held that, under sect. 66, the Lords of the Treasury were not bound to consider only the legal tenure, but might, referring to the circumstances of the case, award compensation as for an office held for life.

The steward had received a small annual sum for holding a corporation court. It was paid by the sheriffs, and not out of the borough fund; but he held the Court as steward. Held, that compensation might be given him in respect of this emolument.

A RULE nisi was obtained in last *Easter* term for a mandamus to the corporation of *Norwich* to execute a compensation bond to *F. Kelly* Esquire, under stat. 5 & 6 *W.* 4. *c.* 76. *s.* 67., for the office of steward of that borough.

It appeared, on affidavit, that he was appointed to that office in *February* 1831, and removed from it by the town council, without reason assigned, in *January* 1836. He thereupon demanded compensation, under sect. 66 of the act, stating the particulars and amount of his claim, which was founded on the assumption that the office was one usually holden for life. The town council passed a resolution, which they communicated to him in answer, declaring that the office was only annual, and fixing the compensation at two thirds of the sum which they considered the amount of one year's salary and emoluments. He thereupon appealed to the Lords of the Treasury, and stated in his memorial, as to the suggestion of the office being only annual, that he was not aware of any thing in the statutes, charters, or usages of the city, supporting such an allegation; but that, if deemed material, its correctness might be tried by a

legal

1838.

The QUEEN *against* The Mayor, &c., of

legal tribunal. He referred, however, to sect 66 of stat. 5 & 6 *W.* 4. *c.* 76., which directs that, in assessing compensation to a person removed from office, regard shall be had "to the manner of his appointment to the said office, and his term or interest therein, and all other circumstances of the case:" and he further cited a minute formerly made by the Lords of the Treasury with reference to that section (*a*), expressing their opinion (as to claims by town-clerks) that, "In all cases where such officer held his office for life, or where the usage has been such as to raise a just expectation that the office should continue for the life of the holder, a compensation of not less than two thirds of his profits may be granted to such officer, estimated upon the principles stated in the commencement of this minute, and calculated upon an average of his just emoluments for the five years previous to the first of *January*, 1835." The memorial alleged that the usage and understanding had always been, that the appointment of steward was for life, or until resignation or promotion: and it further stated that Mr. *Kelly*, when he accepted the office, had been led to believe that the tenure was as above mentioned, and would not otherwise have taken it.

The Lords of the Treasury, after hearing all parties, awarded an annual sum as compensation. Part of their minute was as follows. "It does not appear necessary, so far as the decision of this board is concerned, to investigate what may have been the precise legal tenure of the office. It is admitted by the town council that, whatever may have been the legal right of the corporation, it was not exercised; and no instance is attempted

(*a*) See *Ex parte Lee*, 7 *A.* & *E.* 139.

to

to be adduced of the steward having been removed from office, or ceasing to hold it, except for death or with his own consent. On these grounds, my lords consider that Mr. *F. Kelly* had a just expectation that he would not be deprived of his office except with his own consent." The minute specified the items of claim allowed, among which was a sum received annually for holding the sheriffs' courts. The town council presented a memorial remonstrating against the allowance; but the Lords Commissioners refused to re-open the case. A bond to secure the compensation was then demanded, but withheld under circumstances amounting to a refusal.

The affidavits in opposition stated the practice to have been, that at certain meetings of the corporation, held annually on the 3d of *May*, the recorder, steward, town clerk, and other officers, were elected, their names were read over, and they were considered as appointed till the next 3d of *May*. Entries in the corporation books were also referred to, shewing appointments made for a year; and it appeared that, from the time of Queen *Anne*, re-appointments of the steward from year to year had been regularly minuted. It was further alleged that the sum received by the steward for presiding as assessor in the sheriffs' courts was paid by the sheriffs out of their own, and not the corporate, funds.

B. Andrews, *Austin*, and *Palmer*, now shewed cause. The Lords of the Treasury should have ascertained whether this was an office for life or merely annual. According to sect. 66 of stat. 5 & 6 *W.* 4. *c.* 76., the manner of appointment to the office, and the "term or interest" therein, must be considered in assessing compensation. [Lord *Denman* C. J. The Lords of the Treasury

1838.

The QUEEN *against* The Mayor, &c., of NORWICH.

Treasury are not required to investigate the tenure.] They must make their order conformably to the act. If the tenure may be disregarded, the town council or Treasury have power to enlarge the party's interest. The Treasury order is binding on a mere question of amount; but the act does not make it so as to title. That this office was in fact annual is evident from the affidavits. The payments for holding the sheriffs' courts did not come out of the borough fund, and therefore, according to the judgment of this Court in *Regina* v. *The Corporation of Poole* (a), "there would be an incongruity, almost an injustice, in making that fund chargeable with any compensation for the loss of it."

Sir *J. Campbell*, Attorney-General (with whom were Sir *F. Pollock* and Sir *W. W. Follett*), contrà. The Court cannot now enter into discussion as to the tenure of the office, or the propriety of the compensation ordered by the Lords Commissioners. The whole question is, whether they had jurisdiction; *Regina* v. *The Corporation of Poole* (b), *Regina* v. *The Mayor, &c., of Bridgewater* (c): if they had, their decision as to the quantum is conclusive. The legislature clearly intended that, in a case of this kind, where it has been the understanding of all parties that an office was to be held during life or good behaviour, compensation should be given as if the tenure had been strictly such. [He was then stopped by the Court.]

Lord DENMAN C. J. The judgment of the Lords Commissioners is the same, in effect, as if they had

(a) 7 *A. & E.* 738.
(b) 7 *A. & E.* 730.
(c) 6 *A. & E.* 339.

said,

1838.

The QUEEN *against* The Mayor, &c., of NORWICH.

said, "We do not find that there is a legal tenure of this office for life; but there is an interest equivalent to that:" and they grant compensation accordingly. They have jurisdiction in the case; and therefore I do not know that we should interfere if we thought their decision wrong: but I am of opinion that it was right. As to the sheriffs' court, it was a court of the corporation; and, if the payments in respect of it were an emolument fairly attached to this corporate office, it was a proper subject of compensation.

LITTEDALE J. The Lords of the Treasury are to consider all the circumstances of the case. Here the circumstances were such as enabled them to give compensation, as if the office had been for life. It lay in their discretion to award such compensation if they thought proper.

PATTESON J. I entirely agree that the Lords of the Treasury had jurisdiction, and that they came to a right decision, supposing that this Court had power to review their decision, which I by no means intend to say they have.

WILLIAMS J. concurred.

Rule absolute.

The QUEEN *against* WILLIAM ROBERTS.

Wednesday, *June* 13th.

This case is reported, 7 *A. & E.* 441.

Wednesday, June 13th.

The QUEEN *against* The Recorder of HULL.

In counties of cities, and counties of towns, to which a court of quarter sessions has been granted under stat. 5 & 6 *W.* 4. c. 76., the recorder, by sect. 105, has the powers relating to inspectors of weights and measures, given by sect. 17 of stat. 5 & 6 *W.* 4. c. 63. to the magistrates in quarter sessions assembled.

Although the present jurisdiction of the recorder be limited to a district less extensive than that which the county comprehended up to the time of passing those statutes.

R. C. *HILDYARD* obtained a rule in this term, calling upon the recorder of the borough of *Kingston-upon-Hull* to shew cause why a mandamus should not issue, commanding him to investigate the accounts of *Thomas Oglesby*, inspector of weights and measures for the town and county of *Kingston-upon-Hull*, and to make an order for reasonable remuneration to him for the discharge of his duties as such inspector.

The following facts appeared from the affidavits in support of the rule. At the quarter sessions for the town and county of the town of *Kingston-upon-Hull*, held 20th *October*, 1835, the justices acting for the town and county appointed *Oglesby* inspector of weights and measures for the town and county, directing him to account to the treasurer of the town and county for all fees received by him, and ordering an annual salary of 50*l.* *Oglesby* acted in the office, received and accounted for the fees, and took the salary, up to and including the *April* quarter sessions for the town and county in 1836, the order for the salary being made on the treasurer, and handed to *Oglesby* by the clerk of the peace of the town and county. By the Municipal Corporation Act, stat. 5 & 6 *W.* 4. *c.* 76. *s.* 38., the powers of the then justices ceased on 1st *May* 1836. In *April* 1836, justices were appointed for the town and county, under sect. 98. In *May* 1836, the Crown granted a court of quarter sessions,

1838.

The QUEEN *against* The Recorder of HULL.

sions, and appointed a recorder, under sect. 103. The recorder presided at the *July* quarter sessions, 1836, when *Oglesby* applied to the Court for an order for the payment of his salary; but the clerk of the peace referred him to the town council. The council, from time to time, up to *January* 1837, made orders on the borough treasurer to pay *Oglesby's* salary, and *Oglesby* accounted to the borough treasurer. In *February* or *March* 1837, the property committee of the council declined to order such payment, in consequence of a doubt whether the council could do so without an authority from the recorder. *Oglesby* applied to the recorder at the *April* and *Midsummer* sessions, 1837; but he, from a doubt as to his power, declined to make the order. At the *October* sessions, 1837, the council having appointed a new inspector in the stead of *Oglesby*, application was made to the recorder to confirm their appointment; but the recorder, from the same doubt, declined then to do so. At the *March* sessions, 1838, *Oglesby* again applied to him for an order on the treasurer, and also for an order on himself (*Oglesby*) to pay the fees to the treasurer of the borough; but the recorder declined to act.

Sir *J. Campbell*, Attorney-General, and *Armstrong* now shewed cause. The question is, whether the powers relating to inspectors of weights and measures, which were formerly in the justices of peace, are now vested in the recorder. By sect. 105 of stat. 5 & 6 *W.* 4. *c.* 76., he is sole judge of the court of quarter sessions; and that court "shall be a court of record, and shall have cognisance of all crimes, offences, and matters whatsoever cognisable by any court of quarter sessions of

1838.

The QUEEN *against* The Recorder of HULL.

of the peace for counties." The intention was to give the recorder only such powers as are judicial, or incidental to judicial functions. By sect. 17 of stat. 5 & 6 *W.* 4. *c.* 63., the appointment of inspectors of weights and measures, the fixing of their remuneration, and their suspension or dismissal, are entrusted to "the justices of the peace of every county, riding, or division, or county of a city or county of a town, in general or quarter sessions assembled" (*a*). Such functions, however, are not, properly speaking, imposed upon the magistrates in their character of a court of quarter sessions, although the occasion of their assembling at quarter sessions is prescribed as the proper occasion for exercising the duty. Therefore, although the magistrates can no longer hold a court of quarter sessions in boroughs having a court of quarter sessions and recorder under sect. 103 of stat. 5 & 6 *W.* 4. *c.* 76., they may still assemble and perform the duties imposed on them in their character of justices of peace. Then the "matters whatsoever," mentioned in stat. 5 & 6 *W.* 4. *c.* 76. *s.* 105., must be ejusdem generis with those over which the court of quarter sessions, as such, has jurisdiction; thus a recorder may, in such case, swear sureties of the peace: for that power is akin to his powers as a criminal judge. [*Littledale* J. Why, then was the proviso added in sect. 105, that no recorder by his office shall have power to make county rates, or rates in the nature of county rates, or to license alehouses, or to exercise any of the powers which the

(*a*) By sect. 24 of stat. 5 & 6 *W.* 4. *c.* 63., "every inspector shall, once in every quarter of a year, account to the treasurer of the county, riding, division, county of a city, or county of a town, or to such other persons as shall be duly authorised by those by whom he may have been appointed, for all fees received by him under this act."

act

act specially vests in the council of the borough?] It is not a general rule that every exception to an enactment of a statute refers to something which, but for the exception, would be within the enactment. Moreover, there are powers excepted in the proviso of sect. 105 which might, perhaps, fall within the general scope of the powers of a criminal judge. Thus the recorder, as criminal judge, has power over the expenses of prosecutions which must be defrayed from the rates; and it might be thought that, but for the exception, this would give him some jurisdiction with respect to the rates. By sect. 19 of stat. 5 & 6 *W.* 4. *c.* 63., the powers in question, as to inspectors, are to be exercised, in *Ireland*, by grand juries; which shews that there is no analogy, in the view of the legislature, between such powers and those of a Judge. Indeed, it cannot be said that the grand jurors would exercise the powers in the character even of grand jurors. Sect. 25 of the same statute, in the case of *Berwick-upon-Tweed*, and of "all other places which have been or shall be hereafter authorised" by act of parliament to appoint inspectors, or "which have been or shall be hereafter," by charter, act of parliament, or otherwise, possessed of legal jurisdiction, and shall have been, or be, provided with copies of the imperial standard weights and measures, makes it lawful for the magistrates, or persons so authorised, to appoint inspectors, who shall have the same powers and discharge the same duties as the inspectors appointed by the county justices or grand juries, and shall account as aforesaid to such persons as shall be duly authorised by those who may have appointed such inspectors: and in this section nothing is said as to quarter sessions. It is very improbable that the legislature should have meant to give magistrates juris-

1838.

The QUEEN against The Recorder of HULL.

diction out of quarter sessions in one case, and not in another. [*Patteson* J. Sect. 17 provides for counties, and counties of cities and towns, on the supposition that they must always have courts of quarter sessions.] If so, the provision restricting their acts to what they do in quarter sessions must be understood as applying to boroughs which were counties, so long only as the justices were members of the courts of quarter sessions. [*Patteson* J. The legislature could hardly have contemplated such an interval: chapters 63 and 76 of stat. 5 & 6 *W.* 4. received the royal assent on the same day (*a*).] Then the legislature must be understood to have contemplated both acts at the same time; and sect. 17 of stat. 5 & 6 *W.* 4. *c.* 63. would be inapplicable, from the first, to any case where the magistrates could not meet in quarter sessions. But further, upon the facts of this case, *Hull* is within sect. 25 rather than sect. 17 of c. 63. The town and county of *Kingston-upon-Hull*, which existed at the time when the act passed, is not identical with the present borough, for this, though still a county, has no longer any jurisdiction without the limits of the borough, and the borough has no longer the limits of the ancient town (*b*). The recorder does not act for the district which was comprehended within the county at the time of passing

(*a*) 9th *September* 1835. By sect. 107 of stat. 5 & 6 *W.* 4. *c.* 76. the then existing criminal jurisdictions of boroughs are abolished from 1st *May* 1836. Sect. 101 provides that the justices appointed under the act (sect. 98) shall not act as justices of the peace at any court of gaol delivery or general or quarter sessions, or in making or levying any county rate, or rate in the nature of a county rate.

(*b*) See stat. 5 & 6 *W.* 4. *c.* 76. *s.* 7. and *sched.* A. sect. 1.; stat. 2 & 3 *W.* 4. c. 64. *s.* 35. and *sched.* (O). 40. Also stat. 6 & 7 *W.* 4. *c.* 103. *s.* 1.; and, for the ancient limits of the town and county, see *Appendix to the First Report of the English Municipal Corporation Commissioners*, Part III. p. 1545.

the

the act; a part of that is now in the East Riding of *Yorkshire;* and it cannot be contended that he can appoint inspectors for that part. The present borough, therefore, comes under the words "shall be hereafter" possessed of jurisdiction, in stat. 5 & 6 *W.* 4. *c.* 63. *s.* 25.

Cresswell (with whom was *R. C. Hildyard*) contrà. The alteration of the limits of the county cannot destroy the jurisdiction in the part which remains unaltered. [He was then stopped by the Court.]

Lord DENMAN C. J. I do not see who can execute these powers but the recorder. We must treat the question as if sects. 17 and 25 of stat. 5 & 6 *W.* 4. *c.* 63. and sects. 101, 105, and 107 of stat. 5 & 6 *W.* 4. *c.* 76. were one enactment. There is no inconsistency between sects. 17 and 25 of the first statute. The magistrates are to have power in quarter sessions, by sect. 17, in counties; and in other places, by sect. 25, the power is to be exercised out of quarter sessions. The effect of sects. 101, 105, and 107 of stat. 5 & 6 *W.* 4. *c.* 76. is that the court of quarter sessions, in boroughs where there is a recorder appointed under the act, consists solely of the recorder. The cases in which he is not to act are specified: all other matters cognizable by a court of quarter sessions are within his jurisdiction. The authority, therefore, of the magistrates assembled in quarter sessions is merged in that of the recorder, except in the cases specified in the proviso of sect. 105 of stat. 5 & 6 *W.* 4. *c.* 76.

LITTLEDALE J. concurred.

 PATTESON

1838.

The QUEEN *against* The Recorder of HULL.

PATTESON J. By sect. 17 of stat. 5 & 6 *W.* 4. *c.* 63. the magistrates in quarter sessions assembled are to exercise the powers in question in every county of a city, or county of a town. Here, by the provisions of stat. 5 & 6 *W.* 4. *c.* 76., the magistrates can no longer assemble in quarter sessions. The magistrates appointed under the latter act have a certain jurisdiction: they are different from the justices contemplated by sect. 17 of stat. 5 & 6 *W.* 4. *c.* 63. The only question is, whether any person can now exercise the powers given by that section. I think that sect. 105 of stat. 5 & 6 *W.* 4. *c.* 76. is large enough in its provisions: it gives the recorder cognizance of all matters whatsoever cognizable by any court of quarter sessions of the peace for counties, and not excepted by the proviso, however absurd the consequence may be, and however contrary (as it probably is) to the intention of the legislature. Sect. 25 of stat. 5 & 6 *W.* 4. *c.* 63. speaks of places which have been, or shall be, authorized by act of parliament to appoint inspectors: it seems that this expression relates to places in which persons are so authorized (*a*).

Rule absolute (*b*).

(*a*) *Williams* J. had left the Court.

(*b*) It has since been decided, under stat. 5 & 6 *W.* 4. *c.* 76. *s.* 105., that the recorder of a borough (*Ludlow*) having a commission of the peace, and a court of quarter sessions, though it is not a county, has power to try an appeal against an order made by justices of the borough on parish officers, under stat. 9 *G.* 4. *c.* 40. *s.* 38. *Regina* v. *St. Lawrence, Ludlow. Michaelmas Vacation*, 1839. Post.

Wednesday, June 13th.

The QUEEN *against* The Justices of DERBYSHIRE.

(NEWBOROUGH *against* SWARKSTON.)

This case is reported, 6 *A.* & *E.* 612. note (*b*).

1838.

Thursday, June 14th.

DOE on the several Demises of CLARKE and Another, *against* MARY STILLWELL and Another.

The rule, that an affidavit more than a year old is not to be used, applies only in the case of affidavits to hold to bail.

Where the making and publishing of an award are sworn to, but without fixing the time, the award itself bearing date within the time limited by the order of reference, the Court will not presume that the award was made and published after that time.

So held on motion for an attachment for non-performance.

Where the award directs that *A.* shall pay *B.* 15*l.* for copyhold land; that *B.*, in consideration of that sum, shall at the costs of *A.* surrender the land to *A.*'s use; and that, upon such surrender being made and delivered to *A.*, he shall pay *B.* the 15*l.*; it rests with *B.* to prepare and execute the surrender; and it is a non-performance of the award if *B.* omits, on request, to make the surrender. Or (per *Littledale* J.) if *B.* does not at least give notice to *A.* that he will attend at a certain time before the steward of the manor.

OGLE, in last *Easter* term, obtained a rule nisi for an attachment against the above-named *Mary Stillwell* for non-performance of an award, under the following circumstances.

The cause and all matters in difference between the parties were referred at nisi prius to a barrister, on *June* 18th, 1836, so as he should make and publish his award on or before the fourth day of *Michaelmas* term then next, with liberty to him under his hand at the foot of the order of reference to enlarge the time. The arbitrator recited that he had duly enlarged the time to 1st *January* then next: and awarded that *Clarke* should pay to *M. Stillwell* for a certain piece of land, 15*l.*; and that *M. Stillwell*, "in consideration of the said sum of 15*l.*, shall forthwith, at the costs and charges of the said *T. T. Clarke*," out of court, according to the custom &c., surrender to the use of *Clarke*, his heirs and assigns, the said piece of land, according to the description &c.: "and that, upon such surrender being made and delivered to the said *T. T. Clarke*, he the said *T. T. Clarke* shall pay to the said *M. Stillwell* the aforesaid sums of 15*l*," and 30*l.* and 5*l.*, awarded on certain claims of compensation. The arbitrator then gave

1838.

Doe dem. Clarke against Stillwell.

Stillwell three calendar months from the date of the award to remove from the land, and awarded that she should remove therefrom within that time. The award concluded thus: "In witness whereof I have hereto set my hand this 23d of *December*, in the year of our Lord 1836:" with the arbitrator's name and the following attestation: "Signed and published in the presence of *H. W. Southwell.*" The order of reference was made a rule of Court.

An affidavit in support of the rule stated that the deponent, on *April* 21st, 1838, as the attorney, and in the name and on the behalf, of *Clarke*, required *Stillwell* to perform the award, and that she should forthwith out of court surrender, &c., the piece of land (as directed in the award): and he also required her forthwith to remove from the land. And "that, on the said 21st day of *April*, he informed and told the said *Mary Stillwell* that, upon such surrender being made by her as aforesaid and delivered to the said *T. T. Clarke*, he the said *T. T. Clarke* should and would thereupon pay to her the several sums of 15*l.*, 30*l.*, and 5*l.*, and would also pay the costs and charges of and incident to the making of the said surrender." Another affidavit stated that, on application to the steward of the manor on *May* 9th, 1838, he said that *Stillwell* had not surrendered, or given the steward any intimation of her intending to do so.

As to the execution of the award, affidavit was made by the attesting witness, that he "did see the said" &c. (the arbitrator) "sign, publish, and declare his award in writing hereunto annexed:" and that the names of the arbitrator and attesting witness, subscribed to the award, were respectively of their handwriting.

Knowles

1838.

Doe dem. Clarke against Stillwell.

Knowles now shewed cause. First, it does not appear on affidavit that the award was made in proper time, or when it was in fact made. The attesting witness deposes that he saw the arbitrator sign and publish his award, but does not say when it was either signed or published. The forms of affidavits on the execution of awards in *Tidd* and *Chitty* (*a*) specify the time. *Musselbrook* v. *Dunkin* (*b*) shews what publication is, and the importance of fixing its date. Nothing ought to be presumed on this subject in a penal proceeding. Secondly, the affidavit of execution was more than a year old when it was used in moving for the attachment: it was, therefore, not admissible. *Burt* v. *Owen* (*c*) shews that the rule on this subject is not confined to affidavits of debt. [*Littledale* J. I never heard of such a rule as to other affidavits (*d*). *Wightman*, amicus curiæ, said that he was counsel in *Burt* v. *Owen* (*c*), and that no general rule was there laid down on the subject, the real objection to the affidavit being that the state of facts might have been altered since it was sworn. *Patteson* J. In the case of an affidavit of debt more than a year old, the Court presumes that the debt may have been paid in the mean time. The rule laid down, is usually, with reference to the particular case of affidavits of debt.] Thirdly, there is no sufficient affidavit of a refusal to perform the award. The arbitrator merely directs that *Stillwell* shall surrender at the costs of *Clarke*. It was the business of *Clarke* to bring her before the steward, and tender a

(*a*) *Tidd's Pract. Forms*, 310. ed. 1828. *Chitt. Pract. Forms*, 637. 4th ed.

(*b*) 9 *Bing*. 605.

(*c*) 1 *Dowl. P. C.* 691.

(*d*) The officers on both sides of the Court agreed that the rule did not extend to other affidavits.

1838.

Doe dem. Clarke against Stillwell.

conveyance to be executed by her: *Standley* v. *Hemmington* (*a*).

Sir *J. Campbell*, Attorney-General, and *Ogle*, contrà. *Clarke* has done all that the award required of him, to procure the surrender. He has made a proper demand, offering, upon the snrrender being executed, to pay the 15*l.*, 30*l.*, and 5*l.*, and also the costs of surrender. The onus of preparing the conveyance was thrown by the award upon the defendant. The words, "shall forthwith, at the costs and charges of the said *T. T. Clarke*," "surrender," merely give her a remedy for the costs; the act was to be done by her, and the payment made by him, concurrently. [*Patteson* J. The affidavit is rather short, in not stating what she said when required to make the surrender.] As to the time of executing and publishing the award, the Court will not presume a fraud in the arbitrator. [Lord *Denman* C. J. Surely the presumption will be that the duty was rightly performed. *Littledale* J. referred to *Sinclair* v. *Baggaley* (*b*) and *Barton* v. *Ranson* (*c*).]

Littledale J. (*d*). This rule must be made absolute. As to the time of executing and publishing the award, I think that, although this is a motion for an attachment, we must presume the award to have been made and published according to the arbitrator's authority. Then, it is said that a demand and refusal are not sufficiently sworn to; but it is clear from the affidavit that *Stillwell* was distinctly desired to make the surrender.

(*a*) 6 *Taunt.* 561.

(*b*) 4 *M. & W.* 312. (not then reported). (*c*) 3 *M. & W.* 322.

(*d*) Lord *Denman* C. J., having been absent during part of the discussion, gave no judgment.

Her

1838.

Doe dem. Clarke against Stillwell.

Her answer does not appear; but, on application to the steward afterwards, it was found that she had not complied with the demand. Then a question is made, whose duty it was to prepare the surrender; and it is contended that *Clarke* ought to have done so, because he was to pay the costs. But I think that it rested with *Stillwell* to prepare the surrender, or at all events to give notice that she would attend the steward on such a day. The rule on this subject appears to be as it is stated, in *The Duke of St. Alban's* v. *Shore* (a), by *Marshall* Serjt.: "If it be said that the defendant must prepare the conveyances, because he is to pay the expense of them, the answer is, that the law is otherwise." "Where the grantee is to pay the costs, yet the grantor must prepare the conveyances. *Cro. Eliz.* 517." And *Hallings* v. *Connard* (b), the case cited, seems to bear out that proposition.

Patteson J. In *Hallings* v. *Connard* (b) the Court of Common Pleas held that, where the form of assurance is left to the option of him who has covenanted to make it, he must notify his readiness, and the kind of assurance he intends to make. But *Walmsley* J. said that "there was no difference, whether the manner of the assurance is left to the covenantor, and where he covenants to make one kind of assurance; for in both cases he is to do the first act, and to tender the assurance." This rule must be absolute.

Williams J. concurred.

Rule absolute.

(a) 1 *H. Bl.* 274. (b) *Cro. Eliz.* 517.

1838.

Doe on the Demise of James Hinton Baverstock *against* Rolfe.

In a conveyance of lands a limitation without consideration is void as against a subsequent purchaser for good consideration, being fraudulent under stat. 27 *Eliz.* c. 4.

The concurrence of a necessary party, in the conveyance containing such limitation, does not amount to a consideration where the limitation is shewn, by circumstances apparent on the face of the conveyance, and of other conveyances forming part of the transaction, not to have been made for the benefit, or at the desire, of such party, and the concurrence of such party does not appear to have been a part of the contract at the time.

Therefore, where *H.*, tenant for life of copyhold, and *B.* remainder-man in tail, with remainder to *H.* in fee, intending to join in an absolute sale of the property to *L.*, suffered a recovery to the use of *H.* for life, remainder to *B.* for life, remainder to the right heirs of the survivor; and then joined in surrendering to *L.*, a purchaser for valuable consideration, in fee: it was held, that the contingent remainder was void against *L.*, though, had it been good, it would not have passed to *L.* by the surrender. Especially as, with respect to a moiety, the object of the conveyance appeared to be to effect a sale of the whole interest, in pursuance of an earlier marriage settlement. But

Held that the recovery was not totally void, and therefore that the entail was barred, and *L.* took the use resulting to *B.* in fee.

EJECTMENT for copyhold lands (*a*) in *Essex*. On the trial before *Vaughan* J., at the *Essex* Spring assizes, 1834, the following facts appeared.

James Hinton Baverstock, the lessor of the plaintiff, was the son of *James Baverstock* and his wife *Jane Baverstock*, and was the only son who survived them. *James Rolfe*, the defendant, claimed through *John Letch*, by purchase.

16th *May* 1778. The premises being vested in *John Hinton* for life, remainder to his only child *Jane Baverstock* in tail, remainder to *John Hinton* in fee, *John Hinton*, *James Baverstock*, and his wife the said *Jane Baverstock*, on the day aforesaid (the said *Jane* being first solely and separately examined, &c.), surrendered the same to a tenant, that a recovery might be suffered according to the custom, which tenant was thereon admitted, and a recovery suffered, to the use of *John Hinton* and his assigns for life, and after his de-

(*a*) The action was brought to recover also some freehold lands; but this part of the claim was abandoned.

cease

1838.

Doe dem. Baverstock against Rolfe.

cease to the use of *Jane* for life, and, *after the decease of the survivor of the two, to the use of the heirs of the survivor for ever.* Admission was given accordingly.

16th *May* 1778. Upon the surrender of *John Hinton*, *James Baverstock* and *Jane Baverstock*, in performance of the covenant of *John Hinton* in the marriage settlement of *Jane*, dated 9th *October* 1769 (*a*), a recovery was suffered of one undivided moiety of the premises, to the use of the trustees of that settlement, *Charles Blackstone* and *Thomas Baverstock*, in fee, in trust for the use of *James* for life, remainder in trust for the use of *Jane* for life, remainder in trust for the use of *Thomas Baverstock* (the eldest son of *James* and *Jane*), *John James Baverstock*, *Jane Baverstock*, *Mary Baverstock*, and *Frances Baverstock*, and all other child or children of *James* and *Jane Baverstock*, in such shares, &c., as the survivor of them, *James* and his wife *Jane*, should appoint, and, in default, and subject thereto, in trust for the use of *Thomas*, the eldest son, in tail, remainder to *John James*, the second son, in tail, remainder to the third, fourth, &c., and all other sons successively in tail, remainder in trust for the daughters equally, as tenants in common, and the heirs of their bodies, with cross remainders, remainder to the heirs of *Jane* the wife; with power to the trustees, at the request of *James* and *Jane* his wife, to sell and surrender the said moiety, and apply the proceeds in the purchase of other lands, &c., of equal value, to be conveyed to the said trustees in trust for the same uses as the said surrendered moiety; and with power to *John Hinton*, *James Baverstock*, and the trustees, unanimously, to avoid the uses and create fresh ones by surrender. The trustees were admitted accordingly.

(*a*) P. 654, post.

27th

1838.

Doe dem. Baverstock against Rolfe.

27th *June* 1778. *John Hinton*, *James Baverstock*, and *Jane* his wife, surrendered an undivided moiety of the premises to *John Letch* in fee.

27th *June* 1778. *Charles Blackstone* and *Thomas Baverstock* (the trustees), at the request of *James Baverstock* and *Jane* his wife, surrendered an undivided moiety, and *James* and *Jane* did remise, release, and quit claim thereto, to *John Letch* in fee.

6th *July* 1778. *John Letch* was admitted to both moieties, to hold in fee.

This was a bonâ fide purchase of the whole by *John Letch*; and he, or those claiming through him, had been in possession ever since. *John Hinton* died in 1802, *James Baverstock* in 1815, *Jane Baverstock* in 1835. It was contended, on the part of the defendant, that, as he claimed through a bonâ fide purchase, the contingent remainder reserved to the heir of the survivor of the two, *James Baverstock* and *Jane* his wife, by the limitations of the recovery of 16th *May* 1778, first above mentioned, was voluntary, and therefore fraudulent and void.

The earlier deeds relating to the property were put in, to illustrate the intention of the parties to this recovery. On these deeds, the facts appeared as follows.

26th *April* 1680. *Francis Bridge* was admitted to hold as tenant in fee, and surrendered to the use of himself and *Martha*, his wife, for their lives and the life of the longer liver, remainder to the use of his right heirs. Admission of *Francis* and *Martha* accordingly.

Francis Bridge died, leaving two daughters, co-heiresses, *Mary* the wife of *Edward Hinton*, and *Sarah* the wife of *Philip Betts*. *Martha Bridge*, who survived *Francis*, died at some time before 29th *May* 1732.

As

1838.

Doe dem. Baverstock against Rolfe.

As to *Mary Hinton*'s moiety, the following facts appeared.

29th *May* 1732. *Mary Hinton* was admitted to the moiety, as co-heiress, to hold in fee; and she and her husband *Edward Hinton* surrendered to the use of *Mary Hinton* for life, remainder to the use of *Edward Hinton* for life, remainder to the use of the heirs of the body of *Mary Hinton* by *Edward Hinton*, remainder to the use of the right heirs of *Mary Hinton*. Admission of *Mary* to hold for her life.

Edward Hinton and *Mary Hinton* both died at some time before 19th *May*, 1746, leaving an only child, *Martha Hinton*.

19th *May* 1746. *Martha Hinton* was admitted to the moiety, to hold to her and the heirs of her body.

30th and 31st *July* 1746. By lease and release, reciting an intended marriage between *Martha Hinton* and *John Hinton* (her cousin), *Martha Hinton* covenanted to surrender the copyhold moiety which she had in possession, and also her remainder expectant in the copyhold moiety of *Sarah Betts* (her aunt), to trustees, to certain uses, which corresponded substantially with the limitations of the recovery next herein set out.

1st *August* 1746. *Martha Hinton* suffered a recovery of the copyhold moiety of which she was possessed, to the use of herself until her intended marriage with *John Hinton*, remainder to the use of herself for life, remainder to the use of the said *John Hinton* for life, remainder to the use of the children of the marriage as she should appoint, remainder (in default, &c.) to the heirs of her body by *John Hinton*, remainder to the use of the right heirs of the survivor of the two, *John* and *Martha Hinton*, for ever. Admission of

Martha

1838.

Doe dem. Baverstock against Rolfe.

Martha to hold till the marriage, and afterwards for life.

Martha Hinton married *John Hinton* on 11th *December* 1746. She died in *July* 1761, without having made any appointment, leaving her husband surviving, and two daughters by him, *Jane Hinton* and *Martha Hinton*, both infants.

4th *June* 1762. *John Hinton* was admitted tenant for life of the moiety.

9th *October* 1769. By indenture of this date, reciting an intended marriage between *Jane Hinton* and *James Baverstock*, *John Hinton*, her father, covenanted, when *Jane Hinton* should have attained the age of twenty-one, to surrender a moiety of the copyhold to the use of *James Baverstock* for life, remainder to the use of *Jane Hinton* for life, remainder to the use of the children of the marriage, as the survivor of the two, *James Baverstock* and *Jane Hinton*, should appoint, remainder to the use of the heirs of the body of *Jane Hinton* by *James Baverstock*, remainder to the use of the right heirs of *Jane Hinton*; with power to the trustees, parties to the indenture (*Charles Blackstone* and *Thomas Baverstock*), at the request of *James* and *Jane*, to sell the copyhold, and apply the proceeds in the purchase of other lands, &c., of equal value, to be conveyed to the said trustees, for the like trusts as before limited; and with power to *John Hinton*, *James Baverstock*, and the trustees, unanimously, to avoid the uses and create fresh ones. *Jane Hinton* was not a party to this deed. The surrender of 16th *May* 1778 (antè, p. 651.) was stated, in the conveyance to trustees of that date, to have been made in pursuance of the above mentioned covenant.

Jane Hinton married *James Baverstock* on 10th *October*

1838.

Doe dem. Baverstock against Rolfe.

ber 1769. *Martha Hinton*, her sister, died an infant and unmarried, in *June* 1776.

16th *May* 1778. *Jane Baverstock* was admitted to the moiety, to hold to her and the heirs of her body after the death of *John Hinton*.

The effect of which was, that this moiety was limited to *John Hinton* for life, remainder to *Jane Baverstock* in tail, remainder to *John Hinton* in fee.

As to *Sarah Betts's* moiety, the following facts appeared.

29th *May* 1732. *Sarah Betts* was admitted to hold the moiety in fee. After which she and her husband *Phiilp Betts* surrendered to the use of *Sarah* for life, remainder to the use of *Philip* for life, remainder to the use of the heirs of the body of *Sarah* by *Philip Betts*, remainder to the use of the right heirs of *Sarah*. Admission of *Sarah Betts* to hold for life.

14th *June* 1736. *Philip Betts* and *Sarah Betts* suffered a recovery of the moiety, to the use of *Quarles Harris* to secure 550*l.* and interest (*a*); and, subject thereto, to the use of *Sarah* for life, remainder to *Philip* for life, remainder to the right heirs of *Sarah* for ever. Admission of *Philip* and *Sarah Betts* accordingly.

11th *January* 1739. *Philip Betts* and *Sarah Betts* surrendered the moiety to the use of *Sarah* for life, remainder to the use of *Philip* for life, remainder to the use of the before mentioned *Edward Hinton* and his wife *Mary Hinton* (only sister of *Sarah Betts*) in fee.

Philip Betts and *Sarah Betts* both died before 19th *May* 1758; before which time, also, *Edward Hinton* and *Mary Hinton* died, leaving only one child, the before mentioned *Martha Hinton*, wife of *John Hinton*.

(*a*) It did not appear what became of this mortgage; probably payment was presumed.

1838.

Doe dem. Baverstock *against* Rolfe.

19th *May* 1758. *Martha Hinton* was admitted to the moiety to hold in fee.

Martha Hinton died in *July* 1761, leaving only two children, the before mentioned *Jane Hinton* and *Martha Hinton*, infants, her co-heiresses.

4th *June* 1762. The daughters, *Jane Hinton* and *Martha Hinton*, were admitted to the moiety, by guardian, to hold each a moiety of the moiety in fee.

Jane Hinton married the before mentioned *James Baverstock* 10th *October* 1769. *Martha Hinton* died an infant, and unmarried, in *June* 1776.

7th *July* 1777. *Jane Baverstock* (late *Hinton*) was admitted to her sister *Martha Hinton*'s moiety of the moiety, to hold in fee.

16th *May* 1778. *James Baverstock* and his wife *Jane Baverstock*, in performance of the covenants, &c., of *Jane Baverstock's* mother, *Martha Hinton*, in her marriage settlement of 31st *July* 1746 (for which see p. 653. antè), surrendered the moiety to the use of the father of *Jane Baverstock*, *John Hinton*, for life; remainder to *Jane Baverstock* and the heirs of her body; remainder to the heirs of *John Hinton* for ever. Admissions of *John Hinton* and *Jane Baverstock* accordingly.

The effect of which was that this moiety, like the other, was limited to *John Hinton* for life, remainder to *Jane Baverstock* in tail, remainder to *John Hinton* in fee.

Then followed the deed of 16th *May* 1778, above first mentioned.

A verdict was found for the plaintiff; and leave was reserved to move to enter a nonsuit. In *Easter* term 1836, *Spankie* Serjt. obtained a rule accordingly.

In *Michaelmas* term last (*a*),

(*a*) *November* 17th and 18th, 1837, before Lord *Denman* C. J., *Patteson*, *Williams*, and *Coleridge* Js.

Thesiger,

1838.

Doe dem. Baverstock against Rolfe.

Thesiger, *Platt*, and *C. R. Turner* shewed cause. First, by the uses of the recovery of 16 *May* 1778, *Jane Baverstock* had a contingent remainder in fee. That contingent remainder did not pass, either, as to one moiety, to the trustees by the surrender of the same date (and therefore not by their surrender to *Letch* on 27th *June* 1778), or, as to the other moiety, by the surrender of *John Hinton*, *James Baverstock*, and *Jane Baverstock*, to *Letch*, of 27th *June* 1778. Afterwards, upon the death of *James Baverstock*, this remainder became vested in *Jane*. Therefore, upon *Jane*'s death in 1835, her heir at law, the lessor of the plaintiff, became entitled. *Doe dem. Blacksell* v. *Tomkins* (*a*) shews that a surrender cannot operate upon an interest merely contingent, and that it does not pass such interest by estoppel. *Doe dem. Dormer* v. *Wilson* (*b*) confirms this, and is a case closely resembling the present.

Secondly, it will be argued for the defendant that the creation of a contingent remainder to the survivor of the two, *James Baverstock* and *Jane Baverstock*, was void as against purchasers for valuable consideration; and that the trustees to the conveyance of 16 *May* 1778, and *Letch*, were such purchasers. One argument, to shew that this contingent remainder was void, will be that, as the limitations of uses of the recovery of 16 *May* 1778 were merely intended as the machinery to carry into effect the sale of the property, and as the creation of the contingent remainder defeated this intention of the parties, this part of the limitation was a mere mistake, and so without consideration. But the mistake, if any, is one of law, and not of fact. Courts of law hold

(*a*) 11 *East*, 185.

(*b*) 4 *B. & Ald.* 303.

1838.

Doe dem. Baverstock against Rolfe.

parties cognizant of the legal effect of facts as to which there is no mistake; *Bilbie* v. *Lumley* (*a*), *Brisbane* v. *Dacres* (*b*); and even courts of equity refuse to relieve against mistakes of law; *Worrall* v. *Jacob* (*c*). If any other rule were adopted, the Courts would be called upon to remodel limitations according to the presumed intentions of parties. But there is no ground, here, for assuming that any mistake has been committed. The sale to *Letch* did not take place till 27th *June* 1778: it does not appear that this sale was contemplated at the time of the conveyances of 16th *May* 1778. It will be said that, as to *Hinton*'s moiety, the design of the limitations of uses in the first mentioned recovery of 16th *May* 1778 was to carry into effect the provisions of the antenuptial deed of 9th *October* 1769; and that the creation of the contingent remainder was inconsistent with the provisions of that deed. But it does not appear that, even as to this moiety, there has been any mistake. *Jane Hinton* (afterwards *Baverstock*) was no party to the antenuptial deed. She had then a vested remainder in tail; and *John Hinton*, her father, was tenant for life, and was dealing merely with his own life estate: the disposal of the remainder expectant upon his death seems not to have been contemplated by the deed of 1769. It is observable, also, that the limitation of the contingent remainder, by the recovery of 16th *May* 1778, agrees with the limitation of the same property in the earlier deed of 1st *August* 1746; so that there is no appearance of a mistake. At any rate, this objection applies to one moiety only. But, further, the uses to which the copyhold was limited could not, at the time of the recovery

(*a*) 2 *East*, 469. (*b*) 5 *Taunt.* 143.
(*c*) 3 *Mer.* 256. See p. 271.

of

1838.

Doe dem. Baverstock against Rolfe.

of 16th *May* 1778, be varied, as to *Jane Baverstock's* interest, without her concurrence: her joining in the deed, therefore, raises a good consideration; *Myddleton* v. *Lord Kenyon* (a), *Scot* v. *Bell* (b), *Osgood* v. *Strode* (c), *Roe dem. Hamerton* v. *Mitton* (d), *Pulvertoft* v. *Pulvertoft* (e), *Hill* v. *The Bishop of Exeter* (g). *Nunn* v. *Wilsmore* (h) is an instance of settlements being held good against creditors, without pecuniary consideration, sufficient motive arising from the legal position of the parties with respect to each other (i).

Spankie Serjt., *Channell* and *Tomlinson* contrà. The limitation of the contingent remainder in the first recovery of 16th *May* 1778 was voluntary, and therefore, legally speaking, fraudulent, under stat. 27 *Eliz.* c. 4. (which applies to copyholds, *Doe dem. Tunstill* v. *Bottriell* (k)), against purchasers for valuable consideration, or creditors; *Humberton* v. *Howgil* (l), *Doe dem. Otley* v. *Manning* (m). The latter case shews that even notice to *Letch* would not have prevented the limitation from being fraudulent as against him. The conveyances of 16th *May* 1778 were the first attempt to carry out the inten-

(a) 2 *Ves.* jun. 391. See p. 410. See 3 *Sugd. Vend. & P.* 295. (10th ed.).

(b) 2 *Lev.* 70.

(c) 2 *P. Wil.* 245. See p. 256.

(d) 2 *Wil.* 356.

(e) 18 *Ves.* 84. See p. 92.

(g) 2 *Taunt.* 69.

(h) 8 *T. R.* 521.

(i) In addition to the objections here answered, two other points were made for the defendant, but ultimately abandoned. First, that *James H. Baverstock*, the lessor of the plaintiff, had not been admitted; as to which *Co. Lit.* 378 b. (cited, *Fearne, Cont. Rem.* 30. 9th ed.) and *Phypers* v. *Eburn*, 3 *New Ca.* 250., were referred to. Secondly, that there was an adverse possession against the lessor of the plaintiff; as to which *Doe dem. Dormer* v. *Wilson*, 4 *B. & Ald.* 303. was cited. See p. 670., post.

(k) 5 *B. & Ad.* 131.

(l) *Hob.* 72. (5th ed.).

(m) 9 *East*, 59.

 tion

1838.

Doe dem. Bavenstock against Rolfe.

tion of the settlement of 1769. But the limitation of the contingent remainder is inconsistent with that intention. In the cases where the consideration has been held sufficient, it will be found that it was one either of money or money's worth, or marriage, or the concurrence of parties not bound, as here, by previous contract. And the limitations are supported to the extent only of the consideration. The concurrence of a necessary party is a consideration, only where the joining of such party is the result of the contract then made; where that is not the case, the conveyance is void; *Goodright dem. Humphreys* v. *Moses* (*a*). And, further, such concurrence is a good consideration only for limitations made in favour, or at the desire, of such party; but here the limitation defeated the object of the party. In *Roe dem. Hamerton* v. *Wilson* (*b*) the reservation was in favour of sons of the party concurring, and the Court treated it as part of the bargain made by her. In *Johnson* v. *Legard* (*c*) a party, in consideration of his intended marriage and the marriage portion, settled land (after certain limitations in favour of the wife and the issue of the marriage, and the sons of the settlor by any future marriage) to the use of the brothers of the settlor and their issue; and, as to this limitation, the settlement was held void as against purchasers for value, being so far without consideration, and foreign to the purposes of the deed. Indeed, in *Clayton* v. *The Earl of Wilton* (*d*), it was attempted unsuccessfully to carry the principle still further, and to avoid limitations made in favour of the issue of the settlor by a second marriage.

(*a*) 2 *W. Bl.* 1019.
(*b*) 2 *Wils.* 356.
(*c*) 6 *M.* & *S.* 60.
(*d*) 6 *M.* & *S.* 67.

1838.

Doe dem. Baverstock against Rolfe.

riage (*a*). *Myddleton* v. *Lord Kenyon* (*b*) was not a decision on stat. 27 *Eliz. c.* 4., and is inapplicable here. In *Scot* v. *Bell* (*c*) the lands newly settled, in consideration (as was held) of the wife's concurrence, were limited to the uses of the old marriage settlement. In *Osgood* v. *Strode* (*d*) the limitation which was held good was considered to be the real object of the transaction between the parties, and was upheld against the heirs and devisees of the parties. In *Hill* v. *The Bishop of Exeter* (*e*), where the release of an adverse claim was held to be a good consideration, the party releasing took the benefit which was contemplated; and the limitation to him was therefore upheld against a grant made to the releasor's son in consideration of natural love and affection. In the present case, the limitation has an effect which could not have been contemplated as to either moiety. With respect to *Hinton*'s moiety, the intention clearly was, in pursuance of the deed of 9th *October* 1769, to sell the land absolutely and invest the proceeds in other estates, to be limited to the same uses as those in the deed of 9th *October* 1769. And, as to *Betts*'s moiety also, the intention of the parties evidently was that it should be dealt with in the same way as the other moiety; and, in this case also, an absolute sale must have been contemplated by *Hinton* and *James* and *Jane Baverstock*, who, among them, had the whole interest. The first recovery of 16th *May* 1778 must, for the purpose of the present question, be treated as forming one conveyance with those by which it was followed

(*a*) See remarks on this case, 3 *Sugd. V. & P.* 291. (10th ed.).

(*b*) 2 *Ves.* jun. 410.

(*c*) 2 *Lev.* 70.

(*d*) 2 *P. Wms.* 245. See p. 256.

(*e*) 2 *Taunt.* 69.

up,

1838.

Doe dem. Baverstock against Rolfe.

up, according to the principle of *Selwyn* v. *Selwyn* (*a*), *Roe dem. Noden* v. *Griffits* (*b*), and *Doe dem. Odiarne* v. *Whitehead* (*c*). In *Pulvertoft* v. *Pulvertoft* (*d*) the Court of Chancery refused to restrain parties from a sale which went to defeat the limitations of a voluntary conveyance. *Buckle* v. *Mitchell* (*e*) goes further still. There Sir *William Grant* M. R. decreed a specific performance, against the parties claiming under a voluntary settlement, in favour of a purchaser with notice.

Cur. adv. vult.

Lord Denman C. J., in the ensuing term, mentioned this case, and said that the Court wished it to be re-argued by one counsel on each side, as to the following point. *John Hinton* being tenant for life, remainder to Mrs. *Baverstock* in tail, remainder to *John Hinton* in fee, a surrender is made and recovery suffered (16th *May* 1778) to the use of *John Hinton* for life, remainder to the use of Mrs. *Baverstock* for life, remainder to the use of the right heirs of the survivor. The lessor of the plaintiff is heir to the survivor, and also issue in tail. If that recovery be void, he is entitled as issue in tail, because his mother's estate tail was never barred; if that recovery and the uses of it stand good, he is entitled as heir to the survivor, because the contingent remainder could not pass to *Letch*. Therefore, to entitle the defendant to a verdict, it must be shewn that the recovery is good so as to bar the entail, and yet the uses void.

(*a*) 2 *Burr.* 1131. See p. 1134.
(*b*) 4 *Burr.* 1952. See p. 1962.
(*c*) 2 *Burr.* 704. See p. 711.
(*d*) 18 *Ves.* 84.
(*e*) 18 *Ves.* 100.

Accordingly,

Accordingly, the case was further argued in *Easter* term 1838 (*a*).

C. R. Turner for the plaintiff. [*Patteson* J. Supposing the declared uses to be void, can the recovery stand? And, if the recovery fails with the uses, the tenancy in tail remains.] If no uses were declared of which the Court can take notice, the recovery is ineffectual, and there is no fee simple. [*Patteson* J. Is there any authority to shew whether, where uses have actually been declared, which prove void, the whole conveyance is avoided?] In *Fitzjames* v. *Moys* (*b*) tenant in tail suffered a recovery and declared the use by deed to his cousin (through whom plaintiff claimed) and her heirs after his death; afterwards he sold the lands to another cousin, the defendant, for 1000*l.*, without notice of the first conveyance, and, on a trial at bar, the Court said that the first conveyance might be fraudulent within the statute of *Elizabeth*, and it was so found. [*Patteson* J. Was any person party to that suit, who could have taken under the entail? If nothing is stated on that subject, it does not appear that the defendant may not have had sufficient title, although no valid recovery had been suffered.] It is sufficient for the lessor of the plaintiff here to stand upon the uses declared. The recovery and surrender to uses constitute one entire conveyance; *Stevens dem. Costard* v. *Winning* (*c*), 5 *Cruise's Dig.* 461, 4th ed. If therefore the conveyance stands good, its operation will be determined by the intention of the parties, as disclosed by the deed of uses. If the

(*a*) *May* 4th. Before Lord *Denman* C. J., *Patteson* and *Coleridge* Js.

(*b*) 1 *Sid.* 133.

(*c*) 2 *Wils.* 219.

1838.

Doe dem. Baverstock against Rolfe.

uses are void, the Court will not suppose a resulting use which would supersede the expressed ones, and the clear intention. The conveyance is wholly good, or wholly void. But the uses are good at law; though, if the parties have declared such uses that a sale cannot be effected, that may be a ground for applying to a court of equity.

Spankie Serjt. contrà. The declaration of void uses does not make the recovery invalid for the purpose of giving title to the defendant. The statute of *Elizabeth* renders fraudulent conveyances void only as against those who may be prejudiced by them; it does not alter the law in other respects, as between the parties to the conveyance. Many authorities shew that a deed may be good for some purposes, though bad for others; *Pigot's* case (*a*); 1 *Shepp. Touchst.* 71. *c.* 4. 8th ed.; *Greenwood* v. *Bishop* of *London* (*b*); *Doe dem. Thompson* v. *Pitcher* (*c*); *Winchcombe* v. *Bishop of Winchester* (*d*); *Anonymous* case in *Style* (*e*); *Veale* v. *Priour* (*g*); in which last three cases fraudulent conveyances are expressly adverted to. The recovery is independent of the declaration of uses; it is from the recovery that the uses are to arise; and, if none or void ones only are declared, a fee-simple results to the tenant in tail. *Lee* C. J. says, in *Martin dem. Tregonwell* v. *Strachan* (*h*), " An absolute, unfettered, pure fee-simple passes by the common recovery;" " it is this use of the fee-simple that passes to the recoveror from the tenant in tail, and which

(*a*) 11 *Rep.* 27 *b.*

(*b*) 5 *Taunt.* 727.

(*c*) 6 *Taunt.* 359.

(*d*) *Hob.* 166. (5th ed.).

(*e*) *Style*, 428.

(*g*) *Hardr.* 353, 354.

(*h*) Note (*b*) to *Roe dem. Crow* v. *Baldwere*, 5 *T. R.* 110.

results

1838.

Doe dem. Baverstock against Rolfe.

results to him and his heirs if no use is declared." [*Patteson* J. If the recoveror takes the estate independently of the declaration of uses, it would appear that the nominal recoveror would have the legal estate]. The use would result according to the actual interests of the parties. And in *Fearne, Cont. Rem.* 48. it is laid down (referring to *Co. Litt.* 22 *b*, 23 *a*.) that "in a conveyance to uses without valuable consideration, so much of the use as is not disposed of remains in the grantor." The recovery therefore, in the present case, would take its effect out of the resulting use, regulated by the interest remaining in the grantor. In *Gilbert on Uses*, 119. (*a*), 3d (*Sugden's*) ed., it is said that, "if a man seised of lands in tail, levies a fine, or suffers a recovery, and declares no uses, the use results to the tenant in tail, and he becomes seised *in fee* by virtue of the recovery, because the recoveror is tenant in fee." *Com. Dig. Uses* (D 2.) also states the doctrine on this subject. And in 1 *Preston on Conveyancing*, 196, 3d ed., the author cites the following opinion given by Mr. *Fearne*. "I conceive that where a tenant in tail is vouched in a common recovery, it bars the estate tail, and all remainders and reversions thereon depending and expectant, and expands the estate into a fee-simple, abstracted from the declaration of the uses of such recovery, because a fee-simple is recovered. And therefore where no use of the fee is declared in such a case, and there is no consideration to raise the use in the recoveror, it results to the tenant in tail in fee, 2 *Roll. Abr.* 789. pl. 1., *Godbolt*, 180. *Bury* v. *Taylor* (*b*). *Gilb. Law of Uses*,

(*a*) Page 64. of 1st ed.

(*b*) See *Beckwith's Case*, 2 *Rep.* 56 *b*, there cited.

61,

1838.

Doe dem. Baverstock against Rolfe.

61, 64. And if such recovery be with the concurrence of a preceding tenant for life, then the use also results to him for his life. Vide *Waker* v. *Snow*, *Palm.* 359. And consequently, I apprehend, that where the use of such recovery is only partially, and not completely limited, as far as the limitation fails, that is, the unlimited use results in the same manner as the whole use would have done, if there had been no limitation of any part of it." In the present case the limitation failed as to the contingent remainder. No other use was expressly declared, inconsistent with those which would have resulted if there had been no declaration of uses. The recovery, then, passed over, in its operation, the contingent remainder, though it took effect by barring the estate tail of Mrs. *Baverstock*. The contingent remainder was like one of the impossible or absurd uses treated of in 22 *Vin. Abr.* 247, *Uses* (E. a) pl. 4. As to *Fitzjames* v. *Moys* (*a*); if the recovery in that case was void, the tenancy in tail was not barred; and it does not appear that any of the parties in that suit claimed under the entail. No question was made whether the recovery was void or not, but only whether the uses first declared were void by the statute, as if the case had been that of a conveyance to uses by a party having the fee-simple. The recovery held good for the purpose of giving title to a bonâ fide purchaser. Had it not barred the entail, no title could have been made to the purchaser. As soon as the sale took place, the limitation to uses disappeared by force of the statute, and the bonâ fide conveyance remained effectual. So, in the present case, the conveyance to *Letch* takes effect

(*a*) 1 *Sid.* 133.

by

1838.

Doe dem. Baverstock against Rolfe.

by virtue of the recovery, and the contingent remainder is as if it had never existed. The principle on which the Courts have always acted in such cases has been to give the utmost possible effect to the statute of *Elizabeth*; *Burrel's Case* (a), *Thorne* v. *Newman* (b).

Cur. adv. vult.

Lord Denman C. J. in this term (*June* 14th) delivered the judgment of the Court.

This was an ejectment to recover certain copyhold premises in the county of *Essex*. The lessor of the plaintiff claimed as heir at law of Mrs. *Jane Baverstock*. The defendant held under *John Letch*, who had purchased the premises many years ago.

A verdict was found for the lessor of the plaintiff, with liberty to move to enter a nonsuit. A rule nisi to that effect having been obtained, the case was argued in *Michaelmas* term last, when the facts appeared to be as follows.

On the 29th of *May* 1732, *Mary Hinton*, the wife of *Edward Hinton*, was admitted to a moiety of the premises in fee, as coheiress of her father *Francis Bridge*; which moiety, and on the same day, she and her husband surrendered, to the use of *Mary Hinton* for life; remainder to the use of *Edward Hinton* for life; remainder to the use of the heirs of the body of *Mary Hinton*, by *Edward Hinton*; remainder to the use of the right heirs of *Mary Hinton*. On the 19th of *May* 1746, *Martha Hinton*, the only child of *Edward* and *Mary* (they being both dead), was admitted to this moiety as tenant in tail.

(a) 6 *Rep.* 72 a.

(b) 2 *Reports in Chancery*, 37.

1838.

Doe dem. Baverstock against Rolfe.

tail. On 1st of *August* 1746, *Martha Hinton* surrendered in order that a recovery might be suffered, which was done, and the moiety afterwards surrendered and settled to the use of *Martha Hinton* for life; remainder to the use of her intended husband, *John Hinton*, for life; remainder to the use of the children of the marriage, according to appointment; remainder to the use of the heirs of the body of *Martha Hinton* by *John Hinton;* remainder to the use of the right heirs of the survivor of *John* and *Martha Hinton* in fee. On the 4th *June* 1762, *John Hinton* was admitted tenant for life on the death of his wife. On the 16th *May* 1778, *Jane Baverstock*, the wife of *James Baverstock*, the only surviving child of *John* and *Martha Hinton* (her sister *Martha* having died an infant unmarried), was admitted tenant in tail in remainder.

This moiety then stood settled to *John Hinton* for life; remainder to *Jane Baverstock* in tail; remainder to *John Hinton* in fee; for the contingency of survivorship between him and his wife had happened in his favour.

The other moiety, on the death of Mrs. *Sarah Betts* (who was the sister of *Mary Hinton* and coheiress of *Francis Bridge*) and her husband, descended to *Martha Hinton*, who was admitted in fee 19th *May* 1758. She, by her marriage settlement in 1746, covenanted to settle this moiety in the same way as the other was settled; but died without doing so. After her death, on 4th *June* 1762, her daughters *Jane* and *Martha* were admitted each to a fourth in fee. On 7th *July* 1777, on the death of *Martha*, *Jane Baverstock* her sister was admitted to her share. On 16th *May* 1778, *Jane Baverstock*, in pursuance of the covenant in her mother's settlement, surrendered

surrendered the whole moiety to the use of her father *John Hinton* for life; remainder to the use of her, *Jane Baverstock*, in tail; remainder to the use of the heirs of *John Hinton* for ever.

Whereby this moiety, as well as the other, became settled in *John Hinton* for life; remainder to *Jane Baverstock* in tail; remainder to *John Hinton* in fee.

On the same day, *John Hinton* and *Jane Baverstock* surrendered the entirety for the purpose of suffering a recovery, which was accordingly suffered, and then the premises surrendered to the use of *John Hinton* for life; remainder to *Jane Baverstock* for life; remainder to the heirs of the survivor.

On the same day, *John Hinton*, in performance of his covenant in his daughter's marriage settlement, dated 9th *October* 1769, and *James Baverstock* and *Jane* his wife, surrendered a moiety of the premises to the use of the trustees of that settlement, *Charles Blackstone* and *Thomas Baverstock*, their heirs and assigns, in trust for *James Baverstock* for life, remainder to *Jane Baverstock* for life, remainder to *Thomas Baverstock* their eldest child, and four others by name, as *James* and *Jane* should appoint; and, in default of appointment, to *Thomas* the eldest in tail; remainder to *John James* the second son in tail; remainder to the third, fourth, and other sons; remainder to the daughters in tail; remainder to the heirs of *Jane Baverstock* for ever: with a power to the trustees, at the request of *James* and *Jane*, to sell the moiety and invest the proceeds in other estates to be settled to the same uses; and with a power to *John Hinton*, *James Baverstock*, and the trustees, unanimously, to alter or make void all the uses and to create new and other uses.

On

1838.

Doe dem. Baverstock against Rolfe.

On the 6th *July* 1778, *John Hinton*, *James Baverstock*, and *Jane* his wife, surrendered one moiety to *John Letch* in fee. And the trustees, at the special instance and request of *James Baverstock* and *Jane* his wife, testified by their joining in the surrender, surrendered the other moiety to *John Letch* in fee.

This was a bonâ fide purchase by *John Letch*, for an adequate consideration; and the possession has gone along with it ever since. *John Hinton*, the father of Mrs. *Baverstock*, died in 1802. *Jane Baverstock* died in 1835.

It was contended by the defendant, first, that the lessor of the plaintiff had never been admitted; but this point was given up on the argument, it being clear that he claimed as heir.

Secondly, that the Statute of limitations applies; but it is plain that Mrs. *Baverstock*'s life interest, at all events, passed to the defendant. She, therefore, could never enter; and the lessor of the plaintiff had no right of entry till her death.

Thirdly, that the contingent remainder created by the settlement of 16th *May* 1778 was void as against a bonâ fide purchaser, being a voluntary conveyance.

It seems most probable that the parties in the surrender to *Letch* acted under a mistaken supposition that the contingent remainder would pass to him. The cases of *Doe dem. Blacksell* v. *Tomkins* (*a*) and *Doe dem. Dormer* v. *Wilson* (*b*) shew that it would not. But, if such a mistake was made, the Court has no power to remedy it. And, inasmuch as Mrs. *Baverstock* did not, after the fee had vested in her by survivorship on

(*a*) 11 *East*, 185. (*b*) 4 *B. & Ald.* 303.

the

1838.

Doe dem. Baverstock against Rolfe.

the death of her father, make any further surrender of the premises, it seems clear that, if the uses of that surrender to Mr. *Hinton* for life, remainder to Mrs. *Baverstock* for life, remainder to the heirs of the survivor, are held valid, the lessor of the plaintiff must be entitled to recover. On the other hand, if those uses, *and the recovery under which they are declared*, be held void under stat. 27 *Eliz. c.* 4., as against a purchaser, then the surrender to *Letch* must be treated as made by tenant for life, tenant in tail in remainder, and tenant in fee in remainder. Neither that surrender, nor any subsequent one, barred the estate tail of Mrs. *Baverstock*; therefore *Letch* took only for the lives of Mr. *Hinton* and Mrs. *Baverstock*; and the lessor of the plaintiff, as issue in tail, is entitled to recover.

If this view of the case be correct, the only mode by which the defendant can succeed is, by satisfying the Court that the recovery suffered by Mr. *Hinton* and Mrs. *Baverstock* is valid, so as to bar her estate tail, though the uses declared upon it are void as a voluntary settlement; in which case an use would result to Mrs. *Baverstock* in fee, as for want of any declaration of uses, those declared being held void.

The Court had some doubt as to this last point, and in consequence directed a second argument; upon which we are satisfied, on reference to the cases cited, particularly that of *Fitzjames* v. *Moys* (*a*), that such use would result.

The single question therefore is, whether the contingent remainder be void under stat. 27 *Eliz. c.* 4.

Many cases were cited upon the argument, most of

(*a*) 1 *Sid.* 133.

which

1838.

DOE dem. BAVERSTOCK *against* ROLFE.

which will be found collected in the case of *Johnson* v. *Legard* (*a*). On the one hand, it is said that, as the limitations of the estate could not be changed without the consent of all parties, the joining of those parties, namely, Mr. *Hinton* and Mrs. *Baverstock*, is itself a sufficient consideration to prevent the new settlement from being voluntary. On the other hand it is argued that such joinder is not in itself sufficient, unless the terms of joining be matter of contract and bargain; and for this point *Goodright dem. Humphreys* v. *Moses* (*b*) was cited, also *Pulvertoft* v. *Pulvertoft* (*c*), and, in the same volume, *Buckle* v. *Mitchell* (*d*). It is further argued that no contract appears in this case, either upon the face of the documents, or in any other manner; nor is any valuable consideration necessarily implied from the circumstances; and that the plain object of the parties was to effectuate a valid sale of the premises.

It is difficult to reconcile all the cases upon this subject, or rather to extract from them any clear principle for our guidance. The inclination of the Courts appears to have been always to support a fair settlement in favour of the persons intended to be benefited by that settlement, and to treat nearly any consideration as sufficient for that purpose; that inclination, however, cannot operate on the present occasion, inasmuch as the lessor of the plaintiff is clearly not one of the persons intended to be benefited.

Upon the whole, we are of opinion that the uses declared upon the recovery in question were voluntary, and void within stat. 27 *Eliz.* c. 4. as against purchasers, no sufficient consideration having been shewn to us: and

(*a*) 6 *M.* & *S.* 60.

(*b*) 2 *W. Bl.* 1019.

(*c*) 18 *Ves.* 84.

(*d*) 18 *Ves.* 100.

the

the more so, as we cannot but see that the plain intention, both of Mr. *Hinton* and Mrs. *Baverstock*, was to sell the premises, and that the different surrenders were made under the supposition of their being necessary in order effectually to make that sale.

The rule for a nonsuit must, therefore, be made absolute.

Rule absolute (*a*).

(*a*) See 2 *Sugd. Vend. and Pur.* p. 294. (10th ed.)

CORBETT *against* SWINBURNE.

It is a good plea, in assumpsit, that, as to 50*l.*, parcel &c., plaintiff ought not *further* to maintain &c., because, after the commencement of the action, defendant indorsed and delivered to plaintiff a bill of exchange for 82*l.* drawn by *C.* and accepted by *B.* (or that defendant paid plaintiff 50*l.*), in full satisfaction and discharge of defendant's promise as to 50*l.*, and of all damages by plaintiff sustained by reason of the non-performance of such promise (not mentioning costs), which bill plaintiff took and received in such full satisfaction and discharge.

ASSUMPSIT by indorsee against drawer and indorser of a bill of exchange for 126*l.* 17*s.* 6*d.*, averring non-payment by the drawee, and notice thereof to defendant. The second count was for 200*l.* on an account stated. Damages 200*l.*

Pleas. 1. To first count, that defendant had not notice. Issue thereon.

2. A plea in bar as to 76*l.* 17*s.* 6*d.* parcel of the money in the first count mentioned, and 76*l.* 17*s.* 6*d.* parcel of the money in the last count mentioned; alleging them to be the same debt. The plea was traversed, and issue joined on the traverse.

3. As to 50*l.* residue of the sum in the first count mentioned, and 50*l.* parcel of the sum in the last count mentioned, other than the 76*l.* 17*s.* 6*d.*, that the plaintiff *ought not further to maintain* his action thereof, because &c.; averment of the identity of the two sums of 50*l.*; and that, after the making of plaintiff's said promise re-

 lating

1838.

CORBETT *against* SWINBURNE.

lating to the said sum of 50*l.*, residue &c., and after the commencement of this action, defendant indorsed and delivered to plaintiff a bill of exchange, made and drawn, to wit on 28th *September* 1836, by *C. S.*, upon and accepted by *B.* and *N. S.*, payable at one month's date, for 82*l.* 10*s.*, in full satisfaction and discharge of the said promise of defendant as to the said sum of 50*l.* residue &c., and of all damages by plaintiff sustained by reason of the non performance &c.; which bill plaintiff then took and received from defendant in such full satisfaction and discharge as aforesaid: verification. Replication; that plaintiff ought not to be barred from further maintaining &c., because defendant did not indorse and deliver to plaintiff the supposed bill in full satisfaction and discharge &c.; and plaintiff did not take or receive it from defendant in such full satisfaction and discharge &c.: conclusion to the country. Issue thereon.

4. As to 76*l.* 17*s.* 6*d.* parcel of the sums in the first and second counts and second plea mentioned, actionem non; alleging payment of 76*l.* 17*s.* 6*d.*, and acceptance thereof, before the commencement of the suit, in full satisfaction and discharge of the promise and of all damages &c.: verification. Replication, denial of such payment or acceptance in full satisfaction &c.: conclusion to the country. Issue thereon.

5. As to the 50*l.* in the third plea mentioned, that plaintiff *ought not further to maintain* &c.; averment that, after the commencement of the action, to wit on &c., defendant paid plaintiff, and plaintiff accepted and received from defendant, 50*l.* in full satisfaction and discharge of the promise of defendant as to the 50*l.* pleaded to, and of all damages sustained by reason of the non performance &c.: verification. Replication, denying the

1838.

Corbett *against* Swinburne.

the payment or acceptance in full satisfaction &c. Issue thereon.

6. To the last count, non assumpsit. Issue thereon.

On the trial before *Patteson* J., at the *Middlesex* sittings in *Trinity* term, 1837, a verdict was found for the plaintiff on the first issue, and for the defendant on the other five. In the same term, *Platt* obtained a rule for judgment, non obstante veredicto, with respect to the 50*l.* as to which the third and fifth pleas were pleaded. In this term (*a*),

Alexander and *Busby* shewed cause. The third and fifth pleas are pleaded in bar of the further maintenance of the action. Had the plaintiff admitted them, he might have had his costs up to the pleading of the pleas, so far as relates to the matter pleaded to in the third and fifth: but he has denied them; and, the jury having found that they are true, the defendant must have judgment. The pleas furnish a good answer; for they shew that the plaintiff has received satisfaction for the damages sustained by reason of the non performance of so much of the promises as the pleas relate to. Such damages include costs. If the pleas had been pleaded in this form to the whole action, there can be no doubt that they would have been a good answer; *Le Bret* v. *Papillon* (*b*).

Cottingham contrà. The third plea does not shew that the defendant had any power to indorse the bill.

(*a*) *Thursday, June* 7th, before Lord *Denman* C. J., *Littledale*, *Patteson*, and *Williams* Js.

(*b*) 4 *East*, 502.

1838.

Corbett *against* Swinburne.

[*Patteson* J. It states that the plaintiff accepted it in satisfaction.] Neither plea shews that the costs are satisfied: but from the language of each plea it appears that costs must have been incurred in the action before the supposed satisfaction was accepted. "Damages" are always understood as distinct from "costs."

Cur. adv. vult.

Lord Denman C. J., in this term (*June* 9th), delivered the judgment of the Court.

We are of opinion that the pleas in this case are good. They are pleaded in bar of the *further* maintenance of the action, and are not open to the objection taken in the case of *Le Bret* v. *Papillon* (*a*). They also state that the bills therein mentioned were accepted by the plaintiff in full satisfaction and discharge of the causes of action to which they are pleaded. They would have been good in that form if the transaction had been prior to the action, and they had been pleaded in bar generally; and we cannot see any reason why they are not equally good in the same form as a bar to the *further* maintenance. This being our opinion, it is unnecessary to notice the other matters which were discussed on the argument (*b*).

Rule discharged.

(*a*) 4 *East*, 502.

(*b*) It was argued, for the defendant, that the objection could not be taken for the plaintiff, in this form, at the present stage of the proceedings. *Rand* v. *Vaughan* (1 *New Ca.* 767.), *Clement* v. *Lewis* (3 *Br.* & *B.* 297.), *Hall* v. *Cole* (4 *A.* & *E.* 577.), *Putney* v. *Swann* (2 *M.* & *W.* 72.), were cited. And a discussion took place on right of the parties with regard to costs as in the case of a plea pais darrein continuance.

HAMLIN *against* CROSSLEY.

By stat. 7 *G.* 4. *c.* 57. *ss.* 10, 50., the Insolvent Debtors' Court has power to discharge a party from custody under a capias utlagatum upon a judgment for damages and costs.

THE plaintiff obtained a verdict against the defendant, for 20*l.* damages, in an action of trespass for criminal conversation. In *Easter* term, 1835, final judgment was signed for 288*l.* damages and costs. The defendant was proclaimed an outlaw in this cause, on 7th *October*, 1835; and the outlawry was entered of record in *Michaelmas* term 1835. On 3d *November*, 1837, a writ of *capias utlagatum* issued in the cause, directed to the sheriff of *Hertfordshire*, under which the defendant was captured and committed to the prison of that county. The defendant petitioned the Court for the relief of Insolvent Debtors on 10th *November*, 1837, and came up for hearing on 13th *December* in that year, before the Chief Commissioner, at *Hertford*. The plaintiff opposed the discharge, and took a preliminary objection, that the defendant, being an outlaw, had no *locus standi* in Court. The Chief Commissioner overruled the objection: the cause was heard, under protest on the part of the plaintiff; and the defendant was ordered to be discharged after he should have remained in custody four months from the filing of his petition. An order to the above effect was made out, and handed to the gaoler. *Crowder*, in *Hilary* term last, obtained a rule calling on the defendant and the Commissioners of the Court for the Relief of Insolvent Debtors to shew cause why a writ of prohibition should not issue, to prohibit

 the

1838.

HAMLIN *against* CROSSLEY.

the Commissioners from further proceeding on the said order. In the same term (*a*),

Sir. *W. W. Follett* shewed cause. The first question is, whether this Court has power in the present case to grant a prohibition. The question was raised in *Ex parte Battine* (*b*), but not decided, this Court considering the proceeding of the Insolvent Court to have been correct. What is to be prohibited here? The order complained of is made; and the Insolvent Court has no more steps to take. But the objection to the proceeding of the Insolvent Court is untenable. That Court has jurisdiction, under stat. 7 G. 4. c. 57. s. 10., in the case of any person in actual custody within the walls of any prison in *England*, "upon any process whatsoever, for or by reason of any debt, damage, costs, sum or sums of money, or for or by reason of any contempt of any court whatsoever for non payment of any sum or sums of money, or of costs taxed or untaxed, either ordered to be paid or to the payment of which such person would be liable in purging such contempt, or in any manner in consequence or by reason of such contempt." Sect. 50 enacts, "that the discharge of any prisoner so adjudicated as aforesaid shall and may extend to all process issuing from any Court, for any contempt of any Court, ecclesiastical or civil, for non payment of money or of costs or expenses in any Court, ecclesiastical or civil; and that in such case the said discharge shall be deemed to extend also to all costs which such prisoner would be liable to pay in consequence or by reason of such con-

(*a*) *January* 30th, 1838, before Lord *Denman* C. J., *Littledale* and *Williams* Js.

(*b*) 4 *B. & Ad.* 690.

tempt

1838.

HAMLIN *against* CROSSLEY.

tempt, or on purging the same." (*a*) The outlawry here is a consequence of the judgment for damages and costs. Taking the custody to be in the nature either of process to compel payment, or of attachment for contempt in not paying, the case is within the act. From *Castelman's Case* (*b*) it appears that an outlaw may apply for his discharge under a clause like sect. 10 of this act. In *Dickson* v. *Baker* (*c*) the power of the Insolvent Court to hear the petition was not denied.

Crowder contrà. As to the more general question, the plaintiff has no remedy but prohibition. The superior Courts have power to control by prohibition all inferior Courts acting under statutes which prescribe their jurisdiction, and exceeding that jurisdiction; 6 *Bac. Abr.* 588 (7th ed.), *Prohibition*, (I). Here the rule is to prohibit the Insolvent Court from proceeding on the order made by them; and it follows the precedent of the rule in *Ex parte Battine* (*d*). There the Court merely refused to interfere, because the Insolvent Court had proceeded correctly: they expressly abstained from entering into the general question as to their power to prohibit that Court; but no objection was raised on the ground that the order had been already made. In *Ex parte Smyth* (*e*) the power of the Court to control the judicial committee of the Privy Council by prohibition was the preliminary question. [*Littledale* J. It was not definitively conceded (*g*).] In *Roberts* v. *Humby* (*h*),

(*a*) The language of stat. 7 *G.* 4. *c.* 57. *ss.* 10, 50. corresponds with that of sects. 35, 79. of stat. 1 & 2 *Vict. c.* 110. respectively.

(*b*) 4 *Bur.* 2119.; and *Rex* v. *Castelman*, 4 *Bur.* 2127.

(*c*) 1 *A.* & *E.* 853.

(*d*) 4 *B.* & *Ad.* 690.

(*e*) 2 *Cr. M.* & *R.* 748. *S. C. Tyrwh.* & *Gr.* 222.

(*g*) See *Ex parte Smyth*, 3 *A.* & *E.* 719, 724.

(*h*) 3 *M.* & *W.* 120.

 where

1838.

HAMLIN *against* CROSSLEY.

where the motion was for a prohibition to a Court of Requests, it was argued that, as that Court had pronounced judgment, the superior Court could not interfere: but it was held that the interference might take place at that stage, where the defect of jurisdiction appeared on the face of the proceedings; and 2 *Inst.* 602 was cited. And it rather seems, from the language of the learned judges in that case, that this may be done also where the party asking for the prohibition has had no earlier opportunity of applying. In *In the matter of Poe* (*a*) this Court refused to prohibit a Court Martial the sentence of which had been pronounced, ratified by the Crown, and carried into execution; and they distinguished the case from *Grant* v. *Gould* (*b*), where, the sentence not having been executed, the Court of Common Pleas considered that the prohibition would have lain if the Court Martial had exceeded their power. Here the order of the Insolvent Court will not be executed till the defendant is discharged. It may be asked what remedy a party in such custody can have; but the only point before this Court, as in *Ex parte Deacon* (*c*), is, whether the Insolvent Court have power to discharge.

Then as to the proceedings of the Insolvent Court. An outlaw cannot be heard, except for the purpose of reversing his outlawry, having no *locus standi* in Court (*d*). He is *extra legem positus; Co. Lit.* 122. *b.*, 128. *b.*, *Aldridge* v. *Buller* (*e*), *Loukes* v. *Holbeach* (*g*), *Griffith* v. *Mid-*

(*a*) 5 *B.* & *Ad.* 681. (*b*) 2 *H. Bl.* 69. See p. 100—102.

(*c*) 5 *B.* & *Ald.* 759. See *Defries* v. *Davis*, 1 *New Ca.* 692.

(*d*) See judgment of *Littledale* J. in *Dickson* v. *Baker*, 1 *A.* & *E.* 855.; 22 *Vin. Abr.* 374, 376, 378. *Utlawry*, (U. a), (X. a), (Y. a).

(*e*) 2 *M.* & *W.* 412. (*g*) 4 *Bing.* 419.

dleton

1838.

HAMLIN *against* CROSSLEY.

dleton (*a*); in which last case *Montague* C. J. said, "that where the action is *ad lucrandum*, there ought to be ability in the person: and it is all one to gain by way of discharge, as by way of perquisition." The process of the Insolvent Court is "by way of discharge." The words of stat. 7 *Geo.* 4. *c.* 57. *ss.* 10, 50. are relied on: but here the defendant is not in contempt for nonpayment of money, but in contempt of the *lex terræ*. Thus in *Ex parte Lawrence* (*b*) the Court of Common Pleas refused to discharge an insolvent (under stat. 34 G. 3. *c.* 69. *s.* 31., the material words there being "contempts for nonpayment of money") who was in contempt for not putting in an answer in Chancery, and whom the Court of Chancery had refused to discharge except upon payment of fees. In *Beauchamp* v. *Tomkins* (*c*) the Court inclined to think that a bankruptcy and certificate did not discharge a prisoner in custody on an *utlagatum capias*. The ground of the decision in *Castelman's Case* (*d*) was the form of the order of the magistrates. In *Dickson* v. *Baker* (*e*) the party had not been discharged from custody under an outlawry, but only from the debt: and the question was, whether this Court would thereupon reverse the outlawry; which they refused to do.

Cur. adv. vult.

Lord DENMAN C. J., in this term (*June* 8th), delivered the judgment of the Court.

A rule was obtained, and has been argued, to shew cause why a prohibition should not go to the Insolvent

(*a*) *Cro. Jac.* 425.

(*b*) 1 *B.* & *P.* 477.

(*c*) 3 *Taun.* 141.

(*d*) 4 *Bur.* 2119; and *Rex* v. *Castelman*, 4 *Bur.* 2127.

(*e*) 1 *A.* & *E.* 853.

Court,

1838.

HAMLIN *against* CROSSLEY.

Court, prohibiting them from proceeding to discharge a defendant who has been outlawed in an action for criminal conversation, upon the general ground that an outlaw cannot be heard in any Court except for the single purpose of reversing his outlawry. And this is an undoubted rule of law, laid down in numerous cases and text-books, the authority of which is fully recognised, and was acted upon by the Court of Common Pleas in *Loukes* v. *Holbeach* (a). My brother *Park* there pronounced a learned judgment, affirming the principle, and applying it to a motion for setting aside an annuity in that Court, made by a person outlawed in the Court of King's Bench in an action to recover arrears of that annuity.

Whether the words of the Insolvent Act (7 *Geo.* 4. *c.* 57. sects. 10, 50.), which were cited in the argument as creating an exception from the general rule, ought to have that effect, is the question which we are now called upon to decide. But, in truth, we cannot consider it an open question. The words "upon any process whatsoever," "by reason of any" "damage," are undeniably extensive enough to embrace a person outlawed in an action. Whether it be an action of tort, or in debt or assumpsit, appears to make no difference in this case. There may be some ground for contending that persons outlawed were not in the contemplation of the act: but, in Lord *Mansfield*'s time, this Court expressly declared its unanimous opinion on two different occasions, 4 *Bur.* 2119, 2127 (a), that an outlaw fell within the clause of the then existing act, the terms of which exactly corresponded with the present. We hold ourselves bound

(a) 4 *Bing.* 419. (b) *Castelman's Case* and *Rex* v. *Castelman.*

by

by that opinion, and think that we must discharge the present rule. In the case of *Loukes* v. *Holbeach* (a) no reference was made to the report in *Burrow*, which indeed could not have been brought to bear on the question there decided.

1838.

HAMLIN *against* CROSSLEY.

Rule discharged.

(a) 4 *Bing.* 419.

ABERCROMBIE, W. T. HARDY, BLISS, and MAN, *against* HICKMAN, Executor of POCOCK.

The provisional assignee of the Insolvent Court, under stat. 1 *G.* 4. *c.* 119. *s.* 7., assigned the estate of an insolvent to an assignee, who assented to such assignment, and acted under it as tenant of premises which the insolvent held as lessee for years after the death of such last-mentioned assignee. Held that his executor was liable to the lessor for breaches of covenants in the lease subsequent to the testator's death, it not appearing that the Insolvent Court had appointed fresh assignees.

Action for breach of covenants to pay rent and repair, contained in a lease, the reversion on which was vested, by the provisions of a will, in plaintiffs, upon trust (among others) to pay an annuity to the separate use of a married woman for life, and, after her death, to pay certain annuities to the use of her children. Held, that her husband was a competent witness, though other part of the trust property had been sold because the rents were not sufficient for the purposes of the will.

COVENANT. The declaration stated that *Charles Wilmot*, being possessed of certain premises for the residue of a term of ninety-six years, commencing in 1793, demised the same, by indenture of 12th *April* 1804, to *Thomas Tasker*, his executors, administrators, and assigns, for forty-one years from 24th *June* then next, at an annual rent of 21*l.*; and *Tasker* did, for himself, his executors, administrators, and assigns, covenant, &c., with *Wilmot*, his executors, administrators, and assigns, that he, *Tasker*, his executors, &c., should and would pay the rent to *Wilmot*, his executors, &c., and that he, *Tasker*, his executors, &c., should and would, during the term thereby granted, repair &c. the premises (as specified in the indenture recited in the declaration): that, by virtue of the demise, *Tasker*, on 24th *June* 1804, entered and was possessed for the term granted:

1838.

ABERCROMBIE *against* HICKMAN.

granted: that *Wilmot* afterwards, to wit 1st *January* 1805, granted, &c., the reversion for all the residue of the first-mentioned term to the plaintiffs, their executors and administrators; whereby plaintiffs became, and thence hitherto had been, and still were, possessed of the reversion: that, after the making of the indenture of 1804, to wit 1st *December* 1822, and after the grant of the reversion to plaintiffs, all the estate, interest, and term of years unexpired &c. whatsoever, of *Tasker*, of and in the demised premises, by assignment thereof, came to and vested in *John Thomas Pocock* (the testator), who continued possessed thereof for a long &c., to wit from thence till 1st *January* 1832, when *Pocock* died; on whose death all the estate and interest of *Pocock* came to and vested in defendant, as his executor; by reason whereof defendant, as executor, became possessed, and thence hitherto had been, and still was, possessed for the residue of the term granted to *Tasker*. Breach; that, during the term so granted by *Wilmot* to *Tasker*, and after *Pocock's* death, and after defendant, as executor, became assignee as aforesaid, and while he continued such assignee, and after the grant by *Wilmot* to the plaintiffs, and whilst the plaintiffs were possessed of the reversion, to wit on 25th *March* 1836, a large &c., to wit 47*l.* 5*s.*, of the rent, for two years and a quarter, became and still was in arrear to the plaintiffs, and, during the term &c. (laying the time as in the preceding breach), the defendant did not repair &c. (following the language of the covenant to repair), but, on the contrary, the defendant, as executor &c., suffered and permitted &c. (laying want of repair during a part of the same time): conclusion; that defendant, as executor as aforesaid, hath not kept the said

1838.

ABERCROMBIE *against* HICKMAN.

said covenants by *Tasker* for himself and his assigns made, &c.

Pleas. 1. That *Pocock* never was assignee of the lease, in manner &c. 2. That defendant was not, nor ever had been, assignee of the lease, in manner &c. 3. That the demised premises did not come to, or vest in, the defendant as executor as aforesaid, in manner &c.

Issue on all the traverses.

On the trial before *Patteson* J., at the *Middlesex* sittings in *Hilary* term, 1837, the plaintiffs proved *Wilmot*'s possession of the term, the demise to *Tasker*, and that, in 1815, the plaintiffs became possessed of the reversion; that, in 1822, *Tasker* was discharged from prison by the Insolvent Debtors' Court; that, on 18th *November* 1822, the provisional assignee assigned the estate and effects of *Tasker* to *Pocock*, the assignment, however, not being executed by *Pocock;* and that *Pocock* had, on the 15th of that month, filled up with his name &c. the following form, which was deposited in the office of the Insolvent Debtors' Court.

"Court for Relief of Insolvent Debtors.—In the matter of the petition of *Thomas Tasker*, I, *John Thomas Pocock*, of *Saint Bride's Wharf*, coal merchant, do hereby signify to the said Court my acceptance of the appointment of assignee herein. Dated the 15th day of *November* 1822."

That *Pocock* died 13th *August* 1832; and that defendant was his sole executor: that 47*l.* 5*s.* was due for rent up to *Lady-day* 1836; and that the dilapidations accrued since 1st *January* 1833 amounted to 27*l.* 15*s.*

To prove that *Pocock* had taken to the lease, the plaintiffs called *Robert Hardy*, who, being examined on the

1838.

ABERCROMBIE *against* HICKMAN.

the voir dire, stated that he had married a daughter of *Charles Wilmot*, that the premises in question were vested in the plaintiffs as trustees (*a*), and charged with an annuity to the separate use of *R. Hardy's* wife for life, and that 50*l.* per annum was, in the event of her decease, to be paid for the maintenance of each of her children into the hands of the other parent if surviving, or otherwise for the trustees to superintend the application thereof: and he stated that other part of the trust property had been sold, because the rents were not sufficient according to the directions of *Charles Wilmot's* will (*a*), and that the rent to be recovered in the present action would go to the general fund. It was objected that *R. Hardy* was incompetent by reason of interest; but the learned Judge received his evidence, giving leave to move for a nonsuit, if the Court should think that the evidence was inadmissible, and that there was no case without it. *R. Hardy* then stated that he collected the rents of the estates; and that, after the assignment to *Pocock*, the witness had asked him whether he would take the lease; to which *Pocock* answered that he would, adding that there was no occasion for an assignment, because he took under the Insolvent Court; that *Pocock* had directed the witness to demand the rent of a person whom he, *Pocock*, should put in possession; that the witness had done so, and received rent accordingly, till *Christmas* 1833, at the rate of 21*l.* per annum, and had given *Pocock* a receipt for the rent, during his life. The counsel for the plaintiffs contended that the executor of *Pocock* was not liable for breaches after the testator's death. The learned Judge left it to the jury to say

(*a*) The plaintiffs in the present action, stated on the record to be grantees of *Charles Wilmot*, were in fact trustees under his will.

whether

1838.

ABERCROMBIE *against* HICKMAN.

whether *Pocock* took to the lease on his own account; and directed them, if they thought he did, to find for the plaintiffs; giving leave to move for a nonsuit. Verdict for the plaintiffs. In *Hilary* term, 1837, *Platt* obtained a rule according to the leave reserved. In this term (*a*),

Channell shewed cause. First, *R. Hardy* was a competent witness. Mrs. *Hardy* herself would have been so; for she has, at the most, only a charge to a definite amount. It is not as if she were residuary legatee, where, inasmuch as the event of the suit would affect the amount of the residue, she would be interested in such event. In *Nowell* v. *Davies* (*b*), on assumpsit brought against executors, and non assumpsit pleaded, it was held that a legatee of an annuity under the will, no proof being given of the sufficiency or insufficiency of the funds, was a competent witness for the defence. It makes no difference whether the witness comes, as there, to prevent a diminution of the funds, or, as here, to increase them. But, further, the interest of Mrs. *Hardy* does not make her husband a party immediately interested; for the annuity is to her separate use, and, after her death, the husband could receive only to the use of the children. Therefore, even if Mrs. *Hardy* would be incompetent, her husband would not be so. This is merely an action of covenant between third parties. Secondly, supposing the evidence admissible, it shews the liability of the defendant. At the time of these transactions, the Insolvent Debtors' Act in force was

(*a*) *Thursday, June* 7th, 1838, before Lord *Denman* C. J., *Littledale, Patteson*, and *Williams* Js.

(*b*) 5 *B. & Ad.* 368.

stat.

1838.

ABERCROMBIE *against* HICKMAN.

stat. 1 *G.* 4. *c.* 119. By sect. 7 the Insolvent Court is to appoint an assignee or assignees of the insolvent's estate, and, when he or they shall have signified his or their acceptance of the appointment, the provisional assignee is immediately to assign over the estate to them. Here the testator, *Pocock*, did signify his assent; and the assignment was made. He afterwards elected to take the particular property: so that the only question is, whether he could take it. He did not indeed execute the assignment; but that is unnecessary. A lease passes the property to the lessee, if executed by the lessor though not by the lessee: to create a liability as to particular covenants, on the part of the lessee, it must indeed be shewn that he accepts the lease, as by entry, &c. (*a*); but here that took place. Then, the estate being in the testator, to whom did it come upon his death? Sect. 14 of stat. 1 *G.* 4. *c.* 119. enables the Insolvent Court, upon such an event, to appoint new assignees; but no such appointment was here shewn. And the estate cannot be in the provisional assignee; for he has assigned it away. It must therefore be in the executor of the testator.

Platt contrà. First, by obtaining judgment in this suit the plaintiffs will improve the property upon which Mrs. *Hardy*'s annuity is charged, and will also recover rent which is to contribute to that annuity. Therefore, during her life, her husband is directly interested in the event of the suit. Secondly, *Pocock* could not have sued upon the covenants in this lease, not having executed it; neither then could he be sued. [*Patteson* J. It is very

(*a*) See *Co. Lit.* 231 *a.* *Burnett* v. *Lynch*, 5 *B.* & *C.* 589.

common

common indeed to bring actions against assignees of leases who have not executed: and *vice versâ.*] A man cannot be made assignee without his consent. By the recent act, 7 *G.* 4. *c.* 57, *s.* 19., a counterpart of the assignment by the provisional assignee must be filed of record in the Insolvent Court. [Lord *Denman* C. J. There is no such provision as to filing in stat. 1 *G.* 4. *c.* 119. It seems that any mode of signifying assent was enough.] On the death of the assignee, if no fresh assignee be appointed, the property reverts to the provisional assignee: if it did not, it must revert to the insolvent himself, which would lead to absurd consequences, in respect of his liability and power.

1838.

ABERCROMBIE *against* HICKMAN.

Cur. adv. vult.

Lord DENMAN C. J., in this term (*June* 14), delivered the judgment of the Court.

This was an action of covenant by a lessor against the executor of the assignee of his lessee, an insolvent, for nonpayment of rent accrued due since the testator's death. We felt some doubt whether the action could be maintained against the executor, from a provision in the Insolvent acts, which may be thought to import that the appointment of such assignee is a mere personal trust; we mean the power vested in the Insolvent Commissioners to appoint a new assignee on the death of him first appointed. But, upon full consideration, and on referring to *Bloxam* v. *Hubbard* (*a*), *Aldritt* v. *Kittridge* (*b*), and *Ex parte Bainbridge* (*c*), decided under the Bankrupt Act, 5 *G.* 2. *c.* 30., we think that the

(*a*) 5 *East*, 407.

(*b*) 6 *B. Moore*, 569. See *Aldritt* v. *Kettridge*, 1 *Bing.* 355.

(*c*) 6 *Ves.* 451.

1838.

ABERCROMBIE *against* HICKMAN.

executor is liable, as representing the assignee, if the latter acted as tenant of the premises demised, as well as assented to the assignment.

But the evidence by which this fact was established was objected to, as proceeding from a witness who was said to be inadmissible, by reason of his interest in the event of the suit. That witness was the husband of a lady who was entitled to an annuity charged on the premises which were vested in the plaintiffs as trustees. The annuity was settled to the separate use of the wife, and afterwards for the benefit of the children. It was argued that the witness, therefore, through the interest of his wife in these premises, was interested in fixing the defendant with this rent, that the security for the annuity might be the ampler. But this objection is obviously untenable; for, in whatever person the lease may be vested, the rent must be paid; and the interest of the witness, if any, is far too remote to render him incompetent. This rule must be discharged.

Rule discharged.

Doe on the several Demises of Rowlandson, Assignee of Margaret Williams an Insolvent Debtor, of Margaret Williams, and of Jeremiah Williams, *against* Wainwright and Ledgerwood (*a*).

On the trial of an ejectment upon demise of *J.*, the defendant, to prove that the premises had passed by a deed conveying a messuage *with the appurtenances*, offered in evidence another deed by which *M.*, for whom *J.*, if the plaintiff recovered, would be trustee during *M.*'s life, conveyed the messuage by a description which (as contended) disposed of the premises in question as appurtenant thereto. *M.*'s conveyance recited a previous unsatisfied mortgage of the messuage, by her late husband, (who had devised to her for her life), and purported to be made in consideration of the forbearance of certain sums owing by her as her husband's executrix, and of further advances then made to her. The defendant offered *M.*'s deed, first, as a *declaration made by* the cestui que trust of the lessor of the plaintiff, and therefore *a party equitably represented* by *the party on the record*, secondly, as an act of *user* of the premises, as appurtenances, *by the occupier*.

Held, that *M.*'s conveyance was not admissible, inasmuch as *M.*, in *her conveyance*, appeared, not only to admit a fact in derogation of her own title, but to gain a benefit by the forbearance and advance of money.

EJECTMENT for messuages in *Liverpool*. On the trial before *Coleridge* J., at the *Liverpool* summer assizes, 1836, no evidence was offered in support of *Rowlandson*'s demise. It was proved, for the plaintiff, that one *Oldham* was formerly owner of the premises; and the last two lessors of the plaintiff claimed under an indenture of feoffment of 9th *July* 1807, between one *Rogers* of the first part, *Oldham* of the second, *Michael Williams* of the third, and *Jeremiah Williams*, the last lessor of the plaintiff, of the fourth; by which *Rogers* and *Oldham* granted, bargained, sold, enfeoffed, and confirmed a parcel of ground, comprehending the premises in question, to *Michael* and *Jeremiah* in fee, habendum to *Michael* and *Jeremiah*, and the heirs and assigns of *Michael*, to the use of *Michael* and *Jeremiah*, and the heirs and assigns of *Michael*, in trust, as to *Jeremiah*'s estate, for *Michael*, his heirs and assigns. That *Mi*-

(*a*) For the points previously decided in this case, see *Doe dem. Rowlandson* v. *Wainwright*, 5 *A. & E.* 520.

1838.

Doe dem. Rowlandson *against* Wainwright.

chael Williams was in possession at the time of his death, *October* 17th, 1821; that he devised all his real and personal estate to his widow, *Margaret Williams*, the second lessor of the plaintiff, for life, and, after her death, to her children, to be divided equally; and that she had occupied from *Michael's* death down to and at the time of the conveyance of 1824, hereinafter mentioned.

The defendants proved an indenture of mortgage, dated 15th *October* 1808, between *Michael Williams* of the first part, *Jeremiah Williams* of the second part, and two persons named *Holden* and *Gordon* of the third part, reciting the indenture of feoffment of 9th *July* 1807, and that *Holden* and *Gordon* had agreed to advance *Michael Williams* 150*l*. on the security in the present indenture contained: and witnessing that, in consideration of such advance, and of 5*s*. paid by *Holden* and *Gordon* to *Jeremiah Williams*, *Michael Williams*, and *Jeremiah Williams* granted, bargained, sold, aliened, remised, released, and enfeoffed, unto *Holden* and *Gordon*, their heirs and assigns, all that piece of land, with the messuage or dwelling-house and buildings thereon erected, situate &c. (setting out bounds and metes), now in the possession of *Michael Williams*, *together with all and singular houses, outhouses, edifices, buildings, ways, waters, water-courses, paths, passages, lights, liberties, easements, commodities, privileges, advantages, hereditaments and appurtenances whatsoever, to the said piece or parcel of land, messuage, or dwelling-house, belonging or in anywise appertaining*: habendum to *Holden* and *Gordon* in fee, to the use of themselves in fee, in trust to permit *Michael Williams*, his heirs, and assigns, to hold &c. till default of payment of 150*l*. on 15th of *April* then next

1838.

Doe dem. ROWLANDSON against WAINWRIGHT.

next, with interest; with power to *Holden* and *Gordon* to sell, &c., and apply the proceeds to satisfy the debt and interest, &c., and pay the surplus to *Michael Williams*, his heirs, executors, administrators, or assigns.

The premises claimed in the present action were a yard and outhouses; and it appeared that they were not comprehended within the bounds and metes specified in the last-mentioned deed. For the defendant it was contended that the premises in question would pass by the last-mentioned deed as houses, outhouses, &c., appertaining to the messuage. Parol evidence was given to shew that the premises had, in fact, been used as such appurtenances.

The defendants also proposed to put in indentures of lease and release, dated 26th and 27th *October* 1824, between *Margaret Williams*, widow and executrix of *Michael Williams*, of the first part, *Holden* and two persons named *Pye* and *Lepp*, of the second part, and one *Etches*, of the third part, reciting the indentures of 1807 and 1808, and *Michael Williams*'s will, and that *Gordon* was dead, and that *Pye* and *Lepp* (who represented the mortgagees in the deed of 1808) had applied to *Margaret Williams* for payment of 150*l.* and interest, which she was unable to pay, and that she had therefore applied to *Etches* to advance it, which he had agreed to do; reciting also that *Michael Williams* had borrowed 100*l.* of *Etches* in his lifetime, and that *Etches* had applied to *Margaret Williams* to repay it, which she was unable to do, and that *Etches* had thereupon commenced legal proceedings against her; and that, to put an end to such proceedings, she had agreed to make the present assignment as a security to him, his heirs and assigns; and that she had applied to *Etches* to advance

 her

1838.

Doe dem. Rowlandson against Wainwright.

her the further sum of 50*l.*, which he had agreed to do on having the premises assigned to him: after which recitals it was witnessed that *Pye* and *Lepp*, in pursuance of such agreement, and in consideration of 158*l.* paid by *Etches* to *Pye* and *Lepp*, and 5*s.* paid by *Etches* to *Holden*, with the consent and approbation and at the request of *Margaret Williams*, bargained, sold, &c., and also *Margaret Williams*, in consideration of the 100*l.* advanced by *Etches* to *Michael Williams*, and the 50*l.* paid by him to *Margaret Williams*, bargained, sold, &c., to *Etches*, in fee, all that piece or parcel of land, together with the messuage or dwelling-house and buildings thereon erected, situate &c., now in the occupation of the said *Margaret Williams*, bounded &c. (setting out bounds and metes), *and all and singular houses, outhouses, edifices, buildings, yards, walls, ways, waters, watercourses, paths, passages, lights, liberties, privileges, profits, advantages, and appurtenances to the same hereditaments and premises belonging or appertaining*; with a proviso for redemption by *Margaret Williams*, on payment &c.

The messuage mentioned in the above conveyance was the same as the messuage mentioned in the deed of 1808. It was objected, for the plaintiff, that *Margaret Williams*, at the time of this conveyance, appeared to have only an equitable estate, and therefore the conveyance was not evidence to shew an outstanding legal estate. The learned Judge ruled that, as *Margaret Williams* was one of the lessors of the plaintiff, the deed was evidence, unless the plaintiff's counsel abandoned that demise. The plaintiff's counsel having elected to do so, the defendants proposed to shew that the parcels in the deed of 1824 comprehended a passage which was the only way to the premises in question, and

1838.

Doe dem. Rowlandson against Wainwright.

and contended that the deed would so become evidence to prove that the premises in question were in fact appurtenant to the messuage and building, and that the conveyance by *Margaret* was in the nature of an act of user or declaration by *Margaret Williams*, the occupier at the time of the conveyance, and the party beneficially entitled in the subject of the present action, since *Jeremiah Williams*, if the plaintiff obtained a verdict, would hold in trust for *Margaret* during her life. The learned Judge rejected the deed, and left it to the jury whether, upon the facts proved, they were of opinion that the premises in question were comprehended in the deed of 1808. Verdict for the plaintiff.

Nevile, in *Michaelmas* term, 1836, obtained a rule for a new trial, on the ground of rejection of evidence. In *Easter* term last (*a*),

Cresswell and *Cowling* shewed cause. If this evidence be admitted, the effect will be that a party having only an equitable and partial interest may, by his declarations, defeat the estate of others having a legal interest in the whole, or an equitable interest in the residue. If *Jeremiah Williams*, the lessor of the plaintiff, fail in this action, the consequence may be an adverse possession, and the trusts to be executed after the death of *Margaret Williams* may fail. It is very doubtful whether the declaration of a party having the whole equitable interest could be admitted to this extent. But, at any rate, a party having only a partial equitable interest could not by his formal act bind the claims of those interested in the residue: here it is sought to effect that by his mere declaration.

(*a*) *Saturday*, 5th *May* 1838, before Lord *Denman* C. J., *Littledale*, *Patteson*, and *Coleridge* Js.

E. Perry,

1838.

Doe dem. Rowlandson *against* Wainwright.

E. Perry, contrà. This evidence was admissible on two grounds. First, it was the declaration by *Margaret Williams* that the premises in question were appurtenant to the messuage and buildings described and conveyed by the deed of 1808. *Margaret Williams* will have an equitable interest for life in the premises in question, if *Jeremiah Williams*, the lessor of the plaintiff, succeed in this action. He is her trustee for her life. The question therefore is, whether, in an action of ejectment, the declaration of a party interested, as cestui que trust of the lessor of the plaintiff, in the success of the suit, be evidence against the plaintiff. In *Fenn dem. Pewtriss* v. *Granger* (*a*) it was held that one of two several lessors of the plaintiff could not be compelled to give evidence for the defendant, although the evidence shewed that the title was exclusively in the other lessor. It follows that the declaration of such lessor would have been evidence against the plaintiff; and this, in principle, shews that the declarations of parties who, though not actual plaintiffs, are in fact represented by the plaintiff are admissible for the defendant. [*Coleridge* J. Do you say that the declaration of any living party who has any interest in the event of the suit is admissible against his interest?] It is not necessary to carry the argument beyond the case of lessors of the plaintiff in ejectment, or parties for whom a plaintiff, or the lessor of a plaintiff in ejectment, would, if successful in the suit, be a trustee. In *Gilbert's Evidence*, 108. (6th ed.), it is said, "Nor can the equitable *cestui que trust* be sworn to the title, for equity is part of the law of *England*, and therefore the law ought so far to take notice of the equitable interest as to exclude the owners of

(*a*) 3 *Campb.* 177. See *King* v. *Baker*, 2 *A.* & *E.* 333.

such

1838.

Doe dem. Rowlandson against Wainwright.

such interest, who do really enjoy the benefit of the estate from any attestation." Whatever excludes a cestui que trust from giving evidence for the title must make his declarations evidence against the title. [Lord *Denman* C. J. referred to *Rex* v. *Woburn* (*a*).] In 2 *Stark. Ev.* 23., it is said, "So the admissions of the party really interested, although he be no party to the suit, are evidence against him; for the law, with a view to evidence, regards the real parties:" and *Hanson* v. *Parker* (*b*), *Dowden* v. *Fowle* (*c*), *Bell* v. *Ansley* (*d*), are cited. It is said that the interest of *Margaret Williams* was only partial: but that objection would apply to all cases of equitable interests, and wherever the party making the declaration was not the party on the record. [*Coleridge* J. There may be an equitable interest in the whole.] The objection would exclude declarations by legal tenants for life being lessors of the plaintiff in ejectment, and indeed those of actual parties on the record having only a partial interest. It is a fallacy to treat this as an attempt to bind the interest of the trustee, or the equitable remainder man, by the act or word of the equitable tenant for life; the question is as to the admissibility of a declaration offered, not as passing an interest, but as suggesting an inference of fact, which the jury may adopt or reject. *Doe dem. Daniel* v. *Coulthred* (*e*) is an instance of a declaration admitted on an analogous principle, that of its being against the interest of the party at the time when it was made. [Lord *Denman* C. J. referred to *Woolway* v. *Rowe* (*g*); and *Coleridge* J. to *Davies* v. *Ridge* (*h*).]

(*a*) 10 *East*, 395.
(*b*) 1 *Wils.* 257.
(*c*) 4 *Campb.* 38.
(*d*) 16 *East*, 141. See p. 143.
(*e*) 7 *A. & E.* 235.
(*g*) 1 *A. & E.* 114.
(*h*) 3 *Esp.* 101.

There

1838.

Doe dem. Rowlandson against Wainwright.

There the declaration of one of several trustees, joint defendants, who were not personally liable, was held not admissible to bind the others, the Court looking to the real interest, not the nominal liability on the record. That is in favour of the defendant. Secondly, the fact that *Margaret Williams* conveyed the premises in question as appurtenances was evidence that they were so used. Much of the evidence which went to the jury was on the question, whether they had been used as appurtenances. For this purpose, the act of any occupier dealing with the property was evidence. It was a strong fact that the parcels had all gone together in a conveyance made by a party in actual occupation. But, however slight its effect may be, the rejection of any evidence bearing on the issue, entitles the defendant to a new trial; *De Rutzen* v. *Farr* (a), *Crease* v. *Barrett* (b). [*Cresswell*. As to *Woolway* v. *Rowe* (c), the party making the declaration there was identified in interest with the party to the suit.]

Cur. adv. vult.

Lord Denman C. J., in this term (*June* 13th), delivered the judgment of the Court.

The question in this case arose on the following state of facts. (His Lordship, after stating the effect of the feoffment of 9th *July* 1807, and the mortgage of 15th *October* 1808, and that the question in the cause ultimately was, whether the premises sought to be recovered passed by this latter deed, proceeded as follows.) *Michael*, the mortgagor, died in 1821, having first duly executed a will, and devised all his

(a) 4 *A.* & *E.* 53.

(b) 1 *Cr. M.* & *R.* 919. *S. C.* 5 *Tyrwh.* 458. See also *Wright* v. *Doe dem. Tatham*, 7 *A.* & *E.* 313.

(c) 1 *A.* & *E.* 114.

real

1838.

Doe dem. ROWLANDSON *against* WAINWRIGHT.

real and personal estate to his wife *Margaret* for life. He had continued in possession of the whole property down to his death; and she in like manner had occupied the whole, and continued so to do, down to and at the time of her executing the deed next to be mentioned, the propriety of rejecting which, as evidence for the defendant, is the matter now to be determined. It was a deed between *Margaret* of the first part, *Holden, Pye* and *Lepp* (who represented *Holden* and *Gordon* the mortgagees), of the second, and one *George Etches* of the third: it recited the prior deeds of 1807 and 1808, and the will and death of *Michael*, and was a conveyance in fee of the mortgaged premises, in consideration of the payment of the mortgage money, by *Etches*, to *Holden, Pye*, and *Lepp*, *the forbearance by him of a prior loan of* 100*l. to* Margaret, *and the further advance to her of* 50*l.* The conveying parties were *Holden, Pye*, and *Lepp*, and *Margaret*, who professed to convey in fee.

This deed was tendered in evidence, because it was said that, from its language, it would appear that the premises in dispute were contained in the mortgage of 1808: and it was contended to be admissible for that purpose, being a declaration by *Margaret* against her interest. For, being devisee for life of all the real estate of her deceased husband, an admission that a certain portion had been mortgaged by him went to reduce the amount of that to the beneficial occupation of which she was primâ facie entitled. Against the reception of the evidence, it was argued that the declarations of the cestui que trust for life could only be evidence to affect her own interest, and therefore were receivable against the trustee in those cases only in which

1838.

Doe dem. Rowlandson against Wainwright.

which the interests were commensurate and the trustee really suing only for the benefit of such cestui que trust; which state of things made the latter substantially the party in the cause: *Hanson* v. *Parker* (a) is a case of this sort: but that in the present case the trustee was suing for all parties concerned; and this evidence, if received, would be binding on the remainder in fee, which would be, in effect, to allow the cestui que trust for life to affect, by her declarations, the estate, which certainly she could not prejudice by her acts; a strange inconsistency, that, as an act of conveying, *Margaret* should pass nothing beyond her own interest for life, but that the same instrument, considered as a declaration by her, should operate prejudicially on the remainder in fee.

It is not necessary for us to decide upon the entire soundness of this argument in all its parts. Considering the vast importance of the system of trusts, and how essential a part of that system it is to protect the estates of cestui que trusts from the consequences even of their own acts, by the intervention of trustees, the question which this argument raises is one of very serious consideration and not a little difficulty; upon which at present we express no opinion.

But, upon the statement of the facts in this particular case, we cannot see that this was a declaration *clearly* and unambiguously against the interest of her who made it. By saying that certain premises had passed under a previous mortgage, she undoubtedly divested herself of the beneficial occupation of them until the mortgage was paid off; but, at the same time, and by the same declaration, she procures to herself the forbearance of a

(a) 1 *Wils.* 257.

loan

loan of 100*l.* and the advance of 50*l.* more: it is therefore a balance of interests. The latter may have been more than an equivalent advantage to what was lost by the former; but whether it were or not we cannot inquire: if there were an interest both ways, she stood legally indifferent, and the ground on which the evidence was tendered fails.

We are of opinion, therefore, on this ground, that the deed was rightly rejected, and the rule must be discharged.

Rule discharged.

G. GREEN, M. WIGRAM, H. L. WIGRAM, and R. GREEN, *against* BICKNELL and WARD.

In a special case it was stated that, by contract between *B.* and *G.*, *G.* had agreed to sell to *B.* all the oil which should arrive by a certain ship, which *B.* was to receive within fourteen days after the landing of the cargo, and pay for, at the expiration of that time, by bills or money, at a specified price per tun, with customary allowances: that the ship arrived, and the cargo was landed, and *G.* tendered the oil to *B.* at the end of the fourteen days: that the quantity of oil, after allowances &c., was a certain number of tuns stated in the case; that, at the time of the tender, the market price of oil was lower than the contract price by an amount stated: that *B.*, on the tender being made, refused to accept; and that the difference of prices was within the knowledge of the parties.

Held that, *B.* having become bankrupt after the refusal, *G.* could not prove for this breach of contract under the commission: for that, although *G.*'s claim would be measured by the difference between the contract and market prices at the time when *B.* should have fulfilled his contract, yet the case did not shew that the data on which the calculation must proceed were so settled as to admit of no dispute, and render the intervention of a jury unnecessary; and consequently the claim of *G.* was not for a debt but for damages.

ASSUMPSIT on a special contract. Issue being joined, a case was stated by consent, according to stat. 3 & 4 *W.* 4. *c.* 42. *s.* 25., substantially as follows.

On 4th *November* 1831, Messrs. *John Field*, *Charles Field*, *John Field* the younger, and *John Thompson*, then carrying on the business of oil merchants in *London*, under the firm of *Fields and Thompson*, entered into the following contract with the plaintiffs under the firm of *Wigram and Green*.

"Bought

1838.

GREEN *against* BICKNELL.

"Bought for Messrs. *Fields and Thompson*, of Messrs. *Wigram and Green*, one half quantity of all the sperm oil and head matter of merchantable quality that may arrive by the *Harponeer*, Captain *Clark*, now on her voyage, at 68*l.* per tun, to be received by the buyers within fourteen days after the ship has landed her cargo on a wharf in *London*, and paid for, at the expiration of that period, by approved bills at six months, or in money, deducting 2½ per cent. discount, at the buyers' option: customary allowance for dirt and water.

"*London*, 4th *November* 1831. Signed, *William* and *John Beale*, brokers."

The *Harponeer* was, at the time of the contract, engaged on a fishing voyage, on account of the plaintiffs, to the *South Seas*, and back to the port of *London*.

On 5th *April* 1832, and before the arrival of the ship, Messrs. *Fields and Thompson* entered into the following contract with the plaintiffs for the purchase of the residue of the sperm oil and head matter which might arrive in the said ship.

The case then set out a second contract for half the oil &c., which was in the same terms as the former, except that the price specified per tun was 63*l.*, that the bills were to be at four months, and that the following clause was added. "A fair allowance in price for unmerchantable oil and head matter (if any) to be made by the brokers."

The *Harponeer* arrived at the port of *London*, thereby completing her said voyage, on 8th *April* 1833, having on board a cargo of sperm oil and head matter of a merchantable quality. The cargo was thereupon landed by the plaintiffs on a wharf in *London*, and notice thereof was given to *Fields and Thompson*; the quantity

1838.

GREEN *against* BICKNELL.

quantity was, within fourteen days after landing, ascertained to be 254 tuns and 93 gallons; and the price of the whole, taking half at 68*l.* per tun and the residue at 63*l.* per tun, was ascertained to be 16,661*l.* 1*s.* 10*d.*, after making the allowances contracted for.

On the expiration of the prompt, that is to say on the fourteenth day after the ship had landed her cargo (2d *May* 1833), the plaintiffs tendered to *Fields and Thompson* the said several quantities of sperm oil and head matter purchased by them, and required *F. and T.* to accept and pay for the same, respectively, by approved bills, or in money, according to the contracts.

At the time of such tender nothing remained to be done by the plaintiffs to complete the contracts, except the actual delivery of the oil and head matter to *Fields and Thompson:* nor did any thing remain to be done by *F. and T.* except the payment of the stipulated prices. *Fields and Thompson* refused to accept or pay for the oil and head matter, or any part thereof; and never have accepted or paid for it.

When the *Harponeer* arrived and the cargo was landed, and when the same was tendered to and refused by *Fields and Thompson*, the market price of oil and head matter, of the quality of the oil and head matter contracted to be purchased, was, within the knowledge of all the parties, only 51*l.* 10*s.* per tun, which price, and no more, the said oil and head matter would have produced, had it been sold on the day it was so tendered to *F. and T.* The difference, therefore, between the prices contracted for (deducting the specified discount), and the market price, at the time of the tender and refusal, was 3472*l.* 1*s.* 3*d.*

Fields and Thompson being embarrassed in their circumstances,

1838.

GREEN *against* BICKNELL.

cumstances, a meeting of their creditors took place on 10th *May* 1833. The plaintiffs and defendants attended: and, in consideration of plaintiffs foregoing legal proceedings against *F. and T.* in respect of the above contracts, and agreeing that the defendants, who were at such meeting appointed trustees of *F. and T.*'s estate, should be allowed to receive and distribute *F. and T.*'s property and assets, the defendants agreed to pay the plaintiffs whatever debt or damages they would have been entitled to prove in respect of those contracts, or either of them, against the estate of *F. and T.*, supposing them on that day to have committed an act of bankruptcy, and a fiat to have then issued thereupon.

The question for the opinion of the Court was, supposing that *Fields and Thompson* had committed an act of bankruptcy on 10th *May* 1833, and a fiat had thereupon issued against them, under which they had been adjudged bankrupts, would the plaintiffs have been entitled to prove any sum against their estate in respect of the above contracts or either of them?

If they could so prove, could they prove the said sum of 3472*l.* 1*s.* 3*d.*, or what other sum?

If the Court should be of opinion that they might have so proved, judgment was to be entered by confession, for such sum as the Court should think might have been so proved. If the Court should think the plaintiffs could not have proved, a nolle prosequi was to be entered.

The case was argued in *Easter* term last (*a*).

(*a*) *Tuesday* and *Wednesday*, *May* 1st and 2d, 1838. Before Lord *Denman* C. J., *Littledale*, *Patteson*, and *Coleridge* Js.

F. Robinson

1838.

GREEN *against* BICKNELL.

F. Robinson for the plaintiffs. The plaintiffs are entitled to prove for the debt which arises from their damage by the breach of the contract; and that is measured by the excess of the contract price above the price in the market at the time when the contract ought to have been performed. The general principle is that, wherever a creditor has sustained a clear damage, the amount of which can be computed without the aid of a jury, such amount constitutes a debt for which he may prove. *Boorman* v. *Nash* (*a*) is distinguishable. There it was held that a bankrupt, notwithstanding his certificate, was liable on a contract like the present for damages estimated as here claimed, the contract having been made before the bankruptcy, but the time for performance being after it. The ground there taken was that proof could not be made, inasmuch as, before the time for performing arrived, it could not be known what the damage would be, nor whether there would be any damage at all, nor that the contract would be broken. Here that objection does not exist, because the time for performing is before the bankruptcy. Nothing can turn on the question whether this was, technically speaking, a debt. The Courts always interpret the bankrupt acts liberally for the protection of creditors; the want of a remedy in a case something like the present, was regretted by Lord *Hardwicke* in *Ex parte Groome* (*b*). In *Whitmarsh's Bankrupt Laws*, p. 266. c. 12. s. 17. (2d edit.), it is said, "If a demand in the nature of damages be capable of being liquidated and ascertained at the time of the bankruptcy taking place, so that a creditor can swear to the amount, he

(*a*) 9 *B. & C.* 145. (*b*) 1 *Atk.* 115.

1838.

GREEN *against* BICKNELL.

may prove it as a debt under the commission." In *Hammond* v. *Toulmin* (*a*), where damages accruing to a party by reason of the bankrupt having sold him a ship with a covenant for good title, which the bankrupt had not, were held not to be barred by the certificate or proveable under the commission, *Ashhurst* J. said, "I have always understood that, where the plaintiff's demand rested in damages, and could not be ascertained without the intervention of a jury, it could not be proved under the defendant's commission." It seems to have been at one time understood that proof could be made in cases only where indebitatus assumpsit lay: but that restriction cannot now be supported. Thus a loss on a policy of assurance may now be proved by the assured, under stat. 19 *G.* 2. *c.* 32. *s.* 2. Debts arising on guarantees are now proveable. [*Patteson* J. By express provision (*b*).] In *Johnson* v. *Spiller* (*c*) *Buller* J. said, "It is not to be taken for granted, that a demand in trover cannot be proved under a commission of bankruptcy; where the demand can be liquidated, it may." Mesne profits may be recovered by waiving the tort and proving for use and occupation. Cases of loan of stock, to be replaced, are similar: yet indebitatus assumpsit would not lie in those; *Nightingal* v. *Devisme* (*d*). [*Patteson* J. The greater number of the cases have arisen upon bond, where the action, if brought, would have been debt.] The decisions do not, however, appear to rest upon the fact of there having been a bond. If the damage be really unliquidated, there can

(*a*) 7 *T. R.* 612.

(*b*) See stat. 6 *G.* 4. *c.* 16. *ss.* 52, 53, 56. See, before the statute, *Hoffham* v. *Foudrinier*, 5 *M.* & *S.* 21.

(*c*) Note to *Alsop* v. *Price*, 1 *Doug.* 168.

(*d*) 5 *Bur.* 2589.

be

1838.

GREEN *against* BICKNELL.

be no proof, even where there is a bond; *Taylor* v. *Young* (*a*). In *Utterson* v. *Vernon* (*b*) it was finally held that proof could not be made in respect of an agreement to replace stock on request, where no request had been made before the bankruptcy. That case therefore resembles *Boorman* v. *Nash* (*c*). But, where a bond was given, conditioned to replace stock on or before a day named, and pay all dividends in the mean time, it was held that proof might be made, under a bankruptcy taking place after the day named, for the dividends and the value of the stock at the date of the commission; *Ex parte Day* (*d*): and, on the other hand, where no default either as to the dividends or the capital stock had been made before the bankruptcy, it was held that there could be no proof in respect of such a bond; *Ex parte King* (*e*). In *Ex parte Campbell* (*g*) a bankrupt had covenanted to assign stock to the trustees of his marriage settlement upon their request; and Lord *Eldon* decided that proof might be made or not, according as there had or had not been a request before the bankruptcy. *Parker* v. *Ramsbottom* (*h*), where the agreement was by covenant, turned on the same principles. [*Patteson* J. Cases of loans of stock are not exactly similar to cases upon contracts to transfer stock at a future day.] In *Bowles* v. *Rogers* (*i*) it was decided that a party who has sold a real estate to a bankrupt may, if the bankrupt has made default in payment before the bankruptcy, resell, and prove for the loss, if any: there the resale took place

(*a*) 3 *B. & Ald.* 521.

(*b*) 3 *T. R.* 539. 4 *T. R.* 570. See *Ex parte Coming*, 9 *Ves.* 115.

(*c*) 9 *B. & C.* 145.

(*d*) 7 *Ves.* 301.

(*e*) 8 *Ves.* 334.

(*g*) 16 *Ves.* 244.

(*h*) 3 *B. & C.* 257.

(*i*) 1 *Co. B. L.* 146. (8th ed.)

 after

1838.

GREEN *against* BICKNELL.

after the bankruptcy. *Ex parte Hunter* (*a*) was a similar case, except that the resale was before the bankruptcy. No argument can be urged here from any supposed uncertainty respecting the market price, which might not equally have been urged in the cases of loan of stock. The market price of goods would form as definitive a guide for a jury as any that can be suggested. [Lord *Denman* C. J. Can you prove for breach of warranty of a horse?] Perhaps, in that case, there might be a difference of opinion as to the value to be proved, although the rule to be applied would be definite. [Lord *Denman* C. J. It might be convenient to make the form of action the criterion; but even that leaves room for a difference of opinion as to the amount.] There is a large class of cases in which the party may elect between tort and contract. The measure of damages now suggested was adopted in assumpsit for not delivering according to contract, in *Gainsford* v. *Carroll* (*b*), which accords with *Leigh* v. *Patterson* (*c*). *Startup* v. *Cortazzi* (*d*) shews, in substance, that the principle is not only correct, but the only proper one: *Alderson* B. there lays it down that the damages are not to be measured by the value at any time earlier than that at which the contract ought to be performed. Here the case finds precisely all the items required for the computation. It is, indeed, not absolutely impossible that a dispute might arise as to these; but the same might have been said in all the cases on this point where the proof has been allowed. In the case of a claim upon an insurance, for a partial loss before the bankruptcy, there might possibly be a difference of opinion. [*Patteson*

(*a*) 6 *Ves.* 94. (*b*) 2 *B.* & *C.* 624.
(*c*) 8 *Taunt.* 540. (*d*) 2 *C. M.* & *R.* 165. *S. C.* 5 *Tyrwh.* 697.

teson J. Or on a claim for use and occupation, where, if there were an action, the jury would fix the amount.] Wherever the Judge would direct the jury positively as to the amount, and the verdict, if the jury gave a different amount, would be set aside, there the claim is sufficiently definite to be admitted in proof. In most of the cases where the proof was not allowed there was no breach before the bankruptcy; but in such cases it has been tacitly admitted that the proof must have been allowed if the breach had been before bankruptcy. Such are *Ex parte Thompson* (a), *Ex parte Marshall* (b), *Ex parte The Lancaster Canal Company.* (c)

R. V. Richards, contrà. The damages here were not ascertained so as to make the amount proveable. It is said that the parties knew of the market prices; but that does not conclude the assignees, who might still dispute the items. *Boorman* v. *Nash* (d) substantially decides this case. It is true that the breach there occurred after the bankruptcy; but, if that had been the only objection, the debt might have been proved under stat 6 *G.* 4. *c.* 16. *s.* 56., inasmuch as the contract was made before the bankruptcy. The measure suggested for ascertaining the damages cannot apply. Where, indeed, the breach of contract is in non-delivery, the difference of the market and contract prices is a fair measure of damage; but that is because the party to whom the delivery is to be made has the purchase-money in his hands, and, if he purchased elsewhere, would be a loser by exactly the difference: the party who ought to deliver would have to make the contract good at the

(a) 1 *Mont.* & *Bl.* 219.
(b) 2 *Deac.* & *Ch.* 589.
(c) *Mont. C. B.* 27.
(d) 9 *B.* & *C.* 145.

1838.

GREEN *against* BICKNELL.

market price. But a party who was bound to receive has not subjected himself to the risk of the market in this manner. Even this, too, assumes a known and definite market price; but the mere purchase or sale of so large a quantity as was the subject of this contract would affect the market materially. The whole could not be sold at the price which was the market price before the sale. In the case of stock nothing is necessary but a computation of figures. [Lord *Denman* C. J. Your argument would apply there: a party might influence the market by sale or purchase of stock.] The case of stock has always been understood to be peculiar. In *Bowles* v. *Rogers* (*a*) the Chancellor, having the assignees before him, could treat the prices as admitted; and indeed the resale had taken place before the decision ordering proof, so that the sums were not contingent. As to insurance cases, no difficulty could of course arise where the loss was total, and where the policy was a valued one: in the case of partial losses, too, it has become an almost universal custom to adjust the amount out of Court. In the case of bonds, the whole penalty of the bond is properly the debt; only the claimants are allowed to prove for less; and this seems to be Lord *Eldon*'s view in *Ex parte Day* (*b*). In *Ex parte Campbell* (*c*) the contract was by covenant: there the Chancellor treated the stock as money, into which stock is always convertible at the market price. In guarantees, where the sum of money is specific, and *A.* is to pay what *B.* owes if *B.* do not, then *B.*'s debt may be proved for: but no proof could be made upon a guarantee to do an act. In 1 *Deacon's Bankrupt*

(*a*) 1 *Co. B. L.* 146. (8th ed.).

(*b*) 7 *Ves.* 301.

(*c*) 16 *Ves.* 244.

Laws,

1838.

GREEN *against* BICKNELL.

Laws, p. 284., the rule is thus laid down. "Unliquidated damages, though arising on a *contract*, cannot be proved, if there is any *uncertainty* in the mode of estimating them. Thus damages sustained from a breach of covenant, in not building a certain number of houses within a given time (*a*), in not having full power and authority to sell a ship (*b*), or in not indemnifying the assignor of a lease from the covenants contained in it (*c*), have been in each of these cases held not proveable under a commission. For in all such cases a variety of circumstances must be taken into consideration, which may either increase, or mitigate, or even sometimes altogether excuse the damages, and which it is the peculiar province of a jury to determine." How could the commissioners here take the account? As soon as it appeared that the oil had not been sold, they would be without data. The case is like *Banister* v. *Scott* (*d*), where the value of a covenant to build houses was held not to be proveable: the commissioners might have taken the account there as well as here. *Hammond* v. *Toulmin* (*e*) cannot be distinguished in principle from the present case; the authorities there cited in the argument for the plaintiffs shew that nothing is proveable which is not in the nature of a debt. Though the second decision in *Utterson* v. *Vernon* (*g*) is contrary to the first (*h*), yet both assume the above principle. A general contract to indemnify could not become the

(*a*) Citing *Banister* v. *Scott*, 6 *T. R.* 489.

(*b*) Citing *Hammond* v. *Toulmin*, 7 *T. R.* 612.

(*c*) Citing *Mayor* v. *Steward*, 4 *Bur.* 2439. *Ludford* v. *Barber*, 1 *T. R.* 90. *Mills* v. *Auriol*, 1 *H. Bl.* 433. *Aurioli* v. *Mills*, 4 *T. R.* 94. See *S. C.* 1 *Smith's Leading Cases*, 436.

(*d*) 6 *T. R.* 489.

(*e*) 7 *T. R.* 612.

(*g*) 4 *T. R.* 570.

(*h*) 3 *T. R.* 539.

 subject

1838.

GREEN *against* BICKNELL.

subject of proof; *Taylor* v. *Young* (a), *Atwood* v. *Partridge* (b), *Yallop* v. *Ebers* (c): yet the commissioners might take the account in such a case as easily as here. The damages could not here be ascertained without a jury; and therefore there was no definite debt. An action of trespass for mesne profits is not barred by a certificate, *Goodtitle* v. *North* (d): it is only by claiming for use and occupation that the money can be proved as a debt. *Parker* v. *Norton* (e) was an action of trover brought for a cause of action which substantially was a contract; yet it was held that the certificate was no bar, though it would have been a bar if the action had been shaped in assumpsit. In *Forster* v. *Surtees* (g) the certificate was held a bar to assumpsit on a special count, because there was substantially a debt, for which indebitatus assumpsit would have lain. But in *Parker* v. *Crole* (h) it was held that a certificate did not bar an action of tort for selling stock contrary to the Plaintiff's orders. Yet there the action was in the nature of assumpsit; and the damages might have been estimated as precisely as here.

F. Robinson, in reply. The cases on replacing stock have not been distinguished. [*Patteson* J. Does it appear for how much the party proved, in the cases of loan of stock? Might he not prove for the value of the amount lent, without reference to the subsequent state of the market?] *Ex parte Campbell* (i) was not a case of loan of stock. The influence which a sale of oil would produce

(a) 3 *B. & Ald.* 521.
(b) 4 *Bing.* 209.
(c) 1 *B. & Ad.* 698. See *Clements* v. *Langley*, 5 *B. & Ad.* 372.
(d) 2 *Doug.* 584.
(e) 6 *T. R.* 695.
(g) 12 *East*, 605.
(h) 5 *Bing.* 63.
(i) 16 *Ves.* 244.

on

1838.

GREEN against BICKNELL.

on the market does not affect the question. The party who was entitled to deliver has, instead of the money, what is worth less at the then market price. He could not sell the oil till the contract was broken: if he did, and that lowered the market price, his claim would be so much greater. Therefore the loss cannot be less than that now claimed; and consequently the cases of non-delivery are not distinguishable. [*Coleridge* J. Does the statement in the case mean that the parties could not, when before the commissioners, dispute the market price, or any other matter, such as the quantity of oil, the quality, or how much dirt was in the casks?] It must be taken that the facts are precisely as stated, and that they would so appear before the commissioners. If by "unliquidated damages" be meant damages where the balance has not actually been struck, there are many cases to shew that the rule against receiving proof of unliquidated damages is not general. The cases of bonds do not rest upon the penalty being the real debt, as suggested for the defendants. In *The Overseers of St. Martin* v. *Warren* (a) *Holroyd* J. said, "The only thing proveable under the commission, where the penalty is considered as the debt, is the amount of the injury sustained by the breach of the condition of the bond. In a case, therefore, where this cannot be estimated, you cannot prove under the commission." The cases cited for the defendants are cases where either there has been no breach before bankruptcy, or no means of estimating its amount without a jury. The former class comprehends *Atwood* v. *Partridge* (b),

(a) 1 *B. & Ald.* 491.

(b) 4 *Bing.* 209. See *S. C.* 12 *B. Moo.* 431.

and

1838.

GREEN against BICKNELL.

and *Yallop* v. *Ebers.*(a); the latter comprehends *Banister* v. *Scott* (b), *Hammond* v. *Toulmin* (c), and *Taylor* v. *Young* (d). [*Patteson* J. *Hammond* v. *Toulmin* (c) would have been strongly against you had there been absolutely no title: but there was only an incumbrance. What is reported to have been said by Lord *Eldon* in *Ex parte Coming* (e), seems to shew that, if money be advanced on a condition not fulfilled, it may be considered a loan. Perhaps that principle may run through the cases on the loan of stock.] Such a principle would not explain *Ex parte Campbell* (g).

Cur. adv. vult.

Lord DENMAN C. J., in this term (*June* 14th), delivered the judgment of the Court.

The question was, whether the difference between the contract price of a cargo of whale oil of merchantable quality which certain persons had agreed to purchase of the plaintiffs, but had refused to accept, and the market price of the oil at the time of refusal, can be proved under a fiat of bankruptcy issued against those persons upon an act of bankruptcy committed subsequent to the refusal.

The case of *Boorman* v. *Nash* (h), cited on the plaintiffs' behalf, is not decisive of the present, because there the breach did not take place till after the act of bankruptcy and the commission. But, independently of all authority, we must inquire whether the difference of price before stated, which is undoubtedly the true mea-

(a) 1 *B. & Ad.* 698.
(b) 6 *T. R.* 489.
(c) 7 *T. R.* 612.
(d) 3 *B. & Ald.* 521.
(e) 9 *Ves.* 115.
(g) 16 *Ves.* 244.
(h) 9 *B. & C.* 145.

sure

1838.

GREEN *against* BICKNELL.

sure of the damages sustained by the plaintiffs, was a debt due from the bankrupt.

In many cases in Chancery, proof has been admitted of the value of stock agreed to be transferred at a given day. Most of them are cases of loans of stock; but there is one instance of allowing the value of a sum of stock to be proved, which was covenanted to be transferred by a marriage settlement (*a*).

We were strongly pressed with these authorities, as establishing the principle that any right to recover money, or money's worth, may be treated as a debt, when its amount can be fixed by calculation. But we think that those cases must be regarded as exceptions to the rule, which is, generally speaking, that no claim of this nature shall be proveable as a debt, for which the intervention of a jury is necessary. That it was so here is undeniable; for every one of the data which form the basis of the calculation may be denied and disputed, and is the subject of opinion rather than direct decision of facts. And, although the case finds the quantity of the oil, and that it was of merchantable quality, and that customary allowances were offered to be made, and what was the market price of oil of that quality at the time of refusal, and that such price was in the knowledge of all parties, yet it does not find that any settlement was made, or account agreed to, by the bankrupts, nor anything which would have precluded them from disputing every one of those facts before a jury; on the contrary, it states that the bankrupts positively refused to accept or pay for the oil, and no reason is assigned for their so doing.

(*a*) *Ex parte Campbell*, 16 *Ves.* 244.

For

1838.

GREEN *against* BICKNELL.

For these reasons, we are of opinion that the sum claimed is not a debt, but damages, and cannot be proved. Therefore our judgment must be for the defendants, that a nolle prosequi be entered.

Nolle prosequi to be entered.

The QUEEN *against* The Marquis of SALISBURY.

A wooden bridge was constructed across a river which divided the parishes of *W.* and *A.* from each other, one bank and part of the bridge being in *W.*, the other bank and other part of the bridge in *A.* The bridge was supported by piles driven into the ground at the bottom of the river, and by abutments of brick-work on each bank. On the *A.* side of the bridge was a toll house supported on piles also driven into the soil of the river. Tolls were taken, at this house only, for carts with merchandize passing the bridge. *S.* was the owner of the tolls, deriving title from a grant from the duchy of *Lancaster*. In a document of the reign of *Ed.* 2., and in other documents down to the time of *Charles* 1., the tolls were called traverse; and it appeared that the tolls had passed by grants conveying likewise the manor and castle of *H.*, of which *S.* and those preceding him were also owners. *S.*, and those preceding him, had for twenty years performed the repairs of the bridge, including excavations in the soil at the bottom of the river, and the planking of the carriage way, but had not repaired the carriage way. Held,

1. That this was primâ facie evidence that *S.* had the tolls as tolls traverse, in respect of ownership of the soil on which the bridge stood.

2. That this was a beneficial occupation by him of land in *W.* for which he was rateable in *W.*

The tolls were actually received by *E.*, who paid rent for them to *S.*, under a parol agreement by which *E.* contracted with *S.* for the receipt of the tolls at such rent. Held, That *S.* was nevertheless the rateable party, since the agreement did not profess to demise the lands, and the tolls, as such, could not pass from him without deed.

BY a rate for the relief of the poor of the parish of *Ware*, in *Hertfordshire*, the Marquis of *Salisbury* was rated as the owner and occupier of "land," designated as "*Ware Bridge*." He appealed, on the following grounds. 1. That he was not the owner or occupier of any land or rateable property in the parish. 2. That he was not the occupier or owner of *Ware Bridge*. 3. That *Ware Bridge* was not land, and was not beneficial or rateable property. 4. That the rate did not shew that *Ware Bridge* was in any, and what, respects beneficial or rateable property, or beneficially occupied by him. 5. That *Ware Bridge* was not within the parish of *Ware*. 6. That he, not being an in-

habitant

habitant of the parish, was not liable to the rate. The sessions confirmed the rate, subject to the opinion of this Court on the following case. 1838.

The QUEEN *against* The Marquis of SALISBURY.

Ware Bridge is situate on the highway of the *Great North Road*, across the navigable river *Lea*, connecting the town of *Ware* with a street partly in the parish of *Ware* and partly in that of *Great Amwell*; and is itself in the several parishes of *Ware* and *Great Amwell*. It is a wooden and very ancient structure, resting upon piles driven into the soil of the bottom of the river, and on abutments of brick work on the bank on either side. Attached to the bridge, and resting on piles driven also into the bed of the river, is a stand or house used by the person who collects the tolls hereinafter described, and which is in *Great Amwell*. The occasional repairs necessary to the wood-work and frame of the bridge have, during the last twenty years, been executed by the orders and at the cost of the present Marquis and his father; amongst which have been excavations of the soil in the bed and banks of the river, for the purpose of driving piles, and strengthening the abutments and land-ties. The planking of the carriage way has, in the same manner, been repaired by the Marquis and his father; but the road itself has never been repaired by either. The tolls are regulated according to a fixed scale set out in the deeds relating to them, hereinafter mentioned. They are collected by one *J. Kent*, residing in the toll house, on behalf of *Robert Everett*, who, by a parol agreement with the Marquis of *Salisbury*, has contracted for the receipt of these and other tolls, for one year from 1st *April* 1835, at the rent of 261*l.*, the payment of which, by monthly instalments, was secured by warrant of attorney; but no grant

1838.

The QUEEN *against* The Marquis of SALISBURY.

grant or demise of the tolls to *Everett* has been executed by the Marquis. The Marquis is entitled to the tolls by grant made to his ancestors in 6 *Ch.* 1. The following evidence of their nature and quality was produced on the hearing of the appeal (*a*).

17 *Ed.* 2. — An inquisition post mortem, on the oath &c., who say that *Aymare de Valence*, late Earl of *Pembroke*, was seised in his demesne as of fee, on the day of his decease, of the castle and town of *Hertford*, with appurtenants; and there are in the same castle certain ruinous buildings &c.; also there is there a certain custom for feeding &c., it is worth by the year 10*s.*; also there is there a certain payment at the feast of *Saint Martin*, which is called Stallpence, for the stalls situate &c.: also they say that the tolls of the market and the traverse, within the borough of *Hertford*, together with the tolls of the fairs there, is worth &c.: also *the traverse at the bridge of* Ware *and at the bridge of* Thele, pertaining to the said borough of *Hertford* (*b*), with the flow of the water from the town of *Waltham Cross* as far as to the town of *Hertford*, is worth by the year 8*l.*: also the pleas and perquisites of the Courts, with one leet there, are worth &c. And they say the aforesaid Earl held the aforesaid castle and town of *Hertford*, with the manors of *Essenden* and *Bayford* pertaining, and other their appurtenances, of the gift of the now Lord the King, by what service they know not.

(*a*) The deeds, &c., were in most instances fully set out in the case; but it is thought sufficient to state the parts relied on. The original language of the documents not in *English*, having been referred to in the argument, though translations only were used in the case, is occasionally added in the notes to this report.

(*b*) Item transversum ad pontem de *Ware* et ad pontem de *Theis* pertinens ad dictum burgum de *Hertford*.

E Registro

1838.

The QUEEN *against* The Marquis of SALISBURY.

E Registro Ducatus *Lancastriæ* temp. Henry 5. folio xlix.

For the Tenants of *Hertford.* } *Henry*, &c., To all to whom &c., greeting. Know ye that we, considering the poverty of our tenants of our town of *Hertford*, and others dwelling in the same town, of our especial grace have pardoned and releasedun to our said tenants, and the other inhabitants, all manner of toll to us pertaining, of and for all kind of merchandize, which shall be brought at the fairs and markets in the town above said, for the term of ten years next to come, saving always to us the custom to us due of and for all kind of merchandize which shall pass (*a*) over the water of *Lea* by the town above said, *in the same manner as we have at the bridge of Ware.* Dated 30th *January*, 3 *H.* 5.

By the King himself and the council.

The Counties of { *Hertford*, *Middlesex*, *Surrey.* } The accounts of all and singular the ministers of the King's Majesty, there accountable from the feast of *St. Michael* the Archangel, in the 35th year of the reign of his Majesty *Henry* the 8th, by the grace &c., unto the feast of *St. Michael* the Archangel then next ensuing, in the 36th year of his said Majesty's reign.

The town of *Hertford.* } The account of *John Kelyng*, &c.

(*a*) La custume a nous due de toute manere de marchandize qui passera &c.

The

1838.

The QUEEN *against* The Marquis of SALISBURY.

The Farm of the Toll or Passage of the Bridge of *Ware* (*a*).	For 27*l*, lately received from the issues of *the toll travers*

of the bridge of Ware (*b*), so lately approved by the collector of the customs and tolls, daily, weekly, and quarterly, he does not answer here, because the profit thereof is demised unto *William Graves*, by indenture, and as charged below, under &c. But he does answer for 34*l*. from the farm of the toll, otherwise called the travers, and custom (*c*) of the castle and honour *Hertford*, parcel of the duchy of *Lancaster*, to be taken in the accustomed manner, viz. of and for all things vendible, passing (*d*) as well by the town of *Hertford* as by the town of *Ware*, *Bishop's Hatfield*, &c., and elsewhere in divers places in the county of *Hertford*, viz. of and for every cart laden with wools, &c., and being vendible, passing over (*e*) the bridge of *Ware* and *Hertford* or elsewhere in the several places above said, 2*d*.; and of and for every horse &c., and of and for every man carrying &c., passing over the bridges aforesaid, or elsewhere, as is above said, ½*d*.: as also from the farm of the fishery of the demesne water of *Hertford*, now in the occupation of the said *William Greaves*; rendering therefore yearly to the aforesaid Lord the King &c.: namely, for the said toll, with its appurtenances, 32*l*. 13*s*. 4*d*.; and for the said fishery 20*s*. 8*d*.; and for &c.

(*a*) Firma tolneti sive passagii pontis de *Ware*.

(*b*) Tolneti transeunt' pontis de *Ware*.

(*c*) De firma theolonii alias transvers ac custum'.

(*d*) De omnibus rebus venalibus transeunt'.

(*e*) Transeunt' ultra.

Duchy

1838.

The QUEEN *against* The Marquis of SALISBURY.

Duchy of *Lancaster* (a).

E Bund. certificates and depositions 33 *Eliz.*

Elizabeth, by the grace &c., to our trusty and well-beloved *Thomas Sadler*, Esquire, *William Pursey* our auditor of our possessions, parcel of our duchy of *Lancaster* in the south parts (and others): whereas we are credibly informed that *our toll belonging to our bridges of Hertford, Ware, and Stanstead*, parcel of our said duchy, is greatly decayed and impaired by reason of the number of barges, &c., going upon the river of *Lee*, used for the carrying and recarrying of corn, &c., to and from *London* or elsewhere, to and from the towns of *Ware*, *Hertford*, and *Stanstead*, all which carriages in the most part were of late made and conveyed by carts, and on horsebacks, by and through the said towns of *Hertford*, *Ware*, and *Stanstead*, *and over the bridges of the same towns, whereof we have used to have toll at the said bridges*, (reciting the consequent falling off of the toll, and directing an inquiry by witnesses, or otherwise, of the decays of the toll; the return to be made to the chancellor and council of the duchy). Dated 15th *May*, 33 *Eliz.* Indorsed. A commission to inquire of toll over *Ware Bridge* &c., in the county of *Hertford* (33 *Eliz.*).

The case then set out the return by the commissioners, stating that depositions had been taken before them on 17th *September* 1591, whereby it appeared that the toll of the said bridges was decayed by reason of the barges &c., and that the toll of the said three bridges was not then worth, to be letten, above forty marks by the year.

(a) This was the only deed in *English*, and is given here without alteration (so far as it is set out) except in the spelling.

 The

The Counties of Essex, Hertford, Middlesex. — The accounts of all and singular the ministers of the Lord King of his duchy of *Lancaster* there accountable, from the Feast of *St. Michael* the Archangel, in the first year &c. (1 *Ch.* 1.), unto the same feast &c. (*Mich.* 2 *Ch.* 1.).

The Town of *Hertford.* — The account of *Thomas Wright*, &c.

(No arrears.)

The Farm of the Toll of the Bridges, with certain meadows, and the fishery there. — And he answers for 16*l.* from *the farm of the toll travers and customs of the lordship, castle, and honor of Hertford, of all things for sale passing over the bridges* (*a*) *of Hertford, Ware, Hatfield, Stanstead,* and elsewhere, in divers places in the county of *Hertford*, demised unto *Nathaniel West* for a term of years, &c.

The Counties of *Essex*, *Hertford*, *Middlesex.* — The accounts &c. (as before, from *Michaelmas* 6 *Ch.* 1. to *Michaelmas* 7 *Ch.* 1.).

The Town of *Hertford.* — The account of *William*, Earl of *Salisbury*, and the other farmers there, during the period aforesaid.

(No arrears.)

The Fee Farms there. — But they answer for 49*l.* 2*s.* 5½*d.* from the fee farms, with their rights, members, and appurtenances, so granted unto the aforesaid accountants by letters patent of his Majesty King *Charles*, as in the same appears.

By letters patent, duly sealed and enrolled in the Duchy Court of *Lancaster*, dated 6 *Ch.* 1., after recit- ing

(*a*) De firma transvers' ac custum' dominii castri et honoris de *Hertford* cum omnibus rebus vend' transeun' per pontem &c.

1838.

The QUEEN *against* The Marquis of SALISBURY.

ing that, by indenture of 17 *James* 1., between his said late Majesty *James* 1. of the one part, and Sir *Henry Hobart* Knt. and Bart., Sir *John Walter*, and others named, on the other part, his said late Majesty did, of his special grace, certain knowledge, and mere motion, and at the request and nomination of his then present Majesty King *Charles*, being then Prince of *Wales* &c., and for his sole use and benefit, lease, grant, and to farm let to the said Sir *Henry Hobart* &c. (amongst other things), all those the honor, castle, lordship, manor, town, grange, farms, rents, revenues, lands, tenements, and hereditaments of *Hertford*, whether called *Hertford*, or lying, growing, and being in *Hertford*, with their rights, members, and appurtenances, in the said county of *Hertford* (except certain mills), in the deed specified; and all those lordships, manors, &c., of *Hertingfordbury* &c., which said manors of *Hertford* and *Hertingfordbury* are parcel of the lands belonging to the ancient duchy of *Lancaster*, for the term of ninety-nine years, commencing from the Feast of the Annunciation last past before the date of the said indenture; And reciting that the said Sir *John Walter*, and two others, being survivors, and in possession by virtue of the said demise of and in the said lordships, castle, manors, and premises, with the appurtenances (among other things), by right of accruer for the residue of the said term, by indenture of 20th *September*, 3 *Ch.* 1., between the said Sir *John Walter* and the two other grantees of the one part, and *Christopher Kighley* and *John Southworth* of the other part, by his said Majesty's special warrant, and by the direction of *James*, Earl of *Marlborough*, his Majesty's treasurer of *England*, and other his Majesty's commissioners for the sale of lands,

 and

1838.

The QUEEN against The Marquis of SALISBURY.

and for and in consideration of a certain annual rent by the indenture reserved, payable by *Kighley* and *Southworth*, and of a competent sum paid by them to his Majesty's use and for other causes &c. the said Sir *J. Walter* &c. moving, did grant and assign to *Kighley* and *Southworth* all that the castle and manor of *Hertford*, with all their rights, members, and appurtenances in the said county of *Hertford*, and all that the fishery of the demesne water of *Hertford*, then late in the tenure &c., and also all that meadow &c., and all those ozier beds or islands within the river of *Hertford*, with divers other messuages therein described, *and all those tolls, otherwise called transverse, and customs* (*a*), of the lordship, castle, and manor (*b*) of *Hertford*, parcel of the duchy of *Lancaster*, to be taken and received as heretofore had been accustomed, (that is to say) for all saleable things passing through the town of *Hertford*, and also through the towns of *Ware, Bishop's Hatfield, Thele*, otherwise *Therle*, and *Belbar*, and elsewhere in divers places in the said county, for every cart or waggon &c. passing (*c*) as aforesaid, or elsewhere in divers places above mentioned, 2*d*.; for every horse carrying &c., passing (*c*) as aforesaid, or elsewhere, as is above mentioned &c., and all and singular houses, edifices, buildings, barns, &c., lands, &c., waters, watercourses, *rivers*, lakes, fisheries, &c., profits, commodities, emoluments, and hereditaments whatsoever to the aforesaid manor, castle, and premises, or to any part thereof, belonging or appertaining; which said castle, lordship, and manor of *Hertford*, and other the lands in *Hertingfordbury*, above mentioned to be granted and assigned by the particular

(*a*) Et tot' ill' tolnet' alias vocat' transvers' et custum'.

(*b*) Honoris. (*c*) Transeun'.

thereof

1838.

The QUEEN *against* The Marquis of SALISBURY.

thereof were mentioned to be parcel of the ancient possessions of the duchy of *Lancaster;* and all the estate, right, title, interest, term of years to come, reversion and reversions &c. of the said Sir *J. Walter*, and the other grantees, in and to the aforesaid castle, manor, and other the premises &c., except &c. (certain parcels not here material), to have and to hold the aforesaid manor, castle, and all other the premises above mentioned to be granted and assigned, with their rights, members, and appurtenances (except as before excepted), to the said *Kighley* and *Southworth*, their executors, administrators, and assigns, for and during the residue of the term of ninety-nine years, rendering and paying therefore yearly to the said Sir *J. Walter*, and the two other parties of the first part, their executors, administrators, and assigns, to the use of his Majesty, his heirs and successors, for the said manor, castle, and premises in *Hertford* aforesaid, the yearly rent of 32*l.* 15*s.* 1½*d.*:— It was, by the now stating letters patent, made known that King *Charles*, of his special grace and certain knowledge and mere motion, approving, accepting, and ratifying the said indenture of 20th *September*, and all and singular the grants &c. therein mentioned, did, for himself, his heirs and successors, ratify and by these presents confirm the same, and the said manor, castle, messuages, lands, tenements, and hereditaments, and all and every thing in the same contained, under the rents, profits &c., and during the term, in the said indenture specified, to *Kighley* and *Southworth*, their executors, &c.; And further, that his Majesty, in consideration of 292*l.* 16*s.* 8*d.* paid by *William* Earl of *Salisbury*, did give and grant to the said earl, his heirs and assigns, for ever, his Majesty's reversion and reversions, re-

1838.

The Queen *against* The Marquis of Salisbury.

mainder and remainders whatsoever, of the aforesaid manor and castle of *Hertford*, and of the aforesaid lands, tenements, and hereditaments, and all and singular other the premises by the said indenture of 20th *September* granted and assigned &c., with all their rights, members, and appurtenances, and also all his Majesty's manor (*a*) and castle of *Hertford*, in his county of *Hertford*, with all the rights, members, and appurtenances, and all those his rents of assize there &c., and all those his new rents &c., and all those issues of lands &c., and all those his works and customs there &c., and all those issues of the manor &c., and all those the perquisites and profits of the courts of the manor aforesaid &c., and all that his Majesty's fishery of the demesne water of *Hertford* aforesaid &c., and all those islands of osiers and osier-beds within the river of *Hertford* aforesaid &c., and also all that the ruinous and dilapidated castle of *Hertford*, in the county of *Hertford*, with the appurtenances, as thereinafter particularly mentioned, that is to say, all that &c. (the tower, walls, and the ground and soil of, in, and within the walls), and and also *all that toll, and all those tolls called traverse, and customs of the lordship and honor* (*b*) of *Hertford*, in the said county of *Hertford*, to be taken in manner accustomed, that is to say, of all saleable things passing through the town of *Hertford* (*c*), and also through the town of *Ware*, *Bishop's Hatfield*, *Thele*, otherwise *Therle*, *Belbar*, and elsewhere in divers places in the said county, that is to say, for every cart carrying or laden

(*a*) Manerium.

(*b*) Tot' ill' theolon' ac' omn' ill' theolon' vocat' transversa' ac custom' dominii et honoris.

(*c*) De omnibus reb' venal' transeun' per vill' de *Hertford*.

with

1838.

The QUEEN *against* The Marquis of SALISBURY.

with wool, flax, corn, leather, wine, or other wares and saleable things, *passing over the bridges* (*a*) aforesaid, or elsewhere, in divers places above mentioned, 2*d.*; for every horse &c. passing over the bridges aforesaid, or elsewhere, &c.; which said manor and castle &c., and all and singular other the premises above by those presents (granted), were by the said particular mentioned to be parcel of the ancient possessions of his Majesty's duchy of *Lancaster* in the county aforesaid: And his Majesty did also by those presents, for himself, his heirs and successors, give and grant to the said earl, his heirs and assigns, all and singular his Majesty's messuages, mills, houses, edifices, buildings, barns, &c., lands, tenements, &c., demesne lands, &c., profits, fruits, waters, watercourses, ponds, fishponds, aqueducts, lakes, rivers, fisheries, fishings, suits, sokome, multures, warrens, mines, quarries, rents, revenues, and profits, rents charge, rents seck, and rents and services, &c., courts leet, &c., fairs, markets, *tolls, tollage, customs* (*b*), jurisdictions, franchises, liberties, privileges, profits, commodities, advantages, emoluments, and hereditaments whatsoever, with all their rights, members, and appurtenances, of what kind &c., or by whatsoever names &c., situate, &c., coming, growing, renewing, or arising within the county, towns, fields, places, parishes, or hamlets aforesaid, or either or any of them, or elsewhere wheresoever, to the said manor, messuages, lands, tenements and hereditaments, and other the premises above granted, or any or either of them, or any part or parcel thereof, in any manner belonging, appertaining, incident, appendant or incumbent,

(*a*) De qualibet carectâ' careat' sive onerat' cum lan' &c. vel al' mercimon' et rebus venal' transeun' pontes præd'.

(*b*) Tolnet' theolon' custum'.

1838.

The QUEEN *against* The Marquis of SALISBURY.

bent, or as members, parts or parcels of the aforesaid manor, messuages, &c., and other the premises &c., or to any or either of them, being theretofore had, known, accepted, occupied, used, or reputed; and also his Majesty's reversion and reversions, &c., of the said manor, &c., and other &c.: And further, of his more ample especial grace, and of his certain knowledge &c., his Majesty, by those presents, for himself, his heirs and successors, did grant to the said earl, his heirs and assigns, to have, hold, &c., from thenceforth for ever, within the aforesaid manor, messuages, &c., all and singular other the granted premises, and every parcel thereof, so many, so great, the like, the same, such and similar courts leet, &c., waifs, estrays, &c., free-warrens, &c., and all rights, jurisdictions, liberties, franchises, customs, privileges, profits, commodities, advantages, and emoluments whatsoever, as and which, and as fully, &c., as any other person or persons theretofore having possessed or being seised of the aforesaid manor &c., at any time had, or ought to have had, holden, &c., in the premises above &c., by reason or force of any charter &c., prescription, usage, or custom, or otherwise, and as fully, &c., and in as ample manner and form, as his Majesty, or any of his progenitors or ancestors, then late Kings or Queens of England, had and enjoyed, or ought to have had and enjoyed, the aforesaid manor, &c.: and his Majesty did give further, and did by those presents, for himself, &c., grant to the said earl, his heirs and assigns, all and singular the aforesaid manor, &c., and the other before granted premises, with all their appurtenances, as fully, &c., and in as ample manner as the same or any parcel thereof came or ought to have come to his Majesty's hands, or to the hands of any of

his

1838.

The QUEEN *against* The Marquis of SALISBURY.

his progenitors or predecessors, &c., by reason or force of any dissolution, surrender, or relinquishment &c. of the late monastery of *St. Peter*, *Westminster*, or by reason or force of any act of parliament &c., or purchase, or of any gift or grant &c., or of any other lawful means, right, or title whatsoever, and in his Majesty's hands then were or ought to be, or might be, except &c. (certain market tolls): To have, hold, and enjoy the aforesaid manor, castle, messuages, lands, tenements, &c., profits, commodities, liberties, pre-eminences, advantages, emoluments and hereditaments, and all and singular other the premises above by those presents granted, or mentioned to be granted, with all their rights, members, and appurtenances (except as before excepted), to the said Earl, his heirs and assigns, to the only and proper use and behoof of him the said earl, his heirs and assigns, for ever: to hold the aforesaid manor and castle of *Hertford*, and all and singular other the premises in *Hertford* aforesaid, of his Majesty, his heirs and successors, in chief, by knight's service, that is to say, by the service of one entire knight's fee: and to hold the rest of the premises mentioned to be parcel of the aforesaid manor of *Hertingfordbury* &c. (in free socage), without any rent for all of the premises before granted to be rendered to his Majesty, his heirs or successors, during the residue of the term of ninety-nine years; and, after the end of the said term or other determination thereof, rendering yearly to his Majesty, his heirs &c., out of and for the said manor, castle of *Hertford*, and other the premises there, 32*l.* 15*s.* 1½*d.*; and out of and for the premises, parcel of the said manor of *Hertingfordbury*, 22*s.* &c.

The

1838.

The QUEEN *against* The Marquis of SALISBURY.

The castle of *Hertford* belongs to the present Marquis of *Salisbury*. It is the practice to charge all waggons and carts laden with merchandise, passing over the bridge, with the toll: but, if they pass through the town, and not over the bridge, no toll is demanded.

The case was argued in *Hilary* term last (*a*).

Thesiger, *A. S. Dowling*, and *Calvert*, in support of the order of sessions. First, assuming that the Marquis of *Salisbury* is the owner and occupier of the land, by means of the bridge which is fixed in the river, that is a beneficial occupation for which he should be rated. The bridge stands partly in *Ware*, partly in *Great Amwell*: the case is therefore precisely similar to *Rex* v. *Barnes* (*b*). The tolls are here collected in the parish of *Amwell*; but they are paid for passing over the bridge. In *Rex* v. *Barnes* (*b*) the tolls were collected only in *Hammersmith*; and it was urged that, as any one might go from the *Barnes* side of the river into *Hammersmith*, and up to the *Hammersmith* gate, and return without paying, provided he did not actually pass through the *Hammersmith* gate, the tolls were payable for passing through the gate, and not for traversing the bridge, and therefore the proprietors of the bridge were not rateable in *Barnes*: but the Court would not adopt this view; and *Bayley* J. asked, how tolls could be obtained if the part of the bridge in *Barnes* were away. There is here a beneficial occupation of land, by means of the tolls; and therefore the case does not fall

(*a*) *Wednesday*, 17th *January* 1838, before Lord *Denman* C. J., *Littledale*, *Williams*, and *Coleridge* Js.

(*b*) 1 *B. & Ad.* 113.

within

1838.

The QUEEN *against* The Marquis of SALISBURY.

within the rule in *Rex* v. *Liverpool* (a) and *Rex* v. *The Commissioners for lighting Beverley* (b). The emolument from the tolls is derived by the Marquis of *Salisbury* in a personal and private respect; he therefore is rateable within the principles laid down by Lord *Ellenborough* in *Rex* v. *Terrott* (c).

But, secondly, it will be argued that the Marquis of *Salisbury* is not an owner or occupier of land, but only of the tolls: and that tolls are not rateable per se. But the facts stated shew that he takes the toll as a toll traverse, in respect of his ownership of the land. By the accounts of 35 *H.* 8. it appears that the profits of the "toll traverse" of the bridge had been demised. In the commission of inquiry of 33 *Eliz.* the toll is spoken of as "belonging to *our* bridges of *Hertford, Ware*," &c. The accounts of 1 *Ch.* 1. mention the "toll travers" for "passing over the bridges." From the recital in the letters patent of 6 *Ch.* 1. it appears that *James* 1. had leased the honour, castle, lordship, manor, &c., of *Hertford* for ninety-nine years; and that in 3 *Ch.* 1. the representatives of the lessees assigned over the castle and manor of *Hertford*, "and all those tolls otherwise called transverse;" and, by the letters patent, *Charles* 1., "of his certain knowledge and mere motion," confirmed the assignment, and granted the reversion to *William* Earl of *Salisbury* in fee, and all the King's manor and castle of *Hertford*, and "all that toll, and all those tolls called traverse," of the lordship and honour for (among other things) "passing over the bridges" of *Ware* &c., and all edifices, buildings, lands,

(a) 7 *B.* & *C.* 61.
(b) 6 *A.* & *E.* 645.
(c) 3 *East*, 506.

tenements,

1838.

The QUEEN *against* The Marquis of SALISBURY.

tenements, tolls, tollage, customs, privileges, profits, commodities, advantages, emoluments, and hereditaments, with all their appurtenances, by whatsoever names called, to the manor, &c., or any part thereof, appertaining, &c., as fully and amply as the King and his predecessors had enjoyed them. In *Com. Dig. Grant*, (G 12.), it is said, "If the King's grant be *ex certâ scientiâ et mero motu*, it shall be taken more strongly against the King, and beneficial for the subject." Now here it clearly appears that the King, being owner of the bridge, had a toll traverse: the grant will therefore be construed to pass the ownership of the bridge and the toll traverse incident thereto. The fact that the repairs have been performed by the owners of the toll shews also that the edifice repaired was their property. If the bridge had remained in the Crown, the owners of the tolls would not have held them so fully as the Crown: for the Crown might neglect to repair, and then the bridge would go to decay, and the tolls be lost. If the repairs were performed by the owners of the toll in consequence of their having a mere toll thorough, the toll and the liability should be shewn by some grant; if it was in the character of tenants under the Crown, or ratione tenuræ, that might have been shewn; and it is not open to the party letting the toll to say that he has repaired the bridge, which is an act of ownership, under a wrongful possession, adverse to the Crown. But, even if the occupation of the bridge were under a wrongful possession, the owners of the toll, having had it for twenty years, might retain the possession till judgment for the Crown on an information of intrusion, by stat. 21 *Ja.* 1. *c.* 14. *s.* 1., and might maintain trespass against any third party. No other party then can be named as occupier. Nothing is

1838.

The QUEEN *against* The Marquis of SALISBURY.

is attempted to be demised to *Everett* but the tolls; and they could not pass by parol, being an incorporeal hereditament; *Gardiner* v. *Williamson* (*a*), *Bird* v. *Higginson* (*b*). In *Rex* v. *Snowdon* (*c*) it was held that the lessee of a toll traverse was not rateable for the toll: but that only shews that *Everett* could not be rated here: the Marquis is rated as owner and occupier of the land on which the bridge stands, which is beneficial to him by means of the tolls. The appellant also objects on the ground that he is not an inhabitant; but that is not necessary in the case of the beneficial occupation of visible property; *Rex* v. *Barnes* (*d*) is an instance of this.

Platt and *E. F. Moore*, contrà. The Marquis is not an occupier of visible beneficial property in *Ware*. All that appears is that tolls are taken by another party under a parol agreement with the Marquis. It is said that this is a toll traverse: but the documents do not shew that it is other than a toll thorough. In the letters patent of *Charles* 1., the toll is called *transverse, for saleable things passing through the town; theolonia vocata transversa, de omnibus rebus venalibus transeuntibus.* This does not show a toll traverse, technically so called, but rather a toll so called *à transeundo*, that is, because levied upon things passing along what the case expressly states to be a highway. Now "toll-thorough is a sum demanded for a passage through an highway," "or, for a passage over a ferry, bridge, &c."; *Com. Dig. Toll*, (C): but "toll-traverse is a sum demanded for passage over the private soil of another;" *Ib.* (D). This

(*a*) 2 *B.* & *Ad.* 336. (*b*) 2 *A.* & *E.* 696.; 6 *A.* & *E.* 824.
(*c*) 4 *B.* & *Ad.* 713. (*d*) 1 *B.* & *Ad.* 113.

is

1838.

The QUEEN against The Marquis of SALISBURY.

is in fact a grant of a species of pontage. The bridge is not granted: though it is true that the tolls are granted in the character of appurtenances. If the grant of the toll be interpreted as a grant of the land (which is the suggestion on the other side), then land is granted as appurtenant to land, which cannot be. But, if the grant be simply of tolls, this is the case of a toll taken for passing the bar, and not in respect of property in land: then the rate must be, if at all, to *Amwell*, where the bar is. But tolls, as such, are not rateable at all; *Rex* v. *Nicholson* (a), *Williams* v. *Jones* (b), *Rex* v. *Eyre* (c). *Rex* v. *Barnes* (d) is rather an authority against than for the rate: for there the rate was laid upon the party actually receiving the tolls; and, if the grant of *Ch.* 1. passed the bridge by the grant of the tolls, *Everett* would take the bridge under the Marquis's demise of the tolls. The tolls appear to have been collected in consideration of the repair of the bridge, and at the bridge only: that is consistent with a toll thorough: they could not be collected elsewhere for want of such consideration; *Brett* v. *Beales* (e). A toll-traverse must be coeval with the ownership of the land: to assume here that the grant of toll traverse is a grant of the land is, in fact, begging the question: unless the land and toll were granted together, the toll would not be toll traverse. Probably all toll originated in the lord's power over those who held in villenage and could be removed at will; 2 *Bla. Com.* c. 6. From *Ellis's General Introduction to Domesday Book*, vol. i. p. 256., it appears that, in the language of the Domesday survey, *toll* signified the liberty of selling and

(a) 12 *East*, 330.
(b) 12 *East*, 346.
(c) 12 *East*, 416.
(d) 1 *B.* & *Ad.* 113.
(e) *Moo.* & *M.* 426. *S. C.* in Banc, 10 *B.* & *C.* 508.

buying

1838.

The QUEEN *against* The Marquis of SALISBURY.

buying in one's own soil, as stated in *Wilkins, Leg. Ang. Sax.* p. 202., and of keeping a market; and also the dues paid to the lord for his profits of fair or market, and a tribute or custom for passage. For this the author cites *Kennett's Parochial Antiquities, Glossary*, tit. *Toll*, and *Bracton* (*a*). Generally, toll seems to have been considered due for passage, without reference to the tenure of the soil on which the transit took place. All highways appear to be treated as the property of the lord in the statute of *Winton*, 2 stat. 13 *Ed.* 1. *c.* 5., which is the earliest act relating to highways. Tolls for passing along highways are mentioned, probably for the first time, in a statute of 20 *Ed.* 3. (A. D. 1346), which is not in the Statutes at large, but is given in *Rymer's Fœdera*, vol. v. p. 520., *De viis regiis reparandis*, and the expression there is only *consuetudines de rebus venalibus*, &c., *per easdem vias*, &c., *transeuntibus*. The distinction between toll thorough and toll traverse does not seem to be noticed earlier than 22 *Ed.* 3. (22 *Assis.* fol. 98 B. pl. 58.). The foundation of all the modern law on the subject is *Smith* v. *Shepherd* (*b*). It may be inferred that it is not safe to apply the modern distinctions beween toll traverse and toll thorough strictly to ancient deeds (*c*), or to assume that a party granting a traverse

(*a*) Lib. 2. c. 24. s. 3.; but the passage does not appear to be in point.

(*b*) *Cro. Eliz.* 710. *S. C. Moor.* 574.

(*c*) From records in the office of the duchy of *Lancaster*, it appears that in very early times the thorough toll was distinguished from the toll of the bridge. The following are extracts.

The earliest lease of the toll and passage of the bridge of *Ware*, to be found in the office, is of 46 *Ed.* 3. (1372). By it, *John* Duke of *Lancaster* grants to *Roger Syward de Ware* "le tolnue et le passage del pount de *Ware Thele* & *Haitfeld* barre," for seven years.

In the ministers' accounts of 7 & 8 *R.* 2. this is distinguished from the toll thorough as follows. "Idem reddit compotum de 22d de carectis

1838.

The QUEEN *against* The Marquis of SALISBURY.

a traverse or *transverse* toll meant to grant the land with it. In 2 *Jacob's Law Dictionary*, *traversum* is translated "a ferry," and reference is made to 2 *Monast. Angl.* 1002 (*a*). That the toll was actually taken in land belonging to the Crown would prove nothing: a man may have toll thorough in his own land; *Webb's Case* (*b*).

---

carectis extraneis trans' per villam vocat' Thourtol" &c. — "Idem reddit compotum de 16*l.* 6*s.* 8*d.* receptis de tholon' pontis de *Ware*, *Thele*, et barre de *Hatfeld*" &c.

In those of 21 & 22 *R.* 2., "Et de 3*s.* 6*d.* provenient' de quadam consuetudine vocata Thorughtoll de carectis trans' per villam" &c. — "De tolneto pontis de *Ware Thele* cum barr' de *Hatfeld*" &c.

In those of 2 & 3 *H.* 4., "Et de 9*s.* 8*d.* de quadam consuetudine vocata Thorugtoll hoc anno de carectis transeuntibus per villam." — "Et de 33*l.* 6*s.* 8*d.* de firma tolneti pontis de *Ware Thele* et *Neveles-bare*" &c.

By indenture of 14th *July*, 15 *H.* 6. (1437), the King demised to *Thomas Hoddesdon*, of *Amwell*, "transversum et custumam eidem domino regi debit' ratione dominii castri et honoris sui de *Hertford* capiend' modo consueto de omnibus rebus venalibus transeuntibus per villam de *Hertford* ac per villas de *Ware Hatfeld Episcopi Thele* et alibi", for nine years, at 38*l.* per annum. That this was a demise of both the toll thorough and the toll of the bridge, appears from the following extract from the ministers' accounts of 20 & 21 *H.* 6., before which time, however, the lease seems to have been surrendered.

"De quadam consuetudine vocata Thoroughtoll ut de carectis transeuntibus per villam *Hertford* nihil hoc anno quia dimittitur cum firma pontis de *Ware* inferius specificata" &c.

"Firma tolneti pontis de *Ware* } Et de 38*l.* de firma tolneti sive transversi et custumæ regis castri dominii et honoris sui de *Hertford*" &c. "de omnibus rebus venalibus transeunt' per villam de *Hertford* necnon et villas de *Ware Hatfeld Episcopi Thele* et alibi in diversis locis in com *Hertford* videlicet de qualibet carecta lanis pannis coriis vino et aliis mercimoniis et rebus venalibus transeunt' ultra pontes de *Ware* et *Hertford* vel alibi in locis supradictis" &c., demised to *John Campswell* de *Hertford* and others, as long as the king should please, by letters patent of 14th *November*, 20 *H.* 6.

(*a*) Vol. vi. p. 1105, 1106. of ed. 1830. But the word *traversum* does not there occur. Reference was also made to an inquisition of 5 *Ed.* 3., for which *Chauncy's Hertfordshire*, p. 238., was cited, as shewing that "transversum pontis de *Ware*" meant merely passage; but the Court did not notice the work as authority.

(*b*) 8 *Rep.* 46 *b*.

Then,

1838.

The QUEEN *against* The Marquis of SALISBURY.

If there be merely an ambiguity here, the interpretation should be in favour of the Crown; 2 *Bl. Com.* 347.; and the land will not be taken to pass. But, in fact, the documents do not distinctly shew a right to the land in the Crown. [*Littledale* J. inquired if there were any Latin words, for toll thorough and traverse, in *Rolle* or *Fitzherbert*.]

Cur. adv. vult.

Lord DENMAN C. J., in this term (*June* 2d.), delivered the judgment of the Court. After stating the facts detailed in the outset of the special case, pp. 717, 718, 730, antè, his Lordship said,

Upon these facts, if there were nothing more in the case, there would be clearly quite enough to warrant the sessions in finding that there was an occupation of land in the parish of *Ware* by the Marquis, and an occupation beneficial in respect of the tolls. The actual perception of the tolls in the parish of *Great Amwell* alone would be immaterial, because the land in *Ware* would appear to contribute towards the earning them; and the case would seem to be almost identical with that of *Rex* v. *Barnes* (a): the difference that a road-way was placed upon the planking of the bridge, and kept in repair by others than the Marquis, whereas, in the case cited, the bridge company made and repaired the carriage-way as well as the bridge, could not be considered material, because it would not rebut the presumption of ownership and occupation of the bridge itself and the land on which it stands, arising from the facts before stated.

(a) 1 *B. & Ad.* 113.

1838.

The QUEEN *against* The Marquis of SALISBURY.

Two circumstances, however, were relied on to relieve the Marquis from the present assessment; the first, that, by reason of a demise, another person was the occupier; the second, that the nature of the toll itself, and the title under which the Marquis held it, when examined into, shewed conclusively that he was not the owner of the bridge, or land on which it stands, but that he had repaired the bridge only in respect of the toll granted to him.

With regard to the former, the case states the tolls to be collected by *J. Kent*, who resides in the toll-house, on behalf of *Everett*, and that *Everett* receives them under a parol agreement with the Marquis, for one year, at a yearly rent or sum to be paid by monthly instalments, secured by a warrant of attorney; and that the Marquis has executed no grant or demise of the tolls. Assuming, then, that the tolls are claimable in respect of the ownership of the land, there is no evidence here that the land *eo nomine* is professed to be demised at all: there is nothing to shew that at this moment the Marquis is not in the possession of the land for the purpose of doing the repairs, indeed for every purpose consistent with the bare collection of the tolls by *Everett* at the toll-house; on the other hand, though there is an agreement for a demise of the tolls *eo nomine*, yet, as by their nature they can only pass by deed, no interest at law has passed out of the Marquis, who must, therefore, be still considered in possession of them, his intended tenant being, in truth, only his bailiff for the collection of them.

We pass to the consideration of the remaining point of the case. The question intended here to be raised is, whether the toll claimed by the Marquis be toll

traverse,

1838.

The QUEEN *against* The Marquis of SALISBURY.

traverse, or toll thorough. In the former case, it would imply the ownership of the land; and then the repairs before mentioned would still be referable, as before they appeared to be, to the ownership of the bridge and land: in the latter, no such inference would arise; and he repairs of the bridge would be explainable as done in respect only of the toll, and as the necessary consideration to render the grant of it valid. The sessions have not found all the facts from which we might draw the legal inference; but, in addition to some facts stated, have supplied us with a considerable portion of documentary evidence. This is not the proper mode of submitting a case for our consideration; and it must not be assumed, because we enter into the examination of these documents, that we will upon all occasions enquire into matters of fact properly cognisable by the sessions only.

From the documentary evidence, it appears that the Marquis derives title to this toll under a grant from the Crown of the reversion, expectant on a lease, of the honour, castle, lordship, manor, town, &c., of *Hertford*. Among the parcels of the grant specially set forth are these, "all that toll, and all those tolls called traverse, and customs *of the lordship and honor of Hertford*, in the said county of *Hertford*, to be taken in manner accustomed, that is to say, of all saleable things passing through the town of *Hertford*, and also through the town of *Ware*, *Bishop's Hatfield*, *Thele* otherwise *Therle*, *Belbar*, and elsewhere in divers places in the said county, that is to say, for every cart" &c., passing over the bridges aforesaid, &c.

The Marquis therefore takes this by the description of a toll called traverse, and belonging to the lordship

1838.

The QUEEN against The Marquis of SALISBURY.

and honour of *Hertford*. This grant is of the date 6 *Ch.* 1.

We are also supplied with an inquisition after the death of *Aymare de Valence, Earl of Pembroke* (17 *E.* 2.), in which the toll is connected with the castle and town of *Hertford*, and called "the traverse at the bridge of *Ware*." A minister's account for *Hertford*, of the 35 & 36 of *H.* 8., describes it as "the toll travers of the bridge of *Ware*;" and, in another account of the 1st & 2d *Charles* 1st, the minister answers for 16*l.* from the farm "of the toll traverse and customs of the lordship, castle, and honour of *Hertford*, of all things for sale passing over the bridges of *Hertford*, *Ware*," &c.

It cannot be denied that this is strong evidence to shew that the toll in question is in its nature toll traverse (*a*). It raises a strong probability that *Ware* is a manor within the honour of *Hertford*, and that the Marquis is the owner of the wastes in it; the soil therefore may well be in him; and, that it is so, is consistent with the fact of repairs before stated. We think that, after this evidence, the burthen was cast upon the Marquis of meeting it by contrary evidence; and that, in default of of his doing so, the sessions were well warranted in considering it a toll traverse, and in confirming the rate upon him. The order of sessions, therefore, will be confirmed.

Order of sessions confirmed.

(*a*) The early history of the toll appears from the inquisition of 5 *Ed.* 3., referred to in p. 736, *note* (*a*), antè.

END OF TRINITY TERM.

CASES

ARGUED AND DETERMINED

IN THE

Court of QUEEN's BENCH,

AND

UPON WRITS OF ERROR FROM THAT COURT TO THE

EXCHEQUER CHAMBER,

IN

Michaelmas Term,

In the Second Year of the Reign of Victoria.

1838.

The Judges who usually sat in Banc in this term were

Lord Denman C. J.	Williams J.
Patteson J.	Coleridge J.

REGULA GENERALIS.

(Read in Court, *Monday, November* 5th.)

Michaelmas Term, 2 *Vict.*

Whereas it is provided by the act of the 1 & 2 of her present Majesty, *c.* 45. *s.* 3., that, after the 1st day of *November*, 1838, any person entitled to be admitted an attorney of any of the superior courts of common law at *Westminster* shall, after being sworn in and admitted as an attorney of any one of the said courts, be

 entitled

1838. entitled to practise in any other of the said courts upon signing the roll of such court, and not otherwise, in like manner as if he had been sworn in and admitted an attorney of such court, provided that no additional fee besides those payable under the act of the 1st year of the reign of her present Majesty, *c.* 56. (*a*), shall be demanded or paid; and that the fees payable for such admission shall be apportioned in such manner as the Judges of the said courts, or any eight of them, shall, by any rule or order made in term or vacation, direct and appoint:

We therefore direct and appoint that the fees payable by virtue of the said last-mentioned act for the Judge's fiat be received in the first instance by the clerk of the Judge granting the fiat, and paid over by him to the clerk of the Chief Justice or Chief Baron of the court, as the case may be: and the day after each term all the fees so received shall be divided into fifteen portions, one of which shall be paid to the clerk or clerks of each Judge. And, further, that the fees payable by virtue of the said act to the ushers shall be received, in the first instance, by one of the ushers of the court in which the admission shall take place, and shall, on the day after each term, be divided into three equal portions, one of which shall be paid to the ushers of each court.

(Signed)	DENMAN.	J. B. BOSANQUET.
	N. C. TINDAL.	E. H. ALDERSON.
	ABINGER.	J. PATTESON.
	J. A. PARK.	J. GURNEY.
	J. LITTLEDALE.	J. WILLIAMS.
	J. VAUGHAN.	J. T. COLERIDGE.
	J. PARKE.	T. COLTMAN.

(*a*) 7 *W.* 4. & 1 *Vict.* *s.* 3, and schedule.

1838.

BAINBRIDGE *against* FIRMSTONE.

Friday, November 2d.

Declaration, in assumpsit, stated that, in consideration that plaintiff, at defendant's request, had consented to allow defendant to weigh two boilers of plaintiff, defendant promised to give them up, after weighing, in as perfect condition as they were in at the time of the consent: breach, that defendant did not give up &c.

On motion in arrest of judgment, on the ground of want of a consideration shewing detriment to plaintiff or benefit to defendant, and also of ambiguity in the word "weigh:" Held, that the declaration was sufficient.

ASSUMPSIT. The declaration stated that, whereas heretofore, to wit &c., in consideration that plaintiff, at the request of defendant, had then consented to allow defendant to weigh divers, to wit two, boilers of the plaintiff, of great value &c., defendant promised that he would, within a reasonable time after the said weighing was effected, leave and give up the boilers in as perfect and complete a condition, and as fit for use by plaintiff, as the same were in at the time of the consent so given by plaintiff; and that, although in pursuance of the consent so given, defendant, to wit on &c., did weigh the same boilers, yet defendant did not nor would, within a reasonable time after the said weighing was effected, leave and give up the boilers in as perfect &c., but wholly neglected and refused so to do, although a reasonable time for that purpose had elapsed before the commencement of this suit; and, on the contrary thereof, defendant afterwards, to wit on &c., took the said boilers to pieces, and did not put the same together again, but left the same in a detached and divided condition, and in many different pieces, whereby plaintiff hath been put to great trouble &c. Plea, Non assumpsit.

On the trial before Lord *Denman* C. J., at the *London* sittings after last *Trinity* term, a verdict was found for the defendant.

1838.

BAINBRIDGE *against* FIRMSTONE.

John Bayley now moved in arrest of judgment. The declaration shews no consideration. There should have been either detriment to the plaintiff, or benefit to the defendant; 1 *Selwyn's N. P.* 45. (*a*). It does not appear that the defendant was to receive any remuneration. Besides, the word "weigh" is ambiguous.

Lord DENMAN C. J. It seems to me that the declaration is well enough. The defendant had some reason for wishing to weigh the boilers; and he could do so only by obtaining permission from the plaintiff, which he did obtain by promising to return them in good condition. We need not enquire what benefit he expected to derive. The plaintiff might have given or refused leave.

PATTESON J. The consideration is, that the plaintiff, at the defendant's request, had consented to allow the defendant to weigh the boilers. I suppose the defendant thought he had some benefit; at any rate, there is a detriment to the plaintiff from his parting with the possession for even so short a time.

WILLIAMS and COLERIDGE Js. concurred.

Rule refused.

(*a*) 9th ed.

1838.

In the Matter of The Examiners of Attorneys.

Saturday, November 3d.

If a party applying to be admitted an attorney undergo the examination under R. *H.* 6 *W.* 4., but fail to obtain his certificate, he cannot be examined again without giving a fresh term's notice.

KELLY moved for an order to the examiners, appointed under R. *Hil.* 6 *W.* 4. (*a*), to examine a party desirous of being admitted an attorney. It appeared that he had already, upon giving due notice and complying with the other requisites, undergone an examination, but had failed to obtain a certificate of fitness, the examiners not being satisfied as to his knowledge; that he considered himself now capable of satisfying the examiners; but that he had not given a fresh term's notice. *Kelly* contended that the requisite of a term's notice, as prescribed by sect. 4 of the rule (*b*), was satisfied by the notice given in the first instance, the question now being only as to the competency of the applicant in point of knowledge.

Per Curiam (*c*). We consider it to be clear that there must be a new notice of a full term. It is as if nothing whatever had taken place.

Application refused.

(*a*) 4 *A.* & *E.* 744. (*b*) 4 *A.* & *E.* 746.

(*c*) Lord *Denman* C. J., *Patteson*, *Williams*, and *Coleridge*, Js.

Monday, November 5th.

Cooper *against* Lawson.

Case for libel. The alleged libel stated that plaintiff, a tradesman in *London*, became surety for the petitioner on the *Berwick* election petition, and stated himself, on oath, to be sufficiently qualified in point of property, when he was not in fact qualified, nor able to pay his debts. It then asked, why the plaintiff, being unconnected with the borough, should take so much trouble, and incur such an exposure of his embarrassments; and proceeded: "*There can be but one answer* to these very natural and reasonable queries; *he is hired for the occasion.*" The defendant justified, stating that the above-mentioned allegations in the libel (except the hiring, which was not specifically noticed,) were true, and that the publication was a correct report of proceedings in a legal court, "*together with a fair and bonâ fide commentary thereon.*" Replication de injuriâ. Issue thereon.

Held, that the concluding observation in the libel, not being a mere inference from the previous statement, but introducing a substantive fact, required a distinct justification; and therefore that, on trial of the above issue, it was properly left to the jury to say, not only whether the evidence made out the facts first alleged, but also whether the imputation, that the plaintiff had been hired, was a fair comment.

CASE. The declaration stated that defendant, intending to cause it to be believed that plaintiff had been guilty of perjury and of the other offences and misconduct after-mentioned, and that he was in bad circumstances and could not pay his creditors, and to vex, harass, &c., published a libel in *The Times* newspaper of and concerning plaintiff, and of and concerning him as surety on the *Berwick* election petition, and in his business of a tailor. The libel, as set out in the declaration, stated that the sureties proposed on the petition were a tailor (the plaintiff) and a printer, neither the one nor the other having any connexion with *Berwick*, "but both procured for the job, no doubt for a consideration." It then recited the affidavit of qualification made by the plaintiff as one of the sureties; and alleged that the plaintiff was known to be in circumstances which rendered him unfit to be a surety in in any such case; and it set forth affidavits put in by the agent for the sitting members before the examiners appointed under stat. 9 *G.* 4. *c.* 22. *s.* 7., stating circumstances to shew that the plaintiff was embarrassed in his affairs, unable to pay his debts, and an insufficient surety. It likewise detailed a counter-affidavit put in by the plaintiff, and stated that the agent for the sitting

members

members had asked for time to answer such affidavit, which he could have done, but which was refused, and the surety admitted. The following passage was then added: "But why, it may be asked, does this cockney tailor take all this trouble, and subject himself to all this exposure of his difficulties and embarrassments? He has nothing to do with the borough of *Berwick-upon-Tweed* or its members. How comes it then that he should take so much interest in the job? There can be but one answer to these very natural and reasonable queries: he is hired for the occasion. The affair in fact is a foul job throughout, and it is only by such aid that it can possibly be supported." And the declaration stated that by reason of the committing &c. divers persons believed plaintiff to have been guilty of perjury, and the said other offences and misconduct above mentioned, and to have been and to be unable to pay his creditors their just demands. Special damage to the plaintiff in his credit and trade was alleged.

Pleas. 1. Not Guilty. 2. Justification, alleging that affidavits were put in, and other proceedings taken before the examiners of sureties, as stated in the alleged libel; that the statements made on affidavit for the sitting members were true; that the plaintiff, at the time of making his affidavits and becoming surety, was not a fit person to become surety; and that a principal averment in his affidavit before the examiners was not true. The plea further stated as follows.

"That the said several affidavits in the said declaration and in this plea above mentioned were made, sworn, and publicly exhibited to and before the said *William Ley* and *Francis Cross*" (the examiners), "and are respectively proceedings publicly had and taken before

1838.

Cooper *against* Lawson.

before a legal court, jurisdiction, and tribunal, competent to entertain, examine, and determine upon the same (*a*), for the purpose of their being examined and determined upon by the said tribunal; and that the said supposed libellous matter in the said declaration mentioned, so far as the same alludes to or concerns the plaintiff, was and is a just, fair, honest, impartial, and a substantially and, in every thing therein material of and concerning the plaintiff, a strictly true account, narrative, and report of the said proceedings, *together with a fair and bonâ fide commentary thereon*: and that the subject matters of the said supposed libel, so far as the same alludes to or concerns the plaintiff, as being such an account, narrative, and report of the said proceedings, *together with the said commentary thereon*, were and are matters which it was lawful, fit and proper, and useful for the public, for him the defendant to publish, and cause and procure to be published in the said newspaper as and being such an account, narrative, and report of the said proceedings, and such commentary thereon." There was no specific justification of the charge that the plaintiff was hired. Verification.

Replication, de injuriâ. Issue thereon.

On the trial before Lord *Denman* C. J., at the sittings in *London* after last *Trinity* term, evidence was given by the defendant in support of the second plea; but no proof was offered of the plaintiff having been hired to become surety. The Lord Chief Justice, in summing up, said that, on the second plea, the opinion of the jury was to be taken, first, on the truth of the facts, the principal question of fact being, whether the plaintiff

(*a*) See stat. 9 *G.* 4. *c.* 22. sects. 7, 8.

was

1838.

COOPER against LAWSON.

was or was not fit to be surety. If the jury should think he was, the plaintiff would be entitled to damages. If the jury should be of opinion that he was not fit, they were then to say whether the comments which imputed to him that he was a hired swearer, and which would make him liable for a wilful false statement of facts, were fair comments. If the jury should think them not fair comments, the plaintiff would be entitled to such damages as they considered reasonable. Verdict for the plaintiff; damages 100*l.*

Sir *J. Campbell*, Attorney-General, now moved for a new trial on the ground of misdirection. The observation that the plaintiff must have been hired was a mere inference from the preceding statements, which were justified in pleading, and the justification proved. It was unnecessary to plead that this was a fair comment; the plea would have been good if it had only justified the other statements. [Lord *Denman* C. J. Suppose it were published that a thief had been bailed by some person, and that no one would have become bail but a receiver. Would not the last averment, if applied to any individual, be libellous?] There a new fact is introduced, unconnected by inference with that which precedes. If the publication were, "He murdered his father, and therefore is a disgrace to human nature," the latter words there would be a fair comment on the previous ones; and nothing material could turn upon them in an action. [Lord *Denman* C. J. The comment here involves a new fact, which may or may not be connected with the previous ones.] Both sides, at the trial, treated it as matter of inference. The plaintiff, by his pleading to the justification, admits that

1838.

Cooper *against* Lawson.

that the facts there stated, if proved, are a sufficient defence. The words, "there can be but one answer," "he is hired for the occasion," mean, in effect, that any person who becomes surety on an election petition under the circumstances before stated, that is, owing money which he cannot pay, and having no connection with the place to be represented, must have been hired for the occasion. [*Patteson* J. Suppose the declaration had been upon the comment only. Would it be a sufficient defence, that the words were a comment on certain facts?] The facts might be alleged in justification; and, if they were proved, and the words declared upon were merely a comment upon them, no question for the jury could arise upon the mere expression of opinion. *Clarke* v. *Taylor* (*a*), and *Edwards* v. *Bell* (*b*) there cited, shew that it is not necessary to justify every part of an alleged libel, but that, if the material assertions are justified, passages consisting of mere comment, or not amounting to a substantive allegation of crime or misconduct, may be left unnoticed. Here the Lord Chief Justice left it to the jury to say whether the comments were fair; so that, if any part of them, in the jury's opinion, was not so, they would have thought the plaintiff entitled to recover. [Lord *Denman* C. J. I put it to them, whether the comments which imputed to the plaintiff that he was a hired swearer and wilfully stated falsehood were fair. To shew that that was wrong, you must argue that it is immaterial what comment a writer makes, if the facts commented upon be true. Here the comment was an averment of fact.] If this was a distinct allegation of fact, which might be a libel, the plaintiff must contend that, if the verdict had

(*a*) 2 *New Ca.* 654.

(*b*) 1 *Bing.* 403.

been

been against him he might have demanded judgment non obstante veredicto, part of the libel on the record not being justified.

PATTESON J. The only doubt in my mind arose from the case of *Clarke* v. *Taylor* (a); but that is not in point. There the plaintiff declared upon a long publication which he alleged to be a libel upon him. The defendants justified some paragraphs, but not others. A verdict being found for the defendants, a rule nisi was obtained for entering a verdict with nominal damages for the plaintiff on the parts of the publication not justified. *Tindal* C. J. said, "There can be no doubt that a defendant may justify part only of a libel containing several distinct charges." "But if he omits to justify a part which contains libellous matter, he is liable in damages for that which he has so omitted to justify. The plea in the present instance does not affect to justify the whole of the publication, and we are to see whether the part omitted would, by itself, form a substantive ground of an action of libel. I cannot say that it is of that description." Therefore, the part omitted in the justification not being matter on which an action would lie, it was held that the plaintiff could not have a verdict. But in the present case, if the plea had omitted to justify the comment, there is no doubt that the plaintiff would have been entitled to recover. The comment is, in substance, that the plaintiff would not have become surety unless he had been hired. That alone would be sufficient, if not answered, to give the plaintiff a verdict. *Clarke* v. *Taylor* (a), therefore, does

(a) 2 *New Ca.* 654.

not

1838.

Cooper against Lawson.

not apply. I do not say that, in all cases where an alleged libel consists partly of comment, it should be left to the jury to say whether the comment is fair, because, if, as the *Attorney-General* has put it, the words were, "he has murdered his father, and therefore is a disgrace to human nature," it would be ridiculous to ask whether the observation was or was not a fair comment. But, where the comment raises an imputation of motives which may or may not be a just inference from the preceding statement, it is a distinct libel. That is so here; and therefore the question put to the jury related to a material part of the issue. If the defendant had meant to justify as to the facts first alleged, and those only, he should have contented himself with shewing that the statements contained in the affidavits for the sitting members were true, and should have left his case there, which, according to the *Attorney-General*, would have been a sufficient plea. But he has gone on to say that the comment was fair; and wisely, in my opinion; for, if not justified, it is libellous. Then it was necessary that the question which he himself raised should be put to the jury. The direction, therefore, was right.

Williams J. Mr. *Attorney-General* assumes that the comment suggesting that the plaintiff was hired makes no addition to the previous statement. But, where a question is raised on the conduct of a party who becomes security when in a state of ambiguous solvency, such an allegation must have a material effect in testing the character of the principal transaction. And, a justification of this statement being put on the record, and properly, the opinion of the jury must necessarily have

been

been taken upon it. Where a libel has been justified as being the report of a trial, a mere interjectional remark has been held to deprive it of protection. The comment supposed by the *Attorney-General* on the fact of a man murdering his father is a mere conclusion upon which none could differ; it adds no fact or feature to the suggested case. Here the comment does add a fact, which gives character to the whole transaction previously stated, if its nature were uncertain before.

COLERIDGE J. The libel here imputes perjury to the plaintiff in representing himself as a fit surety, and adds, as a conclusion, that he must have been hired. The question, then, is, first, whether the propriety of such a comment can, in any case, be put to the jury. The *Attorney-General* says it cannot, if the preceding facts are justified. Yet it often happens that the whole sting and injury of the libel are in the comment. This proposition, therefore, is too strong. But it would be as much too strong to say that all such comments are to be submitted to the jury; for there are cases, one of which has been put, where the inference is so fair, that, if you prove the fact, you prove the correctness of the comment. But this was not such a case. The comment introduced an additional fact, and then it was for the jury to say whether that was fairly done, or not. I think therefore that, in this particular case, the comment was properly submitted to the jury.

Lord DENMAN C. J. It would be extravagant to say that, in cases of libel, every comment upon facts requires a justification. But a comment may introduce independent facts, a justification of which is necessary.

1838.

Cooper *against* Lawson.

The plea is perfectly good, justifying the libel, partly as the report of proceedings before a court, partly as stating that which is in itself true, and partly as giving a fair and bonâ fide commentary on the proceedings stated. Now a comment may be the mere shadow of the previous imputation; but, if it infers a new fact, the defendant must abide by that inference of fact, and the fairness of the comment must be decided upon by a jury. The defendant here cannot say that, if the plaintiff became bail under the circumstances stated, it followed as a necessary inference that he was hired.

Rule refused.

Tuesday, November 6th.

John Murley *against* Sherren, Greenham, and Parker.

It is no objection in law to a conveyance, that the grantor acquired the property by a fraud, and that the grant tends (and was designed, as the adverse party alleges,) to defeat the equitable right of third persons to relief against such fraud.

As the right (if any) of an heir at law to relief against a fine levied by a lunatic during his lunacy.

TRESPASS for breaking and entering plaintiff's closes. Plea, that the closes were and are the closes, soil, and freehold of defendant *Greenham;* wherefore *Greenham* in his own right, and the other defendants as his servants &c. Replication, that the closes were the closes, &c., of plaintiff, and not of *Greenham:* and issue thereon.

On the trial before *Coltman* J., at the last *Somersetshire* assizes, it appeared that the locus in quo had formerly belonged to *Edward Thomas Murley*, to whom the plaintiff was heir at law. In 1805, *E. T. Murley* conveyed the locus in quo, with other property, to a person named *Templeman*, in fee by a fine. In 1822 it was found, upon a commission of lunacy, for which *Greenham* had applied, that *E. T. Murley* was, and had been ever since 1792, of unsound mind; and *Greenham*

1838.

MORLEY against SHEREEN.

ham was appointed committee. *Greenham* afterwards instituted proceedings in equity to recover the property from *Templeman;* but the suit was compromised in 1828, on the terms that *Templeman* should retain some portion and convey the residue of the property claimed to *Greenham.* In 1828 *Templeman* accordingly conveyed the residue, which included the locus in quo, to *Greenham.* The plaintiff's counsel contended that *Greenham* could not make title under this conveyance, if the jury, under the circumstances, considered that the transaction was concerted between *Templeman* and *Greenham* in order to defraud the lunatic. The learned Judge was of opinion that the lunatic had no legal title after the fine of 1805, and that, consequently, assuming the transaction to have been concerted as said by the plaintiff's counsel, the right of the lunatic, against which the fraud was practised, was only equitable; and that such fraud could not be insisted upon at law to defeat the conveyance: he therefore directed the jury to find for the defendants. Verdict accordingly.

Erle now moved for a new trial, on the ground of misdirection. It is true that a fine levied by a lunatic is valid at law; 3 *Bac. Abr.* 645, 646; *Fines and Recoveries* (C) (*a*). But a court of equity will decree a reconveyance; *Addison* v. *Dawson* (*b*). There was therefore an equitable right, which the conveyance of 1828 was intended to defeat. That avoided the transaction at law: for the principle is, that no effect shall be given to a fraudulent transaction; and, for this

(*a*) 7th ed.

(*b*) 2 *Vern.* 678.

1838.

MURLEY *against* SHERREN.

purpose, it can make no difference whether the fraud be proved by shewing that it is directed against legal or against equitable rights.

Cur. adv. vult.

Lord DENMAN C. J., in this term (*November* 22d), delivered the judgment of the Court.

In this case a rule was moved for a new trial, on the ground of misdirection, under the following circumstances. The action was in trespass; and the plea, the soil and freehold of *Greenham*, one of the defendants. The land had originally belonged to one *Murley*, who, by a deed of 1805, had conveyed it to *Templeman*, and levied a fine thereupon to the use of *Templeman*. In 1822 *Greenham* applied for a commission of lunacy; under which *Murley* was found to have been a lunatic for thirty years preceding, and *Greenham* was appointed the committee of the estate. He then proceeded in equity against *Templeman*, but finally compromised with him, and himself took a conveyance from him in 1828. On this title the defendants relied to make out their plea, it being settled law, that, if a lunatic levies a fine, neither he, nor those who represent him, shall avoid it; *Beverley's Case* (a). Mr. *Erle*, for the plaintiff, contended that he might impeach these transactions by shewing fraud practised on the alleged lunatic; the learned Judge, however, stated that no effect was to be given to any such evidence, unless he was prepared to shew fraud practised by *Greenham* on *Templeman*; for that *Templeman*'s title under the fine must be taken to be good in law, and therefore the only deed open to

(a) 4 *Co.* 123. b.

impeachment

1838.

MORLEY against SHERREN.

impeachment was the conveyance from *Templeman* to *Greenham*.

This ruling, upon which the learned Judge acted in his summing up, was the ground of the application; and it was argued that, although at law the fine of the lunatic might not be liable to impeachment on the ground of the lunacy of the conusor, yet, as this might in effect be done in equity (for which *Addison* v. *Dawson* (*a*) was cited), the plaintiff ought to have been permitted to shew that the whole transaction was void.

We are of opinion, however, that the ruling of the learned Judge was perfectly right. We express no opinion as to the relief which a court of equity may be competent to give. But it is of great importance that a court of law should proceed on legal principles, and not be induced to depart from them by any hardship in the particular case. At law the fine is valid, and nothing has been done to avoid it: full effect, therefore, must be given to it. The result is, that *Templeman* was competent to convey a good legal title to *Greenham*; and no evidence was tendered to shew that, as between these two, he had not done so. There must be, therefore, no rule.

Rule refused.

(*a*) 2 *Vern.* 678.

Friday, November 9th.

GROOM and Others, Assignees of RAVEN, a Bankrupt, *against* WEST.

Declaration, by assignees of *R.*, a bankrupt, stated that defendant, in consideration that *R.* would sell and deliver to him sugars at the rate and price of &c., agreed to pay him for the same, prompt two months, or an acceptance at seventy days if required; that the goods were delivered to and received by defendant, before the bankruptcy, on the terms aforesaid, but he did not, though required before the bankruptcy, pay, then or since, by an acceptance, nor did he otherwise pay; whereby *R.* before his bankruptcy lost the use and benefit of such acceptance, and the benefit which would have accrued to him from having it discounted and raising money on it for his use in the way of his trade, and was put to loss and inconvenience by not having such acceptance to negotiate, *and his estate applicable to the payment of his just debts was, by reason of the non-payment for the goods in manner aforesaid, diminished in value, to the damage of the assignees and creditors.* Plea, set-off for a debt due from *R.* before bankruptcy. Demurrer.

Held, that the concluding averments of the declaration did not shew a special damage to the plaintiffs, but only a common pecuniary loss: that the case appearing on the declaration was one of mutual credit, within stat. 6 *G.* 4. *c.* 16. *s.* 50., and that a set-off might be pleaded.

ASSUMPSIT. The first count of the declaration stated that heretofore, and before *Raven* became bankrupt, viz. on 23d *June* 1835, in consideration that *Raven*, at defendant's request, would sell and deliver to him a certain quantity, viz. five hogsheads, of *Demerara* sugar, tares as settled with the merchant, at a certain rate or price then agreed upon between *Raven* and defendant, viz. at the rate or price of 2*l.* 15*s.* for each and every hundred weight of the said sugar, amounting in the whole to a large sum, viz. 175*l.* 0*s.* 4*d.*, defendant promised *Raven* to accept the said sugars, and pay him for the same in manner following, that is, prompt two months, or an acceptance, that is to say of a bill of exchange, for the amount thereof, payable seventy days after the date of such bill, if such acceptance should be required by *Raven*, the said seller. Averment that *Raven*, confiding &c., did afterwards and before he became bankrupt, viz. on &c., sell and deliver the said quantity of goods to defendant on the terms aforesaid, and defendant then accepted the same. And that, although *Raven* afterwards and before he became bankrupt, viz. on &c., required defendant to pay him

for

for the said sugars by an acceptance according to the terms of the said sale, yet defendant, not regarding &c., did not nor would, when he was so required, or at any time before or afterwards, pay *Raven* before he became bankrupt, or the plaintiffs, assignees as aforesaid, the said price of the said goods, or any part thereof, by an acceptance or otherwise howsoever, but has hitherto wholly neglected and refused, and still neglects &c., so to do; and by reason thereof *Raven*, before he became a bankrupt, lost and was deprived of the use and benefit of an acceptance of and by defendant for the said price of the said sugars, and all the benefit and advantage which would have accrued to him from having the said acceptance discounted, and raising money thereby for his use and accommodation in the way of his trade and business, and was thereby also put to great loss, trouble, and inconvenience, by reason of not having the said bill to negotiate; and the personal estate and effects of *Raven*, applicable to the discharge of his just debts, were thereby and by reason of the non-payment of and for the said goods or any part thereof, in manner aforesaid, much diminished in value, to the great damage of plaintiffs as assignees, and of the creditors seeking relief under the fiat, &c.

The second count stated that defendant had bought of *Raven*, and *Raven* had sold to him, goods at a certain price, viz. &c., to be paid for prompt two months, or by an acceptance at seventy days, if required, and other goods at a certain price &c., to be paid for on delivery, the proceeds and value of which several quantities of goods amounted in the whole to a large &c., viz. 615*l.*, which goods respectively had been delivered to and accepted by defendant before the bankruptcy, but neither the acceptance had been given, though required, nor had

1838.

GROOM *against* WEST.

the payment been made in any way: and that, in consideration thereof, and of an agreement that the goods should be paid for by, and that *Raven* should take, defendant's acceptance as after-mentioned, defendant promised *Raven* to accept a bill for the amount of all the last mentioned goods when requested; that, before the bankruptcy, *Raven* consented to take such acceptance, and, to wit on &c., requested defendant to pay him for the last mentioned goods by such acceptance. Averment of breach and damages substantially as in the first count.

Plea, that before and at the time of the fiat, to wit &c., *Raven* was indebted to defendant in 1000*l.* for goods before then sold and delivered, and money before then lent, by defendant to *Raven*, without notice to defendant, when he gave credit to *Raven* for the said sum &c., of any act of bankruptcy, &c.: set-off.

Demurrer, assigning for causes: that the set-off is pleaded to a declaration for unliquidated damages; that there does not appear by the plea to have been any mutual credit between *Raven* and the defendant before or at the time of making the several contracts mentioned in the declaration, but, on the contrary, it appears by the declaration that the several goods therein respectively mentioned were to have been paid for by the defendant by acceptances to be immediately given by the defendant to *Raven*, and which he might negotiate and get discounted for the purposes of his trade; and each of the dealings and transactions in the declaration mentioned was a distinct and independent dealing and transaction, made and effected as such, and not with reference to the general state of accounts, debts, or credits, or any mutual credit between *Raven* and the defendant: That it does not appear by the plea that, when

when the contracts mentioned in the declaration were entered into, *Raven* was indebted to the defendant; and his becoming so after breach of those contracts (which ought to have been immediately fulfilled by defendant) can be no answer to the breach of such contract at the periods when such breaches were respectively committed: and that the plea attempts to substitute for the mode of payment contracted for in respect of the goods mentioned in the declaration, a different mode, more prejudicial to the seller, and not appearing to have been assented to by him or the assignees. It was also stated, in the margin of the paper-book, as an objection by the defendant, that neither count of the declaration averred any tender of the bill to be accepted, or waiver of such tender. Joinder in demurrer.

Sir *F. Pollock*, for the plaintiff. The object of this demurrer is to defeat a practice resorted to for obtaining more than a proportional payment out of a bankrupt's estate. A trader being likely to fail, one of his creditors, knowing him to be in that situation, contracts with him for goods, undertaking to pay or give a bill immediately; but, having the goods, he either presents in payment a bill of the bankrupt's own, or refuses to pay or give any bill, leaves the assignees to their action, and then sets off the debt due from the bankrupt to him, thus securing to himself, if the set-off be allowed, 20*s.* in the pound, as in a case of mutual credit. *Fair* v. *M'Iver* (a) furnishes an example of this kind of contrivance. [*Patteson* J. In that case facts shewing fraud were before the Court. We cannot assume that this is such a transaction.] If the contract

(a) 16 *East*, 130.

with

1838.

Groom *against* West.

with the bankrupt was not made for the purpose of fraud, still this use of it is a fraud. On the question, whether this be a case of mutual credit, *Rose* v. *Sims* (*a*) is decisive. *Taunton* J. says there, "A mutual credit may be said to exist where there is a debt, or something which will end in a debt. Here neither was shewn, but only a cause of action, namely, the failure of the defendant to indorse pursuant to his engagement. Immediately upon that failure, a right of action accrued to the plaintiff, but not a debt. The damages were unliquidated, and their amount dependent on circumstances." In a note at the end of that case, it is stated that "A party cannot avail himself of his own wrongful act as establishing a mutual credit within the statute; as where a creditor, with whom bills of exchange are deposited by his debtor for a specific purpose, detains them against good faith." *Key* v. *Flint* (*b*), *Ex parte Flint* (*c*), and *Buchanan* v. *Findlay* (*d*) are cited. It is true, that where a bill has become due it constitutes a debt; and that on a contract to pay for goods sold by a bill the seller may declare as for goods sold: but it is not necessary that he should do so; and the contract is not, necessarily, part of a mutual credit. It clearly would not be so if the parties agreed that a bill should be given and taken, and that that transaction should stand apart from all others; or, in express terms, that it should not be a matter of mutual credit. It is the same where the obvious sense of the transaction is that it shall stand by itself. At least the wrongdoer, who has engaged to give a bill, and failed, cannot insist that the transaction constitutes a debt: the assignees may, if they choose,

(*a*) 1 *B. & Ad.* 521.

(*b*) 8 *Taunt.* 21.

(*c*) 1 *Swanst.* 30.

(*d*) 9 *B. & C.* 738.

waive

1838.

GROOM *against* WEST.

waive the more beneficial contract and proceed as for a common debt; but he cannot compel them to do so. [*Patteson* J. If a person takes goods on a contract that he shall give, and the seller receive, an acceptance for them, how can it be said that that is not a credit? If the acceptance were given and received, would not that be a credit; unless you set up the fraud? The test mentioned in *Rose* v. *Sims* (*a*) is, that there shall be a debt, or something which will end in a debt. Is not that so here?] Credit does not mean simply trusting. Suppose there were a special agreement that a certain supply of merchandise should be paid for in goods; that would not be a mutual credit within sect. 50 of stat. 6 *G.* 4. *c.* 16. Yet in principle it can make no essential difference whether the payment is to be by a specific payment of money, or by goods. The agreement to pay by a bill is like an agreement to give goods. Suppose the acceptance to be given and received were that of a third person; there would be *a credit* to the party giving the acceptance; but no one would say it was a case of mutual credit within the statute. The bankrupt is entitled to treat this transaction as one of barter; to look upon the bill merely as a thing in respect of which trover would have lain, as in *Key* v. *Flint* (*b*). There the bankrupts, whose assignees sued in trover, had deposited a bill with the defendant in order that he might get it discounted; he advanced a part only of the amount, and kept the bill, promising further advances; and it was held that the assignees, paying back what had been advanced, might recover for the amount of the bill, though the bankrupts were indebted to the defendant at the time of depositing the bill with him.

(*a*) 1 *B. & Ad.* 526. (*b*) 8 *Taunt.* 21.

The

1838.

GROOM *against* WEST.

The Court of Common Pleas did not consider this a case of mutual credit, the bill having been deposited for a specific purpose, with an understanding that it was not to go into the general account. In *Olive* v. *Smith* (a) the law of mutual credit was considered as extending to deposits which might be the subject of trover; but that doctrine was corrected in *Rose* v. *Hart* (b) and *Buchanan* v. *Findlay* (c). In the latter case the bankrupts had sent bills to the defendants, who were their creditors, to be discounted, and applied to particular purposes; the defendants held the bills till they were due, and then received and kept the proceeds; and it was decided that an action of money had and received lay against them for the amount, at the suit of the assignees, though the bankrupts were still debtors to the defendants. Yet there, if in any such case, it might have been said that the transaction was one terminating in a debt on the part of those dealing with the bankrupts. The law, then, as applicable to the present case is, that, where a bill which should have been given has been withheld contrary to the faith on which the particular dealing took place, a special action on the case lies; and mutual credit cannot be alleged, nor a set-off pleaded. [Lord *Denman* C. J. Is there any damage really shewn here beyond the loss of the money?] It must be admitted that, for the mere non-payment of money, damages cannot be recovered beyond the interest; but, where a trader loses the benefit of a bill which he contemplated turning into money, he is entitled to damages, without a more specific allegation of inconvenience than is made here. [*Patteson* J. Does any inconvenience appear which can give a right

(a) 5 *Taunt.* 56.
(b) 8 *Taunt.* 499.
(c) 9 *B. & C.* 738.

of

of action to the assignees? There is an averment of injury to the estate, but it is strangely alleged.] In *Gibson* v. *Bell* (*a*), where it was held that a demand for money lent might be set off against a claim by assignees for not accepting a bill and delivering it to the bankrupt pursuant to agreement, one ground of the judgment was, that no special damage was alleged; the Lord Chief Justice observing that the bill to be accepted would have been a security for a settled and ascertained balance on account of goods. [*Patteson* J. The same observation seems applicable to the second count here.] If it becomes necessary, that count may be abandoned. The whole transaction in *Gibson* v. *Bell* (*a*) turned upon mutual credit; the acceptance was to be given merely to secure a balance, and not as a specific mode of payment to be made available in a peculiar manner. Here the bill was to be used by paying it away, and there was, in the particular transaction, no mutual credit. Goods were bartered for a bill. Lastly, it is suggested that the declaration does not aver any tender of a bill for acceptance; but, supposing that this objection would have been good if specified as a ground of demurrer, which it is not, it is cured by pleading over.

Bramwell, contrà. No question of fraud can arise on these pleadings. If the mere fact of nonpayment by the defendant could raise it, such a question might arise on every plea of set-off. The judgment in *Fair* v. *M'Iver* (*b*) did not turn simply on the fraud; the ground of decision was, that the defendants were not bonâ fide holders of the bill: but that point would have been immaterial, if the fact of taking with intent to set it off had been

(*a*) 1 *New Ca.* 743. (*b*) 16 *East*, 130.

sufficient

1838.

GROOM *against* WEST.

sufficient to invalidate their claim. *Hankey* v. *Smith* (*a*) shews that, where parties holding a bill buy goods of the acceptor for the purpose of covering the bill, a mutual credit is created, and on his bankruptcy the bill may be set off in account with his estate, though he was not informed, at the time of the purchase, that the buyers held his acceptance. The Court, then, cannot say judicially on these pleadings that there is fraud on the defendant's part. [Lord *Denman* C. J. Clearly not: there is no doubt of that.] Then, the claim in the declaration is a "debt *or demand*" which may be the subject of set-off under stat. 6 *G.* 4. *c.* 16. *s.* 50. The comprehensive effect of the word "demand" is shewn by various instances in *Com. Dig. Release* (E. 1.). A claim like that now sued upon by the assignees might also, by a party having such claim, have been proved against the estate as a debt: and, therefore, when the assignees proceed upon it, a debt may be set off against it. In *Forster* v. *Surtees* (*b*) the plaintiffs and defendants were bankers, and the declaration (in assumpsit) stated their practice to have been, that the plaintiffs should weekly, on *Saturday*, forward to the defendants, for their use, all bank notes payable on demand by the defendants which had come to the plaintiffs' hands during the week, and that the defendants, having received the same, should, on or before *Friday*, weekly, forward to the plaintiffs, for their use, all the bank notes payable on demand by the plaintiffs which should be in the defendants' possession on such *Friday*; that, if such last-mentioned notes should amount to a less sum that those received by the defendants from the plaintiffs on the previous *Saturday* (after deducting any sums with which the plaintiffs might

(*a*) 3 *T. R.* 507. note (*a*).

(*b*) 12 *East*, 605.

on

on that day have debited themselves in account), the defendants should, on such *Friday*, send the plaintiffs a bill of exchange drawn by the defendants on a banker in *London* for the balance, payable to the plaintiffs or their order twenty days after date: that there was a corresponding arrangement in case of a balance against the plaintiffs: that, in consideration of the plaintiffs having on *Saturday* &c. forwarded to the defendants bank notes of the defendants to the amount of 1984*l.* (according to the practice), the defendants promised to send them, on *Friday* &c., all the bank notes payable by the plaintiffs &c. (according to the practice), or, if they should not equal 1984*l.*, then to send the plaintiffs, on such *Friday*, with such notes, a bill (as before described) for the balance: and the declaration alleged, as a breach, the omission to send such notes of the plaintiffs, or a bill for such balance. The defendants pleaded that they became bankrupt after the causes of action accrued, and after the bill, if given, would have been payable, and that they obtained their certificate: and on general demurrer it was held that the pleas were good, the cause of action being a debt, which was discharged by certificate. There the contract declared upon was prior to any actual debt; the case, therefore, is not affected by the observation on *Gibson* v. *Bell* (*a*), that the contract had reference to an ascertained balance. Lord *Ellenborough* said, in *Forster* v. *Surtees* (*b*), "This is substantially the subject-matter of a debt, and not the case of a mere breach of duty for which the plaintiffs could have declared for or recovered any special damage ultra the debt for which the bill was to be given." The declaration here brings the present

1838.

GROOM *against* WEST.

(*a*) 1 *New Ca.* 743.

(*b*) 12 *East*, 605.

case

1838.

Groom *against* West.

case precisely within that remark. As to special damage, there is no averment here under which it could be recovered. The injury complained of is merely such, in substance, as might be alleged on a count for goods sold; that the plaintiff was prejudiced by not being paid. The contract is called a barter; but the declaration treats it as a contract for payment. It states that the defendant promised to *pay* for the sugars, prompt two months, or an acceptance, and that he was afterwards required by the bankrupt to *pay* by an acceptance. An action in the common form, for goods sold, would have lain on such a contract. There is, therefore, no essential distinction between this case and *Gibson* v. *Bell* (*a*); and there the Court of Common Pleas adopted the principle acted upon in *Rose* v. *Sims* (*b*), where *Taunton* J. observed: "A mutual credit may be said to exist where there is a debt, or something which will end in a debt. Here neither was shewn, but only a cause of action." "The damages were unliquidated, and their amount dependent on circumstances. How could the commissioners, in such a case, have stated an account between the parties, as directed by the act?" Here the damages are liquidated. The commissioners might, at any rate, have put a value on the undertaking to give an acceptance; that value would have been the amount of the bill, minùs discount. As to the objection that *Raven* does not appear by the plea to have been indebted to the defendant when the contracts declared upon were made, it is not necessary to a mutual credit that both parties should have given credit at the same time. That was not so in *Hankey* v. *Smith* (*c*). It is sufficient if both parties had given credit at any time

(*a*) 1 *New Ca.* 743. (*b*) 1 *B. & Ad.* 521.

(*c*) 3 *T. R.* 507. note (*a*).]

before

1838.

GROOM *against* WEST.

before the fiat. It is also objected that the plea attempts to substitute another mode of payment for that agreed upon, without consent of the creditor. But that might be said in other cases of set-off, where no such objection has ever been recognised. And this is not such a substitution. The plea admits a breach of the contract, but sets up in defence something which has happened since. The declaration is faulty in not sufficiently averring tender of a bill for acceptance. *Read* v. *Mestaer* (*a*) shews that such tender was necessary on the bankrupt's part. And the plea does not cure this defect; for it does not allege anything which could not be true unless the fact omitted in the declaration had taken place. [*Coleridge* J. Is not there an averment, in substance, that the necessary demand of an acceptance was made? *Patteson* J. Suppose you had traversed that averment, must not they, on the trial, have proved a proper demand?] The defendant has traversed it in one of his pleas (*b*), and is content if the traverse will have the effect suggested; but the averment, that he was required to pay by an acceptance, and refused, does not seem to imply the tender of a bill.

Sir *F. Pollock*, in reply. *Hankey* v. *Smith* (*c*) shews that there *may* be a mutual credit though it was not contemplated by both parties. But if the plaintiffs here were entitled to sue as for a debt, they may also insist wholly on the special contract, and, electing to do so, they exclude the plea of set-off. So *Parke* J., in *Thorpe* v. *Thorpe* (*d*), says, "If the plaintiff had chosen, instead of assumpsit for money had and received, to bring

(*a*) *Comyn on Contracts*, 181. 2d ed.

(*b*) Not in the paper-book.

(*c*) 3 *T. R.* 507. note (*a*).

(*d*) 3 *B. & Ad.* 584.

1838.

GROOM *against* WEST.

a special action for the breach of duty, there could have been no set-off, because it would have been an action for unliquidated damages. But by bringing assumpsit for money had and received, he lets in the consequences of that form of action, one of which is the right of set-off." [*Patteson* J. Has *Eland* v. *Karr* (*a*) ever been over-ruled? The plaintiff there declared for goods sold; the defendant set off bills of exchange; the plaintiff replied an agreement to pay in ready money; and the Court held, on demurrer, that the plea of set-off was not answered. That seems a very strong decision.] If no express contract for ready money was mentioned in the declaration, the replication was a departure. And Lord *Ellenborough* said in *Fair* v. *M'Iver* (*b*), "As to the case of *Eland* v. *Karr* (*a*), where a party upon a sale of goods had stipulated for ready money payment only, which was held to be satisfied by a payment made with his own bill, I defer to the authority, but am not convinced by it." [*Bramwell* referred to the following passage of the judgment of *Littledale* J. in *Clarke* v. *Fell* (*c*). "If, indeed, the defendants had delivered the stanhope without insisting on the agreement for ready money, and afterwards brought an action, the set-off on the other side would have been let in, *Cornforth* v. *Rivett* (*d*)."]

Lord DENMAN C. J. The plaintiffs declare on breach of an agreement to pay for goods sold, prompt two months, or by an acceptance. And the only important question is, whether a debt can be set off against the claim as declared upon. I think there was clearly a mutual

(*a*) 1 *East*, 375.
(*b*) 16 *East*, 138.
(*c*) 4 *B. & Ad.* 407.
(*d*) 2 *M. & S.* 510.

credit,

1838.

GIBSON against WEST.

credit, and that the stipulated mode of payment is of no essential importance to the consideration whether stat. 6 *G.* 4. *c.* 16. *s.* 50. attached, and the debtor acquired a right to set off at his option. *Forster* v. *Surtees* (*a*), *Gibson* v. *Bell* (*b*), and *Rose* v. *Sims* (*c*), support this opinion; and there is no case inconsistent with it. *Parke* J. said, in *Thorpe* v. *Thorpe* (*d*), that, if the plaintiff, instead of assumpsit for money had and received, had brought a special action for breach of duty, there could have been no set-off, because the damages would have been unliquidated. But the case there was, that *B.* received from *A.* a bill, to be paid on *A.*'s account, and for a debt due from *A.* to *C.*; and *B.* obtained discount of the bill, but did not pay over the proceeds. *A.* sued for money had and received, and therefore treated the liability as a debt; consequently a set-off was admissible. If he had brought his action for the breach of duty, there could have been no set-off to what would then have been a demand for unliquidated damages. It would have been as if *A.* had employed a carrier to deliver a letter containing a bill of exchange with which a debt of *A.*'s was to be paid, and the carrier had converted the bill, in consequence of which *A.* had been arrested for the debt. Such a case is entirely different from that of money had and received. I doubt whether in any instance a mere pecuniary loss from breach of contract can be deemed such a special damage as excludes a set-off. There are a thousand cases where a pecuniary damage is the occasion of great loss, owing to particular circumstances; but we never hear of its being treated, on that account, otherwise than as pecuniary damage. To say that the

(*a*) 12 *East*, 605.

(*b*) 1 *New Ca.* 743.

(*c*) 1 *B.* & *Ad.* 521.

(*d*) 3 *B.* & *Ad.* 584.

1838.

GROOM *against* WEST.

bankrupt's personal estate and effects were diminished in value is stating that which, in contemplation of law, is merely a pecuniary loss. I therefore think that the plea is good.

PATTESON J. I disclaim any argument from the inconvenience which, it is said, this demurrer was intended to meet. The rule that, on demurrer, the Court can look only at the facts stated on the record, is a salutary one; and to depart from it introduces much mischief. We are bound to observe it to the greatest possible extent. Any consideration of fraud, therefore, in the present case, must be excluded. Then the question is, whether this record shews a mutual credit. Now, it is not possible to say that, where goods are sold for money, at a price to be paid by bill, or however else, that contract does not admit of a mutual credit; though it is true that, if a party sends another bills to be applied to a specific purpose, the receiver cannot, by applying them to his own needs, alter the purpose, and make the trust a debt. That appears from *Buchanan* v. *Findlay* (*a*) and other cases. A mutual credit exists (as was said in *Rose* v. *Sims* (*b*)) where there is a debt or something which will end in a debt. Apply that to the present case. Goods are sold, to be paid for, prompt, or by acceptance of a bill at seventy days. Must not this, of necessity, end in a debt? If the buyer accepts, he will be indebted on his acceptance to the holder of the bill; if he does not, he remains debtor for the goods. This is different from a case where, as in *Rose* v. *Sims* (*c*), the defendant has merely agreed to indorse over another person's bill to the

(*a*) 9 *B. & C.* 738.

(*b*) 1 *B. & Ad.* 526. So, per *Gibbs* C. J. in *Rose* v *Hart*, 8 *Taunt.* 506.

(*c*) 1 *B. & Ad.* 521.

the plaintiff; for such a contract does not necessarily end in a debt on the part of the defendant. *Gibson* v. *Bell* (*a*) was a case precisely resembling this, except in one respect. The plaintiff there declared on a breach of promise to accept a bill of exchange in payment of a balance due for goods; and a set-off was held admissible. The only distinction that can be drawn between that case and the present is, that no special damage was alleged there. The question, then, comes to this point, whether the allegation of what is here called special damage makes any difference. I think it makes none. The inconvenience suffered by the bankrupt is not to the purpose in this action. The only damage to the assignees is a damage to the estate; that " the personal estate and effects " of the bankrupt, " applicable to the discharge of his just debts," was, by reason of the non-acceptance and non-payment, much diminished in value." I do not see how the bankrupt's estate, in the hands of the assignees, could sustain any special injury by the non-acceptance and non-payment, otherwise than that the defendant, by reason of them, is now enabled to plead a set off. But the declaration cannot mean that; it means that the estate suffered injury at the time of the breach. And, if any such injury could have accrued, it is not sufficiently alleged; the declaration should have shewn how it accrued, and we might then have seen whether it took the case out of the general rule of mutual credits. Here is nothing, in substance, but the ordinary allegation of damage by non-payment for goods; the case, therefore, is that of a common money transaction. If this were not so, then, wherever a seller of goods became bankrupt, and his assignees sued the buyer, the case might be taken out of

(*a*) 1 *New Ca.* 743.

1838.

GROOM against WEST.

the Bankrupt Act by pleading. If the defendant had promised to pay in six months, and had not done so, the bankrupt's estate would be as much injured as by the omission to accept a bill at six months' date; if a set-off were excluded in the one case, it might be so in the other; and thus the effect of a bankrupt's certificate might be constantly defeated by an allegation, in form, of special damage. I think that *Forster* v. *Surtees* (a) is a material authority here; and that this is a mere money transaction, and the declaration only a mode of suing for the price of goods.

WILLIAMS J. My only doubt was, whether, on the face of this declaration, the action was for special damage or not. It seems admitted that, unless this be so, the case is not distinguishable from *Gibson* v. *Bell* (b). Now I am satisfied, by the reasons which my Lord and my brother *Patteson* have given, that this declaration, though it appears to sound in special damage, is, substantially, for no such thing. If it could be so considered, then special damage might be alleged if the payment had been to be made in money. I am considerably influenced by the indeterminate manner in which the special damage is alleged: it appears rather nominal than real. We must abide by *Gibson* v. *Bell* (b), which does not substantially differ from the present case.

COLERIDGE J. I agree that we must adhere to the state of facts presented by the pleadings, and disregard any inconvenience which they do not bring under

(a) 12 *East*, 605.

(b) 1 *New Ca.* 743.

our

1838.

GROOM *against* WEST.

our consideration; though I also agree that much injury may result from the breaking of contracts under such circumstances as were suggested on behalf of the plaintiffs: and, had the facts been pleaded specifically as they were represented in argument, I own there might have been difficulty in the case. It seems a condition precedent to the operation of stat. 6 *G.* 4. *c.* 16. *s.* 50., as to mutual credit, that the commissioners of bankrupt should be able, in taking an account, to satisfy the claims of both parties; if the circumstances are such that they cannot, it goes far to shew that the case is not within the section. But here no peculiar circumstances are shewn; nothing specific is stated, but merely a common money loss. On a trial, I think a Judge would say that no question of special damage was raised on the allegations which are relied upon as having that effect. It is admitted that, where the transaction must end in a debt, the case is one of mutual credit. Now here, whether the defendant failed to pay either by money or acceptance, or gave an acceptance which was not honoured, a debt would be created. The case, therefore, is distinctly within the statute, and the set-off maintainable.

Judgment for the defendant.

BINGLEY *against* DURHAM.

Tuesday, November 13th.

In debt on an account stated, it is a sufficient averment of time to say that defendant, on &c., was indebted to plaintiff for money found due to him from defendant on an account "*before then*" stated between them.

DEBT. The declaration stated that defendant, on &c., was indebted to plaintiff in 40*l.*, "for money found to be due from the defendant to the plaintiff on an

1838.

BINGLEY *against* DURHAM.

an account *before then stated* between them." Demurrer assigning for cause that the count does not mention the specific time, or any particular day, on which the account is supposed to have been stated. Joinder.

Mansel, for the defendant. It was expressly held in *Ferguson* v. *Mitchell* (*a*) that the omission of time in the count on an account stated is a good ground of objection; and *Spyer* v. *Thelwell* (*b*) accords with that decision. In those cases the count said nothing as to a time of stating the account. But "before then" is not sufficient. The particular time ought to be stated in terms, or by reference. The form given under the head "Common Counts," in *Reg. Gen. Trin.* 1 *W.* 4. (*c*), is, "And in £—— for money found to be due from the defendant to the plaintiff on an account *then* and there stated between them." [Lord *Denman* C. J. mentioned *Debenham* v. *Chambers* (*d*).] The allegation of time ought to be more precisely made in the count on an account stated than in the other money counts (*e*). "Before then" is not, in this count, a proper substitute for "then."

G. T. White, for the plaintiff. In *Ferguson* v. *Mitchell* (*a*) the judgment did not ultimately turn on the point now before the Court. The account stated is subject only to the same rules which apply to the other indebitatus counts. It is observed in note (2) to *Peeters* v. *Opie* (*g*) that the indebitatus count in assumpsit, for

(*a*) 2 *Cro. M. & R.* 687. *S. C. Tyr. & Gr.* 179.
(*b*) 2 *Cro. M. & R.* 692. *S. C. Tyr. & Gr.* 191.
(*c*) 2 *B. & Ad.* 787. (*d*) 3 *M. & W.* 128.
(*e*) See *Leaf* v. *Lees*, 4 *M. & W.* 579.
(*g*) 2 *Wms. Saund.* 350.

work

1838.

BINGLEY against DURHAM.

work and labour generally, was not held to be maintainable till some time after the decision of that case (*a*); and the other common counts were also of late introduction; note (1) to *Tate* v. *Lewen* (*b*). In *Hibbert* v. *Courthope* (*c*) it is said that a declaration in the general form for work and labour was objected to, but held good, because "the only reason why the plaintiff is bound to shew wherein the defendant is indebted, is, that it may appear to the Court that 'tis not a debt on record or specialty, but only upon simple contract; and any general words, by which that may be made to appear, are sufficient." It is enough, on any of the indebitatus counts, even in assumpsit, if the cause of action be disclosed, and appear not to be on a record or specialty, but on simple contract. In the present form, debt, it is not even material that the cause of action should appear not to be on record or specialty. And, as to the stating of a contract, in *Emery* v. *Fell* (*d*) the plaintiff declared that the defendant, on &c., at *Westminster* &c., was indebted to him in 2*l*. 12*s*. 6*d*. for goods by the plaintiff before that time sold and delivered to the defendant at his request; and on demurrer, alleging that the contracts were not sufficiently stated, and that it did not appear when or where the contracts or causes of action arose, judgment was given for the plaintiff. It is not mentioned that the declaration there contained any count on an account stated; but the judgment of the Court would have applied to that, as well as to a count for goods sold and delivered. In *Ferguson* v. *Mitchell* (*e*) *Parke* B., in finally delivering his opinion, said only

(*a*) 23 *Car*. 2. (*b*) 2 *Wms. Saund.* 374.
(*c*) *Carth*. 276. *S. C. Skinn*. 409. (5 *W*. & *M*.)
(*d*) 2 *T. R*. 28.
(*e*) 2 *Cro. M. & R*. 687. *S. C. Tyr. & Gr*. 179.

that

1839.

BINGLEY against DURHAM.

that the objection to the *omission* of time in the account stated was certainly valid, and that the defendant would have been entitled to judgment, if his demurrer had been confined to that count. In that case there was no reference at all to a time of stating an account. The same observation applies to *Spyer* v. *Thelwell* (a). Here the account is said to have been "before then" stated. [*Coleridge* J. According to your argument, even these words are unnecessary.] At all events the insertion of them distinguishes the present case from those just cited.

Lord DENMAN C. J. In those cases all notice of time was omitted. Here the account is said to have been "before then stated." The defendant insists that the expression should have been "then stated." We think that the distinction taken between this case and *Ferguson* v. *Mitchell* (b) is sufficient, and that the plaintiff must have judgment.

PATTESON, WILLIAMS, and COLERIDGE Js. concurred.

Judgment for the plaintiff (c).

(a) 2 *Cro. M. & R.* 692. *S. C. Tyr. & Gr.* 191.
(b) 2 *Cro. M. & R.* 687. *S. C. Tyr. & Gr.* 179.
(c) See *Webb* v. *Baker*, 7 *A. & E.* 841. *Leaf* v. *Lees*, 4 *M. & W.* 579.

NOTE on the Case of

BAILEY *v.* APPLEYARD. Antè, p. 161.

SINCE the publication of this case, the following passage has appeared in *A Treatise on the Law of Easements*, by *C. J. Gale*, Esq., and *T. D. Whatley*, Esq. 1838.

"It is certainly by no means clear what the intention of the legislature was" (in stat. 2 & 3 *W.* 4. *c.* 71. sects. 1—4.); "but it appears hardly possible that it should have been intended to confer a right by user during the prescribed period, however 'contentious' or 'litigious' such user may have been (*a*). In the recent case of *Bailey* v. *Appleyard* (*b*), the erection of a rail by the owner of the servient tenement within the shorter period of the statutory prescription was held sufficient to prevent the acquisition of the right; and it was decided that it was incumbent on the plaintiff to prove an enjoyment not interrupted, every interruption being presumed to be hostile until the contrary was shewn. It does not appear from the report that in this instance the interruption was acquiesced in, or even continued for a year." (P. 123.)

(*a*) See *Wright* v. *Williams*, 1 *M.* & *W.* 100.
(*b*) 3 *Nev.* & *P.* 257.

The learned Judge who tried the cause of *Bailey* v. *Appleyard* has favoured the reporters with a note of the facts proved before him, from which it appears that the report of the case, above referred to, and that in the present volume (page 161.), are incorrect in representing that, on the trial, any question ultimately turned upon an interruption within thirty years.

The plaintiff endeavoured to shew that the tenant of *Upper-house Farm* (in respect of which the plaintiff claimed) had for more than thirty years pastured his cattle in *Toadholes Lane* as far as a close called *Potover Lane*. But it was proved that a stang, or rail, sufficient to prevent cattle from passing, had been erected across *Toadholes Lane*, between *Upper-house Farm* and *Potover Lane*. *It did not appear when the stang was put up*; but it had stood much more than two years before its

1838. its removal in 1809. A neighbouring proprietor had been accustomed to turn his cattle into *Toadholes Lane* from the *Potover Lane* end; and the stang obstructed the passage of his cattle towards *Upper-house Farm*, as well as the passage of cattle from *Upper-house Farm* into the part of *Toadholes Lane* between the stang and *Potover Lane*. By agreement between the two proprietors in 1809, a gate was put up at the end of *Potover Lane;* the stang was then removed; and from that time the cattle of the plaintiff's predecessor depastured the whole of *Toadholes Lane* up to the gate. The plaintiff's counsel argued that the stang was not necessarily an interruption of the plaintiff's enjoyment of pasture over the locus in quo; and that, if it was not, the evidence shewed an enjoyment of many years before 1809. The learned Judge left it to the jury to say whether the stang had *prevented the exercise of the right*. Verdict for the defendant.

No question, therefore, at the trial, turned on the effect of an *interruption;* but, if the stang was erected adversely to the right insisted on by the plaintiff, he failed in proving a thirty years' enjoyment, because the evidence, as far as it went, shewed that the enjoyment, as claimed, had not begun till 1809, and the plaintiff had been excluded, and not interrupted, during the first two years of the thirty. And even if it had appeared that the stang ought to have been treated as an "interruption," it was plain that it had existed and been acquiesced in for more than a year. On the motion, reported at page 161, antè, the term "interruption" was used; but it was evidently unnecessary, for the purpose of the decision, to employ it in any other sense than that of obstruction.

1838.

Tuesday, November 13th.

DOE on the several and joint demises of WILLIAM OSBORN TAYLOR and JOHN WILLIAM TAYLOR, *against* JOHN CRISP.

T., seised in fee of copyhold, devised it to his daughter-in-law for life, remainder in fee to her son *A.*, *T.*'s grandson, in fee, "upon this express condition, and not otherwise," that *A.* should, within three months next after *T.*'s decease, convey three specific leasehold messuages severally to *A.*'s three sisters; but, in case *A.* should "object or refuse to make such conveyances," "then, and in that case, and upon failure thereof," *T.* thereby revoked and made void the devise to *A.*, and did thereby give, &c., immediately after the decease of the daughter-in-law, tenant for life, the copyhold to the three sisters, as tenants in fee in common; but, in case of any one or more dying under twenty-one, then to the survivors or survivor, in fee.

The daughter-in-law, tenant for life, entered on *T.*'s death, and held for several years, till her death. She survived *A.* *A.* was heir at law to *T.* Held, that *A.*'s heir might recover in ejectment on this title, without shewing a conveyance of the leaseholds, or tender, by *A.*, it not being shewn that *A.* had knowledge or notice of the will, or proviso, or had been requested to convey.

Admitted, that the proviso was a conditional limitation, not a condition.

Held, that it made no difference that neither the tenant for life, nor *A.*, nor his heir, had been admitted, and that the three sisters had been admitted, and had entered, and that the defendant claimed through them.

On a special case the Court will not infer such a fact as notice, where not stated expressly in the case, from other facts, unless a power to draw such inference be reserved by the case, and accepted by them.

EJECTMENT for copyhold lands, parcel of and situate in the manor of *Ightham*, in *Kent*, whereof *Thomas Taylor*, at the time of making his will, after mentioned, and of his death, was seised according to the custom of the manor. The custom, as regards descent, was the custom of gavelkind. On the trial at the assizes for *Kent*, a verdict was found for the plaintiff, subject to the opinion of this Court on a case substantially as follows.

The lessors of the plaintiff were proved to be the great grandsons and customary co-heirs of the said *Thomas Taylor*, who made his will, dated 9th *April* 1801, duly executed &c.: of which the following is an extract.

Whereas I am seised in fee of a moiety or half part of a certain freehold messuage, &c., situate in or near *Parsonage Lane*, in the parish of *Sevenoaks*, in *Kent*,

and

1838.

Doe dem. Taylor against Crisp.

and also to certain copyhold lands and premises, situate in the parish of *Ightham*, in *Kent*; and whereas my late son *Thomas Taylor*, some short time since, departed this life intestate, being seised in fee of the other or remaining moiety or half part of the said freehold messuage, &c., in *Parsonage Lane* aforesaid, and also possessed of three leasehold messuages, &c., situate at *Lewisham*, and to other personal estate, and leaving his widow *Sarah Taylor*, and his son *Thomas Taylor*, and three daughters, namely, *Lucy*, *Ann Mary*, and *Eleanor Morgan Taylor*, him surviving, and who are all now living; upon whose decease the said *Thomas Taylor* (the grandson) became entitled to the moiety or half part of the said freehold premises of his said late father, as well as to share of the personal estate; and whereas the said *Thomas Taylor*, deceased, before his death, declared his intention that his said son *Thomas* should have his freehold estate at the time of his decease, and that his said three daughters, *Lucy*, *Ann Mary*, and *Eleanor Morgan*, should have and be entitled to the said three leasehold messuages equally, subject nevertheless to the estate for life therein of the said *Sarah*, the wife, and now the widow, of the said *Thomas Taylor*, deceased; and whereas the said *Thomas Taylor*, the party hereto, in order, if possible, to confirm the intentions of the said *Thomas Taylor*, deceased, is desirous of devising his said moiety of the said freehold premises and the entirety of the said copyhold premises to his said grandson *Thomas Taylor*, son of the said *Thomas Taylor*, deceased, upon the condition hereinafter mentioned concerning the same: now I, the said *Thomas Taylor*, do hereby give and devise all that my moiety or half part, the whole into two equal parts to be divided, of and in all

1838.

Doe dem. Taylor against Crisp.

all that freehold messuage, &c., situate in *Parsonage Lane*, and also all and every my said copyhold premises situate in the parish of *Ightham*, and also all and every other my freehold and copyhold premises situate in *Sevenoaks* and *Ightham*, or elsewhere in *Kent*, unto my daughter-in-law, the said *Sarah Taylor*, and her assigns, for and during the term of her natural life; and, from and immediately after her decease, I give and devise the said moiety or half part of the said freehold and copyhold premises, so given to her for life, unto my said grandson, the said *Thomas Taylor*, to hold to him, the said *Thomas Taylor*, his heirs and assigns, for ever, "upon this express condition, nevertheless, and not otherwise, that he, my said grandson, *Thomas Taylor*, shall and do, within three months next after my decease, by good and sufficient conveyances, assignments, or other assurances, assign over, release, exonerate, and discharge the said leasehold premises, late of my said son *Thomas Taylor*, deceased, and situate in *Lewisham* aforesaid, and all his right, claim, and demand whatsoever in and to the said leasehold premises, unto and for the benefit of his said three sisters, *Lucy*, *Ann Mary*, and *Eleanor Morgan*, in the manner following; (that is to say) to his said sister *Lucy*, all the estate, right, title, and interest of him the said *Thomas Taylor*, of and in the leasehold messuage" (describing it), "to his said sister *Ann Mary* all his estate," &c. (as before, describing another leasehold messuage), "to his said sister *Eleanor Morgan*," &c. (as before, describing another leasehold messuage); "but, in case he my said grandson, *Thomas Taylor*, shall object or refuse to make and execute such conveyances, assignments, or other assurances of his respective estates, rights, and

interest,

1838.

Doe dem. Taylor against Crisp.

interest, of, in, and to the said leasehold premises before described, unto and for the benefit of his said three sisters respectively, in the manner above mentioned and described, then, and in that case, and upon failure thereof, and immediately upon such failure, I do hereby revoke and make void the devise of the said freehold and copyhold estates heretofore by me given and devised to my said grandson; and I do hereby give, devise, and bequeath the same freehold and copyhold estates, from and immediately after the decease of his said mother, unto his said three sisters," "and to their heirs and assigns for ever, equally, share and share alike, as tenants in common, and not as joint tenants: but, in case any one or more of them shall die under the age of twenty-one years, then I give and devise the part or share of such one or more dying under that age to the survivors who shall live to attain the said age, and to their heirs and assigns, as tenants in common, and not as joint tenants; and, if but one shall live to attain that age, then I give and devise the same freehold and copyhold estates unto such one only, and to her heirs and assigns for ever: and, as to all and every the rest, residue, and remainder of my estate and effects whatsoever and wheresoever," &c. (to his daughter-in-law, *Sarah Taylor*, who was made executrix).

The testator died in 1808, leaving his daughter-in-law, the said *Sarah Taylor*, his said grandson *Thomas Taylor*, and also his grandaughters, the three sisters of his said grandson, *Lucy*, *Ann Mary*, and *Eleanor Morgan*, him surviving. *Sarah Taylor* entered into possession of the premises, and continued possessed till her death, which happened in *August* 1827; *Thomas Taylor*, the

1838.

Doe dem. Taylor against Crisp.

the grandson, died in *February* 1817, intestate, leaving his two sons, the lessors of the plaintiff, him surviving.

The grandaughters of the testator, *Lucy*, *Ann Mary*, and *Eleanor Morgan*, are still living. On their mother's death, they were admitted in the Lords' court to the premises in question: and the defendant claims by conveyance from them.

Neither *Sarah Taylor*, nor *Thomas Taylor* the grandson, was ever admitted to the premises in question; nor have the present lessors of the plaintiff been admitted.

The defendant objected, 1. That, as there was no evidence of the execution by the grandson of any such conveyances or releases for the benefit of his sisters as required by the will, nor evidence of any tender or offer by the grandson to execute such conveyances or releases, the lessors of the plaintiff were not entitled to recover: 2. That the lessors of the plaintiff had not shewn any sufficient admission to entitle them to recover.

The plaintiff contended that it was not incumbent on him to offer evidence on either of the above points; and that, there being no evidence of any objection or refusal by *Thomas Taylor* the grandson to execute such conveyances or releases, the plaintiff was entitled to recover.

If the Court should be of opinion that neither of the above objections was valid, the verdict was to stand: if the Court should be of opinion that the first objection was valid, the verdict was to be for the defendant: if the Court should be of opinion that the last objection was valid, a nonsuit was to be entered.

Thesiger for the plaintiff. It must be admitted that this is not a condition but a conditional limitation. The

1838.

Doe dem. Taylor against Crisp.

The devisee over would clearly take advantage of it, not the heir at law; *Avelyn* v. *Ward* (*a*), *Fearne's Cont. R.* 272 (9th ed.). But the event on which the limitation depends has not taken place. The conditional limitation, as it defeats an estate, will be construed strictly; *Co. Lit.* 219. b., *Fraunces's Case* (*b*). Now here the estate is carried over, in case *Thomas Taylor*, who was also heir at law, "shall object or refuse to make and execute such conveyances," &c. These words do not apply to mere passive neglect, where there has been no demand or notice. In *Doe dem. Kenrick* v. *Lord W. Beauclerk* (*c*) Lord *Ellenborough* said, "If it were necessary, we might lay some stress upon the wording of the proviso, which speaks of a *refusal* to reside, &c.," "not of a mere *neglect*; and a refusal imports that the thing refused was proposed to the *refusing* party." Here, indeed, the proviso adds that "then, and in that case, and upon *failure* thereof, and immediately upon such *failure*," the devise is revoked, and the estate is to go over; and it will be said that this comprehends any non-performance of the condition. But *Doe dem. Kenrick* v. *Lord W. Beauclerk* (*c*) shews that a party, who would have title if there were no such instrument as that which contains the condition, is not to lose the estate by a breach of the condition, unless he has notice of the instrument; and this is in accordance with *Fraunces's Case* (*d*), *Malloon* v. *Fitzgerald* (*e*), *Burleton* v. *Humfrey* (*g*). And this was admitted in *Williams dem. Porter* v. *Fry* (*h*), where it was held that notice was not necessary in the

(*a*) 1 *Ves.* sen. 420. See the argument in *The Earl of Scarborough* v. *Doe dem. Savile*, 3 *A.* & *E.* 906., &c.

(*b*) 8 *Rep.* 90 b., 91 a.

(*c*) 11 *East*, 657. See p. 667.

(*d*) 8 *Rep.* 89 b. See 92 a.

(*e*) 3 *Mod.* 28.

(*g*) *Amb.* 256. See p. 259.

(*h*) 1 *Mod.* 86.

case

1838.

Doe dem. Taylor against Caise.

case of a party not being heir. Here it does not appear that *Thomas Taylor*, the grandson, knew of the devise, or even of the death of the devisor. The condition was to be performed within three months of the devisor's death. It may, perhaps, be said that the fact of notice is to be inferred from *Thomas Taylor* having left his mother in possession. But it does not appear that he even knew that she was in possession; and, if he did, that would not shew knowledge of the devise to himself, and the conditional limitation attached to it. It does not appear that he did not consider his mother an abator. The only question is as to notice within three months from the devisor's death. How can the entry of a stranger be treated as notice of a devise and a conditional limitation? But, further, in *Malloon* v. *Fitzgerald* (*a*) it was held that even knowledge was not sufficient without express notice from the party who was to require performance.

Another question will be raised; whether the lessors of the plaintiff can maintain ejectment before admittance. But admittance is not necessary to entitle an heir to devise; *Right dem. Taylor* v. *Banks* (*b*): and therefore he may maintain ejectment without it. Here the lessors are co-heirs of the devisor. Their father, the devisee, *Thomas Taylor*, never claimed as devisee; nor indeed does he appear to have dealt with the reversion at all. The lessors of the plaintiff claim as heirs to their great grandfather, the party last seised in fee.

Sir *J. Campbell*, Attorney-General, contrà. As to the last point, the general rule certainly is that the heir may

(*a*) 3 *Mod.* 28.

(*b*) 3 *B.* & *Ad.* 664. See *Doe dem. Perry* v. *Wilson*, 5 *A.* & *E.* 321.

 maintain

1838.

Doe dem. Taylor against Crisp.

maintain ejectment without admittance. Here, if the proviso did not operate in favour of the granddaughters, it may perhaps be difficult to shew that the rule does not apply. If, however, *Thomas Taylor*, the grandson, took under the devise, he would be a purchaser, and the descent would be broken. His mother never was admitted (*a*).

As to the principal question, this is a conditional limitation, and not a condition, as appears from the authorities cited on the other side, and from *Newis* v. *Lark* (*b*), commonly cited as *Scolastica's Case*. It is not to be so strictly construed as a condition, which is in the nature of a mere defeasance, whereas a conditional limitation is in the nature of a creation of an interest. The clear intention of the devisor was that, either by conveyance of the leasehold from his grandson, *Thomas Taylor*, or, in default of that, by the clause carrying the freehold and copyhold over, the three granddaughters should be provided for. The words "object or refuse" do not necessarily express a positive act; it was assumed by the devisor that the grandson would convey if he did not object. That does not imply a request on the other side. Which of the granddaughters was to make the request? Would a request by one enure to all? If not, to what extent would the proviso take effect? The devise provides for none of these cases, and therefore clearly did not contemplate a request. Then, as to notice and knowledge, the Court will, from the facts stated, infer both. It is true that, if, as in *Fraunces's Case* (*c*) and *Malloon* v. *Fitzgerald* (*d*), it was to be assumed that the heir had no notice or knowledge, the

(*a*) See *Doe dem. Winder* v. *Lawes*, 7 *A.* & *E.* 195.
(*b*) *Plowd.* 408.
(*c*) 8 *Rep.* 89 b.
(*d*) 3 *Mod.* 28.

non-

1838.

Doe dem. Taylor against Camp.

non-performance of the condition would not defeat his estate. Thus in *Doe dem. Kenrick* v. *Lord W. Beauclerk* (*a*) the question arose on a special verdict, where, in the absence of a direct finding, the Court could not assume the fact. On a special case, they may draw obvious inferences of fact. The heirs at law must, at the trial, have produced the will to get rid of the statute of limitations. Without that, the mother's possession would have been adverse; for, since her husband was not seised, there could have been no free-bench.

Thesiger in reply. No inference can be drawn from the length of time. That the lessors of the plaintiff knew of the will at the time of the trial, does not afford any inference that *Thomas Taylor*, the grandson, knew of it within three months of the devisor's death. [Lord *Denman* C. J. I do not see how we can draw any inference of fact. The case reserves no such power to us; and, when such a power is reserved, we are often compelled to decline it.] Then, as to the intention of the devisor. Although it is true that he meant to provide for his granddaughters, it does not follow that he meant the grandson to take notice of the conditional limitation at his peril. It is asked, what the effect of a request by one or two of the granddaughters would have been. Probably it would have enured to all; for they take cross remainders.

Lord DENMAN C. J. If the question turned simply on the meaning of the proviso, the point might be open to much argument. But it is laid down in many cases, especially in *Doe dem. Kenrick* v. *Lord W. Beauclerk* (*a*),

(*a*) 11 *East*, 657.

that

1838.

Doe dem. Taylor against Caser.

that the heir is not to be defeated by a condition of which he had not notice. This is admitted by the Attorney-General. Then the only question is, whether we are justified in inferring the fact of notice. The Attorney-General reminds us that in *Doe dem. Kenrick* v. *Lord W. Beauclerk* (a) there was a special verdict. But I consider the rule to be the same where there is a special case, unless a power to infer facts be given in the case, and accepted by the Court. The Court could not exercise such a power upon a statement like this; there would be merely a question for a jury, who would take into consideration the circumstances of acquiescence, age, and ten thousand others; where no such consideration can be had, it would be idle to attempt to draw an inference.

Patteson J. I agree in the general rule, as to the necessity of notice to defeat the heir's estate. We need not enquire from whom a notice would be valid; for here none at all was given; nor should he be justified even in assuming that there was knowledge. As to the other point, it is conceded that admittance was not necessary unless the conditional limitation took effect by breaking the descent.

Williams J. The Attorney-General admits that, if this were a special verdict, the rule laid down in *Doe dem. Kenrick* v. *Lord W. Beauclerk* (a) must apply. But we can draw no inference of fact here. Even if the power to do so were expressly reserved, I do not see on what we could found such an inference as he suggests.

(a) 11 *East*, 657.

Coleridge

1838.

Doe dem. Taylor against Crisp.

COLERIDGE J. It is admitted that, unless there was a notice, the case cited by Mr. *Thesiger* shews that the descent is not broken. And, as to inferring the fact of notice, I agree with my Lord that we have no power to do so. But, on this statement, I should not draw the conclusion suggested; for it would have been very easy to give, I do not say positive, but circumstantial evidence of notice, had there been notice in fact.

Verdict for the plaintiff to stand.

CHARLES FEW *against* BACKHOUSE.

Tuesday, November 13th.

Declaration in covenant on an annuity deed (dated *June* 15th, 1832, payments to be made half-yearly) for payments in arrear to *June* 15th 1834. Plea, judgment recovered by plaintiff against defendant in *Michaelmas* term 1832, for 2000*l.* in an action of debt (prout patet &c.) for the same causes of action. In the margin of the plea: "*Michaelmas* term, 1832. Roll 1146." Replication, that the causes of action were not the same (with other averments). On demurrer to the replication, Held that the plea was bad.

Grant of annuity, charged on lands, in consideration of 1000*l.*: demise of the lands by the same deed, in consideration of the 1000*l.*, and of 10*s.* paid by the lessee (a third party), in trust to secure payment of the annuity.

Held that the memorial need not mention the 10*s.* as part of the consideration.

COVENANT by grantee of an annuity or rent-charge of 114*l.* against the grantor. Breach, "that, after the making of the said indenture, and before the commencement of this suit, to wit on the 15th day of *June* A. D. 1836, a large" &c., "to wit the sum of 245*l.* of the said annuity for two years, and parcel of the said annuity for one other half year ending on the 15th day of *June* A. D. 1834, and then last elapsed," (the residue for the said half year having been paid) became due and still is in arrear &c. By the deed (set out on oyer), bearing date *June* 15th, 1832, between defendant of the first part, *Charles Few*, the plaintiff, of the second part, and *Robert Few* of the third part, it was witnessed that the defendant, in consideration of 1000*l.* paid to him by the plaintiff as therein after mentioned, did grant, &c., to the plaintiff an annuity of 114*l.*, for ninety-five years if

1838.

FEW *against* BACKHOUSE.

if the defendant should so long live, payable on *June* 15th and *December* 15th, beginning on the next 15th of *December*, charged upon, and payable out of, certain messuages, lands, &c., stated to be thereinafter mentioned and demised. And it was afterwards witnessed that, in consideration of the said sum of 1000*l.* paid as before mentioned, and for the more effectually securing payment of the said annuity, "and also in consideration of the sum of 10*s.* of lawful" &c. "to the said *Thomas Backhouse* paid by the said *Robert Few* at or before the sealing and delivery of these presents," *Backhouse* granted, bargained, sold, demised and confirmed the messuage, lands, &c., to *Robert Few* for ninety-five years, on trusts for satisfying arrears, &c.

Pleas. 1. "That the said plaintiff heretofore, to wit in *Michaelmas* term A.D. 1832, in the Court of our said Lord the King before the King himself, impleaded the said defendant in a certain action of debt of 2000*l.* for the very same identical causes of action as are in the said declaration above mentioned; and such proceedings were thereupon had in the said action, that afterwards, to wit in the same *Michaelmas* term in the year last aforesaid, the said plaintiff, by the consideration and judgment of the said Court, recovered in the said action against the said defendant 2000*l.* debt, and also 65*s.*, as well for his damages which he had sustained by reason of the detention of the said debt (being the same causes of action as in the said declaration mentioned), as for his costs and charges by him about his suit in that behalf expended, whereof the said defendant was convicted, as by the record and proceedings thereof still remaining in the said Court fully appears, and which said judgment is in full force and unreversed and unsatisfied

satisfied; with this, that the said causes of action in the said judgment so had and obtained are the same causes of action as the causes of action in the said declaration mentioned. And this the defendant is ready to verify by the said record," &c. In the margin of the plea were given the date of the judgment, and a reference to the roll, as follows: "*Michaelmas* term, 1832. Roll 1146." (*a*)

Plea 2. No proper memorial enrolled according to the statute. Verification.

Replication. 1. That the causes of action in the declaration mentioned were not, nor was any or either of them, the same or any one of the identical causes of action in the first plea mentioned, and in respect whereof plaintiff impleaded defendant and recovered the said judgment against him as in that plea respectively mentioned: but, on the contrary thereof, the said action of debt in the said first plea mentioned was brought, and judgment therein recovered by plaintiff against defendant, for a large &c., viz. 2000*l*., which defendant, before the commencement of that suit, viz. 15th *June* 1832, had borrowed of plaintiff, and which was to be paid by defendant to plaintiff whenever afterwards defendant should be thereunto requested; which last-mentioned causes of action were and are other and different from the causes of action in the declaration mentioned. Verification.

2. Setting out a memorial and alleging its sufficiency. The last column but one was as follows. "Consideration and how paid. — One thousand pounds in notes of the Governor and Company of the Bank of *England*." Verification by the enrolment on record.

(*a*) See p. 794., note (*a*), post.

Demurrer

1838.

Few *against* Backhouse.

Demurrer to the replication first pleaded, assigning for causes that it neither confesses and avoids, nor denies, &c., and that, if pleaded as a denial of the identity of the causes of action in the first plea mentioned, it should have concluded to the country: and that it is double &c. Joinder. To the replication secondly pleaded, general demurrer. Joinder.

W. H. Watson, for the defendant. First, the memorial states the annuity to have been granted in consideration of 1000*l.*, and omits to notice the payment of 10*s.* by *Robert Few* to the defendant, which was part of the consideration. It does not, therefore, conform to stat. 53 *G.* 3. *c.* 141. *s.* 2., which requires that, in the memorial of an annuity, "the pecuniary consideration or considerations for granting the same" shall be stated, otherwise the deed shall be null and void. The smallness of the sum left out cannot excuse the omission. In *Ince* v. *Everard* (*a*) (under stat. 17 *G.* 3. *c.* 26.) the consideration of 10*s.* paid by the grantee on a conveyance of premises to secure the annuity was omitted, and the defect held immaterial: but there the payment was to a third person as trustee; here it is to the grantor. [*Coleridge* J. In point of practice, these considerations are never paid. In the form of memorial in stat 53 *G.* 3. *c.* 141. *s.* 2. the column as to consideration is headed "consideration *and how paid.*" Lord *Denman* C. J. Suppose the 10*s.* never were paid.] The memorial should state the fact as it was. [*Patteson* J. The payment of 10*s.* is mentioned in the deed as a consideration, not for granting the annuity, but for conveying the land. Under this

(*a*) 6 *T. R.* 545.

deed

1838.

FEW *against* BACKHOUSE.

deed the grant of annuity would have been good if there had been no express consideration for conveying the land.] The provision for a memorial relates to the whole "deed, bond, instrument, or other assurance," and to all the pecuniary consideration mentioned in it: and the practice has been to construe this section strictly. Secondly, the first plea alleges that the causes of action now declared upon are the same as those upon which the plaintiff formerly recovered judgment against the defendant; that is a material and issuable averment, and the plaintiff should have traversed the identity of the causes of action and concluded to the country, or should have pleaded nul tiel record, as in the precedents, *Chitt. Pract. Forms*, 303, 4., 4th ed.

Wightman, contrà. The first plea is bad. The plaintiff declares on a breach of covenant in 1834, by nonpayment of portions of an annuity for two years and a half, ending *June* 15th in that year. The defendant pleads a judgment recovered in an action of debt in *Michaelmas* term, 1832. That cannot be an answer, though the causes of action are alleged to be the same. Even assuming the dates to be immaterial, a judgment recovered in debt would not be a satisfaction for damages claimable on breach of covenant. And, if it would, the defendant should have pleaded satisfaction.

W. H. Watson, in reply. As to the first objection; the defendant was not apprised of it: it is not stated in the marginal note to the paper-book. [Lord *Denman* C. J. Those notes are required for the information of the Court, not of the opposite counsel.] The defendant is not concluded by the averment as to the time

1838.

Few *against* Backhouse.

time of recovering the judgment. At Nisi Prius it would have been sufficient to prove a judgment recovered in 1834. [*Patteson* J. If they had replied nul tiel record, could you have proved a judgment of another term than *Michaelmas* 1832? If so, what is the use of requiring that, where a plea of judgment recovered is pleaded, the defendant shall give the date of the judgment and number of the roll? (*a*)] This is a regulation made to prevent sham pleading: but it does not affect the rule of evidence, that, where pleadings state the substance of a record, not professing to give the tenor, a variance is not fatal: 1 *Phill. on Ev.* 213. (*b*); *Purcell* v. *Macnamara* (*c*). It was sufficient here that the date was laid before the commencement of the action. [*Patteson* J. In *Rastall* v. *Straton* (*d*) the plaintiff declared in debt on a judgment recovered in K. B. in *Trinity* term, 1787; nul tiel record was pleaded; the record being brought into the Court of Common Pleas by mittimus, it appeared that the judgment was of *Easter* term, 1788: and, on this and another ground, judgment was given for the defendant.] Unless the time of recovering this judgment is an essential part of the pleading, *Stoddart* v. *Palmer* (*e*) is an authority for the defendant. [*Patteson* J. I can see no sound distinction between a plea of judgment recovered, like this, and a declaration on a judgment as in *Rastall* v. *Straton* (*d*).] If the defendant here produced, on trial, a record vary-

(*a*) See, as to pleas of judgment in another Court, *Reg. Gen. Hil.* 4 *W.* 4. 8. 5 *B. & Ad.* xv. As to pleas of judgment in the same Court, 2 *Tidd's Pract.* 742. 9th ed.

(*b*) 7th ed. (Vol. ii. page 860. ed. 8.)

(*c*) 9 *East*, 157. As to the effect of a prout patet (which was pleaded in the present case), see Lord *Ellenborough's* judgments in *Purcell* v. *Macnamara*, 9 *East*, 160, and in *Phillips* v. *Bacon*, 9 *East*, 304, and the judgment of *Abbott* C. J. in *Stoddart* v. *Palmer*, 3 *B. & C.* 2.

(*d*) 1 *H. Bl.* 49. (*e*) 3 *B. & C.* 2.

ing

ing from that stated in the plea, it might be a failure of record; but the attempt is to raise the objection on demurrer to the replication. The plaintiff should have demurred specially, and not pleaded over. As to the other objection, debt lies, as well as covenant, on an annuity deed.

1838.

FEW *against* BACKHOUSE.

Lord DENMAN C. J. We think this plea is bad.

PATTESON, WILLIAMS, and COLERIDGE Js., concurred.

Judgment for the plaintiff.

MATTOCK, Executor of SOUTHWOOD, *against* KINGLAKE.

Tuesday, November 13th.

S., the lord of a manor, appointed K. by parol to the offices of steward of the manor, and clerk of a castle therein; K., in consideration of S. permitting him to hold the offices at the will of S. as lord, promised S. to pay, out of the fees of the offices, an annuity to G. during G.'s life, for the payment of which S. had bound himself, his heirs and executors, and to indemnify S. from such payment, so long as K. should execute the offices either by himself or by deputy to be approved of by S. Afterwards S., as lord, granted the same office to K. by deed-poll (not reciting any special consideration) for K.'s life, and died.

Held that K. remained liable to pay G.'s annuity; that the consideration for K.'s promise in that respect still continued; that the grant by deed did not affect the parol contract on his part; and that, although, since the death of S., K. could not execute the office by deputy to be approved by him, it was sufficient that K. could execute it in person.

ASSUMPSIT. The first count of the declaration stated that, before and at the time of the promise, *Thomas Southwood*, the testator, was lord of the manor of *Taunton Dean* in *Somersetshire*: and that there were, and immemorially had been, attached and incident to the said manor certain offices of great profit and emolument, viz. the offices of clerk of the Castle of *Taunton*, and steward of the said manor; and the right and power of appointment of persons to fill the said offices then was, and immemorially had been, vested in the lord of the said manor for the time being, who had

1838.

MATTOCK *against* KINGLAKE.

power to exercise, and exercised, the said right by the appointment of such person as to the said lord seemed fit to hold the said offices, either by patent for the life of the person so appointed, or during the will and pleasure of the said lord for the time being, as to the said lord seemed meet. That, before and at the time of the making of the bond after-mentioned, *John Henry Gell* held the said offices under an appointment by patent from the lord for *Gell's* life, and was in the possession, receipt, and enjoyment of the emoluments, fees, and profits. That *Southwood* had applied to *Gell* to surrender his interest in the offices and emoluments into the hands of *Southwood*, which *Gell* had agreed to do on *Southwood's* securing to him by his bond an annuity of 50*l*. for *Gell's* life. That *Southwood* agreed so to do, and, in pursuance of the premises, executed and delivered to *Gell* his bond in 500*l*. conditioned for the payment of an annuity (as above described) by *Southwood*, his heirs, executors &c., to *Gell* or his assigns; and *Gell* accepted such bond, and surrendered to *Southwood*, as lord, all his right and claim to the offices, and to the emoluments &c.; and the offices became vacant, and the right of appointment vested in *Southwood*, then being, and as, such lord of the manor. That afterwards, to wit on &c., "in consideration of the premises, and also in consideration of the said *Thomas Southwood's* permitting the said defendant to hold the said offices at the will of the said *Thomas Southwood* as, and being, lord of the said manor, he the defendant promised the said *Thomas Southwood* in his life-time to pay out of the fees of the said offices the said annuity of 50*l*. so as aforesaid secured by the said bond of the said *Thomas Southwood* to the said *John Henry Gell* (by the description

tion of Mr. *Gell*) during the life of the said *John Henry Gell* and to indemnify the said *Thomas Southwood* from the payment of the said annuity so long as he, the defendant, should execute the said offices either by himself or deputy to be approved of by the said *Thomas Southwood*." Averment, that *Gell* is still living, and that defendant from the time of his appointment hitherto hath continually executed the offices and received the fees, profits, and emoluments to his own use. Breach, nonpayment of the annuity for four years last past, since the death of *Southwood* (though the fees have exceeded 50*l.* a year), and neglect to indemnify plaintiff, who, by reason of such non-payment, was compelled, as executor, to pay the arrears.

Fourth plea. That, after the making of the promise, and in *Southwood*'s life-time, viz. on &c., *Southwood* by his deed poll, bearing date &c. (profert), "for divers good causes and considerations him in that behalf specially moving, gave and granted to the defendant the offices of steward and clerk, or the clerkship of his the said *Thomas Southwood*'s castle, town, and lordship or manor of *Taunton* and *Taunton Dean* in the county of *Somerset*, with all and singular the hundreds and members of the said castle, town, and lordship or manor, to have, occupy, and exercise the offices aforesaid to the defendant during his the defendant's life, and to receive for exercising the same all and singular the profits, commodities, and emoluments to the said offices in any manner belonging or appertaining; that defendant thereupon then accepted and agreed to the said deed poll and to the grant of the said offices therein contained; and that, from the time of the making of the

1838.

MATTOCK *against* KINGLAKE.

said deed poll hitherto, he, the defendant, has exercised the offices therein mentioned, being the same offices as in the declaration mentioned, under and by virtue of the grant in the said deed poll contained, and under no other appointment, right, title or authority whatsoever." Verification.

Demurrer, assigning for causes that the plea attempts to raise an immaterial issue; for that the matter of the plea, if true, is compatible with the liability alleged in the declaration; that the plea does not traverse, or sufficiently confess and avoid, the count pleaded to, for that it does not shew how plaintiff has been discharged from the promise declared upon, or that he has ceased to execute the offices; that the interest of defendant in the offices is not shewn to have determined at the time of the making of the grant pleaded; and that the grant, admitting that it applied to the said offices, operated merely by way of confirmation, not as creating any new estate or interest. Joinder in demurrer.

Bere for the plaintiff. The plea furnishes no answer to an action on the contract. The declaration states that, in consideration of the "premises" mentioned in the inducement, and of *Southwood*'s permitting the defendant to hold the offices at the will of *Southwood* as lord, the defendant promised *Southwood* to pay *Gell*'s annuity out of the fees, during *Gell*'s life, and to indemnify *Southwood* from such payment so long as the defendant should execute the offices. The contract to pay embraced a period co-extensive in duration with the holding of the offices, and not longer. It will be argued that, because

1838.

MATTOCK *against* KINGLAKE.

because the defendant, after making the agreement, ceased to hold at will, and received an appointment, by deed, for his life, he no longer holds subject to the contract. But the parties are not likely to have contemplated that the defendant's guarantee should cease, and the grant so become gratuitous, while the grantee still enjoyed the benefit of *Gell's* resignation (and that under a more durable arrangement), and *Southwood* remained liable to *Gell* for the annuity. The grant enlarging the estate at will into an estate for life did not merge the defendant's promise; his engagement to pay was not dependent on, but collateral to, that grant. It is not necessary, in assumpsit, that the consideration should be co-extensive, in point of duration, with the subject-matter of the promise. A grant of the office for a year would, in this case, have been a sufficient legal consideration. And the consideration here was not merely the grant of the office to hold at will, but the fact, also, of *Gell* having given up the offices now held by the defendant, on *Southwood's* application, for an annuity payable by *Southwood*. The grant by deed may probably have been made in consequence of the defendant's promise to pay the annuity, although that might not appear by the deed itself, the consideration not being usually stated in the grant of an office. The deed did not create a new office, but operated in confirmation and enlargement of the former grant, as in the cases put in *Shepp. Touchst.* 315., where estates in land are enlarged by confirmation. It cannot be said that the contract expired on *Southwood's* death; for the liability to *Gell* continued in his representatives, and, while it did so, the defendant's guarantee remained in force.

 Manning,

1838.

MATTOCK *against* KINGLAKE.

Manning, contrà. The consideration for this contract was, in reality, the appointment to hold at will. The words "in consideration of the premises" are merely formal, and signify only "in that state of things." *Southwood's* obtaining a surrender from *Gell* would be no legal consideration for a promise by the defendant, unless it had been done at his request, which is not averred. The declaration does not shew a promise by the defendant to pay the annuity for *Gell's* life. The undertaking alleged is, "to pay" "during the life of the said *J. H. Gell*, and to indemnify the said *Thomas Southwood* from the payment of the said annuity, so long as he, the defendant, should execute the said offices." The words "so long" &c. over-ride and qualify all the preceding part of the promise. And the payment is to be "out of the fees of the said offices;" it was, therefore, intended to continue so long only as the offices were held. Nor was it to continue longer than the offices should be held under that appointment. *Southwood* was to permit the defendant to hold at his will, and the defendant to pay and indemnify, so long as he "should execute the said offices either by himself, or deputy to be approved of by the said *Thomas Southwood*." The offices, therefore, would cease, either by the determination of *Southwood's* will, or by the determination of his power to approve of a deputy; the latter event, of course, took place on *Southwood's* death, and that, but for the deed, would have terminated the appointment. [*Patteson* J. The words of the agreement are not "so long as he should execute the offices under the same appointment."] That is their effect. If *Southwood* had died, and his heir had reappointed the defendant, he could not have executed the offices by a deputy

1838.

MATTOCK *against* KINGLAKE.

deputy to be approved of by *Southwood;* and, therefore, the terms of the original appointment would no longer have applied. It is contended that the grant for life did not affect the defendant's contract, because the former appointment was only confirmed; but the analogy from estates in land is against this proposition. Thus it has been laid down that, if tenant by statute-merchant, or the like, brings assize, and, pending the writ, the fee simple descends to him, that shall abate the writ, for the descending of the greater estate extinguishes the lesser; *Bro. Abr. Extinguishment et Suspencion*, pl. 56. (*a*). And, if a man grants a lease to commence after the determination of a prior lease, and then infeoffs the first lessee, that is a determination of his lease, and the second lessee may enter; per *Crook* J., *Northen's Case* (*b*). Further, the appointment to hold an office at *Southwood*'s will was no sufficient consideration for a promise to pay an annuity during *Gell*'s life. The will might be determined at any moment; such a contract, therefore, on the defendant's part, was unilateral, like a contract in consideration of forbearance to sue where no time is specified for the forbearance. At most it could only bind so long as *Southwood*'s will could continue. It may be that a grant of the offices for a year would have been a sufficient consideration; but here the time is indefinite. Again, the second appointment was by deed. For the terms of that appointment the writing itself must be looked to; and no promise to pay an annuity is there stated. It is argued that the lord is not likely to have substituted a gratuitous grant for one which bound the defendant to pay the annuity; but the

(*a*) See 11 *Vin. Abr.* 439. *Extinguishment* (A). (*b*) *Hetley*, 55.

1838.

MATTOCK *against* KINGLAKE.

appointment to an office, in its nature judicial, ought to be gratuitous; and at any rate it cannot be decided whether this grant was or was not so, from the mere silence of the deed, because it is not necessary that a deed should express the consideration. [Lord *Denman* C. J. When the office was granted, the execution of it would be the proper consideration; and that makes it doubtful whether the contract for such a grant on a pecuniary consideration would be lawful. But, if, as you argue, nothing but the contract under seal is to be looked to, no question turns on the consideration.] The Court cannot look beyond the deed for the terms on which the second appointment was made, and on which the offices were from thenceforth to be held. But, if they could see that the contract was grounded on an unlawful consideration, they ought to take notice of the objection, though not regularly brought before them (*a*), and not give effect to such a bargain. It is contended that the agreement to pay was collateral to the engagement of *Southwood* to continue the defendant in his offices. But, if so, that continuance could not be a consideration for the future payments; the objection tends rather to defeat the action than the plea.

Bere, in reply. The matters stated before the words "in consideration of the premises" were a sufficient benefit to the defendant to form a consideration. And, further, it is conceded that the appointment, if for a year, would have been a consideration. But it would be so here, if even for a shorter period. The fact of its being determinable at will made no difference, the payment

(*a*) The objection was not pointed out in the defendant's paper-book.

being

1838.

MATTOCK *against* KINGLAKE.

being promised only so long as the defendant should execute the offices. Those words shew also that the contract was not limited to *Southwood*'s lifetime; his executors remained liable for the annuity; and the intention was to indemnify his estate so long as *Gell* should live, if the defendant should so long execute the offices. As to the term "collateral," the contract for payment was so, inasmuch as that and the appointment by deed had no dependence on each other. The second grant did not create any new engagement on the part of the plaintiff: it was by deed-poll. The cases cited for the defendant as to extinguishment of a lesser estate do not interfere with the proposition that when the estate is enlarged former incidents of it may continue. The question on the legality of the contract cannot regularly be gone into; and the defendant has no ground for saying that the will of the lord is determined, for he holds under the lord, and by an exercise of his will, at this moment; and the lord has not now any interest in the fees.

Lord DENMAN C. J. The only question is, whether the change of tenure put an end to the agreement for paying the annuity. I am of opinion that that effect did not follow. The defendant is appointed to certain offices, and agrees to pay, so long as he shall execute the same, an annuity for which the appointor was liable during *Gell*'s life. The appointment was originally at will; but, as Mr. *Bere* has said, the will is now exercised in favour of the appointee as much as it was before, by means of the deed which has prevented the lord or his representatives from turning out the party as they might have done at first. They are now bound; but

1838.

MATTOCK *against* KINGLAKE.

but it cannot be said that the will is determined. The defendant executes the office and receives the fees. All the material circumstances continue as at first.

PATTESON J. The vice of Mr. *Manning's* argument lies in his contending that the defendant's agreement was to pay while he held under the original appointment. But it was, to pay so long as he "should execute the said offices either by himself or deputy to be approved of by the said *Thomas Southwood*." It is true that, after the execution of the deed, he held under that, and not by the original grant; but he did not the less hold the offices according to the agreement, because the lord had parted with his power to turn out the grantee. If, indeed, *Southwood* had died without making such grant, Mr. *Manning's* argument would have applied, because the defendant's right in the office would have been at an end for a moment, though he might afterwards have been re-appointed. But here no such interval occurred. With respect to the merger, an estate may merge, and so may a contract, as where a person lends money on a simple promise to pay, and afterwards takes a bond for the same sum; there the lower kind of security is merged in the higher. But here the grant by deed states no contract. It is a deed-poll, and does not comprise any engagement on the defendant's part. It was ingeniously argued that the consideration for the defendant's promise was his being permitted to hold the offices at the will of the lord, and that when he ceased to hold at will the consideration was at an end. But, although he no longer holds at will, he still holds by the lord's permission, and more beneficially to himself than before, because he cannot be turned out.

Therefore

Therefore the consideration virtually continues. I do not proceed upon the ground that the matters stated in the introductory part of the count can be taken as part of the consideration; for it is not sufficiently averred that such things had happened, and that the defendant had notice of them.

WILLIAMS J. I think that, in this case, there was a continuing consideration. The deed making the offices permanent is treated, on the defendant's part, as if it had an effect on the previous promise, by substituting a higher security. This deed, however, did not put an end to the consideration, which was the holding of the offices, but furthered it by substituting a higher and better title.

COLERIDGE J. I am of the same opinion. The only question is, whether the plea gives a sufficient answer. My decision proceeds on this ground; that, in consideration of being permitted to hold these offices, the defendant promised to indemnify, not so long as he should hold the offices in the way in which he then held them, but so long as he should execute them by himself or by deputy to be approved of by the lord. Waiving the question of legality, this is a consideration for the specific promise. Then the plea is, not that the defendant has ceased to execute the office, but that he does not hold it under the same grant. I think, therefore, that it goes beside the declaration. And I must say I am glad that we can come to this conclusion, because the defendant has not only the same thing as when he made the promise, but something better. I was struck with the observation that, since the death of *Southwood*, there could no longer be

1838.

MATTOCK *against* KINGLAKE.

be a deputy approved of by him. But the promise is to pay so long as the defendant shall execute the offices, either by himself or by such deputy; not so long as both incidents may continue.

Judgment for the defendant.

Wednesday, November 14th.

The QUEEN *against* The Inhabitants of YEOVELEY.

1. On appeal against an order of removal, in 1837, the appellants, to prove an order of the sessions for the same county in 1824, discharging a former order of removal, produced the original sessions book, which was in paper, containing the orders and other proceedings of the Court (among which was the order of sessions now in question), made up and recorded after each session by the clerk of the peace from minutes taken by him in court, which book he considered, and stated to be, the record itself. No other record was kept. The minutes of each session were headed with an entry containing the style and date of the sessions and the names of the justices in the usual form of a caption. The minute in question stated the subject of the appeal then brought, and the order made on hearing. The book was signed, at the end of the proceedings of the session, "By the court. *John Charge*, clerk of the peace."

Held proper evidence of the order of sessions.

2. Pauper's father was born in the parish of *S.*; and pauper's mother and her family, after the father's death, were relieved by *S.* (while resident in another parish) down to 1817, when pauper was apprenticed, but not so as to gain a settlement. In 1824, the mother was removed, by order describing her as the widow of pauper's father, to *S.*; but the order was quashed on appeal. Pauper was then twenty-six years old; he was not named in the order of 1824; nor did it appear where he had resided since 1817, except as abovementioned.

Held that, on appeal against a subsequent order of justices removing pauper to *S.*, the discharge of the order made in 1824 was material evidence for *S.*

That, in the absence of proof to the contrary, it must be presumed that the order of 1824 was discharged on the merits as to settlement.

And that it could not be presumed, in the absence of proof, that the pauper was at that time emancipated.

ON appeal against an order of justices (4th *February* 1837) removing *Edward Smith*, his wife, and their five children, the eldest aged twelve, from the township of *Yeoveley*, in the county of *Derby*, to the parish of *Shirley*, in the same county, the sessions (*June* 1837) quashed the order, subject to the opinion of this Court on the following case.

The pauper was the son of *Edward* and *Millicent Smith*, and was born at *Yeoveley*, in 1798. The respondents, to shew a settlement in the appellant parish

of

1838.

The QUEEN *against* The Inhabitants of YEOVELEY

of *Shirley*, proved that *Edward Smith*, the pauper's father, who died at *Yeoveley* in 1811, was born at *Shirley*, and that, after his death, his widow and family received relief weekly, for several years previous to 1817, from *Shirley*, whilst residing in the township of *Yeoveley*; and that the pauper, in 1817, being then under age and unemancipated, was bound apprentice to one *William Walker*, under such circumstances that no settlement was gained thereby.

In answer to this case, the appellants offered in evidence an order of removal of *Millicent Smith*, the pauper's mother, from *Yeoveley* to *Shirley*, dated 6th *October* 1824, in which order the said *Millicent Smith* was described as widow of the late *Edward Smith*, who was the father of the pauper: and, for the purpose of proving that such order was quashed on appeal, they offered in evidence the original sessions book, being a paper book containing the orders and other proceedings of the Court, made up and recorded after each sessions by the clerk of the peace from minutes taken by him in Court, which book he considered and stated to be the record itself of the proceedings of the Court. It was headed at each sessions in the manner following. "*Derbyshire* to wit. At the general quarter sessions of the peace of our sovereign lord the king for his county of *Derby*, holden at *Derby*, in the said county, on *Monday*, in the first week after the eleventh day of *October*, to wit" &c. (stating the day of the month and the year), "before *John Balguy*, Esquire, chairman," &c. (setting out the names of the justices present), "assigned to keep the peace in the said county, and also to hear and determine divers felonies, trespasses, and other misdemeanors in the said county committed;" and it contained, under the above heading

for

1838.

The QUEEN against The Inhabitants of YEOVELEY.

for the *October* sessions, 1824, amongst other orders made at the same sessions, the following.

"Upon an appeal brought this sessions by the churchwardens and overseers of the poor of the parish of *Shirley*, in this county, against an order of removal under the hands and seals of *Richard Arkwright* the younger and *William Webster*, Esq., two of his Majesty's justices of the peace for the said county (one whereof is of the quorum), whereby *Millicent Smith*, widow of the late *Edward Smith*, and her grandson, *Thomas Smith*, actually become chargeable, were removed from the township of *Yeoveley*, in the said county, to the township of *Shirley* aforesaid, as the place of the lawful settlement of them the said *Millicent Smith* and *Thomas Smith*, and upon hearing counsel and witnesses examined upon oath on both sides: this Court doth order that the said order of the said two justices be, and the same is, hereby, discharged, and doth further order that the churchwardens and overseers of the poor of the township of *Yeoveley* aforesaid do pay to the churchwardens and overseers of the poor of the parish of *Shirley* aforesaid the sum of 40*s*. for their costs of this appeal, and also the sum of for the maintenance of the paupers."

The book, at the termination of the proceedings of the sessions, is signed } By the Court, *John Charge*, Clerk of the peace.

Every order, when copied out to deliver, is always signed in the same manner. No other record was kept of the proceedings of the sessions than the said sessions book; and it had always been received in evidence in the court for the purpose of proving them. This evidence was objected to on the part of the respondents, on the ground

ground that it was not material to the issue between the parties, and also that the order of the sessions, if material, could not be proved by such evidence. The Court received the evidence.

If this Court should be of opinion that the evidence was material to the issue between the parties, and afforded an answer to the respondents' case, and that the order of sessions might be proved by such evidence, the present order of sessions was to be confirmed. If the Court should be of opinion that the order of sessions could not be proved by such evidence, or that it was not an answer to the respondents' case, the present order of sessions was to be quashed.

Wildman and *Willmore* in support of the order of sessions. First, the evidence was material. The respondents proved a birth settlement of the pauper's father in *Shirley*, and relief given by *Shirley* to the family when resident in *Yeoveley*. That relief would be attributable, in the absence of other proof, to the father's birth settlement. Then it was a sufficient answer, on the part of the respondents, to shew that the father did not continue settled in *Shirley* till his death. If he did not, the pauper's settlement would shift with his; and a Court would not presume, without proof, that the mother acquired a settlement of her own at any subsequent period. If she did, the order of sessions in 1824 proves that at that time she had no settlement in *Shirley*; and the conclusion drawn as to her settlement would apply equally to that of her son. He was not emancipated in 1824, either by reason of his age, *Rex* v. *Sowerby* (a), or of the attempt to bind

(a) 2 *East*, 276.

him

1838.

The Queen *against* The Inhabitants of Yeovelet.

him apprentice, *Rex* v. *Edgeworth* (*a*): and, even if he had been so, *Rex* v. *Catterall* (*b*) shews that the order was conclusive as to his settlement, no proof being given that he had acquired one in his own right. There the order relied upon had been confirmed; but an order quashed is also conclusive between the same parties. The ground of quashing may be explained by evidence, but primâ facie it will be supposed that the order was quashed because the party was not settled; *Rex* v. *Wick St. Lawrence* (*c*). The order here described the pauper's mother as *Millicent Smith*, widow of *Edward Smith*; that shews that she was removed as his widow, and that her settlement, acquired through him, was in question. In *Rex* v. *Hinxworth* (*d*), where a pauper had been named, in an order of removal, the wife of *Joseph Griffin*, the Court presumed that she had been removed as to her husband's settlement, nothing being proved to the contrary. In *Rex* v. *Rudgeley* (*e*) the wife of a pauper, *Emanuel Smith*, was removed by the name and description of *Elizabeth Smith*, widow; and the order, not having been appealed against, was held conclusive as to the settlement of both. *Rex* v. *Knaptoft* (*g*) may be cited, but is not applicable. There the attempt was to give in evidence the quashing of an order by which the pauper's brother was adjudged to be settled in the appellant parish. But a brother is not privy to his brother's settlement; a son is privy to that of his father.

Secondly, as to the admissibility of the evidence. The document put in was a record of the sessions, having a regular caption according to 2 *Hale's P. C.*

(*a*) 3 *T. R.* 353.
(*b*) 6 *M. & S.* 83.
(*c*) 5 *B. & Ad.* 526.
(*d*) *Cald.* 42.
(*e*) 8 *T. R.* 620.
(*g*) 2 *B. & C.* 883.

165,

1838.

The QUEEN *against* The Inhabitants of YEOVELEY.

165 (*a*), and in this respect the case differs from *Cooke* v. *Maxwell* (*b*), *Rex* v. *Bellamy* (*c*), and *Rex* v. *Smith* (*d*). In all those cases the document was produced as the record of another court than that in which the evidence was offered; here it was of the same court, and therefore admissible according to the decision in *Rex* v. *John Horne Tooke* (*e*), where the acquittal of *Hardy* was proved, before the Court sitting under a special commission of oyer and terminer, by the minutes of the same court. It was not necessary that the record here in question should have been engrossed on parchment. In *Co. Litt.* 260 a. it is said that a record is "a memorial or remembrance in rolls of parchment;" but that is only general description; the author gives no reason here for the employment of a specific material, though he does so in the case of a deed (*g*); and his observation is confined to the records of superior courts. Records are spoken of in *Bull. N. P.* 228. as "brought into court in parchment:" but no authority is cited as to the material. *Rex* v. *Bellamy* (*c*) is referred to in *Roscoe on Evidence* (*h*), as shewing that "records are not complete until delivered into court in parchment;" but the language of *Abbott* C. J. there rather leads to a contrary inference as to the records of quarter sessions. In 5 *Burn's Justice*, tit. *Recognizance* (*i*), it is said that, from *Co. Litt.* 260 a. (above cited), "it seemeth that a

(*a*) Part 2. c. 23.

(*b*) 2 *Stark. N. P. C.* 183.

(*c*) *Ry. & M.* 171.

(*d*) 8 *B. & C.* 341.

(*e*) 25 *How. St. Tr.* 446—449.

(*g*) *Co. Litt.* 35 b. 229 a.

(*h*) Under the head "Proof of Records," p. 71. 4th ed. The context is altered in the 5th edition, but it is said, p. 75., that "records are not complete until enrolled on parchment," and *Glynn* v. *Thorpe*, 1 *B. & Ald.* 153. and *Bull. N. P.* 228. are cited.

(*i*) 5 *D'Oyly & Williams's Burn*, 643. 5 *Chitty's Burn*, 28th ed. 324.

1838.

The Queen against The Inhabitants of Yeovelsy.

recognizance ought to be ingrossed on parchment, perhaps for this reason, because parchment is more durable than paper: but since there is no law which prohibits it to be ingrossed on paper, it seemeth that if it shall be on paper only, and not on parchment, it is good in law" (*a*). And, however this may be as to proceedings of the superior courts, and judgments in criminal matters even at quarter sessions, the rule which may prevail in those cases does not necessarily extend to adjudications on appeal against orders of removal. The jurisdiction there is given by statute (13 & 14 *Car.* 2. *c.* 12. *s.* 2.) to "the justices of the peace of the said county at their next quarter-sessions." This is a new jurisdiction, given to the *justices at sessions*, and different from that which the sessions exercise for other purposes; *Rex* v. *Colliton* (*b*). "The justices do not hold their sessions for the examination and judging of matters relating to the poor by force of their commission of oyer and terminer"; and therefore the caption of an order of sessions, describing the justices as justices of the peace only, was held sufficient; *Anonymous* case in *Viner* (*c*). Lord *Hardwicke* takes a like distinction, in *Rex* v. *Reading* (*d*), between the justices exercising a statutory jurisdiction in their sessions, and the sessions acting as a common law court of record. He says,

(*a*) In *Burn's Justice*, tit. *Justices of the Peace*, 5 *D'Oy.* & *Wms. Burn*, 34., 3 *Chitt. Burn*, 28th ed., 562., it is said in a note: "Generally speaking, all records ought to be on parchment, but there does not appear to be any positive law to this effect, and, therefore, they are good if written on paper."

In 2 *Lilly's Pract. Reg.* 69. (cited, 4 *Cruise's Dig.* 462. 4th ed.) it is said that "A record is the entry in parchment of judicial matters controverted in a court of record." See 3 *Bl. Com.* 24. 3 *Inst.* 71.

(*b*) *Carth.* 221. (*c*) 19 *Vin. Abr.* 355. *Sessions of the Peace*, (R), pl. 4.

(*d*) *Ca. temp. Hard.* K. B. 79.

"It

1838.

The QUEEN *against* The Inhabitants of YEOVELEY.

"It does not seem that there ever was any determination in this court, that it is necessary for the justices in their quarter-sessions in the execution of any jurisdiction given by statute to make formal and regular continuances, as the courts above do. It must indeed be agreed, that upon indictments where they proceed as a court of record at common law, they must make regular continuances. But it seems that upon orders no such formal adjournment is necessary." The style of the justices as a court of quarter sessions, is "justices assigned to keep the peace in the said county, and also to hear and determine divers felonies, trespasses, and other misdemeanors in the said county committed;" not noticing the jurisdiction over appeals. In *Rex* v. *The Nottingham Old Waterworks Company* (a) a distinction was taken between the ordinary records of the quarter sessions, and judgments of the sessions given and enrolled under a local act of parliament, which ordered that they should "be deemed records to all intents and purposes." In the present case the entry produced had a proper caption, and was regular in its form; and the clerk of the peace deposed that the book was "the record itself of the proceedings of the court." The minute, therefore, being made according to the practice, and no other record kept, *Doe dem. Bassett* v. *Mew* (b) and *Doe dem. Edwards* v. *Gunning* (b) shew that it was proper evidence. *Rex* v. *Ward* (c) may be cited on the other side. There, on indictment for perjury upon the trial of an appeal, the sessions book was held not to be regular proof of the appeal having been heard;

(a) 6 *A. & E.* 355. See judgment of *Patteson* J., p. 369.

(b) 7 *A. & E.* 240. Same cases, 2 *Nev. & P.* 260, 266 note (*f*). *Will. Woll. & Dav.* 460, 463.

(c) 6 *C. & P.* 366.

it

1838.

The QUEEN *against* The Inhabitants of YEOVELEY.

it did not appear, however, as here, that a record was never made up on parchment, but the contrary.

Clarke, contrà. On the first point the only important case relied upon by the appellants is *Rex* v. *Rudgeley* (*a*). But the order here offered in evidence was only an order generally discharged; there the order was unappealed against. And in that case the pauper's settlement was held to be decided by an order removing his wife as "widow" of the pauper: it appears by the order itself that the parish receiving the wife was called upon, if it could, to dispute the husband's settlement; the case, therefore, is very different from this. [Lord *Denman* C. J. *Le Blanc* J. there grounds his judgment on a different reason from those of the other Judges.] He considers it sufficient that the order was unappealed against, and holds it to have been conclusive on that account, though the woman was removed by a wrong addition. In *Rex* v. *Knaptoft* (*b*), after evidence given of the pauper's father having been settled in the appellant parish down to 1815, the appellants offered to prove, in answer to that case, that on a subsequent appeal, an order, adjudging the pauper's brother to be settled in that parish, had been quashed: the evidence was rejected, and, as this Court held, rightly. *Bayley* J. said there (referring to the judgment of *De Grey* C. J. in *Rex* v. *The Duchess of Kingston's*(*c*)) that the point decided on the trial of the brother's settlement was not necessarily the same as that which the sessions had been required to adjudicate upon in the case then before the Court. He observed that, "where the order of removal

(*a*) 8 *T. R.* 620. (*b*) 2 *B. & C.* 883.
(*c*) 20 *How. St. Tr.* 538. note.

is

1838.

The QUEEN *against* The Inhabitants of YEOVELEY.

is quashed, the sessions only adjudge negatively that the pauper is not settled in the appellant parish." Proof had been offered that, on the appeal respecting the brother's settlement, the point actually determined was that the father had none, and therefore could not communicate any to the brother. But *Bayley* J. said, "Without deciding whether such evidence was admissible to explain the ground of the judgment, it is sufficient to say, that that was a point which arose collaterally, and, therefore, upon the principle laid down by Lord Ch. J. *De Grey*, the order of sessions would not be evidence to prove that fact in another case between the same parties." So here, when the order removing *Millicent Smith* was quashed, it cannot be said that her husband's settlement necessarily came in question. She might have acquired a subsequent settlement of her own; and, primâ facie, her maiden settlement was the proper one, though she was removed as a widow; *Rex* v. *Hedsor* (a), *Rex* v. *Woodsford* (b). As *Parke* J. said in *Rex* v. *Wick St. Lawrence* (c), "the point adjudicated was merely that, at the time when the order of removal was made, the appellant parish was not bound to receive the pauper." Besides, it does not appear that, at that time, the pauper *Edward* was a member of his mother's family; the facts rather lead to a contrary inference. According to the case stated, the mother was settled in *Shirley* down to 1817; but in 1824, as the appellants contend, she was not settled there. The pauper, in the latter year, was twenty-six years old. To affect him with the mother's change of settlement, the appellants ought

(a) *Cald.* 371. *S. C.* 2 *Bott.* 75. pl. 119. 6th ed.
(b) *Cald.* 236. *S. C.* 2 *Bott.* 75. pl. 118. 6th ed.
(c) 5 *B.* & *Ad.* 536.

1838.

The QUEEN *against* The Inhabitants of YEOVELEY.

to have shewn that, after leaving her family in 1817, he returned to it under age. At any rate, the mere negative evidence, that the mother was not then settled in *Shirley*, proves nothing as to the settlement of the present pauper. He does not derive his settlement from her; and the quashing of the former order can be evidence only as to her own settlement. The ground of quashing may have been that she was not removeable, or not chargeable. [Lord *Denman* C. J. That is true; but on the case, as sent up, the Court will presume that the merits have been tried as to the settlement. Your argument would shew that the former decision was no evidence even as to the mother's settlement; but that cannot be contended.] The matter supposed to be proved by a former judgment must be such as necessarily must have come in issue upon that occasion. Here the father's settlement did not come in issue on the former adjudication, necessarily or directly. [Lord *Denman* C. J. In *Rex* v. *Knaptoft* (*a*) there was no need to lay down that the former adjudication was inadmissible unless the point decided was *necessarily* the same as the point then before the Court. And in *Rex* v. *Wheelock* (*b*) *Bayley* J. said that, on appeal against a second order removing the same party, the respondents might explain by evidence the ground on which the former order was quashed.] If it were explained here that the quashing of the former order turned upon the father's settlement, that, for the reasons already given, could not conclude the respondents: though it ought to do so if the dictum of *De Grey* C. J. were applicable.

Secondly, the judgment here ought to have been proved as in other cases. There is no authority for denying

(*a*) 2 *B.* & *C.* 883.

(*b*) 5 *B.* & *C.* 511.

1838.

The QUEEN *against* The Inhabitants of YEOVELEY.

denying that the quarter sessions, sitting on appeals, are a court of record. *Rex* v. *J. H. Tooke* (a) does not apply, because there the entry read to the Court was the minute of the same Court, sitting under the same commission. Here the justices were sitting under a new commission, the former appeal having been tried in 5 *G.* 4., and this in 1 *Victoria*. In *Rex* v. *Smith* (b) an entry like the present was offered, not, as here, to prove a judgment of the quarter sessions, but merely to shew the caption of an indictment, and even for this purpose it was held not admissible. [*Williams* J. What do you say the proper evidence would have been in this case? An entry on parchment?] It is not necessary to say; but at all events there should have been a record made up of the particular proceeding, with its own caption. Here nothing is produced but a general book. *Rex* v. *Ward* (c) is in point. There the sessions book, produced by the clerk of the peace, was held insufficient to prove that an appeal was heard. *Porter* v. *Cooper* (d) does not add anything material to that decision. [*Patteson* J. That case was very different]. If this adjudication might be proved in the manner proposed, so might a judgment of transportation. [*Coleridge* J. Did you ever see a record drawn up of an order of quarter sessions? Yet it is clear they have records of their indictments].

Lord DENMAN C. J. The first question is on the admissibility of evidence. [After stating the principal facts on this point, his lordship said:] I have no doubt

(a) 25 *How. St. Tr.* 446—449.

(b) 8 *B.* & *C.* 341.

(c) 6 *Car.* & *P.* 366.

(d) 6 *Car.* & *P.* 354. *S. C.* (but no argument or decision on this point) 1 *Cro. M.* & *R.* 387. 4 *Tyr.* 456.

 that

1838.

The QUEEN *against* The Inhabitants of YEOVELEY.

that this evidence was properly received. It appears that no other record was ever made at the sessions. Unless parchment is necessary, I think that this record was good, and perfectly well proved. It contains a caption, and the decision of the sessions; and their decision is the only fact to be proved; the case therefore is not like that in which the minute-book was offered to prove the finding of a bill of indictment (*a*). In holding this evidence admissible I do not think that we interfere with *Rex* v. *Ward* (*b*). It is not stated there what the form of the minute was: and *Park* J. said, "If it" (the appeal) "was not heard before a court of competent jurisdiction, perjury cannot be committed on the hearing of it." I should infer from that that the minute was one made only for the convenience of the clerk, and that the caption, which was necessary to shew that a court of competent jurisdiction had tried the appeal, did not appear. Then as to the effect of the evidence. Notwithstanding the case of *Rex* v. *Knaptoft* (*c*), where *Bayley* J. used some larger expressions than were necessary, I think that the discharge of the order in 1824 was evidence of the mother not being then settled in *Shirley*. It is true that the order may have been discharged because she was irremoveable or not chargeable: but that should have been shewn by the present respondents, in order to take off the primâ facie presumption, arising from the evidence, that the decision turned upon the settlement. Then, did the mother's settlement, if proved, affect the son's? I think it was evidence as to his. In 1817 he was unemancipated; and an attempt was then made, without effect, to bind him

(*a*) *Rex* v. *Smith*, 8 *B.* & *C.* 341.

(*b*) 6 *Car.* & *P.* 366.

(*c*) 2 *B.* & *C.* 883.

apprentice.

1838.

The QUEEN against The Inhabitants of YEOVELEY.

apprentice. There was no evidence of his being afterwards emancipated. At the time of the order of sessions in 1824, the mother appears to have obtained a subsequent settlement, and not by marriage. Then, if the pauper was not emancipated in 1824, though he was then twenty-six years old, it resulted, as a primâ facie case, that his settlement had changed with hers.

PATTESON J. As to the reception of evidence, I observe, though I do not rest my decision on that ground, that in *Rex* v. *Ward* (*a*) it was stated not to be the practice to draw up a record on parchment *unless it was bespoke;* here the practice, as stated in the case, is to keep no other record of the proceedings at sessions than the sessions book. We come, therefore, to the question, whether it was necessary that the proceeding of the quarter sessions should be entered on parchment. In the absence of authority, and finding in this document every necessary statement, I think we must take it to be sufficient. As to the other point, there is strong evidence that the pauper's mother was settled in *Shirley* down to 1817. Then the pauper was put out apprentice, but not so as to gain a settlement; and there the case is left as to him. There is nothing to shew that he was at any time emancipated. It is said that, to acquire the new settlement of his mother, he must have returned to her before he was of age, and that he is not proved to have done so. But *Rex* v. *Edgeworth* (*b*) shews that a return to his mother was not necessary. In that case the father's settlement changed before the son was of age; but I do not find any authority for a distinction on

(*a*) 6 *Car. & P.* 366.

(*b*) 3 *T. R.* 353.

1838.

The QUEEN *against* The Inhabitants of YEOVELEY.

that account. And here the onus of proof lay on those who relied upon the pauper's emancipation; but no facts tending to that result were proved. And, as to the mother's settlement, we must take it that the sessions in 1824 discharged the order of removal to *Shirley*, on the ground, either that the father had not been settled in the appellant parish, or that he had been so, but the mother had acquired a new settlement. In either case, if the pauper was unemancipated, the mother's settlement was his; therefore the former decision upon that point was of the utmost importance here.

WILLIAMS J. No instance has been adduced in which it has been held necessary to make up a formal record of the judgment of quarter sessions on an appeal. It is said that, if such an adjudication may be proved as it was here, a judgment of transportation might be proved in the same manner; but the indictment with a minute indorsed upon it would be no proof of a valid judgment, for reasons which do not apply to this case. And in the case of an indictment for perjury (*a*) the possibility of the offence having been committed would depend upon the Court having had jurisdiction; consequently there must, in that instance, be such a record as would shew jurisdiction. But here the whole question was as to the order made at sessions; and it is stated that the minute entered by the clerk of the peace was the only thing ever done at the sessions for the purpose of recording such an order. Then as to the effect of the order; it stands on very early principles that an

(*a*) *Rex* v. *Ward*, *Car. & P.* 366.

order

1838.

The QUEEN against The Inhabitants of YEOVELEY.

order unappealed against is conclusive upon all persons as to the facts decided, and an order quashed is conclusive as between the parties to the appeal. Here, therefore, the order of sessions in 1824 was decisive as to the mother's settlement at that time. And it clearly lay on the respondents to shew, if they relied upon the fact, that, when the sessions quashed the order of removal in 1824, the pauper had ceased to be part of her family. The last account of him before that time shews him to have been still unemancipated. It was to be presumed, till the contrary was proved, that that state of things continued. [*Clarke* here observed that, as one of the pauper's children was stated in the present order of removal to be twelve years old, and that order was dated *February* 4th, 1837, the pauper must have been married, and consequently emancipated, in *October* 1824.]

COLERIDGE J. The quashing of the order of removal in 1824 is conclusive against a settlement of the mother in *Shirley* at that time. Then, as the unemancipated children of a widow follow their mother's settlement, the pauper must also have been settled elsewhere than in *Shirley* at the time of that order. On the facts stated, he must be taken to have been then unemancipated. The onus of shewing the contrary lay on those who relied upon a different state of things from that already proved. Mr. *Clarke* has made a calculation, with reference to the statement in the present order of removal, to shew that the pauper must have been emancipated by marriage in 1824; but it is sufficient to say that the case states nothing on that subject. The evidence of the former order of sessions, therefore,

was

1838.

The QUEEN *against* The Inhabitants of YEOVELEY.

was cogent, and ought to have been received. As to the sessions book, taking it to be proved that no other record existed, I think the original entry of the caption and order was sufficient. Mr. *Clarke* does not say that he, in the course of a long practice, has ever seen a parchment record of the proceedings of quarter sessions on a settlement case: nor have I.

Order of sessions confirmed (*a*).

(*a*) See, as to the conclusiveness of a former order of sessions, *Rex* v. *Church Knowle*, 7 *A.* & *E.* 471.; *Rex* v. *Wye*, 7 *A.* & *E.* 761. As to the record of an indictment at sessions, *Rex* v. *Hewes*, 3 *A.* & *E.* 725.

Thursday, November 15th.

The QUEEN *against* FROST.

The Court will not grant a mandamus commanding a party to pay money to the treasurer of a borough, under stat. 5 & 6 *W.* 4. c. 76. s. 92., unless the application be made, either by the treasurer, or after he has been required to demand the payment.

Though the party applying for the mandamus be ultimately entitled to the money.

MAULE had obtained a rule, in *Michaelmas* term last, calling upon *John Frost*, late mayor, and one of the councillors, of the borough of *Newport*, in *Monmouthshire*, to shew cause why a mandamus should not issue, commanding him to pay over to the treasurer of the said borough all sums of money received by him for and on account of the rents of the corporation property of the said borough.

The rule was obtained on the affidavit of *James Goold*. It referred to a charter of 21 *Jac.* 1., granted to, and accepted by, the mayor, bailiffs, and inhabitants of the borough of *Newport*, whereby they were incorporated by the name of the mayor, aldermen, and burgesses of the borough of *Newport*, in the county of *Monmouth*; and power was given them to hold lands, &c. The affidavit stated that, for many years before, and at, the passing of stat. 5 & 6 *W.* 4. *c.* 76., and from thence

thence hitherto, the corporation had been, and still were, seised, or entitled to receive the rents and profits, of certain lands, as to which the affidavit stated some particulars. That, on 26th *December* 1835, *Frost* was elected, and still continued to be, a councillor, and that he was elected mayor on 9th *November* 1836, and continued to be mayor at the date of the affidavit, 6th *November* 1837. That, both before and since he was elected councillor, and while he had been mayor, he had received various sums, specified in the affidavit, in respect of the rents of the said lands. That, on 1st *January* 1836, the council appointed *Phillip Jones* treasurer, and he had since continued to be treasurer. That the rents so received by *Frost* had not been paid to *Jones* or otherwise accounted for by *Frost*. That *Goold*, on 27th *October* 1837, served *Frost* with the following notice, addressed to him as mayor and one of the councillors. "I, the undersigned *James Goold*, of *Newport* aforesaid, being a freeman of the said borough, duly enrolled upon the freemens' roll thereof, and also a burgess of the said borough, and member of the body corporate of the mayor, aldermen, and burgesses thereof, and an inhabitant of the said borough, liable to contribute to the borough rate thereof, do hereby require you forthwith to pay to *Phillip Jones*, Esquire, the treasurer of the said borough, all monies belonging to the mayor, aldermen, and burgesses of the said borough, now in your possession or custody, or which have been received by you and not paid to the treasurer of the borough aforesaid; and particularly all and every the rents, profits, and proceeds of the lands, tenements, and hereditaments, or any of them, of the said mayor, aldermen, and burgesses, which at any time heretofore

1838.

The QUEEN against FROST.

heretofore have come to your hands." (The notice further stated that, in default of compliance, *Goold* would move for a mandamus, or take such other proceedings as might be advised, to enforce payment.) The notice was dated 26th *October* 1837, and signed "*James Goold.*" The affidavit stated that *Frost* had not answered this application, and that the rents had not, as deponent was informed and believed, been paid over to the treasurer. And that deponent was a freeman, &c. (as he styled himself in his notice).

The affidavit of *Frost*, in answer, stated that, long before and at the time of the granting the charter of *James* I., the mayor, bailiffs, and burgesses, were reputed to have been, and, as deponent believed, were, a body corporate, enjoying divers rights, &c., and that all their privileges were confirmed by that charter. Facts were then stated for the purpose of shewing that it was matter of dispute whether the lands in question were the property of the corporation, or whether (as the deponent believed to be the case) the freemen, meaning thereby the burgesses under the charter of *James* I., were entitled to the enjoyment or profit of the lands, as freemen, for their private benefit. And it was sworn that, at a meeting of the freemen, including *Goold*, held on 14th *November* 1836, it was resolved, with *Goold's* full concurrence and consent, that *Frost* should "be requested to demand the payment of the rents from the different tenants, and to pay the same into the bank, in his own name, to remain there until the claim of the burgesses thereto be decided." That *Frost* had collected certain of the rents accordingly, and had paid the amount in his own name into the bank, where it now was.

Sir

Sir *W. W. Follett* now shewed cause. The Court will not grant this mandamus at the instance of an individual. The town council, or the treasurer, should apply. If the money were paid to the treasurer, the corporation might possibly decline to claim it. Besides, on the facts, the corporation have no title.

Maule, contrà. If there be a question as to the title, the Court will not determine that upon affidavit, but will at least put the party to a return. But, even supposing the right of the freemen to be as alleged, still, under stat. 5 & 6 *W.* 4. *c.* 76. *ss.* 2, 92., this money, being corporate property, to the benefit of which the freemen are entitled as individuals, should in the first instance go to the borough fund, and be paid to the treasurer, subject to the claims of the individual freemen. There is no pretence for saying that the freemen form a corporation distinct from the corporation of the borough. [Lord *Denman* C. J. Does it appear that *Goold* has made any application to the treasurer?] It does not; but *Goold* is entitled to make this application in the first instance, since he is interested in the property on each supposition; and *Frost* has clearly no right to retain it.

Lord DENMAN C. J. This application cannot be supported. *Goold*, having voted the money into Mr. *Frost*'s hands, should at any rate shew that the treasurer has been properly required to take possession of the fund. We do not know that Mr. *Frost* might not, upon application by the treasurer, have paid him the money. If we were to accede to this application, we should entitle every person, who has an interest, to set the Court

1838.

The Queen against Frost.

Court in motion before he has required the proper party to do his duty.

Patteson J. I agree that this application ought to have been made by the treasurer.

Williams and Coleridge Js. concurred.

Rule discharged.

Thursday, November 15th.

The Queen *against* The Justices of Cheshire.

This case is reported, antè, p. 398.

Thursday, November 15th.

The Queen *against* The Committee Men for The South Holland Drainage.

This case is reported, antè, p. 429.

Friday, November 16th.

The Queen *against* Harland and Others.

Under stat. 8 *H.* 6. *c.* 9., if an indictment for forcible entry and detainer be found by the grand jury at the assizes, and application be thereon made to the judge of assize to grant a warrant of restitution, it is in his discretion whether he will grant it or not.

Therefore, when the judge, upon such application, made on affidavit, granted a rule nisi, which he afterwards, upon cause shewn on affidavit, discharged, and a motion was made to this Court (but without removing the indictment) for a mandamus to the Judge, or a warrant of restitution, the Court refused to interfere; nor would they enter into the question whether the judge had exercised the discretion rightly.

At the last *Yorkshire* assizes, a bill was found against the defendants for a forcible entry and detainer. The prosecutor thereupon applied, on affidavit of the facts relating to the entry and detainer, to *Williams* J., one

1838.

The QUEEN *against* HARLAND.

one of the judges of assize for the county, for a warrant of restitution of possession. The learned Judge refused to grant the warrant at once; but he granted a rule calling on the defendants to shew cause why it should not issue. Cause was shewn before his Lordship during the assizes, upon affidavit, when the rule was discharged, the learned Judge saying that he considered the granting of the warrant discretionary, and that he determined not to grant it. On affidavit of the above facts,

Newton now moved, either for a mandamus commanding the learned Judge to issue the warrant, or for a warrant from this Court. The power of the judge of assize is not discretionary. By stat. 8 *H.* 6. *c.* 9. *s.* 3., if it be found before justices that any one doth contrary to the statute, they shall put the party aggrieved into possession. Here the indictment was found before the learned Judge by the inquisition of the grand jury (*a*). The defendants not having traversed the force, or alleged a three years' possession (*b*), the statute leaves no discretion in the judge any more than in the local magistrate, who clearly has none, per *Holt* C. J. in *Regina* v. *Goodenough* (*c*). In *Rex* v. *Hake* (*d*) an order of restitution was granted by the judge of assize upon the finding of an indictment by the grand jury. So, if the conviction of forcible entry be quashed, the Court has no discretion, but must

(*a*) See 3 *Bac. Abr.* 723. (ed. 7.), *Forcible Entry and Detainer*, (F): *Anonymous* case, *Savile*, 68. pl. 141.

(*b*) 3 *Bac. Abr.* 724, 5. (ed. 7.), *Forcible Entry and Detainer*, (G). It did not appear by the affidavits whether any or what steps were taken in the prosecution after the finding of the bill.

(*c*) 2 *Ld. Raym.* 1036.

(*d*) Note (*a*) to *Rex* v. *Williams*, 4 *Man. & R.* 483.

 award

1838.

The Queen against Harland.

award re-restitution; *Rex* v. *Jones* (a), *Rex* v. *Wilson* (b). [Lord *Denman* C. J. In *Rex* v. *Wilson* (b) the proceeding was altogether different: the conviction was by local justices.] There is no distinction in this respect between a justice of peace and a judge of assize, as appears, for instance, by stat. 21 *Jac.* 1. *c.* 15. In *Rex* v. *Marrow* (c) an indictment for forcible entry was found at quarter sessions, and removed to this Court by certiorari; there the Court, apparently upon the equity of the statutes, held that they had a discretionary power as to awarding restitution, and put the defendant under terms as to his plea. The discretion appears to have arisen only from the prosecutor choosing to remove the indictment. In an earlier case of *Rex* v. *Wilson* (d) the question was whether an indictment for forcible entry lay at common law; and Lord *Kenyon* said that it did, "though the statutes give other remedies to the party grieved, restitution and damages." As for the remedy at this stage, a mandamus would put the learned Judge to no personal inconvenience; costs can be given only against parties interested, under stat. 1 *W.* 4. *c.* 21. *s.* 4. (e). Or this Court may now issue the warrant. The prosecutor has no other remedy.

Lord Denman C. J. In ancient times violent acts were committed in taking possession of property, sometimes by those who were really the owners of the property, sometimes by those who were not. The statutes which were passed to meet this mischief gave a great, and indeed violent, power to the magistrates;

(a) 1 *Str.* 474. (b) 3 *A.* & *E.* 817. See p. 838.

(c) *Ca. K. B. temp. Hardw.* 174. (d) 8 *T. R.* 357.

(e) See stat. 1 & 2 *W.* 4. *c.* 58. *s.* 8.

but

1838.

The QUEEN *against* HARLAND.

but the party against whom the proceeding takes place has the right of traversing the conviction, and, if he succeeds, is entitled to a writ of re-restitution. The proceeding under these statutes is peculiar; and furnishes the only instance, known to the law of England, in which a party may be turned out of possession by ex parte steps taken. Such a power is not to be extended by implication. I think that it is a mistake to suppose that the rule compelling the magistrate to act applies to the case of the inquisition of a grand jury. *Rex* v. *Hake* (a) shews that, in 1827, a Judge, upon such an inquisition, granted a writ of restitution, not as a matter of right, but in the exercise of his discretion. The reporter there says that the finding of a bill of indictment is necessary to give the Court jurisdiction, but that the Court will not award restitution upon an indictment found, unless a sufficient case for their interference be made out on affidavit. In the same report there is a reference to *Rex* v. *Marrow* (b), where it was laid down that, when an indictment is removed by certiorari into this court before it is pleaded to, the Court has a discretionary power to award a writ of restitution, and may therefore put the defendant under terms as to his pleading. Lord *Hardwicke* there cites *Dalton's Justice*, to shew that the Court, upon the indictment being brought up by certiorari, may award restitution (c), and that restitution is a thing in the discretion of the Court. It is therefore clear that the Court has a discretion whether or not it will exercise its power. Here the learned Judge, constituting the Court upon the occasion, heard the affida-

(a) Note (a) to *Rex* v. *Williams*, 4 *Man. & R.* 483.

(b) *Ca. K. B. temp. Hard.* 174.

(c) See *Dalt. Just.* c. 22, 80, 81, 82.

 vits,

1838.

The QUEEN against HARLAND.

vits, and, in his discretion, refused the writ. The learned counsel admits that the application was entirely ex parte: all must feel that an ex parte proceeding is to be deprecated where we are not absolutely compelled to entertain it. A discretion, therefore, has been exercised, and, no doubt, rightly; though into that we cannot enquire, for it is sufficient that the learned Judge had the discretion.

PATTESON J. The sole question is, whether it be imperative on the judge of assize to grant this warrant, or be in his discretion. If he had a discretion, no doubt he exercised it rightly. The learned counsel admits that, when an indictment is removed by certiorari, the power of this Court is discretionary: but he says that the prosecutor there, by removing the indictment, gives the Court a discretion which otherwise would not exist. I do not find this laid down; and I think the same principle applies to a judge of assize as to this Court in the case alluded to; namely that, the proceeding being ex parte, a discretion must be exercised. In the case of local magistrates, who are to go to the spot and make enquiry by the inquisition of a jury, witnesses may be called on both sides: whether the prosecutor would be a good witness I do not know; I rather think he would (a). There, if the jury find the facts, it is imperative on the magistrate to grant restitution; and the reason is that there has been a fair enquiry. In the present case the enquiry had been only ex parte; and the proceeding was consequently discretionary. We therefore cannot interfere.

(a) As to the competency of the aggrieved party on *indictment* for forcible entry, see *Rex* v. *Beavan*, *Ry. & M.* 242. *Rex* v. *Williams*, 9 *B. & C.* 549.

COLERIDGE

1838.

The QUEEN *against* HARLAND.

COLERIDGE J. (*a*). I am of the same opinion: and I should have regretted if any authority had appeared, compelling us to come to a different conclusion. If we understand this to be an application for a mandamus, the answer is, that the judge of assize had a discretion. It is said that, under stat. 8 *H.* 6. *c.* 9. *s.* 3., the law is imperative. That statute prescribes that the justices shall enquire by the people of the same county, and, if it be found that any doth contrary to the statute, shall cause to reseise the lands, and put the party in full possession. It is a mockery of common sense to say that, in the absence of such enquiry, on evidence furnished only by one party, that party is to be absolutely entitled to the writ. The case can therefore be only one for discretion. In my opinion, the discretion was here wisely exercised; and, as to the alleged absence of other remedy, why did not the party go before a justice of peace? If, again, this be considered as an application to this Court now to issue the writ, I think we have no authority to do so. The indictment is not removed; and I cannot see what jurisdiction we have.

Rule refused.

(*a*) *Williams* J. took no part in the discussion.

The QUEEN *against* SULLIVAN and Others.

Saturday, November 17th.

On trial of an indictment for misdemeanor by a special jury, a juryman, after being sworn, stated himself to have been one of the grand jury who found the bill. He continued, however, in the box, the defendant not consenting to his being withdrawn. It did not appear whether the defendant knew of the objection before the juror stated it. On motion for a new trial by the defendant after conviction,

Held not a mistrial.

INDICTMENT for a conspiracy. The case was tried before Lord *Denman* C. J. and a special jury, at the sittings after last *Trinity* term, at *Westminster*. After the jury had been sworn and the case for the

 prosecution

1838.

The Queen *against* Sullivan.

prosecution partly opened, the foreman of the jury stated to the Court that he had been on the grand jury which found the bill. The counsel for the prosecution offered to consent that this juror should withdraw and the trial proceed with eleven; but, the defendants not consenting, the case went on before the jury as at first composed, and the defendants were convicted. In this term (*a*),

Platt moved for a new trial, on the ground that the case had been mistried. No man ought to be convicted of a crime on the finding of less than twenty-four different jurors. *Blackstone* says (4 *Bla. Com.* 306.) that "no man can be convicted at the suit of the King of any capital offence, unless by the unanimous voice of twenty-four of his equals and neighbours: that is, by twelve at least of the grand jury, in the first place, assenting to the accusation; and afterwards, by the whole petit jury, of twelve more, finding him guilty upon his trial." The authorities shew that there is no distinction in this respect between felony and misdemeanor (*b*). Stat. 25 *Ed.* 3. *st.* 5. *c.* 3. enacts "That no indictor" (that is, no one who found the bill as a grand juryman) "shall be put in inquests upon deliverance of the indictees of felonies or trespass, if he be challenged for that same cause by him which is so indicted" (*c*). Here the objection was not taken by

(*a*) *November* 7th. Before Lord *Denman* C. J., *Patteson*, *Williams*, and *Coleridge* Js.

(*b*) See 21 *Vin. Abr.* 256. *Trial*, (B. d), pl. 14. in marg. and *Co. Litt.* 157 b. there cited. In *Rex* v. *Oates*, 10 *How. St. Tr.* 1079. it seems to have been held a good objection to a petit juryman, on indictment for perjury, that he was one of the grand jury who found the bill: p. 1081. See also *Rex* v. *Percival*, 1 *Sid.* 243.

(*c*) *Staundford*, in *Pl. Cor.* f. 158. (lib. iii. c. 7.), says that the statute was passed in affirmance of the common law. *Britton*, f. 12. (there cited to this point), speaks of the objection being allowable, "en peril de mort."

challenge;

1838.

The QUEEN against SULLIVAN.

challenge; but the defendants were not aware of it till after the jury were sworn. [Lord *Denman* C. J. How do we know that? The jury was special; the defendants had an opportunity of inquiring when they reduced the list.] It cannot be said that in every possible case the omission to challenge at the proper time shall exclude any objection to a juror; as, for instance, if it turned out, in the course of a trial for forcible entry, that a juryman had a direct interest in the lands. It is true that stat. 6 *G.* 4. *c.* 50. *s.* 30. enacts that, where a special jury is struck as there directed, "every jury so struck shall be the jury returned for the trial of such issue:" but that means only that the panel shall contain those names; not that the jury struck and no others shall be competent to serve. If that were so, a tales could not be prayed, nor a juror taken from the common jury panel. [Lord *Denman* C. J. Have you any authority for this application?] It is founded in principle. *Blackstone*, 3 *Com.* 363., states several grounds of objection to jurors in civil cases, and, among them, that of having formerly been a juror in the same cause: and he adds, as the ground of such objections, that jurors ought to be "omni exceptione majores." [Lord *Denman* C. J. I am not disposed to say whether the challenge, if taken, would have been available or not; but, at any rate, the objection should have been stated at the proper time. If it had been mentioned before the trial, all of us probably would have agreed to exclude the juryman. But these questions are so important that we will not decide without looking into the statute.]

Cur. adv. vult.

 Lord

1838.

The QUEEN *against* SULLIVAN.

Lord DENMAN C. J. now delivered the judgment of the Court. In this case we grant no rule. We think that the old statute does not apply: but that statute itself requires that the objection should be taken by way of challenge. The defendants here did not challenge; and, when the objection was pointed out and it was proposed that the juror should withdraw, they declined assenting to that course, and preferred to stand upon the strict law. There is no ground for a rule.

Rule refused (a).

(a) See, as to the point here decided, *Rex* v. *Sutton*, 8 *B. & C.* 417. Also, as to the proper time for challenging, and the inadmissibility of a challenge afterwards, 21 *Vin. Abr.* 274. *Trial*, (L. d); *Rex* v. *Oates*, 10 *How. St. Tr.* 1081; *Rex* v. *Layer*, 16 *How. St. Tr.* 135.; *Rex* v. *Brandreth*, 32 *How. St. Tr.* 770. This latter point was likewise much discussed in the case of *Rex* v. *Frost*, tried under the special commission at *Monmouth*, *December* and *January* 1840. See pp. 42. et seq., and p. 769. of the Report published by Messrs. *Gurney*.

In a case, *Lib. Assis.* 40 *Ed.* 3. f. 241 A. pl. 10. (See *Bro. Abr.*, *Challenge* 142., 21 *Vin. Abr.* 256., *Trial*, (B. d), pl. 14.), *J.* was indicted for battery of *R.*, and sued *R.* in trespass for the same battery; plea, son assault demesne, and issue thereon. *T. H.*, one of those who indicted (found the bill), was of the inquest on the trial of the action of trespass, and gave a verdict for the plaintiff with twenty shillings damages: and *T. H.* was committed to the custody of the marshal, and fined, for two causes, one of which was, that he was one of the indictors of the said *J.*, whom now he has acquitted, and did not challenge himself.

FENTON *against* The City of DUBLIN Steam Packet Company.

Wednesday, November 21st.

CASE. The declaration stated that the plaintiff, before and at &c., was possessed of a vessel of great value, to wit &c., then lawfully being in the river *Humber*, and the defendants were also then possessed of a certain steam vessel, in the said river, and then by their servants and mariners had the care, direction, and management thereof: yet defendants, not regarding &c., whilst the vessel of the plaintiff so was in the river *Humber*, to wit on &c., by their said servants and mariners took so little and such bad care of their said steam vessel, in the direction and management of the same, that the same, by and through the carelessness, misdirection, and mismanagement of the said servants and mariners of the defendants in that behalf &c. (charging that the vessel of the defendants ran foul of, and sank, the vessel of the plaintiff). Pleas. 1. Not Guilty. 2. That the defendants had not the possession of the said steam vessel, and the care, direction, and management of the same, by their servants and mariners, or otherwise, in manner and form &c.: conclusion to the country. Issue thereon.

Case for sinking plaintiff's vessel by a steam boat, of which defendants were possessed and had the care, management, and direction by their servants and mariners, through the mismanagement of the said servants and mariners. Plea, that defendants had not the possession and care, &c., by their servants and mariners, or otherwise.

Defendants, being owners of the steam vessel, chartered her to *D.*, for six months, at 20*l.* per week, the owners to keep her in good and sufficient order for the conveyance of goods, &c., to and from *Newcastle* and *Goole*, or any other coasting station which *D.* might employ her in: *D.* to pay all disbursements, including harbour dues, pilotages, seamen's and captain's wages, and coals, oil, tallow, &c., for engines, and to insure the vessel; the policy to be deposited with the owners.

Held, that the issue ought to be found for plaintiff upon the interpretation of the charter party alone.

A fortiori, upon proof, in addition, that *D.* had no power to appoint or dismiss the officers and crew, and did not interfere in the arrangements of the ship.

On the trial before *Alderson* B., at the *Yorkshire* Spring assizes, 1837, it appeared that the defendants

were

1838.

Fenton against The City of Dublin Steam Packet Company.

were owners of the steam vessel, which, at the time of the accident, was, and for some time had been, chartered to *John Dails*, under the following instrument.

Memorandum for charter, 22d *September* 1834.

It is mutually agreed between the City of *Dublin* Steam Packet Company, owners of the good steam ship or vessel called the *Kingstown*, now at *Liverpool*, on the one part, and *John Dails*, of &c., on the other part, that the said company agree to charter with *J. D.* the said steamer, for the space of six months, to be paid for same at and after the rate of 20*l*. per week, the owners to keep the vessel in good and sufficient order, for the conveyance of goods, merchandise, and passengers to and from *Newcastle* and *Goole*, or any other coasting station which the said *J. D.* may from time to time employ the said vessel in. The said *J. D.* to pay all disbursements, including harbour dues, pilotages, seamens' and captain's wages, and coals and oil, tallow &c., for engines, and to insure the vessel for 3000*l*., the policy to be deposited with the company before-mentioned. And it is further agreed that, if, at the expiration of the six months above stated, the said *J. D.* should wish to retain the vessel for a further period, he shall be allowed to do so for six months longer, at the rate of 25*l*. per week, subject to the same payments and conditions as before named. The period at which the present engagement is to commence is from and after the time when the *Kingstown* shall have arrived at *Newcastle*, and Captain *Batly* have given notice to Messrs. *Shield* and *Parker* of her being ready to take in a cargo.

Dails, being called as a witness, stated that he had no power to appoint or dismiss any of the officers or crew, nor

1838.

FENTON against The City of Dublin Steam Packet Company.

nor did he interfere in the arrangements of the ship, but paid the crew so long as she was chartered. At the time of the accident the ship was under the management of a captain appointed by the company. *Dails* was on board. *Alderson* B. was of opinion that the defendants were liable; and he left the case to the jury on the question of negligence only. Verdict for the plaintiff. Leave was reserved to move for a nonsuit. In *Easter* term, 1837, *Atcherley* Serjt. obtained a rule accordingly.

Alexander, *Baines*, and *Wortley*, now shewed cause. The defendants, being the owners of the vessel, are the parties liable, and not the charterer. In *Fletcher* v. *Braddick* (a) the owners of a vessel chartered to the commissioners of the navy were held liable for an injury done to another vessel by persons on board. That case was less strong than the present; for there the commander was appointed by the crown, and there was a king's pilot on board, though the master and crew were appointed by the owners, as here. There *Mansfield* C. J. said that, except as between the owners and commissioners, the ship must be taken to belong to the owners, and that third parties could not be supposed to know of the contract between the owners and commissioners. The principle of that case applies to the present; and it can make no difference that the charterer paid the wages while he used the ship. That was only in the nature of price paid for the hire of the ship, like payment of rates by a tenant, which diminishes the sum named for rent. The clause that the charterer shall pay the wages shews merely a contract between him and the owners, and indeed proves that the mariners,

(a) 2 *N. R.* 182.

&c.,

1838.

FENTON *against* The City of DUBLIN Steam Packet Company.

&c., are servants of the owners; else it would be superfluous. The language of Lord *Mansfield* in *Rich* v. *Coe* (a) confirms the principle here contended for; though it may be questionable whether the application of it would now be deemed correct under the particular circumstances of that case. How can it be said that the crew, &c., are not the servants of the defendants, who have power to remove them at any time? The law as to the liability of owners is laid down in an unqualified manner in *Abbott on Shipping*, 132 (b). The owners would be liable to the charterer for any losses occasioned by the negligence of the crew; and, if this action lay against the charterer, there would be a circuity of action. The passages cited from *Pothier* (c) and *Molloy* (d), in the argument in *Laugher* v. *Pointer* (e), shew that liability accrues to the owners on the ground of the master and crew being appointed by them. In *Lane* v. *Cotton* (g) the postmaster general was held not liable for the loss of exchequer bills delivered to his clerk. There *Holt* C. J., who differed from the rest of the court, held that he would be liable, on the ground that he appointed the clerk (h); and the grounds on which the other Judges decided that he was not liable were the peculiar nature of his office, or that the bills should not have been sent by the post. That case, therefore, is really in favour of the present plaintiff here. In *Laugher* v. *Pointer* (e) the Judges of this Court were equally divided on the question whether the owner of a carriage, having hired horses of a party who also provided

(a) 2 *Cowp.* 636.

(b) 5th ed.

(c) *Traités*, &c. tom. i. p. 54. ed. 2. part 1. ch. 1. s. 2. § 2. 121. *Pothier on Obligations*, vol. i. p. 72. *Evans's* transl.

(d) Vol. i. p. 358. 9th ed. b. 2. ch. 3. § 13.

(e) 5 *B. & C.* 549.

(g) 12 *Mod.* 472. *S. C.* 1 *Salk.* 17.; *Carth.* 487.

(h) See 12 *Mod.* p. 488, 9.

1838.

FENTON *against* The City of DUBLIN Steam Packet Company.

vided the driver, was liable for damage occasioned by negligent driving. There *Abbott* C. J., who held for the defendant, argued partly upon what he considered undisputed, that the charterer of a ship had never been thought answerable; and *Littledale* J. took the same line of argument. And it seems that, but for the doubt who had the controul of the driver, there would have been no difference of opinion. Here no such doubt exists; the charterer could not controul the navigation by the commander and crew; he was merely entitled to insist on the voyage being effected by them. Further, the doubt which existed in *Laugher* v. *Pointer* (a) may be considered as removed by the later case of *Smith* v. *Lawrence* (b). There it was held that a livery stable keeper, who let out posthorses and postboys for the day to the owner of a carriage, was liable for damage done in the course of the employment. [*Patteson* J. I do not understand that, in *Laugher* v. *Pointer* (a), any Judge expressed an opinion that the owner of the horses and master of the driver was not liable: the then defendant might be liable also.] The principle agreed on there seems to have been that the party who had the controul of the driver was liable. Another principle insisted upon, by the counsel who contended that the owner of the carriage was not liable, was the facility of discovering the party against whom the remedy was to lie. Here the notoriety of ownership is very strong, especially under the Registration Acts. In *Dean* v. *Hogg* (c) one of the defendants (*Lewis*) hired a steam boat for a specific voyage, the captain and crew being employed by the owner; and it was held that *Lewis*, or the other

(a) 5 *B.* & *C.* 547. (b) 2 *Man.* & *R.* 1. (c) 10 *Bing.* 345.

defendant

1838.

Fenton against The City of Dublin Steam Packet Company.

defendant by his authority, could not justify turning out a stranger on the ground that the vessel was in *Lewis's* possession. [*Coleridge* J. Did not that case turn on the language of the plea?] The question turned on the possession; and *Tindal* C. J. said, that, with reference to the owner's contract, "the merely putting *Lewis* in possession of the vessel would have been nothing; the main part of the contract remained to be performed by the captain and crew; viz., the carrying them to *Richmond* and back again: for which purpose it was essential they should remain on board, and retain the management and conduct of the vessel." In *Newberry* v. *Colvin* (a) it was held that the owners of a ship were not liable for the non-delivery of goods, the privity of contract (which was held to be the substantial ground of the action, though shaped in tort,) being merely between the shipper of the goods and the commander of the vessel, under the particular form of the instrument appointing the captain, of which the shippers had notice; and in *Hutton* v. *Bragg* (b) it was held that the owner had no lien upon the charterer's goods, the possession having been always in the charterer. These cases, which rest entirely on the relation between contracting parties, are inapplicable to actions of tort brought by strangers. So in *Reeve* v. *Davis* (c) the charterer was held to be the only party liable for repairs ordered by himself for his own benefit, and performed by persons who knew of no owner but the charterer; *James* v. *Jones* (d) belongs to the same class of cases.

(a) 7 *Bing.* 190., in Exch. Ch., reversing judgment of K. B. in *Colvin* v. *Newberry*, 8 *B.* & *C.* 166.

(b) 7 *Taunt.* 14. *S. C.* 2 *Marsh. Rep.* 339. (c) 1 *A.* & *E.* 312.

(d) *Abb. Shipp.* 20. (5th ed.). *S. C.* 3 *Esp. N. P. C.* 27.

Atcherley

1838.

Fenton against The City of Dublin Steam Packet Company.

Atcherley Serjt. and *Wightman*, contrà. The relation of the parties depends, not upon the greater or less facility of proof, but upon the duties which are created by the position in which they are placed. And these depend, not on the understanding of a particular witness, but on the legal result of what has taken place. Here the issue on the second plea raises the whole question. The charterer has the possession and controul of the vessel for his own benefit. He is therefore the wrongdoer, the wrongful act being done immediately by those whom he employs. In *Fletcher* v. *Braddick* (*a*) the owners paid the crew, as the charterer does here; and Sir *James Mansfield* said, "As far as appearances went the defendants continued the owners at the time of the loss, *for they paid* the master and sailors which they had put on board." In *Dean* v. *Hogg* (*b*) the owner of the steam boat had never parted with the possession. *Hutton* v. *Bragg* (*c*) was decided upon the express ground that the charterer had the possession. If a fraudulent deviation be made without the knowledge of the owners, it is barratry; otherwise, not: but the knowledge of an owner who has let out the ship will not prevent the deviation from being barratry, though the knowledge of the freighter would; *Vallejo* v. *Wheeler* (*d*). In *Scott* v. *Scott* (*e*) the opinion of *Best* J. appeared to be that the owner of a vessel, navigated by the servants of a party to whom the vessel was lent, was not liable for mischief done in the course of such navigation. The utmost that could be said here is, that the vessel was in the charterer's possession by the servants of the owners. But, in fact, the crew were the charterer's servants.

(*a*) 2 *N. R.* 182.

(*b*) 10 *Bing.* 345.

(*c*) 7 *Taunt.* 14. *S. C.* 2 *Marsh. Rep.* 339.

(*d*) 1 *Cowp.* 143.

(*e*) 2 *Stark.* 438.

1838.

FENTON *against* The City of DUBLIN Steam Packet Company.

servants. It is true, the witness said that he could not dismiss the crew; but the charterparty appears to give him that power: if any had deserted, he would have been the person to procure fresh hands. The fact that the mariners were originally appointed by the owners is unimportant: they are the servants of the party who pays them, as in the case of a man hiring a house, and retaining in his service the domestic servants whom he may find there, put in originally by the lessor. It is said that the charterer here had not the controul of the navigation: but the contrary is clear; he might have altered the hour of starting, or varied the coasting stations. If (as indeed was alleged at the trial) the vessel was under way at an hour which was improper, that was caused by the charterer, not the owners. *Parish* v. *Crawford* (*a*) is an authority against the defendants; but it has been frequently overruled, as was said by *Park* J. in *Hutton* v. *Bragg* (*b*).

Lord DENMAN C. J. The question is, not whether the charterer is liable, but whether the owners, who have let him have the benefit of the vessel, are liable for the negligence of the servants whom they have put on board for him. We must take it that this accident has occurred by the negligence of the crew in the ordinary course of the vessel's employment. If so, there can be no doubt that for that the owners are liable. It does not turn on the other question; the charterer may be answerable also: but, unless the charterparty has interfered with the general controul of the owners, they are clearly liable. Now here it appears that the charter-

(*a*) *Abb. Shipp.* 19. *S. C.* 2 *Str.* 1251.

(*b*) 7 *Taunt.* 27. *S. C.* 2 *Marsh. Rep.* 339. And see *Abb. Shipp.* 21, 22.

party

1838.

FENTON *against* The City of DUBLIN Steam Packet Company.

party binds the charterer only to pay for that which the owners are to provide.

PATTESON J. The question is, whose servants were the crew? For their negligence has occasioned the accident. I do not say that they are not the servants of the charterer. *Laugher* v. *Pointer* (*a*) does not bear on the point. To hold that the hirer is liable is not inconsistent with holding the letter liable also; and, since that case, it has been held that the letter is liable (*b*). The issue is, whether the defendants had the possession and care of the vessel by their servants; which brings us back to the question, whose servants were the crew? Now, on the charter-party alone, I have no difficulty in saying that they were the servants of the owners. The charterer hires the steam vessel for six months, with the option of retaining her six months longer; but the owners are to keep her in good order; and the charterer is not to find seamen, coals, &c., but to pay for all disbursements in these and other respects. Therefore I think it clear that the owners are to have their own engineer and servants on board, and that the charterer is to pay for them. These are therefore the servants of the owners.

WILLIAMS J. It is always a question of fact under whose direction and controul the vessel is at the time of the occurrence complained of. That question is solved by another, — whose are the crew? On the charter-party alone the fair construction is that they are the servants of the owners. When I find a specific clause intro-

(*a*) *5 B. & C.* 547.

(*b*) Referring apparently to *Smith* v. *Lawrence*, 2 *Man. & R.* 1.

1838.

FENTON against The City of DUBLIN Steam Packet Company.

duced, binding the charterer to pay for the seamen, and even for the materials to be consumed by the engines, the reasonable inference is, not merely that the owners furnished the crew, but that they had the controul.

COLERIDGE J. The question is as the issue expresses it: it is a pure question of fact. How can we exclude evidence, whatever may be the relation of the parties to each other on paper, of the vessel being, in fact, in the controul of the owners? Now it appears, on the evidence, that the vessel was navigated by a crew appointed by the owners. If I am to shut that out, I must, in examining the charter-party, at any rate take into consideration the nature of the ship, of the voyage, and every other particular; and I think the reasonable interpretation of the charter-party is that the owners meant to keep the controul of the vessel in their own hands. They are therefore liable.

Rule discharged (*a*).

(*a*) See *Randleson* v. *Murray*, antè, p. 109.

Wednesday, November 21st.

BUCKTON and WRAY, Assignees of MASON, a Bankrupt, *against* FROST, LIDDELL, and WHITTAKER.

In trover by assignees of a bankrupt, laying the possession in themselves as assignees, pleas that the plaintiffs are not assignees, and were not possessed as assignees, put in issue the trading, the petitioning creditor's debt, and the act of bankruptcy; and these must be proved, if notice to dispute them be given. It is not enough to prove the fiat and assignment to the plaintiffs.

TROVER, laying the possession in the plaintiffs as assignees of the bankrupt. Pleas. 1. That the plaintiffs are not assignees of *Mason*. 2. That the plaintiffs were not lawfully possessed as assignees; 3. Not guilty. Issues thereon.

On

1838.

BUCKTON *against* FROST.

On the trial before *Alderson* B., at the *Yorkshire* Spring assizes, 1837, it appeared that the defendants had given notice of their intention to dispute the petitioning creditor's debt, the trading, and the act of bankruptcy. The plaintiffs proved the fiat and their appointment as assignees; but gave no proof of the debt, trading, or act of bankruptcy. The defendants' counsel applied for a nonsuit; and the learned baron expressed his opinion that the objection was fatal; but he declined to stop the cause, and reserved leave to move for a nonsuit. Verdict for the plaintiffs. In *Easter* term 1837 *Cresswell* obtained a rule nisi for a nonsuit.

Alexander, *Wightman*, and *Tomlinson*, now shewed cause, and mentioned *Scott* v. *Thomas* (*a*); but they admitted that the point was identical with that decided in *Butler* v. *Hobson* (*b*), and that, if the latter case was upheld, the rule must be made absolute.

Per Curiam (*c*). We must be bound by *Butler* v. *Hobson* (*b*).

Rule absolute.

Cresswell and *Martin* were to have supported the rule.

(*a*) 6 *C. & P.* 611. On the argument in the present case, *Patteson* J. remarked that it did not appear in *Scott* v. *Thomas* that notice was given.

(*b*) 4 *New Ca.* 290.

(*c*) Lord *Denman* C. J., *Patteson*, *Williams*, and *Coleridge* Js.

Wednesday, November 21st.

THOMAS RAIKES, and ROBERT RAIKES the Younger, *against* TODD.

Under the Statute of Frauds, 29 *C.* 2. *c.* 3. *s.* 4., to charge a party on a promise to answer for the debt of another, the written agreement or memorandum must shew the consideration expressly or by necessary inference.

Memorandum in writing: — "I undertake to secure to you the payment of any sums you have advanced, or may hereafter advance, to *D.* on his account with you, commencing 1st *November* 1831, not exceeding 2000*l.*"

Declaration thereupon, stating that plaintiff had opened an account with, and thereon made advances to, *D.*, commencing on &c., and that the guarantee was given in consideration of the premises, and also in consideration that plaintiff, at the request of the party guaranteeing, would continue to advance further sums to *D.* on his said account with plaintiff. Held, that the consideration did not sufficiently appear by the written instrument to support such declaration.

If a creditor receive dividends upon a debt partly secured by guarantee of a third person, the dividends must not be appropriated to the excess of the debt above the sum guaranteed, but must be applied rateably to the whole debt, and the surety is relieved from liability by the amount of dividend on the part which is secured.

ASSUMPSIT. The declaration stated that before and at the time of the promise &c. the plaintiffs had been, and still are, bankers, and, as such bankers, had opened an account with one *Henry Davenport* (using the name, style, and firm of Messrs. *Henry Davenport* and Co.), commencing on 1st *November* 1831, and had advanced to *H. D.*, on his said account with them, commencing as aforesaid, certain sums of money, amounting together &c., viz. to 1600*l.*, which sum afterwards, viz. on 19th *October* 1832, was wholly due and owing by *H. D.* to plaintiffs, whereof defendant had notice; and thereupon, afterwards, viz. on &c., *in consideration of the premises, and in consideration that the plaintiffs, at the request of the defendant, would continue from time to time to advance further sums of money to the said* H. D. *on his said account with them, commencing as aforesaid*, defendant undertook to secure to plaintiffs the payment of any sums of money they might then have advanced, or might thereafter advance, to *H. D.* on his said account with them, commencing as aforesaid, not exceeding 2000*l.* Averment, that plaintiffs, confiding &c., afterwards, viz. 19th *October* 1832, and on divers other days between that day and 1st *May* 1833, did further, from

time

1838.

RAIKES *against* TODD.

time to time, advance to *H. D.*, on his said account with them, commencing as aforesaid, other sums, amounting altogether to a further large sum, viz. 1300*l.*; and that *H. D.*, although he was afterwards, to wit on &c., requested so to do, hath not as yet paid the said several sums of 1600*l.* and 1300*l.*, or either &c., but hath hitherto wholly neglected &c.; of which defendant afterwards, viz. on &c., had notice. Breach, non-payment by defendant of 2000*l.*, parcel of the said sums of 1600*l.* and 1300*l.*, and that the 2000*l.* is still wholly due &c.

Pleas, 1. As to so much of the declaration as alleges that defendant undertook to secure to plaintiffs the payment of any sum of money they might then have advanced, that defendant did not promise in manner &c. 2. As to the residue, payment into Court of 1146*l.* 7*s.* 6*d.*, with averment that plaintiffs had not sustained damages to a greater amount. 3. A set off, on which nothing turned.

The plaintiffs joined issue on the first plea, traversed the third, and, as to the second, accepted the 1146*l.* in satisfaction and discharge of the cause of action in the introduction thereof mentioned.

On the trial before *Alderson* B., at the *Yorkshire* Spring assizes, 1837, the plaintiffs put in the guarantee, which was addressed to themselves, and was as follows.

"Messrs. *Raikes*. "*October* 19th, 1832.

"Gentlemen,

"I hereby undertake to secure to you the payment of any sums of money you have advanced, or may hereafter advance, to Messrs. *Henry Davenport* and Co. on their account with you, commencing the 1st *November* 1831, not exceeding 2000*l.*

"*John Todd.*"

 Henry

1838.

RAIKES against TODD.

Henry Davenport, the person mentioned in the declaration, was the person described in the guarantee as Messrs. *Henry Davenport* and Co. The whole sum advanced to him by the plaintiffs, before and after the giving of the guarantee, was 2426*l.* 17*s.* 11*d.*, of which 1305*l.* 1*s.* 3*d.* had been advanced since the giving of the guarantee. *Davenport* had become bankrupt; and the plaintiffs had proved their whole debt against the estate. A dividend of 2*s.* 5$\frac{7}{16}$*d.* had been paid to the plaintiffs, producing 297*l.* 13*s.* 5*d.* on the 2426*l.* 17*s.* 11*d.* The plaintiffs contended that, as this left more than 2000*l.*, the amount of the guarantee, unsatisfied, they were entitled to the difference between the 2000*l.* and the 1146*l.* 7*s.* 6*d.* taken out of Court, being 853*l.* 12*s.* 6*d.* The defendant contended that the guarantee did not cover past advances at all, and that, at any rate, the consideration for giving it was not correctly described in the declaration. And further (supposing that the guarantee was properly declared upon, and did cover past advances), first, that at all events the pleadings confined the plaintiffs' claim to the difference between the 1305*l.* 1*s.* 3*d.*, advanced since the guarantee, and covered by the second plea, and the 2000*l.*, namely to 694*l.* 18*s.* 9*d.*; but that, secondly, the dividends received were to be distributed rateably over the whole balance; that the dividend of 2*s.* 5$\frac{7}{16}$*d.* in the pound, so distributed over 2426*l.* 17*s.* 11*d.*, would produce, on the 2000*l.*, 245*l.* 1*s.* 5*d.* (*a*); and, therefore, that no damages could be recovered beyond the excess of the 2000*l.* above the aggregate of the 245*l.* 1*s.* 5*d.* and the 1146*l.* 7*s.* 6*d.* taken out of Court; which would reduce the claim to 608*l.* 11*s.* 1*d.* The learned Baron, after stating his

(*a*) Apparently a miscalculation for 245*l.* 6*s.* 3*d.*

opinion

1838.

RAIKES *against* TODD.

opinion that the word "secure" implied a forbearance, directed a verdict for the plaintiffs for 853*l.* 12*s.* 6*d.*, reserving leave to move to enter a verdict for the defendant, or to reduce the damages. In *Easter* term, 1837, *Alexander* obtained a rule accordingly.

Cresswell and *Wharton* now shewed cause. First, the guarantee in its terms covers future advances, and the consideration is sufficient. It is not necessary that the consideration for a guarantee should appear in express terms upon the face of the instrument: it is sufficient if it can be collected from the whole of the instrument (*a*). The Courts will not be strict in the construction of such instruments; per *Tindal* C. J. in *Newbury* v. *Armstrong* (*b*): they are "to be taken as strongly against the party giving the guarantee as the sense of them" will admit of; *Mason* v. *Pritchard* (*c*). The consideration here was the keeping open *Davenport's* account to the extent of the guarantee, viz. 2000*l.* The advance of future sums is a good consideration; and this consideration appears on the face of the instrument. The attempt on the other side will be to apply that consideration to the guarantee of the future advances only. But such a consideration will support a promise to guarantee, not merely future, but past advances. It is not necessary that the consideration and promise should be coextensive in this respect. The contract cannot be divided, so as to leave one part of the guarantee without consideration: the whole constitutes one agreement, and the consideration goes to all. There could be no doubt of this if the

(*a*) See the cases in *Smith's Compendium of Mercantile Law*, p. 382., &c. (2d ed.).

(*b*) 6 *Bing.* 201.

(*c*) 12 *East*, 227.

 instrument

1838.

RAIKES *against* TODD.

instrument had expressly guaranteed past and future advances, in consideration of advances to be made; and it can make no difference that the consideration is collected from the whole instrument instead of being expressly stated. In *Jenkins* v. *Reynolds* (a) it was held, in the Common Pleas, that the words, "To the amount of 100*l.*, be pleased to consider me as security on Mr. *James Cowing* and Co.'s account," did not satisfy the Statute of Frauds, 29 *C.* 2. *c.* 3. *s.* 4., for want of consideration. In that case there was no ground for inferring that any future advances were to be made. Soon after, in *Russell* v. *Moseley* (b), the same Court held the following sufficient: — "I hereby guarantee the present account" of *H. M.*, "and what she may contract from this date to the 30th *September* next." That case cannot be distinguished from the present. *Wood* v. *Benson* (c) will perhaps be relied upon, as shewing that a contract to guarantee past and future advances may be divided, and the consideration applied to the future advances only. But there the instrument first guaranteed the future supply, and then followed a distinct clause as to the past supply, which the Court treated as altogether separate, Lord *Lyndhurst* saying, "if it is distinct and separate, it cannot be supported for want of consideration apparent on the instrument. The question then arises on the first engagement," &c. The ruling as to the second need not be disputed here, the whole promise, in this case, clearly springing from a single motive, and the clauses not being distinct. Further, the consideration, as laid, cannot be disputed on

(a) 3 *Brod. & B.* 14.

(b) 3 *Brod. & B.* 211.

(c) 2 *Tyrwh.* 93. *S.C.* 2 *Cr. & J.* 94. See *Head* v. *Baldrey*, 6 *A. & E.* 459. *Mechelen* v. *Wallace*, 7 *A. & E.* 49.

this

this record: it should have been specially traversed; *Passenger* v. *Brookes* (*a*). Secondly, the defendant will contend that the dividends received are to be distributed rateably over the whole debt. But the guarantee is to protect the plaintiffs to the extent of 2000*l.*: this would not be effected on the principle contended for by the defendant. If the guarantee limited the credit which was to be given, it might perhaps be said that the security was specifically appropriated to the particular sum advanced, and that therefore the liability was diminished by the dividend on so much. That was the case in *Bardwell* v. *Lydall* (*b*), where the guarantee, in consideration of credit being given to the principal, was of "a running balance of account to any amount not exceeding 400*l.*;" and it was held that the liability was to be diminished by the dividends payable in respect of the 400*l.* *Paley* v. *Field* (*c*) is a similar case. Here no such appropriation can be made; for the guarantee does not limit the credit to be given, but merely secures 2000*l.* out of advances to be made to any amount. The payment of the dividend is as if the principal debtor had reduced the balance of 2426*l.* 17*s.* 11*d.* by any other mode of payment.

Alexander and *Tomlinson*, contrà. It is now undoubted law that, under 29 *Car.* 2. *c.* 3. *s.* 4., to charge a party upon any special promise to answer for the debt of another, there must be a written agreement or memorandum thereof, which will not be valid unless it shew a consideration. It is true that the consideration need not be expressly and formally stated; but it must at least

(*a*) 1 *New Ca.* 587. (*b*) 7 *Bing.* 489.
(*c*) 12 *Ves.* 435.

appear

1838.

RAIKES *against* TODD.

appear clearly and without ambiguity; *James* v. *Williams* (*a*), *Cole* v. *Dyer* (*b*). In *Wain* v. *Warlters* (*c*) it might have been fairly conjectured that the guarantee was given in consideration of forbearance to enforce against the principal the bill which the plaintiffs held: and a similar conjecture might have been made, and was pressed on the Court, in *Hawes* v. *Armstrong* (*d*). But, in each case, the Court held the agreement invalid for want of shewing a consideration. In *Stadt* v. *Lill* (*e*) the guarantee was merely for payment of goods *to be* delivered; and the Court held that the agreement shewed clearly that the delivery of goods was the consideration. That construction arises naturally where the guarantee extends merely to future advances. But the consideration, on this instrument, is only matter of conjecture; and different minds might, on the perusal, reasonably form different conjectures as to the true consideration. It is contended by the plaintiffs' counsel that the consideration for the guarantee of both past and present advances is the future advance: and that is the consideration alleged on the record. But it might more reasonably be contended that the consideration was the forbearance of the sum already due, since otherwise the advance of a single shilling, though followed immediately by an arrest for the old balance, and the consequent destruction of *H. D.*'s commercial credit, would impose on the defendant a liability for all the old balance: and this appears to have been the interpretation adopted at Nisi Prius by the learned Judge, who treated the word "secure" as implying a state of ease and quiet, and obviously

(*a*) 5 *B. & Ad.* 1109.
(*b*) 1 *Cr. & J.* 461. *S. C.* 1 *Tyrwh.* 304.
(*c*) 5 *East*, 10.
(*d*) 1 *New Ca.* 761.
(*e*) 9 *East*, 348.

therefore,

1838.

RAIKES against TODD.

therefore indicating forbearance of the existing debt. It is sufficient, however, to invalidate the agreement that there should be any reasonable ground for doubting what the consideration is; since the consideration, if not formally expressed, must at least appear unambiguously. If it were urged that the Court may infer a consideration made up of forbearance as to past advances and the prospect of future ones, from the guarantee being given as to both (and this is perhaps the most reasonable conjecture, the probable inducement being the support of *H. D.* generally in his business, which might require both indulgence for the existing debt and future accommodation), then the answer is that no such consideration is alleged in the count. [Lord *Denman* C. J. The declaration says, "in consideration of the premises," that is, of the past advances as well as future credit.] These are mere words of form. A past consideration is good only when laid with a request, which request is a material averment. The defendant does not, as was suggested, insist that the consideration must be coextensive with the promise: any consideration *clearly expressed* would of course support the promise as to both past and future advances; but, when a plaintiff relies on a promise to be collected by implication, the extensiveness of the benefit resulting from the promise becomes a material test as to the extent of the consideration. *Russell* v. *Moseley* (a) cannot be relied upon. It is very shortly reported in *Broderip and Bingham:* from the report in 6 *B. Moore* (b) it appears that the attention of the Court was principally directed to the question of the

(a) 3 *Br. & B.* 211. (b) 6 *B. Moore*, 521.

extent

1838.

RAIKES *against* TODD.

extent of the promise: and the rule was finally made absolute by consent: there was no express decision on the point now in dispute. The promises here are as distinct as those in *Wood* v. *Benson* (a). The collocation of the words cannot make a material difference.

It is contended, also, that the absence of consideration, or variance as to the statement of it, should be specially pleaded; but *Passenger* v. *Brookes* (b), as reported in *Bingham's New Cases*, is overruled by *Bennion* v. *Davison* (c), where the Court relied on the report of *Passenger* v. *Brooks* in 1 *Scott* (d); and from the latter report it appears that the defendant sought, not to deny the consideration alleged in the declaration, but to prove facts which established a kind of confession and avoidance. [Lord *Denman* C. J. If you disprove the consideration laid, you of course disprove the contract.]

As to the second point, the plaintiffs appear already to have impliedly admitted the principle insisted on by the defendant. The sum advanced since the guarantee was 1305*l.* 1*s.* 3*d.*; the money paid into Court, and accepted by the plaintiffs, is 1146*l.* 7*s.* 6*d.*: the difference between these two sums is 158*l.* 13*s.* 9*d.*, which is almost exactly the dividend of 2*s.* $5\frac{7}{16}$*d.* upon 1305*l.* 1*s.* 3*d.* The declared dividend is appropriated, so much for every distinct pound. By the Bankrupt Act, stat. 6 *G.* 4. *c.* 16. *s.* 52., a surety who pays the debt may stand in the place of the creditor who has proved against the principal. But according to the rule contended for by the plaintiffs, if the creditor had a demand exceeding the sum secured, he might receive

(a) 2 *Cr. & J.* 94. *S. C.* 2 *Tyrwh.* 93.
(b) 1 *New Ca.* 587.
(c) 3 *Mee. & W.* 179.
(d) 1 *Scott*, 560.

the

1838.

RAIKES *against* TODD.

the dividend on his own proof, and apply the whole in reduction of that part of the debt which was not covered by the guarantee; and so the surety would lose the benefit of the enactment. By the same section, if the creditor has not proved, the surety may prove his payment as a debt, and receive the dividend on such debt. The principle of both these provisions is that the surety is to pay only the excess of the sum which he guarantees above the dividend paid *in respect of such sum*. *Bardwell* v. *Lydall* (a) cannot be substantially distinguished. [Lord *Denman* C. J. We quite agree with you on the second point.]

Lord DENMAN C. J. The question is, whether the plaintiff has made out the contract laid in the declaration; namely, whether the defendant made the agreement in consideration of the premises (that is, of the previous advances, which part of the consideration must certainly be disregarded), and also that the plaintiffs would advance further sums. For the plaintiffs it is urged that the consideration need not be coextensive with the promise. But we are to see that the contract entered into by the parties is placed on the record. I adhere to what the Court said in *Mason* v. *Pritchard* (b): but I also agree in the remarks of my brother *Patteson* in *James* v. *Williams* (c): — "The consideration need not be stated in express words on the face of the instrument; it may be collected or implied from the instrument itself, but then it must be collected not as matter of conjecture, but with certainty." In a late case (d) the Lord Chief Justice of the Common Pleas said, "It is not, however,

(a) 7 *Bing.* 489.
(b) 12 *East*, 227.
(c) 5 *B. & Ad.* 1109.
(d) *Hawes* v. *Armstrong*, 1 *New Ca.* 761.

necessary

1838.

Raikes against Todd.

necessary that such consideration should appear in *express terms*: it would undoubtedly be sufficient in any case, if the memorandum is so framed that any person of ordinary capacity must infer from the perusal of it, that such, and no other, was the consideration upon which the undertaking was given. Not that a mere conjecture, however plausible, that the consideration stated in the declaration was that intended by the memorandum, would be sufficient to satisfy the statute: but there must be a well grounded inference to be necessarily collected from the terms of the memorandum, that the consideration stated in the declaration, and no other than such consideration, was intended by the parties to be the ground of the promise." I must confess that here I cannot sufficiently see what the consideration is. If I were to conjecture, I should say that it was made up of two considerations; first, a forbearance to sue for the advances already made; secondly, the future advances. But such a consideration is inconsistent with the agreement set out in the declaration. According to the best construction I can put on this instrument, the declaration does not describe the contract correctly. It would, however, be a sufficient ground for making this rule absolute, if it were merely uncertain what the consideration is.

Patteson J. I have had some difficulty in coming to a conclusion; but, upon the whole, this instrument does not contain enough to satisfy me what the consideration is. If the guarantee were merely for future advances, then such future advances might be considered as the consideration for the guarantee; but that does not apply to a guarantee comprehending also past advances. All

All these cases are difficult to determine: the Court is obliged to look closely at the instrument, and is not at liberty to form conjectures. I cannot myself perceive an engagement here to forbear suing on the past advances. But, supposing the instrument to contain such an engagement, there would be an equally fatal defect, since that consideration does not appear in the declaration. The Statute of Frauds is therefore not satisfied: and the rule must be made absolute for entering a verdict for the defendant.

WILLIAMS J. It is admitted, in argument, that a consideration must appear on the face of the instrument. The main question therefore is, whether we can discover the real consideration without a conjecture, and that a hazardous one. The learned Judge who tried the cause appears to have been of opinion that the document raises an implication that there should be a forbearance, whence it might be inferred that forbearance formed a part of the consideration. To me the instrument seems too uncertain in its construction to warrant us in holding it to be a good guarantee.

COLERIDGE J. Mr. *Tomlinson* appears to me to have laid down, in his very able argument, the real rule. A consideration must appear, either expressly, or by necessary inference; if not, the Statute of Frauds is not satisfied. Is that so here? As to future advances, the case is clear; but, as to the rest of the guarantee, I do not see so clearly. From the word "secure" I should rather be disposed to infer a reference to bygone advances, and a consideration of forbearance. If that

be

1838.

RAIKES *against* TODD.

be correct, the plaintiffs cannot succeed; for that consideration is not alleged on the record. I may be wrong in my interpretation of the instrument; but can I say that the consideration alleged on the record must be necessarily inferred?

Rule absolute for entering verdict for defendant (*a*).

(*a*) See *Haigh* v. *Brooks*, *Trin.* T. 1839, post.

The QUEEN *against* The Lady and Steward of the Manor of DULLINGHAM.

K., copyholder in fee, devised to *R.* for life, who was admitted, and paid, in respect of her admittance to hold for life, as large a fine as if she had been admitted tenant in fee. During *R*'s life, *K.*'s heir at law surrendered to such uses as *L.* should appoint, and, in default &c., to the use of *L.* in fee. *K.* had not been admitted or paid any fine.
Held, that the lord could not be compelled on the application of the heir, nor, à fortiori, on that of *L.*, to receive and enrol the surrender without payment of the fine for the descent of the reversion to the heir.

MANDAMUS to *Harriet Pigott*, the wife of *William Pigott*, Esq., lady of the manor of *Dullingham*, in *Cambridgeshire*, and to *Edward Weatherby*, her steward of the said manor.

The writ recited that the manor of *Dullingham* is, and from time whereof &c. hath been, an ancient manor, within which there are various copyhold tenements, parcel of the said manor, granted by and held of the lord or lady, according to the custom, and demised and demisable by copy of court-roll, by the lord or steward, according to the custom &c., at the will of the lord or lady, according to the custom &c.; and that, during all the time aforesaid, by the custom &c., copyhold hereditaments and premises, held of the lord or lady, according to the custom &c., have been, and might and may be, surrendered out of court before two copyholders of the manor; and in which manor, during all the time aforesaid, the lord or lady, and the steward for the time being, have accepted, and of right ought to

accept,

1838.

The QUEEN against The Lady of the Manor of DULLINGHAM.

accept, all surrenders duly tendered for enrolment, and once or oftener in every year have held, and of right ought &c., and still of right ought &c., customary courts for the manor, and have accepted, and of right ought &c., and still of right ought to accept and to enrol all such surrenders of any of the said customary tenements as have been and are duly tendered for acceptance, according to the custom &c.

The writ further stated that *Robert King*, deceased, was in his lifetime seised to him and his heirs of certain copyhold hereditaments and premises, parcel of the said manor, and had been duly admitted thereto, and had paid all fines, and performed all services, which, of right and according to the custom &c., ought to be paid to the lady of the said manor in respect of the said hereditaments and premises; that he died seised of the same in *June* 1834, leaving *Robert William King*, his eldest son and heir, according to the custom &c., him surviving; that the said *Robert K.*, in his lifetime, duly made and published his will, according to the custom &c., and thereby devised all his copyhold estates in the said manor to *Rebecca*, his wife, for the term of her natural life; and the said *Rebecca*, upon the death of *Robert K.*, was duly admitted to all his copyhold estates at the time of his death within the said manor, to hold &c. (as devised), according to the custom &c., at the will &c.; and she, upon such admission, paid a full fine to the steward, that is to say, a fine to the same amount as if she had been admitted to an estate in fee simple in the said premises.

The writ then stated that *R. W. King*, being the eldest son and heir of *Robert K.*, according to the custom &c., did

1838.

The Queen against The Lady of the Manor of Dullingham.

did afterwards, viz. on 31st *October* 1835, duly surrender, by the rod, into the hands of the lady of the said manor, by the hands and acceptance of &c. (one copyholder of the manor, in the presence of another), according to the custom &c., all the said copyhold hereditaments and premises to which his said father had been admitted, upon the terms and conditions in such surrender mentioned, and which said surrender is in the words &c. The writ then set out the surrender, which recited the title of *Robert King* to the several parcels of his copyhold estate; his death on or about 19th *June* 1834, seised of the premises; his will, and the admittance of *Rebecca* under the will, to hold for life; and that *R. W. King* was *Robert's* eldest son and heir, according to the custom &c.; and it set forth that, on 31st *October* 1835, *R. W. King*, in pursuance of his covenant contained in an indenture dated the day of the passing of the surrender, between *R. W. King* of the first part, *Rebecca King* of the second part, and *James King*, *John Lyles King*, and *John King*, of the third part, did out of Court &c. surrender &c. the premises, subject to the life estate of *Rebecca K.*, to the use of such person or persons, for such estate or estates, upon and for such trusts, intents, and purposes, and with, under, and subject to such powers, provisos, and declarations as the said *James K.*, *John Lyles K.*, and *John K.*, or the survivor of them, or the heirs of the survivor of them, by any deed &c., should from time to time, and at any time or times thereafter, during the life of *Rebecca* (but, if during her life, with the consent in writing of the said *Robert William K.*, his executors, administrators, or assigns), or within twenty-one years from the

1838.

The QUEEN against The Lady of the Manor of DULLINGHAM.

the time of her decease, direct, limit, or appoint; and, in the meantime, and until, and also in default of, any such direction &c., and so far as the same, if incomplete, should not extend, to the use of *James K.*, *John Lyles K.*, and *John K.*, in fee, to be holden at the will of the lady, according to the custom &c., by and under the rents and services theretofore due and of right accustomed in respect of the said premises; but, nevertheless, upon and for the trusts, intents, and purposes, and with and subject to the powers, provisos, and declarations, in and by the before-mentioned indenture declared.

The writ then stated that the said *James K.*, *John Lyles K.*, and *John K.*, being desirous of having the said surrender enrolled by the lady of the said manor or her steward thereof, did cause application to be made on their behalf to the said lady and her steward to receive and enrol the said surrender, for the purposes therein mentioned, according to the custom &c.; and that the lady and steward had refused to receive and enrol the surrender, to the great damage of *James K.*, *John Lyles K.*, and *John K.*, and to the manifest injury of their estate. The writ then commanded the lady and steward that they, or one of them, should receive and enrol the said surrender of *R. W. King*, or shew cause &c.

Return. That on the death of *Robert King* the reversion of the messuages, lands, &c., described in the surrender, expectant on the determination of the life estate devised to *Rebecca* by the said *Robert K.*, descended to *Robert William K.*, his heirs and assigns, he being the eldest son and heir, according to the custom &c., of *Robert K.*; but that the said *Robert William K.* has never been admitted, nor requested, nor tendered himself to be

 admitted

1838.

The QUEEN *against* The Lady of the Manor of DOLLINGHAM.

admitted, to the said reversion of the said messuages, lands, &c., or any part thereof: aud, further, that the fine within mentioned to have been paid by *Rebecca* was assessed, and by her paid, in respect only of the life estate devised to her by *Robert King*; and that, besides that fine, the said *Harriet Pigott* claimed, and there became and was, on the said surrender being made as within mentioned, due to her the said *H. P.*, being the lady &c., from the said *Robert William K.*, in respect of his said reversion in the messuages, &c., and the said descent thereof to him, a reasonable fine, to be fixed and assessed by her the said lady, or on her behalf by her steward, at her or his will and pleasure, and to be paid to or for her, the said lady &c.: and, further, that the fine so due in respect of the said reversion and the said descent thereof to *Robert William K.*, had never been paid, but that the said *Robert William K.*, the within-mentioned *James K.*, *John Lyles K.*, and *John K.*, have always refused to pay or agree to pay, or become answerable for the payment of, and have not in fact paid &c., such fine, or any fine, so in respect of the said reversion due &c., on the said surrender: and, further, "that we have always been and are ready and willing, and, when application was made to us to receive and enrol the said surrender as in the said writ mentioned, we offered to the said *James K.*, and *John Lyles K.*, and *John K.*, to receive and enrol the said surrender for the purposes therein mentioned, according to the custom of the said manor, on the fine so as aforesaid due to me the said *Harriett Pigott* from the said *Robert William K.*, in respect of the said reversion and the said descent thereof upon him, being paid, or on the said *James K.*, *John Lyles K.*, and *John K.* agreeing to pay such

1838.

The QUEEN against The Lady of the Manor of DULLINGHAM.

such fine:" but that *James K.*, *John Lyles K.*, and *John K.* refused the offer, or to pay or agree to pay such fine, and declined to entertain the question of the claim of the lady of the manor to a fine from the said *Robert William K.* in respect of the reversion and the descent thereof: whereupon the lady, by her steward, refused to receive or enrol the surrender unless the fine in respect &c., due from *Robert William K.* on the said surrender, were paid, or the said *James K.*, *John Lyles K.*, and *John K.* would agree to pay such fine: and, further, that the lady and steward have always been ready and willing to accept, as and for such fine, "half the fine which might have been reasonably assessed, and, according to the custom of the manor, would have been payable, on the admittance of a tenant in fee simple in possession to the messuages" &c.; and that, save as aforesaid, they have not, nor has either of them, neglected or refused to receive or enrol &c.

The case was set down for argument in the Crown paper, and argued in *Trinity* term last (*a*).

Sir *F. Pollock* against the return. During the life of the tenant for life, who has paid a full fine, no fine is due from the reversioner. The lord has a tenant on the roll who has paid the full amount due for the fee simple; and no more can be required. If the person last seised had died without a will, the heir might have surrendered without being admitted; and, till the admittance, the lord could have claimed no fine; *Rex* v. *The Lord of the Manor of Hendon* (*b*). In 2 *Bac. Abr.* 223

(*a*) *Saturday, June* 2d. Before Lord *Denman* C. J., *Littledale*, *Patteson*, and *Williams* Js.

(*b*) 2 *T. R.* 484.

1838.

The Queen against The Lady of the Manor of Dullingham.

(7th ed.), *Copyhold* (I) 1., it is said, "If a copyholder in fee surrenders to the use of one for life, the remainder to another for life, remainder to another in fee, by this but one fine is due, for the particular estates and remainders are but one estate." The admittance of the wife, therefore, was also an admittance of the heir. The heir might devise without being admitted or paying the fine due on admittance; *Right dem. Taylor* v. *Banks* (*a*), *King* v. *Turner* (*b*), *Doe dem. Perry* v. *Wilson* (*c*). In *The Dean and Chapter of Ely* v. *Caldecot* (*d*) *Tindal* C. J. adopted the law laid down in *Barnes* v. *Corke* (*e*), that no fine is due on the admittance of a remainder-man after admittance and payment of a fine by the tenant for life, unless there be a special custom; and here no special custom appears. Even if the fine be due here, it cannot be enforced by a refusal to enrol the surrender, but only upon the claim of the surrenderee to be admitted in pursuance of the surrender.

B. Andrews contrà. It is true that no fine would be here payable by the surrenderee before admittance. But the question is, whether the lord can be compelled to enrol the surrender of the heir at law without the fine being paid. If he did, he might be compelled to admit without payment of fine. [*Patteson* J. Perhaps it will be contended that the lord, in such a case, might have his remedy by action against the heir, as having been virtually admitted through the admittance of his surrenderee.] He would, at any rate, lose a remedy. If he accepted the surrender, he could not seise the land

(*a*) 3 *B. & Ad.* 664.
(*b*) 1 *Mylne & K.* 456., reversing *King* v. *Turner*, 2 *Sim.* 545.
(*c*) 5 *A. & E.* 321.
(*d*) 8 *Bing.* 447, 448.
(*e*) 3 *Lev.* 308.

1838.

The QUEEN *against* The Lady of the Manor of DULLINGHAM.

as belonging to the heir; and he might be barred by the Statute of Limitations. The admittance of a tenant for life enures to a remainder-man, but not to a reversioner: the remainder and life estate make up one fee: the reversioner does not come in under the devise creating the life estate (*a*). The fine, therefore, paid by the tenant for life does not aid the reversioner. It is as if the devisor had, in his lifetime, surrendered to his wife for her life, and she had survived him. *The Dean and Chapter of Ely* v. *Caldecot* (*b*) was the case of a remainder. It is said that the tenant for life here paid a fine answering in amount to the whole fee; but the return shews that it was paid in respect only of the life estate. Here the lord does not call upon the heir to be admitted; but he insists upon the heir not acting through or in his court without becoming a tenant and paying the fine. In *Watkins on Copyholds*, 245. (vol. i. p. 305. of 4th ed., *Coventry's*), it is said, "Though the heir before admittance may maintain an action in the common law courts, as an action for trespass or ejectment, yet he cannot sue in the court of the manor: and therefore he shall not have plaint in the nature of an assize. So he cannot sit on the homage." From *Watkins's* note 136. to *Gilbert on Tenures* it may be inferred that the approbation of the lord is equivalent to admittance. In *Coke's Compl. Copyholder*, s. 41., it is said, "In admittances upon descents the heir is tenant by copy immediately upon the death of his ancestor, not to all intents and purposes: for peradventure he cannot be sworn of the homage before, neither can he maintain a

(*a*) See *Doe dem. Winder* v. *Lawes*, 7 *A. & E.* 195., and the judgment there, p. 210.

(*b*) 8 *Bing.* 439.

1838.

The QUEEN against The Lady of the Manor of DULLINGHAM.

plaint in the nature of an assise in the lord's court before, because till then he is not complete tenant to the lord, no farther forth than the lord pleaseth to allow him for his tenant. And therefore if there be grandfather, father and son, and the grandfather is admitted, and dieth, and the father entereth, and dieth before admittance, the son shall have a plaint in the nature of a writ of ayel, and not an assise of mort d'auncestor. So that to all intents and purposes the heir, till admittance, is not complete tenant; yet to most intents, especially as to strangers, the law taketh notice of him as of a perfect tenant of the land instantly upon the death of his ancestor: for he may enter into the land before admittance, take the profits, punish any trespass done upon the ground, surrender into the hands of the lord to whose use he pleaseth, *satisfying the lord his fine due upon the descent.*" And in an opinion of Mr. *Fearne*, *Posthumous Works*, p. 103—107, the principle for which the defendants now contend is expressly laid down. [*Littledale* J. In 1 *Scriven on Copyholds*, 171 (*a*) it is said that *Doe dem. Tofield* v. *Tofield* (*b*) has decided that the steward's acceptance of a surrender from the first surrenderee is not an admittance of him.] *Right dem. Taylor* v. *Banks* (*c*), *King* v. *Turner* (*d*), and *Doe dem. Perry* v. *Wilson* (*e*), shew only that a devise by an heir is good without his admittance. In the last case, Lord *Denman* C. J., referring to Mr. *Fearne's* opinion, above noticed, said (*g*), "That shews only that the lord may refuse to accept the surrender till the fine is paid, but is bound if he accept it without payment."

(*a*) 3d ed.
(*b*) 11 *East*, 246.
(*c*) 3 *B. & Ad.* 664.
(*d*) 1 *Myl. & K.* 456.
(*e*) 5 *A. & E.* 321.
(*g*) Page 324.

Sir

1838.

The QUEEN against The Lady of the Manor of DULLINGHAM.

Sir *F. Pollock*, in reply. The argument that the lord, if he enrolled the surrender, would be bound to admit, is unfounded: the effect of the enrolment is merely that evidence of the surrender is secured. The estate is in the surrenderor till admittance; *Rex* v. *Wilson* (a). [*Patteson* J. In *Rex* v. *Dame Jane St. John Mildmay* (b), where the custom was that a copyholder convicted of felony forfeited to the lord, it was held that the forfeiture took place though the conviction was after the convict had surrendered, it being before the admittance of the surrenderee.] "No fine is due, either upon a descent or surrender, till admittance, for that is the cause of the fine; and therefore, if after admittance, the tenant deny to pay, it is a forfeiture:" 2 *Bac. Abr.* 224. (7th ed.). *Copyhold* (I.) 2.

Cur. adv. vult.

Lord DENMAN C. J., in this term (*November* 3d) delivered the judgment of the Court. After stating the substance of the writ, his Lordship proceeded as follows.

The return in substance states that the said lady of the manor and steward have refused to do what is required, because the said *Robert William King* and the said *James King*, *John Lyles King*, and *John King* refuse to pay any fine for the acceptance and enrolment of the said surrender. And whether any fine be lawfully due to the said lady of the manor, under these circumstances, is the question.

Against the return, and in support of a peremptory mandamus being awarded, it was contended that the lady has a tenant upon the roll who has paid a full fine;

(a) 10 *B. & C.* 80. (b) 5 *B. & Ad.* 254.

that

1838.

The Queen against The Lady of the Manor of Dullingham.

that the admittance of tenant for life is the admittance of him or them in remainder; that nothing was required by the acceptance and enrolment of the surrender but safe custody; and that, if any fine be due and payable, it becomes so only upon a tenant being presented for admittance, and after such admittance. Which several propositions, with the exception of one, may, as it seems to us, be admitted, without affecting the conclusion which they were advanced to establish. The exception to which we allude is, that the present was incorrectly assumed to be a case of tenancy for life, with a remainder or remainders dependent thereon; whereas we are apprised of no provision of the will of *Robert King*, except the devise of a life estate to his wife; and therefore the interest of the heir was clearly reversionary, and not a remainder. For reasons, however, which will appear presently, we do not consider it necessary to pursue this distinction. Still less is it requisite, for the purposes of the present discussion, to consider the nature and extent of the heir's interest in a copyhold before admittance. This subject was very fully entered into by this Court in the case of *Right dem. Taylor* v. *Banks* (*a*), and by the Lord Chancellor *Brougham* in *King* v. *Turner* (*b*). That the heir is, for many purposes, perfect tenant of the land before admittance, especially as to strangers, is true; but he is not *as to all*. The general rule and the exception are given with sufficient distinctness in *Coke's Copyholder*, section 41. (His lordship here read the passage cited in argument, antè, p. 865.) Again in *Brown's Case* (*c*) we find

(*a*) 3 *B. & Ad.* 664.

(*b*) 1 *Mylne & K.* 456.

(*c*) 4 *Rep.* 22 *b.*

that

1838.

The QUEEN against The Lady of the Manor of DULLINGHAM.

that the "heir may surrender to the lord to the use of another before admittance, as any other copyholder may, *but it cannot prejudice the lord of his fine due to him* by the custom of the manor upon the descent." Also in *Brown* v. *Dyer* (*a*) it is said, "The heir may surrender before admittance, because he has a title by descent. *But the lord in this case shall have a fine.*" In *Morse* v. *Faulkner* (*b*) it is said, "In copyholds the heir takes without actual admittance, and may surrender and convey without it, which he could not do if he were not seised; *but the lord is in that case entitled to the double fine on the surrender.*" See *Fearne's Posthumous Works*, p. 106. (*Cases and Opinions.*)

The lady of the manor, it is to be observed, in the present instance, seeks for nothing. There is no demand, on her part, to the heir to come in and be admitted, in order that she may become entitled thereby to the accustomed fine. The demand is *upon her* to do an act; and she insists that the demand can only be made by one who is (in the language of Lord *Coke*) "to all intents and purposes" a tenant of her manor. This case, therefore, has no resemblance to those in which a question has arisen between the heir and a stranger. Here it is a mere question of right between the lady of the manor and the heir; and, upon such a question, we think she is entitled to have (as we find him called) a "*complete tenant.*" The payment of a fine is the method by which, according to all the authorities above referred to, a recognition is made of the title under which he holds, and, according to all of them, a fine becomes due upon an act being done like the pre-

(*a*) 11 *Mod.* 73.

(*b*) 1 *Anst.* 11. See p. 13.

sent.

1838.

The QUEEN *against* The Lady of the Manor of DULLINGHAM.

sent. In conformity hereto also, it seems, was the opinion of Mr. *Fearne*, which, in addition to the weight justly due to it from his great and acknowledged accuracy and precision, in the recent case of *Doe dem. Perry* v. *Wilson* (a) was recognised by this Court as to the point now immediately under consideration. The subject is thus treated: "There can be no question, that the heir is compellable (if the lord please) to come in and pay the fine due on a descent; and it is said, that where the lord is to have a fine, there must be a new admittance; vide *Moor*, 465. (b) If so, I should think the lord may (if he please) refuse a surrender by the heir, until he has paid the fine on the descent. Indeed, if he could not, the lord might be disappointed of his fine; for after the accepting of the surrender tendered by the heir, though a conditional one, and the surrenderee's being admitted on the forfeiture of the condition, who of course could be liable to only the alienation fine on such an admission, where would be the lord's remedy for his fine upon the descent? And though the lord cannot compel the heir to come in and be admitted, and pay his fine, during the life of the tenant for life, yet if the heir require to surrender before, I apprehend, the lord may refuse accepting his surrender until he pay such fine; for otherwise he may be disappointed of it, by accepting the surrender from the heir to the use of a stranger, who would be entitled to admission under it (even though conditional, if forfeited), upon payment of the alienation fine only."

The question, it will be perceived, has been hitherto considered as if the application had been made by the heir

(a) 5 *A. & E.* 321. See p. 324. (b) Pl. 658. *Tiping* v. *Bunning*.

of

1838.

The QUEEN *against* The Lady of the Manor of DULLINGHAM.

of the party last seised. If, however, it ought rather to be deemed an application by mere strangers, our observations will be applicable à fortiori. And in the writ of mandamus itself it is stated that the said parties of the third part to the said indenture to lead the uses of the said surrender, being desirous of having the said indenture enrolled by the said lady of the said manor, did cause application to be made to the said lady to receive and enrol the said surrender, for the purposes therein (that is, in the said surrender) mentioned. That is, persons wholly unconnected with the lady of the manor (so far as appears), either by duty or service, without any offer to acknowledge her as lady, but expressly refusing so to do, require her to do an act which none but a tenant is entitled to ask. Which act, it is moreover to be observed, is not calculated, or intended, in any degree to confirm or establish the life estate of the said widow, to which she had been admitted regularly, and had paid her fine accordingly, but for purposes wholly unconnected with and independent of it.

Upon the whole, therefore, we are of opinion that the return is good, and that a peremptory writ of mandamus ought not to go.

Return good (*a*).

(*a*) In the same term *B. Andrews* obtained a rule to shew cause why the Court should not give the defendants the costs of the mandamus and of that motion. In *Hilary* term following (*Thursday, January* 31st, 1839) *Wightman* shewed cause, and *B. Andrews* was heard in support of his rule. The Court (Lord *Denman* C. J., *Littledale*, *Williams*, and *Coleridge* Js.) discharged the rule, saying that it was a matter of discretion, and that the point decided in the principal case was a very doubtful one. See *Rex* v. *The Commissioners of the Thames and Isis Navigation*, 5 *A.* & *E.* 804, 816.; *Regina* v. *St. Saviour's, Southwark*, 7 *A.* & *E.* 925, 948.

1838.

Wednesday, November 21st.

CARNABY *against* WELBY, WINDOVER, and Others.

In trespass for breaking and entering plaintiff's house and taking his goods, defendants pleaded, as to the house, that plaintiff was not possessed thereof; and, as to the goods, that they were not plaintiff's property. Issues were joined on these pleas. Defendants also pleaded, as to the breaking and entering, two other pleas, justifying under a fi. fa. and warrant of execution against the goods of one *B.*, which warrant was duly delivered to one of the defendants, a bailiff, to be executed; that goods of *B.* liable to be taken under the execution were in the house, and that, by virtue of the writ and warrant, defendants, being the sheriff, bailiff, &c, broke and entered &c. Replication, that although the writ issued and was delivered to the sheriff, and the warrant was made by him and delivered to the bailiff, in manner and form &c., nevertheless defendants, *of their own wrong and without the residue of the cause in their plea alleged*, committed the trespasses &c. Issue thereon.

On the trial, plaintiff proved that he was in possession of the house and goods, which had been conveyed to him by *B.*, and that the house was entered and the goods taken by defendants, as under the process of execution against *B.* The case for the defendants was, that the conveyance was fraudulent. The Judge, in summing up, told the jury that on the pleadings it was admitted that the goods were bonâ fide taken in execution under the writ; on which point, therefore, he did not ask their opinion; and that the main question was, whether or not the property was in plaintiff, the burden of proving which fact lay on him: Held a misdirection. For

1. The replication de injuriâ suâ absque residuo causæ admitted the issuing of the writ and warrant, and the delivery of the warrant to the bailiff, but not that the seizure was under the warrant.

2. The fact that the seizure was under the warrant was traversable.

3. That fact not being admitted on the record, and no evidence of it having gone to the jury, the defendants were in the situation of wrongdoers, against whom possession alone was a sufficient title.

4. That the plaintiff, having proved possession, might recover in respect of the goods as well as the house, though he had, by his pleading, claimed *property* in the goods.

TRESPASS for breaking and entering plaintiff's dwelling-house and closes, and expelling him from the same, breaking open the outer and other doors of the house, making a noise therein, and continuing &c., and carrying away and converting goods &c., being in and about the said dwelling-house and closes.

Pleas. 1. Not Guilty. 2. As to breaking and entering the house and closes, &c., that plaintiff was not possessed of the said house, closes, &c. Conclusion to the country. Issue thereon. 3. As to the same trespasses, That the house and closes were the dwelling-house &c., soil and freehold, of *E. W.* Justification as servants of *E. W.* Verification. To this plea the plaintiff replied that the house &c. were his, and not

the

1838.

CARNABY against WELBY.

the house, soil, and freehold of *E. W.* Issue was joined on the traverse. 4. Plea, as to the goods, that the same were not the property of plaintiff. Conclusion to the country. Issue thereon. 5. As to breaking and entering the dwelling-house and closes, making a little noise &c., and continuing &c., and forcing the outer door &c., that a writ of fi. fa. had issued to the sheriff of *Lincolnshire* to levy on the goods of one *Bower* a debt and damages recovered against him in K. B., which writ was delivered to the said sheriff, the defendant *Welby*, to be executed; by virtue of which writ *Welby*, as such sheriff, made his warrant to the defendant *Windover*, then being his bailiff, commanding him to cause to be levied of the goods of *Bower* within the bailiwick the said debt &c., which warrant duly indorsed was delivered to *Windover*, being such bailiff, to be executed in due form of law. That, before and at the times when &c., divers goods of *Bower* liable to be taken in execution under the writ and warrant were in the said dwelling-house and closes in which &c. And that thereupon, under and by virtue of the said writ and warrant, *Welby*, being sheriff, and *Windover*, being such bailiff as aforesaid, and the other defendants in aid of the said sheriff and bailiff, and by command of the latter, at the times when &c., peaceably and quietly broke and entered &c., to seize, and did seize and take in execution, the goods of *Bower* so then being in the said dwelling-house and closes &c., for the purpose of levying &c. There was also a special justification, not material here, as to the breaking of the outer door. Averment that the trespasses were committed within the bailiwick, and before the return of the writ. Verification. 6. A similar plea as to breaking the doors other

1838.

Carnaby against Welby.

other than the said outer door, averring that the defendants necessarily forced and broke open the same, in order to take *Bower's* goods in execution under the said writ and warrant, and that they did within the said bailiwick seize the said last-mentioned goods in execution under and by virtue of the said writ and warrant, as they lawfully &c. Verification.

Replication to plea 5. That, "though a writ called a fi. fa. issued out of the Court of our Lord the King before the King himself, directed to the sheriff of *Lincolnshire*, and was, being duly indorsed, delivered to the said sheriff to be executed, who made his certain warrant, and delivered the said warrant to the said defendant *Charles Windover*, in manner and form as the said defendants in their said fifth plea have alleged, for replication nevertheless in this behalf, the said plaintiff says that the said defendants, at the said several times when &c., committed the said trespasses in the introductory part of the said plea mentioned, of their own wrong, and without the residue of the cause in their said fifth plea alleged, in manner and form as the said plaintiff hath above in his declaration complained" &c. Conclusion to the country. Issue thereon.

Same replication (mutatis mutandis) to the sixth plea. Issue thereon.

On the trial before Lord *Abinger* C. B., at the *Lincolnshire* Spring assizes, 1837, it appeared that the plaintiff, at the time of the alleged trespasses, was in possession of the premises and goods mentioned in the declaration, which had previously belonged to *Bower*, but had been conveyed by him to the plaintiff in 1835, by an agreement, under which the plaintiff now claimed. Evidence was given of the seizure, which appeared to have

1838.

CARNABY *against* WELBY.

have been made conformably to the process. The defendants called no witnesses, but endeavoured to shew, on the plaintiff's case, that the agreement was merely colourable, and that the plaintiff really held the premises and goods for the use of *Bower*. The Lord Chief Baron, in summing up, told the jury that, on these pleadings, the goods were admitted to have been bonâ fide taken under the execution, but the great question was, whether or not the property was the plaintiff's; whether there had been a bonâ fide transfer, or whether the plaintiff held under a secret trust for *Bower?* And he said that the plaintiff had the burthen cast on him of shewing the property to be in himself; and, if the jury were not fully satisfied on that point, they ought to find for the defendants. Verdict for defendants. In the ensuing term, a rule nisi was obtained for a new trial, on the ground of misdirection.

Balguy and *Goulburn* Serjt. now shewed cause. The plaintiff undertook to shew title, and not mere possession; the case, therefore, was rightly left to the jury. The second plea denies that the plaintiff was possessed of the house and closes; the fourth plea, that the goods were his property. These, therefore, virtually put in issue the validity of the transaction by which the premises and goods were transferred. [*Coleridge* J. If these had been the only pleas, the answer upon the evidence was that the plaintiff appeared to be in possession, and you to be wrong-doers. *Patteson* J. In *Heath* v. *Milward* (a), which was an action of trespass for breaking a close, the defendant pleaded that the close was not the plaintiff's:

(a) 2 *New Ca.* 98. See *Fleming* v. *Cooper*, 5 *A.* & *E.* 221.

 and

1838.

Carvalho against Welby.

and that plea was held to put only the possession in issue.] In this case the plaintiff, at the trial, stood on his title as under a bonâ fide conveyance; and therefore he ought not now to have the advantage of restricting himself to the possession. [*Patteson* J. In *Heath* v. *Milward* (*a*) the plaintiff, at the trial, did not stand upon a mere possession.] There the jury would not say whose the land was. Here they have, in effect, said that there was no bonâ fide transfer, thus negativing both property and, if there was fraud, even possession. The replication to the fifth and sixth pleas admits that the writ was issued, and the warrant made and delivered to *Windover* the bailiff, "in manner and form" as in the pleas alleged, but avers that the defendants committed the trespasses of their own wrong, and without the residue of the cause &c. That is, in effect, an acknowledgment that the entry was made and the goods taken under the writ and warrant: it was not necessary, therefore, for the defendants to prove that fact; and it lay on the plaintiff to shew that he had title under a bonâ fide conveyance.

Adams Serjt., *Hildyard* and *Humfrey*, contrà. The summing up was wrong, inasmuch as it excluded any inquiry as to the mere possession, and made the result of the case depend on the property. The second plea in terms put the possession in issue; and, as to the fourth, a plea of property in goods means property as against a wrong-doer, *Nicolls* v. *Bastard* (*b*); and, if so, the plaintiff, by merely being in possession, had sufficient property as against the defendants, unless their proceeding was covered by the writ and warrant. The learned Judge was incorrect in treating it as established that the

(*a*) 2 *New Ca.* 98.

(*b*) 2 *Cro. M. & R.* 659. *S. C. Tyrwh. & Gr.* 156.

goods

1838.

CARNABY *against* WELBY.

goods were bonâ fide taken under the execution; that was not proved, nor was it admitted by the replication to the fifth and sixth pleas. There was no admission on the record which connected the taking with the writ: if a bonâ fide seizure under the writ was not admitted by the replication to the fifth and sixth pleas, the defendants appear, on that part of the pleadings, to be wrongdoers. [Lord *Denman* C. J. The question is, what is put in issue by "de injuriâ absque residuo causæ"? In *Lucas* v. *Nockells* (*a*) it was admitted that the goods in respect of which the plaintiff sued were taken under the writ, but it was said the writ was made use of colourably. You would contend here that there was no seizure under the writ at all.] The question as to seizing by colour of the writ does not arise, unless the sheriff acted under the writ in taking the goods. *Lucas* v. *Nockells* (*a*) shews that, on pleadings like those upon the fifth and sixth pleas, it may be proved that the acts were not really done in execution of the writ, but under another claim, though that case is not strictly in point, because here the plaintiff contends that the seizure is not shewn to have been under the writ; there, from the particular circumstances, it was only necessary to contend that the seizure, if under the writ, was not bonâ fide made for the purposes of the writ. If the sheriff was not justified by the process in taking the goods, the plaintiff is entitled to recover on the fourth issue, according to *Nicolls* v. *Bastard* (*b*). And in *Ashmore* v. *Hardy* (*c*) *Patteson* J. held that, in trespass for taking goods, where the de-

(*a*) 4 *Bing.* 729. *S. C.*, on error, in *Dom. Proc.* 10 *Bing.* 157. See the pleadings more fully stated, *Lucas* v. *Nockells*, 1 *Mo. & P.* 783., 3 *Mo. & Scott*, 627.

(*b*) 2 *Cro. M. & R.* 659. *S. C. Tyrwh. & Gr.* 156.

(*c*) 7 *Car. & P.* 501.

1838.

CARNABY against WELBY.

fendant pleaded that they were not the goods of the plaintiff, it was sufficient for the plaintiff to prove possession without shewing title. The judgment of *Tindal* C. J. in *Heath* v. *Milward* (a) is to a like effect. It is observed that the jury there would not say whose land the close in question was: but that suggestion will not reconcile the judgment with the present decision; because the Lord Chief Baron here said that the burthen of proving property lay on the plaintiff. [Lord *Denman* C. J. The question still turns on the meaning of "absque residuo causæ," with the inducement. If that admits that the sheriff acted under the writ and warrant in making the seizure, he was not a wrong-doer.] The argument assumes that that point will be decided in the plaintiff's favour.

Lord DENMAN C. J. I come unwillingly to a conclusion in favour of making this rule absolute, because the case has been tried and decided on the merits. The Lord Chief Baron thought that the words "absque residuo causæ" in the replication to the fifth and sixth pleas put in issue nothing less than the actual right of property. *Lucas* v. *Nockells* (b) is a binding authority, and obliges us to hold the contrary. The Lord Chief Baron's view of that point was, therefore, incorrect. It occurred to me, as a distinction between this case and *Lucas* v. *Nockells* (b), that the only question entertained there was, whether the seizure was colourable, not whether it took place under the writ at all. But this distinction cannot be borne out. The rule must be absolute.

PATTESON J. I am of the same opinion. *Heath* v. *Milward* (a) decides that it was sufficient, in an action

(a) 2 *New Ca.* 98. (b) 4 *Bing.* 729.; 10 *Bing.* 157.

of

1838.

CARNABY *against* WELBY.

of this kind, as against wrong-doers, if the plaintiff had possession; and, if there had been any doubt on this point, it would have been a proper subject for inquiry by the jury. But the plaintiff clearly had possession; and the only question raised was, whether or not he had it by fraud? On the second issue, as to the house and closes, it was not competent to the defendants to go into that question. On the third issue there was no evidence. The fourth issue was, whether the goods were the property of the plaintiff, not merely, as on the issue respecting the house, whether he was possessed? Possession is evidence of property, but evidence only. In the present case it would have been better for the plaintiff to rely on that, nakedly, than to set up a lawful title, although this latter case, if established, was stronger. But the plaintiff does not now put his case as a case of title proved; he says that the fraud was at any rate a matter of doubt, and, if so, the jury should have been directed to find according to the actual possession; and in so putting it I think he is right. The defendants are not entitled to a verdict as against an actual possessor, while they stand in the situation of wrong-doers. Then as to the effect, on this point, of the replication to the fifth and sixth pleas. It might have been said that, when the delivery of the writ and warrant to the bailiff for execution, as mentioned in the pleas, was admitted by the replication, there was strong evidence to connect the seizure, as proved, with the warrant. That, however, is not relied upon; but it is said that the pleadings admit a seizure under the writ and warrant. Now *Lucas* v. *Nockells* (a) shews that a replication, admitting

(a) 4 *Bing.* 729.; 10 *Bing.* 157.

1838.

CARNABY against WELBY.

a writ and warrant, and adding "de injuriâ absque residuo causæ," admits no more than it does in terms admit. According to that case, the plaintiff, on such a replication, might shew that the seizure was merely colourable; but, if colourable, it was as no seizure; the plaintiff therefore might give in evidence on the present pleadings, that there was no seizure under the writ at all. And, if the plaintiff would be at liberty to shew such a state of things, did it lie on the plaintiff or the defendant here to shew that there had been a bonâ fide seizure under the writ? Clearly the party asserting that fact ought to have proved the affirmative on which he relied.

WILLIAMS J. It is sufficient, for the purpose of deciding as to a new trial, to look at the issue respecting the possession of the house: if the plaintiff is entitled to some damages on that, though the merits of the case may, upon the whole, have been disposed of, the rule must be made absolute. As for the replication to the fifth and sixth pleas, granting that that admitted no more than it professed in terms to admit, still there was some evidence that the seizure was made under the process. But the learned Judge, instead of relying on that, said that the fact was admitted on the pleadings. Then, there being nothing either on the record, or on the evidence left to the jury, to connect the seizure and process, the defendants were wrong-doers, against whom possession alone was a sufficient title.

COLERIDGE J. Every thing turns on the ruling as to the effect of the replication; and, for the reasons already given by the Court, I think the direction on that point was wrong. If the seizure under the warrant was traversable,

1838.

CARNABY *against* WELBY.

versable, and was not admitted on the pleadings, no evidence of it was submitted to the jury: I do not say there was none in the cause. The fifth and sixth pleas, therefore, may be laid out of consideration. Then no issue remains on which any evidence was tendered for the defendants. The case stood upon possession on the one hand, and an entry without lawful warrant on the other. On the fourth issue, the property in the goods must be looked at with reference to the situation of the parties in this state of the case. As against a wrong-doer there was property enough. There was clearly a sufficient possession of the house to bear out the plaintiff's case on the issue; but I think there was also a case as to the goods.

Rule absolute.

The QUEEN *against* LEWIS.

Thursday, November 22d.

An order of maintenance on the father of a bastard, under stat. 4 & 5 *W.* 4. c. 76. s. 72., need not shew, on its face, that the application was made to the next practicable general quarter sessions after the child had become chargeable. An order was held good, purporting to be made at the sessions held 29th *June* 1837, and stating that the child, on 6th *March* then last, by reason of the mother's inability, became and thence had been and still was chargeable.

The order recited as follows, "It being now duly proved to this Court," &c., that the child was on &c., at the parish aforesaid, born a bastard of the body of *E. J.* (not giving any further account of *E. J.*), and, on &c., by reason of the inability of the mother to provide for its maintenance, became and from thence hath been and still is chargeable to the said parish, "and that he, the said *R. L.*, is the father," and the evidence of *E. J.* having been corroborated &c., and the Court "*having heard all parties, and being satisfied* that the said *R. L.* is really and in truth the father of the said child, and it appearing to this Court to be just," &c., that *R. L.* should pay &c. The order then proceeded, "This Court doth therefore hereby order that the said *R. L.* do forthwith pay" &c. Held good, under stat. 4 & 5 *W.* 4. c. 76. ss. 71, 72., without any statement as to the mother's settlement, or any more express adjudication that *R. L.* was the father.

AT the *Montgomeryshire* quarter sessions, held 7th *April* 1837, the following order was made.

"In the matter of the application of the overseers of the poor of the parish of *Penstrowed*, for an order upon

1838.

The QUEEN against LEWIS.

Richard Lewis of" &c., "to reimburse the said overseers for the maintenance and support of the female bastard child of one *Elizabeth Jones*, chargeable to the said parish, and born on the 3d day of *October* last. Whereas it appears to this Court that, owing to the said *Richard Lewis* having keept out of the way to avoid being served with fourteen days' notice of this application, the said overseers have not had sufficient time to give such notice, it is ordered that the hearing of such application be, and the same is, hereby, deferred to the next general quarter sessions of the peace to be holden for this county."

At the quarter sessions for the same county, holden 29th *June* 1837, the following order was made.

"Whereas the overseers of the poor of the parish of *Penstrowed*, in the said county, did, on the 2d day of *May* last, give due notice to *Richard Lewis*, late of" &c., "of their intention to apply to this Court for an order upon him, the said *Richard Lewis*, as the putative father of a certain female bastard child, of which one *Elizabeth Jones* was then lately delivered, and which had then lately become chargeable to the said parish, to reimburse the said parish for the maintenance and support of the said child, and the said overseers having now made such application accordingly, and the said *Richard Lewis* being at the same time here present, and it being now duly proved to this Court, in the presence and hearing of the said *Richard Lewis*, that the said child was, on the 25th day of *October* last, at the parish aforesaid, born a bastard of the body of the said *Elizabeth Jones*, and that the said child, on the 6th day of *March* last, by reason of the inability of the said mother to

1838.

The QUEEN *against* LEWIS.

to provide for its maintenance, became and from thence hitherto hath been and still is chargeable to the said parish, and that he, the said *Richard Lewis*, is the father of the said child, and the evidence of the said *Elizabeth Jones* having been corroborated in divers material particulars by other testimony, and this Court having heard all parties, and *being satisfied* that the said *Richard Lewis* is really and in truth the father of the said child, and it appearing to this Court to be just and reasonable, under all the circumstances of the case, that the said *Richard Lewis* should pay unto the overseers of the poor of the said parish for the time being such sum or sums of money as they have expended, or may from time to time hereafter, during the time hereinafter limited, expend, for the maintenance and support of the said bastard child, not exceeding the sum of 1*s.* 4*d.* per week: This court doth therefore hereby order that the said *Richard Lewis* do forthwith pay unto the said overseers the sum of 1*l.* 8*s.* 4*d.*, by them expended for the maintenance and support of the said child from the 6th day of *March*, when the said child first became chargeable as aforesaid, to the present day; and that the said *Richard Lewis* do also pay unto the overseers of the said parish for the time being, weekly and every week from thenceforth until the said child shall attain the age of seven years, if the said child shall so long live and continue to be chargeable to the said parish, such sum or sums of money as shall be weekly expended" &c.

These orders having been brought up by certiorari, *Busby*, in *Michaelmas* term, 1837, obtained a rule for quashing the order of 29th *June* 1837. Cause was shewn

1838.

The QUEEN *against* LEWIS.

shewn in this term (*a*), when the Court desired to hear the objections to the order in the first instance.

Busby, against the order. First, the order contains no adjudication that *Lewis* is the father of the bastard. It merely recites, "it being now duly proved" to the Court that he is the father, and the Court, "being satisfied that the said *Richard Lewis* is really and in truth the father of the said child;" and then the Court "doth therefore hereby order" that he pay &c. Under stat. 18 *Eliz. c.* 3. *s.* 2. such an order would clearly be bad, for want of express adjudication; *Rex* v. *Pitts* (*b*). Then stat. 4 & 5 *W.* 4. *c.* 76. *s.* 72. provides that, if the Court "shall be satisfied" "that the person so charged is really and in truth the father of such child," it shall make the order. The order here follows the words of sect. 72: but that section does not prescribe the form of the order; nor does it interfere with the rule requiring an express adjudication. It merely points out the course of investigation which the Court is to pursue. The form given in 1 *D'Oyly* and *Williams's Burn's Just.* p. 388. *Bastards*, (*Forms*), contains an express adjudication. *Rex* v. *Kenworthy* (*c*) shews that the want of an express adjudication cannot be supplied. Secondly, the order shews no jurisdiction. In the first place, it does not appear that the child was legally chargeable to the parish which made the application. The chargeability is on the parish of the mother's settlement. [*Patteson* J. Suppose the mother had no settlement, or one a hundred miles from the place where the child was maintained in the

(*a*) *Saturday, November* 10th, before Lord *Denman* C. J., *Patteson*, *Williams*, and *Coleridge* Js.

(*b*) 2 *Doug.* 662.

(*c*) 1 *B.* & *C.* 711.

mean

1838.

The Queen against Lewis.

mean time.] The mother's inability produces a charge upon a parish only by the parish being bound to support the child; and that depends upon the mother's settlement (*a*). In the second place, the order fails to shew jurisdiction, because it appears that it was not made at the next general quarter sessions after the chargeability. [*Coleridge* J. Was not that a point entirely for the sessions? The question, what were the next practicable quarter sessions, involves many facts.] *Rex* v. *Heath* (*b*) shews that it must appear that the sessions were the next practicable sessions; here that is not apparent, even assuming that the language of sect. 72 is to be extended to the next practicable sessions (*c*). [*Coleridge* J. It appeared distinctly there that no evidence had been required at sessions of the application being made as soon as was practicable. Here, I suppose, the officers did make that appear to the sessions. *Patteson* J. The recital in the order of 29th *June* 1837 seems framed on a misunderstanding of sect. 73. It is said the overseers gave notice in *May* "of their intention to apply:" it should have been "of their having applied."] The order of 7th *April* 1837 cannot be looked to; for there is nothing to identify the persons named in the two orders.

Jervis in support of the order. This would certainly not have been a good order of filiation under stat. 18 *Eliz. c.* 3. *s.* 2., for want of an express adjudication that *Lewis* was father of the child; *Rex* v. *Pitts* (*d*), *Rex* v. *Perkasse* (*e*). It would also be bad under stat. 49

(*a*) See stat. 4 & 5 *W.* 4. c. 76. *s.* 71. *Rex* v. *Wendron*, 7 *A.* & *E.* 819.

(*b*) 5 *A.* & *E.* 343.

(*c*) See *Rex* v. *The Justices of Oxfordshire*, 5 *Dowl. P. C.* 116.

(*d*) 2 *Doug.* 662.

(*e*) 2 *Sid.* 363.

G. 3.

1838.

The QUEEN against LEWIS.

G. 3. *c.* 68. *s.* 1. But it follows the words of stat. 4 & 5 *W.* 4. *c.* 76. *s.* 72. [*Patteson* J. In the form in 1 *Chitty's Burn*, 385. (*a*) there is an express adjudication.] As to the first objection to the jurisdiction, a child may be chargeable to the parish where it is born before it is removed to its mother's settlement. [*Coleridge* J. The order is for payment till the child attain the age of seven years: can it be a case of casual poor?] The Court will construe liberally, as in *Regina* v. *Toke* (*b*). Even under the old acts it was not necessary to shew how the sessions came to their conclusion: here it is enough to find that the child is chargeable to the parish in question. [*Coleridge* J. The place of the birth was always stated.] Perhaps that was with a view of shewing the settlement hereafter. Who is to contest the settlement here, if stated? *Lewis* has no interest in doing so: he must pay to some parish. The order cannot be evidence against a party who has no opportunity of disputing it. The last objection taken to the jurisdiction assumes that the sessions must appear by the order to have been the first practicable ones: but the rule is, only, that this must be shewn in proof.

Busby, contrà. No distinct fact giving jurisdiction can be intended; *Rex* v. *Hulcott* (*c*), *Rex* v. *Davis* (*d*), *Day* v. *King* (*e*).

Cur. adv. vult.

Lord DENMAN C. J. now delivered the judgment of the Court. We are of opinion that this order of filia-

(*a*) Ed. 28. *Bastards*, s. 8. See *Archbold* on *The Act for the Amendment of the Poor Laws*, p. 28. 5th ed.

(*b*) Antè, p. 227.

(*c*) 6 *T. R.* 583.

(*d*) 5 *B. & Ad.* 551.

(*e*) 5 *A. & E.* 359.

tion

1838.

The QUEEN *against* LEWIS.

tion made by the court of quarter sessions is good. It recites that the child was born a bastard of *Elizabeth Jones*: "that the said child, on the 6th day of *March* last, by reason of the inability of the said mother to provide for its maintenance, became and from thence hitherto hath been and still is chargeable to the said parish;" that the defendant was the father, and the mother's evidence to prove him such had been corroborated. "And this Court having heard all parties, *and being satisfied that the said Richard Lewis* is really and in truth the father of the said child," proceeds to order him to reimburse the parish for the expenses already incurred, and make payments weekly for its support.

We disposed of the objection that the Court did not appear to be the next session, during the argument; but two others remain for consideration.

The first is founded on the authority of *Rex* v. *Pitts* (*a*), which requires an express adjudication by the justices of peace of every fact material to give them jurisdiction: the second is that, though the child is said to have become chargeable by reason of the mother's inability to maintain, the particular facts from which the inability results are not found by the Court.

The first objection is twofold. First: it does not *adjudge* defendant the father, but only states the Court *to be satisfied* of that fact. We think the words of the statute an answer to this objection. However strictly it may be proper to employ the regular legal terms in the proceedings of courts of justice, these are what the statute supplies for that purpose. But, secondly: this

(*a*) 2 *Doug.* 662.

satisfaction

1838.

The QUEEN *against* LEWIS.

satisfaction is not directly alleged, the order only saying that the Court, "being satisfied," makes the order. This we think a sufficient allegation. *Rex* v. *Pitts* (a) and the earlier cases do not depend on the grammatical form in which facts are found, but on their not being found at all (b).

The objection, that the circumstances which prove the mother's inability (which may be various) do not appear in the order, is also removed, we think, by the statute. The Court of quarter sessions must receive credit for having been convinced by proof of some such circumstances. It might be more convenient for parties to be apprised of the means by which they arrive at their conclusion; but the act mentions the conclusion of fact only, and does not require these particulars to be set out.

Rule discharged.

(a) 2 *Doug.* 662.

(b) See *Rex* v. *The Justices of Cambridgeshire*, 4 *A.* & *E.* 111.; *Rex* v. *The Marquis of Downshire*, 4 *A.* & *E.* 698.; *Rex* v. *Milverton*, 5 *A.* & *E.* 841.

The QUEEN *against* The Select Vestrymen of the Parish of ST. MARGARET, in the Borough and County of LEICESTER.

Thursday, November 22d.

BALGUY had obtained a rule nisi, in *Trinity* term last, for a mandamus commanding the select vestrymen of the parish of *St. Margaret*, in the borough and county of *Leicester*, to lay a rate for the support and repair of the churches and burial ground of the said parish, and for defraying all expenses incident thereto, and for other purposes to which church rates are by law applicable, for the present year.

The rule was obtained on the affidavit of the present churchwardens, which stated that certain persons therein named had been appointed Select Vestrymen of the parish under stat. 2 *W.* 4. *c.* x. (local and personal, public (*a*)), by order of justices in petty sessions, dated 30th

Where an act of parliament directs a body, created by the act, to levy church rates, this Court will compel them, by mandamus, to levy the rate, and will not confine the writ to ordering the body to assemble for the purpose of determining whether they will levy the rate or not.

And this, although the act contain a clause reserving all ecclesiastical jurisdiction, if it appear, from the rest of the act, that the temporal court was intended to have at least concurrent jurisdiction. As in the act for *St. Margaret's, Leicester*, stat. 2 *W.* 4. *c.* x., which gives powers of laying the rates to an annually chosen select vestry (excluding the ordinary authorities), and of levying the rates by distress and sale, authorises the select vestry to rate other than occupiers, and to compound and make allowances with certain parties rated, and gives an appeal against rates, &c., first to such select vestry, then to quarter sessions.

The churchwardens required the select vestry to lay a rate, *or* to do another act, which last was illegal. Held, nevertheless, a good demand of the rate.

The select vestry adjourned from time to time, on pretexts which the churchwardens alleged, upon affidavit, to be, as they believed, colourable and merely intended to evade laying the rate, requiring details which could not be furnished for want of funds to pay a surveyor, and fixing an adjournment day after which a mandamus could not have been obtained for some months. It appearing that a previous select vestry had pursued the same course, and the present select vestry not satisfactorily denying the imputed motive, this Court held the adjournments colourable, and equivalent to a refusal.

(*a*) "For better assessing and collecting the Poor and other Parochial Rates, and for the better Maintenance and Employment of the Poor, of the Parish of *St. Margaret* in the Borough and County of *Leicester*." Sects. 4 & 5 provide for the election by the inhabitants of the parish, qualified as in the act mentioned, on any fourth *Thursday* in *April*, of thirty persons,

1838.

The QUEEN *against* The Select Vestrymen of ST. MARGARET, LEICESTER.

30th *April* 1838, to continue in office till the fourth *Thursday* in *April* 1839, and until another vestry should be appointed. At a meeting of the Select Vestry on 21st

sons, qualified as in the act mentioned, of whom the justices in petty sessions shall appoint twenty, by writing under hand and seal, to be vestrymen; which twenty, with the vicar, churchwardens, overseers, and surveyors of highways, shall be the select vestry, to continue in office until the fourth *Thursday* in the *April* of the following year, and until another vestry shall be duly appointed. Sect. 13 makes five a quorum of the select vestry, of which five three are to be neither churchwarden, overseer, nor surveyor.

Sect. 32, and others following, provide for the making of surveys and valuations of houses, &c., in the parish, by the select vestry. Sect 39 enacts "That it shall be lawful for the select vestry for the time being of the said parish, and they are hereby authorised and required, from time to time as often as occasion shall require, to lay and assess upon all and every the tenants and occupiers of houses, lands, tenements, and other hereditaments and premises within the said parish, according to the respective annual value thereof, rates for the maintenance and relief of the poor of the said parish, and for defraying all expenses incident thereto or connected therewith, or for any purpose to which poor rates are or shall by law be applicable, and rates for the support and repair of the churches and burial ground of the said parish, and for defraying all the expenses incident thereto or connected therewith, or for any purpose to which church rates are or shall by law be applicable, and also rates for defraying the expenses to be incurred in repairing the highways, streets, and roads within the said parish, and all other expenses incident thereto or connected therewith, or for any purpose to which highway rates are or shall by law be applicable, such last mentioned rates not to exceed" &c. Sect. 40 enacts that four days' notice of any meeting for levying a rate be given to every select vestryman. Sect. 42 enacts that "no poor rate, church rate, or highway rate shall be made or raised within the said parish by any other ways or means than are directed by this act."

Sect. 62 empowers the select vestry to elect or remove the sexton, and from time to time to fix his remuneration or salary.

Sect. 63 enacts that the monies to be received under the church rates shall, after payment of expenses of collecting, &c., "be paid over by the said select vestry, and they are hereby required to pay over the same, to the churchwardens, or one of them, for the time being, to be by them or him applied and accounted for in manner as by law established." Sect. 65 enacts that the select vestry, on demand, shall pay and advance to

21st *May* 1838, the churchwardens delivered a written demand, reciting certain sections of the local act, and that the select vestry for the year then last past refused or

---

to the churchwardens and overseers of the poor, or reimburse to them, out of the poor-rates, "all sums of money to the payment of which the said churchwardens and overseers of the poor shall and may be liable by law, or which they shall have lawfully incurred or paid in the execution of their office, and for the payment and reimbursement of which the said churchwardens and overseers might lawfully have raised any special and distinct rate if this act had not been passed, or might have applied any money raised by them for the relief of the poor." Sect. 67 enacts, that it shall not be lawful for the churchwardens and overseers, or surveyors of highways, to levy or raise any rate within the parish for any purpose whatsoever.

Sect. 68 enacts, that all rates shall be paid by the tenant or occupier rated for the several lands, &c.; and, if any such tenant or occupier, or any other person made liable to pay, shall neglect to pay for seven days after demand, he shall be summoned before a justice, and, in case such party shall not attend and prove that he is not liable, he shall pay the rate, and, if the rate be not paid as therein mentioned, the rate and costs are to be levied by distress, under a justice's warrant, and sale of the goods. Sect. 69 enacts that, in case of sufficient distress not being found, the party shall be committed under a justice's warrant, &c. Sect. 70 gives power to proceed against parties quitting the lands, &c., by distress and sale, or imprisonment. Sect. 71 distributes the rate among successive occupiers in proportion to the time of occupation. Sect. 72 enacts that lessors, landlords, and owners, of houses, lands, &c., under certain circumstances, may be rated, instead of the actual occupiers: and the select vestry may compound with such lessors, &c., or make allowance for the houses, &c., having remained unoccupied. Sect. 75 enacts that, where the lessor, &c., is rated, the occupier, though not rated, shall still be liable, for the rates, to distress and sale, to the amount of his rent due, and may deduct sums paid or levied, &c., from the rent. Sect. 80 enacts that, when sufficient distress cannot be found, the select vestry may bring an action of debt, or special action on the case, for the rates, in any of the courts of record at *Westminster*.

Sect. 92 enacts, "That if any person shall think himself or herself aggrieved by any survey or valuation, or by any rate, or by any other act or matter made or done or arising under or in pursuance of this act, such person may appeal to the select vestry by or from whom or by or from whose act or order such cause of complaint shall arise, at any of their

1838.

The QUEEN *against* The Select Vestrymen of ST. MARGARET, LEICESTER.

or neglected to raise any monies by virtue of the said act, under church rates, or to pay and advance to the churchwardens for the year any money for defraying the expenses which they incurred in the execution of their office, and for which such churchwardens might have lawfully raised a special and distinct rate, if the act had not been passed: reciting also that the present churchwardens had necessary and immediate occasion for money for the repairs of the churches, and for such purposes as a church rate was by law applicable to for

---

their meetings," giving certain notice; "and such select vestry may examine any appellant and any witnesses touching the matter of such appeal, and may grant or refuse relief to the person or persons appealing, and make such order therein as to them shall seem meet." Sect. 93 enacts that, if any person shall think himself aggrieved by any survey &c., or rate &c. (as in the preceding section), "or by any order or conviction of any justice or justices of the peace, it shall be lawful for such person to appeal to some general or quarter sessions," &c., "within six calendar months next after the cause of complaint shall have arisen, or in case of an appeal against the confirmation of any rate by the said select vestry, then, on having paid such rate, to such general or quarter sessions of the peace within six calendar months next after such confirmation shall have been notified to the party," &c., either of which courts of session may hear and finally determine &c.; but the sessions are not to inquire into any appeal against any rate or thing made or done by the special vestry, unless complaint shall have been made to the select vestry by whose act or order the cause of complaint shall have arisen, and such select vestry shall have refused to give satisfaction, or have neglected to do so for ten days after notice, and to notify the same to the appellant. Sect. 94 gives power to the sessions to amend or quash the survey, valuation, or rate, and order new ones.

Sect. 103 enacts, "That this act or any thing herein contained shall not extend or be construed to extend to invalidate or avoid any ecclesiastical law or constitution of the Church of *England*, or to destroy or in anywise abridge or control any of the rights or powers of the Lord Bishop of *Lincoln* or the prebendary of the prebendal church of the said parish of *St. Margaret*, or of any other person or persons having ecclesiastical jurisdiction in or over the said parish, or in any manner to affect the jurisdiction of them or any of them in or over the said parish, or in or over any matter or thing concerning the churches of the said parish, or the ministers thereof."

the

1838.

The QUEEN against The Select Vestrymen of St. MARGARET, LEICESTER.

the present year: and requiring the select vestry forthwith to make a church rate and assessment upon the persons and premises liable to be rated to church rates, at the rate of 2*d.* in the pound on the annual value, or at and after such other rate as the select vestry should see fit, to the intent that the monies to be raised under such church rate might (after payment of attendant costs, &c.) be paid over to them the churchwardens, to be by them applied and accounted for in manner as by law established; "or we do hereby demand and require the select vestry of the said parish to pay and advance to us, as such churchwardens, out of the rates for the relief of the poor raised or received by virtue of the said act, an adequate sum for the necessary repairs of the churches, and for such other purposes as a church rate is by law applicable to, for the present year." Then followed a notification that, in case of refusal, a mandamus would be applied for. There not being a sufficient notice under sect. 40, the requisition was not taken into consideration at the meeting; and the select vestry adjourned to *Monday*, 4th *June*. On *May* 28th the churchwardens, as ex officio members of the select vestry, gave notice to all the select vestrymen that, on the said *Monday*, a meeting would be holden to lay a rate for the church. On that day, only four select vestrymen attended, being the two churchwardens, the vicar, and an overseer, all ex officio members. There not being a quorum under sect. 13, the clerk adjourned the meeting till 8th *June*, for which day a notice was given as before. The meeting took place on 8th *June*, when it was proposed and seconded that a church rate of 2*d.* in the pound should be laid; to which the following amendment was carried, "That, as, for several years,

 fresh

1838.

The QUEEN *against* The Select Vestrymen of ST. MARGARET, LEICESTER.

fresh charges have been introduced into the churchwardens' accounts which this vestry consider to have been illegal, the churchwarden be now requested to furnish each member of this vestry with a copy of the items of the expenditure he contemplates in the rate he now asks for, and that this vestry, at its rising, do adjourn, for the further consideration of this question, to *Monday* evening, the 18th *June* instant, at 6 o'clock." Before the amendment was put, the churchwardens stated that they were unable to enter into a minute detail of the particulars of the expected expenditure, and referred to an estimate delivered to the select vestry in the preceding *December*, adding that, from the want of supplies by the preceding select vestry, probably 200*l.* or a greater sum would now be wanted, and that the churchwardens could not employ a surveyor to make an estimate without incurring expense. The churchwardens deposed that, to the best of their knowledge, judgment, and belief, less than a rate of 2*d.* in the pound would not cover the expected expenditure (as to which they entered into some details); that they suspected that the select vestrymen, who did not attend on the 4th *June*, collusively absented themselves to prevent a quorum being formed, and for the purpose of delay; and that they believed that a majority of the present select vestry were desirous of procrastinating the matter without coming to a distinct refusal to lay a church rate, with a view of defeating the requisition, as had been done in the previous year; and one of the churchwardens, who had also been churchwarden for the preceding year, stated that similar applications to the preceding select vestry had been met by repeated adjournments, which he detailed, one of which was on the

1838.

The QUEEN *against* The Select Vestrymen of ST. MARGARET, LEICESTER.

the alleged ground of an illegality in some items of an estimate of the expected expenditure submitted by the deponent to the then select vestry: and that the then churchwardens had, in consequence of the repeated postponements, been induced to make a demand for an advance out of the poor rate, under a special clause in the act, which demand, however, had not been complied with.

The affidavits in answer, by sixteen of the select vestry elected under the act, stated (amongst other allegations not materially differing from the statement on the other side) that *Monday*, 4th *June* 1838, was *Whit-Monday*, and deponents believed that, when that day was named, this did not occur to any of the select vestrymen then present; but that, from the day falling on *Whit-Monday*, many of the deponents had engagements, and it was generally inconvenient to the members to attend. That nineteen select vestrymen attended on 8th *June*. That the deponents conceived it to be their duty, before levying a rate, to obtain some kind of detailed statement or estimate, and not to act simply on the suggestion of the churchwardens: that a minute statement had never been required, but only a copy of the items of the expenditure contemplated; but that the churchwardens merely referred to a statement which they alleged to have been previously delivered to the select vestry of the preceding year, accompanied by a demand for an advance out of the poor rates, and required that a rate of 2*d.* in the pound should be forthwith levied, stating that probably 200*l.* would be required. That deponents were informed and believed that a rate of 2*d.* in the pound would produce about 436*l.* That they believed that the churchwardens could readily have furnished the account required from the accounts

 of

1838.

The QUEEN *against* The Select Vestrymen of ST. MARGARET, LEICESTER.

of former churchwardens; and that they had reason to, and did, believe that in preceding years illegal items of expenditure had been defrayed from the church rate. That, although the appointment of the sexton, and fixing of his salary, was in the select vestry (under sect. 62), the churchwardens had been in the practice of paying him out of a salary from the church rate, in addition to his fees, which fees the deponents considered to be a sufficient remuneration; and that the sexton had agreed with them that his remuneration should be confined to such fees. That they were advised that they were not authorised to make the advance out of the poor rate, under the clause referred to (sect. 65). That the deponents, being of opinion that further informaation was necessary, "did adjourn the consideration of the said question for a period of ten days only in order to afford an opportunity for the said churchwardens to furnish such information," and that the vestry broke up under the impression, entertained, as deponents believed, by the majority, that the churchwardens were content with the resolution, and could furnish the information by the next meeting. That the information was not furnished, but a copy of the present rule nisi was served on the select vestry at the meeting on 18th *June;* and the deponents pointed out that the affidavit, on which the rule was obtained, was sworn on 9th *June*, the day after the adjournment. That the deponents had not refused to take the requisition into consideration, and had been perfectly willing to enter into the consideration of it, provided the churchwardens would have supplied them with proper estimates and information.

Sir *J. Campbell*, Attorney-General, *Waddington*, and *Mellor*, now shewed cause. First, this is not a case for a mandamus

1838.

The QUEEN against The Select Vestrymen of St. MARGARET, LEICESTER.

a mandamus, but is merely matter of ecclesiastical jurisdiction. This is clearly so as to church rates in general; *Rex* v. *The Churchwardens of St. Peter's, Thetford* (a) (where *Thursfield* v. *Jones* (b) was cited), *Rex* v. *Wilson* (c). It is true that, in general, where a statute requires a rate to be laid, this Court has jurisdiction: but here, though sects. 39 and 42 impose the duty of laying the rate upon the select vestry, yet sect. 103 saves the ecclesiastical jurisdiction. The utmost that the Court will do will be to order the select vestry to assemble *in ordine ad*, to take the subject into consideration; *Rex* v. *The Churchwardens of St. Margaret* (d). Further, this application must be refused on the merits. A mandamus is granted only when other means fail. Here the churchwardens need only furnish a proper estimate, to have this demand taken into consideration. There has been no refusal, but merely an adjournment of the question: and, in default of specific information, the select vestry could perform their duty no otherwise than by adjourning, especially as they had reason to apprehend that the calculation of the churchwardens was founded on illegal items, as, for instance, the salary of the sexton. The only pretext for treating the adjournment as colourable is founded on the proceeding of the previous select vestry; but that affords no fair inference as to the motives of the present one. Again, there has been no legal demand; for the demand of the rate was accompanied by an illegal alternative, namely, an advance from the poor rate. This, at least, justified an adjournment for the purpose of consideration. And the rate demanded appears, on affidavit, to be much beyond what was required.

(a) 5 *T. R.* 364.
(b) 1 *Vent.* 367.
(c) 5 *D. & R.* 602.
(d) 4 *M. & S.* 250.

Balguy,

1838.

The Queen against The Select Vestrymen of St. Margaret, Leicester.

Balguy, contrà. The adjournment was colourable: the whole series of facts shews this: and the motive is not denied by the affidavits in opposition. The demand is not absolutely of the twopenny rate, but of that or such other as the select vestry think fit to lay. Instead of determining the amount, the vestry attempt to evade the consideration altogether. As for the improper item mentioned, it was competent to the select vestry to frame the rate in proportion to the legal expenditure. (He was then stopped by the Court.)

Lord Denman C. J. One purpose of this act appears to have been to provide for the maintenance of the churches and burial ground of the parish. A preceding select vestry refused to comply with the act; and the present one has adopted the same system. An application is made for a rate, accompanied, indeed, by a demand of something else, in the alternative, but which alternative may be rejected. The question then is, whether there has been a refusal of the church rate. It does not seem to be denied that, if the refusal be merely colourable, the writ must go. Now here the imputation is that the present select vestry are pursuing the same course as the preceding one: if this were denied, the case might be different. Their excuse is, that the churchwardens refused to give them a detail of the items of the expected expenditure. That refusal was capable of explanation; and I think the explanation given by the churchwardens is perfect. They say, the church wants repair, and we have no money to pay a surveyor for estimating the amount. Had they employed the surveyor, a rate laid for the purpose of paying him might, at a future time, have been

1838.

The QUEEN *against* The Select Vestrymen of ST. MARGARET, LEICESTER.

been objected to, as retrospective. The churchwardens, therefore, applied for the means of taking the initiative step. Then the meeting adjourn to a day, after which, as they knew, there would be no opportunity, for a long time, of applying for a mandamus. I think, upon this, the churchwardens were justified in applying to this Court for a rule. Then comes the question, to what extent the rule is to go. For, if *Rex* v. *The Churchwardens of St. Margaret* (a) be good law, and applicable here, we can only order the select vestry to assemble and come to such resolution as they think right. But, here I think we are not so limited. The act directs that the rate shall be laid; and we have full power to enforce a compliance with the act, whether the Ecclesiastical Courts have jurisdiction or not.

PATTESON J. I cannot avoid the conclusion that the adjournment was colourable merely. With respect to *Rex* v. *The Churchwardens of St. Margaret* (a), to which my Lord has adverted, I will only add that, in that case, there was no select body. All that the acts of parliament had done there was to carve out a new parish: but the rate was still to be made by those who had the power to make it at common law: and there, accordingly, the Court said that they would not compel the making of a church rate. But here, whether an Ecclesiastical Court would have jurisdiction or not, the merely saving their power cannot exclude ours. We have, therefore, jurisdiction.

WILLIAMS J. The argument raised from the fact that the demand was for a twopenny rate, which is said

(a) 4 *M. & S.* 250.

to

1838.

The Queen *against* The Select Vestrymen of St. Margaret, Leicester.

to be more than was wanted, has been answered: the demand was of that rate or such other as might be considered requisite on the occasion. I think the churchwardens were entitled to demand a rate at this stage: they had no means, without it, of paying the surveyor; that is not denied. The whole proceeding savours of affected delay in order to get rid of the rate. As to the question of jurisdiction, the act shews that this was an affair of temporal cognisance. There is an appeal given to the quarter sessions in the event of failure on an appeal to the vestry.

Coleridge J. The question as to the refusal has been already exhausted: I will only add that it would have been satisfactory if, during the long interval which has taken place since this rule was obtained, the select vestry had taken some step towards doing that which they do not deny to be necessary, and to have long been necessary. I am satisfied that the adjournment was merely colourable. As to the demand having contained an alternative which is said to be illegal, I could understand the objection if the demand had been to do the whole, a part being illegal: but no objection of the sort can arise when the demand is only to do one of several things, provided any be legal. The question as to the jurisdiction is of more importance. The case does not resemble *Rex* v. *The Churchwardens of St. Margaret* (a). I do not, as to this, rely on any possible peculiarity in the saving clauses of the two acts; for I think it better not to rest upon subtle distinctions, and will assume that the saving clause is the same in each. But, in each, the saving clause must be

(a) 4 *M. & S.* 250.

interpreted

1838.

The QUEEN *against* The Select Vestrymen of St. Margaret, Leicester.

interpreted with reference to the whole of the act. Now, in the present act, when I find that the matter is made throughout one of temporal jurisdiction, I must infer that sect. 103 had some other purpose than that of excluding temporal jurisdiction. Sect. 39 authorises and requires the select vestry to lay the rates. Sect. 68 gives powers of enforcing the rate different from those which exist in ordinary cases. Sect. 72 also gives powers which the Ecclesiastical Court does not possess. Sect. 93 gives to any person thinking himself aggrieved by any rate an appeal, first to the select vestry, next to the quarter sessions. If any effect whatever is given to those clauses, how can it be said that the ecclesiastical jurisdiction is not interfered with (*a*)? Construing, therefore, sect. 103 with the rest of the act, whether or not the Ecclesiastical Courts have a concurrent jurisdiction, this Court, at all events, has jurisdiction.

Rule absolute (*b*).

(*a*) See *Regina* v. *St. Saviour's, Southwark*, 7 *A. & E.* 935. note (*a*).

(*b*) The following case was decided in *Easter* term, 1839.

The QUEEN *against* The Commissioners of the Navigation of the Rivers THAMES and ISIS.

Tuesday, May 7th, 1839.

By an inland navigation act, 35 *G.* 3. *c.* 106., it was enacted, that any person aggrieved by the works might complain to the commissioners of the navigation at one of their meetings, and they should hear such complaint, and report upon it to a subsequent meeting, which should make such order and give such satisfaction as should be thought just and reasonable; with an appeal to quarter sessions, by any party dissatisfied with any judgment of the commissioners.

A party aggrieved required satisfaction of the commissioners (*October* 6th), and had several communications with them, but received no definite answer. He then (*January* 18th) demanded, in the manner prescribed by the act, that the commissioners should, at their next meeting, hear and report upon his complaint, stating that he would, on that occasion, be prepared with evidence of the alleged injury. His agent attended the meeting (*February* 8th) with the witnesses, but they were ordered to withdraw, and no adjudication was made on his complaint, the previous question being moved and carried. No explanation was given to the complainant. The commissioners had, on his first application, laid a case before counsel, but had not been able to obtain the opinion by *February* 8th, for which reason they made no communication to the complainant, fearing that, if made, it might be treated as an adjudication. The opinion was obtained (*March* 24th)

A rule nisi was obtained, in *Easter* term (16th *April*), 1839, for a mandamus to the above-named commissioners to hear, report, and adjudicate upon the complaint and claim of *George* Lord *Boston*, for compensation

1838.

The QUEEN *against* The Select Vestrymen of St. MARGARET, LEICESTER.

24th) too late, as the commissioners alleged, for notice to be given to the complainant of a hearing at their next meeting (*March* 30th). After that meeting, and before the subsequent one, the complainant moved for a mandamus to the commissioners to hear and report upon his complaint.

Held, that the conduct of the commissioners was a virtual refusal to hear. Rule absolute, with costs.

pensation for injury sustained by him, and which he might thereafter sustain, by the erection of a certain weir &c. The facts relative to the refusal to hear, &c., (which alone came in question) appeared, by the affidavits in support of the rule, to be as follows.

The commissioners completed the weir on 20th *September* 1837, on which day Lord *Boston*'s agent complained on his behalf that it would impede the navigation of the *Thames*, and thereby injure him, and required that it should be removed. This was refused. At a general meeting of the commissioners, held 6th *October* 1838, Lord *Boston* gave them notice in writing, dated 5th *October* 1838, that he thought himself aggrieved by the erection of the weir, and did, by that notice, complain thereof to them, according to the statute &c., and require them to make him reasonable satisfaction for the injury he had sustained, and might thereafter sustain, by the loss of the trade &c. The complaint was read at the meeting; but nothing done. On 20th *October* 1838, the clerk of the commissioners, in answer to an inquiry by Lord *Boston*'s agent when the next general meeting would be holden, stated that it would be holden on 9th *November* (as specifically appointed by act of parliament), and that there was no chance of the matter being then reported upon. Several communications afterwards passed, as to the time when it was probable that Lord *Boston*'s claim would be considered, in one of which the clerk assured Lord *Boston*'s agent that there was no intention of taking him by surprise, and that he should be furnished with information a sufficient time before the meeting. On 29th *December*, the commissioners, in answer to an inquiry by Lord *Boston*'s agent, informed him that they did not intend to adjudicate on the claim then, and could not anticipate the business of the next meeting. On 18th *January* 1839, Lord *Boston* gave a written notice, dated 15th *January* 1839, to the commissioners at their general meeting, stating some of the above facts, and that he was further injured by the delay, and apprising them that he should be prepared with, and offer, evidence, at their next general meeting, of the injuries he had sustained and was likely to sustain by the weir &c.; and that he required the commissioners of the navigation, to be assembled at the next general meeting to be holden, &c., on 8th *February* next, to hear and report upon his said complaint, and to make such order, determination and judgment thereon as was just, and give such satisfaction to him as was reasonable; and that, on neglect or refusal, he should take such legal steps as should be advised. Lord *Boston*'s agent attended with witnesses at the meeting on 8th *February*, when the commissioners resolved that all persons not qualified to act should leave the room. Lord *Boston*'s agent, after demanding an adjudication, left the room. One of the commissioners then moved that the meeting should adjudicate on Lord *Boston*'s claim; upon which the previous question was put and carried. A commissioner then moved that the claim should be referred to a general committee, with a request that they should report at the next general

1838.

The QUEEN *against* The Select Vestrymen of ST. MARGARET, LEICESTER.

general meeting; upon which the previous question was again put and carried.

Stat. 35 *G.* 3. *c.* 106. *s.* 22. enacts that, if any person shall think himself aggrieved, damaged, or injured by any work made by the commissioners (acting under that and prior statutes for the improvement of the navigation), or by the operation or effect of such work, and shall make complaint thereof in writing to the commissioners at any district meeting, or at any general meeting, under his hand, the commissioners shall hear and report on such complaint to the next or some other subsequent general meeting; and, at such next or subsequent general meeting, the commissioners shall make such order, determination, and judgment thereon as to them shall seem just, and give such satisfaction to the party complaining as they shall think reasonable; and an appeal is given to the sessions if the party shall be dissatisfied with such order, judgment, or determination.

In opposition to the rule, it was deposed that the notice of 5th *October* 1838 was handed to the commissioners at the meeting of 6th *October* 1838, and was, at the next general meeting, referred to a general committee, who instructed their attorney to lay a case before counsel for his opinion, which was done. That, on receiving the notice of 15th *January* 1839, the general committee directed the attorney to endeavour to procure the opinion before *February* 8th. That he endeavoured to do so, but could not, in consequence of the illness of their counsel. That the commissioners were in doubt whether the subject-matter of the complaint was within the act, but had endeavoured to defer considering the complaint until they should have obtained the opinion, without actually refusing to hear; it having been decided, in *Rex* v. *The Commissioners of the Navigation of the Rivers Thames and Isis* (5 *A* & *E.* 804.), that such a refusal to hear was an order, determination, and judgment, from which an appeal lay to the sessions; for which reason, the previous question was moved: that counsel's opinion was not obtained by the clerk until after 24th *March* 1839, the then next general meeting being on the 30th *March* 1839, before which day sufficient notice could not be given to Lord *Boston*'s agent, according to the promise made to him by the clerk; and the complaint was therefore not taken into consideration on 30th *March*. That the next meeting after that would be on 8th *May* 1839; and the clerk deposed that he intended to advise the commissioners, at that meeting, to hear and report, and had no reason to doubt that they would do so; that on 25th *April* 1839 the attorney for the commissioners, after being served with the present rule, had stated to Lord *Boston*'s attorney that it was not intended on *February* 8th to refuse an adjudication, but that the commissioners had waited for counsel's opinion, which had since been obtained: and the attorney proposed that the rule should stand over until after the meeting of *May* 8th.

Kelly and *T. F. Ellis* now shewed cause. The application is premature, for there has been no refusal to hear. The reason for moving the previous

1838.

The QUEEN *against* The Select Vestrymen of ST. MARGARET, LEICESTER.

previous question on *February* 8th is explained by the affidavits on behalf of the commissioners. It would have been a breach of their duty to decide upon a course of proceeding without having obtained counsel's opinion; and they were anxious to avoid giving any answer to Lord *Boston* in the mean time, lest it should be construed into an adjudication, or refusal to adjudicate. *Rex* v. *The Brecknock and Abergavenny Canal Company* (3 *A. & E.* 217.), and particularly the judgment of Lord *Denman* C. J. there, shews that facts like those now before the Court do not amount to a refusal. Had the postponement been merely colourable, it might have been treated as substantially a refusal, as in *Regina* v. *The Select Vestrymen of St. Margaret, Leicester* (antè, p. 889.); but the facts here negative that construction. Nothing previous to the 8th of *February* can be properly taken into consideration; for Lord *Boston*'s first notice, requiring the commissioners at once to make him satisfaction, was one which they could not legally comply with. Supposing that the commissioners ought to have given some explanation to Lord *Boston* on *February* 8th, which was omitted, the neglect in that particular cannot change the nature of the transaction, and make the postponement colourable in itself, so as to amount to a refusal.

Sir *J. Campbell*, Attorney-General, *Barnewall*, and *Hoggins*, contrà, were stopped by the Court.

Lord DENMAN C. J. No rule can be laid down for determining whether there has been a refusal or not. It is a waste of time to cite former decisions on the subject, as if the want of some one circumstance which existed in a former case would decide this. In the present instance Lord *Boston*'s agent attends the commissioners at their meeting of the 8th of *February*, with his witnesses; they are turned out of the room, and no explanation given. Afterwards comes the communication of *April* 25th. I think that Lord *Boston* could only understand from what had taken place that he must be put to his legal remedy. No satisfactory communication had been made to him, nor any time pointed out at which the commissioners would be willing to proceed. I think that he is entitled to have the rule made absolute.

LITTLEDALE J. I am of the same opinion. The commissioners, when applied to, might, as individuals, feel a difficulty in giving reasons for not proceeding; but that was nothing to Lord *Boston*. There may be a refusal by continued silence as well as by words.

PATTESON J. I do not see how Lord *Boston* could treat the conduct of the commissioners otherwise than as a refusal, no communication being made to him. It is represented to us that they would have heard the application on *February* 8th, but had not obtained counsel's opinion.

All

1838.

The QUEEN *against* The Select Vestrymen of ST. MARGARET, LEICESTER.

All this, however, turns on matter occurring behind the back of Lord *Boston*. He had his witnesses in attendance at the meeting of *February* 8th. I do not think much of their having been sent out of the room, where perhaps other business was to be done; but he was entitled to some answer, and none was given, the previous question having been moved on a proposal to adjudicate upon his claim. The commissioners had not then obtained counsel's opinion; but they had it before the next meeting; and they might then have made a communication to Lord *Boston*: that, however, they did not do. No sensible man could treat this otherwise than as a refusal.

(COLERIDGE J. was in the Bail Court.)

Sir *J. Campbell*, Attorney-General, moved for costs.

Kelly, contrà. The practice is to make that a separate application.

Lord DENMAN C. J. That may be so where a mandamus has been tried; but I think that the costs of this rule must be granted now.

Per Curiam,

Rule absolute with costs.

DOE on the Demise of HENRY HAMPTON *against* SHOTTER.

Thursday, November 22d.

Devise of freehold to testator's wife, during her life; and, after her decease, "my will is that my said freehold," "shall be then sold by my executors in trust" (parties before named), "and all the money to be equally divided between all my children or their heirs," "by my said executors." Held, that the executors took a power, not a legal estate.

ON the trial of this ejectment before Lord *Denman* C. J., at the last Summer assizes for *Surrey*, it appeared that the lessor of the plaintiff claimed as surviving executor and devisee under the will of his father, *William Hampton*, made in *August* 1800. The defendant insisted that, by that will, no legal estate passed to the executors. The will was as follows.

After appointing his sons *Henry* (the lessor of the plaintiff) and *William* joint executors in trust of the will, the testator proceeded. "I give, devise, and bequeath unto my wife *Elizabeth Hampton* all that my freehold

1838.

Doe dem. Hampton against Shotter.

freehold called *Moor's Platt*" (the premises in question), "in the parish of *Frensham*, in the county of *Surrey*, where I now dwell, with dwelling-house and all out-building, garden, lands, and premises, and all the appurtenances thereunto belonging, during the term of her natural life; and, after the decease of my said wife *Elizabeth Hampton*, my will is, that my said freehold called *Moor's Platt*, where I now dwell, shall be then sold by my executors in trust, and all the money to be equally divided between all my children or their heirs, and their names are as follows," *J. H.*, *E. H.*, *H. H.*, &c., "in equal parts, as equal as possible can be done, by my said executors in trust." *Elizabeth Hampton* and *William Hampton* died before the commencement of this action.

The Lord Chief Justice, being of opinion that a power only was given by the will, directed a nonsuit, but with leave to move to enter a verdict for the plaintiff.

Wordsworth (*a*), in this term, moved accordingly. The lessor of the plaintiff took a legal estate. Where lands are devised *to the executors to sell*, they acquire an interest in the lands; where the devise is merely *that the executors shall sell*, a power only is given; 1 *Sugd. on Powers*, 128, &c. (*b*). The present case falls within the first of these descriptions. The doctrine on this subject is further explained by *Barrington* v. *The Attorney-General* (*c*), *North* v. *Crompton* (*d*), and other authorities, cited in 1 *Sugd. on Powers*, 128—133. (*b*);

(*a*) *November* 6th. Before Lord *Denman* C. J., *Patteson*, *Williams*, and *Coleridge* Js.

(*b*) 6th ed. (*c*) *Hardr.* 419. (*d*) 1 *Ca. Chanc.* 196.

2 *Watkins*

1838.

Doe dem. Hampton against Shotter.

2 *Watkins on Conveyancing*, Part 2. 363. note (*a*); *Doe dem. Tomkyns* v. *Willan* (*b*).

Cur. adv. vult.

Lord DENMAN C. J. now delivered the judgment of the Court. We are of opinion that in this case nothing more than a power was given to the executors. The testator merely devised, in substance, that the lands should be sold by the executors. There will consequently be no rule.

Rule refused (*c*).

(*a*) 8th ed. (*Morley, Coote, Coventry* and *White*). (*b*) 2 *B.* & *Ald.* 84.

(*c*) See *Doe dem. Keen* v. *Walbank*, 2 *B.* & *Ad.* 554.; *Doe dem. Gratrex* v. *Homfray*, 6 *A.* & *E.* 206.; *Doe dem. Cadogan* v. *Ewart*, 7 *A.* & *E.* 636, 666.

The QUEEN *against* GREGORY.

Thursday, November 22d.

Libels were published, alleging that the Marquis of *B.*, then married and having children, had, at the time of such marriage, a former wife living, and issue by her; and that their claim to succeed him was in a course of litigation, the result of which would be to annul the present marriage, and bastardise the children.

A criminal information was moved for; and the marquis, his eldest son, his wife's brother, and other persons, made affidavit in support of the rule. The marquis admitted that he had cohabited with the lady said to have been his first wife, but his marriage with her, and all the other material statements in the libels, were negatived. Affidavit was made in answer, not confirming those statements, but throwing great blame on the marquis's conduct in his connection with the lady alluded to.

Held that, although the marquis himself might be too much inculpated to demand a criminal information, the rule should nevertheless be made absolute for the protection of his family.

A RULE nisi was obtained, in this term, for a criminal information against the defendant for libels published in a newspaper called *The Satirist*. The libels were contained in papers published on three successive *Sundays* in this year. They stated that the present Marquis of *Blandford* had, twenty years ago, eloped with a lady, and lived with her in *Scotland*, where she was introduced by him, and received, as his wife; that she was still living; that a marriage had taken place

between

1838.

The Queen *against* Gregory.

between them by recognition in *Scotland*, and could be established beyond doubt; that the matter was in a course of litigation; that there was issue of the *Scotch* marriage, and that, on its validity being proved, that issue would claim to inherit the dukedom of *Marlborough* after the marquis, and his marriage with the present marchioness would be annulled, and his offspring by her bastardized. The marquis and several other persons made affidavits in support of the rule, by which it appeared that, although the marquis had (as he admitted) cohabited with a lady, alluded to in the libels, from whom he separated himself before his present marriage, he had never married her or introduced her as his wife, nor had she been so received; and that no litigation had been commenced or contemplated on the subject, nor if such marriage had existed, would the issue have been entitled to inherit the dukedom. The marquis's eldest son, the Earl of *Sunderland*, made an affidavit stating his belief that the libel was intended falsely to impute that he, and his brothers and sister, were illegitimate; and another affidavit, contradicting some assertions in the libels, was sworn by the Earl of *Galloway*, brother of the Marchioness of *Blandford*. Affidavits in answer were put in, not supporting the abovementioned statements in the libels, but throwing great reproach upon the conduct of Lord *Blandford* towards the lady alluded to, by whom one of these affidavits was sworn.

Sir *J. Campbell*, Attorney-General, now shewed cause, and contended that, whatever might be the merits of the case as to the particular allegations of the libels, the Marquis of *Blandford* did not come before the Court blameless

blameless as to the matters therein referred to, and therefore could not demand a criminal information.

Sir *W. W. Follett* and *R. V. Richards*, contrà. The affidavits in answer do not justify the libels; and they state facts which the prosecutor has no opportunity of answering, and was not called upon to answer in the first instance by the publications complained of. And, further, this is not an application merely on behalf of the marquis. The scandal does not only affect his character, but attacks the fortune and station of his family. The rule ought to be granted at his instance: but they at least are entitled to redress.

Lord DENMAN C. J. This is an important application, and interesting both as to the parties whom it affects and the principles on which informations of this kind are to be granted. I have no difficulty in saying that, if it concerned Lord *Blandford* alone, I would not have consented to the present rule being made absolute. His own affidavit throws the greatest imputation upon his conduct towards the lady mentioned in these publications; and I cannot pronounce that her statements on the subject are perjured. But Lord *Blandford* is not the only party before us. His wife and family complain of an attack made upon them in their dearest interests and tenderest feelings, and that by a series of libels. The application brings before us a slander, which the affidavits in answer do not support. There is no pretence for saying that the marriage alleged in these libels ever took place. Considering both the interests of individuals, and the importance of warning those who traffic with character that they shall not do so with impunity, I think that we are bound to comply with this

 application;

1838.

The QUEEN *against* GREGORY.

application; and that Lady *Blandford*, and Lord *Sunderland* and the rest of the issue of that marriage, are entitled to have this rule made absolute.

PATTESON, WILLIAMS, and COLERIDGE Js. concurred.

Rule absolute (*a*).

(*a*) As to the circumstances under which, technically, a person may be considered party to a motion for a criminal information, see *Regina* v. *Thomas*, 7 *A. & E.* 608.

Thursday, November 22d.

The QUEEN *against* The DEPTFORD Pier and Improvement Company.

The *Deptford* Pier Company were authorised, by stat. 5 *W.* 4. c. xiii., to take lands for the purposes of the act, the compensation money to be assessed by a jury, on refusal by the proprietor to treat after notice, and in some other cases. If the company should not, within three years after the passing of the act, agree for or cause to be valued and paid for, according to the act, the premises to be purchased, the powers given them were to cease, except with consent of the owners and occupiers. Sect. 68 directed that, on payment of the purchase money assessed, either to the proprietor, or, if he should "not be able to make a good title," then into the Bank of *England*, in the manner and for the purposes specified by the act, it should "be lawful" for the company to enter, and the lands should from thenceforth vest in them. Sect. 80 empowered them to resell lands purchased but found unnecessary.

The company gave notice of treating for lands in the possession of *C.* A jury was summoned, and assessed the purchase money. *C.* offered to convey and give possession, but was unable to deduce a complete title, though he offered one which, as he contended, ought to be satisfactory. The company refused to complete the purchase. On motion by *C.* for a mandamus to them to pay the purchase money to *C.* or into the Bank:

Held, that an affidavit by *C.*, shewing merely that he was *not in a situation to complete the title*, and had suggested a payment into the Bank to save expense, was not sufficient for the writ.

Writ granted on affidavit shewing that *C.* had endeavoured to obtain a complete title, but could not.

After the assessment, and during the dispute on title, three years from the passing of the act expired: Held no ground for refusing the writ.

A RULE nisi was obtained, last *Trinity* term (*June* 13th), for a mandamus calling on the above-named company to pay *Christopher William Collier* the sums of 1320*l.* and 750*l.*, assessed by a jury on inquisition, as compensation to him for certain lands, or to pay him 750*l.*, and pay 1320*l.* into the Bank of *England* in the name and with the privity of the Accountant-General of the Court of Exchequer, to be placed to his account to the credit of the parties interested in

such

such lands, and to be subject to the order of the said Court.

1838.

The Queen *against* The Deptford Pier Company.

The company was incorporated, and empowered to make certain works, and to purchase lands, houses, &c. (including the premises here in question), by stat. 5 *W.* 4. *c.* xiii. local and personal, public (*a*); the purchase-money,

(*a*) "For making and maintaining a pier and other works at *Deptford* in the county of *Kent*." (Royal Assent, 12th *June* 1835.)

Sect. 53 enacts that, if the company shall not within three years next after the passing of the act agree for, or cause to be valued and paid for, as directed by the act, the premises thereby authorized to be purchased, or so much thereof as they shall deem necessary or proper for the purpose of the act, the powers thereby given them for such purpose only shall from thenceforth cease, except with the consent of the owners and occupiers respectively.

Sect. 60 provides for the assessment by a jury, if necessary, of "the sum of money to be paid for the purchase" of lands, &c., and the separate and distinct sums to be paid as compensation for damage, &c., as in case of refusal to treat after notice.

Sect. 68 enacts, "That upon payment or legal tender of such sum of money as shall have been contracted or agreed for between the parties, or assessed by any jury in manner aforesaid, for the purchase of any lands, tenements, or hereditaments," "or as a satisfaction or compensation for damages, as hereinbefore mentioned, to the proprietor of such lands" &c., "or such person as shall be interested therein or entitled to receive such compensation, within twenty-one days after the same shall have been so agreed for, determined, or awarded, or if the person so entitled or interested cannot be found, or shall refuse to receive the same, or shall not be able to make a good title to, or shall refuse to execute a conveyance or conveyances of the premises which shall be required for the purposes of this act, then upon payment of the said sum of money into the Bank of *England*, as hereinafter directed and required, for the use of such body or person as is interested or entitled as aforesaid, it shall be lawful for the said company, and their directors, agents" &c. "thereupon, and not before, to enter upon and take and use such lands" &c. "respectively, and then and thereupon the said lands" &c., "and the fee simple and inheritance thereof, or such part thereof as is or shall be of fee simple or freehold tenure, and the absolute estate and interest of such as shall be leasehold or of any other tenure, according to the nature and tenure of the same respectively, together with the yearly profits thereof, and all the estate, use, trust, and interest of any body or person therein, shall from thenceforth become vested in and be the sole property of the said company to and for the

1838.

The QUEEN *against* The DEPTFORD Pier Company.

money, or compensation for damage, to be assessed, if necessary, by a jury, as particularly directed by the act. On *November* 9th, 1837, the company gave *Collier* and some

---

the purposes of this act for ever; and such tender, payment, or investment shall not only bar all right, title, interest, claim, and demand of the person by whom the same shall or ought to have been made, but also" dower, estates tail, reversions and remainders. Provided that, until such payment, tender, or investment, the company shall not dig or cut any land, or take down, remove, or alter any messuage &c. for the purposes of the act, without leave of the proprietor entitled to such payment.

Sect. 74 enacts, "That if any money shall be paid, or agreed, or adjudged, or awarded to be paid, for the purchase of or damage to any lands" &c. taken for the purposes of the act, "which shall belong to any body politic, corporate, or collegiate, or to any feoffee in trust, executor," guardian, &c., "or other trustees for or on behalf of any infant," &c., "or other cestui que trust," &c., "such money shall, in case the same shall amount to or exceed the sum of 200*l*., with all convenient speed be paid into the Bank of *England* in the name and with the privity of the Accountant-General of the Court of Exchequer, to be placed to his account there *ex parte* 'The *Deptford* Pier and Improvement Company,' pursuant to" stat. 1 *G.* 4. *c.* 35. and the general orders of the said Court, to be applied, under the direction of the Court, on petition by the body or person who would have been entitled to the rents and profits, in purchase of the land-tax, discharge of debts &c., or otherwise, as by this clause is particularly directed. Sect. 75 provides for the disposal of purchase or compensation money below 200*l*. and above 20*l*., and gives an option to bodies or persons entitled to the rents and profits, to have the money paid into the Bank as above, or to trustees. Sect. 76 regulates the application of sums under 20*l*.

Sect. 77 enacts, "That in case the body or person to whom such sum of money shall be so ordered, awarded, or agreed to be paid for the purchase of any lands" &c., "to be purchased, taken, or used under or by virtue of the powers of this act, as aforesaid, shall refuse to accept the same, or shall not be able to make a good title to the premises, or shall refuse to execute such conveyance, or in case the person to whom such sum of money shall be so awarded to be paid as aforesaid cannot be found, or if the person entitled to such lands" &c. "be not known or discovered," it shall be lawful for the company to order such sum of money "to be paid into the Bank of *England* in the name and with the privity of the Accountant-General of the said Court of Exchequer, to be placed to his account to the credit of the parties interested in the said lands, tenements, and hereditaments (describing them,) subject to the order, control, and disposition

1838.

The QUEEN *against* The DEPTFORD Pier Company.

some other persons notice that a jury would be summoned to attend before the sheriff at &c., on &c., to assess the purchase-money for "all the estate and interest of you or any or either of you, or of any other person or persons, of and in all that messuage" &c. (including the premises in question), required by the company under the authority and for the purposes of the act: and also the satisfaction for damage &c. by reason of the company's works. *Collier* deposed, in his affidavit on the present motion, that he was, at the time of the notice, and of the inquisition and verdict after mentioned,

disposition of the said Court of Exchequer," which Court, on application by any claimant, may, in a summary way of proceeding, make order concerning the same.

Sect. 78 enacts, "That when any question shall arise touching or concerning the title of any body politic, corporate, or collegiate, or person, to any money to be paid into the Bank of *England* in the name and with the privity of the said Accountant-General of the said Court of Exchequer, in pursuance of this act, for the purchase of or in satisfaction for any damage to be done to any lands" &c., "or of any estate, right, interest, title, or charge in, to, or upon any lands" &c. "to be purchased, taken, or used for the purposes of this act, or to any bank annuities to be purchased with any such money, or to any dividends or interest of any such bank annuities, the body or person who shall have been in possession and enjoyment of such lands, tenements, or hereditaments, parts or shares, estates, interests, or charges, at the time of such purchase by the said company, and all bodies politic" &c. "or persons claiming under such bodies or persons, shall be deemed and taken to have been lawfully entitled to such lands" &c., "according to such possession, until the contrary shall be shown to the satisfaction of the said Court of Exchequer; and the dividends or interest of the bank annuities to be purchased with such money, and also the capital of such bank annuities, shall be paid, applied, and disposed of accordingly, unless it shall be made to appear to the said Court that such possession was a wrongful possession, and that some other body or persons was lawfully entitled to such lands, tenements, or hereditaments, or to any part or parts thereof, or to some estate or interest therein or charge thereon."

Sect. 80 empowers the company to resell lands which may be purchased by and conveyed to them but shall not be wanted for the purposes of the act.

1838.

The Queen against The Deptford Pier Company.

tioned, "well and sufficiently entitled as owner thereof" to the premises in question. The inquisition was holden, and a verdict given for 1320*l.* purchase-money, and 750*l.* compensation for damage. On the 15th *January* 1838, *Collier* sent his abstracts of title to the company. They insisted that, to complete such title, the pedigree of one *James Stephens* ought to be traced. *Collier* (as his solicitor now deposed) "not being in a situation to furnish" the required evidence, his solicitor wrote to the company stating this fact, and suggesting that the purchase-money should be paid into the Bank under sect. 77 of the act, which, he observed, would save expense, and afford protection to all parties. He added that, although the vendor was "unable to furnish the necessary documentary evidence to establish *James Stephens*'s pedigree," he considered *Collier*'s title to be such as the company ought to be satisfied with, assigning reasons for this opinion. After some further correspondence, in which the company still insisted upon proof of the pedigree, *Collier* gave them notice to pay the sums assessed, according to the terms of the present motion, stating that, on refusal, proceedings would be taken against the company, and that, on compliance, *Collier* was ready and willing to convey the premises to them, and give them possession. No payment was made or offered. *Collier* now deposed that he had always been, and still was, ready and willing so to convey and give possession on payment as before stated; and that he was, and had for several years been, "in possession, as the owner thereof," of the premises in question, and of the title-deeds. He also stated that a part of the property was ground on which he had been preparing to build; but that the company, in *January* 1836, gave him

1838.

The QUEEN against The DEPTFORD Pier Company.

him notice not to do so, as the land would be required for their purposes; whereupon he desisted. In answer to the above-mentioned notice, the company stated that they were ready and willing to complete the purchase on receiving the information before required. *Collier's* solicitor, in reply (*June* 12th, 1838), referred to his former observations.

Thesiger and *Twells* now shewed cause. Sect. 77 is not imperative, but only enacts that it "shall be lawful" for the company to pay the purchase-money into the Bank, if the vendor cannot make a good title. In sect. 74, which is meant to be imperative, the language is different. It is not reasonable that the company should be obliged to pay in this money without the certainty of obtaining a title. Sect. 80 empowers them to resell: the company in fact do not want this land, and would resell it; but if the title is not perfected they may be unable to resell. The claimant here ought to shew that he has made every effort in his power to complete the title, and is unable to do so. But he does not allege this; his objection appears to be only that it would be inconvenient and expensive. That is not a sufficient ground for insisting upon the extraordinary course pointed out by sect. 77. [*Patteson* J. referred to sect. 68.] That section vests the purchased lands in the company *on their entering*. Here they have not entered. [*Patteson* J. It does not matter to the company whether the vendor makes a good title or not, if, upon entering, they are protected against all the world.] That is a provision for the benefit of the company; they cannot be forced to take advantage of it by a vendor whose land is not wanted. [*Coleridge* J. Your objection to completing

1838.

The QUEEN *against* The DEPTFORD Pier Company.

completing the purchase is removed, if your title becomes good the moment you enter.] By sect. 53, the powers given by the statute cease if the company do not, within three years of its passing, agree for or cause to be valued and paid for, the lands authorised to be purchased. Both must be done within the three years. Here, therefore, the three years having expired, payment of the purchase-money, and entry, would no longer vest the land. The company, it is true, have given notice that the land would be required; but they have not touched any part of it (*a*).

Platt, contrà. Sect. 60 empowers a jury, summoned at the instance of the company, to assess "the sum of money to be paid for the purchase," that is, acquisition, of the lands required. Then several subsequent clauses protect the company against the consequences of making payment without receiving a sufficient title. [*Patteson* J. You do not shew that you are unable to make a good title, but only that it will cost you money.] It may be questioned whether the act obliges vendors to make a title. In the cases pointed out by sect. 78 the party in possession at the time of purchase is to be deemed lawfully entitled till the contrary is shewn. It is said that the company, if now obliged to take the land, will lose the protection of sect. 68, because three years have elapsed since the act passed; but the delay was their own fault. [Lord *Denman* C. J. Your difficulty is, that your affidavit does not shew inability to make a title. It rather appears that you could, but for the expense.

(*a*) See *Rex* v. *The Hungerford Market Company*, 4 *B.* & *Ad.* 327.; *Rex* v. *The Commissioners for improving Market Street, Manchester*, 4 *B.* & *Ad.* 333. note (*a*).

Patteson

1838.

The QUEEN against The DEPTFORD PIER Company.

Patteson J. The provision of sect. 68 seems confined to cases where the vendor is unable to make a title. *Coleridge* J. Waiving any question as to the lapse of the three years, I think the company is obliged to take a bad title, only where the vendor cannot make a good one. Here no evidence of that appears, except from the vendor's own letter]. At least the company should be required to state their excuse on a return.

Lord DENMAN C. J. No; the rule must be discharged.

PATTESON and COLERIDGE Js. concurred (*a*).

Rule discharged.

On a subsequent day of this term (*November* 26th) a rule nisi was again obtained, in the same form, upon affidavit stating the circumstances under which *Collier* became possessed of, and now claimed, the premises conveyed to him by *Stephens*, and reasons for which he believed *Stephens* to have been entitled to it, by inheritance from one *John Roe*; but *Collier* stated that, in consequence of advice received from his solicitors in *March* 1836, he had, after the passing of the company's act, made inquiry of *Stephens* and his agent as to the pedigree of *Stephens* and his relationship to *Roe*; and "that the result of such inquiries is that the said *James Stephens* could not satisfactorily make out his pedigree," or prove that he had title when he conveyed to *Collier*; wherefore *Collier* "hath always been, and still is, unable to make a good title" to that property. But he stated

(*a*) *Williams* J. had left the Court.

that

1838.

The QUEEN *against* The DEPTFORD Pier Company.

that he was still ready and willing to convey and give possession to the company on their paying &c., which they had not done. In *Hilary* term 1839 (*January* 30th),

Twells shewed cause, and again urged the difficulty the company would be under in reselling, especially by the operation of sect. 53 of the act, three years having expired since the act passed. If the company, knowing the defect of title, had gone before a jury, they might not now have had any excuse for resisting payment; but such is not the case. It is as if the difficulty had arisen on a common bargain between the parties. The Court, therefore, will not interfere by mandamus, but leave the applicant to such remedy as he may have, by a bill for specific performance, or otherwise, independently of the act.

Platt, contrà, was not heard.

Lord DENMAN C. J. The company has required this property, and the jury has assessed the value. *Collier*, then, stands in the situation of a proprietor entitled to payment under the act. The suggestion before was, that he did not shew his inability to make a title. That objection is now met. If the company has any further ground for withholding payment, it must be returned to the mandamus.

LITTLEDALE and WILLIAMS Js. concurred (*a*).

Rule absolute.

(*a*) *Coleridge* J. was in the bail court. *Patteson* J. at *Guildhall*.

The Queen *against* The Mayor of Harwich.

Friday, November 23d.

When a party whose name has been expunged from the burgess roll of a borough by the mayor on revision applies to this Court, under stat. 7 *W.* 4. & 1 *Vict. c.* 78. *s.* 24., for a mandamus to replace it, the Court is bound to inquire into his title.

It is not therefore sufficient for him to shew that his name was inserted by the overseers, and was expunged by the mayor on an objection which, for want of legal notice under stat. 5 & 6 *W.* 4. *c.* 76. *s.* 17. (as the party alleges), ought not to have been heard.

A RULE nisi was obtained, in this term (*November* 8th), for a mandamus to the mayor of *Harwich* to insert the name of *William Middleton* in the burgess roll of that borough. In the burgess list delivered to the town clerk by the overseers of the parish of *St. Nicholas, Harwich*, on *September* 5th, 1838, the name and description of this applicant were inserted as follows. "*Middleton, William.* House, *West Street.*" Notice of objection was given, under stat. 5 & 6 *W.* 4. *c.* 76. *s.* 17., signed "*Edgar Alexander, King's Quay Street, Harwich.*" On the revision, it was urged, on behalf of *Middleton*, that the notice of objection deviated from the form given in schedule D. No. 3. to the statute, in not stating the property for which the objector was rated, or shewing in any way that he was on the burgess list. The mayor and assessors, being satisfied that the objector's place of abode was as stated, "that the property for which he is said to be rated in the burgess list is situate in *King's Quay Street, Harwich*," and that, from his subscription and from the provisions of the statute, sect. 17, it must be inferred that his name was on the burgess list, admitted the objection: and, the qualification of *Middleton* to have his name retained on the list not being proved to their satisfaction, they expunged it. The town clerk deposed, in opposition to this rule, that there was only one *King's Quay Street* in the borough; that no person named *Edgar Alexander* but the objector had been resident within, an inhabitant householder of, or rated to any rate of, the said parish during the time required

1838.

The Queen against The Mayor of Harwich.

required to entitle a person to be on the burgess roll; and that there had been no other person of the name of *Alexander* on the burgess lists.

Middleton stated in his affidavit that, by the insertion of his name in the list as above mentioned, he (as he was advised and believed) was qualified, and by such insertion entitled, to vote as a burgess; but he did not add any particulars of his claim.

Thesiger now shewed cause. [Lord *Denman* C. J. Is not there a preliminary objection to this rule, that the expunging of *Middleton's* name was a judicial act of the mayor on a point submitted to his decision by the statute?] That is so. No other person can determine whether or not the description was sufficient. And sect. 142 of stat. 5 & 6 *W.* 4. *c.* 76. enacts "that no misnomer or inaccurate description of any person, body corporate, or place named in any schedule to this act annexed, or in any roll, list, notice, or voting paper required by this act, shall hinder the full operation of this act with respect to such person, body corporate, or place, provided that the description of such person" "be such as to be commonly understood." [Lord *Denman* C. J. Here is a complete omission. The situation of the objector's property is not described at all.] The affidavits sufficiently shew that it is in *King's Quay Street*. Separate descriptions as to the residence and property can be required (if at all) only where they are situate in different places. The object in requiring the particulars mentioned in the schedule, as to dwelling and property, is that the objector may be identified; and that is sufficiently done here. In *Tadman* v. *Wood* (a), where the indorsement on process described

(a) 4 *A.* & *E.* 1011.

the

the attorney as "of 40 *Stamford Street*," and it was contended that such description was insufficient under stat. 2 *W.* 4. *c.* 39. *s.* 12. and sched. No. 1., the description was held bad by a Judge at chambers; and, on a subsequent motion to this Court, the same objection being taken, it was said that the sufficiency or insufficiency was a matter in the discretion of the Judge, and that his decision ought to be final. The same may be said here as to the decision of the mayor and assessors. It is true that stat. 7 *W.* 4. & 1 *Vict.* *c.* 78. *s.* 24. makes it lawful for any person whose name shall have been expunged to move for a mandamus to the mayor to insert his name on the burgess-roll, "and thereupon for the Court to inquire into the title of the applicant to be so enrolled;" and it enacts that, if the Court shall award such mandamus, the mayor shall be bound to insert the name, and shall add the words "By order of the Court of King's Bench," subscribing his name thereto; and thereupon the party shall be deemed a burgess (*a*). But the party making such motion for a mandamus must satisfy the Court of his qualification.

(*a*) Stat. 7 *W.* 4. & 1 *Vict.* *c.* 78. *s.* 24. "And be it enacted, that it shall be lawful for any person whose claim shall have been rejected, or name expunged at the revision of the burgess roll of any of the said boroughs to apply, before the end of the term then next following, to the Court of King's Bench for a mandamus to the mayor for the time being of that borough to insert his name upon the burgess roll, and thereupon for the Court to inquire into the title of the applicant to be so enrolled; and if the Court shall award such mandamus, the mayor shall be bound to insert the name upon the burgess roll, and shall add thereunto the words "By order of the Court of King's Bench," and shall subscribe his name to such words; and thereupon the person whose name shall be so added to the burgess roll shall be deemed a burgess, and entitled to vote and act as a burgess in all respects as if his name had been put upon the burgess roll by the mayor and assessors; and upon every such application the Court shall have power to make such order with respect to the costs as to the Court shall seem fit."

Wordsworth,

1838.

The QUEEN against The Mayor of HARWICH.

Wordsworth, contrà. The inquiry for this Court on such a motion is, what title the party had at the time of the revision. Now it appears, here, that there was no obstacle at that time to the placing of *Middleton* on the roll, except an inadmissible objection. As to the defect in the notice, a similar omission was held fatal by a Committee of the House of Commons in the case of *Bedford Town* (*a*), under the Parliamentary Reform Act, 2 *W*. 4. *c*. 45. *s*. 47. and sched. (I.) No. 5. The argument for the sitting member on that point applies to the present case. [Lord *Denman* C. J. You say that you are entitled if the objector was not in a situation to interpose. But, if your affidavit shews no title, how can this Court act?] Under stat. 7 *W*. 4. & 1 *Vict*. *c*. 78. *s*. 24. this Court gives judgment as a court of appeal from the mayor and assessors; and no other mode exists of correcting any erroneous decision given by them. [*Coleridge* J. The Court cannot act as a court of appeal except under the statute, and conformably, therefore, to the terms prescribed by it.] If the objection was bad, the mayor was not justified in striking out the name: the right, as it came before him, was indefeasible, and is not subject to further inquiry. The qualification was not impeached, and that is sufficient. It will not be presumed that the overseers acted improperly in placing this name on the list. The act says that "it shall be lawful" for the Court, on motion for a mandamus, to inquire into the title, but uses no imperative words.

(*a*) Case of *Thomas Flight's* vote, *Perry and Knapp's Election Cases*, 116.

Lord

1838.

The Queen *against* The Mayor of Harwich.

Lord Denman C. J. This is not an application under sect. 18 of stat. 5 & 6 *W.* 4. *c.* 76., grounded on the want of a proper objection, but a motion calling upon us to act under stat. 7 *W.* 4. & 1 *Vict. c.* 78. *s.* 24., on the ground of an improper exercise of jurisdiction by the mayor and assessors. [His Lordship here read sect. 24.] Now, if the legislature had intended, by the section which we are here called upon to construe, that the mere discovery of an objection being bad should entitle the party applying to have his name put on the burgess-roll, they would probably have used words to that effect. There is good reason for considering that this was not intended; for, if such were the meaning of the act, great abuse might arise from parties appealing in the confidence that an objection would not be followed up in this Court; or procuring a friendly opponent to set up an objection before the mayor and assessors, which would be over-ruled in this Court. The words in stat. 7 *W.* 4. & 1 *Vict. c.* 78. *s.* 24., "that it shall be lawful" "for the Court to inquire into the title," require us to see, not only that the objection is bad, but that a title is shewn. In this case, therefore, proof of the title should have been given; none is produced, and the rule must consequently be discharged. When the name is placed on the burgess-roll in obedience to a mandamus, the mayor is to add the words "By order of the Court of King's Bench." We should not be justified, here, in ordering such an insertion.

Patteson J. Under sect. 18 of stat. 5 & 6 *W.* 4. *c.* 76., the mayor is bound to retain on the burgess list the names of all persons to whom no objection shall have

 been

1838.

The QUEEN *against* The Mayor of HARWICH.

been duly made: and there is no objection duly made, if there is an invalid notice. But Mr. *Wordsworth* seeks to shew that, when the mayor and assessors have determined against a claim notwithstanding an invalid notice, then, by the subsequent statute, this Court has only to revise what they have done. I thought at first that there was strong reason for this construction: but I believe the meaning of the act to be that it shall be lawful for the party whose name is expunged to apply to this Court if he thinks proper, and that, when he does so, the Court shall inquire into the title. I think it is intended that the party may come here, notwithstanding any decision below; but, if he does so, he must come prepared in all respects to prove his title.

WILLIAMS J. This Court has power to award a mandamus under sect. 24 of stat. 7 *W.* 4. & 1 *Vict. c.* 78, and that only; and we must see that clause complied with, both in form and in substance, before we grant the writ. The present application treats the words, "and thereupon for the Court to inquire into the title," as if they could be left out of the clause which gives us jurisdiction.

COLERIDGE J. Before the late statute the mayor's decision was conclusive: under sect. 24 of the act, this Court acts as in execution of a power; and one of the conditions under which the power is exercised is inquiry into the title. It is said that we must not presume that the overseers acted improperly. We must, it is true, assume the objection to be bad; but we cannot exclude all the facts of the case; among which

it

1838.

The QUEEN *against* The Mayor of HARWICH.

it appears that, on the merits, the mayor and assessors expunged this name. If we give credit to the overseers for having acted rightly, we must make the same assumption in favour of the mayor and assessors. But, laying aside both assumptions, this act requires that the Court, on motion for a mandamus, should inquire into the title. And it is to be observed that the applicant, on this proceeding, acquires a new title, because, when the name is inserted, the mayor is d ire [illegible] tod that it is, "by order of the Court of King's Bench."

Rule discharged, without costs (*a*).

(*a*) Several other rules, moved for by persons claiming to be burgesses of the same borough, under similar circumstances, were discharged without argument.

BODDINGTON *against* WOODLEY.

Friday, November 23d.

Where a defendant, arrested on mesne process for 9000*l.*, claimed to be discharged under stat. 1 & 2 *Vict.* c. 110. s. 7., having entered a common appearance, and application was made to a Judge to detain him under s. 7., on the ground that he was likely to quit *England*: Held, that an order by the Judge for detaining him till he should give bail for 9000*l.*, or *till further order*, was invalid.
And on motion to this Court that the order might be set aside and the defendant discharged out of custody, the rule was made absolute.

SIR *W. W. FOLLETT* in this term (*November* 19th) obtained a rule calling upon the plaintiff to shew cause why an order made by *Coltman* J. in this cause should not be set aside, and the defendant discharged out of the custody of the warden of the *Fleet* prison as to this action.

The defendant was arrested, *July* 31st, 1838, on mesne process at the plaintiff's suit for 9000*l.*, and committed to the *Fleet* prison. After the passing of stat. 1 & 2 *Vict.* c. 110., for abolishing arrest on mesne process in civil actions, he, being still in the same custody, obtained a summons to shew cause why he should not be discharged on entering an appearance pursuant to

1838.

BODDINGTON *against* WOODLEY.

to sect. 7 of the statute (*a*). The learned Judge before whom the parties attended, at chambers, ultimately made the following order.

"Upon

(*a*) Stat. 1 & 2 *Vict.* c. 110. *s.* 1. enacts, "that from and after the time appointed for the commencement of this act" (1st *October* 1838) "no person shall be arrested upon mesne process in any civil action in any inferior court whatsoever, or (except in the cases and in the manner hereinafter provided for) in any superior court." Sect. 2 enacts that all personal actions in the superior courts of law at *Westminster* shall be commenced by writ of summons.

Sect. 3 enacts, "that if a plaintiff in any action in any of her Majesty's superior courts of law at *Westminster*, in which the defendant is now liable to arrest, whether upon the order of a Judge, or without such order, shall, by the affidavit of himself or of some other person, shew, to the satisfaction of a Judge of one of the said superior courts, that such plaintiff has a cause of action against the defendant or defendants to the amount of 20*l.* or upwards, or has sustained damage to that amount, and that there is probable cause for believing that the defendant or any one or more of the defendants is or are about to quit *England* unless he or they be forthwith apprehended, it shall be lawful for such Judge, by a special order, to direct that such defendant or defendants so about to quit *England* shall be held to bail for such sum as such Judge shall think fit, not exceeding the amount of the debt or damages; and thereupon it shall be lawful for such plaintiff, within the time which shall be expressed in such order, but not afterwards, to sue out one or more writ or writs of capias into one or more different counties, as the case may require, against any such defendant so directed to be held to bail, which writ of capias shall be in the form contained in the schedule to this act annexed," &c.

The form of capias in the schedule (No. 1.) commands the sheriff to take *C. D.* "and him safely keep until he shall have given you bail, or made deposit with you according to law in an action on promises [*or of* debt, *&c.*] at the suit of *A. B.* , or until the said *C. D.* shall by other lawful means be discharged from your custody." Among the "Indorsements to be made on the writ" is "Bail for pounds by order of [*naming the Judge making the order*] dated this" &c.

Sect. 4 enacts, "that the sheriff or other officer to whom any such writ of capias shall be directed shall, within one calendar month after the date thereof, including the day of such date, but not afterwards, proceed to arrest the defendant thereupon; and such defendant when so arrested shall remain in custody until he shall have given a bail bond to the sheriff, or shall have made deposit of the sum endorsed on such writ of capias, together with 10*l.* for costs, according to the present practice of the said superior courts; and all subsequent proceedings as to the putting

in

1838.

BODDINGTON *against* WOODLEY.

"Upon hearing counsel on both sides, and upon reading the joint affidavit of the plaintiff and" *F. S. G.* &c., "it appearing to my satisfaction that there is probable cause for believing that the defendant is about to quit *England*, I order that he be detained in the custody of the warden of the *Fleet* prison until he shall give bail in the sum of 3000*l.* in this action, or until further order. Dated the 10th day of *October* 1838."

It was sworn, in support of the present rule, that the defendant had entered an appearance to the writ of capias, and was now detained in the *Fleet* solely by virtue of the above order, which had been served on the warden; and that he had not petitioned to be discharged under the laws for the relief of insolvent debtors.

Sir *J. Campbell*, Attorney-General, and *F. Robinson*, now shewed cause. The first objection is, that the defendant cannot, under sect. 7, be "detained" simply by virtue of the Judge's order. But the clause does not mean that there should be a detainer in the technical sense. If any process ulterior to the Judge's

---

in and perfecting special bail, or of making deposit and payment of money into court instead of putting in and perfecting special bail, shall be according to the like practice of the said superior courts, or as near thereto as the circumstances of the case will admit."

Sect. 7 enacts, "that every prisoner who at the time appointed for the commencement of this act shall be in custody upon mesne process for any debt or demand, and shall not have filed a petition to be discharged under the laws now in force for the relief of insolvent debtors, shall be entitled to his discharge upon entering a common appearance to the action: provided nevertheless, that every such prisoner shall be liable to be detained, or after such discharge to be again arrested, by virtue of any such special order as aforesaid, at the suit of the plaintiff at whose suit he was previously arrested, or of any other plaintiff."

1838.

BODDINGTON *against* WOODLEY.

order is contemplated, no mode is given in which it can be sued out. The proceeding under sect. 3 applies to the commencement of a suit; so also does the process of detainer under stat. 2 *W.* 4. *c.* 39. *s.* 8. The clause now in question must be construed so as to accomplish the object evidently contemplated by the legislature (*a*). It is further objected, that an order to detain until bail be given, "or until further order," is illegal. To assert this is, in effect, to argue that the special order mentioned in sect. 7 must be adapted, throughout, to the form of capias in sched. No. 1. But nothing renders it necessary for the Judge to specify in his order that the party will be discharged on making deposit; it is implied in the present order that, if he deposits or pays the requisite sum, he will be discharged; a "further order" will then be made to that effect. If these are terms necessarily engrafted upon the order by stat. 43 *G.* 3. *c.* 46. *s.* 2., or 7 & 8 *G.* 4. *c.* 71. *s.* 2., it cannot be necessary for the Judge to state them.

Sir *W. W. Follett*, *C. Thompson*, and *Dowdeswell*, contrà. Stat. 1 & 2 *Vict.* *c.* 110. does not give the Judge power to detain by his order merely. The cases in

(*a*) On the motion for a rule nisi, in the Bail Court, *Littledale* J. said that it was a matter of much doubt what proceeding was meant by the word "detained" in sect. 7. No decision having been given on this point, the argument upon it is noticed so far only as appears necessary to explain the reference to it in the judgments delivered. Other objections, not mentioned in the text, were taken to the form of the order; particularly that it did not, by recital or otherwise, shew jurisdiction in the learned Judge to make an order under sect. 3. The case was likewise argued on the merits; and it was also made a question whether the learned Judge's adjudication upon them was open to review. But no decision was pronounced on any of these points.

1838.

BODDINGTON *against* WOODLEY.

in which detention is contemplated are those pointed out by sect. 3. And, if it had been intended that a Judge should by his mere order, as in the present case, authorise a detention, some provision would have been made as to the taking of bail. Here the party is arrested for 9000*l.*, and the learned Judge orders him to be detained till he shall give bail for 3000*l.* If it were meant that the order should operate as process to detain, it should at least be framed according to the form of capias given in the schedule. According to sect. 4, the party arrested on such capias is to remain in custody "until he shall have given a bail-bond to the sheriff, or shall have made deposit of the sum endorsed on such writ of capias." And under the previous acts the defendant would have been discharged by the sheriff on making a deposit in lieu of bail, without any Judge's order. Here the learned Judge directs that the party shall be detained till he gives bail, or till further order: he could not, therefore, be discharged on making deposit, or on payment, or by laches in the plaintiff, without a new order of the Judge. But it does not seem to have been intended by the act to put defendants in a worse situation than before in this respect. [*Patteson* J. You argue on an assumption that the Judge's order is supposed to be the operative process. May it not be intended that the party shall remain in custody under the process already issued?] Then the order here is irregular in altering the amount of bail. If the order be not an operative process, the defendant is entitled to be discharged, nothing else having been done. If it be the operative process, it should be shaped as an order to detain under the process already in force, or should follow the form of capias in the schedule, so

that

1838.

BODDINGTON *against* WOODLEY.

that the defendant might have the advantages which he would have enjoyed under the former acts.

Lord DENMAN C. J. On one of the grounds of objection, whatever we may think of the rest, this order is not sustained. It directs an imprisonment until the party shall give bail, or until further order. That is illegal in any view of the case. The learned Judge had no right to make his own or another Judge's order a condition of the discharge. That objection applies equally, whether the Judge's order gives the power to detain, or not.

PATTESON J. I am of the same opinion upon this point; and it is unnecessary to give any decision on the others. In the writ of capias which was in force before this statute, the direction to the sheriff was to keep the defendant " until he shall have given you bail, or made deposit with you according to law," or " shall by other lawful means be discharged from your custody." So the detainer, under stat. 2 *W.* 4. *c.* 39. (sched. No. 5.), ordered the marshal or warden to keep the party " until he shall be lawfully discharged from your custody." Whether the Judge's order in this case be of itself operative for the purpose of detention or not, the direction, in either view of the case, should have been to detain, not until further order, but until the defendant should be lawfully discharged.

WILLIAMS J. The Judge's order seems to negative the supposition that the defendant is detained under the old process, by requiring a different amount of bail. If he is kept in custody by virtue of the order, that expresses

1838.

BODDINGTON *against* WOODLEY.

expresses no condition of discharge but the giving bail, or a further order. But there were other circumstances than his giving bail, under which he would by law have been entitled to his discharge. The order, therefore, is in this respect bad.

COLERIDGE J. concurred.

Sir *W. W. Follett* then contended that the defendant was entitled, by the act, and under the terms of the rule nisi, to be at once discharged, having entered an appearance to the writ of capias.

The Attorney-General argued that the rule ought to be merely that the Judge's order should be rescinded, for that the Court was not exercising a jurisdiction under sect. 7 of stat. 1 & 2 *Vict. c.* 110., and would not therefore enter into the question of discharge or detainer under that clause. [*Coleridge* J. If the Judge's order is out of the way, what prevents the discharge?]

Rule absolute.

Saturday, November 24th.

The QUEEN *against* The Justices for the Liberty of ST. ALBAN'S.

Under sect. 6 of the Parochial Assessment Act (6 & 7 *W.* 4. *c.* 96.), which enacts that the decision of special sessions on appeal against a poor rate shall be conclusive unless the party impugning such decision give notice as therein prescribed, to the opposite party, and, within five days afterwards, enter into a recognisance before a justice of the peace to try at the quarter sessions, it is sufficient that the recognisance be, within the five days, verbally acknowledged before a justice; the record of the recognisance may be perfected afterwards from the minute then made.

RYLAND had obtained a rule, in this term, calling upon the justices of the peace for the liberty of *St. Alban's*, in *Hertfordshire*, to shew cause why a mandamus should not issue, commanding them to enter continuances and hear the appeal of the churchwardens and overseers of the parish of *Watford*, against the after-mentioned order of special sessions.

The rate was made on 5th *June* 1838, and signed by the churchwardens and overseers of *Watford*, which is within and part of the liberty of *St. Alban's*. The rate was allowed by two justices of the liberty, and notice thereof duly given. The Honourable and Reverend *William Capel*, a party rated, appealed at the petty sessions of *St. Alban's*, holden 24th *July* 1838, when it was ordered that the rate should be amended by reducing the rate or assessment on certain hereditaments occupied by the appellant. Notice of appeal against this order, signed by two churchwardens and four overseers of *Watford* (which has, in all, five churchwardens and four overseers), all being rated inhabitants of *Watford*, was served on Mr. *Capel*, on 6th *August* 1838; and, on 7th *August*, the parties signing entered into a recognisance (*a*) with two sufficient sureties, before three

(*a*) By the Parochial Assessment Act, 6 & 7 *W.* 4. *c.* 96. *s.* 6. special sessions are to be held four times a year at least for hearing appeals against rates, on the grounds specified in the section, and the decision of such special sessions "shall be binding and conclusive on the parties, unless

1838.

The QUEEN *against* The Justices of St. ALBAN'S.

three justices of *St. Alban's* in petty sessions (at whom they appeared personally), conditioned to try the appeal at the next quarter sessions, abide the order there made, and pay such costs as should be awarded. The next quarter sessions for the liberty were holden on 18th *October* 1838; and these were the first quarter sessions after 24th *July*. The deputy clerk of the justices, who acted as clerk at the petty sessions on the 7th of *August*, made an entry of the recognisance in a minute book of the evidence taken at the sessions, which minute book was then signed by the chairman of the petty sessions; and the deputy clerk also, on the same day, made another entry and memorandum of the recognisance in another book used at the petty sessions, called the petty sessions minute book; and the same clerk deposed that it is the usual practice of justices of the peace, in taking recognisances, to make minutes thereof at the time of taking them, and from such minutes to make out records afterwards. Some weeks after making these entries, the deputy clerk drew up the record of the recognisance, ready for signature of one of the justices before whom it was taken; and, about the 3d of *October* 1838, sent it to the chief clerk of the justices for him to get it so signed, and to return

---

unless the person or persons impugning such decision shall within fourteen days after the same shall have been made cause notice to be given in writing of his, her, or their intention of appealing against such decision, and of the matter or cause of such appeal, to the person or persons in whose favour such decision shall have been made, and within five days after giving such notice shall enter into a recognizance before some justice of the peace, with sufficient securities, conditioned to try such appeal at the then next general sessions or quarter sessions of the peace which shall first happen, and to abide the order of and pay such costs as shall be awarded by the justices at such quarter sessions, or any adjournment thereof."

it

1838.

The QUEEN *against* The Justices of ST. ALBAN'S.

it to the clerk of the peace of the liberty, that it might be in Court on the hearing of the appeal. The chief clerk gave it to the clerk of the peace about the 10th of *October*, having inadvertently omitted to get it signed. The appeal was called on at the *October* quarter sessions; when the respondents' counsel called for the notice of appeal, which was produced; and he then required proof of the recognisance being entered into; whereupon the clerk of the peace produced the record unsigned. The counsel for the appellants proposed to prove that the recognisance had been entered into, by parol evidence, and also by the minute book signed by the chairman of the petty sessions; and he also proposed to obtain the signature of one of the justices then present, being also one of the justices before whom the recognisance was taken at petty sessions, and to give in evidence the record so signed. The quarter sessions decided that they could not receive any evidence but a record of the recognisance perfected within five days after notice of appeal; and that they had therefore no jurisdiction; and they refused to hear the appeal, and dismissed it. About the 8th of *November*, the record was signed by the chairman of petty sessions before whom the recognisance was entered into, and it was afterwards transmitted to the clerk of the peace.

Wordsworth now shewed cause. Under sect. 6 of stat. 6 & 7 *W.* 4. *c.* 96., the recognisance should have been complete within five days of the notice of appeal; the quarter sessions were therefore right in rejecting the evidence of a record signed after the five days, as this would have been if the signature of the magistrate had been

1838.

The QUEEN against The Justices of ST. ALBAN'S.

been affixed at the quarter sessions. Then the quarter sessions had before them nothing to give jurisdiction except the minute of the petty sessions, which is not the recognisance, but only a memorandum of something done preparatory to a recognisance being perfected. *Glynn* v. *Thorpe* (a) and *Rex* v. *Smith* (b) are in point.

Platt and *Ryland*, contrà, were stopped by the Court.

Lord DENMAN C. J. This rule must be made absolute. In point of fact the recognisance was entered into within the five days. A recognisance is no more than an acknowledgment. The clerk did not perfect the record: if he had perfected it at any time before the quarter sessions, the parties to it could not have objected that they were not bound. Their objection to the jurisdiction, therefore, fails, even on the assumption (as to which we pronounce no opinion) that the quarter sessions could enquire whether the recognisance had been entered into or not.

PATTESON, WILLIAMS, and COLERIDGE Js. concurred.

Rule absolute (c).

(a) 1 *B. & Ald.* 153.

(b) 8 *B. & C.* 341. And see *Rex* v. *Bellamy*, *Ry. & Moo.* 171.

(c) See *Reg.* v. *Yeoveley*, p. 806, antè.

1838.

Saturday, November 24th]

In the Matter of JAMES LAWRENCE DAWS.

An inquest was held on a person deceased, in the coroner's absence, by *C. A.*, his clerk, who signed the inquisition, "*C. A.*, coroner." Other irregularities took place in the proceedings, but did not appear on the face of the inquisition.

On application by the father of the deceased, eight months after the inquest, to have the inquisition brought up by certiorari to be quashed, that a new inquest might be held, on affidavit of the above facts, and on a suggestion that the cause of death had not been properly investigated: The Court refused to interfere.

CLARKSON moved for a certiorari, to be directed to the coroner for the rape of *Hastings* in *Sussex*, to bring up an inquisition taken on view of the body of *James Lawrence Daws*, in order to such inquisition being quashed.

The inquest was held *April* 3d, 1838. It did not appear by whose authority the jury were summoned. The coroner did not attend (*a*); but his clerk, *Charles Arnold*, acted as coroner, and swore the jury and witnesses. The inquisition (a copy of which was annexed to the affidavits now put in) purported to be taken "before *Charles Arnold*, coroner for the said rape," and was signed, "*C. Arnold*, coroner." Some of the jurors did not sign the inquisition, or make their marks; but their names were subscribed by the constable. Other irregularities were stated to have taken place in conducting the inquest. The affidavits gave the substance of the depositions, by which it appeared that the deceased had died suddenly, in a state of intoxication. The verdict was, that he died of apoplexy or other sudden visitation of God. The father of the deceased made an affidavit, alleging, on information and belief, that the circumstances of the death had not been properly investigated; and that, if they had, it would have appeared that the death was caused by

(*a*) It was stated on moving, that he was since dead.

improper

1838.

In the Matter of DAWS.

improper treatment: and he stated that he was desirous of having a fresh inquest held.

Clarkson now stated the facts, and the object of the application, namely, that another inquest might be held. [Lord *Denman* C. J. The application might have been made much sooner. Is it clear that we ought to quash every inquisition which we know to be bad? The proceeding, as it stands, is a mere nullity. I do not think public justice is so far concerned that we should interfere]. The inquisition, though bad, would, until it is quashed, prevent another inquest being holden, since it purports to have been taken by the proper officer, and is not defective in form. "If it appear, that a coroner hath been guilty of any corrupt practice in the taking of an inquisition, it seems that a *melius inquirendum* shall be awarded." "But where his inquisition is quashed for a defect in point of form only, he may and ought to take a new one, in like manner as if he had not taken any before." 3 *Hawk. P. C.* 122. *B.* 2. *c.* 9. *s.* 56 (*a*). Here a melius inquirendum is necessary; but the inquisition must first be quashed for the irregularity shewn by the affidavits. [*Patteson* J. That is where the inquest is held by a proper person, but the proceedings are bad. Here the coroner's clerk has held the inquest, and signed his own name].

Lord DENMAN C. J. If you wish to take any further proceeding and have a right to do so, how can you be prevented by the act of a person calling himself the coroner, but really a stranger? I think that to grant

(*a*) *Leach's* (7th) ed. Vol. ii. p. 89, of *Curwood's* (8th) ed.

this

1838.

In the Matter of DAWS.

this rule would be doing a very unnecessary act, to set on foot a very undesirable proceeding; for such it would be to hold a new inquest on the body of this person. There is nothing to prevent an indictment against any accused parties, if there be sufficient cause.

PATTESON and WILLIAMS J. concurred (a).

Rule refused (b).

(a) *Coleridge* J. was in the bail court.

(b) See *In re Culley*, 5 *B. & Ad.* 230.

Monday, November 26th.

The QUEEN *against* The Sheriff of MIDDLESEX.

A sheriff, attached for not bringing in the body, moved to have the attachment set aside, on an affidavit stating, as to the sheriff's interest in the motion, that it was made "on his behalf, at his expense, and for his protection, without collusion with the plaintiff or defendant, or any other person or persons whomsoever." Held, not a sufficient affidavit within *Reg. Gen.* K. B. *Mich.* 59 *G.* 3. And the Court discharged the rule for this defect, though the application was made after stat. 1 & 2 *Vict.* c. 110. came into operation; the contempt having taken place before that time.

A RULE nisi was obtained this term (*November* 8th) for setting aside an attachment against the sheriff, on payment of costs. The sheriff, on *June* 15th, 1838, returned to a writ of capias that he had taken the defendant, and kept her until she gave bail &c. On *June* 21st, the sheriff was ordered to bring in the body; but the order was not complied with; and the plaintiff, in consequence of this, as he alleged, did not declare, and lost a trial at the assizes. Bail above was put in on *June* 27th; the defendant rendered in discharge of the bail, *October* 31st, was discharged, *November* 1st, on entering a common appearance, and about the same time became bankrupt. The affidavit in support of the present rule stated, "That the application of the sheriff is made on his behalf, at his expense, and for his protection, without collusion with the plaintiff or defendant, or any other person or persons whomsoever."

Hodges

1838.

The QUEEN *against* The Sheriff of MIDDLESEX.

Hodges now shewed cause. The affidavit is insufficient, because it does not state, as the rule of Court *Mich.* 59 *G.* 3. (*a*) requires, that the application "is really and truly made on the part of the sheriff, or bail, or officer of the sheriff, (as the case may be) at his or their own expense and for his or their only indemnity;" *Rex* v. *Sheriff of Surrey* (*b*), *Call* v. *Thelwell* (*c*), *Regina* v. *Sheriff of Cheshire* (*d*).

Kennedy, contrà. The rule of Court is in effect superseded by stat. 1 & 2 *Vict. c.* 110. The form of affidavit now insisted upon was material when the proper mode of purging such a contempt as the present was to bring in the body. But, since the late act (which, by sect. 123, came into operation on 1st *October* 1838), bringing in the body would be a mere form, for the defendant, under sect. 7, would be entitled to an immediate discharge on entering a common appearance. [*Patteson* J. Here the contempt had taken place, and the sheriff was fixed, before the act came into operation. It is one thing to say that a party arrested shall, after a certain day, be entitled to his discharge, and another to say that a contempt previously incurred by the sheriff shall, after that day, be purged.] The affidavit does, in substance, allege all that the rule requires. And, if the Court think other-

(*a*) 2 *B.* & *Ald.* 240. See *Reg.* v. *The Sheriff of Cheshire*, 3 *M.* & *W.* 605. by which it appears that the words "only indemnity," are, in the original rule, "indemnity only."

(*b*) 1 *Cro. M.* & *R.* 581. *S. C.* 5 *Tyr.* 184.

(*c*) 1 *Cro. M.* & *R.* 780. *S. C.* 5 *Tyr.* 231.

(*d*) 3 *Mee.* & *W.* 605. The rule, Exch. *Hil.* 7 *W.* 4. (2 *M.* & *W.* 219.), which is the same as that of *Mich.* 59 *G.* 3. (except that it has the words "his and their own," instead of "his or their," before the words "indemnity only"), was prior to this case, and subsequent to the two last above cited.

 wise,

1838.

The Queen against The Sheriff of Middlesex.

wise, time may be granted to produce an amended affidavit, as was done in *Rex* v. *Sheriff of Surrey* (a) and *Call* v. *Thelwell* (b), where the defects were not less important than in the present case. [Lord *Denman* C. J. We wish to avoid such arguments on the importance of defects.] In *Merryman* v. *Quibble* (c), where a motion on behalf of bail was objected to, under the rule of *Mich.* 59 *G.* 3., for not stating that the application was made bonâ fide on behalf of the bail, the rule was made absolute, subject to the production of an amended affidavit containing the necessary statement. In *Rex* v. *The Sheriff of London* (d) the Court of Common Pleas relieved the sheriff from an attachment for not bringing in the body, on an affidavit which stated that the application was made at the instance of the bail, and without collusion with, or indemnity from, the defendant; though it omitted to state (as the Court thought it properly should) that the application was at the expense of the bail. [*Patteson* J. There was no direct rule of the Court of Common Pleas opposed to the form used in that case. Here an express rule of Court exists, and it ought to be followed. I am never disposed to give indulgence in such cases. The present is a strong example of the inconvenience resulting from such a practice. Our time is taken up with ascertaining whether "protection" means "indemnity."] (e).

Lord Denman C. J. The question we have to consider is, whether the rule of *Mich.* 59 *G.* 3. is super-

(a) 1 *Cro. M. & R.* 581. *S. C.* 5 *Tyr.* 184.

(b) 1 *Cro. M. & R.* 780. *S. C.* 5 *Tyr.* 231.

(c) 1 *Chitt. Rep.* 127.

(d) 4 *Bing.* 427.

(e) Another point was discussed in the case; but the decision renders it immaterial.

seded

seded by the late act, as has been suggested. We think it is not, and that parties are not excused for omitting to comply with it, because they thought it superseded. The rule must therefore be discharged.

PATTESON, WILLIAMS, and COLERIDGE Js. concurred.

Kennedy asked if an amended affidavit might be filed; but

The Court refused permission.

Rule discharged, without costs.

WELLS *against* DAY.

Monday, November 26th.

No Judge's order is necessary, under *Reg. Gen. Hil.* 4 *W.* 4. 18., for amending the day of the teste and return of the distringas &c., or of the clause of nisi prius, in a cause which has been made a remanet and continues in the paper. It is sufficient if the jury process and nisi prius record be resealed as before the rule. A Judge's order for amendment, as mentioned in the rule, is required only in cases where it was formerly necessary to repass the record.

SIR *J. CAMPBELL*, Attorney-General, in this term (*November* 16th), obtained a rule to shew cause why the venire and distringas, nisi prius record, verdict, postea, judgment, and all subsequent proceedings in this cause, should not be set aside for irregularity.

Notice of trial had been given for the *Middlesex* sittings after last *Trinity* term; but the cause was made a remanet to the first sittings in this term, when it was tried, and a verdict found for the plaintiff. On taxation of costs it was found that no Judge's order had been obtained to amend the jury process or nisi prius record; and on that ground the defendant's attorney objected to the taxation proceeding. He contended that it became necessary, in consequence of the cause being made a remanet, to amend the days of the teste, return of dis-

tringas,

1838.

WELLS against DAY.

tringas, and clause of nisi prius, and that this could not be done without a Judge's order, according to the rule *Hil.* 4 *W.* 4., *Regulæ Generales*, 18. (*a*), which is as follows.

"It shall not be necessary to repass any nisi prius record which shall have been once passed, and upon which the fees of passing shall have been paid. And if it shall be necessary to amend the day of the teste and return of the distringas or habeas corpora, or of the clause of nisi prius, the same may be done by the order of a Judge, obtained on an application ex parte."

The Master proceeded with the taxation, and made his allocatur. The defendant's attorney stated, by his affidavit in support of this rule, that he saw at the trial that the nisi prius record appeared to have been altered so as to adapt it to a trial at the sittings after term; that he now believed the jury process to have been altered as above stated without a Judge's order; that he did not know, and had no reason to suspect, until the taxation, that the several amendments had been made without such order; and that he believed there were no means of ascertaining at the Judges' chambers, whether such order had been obtained or not. The venire and distringas were resealed. Nothing further appeared in the affidavits as to resealing. The nisi prius record had been passed and entered for trial for the sittings after *Trinity* term, but not repassed for the sittings in this term. The plaintiff's attorney, in his affidavit in opposition to the rule, stated, on information and belief, that, before the late rule of Court, it was not necessary to repass the record where the cause was made a remanet,

(*a*) 5 *B.* & *Ad.* xvii.

but

1838.

WELLS *against* DAY.

but only where the cause was for some reason struck out of the paper, and again set down for trial, or where a second trial was had. He also stated that, on enquiry at the Marshals' offices of this Court and the Common Pleas, the opinion stated to him was, that the rule as to obtaining a Judge's order to amend applied only to cases where, before the rule, it would have been necessary to repass the record; that such order was a substitution for repassing; that it had sometimes been applied for in the case of a remanet, but was not considered necessary; and that, if it were so, the rule would in such cases increase, instead of lessening, expense. On the day on which the present rule was obtained, the plaintiff took out a summons to shew cause why an order for amending the jury process and nisi prius record should not be made nunc pro tunc; but *Littledale* J. refused to grant such order.

Platt now shewed cause. The rule does not apply where the cause is merely made a remanet; it was intended to lessen expense in the case of a new trial. In that case, the practice in this Court, before the rule, was, according to 2 *Tidd*, 917. (*a*), that the record "must be passed again, with an alteration of the term in the second *placita*, and of the return of the *distringas* in the *jurata*, and a new notice of trial given; after which, another *venire* and *distringas* must be sued out and returned, and the cause set down anew." It does not appear by any affidavit that the nisi prius record in this case was not resealed.

(*a*) 9th ed.

1838.

Wells *against* Day.

Sir *J. Campbell*, Attorney-General, and *Peacock*, contrà. The alteration was not warranted, either by the old or by the recent practice. The nisi prius record, as is stated in 2 *Tidd's Pract.* 775, 6. (*a*), is "in the nature of a commission to the Judges at *nisi prius*, for the trial of the cause:" it is to be sealed and passed on or before the day appointed for trial; and "in causes which stand over from one sitting to another, the records should be regularly resealed, previous to the sitting to which they stand over; or in default thereof, the causes cannot be tried." The late rule enables parties to alter the teste and return of the distringas, and the clause of nisi prius, without repassing the record, or resealing, provided a Judge's order be obtained for the amendment, not otherwise. [*Patteson* J. There was no necessity in this case for the record being repassed: the rule, as to amending by a Judge's order, applies only to cases where it would formerly have been necessary to repass the record. This case, then, stands upon the old practice.] On principle, the nisi prius clause should correspond with the time when the trial is actually to take place. If an alteration be necessary, it should be sanctioned either by resealing, which is the act of the Court, or by a Judge's order. The present case is like *Crowder* v. *Rooke* (*b*). [The *Attorney-General*, in answer to the objection by *Platt* that the omission to reseal the nisi prius record was not sworn to, produced the record itself; but *The Court* said that, not being verified by affidavit, it could not be noticed.]

(*a*) 9th ed.

(*b*) 2 *Wils.* 144.

Lord

1838.

WELLS *against* DAY.

Lord DENMAN C. J. It only appears, in this case, that the nisi prius record was altered; there is no proof that it had not been resealed. Then, as far as the statements go, the alteration was made in the ordinary way, which is without a Judge's order.

PATTESON J. This is quite different from a case where it would have been necessary to repass the record. Here there was no occasion to do so. The rule as to obtaining a Judge's order says nothing of alteration in the nisi prius record. The case is the plainest I ever saw.

WILLIAMS and COLERIDGE Js. concurred.

Rule discharged (*a*).

(*a*) The following case was decided in *Hilary* term, 1840.

DUBOIS *against* KEATS.

Friday, January 31st, 1840.

When a cause made a remanet has been tried, a verdict found for the plaintiff, and judgment signed by him, it is too late to object that the jury process was altered before the trial, without proper authority. Though the defendant swears that he did not discover the supposed irregularity till the taxation of costs.

MARTIN, in this term, (*January* 22d), obtained a rule to shew cause why the resealing of the jury process, and all subsequent proceedings in this cause, should not be set aside for irregularity. The rule was obtained on an affidavit by the clerk to the defendant's attorneys, stating as follows. The cause was made a remanet from the adjourned sittings in *London* after last *Trinity* term to the adjourned sittings after last *Michaelmas* term. On taxation of costs (*January* 21st, 1840), the plaintiff's bill of costs being produced, it appeared that the teste and return of the venire and distringas, and the clause of nisi prius, had been amended, but no Judge's order obtained for so doing. The deponent had not, until that time, any knowledge that the order had not been obtained; and he objected to the taxation proceeding; whereupon it was adjourned. The ground alleged for this application was, that, by the practice of the Court, a Judge's order was requisite for making the amendments. By the affidavits in opposition to the rule, it appeared that the objection taken before the Master was, that no Judge's order had been obtained for resealing. A clerk to the plaintiff's agents deposed that, upon the cause not being tried at the sittings after *Trinity* term, he, in the following *October*, attended at the Marshal's office and had the cause marked a remanet, and the Marshal's clerk then delivered to him the jury process to alter and get the same resealed and returned, which he did as directed, and every thing was done, in making the cause a remanet, and getting the jury process altered, resealed, and returned, that

1838.

Wells *against* Day.

that was necessary and proper according to the practice of the Court, as the deponent was informed and believed. That, on the trial, the defendant appeared by counsel, and a verdict was returned for the plaintiff, who signed final judgment on *January* 21st. That on *January* 20th the plaintiff's bill of costs was delivered to the defendant's attorneys, with notice of taxation, such bill containing no charge for a Judge's order to amend the jury process and nisi prius clause. And "that it is not the practice at the Marshal's office or at the Seal office to require the production of a Judge's order for amending the record and resealing the jury process on causes being made remanets."

Sir *F. Pollock* (with whom was *Hoggins*) now shewed cause, and contended that the objection, even if valid, was taken too late; but that where a cause was made a remanet, and not re-entered, resealing was sufficient, and the rule, *Reg. Gen. Hil.* 4 *W.* 4. 18. (suprà, p. 942.), did not require more. On this point he relied upon the affidavit in support of the rule, as to the practice. [*Littledale* J. I do not recollect ever making an order to reseal. Before the new rule it was never thought of.]

Martin, contrà, was called upon by the Court. A rule of the Court cannot be set aside by practice. [*Coleridge* J. Would this, at any rate, be more than an irregularity? and, if not, are not you too late?] The defendant has taken no step since the amendment, except by compulsion; and he made this application as soon as he knew of the omission. [*Littledale* J. You might have seen at the time of the trial that the jury process had been altered. You should have enquired then whether the alteration was made with proper authority]. The application to amend is ex parte by the rule of Court. The defendant was not entitled to presume that the amendment was made without due sanction. That fact would not appear by the proceedings. [*Littledale* J. I suppose the rule of Court was made to prevent the necessity of repassing the record where it was formerly the practice to do so. Sir *F. Pollock* referred to *Wells* v. *Day*, suprà.] This case is within the words of the rule, since "the day of the teste and return of the distringas" and "of the clause of nisi prius" is amended.

Littledale J. There is no doubt that the defendant knew nothing of the mode in which the amendment was made; but it was in his power to make enquiry. He applied to the Court as soon as he knew of the objection which he alleges; but he might have known of it sooner. The rule must be discharged.

Williams and Coleridge Js. concurred.

Lord Denman C. J. had left the Court.

Rule discharged.

1838.

The QUEEN on the Prosecution of Sir GEORGE DUCKETT *against* BALDWIN.

Monday, November 26th.

A peremptory mandamus will not be awarded until the proceedings on the first mandamus are complete: and therefore, where, a mandamus having issued requiring payment of two distinct sums, the prosecutor traversed the return, and the issues were found for him as to one sum, and substantially in his favour as to the other, but a rule nisi had been obtained to enter a verdict for the defendant as to this, the Court would not award a peremptory mandamus to enforce payment of the first sum, pending the rule as to the second.

SIR *J. CAMPBELL*, Attorney-General, on a former day in this term, obtained a rule nisi to set aside with costs the peremptory writ of mandamus issued by the prosecutor, under the following circumstances. In *Trinity* term 1836, the prosecutor obtained a rule calling on the defendant, who was then surveyor of the highways of the parish of *St. John Clerkenwell*, to shew cause why a mandamus should not issue, requiring him to pay to the prosecutor the arrears of two several rents or annual sums, one of 18*l.* and the other of 9*l.*, which rule was afterwards made absolute, the Court thinking that enough was shewn on the affidavits to call upon the parish to make a return.

The writ accordingly issued, setting out certain parts of stat. 29 *G.* 2. *c.* 88., for making "a new road from the Great Northern Road at *Islington*, to the *Edgeware* Road near *Paddington*," &c., and of several other local and personal public acts, amongst others of stat. 7 *G.* 4. *c.* cxlii. (Metropolitan Turnpike Act); under which it was contended by the prosecutor that two pieces of land, one containing three acres, the other one acre and a half, belonging to the late Mr. *Penton*, situate in the parish of *St. John, Clerkenwell*, had at several times been taken by the trustees for carrying the act of 29 *G.* 2. into execution, under contracts with Mr. *Penton* or his family, which entitled them (through the prosecutor their trustee) to receive from that parish the annual rents now in question.

The

1838.

The Queen *against* Baldwin.

The defendant made a return denying the material facts alleged in the writ; which return being traversed, eleven distinct pleas were pleaded to the traverse, and issues joined upon them. The issue taken on the eighth plea was, whether the said three acres of land, and the said one acre and a half of land, and the said road rents, were settled and stand now limited to the said Sir *G. Duckett* as such surviving trustee as in the said writ mentioned. The issue joined on the ninth plea was, whether the said annual rents were, at the time of the passing of stat. 7 *G.* 4. *c.* cxlii., subsisting rents and charges, chargeable upon and payable out of the tolls taken on certain roads made over the *Pentonville* estate. The issue joined on the eleventh plea was, whether the said two annual rents were in arrear, and not paid to Sir *G. D.*

The issues were tried before Lord *Denman* C. J., at the sittings after *Michaelmas* term 1837, when the prosecutor proved a lease of three acres of land, at the annual rent of 18*l*., as stated in his pleadings; and he also proved payment of the two annual rents for some years by the parish. The defendant contended that, as to the one acre and a half, there was no proof of any binding contract to make the annual sum of 9*l*. chargeable on the tolls within stat. 7 *G.* 4. *c.* cxlii.; nor sufficient evidence of Sir *G. D.* being the surviving trustee of the *Penton* estates, and so entitled to receive the rents if chargeable on the tolls. A deed bearing date 25th *May* 1808, and purporting to vest those estates in Sir *G. Duckett* and another trustee (since dead), was offered in evidence, but rejected, the attesting witness not being present. A verdict was found for the defendant on the eighth issue, and for the prosecutor

secutor upon all the others, with liberty to either party to move as after-mentioned.

In *Hilary* term 1838, cross rules nisi were obtained: by the prosecutor, to have the verdict on the eighth issue entered for him; by the defendant, to have the verdict on the ninth issue entered for him, on the ground that the 9*l.* rent was not charged on the tolls. In *April* 1838 the defendant ceased to be surveyor; and a board was appointed for superintending the parish highways under stat. 5 & 6 *W.* 4. *c.* 50. *s.* 18. In *Trinity* term 1838, the prosecutor obtained a rule nisi for a peremptory mandamus directed to the board so appointed, requiring them to pay the arrears of one of the annual sums (18*l.* per annum), on affidavit that the liability of the parish as to *that* rent was admitted by the defendant's counsel on the trial as soon as the lease for the three acres of land was produced; that the defendant's counsel had only contended against the parish being liable to the rent of 9*l.*; and that, although it was true that the finding on the eighth issue was for the defendant, that merely arose from the accidental absence of the attesting witness to the deed: that, when the rules as to entering the verdict were moved for, the defendant's counsel had engaged that the arrears of the 18*l.* rent should be paid; but that nevertheless the defendant and the board had refused to pay it. This rule was discharged by *Coleridge* J. in the Bail Court, *June* 14th, on the ground that the board had not hitherto been parties to the proceedings, and that it was irregular to issue a peremptory mandamus against them in the first instance. But, on the suggestion of the prosecutor's counsel, his Lordship made an ex parte order for a peremptory writ against the defendant *Baldwin*, though out of office. The writ now in question was thereupon issued.

Sir

1838.

The QUEEN *against* BALDWIN.

Sir *W. W. Follett* and *Byles* now shewed cause on affidavits alleging in substance the facts before stated; and, further, that, although out of office, the defendant had retained money in his hands sufficient to pay this demand, and for the very purpose of paying it if necessary, although it was true the parish had required him *not* to pay it. They contended that on the facts stated there was no reasonable doubt as to the prosecutor's right to one, at least, of the annual sums included in the mandamus (that for 18*l.*), and that the peremptory writ of mandamus affected the arrears of that only. [Lord *Denman* C. J. Is there any instance of a peremptory writ of mandamus being awarded whilst the proceedings on the first mandamus remained incomplete?] They are not substantially incomplete so far as concerns the 18*l.* Even if the rule for setting aside the verdict on the eighth issue should be discharged, that is a mere question as to the costs of the trial. It being admitted, now, that the prosecutor was, in justice, entitled to the arrear of the 18*l.*, the Court will not allow the parish vexatiously to withhold it for the purpose of delay. [*The Attorney-General*, for the defendant, referred to *Buckly* v. *Palmer* (*a*), and an *Anonymous* case in *Salkeld* (*b*), as shewing that a peremptory mandamus could not be regularly awarded until the prosecutor had obtained judgment on the mandamus.] The granting of a peremptory mandamus is in the discretion of the Court: *Rex* v. *Griffiths* (*c*).

Sir *J. Campbell*, Attorney-General, (with whom was *F. Robinson*) contrà, was stopped by the Court.

(*a*) 2 *Salk.* 430.

(*b*) 2 *Salk.* 428.

(*c*) 5 *B.* & *Ald.* 731.

Lord

1838.

The QUEEN *against* BALDWIN.

Lord DENMAN C. J. We have enquired of the officers; and they inform us they know of no instance where the Court has awarded a peremptory mandamus on part of a record. We are not inclined to make a precedent to that effect. The regular course is to wait until the whole record comes before the Court.

PATTESON, WILLIAMS, and COLERIDGE Js. concurred.

Rule absolute without costs.

The QUEEN *against* RICKETTS.

Monday, November 26th.

By a writ of capias cum proclamatione (for contempt in not paying costs in the ecclesiastical court) it appeared that a writ de contumace capiendo had issued in the same cause, returnable *January* 11th, 1838, and had been duly returned, non est inventus: wherefore, the present writ commanded the sheriff to take the defendant if found in his bailiwick, and him safely keep &c., and, if he were not found, then to cause proclamation to be made, according to stats. 5 *Eliz.* c. 23., and 53 *G.* 3. *c.* 127. The latter writ was tested *May* 24th, 1838, and did not shew any continuance of process from *January* 11th to *May* 24th. The return of the writ de contumace capiendo was "of *Trinity* term" 1838, and contained this memorandum, "Received 13th *June* 1838." On application to set aside the capias, it appeared by affidavit that there had not in fact been any continuance: that the first writ had not been lodged with the sheriff till after the return day; that he made the return on *June* 13th, after he was out of office; and that the capias issued on *June* 21st.

Held that the writ was irregular, because the proceedings did not shew a proper continuance; and, per *Patteson* J., that, if the facts could be looked at, the proceedings would still appear to be irregular.

Semble, per *Williams* J., that the direction in the capias, to make proclamation if the defendant were not found, was improper, for that the statutes require proclamation absolutely.

SIR *F. POLLOCK*, in this term (*November* 2d), obtained a rule to shew cause why a writ of capias cum proclamatione issued in this cause, on a significavit from the Arches Court of *Canterbury* (*a*), should not be set aside for irregularity, with costs. The defendant had appealed to the Arches Court from a sentence of the Consistory Court of *Hereford* in a cause concerning church-

(*a*) A like motion was made in the same cause, and under circumstances not materially different, as to a capias on significavit from the High Court of Delegates.

1838.

The QUEEN *against* RICKETTS.

church-rate. The Court of appeal made a decree affirming the sentence with costs; which decree, and the sentence of the Consistory Court, were affirmed, on further appeal, by the High Court of Delegates. In *Michaelmas* term 1837, a writ de contumace capiendo (tested *November* 25th, 1837,) was issued against the defendant, on significavit from the Arches Court, for non-payment of the costs in that Court, returnable *January* 11th, 1838. The sheriff indorsed his return on the writ, as follows. "Of *Trinity* term, in the first year of Queen *Victoria*. The within named *Thomas Bourke Ricketts* is not found in my bailiwick. The answer of *Thomas Monington*, Esq., late sheriff. Received 13th *June*, 1838." A writ of capias cum proclamatione, founded on this return, then issued, bearing teste *May* 24th, 1838, returnable *November* 2d, to enforce payment of the costs. The writ recited the significavit, and the writ de contumace capiendo, which, by the recital, was stated to have been returnable on *January* 11th, and to have been returned, in obedience to the said writ, non est inventus (*a*). Therefore, the present writ commanded the sheriff, "that you do not forbear" &c., "but that you take the said *Thomas Bourke Ricketts*, if he shall be found in your bailiwick, and him safely keep, so that he make satisfaction for the said contempt. And, *if the said* T. B. R. *shall not be found in your bailiwick, that then*

(*a*) This recital was as follows. "We lately, by our writ directed to you, commanded you that you should attach the said *Thomas Bourke Ricketts* by his body until he should have made satisfaction for the said contempt, and how you should execute this our precept you were to notify to us on the 11th day of *January* then next, wheresoever we should then be in *England*, and to have there that writ: And whereas in obedience to the said writ you returned to us that the said *T. B. R.* was not found in your bailiwick, as in our Court before us it appears upon record: Therefore" &c.

you

1838.

The QUEEN *against* RICKETTS.

you cause open proclamation to be made" &c., according to the form of the statutes, for the said *T. B. R.* to yield himself to prison within six days, &c. This writ was made returnable *November* 2d, 1838. It was stated, on affidavit in support of the rule, that no writ continuing the said writ de contumace capiendo had issued against *T. B. R.* at any time between the said 11th *January* and 24th of *May*; and that the writ de contumace capiendo was not lodged with the sheriff at any time between the teste and return day thereof; but that, after the return day, and after the sheriff was out of office, namely, on *June* 13th, 1838, he made the return of non est inventus at the instance of the prosecutors; and the capias, founded on such return, issued from the Crown Office on *June* 21st, though tested on 24th *May*. It was also stated that the defendant could have been found within the bailiwick between the teste and return day of the writ de contumace capiendo.

The objections chiefly relied upon for the defendant were as follows. 1. That the sheriff could not receive the writ de contumace capiendo, for the purpose of executing it, after the day of the return, such a course being irregular, more especially in a case affecting liberty. 2. That a return, stating that the party "is not" found, was incorrect, the proper return being that he "cannot be" found. 3. That the defendant could have been found in the bailiwick between the teste and return day of the writ de contumace capiendo. 4. That the last mentioned writ was, in point of fact, issued in vacation, and was returned by the sheriff when he was out of office. 5. That no continuances appeared to have been entered between the return day of that writ (*January* 11th) and the teste of the capias cum proclamatione

1838.

The Queen against Ricketts.

clamatione (*May* 24th). 6. That, on the return non est inventus, proclamation should be ordered peremptorily, whereas the capias here directed it in the alternative only "if the said *T. B. R.* shall not be found" &c. The enactments referred to were 53 *G.* 3. *c.* 127. *ss.* 1, 2, 3., and 5 *Eliz. c.* 23. *ss.* 2, 3, 4.

Sir *W. W. Follett* and *Stammers* now shewed cause (*a*). The writ de contumace capiendo, as recited, appears to have been tested and made returnable at proper times, and regularly returned. By stats. 53 *G.* 3. *c.* 127. *s.* 1., and 5 *Eliz. c.* 23. *s.* 2., the writ is "delivered of record" to the sheriff, in Court, and the return appears of record. The delivery was the act of the Court; and the proceedings, being of record, cannot be averred against. Besides, "where the teste of the writ is in support of justice, no averment shall be made against it;" *Mason* v. *March* (*b*); which is consistent with the doctrine of Lord *Mansfield* in *Johnson* v. *Smith* (*c*). And, taking this return as made by a late sheriff, it is not bad on that account: a return may be so made (*d*). Nor is it a substantial objection that the writ de contumace capiendo was issued in vacation. The teste in term is a mere fiction. As to the delivery of the writ, the first writ was not one to be delivered for the purpose of execution, but merely, according to stat. 5 *Eliz. c.* 23. *s.* 3., to ground further process: therefore it was not necessary that it should actually have been delivered to the sheriff, or non est inventus returned, before the

(*a*) The Court not having given judgment on all the objections, the report is confined, as much as possible, to that part of the argument which bears upon the points decided, or on which an intimation of opinion was given.

(*b*) 3 *Salk.* 397.

(*c*) 2 *Burr.* 950.

(*d*) See *Rex* v. *The late Sheriff of Middlesex*, 4 *East*, 604. Stat. 3 & 4 *W.* 4. *c.* 99. *s.* 7.

ulterior

1838.

The QUEEN *against* RICKETTS.

ulterior process issued, so that the proceedings were regularly entered up at last. [*Patteson* J. If we had been called upon to issue the second writ under the circumstances mentioned, we should not have done it. These fictions are not to be encouraged, especially in cases affecting liberty.] The same objection, if valid, might have prevailed in *Taylor* v. *Gregory* (*a*). [Lord *Denman* C. J. There the object of the proceeding was to save the Statute of Limitations. Here it is to take away liberty.] In that case the defendant was arrested on the process, as continued (*b*). It is sufficient, here, that a writ appears, upon which the capias cum proclamatione might be grounded, such prior writ being properly tested and returned. [*Patteson* J. Such an argument may be good where a regular proceeding has been taken, and back writs are issued to warrant it in point of form; but here the acts of parliament expressly provide that the writ de contumace capiendo shall be returned before the writ of capias issues (*c*); and you take upon you to issue the capias in the first instance.] There is no reason that the continuances between the return of the first writ and issuing of the second should not be entered now. The rule *Hil.* 4 *W.* 4., *General Rules and Regulations*, 2. (*d*), does not affect the practice in cases of this kind. As to the proclamation, it is sufficient that the direction in the writ fulfils the intention of the statute, though not strictly accordant with it in point of mere form. It cannot have been intended that, if the defendant was in custody after

(*a*) 2 *B.* & *Ad.* 257. (*b*) See 2 *B.* & *Ad.* 260.
(*c*) 5 *Eliz.* c. 23. ss. 2, 3, 4.; 53 *G.* 3. c. 127. s. 1.
(*d*) 5 *B.* & *Ad.* ii.

 the

1838.

The Queen against Bickers.

the return of non est inventus, proclamation should be made for him to yield himself to the gaol.

Sir *F. Pollock* and *J. W. Smith*, contrà. The return is irregular, the sheriff having received the writ after the return day named, and after he was out of office. Returns should be on the day named in the writ, or before; *Com. Dig. Return* (C 1.). No relaxation will be allowed in a penal case. It is said that the only object of the writ is to lay a foundation for the capias cum proclamatione; but in *John Parker's Case* (a) a party taken under a writ de excommunicato capiendo was discharged on habeas corpus because the writ had not been brought into K. B. and enrolled there, and delivered in convenient time to the sheriff. Stat. 5 *Eliz.* c. 23. s. 2. prescribes strictly the time of bringing the writ into Court, delivering it of record, &c.; which shews that the steps are not fictitious, and that the allegations on the return must correspond with the facts. It is argued that the return cannot be controverted; but, upon the face of it, there is a memorandum shewing the date of the receipt. If that be not taken as part of the sheriff's return, he will be liable to an action for a false return. Under stat. 5 *Eliz.* c. 23. ss. 5, 6, 7. there are cumulative penalties on successive defaults in paying obedience to writs of capias. Could a party keep the process in his own hands for a long time, and then enter up the successive steps fictitiously, so as to render the opposite party liable? No analogy exists between a penal statutory proceeding like this and writs at common law where steps may be supplied to

(a) *Cro. Car.* 582.

make

1838. The QUEEN *against* RICKETTS.

make proceedings appear regular. An *Anonymous* case, *Cro. Jac.* (*a*), shews the strictness required in returning the capias. There is here, independently of the facts supplied by affidavit, and of the memorandum, a discontinuance on the face of the writ. In *Willett* v. *Archer* (*b*) it was held, even in the case of a bill of *Middlesex*, that a term must not intervene between the return of the alias and issuing of the pluries. And in *Com. Dig. Pleader* (V 3.) it is said, "A *capias* cannot be continued intermitting a term:" "nor, a *capias utlagatum*:" "So, in an appeal, if the process leaves a day between, it will be a discontinuance." The words of stat. 5 *Eliz.* c. 23. s. 4., "upon every such return," shew that the omission here is a discontinuance and an irregularity. The capias cum proclamatione is merely a continuance of the writ de contumace capiendo. Further, the statute directs that the capias shall issue with order for proclamation absolutely, not, as here, contingently. The statute is precise; and, being penal, must be strictly followed. Sect. 14 shews that the legislature intended proclamation to be made in the bailiwick where the defendant is. It is said that, if the defendant be found in the bailiwick, the proclamation is unnecessary. But it does not follow, from his being in the bailiwick, that he should be found there. And the object of the proclamation is to give the party notice to come in. Besides, it cannot be known, before the return, that the defendant will not be found; and the statute requires that the proclamation should be made ten days before the return. [*Patteson* J. Sect. 14 provides only for the case where the addition is not

(*a*) *Cro. Jac.* 566.

(*b*) 1 *Man. & R.* 317.

good.]

1838.

The QUEEN *against* RICKETTS.

good.] The meaning is that the addition of *nuper* is to be given where the party was recently of another county.

Lord DENMAN C. J. The sheriff has not made a proper return. There is a discontinuance on the face of the proceedings. Whether this defect could be supplied or not, it must not appear. The rule must therefore be made absolute on this ground; and it is not necessary to discuss the other points.

PATTESON J. I am satisfied that this writ is irregular. The writ was brought hither and delivered of record in *Michaelmas* term, 1837, returnable in *January* 1838. Now, according to the memorandum, it was not put into the sheriff's hands till *June*, at which time the writ was out, and the sheriff no longer in office. But, if we look to the proceedings alone, we find an interval which is quite fatal. The act of parliament requiring that the successive steps should be taken after each return, the proceedings ought to shew when the return was made; but they shew only an hiatus. And, if this is to be supplied by affidavit, the facts will be brought before us which shew that in truth the sheriff received the writ too late. That the sheriff did not make the return in proper time was the fault of the party who sued the writ out, and who cannot now cure the defect.

WILLIAMS J. I am of the same opinion. In a proceeding tending to such penal consequences, and founded on statute, we cannot supply matter by intendment. I must also say that, where the statute expressly requires proclamation to be made before the return of the writ, it is too much to consider that an idle ceremony.

1838.

The QUEEN *against* RICKETTS.

ceremony. There may well be an intelligible meaning. I do not know, or think, that it follows, as a matter of course, from a party being within the bailiwick, that the sheriff can take him. Peradventure the proclamation might bring him in. At all events that is a formidable objection; and, as to the other, I am satisfied that it is fatal.

COLERIDGE J. concurred.

Rule absolute.

Ex parte BODENHAM, Under-sheriff of HEREFORDSHIRE.

Monday, November 26th.

In the Matter of JEPHSON, a Lunatic (*a*).

Where an attorney, attending a commission of lunacy for the petitioner, promised the under-sheriff to pay the fees due to him, the commissioners and the jury, on the inquisition being returned, but failed to do so on the return and on request, this Court granted a rule calling upon him to pay such fees, on the ground that, when his undertaking was accepted, credit was given to him in his professional character. And it was held no objection to such rule, that the proceedings in respect of which the obligation was incurred took place in another Court.

BUSBY had obtained a rule calling upon *William Parker*, an attorney of this Court, to shew cause why he should not pay to Mr. *Bodenham*, the under-sheriff of *Herefordshire*, several sums of money pursuant to his undertaking. By the affidavit of Mr. *Bodenham*, upon which the rule had been granted, it appeared that a commission de lunatico inquirendo directed to certain persons in the county of *Hereford*, had been issued to ascertain the state of mind of *John Jephson*, an alleged lunatic: that *Bodenham*, as under-sheriff, by virtue of the commissioners' precept, summoned the jury: that the inquiry lasted several days: that the fees payable to the commissioners, the jury, and *Bodenham* as under-sheriff, amounted to 376*l.*: that at the last meeting

(*a*) The arguments and judgments in this case are ex relatione *Busby*.

1838.

Ex parte Bodenham.

Mr. *Parker*, who had attended the inquiry as solicitor for the petitioner, stated that he was unprepared with money to pay the commissioners and jury, but offered his undertaking to discharge all the fees when the inquisition should be returned; that *Bodenham* thereupon communicated with the commissioners and jury, who instructed him to make such terms with *Parker* as would insure payment, and that *Parker* then gave him the following written undertaking. "*Ross*, 9th *March* 1838. *In the Matter of Jephson*, a supposed lunatic. I hereby undertake to pay to *Francis Lewis Bodenham*, gentleman, under-sheriff of the county of *Hereford*, the several fees payable to the commissioners, jury, under-sheriff, and bailiffs, for the execution of this commission, upon the inquisition being returned and delivered to the proper authority. *Wm. Parker*." The inquisition was returned, and filed in the petty bag office; but *Parker* refused, on request, to pay the fees. *Parker* stated, in his affidavit in answer, that he had always said, when requested to pay the fees, that he would pay what was justly due when he received the amount from his client; but he added that the client had not yet paid him such amount.

W. H. Watson now shewed cause. This is a novel application, and goes further than any that can be cited. It is very doubtful whether the Court has jurisdiction: for, in the first place, all the proceedings in respect of which the present claim arises occurred in another court, namely, the Court of Chancery; secondly, there was no privity between *Parker* and *Bodenham*. If there was, the Court of Chancery should be applied to. It is true that *Parker* is an attorney of this Court; but the

the correct test of jurisdiction is, in what court the undertaking was given.

Busby, contrà. The application is not new in principle. First, the jurisdiction of this Court is clear. *In the Matter of Aitkin* (a) and *In the Matter of Knight* (b) shew the principle upon which the courts entertain summary applications like the present. It is that, where a reasonable presumption exists that the attorney was trusted in consequence of his professional character, and he does not shew any sufficient excuse for not fulfilling the trust, he ought to be compellable forthwith to do his duty, and the complaining party should not be put to an action or bill in equity. Here, the professional character in which *Parker* appeared before the commissioners was the sole ground of the confidence reposed by *Bodenham* in his undertaking: and no excuse is alleged for the nonperformance. The fact that these proceedings took place in another court cannot defeat the general jurisdiction which the courts have over their officers. *Evans* v. *Duncombe* (c) and *In re Greaves* (d) shew that this application is properly made here. Secondly, this is a fit case for the exercise of the jurisdiction, not only because it falls within the principle, but also because, if the rule be discharged, there may be a failure of justice, inasmuch as it is doubtful whether the undertaking would support an action, though in fairness, and according to the obvious meaning of the parties, it ought to be fulfilled. (He also stated that the reason for not applying to the Lord Chancellor was that a

(a) 4 *B. & Ald.* 47. (b) 1 *Bing.* 91.
(c) 1 *Cro. & J.* 372. *S. C.* 1 *Tyrwh.* 283.
(d) 1 *Cro. & J.* 374. note (a).

1838.

Ex parte BODENHAM.

member of the Chancery Bar had given an opinion that his Lordship had no jurisdiction.)

Lord DENMAN C. J. It seems to me that this rule should be made absolute. The authorities cited shew that our jurisdiction is not taken away by reason of the undertaking having been given in a proceeding in another court; and, that being so, the case is certainly within the principle upon which we act on similar occasions.

PATTESON J. I am of the same opinion. *In the Matter of Aitkin* (a) is an authority in support of the rule. That case proceeded on the principle of the trust and confidence necessarily reposed in attorneys in their professional character; and, though it carried the principle a great way, I am perfectly satisfied that the decision was a sound one. In the present case, what was the inducement to the party to accept Mr. *Parker's* undertaking? Clearly the circumstance that he was an attorney acting professionally for the petitioner. Confidence, therefore, was placed in him in that character; and the case falls within the principle I have mentioned.

WILLIAMS and COLERIDGE Js. concurred.

Rule absolute (b).

(a) 4 *B. & Ald.* 47.

(b) See *In the Matter of Morris*, 2 *A. & E.* 582.

Pozzi *against* James Shipton and Maurice Shipton.

CASE. The declaration stated that, on &c., the plaintiff caused to be delivered to the defendants, and the defendants then accepted and received of and from the plaintiff, a certain package containing a looking-glass of the plaintiff, of great value, to wit &c., to be taken care of, and carried and conveyed by the defendants from *Liverpool* to *Birmingham* in the county of *Warwick*, and there, to wit at *Birmingham*, to be delivered to one *Peter Pensey* for the plaintiff, for certain reasonable reward to the defendants in that behalf; and thereupon it then became and was the duty of the defendants to take due care of the said package and its contents whilst they so had the charge thereof for the purpose aforesaid, and to take due and reasonable care in and about the conveyance and delivery thereof as aforesaid; yet the defendants, not regarding their duty in that behalf, but contriving and fraudulently intending to deceive and injure the plaintiff in that behalf, did not nor would take due care of the said package and its contents aforesaid, whilst they had the charge thereof for the purpose aforesaid, or take due and reasonable

Declaration stated that plaintiff delivered to defendants, and they accepted and received from him, goods to be taken care of and carried and conveyed by defendants from *L.* to *B.* and there delivered to *P. P.* for plaintiff, for reasonable reward to defendants in that behalf, and thereupon it became the duty of defendants to take due care of such goods while they so had the charge thereof for the purpose aforesaid, and to take due and reasonable care in and about the conveyance and delivery thereof as aforesaid; yet defendants, not regarding their duty in that behalf, but contriving &c., did not nor would take due care &c., but on the contrary, whilst they had the charge &c., took such bad care &c. that the goods were injured, to plaintiff's damage &c. Pleas, Not Guilty, and traverse of the delivery and acceptance modo et formâ.

On the trial, the plaintiff gave no proof of an express contract, but endeavoured to shew that the defendants were common carriers. No objection was taken to the course of evidence. The case was proved as to one defendant only, who was shewn to be a common carrier, and a verdict was taken against him and for the other defendant. On motion to enter a nonsuit, on the ground that the action was founded in contract, and therefore a verdict could not pass against one defendant only:

Held that the declaration might, and therefore must after verdict, be read as a declaration against carriers on the custom of the realm, and consequently that the verdict was maintainable.

Quære whether such declaration against carriers on the custom would have been sufficient on special demurrer?

care

1838.

Pozzi *against* Shipton.

care in and about the conveyance and delivery thereof as aforesaid; but, on the contrary thereof, the defendants, whilst they had the charge of the said package and its contents for the purpose aforesaid, to wit on &c., took so little and such bad and improper care of the said package and its contents, and such bad and unreasonable care in and about the conveyance and delivery thereof as aforesaid, and so carelessly and negligently conducted themselves in the premises, that the said looking-glass, being of the value aforesaid, afterwards, to wit on &c., became and was broken and greatly damaged. To the damage of the plaintiff of 10*l.* &c.

Pleas: 1. Not guilty. 2. That plaintiff did not cause to be delivered to defendants, nor did defendants accept from plaintiff, the said package &c., to be taken care of and carried &c., and safely to be delivered &c., for reward in that behalf, in manner and form &c. Conclusion to the country. Joinder.

On the trial before *Coleridge* J., at the *Liverpool* Summer assizes 1836, the plaintiff failed to establish his case against one defendant, but obtained a verdict under the direction of the learned Judge against the other, who was proved to be a common carrier. *Atcherley* Serjt., in the ensuing term, moved for a rule to shew cause why a nonsuit should not be entered, on the ground that the action was founded on a contract; that, if the declaration had been framed in assumpsit, the plaintiff could not have recovered against one only of the defendants; and that the rights of parties in this respect were not to be changed by varying the form of declaration. A rule nisi having been granted,

Alexander

1838.

POSSI against SHIPTON.

Alexander shewed cause, in last *Easter* term (a). The verdict against one party is maintainable, because the defendants here were substantially, though not in form, charged by the declaration as common carriers, and were made liable, not on contract, but by the custom or common law of the land. This was the principle of *Bretherton* v. *Wood* (b). The declaration there stated that the defendants were proprietors of a stage-coach for the conveyance of passengers for hire (which the Court construed to mean common carriers), and received the plaintiff to be safely carried for hire from *A.* to *B.*, and by reason thereof ought to have safely carried him, but that they, not regarding their duty, conducted themselves so carelessly in that behalf that the plaintiff, by their carelessness, while being so conveyed, was injured. A second count stated that the plaintiff became a passenger at the special instance of the defendants, an averment not made here. But in that case it was held that a verdict against eight of ten defendants, the other two being found not guilty, was good. In *Ansell* v. *Waterhouse* (c) the defendant pleaded in abatement to a similar declaration, that there were parties jointly liable, who were not sued; and the plea was held bad. *Bayley* J. there adverts to *Govett* v. *Radnidge* (d), where the declaration stated that three defendants had the loading of a hogshead of treacle of the plaintiff, for reward to be paid by him to them, but so carelessly conducted themselves in the loading that, by reason thereof, the hogshead was broken; and a verdict against one defendant only was held good; and he says that, if it were necessary to choose between conflicting cases (which necessity,

(a) *May* 3d. Before *Littledale*, *Patteson*, and *Coleridge* Js.

(b) 3 *Brod.* & *B.* 54.

(c) 6 *M.* & *S.* 385.

(d) 3 *East*, 62.

1838.

Possi against Shipton.

necessity, however, he thinks does not arise), he should be disposed to adhere to *Govett* v. *Radnidge* (a). But the decision there, as well as those before cited, must be over-ruled, if the defendants succeed here; and yet the present is a stronger case for the plaintiff than that; for there the averments of the declaration tended more directly to shew a contract with the party against whom a verdict was found. The principle of the decision in that case is illustrated by *Mast* v. *Goodson* (b) and *Brown* v. *Dixon* (c). The general result of the authorities is thus stated in note [e] to *Cabell* v. *Vaughan* (d); "Where the action is maintainable for the tort simply without reference to any contract made between the parties, no advantage can be taken of the omission of some defendants, or of the joinder of too many, as for instance in actions against carriers, which are grounded on the custom of the realm. But where the action is not maintainable without referring to a contract between the parties, and laying a previous ground for it by shewing such contract, there, although the plaintiff shapes his case in *tort*, he shall yet be liable to a plea in abatement, if he omit any defendant, or to a nonsuit, if he join too many: for he shall not by adopting a particular form of action alter the situation of the defendant."

As to the cases which may be relied upon on the other side. In *Powell* v. *Layton* (e) the declaration had words evidently referring to a contract, and was substantially in assumpsit, as was observed by *Dallas* C. J. in delivering the judgment of the Court of Common Pleas in

(a) 3 *East*, 62.

(b) 3 *Wils.* 348.

(c) 1 *T. R.* 274.

(d) 1 *Wms. Saund.* 291 e, 5th ed.

(e) 2 *New Rep.* 365.

Bretherton

Bretherton v. *Wood* (*a*). *Max* v. *Roberts* (*b*) follows up the decision in *Powell* v. *Layton* (*c*). *Bayley* J. refers to these cases in *Ansell* v. *Waterhouse* (*d*), when stating that, if there were a conflict of decisions, he should adhere to *Govett* v. *Radnidge* (*e*). In *Weall* v. *King* (*g*), where it was held that one of the two defendants could not be found guilty as for a tort, the joint warranty declared upon was inseparable from a joint contract, which not being proved, the whole case failed. Lord *Ellenborough* said that the Court thought it better to decide the case on this ground than by "a reference to any cases either of doubtful authority, or in which the particular facts may seem to afford a special rule of construction;" *Powell* v. *Layton* (*c*) having been cited in the argument. In *Green* v. *Greenbank* (*h*) the ground of action was substantially contract; and the point really decided was that, in such a case, the plaintiff could not, by declaring in tort, exclude the defence of infancy. In *Buddle* v. *Willson* (*i*) nothing was judicially determined (though an opinion was expressed) on the point now in question. In *Boson* v. *Sandford* (*k*) the declaration charged the defendants on an undertaking to carry safely; and the judgment, which was for the defendants by reason of non-joinder, proceeded on the ground that they were charged upon contract. The case, therefore, is not in point; and its authority has been questioned in some material respects;

(*a*) 3 *B.* & *B.* 54.

(*b*) 2 *New Rep.* 454. *S. C.* (but no decision on this point), in error, 12 *East*, 89.

(*c*) 2 *New Rep.* 365.

(*d*) 6 *M.* & *S.* 385.

(*e*) 3 *East*, 62.

(*g*) 12 *East*, 452.

(*h*) 2 *Marsh*, 485.

(*i*) 6 *T. R.* 369.

(*k*) 2 *Salk.* 440; 3 *Salk.* 203; and in several other reports. See the declaration in *Carth.* 59. and 2 *Show.* 478.

Govett

1839.

Possy against Shipton.

Govett v. *Radnidge* (a). In *Dale* v. *Hall* (b) this Court appears to have considered an action against carriers on the custom of the realm in the same light as an action ex contractu; but the declaration there was expressly in assumpsit. The declaration, in the present case, does not allege that the defendants were common carriers; but it is usual now to omit the circumstantial allegations formerly introduced; and the plaintiff may (as is laid down in 1 *Selw. N. P.* 414. (9th ed.),) "adopt a more general form (omitting the recital of the custom,) and allege his gravamen as consisting in a breach of duty arising out of an employment for hire, and may consider that breach of duty as a tortious negligence." And, if upon the whole the declaration appears to be founded on the custom, the Court, after verdict, will lean to that construction which supports the plaintiff's claim. If the objection be merely that the declaration is faulty in itself, that is no ground for the present application.

Atcherley Serjt., and *Crompton*, contrà. The nonjoinder in this case was fatal. The declaration is, by its terms, evidently founded on contract: and, if this were not so, the count should have distinctly charged the defendant with liability on some ground of duty, as by office, public or otherwise, or custom. [*Coleridge* J. If the declaration is on contract, why did not you plead non assumpsit?] That might perhaps have been done; but the question is upon the case as now situated. If a duty independent of contract can be inferred from this declaration, any person undertaking to carry goods, though not a public carrier, may be charged on the ground of duty. [*Patteson* J. You would say that, even if both defendants had been proved to be com-

(a) 3 *East*, 62. See p. 69.

(b) 1 *Wils.* 281.

mon

mon carriers, they were both entitled to a verdict, unless a contract was proved]. At any rate a nonsuit may be demanded. The general rule is that, where an action appears on the pleadings to be really founded in contract, though formally in tort, the incidents of an action on contract apply; one of which is that all the contracting parties must be fixed at nisi prius. The only incident of an action on contract not applicable in such a case is the right of adding a count in assumpsit; and the rules on this subject, if settled, are anomalous. Where the action is framed as in tort, but is founded on contract, the plaintiff has been held for that reason entitled to nominal damages, though no real injury had been sustained: *Marzetti* v. *Williams* (a), *Godefroy* v. *Jay* (b). In *Ansell* v. *Waterhouse* (c) the judgment (whether founded on a right view of the declaration or not) proceeded on the ground that the defendant was in fact charged on the custom of the realm as a common carrier. The same observation applies to *Bretherton* v. *Wood* (d); and *Dallas* C. J. there points out that in *Powell* v. *Layton* (e) the action was against owners of a ship, not stated to be a general ship carrying the goods of all who chose to send them; the employment was stated to be a particular employment, at the special request of the defendants; the action was therefore founded on a particular contract; and, that being so, he does not deny the case to be good law. He makes similar observations on *Max* v. *Roberts* (g). But he says, as to the duty of a common carrier, "a breach of this duty is a breach of the law, and for this breach an action lies, founded on the common law, which action

(a) 1 *B. & Ad.* 415.
(b) 7 *Bing.* 413. See p. 419.
(c) 6 *M. & S.* 385.
(d) 3 *Brod. & B.* 54.
(e) 2 *New. Rep.* 365.
(g) 2 *New Rep.* 454.

wants

1838.

Pozzi *against* Shipton.

wants not the aid of a contract to support it." Here the declaration states that the plaintiff delivered to the defendants, and they accepted and received from him, a package to be taken care of and carried and conveyed by them from *Liverpool* to *Birmingham*, and there delivered, for reasonable reward to the defendants in that behalf, and thereupon it became their duty to carry safely. That alleges no duty on the custom; it states either a particular contract or no ground of obligation at all. [*Coleridge* J. Under the general words of the declaration the plaintiff offered evidence to shew that he stood in a relation to the defendants which would have created a duty. Does your objection amount to more than pointing out a fault in the declaration? Or should not you have contended at the trial that the evidence was improper? And, not having done so, can you claim to enter a nonsuit?] The question is not as to the medium of proof, but what the plaintiff undertakes by his pleading to prove. If a contract is alleged, it may be proved by shewing that the defendants received the goods as common carriers, from which fact a contract would be inferred. [*Patteson* J. That is contrary to the doctrine of *Bretherton* v. *Wood* (a)]. The question there (and in *Ansell* v. *Waterhouse* (b)) was, not whether any contract subsisted, but whether the action was necessarily founded in contract. If there was a tort on which the action might be founded, the incidents of an action of tort were applicable, although there might in point of law have been a contract also, as indeed there is in every case of bailment in which tort may be brought. But, where there is a contract, that may be sued upon, though there be a tort also; and here, if the contract was to be proved through the medium of shew-

(a) 3 *B.* & *B.* 54.

(b) 6 *M.* & *S.* 385.

ing

1838.

Pozzi *against* Shipton.

ing the parties to be common carriers, complete proof should have been given as to both, or the action failed.

There is no case really adverse to the present defence except *Govett* v. *Radnidge* (*a*). That case, however, is inconsistent with the other decisions, particularly *Boson* v. *Sandford* (*b*), which (on very full consideration) was upheld, and *Govett* v. *Radnidge* (*a*) in effect overruled (note (4) to *Cabell* v. *Vaughan* (*c*), in *Powell* v. *Layton* (*d*). [*Patteson* J. It is strong to say "overruled," because it is clear that *Powell* v. *Layton* (*d*) would itself have been over-ruled, if brought into the King's Bench on error.] In the note [*e*] to the passage of *Wms. Saund.* just cited, it is said that the incidents of an action of tort, as to joinder, apply "where the action is maintainable for the tort simply without reference to any contract;" otherwise, "where the action is not maintainable without referring to a contract between the parties, and laying a previous ground for it by shewing such contract," for the plaintiff "shall not by adopting a particular form of action alter the situation of the defendant. On this last ground undoubtedly the case of *Green* v. *Greenbank* (*e*) was determined, in which it was held that infancy was a good plea to an action on the case on a warranty." *Jennings* v. *Rundall* (*g*) is to the same effect. In *Buddle* v. *Willson* (*h*) the defendant was, in form, charged in tort for neglect of duty as a common carrier, and pleaded in abatement the non-joinder of his partners; and the Court thought that such a plea, if pleaded in time, would have been good, the cause of

(*a*) 3 *East*, 62.
(*b*) 2 *Salk.* 440. 3 *Salk.* 203.
(*c*) 1 *Wms. Saund.* 291 *e.* 5th ed.
(*d*) 2 *New Rep.* 365.
(*e*) 2 *Marsh.* 485.
(*g*) 8 *T. R.* 335.
(*h*) 6 *T. R.* 369.

1838.

PENN against SMIRSON.

action arising quasi ex contractu. [*Coleridge* J. How is that reconcileable with *Bretherton* v. *Wood* (a)? *Patteson* J. The opinion expressed in *Buddle* v. *Willson* (b) is a mere dictum. The plea was held bad, as having been pleaded after a general imparlance.] *Weall* v. *King* (c) is in point. The declaration there stated that the defendants exposed lambs to sale as "stock," and that the plaintiff bargained with them for the said lambs as and for stock, at a certain price to be therefore paid by plaintiff to defendants; and that defendants, by falsely warranting the said lambs to be stock, deceitfully sold the same to plaintiff as and for stock, for a price &c., whereas at the time of the warranty they were not stock, &c. The plea was Not Guilty; and on the trial no evidence was given to affect more than one defendant. It was contended that a verdict might pass against one, the action being on the tort, not the contract; but *Heath* J. directed a nonsuit, saying that, if that reasoning were to prevail, every breach of promise might be converted into a tort. And he referred to *Powell* v. *Layton* (d) and *Max* v. *Roberts* (e), as lately decided against the authority of *Govett* v. *Radnidge* (g). Lord *Ellenborough* said, in delivering the judgment of this Court in *Weall* v. *King* (c), — "It cannot be questioned that the allegation of a joint contract of sale was not only material, but essentially necessary to a joint warranty alleged upon record to have been made by the supposed sellers, by whatever circumstances, and in whatever action, be the same debt, assumpsit, or tort, the allegation of a contract becomes necessary to be

(a) 3 *B.* & *B.* 54.
(b) 6 *T. R.* 369.
(c) 12 *East*, 452.
(d) 2 *New Rep.* 365.
(e) 2 *New Rep.* 454.
(g) 3 *East*, 62.

made:"

1838.

POZZI against SHIPTON.

made:" and "such allegation requires proof strictly corresponding therewith." *Ansell* v. *Waterhouse* (*a*) and *Bretherton* v. *Wood* (*b*) are, in principle, authorities for the plaintiff, because in each of those cases the defendants were charged, substantially at least, as common carriers: a duty therefore was shewn, for the violation of which an action of tort lay. In the present case no such duty appears; for the mere allegation of it is not sufficient, unless the circumstances are stated from which a duty arises. Had it been averred here, with or without a subsequent allegation of duty, that the defendants were common carriers, the case would have been different. The action, therefore, is grounded merely on contract, and subject to the incidents of an action of assumpsit; and the same would evidently have holden in the two last-cited cases, if the circumstances had been similar. *Max* v. *Roberts* (*c*), in the Court of Common Pleas, was decided, as this case must be, on the ground that no duty appeared unless by contract. The position, that the real ground of the action, and not the mere form, must be looked to, is clearly recognized by *Parke* and *Patteson* Js. in *Marzetti* v. *Williams* (*d*), and *Tindal* C. J. in *Godefroy* v. *Jay* (*e*).

Cur. adv. vult.

PATTESON J., in this term (*November* 3d), delivered the judgment of the Court.

This is an action against carriers for negligence. A verdict was found for the plaintiff against one of the de-

(*a*) 6 *M.* & *S.* 385.
(*b*) 3 *B.* & *B.* 54.
(*c*) 2 *New Rep.* 454.
(*d*) 1 *B.* & *Ad.* 415.
(*e*) 7 *Bing.* 413.

1838.

Pozzi against Shipton.

fendants only; and, upon a rule for a new trial having been obtained, the case was argued in last *Easter* term before my Brothers *Littledale*, *Coleridge*, and myself.

The form of the declaration is in case, and differs from that used in *Bretherton* v. *Wood* (*a*) in this, that it contains no positive averment that the defendants were carriers; whereas in *Bretherton* v. *Wood* (*a*) there was an averment that the defendants were proprietors of a stage coach for the carriage and conveyance of passengers for hire from *Bury* to *Bolton*. The present declaration states simply that the plaintiff delivered to the defendants, and the defendants received from the plaintiff, goods to be carried for hire from *A.* to *B.* It is therefore consistent with the defendants being common carriers, or being hired on the particular occasion only. Upon the trial it was proved satisfactorily that the defendant against whom the verdict was found was a common carrier; and it does not appear to have been objected, at that time, that proof of an express contract between the plaintiff and the defendants was necessary in order to sustain the declaration. If such proof was not necessary, it can only be because the declaration may be read as founded on the general custom of the realm; and, if it *may* be so read, the Court after verdict *must* so read it; and then the case of *Bretherton* v. *Wood* (*a*) is directly in point in favour of the plaintiff.

Upon consideration, we are of opinion that the declaration may be so read. The practice appears to have been in former times to set out the custom of the

(*a*) 3 *B.* & *B.* 54.

realm;

1838.

Pozzi against Shipton.

realm; but it was afterwards very properly held to be unnecessary so to do, because the custom of the realm is the law, and the Court will take notice of it, and the distinction has for many years prevailed between general and special customs in this respect. Afterwards the practice appears to have been to state the defendants to be *common carriers for hire*, totidem verbis. That however was departed from in *Bretherton* v. *Wood* (*a*) to a considerable extent, and certainly still farther upon the present occasion.

It may be that the present declaration could not have been supported on special demurrer for want of some such averment; but on this point we are not called upon to give any opinion. It does not state that the goods were delivered to the defendants at their special instance and request, nor contain any other allegation necessarily applicable to an express contract only, or even pointing to any express contract. We cannot therefore say that it shews the action to be founded on contract: and it is sufficient for the present purpose, if the language in which it is couched is consistent with its being founded on the general custom as to carriers.

Taking this declaration, therefore, to charge the defendants as common carriers, it follows that it is strictly an action on the case for a tort, and that one of several defendants may be found guilty upon it according to the doctrine established in *Bretherton* v. *Wood* (*a*). The evidence warrants the verdict which has been found, and we cannot disturb that verdict. We purposely abstain from giving any opinion, whether the doctrine

(*a*) 3 *B.* & *B.* 54.

1838.

Pozzi *against* Shipton.

in *Govett* v. *Radnidge* (*a*) or that in *Powell* v. *Layton* (*b*) be the true doctrine, as we do not feel ourselves called upon to decide between them, supposing them to differ.

The rule must be discharged.

Rule discharged.

(*a*) 3 *East*, 62. (*b*) 2 *N. R.* 365.

Monday, November 26th.

The Queen *against* The Manchester and Leeds Railway Company.

This case is reported, antè, p. 419.

END OF MICHAELMAS TERM.

AN

INDEX

TO

THE PRINCIPAL MATTERS.

the event of her not arriving at *Constantinople* before 15th *November*, to exercise the option of annulling the contract, and that the option should be exercised in a reasonable time after the ship's arriving at *Constantinople* and notice thereof to the agents of *S.* or defendant there: Averment, that she arrived after 15th *November* at *Constantinople*, and was ready to proceed to *Odessa* or the *Crimea*, as plaintiff should be ordered by *S.*, or defendant or their agents: that plaintiff, on the ship's arriving at *Constantinople*, made due search to find, but could not find, *S.*, or any agent of *S.*, or defendant, nor could discover any orders, or information whether the option would be exercised: that the ship remained at *Constantinople*, waiting for orders or notice, for a long and reasonable time, after which plaintiff received notice from *S.* that he cancelled the contract: that this notice was not given in a reasonable time after the ship's arrival at *Constantinople* and the period at which plaintiff would and could have given notice of the arrival had *S.*, or any agent of *S.*, or defendant been at *Constantinople*, or could plaintiff have discovered them: that plaintiff was ready to receive a cargo, but, by reason of defendant's neglect in not having *S.*, or an agent at *Constantinople*, and of the option not being exercised *by reason thereof* in a reasonable time, plaintiff was prevented from proceeding to *Odessa*, or the *Crimea*, and there receiving such a cargo as aforesaid, or seeking a cargo elsewhere.

Pleas, 1. Non assumpsit. 2. That notice was given by *S.* in reasonable time after the ship's arrival at *Constantinople*. 2. That she did not remain at *Constantinople* waiting for such orders or notice, from the time of her arrival, for a reasonable time. Issues thereon.

On the trial, no evidence was given of any express promise that *S.* or any agent, should be at *Constantinople*, or that the option should be exercised in a reasonable time after the vessel's arrival. Defendant objected that such promise did not arise from the charter-party, and applied for a nonsuit. The Judge left it to the jury, whether the notice of the exercise of option was reasonable; and, upon their finding in the negative, directed a verdict for plaintiff, and allowed him to amend the declaration by substituting a promise that defendant, or *S.*, in a reasonable time after the ship's arrival at *Constantinople* and notice thereof, would give orders whether she was to load at *Odessa* or the *Crimea*, or, if she arrived after 15th *November*, would, in a reasonable time after her arrival and notice thereof, communicate to plaintiff the exercise of the option: and the Judge reserved to the full Court the question whether he had the power to allow the amendment, and on what terms it should be made.

Held, that, the allegation of the promise being intended only as a statement of the legal effect of the charter-party, the Judge had power, under stat. 3 & 4 *W.* 4. *c.* 42. *s.* 23., to amend, by either striking out the allegation, or substituting a correct statement of the legal effect; that the promise as amended was such a correct statement; and that the amendment should be allowed, without any terms as to costs.

Although affidavit was made that defendant had gone to trial with the intention and expectation (grounded on circumstances which were stated) of contesting the allegation as it stood originally. *Whitwill* v. *Scheer*, 301.

II. Of N. P. record where cause made a remanet, 941. 945. n. *Remanet.*

III. Of proceedings in Ecclesiastical Court, 610. *Prohibition*, III.

AMOUNT.

Effect of not specifying in acknowledgment of a debt, 225. n. *Statute*, XLIV. 2.

ANCIENT DOCUMENT.

Proper custody, 151. *Evidence*, XV. 3.

ANNUITY.

I. Memorial.

Nominal consideration for a collateral security by the same deed, 789. *Judgment*, VIII.

II. Interest of husband, 683. *Evidence*, V. 4.

ANSWER.

ANSWER.

APOTHECARY.

What charges he may make.

There is no rule of law which prevents an apothecary from making distinct charges for attendances and for medicines.

Whether the patient be liable to a separate demand for attendances, is a question to be decided by the jury in each case, on the facts proving or disproving a contract to that effect; as the prior dealing between the same parties; or the reasonableness or unreasonableness, under the circumstances in the particular case, of making a charge for attendances, as well as for medicines. *Morgan* v. *Hallen*, 489.

APPEAL.

I. Not given by implication.

The church-building act, 59 *G.* 3. *c.* 134. *s.* 39., empowers the commissioners to order the stopping up of footways, which appear to them unnecessary, in churchyards, provided the same be done with the consent of two justices, and on notice being given in the manner and form prescribed by stat. 55 *G.* 3. *c.* 68. Schedule (A.) of that statute gives a form of notice of an order for stopping up a useless road; and the form states that such order will be enrolled at sessions, unless, *upon an appeal against the same to be then made*, it be otherwise determined. Sect. 3 of the same act empowers any party aggrieved by such order to appeal to the sessions, upon giving ten days' notice to the *surveyor of the highways*.

Held, that stat. 59 *G.* 3. *c.* 134. *s.* 39., though incorporating the form of notice annexed to stat. 55 *G.* 3. *c.* 68., did not thereby give an appeal against an order of the commissioners for stopping a footway: for that an appeal cannot be given by implication only.

Held also, that, if such power had been given by reference to stat. 55 *G.* 3. *c.* 68., the repeal of that statute would not have taken it away. *Regina* v. *Stock*, 405.

APPLICATION.

APPOINTMENT.

APPORTIONMENT.

APPROBATION.

ARBITRATION.

II. Power

II. Power of arbitrator, 290. *Post*, VII. 1.

III. Proceedings.

Presumption of regularity, 645. *Post*, IV.

IV. Construction of award.

The rule, that an affidavit more than a year old is not to be used, applies only in the case of affidavits to hold to bail.

Where the making and publishing of an award are sworn to, but without fixing the time, the award itself bearing date within the time limited by the order of reference, the Court will not presume that the award was made and published after that time.

So held on motion for an attachment for non-performance.

Where the award directs that *A.* shall pay *B.* 15*l.* for copyhold land; that *B.*, in consideration of that sum, shall at the costs of *A.* surrender the land to *A.*'s use; and that, upon such surrender being made and delivered to *A.*, he shall pay *B.* the 15*l.*; it rests with *B.* to prepare and execute the surrender; and it is a non-performance of the award if *B.* omits, on request, to make the surrender. Or (per *Littledale* J.) if *B.* does not at least give notice to *A.* that he will attend at a certain time before the steward of the manor. *Doe dem. Clarke* v. *Stillwell*, 645.

V. Conformability, 290. *Post*, VII. 1.

VI. Particularity.

Where distinct matters are referred, 235. *Post*, VII. 2.

VII. Finality.

1. *A.* agreed to purchase land of *B.*, the title to be made out to the satisfaction of *B.*'s attorney. The agreement being uncompleted, and disputes arising, all matters in difference between the parties, and the settlement of all questions on the agreement, were referred to arbitration. The arbitrator awarded that *B.* should convey to *A.* the title to the above land, contained in two abstracts given in evidence on the arbitration; he also prescribed the boundary of the land so to be conveyed, and ordered that *B.* should execute an indemnity bond to *A.*, to be forfeited if *A.* should be evicted by reason of defect in the title; and that on execution of the premises, *A.* should pay the purchase-money. Nothing further was awarded as to the validity of the title. The goodness of the title had been a matter of dispute before the arbitrator.

Held, that the award was bad, as not finally determining the questions referred. *Ross* v. *Boards*, 290.

2. On motion to set aside a judgment on an award, advantage may be taken of objections apparent on the face of the award, but of none other.

Ejectment being brought on two demises, all matters in difference in the cause were referred by a Judge's order, which directed that the costs of the suit and of the reference and award should abide the event of the award; that the party in whose favour the award should be might sign judgment in the same manner as if the cause had been tried at Nisi Prius; and that, if it was in plaintiff's favour, he might issue a writ of possession thereon and proceed in the usual way for costs on such judgment.

The arbitrator awarded that the plaintiff was entitled to the possession "of a certain part of the lands sought to be recovered," which he set out by boundaries. The award stated nothing as to the residue, did not say on which demise the plaintiff was entitled; and gave no damages. Held,

(1.) That the award was bad for not stating on which demise the plaintiff was entitled.

(2.) Also for not expressly deciding as to the residue. Per *Littledale* and *Patteson* Js., dubitante *Coleridge* J.

(3.) But not for giving no damages. Per *Coleridge* J. *Doe dem. Madkins* v. *Horner*, 235.

3. In trespass, quare clausum fregit, &c., defendant pleaded several pleas, to some of which plaintiff replied, and issue was joined on the replication; as to others, the plaintiff new assigned, and signed judgment for want of a plea. The cause went to the assizes for an assessment of damages on the new assignment, and for trial on the issues joined. A verdict was taken for the plaintiff, subject to a reference of the cause and all matters in difference; the costs to abide the event of the award. The

The arbitrator awarded in defendant's favour as to the matter disputed on the issues, and directed a verdict to be entered for him, instead of the former verdict; but he took no notice of the new assignment.

Held, that the award was therefore bad, and that the Court could not remedy the defect. *Wykes* v. *Shipton*, 246. n.

VIII. As to damages, 235. 246. n. *Antè*, VII. 2, 3.

IX. As to costs, 235. *Antè*, VII. 2.

X. Affidavit of publication, 645. *Antè*, IV.

XI. Performance.

1. Notice of intention to perform, 645. *Antè*, IV.
2. What is a non-performance on request, 645. *Antè*, IV.

XII. Motion to set aside award, 246. n. *Antè*, VII. 3.

XIII. Attachment for non-performance. On old affidavit, 645. *Antè*, IV.

XIV. Objections how available.

1. On motion to set aside award, 246. n. *Antè*, VII. 3.
2. On motion to set aside judgment, 235. *Antè*, VII. 2.

XV. Power of Court to remedy defects, 246. n. *Antè*, VII. 3.

ARREST.

I. What constitutes, 351. *Costs*, II.

II. 1. Irregularity, 275. *Practice*, XVI. 1.

2. Trespass for irregular, 449. *Attorney*, V. 1.

III. On mesne process.

1. Form of judge's order for detainer.

Where a defendant, arrested on mesne process for 9000*l*., claimed to be discharged under stat. 1 & 2 *Vict*. *c*. 110. *s*. 7., having entered a common appearance, and application was made to a Judge to detain him under *s*. 7., on the ground that he was likely to quit *England*:

Held, that an order by the Judge for detaining him till he should give bail for 3000*l*., or *till further order*, was invalid. And on motion to this Court, that the order might be set aside and the defendant discharged out of custody, the rule was made absolute. *Boddington* v. *Woodley*, 925.

2. Attachment for not bringing in the body, 938. *Sheriff*, IV.

IV. Remedies for.

1. Trespass, 449. *Attorney*, V. 1.
2. Defendant not entitled to costs for excessive arrest, unless there has been an arrest in fact, 351. *Costs*, II.
3. Discharge on motion, 925. *Antè*, III. 1.

ARREST OF JUDGMENT.

Judgment.

ASSAULT.

What is a battery, 602. *Costs*, VIII. 2.

ASSENT.

I. By taking part in proceedings under protest, 413. *Certiorari*, II.

II. To assignment under Insolvent Debtors Act, 1. *G*. 4. *c*. 119. *s*. 7., 683. *Evidence*, V. 4.

ASSIGNEE.

I. Of insolvent debtor.

1. Assent to assignment under 1 *G*. 4. *c*. 119. *s*. 7., 683. *Evidence*, V. 4.
2. Liability of executor for breach of covenant subsequent to assignee's death, 683. *Evidence*, V. 4.

II. Of bankrupt. *Bankrupt*.

ASSUMPSIT.

I. Whether it lies against widow for goods supplied to her during coverture, 467. *Pleading*, XIII.

II. Consideration.

Declaration, in assumpsit, stated that, in consideration that plaintiff, at defendant's request, had consented to allow defendant to weigh two boilers of plaintiff, defendant promised to give them up, after weighing, in as perfect condition as they were in at the time of the consent: breach, that defendant did not give up, &c.

On motion in arrest of judgment, on the ground of want of a consideration shewing detriment to plaintiff or benefit

benefit to defendant, and also of ambiguity in the word "weigh:" Held, that the declaration was sufficient. *Bainbridge* v. *Firmstone*, 743.

III. For money paid.

By surety to a promissory note after an addition to the note, 136. *Bills*, II. 1.

IV. For money had and received.

On sale rescinded by option.

A. bought horses of *B.*, paying 80*l.*, with liberty to return them within a month, allowing *B.* 10*l.* out of the 80*l.*, and with a stipulation that, if he kept them beyond the month, he should pay *B.* 10*l.* above the 80*l.*

Held, that *A.*, on returning the horses within a month, might recover the 70*l.* in an action for money had and received. *Hurst* v. *Orbell*, 107.

V. Pleading.

1. Plea, that plaintiff's demand vested in the assignees under his second bankruptcy, by reason of his not having paid 15*s.* in the pound, 470. *Bankrupt*, VI.
2. Amendment by substituting legal effect of contract for express promise, 301. *Amendment*, I.

ATTACHMENT.

I. Arrest redeundo after discharge from custody, 275. *Practice*, XVI. 1.

II. Time for taking advantage of irregularity, 275. *Practice*, XVI. 1.

III. Against sheriff, 938. *Sheriff.*

IV. For non-performance of award, 645. *Arbitration*, IV.

ATTESTATION.

Proof by witness, when dispensed with, 582. *Landlord and Tenant*, XII.

ATTORNEY.

I. Examination. Term's notice.

If a party applying to be admitted an attorney undergo the examination under *Reg. H.* 6. *W.* 4., but fail to obtain his certificate, he cannot be examined again without giving a fresh term's notice. *In re Examiners*, 745.

II. Admission.

Apportionment of fees, 741. *Reg. Gen.*

III. Use of his name without sanction, 275. *Practice*, XVI. 1.

IV. Delivery of bill.

Month how reckoned.

Under stat. 2 *G.* 2. *c.* 23. *s.* 23., which directs that no attorney shall commence an action for his fees until *the expiration of one month or more after* he shall have delivered his bill, the month is to be reckoned exclusively of the days on which the bill is delivered and the action brought. *Blunt* v. *Heslop*, 577.

V. Liability and remedies.

1. Trespass for irregular arrest.

Where an arrest is made under process which is afterwards set aside for irregularity, the attorney in the suit is liable in trespass, as well as the plaintiff.

And if, in an action of trespass, he justifies under the process, it is a good replication, that the process was irregularly sued out, and was afterwards set aside, by rule of Court, for irregularity.

Where issues are joined in fact and in law on the same count, and the plaintiff obtains judgment on the issue in law, and then proceeds to try the issue in fact, the jury process must be awarded to assess damages on the issue in law as well as to try the issue in fact; although the latter issue goes to the whole cause of action in the count.

Where the plaintiff in such a case delivered an issue and notice of trial with a venire only to try the issue in fact, the Court set them aside for irregularity, with costs. *Codrington* v. *Lloyd*, 449.

2. For representations respecting his client's ability, 457. *Statute*, XLIV. 3.

3. Where credit given in professional character.

Where an attorney, attending a commission of lunacy for the petitioner, promised the under-sheriff to pay the fees due to him, the commissioners and the jury, on the inquisition being returned, but failed to do so on the return and on request, this Court granted a rule calling upon him to pay such fees, on the ground that, when his

his undertaking was accepted, credit was given to him in his professional character. And it was held no objection to such rule, that the proceeding in respect of which the obligation was incurred took place in another court. *Ex parte Bodenham*, 959.

VI. Pleading.
Replication of irregularity to plea of process, 449. *Antè*, V. 1.

VII. Administration by, 624. *Executor*, II.

ATTORNMENT.

I. Acknowledgment in the nature of, 255. *Stamp*, II. 3.

II. Stamping, 255. *Stamp*, II. 3.

AUTHORITY.

I. To issue commission to ascertain boundaries, 198. *Evidence*, XXV. 1.

II. To grant alehouse licences, 281. *Quo Warranto*, II. 1.

III. Use of attorney's name without, 275. *Practice*, XVI. 1.

IV. To give notice to quit, under 4 *G*. 2. *c*. 28. *s*. 1., 582. *Landlord and Tenant*, XII.

V. To inform for trespass in search of game, 155. *Game*.

VI. Of servant to do an illegal act must be proved, 512. *Master and Servant*, I. 1.

AVERMENT.

By reference, 227. *Poor*, XIII.

AVOWRY.

Replevin.

AWARD.

Arbitration.

BAIL.

I. Putting in, when not equivalent to an arrest in fact, 351. *Costs*, II.

II. Render in discharge.
How soon defendant not charged in execution becomes supersedeable after a render in vacation, 195. *Execution*, III. 1.

BAILMENT.

Carrier.

BAILIFF.

I. Parol lessee of tolls, 716. *Poor*, II. 2.

II. Misconduct of, 565. 568. n. *Sheriff*, II.

BANK OF ENGLAND.

Payment of purchase-money into, 710. *Compensation*, II. 1.

BANKRUPT.

I. Statutes.
Retrospective operation of 6 *G*. 4. *c*. 16. *s*. 127., 470. *Post*, VI.

II. Mutual credit.
Declaration by assignees of *R*., a bankrupt, stated that defendant, in consideration that *R*. would sell and deliver to him sugars at the rate and price of &c., agreed to pay him for the same, prompt two months, or an acceptance at seventy days if required; that the goods were delivered to and received by defendant, before the bankruptcy, on the terms aforesaid, but he did not, though required before the bankruptcy, pay, then or since, by an acceptance, nor did he otherwise pay; whereby *R*. before his bankruptcy lost the use and benefit of such acceptance, and the benefit which would have accrued to him from having it discounted and raising money on it for his use in the way of his trade, and was put to loss and inconvenience by not having such acceptance to negotiate, *and his estate applicable to the payment of his just debts was, by reason of the non-payment for the goods in manner aforesaid, diminished in value, to the damage of the assignees and creditors*. Plea, set-off for a debt due from *R*. before bankruptcy. Demurrer.

Held, that the concluding averments of the declaration did not shew a special damage to the plaintiffs, but only a common pecuniary loss; that the case appearing on the declaration was one of mutual credit, within stat. 6 *G*. 4. *c*. 16. *s*. 50., and that a set-off might be pleaded. *Groom* v. *West*, 758.

III. What claim proveable.

Distinction between debt and damages.

In a special case it was stated that, by contract between *B.* and *G.*, *G.* had agreed to sell to *B.* all the oil which should arrive by a certain ship, which *B.* was to receive within fourteen days after the landing of the cargo, and pay for, at the expiration of that time, by bills or money, at a specified price per tun, with customary allowances: that the ship arrived, and the cargo was landed, and *G.* tendered the oil to *B.* at the end of the fourteen days: that the quantity of oil, after allowances, &c., was a certain number of tuns stated in the case; that, at the time of the tender, the market price of oil was lower than the contract price by an amount stated: that *B.*, on the tender being made, refused to accept; and that the difference of prices was within the knowledge of the parties.

Held that, *B.* having become bankrupt after the refusal, *G.* could not prove for this breach of contract under the commission: for that, although *G.*'s claim would be measured by the difference between the contract and market prices at the time when *B.* should have fulfilled his contract, yet the case did not shew that the data on which the calculation must proceed were so settled as to admit of no dispute, and render the intervention of a jury unnecessary; and consequently the claim of *G.* was not for a debt but for damages. *Green* v. *Bicknell*, 701.

IV. Liability for rent.

A lessee, under an unwritten contract reserving rent on 6th *April* and 6th *October*, became bankrupt, and a fiat issued in *March*, the rent due in the previous *October* having been paid. Upon the assignees refusing to accept the premises, the bankrupt offered, within fourteen days after his receiving notice of such refusal, and one day before 6th *April*, to deliver up possession to the lessor. Held that, under stat. 6 *G.* 4. *c.* 16. *s.* 75., he was not liable in assumpsit for use and occupation to pay any thing in respect of the time subsequent to 6th *October*.

Where the bankrupt holds by an unwritten lease, offering possession is a delivery within sect. 75. *Slack* v. *Sharpe*, 366.

V. Dividend.

Application of, as between creditor and partial guarantor, 846. *Guarantee*, I. 1.

VI. Second bankruptcy.

To an action for money had and received, it is a good plea (under stat. 6 *G.* 4. *c.* 16. *s.* 127.), that plaintiff became bankrupt and obtained his certificate in 1822; that a second commission issued against him, *May* 20th, 1825, under which his effects were assigned in *July* 1825, and he obtained his certificate in 1826, but did not pay 15*s.* in the pound, whereby, and by force of the statute, the debt demanded in the declaration hath vested in the assignees.

Stat. 6 *G.* 4. *c.* 16. *s.* 127. (*September* 1, 1825) operates in such a case retrospectively.

Where the estate of a bankrupt after certificate is vested in the assignees by stat. 6 *G.* 4. *c.* 16. *s.* 127., he cannot sue for an after-accruing debt, though the assignees do not interpose. *Young* v. *Rishworth*, 470.

VII. Pleading.

1. Ingredients of the bankruptcy how put in issue.

In trover by assignees of a bankrupt, laying the possession in themselves as assignees; pleas, that the plaintiffs are not assignees, and were not possessed as assignees, put in issue the trading, the petitioning creditor's debt, and the act of bankruptcy; and these must be proved, if notice to dispute them be given. It is not enough to prove the fiat and assignment to the plaintiffs. *Buckton* v. *Frost*, 844.

2. Plea that plaintiff's property is vested in his assignees under 6 *G.* 4. *c.* 16. *s.* 127., 470. *Antè*, VI.

BARON AND FEME.

I. Revocation of will by marriage, &c.

1. Parol evidence, when not admissible to shew husband's intentions that his will should stand good, notwithstanding subsequent marriage and birth of issue, 14. *Will*, V. 2.

2. What

2. What provision for wife and issue necessary to prevent the revocation, 14. *Will*, V. 2.

3. How the question is affected by descent of after-acquired property or mere legal estate, 14. *Will*, V. 2.

II. Proper custody of marriage settlement, 151. *Evidence*, XV. 3.

III. Feme.

1. Promise by when void, 467. *Pleading*, XIII.

2. When liable after husband's death for goods supplied to her during coverture, whilst living separate in adultery, 467. *Pleading*, XIII.

3. Wife's remedy for libel disputing the marriage, 907. *Libel*, V. 1.

BASTARD.

pp. 881. 907. *Poor*, XII. *Libel*, V. 1.

BATTERY.

What is, 602. *Costs*, VIII. 2.

BEER.

Form of conviction under beer-selling acts, 124. *Conviction*, I. 1.

BENEFIT.

How far essential to considerations, 743. *Assumpsit*, II.

BILL.

Attorney's. *Attorney*, IV.

BILL OF EXCEPTIONS.

Evidence, VIII.

BILLS OF EXCHANGE AND PROMISSORY NOTES.

I. Joint and several.

Payment by surety when not voluntary, 136. *Post*, II. 1.

II. Alteration.

1. What addition not an alteration.

Defendant and plaintiff gave a joint and several promissory note to *A.*, plaintiff signing as defendant's surety. Afterwards, *A.* pressing defendant for payment, time was allowed upon *L.* adding his signature as additional security. No new stamp was put on the note. Plaintiff afterwards paid *A.* the money.

Held, that he might sue defendant for money paid, and that the payment was not voluntary, the addition of *L.*'s name not annulling plaintiff's original liability on the note. *Catton* v. *Simpson*, 136.

2. Evidence of the time.

Where a bill of exchange, produced on a trial, appears to have been altered, the jury cannot, on inspection of such bill, without other proof, decide whether it was altered at the time of making or at a subsequent period.

Where a bill was drawn upon a two months' stamp, and had begun with the words "*Three* months after date," but the word "three" had been defaced (as if blotted while the ink was wet), and "two" written upon it, and "two" written again underneath, and the plaintiff, who put in the bill at nisi prius, offered no evidence to account for these alterations: Held, that the document, by itself, was no evidence to go to the jury of the alterations having been made at the original writing of the bill. And (issue having been joined on a plea of non accepit), that the plaintiff must be nonsuited. *Knight* v. *Clements*, 215.

III. Stay of proceedings on payment, 277. *Reg. Gen.*

IV. Pleading.

Indorsement and acceptance in satisfaction pleaded against further maintaining action, 673. *Plea*, II.

V. Evidence.

Inspection when no evidence, 215. *Antè*, II. 2.

BOND.

I. Obtained by collusion, 565. *Sherif*, II. 2.

II. Effect of compounding action against one of several co-obligors, 90. *Composition*.

BOOK.

I. Of quarter sessions, 806. *Poor*, IX. 2.

II. Official, 170. *Evidence*, XVIII. 3.

BOUNDARY.

I. Commission to ascertain, 198. *Evidence*, XXV. 1.

II. Evidence in questions of, 198. *Evidence*, XXV. 1.

BREACH.

I. Of contract, when not proveable under bankruptcy, 701. *Bankrupt*, III.

II. In declaration on covenant in a lease, bad for not noticing exceptions, 144. *Covenant*, IV. 1.

BRIDGE.

I. Repair ratione tenuræ.

On indictment for non-repair of a bridge, charging the defendants ratione tenuræ, they produced at the trial a record setting forth a presentment, in time of *Ed.* 3., against a Bishop of *L.* (not connected with the present defendants), who was thereby charged with non-repair of the same bridge, and liability to repair. The record stated a trial of this presentment at the Spring assizes, in the year 20 *Ed.* 3., and an acquittal of the Bishop as not liable; it further stated that the jury, being asked who was bound to repair, said they did not know; and, being asked when and by whom it was first built or repaired, said, about sixty years since, and then of alms, and that a Bishop of *L.* bestowed 40*s.* on the workmen repairing it, of his alms, and not otherwise.

In addition to this record, the defendants put in a writ of privy seal of *June* 28th, 20 *Ed.* 3., for a grant of pontage to the town of *K.* (where the bridge was), reciting, as the cause of the grant, that the bridge was ruinous, and no person bound to repair in certain, according to that which was found by inquest. They also put in the grant of pontage, dated in the same year.

Held, that the evidence was admissible on behalf of the present defendants.

Semble, that the special findings of the jury may have been regular, according to the practice in the time of *Ed.* 3. But,

Held, that at all events the acquittal of the Bishop, followed by the writ and grant of pontage, was evidence to negative the existence of a prescriptive liability in any person. *Regina* v. *Sutton*, 516.

II. Repair of approaches.

A party who is liable, by prescription, to repair a bridge, is also primâ facie liable to repair the highway, to the extent of 300 feet from each end.

Such presumption is not rebutted by proof that the party has been known only to repair the fabric of the bridge, and that the only repairs known to have been done to the highway have been performed by commissioners under a turnpike road act. *Regina* v. *Lincoln*, 65.

III. Toll, 716. *Poor*, II. 2.

BURGESS ROLL.

Municipal Corporation, II.

BURNING.

Attempt to burn will, when a sufficient revocation, 1. *Will*, V. 1.

CAMBRIDGE.

I. University.
Authority over alehouse licences, 281. *Quo Warranto*, II. 1.

II. Gas company, 73. *Poor*, II. 3.

CANCELLATION.

Of will, 1. *Will*, V. 1.

CAPIAS.

I. Ad respondendum, 449, 925. *Attorney*, V. I. *Arrest*, III. 1.

II. Utlagatum, 677. *Outlawry*.

III. Cum proclamatione, 951. *Writ*, I.

CARRIER.

Declaration against.

Declaration stated that plaintiff delivered to defendants, and they accepted and received from him, goods to be taken care of and carried and conveyed by defendants from *L.* to *B.* and there delivered to *P. P.* for reasonable reward to defendants in that behalf, and thereupon it became the duty of defendants to take due care of such goods

goods while they so had the charge thereof for the purpose aforesaid, and to take due and reasonable care in and about the conveyance and delivery thereof as aforesaid; yet defendants, not regarding their duty in that behalf, but contriving &c., did not nor would take due care &c., but on the contrary, whilst they had the charge &c., took such bad care &c., that the goods were injured, to plaintiff's damage &c. Pleas, Not guilty, and traverse of the delivery and acceptance modo et forma.

On the trial, the plaintiff gave no proof of an express contract, but endeavoured to shew that the defendants were common carriers. No objection was taken to the course of evidence. The case was proved as to one defendant only, and a verdict was taken against him and for the other defendant. On motion to enter a nonsuit, on the ground that the action was founded on contract, and therefore a verdict could not pass against one defendant only,

Held, that the declaration might, and therefore must after verdict, be read as a declaration against carriers on the custom of the realm, and consequently that the verdict was maintainable.

Quære, whether such declaration against carriers on the custom would have been sufficient on special demurrer? *Pozzi* v. *Shipton*, 963.

CASE.

CERTAINTY.

CERTIFICATE.

CERTIORARI.

II. Objections to inquisition of compensation jury.

A certiorari will not be granted to to bring up the inquisition of a compensation jury, unless defects in the inquisition be positively sworn to.

Thus, where a statute (6 & 7 *W*. 4. *c*. cxi.) directed that a railway company should not take lands, unless set out in a schedule to the act, or certified by justices to have been omitted by mistake, it was held not sufficient to shew that lands which were the subject of the inquisition were not in the schedule, without negativing the fact of the certificate.

Nor to assert generally, in addition to such statement, that the act did not authorise taking the lands.

Nor to allege further, that certain objections were made in a protest delivered before the taking of the inquisition, which were now in general terms sworn to be true.

If the objection be to the form of the inquisition, a copy should be set out, or it should be sworn that the deponent could not procure a copy; and he should in the latter case swear positively on information and belief.

It is not enough to swear that he "objects" that the inquisition does not contain certain requisites pointed out.

The granting a certiorari is matter of discretion, though there are fatal defects on the face of the proceedings which it is sought to bring up.

It is an almost invariable rule, that, where a party applying for a certiorari fails from incompleteness in his affidavits, he will not have a certiorari granted to him upon fresh affidavits supplying the defect; as in the case of the defects above mentioned.

Especially if he appears to have suffered no injury;

Or to have assented to the proceeding below.

Semble, per Lord *Denman* C. J., that the rule requiring that, in proceedings by an inferior jurisdiction, the facts giving the jurisdiction should appear on the face of such proceedings, is not confined to facts necessarily within the knowledge of the party exercising the jurisdiction. *Regina* v. *Manchester and Leeds Railway Co.*, 413.

III. To

IX. The conduct of the party applying.

1. On application for a certiorari, the Court will take into consideration the conduct of the party applying.

A party, whose land had been taken under the *South Holland* Drainage Act (57 *G.* 3. *c.* lxix.), applied for a certiorari to bring up the inquisition held before a compensation jury, on the grounds, 1. That the inquisition did not state such a notice to treat for compensation as was requisite under the act to give jurisdiction; 2. That the jury had ordered a fence to be erected for the benefit of the applicant, in addition to a money compensation, instead of giving him the whole compensation in money; 3. That the applicant held in right of his wife, and that the tenure was copyhold, and no compensation was made to the wife or lord.

This Court refused a certiorari, it appearing, on affidavit, 1. That the applicant had consented to waive the notice, and requested that the jury might be summoned for a day too near to admit of proper notice under the act; 2. That he had discussed the amount of compensation proper to be given, upon the supposition of the fence being erected, and, 3. That he did not now swear to his belief that the jury had awarded less money in consequence of the award as to the fence; 4. That, in the dispute respecting the land, he had not mentioned his wife's interest, or the nature of the tenure, but had acted as if the property was his own freehold. *Regina* v. *South Holland Drainage*, 429.

CHURCHWARDEN.

Election of.

In the election of churchwardens, if a poll be demanded, the votes are to be given by the qualified inhabitants present; but all qualified inhabitants (whether they were present or not at the shew of hands) have a right to be admitted into the vestry-room and vote during such poll: Although the qualified inhabitants present at the time of granting the poll resolve that the poll shall be confined to those then present.

It is not a sufficient ground for impeaching such election (on motion for a mandamus to elect), that the poll was taken with closed doors, unless it be expressly sworn that some qualified person who meant to vote was thereby prevented from doing so.

Semble, per Lord *Denman* C. J., that, if such an instance were shewn, the Court would grant a mandamus, without inquiring strictly whether the number of persons excluded was in fact such as to affect the result of the election. *Regina* v. *Lambeth, Rector*, 556.

CHURCHYARD.

CLERK.

CO-DEFENDANT.

COGNIZANCE.

COLLATERAL ENQUIRY.

COLLUSION.

COLOUR.

COMMENT.

COMMISSION.

COMMISSIONERS.

COMMITTEE.

COMMON.

COMPENSATION.

II. Under acts for public works.

1. Payment into bank on defective title.

The *Deptford* Pier Company were authorised by stat. 5 *W*. 4. *c*. xiii. to take lands for the purposes of the act, the compensation money to be assessed by a jury, on refusal by the proprietor to treat after notice, and in some other cases. If the company should not, within three years after the passing of the act, agree for or cause to be valued and paid for, according to the act, the premises to be purchased, the powers given them were to cease, except with consent of the owners and occupiers. Sect. 68 directed that on payment of the purchase money assessed, either to the proprietor, or if he should "not be able to make a good title," then into the Bank of *England*, in the manner and for the purposes specified by the act; it should "be lawful" for the company to enter, and the lands should from thenceforth vest in in them. Sect. 80 empowered them to resell lands purchased, but found unnecessary.

The company gave notice of treating for lands in the possession of *C.* A jury was summoned, and assessed the purchase money. *C.* offered to convey, and gave possession, but was unable to deduce a complete title, though he offered one which, as he contended, ought to be satisfactory. The company would not complete the purchase. On motion by *C.* for a mandamus to them to pay the purchase money to *C.* or into the Bank:

Held, that an affidavit by *C.*, stating that he was not in a situation to complete the title, and had suggested a payment into the Bank to save expense, was not sufficient for the writ.

Writ granted on affidavit showing that *C.* had endeavoured to complete the title, but could not.

After the assessment, and during the dispute on title, three years from the passing of the act expired: Held, no ground for refusing the writ. *Regina* v. *Deptford Pier Company*, 910.

2. Virtual refusal to hear complaint, 901. n. *Refusal*, I.

3. Mandamus, 910. *Antè*, 1.

4. Certiorari to remove inquisition, 413. 429. 439. *Certiorari*, II. IX. 1. *Inquisition*, III. 2.

COMPETENCY.

Of witness. *Evidence*, V.

COMPOSITION.

Of action against one of several co-obligors.

Plaintiffs, on becoming sureties for defendant, took a joint and several indemnity bond from defendant and *J.* Plaintiffs afterwards became liable, as such sureties, to pay, and paid, 1098*l.* They then sued *J.* on the indemnity bond, and obtained a verdict for 1098*l.*, but accepted 215*l.* from him in compromise, giving him a receipt as follows:—"Received of *J.* 215*l.*, being the sum we have agreed to accept in discharge of the damages and costs in this action." Plaintiffs afterwards sued defendant on the same bond, and he pleaded payment by *J.* of 215*l.* in full satisfaction.

Held, that proof of the compromise with *J.*, as above stated, did not support the plea. *Field* v. *Robins*, 90.

COMPROMISE.

Composition.

COMPUTATION.

Of time, 173. *Poor*, VIII.

CONDITION.

I. Annexed by the law to a will before marriage, 14. *Will*, V. 2.

II. Conditional acknowledgment of debt, 221. 225. *Statute*, XLIV. 1, 2.

III. Onus of proof of performance or breach, 779. *Devise*, I. 1.

CONDITIONS OF SALE.

When evidence to apply the language of the conveyance, 138. *Party Wall*, I.

CONDITIONAL LIMITATION.

p. 779. *Devise*, I. 1.

CONFESSION.

In pleading. *Pleading*, II.

CONFIRMATION.

Of alterations in rules of Friendly Societies, 358. *Friendly Society*.

CONSENT.

To admit counterpart, effect of, 255. *Stamp*, II. 3.

CONSIDERATION.

I. Moral, 467. *Pleading*, XIII.

II. Temporary detriment, 743. *Assumpsit*, II.

III. Of guarantee, 846. *Guarantee*, I. 1.

IV. For promise by widow, 467. *Pleading*, XIII.

V. Continuing.

S., the lord of a manor, appointed *K.* by parol to the offices of steward of the manor, and clerk of a castle therein; *K.*, in consideration of *S.* permitting him to hold the offices at the will of *S.* as lord, promised *S.* to pay, out of the fees of the offices, an annuity to *G.* during *G.*'s life, for the payment of which *S.* had bound himself, his heirs and executors, and to indemnify *S.* from such payment, so long as *K.* should execute the offices either by himself or by deputy to be approved of by *S.* Afterwards *S.*, as lord, granted the same office to *K.* by deed-poll (not reciting any special consideration) for *K.*'s life, and died.

Held, that *K.* remained liable to pay *G.*'s annuity; that the consideration for *K.*'s promise in that respect still continued; that the grant by deed did not affect the parol contract on his part; and that, although, since the death of *S.*, *K.* could not execute the office by deputy to be approved by him, it was sufficient that *K.* could execute it in person. *Mattock* v. *Kinglake*, 795.

VI. Nominal, 789. *Judgment*, VIII.

VII. What not sufficient to support the limitation of a contingent remainder to a necessary party, 650. *Fraud*, VII.

VIII. Failure of one alternative, 795. *Antè*, V.

CONSTRUCTION.

I. Of statute.

1. In cases affecting liberty, 951. *Writ*, I.
2. Of ancient statutes, with respect to the conciseness of their language, 335. *River*.
3. Of forms incorporated by reference to another statute, 405. *Appeal*, I.
4. As one enactment, 638. *Statute*, LIII. 7.
5. Effect of repeal on clauses incorporated by reference into another statute, 405. *Appeal*, I.
6. Of repeal clauses, 496. *Statute*, XXII.
7. Directory, 259. *Inquisition*, III. 2.
8. Strict, 375. *Poor*, VII.
9. Not restrained, 155. *Game*.
10. Not extended, 351. *Costs*, II.
11. Liberal, 176. *Statute*, LIII. 3.
12. Enlarged, 566. *Bankrupt*, VI.
13. Cumulative, 168. *Libel*, I.
14. Contrary to probable intention, 386. 405. 496. 638. *Turnpike*. *Appeal*, I. *Statute*, XXII. LIII. 7.
15. Not by implication, 405. *Appeal*, I.
16. Reasonable, 481. *Statute*, XLIII.
17. Not literal, 555. *Stamp*, I.
18. Not merely ejusdem generis, 638. *Statute*, LIII. 7.
19. Retrospective, 470. *Bankrupt*, VI.
20. Controlled by precedent, 173. 598. *Poor*, VIII. *Costs*, VII.
21. Clause saving ecclesiastical jurisdiction, 889. *Rate*, II. 2.
22. Compensation clauses, 910. *Compensation*, II. 1.

II. Order of justices.

Allegation of defendant's residence, 227. *Poor*, XIII.

III. Of deed.

1. By reference to circumstances apparent on the face of it, 650. *Fraud*, VII.
2. Distinction between evidence to apply the language of a deed and evidence to control or construe it, 138. *Party Wall*, I.
3. As to time of payment of rent, 463. *Landlord and Tenant*, VIII. 1.

IV. Of written memorandum.

1. Whether a question for the court or one for the jury, 221. 225. *Statute*, XLIV. 1, 2.
2. Of option to annul charter-party, on non-arrival by a certain day, 301. *Amendment*, I.

V. Of pleadings.

1. Of plea that an indemnity bond was obtained by plaintiff (sheriff) and others in collusion, 565. *Sheriff*, II. 2.
2. Of a justification as to assaulting plaintiff and wetting his clothes, 602. *Costs*, VIII. 2.
3. Of the words absque residuo causæ, 872. *Evidence*, XX. 3.

VI. Of finding of jury on issues not necessarily inconsistent, 296. *Postea*, I.

VII. Par-

CONTINGENT REMAINDER.

CONTINUANCES.

CONTRACT.

inquest might be held, on affidavit of the above facts, and on a suggestion that the cause of death had not been properly investigated.

The Court refused to interfere. *In re Daws*, 936.

II. Inquisition taken by a stranger, 936. *Antè*, I.

COSTS.

I. Generally.

1. Construction of award that *A.* shall surrender to *B.* at the costs of *B.*, 645. *Arbitration*, IV.
2. Whether the word "damages" in a pleading includes costs, 673. *Plea*, II.

II. For defendant on excessive arrest.

To entitle a defendant to costs under stat. 43 *G.* 3. *c.* 46. *s.* 3., there must have been an arrest in fact. It is not sufficient that the sheriff's officer called on defendant's attorney with a warrant, and required special bail to be put in, which was done after communication between such attorney and the defendant. *James* v. *Askew*, 351.

III. Security for.

Time of application.

Defendant, on the eve of trial at the assizes, *March* 1836, obtained leave to add a plea. Plaintiff thereupon countermanded notice of trial, and demurred to the plea; and the demurrer was set down for argument, *May* 1836. Plaintiff, in *October* 1836, became insolvent, and in *December* obtained his discharge. In the beginning of *Michaelmas* term, 1837 (the demurrer then standing near the head of the special paper), defendant moved that plaintiff might give security for costs. Held, too late. *Young* v. *Rishworth*, 479. n.

IV. On new assignment, 246. n. *Arbitration*, VII. 3.

V. With reference to the issues.

1. Of issue joined on a justification on which, becoming unnecessary, no evidence is offered, 296. *Postea*, I.
2. On distributable issue.

Trespass for breaking and entering plaintiff's house, and taking and converting his goods, which were described by distinct parcels. Pleas. 1. Not guilty. 2. That the house and goods were not plaintiff's. Issues thereon. 3. That the goods were not plaintiff's, but the goods of a bankrupt; justifying the seizure under a warrant of the commissioners. Replication, traversing the pleas. Issue thereon. Verdict for plaintiff as to the trespasses in entering the house, and taking parcel *A.* of the goods, with 100*l.* damages; for defendant as to parcel *B.* of the goods:

Held, that the second and third issues were divisible, and that the verdict must be entered up distributively, according to the special finding, for the purpose of an apportionment of costs according to *Reg. Gen. Hil.* 2 *W.* 4. I. 74. *Routledge* v. *Abbott*, 592.

3. Different issues, under 4 *Ann. c.* 16. *s.* 5.

Since the rules of *Hil.* 4 *W.* 4. a Judge may still certify, under stat. 4 *Ann. c.* 16. *s.* 5., that a defendant (who succeeds on an issue that goes on to the whole action) had probable cause to plead one of several pleas, which is found against him. *Robinson* v. *Messenger*, 606.

VI. Of amendment under 3 & 4 *W.* 4. *c.* 42. *s.* 23., 301. *Amendment*, I.

VII. Under 43 *Eliz. c.* 6. *s.* 2.

Trespass for breaking and entering plaintiff's house, and taking away a sign-board affixed thereto, and goods not affixed. Pleas. 1. Not guilty. 2. As to the breaking, &c., and taking away the sign-board, that the house and sign-board were not the plaintiff's. 3. As to the same trespasses, that the house and sign-board were defendant's. Replication, that defendant demised the house, with the sign-board affixed, to plaintiff, who entered and was possessed, and that defendant during the continuance of the demise committed the trespasses. Rejoinder, traversing the demise. Issues on the pleas and rejoinder. Verdict for plaintiff on all the issues, with 20*s.* damages.

Held, that the Judge could not certify to deprive plaintiff of costs under stat. 43 *Eliz. c.* 6. *s.* 2., and that the plaintiff might recover full costs without a certificate from the Judge, the case not being within stat. 22 & 23 *Car.* 2. *c.* 9. *s.* 136. *Thomas* v. *Davies*, 598.

VIII. Under

COUNTERPART.

COUNTY.

COURT.

COVENANT.

the demise and of their possession, and until the determination of the term as aforesaid, they suffered the premises to be out of repair, and so left the same &c., contrary to the indenture, whereby &c.

Plea, payment of money into court generally. Replication of damages ultrà. Issue thereon: Held:

1. That the declaration would have been bad on special demurrer (but was not so after verdict) for mixing the claim of damages on the breach of covenant to repair after notice with the claim for breach of the covenant to repair generally.

2. That the breach was demurrable (though sufficient, *semble*, after verdict) for not noticing the exception of reasonable wear and tear.

3. and 4. That the averments of notice were demurrable for not stating that the notices were in writing. But,

5. That the defendants, by pleading payment into court generally, had acknowledged something to be due on every part of the breach, and could not, therefore, allege the last three objections in arrest of judgment. *Wright* v. *Goddard*, 144.

2. What cured after verdict, 144. *Antè*, 1.

3. Effect of pleading payment into Court generally, 144. *Antè*, 1.

4. Arrest of judgment, 144. *Antè*, 1.

COVERTURE.

Baron and Feme.

CREDIT.

I. Representations as to, 457. *Statute*, XLIV. 3.

II. Mutual, 758. *Bankrupt*, II.

CREDITOR.

Sale fraudulent against creditors, 121. *Plea*, IV. 6.

CREW.

Misconduct of, 835. *Shipping*, I. 2.

CRIMINAL INFORMATION.

I. When not refused.

On account of the culpability of the principal party libelled, other innocent parties being implicated, 907. *Libel*, V. 1.

II. Rule when discharged.

1. Defects in prosecutor's affidavits, when not cured by statements in those of defendant, 168. *Libel*, I.

2. Proof of publication of libel, what insufficient, 168. *Libel*, I.

CRIMINAL LAW.

I. Indictment.

Statement of property when necessary, 481. *Statute*, XLIII.

II. Obtaining goods under false pretences, 481. *Statute*, XLIII.

III. Forcible entry. *Forcible Entry.*

IV. Verdict.

What defects not cured by, 481. *Statute*, XLIII.

V. Judgment.

When judgment cannot be given on an indictment founded on process given by a statute repealed pendente lite, 496. *Statute*, XXII.

V. Convictions. *Conviction.*

CRIMINAL PRACTICE.

Practice, XX. to XXVIII.

CROWN.

I. Rights of, as to navigable rivers, 314. *River.*

II. Its power to authorise theatrical entainments, how limited; 129. *Stage.*

III. Practice. *Practice*, XX. to XXVIII.

CUSTODY.

I. Detainer in, 925. *Arrest*, III. 1.

II. 1. Of documents, 151. *Evidence*, XV. 3.

2. Of voting papers, 535. *Statute*, LIII. 3.

CUSTOM.

CUSTOM.

DAMAGE FEASANT.

DAMAGES.

DAYS.

DE INJURIA.

DEBT.

DEBTOR AND CREDITOR.

DEBTOR, INSOLVENT.

DECLARATION.

DEDICATION.

DEED.

DEFECT

DEVISE.

I. Conditional limitation.

1. Onus of proof.

T., seised in fee of copyhold, devised it to his daughter-in-law for life, remainder to her son, *A.*, *T.*'s grandson, in fee, "upon this express condition, and not otherwise," that *A.* should, within three months next after *T.*'s decease, convey three specific leasehold messuages severally to *A.*'s three sisters; but, in case *A.* should "object or refuse to make such conveyances," "then, and in that case, and upon failure thereof," *T.* thereby revoked and made void the devise to *A.*, and did thereby give, &c., immediately after the decease of the daughter, tenant for life, the copyhold to the three sisters, as tenants in fee in common; but, in case of any one or more dying under twenty-one, then to the survivors or survivor, in fee.

The daughter, tenant for life, entered on *T.*'s death, and held for several years, till her death. She survived *A.* *A.* was heir at law to *T.* Held, that *A.*'s heir might recover in ejectment on this title, without shewing a conveyance of the leasehold, or tender, by *A.*, it not being shewn that *A.* had knowledge or notice of the will, or ot the proviso, or had been requested to convey.

Admitted, that the proviso was a conditional limitation, not a condition.

Held, that it made no difference that neither the tenant for life, nor *A.*, nor his heir, had been admitted, and that the three sisters had been admitted, and had entered, and that the defendant claimed through them.

The Court will not, on a special case, infer such a fact as notice, where not stated expressly in the case, from other facts,

facts, unless a power to do so be reserved to them by the case, and accepted by them. *Doe dem. Taylor* v. *Crisp*, 779.

2. What is, 779. *Antè*, 1.

II. Notice to heir, 779. *Antè*, I. 1.

III. What words give only a power.

Devise of freehold to testator's wife, during her life; and, after her decease, "my will is that my said freehold," "shall be then sold by my said executors in trust," (parties before named), "and all the money to be equally divided between all my children or their heirs," "by my said executors."

Held, that the executors took a power, not a legal estate. *Doe dem. Hampton* v. *Shotter*, 905.

DIRECTION.

In writ, varying from the statute under which it is issued, 951. *Writ*, I.

DISCHARGE.

I. Of outlaw, under Insolvent Debtors Act, 677. *Outlawry*.

II. Of bail, render in vacation, 195. *Execution*, III. 1.

III. From arrest, 925. *Arrest*, III. 1.

IV. Of surety, by addition to promissory note, 136. *Bills*, II. 1.

V. Of one of several co-obligors, 90. *Composition*.

VI. Of order of removal, effect in evidence, 806. *Poor*, IX. 2.

DISCRETION.

Of court, 418. 429. 439. 826. *Certiorari*, II. IX. 1. *Inquisition*, III. *Statute*, VII.

DISTRESS.

I. Proper pound.

In an action for abusing a distress, by putting the animals distrained into a muddy pound, whereby they were injured, it is no defence that the place was the manor pound, and was *generally* in a proper state. The distrainer must, at his peril, put the distress into a pound which is, not only in general, but at the particular time, fit for it. And, if the common pound be unfit (though by reason of a casualty, as rain or snow), he must find another.

To trespass for distraining sheep, and injuring them by impounding them in a muddy pound, defendants pleaded distress damage-feasant, and that the sheep were impounded in a common pound, with no unnecessary damage to them. Replication, that defendants, after the distress, at the time when &c., impounded them in the pound in the declaration mentioned, which was *then* too small, and which was *then* muddy, and thereby injured them. Rejoinder, that the pound was not too small, nor muddy *in manner* &c. Held, that this was an issue on the state of the pound *at the time of the impounding;* and that, on proof that the pound was *then* muddy, plaintiff was entitled to recover. *Wilder* v. *Speer*, 547.

II. Pleadings in trespass for abusing, 547. *Antè*, I.

DIVIDENDS.

Application of, where there is a partial guarantee, 846. *Guarantee*, I. 1.

DOCUMENTS.

Admitting by consent, 255. *Stamp*, II. 3.

DOCUMENTARY EVIDENCE.

Evidence, XIV. to XVIII.

DOUBLE VALUE.

p. 582. *Landlord and Tenant*, XII.

DRAINAGE.

South Holland, 429. *Certiorari*, IX. 1.

DUCHY OF LANCASTER.

Authority to issue boundary commission, 198. *Evidence*, XXV. 1.

DUTY.

Stamp.

When

ESTOPPEL.

EVIDENCE.

solvent Court, under stat. 1 *G.* 4. *c.* 119. *s.* 7., assigned the estate of an insolvent to an assignee, who assented to such assignment, and acted under it as tenant of premises which the insolvent held as lessee for years after the death of such last-mentioned assignee.

Held, that his executor was liable to the lessor for breaches of covenants in the lease subsequent to the testator's death, it not appearing that the Insolvent Court had appointed fresh assignees.

Action for breach of covenants to pay rent and repair, contained in a lease, the reversion on which was vested, by the provisions of a will, in plaintiffs, upon trust (among others) to pay an annuity to the separate use of a married woman for life, and, after her death, to pay certain annuities to the use of her children. Held, that her husband was a competent witness, though other part of the trust property had been sold because the rents were not sufficient for the purposes of the will. *Abercrombie* v. *Hickman*, 683.

VI. Objections when to be taken.
1. *Regina* v. *Lady Sutton*, 526.
2. See also, 314. 963. *River*, II. *Carrier*.

VII. Decision by sessions on insufficient, 398. *Poor*, XI. 1.

VIII. Bill of exceptions.
Effect of not stating for what purpose the evidence was tendered, 14. *Will*, V. 2.

IX. In particular proceedings.
1. Criminal information for libel, 168. *Libel*, I.
2. On rule for quo warranto, 183. *Office*, II.
3. Mandamus to levy church rate, 889. *Rate*, II.
4. On collateral inquiries, 198. *Post*, XXV. 1.

X. With reference to the pleadings.
1. Under declaration against carrier, stating neither an express contract, nor that defendant was a common carrier, 963. *Carrier*.
2. Reference to distinct pleas. *Lyons* v. *Martin*, 512.
3. Under plea bad on demurrer, as being too indefinite, 161. *Prescription*, I.
4. In reply to plea of statute of limitations, 221. 225. n. *Statute*, XLIV. 1, 2.
5. Under issue whether defendant was duly elected town councillor, 535. *Statute*, LIII. 1.
6. Under traverse of a public right to navigate certain part of a river when the rest was choked up, 314. *River*, II.
7. Plea of prescription: proof of a more extensive right, 161. *Prescription*, I.
8. Plea of general right to turn cattle into a close, 161. *Prescription*, I.
9. On issue as to property of a party wall, 138. *Party Wall*, I.
10. Under plea denying plaintiff's property in goods, 121. *Plea*, IV. 6.
11. Under general issue by statute, 279. *Reg. Gen.*

XI. Presumption. *Presumption*, I.

XII. Presumption, when refused.
1. Authority of servant to do an unlawful act, 512. *Master and Servant*, I. 1.
2. Emancipation of pauper, 806. *Poor*, IX. 2.

XIII. How rebutted. *Presumption*, X.

XIV. Documentary, notice to produce.
1. What proof dispensed with on non-compliance, 582. *Landlord and Tenant*, XII.
2. Has no effect beyond making secondary evidence admissible, 571. *Antè*, II. 6.

XV. Documentary, generally.
1. For collateral purposes, 555. *Stamp*, I.
2. Want of stamp. *Stamp*.
3. Proper custody of marriage settlement.

A document more than thirty years old is admissible in evidence without proof of execution, if produced by persons whose possession of it may be reasonably accounted for, although their custody be not the strictly proper one.

A. conveyed lands to trustees by way of

of marriage settlement, the deed containing a proviso that it should be void if the marriage did not take place in six months. The marriage did so take place. Afterwards *A.* executed a mortgage of the same lands in fee. On his death, the mortgagee brought ejectment against *A.*'s son, then in possession. The son, in defence, produced the deed of settlement, which appeared to have remained among his father's papers ever since the execution, and was more than thirty years old.

Held, that the deed might be read in evidence without proof of the execution. *Doe dem. Neale* v. *Samples*, 151.

4. Custody and identification of voting papers, 535. *Statute*, LIII. 1.

XVI. Documentary, proof of execution.

1. Order by consent to admit execution, its effect, and what inspection presumed, 255. *Stamp*, II. 3.
2. Proof by subscribing witness, when dispensed with, 582. *Landlord and Tenant*, XII.
3. More than thirty years old, 151. *Antè*, XV. 3.

XVII. Documentary, copies generally.

1. When the objection is to be taken that due search for the originals has not been proved, 314. *River*, II.
2. When admissible without proof by attesting witness to original, 582. *Landlord and Tenant*, XII.

XVIII. Particular documents.

1. Affidavits of party shewing cause, for what purposes they cannot be used by the party moving, 168. *Libel*, I.
2. Agreement with a stranger explaining permissive user of road, 99. *Highway*, I. 1.
3. Official books.

A register of attendances, &c., kept by the medical officer of a poor-law union, and laid before the board of guardians weekly for inspection, in obedience to rules made by the commissioners under stat. 4 & 5 *W.* 4. *c.* 76. *s.* 15., is not receivable in evidence for the party making it as a public official book. *Merrick* v. *Wakley*, 170.

4. Conditions of sale.

To apply the language of the conveyance, 158. *Party Wall*, I.

5. Counterpart of lease, 255. *Stamp*, II. 3.
6. Record of sessions, 806. *Poor*, IX. 2.
7. Recognizance, 932. *Poor*, III.
8. Removal order, 806. *Poor*, IX. 2.
9. Statement signed by deceased parishioners at a public meeting, 99. *Highway*, I. 1.
10. Ancient verdict with special findings, 516. *Bridge*, I.
11. Finding of jury summoned to determine boundaries, 198. *Post*, XXV. 1.
12. Finding of jury summoned under commission of *Duchy* Court, 198. *Post*, XXV. 1.
13. Former wills of same testator, 14. *Will*, V. 2.

XIX. Parol.

1. To apply the language of deeds, 158. *Party Wall*, I.
2. That the purchaser of real estate was only agent, 14. *Will*, V. 2.

XX. Admission on the pleadings.

1. Dates. *Poole* v. *Warren*, 582.
2. By pleading payment into court generally, 144. *Covenant*, IV. 1.
3. By replication de injuriâ absque residuo causæ.

In trespass for breaking and entering plaintiff's house and taking his goods, defendants pleaded, as to the house, that plaintiff was not possessed thereof; and as to the goods, that they were not plaintiff's property. Issues were joined on these pleas. Defendants also pleaded, as to the breaking and entering, two other pleas, justifying under a fi. fa. and warrant of execution against the goods of *B.*, which warrant was duly delivered to one of the defendants, a bailiff, to be executed; that goods of *B.* liable to be taken under the execution were in the house, and that by virtue of the writ and warrant, defendants, being the sheriff, bailiff, &c., broke and entered &c. Replication, that

that although the writ and warrant issued, and the warrant was delivered to the bailiff in manner and form &c., nevertheless defendants *of their own wrong, and without the residue of the cause in their plea alleged*, committed the trespasses &c. Issue thereon.

On the trial, plaintiff proved that he was in possession of the house and goods, which had been conveyed to him by *B.*, and that they were taken by defendants, as under process of execution. The case for the defendants was, that the conveyance was fraudulent. The Judge, in summing up, told the jury that on the pleadings it was admitted that the goods were boná fide taken in execution under the writ; on which point, therefore, he did not ask their opinion; and that the only question was, whether or not the property was in plaintiff, the burden of proving which fact lay on him.

Held a misdirection. For

1. The replication de injuriâ suâ absque residuo causæ admitted the issuing of the writ and warrant, and the delivery of the warrant to the bailiff, but not that the seizure was under the warrant.

2. The fact, that the seizure was under the warrant was traversable.

3. That fact not being admitted on the record, and no evidence of it having gone to the jury, the defendants were in the situation of wrong-doers, against whom possession alone was a sufficient title.

4. That the plaintiff, having proved possession, might recover in respect of the goods as well as the house, though he had by his pleading claimed *property* in the goods. *Carnaby* v. *Welby*, 872.

XXI. Other admissions.

1. Of deed as a counterpart, effect of, 255. *Stamp*, II. 3.

2. Effect of acknowledgment of debt offering a particular mode of satisfaction, 221. *Statute*, XLIV. 1.

3. Effect of better acknowledging debt and regretting non-inclosure of the amount, 225. n. *Statute*, XLIV. 2.

XXII. Declarations against interest.

1. Where not *clearly* against interest.

On the trial of an ejectment upon demise of *J.*, the defendant, to prove that the premises had passed by a deed conveying a messuage *with the appurtenances*, offered in evidence another deed by which *M.*, for whom *J.*, if the plaintiff recovered, would be trustee during *M.*'s life, conveyed the messuage by a description which (as contended) disposed of the premises in question as appurtenant thereto. *M.*'s conveyance recited a previous unsatisfied mortgage of the messuage, by her late husband (who had devised to her for her life), and purported to be made in consideration of the forbearance of certain sums owing by her as her husband's executrix, and of further advances then made to her. The defendant offered *M.*'s deed, first, as a *declaration made by* the cestui que trust of the lessor of the plaintiff, and therefore *a party equitably represented* by *the party on the record;* secondly, as an act of *user* of the premises, as appurtenances, *by the occupier*.

Held, that *M.*'s conveyance was not admissible, inasmuch as *M.*, *in her conveyance*, appeared, not only to admit a fact in derogation of her own title, but to gain a benefit by the forbearance and advance of money. *Doe dem. Rowlandson* v. *Wainwright*, 691.

2. By occupier, 691. *Antè*, 1.

3. Of deceased parishioners, 99. *Highway*, I. 1.

XXIII. Other declarations.

1. Intention to revoke will, 1. *Will*, V. 1.

2. Testator's directions on purchasing property, when admissible in a will cause, 14. *Will*, V. 2.

XXIV. By particular acts.

1. Permissive user, how explained, 99. *Highway*, I. 1.

2. Acts tantamount to declarations, 1. *Will*, V. 1.

3. User by occupier, 691. *Antè*, XXII. 1.

4. Possession of goods, under plea of property, 872. *Antè*, XX. 3.

XXV. Res inter alios actæ.

1. Verdict of jury summoned to determine boundaries.

In trespass for breaking plaintiff' close, issues were joined on two pleas 1. That the close was not the plaintiff's:

tiff's: 2. That the close was parcel of the manor of *O.*, and the close of the lord of the said manor. Plaintiff was owner of an estate conterminous with the manor of *W.* in *Yorkshire.* Manor *O.* was in *Lancashire;* the boundary between manors *W.* and *O.* was the boundary between *Yorkshire* and *Lancashire;* another manor, *I.*, was in *Yorkshire*, next adjoining to *W.*, and also abutting on *O.;* and the boundary between manors *I.* and *O.* was also the boundary between *Yorkshire* and *Lancashire.*

Plaintiff's case was, that the boundary between manors *W.* and *O.* was the ridge of a mountain, from which the waters descended in opposite directions. Held.

1. That he might shew, in support of this, that the boundary between manors *O.* and *I.* was the ridge of the same line of mountain from which the waters descended in opposite directions.

2. That he might prove this fact by the finding of a jury summoned under a commission from the Duchy Court of *Lancaster*, for the purpose of determining the boundary between manors *I.* and *O.*, on the petition of former owners of *I.* and *O.*, who had represented that the boundary was uncertain, and that suits were likely to grow between them. And this, though it did not appear that any steps had been taken after the return of the verdict to the Duchy Court, and though another commission had issued in the next year to ascertain the boundary of *O.* For that on a question of boundary, reputation was evidence; and, where reputation is evidence, a verdict between third parties is evidence; and the Duchy Court must be taken to have had authority to issue the commission. *Brisco* v. *Lomax*, 198.

2. Ancient verdict, 516. *Bridge*, I.

XXVI. Post litem motam.

Verdict inter alios, when not objectionable on this ground, 198. *Antè*, XXV. 1.

XXVII. Reputation.

1. Statement signed by deceased parishioners at a meeting, 99. *Highway*, I. 1.
2. Conditions of sale, to shew what was "known and reputed to be parcel," 138. *Party Wall*, I.
3. Verdict inter alios, how far in the nature of, 198. *Antè*, XXV. 1.

XXVIII. Payment not admissible in reduction, 280. *Reg. Gen.*

XXIX. Of particular facts.

1. Agency, 14. *Will*, V. 2.
2. Appointment of receiver, 582. *Landlord and Tenant*, XII.
3. Appurtenances under general words, 691. *Antè*, XXII. 1.
4. Authority of Duchy Court to issue commission of boundaries, 198. *Antè*, XXV. 1.
5. Boundary of adjacent manors, 198. *Antè*, XXV. 1.
6. Breach of covenant to insure, 571. *Antè*, II. 6.
7. Easement, as distinguished from a profit à prendre, 161. *Prescription*, I.
8. Of adjournments being merely colourable, 889. *Rate*, II. 2.
9. Of franchise to license alehouses, 281. *Quo Warranto*, II. 1.
10. Of fraud in vendee paying with a cheque not duly stamped, 555. *Stamps*, I.
11. That sheriff obtained an indemnity bond by collusion, 565. *Sheriff*, II. 2.
12. Of payment of a smaller sum in satisfaction by one of several co-obligors, 90. *Composition.*
13. Prescription, 161. *Prescription*, I.
14. Publication, 168. *Libel*, I.
15. To negative liability to repair ratione tenuræ, 516. *Bridge*, I.
16. Of signature of will by marksman, 94. *Will*, I.
17. Time of alteration of bill, 215. *Bills*, II. 2.
18. Toll traverse, 716. *Poor*, II. 2.
19. Uninterrupted enjoyment, 161. *Prescription*, I.
20. To rebut presumption of dedication, 99. *Highway*, I. 1.
21. Ancient grant of weir, 314. *River*, II.

22. Will,

22. Will, revocation and revival, 1. *Will*, V. 1.

XXX. Fraud.

Evidence of, when admissible under plea denying property, 121. *Plea*, IV. 6.

XXXI. Effect of.

Sometimes causes the construction of a document to be a question for the jury, 221. *Statute*, XLIV. 1.

XXXII. Variance. *Variance*.

XXXIII. Pleading matter of, 314. *River*, II.

EX PARTE PROCEEDING.

p. 826. *Statute*, VII.

EXAMINATION.

Of parties applying to be admitted attornies, 745. *Attorney*, I.

EXCEPTIONS, BILL OF.

Evidence, VIII.

EXECUTED CONTRACT.

p. 118. *Landlord and Tenant*, XI.

EXECUTION.

I. Of document. *Evidence*, XVI.

II. Of office, 795. *Consideration*, V.

III. Under judgment.

1. Time for charging.

Plaintiff signed judgment against defendant in *Michaelmas* term, 1836. Defendant rendered in discharge of his bail in the vacation after *Michaelmas* term, 1837, and gave notice to plaintiff. He was not charged in execution in *Hilary* term, 1838: Held, that he was supersedeable under R. *Hil.* 2 *W.* 4. I. 85.

Semble, per *Patteson* J., that, if a trial be had, and judgment entered, in vacation, and afterwards the defendant render in the same vacation, the plaintiff has the two following terms for charging the defendant in execution. *Thorn* v. *Leslie*, 195.

2. Costs of abortive fi. fa., 272. *Practice*, XIV.

EXECUTORS AND ADMINISTRATORS.

I. What words give only a power of sale to, 905. *Devise*, III.

II. Administration by attorney.

K. being left executor, *M.*, as his attorney, obtained letters of administration to the testator's effects, with the will annexed, for the benefit of *K.*, who never took out probate. *K.* died, having appointed an executor, and *S* took out administration with the will of the first testator annexed, and also administration with the will of *K.* annexed, for the benefit of *K.*'s executor, till that executor should himself obtain probate. *M.* was still living, and the goods of the first testator were not fully administered.

Held, that during the life-time of *K* the goods of the first testator vested, not in him, but in *M.*, as the personal representative of the first testator: but that after *K.*'s death *M.* ceased to be such representative.

And consequently, that arrears of interest, becoming due to the estate of the first testator in *K.*'s life-time, were not recoverable in assumpsit by *S.* as his personal representative: but that *S.* might, by virtue of the administration taken out by him, bring assumpsit for such arrears accruing after the administration was granted. *Suwerkrop* v. *Day*, 624.

III. Liability for funeral expenses

1. Where extravagant.

If an executor ratifies orders given by another person for an extravagant funeral, he may be sued by the undertaker individually, and not as executor, for the whole expense. *Brice* v. *Wilson*, 394. n.

2. See also, 348. *Evidence*, V. 3.

IV. Administrator de bonis non.

What he may recover in assumpsit, 624. *Antè*, II.

V. Liabilities of executor of assignee of insolvent lessee, 683. *Evidence*, V. 4.

EXEMPTION.

From toll, 386. *Turnpike*.

II. Of inquisition of compensation jury, 429. 439. *Certiorari*, IX. 1. *Inquisition*, III. 2.

FRANCHISE.

Degree of doubt to obtain a quo warranto, 281. *Quo Warranto*, II. 1.

FRAUD.

I. Fraudulent representation of ability, 457. *Statute*, XLIV. 3.

II. Of original purchaser, 555. *Stamp*, I.

III. When it does not vitiate.

It is no objection in law to a conveyance, that the grantor acquired the property by a fraud, and that the grant tends (and was designed, as the adverse party alleges,) to defeat the equitable right of third persons to relief against such fraud.

As the right (if any) of an heir at law to relief against a fine levied by a lunatic during his lunacy. *Murley* v. *Sherren*, 754.

IV. Liability of sheriff for his officer's fraud, 565. *Sheriff*, II. 2.

V. Plea of collusion to action on sheriff's indemnity bond, 565. *Sheriff*, II. 2.

VI. Evidence.

1. Onus of proof, 872. *Evidence*, XX. 3.

2. Evidence of, when admissible under plea denying property, 121. *Plea*, IV. 6.

VII. Fraudulent conveyance.

In a conveyance of lands a limitation without consideration is void as against a subsequent purchaser for good consideration, being fraudulent under stat. 27 *Eliz. c.* 4.

The concurrence of a necessary party, in the conveyance containing such limitation, does not amount to a consideration where the limitation is shewn, by circumstances apparent on the face of the conveyance, and of other conveyances forming part of the transaction, not to have been made for the benefit, or at the desire, of such party, and the concurrence of such party does not appear to have been a part of the contract at the time.

Therefore, where *H.*, tenant for life of copyhold, and *B.*, remainder-man in tail, with remainder to *H.* in fee, intending to join in an absolute sale of the property to *L.*, suffered a recovery to the use of *H.* for life, remainder to *B.* for life, remainder to the right heirs of the survivor; and then joined in surrendering to *L.*, a purchaser for valuable consideration, in fee: it was held, that the contingent remainder was void against *L.*, though, had it been good, it would not have passed to *L.* by the surrender. Especially as, with respect to a moiety, the object of the conveyance appeared to be to effect a sale of the whole interest, in pursuance of an earlier marriage settlement. But,

Held, that the recovery was not totally void, and therefore that the entail was barred, and *L.* took the use resulting to *B.* in fee. *Doe dem. Baverstock* v. *Rolfe*, 650.

FRAUDS, STATUTE OF.

Statute, XV.

FRAUDULENT CONVEYANCE.

Fraud, VII.

FREEMAN.

Municipal Corporation, I.

FRIENDLY SOCIETY.

Alteration of rules acted on but not enrolled.

A Friendly Society enrolled its rules in 1794, under stat. 33 *G.* 3. *c.* 54. In 1804, alterations were made in them, but, by a neglect for which the society was not to blame, the altered rules were never enrolled. They were, however, acted upon, and the original ones disused, till 1835, when the omission to enrol was for the first time discovered. On motion for a mandamus to justices to hear the complaint of a member who had been expelled in 1836,

Held: 1. That the rules as altered could not legally be acted upon.

2. That it was at least doubtful whether the original rules continued in force, and, consequently, that the Court could not issue a mandamus to the justices, but must leave the applicant

HIGHWAY.

I. What is.

1. How far permissive user is evidence of dedication.

On an issue whether or not certain land, in a district repairing its own roads, was a common highway, it is admissible evidence of reputation (though slight), that the inhabitants held a public meeting to consider of repairing such way, and that several of them, since dead, signed a paper on that occasion, stating that the land was not a public highway; there being at the time no litigation on the subject.

In determining whether or not a way has been dedicated to the public, the proprietor's intention must be considered. If it appear only that he has suffered a continual user, that may prove a dedication; but such proof may be rebutted by evidence of acts shewing that he contemplated only a licence resumable in a particular event.

Thus, where the owner of land agreed with an Iron Company, and with the inhabitants of a hamlet repairing its own roads, that a way over his land, in such hamlet, should be open to carriages, that the company should pay him *5s.* a year and find cinder to repair the way, and that the inhabitants of the hamlet should lead and lay down the cinder, and the way was thereupon left open to all persons passing with carriages for nineteen years, at the end of which time, a dispute arising, the passage was interrupted, and the interruption acquiesced in for five years: Held, that the evidence shewed no dedication, but a licence only, resumable on breach of the agreement. *Barraclough* v. *Johnson*, 99.

HUSBAND.

IDENTITY.

ILLEGALITY.

ILLEGITIMATE.

IMPLICATION.

IMPOSSIBILITY.

IMPRISONMENT.

INCHOATE ACT.

INCORPORATION.

INCORPOREAL HEREDITAMENT.

INDECENT EXPOSURE.

INDEMNITY.

INDICTMENT.

INFERENCE.

INFERIOR COURT.

INFORMATION.

INFORMER.

INHABITANT.

INJURY.

INQUISITION.

III. Of compensation jury.

2. Who may not object to defective statement of preliminaries.

By a statute (6 & 7 *W*. 4. *c*. cxxvi.) empowering trustees of a harbour to purchase lands for certain purposes, it was enacted, that, in case of difference between the trustees and any landholder as to compensation, and if the same could not be agreed for, or the landholder should refuse &c. to treat, after twenty-one days' notice, the trustees might issue their warrant to the sheriff to summon a jury, who should appear before the justices at quarter sessions, and should there assess the compensation, and the justices should accordingly give judgment for the same And that the verdict and judgment should be kept by the clerk of the peace among the records of sessions, and should be deemed records: Also that, if the verdict should be for a sum exceeding, or the same as, that offered by the trustees, they should pay costs to the landholder; if for a less sum, then the costs should be borne equally by the parties: such costs, if necessary, to be recovered under a justice's warrant of distress; the amount to be ascertained by a justice.

The trustees offered money for certain land; the landholder did not accept it, but desired that the amount might be settled by a jury. In the mean time, at their request, he consented that they should take possession, agreeing to pay him interest on the amount of the future compensation. The inquiry was held, and compensation assessed. An inquisition was drawn up, purporting to be taken at sessions

sessions under the statute, and stating that, the trustees and landlord appearing by their counsel, the jurors, being sworn to inquire of the purchase money of the lands (specified), and recompense for damage, did assess and give a verdict for the sum of &c. for the land, and the sum of &c. for damage: whereupon the said Court did adjudge and order the said sums to be paid by the trustees.

On cross motions, for a mandamus to pay, and a certiorari to bring up the inquisition, Held,

That the non-statement in the inquisition of any preliminary requisite to the taking of it (as twenty-one days' notice to treat) could not be insisted upon by the trustees, whose business it was to institute the proceedings.

That the fact of differences having existed sufficiently appeared by the inquisition.

That the inquisition was not irregular in omitting to state whether or not the sum assessed exceeded or equalled the sum offered by the trustees.

The Court granted a mandamus, and discharged the rule for a certiorari. Per *Littledale*, J. The statute requiring no regular form of an inquisition, the enactment that such inquisitions should be kept among the records of sessions, and should be records, did not render it necessary to draw them up with the formality required in setting out the judgment of an inferior court. *Regina* v. *Swansea, Trustees*, 439.

3. When not required to be so formal as judgments, 439. *Antè*, 2.

4. What ought to appear on the face of it, 413. 429. *Certiorari*, II. IX. 1.

5. Finding facts with a view to costs, 439. *Antè*, 2.

6. As to excess of power, 429. *Certiorari*, IX. 1.

7. Defects induced by the conduct of the party, 429. *Certiorari*, IX. 1.

8. Defects how to be stated to obtain certiorari, 413. *Certiorari*, II.

9. Enforcing by mandamus, 439. *Antè*, 2.

INSANE PERSON.

Lunatic.

INSOLVENT DEBTOR.

I. Security for costs, 479. n. *Costs*, III.

II. Court for Relief of.

1. Power to discharge from custody under capias utlagatum, 677. *Outlawry*.

2. Assignment. *Assignee*, I.

INSPECTION.

I. Of documents before consent to admit them, 255. *Stamp*, II. 3.

II. Of bill, no evidence of the time at which it was altered, 215. *Bills*, II. 2.

INSPECTOR.

Of weights and measures, 638. *Statute*, LIII. 7.

INSURANCE.

Evidence of breach of covenant to insure, 571. *Evidence*, II. 6.

INTENDMENT.

When refused in writ founded on statute, 951. *Writ*, I.

INTENTION.

pp. 1. 14. 99. *Will*, V. *Highway*, I. 1.

INTEREST.

I. Partial equitable, 691. *Evidence*, XXII. 1.

II. Of money.

1. By whom recoverable after determination of a defeasible administration, 624. *Executor*, II.

2. Pawnbroker's, 508. *Pawnbroker*.

III. Of parties.

Of administrator after determination of his administration, 624. *Executor*, II.

IV. Of witness. *Evidence*, V.

V. Declarations against, 691. *Evidence*, XXII. 1.

INTERPRETATION.

Construction.

INTER-

Declaration in covenant on an annuity deed (dated *June* 15th, 1832, payments to be made half-yearly,) for payments in arrear to *June* 15th, 1834. Plea, judgment recovered by plaintiff against defendant in *Michaelmas* term, 1832, for 2000*l*. in an action of debt (prout patet &c.) for the same causes of action. In the margin of the plea: "*Michaelmas* term, 1832. *Roll* 1146." Replication, that the causes of action were not the same (with other averments). On demurrer to the replication,

Held, that the plea was bad.

Grant of annuity, charged on lands, in consideration of 1000*l*.: demise of the lands by the same deed, in consideration of 10*s*. paid by the lessee (the grantee of the annuity), in trust to secure payment of the annuity.

Quære, whether the memorial ought to mention the 10*s*. as part of the consideration. *Few* v. *Backhouse*, 789.

IV. Over

JURY.

On trial of an indictment for misdemeanour by a special jury, a juryman, after being sworn, stated himself to have been one of the grand jury who found the bill. He continued, however, in the box, the defendant not consenting to his being withdrawn. It did not appear that the defendant knew of the objection before the juror stated it. On motion for a new trial by the defendant after conviction,

Held not a mistrial. *Regina* v. *Sullivan*, 831.

JUSTICE OF THE PEACE.

JUSTIFICATION.

KING'S BENCH.

KNOWLEDGE.

LACHES.

LANCASTER.

LANDLORD AND TENANT.

II. Tenancy from year to year.

Under unwritten contract, how delivered up, 366. *Bankrupt*, IV.

III. Who tenant.

Master or servant, 379. *Poor*, II. 1.

IV. Attornment.

Acknowledgment of devisee's title does not require agreement stamp, 255. *Stamp*, II. 3.

V. Liabilities of assignee.

Of executor of assignee of insolvent lessee, 683. *Evidence*, V. 4.

VI. Covenants.

1. Liability of lessee, though he does not execute the lease, 683. *Evidence*, V 4.
2. Distinction between covenant for breach and ejectment for forfeiture, 571. *Evidence*, II. 6.
3. Evidence of breach of covenant to insure, 571. *Evidence*, II. 6.

VII. Agreements by landlord.

To pay all taxes, 192. *Poor*, V.

VIII. Rent.

1. Forehand or after expiration of term.

Declaration, in covenant, that, by indenture of 21st *March* 1828, plaintiff demised a messuage to defendant, habendum from 25th *March* then instant for the term of seven years then next ensuing, wanting seven days, *yielding and paying yearly and every year during the term the yearly rent* of 285*l.* by four equal quarterly payments on 25th *March*, 24th *June*, 29th *September*, and 25th *December*, *in every year, commencing from 25th March then instant:* and defendant covenanted to pay the said yearly rent of 285*l.* on the days and in manner appointed. Breach, that in the last year defendant paid only half the yearly rent, and on 25th *March* 1835 two quarters became payable, and were in arrear.

Defendant, paying into Court so much *as became due as and for the first of the two quarterly payments alleged to have become due on 25th March* 1835, demurred to so much of the breach *as respected the non-payment of the second and last quarterly payment alleged to have become due on 25th March* 1835.

Held, that 285*l.* was payable for each year; and that either the first payment was to be made on 25th *March* 1828, or a payment on 25th *March* 1835, though after the expiration of the term.

Judgment for plaintiff. *Hopkins* v. *Helmore*, 463.

2. When due, with reference to bankruptcy, 366. *Bankrupt*, IV.
3. When not apportionable, 366. *Bankrupt*, IV.
4. Acceptance after breach of covenant, 571. *Evidence*, II. 6.

IX. Forfeiture, 571. *Evidence*, II. 6.

X. Notice to quit, 582. *Post*, XII.

XI. Contract to give up possession.

Validity when executed, though less than a regular surrender.

Debt for 63*l.*, rent for two years and one quarter, due 25th *March* 1837, reserved on a demise for forty-five years, at 28*l.* per annum.

Plea, that, before any of the sum claimed became due, and more than two years and a quarter before 25th *March* 1837, and before 25th *December* 1834, viz. 17th *April* 1834, plaintiff and defendant agreed that defendant should give up, and plaintiff take possession of the premises before 25th *December*, 1834, in consideration whereof defendant should be discharged from the rent which would have become due for the occupation after 25th *December* 1834; that possession was given up by defendant and accepted by plaintiff accordingly; and that plaintiff entered on 17th *April* 1834, and had held ever since, and defendant had not held since; "and the said tenancy and the defendant's said interest were thereby then surrendered and extinguished."

Held, that, on this plea, the objection did not arise whether the term was shewn upon the record to be regularly surrendered according to the statute of frauds, 29 *C.* 2. *c.* 3. *s.* 3.; the defence being merely an executed contract that, in consideration of defendant's giving up possession, plaintiff should abandon his claim to the rent: and that such defence was valid. *Gore* v. *Wright*, 118.

XII. Holding over.

Who may give notice under the statute.

Defendant, in an action for double value

value under stat. 4 *G.* 2. *c.* 28. *s.* 1., had notice to produce the original notice to quit, but refused. Plaintiff then produced and proved a copy, by which it appeared that there was an attesting witness. Held, that the attesting witness need not be called.

K., being beneficially interested in the reversion, joined with the trustee, who was legally entitled, in mortgaging it to plaintiff; and *K.*, by the mortgage deed, with the approbation of plaintiff, testified by plaintiff's executing the deed, appointed *G.* to be receiver, agent, and attorney of *K.*, to demand and collect rents, to adjust accounts, to sue or distrain for rent, give notice to quit, and eject on refusal, and to do all that *K.* could have done if the deed not been made. *K.*, the trustees, and plaintiff, executed the deed. Held, that *G.* was an agent lawfully authorised to give the notice required by the statute. *Poole* v. *Warren*, 582.

XIII. Rights of tenant.

When protected after bankruptcy and giving up possession, 366. *Bankrupt*, IV.

XIV. Mortgagee.

Notice by, 582. *Antè*, XII.

XV. Receiver.

Notice by, 582. *Antè*, XII.

XVI. Settlement by renting a tenement, 192. *Poor*, V.

XVII. Pleading.

1. Declaration in action on covenants in lease, 144. *Covenant*, IV. 1.
2. Agreement to abandon rent on possession being given up, 118. *Antè*, XI.
3. Effect of pleading payment into court generally, 144. *Covenant*, IV. 1.

LEASE.

Landlord and Tenant.

LECTURER.

Of a church, 176. *Statute*, LIII. 5.

LEGAL EFFECT.

Pleading, 301. *Amendment*, I.

LEGAL ESTATE.

Estate, I.

LEGATEE.

I. Interest of husband, 683. *Evidence*, V. 4.

II. Residuary, 348. *Evidence*, V. 3.

LETTERS PATENT.

To authorise theatrical entertainments, 129. *Stage.*

LEVY.

Execution.

LIBEL.

I. Evidence of publication.

In moving for a criminal information for libel, a prosecutor need not adopt the statutory mode of proof (see stats. 38 *G.* 3. *c.* 78., 6 & 7 *W.* 4. *c.* 76.); but it is not sufficient to produce an affidavit, stating merely that the defendant, on &c., printed and published a libel in a newspaper, called &c., a copy of which libel is hereunto annexed; and to annex such copy.

The prosecutor cannot use a statement in the defendant's affidavits to supply a defect in his own, where the latter are so imperfect that the Court, if aware of their defectiveness, would not have granted a rule nisi. *Regina* v. *Baldwin*, 168.

II. Fair commentary.

Case for libel. The alleged libel stated that plaintiff, a tradesman in *London*, became surety for the petitioner on the *Berwick* election petition, and stated himself, on oath, to be sufficiently qualified in point of property, when he was not in fact qualified, nor able to pay his debts. It then asked, why the plaintiff, being unconnected with the borough, should take so much trouble, and incur such an exposure of his embarrassments; and proceeded: "*There can be but one answer* to these very natural and reasonable queries; *he is hired for the occasion.*" The defendant justified, stating that the abovementioned allegations in the libel (except the hiring, which was not specifically

MAN-

MANDAMUS.

I. Purposes for which it lies.

1. To lord of manor to enrol surrender, 858. *Copyhold*, I.
2. To corporation to execute compensation bond, 633. *Statute*, LIII. 2.
3. To levy a church rate, when granted, 889. *Rate*, II. 2.
4. To enforce inquisition of compensation jury, 439. 910. *Inquisition*, III. 2. *Compensation*, II. 1.
5. To be inserted in burgess roll, 919. *Statute*, LVI.

II. Peremptory.

Not on part of a record.

A peremptory mandamus will not be awarded until the proceedings on the first mandamus are complete, and therefore, where a mandamus having issued requiring payment of two distinct sums, the prosecutor traversed the return, and the issues were found for him as to one sum, and substantially in his favour as to the other, but a rule nisi had been obtained to enter a verdict for the defendant as to this, the Court would not award a peremptory mandamus to enforce payment of the first sum pending the rule as to the second. *Regina* v. *Baldwin*, 947.

III. Application for.

1. Who must apply, 822. *Post*, IV. 4.
2. Complainant must shew title, 919. *Statute*, LVI.
3. On what refusal, 889. 901. n. *Rate*, II. 2. *Refusal*, I.

IV. When refused.

1. To admit clerk of union, on a suggestion that several guardians who voted for the clerk de facto were not duly elected, 561. *Poor*, I. 4.
2. To elect churchwardens as after a void poll, where the affidavits do not shew that any one was prejudiced, 356. *Churchwarden*.
3. To justices, when jurisdiction doubtful, 338. *Friendly Society*.
4. No previous demand from proper party.

The Court will not grant a mandamus commanding a party to pay money to the treasurer of a borough, under stat. 5 & 6 *W* 4. *c*. 76. *s*. 92., unless the application be made, either by the treasurer, or after he has been required to demand the payment.

Though the party applying for the mandamus be ultimately entitled to the money. *Regina* v. *Frost*, 822.

5. Where it does not appear who are the proper persons to make a return, 561. *Poor*, I. 4.
6. To Judge, to grant writ of restitution, 826. *Statute*, VII.

V. Return.

What defence must be shown on a return, 910. *Compensation*, II. 1.

VI. Costs, 871. n. 901. n. *Refusal*, I.

MANOR.

I. Boundaries, 198. *Evidence*, XXV. 1.

II. Pound, 547. *Distress*, I.

MARK.

Signature by, 94. *Will*, I.

MARRIAGE.

Baron and Feme. *Will*.

MARRIAGE SETTLEMENT.

Baron and Feme.

MASTER AND SERVANT.

I. Liability of master for acts of servant.

1. A master is answerable in trespass for damage occasioned by his servant's negligence in doing a lawful act in the course of his service; but not so if the act is in itself unlawful and is not proved to have been authorised by the master. As if a servant, authorised merely to distrain cattle damage-feasant, drives cattle from the highway into his master's close and distrains them. *Lyons* v. *Martin*, 512.

2. Who sufficiently a servant.

A warehouseman at *Liverpool* employed a master porter to remove a barrel from his warehouse. The master porter employed his own men and tackle; and, through the negligence of the men, the tackle failed, and the barrel fell and injured plaintiff: Held, that the warehouseman was liable in case for the injury. *Randleson* v. *Murray*, 109.

MAYOR.

MEDICINE.

MELIUS INQUIRENDUM.

MEMORANDUM.

MEMORIAL.

MERGER.

MERITS.

MESNE PROCESS.

MINISTER.

MINUTES.

MISCONDUCT.

MISREPRESENTATION.

MISTRIAL.

MONEY HAD AND RECEIVED.

MONEY PAID.

MORTGAGE.

IV. Amount of stamp.

Where redemption subject to a covenant to pay taxes, &c.

Land was mortgaged with a proviso of redemption on payment of principal and interest, and the mortgagor covenanted by the deed to pay all taxes, rates, or assessments upon the premises. The proviso for redemption was made subject to the performance of this covenant.

Held, that such mortgage was not a "security for the repayment of money to be thereafter lent, advanced, or paid," to an amount "uncertain and without any limit," within the Stamp Act 55 G. 3. c. 184. sched. part 1. tit. *Mortgage*. *Doe dem. Merceron* v. *Bragg*, 620.

MOTHER.

MUNICIPAL CORPORATION.

I. Freemen.

NUMBER.

OBJECTION.

OBSTRUCTION.

OCCUPATION.

OCCUPIER.

OFFENCE.

OFFICE.

II. Of clerk of the peace.

Election to.

The borough of *T.*, until *May* 1st, 1836, had its own quarter sessions, and *W.* held the offices of town clerk and clerk of the peace. He resigned; and thereupon, by a resolution of town council on *July* 20th, 1836, *S.* was elected town clerk; but no step was taken towards investing him with the office. At an adjourned meeting of the council, *July* 25th, 1836, a resolution was passed, rescinding that of *July* 20th, and, by another resolution, *T.* was elected town clerk. In *August* 1836, the borough obtained a grant of quarter sessions; and, on *August* 15th, *T.* was, by resolution of the council, elected clerk of the peace: Held, on motion for a quo warranto information against *T.* at the instance of *S.*, for claiming to exercise the two offices,

That *T.* was legally appointed town clerk on *July* 25th, and clerk of the peace on *August* 15th.

That the offices were not full at the times of such respective elections.

That *T.* could not be presumed to claim the office of clerk of the peace as incidental to the office of town clerk, by the appointment of *July* 25th, no specific act appearing to have been done by him in the capacity of clerk of the peace between that time and *August* 15th; though it was alleged generally on affidavit that he had acted as clerk of the peace from *July* 25th.

That the prosecutor could not allege that notice had not been given to him, or to the councillors (according to stat. *5 & 6 W. 4. c.* 76. *s.* 69.), of the business to be done at the meeting of *July* 25th, inasmuch as the prosecutor was bound to prove that fact by his affidavits, and had not done so. And, per *Coleridge* J., because by analogy to the General Rule, *Hil.* 7 & 8 *G.* 4., the objection could not be urged on motion unless specified in the rule nisi, which had not been done here.

That the resolutions rescinding that of *July* 20th, and appointing *T.* town clerk, were, under the circumstances, a

OFFICER.

OMISSION.

ONUS.

OPTION.

ORDER.

OUTLAWRY.

OVERSEER.

OWN ACT.

OWN WRONG.

OWNER.

PARCELS.

PARCHMENT.

PARTY WALL.

I. Considered as one wall.

Effect on plea denying property.

1. Trespass for breaking, &c., a wall of plaintiff, bounded on the north by a workshop of defendant. Plea, that the wall was not the wall of plaintiff. The wall was a party wall, standing partly on plaintiff's and partly on defendant's land. The roof of defendant's workshop rested on the top of the wall on defendant's side, and the trespass was committed partly on the plaintiff's half of the wall. Held, that defendant was entitled to the verdict, for that the plaintiff must be understood to have brought his action for the whole wall, and, even if the party wall were treated as two walls, defendant's part could not be considered as part of the workshop, and therefore the description in the declaration, with the abuttals, comprehended the whole wall, and, consequently, the plaintiff had not proved his property in the wall described in the declaration.

2. Defendant also pleaded, that the wall was a party wall, partly on the land of plaintiff, and partly on the land of defendant. A verdict having been found for the defendant on this plea, *quære*, whether plaintiff was entitled to judgment, non obstante veredicto, for so much of the party wall as belonged to him.

3. On trial of the issues on the above pleas, it appeared that the plaintiff and defendant occupied contiguous premises bounded by the wall, which premises they had severally purchased, at the same auction, from the then owner of the whole. The lots were afterwards conveyed to plaintiff and defendant by separate deeds, in which the premises were described as being in the occupation respectively of *H.* and *R.*, together with all buildings, ways, &c., known or reputed to be parcel thereof. Held, that defendant might give in evidence conditions of sale distributed at the time of the auction, describing the premises by measurement, there being probable evidence that these conditions were seen by the plaintiff's agent at the sale; inasmuch as the conditions were used, not to controul or construe, but to apply, the language of the deeds. *Murly* v. *M'Dermott*, 138.

PAWNBROKER.

His interest how calculated.

Under the pawnbrokers act, stat. 39 & 40 *G.* 3. *c.* 99., where the pledge is redeemed after several months, and the interest, according to the terms of the act, is a sum which is not an exact number of farthings, the pawnbroker is not entitled to calculate the interest on each month separately, taking upon each month the benefit of the fraction of the farthing. *Quære*, whether he be entitled to the benefit of the fraction at all. *Regina* v. *Goodburn*, 508.

PAYMENT.

I. Voluntary.

By surety, what is not, 136. *Bills*, II. 1.

II. Effect of compounding action against one of several co-obligors on part payment by him, 90. *Composition.*

III. Stay of proceedings on, 277. *Reg. Gen.*

IV. Plea of.

1. Payment credited in particulars need not be pleaded, 280. *Reg. Gen.*
2. Against further maintaining action, 673. *Plea*, II.

V. Not admissible in evidence in reduction, 280. *Reg. Gen.*

PAYMENT INTO COURT.

I. Pleaded generally, effect of, 144. *Covenant*, IV. 1.

II. Form of plea, 278. *Reg. Gen.*

III. Proceedings by plaintiff after, 278. *Reg. Gen.*

PENDENTE LITE.

I. Repeal of statute, 496. *Statute*, XXII.

II. Peremptory mandamus not awarded on part of a record, 947. *Mandamus*, II.

PERFORMANCE.

pp. 645. 779. *Arbitration*, IV. *Devise*, I. 1.

PERMISSION.

Dedication by permissive user, 99. *Highway*, I. 1.

PLEA.

I. Several pleas.

1. *D.* and *L.* being defendants in replevin, the Court allowed *D.* to avow, for a distress damage-feasant, in his own right as tenant from year to year to *W.*, tenant in fee, and also to make cognizance as bailiff of *C.*, tenant in fee; and *L.* to make cognizance as bailiff of *D.*, tenant to *W.* as above, and also as bailiff of *C.*, tenant in fee. *Evans* v. *Davies*, 362.
2. Certificate of probable cause, 606. *Costs*, V. 3.

II. Against further maintaining action.

It is a good plea, in assumpsit, that, as to 50*l.*, parcel &c., plaintiff ought not *further* to maintain &c., because, after the commencement of the action, defendant indorsed and delivered to plaintiff a bill of exchange for 82*l.* drawn by *C.* and accepted by *B.* (or that defendant paid plaintiff 50*l.*), in full satisfaction and discharge of defendant's promise as to 50*l.*, and of all damages by plaintiff sustained by reason of the non-performance of such promise (not mentioning costs), which bill plaintiff took and received in such full satisfaction and discharge. *Corbett* v. *Swinburne*, 673.

III. What does not confess a battery, 602. *Costs*, VIII. 2.

IV. Particular pleas.

1. General issue.
   By statute, memorandum in margin, 279. *Reg. Gen.*
2. Payment. *Payment.*
3. Payment into court. *Payment into Court.*
4. That plaintiff's demand vested in the assignees under his second bankruptcy, by reason of his not having paid 15*s.* in the pound, 470. *Bankrupt*, VI.
5. Debt for rent. Plea of agreement to abandon rent on possession being given up, 118. *Landlord and Tenant*, XI.

 6. De-

6. Denying property in goods.

Trespass for taking plaintiff's goods. Plea, that the goods were not plaintiff's. Plaintiff proved that the sheriff had seized the goods, being the property of *B.*, under an execution against *B.*, and had sold them to plaintiff: Held, that defendant might shew, on the issue here joined, that the sale was fraudulent as against creditors, that he himsel had taken the goods under an execution against *B.*, and that this was the alleged trespass. *Ashby* v. *Minnett*, 121.

7. Prescription. *Prescription*, I.

8. To declaration on an agreement to perform plays, that the intended place was so situated that no legal license could be obtained, 129. *Stage.*

9. That defendant's representation of the ability of a third person was not in writing, 457. *Statute*, XLIV. 3.

10. Of collusion by sheriff and others, 565. *Sheriff*, II. 2.

11. Indorsement and acceptance in satisfaction, 673. *Antè*, II.

12. That an alleged libel is a true statement of facts and a fair commentary thereon, 746. *Libel*, II.

13. Judgment recovered, 789. *Judgment*, VIII.

V. Course of proceeding at N. P. on a justification which has become unnecessary, 296. *Postea*, I.

PLEADING.

I. Independence of distinct pleas. *Lyons* v. *Martin*, 512.

II. Confession.

What plea does not confess a battery, 602. *Costs*, VIII. 2.

III. Admission by. *Evidence*, XX.

IV. Effect of pleading over to vague plea, 161. *Prescription*, I.

V. Answer to the whole.

Where a plea to the whole covers only part, *quære*, as to judgment non obstante, 138. *Party Wall*, I.

VI. Certainty.

1. Effects of mixing claim of damages in declaring on several covenants, 144. *Covenant*, IV. 1.

2. Allegation by reference: "the said *A. B.*," 227. *Poor*, XIII.

3. In pleading a prescription to turn cattle into a close, 161. *Prescription*, I.

VII. Particularity.

1. It is sufficient if the pleading disclose the specific proposition contended for, 314. *River*, II.

2. In allegation of special damage, 758. *Bankrupt*, II.

VIII. General pleading.

Effect of pleading payment into court generally, 144. *Covenant*, IV. 1.

IX. What the Court will notice.

Custom of the realm, 963. *Carrier.*

X. Legal effect.

Of option in a charter-party to annul the contract on non-arrival by a certain day, 301. *Amendment*, I.

XI. Averment by implication.

Whether an averment that defendant refused to give his acceptance implies that the necessary tender was made, *Groom* v. *West*, 769.

XII. Evidence, 314. *River*, II.

XIII. Departure.

Replication, in assumpsit, of a distinct promise.

Coverture being pleaded to a declaration in assumpsit for goods sold and delivered, plaintiff replied that defendant was, at the time of the contract, separated from her husband and living in open adultery, that plaintiff did not know of the marriage or adultery, and that defendant, after her husband's death, and before action brought, in consideration of the premises, promised to pay. Held,

1. That no consideration appeared for the promise in the replication.

2. That the replication was a departure, the promise therein being distinct from that alleged in the declaration. *Meyer* v. *Haworth*, 467.

XIV. Presumption.

Not of fraud, 758. *Bankrupt*, II.

XV. Notice.

When it must be averred to be in writing, 144. *Covenant*, IV. 1.

XVI. Time.

1. In debt on an account stated, it is

PLEADING (CRIMINAL).

PLENARTY.

POLL.

PONTAGE.

POOR.

to the office of their clerk, it appeared that *J.* and *R.* had been candidates for the clerkship, but that at a meeting of the persons acting as guardians to elect, *R.* had the majority of votes, and was declared elected. *J.* suggested, as a ground for the rule, that several of the guardians whose votes gave *R.* the majority were themselves not duly elected.

Assuming that the Court would grant a mandamus to admit to this office,

Held, that they would not grant it for the purpose of scrutinizing the elections of guardians who had voted. And that if this enquiry were open, the Court could not grant the writ, since it did not appear who were the proper persons to make a return; and, if the guardians de facto might make it, they might also appoint a clerk.

The Court will not take judicial notice of the rules made by the poor law commissioners, for the government of a union, under stat. 4 & 5 *W.* 4. *c.* 76. *s.* 15. *Regina* v. *Dolgelly, Guardians*, 561.

5. Medical officer of union.

His register of attendances, when not evidence for him, 170. *Evidence*, XVIII. 3.

II. Persons and property rateable.

1. Occupation as servant.

A servant occupying a house cannot be said to hold it *as* servant, if it be not the master's house. *R.*, a brewer, engaged *L.* as clerk, at a yearly salary, and agreed to permit him to occupy a certain house as his residence, free from rent, rates, and taxes, another clerk being also boarded and lodged in the same house if *R.* should require it, but paying for his board: and such salary and house-accommodation were to be in full satisfaction to *L.* for all perquisites, and for his expences in the service. Either party might give the other three months' notice of determining the service. *L.* occupied the house for some time, and then, his health being impaired, he removed to another. *L.* agreed with the landlord for this house, but the latter considered *R.* as his tenant. The furniture of the first house, belonging to *R.*, was removed to the second. *L.* was assessed to the poor-rates and window duty; and these, as well as the rent, were paid by *R.* at the brewery. *L.* once objected to being registered as a voter by reason of occupying the house, but afterwards acquiesced, and voted at the election of a borough member. Subsequently, *L.* appealed against a poor-rate in which he was assessed as the occupier, alleging that he held as servant only; and *R.* appeared on the hearing of the appeal, and claimed to be the party rateable. The sessions confirmed the rate, but stated the above facts for the opinion of this Court.

Held, that *L.*, the clerk, and not *R.*, was the rateable occupier. *Regina* v. *Lynn*, 379.

2. Occupation as owner of toll traverse.

A wooden bridge was constructed across a river which divided the parishes of *W.* and *A.* from each other, one bank and part of the bridge being in *W.*, the other bank and other part of the bridge in *A.* The bridge was supported by piles driven into the ground at the bottom of the river, and by abutments of brickwork on each bank. On the *A.* side of the bridge was a toll-house supported on piles also driven into the soil of the river. Tolls were taken, at this house only, for carts with merchandize passing the bridge. *S.* was the owner of the tolls, deriving title from a grant from the duchy of *Lancaster*. In a document of the reign of *Ed.* 2., and in other documents down to the time of *Charles* 1., the tolls were called traverse; and it appeared that the tolls had passed by grants conveying likewise the manor and castle of *H.*, of which *S.* and those preceding him were also owners. *S.*, and those preceding him, had for twenty years performed the repairs of the bridge, including excavations in the soil at the bottom of the river, and the planking of the carriage way, but had not repaired the carriage way. Held,

1. That this was primâ facie evidence that *S.* had the tolls as tolls traverse, in respect of ownership of the soil on which the bridge stood.

2. That this was a beneficial occupation by him of land in *W.* for which he was rateable in *W.*

The tolls were actually received by *E.*, who paid rent for them to *S.*, under

under a parol agreement by which *E.* contracted with *S.* for the receipt of the tolls at such rent. Held,

That *S.* was nevertheless the rateable party, since the agreement did not profess to demise the lands, and the tolls, as such, could not pass from him without deed. *Regina* v. *Salisbury, Marquis*, 716.

3. Principle on which a gas company occupying land in different parishes is to be rated.

A company, under an act of parliament, erected in the parish of *A.*, in *Cambridge*, a gasometer and other gas apparatus, and laid down mains and pipes in that and other parishes, and also in extra-parochial land belonging to certain colleges in the University. The company supplied light by means of such pipes, &c., to the several parishes and colleges.

Held, that the company were rateable as occupiers of the land in the different parishes by their apparatus, pipes, &c.; and were properly assessed upon the sum which a tenant would pay yearly for the apparatus, pipes, &c., deducting the annual average expence of renovating the same, but not profits of the trade (though profits in trade were not assessed in any of the parishes); and deducting also the annual value of the apparatus and pipes lying in extra-parochial land.

And that the resulting amount was to be distributed among the assessments of the several parishes, in proportion, not to the payments made for lights in the respective parishes, but to the quantity of land occupied by the apparatus, &c., in each parish. *Regina* v. *Cambridge Gas Co.*, 73.

III. Appeal against poor-rate.

Recognizances on appeal from special sessions.

Under sect. 6 of the Parochial Assessment Act (6 & 7 *W.* 4. *c.* 96.), which enacts that the decision of special sessions, on appeal against a poor-rate, shall be conclusive, unless the party impugning such decision give such notice as therein prescribed, to the opposite party; and, within five days after giving such notice, enter into a recognizance before a justice of the peace to try at the quarter sessions, it is sufficient that the recognizance be within the five days verbally acknowledged before a justice; the record of the recognizance may be perfected afterwards from the minute then made. *Regina* v. *St. Albans, Justices*, 932.

IV. Settlement by parentage.

1. Emancipation, 806. *Post*, IX. 2.

2. Mother's settlement, how far evidence of son's, 806. *Post*, IX. 2.

V. Settlement by renting a tenement.

Amount of rent how calculated.

Under stat. 6 *G.* 4. *c.* 57. *s.* 2., a settlement is acquired by renting a tenement for 10*l.*, though the landlord agree to pay, and do pay, tithes to an amount which, if deducted from the rent, would reduce it below 10*l.*; and though it appear that the rent demanded would have been only 9*l.* if the landlord had not so agreed. *Regina* v. *St. John, Bedwardine*, 192.

VI. Order of removal.

Quashed on appeal, effect in evidence, 806. *Post*, IX. 2.

VII. Notice of chargeability.

Where an order of removal has been served upon a parish under stat. 4 & 5 *W.* 4. *c.* 76. *s.* 79., but without notice of chargeability, the parish may take advantage of such omission as a ground of appeal against the order. *Regina* v. *Brixham*, 375.

VIII. Statement of grounds of appeal against order of removal.

Where an act is required by statute to be done so many days *at least* before a given event, the time must be reckoned, excluding both the day of the act and that of the event.

A statement of grounds of appeal under stat. 4 & 5 *W.* 4. *c.* 96. *s.* 81. is not duly served unless fourteen days elapse between the day of service and the first day of the sessions at which the appeal is to be tried. *Regina* v. *Shropshire, Justices*, 173.

IX. Appeal against order of removal.

1. When the sessions have jurisdiction, 398. *Post*, XI. 1.

2. Evidence.

1. On appeal against an order of removal, in 1837, the appellants, to prove an order of the sessions for the same

same county in 1824, discharging a former order of removal, produced the original sessions book, which was in paper, containing the orders and other proceedings of the Court (among which was the order of sessions now in question), made up and recorded after each session by the clerk of the peace from minutes taken by him in court, which book he considered, and stated to be, the record itself. No other record was kept. The minutes of each session were headed with an entry containing the style and date of the sessions and the names of the justices in the usual form of a caption. The minute in question stated the subject of the appeal then brought, and the order made on hearing. The book was signed, at the end of the proceedings of the sessions, "By the Court, *John Charge*, clerk of the peace."

Held, proper evidence of the order of sessions.

2. Pauper's father was born in the parish of *S.*; and pauper's mother and her family, after the father's death, were relieved by *S.* (while resident in another parish) down to 1817, when pauper was apprenticed, but not so as to gain a settlement. In 1824, the mother was removed, by order, describing her as the widow of pauper's father, to *S.*; but the order was quashed on appeal. Pauper was then twenty-six years old; he was not named in the order of 1824; nor did it appear where he had resided since 1817, except as above-mentioned.

Held, that, on appeal against a subsequent order of justices removing pauper to *S.*, the discharge of the order made in 1824 was material evidence for *S.*

That, in the absence of proof to the contrary, it must be presumed that the order of 1824 was discharged on the merits as to settlement.

And that it could not be presumed, in the absence of proof, that the pauper was at that time emancipated. *Regina* v. *Yeoveley*, 806.

3. Competence of rated inhabitant, 502. *Evidence*, V. 1.

4. Decision without proof, when it cannot be rectified, 398. *Post*, XI. 1.

5. Quære as to finality of decision, 398. 403. *Post*, XI. 1.

6. Record how made up, 806. *Antè*, 2.

X. Special case.

What available on certiorari when sessions refuse a case, 394. *Post*, XI. 2.

XI. Certiorari.

1. When the Court will not interfere, the sessions having had jurisdiction.

On appeal against an order of removal, the respondents, at sessions, objected to the statement of grounds, and the Court held the statement bad. The respondents demanded to have the order confirmed, but the sessions quashed it for a defect in the order. On motion for a certiorari to bring up the order of sessions, founded upon affidavit of the above facts: Held,

That the facts did not shew want of jurisdiction in the sessions; and that this Court, therefore, would not notice objections not appearing on the face of the order.

Especially as the respondents, after the statement of grounds had been held insufficient, had asked for a confirmation of the removal.

Although the affidavits shewed that the objection to the order of removal was supported by no proof except an assertion, made at the hearing, by a magistrate on the bench. *Regina* v. *Cheshire, Justices*, 398.

2. What the return ought to set out.

On appeal against an order of removal, the respondents contended that no sufficient notice had been given of the grounds of appeal. The justices in sessions held, assuming that to be so, that the objection had been waived. The respondents then declined to try the appeal, and the order was quashed. The justices refused a case. The respondents then obtained a certiorari to bring up all orders of sessions made in the case, with all things touching the same. The sessions returned the orders, with the notice of grounds and other papers relating to the appeal: and the respondents moved, on the return, and on affidavit, that the order of sessions might be quashed.

Held, that the return was irregular in setting out more than the order of sessions, that this Court could not look to the other matter in the return and affidavits,

affidavits, and that the return ought to be quashed.

But, as a new return, if properly made, would not support a motion to quash the order of sessions, the Court discharged the rule without quashing the return. *Regina* v. *Abergele*, 394.

3. What the Court will notice on affidavit. *Antè*, 1, 2.

XII. Filiation.

Form of order.

An order of maintenance on the father of a bastard need not shew, on its face, under stat. 4 & 5 *W.* 4. *c.* 76. *s.* 72., that the application was made to the next practicable general quarter sessions, *after the child had become chargeable*. An order was held good, purporting to be made at the sessions held 29th *June* 1837, and stating that the child, on 6th *March* then last, by reason of the mother's inability, became and thence had been and still was chargeable.

An order recited as follows: — "It being now duly proved to this Court," &c., that the child was on &c., at the parish aforesaid &c., born a bastard of the body of *E. J.* &c., and on &c., by reason of the inability of the mother to provide for its maintenance, became and from thence had been and still was chargeable to the said parish, "and that he, the said *R. L.*, is the father," and the evidence of *E. J.* having been corroborated &c., and the Court "having heard all parties, and being satisfied that the said *R. L.* is really and in truth the father of the said child, and it appearing to this Court to be just," &c., that *R. L.* should pay &c., and then proceeded: "This Court doth therefore hereby order that the said *R. L.* doth forthwith pay" &c. Held good under stat. 4 & 5 *W.* 4. *c.* 76. *ss.* 71, 72., without any statement as to the mother's settlement, or any more express adjudication that *R. L.* was the father. *Regina* v. *Lewis*, 881.

XIII. Order on child to maintain his parents.

What a sufficient allegation of the child being resident in the jurisdiction.

Under stats. 43 *Eliz. c.* 2. *s.* 7., and 59 *G.* 3. *c.* 12. *s.* 26., which authorise the making of orders upon children, having sufficiency, to maintain their parents, such maintenance to be assessed by justices of the county where the sufficient parties dwell, an order describing the party as *T. G.* "*of*" the parish of *M.*, in the county, &c. (for which the justices act), shews, distinctly enough, that he dwells within that county.

And, where the order recited a complaint made by the parish officers against *T. G.*, described as above, a summons issued against *the said T. G.*, and his appearance before the justices, &c.; and then went on to adjudge that *the said T. G.* is of sufficient ability, and shall forthwith pay &c.; Held, that the dwelling of *T. G.* in the county was sufficiently stated, by reference, in the adjudication.

Absente Lord *Denman* C. J.; dubitante *Littledale* J. *Regina* v. *Toke*, 227.

POOR-RATE.

Poor.

POSITIVENESS.

pp. 415. 881. *Certiorari*, II. *Poor*, XII.

POSSESSION.

I. Against whom a sufficient title, 872. *Evidence*, XX. 3.

II. Delivery of, when equivalent to delivering up lease, 366. *Bankrupt*, IV.

III. Offering, 366. *Bankrupt*, IV.

IV. Giving up, 118. *Landlord and Tenant*, XI.

POSTEA.

I. Form on different issues found for different parties.

Case for publishing a libel. Pleas: 1. Not guilty. 2. Justification, that the supposed libel was true; replication, de injuriâ. The publication was proved, and defendant offered no evidence. The jury found for the defendant on the first issue: Held, that (at any rate, in default of directions to the contrary from the Judge) the verdict should be entered on the postea for the defendant on the first issue, and the plaintiff on the second; such entries not being necessarily inconsistent; and that the

plaintiff

XXII. On shewing cause.

When prosecutor cannot supply imperfections in his own affidavits by statements in those of defendant, 168. *Libel*, I.

XXIII. Irregularity. Waiver, 831. *Jury*, V. 1.

XXIV. Jury, 831. *Jury*, V. 1.

XXV. Certiorari. *Certiorari.*

XXVI. Criminal information. *Criminal Information.*

XXVII. Quo warranto. *Quo Warranto.*

XXVIII. Capias cum proclamatione, 951. *Writ*, I.

XXIX. Costs.

Not given on an error of the court, 420. n. *Quo Warranto*, II. 2.

Thirdly, of other courts.

XXX. Of ecclesiastical court, 610. 951. *Prohibition*, III. *Writ*, I.

PRESCRIPTION.

I. Length of time.

Under stat. 2 & 3 *W.* 4. *c.* 71. *s.* 1., proof of a thirty years' enjoyment of common of pasture is not complete, if proof be given of an enjoyment for twenty-eight years immediately preceding an action in which the right is disputed, and it appear that twenty-eight years back the enjoyment was interrupted, but that the right was exercised before the interruption. And the party disputing the right is not bound to shew that such interruption was adverse: it lies upon the party prescribing, under the statute, to prove thirty years' uninterrupted enjoyment.

Semble, that, under sect. 2 of the statute, prescription for a right, every year, and at all times of the year, to put and turn the party's cattle into and upon a certain close, is too vague, and may be demurred to.

If there be no demurrer, and the issue on such plea be tried, the party prescribing, and relying on sect. 2, must give proof applicable to some definite easement.

And he will fail if the evidence entitle him not to an easement, but to a profit à prendre.

Per *Coleridge* J. A plea of prescription is supported if the party prove a right more extensive than that pleaded; but the right proved must be of such a nature that it may comprehend the right pleaded. *Bailey* v. *Appleyard*, 161.

See note, p. i.

II. Distinction between easement and profit à prendre, 161. *Antè*, I.

III. Repair of bridges and roads, 65. 516. *Bridge*, I. II.

IV. Pleading.

Right when pleaded too vaguely, 161. *Antè*, I.

V. 1. Evidence, 161. *Antè*, I.

2. How negatived by ancient verdict inter alios, 516. *Bridge*, I.

PRESENTMENT.

Of highway, 496. *Statute*, XXII.

PRESUMPTION.

I. Omnia rite esse acta, 516. 645. 381. 919. *Bridge*, I. *Arbitration*, IV. *Poor*, XII. *Statute*, LVI.

II. Not of fraud, 758. *Bankrupt*, II.

III. That officer having two titles acts under the good one, 183. *Office*, II.

IV. That a party inspected a document before consenting to admit it, 255. *Stamp*, II. 13.

V. In cases within the act for shortening periods of prescription, 161. *Prescription*, I.

VI. Revocation of will by subsequent marriage and birth of issue, 14. *Will*, V. 2.

VII. From user.

1. Of dedication of highway, from permissive user, how rebutted, 99. *Highway*, I. 1.

2. From user of franchise, 281. *Quo Warranto*, II. 1.

3. From user of weir, 314. *River*, II.

IX. That a party liable by prescription to repair a bridge is liable to repair 300 feet of highway, 65. *Bridge*, II.

X. Evi-

PRINCIPAL AND AGENT.

PRINCIPAL AND SURETY.

PRISONER.

PRIVILEGE.

PROCESS.

PROFIT A PRENDRE.

PROFITS.

PROHIBITION.

III. Where the proceedings below may be rendered good by amendment.

At a vestry meeting, certain plans were produced for improving the parish church, and were referred to a committee. At a subsequent vestry their report, recommending an enlargement, was received and adopted, and a resolution passed for borrowing money on the parish rates, under stats. 58 *G.* 3. *c.* 45. and 59 *G.* 3. *c.* 134., to carry the plans into execution. The notice of holding the latter vestry, published in pursuance of stat. 58 *G.* 3. *c.* 69. *s.* 1., stated the purpose of it to be "to receive a report from the church committee, and to adopt such measures as may appear necessary for carrying that report into execution."

Held, that this was a sufficient notice of the intention to propose borrowing money on the church rates for the purpose of executing the plans.

Quære, whether it would have been sufficient to give notice of a vestry meeting, "to receive the report of the committee appointed to consider the plans produced to the vestry meeting held on" &c. (the first-mentioned vestry), "for affording additional accommodation to the parishioners desirous of attending divine worship in the said parish church."

A party being libelled in the Spiritual Court for non-payment of a rate made in pursuance of the above resolution, objected to the libel because it stated the notice to have been given in the form last above mentioned, and he obtained a rule nisi for a prohibition. Afterwards the notice really given, which was in the form first above mentioned, and had been lost, was discovered, and was submitted to this Court in shewing cause, with an affidavit that, by the practice of the ecclesiastical court (in the opinion of the deponent, a proctor), leave would be given to amend the libel by an additional article setting out the real notice.

Held that the rule nisi for a prohibition might be enlarged, to give opportunity

PROMISE.

PROMISSORY NOTE.

PROOF.

PROPERTY.

PROTEST.

PROVISO.

PUBLIC.

PUBLIC HOUSE.

PUBLICATION.

PURCHASE.

PUTATIVE FATHER.

QUALIFICATION.

QUARTER SESSIONS.

QUEEN'S BENCH.

QUO WARRANTO.

II. When refused.

1. Sufficient doubt not shewn.

On a motion for a quo warranto information, calling on the Vice-Chancellor of the University of *Cambridge* to shew by what authority he granted alehouse licences within the borough of *Cambridge*, it appeared that the first exercise and origin of the franchise were too remote to be traced; that it had been exercised both within the borough of *Cambridge* and without it to the extent of the University liberties, but not in pursuance of statutory authority, or according to the statutable form

form of granting licences; that the franchise was recognised in stat. 9 *Ann.* c. 23. s. 50., and later statutes, though not in stat. 5 & 6 *Ed.* 6. c. 25.; that, till very recently, no serious dispute had arisen on the subject between the borough and the University, nor had any licences been granted by the charter justices of the borough, or those of the county at large; that in early times the assize of bread and ale was in the borough, not the University; that the Vice-Chancellor, in licensing, had always acted with another head of a house, both being styled justices of peace, but the licence being under the single seal and signature of the Vice-Chancellor; and that his course of proceeding had not been in all respects uniform.

Held, that sufficient doubt not being thrown on the legality of the franchise by these circumstances, the Court would not assist in questioning it by granting an information. *Regina* v. *Archdall*, 281.

2. Refusal of second application.

A rule for a quo warranto information against a mayor, on the ground that he did not reside as the charter required, was discharged on affidavits shewing residence. Afterwards a second rule was obtained, on the same ground, on affidavits impeaching the former opposing affidavits, and tending to shew that the residence was colourable. The rule was discharged, on the ground that a second application ought not to have been made after the former decision; but without costs, as the Court had granted the rule nisi. *Rex* v. *Orde*, 420. n.

III. Evidence for prosecution in quo warranto for acting as councillor though not elected by majority of votes, 535. *Statute*, LIII. 1.

IV. Costs.

Not given on an error of the Court, 420. n. *Antè*, II. 2.

RAILWAY.

p. 413. *Certiorari*, II.

RATE.

I. Poor-rate. *Poor*, II.

II. Church rate.

1. Notice of purposes of vestry meeting, 610. *Prohibition*, III.

2. Mandamus to levy.

Where an act of parliament directs a body, created by the act, to levy church rates, this Court will compel them by mandamus to levy the rate, and will not simply confine the writ to ordering the body to assemble for the purpose of determining whether they will levy the rate or not.

And this, although the act contain a clause reserving all ecclesiastical jurisdiction, if it appear, from the rest of the act, that the temporal court was intended to have at least concurrent jurisdiction. As in the act for *St. Margaret's*, *Leicester*, stat. 2 *W.* 4. c. x., which gives powers of laying the rates to an annually chosen select vestry (excluding the ordinary authorities), and of levying the rates by distress and sale, authorises the select vestry to rate other than occupiers, and to compound and make allowances with certain parties rated, and gives an appeal against rates, &c., first to such select vestry, then to quarter sessions.

The churchwardens required the select vestry to lay a rate, *or* to do another act, which last was illegal. Held, nevertheless, a good demand of the rate.

The select vestry adjourned from time to time, on pretexts which the churchwardens alleged, upon affidavit, to be, as they believed, colourable and merely intended to evade laying the rate, requiring details which could not be furnished for want of funds to pay a surveyor; and fixing an adjournment day after which a mandamus could not have been obtained for some months. It appearing that a previous select vestry had pursued the same course, and the present select vestry not directly denying the imputed motive, this Court held the adjournments colourable, and equivalent to a refusal. *Regina* v. *St. Margaret*, *Leicester*, 889.

3. Jurisdiction as to, 889. *Antè*, 2.

4. Powers of select vestry, 889. *Antè*, 2.

5. Colourable adjournment, 889. *Antè*, 2.

6. What amounts to a refusal, 889. *Antè*, 2.

RATE-

RATE-PAYERS.

RECEIVER.

RECITAL.

RECOGNIZANCE.

RECORD.

RECORDER.

RECOVERY.

REDUCTION.

REFERENCE.

REFUSAL.

I. Virtual refusal to hear a complaint.

By an inland navigation act, 35 *G.* 3. *c.* 106., it was enacted, that any person aggrieved by the works might complain to the commissioners at one of their meetings, and they should hear such complaint, and report upon it to a subsequent meeting, which should make such order and give such satisfaction as should be thought just and reasonable; with an appeal to quarter sessions by any party dissatisfied with any judgment of the commissioners.

A party aggrieved required satisfaction of the commissioners (*October* 6th), and had several communications with them, but received no definite answer. He then (*January* 18th) demanded, in the manner prescribed by the act, that the commissioners should, at their next meeting, hear and report upon his complaint, stating that he would, on that occasion, be prepared with evidence of all the alleged injury. His agent attended the meeting (*February* 8th) with the witnesses, but they were ordered to withdraw, and no adjudication was made on his complaint, the previous question being moved and carried. No explanation was given to the complainant. The commissioners had, on his first application, laid a case before counsel, but had not been able to obtain the opinion by *February* 8th, for which reason they made no communication to the complainant, fearing that, if made, it might be treated as an adjudication. The opinion was obtained (*March* 24th) too late, as the commissioners alleged, for notice to be given to the complainant of a hearing at their next meeting (*March* 30th). After that meeting, and before the subsequent one, the complainant moved for a mandamus to the commissioners to hear and report upon his complaint.

Held, that the conduct of the commissioners was a virtual refusal to hear. Rule absolute, with costs. *Regina* v. *Thames and Isis Navigation Company*, 901. n.

REGULÆ GENERALES.

RELATION.

Of render in discharge of bail, 195. *Execution*, III. 1.

REMAINDER.

Contingent, 650. *Fraud*, VII.

REMANET.

Necessary amendments.

I. No Judge's order is necessary under *Reg. Gen. Hil.* 4 *W.* 4. 18., for amending the day of the teste and return of the distringas, &c., or of the clause of nisi prius in a cause which has been made a remanet, and continues in the paper. It is sufficient if the jury process and nisi prius record be resealed as before the rule. A Judge's order for amendment, as mentioned in the rule, is required only in cases where it was formerly necessary to repass the record. *Wells* v. *Day*, 941.

II. When a cause made a remanet has been tried, a verdict found for the plaintiff, and judgment signed by him, it is too late to object that the jury process was altered before the trial without proper authority. Though the defendant swears that he did not discover the supposed irregularity till the taxation of costs. *Dubois* v. *Keats*, 945. n.

REMOVAL.

I. Of poor. *Poor.*

II. Of officer by rescinding his appointment, 183. *Office*, II.

RENDER.

In discharge of bail, 195. *Execution*, III. 1.

RENT.

Landlord and Tenant. *Poor*, V.

RENTING A TENEMENT.

Poor, V.

REPAIR.

I. Of 300 feet of highway from each end of a bridge, 65. *Bridge*, II.

II. Ratione tenuræ, 516. *Bridge*, I.

III. Deductions for, in rating gas company, 73. *Poor*, II. 3.

IV. Non-repair of defendant's fence replied in trespass for driving cattle, 113. *Fence*.

REPEAL.

I. Pendente lite, 496. *Statute*, XXII.

II. Of statute referred to, 405. *Appeal*, I.

III. *Reg. Hil.* 4 *W.* 4. *General rules*, &c. do not repeal 4 *Ann. c.* 16. *s.* 5. as to certificate of probable cause, 606. *Costs*, V. 3.

REPLEADER.

Refused, 113. *Fence*.

REPLEVIN.

Pleading.

Several avowries, &c., when allowed, 362. *Plea*, I. 1.

REPLICATION.

I. To plea of payment into Court, 279. *Reg. Gen.*

II. De injuriâ absque residuo causæ, effect of, 872. *Evidence*, XX. 3.

III. In trespass for driving cattle, that they escaped into defendant's close through defect of his fence, 113. *Fence*.

IV. Of new promise, when a departure, 467. *Pleading*, XIII.

V. Irregularity in process, 449. *Attorney*, V. 1.

REPRESENTATION.

Of ability.

Plea that it was not in writing, 457. *Statute*, XLIV. 3.

REPUTATION.

Evidence, XXVII.

REQUEST.

I. When necessary to give effect to a limitation over, 779. *Devise*, I. 1.

II. When necessary before application for

RESCINDING CONTRACT.

RESEALING.

RESIDENCE.

RESTITUTION.

RESULTING USE.

RETURN.

REVERSION.

REVISION.

REVIVAL.

REVOCATION.

RIVER.

II. Effect of ancient grant to erect weir in a navigable river.

A weir appurtenant to a fishery, obstructing the whole or part of a navigable river, is legal, if granted by the crown before the commencement of the reign of *Edward* the First.

Such a grant may be inferred from evidence of its having existed before that time.

If the weir, when so first granted, obstruct the navigation of only a part of the river, it does not become illegal by the stream changing its bed, so that the weir obstructs the only navigable passage remaining.

Trespass for breaking down a weir appurtenant to a fishery. Justification, that the weir was wrongfully erected across part of a public and navigable river, the *Severn*, where the king's subjects had a right to navigate, and that the rest of the river was choked up so that defendants could not navigate without breaking down the weir. Replication, that the part where the weir stood was distinct from the channel where the right of navigation existed, and was not a public navigable river. Rejoinder, that the part was a part of the *Severn*, and the king's subjects had a right to navigate there when the rest was choked up, and that the rest was choked up. Surrejoinder, traversing the right. Held, that in support of this traverse plaintiff might show user to raise presumption of such a grant as above, and was not bound, for the purpose of introducing such proof, to set out his right more specifically on the record.

Where the crown had no right to obstruct the whole passage of a navigable river, it had no right to erect a weir obstructing a part, except subject to the rights of the public; and therefore, in such a case, the weir would become illegal upon the rest of the river being so choked that there could be no passage elsewhere.

A party objecting to the production of a copy, on account of due search not having been made for the original, must make the objection, at the time of the trial, distinctly on that ground; if he does not, the Court will not afterwards entertain it. *Williams* v. *Wilcox*, 314.

SELECT VESTRY.

Vestry.

SERVANT.

Master and Servant.

SERVICE.

Of statement of grounds of appeal, 173. *Poor*, VIII.

SESSIONS.

I. Generally.

1. Record not necessarily on parchment, 806. *Poor*, IX. 2.
2. Evidence of order of, 806. *Poor*, IX. 2.
3. Recognizances, 932. *Poor*, III.

II. Quarter sessions.

1. Jurisdiction of recorder, 638. *Statute*, LIII. 7.
2. Next practicable, 881. *Poor*, XII.
3. Form of order of filiation, 881. *Poor*, XII.
4. Adjudication by, 881. *Poor*, XII.
5. Presumption omnia rite esse acta, 881. *Poor*, XII.
6. Effect of absurd decision, 398. *Poor*, XI. 1.
7. Effect of refusing a case, 394. *Poor*, XI. 2.
8. Order of sessions, when not quashed on certiorari, 394. *Poor*, XI. 2.

III. Special, 932. *Poor*, III.

SET OFF.

Mutual credit, 758. *Bankrupt*, II.

SETTLEMENT.

I. Of poor. *Poor.*

II. Marriage, 151. *Evidence*, XV. 3.

SHERIFF.

I. Acts by, after expiration of office, 951. *Writ*, I.

II. Liabilities.

1. For false imprisonment by his officer.

The sheriff is civilly liable for misconduct of his officer in executing a writ, though the act done be contrary to the express terms of the writ; as if he take the person under a fi. fa. *Smart* v. *Hutton*, 568. n.

2. For fraud of his officer.

To an action by a sheriff against an execution creditor, on a bond of indemnity for seizing goods under a fi. fa., defendant pleaded that the bond was obtained from defendant, *by plaintiff and others in collusion with him*, by fraud and misrepresentation: Held, that defendant supported this plea by proof that the sheriff's officer, who executed the process, obtained the bond by fraud and misrepresentation, though the plaintiff did not appear to have been personally cognizant of any part of the transaction. *Raphael* v. *Goodman*, 565.

III. Remedies.

Remedy of under-sheriff for fees on commission of lunacy, 959. *Attorney*, V. 3.

IV. Setting aside attachment.

A sheriff, attached for not bringing in the body, moved to have the attachment set aside, on an affidavit, stating, as to the sheriff's interest in the motion, that it was made "on his behalf, at his expense, and for his protection, without collusion with the plaintiff or defendant, or any other person or persons whomsoever."

Held, not a sufficient affidavit within *Reg. Gen.* K. B. *Mich.* 59 *G.* 3.

And the court discharged the rule for this defect, though the application was made after stat. 1 & 2 *Vict.* c. 110. came into operation; the contempt having taken place before that time. *Regina* v. *Middlesex, Sheriff*, 938.

SHEWING CAUSE.

Rule.

SHIPPING.

I. Charter-party.

1. Legal effect of option to annul on non-arrival by a certain day, 301. *Amendment*, I.
2. Liability for misconduct of crew.

Case for sinking plaintiff's vessel by a steam boat, of which defendant

ants were possessed and had the care, management, and direction, by their servants and mariners, through the mismanagement of the said servants and mariners. Plea, that defendants had not the possession and care, &c., by their servants and mariners, or otherwise.

Defendants, being owners of the steam vessel, chartered her to *D.*, for six months, at 20*l.* per week, the owners to keep her in good and sufficient order for the conveyance of goods, &c., to and from *Newcastle* and *Goole*, or any other coasting station which *D.* might employ her in: *D.* to pay all disbursements, including harbour dues, pilotages, seamen's and captain's wages, and coals and oil, tallow, &c. for engines, and to insure the vessel, the policy to be deposited with the owners.

Held, that the issue was to be found for plaintiff upon the interpretation of the charter-party alone.

A fortiori, upon proof, in addition, that *D.* had no power to appoint or dismiss the officers and crew, and did not interfere in the arrangements of the ship. *Fenton* v. *Dublin Steam Packet Co.*, 835.

3. Declaration on, 301. *Amendment*, I.

II. See *River*.

SIGNATURE.

I. Of minutes of town council, 266. *Statute*, LIII. 5.

II. By mark, 94. *Will*, I.

SOLICITOR.

Attorney.

SOUTH HOLLAND.

Drainage, 429. *Inquisition*, III. 2.

SPECIAL CASE.

pp. 394. 779. *Poor*, XI. 2. *Devise*, I. 1.

SPECIAL DAMAGE.

p. 758. *Bankrupt*, II.

SPECIAL JURY.

p. 831. *Jury*, V. 1.

SPIRITUAL COURT.

Ecclesiastical Court.

STAGE.

Authority to perform.

Entertainments of the stage cannot be exhibited for gain within twenty miles of *Westminster* or *London*, the place of exhibition not being in *Westminster* or its liberties, or some place in which the sovereign resides.

By stat. 10 *G.* 2. *c.* 28., neither the Crown, by letters patent, nor the Lord Chamberlain, by licence, can authorize such performance.

Nor can the the county magistrates, under either stat. 25 *G.* 2. *c.* 36. or stat. 28 *G.* 3. *c.* 30.

No action can be maintained on an agreement to exhibit entertainments of the stage for gain in a place where, by the above statutes, a licence or patent cannot be obtained.

A plea shewing that the intended place of exhibition was so situated is an answer to a declaration on the breach of such an agreement. *Levy* v. *Yates*, 129.

STAGE WAGGON.

What is, 386. *Turnpike.*

STAMPS.

I. Want of.

When the document is offered as evidence of fraud.

In assumpsit for goods sold and delivered, plaintiff's case was, that defendant had received them of *M.*, who had obtained them from plaintiff, the owner, pretending to purchase and pay for them by a cheque drawn on a party who, as *M.* knew, would dishonour the cheque: Held that, in support of this case, the cheque was admissible in evidence, though not duly stamped. *Keable* v. *Payne*, 555.

II. On particular instruments.

1. Attornment, 255. *Post*, 3.

2. Deed not otherwise charged, 248. *Post*, 4.

3. Lease.

S. being in possession of lands, *B.* brought

brought ejectment against him, and recovered; but, at *S.*'s request, forbore taking possession. It was proposed that *S.* should take a lease; but before this was done *B.* died, having devised the lands to *T.* *S.* then signed a paper, reciting the above facts, stating that he thereby attorned tenant to *T.* of the said lands, then in his, *S.*'s, possession, and adding: "And I do become tenant thereof to *T.*, from," &c. "last past." Held, that this instrument did not require to be stamped as an agreement, though it was not strictly an attornment, no attornment being necessary where the new landlord comes in as devisee of the old.

Plaintiff gave defendant notice, under *Reg. Gen. Hil.* 4 *W.* 4. 20., that he might inspect, and would be required to admit, on trial, a "counterpart of lease" from *T.* to *S.*, dated &c.; and a Judge, on summons, made an order, by consent, for admitting the same. The instrument produced on the trial was in the form of a demise from *T.* to *S.* of the date specified, and was indorsed "counterpart," but was executed by landlord as well as tenant. No proof was given that any original or duplicate lease had or had not existed. The stamp was sufficient for a counterpart, but not for a lease.

Held, that the defendant, having consented to admit a counterpart of lease, corresponding in date and parties with that produced, could not now contend that the instrument produced was a lease, and therefore improperly stamped.

And this, whether before such consent he had actually inspected the document mentioned in the notice, or not.

On motion to enter a nonsuit, the plaintiff is not entitled to shew cause in the first instance as a matter of right, even on giving such notice of his intention to the defendant. *Doe dem. Wright* v. *Smith*, 255.

4. Mortgage. Exemption from ad valorem duty.

P. mortgaged land to *L.* for 400*l.* Afterwards *P.* borrowed 1000*l.* more from *L.*, and mortgaged other land to him as a security for the whole 1400*l.* Held, that, under stat. 55 *G.* 3. *c.* 184., the last mortgage required an *ad valorem* mortgage stamp, with progressive duty, on the 1000*l.*, and also a deed stamp on the fresh security upon the 400*l.*, as a deed not otherwise charged for. *Lant* v. *Peace*, 248.

5. Mortgage, where the proviso for redemption is made subject to a covenant by mortgagor to pay all taxes &c. on the premises, 620. *Mortgage*, IV.

STATUTE.

First: Generally.

I. Construction. *Construction*, I.

II. Compliance.

1. Effect of following words of statute, 881. *Poor*, XII.
2. Conditional writ where the statute directs an absolute writ, 951. *Writ*, I.

III. Incorporation of forms by reference to a previous statute, 405. *Appeal* I.

IV. Repeal.

1. Repeal of statute partly incorporated by reference into a subsequent statute not repealed, 405. *Appeal*, I.
2. Effect of repeal pendente lite where the offence is at common law, but the preliminary proceeding was one given by the statute, 496. *Post*, XXII.

V. General issue by, 279. *Reg. Gen.*

Secondly: Decisions on public and general statutes.

VI. 9 *H.* 3. (Magna Charta.)
c. 23. Weirs, 314. 334. *River*, II.

VII. 25 *Ed.* 3. *stat.* 4. *c.* 4. (Weirs.)
Proceedings under, 314. 335. *River*, II.

VIII. 8 *H.* 6. *c.* 9. (Forcible entry.)
Sec. 3. Restitution.

Under stat. 8 *H.* 6. *c.* 9., if an indictment for forcible entry and detainer be found by the grand jury at the assizes, and application be thereon made to the Judge of assize to grant a writ of restitution, it is in his discretion whether he will grant it or not.

Therefore, when the Judge, on such application being made on affidavit, granted a rule nisi, which he afterwards, upon cause shewn on affidavit, discharged, and a motion was made to this Court

Court (but without removing the indictment) for a mandamus to the Judge, or a warrant of restitution, this Court refused to interfere; nor would they enter into the question whether the Judge had exercised the discretion rightly. *Regina* v. *Harland*, 826.

IX. 5 & 6 *Ed.* 6. *c.* 25. (Alehouses), 281. *Quo Warranto*, II. 1.

X. 5 *Eliz.* *c.* 23. (Excommunicato capiendo.)

Sec. 4. Capias cum proclamatione, 951. *Writ*, I.

XI. 27 *Eliz.* c. 4. (Voluntary conveyances.)

Limitation of a contingent remainder to a party whose concurrence was necessary, when void, 650. *Fraud*, VII.

XII. 43 *Eliz.* *c.* 2. (Poor.)

Sec. 7. Order on child to maintain parents, 227. *Poor*, XIII.

XIII. 43 *Eliz.* *c.* 6. (Frivolous suits.)

Sec. 2. Costs, 598. *Costs*, VII.

XIV. 22 & 23 *Car.* 2. *c.* 9. (Proceedings at law.)

Sec. 136. Costs, 598. 602. *Costs* VII. VIII. 2.

XV. 29 *Car.* 2. *c.* 3. (Frauds.)

1. Sec. 3. Executed contract to give up possession of demised premises well pleaded without shewing that it was in writing, 118. *Landlord and Tenant*, XI.
2. Sec. 4. Promise to answer the debt of another: statement of consideration, 846. *Guarantee*, I. 1.
3. Secs. 5, 6. Testator's mark is sufficient, without proving that he could not write at the time, 94. *Will*, I.
4. Sec. 6. Does not extend to wills of copyholds, 1. *Will*, V. 2.
5. Sec. 6. Excludes parol declarations of testator's intention that his will should stand good notwithstanding subsequent marriage and birth of a child, 14. *Will*, V. 2.

XVI. 4 *Ann.* *c.* 16. (Amendment of the law.)

Sec. 5. Certificate of probable cause, 606. *Costs*, V. 3.

XVII. 9 *Ann.* *c.* 23. (Licensing hackney coaches.)

Sec. 50. Salvo of rights of University of *Cambridge*, 281. *Quo Warranto*, II. 1.

XVIII. 2 *G.* 2. *c.* 23. (Attornies.)

Sec. 23. Time in which attorney may commence action, 577. *Attorney*, IV.

XIX. 4 *G.* 2. *c.* 28. (Landlord and tenant.)

Sec. 1. Notice to quit, 582. *Landlord and Tenant*, XII.

XX. 10 *G.* 2. *c.* 28. (Stage plays.)

Sec. 5. Neither the Crown nor Lord Chamberlain can authorise performances within certain limits, 129. *Stage*.

XXI. 25 *G.* 2. *c.* 36. (Stage plays.)

Sec. 2. Authority of justices to grant licences, 129. *Stage*.

XXII. 13 *G.* 3. *c.* 78. (Highway.)

Sec. 24. Presentments by justices.

Under stat. 13 *G.* 3. *c.* 78. s. 24., a magistrate presented the inhabitants of a parish for non-repair of a highway. The proceedings having been removed by certiorari, the defendants pleaded, and issues of fact were joined, which were tried and found against the defendants. The issues were joined before, but the cause was tried after, 20th *March* 1836, on which day stat. 5 & 6 *W.* 4. *c.* 50., repealing stat. 13 *G.* 3. *c.* 78., came into operation.

Judgment was arrested, on the ground that the Court could not now give judgment upon a conviction founded on a magistrate's presentment. *Regina* v. *Mawgan*, 496.

XXIII. 28 *G.* 3. *c.* 30. (Stage plays.)

Sec. 1. Distance from *London*, 129. *Stage*.

XXIV. 33 *G.* 3. *c.* 54. (Friendly Societies.)

Sec. 3. Effect of altering rules without confirmation, 338. *Friendly Society*.

XXV. 38 *G.* 3. *c.* 78. (Newspapers.)

Evidence of publication, 168. *Libel*, I.

XXVI. 39 & 40 *G.* 3. *c.* 99. (Pawnbrokers.)

Sec. 2.

Sec. 2. Rate of interest, 508. *Pawnbroker.*

XXVII. 43 *G.* 3. *c.* 46. (Arrests.)

1. Sec. 3. Defendant not entitled to costs unless arrested in fact, 351. *Costs*, II.

2. Sec. 5. Costs of abortive fi. fa., 272. *Practice*, XIV.

XXVIII. 53 *G.* 3. *c.* 127. (Ecclesiastical courts.)

Sec. 1. Capias cum proclamatione, 951. *Writ*, I.

XXIX. 53 *G.* 3. *c.* 141. (Annuity.)

Sec. 2. Statement of consideration, 789. *Judgment*, VIII.

XXX. 54 *G.* *c.* 170. (Poor.)

Sec. 9. Competency of rated inhabitant, 502. *Evidence*, V. 1.

XXXI. 58 *G.* 3. *c.* 45. (Church building.)

Sec. 58. Consent of vestry, 610. *Prohibition*, III.

XXXII. 55 *G.* 3. *c.* 68. (Highways.)

Sched. A. Effect of repeal of this statute on a statute incorporating the form of notice, 405. *Appeal*, I.

XXXIII. 58 *G.* 3. *c.* 69. (Vestries.)

1. Sec. 1. Notice of special purpose, 610. *Prohibition*, III.

2. Sec. 3. Manner of voting, 356. *Churchwarden.*

XXXIV. 55 *G.* 3. *c.* 184. (Stamps.)

1. Sec. 8. Admissibility in evidence for collateral purposes, 555. *Stamp*, I.

2. Sched. part 1. *Lease.* Evidence that the document is a counterpart, 255. *Stamp*, I.

3. Sched. part 1. *Mortgage.* Stamp on security for repayment of unlimited sum, 620. *Mortgage.*

4. Sched. part 1. *Mortgage.* Stamp on deed giving fresh security, 248. *Stamp*, II.

XXXV. 59 *G.* 3. *c* 12. (Poor.)

Sec. 17. Ejectment by or against parish officers, 502. *Evidence*, V. 1.

XXXVI. 59 *G.* 3. *c.* 12. (Poor.)

Sec. 26. Order on child to maintain parents, 227. *Poor*, XIII.

XXXVII. 59 *G.* 3. *c.* 134. (Church building.)

1. Sec. 14. Consent of vestry, 610. *Prohibition*, III.

2. Sec. 39. Order of commissioners for stopping up a footway, 405. *Appeal*, I.

XXXVIII. 1 *G.* 4. *c.* 119. (Insolvent debtors.)

Sec. 7. Assent to assignment, 683. *Evidence*, V. 4.

XXXIX. 6 *G.* 4. *c.* 16. (Bankrupts.)

Secs. 50. 75. 127. *Bankrupt.*

XL. 6 G. 4. *c.* 57. (Poor.)

Sec. 2. Settlement by a 10*l.* renting where landlord pays the tithes, 192. *Poor*, V.

XLI. 7 *G.* 4. *c.* 57. (Insolvent debtors.)

Sects. 10. 50. Discharge out of custody under a capias utlagatum, 677. *Outlawry.*

XLII. 7 *G.* 4. *c.* 74. (Criminal justice.)

1. Sec. 21. What omission to state property not cured after verdict, 481. *Post*, XLIII.

2. Sec. 23. Costs on indictment for indecent exposure, 589. *Costs*, XII. 1.

XLIII. 7 & 8 *G.* 4. *c.* 29. (Larceny and offences connected therewith.)

Sec. 53. False pretences.

An indictment under stat. 7 & 8 *G.* 4. *c.* 29. *s.* 53., for obtaining goods by false pretences, must state to whom the goods belonged.

Otherwise it will be bad on error; the omission not being cured after verdict by the last clause of stat. 7 *G.* 4. *c.* 64. *s.* 21., that provision relating to the description of the offence, not of the subject-matter. *Regina* v. *Martin*, 481.

XLIV. 9 *G.* 4. *c.* 14. (Written memorandum.)

Sec. 1. Conditional acknowledgment of debt.

1. *J. R.*, a debtor, having sums due to him, handed the accounts to his creditor, and wrote "I give the above accounts to you, so you must collect them and pay yourself, and you and I will then be clear. *J. R.*" Held, that this acknowledgment did not

not imply a promise to pay, and was no answer, under stat. 9 *G.* 4. *c.* 14., to a plea of the statute of limitations.

Per Lord *Denman* C. J. Whether such a written acknowledgment be conditional or unconditional is a question for the Court, not the jury, except where the document is connected with other evidence affecting the construction. *Routledge* v. *Ramsay*, 221.

2. In assumpsit on a bill of exchange, a letter was produced to take the case out of the statute of limitations, from defendant to plaintiff, stating that plaintiff should be informed immediately it was settled how defendant's affairs should be arranged; and adding, "Your account is quite correct, and O! that I were now going to enclose the amount." No amount of debt was stated; and no proof was given, from the letter or otherwise, to what account the letter referred, nor whether the letter applied to the bill.

It being left to the jury whether this was an unconditional acknowledgment of the debt, and they having found that it was: Held, that there was no ground for a nonsuit; for that the acknowledgment was unconditional, and that the jury, if it was a question for them, had decided it rightly.

Quære, whether the plaintiff was entitled to more than nominal damages: And whether the effect of the acknowledgment was a question for the Court or jury. *Dodson* v. *Mackey*, 225. n.

3. Sec. 6. Representation concerning ability.

Declaration, in assumpsit, that defendant, an attorney, requested plaintiff to lend *J.* 300*l.*, and, to encourage plaintiff to do so, and to take no further security than *J.*'s promissory note, falsely and fraudulently represented to plaintiff that she might safely lend *J.* the 300*l.*, and take no further security than such note, *because the title deeds to a certain estate, which defendant then asserted that J. had bought, were in defendant's possession, and nothing could be done without defendant's knowledge, and plaintiff would be perfectly safe in making such loan to J. on the terms aforesaid*; that the defendant by the representation induced plaintiff to lend, and plaintiff did lend, *J.* the 300*l.* on *J.*'s note only, whereas plaintiff could not safely lend, &c. (negativing the representations as above stated); all which defendant, at the time he made such representations, well knew: that *J.* had not paid, or been able to pay, the 300*l.*, and had become bankrupt.

Plea, that defendant's representations were representations concerning the ability of *J.* to repay, and were not in writing.

Held good on demurrer, the representations being within stat. 9 *G.* 4. *c.* 14. *s.* 6. *Swann* v. *Phillips*, 457.

XLV. 11 *G.* 4. & 1 *W.* 4. *c.* 64. (Beer.)

Secs. 14. 25. Conviction for allowing beer to be consumed at improper hours, 124. *Conviction*, I. 1.

XLVI. 1 & 2 *W.* 4. *c.* 32. (Game.)

Sec. 30. At whose instance a conviction for trespass may be, 155. *Game*.

XLVII. 2 & 3 *W.* 4. *c.* 71. (Prescription.)

1. Sec. 1. Onus of proof, 161. *Prescription*, I.

2. Sec. 2. How far the pleading and evidence must apply to some definite easement, 161. *Prescription*, I.

XLVIII. 3 & 4 *W.* 4. *c.* 42. (Amendment of the law.)

1. Sec. 1. Substitution of amended rules, 278. *Reg. Gen.*

2. Sec. 23. Amendment by Judge at N. P., 301. *Amendment*, I.

XLIX. 4 & 5 *W.* 4. *c.* 76. (Poor.)

1. Secs. 71, 72. Form of order of filiation, 881. *Poor*, XII.

2. Sec. 79. Notice of chargeability, 375. *Poor*, VII.

3. Sec. 81. "Fourteen days at least:" construction of, 173. *Poor*, VIII.

L. 4 & 5 *W.* 4. *c.* 85. (Beer.)

Sec. 6. Conviction for allowing beer to be consumed at improper hours, 124. *Conviction*, I. 1.

LI. 5 & 6 *W.* 4. *c.* 50. (Highways.)

1. Sec. 1.

1. Sec. 1. Repeal of 13 *G.* 3. *c.* 78., 496. *Antè*, XXII.

2. Sec. 3. Defeat of prosecutions previously commenced, 496. *Antè*, XXII.

LII. 5 & 6 *W.* 4. *c.* 63. (Weights and measures.)

Sec. 17. Powers of recorder of municipal corporation, 638. *Post*, LIII. 7.

LIII. 5 & 6 *W.* 4. *c.* 76. (Municipal corporations.)

1. Secs. 32. 35. Custody and identification of voting papers.

On trial of a quo warranto information for exercising the office of councillor for a ward having nine, the issue being whether defendant was duly elected, the prosecutor's case was, that nine other candidates at the election had a majority over the defendant: Held, that the prosecutor was not bound to prove, in the first instance, that the nine were qualified to be councillors, but might make a case by shewing simply that they had the actual majority.

Papers, purporting to be voting papers given in at the election, were produced from the town clerk's office; and it appeared that he had been elected town clerk some days after the election, and had not received the voting papers in the first instance, but that they had been delivered to him shortly after his own appointment: Held, that, under stat. 5 & 6 *W.* 4. *c.* 76. *ss.* 32. 35., the papers were not sufficiently identified to be evidence of the votes given. *Regina* v. *Ledgard*, 535.

2. Compensation.

The steward of a borough, removed under stat. 5 & 6 *W.* 4. *c.* 76., demanded compensation under sect. 66, as for an office held for life. The town council allowed compensation as for an annual office only. The Lords of the Treasury, on appeal, and after hearing the parties, awarded compensation on the former principle. On motion for a mandamus to the corporation to execute a compensation bond, there appeared evidence, on the one hand, that the office was not, legally, holden for life, and, on the other, that it had usually been so holden, and that the appointment was accepted on that understanding. Held, that, under sect. 66, the Lords of the Treasury were not bound to consider only the legal tenure, but might, referring to the circumstances of the case, award compensation as for an office held for life.

The steward had received a small annual sum for holding a corporation court. It was paid by the sheriffs, and not out of the borough fund; but he held the court as steward. Held, that compensation might be given him in respect of this emolument. *Regina* v. *Norwich, Mayor, &c.*, 633.

3. Sec. 68. Compensation to ministers of churches.

Stat. 5 & 6 *W.* 4. *c.* 76. *s.* 68., directing that stipends, which, for seven years before *June* 5th, 1835, have been usually paid to *the minister* of any church or chapel, shall be secured by bond under the corporation seal to the person *entitled or accustomed* to receive the same, extends to a person appointed lecturer of a church in such borough by the corporation, and having read prayers, preached, and administered the sacrament of the Lord's Supper, and occasionally solemnized baptisms, marriages, and burials; although there is an incumbent of the same church duly appointed under a local act of parliament, which constitutes him, and not such lecturer, the minister of that church.

It is sufficient, under stat. 5 & 6 *W.* 4. *c.* 76. *s.* 68., that the claimant has performed the duties of minister, according to the general acceptation of that term, and been accustomed for seven years to receive the stipend. *Regina* v. *Liverpool, Mayor, &c.*, 176.

4. Sec. 69. Notice of business to be done at meetings of town council, 183. *Office*, II.

5. Sec. 69. Minutes of proceedings.

Under stat. 5 & 6 *W.* 4. *c.* 76. *s.* 69., the minutes of proceedings in town council should be entered and signed by the chairman at the meeting, and not afterwards. *Regina* v. *Evesham, Mayor, &c.*, 266.

6. Sec. 92. Payment of corporate monies to treasurer, 822. *Mandamus*, IV. 4.

7. Sec. 105. Jurisdiction of recorder.

In counties of cities, and counties of towns, to which a court of quarter ses-

TENANT.

TENANT.

TENDER.

TENURE.

TESTATOR.

THEATRICAL ENTERTAINMENTS.

THAMES.

TIME.

TITHE.

TITLE.

TOLL.

TORT.

TOWN CLERK.

TOWN COUNCIL.

TRANSFER.

TRAVERSE.

TREASURER.

TREASURY, LORDS OF.

TRESPASS.

TRIAL.

TROVER.

TRUSTEE.

TRUSTS.

TURNPIKE.

Exemptions from double toll.

A turnpike act contained a clause giving certain exemptions from toll, but excepted from it, by a proviso, all horses drawing *any stage coach, diligence, van, caravan, or stage waggon, or other stage carriage*, conveying passengers or goods for pay.

R. was a wharfinger and agent to a company, who were carriers of goods by canal. *R.* kept waggons and horses, which he employed in carrying out goods brought by the company to his wharf, situate at *S.*, for persons in the neighbourhood, and bringing goods from the neighbourhood to his wharf, for transit by the canal. For such his conveyance of goods he made charges on each parcel. His waggons were so employed in carrying goods to and from persons residing at or near a place called *L.*, or places intermediate between that and *S.*, almost every day except *Sundays*. The waggons went out and returned at different hours according to circumstances; on some days they made more journeys than on others, and they seldom omitted going alto-

2. By marriage and birth of a child.

In the case of a will made before stat. 7 *W.* 4. & 1 *Vict. c.* 26., the following points were decided by the Judges of the Queen's Bench (absente Lord *Denman* C. J.), Common Pleas, and Exchequer, in the Exchequer Chamber.

Where an unmarried man, without children by a former marriage, devises all the property he has at the time of making his will, and leaves no provision for any child of a future marriage, the law annexes to such will the tacit condition that, if he afterwards marries and has a child born of such marriage, the will shall be revoked.

And evidence (not amounting to proof of republication) cannot be received in a court of law to shew that the testator meant his will to stand good, notwithstanding the subsequent marriage and birth of issue.

Such revocation is not prevented by by a provision in the will, or otherwise, for the future wife only: the children of the marriage must also be provided for.

Semble, that such revocation is not prevented if property acquired by the testator after making his will descend upon the child of such marriage on the testator's death.

It is not prevented if the child takes a legal estate only, and no beneficial interest, in the property so descending.

F. made a will as above-mentioned. Before that event, *J.* had contracted for the purchase of an estate at *M.*; possession was given, but no conveyance executed. *J.* then died intestate, leaving *F.* his heir at law and sole next of kin. *F.* then made his will, and afterwards the estate was conveyed to him. Held, that the estate was not after-acquired property, but that, by reason of *F.*'s equitable interest derived from *J.*, it was one of the subjects of devise in the will made and revoked as above stated.

In an action of ejectment by *F.*'s heir at law against the devisee under such will, for the devised estates: Held, that the plaintiff might give parol evidence that *J.* purchased the property at *M.* as agent for *F.*, the testator, although *J.* had contracted, in writing, for the purchase, in his own name.

Held also, upon bill of exceptions, that the following evidence was admissible for the defendant, the devisee, in the same cause, the bill not stating for what purpose it was tendered.

Two former wills of the testator; the first devising all his estates to *J.*, subject to an annuity to *A. B.* (whom testator afterwards married), for raising which annuity a term in certain lands was granted to defendant; the second devising certain lands to *A. B.* for life, and all the residue of his estates to defendant.

A verbal direction given by the testator, after the will made, and shortly before his marriage, that a clause barring dower should be omitted in the conveyance to him, then preparing, of certain premises. *Marston* v. *Roe dem. Fox*, 14.

3. Not prevented by declarations of intention, 14. *Antè*, 2.
4. What provision for wife and issue necessary to prevent the revocation, 14. *Antè*, 2.
5. How not revived after revocation, 1. 14. *Antè*, 1, 2.

VI. Evidence.

1. Testator's directions in dealing with, his property, 14. *Antè*, V. 2.
2. Former wills, 14. *Antè*, V. 2.
3. Intention to destroy, 1. *Antè*, V. 1.

VII. Residuary legatee, 348. *Evidence*, V. 3.

VIII. Administration. *Executor.*

IX. Office at will, 795. *Consideration*, V.

WITNESS.

Evidence.

WRIT.

I. Capias cum proclamatione.

By a writ of capias cum proclamatione (for contempt in not paying costs in the ecclesiastical court) it appeared that a writ de contumace capiendo had issued in the same cause, returnable *January* 11th, 1838, and had been duly returned, non est inventus: wherefore, the present writ commanded the sheriff to take the defendant if found in in his bailiwick, and him safely keep, &c., and if he were not found, then to cause proclamation to be made according to stats. 5 *Eliz.* c. 23. and 53 *G.* 3. c. 127. The latter writ was tested *May* 24th, 1838, and did not shew any continuance of process from *January* 11th to *May* 24th. The return of the writ de contumace capiendo was "of *Trinity* term" 1838, and contained this memorandum, "Received, 13th *June*, 1838." On application to set aside the capias, it appeared by affidavit that there had not in fact been any continuance: that the first writ had not been lodged with the sheriff till after the return day; that he made the return on *June* 13th, after he was out of office; and that the capias issued on *June* 21st.

Held, that the writ was irregular, because it did not show a proper continuance; and, per *Patteson* J., that if the facts could be looked to, the proceedings would still appear to be irregular.

Semble, per *Williams* J. that the direction in the capias, to make proclamation if the defendant were not found, was improper, for that the statutes require proclamation absolutely. *Regina* v. *Ricketts*, 951.

WRITING.

WRONG-DOER.

END OF THE EIGHTH VOLUME.

London:
Printed by A. Spottiswoode,
New-Street-Square.

Lightning Source UK Ltd.
Milton Keynes UK
UKHW020959020119
334817UK00011B/793/P